Get the Writing Help You Need

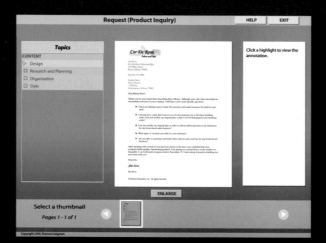

Model Document Practice

In MyCanadianBusCommLab you can see real business-world samples of documents that you will need to write when you begin your career. These "Model Documents" and "Model Document Makeovers" allow you to apply what you have learned.

Help with the Writing Process

MyCanadianBusCommLab provides help with every step of the writing process and will help you prepare to communicate effectively in the business world. Activities include a tutorial on writing formal reports. A "Composing" space provides resources at your fingertips as you research, draft, and revise. You get the help you need when you need it, without ever leaving your writing environment. Improve your writing skills, improve your grade, improve your chances of succeeding in your career.

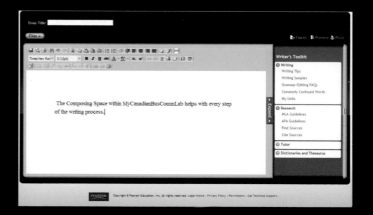

Save Time. Improve Results. www.mycanadianbuscommlab.ca

EXCELLENCE IN BUSINESS COMMUNICATION

EXCELLENCE IN BUSINESS COMMUNICATION

FOURTH CANADIAN EDITION

John V. Thill

Chairman and Chief Executive Officer

Global Communication Strategies

Courtland L. Bovée

Professor of Business Communication

C. Allen Paul Distinguished Chair

Grossmont College

Ava Cross

Department of Professional Communication

Ryerson University

Pearson Canada
Toronto

Library and Archives Canada Cataloguing in Publication

Thill, John V.
   Excellence in business communication / John V.
Thill, Courtland L. Bovée, Ava Cross. — 4th Canadian ed.

Includes index.
ISBN 978-0-13-700399-0

   1. Business communication—Textbooks.
I. Bovée, Courtland L. II. Cross, Ava, 1951– III. Title.

HF5718.2.C3T45 2011   658.4'5   C2009-906912-1

Original edition published by Pearson Education, Inc., Upper Saddle River, New Jersey, USA. Copyright © 2008 Bovée and Thill LLC. This edition is authorized for sale only in Canada.

ISBN 978-0-13-700399-0

Vice-President, Editorial Director: Gary Bennett
Editor-in-Chief: Ky Pruesse
Acquisitions Editor: David S. Le Gallais
Sponsoring Editor: Carolin Sweig
Marketing Manager: Loula March
Senior Developmental Editor: Suzanne Schaan
Production Editor: Richard di Santo
Copy Editor: Ann McInnis
Proofreaders: Nancy Mucklow, Susan McNish
Production Coordinator: Avinash Chandra
Compositor: MPS Limited, A Macmillan Company
Photo Research: Amanda Campbell
Art Director: Julia Hall
Cover Designer: Kerrin Hands
Interior Designer: Peter Papayanakis
Cover Image: James Goldsmith/Getty Images

For permission to reproduce copyrighted material, the publisher gratefully acknowledges the copyright holders listed on pages 643–644, which are considered an extension of this copyright page.

1 2 3 4 5   13 12 11 10 09

Printed and bound in the United States of America.

Brief Contents

Contents

Part II Applying the Three-Step Writing Process 87

4 Planning Business Messages...87

8 Writing Routine and Positive Messages...224

9 Writing Negative Messages...265

10 Writing Persuasive Messages...307

Part IV Preparing Reports and Oral Presentations 346

11 Planning Reports and Proposals…346

12 Writing Reports and Proposals...395

Part V Writing Employment Messages and Interviewing for Jobs   519

15 Building Careers and Writing Résumés...519

16 Applying and Interviewing for Employment...557

Preface

The fourth Canadian edition of *Excellence in Business Communication* offers a collection of contemporary model documents that reflect the entire spectrum of print and electronic communication media. Students entering today's workforce are expected to use a wide range of tools, from instant messaging to blogging to podcasting, and *Excellence in Business Communication* provides the hands-on experience they need to meet employer expectations.

The text offers a set of tools that simplifies teaching, promotes active learning, and stimulates critical thinking. These components work together at four levels to provide seamless coverage of vital knowledge and skills.

> **Previewing.** Each chapter prepares students with clear learning objectives and a brief, compelling vignette featuring a successful professional role model.
> **Developing.** Chapter content develops, explains, and elaborates on concepts with a concise, carefully organized presentation of textual and visual material. The three-step process of planning, writing, and completing is clearly explained and reinforced throughout the text in examples ranging from email messages to blogs to formal reports.
> **Enhancing.** Contemporary examples, many accompanied by the three-step diagram adapted to each message, show students the specific elements that contribute to—or detract from—successful messages.
> **Reinforcing.** Hundreds of realistic business English exercises and activities let students practise vital skills and put their new-found knowledge to immediate use. Communication cases, many featuring real companies, encourage students to think about contemporary business issues as they put their skills to use in a variety of media, including blogging and podcasting.

What's New in This Edition

With business communication evolving so rapidly, textbooks and learning packages need to evolve just as quickly. Key revisions in this edition include the following:

> Icons throughout the text integrate additional resources on MyCanadianBusCommLab, an online site for business communication students, including writing samples, document makeovers, and videos.
> Electronic communication is highlighted throughout the text. A completely new chapter (Chapter 7) on crafting messages for electronic media covers email, instant messaging, blogging, and podcasting. Business applications of Web 2.0 are discussed, including the use of wikis for collaborative communication (Chapter 2) and the value of social networking sites for job searches (Chapter 15). Coverage of organizing and writing online content has also been added to the report section (Chapters 11–13).
> New documents in a variety of media—including blogs, wikis, and podcasts—show both effective and ineffective communication efforts.
> Cases feature virtually every significant medium now used in business, including email, instant messaging, text messaging, social networking, blogging, websites, voice mail, and podcasting. New icons highlight these new media, making it easy to identify appropriate cases to practise specific skills.
> The range of real-world companies referenced has been expanded to include non-profit organizations such as Free the Children ("On the Job" features and model documents in Chapter 6) and Creative Commons ("On the Job" features in Chapter 5). These examples help to highlight corporate social responsibility.
> Expanded coverage of audience psychology (in Chapter 1) gives students important insights into how audiences receive, process, and respond to messages.
> Expanded coverage of visual communication (in Chapter 12) helps students understand the growing importance of visual media in business today. Key topics include visual symbolism, visual design principles, and the ethics of visual design.
> Chapter 15 contains new information on creating employment portfolios and advice on using this course as a way to create work samples to show potential employers. To help students select appropriate projects for their portfolios, "Portfolio Builder" cases are highlighted throughout the book.

Key Features of the Text

Each chapter of *Excellence in Business Communication* includes a number of tools designed to guide students through the process of developing their communication skills and preparing them for the business world. In Chapter 1, yellow bubbles highlight some of these features in practice.

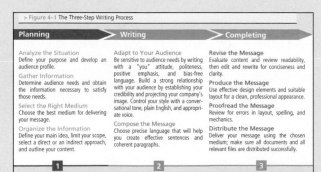

Learning Objectives are listed on the first page of each chapter. This "roadmap" shows what will be covered and what is especially important. Each Learning Objective is repeated in the margin where the material is first covered. The Learning Objectives are summarized at the end of the chapter.

On the Job opens each chapter with a brief story about communications within a real company, such as Royal Bank, Maple Leaf Foods, and Indigo. The chapter itself demonstrates why these communication skills are important to real companies and shows how to apply them. Each chapter ends with the follow-up **On the Job: Performing Communication Tasks** at the featured company. These tasks expand on the chapter's concepts and help students practise real-world decision making.

The **three-step writing process**—planning, writing, and completing—is outlined in Chapters 4–6. This process is also highlighted throughout the chapters with selected sample documents and with the end-of-chapter cases.

Sample documents, many from real companies, provide models in media ranging from printed letters to instant messaging. The **annotations** that accompany every model document help students understand how to apply the principles discussed in the chapter.

> Figure 9–4 Effective Email Advising of a Back Order

One of four types of **themed boxes** appears in each chapter, giving valuable tips for the workplace:

> **Sharpening Your Career Skills** gives tips on improving writing and speaking techniques.
> **Using the Power of Technology** provides help with business communications and technological tools.
> **Achieving Intercultural Communication** offers advice on communicating successfully in the global business world.
> **Promoting Workplace Ethics** examines important ethical issues that face today's employees.

Checklists summarize key points and help students organize their work on communication projects.

Tips for Success give important advice from experts in the field on the chapter's topic. Real people; real experience.

Key Points, highlighted in the margin, emphasize important details from the text and are good tools for reviewing concepts.

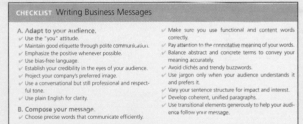

"The most effective writers are those who view what they compose from the reader's vantage point. Ask yourself, Does the intended reader have your background, your education, and your experience with the subject at hand?, If not, adjust your text accordingly."

Ray Dreyfack, systems executive, Fabergé Perfumes, business writer and consultant

Effective teams can pool knowledge, take advantage of diverse viewpoints, and increase acceptance of solutions the team proposes.

Practice is the best way to grasp new business communication techniques and processes. End-of-chapter exercises and cases will help students develop and improve their communication skills.

> **Test Your Knowledge** provides questions that review the chapter topics.

> **Apply Your Knowledge** offers exercises that encourage students to consider the information and apply it to business decisions.

> **Running Cases** present realistic business situations encountered by Noreen and Kwong as they work toward their career goals. Working through these case studies will help students deal with on-the-job tasks.

> **Practise Your Knowledge** provides documents for critique and revision.

> **Exercises** give additional tasks to work through, including teamwork exercises and ethical situations.

> **Cases,** at the end of specific chapters, offer additional opportunities to apply the three-step writing process in work-related situations. Icons highlight cases that use specific media skills—email, blogging, instant messaging, podcasting—as well as "Portfolio Builder" cases, where the projects may be suitable for students' employment portfolios.

Test Your Knowledge

1. Why is it particularly important to adapt your medium and tone to your audience's needs and preferences when writing a bad-news message?
2. What are the main goals in delivering bad news?
3. What are the advantages of using the direct approach to deliver bad news at the beginning of a message?
4. What is the sequence of elements in a bad-news message organized using the indirect approach?
5. What is a buffer? Why do some critics consider it unethical?
6. When using an indirect approach to announce a negative decision, what is the purpose of presenting your reasons before explaining the decision itself?
7. What are the techniques for de-emphasizing bad news?
8. What are the ethical considerations for delivering bad news?
9. What are the characteristics of effective crisis communication?
10. When giving a negative review to an employee, what five guidelines should you follow?

Apply Your Knowledge

1. Why is it important to end negative messages on a positive note?
2. If company policy changes, should you explain those changes to employees and customers at about the same time? Why or why not?
3. If your purpose is to convey bad news, such as refusing a request, should you take the time to suggest alternatives to your reader? Why or why not?
4. When a company suffers a setback, should you soften the impact by letting out the bad news a little at a time? Why or why not?
5. Why is choice of medium important when delivering performance reviews?
6. **Ethical Choices:** Is intentionally de-emphasizing bad news the same as distorting graphs and charts to de-emphasize unfavourable data? Why or why not?

Running Cases

Watch on mycanadianbusresomntlab

> **CASE 1** Noreen

In her role as collections manager, Noreen has to write a letter informing customers with overdue accounts that the interest rate has risen by 1 percent, effective 30 days from the date on the letter. This policy means Petro-Go's current interest rate is 14 percent and in 30 days will increase to 15 percent. Overdue accounts are charged with compounding interest (i.e., interest on both the previous month's balance and the interest already charged on that month's balance).

QUESTIONS
a) What does it mean to use the "you" attitude in this type of message?
b) Is the direct or indirect approach best for this bad-news message? Why?
c) What must be considered to avoid defamation of the customer's character or reputation?
d) How will Noreen end this message on a positive note?
e) Should Noreen suggest ways for the customer to avoid paying late payment charges in this letter?

YOUR TASK
Write the letter. Remember to use company letterhead (create it yourself) and include an enclosure notation. Include a 1-800 number customers can call for further information.
Both the letter and the envelope should indicate the information is confidential. Prepare the envelope. (See Appendix A for letter and envelope formats.)

Practise Your Knowledge

Read the following documents, then (1) analyze the strengths and weaknesses of each sentence and (2) revise each document so it follows this chapter's guidelines.

DOCUMENT 9.A: PROVIDING NEGATIVE NEWS ABOUT TRANSACTIONS

Your spring fraternity party sounds like fun. We're glad you've again chosen us as your caterer. Unfortunately, we have changed a few of our policies, and I wanted you to know about these changes in advance so we won't have any misunderstandings on the day of the party.

We will arrange the delivery of tables and chairs as usual the evening before the party. However, if you want us to set up, there is now a $100 charge for that service. Of course, you might want to get some of the brothers and pledges to do it, which would save you money. We've also added a small charge for cleanup. This is only $3 per person (you can estimate because I know a lot of people come and go later in the evening).

Other than that, all the arrangements will be the same. We'll provide the skirting for the band stage, tablecloths, bar set-up, and, of course, the barbecue. Will you have the tubs of

DOCUMENT 9.B: REFUSING REQUESTS FOR CLAIMS AND ADJUSTMENTS

I am responding to your letter of about six weeks ago asking for an adjustment on your wireless hub, model WM39Z. We test all our products before they leave the factory; therefore, it could not have been our fault that your hub didn't work.

If you or someone in your office dropped the unit, it might have caused the damage. Or the damage could have been caused by the shipper if he dropped it. If so, you should file a claim with the shipper. At any rate, it wasn't our fault. The parts are already covered by warranty. However, we will provide labour for the repairs for $55, which is less than our cost, since you are a valued customer.

We will have a booth at the upcoming trade show there and hope to see you or someone from your office. We have many new models of office machines that we're sure you'll want to see. I've enclosed our latest catalogue. Hope to see you there.

DOCUMENT 9.C: REJECTING JOB APPLICATIONS

I regret to inform you that you were not selected for our summer intern program at Equifax. We had over a thousand

Exercises

9.1 Selecting the Approach: Various Scenarios
Select the approach you would use (direct or indirect) for these negative messages:
a. an email message to your boss informing her that one of your key clients is taking its business to a different accounting firm
b. an email message to a customer informing her that one of the books she ordered over the internet is temporarily out of stock
c. an instant message to a customer explaining that the DVD recorder he ordered for his new computer is on back order and that, as a consequence, the shipping of the entire order will be delayed
d. a blog post to all employees notifying them that the company parking lot will be repaved during the first week of June and that the company will provide a shuttle service from a remote parking lot during that period

Cases APPLYING THE THREE-STEP WRITING PROCESS TO CASES

Persuasive Requests for Action
[Blogging SKILLS] [Portfolio BUILDER]

1. That's the point: Email encouraging your boss to blog
You've tried for months to convince your boss, Will Florence, to start blogging. You've told him that top executives in numerous industries now use blogging as a way to connect with customers and other stakeholders without going through the filters and barriers of formal corporate communications. He was just about convinced—until he looked at the GM Fast-Lane blog site, where General Motors executives and managers write about current GM products and issues.

"Look at this!" he calls from his office. "Some of the most respected executives in the world, and all these people are criticizing them. Sure, a lot of the responses are positive, but quite a few are openly hostile, disagreeing with GM strategy, criticizing the products, criticizing the subjects he chooses for his blog—you name it. If blogging is all about opening yourself up to criticism from every bystander with a keyboard, no way am I going to start a blog."

Your Task: Write Florence an email (w_florence@sprenco.com) persuading him that the freewheeling nature of blog communication is its key advantage, not a disadvantage at all.

mycanadianbuscommlab

MyCanadianBusCommLab is a website that offers videos, sample documents, and interactive exercises to improve communication skills. Throughout the text, icons highlight material where related activities or samples are available on MyCanadianBusCommLab.

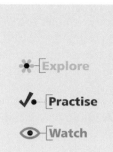

> Explore dozens of **Writing Samples,** from letters to emails to reports, that model effective communication.
> Interactive **Document Makeovers** provide practice in correcting ineffective communication; feedback guides students to understand the problems and find solutions.
> The *Perils of Pauline* **videos** are interactive case studies that follow one employee's workplace communication tasks.

Student Supplements

Grammar-on-the-Go (ISBN 978-0-13-206347-0). *Grammar-on-the-Go* will help you communicate clearly and effectively in any business setting, whether you're working part time, volunteering, or applying for jobs. It keeps its focus on the essential English skills that you need to succeed in today's workplace. See the inside back cover of this text for details.

MyCanadianBusCommLab (www.mycanadianbuscommlab.ca). This state-of-the-art, interactive, and instructive solution for business communication is designed to be used as a supplement to a traditional lecture course or to completely administer an online course. See the opening pages of this text for details.

MyCanadianBusCommLab includes a Pearson eText that gives students access to the text whenever and wherever they have access to the Internet. eText pages look exactly like the printed text, offering powerful new functionality for students and instructors. Users can create notes, highlight text in different colours, create bookmarks, zoom, click hyperlinked words and phrases to view definitions, and view in single-page or two-page view. Pearson eText allows for quick navigation to key parts of the eText using a table of contents and provides a full-text search. The eText may also offer links to associated media files, enabling users to access videos, animations, or other activities as they read.

A student access card for MyCanadianBusCommLab is packaged with every new copy of the text. Access codes can also be purchased through campus bookstores or through the website.

CourseSmart. CourseSmart goes beyond traditional expectations—providing instant, online access to the textbooks and course materials you need at an average savings of 50%. With instant access from any computer and the ability to search your text, you'll find the content you need quickly, no matter where you are. And with online tools like highlighting and note-taking, you can save time and study efficiently. See all the benefits at www.coursesmart.com/students.

Instructor Supplements

MyTest. MyTest from Pearson Education Canada is a powerful assessment generation program that helps instructors easily create and print quizzes, tests, exams, as well as homework or practice handouts. Questions and tests can be authored entirely online, allowing instructors ultimate flexibility and the ability to efficiently manage assessments at any time, from anywhere. MyTest for *Excellence in Business Communication* includes over 1500 multiple-choice, true/false, and fill-in-the-blank questions. To access MyTest, please go to www.pearsonmytest.com.

Instructor's Resource CD-ROM (ISBN 978-0-13-212775-2). This CD-ROM brings together some of the instructor resources for this text, including the following components:

> The *Instructor's Manual* provides chapter outlines, suggests solutions to the exercises, and supplies formatted letters for the cases in the letter-writing chapters. Additional resources include diagnostic tests of English skills and supplementary grammar exercises.
> The *Test Item File* includes all the questions from the MyTest in Microsoft Word format.
> *PowerPoint Presentations* cover the key concepts in each chapter.

The supplements on the Instructor's Resource CD-ROM are also available for download from a password-protected section of Pearson Education Canada's online catalogue (www.pearsoncanada.ca/highered). Navigate to your book's catalogue page to view a list of the available supplements. See your local sales representative for details and access.

CourseSmart for Instructors. CourseSmart goes beyond traditional expectations—providing instant, online access to the textbooks and course materials you need at a lower cost for students. And even as students save money, you can save time and hassle with a digital eTextbook that allows you to search for the most relevant content at the very moment you need it. Whether it's evaluating textbooks or creating lecture notes to help students with difficult concepts, CourseSmart can make life a little easier. See how when you visit www.coursesmart.com/instructors.

Technology Specialists. Pearson's Technology Specialists work with faculty and campus course designers to ensure that Pearson technology products, assessment tools, and online course materials are tailored to meet your specific needs. This highly qualified team is dedicated to helping schools take full advantage of a wide range of educational resources by assisting in the integration of a variety of instructional materials and media formats. Your local Pearson Education sales representative can provide you with more details on this service program.

Acknowledgments for the Fourth Canadian Edition

At Pearson Education Canada, Carolin Sweig offered me the opportunity to work on this fourth edition. Suzanne Schaan guided the manuscript through the development process with professionalism and grace. I am very grateful to them. At Pearson, Richard di Santo served as production editor for this project, and Avinash Chandra served as production coordinator; they shepherded this book through the later stages with great care. Thank you also to Ann McInnis for copyediting and to Nancy Mucklow and Susan McNish for proofreading; I appreciate their proficiency and careful approach.

Many educators in Canada read my manuscript and made thoughtful suggestions. I would like to thank the following instructors, who commented in detail on the manuscript for this new edition: Kathy Cocchio, Northern Alberta Institute of Technology; Elaine Cohen, Concordia University; Dana Hansen, Humber College; Chris Legebow, St. Clair College; Peter Miller, Seneca College of Applied Arts and Technology; Jolene Pattison, Nova Scotia Community College, IT Campus; Sonia Perna, SAIT Polytechnic; Harris Poulis, Concordia University. Thanks also to Janet Fabri, Global Communications, Dell, for reviewing the scenario in Chapter 11.

My love and affection go to my husband, John Cross, and children, Miriam and David, for their good humour and love.

Ava Cross

1

Achieving Success Through Effective Business Communication

LEARNING OBJECTIVES

Learning Objectives are a "roadmap" showing what will be covered in each chapter.

After studying this chapter, you will be able to

1. Explain why effective communication is important to your success in today's business environment
2. Identify eight communication skills that successful employers expect from their employees
3. Describe the five characteristics of effective business communication
4. Discuss six factors that make business communication unique
5. Describe five strategies for communicating more effectively on the job
6. Explain three strategies for using communication technology successfully
7. Discuss the importance of ethics in business communication and differentiate between an ethical dilemma and an ethical lapse

ON THE JOB

Meet real companies and businesspeople communicating at work.

Communicating at Suncor Energy Inc.

WORKING TOGETHER TO FIND SOLUTIONS

www.suncor.com

"Once we understand where our organization wants to go, we communicate, communicate, and communicate some more, with our employees, our shareholders, our communities," says Sue Lee, Suncor Energy's senior vice-president of Human Resources and Communications. A leading North American energy producer, Suncor pursues a dual vision: meeting Canada's need for energy through oil sands development while exploring new energy sources for the future.

The company expects to produce 550 000 barrels per day in 2012 and currently operates two wind power projects, SunBridge in southwestern Saskatchewan and Magrath in southern Alberta. Together, these wind farms can reduce carbon dioxide emissions by approximately 115 000 tonnes each year. Believing in "sharing perspectives, information, and knowledge," Suncor's decision making includes extensive stakeholder consultation. Whether employees work on the oil fields or in laboratories and company offices, the company seeks their input to improve business. And through collaborating with local community and environmental groups, Suncor can respond to their concerns while meeting the demand for energy.

To communicate effectively with 6500 employees, community organizations, government agencies, and the general public, Sue Lee and her staff must tailor

Images are influential communication tools. Suncor Energy uses pictures of alternative power generators in its brochures and on its website to communicate its environmental mission.

Suncor's communications for each audience. Two-page newsletters filled with pho-tos and brief articles update communities on local operations. The extensive annual sustainability report, available through the website, provides detailed information on Suncor's environmental performance. Investor-oriented webcasts and presenta-tions inform shareholders on the company's financial picture. According to Lee, Sun-cor's communication managers "think through and document all our key processes—everything from how we put out a news release to how we develop a comprehensive communication plan."

It's up to Sue Lee to ensure that both internal and external communications not only keep employees and communities informed of Suncor's activities, but also en-gage them in shaping the company's direction. If you were in Sue Lee's position, what would you do to keep communication flowing smoothly and efficiently? How would you overcome the possible barriers to communication as you prepare the mes-sages you send to Suncor's stakeholders?[1]

Achieving Career Success Through Effective Communication

Your career success depends on effective communication.

Organizations such as Suncor Energy understand that achieving success in today's workplace is closely tied to the ability of their employees and man-agers to communicate effectively. Whether competing to get the job you want or to win the customers your company needs, your success or failure depends largely on your ability to communicate. In fact, to stand out from your compe-tition in the job market, improving your communication skills might be the single most important step you take. Employers often express frustration at the poor communication skills of many employees—particularly recent grad-uates who haven't yet learned how to adapt their casual communication style to the professional business environment. If you learn to write well, speak well, listen well, and recognize the appropriate way to communicate in vari-ous business situations, you'll gain a major advantage that will serve you throughout your career.[2]

New terms are defined where bolded in the sentence.

Whether exchanging emails, posting entries on a blog, giving a formal presentation, or chatting with co-workers at lunch, you are engaging in **communication**, the process of transferring information from a sender to a receiver. The essence of communication is sharing—providing data, information, and insights in an exchange that benefits both you and the people with whom you are communicating.[3] However, communication is considered *effective* only when others understand your message correctly and respond to it in the way you want. Effective communication helps you manage your work flow, improves business relationships, enhances your professional image, and provides a variety of other important benefits (see Figure 1–1).

Learning Objectives in the margin identify each stop on the "roadmap."

Objective 1 Explain why effective communication is important to your success in today's business environment.

Communication is vital to every company's success.

Effective communication is at the centre of virtually every aspect of business because it connects the company with all its **stakeholders**—the groups that your company affects in some way and who themselves have some influence on your company. For example, as a customer or an employee of a particular business, you are a stakeholder. Other stakeholders include government regulators, who create guidelines that businesses must observe, and the media, which reports on business and influences public opinion.

Key Points highlight important details from the text and are good tools for reviewing concepts.

> Figure 1–1 The Benefits of Effective Communication

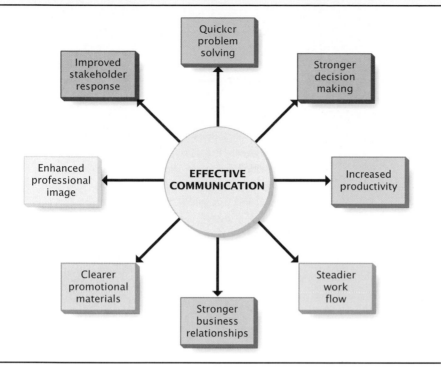

If you want to improve efficiency, quality, responsiveness, or innovation, you'll do so with the help of strong communication skills. Conversely, without effective communication, people misunderstand each other and misinterpret information. "Unclear communication not only results in errors and missed deadlines, but also lies at the root of many other serious workplace issues, such as low morale and poor job performance," says Diane Domeyer, executive director of Office Team, a temporary employment firm.[4] Canada's leading executives believe that 15 percent of each workweek, or almost eight weeks per year, is wasted because of poor communication.[5] At every stage of your career, communication is the way you'll succeed, and the higher you rise in your organization, the more important it becomes. In fact, top managers spend as much as 85 percent of their time communicating with others.[6]

What Employers Expect from You

No matter how good you are at accounting, law, science, or whatever professional specialty you pursue, most companies expect you to be competent at a wide range of communication tasks. Employers spend millions of dollars on communication training every year, but they expect you to come prepared with basic skills, so you can take full advantage of the learning opportunities they make available to you. Check the Employability Skills 2000+ chart, prepared by the Conference Board of Canada (Figure 1–2), for the skills you need for career success. In addition, complete the *Essential Skills Passport* at http://www.hrsdc.gc.ca/eng/workplaceskills/essential_skills/pdfs/learning/passport.pdf, produced by the federal government's Office of Literacy and Essential Skills, to pinpoint your strengths and areas for improvement.

In fact, employers start judging your ability to communicate before you even show up for your first interview, and the process of evaluation never really stops. Improving your communication skills helps ensure that others will recognize and reward your talents and contributions. Fortunately, the specific

Employers are constantly evaluating your communication skills.

> Figure 1–2 Employability Skills 2000+ Chart

Employability Skills 2000+

The skills you need to enter, stay in, and progress in the world of work—whether you work on your own or as a part of a team.

These skills can also be applied and used beyond the workplace in a range of daily activities.

Fundamental Skills	Personal Management Skills	Teamwork Skills
The skills needed as a base for further development	The personal skills, attitudes and behaviours that drive one's potential for growth	The skills and attributes needed to contribute productively

You will be better prepared to progress in the world of work when you can:

Communicate
- read and understand information presented in a variety of forms (e.g., words, graphs, charts, diagrams)
- write and speak so others pay attention and understand
- listen and ask questions to understand and appreciate the points of view of others
- share information using a range of information and communications technologies (e.g., voice, e-mail, computers)
- use relevant scientific, technological and mathematical knowledge and skills to explain or clarify ideas

Manage Information
- locate, gather and organize information using appropriate technology and information systems
- access, analyze and apply knowledge and skills from various disciplines (e.g., the arts, languages, science, technology, mathematics, social sciences, and the humanities)

Use Numbers
- decide what needs to be measured or calculated
- observe and record data using appropriate methods, tools and technology
- make estimates and verify calculations

Think & Solve Problems
- assess situations and identify problems
- seek different points of view and evaluate them based on facts
- recognize the human, interpersonal, technical, scientific and mathematical dimensions of a problem
- identify the root cause of a problem
- be creative and innovative in exploring possible solutions
- readily use science, technology and mathematics as ways to think, gain and share knowledge, solve problems and make decisions
- evaluate solutions to make recommendations or decisions
- implement solutions
- check to see if a solution works, and act on opportunities for improvement

You will be able to offer yourself greater possibilities for achievement when you can:

Demonstrate Positive Attitudes & Behaviours
- feel good about yourself and be confident
- deal with people, problems and situations with honesty, integrity and personal ethics
- recognize your own and other people's good efforts
- take care of your personal health
- show interest, initiative and effort

Be Responsible
- set goals and priorities balancing work and personal life
- plan and manage time, money and other resources to achieve goals
- assess, weigh and manage risk
- be accountable for your actions and the actions of your group
- be socially responsible and contribute to your community

Be Adaptable
- work independently or as a part of a team
- carry out multiple tasks or projects
- be innovative and resourceful: identify and suggest alternative ways to achieve goals and get the job done
- be open and respond constructively to change
- learn from your mistakes and accept feedback
- cope with uncertainty

Learn Continuously
- be willing to continuously learn and grow
- assess personal strengths and areas for development
- set your own learning goals
- identify and access learning sources and opportunities
- plan for and achieve your learning goals

Work Safely
- be aware of personal and group health and safety practices and procedures, and act in accordance with these

You will be better prepared to add value to the outcomes of a task, project or team when you can:

Work with Others
- understand and work within the dynamics of a group
- ensure that a team's purpose and objectives are clear
- be flexible: respect, be open to and supportive of the thoughts, opinions and contributions of others in a group
- recognize and respect people's diversity, individual differences and perspectives
- accept and provide feedback in a constructive and considerate manner
- contribute to a team by sharing information and expertise
- lead or support when appropriate, motivating a group for high performance
- understand the role of conflict in a group to reach solutions
- manage and resolve conflict when appropriate

Participate in Projects & Tasks
- plan, design or carry out a project or task from start to finish with well-defined objectives and outcomes
- develop a plan, seek feedback, test, revise and implement
- work to agreed quality standards and specifications
- select and use appropriate tools and technology for a task or project
- adapt to changing requirements and information
- continuously monitor the success of a project or task and identify ways to improve

The Conference Board of Canada

255 Smyth Road, Ottawa
ON K1H 8M7 Canada
Tel. (613) 526-3280
Fax (613) 526-4857
Internet: www.conferenceboard.ca/education

Download this pamphlet from www.conferenceboard.ca/education/learning-tools/employability-skills.aspx and use it as a reference throughout your schooling and career. Where do you stand now in regard to the three skill areas? Where do you need to improve your skills? How do you plan to do this?

skills that employers expect from you are the very skills that will help you advance in your career:

1. **Organizing ideas and information logically and completely.** You'll often be required to find, process, and organize substantial amounts of raw data and random information, so others can easily grasp its significance.

2. **Expressing and presenting ideas and information coherently and persuasively.** Whenever you're asked to offer an opinion or recommendation, you'll be expected to back it up with solid evidence. However, organizing your evidence well is not all you will need to do; you'll also need to convince your audience with compelling arguments.

3. **Listening to others effectively.** Effective listening is not as easy as you might think. Amidst all the distractions on the job, you'll need to use specific skills to detect the real meaning behind the words. (For a more extensive discussion of listening, see Chapter 2.)

4. **Communicating effectively with people from diverse backgrounds and experiences.** You'll often be called on to communicate with people who differ from you in gender, ethnic background, age, profession, technical ability, and so on.

5. **Using communication technologies effectively and efficiently.** You're already familiar with email, instant messaging, and online research. Increasingly, employers will also expect you to use Web conferencing, electronic presentations, and a variety of other technological tools.

6. **Following accepted standards of grammar, spelling, and other aspects of high-quality writing and speaking.** You and your friends are probably comfortable with informal communication that doesn't put a high value on precision and correctness. However, to be successful in business, you will need to focus on the quality of your communication efforts. Particularly with audiences who don't know you well, careless writing and disregard for accepted standards reflects poorly on both you and your company. Rather than giving you the benefit of the doubt, many people will assume you either don't know how to communicate or don't care enough to communicate well.

7. **Communicating in a civilized manner that reflects contemporary expectations of business etiquette.** Even when the pressure is on, you'll be expected to communicate with courtesy and respect in a manner that is appropriate to the situation.

8. **Communicating ethically, even when choices aren't crystal clear.** Whether you're simply reporting on the status of a project or responding to a complicated, large-scale crisis, you're certain to encounter situations that call for you to make sound ethical choices. (See Promoting Workplace Ethics: Ethical Boundaries: Where Would You Draw the Line?) You'll have the opportunity to practise all these skills throughout this course—but don't stop there. Successful professionals continue to hone communication skills throughout their careers.

Objective 2 Identify eight communication skills that successful employers expect from their employees.

Get workplace advice from the experts.

TIPS FOR SUCCESS

" Make sure your soft skills (communication, teamwork, problem solving) are on par with your technical abilities, as employers look for well-rounded individuals who will integrate well into their companies. "

Paul Hébert, Executive Director, Mining Industry Training and Adjustment Council of Canada

PROMOTING WORKPLACE ETHICS

Four types of boxes link you to today's workplace.

Ethical Boundaries: Where Would You Draw the Line?

At the very least, you owe your employer an honest day's work for an honest day's pay: your best efforts, obedience to the rules, a good attitude, respect for your employer's property, and a professional appearance. Such duties and considerations seem clear-cut, but where does your obligation to your employer end? For instance, where would you draw the line in communication situations such as the following?

> Writing your résumé so an embarrassing two-year lapse won't be obvious.

> Telling your best friend about your company's upcoming merger right after mailing the formal announcement to your shareholders.
> Hinting to a co-worker (who's a close friend) that it's time to look around for something new, when you've already been told confidentially that she's scheduled to be fired at the end of the month.
> Saying nothing when you witness one employee taking credit for another's successful idea.
> Preserving your position by presenting yourself to supervisors as the only person capable of achieving an objective.
> Pirating computer software; that is, using one copy on more than one computer instead of paying for licences to duplicate the product.
> Making up an excuse when (for the fourth time this month) you have to pick up your child from school early and miss an important business meeting.

> Calling in sick because you're taking a few days off and you want to use up some of the sick leave you've accumulated.

The ethics involved in these situations may seem perfectly unambiguous . . . until you think about them. But wherever you are and whatever the circumstances, you owe your employer your best efforts. And time and again, it will be up to you to decide whether those efforts are ethical.

CAREER APPLICATIONS

1 List ethical behaviours you would expect from your employees and compare your list with those of your classmates.
2 As the supervisor of the office filing clerks, you must deal with several workers who have a tendency to gossip about their colleagues. List five actions you might take to resolve the situation.

Characteristics of Effective Communication

Objective 3 Describe the five characteristics of effective business communication.

You can have the best ideas that will help your company run productively, but they're no good to your employer or your career if you can't express them clearly and persuasively. Employers demand oral and written communication skills from all job candidates, from seasonal and entry-level workers to management employees.

To make your messages effective, make them practical, factual, concise, clear about expectations, and persuasive[7]:

SUMMER WILDERNESS CAMP OPPORTUNITIES

Camp Nippising is seeking enthusiastic people with a passion for working with kids and a love of the outdoors.
Applicants will have

- Camping experience
- Excellent oral and written communication skills
- Standard First Aid with Heartsaver CPR
- Lifeguard certificate

Most companies want employees who can communicate effectively, from entry- to high-level positions. What sorts of jobs have you held that required you to communicate with co-workers and with customers or clients? What were your specific communication tasks, both oral and written?

1. **Provide practical information.** Give recipients useful information, whether it's to help them perform a desired action or understand a new company policy.
2. **Give facts rather than impressions.** Use concrete language, specific detail, and information that is clear, convincing, accurate, and ethical. Even when an opinion is called for, present compelling evidence to support your conclusion.
3. **Present information in a concise, efficient manner.** Highlight the most important information, rather than forcing your reader to determine the key points. Most business professionals find themselves wading in a flood of data and information. Messages that clarify and summarize are more effective than those that do not. In today's time-pressured business environment, clear and concise messages are highly valued.
4. **Clarify expectations and responsibilities.** Write messages to generate a specific response from a specific audience. Clearly state what you expect from audience members or what you can do for them. You will see many examples in this book with action requests.

5. Offer compelling, persuasive arguments and recommendations. Show your readers precisely how they will benefit from responding to your message the way you want them to. Including reader benefits is the key to persuading employers, colleagues, customers, or clients to adopt a plan of action or purchase a product.

Keep these five important characteristics in mind as you review Figures 1–3 and 1–4. Both emails appear to be well-constructed at first glance, but Figure 1–3 is far less effective, as explained in the margin comments. It shows the negative impact that poorly conceived messages can have on an audience. In contrast, Figure 1–4 shows how an effective message can help everyone work more efficiently (in this case, by helping them prepare effectively for an important meeting).

Communication in Organizational Settings

In every part of the business organization, communication provides the vital link between people and information. When you join a company such as Suncor, you become a key element in its communication chain. Whether you're a high-level manager or an entry-level employee, you have information that others need to perform their jobs, and others have information

No matter what your level in the organization, you have an important communication role.

Improve your communication skills using the Document Makeover exercises on MyCanadianBusCommLab.

✓• Practise

> Figure 1–3 Ineffective Communication

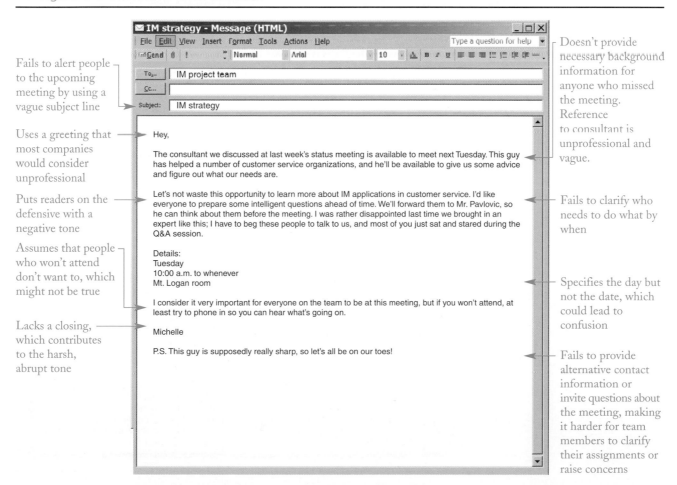

Fails to alert people to the upcoming meeting by using a vague subject line

Uses a greeting that most companies would consider unprofessional

Puts readers on the defensive with a negative tone

Assumes that people who won't attend don't want to, which might not be true

Lacks a closing, which contributes to the harsh, abrupt tone

Doesn't provide necessary background information for anyone who missed the meeting. Reference to consultant is unprofessional and vague.

Fails to clarify who needs to do what by when

Specifies the day but not the date, which could lead to confusion

Fails to provide alternative contact information or invite questions about the meeting, making it harder for team members to clarify their assignments or raise concerns

See the Model Documents on
MyCanadianBusCommLab for more
examples of effective communication.

Explore

that is crucial to you. You exchange information with people inside your organization, called **internal communication**, and you exchange information and ideas with others outside your organization, called **external communication**. This information travels over both *formal* and *informal* channels (see Figure 1–5).

> Figure 1–4 Effective Communication

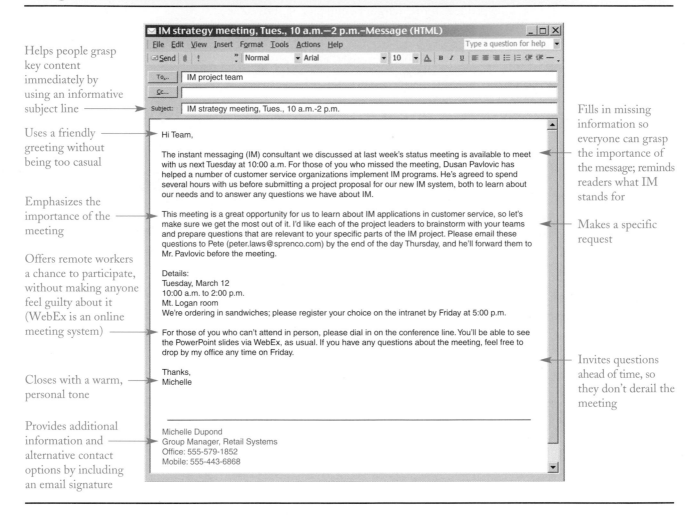

Helps people grasp key content immediately by using an informative subject line

Uses a friendly greeting without being too casual

Emphasizes the importance of the meeting

Offers remote workers a chance to participate, without making anyone feel guilty about it (WebEx is an online meeting system)

Closes with a warm, personal tone

Provides additional information and alternative contact options by including an email signature

Fills in missing information so everyone can grasp the importance of the message; reminds readers what IM stands for

Makes a specific request

Invites questions ahead of time, so they don't derail the meeting

> Figure 1–5 Forms of Communication

	Internal	External
Formal	Planned communication among insiders (such as memos, reports, email, instant messages, executive blogs, conference calls, and presentations) that follows the company's chain of command	Planned communication with outsiders (such as letters, reports, speeches, websites, instant messages, news releases, advertising, and executive blogs)
Informal	Casual communication among employees (such as email, instant messages, face-to-face conversations, phone calls, team blogs, and wikis) that do not follow the company's chain of command	Casual communication with suppliers, customers, investors, and other outsiders (such as face-to-face conversations, email, instant messages, phone calls, and customer-support blogs)

Communicating internally is essential for effective functioning. As an employee, you are in a position to observe first-hand attitudes and behaviours that your supervisors and co-workers cannot see: a customer's reaction to a product display, a supplier's brief hesitation before agreeing to a delivery date, or a slowdown in the flow of customers. Managers and co-workers need such minute information in order to do their jobs. If you don't pass that information along, nobody will—because nobody else knows. Communicating freely helps employees develop a clear sense of the organization's mission and helps managers identify and react quickly to potential problems.

Company websites are designed to project a particular image. What sort of image does the website of TELUS, a telecommunications company, project? Does the TELUS home page encourage you to explore the website? Why or why not?

Like internal communication, external communication is essential for conducting business smoothly. Companies constantly exchange messages with customers, vendors, distributors, competitors, investors, journalists, and community representatives. Whether by letter, Web, phone, fax, or video, good communication is the first step in creating a favourable impression. Extremely careful planning is required for messages such as statements to the press, letters to investors, advertisements, and price announcements. Therefore, such documents are often drafted by a marketing or public relations team—a group of individuals whose sole job is creating and managing the flow of formal messages to outsiders.

Carefully constructed websites convey an important message to outsiders about your organization's products and services. A website's appearance and organization can entice Web surfers to explore it past the home page, and perhaps become your company's customers.

FORMAL COMMUNICATION NETWORK The **formal communication network** is typically shown as an organizational chart such as the one in Figure 1–6. Such charts summarize the lines of authority; each box represents a link in the chain of command, and each line represents a formal **channel**, or route, for the transmission of official messages. Information may travel down, up, and across an organization's formal hierarchy.

> **Downward flow.** Organizational decisions are usually made at the top and then flow down to the people who will carry them out. Most of what filters downward is geared toward helping employees do their jobs and carry out company objectives. From top to bottom, each person must understand each message, apply it, and pass it along.

Information flows up, down, and across the formal hierarchy.

> **Upward flow.** To solve problems and make intelligent decisions, managers must learn what's going on in the organization. Because they must delegate work to be efficient, executives depend on lower-level employees to furnish them with accurate, timely reports on problems, emerging trends, opportunities for improvement, grievances, and performance. Typically, documents generated by lower-level employees for high-level or outside readers are reviewed by a manager. Furthermore, sensitive or complex messages created by upper-level employees are also approved by superiors before being signed off.

> **Horizontal flow.** Communication also flows laterally, from one department to another. This horizontal communication helps employees share information and coordinate tasks. Project teams are one example of horizontal communication: in these teams, employees from different departments work together to solve problems and improve the operation of their company.

> Figure 1–6 Formal Communication

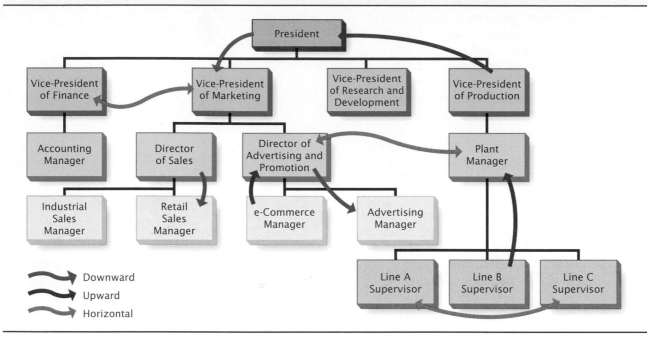

Formal organizational charts illustrate how information is supposed to flow. In actual practice, however, employees across the organizational hierarchy communicate with each other informally.

INFORMAL COMMUNICATION NETWORK Every organization also has an **informal communication network**—a *grapevine*—that operates anywhere two or more employees are in contact, from the lunchroom to the golf course to the company's email and instant messaging (IM) systems. Although many of these conversations deal with personal matters, one study found that about 86 percent of the information that travels along the grapevine pertains to business.[8] Some executives are wary of the informal communication network, possibly because it threatens their power to control the flow of information. However, smart managers tap into the grapevine. It provides them with a sense of employees' concerns and anxieties, and they can use it to spread and receive informal messages.[9] The grapevine also helps employers determine if their formal means of communication are effective: grapevines tend to be most active when employees believe the formal network is not providing the information they want or need.[10]

INFORMAL OUTSIDE COMMUNICATION Although companies often communicate with outsiders in a formal manner, informal contacts with outsiders are important for learning about customer needs. As a member of an organization, you are an important informal channel for communicating with the outside world. In the course of your daily activities, you unconsciously absorb bits of information that add to the collective knowledge of your company. What's more, every time you speak for or about your company to your friends, potential sales contacts, customers, and so on, you send a message. Many outsiders may form their impression of your organization on the basis of the subtle, unconscious clues you transmit through your tone of voice, facial expression, and general appearance. Although these interactions are informal, they can still be vital to the company's success, so they require the same care and skill as formal communication.

In fact, these informal exchanges are considered so important that a new class of technology has emerged to enable them. Just as Facebook, MySpace, and

Grapevines flourish when employees don't receive information they want or need.

Every employee informally accumulates facts and impressions that contribute to the organization's collective understanding of the outside world.

similar **social networking technologies** help students and other individuals connect, software and websites such as Spoke Connect, LinkedIn.com, and Ryze.com help businesspeople connect. These business-oriented solutions typically work by indexing email and IM address books, calendars, and message archives, then looking for connections between names.[11]

THE COMMUNICATION PROCESS Communication doesn't occur haphazardly. Nor does it happen all at once. It is more than a single act. Communication is a dynamic, transactional, or two-way, process that can be broken into seven phases, as shown in Figure 1–7. However, be aware that this is a simplified model; real-life communication is usually more complicated. Both sender and receiver might be talking at the same time, or the receiver might be trying to talk on the phone with one person while instant messaging with another, or the receiver may ignore the sender's request for feedback, and so on.

1. **The sender has an idea.** You conceive an idea and want to share it. The potential success of your communication effort starts here. Its effectiveness depends on the nature of the idea, the composition of the audience and your relationship to these people, and your motivation for wanting to share the idea. For example, if an idea will benefit your department or company and your motivation is to make a contribution, the communication process is off to a strong start. In comparison, if the idea is poorly conceived (perhaps you haven't considered the financial impact of a proposal) or your motivation is suspect (perhaps you're more interested in making an impression on your boss than really contributing), the communication will be more difficult and possibly unsuccessful.

2. **The sender encodes the idea in a message.** When you put your idea into a message (words, images, or a combination of both) that your receiver will understand, you are **encoding** it. Much of the focus of this course is on developing the skills needed to successfully encode your ideas into effective messages. Encoding can fail for a number of reasons, including poor word choices that confuse or anger the audience, imagery that evokes unintended emotional responses, and cultural differences that result in the same words and images meaning different things to different people.

3. **The sender chooses a medium for transmitting the message.** With the appropriate message to express your idea, you now need some way to send that message to your intended audience. As you'll read in Chapter 4, media for transmitting messages can be divided into oral, written, visual, and various electronic forms of the other three. As an experienced user of communication media, you already know that this step requires careful decision making and at least some level of technical skills. Misguided media choices or insufficient technical skills can undermine the best intentions. For instance,

> Senders and receivers connect through a seven-step process.

> Figure 1–7 The Communication Process

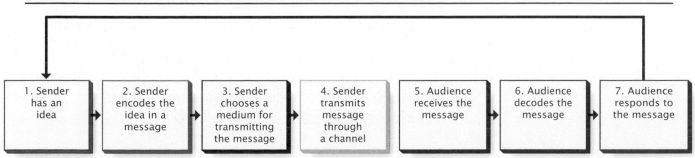

a desire to keep everyone informed of every important detail in a project can lead to email overload—and a breakdown in communication as people struggle to keep track of all the messages and the inevitable response threads. In contrast, many companies now find that a blog is a much better way to keep teams informed because this medium can dramatically reduce the number of messages required.

4. **The sender transmits the message through a channel.** Just as technology continues to multiply the number of media options at your disposal, it also continues to provide new **communication channels** you can use to transmit your messages. The distinction between medium and channel can get a bit murky, but think of medium as the *form* a message takes and channel as the system used to *deliver* the message. The channel can be a face-to-face conversation, the Internet, another company—any system capable of delivering messages.

5. **The audience receives the message.** If your message does not meet any obstacles, such as an unintended email deletion, it arrives at your intended audience. However, mere arrival at the destination is not a guarantee that the message will be noticed or understood correctly. For example, if you're giving a speech, your listeners have to be able to hear you, and they have to pay attention. You have no guarantee that your message will actually get through. In fact, one of the biggest challenges you'll face as a communicator in today's crowded business environment is cutting through the clutter and noise in whatever medium you choose.

6. **The audience decodes the message.** If the message is actually received, the audience must then absorb and understand it, a step known as **decoding**. If obstacles do not block the process, the receiver interprets your message correctly; that is, the receiver assigns the same meaning to your words as you intended and responds in the way you desire.

7. **The audience responds to the message.** After decoding your message, the audience has the option of responding in some way. This **feedback** enables you to evaluate the effectiveness of your message: Feedback often initiates another cycle through the process, which can continue until both parties are satisfied with the result. Successful communicators place considerable value on feedback, not only as a way to measure effectiveness but also as a way to learn.

Understanding Why Business Communication Is Unique

Objective 4 Discuss six factors that make business communication unique.

If you have some experience in the business world, you already know that business communication is far more demanding than the communication you typically engage in with family, friends, and school associates. Expectations are higher on the job, and the business environment is so complex that your messages can fail for many reasons, such as human oversight or a technological glitch. Business communication is affected by factors such as globalization of business and the increase in workforce diversity, the increasing value of information, the pervasiveness of technology, the growing reliance on teamwork, the evolution of organizational structures, and numerous barriers to successful communication.

The Globalization of Business and the Increase in Workforce Diversity

Today's businesses increasingly reach across international borders to market their products, partner with other businesses, and employ workers and executives—an effort known as **globalization**. A number of companies and brands that you may think of as North American (including Ben & Jerry's, Dr. Pepper, and Pillsbury) are in fact owned by organizations based in other countries.[12] Many companies headquartered in North America, such as Boeing, Microsoft, Coca-Cola, and Ford, frequently communicate with customers and colleagues abroad.

Over 2 million North Americans now work for foreign employers.[13] Increased globalization and workforce diversity mean that employees must understand the laws, customs, and business practices of many countries besides being able to communicate with people who speak different languages. Between 1991 and 2001, 1.8 million people immigrated to Canada. Altogether, Canadians come from more than 200 different ethnic backgrounds. In Toronto, which attracts the highest percentage of new immigrants, there are 62 different ethnic groups of at least 10 000 people.[14] It has been said that Canada's multiculturalism is what "makes us so well liked around the world."[15]

As Chapter 3 discusses in more detail, successful companies realize two important facts: (1) the more diverse their workforce, the more attention they need to pay to communication, and (2) a diverse workforce can yield a significant competitive advantage by bringing more ideas and broader perspectives to bear on business challenges.

People with different cultural backgrounds and life experiences may have different communication styles.

The Increasing Value of Business Information

As competition for jobs, customers, and resources continues to grow, the importance of information continues to escalate as well. An organization's information is now every bit as important as its people, money, raw materials, and other resources. Even companies not usually associated with the so-called Information Age, such as manufacturers, often rely on **knowledge workers**: employees at all levels of the organization who specialize in acquiring, processing, and communicating information.

Information has become one of the most important resources in business today.

The valuable information you'll be expected to communicate on the job addresses such key areas as competitive insights, customer needs, and regulations and guidelines:

> **Competitive insights.** Successful companies work hard to understand their competitors' strengths and weaknesses. The more you know about your competitors and their plans, the more able you will be to adjust your own business plans.

> **Customer needs.** Most companies invest significant time and money in an effort to understand their customers' needs. This information is collected from a variety of sources and needs to be analyzed and summarized, so your company can develop goods and services that better satisfy customer needs.

> **Regulations and guidelines.** Today's businesses must understand and follow a wide range of government regulations and guidelines covering such areas as employment, environment, taxes, and accounting. Your job may include the responsibility of researching and understanding these issues and then communicating them throughout the organization.

Less costly than travel, videoconferencing provides many of the same benefits as an in-person meeting. Advanced systems include telepresence and robot surrogates, which use computers to "place" participants in the room virtually, letting them see and hear everyone while being seen and heard themselves. Do you think that such realistic interaction makes meetings more productive? What are the benefits and shortcomings of virtual meetings?

The Pervasiveness of Technology

Technology can help or hinder communication, depending on how it's designed and used.

Technology now has a powerful influence in virtually every aspect of business communication. However, even those technological developments intended to enhance communication can actually impede it if not used intelligently. Moreover, keeping current with technology requires time, energy, and constant improvement of skills. If your level of technical expertise doesn't match that of your colleagues and co-workers, the imbalance can put you at a disadvantage and complicate the communication process.

For a concise overview of the technologies you're most likely to encounter, see "Using Technology to Improve Business Communication" later in this chapter. Throughout this course, you'll learn about numerous technological tools and systems, and it's important to have a general understanding of the internet and its uses.

The Evolution of Organizational Structures

Organizations with tall structures may unintentionally restrict the flow of information.

As Figure 1–6 illustrates, every business has a particular structure that defines the relationships between the various people and departments within the organization. These relationships, in turn, affect the nature and quality of communication throughout the organization. Tall structures have many layers of management between the lowest and highest positions, so they can suffer communication breakdowns and delays as messages are passed up and down through multiple layers.

Flatter organizational structures usually make it easier to communicate effectively.

To overcome such problems, many businesses are now adopting flatter structures that reduce the number of layers. With fewer layers, communication generally flows faster and with fewer disruptions and distortions. On the other hand, with fewer formal lines of control and communication in these organizations, individual employees are expected to assume more responsibility for communication. For instance, you may be expected to communicate across department boundaries with colleagues and team members throughout the company.

In the pursuit of speed and agility, some businesses have adopted flexible organizations that pool the talents of employees and external partners. For instance, when launching a new product, a company might supplement the efforts of internal departments with help from a public relations firm, an ad agency, a marketing consultant, a Web developer, and a product distributor. With so many individuals and organizations involved in the project, everyone must share the responsibility for giving and getting necessary information, or communication will break down.

Corporate cultures with an open climate benefit from free-flowing information and employee input.

Regardless of the particular structure a company uses, your communication efforts will also be influenced by the organization's **corporate culture**, the mixture of values, traditions, and habits that give a company its atmosphere and personality. Successful companies encourage employee contributions by ensuring that communication flows freely down, up, and across the organization chart. Open climates encourage candour and honesty, helping employees feel free enough to admit their mistakes, disagree with their boss, and express their opinions. Since taking the helm at Suncor in 1991, Chief Executive Officer Rick George has fostered an open culture. As the company's leader, he and other members of upper management routinely consult with staff about Suncor's business decisions and performance. This open communication has resulted in early identification of problems and the generation of innovative ideas. Under George's leadership, Suncor's oil production increased from 60 000 barrels a day to more than 271 000, an increase of more than 350 percent.[16]

Of course, as with any honest relationship, sending or receiving negative news is not always easy. In Chapter 9, you'll learn effective strategies for crafting messages that convey bad news in a professional and respectful manner.

The Growing Reliance on Teamwork

Successful companies such as Suncor no longer limit decisions to a few managers at the top of a formal hierarchy. Instead, organizations use teams and collaborative work groups to make the decisions required to succeed in a global and competitive marketplace. You'll probably find yourself on a number of teams throughout your career.

Open cultures promote the flow of information. You may work in an open-plan office designed to encourage casual interaction and impromptu meetings. Does a flexible environment stimulate the flow of information? What are the limits to this sort of workspace?

When teams replace or complement the formal channels in the organization chart, information may no longer be conveyed automatically, so every team member becomes more responsible for communication. This responsibility includes both sending and receiving messages; for example, you might seek out needed information rather than waiting for someone to deliver it to you. In fact, you and your fellow team members may have to invent your own communication processes to ensure that everyone gets the right information at the right time. This extra attention to communication can pay off dramatically in higher performance and a more satisfying work experience.

Working in a team makes you even more responsible for communicating effectively.

The Barriers to Effective Communication

Throughout your career, you'll find that perfectly prepared messages can fail for a variety of reasons. When interference in the communication process distorts or obscures the sender's meaning, it is called a **communication barrier**, or **noise**. Your attempts to transmit and receive messages can be disrupted, distorted, or even blocked by **communication barriers** such as these:

Communication is blocked by various types of barriers.

> **Distractions.** Business messages can be interrupted or distorted by a wide variety of distractions, from uncomfortable meeting rooms to crowded computer screens filled with instant messages and reminders. Physical distractions range from poor acoustics to uncomfortable meeting rooms. Internal distractions are thoughts and emotions that prevent audiences from focusing on incoming messages. For example, people worried about losing their jobs might ignore any message that doesn't apply to their immediate concerns. Poor listening is another kind of distraction. We all let our minds wander now and then, and we are especially likely to drift off when we are forced to listen to information that is difficult to understand or that has little direct bearing on our own lives.

> **Competing messages.** Having your audience's undivided attention in today's technological world is a distinct challenge. In many cases, you must compete with other messages that are trying to reach your audience at the same time. Too many messages can result in **information overload**, which not only makes it difficult to discriminate between useful and useless

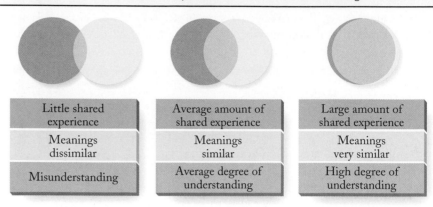

> Figure 1–8 How Shared Experience Affects Understanding

Little shared experience	Average amount of shared experience	Large amount of shared experience
Meanings dissimilar	Meanings similar	Meanings very similar
Misunderstanding	Average degree of understanding	High degree of understanding

information but also amplifies workplace stress.[17] One study found that businesspeople send and receive about 90 email messages a day, and "power emailers" devote more than three hours each day to reading, forwarding, and replying to them.[18]

> **Perceptual differences.** Our minds organize incoming sensations into a mental map that represents our individual **perception** of reality. As a sender, you choose the details that seem important to you. As a receiver, you try to fit new details into your existing pattern; however, if a detail doesn't quite fit, you are inclined to distort the information rather than rearrange your pattern—a process known as **selective perception**.[19] For example, a manager who strongly believes in a particular business strategy might distort or ignore evidence that suggests the strategy is failing. The more your audience members share your experiences—personal, professional, and cultural—the more likely they will be to extract the same meanings that you encode in your messages (see Figure 1–8).

> **Language differences.** The very language we use to communicate can turn into a barrier if two people define a given word or phrase differently. When a boss asks for something "as soon as possible," does that mean within 10 seconds, 10 minutes, or 10 days? When you communicate with non-native speakers of English, you may have to explain such expressions as "he nailed it" and "thinking outside the box."

> **Restrictive environments.** Companies that restrict the flow of information, either intentionally or unintentionally, limit their competitive potential. With their many levels between top and bottom, tall hierarchies often result in significant loss of message quality in both directions.[20] If an organization does not provide an effective means for employees to share their ideas, they will believe management is not interested in them and will avoid conveying their opinions.[21]

> **Deceptive tactics.** Language itself is made up of words that carry values. So merely by expressing your ideas in a certain way, you influence how others perceive your message, and you shape expectations and behaviours.[22] An organization cannot create illegal or unethical messages and remain credible or become successful. Still, some business communicators try to manipulate their receivers by using deceptive tactics: they may exaggerate benefits, quote inaccurate statistics, or hide negative information behind an optimistic attitude. They may state opinions as facts, leave out crucial information, or portray graphic data unfairly. And they may allow personal preferences to influence their own perception and the perception of others.

Communicating More Effectively on the Job

No single solution will overcome all communication barriers. However, a careful combination of strategies can improve your ability to communicate effectively. For example, you can minimize distractions, adopt an audience-centred approach, improve your basic communication skills, make your feedback constructive, and be sensitive to business etiquette.

Objective 5 Describe five strategies for communicating more effectively on the job.

Strategy 1: Minimizing Distractions

Everyone in the organization can help overcome distractions. Start by reducing as much noise, visual clutter, and interruption as possible. A small dose of common sense and courtesy goes a long way. Turn off your cell phone before you step into a meeting. Don't talk across the tops of cubicles when people inside them are trying to work. Be sensitive to your employer's policies about playing music at work: some people may be able to work with soft music playing, but others can't.

Overcome distraction by
> using common sense and courtesy
> sending fewer messages
> informing receivers of your message's priority

Don't let email, IM, or telephones interrupt you every minute of the day. Set aside time to attend to messages all at once, so you can think and focus the rest of the day. Make sure the messages you send are necessary. Email in particular has made it too easy to send too many messages or send messages to the people who don't need them. In fact, one of the reasons that blogging is taking off so quickly in business is that it can significantly reduce internal email traffic.[23]

In addition, if you must send a message that isn't urgent or crucial, let people know so they can prioritize. If a long report requires no action from recipients, tell them up front, so they don't have to search through it looking for action items. Most email and voicemail systems let you mark messages as urgent; however, use this feature only when it's truly needed. Too many so-called urgent messages that aren't particularly urgent will lead to annoyance and anxiety, not action.

Try to overcome emotional distractions by recognizing your own feelings and by anticipating emotional reactions from others.[24] When a situation might cause tempers to flare, choose your words carefully. As a receiver, avoid placing blame and reacting subjectively.

Emotionally charged situations require extra care when communicating.

Strategy 2: Adopting an Audience-Centred Approach

An **audience-centred approach** means focusing on and caring about the members of your audience, making every effort to get your message across in a way that is meaningful to them. This approach is also known as adopting the "you" attitude. Learn as much as possible about the biases, education, age, status, style, and personal and professional concerns of your receivers. If you're addressing strangers and are unable to find out more about them, project yourself into their position by using your common sense and imagination. Remember that your audience wants to know, "What's in it for me?"

UNDERSTAND HOW AUDIENCES RECEIVE MESSAGES Knowing how audiences receive messages will help you fine-tune an audience-centred approach for each situation. For an audience member to actually receive a message, three events need to occur: the receiver has to *sense* the presence of a message, *select* it from all the other messages competing for attention, and *perceive* it as an actual message (as opposed to random, pointless noise).[25]

Today's business audiences are inundated with so many messages and so much noise that they miss or ignore many of the messages intended for them. However, through this course, you will learn a variety of techniques to craft messages that get noticed. In general, follow these five principles to increase your chances of success:

> **Consider audience expectations.** Deliver messages using the media and channels that the audience expects. Of course, sometimes going *against* expectations can stimulate audience attention, which is why companies will advertise in unusual ways to get your attention. However, for most business communication efforts, following the expectations of your audience is the most efficient way to get your message across.

> **Ensure ease of use.** Even if audiences are actively looking for your messages, they probably won't see your messages if you make them hard to find. Poorly designed websites with confusing navigation are common culprits in this respect.

> **Emphasize familiarity.** Use words, images, and designs that are familiar to your audience. For example, most visitors to business websites now expect to see information about the company on a page called "About Us."

> **Practise empathy.** Make sure your messages "speak to the audience" by clearly addressing their wants and needs—not yours. People are much more inclined to notice messages that relate to their individual concerns.[26]

> **Design for compatibility.** With so many messages delivered electronically these days, be sure to verify technical compatibility with your audience. For instance, if your website requires visitors to have the Adobe Flash capability on their computers, you won't reach audience members who don't have that software.

To improve the odds that your messages will be successfully perceived by your audience, pay close attention to expectations, ease of use, familiarity, empathy, and technical compatibility.

UNDERSTAND HOW AUDIENCES DECODE MESSAGES Even though a message may have been received by the audience, it doesn't "mean" anything until the recipient decodes it and assigns meaning to it. Unfortunately, there is no guarantee that your audience will assign the same meaning that you intended. Even well-crafted, well-intentioned communication efforts can fail because assigning meaning is a highly personal process affected by culture, individual experience, learning and thinking styles, hopes, fears, and even temporary moods. Moreover, audiences tend to extract the meaning they *expect* to get from a message, even if it's the opposite of what the sender intended.[27] In fact, rather than extracting *your* meaning, it's more accurate to state that audience members re-create *their* own meaning—or meanings—from the message.

As you'll discover in Chapter 3, culture shapes people's views of the world in profound ways, from determinations of right and wrong to details such as the symbolic meanings attached to specific colours. For example, Canadians tend to admire young professionals who challenge established ways of conducting business. In contrast, in Japan, people generally place a higher value on respect for older colleagues, consensus decision making, and group accomplishment. A younger colleague's bold proposal to reshape business strategy radically could be interpreted more positively in one culture than in the other—quite independent of the proposal's merits alone.

Audiences will likely respond to a message if they remember it, if they're able to respond, and if they're properly motivated to respond.

UNDERSTAND HOW AUDIENCES RESPOND TO MESSAGES After your message is delivered, received, and correctly decoded, will audience members respond in the way you'd like them to? Probably—if three events occur.

First, the recipient has to remember the message long enough to act on it. Simplifying greatly, memory works in several stages: Sensory memory momentarily captures incoming data from the senses; then, whatever the recipient pays attention to is transferred to short-term memory. Information in short-term memory will quickly disappear if it isn't transferred to long-term memory, which can be done either actively (such as by memorizing a list of items) or passively (such as when a new piece of information connects with something else the recipient already has stored in long-term memory). Finally, the information needs to be retrieved when the recipient needs to act on it.[28] In general, people find it easier to remember and retrieve information that is important to them personally or professionally. Consequently, by communicating in ways that are sensitive to your audience's wants and needs, you greatly increase the chance that your messages will be remembered and retrieved.

Second, the recipient has to be able to respond as you wish. Obviously, if recipients simply cannot do what you want them to do, such as paying for a product you are promoting, they will not respond according to your plan. By understanding your audience (see Chapter 4), you can work to minimize these scenarios.

Third, the recipient has to be motivated to respond. You'll encounter many situations in which your audience has the option of responding but isn't required to—the record company may or may not offer your band a contract, the boss may or may not respond to your request for a raise, and so on. In many situations, however, you will have a fair amount of influence over whether the recipient will respond as you'd like. Throughout this course, you'll learn the techniques for crafting messages that motivate readers to respond.

By explaining why audiences will benefit by responding to your messages, you'll increase their motivation to respond.

KNOW AS MUCH AS YOU CAN ABOUT YOUR AUDIENCE The more you know about the people you're communicating with, the easier it will be to concentrate on their needs—which, in turn, will make it easier for them to hear your message, understand it, and respond positively. For example, the presentation slide in Figure 1–9 takes an audience-centred approach. Rather than trying to cover all the technical and legal details that are often discussed in insurance plans, this slide addresses the common fears and worries that employees might have as their company moves to a new health insurance plan. Accessible language and clear organization help communicate the message effectively.

If you haven't had the opportunity to communicate with a diverse range of people in your academic career so far, you might be surprised by the

> Figure 1–9 PowerPoint Slide Showing Audience-Centred Communication

different communication styles you will surely encounter on the job. Recognizing and adapting to your audience's style will improve not only the effectiveness of your communication but also the quality of your working relationship.[29] The audience-centred approach is emphasized throughout this book, so you'll have plenty of opportunities to practise this approach to communicating more effectively.

Strategy 3: Improving Your Business Communication Skills

Work on your communication skills before you start your business career.

Your own skills as a communicator will be as much a factor in your business success as anything else. No matter what your skill level, opportunities to improve are numerous and usually easy to find. As mentioned earlier, many employers provide communication training in both general skills and specific scenarios, but don't wait. Use this course to begin mastering your skills now.

Lack of experience may be the only obstacle between you and effective communication. Perhaps you're worried about a limited vocabulary or uncertain about questions of grammar, punctuation, and style. If you're intimidated by the idea of writing an important document or appearing before a group, you're not alone. Everyone gets nervous about communicating from time to time, even people you might think of as "naturals." People aren't born writing and speaking well; they master these skills through study and practice. Even simple techniques, such as keeping a reading log and writing practice essays, will improve not only your writing skills but also your scholastic performance.[30]

This course lets you practise in an environment that provides honest and constructive feedback. You'll have ample opportunity to plan and produce documents, collaborate in teams, listen effectively, improve nonverbal communication, and communicate across cultures—all skills that will serve your career well.

Strategy 4: Making Your Feedback Constructive

Constructive feedback focuses on improvement, not personal criticism.

You will encounter many situations in which you are expected to give and receive feedback regarding communication efforts. Whether giving or receiving criticism, be sure you do so in a constructive way. **Constructive feedback**, sometimes called *constructive criticism*, focuses on the process and outcomes of communication, not on the people involved (see Table 1–1). In contrast, **destructive feedback** delivers criticism with no effort to stimulate improvement.[31] For example, "This proposal is a confusing mess, and you failed to convince me of anything" is destructive feedback. Your goal is to be more constructive: "Your proposal could be more effective with a clearer description of the construction process and a well-organized explanation of why the positives outweigh the negatives." When giving feedback, avoid personal attacks and give clear guidelines for improvement.

React unemotionally when you receive constructive feedback.

When you receive constructive feedback, resist the immediate urge to defend your work or deny the validity of the feedback. Remaining open to criticism isn't always easy when you've put long nights and much effort into a project, but feedback is a valuable opportunity to learn and improve. Disconnect your emotions from the work and view it simply as something you can improve. Many writers also find it helpful to step back, think a while about the feedback, and let their emotions settle down before making corrections. Of course, don't automatically assume that even well-intentioned

> Table 1–1 Giving Constructive Feedback

How to Be Constructive	Explanation
Evaluate effectiveness	Does the document accomplish its intended purpose with accurate information and clear language?
Think through your suggested changes carefully	Isolated or superficial edits can do more harm than good.
Discuss improvements rather than flaws	Instead of saying, "This illustration is confusing," explain how it can be improved to make it clearer.
Focus on controllable behaviour	Since the writer may not have control over every variable that affected the quality of the message, focus on those elements that the writer can control.
Be specific	Comments such as "I don't get this" or "Make this clearer" don't identify what the writer needs to fix.
Keep feedback impersonal	Focus comments on the message, not the person who created it.
Verify understanding	Ask for confirmation from the recipient to make sure that the person understood your feedback.
Time your feedback carefully	Make sure the writer will have sufficient time to implement the changes you suggested.
Highlight any limitations your feedback may have	If you didn't have time to give the document a thorough edit, or if you're not an expert in some aspect of the content, let the writer know so he or she can handle your comments appropriately.

feedback is necessarily correct. You are responsible for the final quality of the message, so ensure that any suggested changes are valid ones.

Strategy 5: Being Sensitive to Business Etiquette

In today's hectic, competitive world, the notion of **etiquette** (the expected norms of behaviour in a particular situation) can seem outdated and unimportant. However, the way you conduct yourself can have a profound influence on your company's success and your career. When executives hire and promote you, they expect your behaviour to protect the company's reputation. The more you understand such expectations, the better chance you have of avoiding career-damaging mistakes.

In any setting, long lists of etiquette "rules" can be overwhelming. You'll never memorize all of them or remember to follow them in the heat of the moment. Remember three principles that will get you through almost any situation: respect, courtesy, and common sense. Moreover, these principles will encourage forgiveness if you do happen to make a mistake.

Respect, courtesy, and common sense will get you through most etiquette challenges on the job.

As you encounter new situations, take a few minutes to learn the expectations of the other people involved. You can begin with reading travel guidebooks; they are a valuable source of information about norms and customs in other countries. Don't be afraid to ask questions, either. People will respect your concern and curiosity. You'll gradually accumulate considerable knowledge, which will help you feel comfortable and be effective in a wide range of business situations. In Chapter 3, you will learn some rules of etiquette when conducting business with people of other cultures.

> Figure 1–10 Becoming an Effective Business Communicator

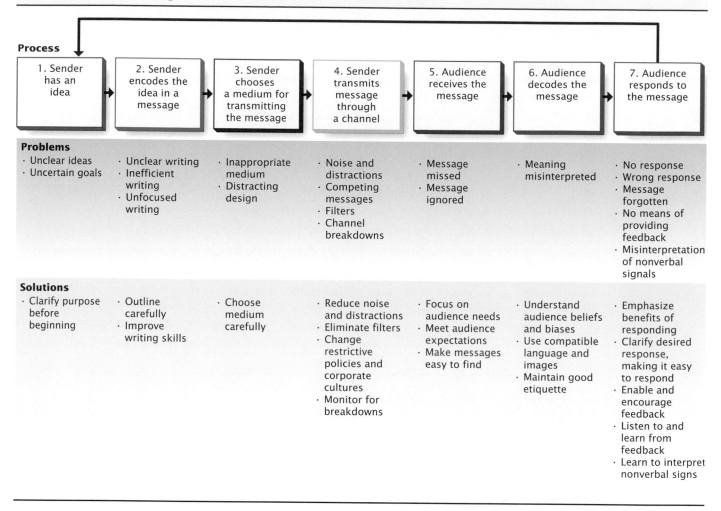

Applying What You've Learned to the Communication Process

With these additional insights into what makes communication succeed, take another look at the communication process model. The communication process presents many opportunities for messages to get lost, distorted, or misinterpreted as they travel from sender to receiver. Fortunately, you can take action at every step in the process to increase your chances of success. Figure 1–10 identifies the key challenges in the process and summarizes the steps you can take along the way to become a more effective communicator.

Using Technology to Improve Business Communication

Communicating in today's business environment nearly always requires some level of technical competence.

Objective 6 Explain three strategies for using communication technology successfully.

Today's businesses rely heavily on technology to improve the communication process. Companies and employees who use technology wisely can communicate more effectively and therefore compete more successfully.

You will find that technology is discussed extensively throughout this book, with specific advice on using common tools to meet communication challenges. While new technologies have the potential to enhance business communication dramatically, anyone who has used a computer knows that the benefits of technology are not automatic. When poorly designed or inappropriately used, technology can hinder communication more than it helps. Communicate effectively by keeping technology in perspective, using technological tools productively, spending time and money on technology wisely, and disengaging from the computer frequently to communicate in person.

Keeping Technology in Perspective

Technology is an aid to interpersonal communication, not a replacement for it. Technology can't think for you or communicate for you, and if you lack some essential skills, technology probably can't fill in the gaps. Your spell checker can run all your words through the dictionary, but it doesn't know whether you're using the correct words or crafting effective sentences.

The sheer number of possibilities in many technological tools can get in the way of successful communication. For example, the content of a message may be obscured if an electronic presentation is overloaded with visual effects. Moreover, if technological systems aren't adapted to user or organizational needs, people won't adapt to the technology—they won't use it effectively or, worse, they won't use it at all. Perhaps even of more concern, some workers are beginning to show signs of information technology addiction—possibly to the point of craving the stimulation of being connected practically around the clock, even while on vacation.[32]

Using Technological Tools Productively

Communication technologies can save time and money, but they can also waste time and money if not used efficiently. You don't have to become an expert to use most communication technologies effectively, but you will need to be familiar with the basic features and functions of the tools your employer expects you to use.

Another major productivity consideration is personal use of IM, blogging, music players, and other technological tools (and toys) on the job. Few companies go to the extreme of banning all personal use of such technologies while at work or of trying to restrict employees' personal blogs, but every company needs to address this issue. For example, inappropriate Web surfing not only distracts employees from work responsibilities but also can leave employers open to lawsuits for sexual harassment if inappropriate images are displayed in or transmitted around the company.[33] In addition, email and instant messages are considered legal documents and can be used as evidence in lawsuits or criminal trials.[34] Blogging has created another set of managerial challenges, given the risk that employee blogs can expose confidential information or damage a firm's reputation in the marketplace. With all of these technologies, the best solution lies in clear policies that are enforced evenly for all employees.[35] Finally, remember that every communication tool, from email to IM to micro-blogging tools such as Twitter, can be used productively or wastefully. Make sure that technology enhances the communication effort rather than overwhelms or disrupts it.

Reconnecting with People Frequently

In spite of technology's efficiency and speed, it may not be the best choice for every communication situation. First, even in the best circumstances, technology can't match the rich experience of person-to-person contact. Suppose you email a colleague asking how her sales presentation to an important client went, and

Online chats with customer service reps are a quick way to get product and service information. Entry level high-tech jobs require effective communication skills, just as mid- and high-level jobs do. What oral communication skills are needed for online service support? What personal qualities are necessary?

Don't rely too much on technology or let it overwhelm the communication process.

Employees who are comfortable using communication technologies have a competitive advantage in today's marketplace.

she simply replies, "Fine." What does *fine* mean? Is an order expected soon? Did she lose the sale? Was the client rude and she doesn't want to talk about it? If you reconnect with her, perhaps visit her in person, she might provide additional information, or you might be able to offer advice or support during a difficult time.

Second, most people need to connect with other people. You can create impressive documents and presentations without ever leaving your desk or meeting anyone in person. But if you stay hidden behind technology, people won't get to know you nearly as well. You might be funny, bright, and helpful, but you're just a voice on the phone or a name on a document until people can interact with you in person. As technological options increase, people seem to need the human touch even more.

No matter how much technology is involved, communication is still about people connecting with people.

Making Ethical Communication Choices

Objective 7 Discuss the importance of ethics in business communication and differentiate between an ethical dilemma and an ethical lapse.

Ethics are the accepted principles of conduct that govern behaviour within a society. Put another way, ethical principles define the boundary between right and wrong. Ethics has been defined as "knowing the difference between what you have a right to do and what is the right thing to do."[36] To make the right choices as a business communicator you have a responsibility to think through not only what you say but also the consequences of saying it.

Of course, people in a society don't always agree on what constitutes ethical behaviour. For instance, the emergence of **stealth marketing**, in which customers don't know they're being marketed to, has raised a new set of concerns about ethics. Two common stealth marketing techniques are sending people into public places to use particular products in a conspicuous manner and then discussing them with strangers—as though they were just regular people on the street, when in fact they are employed by a marketing firm—and paying consumers (or plying them with insider information and other benefits) to promote products to their friends without telling them it's a form of advertising. Critics complain that such techniques are deceptive because they don't give their targets the opportunity to raise their instinctive defences against the persuasive powers of marketing messages.[37]

Any time you try to mislead your audience, the result is unethical communication.

Ethical behaviour is a companywide concern, of course, but because communication efforts are the public face of a company, they are subjected to particularly rigorous scrutiny from regulators, legislators, investors, consumer groups, environmental groups, labour organizations, and anyone else affected by business activities. **Ethical communication** includes all relevant information, is true in every sense, and is not deceptive in any way. In contrast, unethical communication can include falsehoods and misleading information (or can withhold important information). Some examples of unethical communication include:[38]

> **Plagiarism. Plagiarism** is presenting someone else's words or other creative product as your own. Note that plagiarism can also be illegal if it violates a **copyright**, which is a form of legal protection for the expression of creative ideas.[39]

> **Selective misquoting.** Deliberately omitting damaging or unflattering comments to paint a better picture of you or your company is unethical if the picture you create is untruthful.

> **Misrepresenting numbers.** Statistics and other data can be unethically manipulated by increasing or decreasing numbers, exaggerating, altering statistics, or omitting numeric data.

> **Distorting visuals.** Images can also be manipulated in unethical ways, such as making a product seem bigger than it really is or changing the scale of graphs and charts to exaggerate or conceal differences.

An ethical message is accurate and sincere. It avoids language and images that manipulate, discriminate, or exaggerate. On the surface, such ethical practices appear fairly easy to recognize, but deciding what is ethical can be a considerable challenge in complex business situations.

Distinguishing an Ethical Dilemma from an Ethical Lapse

Every company has responsibilities to various groups: customers, employees, shareholders, suppliers, neighbours, the community, and the nation. Unfortunately, what's right for one group may be wrong for another.[40] Moreover, as you attempt to satisfy the needs of one group, you may be presented with an option that seems right on the surface but somehow feels wrong. When people must choose between conflicting loyalties and weigh difficult trade-offs, they face a dilemma.

An **ethical dilemma** involves choosing among alternatives that aren't clear-cut. Perhaps two conflicting alternatives are both ethical and valid, or perhaps the alternatives lie somewhere in the vast grey area between right and wrong. Suppose you are president of a company that's losing money. You have a duty to your shareholders to reduce your losses and to your employees to be fair and honest. After looking at various options, you conclude that you will have to lay off 500 people immediately. You suspect you may have to lay off another 100 people later on, but right now you need those 100 workers to finish a project. What do you tell them? If you confess that their jobs are insecure, many of them may quit just when you need them most. However, if you tell them that the future is promising, you'll be stretching the truth.

> Conflicting priorities and the vast grey areas between right and wrong create ethical dilemmas for an organization's communicators.

Unlike a dilemma, an **ethical lapse** is making a clearly unethical (and frequently illegal) choice. Suppose you have decided to change jobs and have discreetly landed an interview with your boss's largest competitor. You get along great with the interviewer, who is impressed enough with you to offer you a position on the spot. The new position is a step up from your current job, and the pay is much more than what you're getting now. You accept the job and agree to start next month. Then, as you're shaking hands with the interviewer, she asks you to bring along profiles of your current company's 10 largest customers when you report for work. Do you comply with her request? How do you decide between what's ethical and what is not?

> An ethical lapse is knowing that something is wrong and doing it anyway.

Ensuring Ethical Communication

Ensuring ethical business communications requires three elements: ethical individuals, ethical company leadership, and the appropriate policies and structures to support employees' efforts to make ethical choices.[41] Moreover, these three elements need to work in harmony. If employees see company executives making unethical decisions and flouting company guidelines, they might conclude that the guidelines are meaningless and emulate their bosses' unethical behaviour.

Employers have a responsibility to establish clear guidelines for ethical behaviour, including business communication. Many companies establish an explicit ethics policy by using a written **code of ethics** to help employees determine what is acceptable. A code is often part of a larger program of employee training and communication channels that allow employees to ask

> Responsible employers establish clear ethical guidelines for their employees to follow.

Code of Business Conduct

☞ Promptly report violations of the Code or non-compliance with applicable laws, regulations, or company policies or procedures.

2.   Policy details

A. OUR PRINCIPLES OF BUSINESS CONDUCT

2.1   Personal Integrity

We and our shareholders, customers, and suppliers expect honest and ethical conduct in all aspects of our business. Helping the Company meet this commitment is an essential part of our job. It's also a matter of personal integrity. Among other things, personal integrity means performing our job fully and competently in order to meet the Company's business needs and ensure customer satisfaction. It also means being accountable for our behaviour and supporting the shared goal of all of us to uphold the values, principles, and standards upon which our Company's reputation rests.

In addition, the Officers and the Boards of Directors of each of BCE, Inc. and Bell Canada support a culture in which ethical business conduct is recognized, valued, and exemplified. The members of the Boards of Directors, and persons who hold a position of Vice-President or above, certify annually that they have reviewed and follow the Code and encourage and promote the setting of standards needed to ensure that this objective is met each and every day. A copy of these certifications can be found at the end of the Code (See Attachments 1A and 1B).

2.2   Our Responsibility

Many aspects of our business are governed by particular laws, and compliance with such laws is basic to ethical conduct. Ethical behaviour, however, goes beyond compliance with the law. It involves thinking through the possible impact of our decisions on all interested parties – customers, employees and their unions, pensioners, the communities in which we live and work, suppliers, alliance partners, investors, government, and shareholders – even when not required to do so from a legal or regulatory point of view.

Although the Code lays out the fundamental principles of ethical and legal conduct, it cannot anticipate every ethical dilemma or situation we may encounter as we perform our jobs. This would be impossible given that the communications industry is evolving so rapidly and so unpredictably.

Consequently, we may often find ourselves caught in a situation or facing an ethical problem not explicitly covered in the Code. In this case, we must rely on our internal sense of what is right – our moral compass – to guide us in making the right decision.

When faced with a difficult or unclear situation, it may help to ask the following questions such as:

- how would I feel if, rather than initiating this action, I was on the receiving end?
- how would my customer react if he/she knew I was breaking the rules or distorting the facts to make a sale?

6 of 51

Like many Canadian corporations, such as Bank of Montreal, Gildan, and Suncor, BCE posts its code of ethical behaviour on its website. Why does an organization do so? Examine several corporate codes of ethics. What similarities do you find among them? What differences do you see?

questions and report instances of questionable ethics. For example, at Bell Canada Enterprises (BCE), employees can seek advice on matters regarding ethical behaviour and report illegal or unethical behaviour using the Business Conduct Help Line, which is available on a 24/7 basis.[42]

Whether or not formal guidelines are in place, every employee has the responsibility to communicate in an ethical manner. Although ethics can be a murky place to navigate, a good place to start is with the law. Many companies have lawyers on staff or outside attorneys that you can call on for advice when necessary. To ensure ongoing compliance with their codes of ethics, many companies also conduct **ethics audits** to monitor ethical progress and to point out any weaknesses that need to be addressed.

However, the law doesn't cover every situation that you'll encounter in your career. In the absence of clear legal boundaries or ethical guidelines, ask yourself the following questions about your business communications:[43]

> Have you defined the situation fairly and accurately?
> What is your intention in communicating this message?
> What impact will this message have on the people who receive it or who might be affected by it?
> Will the message achieve the greatest possible good while doing the least possible harm?
> Will the assumptions you've made change over time? That is, will a decision that seems ethical now seem unethical in the future?
> Are you comfortable with your decision? Would you be embarrassed if it were printed in tomorrow's newspaper or spread across the internet?

If all else fails, think about a person whom you admire and ask yourself what he or she would think of your decision. If you wouldn't be proud to describe your choice to someone you admire and respect—someone whose opinion of you matters—that's a strong signal that you might be making a poor ethical choice.

If you can't decide whether a choice is ethical, picture yourself explaining it to someone whose opinion you value.

Applying What You've Learned

At the beginning of this chapter, you met Suncor's Sue Lee in "On the Job: Communicating at Suncor Energy Inc." Lee is just one of the many real business professionals you'll meet throughout this book—people who successfully handle the same communication challenges you'll face on the job. Every chapter opens with a similar slice-of-life vignette. As you read through each chapter, think about the person and the company highlighted in the vignette. Become familiar with the various concepts presented in the chapter, and imagine how they might apply to the featured scenario.

At the end of each chapter, you'll take part in an innovative simulation called "On the Job: Performing Communication Tasks." You'll play the role of a person working in the highlighted organization, and you'll face a situation you could encounter on the job. You will be presented with communication scenarios, each with several possible courses of action. It's up to you to recommend one course of action from the simulations as homework, as teamwork, as material for in-class discussion, or in a host of other ways. These scenarios let you explore various communication ideas and apply the concepts and techniques from the chapter.

Now you're ready for the first simulation (page 29). As you tackle each problem, think about the material you covered in this chapter and consider your own experience as a communicator. You'll probably be surprised to discover how much you already know about business communication.

Summary of Learning Objectives

Review the key stops on your "roadmap."

1 **Explain why effective communication is important to your success in today's business environment.** Your ability to communicate can help your company become more efficient, innovative, and responsive. As your career advances and you achieve positions of greater responsibility, your communication skills will gain in importance because you will communicate about increasingly important matters to larger and larger audiences. Employers will recognize your communication abilities and value you as an employee.

2 **Identify eight communication skills that successful employers expect from their employees.** Employers expect their employees to organize ideas and information effectively, express and present ideas coherently and persuasively, and listen carefully for the true meaning behind words. They also want employees to communicate well in a diverse workplace, use communication technologies, and follow the standards of correct writing and speaking. Finally, employers expect their workers to practise courtesy and respect and communicate in an ethical manner.

3 **Describe the five characteristics of effective business communication.** Effective business messages supply information that helps others complete tasks, provide factual support for opinions, and clarify and summarize information to help audiences comprehend documents quickly. Good business writing also states the desired action, so the reader knows how to respond, and persuades audiences by showing benefits.

4 **Discuss six factors that make business communication unique.** Business communication is unique because of teamwork: businesses increasingly rely on teams and expect each member to communicate effectively in a team. Another factor is the evolution toward flatter organizational structures: these structures reduce the number of layers of management, giving employees more responsibility for communication. In addition, the factor of globalization and diversity creates opportunities to learn more about markets and to communicate more effectively with various market segments. For its part, technology provides workers with the challenges of using it intelligently and keeping up to date with innovations. The increasing value placed on business information has created the need to understand evolving regulations and customer needs. Finally, the factor of barriers to effective communication, such as information overload and language differences, can affect the success of message transmission and reception.

5 **Describe five strategies for communicating more effectively on the job.** One method is to reduce distractions caused by technology, sounds, and emotional concerns. Successful communicators also focus on the needs of their audience and adapt to their communication styles. Effective communicators also practise their communication skills at every opportunity, provide constructive feedback, and learn the norms of business etiquette in a variety of situations.

6 **Explain three strategies for using communication technology successfully.** Employees who use communication technology effectively adapt it to their own and their audiences' needs and realize that it does not necessarily supplant traditional communication forms. Employees should also be familiar with the strengths of modern technology as well as its weaknesses. Finally, employees who use communication technology wisely know that face-to-face communication adds the human touch, which is essential for professional relationships.

7 **Discuss the importance of ethics in business communication and differentiate between an ethical dilemma and an ethical lapse.** Ethics are crucial to effective business communication because they can support or damage a company's reputation in the eyes of its stakeholders. Ethical communicators do not deceive their audiences through language, images, and behaviours that manipulate, discriminate, or exaggerate. An ethical dilemma involves choosing between two or more alternatives that are neither clearly ethical nor clearly unethical, such as alternatives that are all ethical but conflicting or alternatives that lie somewhere in the grey areas between right and wrong. An ethical lapse involves choosing an alternative that is clearly unethical or illegal, perhaps placing your own desire or ambition above the welfare of others.

PEARSON
mycanadianbuscommlab

MyCanadianBusCommLab is a website that offers you videos and interactive exercises to improve your communication skills.

Visit www.mycanadianbuscommlab.ca for everything you need to help you succeed in the job you've always wanted! Tools and resources include the following:
- Composing Space and Writer's Toolkit
- Document Makeovers
- Video Case Studies
- Grammar Exercises—and much more!

On the Job PERFORMING COMMUNICATION TASKS AT SUNCOR ENERGY INC. — Join the company and complete your tasks.

As Suncor's senior vice-president of Human Resources and Communications, Sue Lee plays a vital role in keeping communication flowing and ensuring that everyone receives necessary information by helping employees and outside stakeholders overcome potential barriers to effective communication. To assist her with a growing workload of internal and external communication tasks, she has recently hired you as an assistant with special responsibilities for communication. Use your knowledge of communication to choose the best response for each situation. Be prepared to explain why your choice is best.

1 The company's medical insurance plan for the next year contains substantial changes from this year's plan. To maintain Suncor's open communication climate, how should this information be distributed to employees?

   a Have Sue Lee, senior vice-president of Human Resources and Communications, present the information at an all-staff meeting, so employees can give their reactions to the changes.

   b Detail the changes in a single email message sent to all staff.

   c Post the details on the corporate intranet site.

   d Describe the changes in a benefits statement sent to each employee.

2 A manager has asked for your help. Her team is responsible for shipping replacement parts to crews working on the oil rigs in Fort McMurray. Some team members are not filling orders in a timely manner, and she confides that they are not giving their best to the job. As one way

of improving performance, she wants to send a memo to everyone in the department, and she's asked you to recommend an approach.

Which approaches would be the most ethical and effective?

   a Tell employees that the team's performance is not as good as it could be, and ask for ideas on how to improve the situation.

   b Explain that you'll have to fire the next person you see giving less than 100 percent (even though you know company policy prevents you from actually doing so).

   c Ask employees to monitor one another and report problems to their team leader.

   d Tell all employees that if team performance does not improve, wages will be reduced and evaluations will not be positive.

3 A rumour begins circulating that oil production will be reduced and many workers in the oil sands will be laid off. The rumour is false. What is the first action you should take?

   a Put a notice on the company intranet denying the rumour.

   b Publish a denial in a memo asking all managers to tell their employees that the rumour is false.

   c Schedule a meeting with all employees about working at the oil sands. At the meeting have the company CEO explain the facts and publicly state that the rumour is false.

   d Ignore the rumour. Like all false rumours it will eventually die out.

Test Your Knowledge — Review the chapter through questions.

1 Define *stakeholders* and explain why they are important.

2 How is globalization changing communication in the workplace?

3 How does effective communication help employees interact with customers and colleagues in this age of technology?

4 How does internal communication differ from external communication?

5 In what directions can information travel within an organization's formal hierarchy?

6 What is the grapevine? Why should managers know how it works?

7 In which of the seven phases of the communication process do messages get encoded and decoded?

8 Why should communicators take an audience-centred approach to communication?

9 How does corporate culture affect the communication climate within an organization?

10 Define *ethics*. Explain the ethical responsibilities of communicators.

Apply Your Knowledge

Questions that test your critical thinking skills.

1 Why do you think good communication in an organization improves employees' attitudes and performance? Explain.

2 Under what circumstances might you want to limit the feedback you receive from an audience of readers or listeners? Explain.

3 Would written or spoken messages be more susceptible to noise? Why?

4 As a manager, how can you impress on your employees the importance of including both negative and positive information in messages?

5 **Ethical Choices** Because of your excellent communication skills, your supervisor always asks you to write his reports for him. When you overhear the CEO complimenting him on his logical organization and clear writing style, he responds as if he'd written all those reports himself. What kind of ethical choice does this represent? What can you do in this situation? Briefly explain your solution and your reasoning.

Running Cases

Meet, learn, and, grow with Noreen and Kwong on the job.

Watch, learn, and work with the interactive videos of Perils of Pauline.

● Watch on **mycanadianbuscommlab**

> CASE 1 Noreen

Noreen is working toward a Bachelor of Business Administration (BBA) and takes her studies via distance education through a Canadian university. She works full-time at Petro-Go, an international fuel company, in one of their call centres as a customer service representative (CSR). She is the team leader for a group of CSRs located in the "Go Points" program department. Her future career goal is to complete her BBA and obtain a senior management position within a large international firm.

Noreen is on the social committee, and her manager asks her to organize a potluck lunch for 40 employees in her call centre department.

QUESTIONS

a) Suggest an appropriate type of communication (e.g., casual conversation, formal letter, meeting, memo, email, bulletin board notice) and briefly explain your choice.

b) Is this a horizontal flow or a downward flow of communication? Formal or informal?

c) What must Noreen consider when planning this event?

d) What must Noreen consider when communicating the plans?

e) What communication barriers might she encounter and how should she overcome those barriers?

YOUR TASK

Assume all the plans are arranged and now Noreen just needs to notify the guests. Write a memo that she will distribute to the 40 employees in her department. Ensure the necessary details are in the invitation memo. Exchange memos with another student and ask for constructive criticism on how to improve your communication.

> CASE 2 Kwong

Kwong, a new Canadian, is enrolled in a three-year Accounting co-op diploma program at a local college. He is currently in his third semester and will be placed in a co-op position next term. There he will apply what he has learned in his studies and at the same time gain valuable work experience. His future career goal is to complete the CGA (Certified General Accountant) requirements and then open his own accounting firm.

Kwong will be interviewed by a prospective co-op employer. He needs to be successful in the interview to obtain the placement.

QUESTIONS

a) What research should Kwong do before the interview?

b) Which employability skills do you think Kwong may currently possess and which skills may he still need to develop? (Refer to Figure 1–2.)

c) How will he emphasize his strong skills and de-emphasize his weaker skills during the interview?

d) What ethical choices may Kwong have to make?

e) What communication barriers may Kwong be faced with (both oral and written)? Give a specific example.

YOUR TASK

Make a list of the employability skills you believe you possess. Make a list of the employability skills you believe you need to improve. For assistance, consult the charts in the *Essential Skills Passport* available at www.hrsdc.gc.ca/eng/workplaceskills/essential_skills/pdfs/learning/passport.pdf.

Practise Your Knowledge

Read the following document and then (1) analyze the strengths and weaknesses of each sentence and (2) revise the document, so it follows this chapter's guidelines.

It has come to my attention that many of you are lying on your time cards. If you come in late, you should not put 8:00 A.M. on your card. If you take a long lunch, you should not put 1:00 P.M. on your time card. I will not stand for this type of cheating. I simply have no choice but to institute a time-clock system. Beginning next Monday, all employees will have to punch in and punch out whenever they come and go from the work area.

The time clock will be right by the entrance to each work area, so you will have no excuse for not punching in. Anyone who is late for work or late coming back from lunch more than three times will have to answer to me. I don't care if you had to take a nap or if you girls had to shop. This is a place of business, and we do not want to be taken advantage of by slackers who are cheaters to boot.

It is too bad that a few bad apples always have to spoil things for everyone.

Exercises

1.1 Internal Communication: Planning the Flow
For these tasks, identify the necessary direction of communication (downward, upward, horizontal), suggest an appropriate type of communication (casual conversation, formal interview, meeting, workshop, Web conference, instant message, newsletter, memo, bulletin board notice, and so on), and briefly explain your suggestion.
  a. As personnel manager, you want to announce details about this year's company picnic.
  b. As director of internal communication, you want to convince top management of the need for a company newsletter.
  c. As production manager, you want to make sure that both the sales manager and the finance manager receive your scheduling estimates.
  d. As marketing manager, you want to help employees understand the company's goals and its attitudes toward workers.

1.2 Communication Networks: Formal or Informal?
An old school friend suddenly phoned you to say, "I had to call you. You'd better keep this quiet, but when I heard my company was buying you guys out, I was shocked. I had no idea that a company as large as yours could sink so fast. Your group must be in pretty bad shape over there!" Your stomach suddenly turned queasy, and you felt a chill go up your spine. You'd heard nothing about any buyout, and before you could even get your friend off the phone, you were wondering what you should do. Choose one course of action and briefly explain your choice.
  a. Contact your CEO directly and relate what you've heard.
  b. Ask co-workers whether they've heard anything about a buyout.
  c. Discuss the phone call confidentially with your immediate supervisor.
  d. Keep quiet (there's nothing you can do about the situation anyway).

1.3 Ethical Choices: Business Dilemmas
In less than a page, explain why you think each is or is not ethical.
  a. Keeping quiet about a possible environmental hazard you've just discovered in your company's processing plant
  b. Overselling the benefits of instant messaging to your company's management; they never seem to understand the benefits of technology, so you believe that stretching the truth just a bit is the only way to convince them to make the right choice
  c. Telling an associate and close friend that she'd better pay more attention to her work responsibilities or management will fire her
  d. Recommending the purchase of unnecessary equipment to use up your allocated funds before the end of the fiscal year, so your budget won't be cut next year

1.4 The Changing Workplace: Personal Expression at Work
Blogging has become a popular way for employees to communicate with customers and other parties outside the company. In some cases, employee blogs have been beneficial for both companies and their customers by providing helpful information and "putting a human face" on formal and imposing corporations. However, in some other cases, employees have been fired for posting information that their employers said was inappropriate. One particular area of concern is criticism of the company or individual managers. Should employees be allowed to criticize their employers in a public forum such as a blog? In a brief email message, argue for or against company policies that prohibit any critical information in employee blogs.

1.5 Internet: Codes of Ethics

Industry Canada prepares reports for consumers, researchers, and businesspeople. Visit Industry Canada's website and review their report Voluntary Codes: A Guide for Their Development and Use at http://strategis.ic.gc.ca/epic/site/oca-bc.nsf/vwapj/volcodes.pdf/$FILE/volcodes.pdf. Read the section titled Features of Voluntary Codes. Next, find a Canadian corporation that has a code of ethics posted on the internet (other than BCE). Does the code of ethics you found follow the features? Write two or three paragraphs describing the extent to which the code you found follows the features, and describe how it can be improved. Submit your essay to your instructor.

1.6 Communication Process: Know Your Audience

Top management has asked you to speak at an upcoming executive meeting to present your arguments for a more open communication climate. Which of the following would be most important for you to know about your audience before giving your presentation? Briefly explain your choice.

a. How many top managers will be attending
b. What management style members of your audience prefer
c. How firmly these managers are set in their ways

1.7 Ethical Choices: The Go-Between

Your boss often uses you as a sounding board for her ideas. Now she seems to want you to act as an unofficial messenger, passing her ideas along to the staff without mentioning her involvement and informing her of what staff members say without telling them you're going to repeat their responses. What questions should you ask yourself as you consider the ethical implications of this situation? Write a short paragraph explaining the ethical choice you will make in this situation.

1.8 Communication Etiquette: Training for All?

Potential customers frequently visit your production facility before making purchase decisions. You and the people who report to you in the sales department have received extensive training in etiquette issues because you deal with high-profile clients so frequently. However, the rest of the workforce has not received such training, and you worry that someone might inadvertently say or do something that would offend a potential customer. In a two-paragraph email, explain to the general manager why you think anyone who might come in contact with customers should receive basic etiquette training.

1.9 Teamwork: Know Your Audience

Your boss has asked your work group to research and report on corporate childcare facilities. Of course, you'll want to know who (besides your boss) will read your report. Working with two team members, list four or five other factors you'll want to know about the situation and about your audience before starting your research. Briefly explain why the items on your list are important.

1.10 Communication Process: Analyzing Miscommunication

Use the seven phases of the communication process to analyze a miscommunication you've recently had with a co-worker, supervisor, classmate, teacher, friend, or family member. What idea were you trying to share? How did you encode and transmit it? Did the receiver get the message?

Did the receiver correctly decode the message? How do you know? Based on your analysis, identify and explain the barriers that prevented your successful communication in this instance.

1.11 Ethical Choices: Withholding Information

You've been given the critical assignment of selecting the site for your company's new plant. After months of negotiations with landowners, numerous cost calculations, and investments in ecological, social, and community impact studies, you are about to recommend building the new plant on the Lansing River site. Now, just 15 minutes before your big presentation to top management, you discover a possible mistake in your calculations: site-purchase costs appear to be $50 000 more than you calculated, nearly 10 percent over budget. You don't have time to recheck all your figures, so you're tempted to just go ahead with your recommendation and ignore any discrepancies. You're worried that management won't approve this purchase if you can't present a clean, unqualified solution. You also know that many projects run over their original estimates, so you can probably work the extra cost into the budget later. On your way to the meeting room, you make your final decision. In a few paragraphs, explain the decision you made.

1.12 Communication Etiquette: Different Styles

In group meetings, some of your colleagues have a habit of interrupting and arguing with the speaker, taking credit for ideas that aren't theirs, and criticizing ideas they don't agree with. You're the newest person in the group and not sure if this is accepted behaviour in this company, but it concerns you both personally and professionally. Should you adopt their behaviour or stick with your own communication style, even though your quiet, respectful approach might limit your career potential? In two paragraphs, explain the pros and cons of both approaches.

Communicating in Teams and Mastering Listening and Nonverbal Communication

LEARNING OBJECTIVES

After studying this chapter, you will be able to

1. Explain the advantages and disadvantages of working in teams
2. Outline an effective approach to team communication
3. Explain how wiki technology can help teams collaborate
4. Explain how group dynamics can affect team effectiveness
5. Describe how meeting technologies can help participants communicate more successfully
6. Describe the listening process, and explain how good listeners overcome barriers at each stage of the process
7. Clarify the importance of nonverbal communication and list six categories of nonverbal expression

ON THE JOB

Communicating at Royal Bank Financial Group
TAKING CHARGE OF BUSINESS THROUGH TEAMWORK

www.royalbank.com

Guided by the principle of "working together to succeed," Royal Bank Financial Group is a recognized leader in human resources management, earning a place in magazine publisher Mediacorp Canada Inc.'s survey of Canada's Top 100 Employers for 2009. With 70 000 employees serving more than 15 million personal, business, and public sector clients, Royal Bank of Canada counts on teamwork to keep staff productive and satisfied.

Team skills are essential for a job at Royal Bank. An entry-level sales and service representative position seeks "teamwork, cooperation skills, and listening skills." A business analyst/developer must "effectively communicate and build rapport with team members, stakeholders, and business partners" and "facilitate small- to medium-sized group meetings." A technical systems analyst "facilitates small- to large-group meetings for technical design, decision making, problem solving, and task implementation" among other duties. Says Barbara Stymiest, Royal Bank's chief operating officer, "When you think of broader enterprise strategy, you have to think across the entire organization."

Teamwork is an essential component of "flex-work," enjoyed by some 30 percent of Royal Bank employees who work in the 1200 plus Royal Bank branches across

With over 70 000 employees in Canada, the U.S., and more than 30 countries worldwide, Royal Bank Financial Group was recognized as a top corporate employer in Mediacorp Canada Inc.'s 2009 Survey of Canada's Top 100 Employers. Royal Bank helps its employees succeed in their jobs by encouraging teamwork and free-flowing communication throughout the organization.

Canada or in one of 30 global offices. Flex-work is characterized by reduced or varied work hours, job sharing, a modified workweek, or working off-site, from home or a satellite office. For example, four employees at Royal Bank's main Halifax branch co-ordinated schedules, giving each person a long weekend every two weeks. By learning each other's duties and working the occasional longer day, someone is always available to serve clients. Electronic tools play their part, with blogs, intranets, e-newsletters, and other means easing the flow of communication. Executives believe teamwork helps employees perform better, have more energy, and maintain a better life outside their jobs when they have more control over their time.

Teams are an essential part of Royal Bank's culture. If you were a Royal Bank manager, how would you develop effective teams? What would you need to know about getting team members to collaborate? And how could you help your team members improve their listening and meeting skills?[1]

Improving Your Performance in Teams

Your job goal may not be at a bank or other financial institution, but chances are quite good that your career will involve working in teams and other group situations that will put your communication skills to the test. A **team** is a unit of two or more people who share a mission and the responsibility for working to achieve their goal.[2] Companies can create *formal teams* that become part of the organization's structure, or they can establish *informal teams* that aren't part of the formal organization but are created to solve particular problems, work on specific activities, or encourage employee participation.

Whether the task is to write reports, give oral presentations, produce a podcast or a product, solve a problem, or investigate an opportunity, companies look for people who can successfully interact in teams and collaborate with others. Why?

One reason is performance. A study of 232 organizations across 16 countries and more than eight industries revealed that organizations working in teams experience the highest improvement in performance.[3] Another reason is creativity. Teams encourage creativity in workers through **participative management**, involving employees in the company's decision making. At Ryder Integrated Logistics of Mississauga, Ontario, for example, virtual teams of people geographically distant but communicating electronically have replaced the "up–down" hierarchy for serving clients. Doug Harrison, vice-president and managing director, says with the team approach employees "are able to react more quickly to our customers' needs. We're able to get much quicker decision making because everybody's working together as a team."[4]

Team members have a shared mission and are collectively responsible for their work.

Types of Teams

The type, structure, and composition of individual teams vary within an organization. Some teams stay together for years; others may meet their goals in just a few days and then disband.

Three popular types of informal teams are cross-functional teams, quality assurance teams, and task forces.

Cross-functional teams bring together people from different areas—information technology, sales, and manufacturing, for example—to create a new product, computer system, or long-term organizational strategy or to combine their talents on some other assignment. Sometimes as many as eight or more specialties may join a cross-functional team.[5] At Lavalife, a creator of online and mobile dating and networking communities, cross-functional teams comprising human resources, legal, financial, and information technology experts work on complex projects, such as combining its North American call centres.[6]

Quality assurance teams ensure that products and services meet prescribed standards. Typically composed of specialists in a single field, these groups may test automobiles to confirm that they run problem-free before leaving the factory floor or test food products to ensure that they meet safety standards.

Task forces are informal teams that assemble to resolve specific issues and disband once their goal has been accomplished. Similar to cross-functional teams, task forces often include representatives from many departments, so that those who have a stake in the outcome are allowed to provide input. One function of task forces is finding areas where savings can be made. For example, a hospital may bring together people from different departments, such as surgery, nursing, finance, and administration, to find ways to reduce supply costs.[7]

Committees are formal teams that usually have a long lifespan and can become a permanent part of the organizational structure. Committees typically deal with regularly recurring tasks. For example, an executive committee may meet monthly to plan strategy and review results, and a grievance committee may be formed as a permanent resource for handling employee complaints and concerns.

As Chapter 1 points out, being a team member often requires taking on additional responsibility for communication: sharing information with team members, listening carefully to their input, and crafting messages that reflect the team's collective ideas and opinions. Increasingly, this communication takes place long distance, with **virtual teams** connecting from remote locations using a variety of meeting technologies (see "Using Meeting Technologies" on page 48).

Effective communication is essential to every aspect of team performance.

Advantages and Disadvantages of Teams

Teams can play a vital role in helping an organization reach its goals, but they are not appropriate for every situation—and even when they are appropriate, companies need to weigh both the advantages and disadvantages of a team-based approach. A successful team can provide a number of advantages:[8]

Objective 1 Explain the advantages and disadvantages of working in teams.

> **Increased information and knowledge.** By pooling the resources of several individuals, teams have access to more information in the decision-making process.

> **Increased diversity of views.** Team members bring a variety of perspectives to the decision-making process. People have different backgrounds and experiences, which contribute to a deeper and more thorough examination of the issues the team faces. Keep in mind, however, that unless these diverse viewpoints are guided by a shared goal, the multiple perspectives can actually hamper a team's efforts.[9]

> **Increased acceptance of a solution.** Those who participate in making a decision are more likely to support the decision enthusiastically and encourage others to accept it. Because they share in the final product, they are committed to seeing it succeed.

Effective teams can pool knowledge, take advantage of diverse viewpoints, and increase acceptance of solutions the team proposes.

> **Higher performance levels.** Working in teams can unleash new amounts of creativity and energy in workers who share a sense of purpose and mutual accountability. Effective teams can be better than top-performing individuals at solving complex problems.[10] Furthermore, teams fill the individual worker's need to belong to a group, reduce employee boredom, increase feelings of dignity and self-worth, and reduce stress and tension among workers.

Although teamwork has many advantages, it also has a number of potential disadvantages. At their worst, teams are unproductive and frustrating, and they waste everyone's time. Some may actually be counterproductive, because they may arrive at bad decisions. Teams need to be aware of and work to counter the following disadvantages:

Teams need to avoid the negative impact of groupthink, hidden agendas, free riders, and excessive costs.

> **Groupthink.** Like all social structures, business teams can generate tremendous pressures to conform to accepted norms of behaviour. **Groupthink** occurs when these peer pressures cause individual team members to withhold contrary or unpopular opinions. Group members may be influenced by a dominant personality who controls the discussion, or the group may be working under a short deadline so that participants cannot explore all the dimensions of their problem. And, for some people, simply belonging to the team is more important to them than making the right decision. The result can be decisions that are worse than ones the team members might have made individually.
> **Hidden agendas.** Some team members may have a **hidden agenda**—private, counterproductive motives, such as a desire to take control of the group or to undermine someone else on the team. Each person's hidden agenda can detract from the team's effectiveness.
> **Free riders. Free riders** are team members who don't contribute their fair share to the group's activities. Perhaps these members aren't being held individually accountable for their work. Or perhaps they don't believe they'll receive adequate recognition for their individual efforts. The free-ride attitude can lead to certain tasks remaining unfulfilled and damage team morale.
> **Cost.** Another important drawback to teamwork is the high cost of coordinating group activities. Aligning schedules, arranging meetings, and coordinating individual parts of a project can consume time and money.

In many of Canada's businesses, such as Royal Bank Financial Group, employees voluntarily band together to raise funds for charitable causes. Are the dynamics of voluntary teams similar to those of management-imposed teams? How are they different?

Characteristics of Effective Teams

To be effective collaborators in a team setting, you and your colleagues should recognize that each individual brings valuable assets, knowledge, and skills to the team. Strong collaborators are willing to exchange information, examine issues, and work through conflicts that arise. They trust each other, working toward the greater good of the team and organization rather than focusing on personal agendas.[11]

The most effective teams have a clear objective and a shared sense of purpose, communicate openly and honestly, reach decisions by consensus, think creatively, and know how to resolve conflict.[12] Learning these team skills takes time and practice, so many companies now teach teamwork more frequently than any other aspect of business.[13]

In contrast, unsuccessful teamwork can waste time and money, generate lower-quality work, and frustrate both managers and employees. A lack of trust is cited as the most common reason for the failure of teams. This lack of trust can result from team members who are suspicious of one another's motives or ability to contribute.[14] Another common reason for failure is poor communication, particularly when teams operate across cultures, countries, and time zones.[15] Poor communication can also result from basic differences in conversational styles. Some people expect conversation to follow an orderly pattern in which team members wait their turns to speak. Others view conversation as more spontaneous and are comfortable with an overlapping, interactive style.[16]

Collaborative Communication

Collaborating on reports, websites, presentations, and other communication projects gives teams the opportunity to capitalize on each person's unique presentation and communication skills. In other words, you can take the collective energy and expertise of the team to create something that goes beyond what you could do otherwise.[17] However, collaborating on team messages requires special effort; the following section offers guidelines to help you write well as a team.

COLLABORATIVE WRITING GUIDELINES In any collaborative effort, it's important to recognize that team members coming from various backgrounds may have different work habits or concerns: a technical expert may focus on accuracy and scientific standards, whereas an editor might be more concerned about organization and coherence, and a manager might focus on schedules, cost, and corporate goals. In addition, team members will differ in writing styles and personality traits—two factors that can complicate the creative nature of communication.

To collaborate effectively, everyone involved must be flexible and open to other opinions, focusing on team objectives rather than on individual priorities.[18] Successful writers know that most ideas can be expressed in many ways, so they avoid the "my way is best" attitude. The following guidelines will help you collaborate more successfully on team messages:[19]

> **Select collaborators carefully.** Choose a combination of people who have the experience, information, and talent needed for each project.
> **Agree on project goals before you start.** Starting without a clear idea of where you hope to finish inevitably leads to frustration and wasted time. Chapter 4 shows you how to plan messages successfully.
> **Give your team time to bond before diving in.** Even if a virtual team doesn't have the opportunity to meet in person, spend at least some of your time online socializing, so people are more comfortable working together.
> **Clarify individual responsibilities.** Because members will depend on each other, make sure individual responsibilities are clear, including who does what and by when.
> **Establish clear processes.** Make sure everyone knows how the work will be done, including checkpoints and decisions made along the way. For example, if team members will report their progress once a week, make this expectation obvious at the beginning, so that everyone will be prepared. In business, financial success and a firm's reputation depend on meeting deadlines. Supervisors expect their teams to achieve a project's milestones as well as the final submission date. Deadline enforcement is an important part of the team process; appointing a team member to monitor progress will help the team—and the business—accomplish both short- and long-term goals.

Objective 2 Outline an effective approach to team communication.

Successful collaboration requires a number of steps, from selecting the right partners and agreeing on project goals to establishing clear processes and avoiding writing as a group.

TIPS FOR SUCCESS

" Planning is essential to almost any task a team performs. Your knowledge of another team member's strengths and weaknesses . . . allows the team to make adjustments based on past performance and the current situation."

Stephen M. Powell, President, Healthcare Team Training LLC

> **Avoid writing as a group.** The actual composition is the only part of developing team messages that usually does not benefit from group participation. Group writing is often a slow, painful process that delivers bland results. Plan, research, and outline together, but assign the actual writing to one person. If you must divide and share the writing for scheduling reasons, try to have one person do a final review pass to ensure a consistent style.
> **Make sure tools and techniques are ready and compatible across the team.** If you plan to use technology for sharing or presenting materials, test the system before work begins. (See the following section for more on collaboration technologies.)
> **Follow up along the way.** Don't assume everything is working just because you don't hear anything negative. Ask team members how they think the project is going and then fix any problems quickly, so they don't derail the team's efforts.

COLLABORATIVE WRITING TECHNOLOGIES A variety of collaboration tools exist to help teams write, including group review and commenting features in word processors, multiauthor blogs, and **content management systems** that organize and control the content for websites. For example, Google Docs (http://docs.google.com) is a popular, free online collaboration tool where users can share and edit documents with collaborators. These tools addresses specific needs, but none offers the level of direct collaboration as the wiki. A **wiki,** from the Hawaiian word for *quick,* is a website that allows anyone with access to add new material and edit existing material. A telltale sign of a wiki page is the "[EDIT]" links, as shown in Figure 2–1, the online user's manual for the Word-Press blogging system. Anyone who wants to contribute can expand and improve the instructions and advice that benefit the entire community of WordPress users.

Public wikis allow anyone to edit pages; private wikis are accessible only by permission. For instance, Yahoo! uses private wikis to facilitate communication among hundreds of team members around the world involved in creating and documenting new services.[20]

Key benefits of wikis include simple operation—writers don't need to know any of the techniques normally required to create Web content—and the freedom to post new or revised material without prior approval. This approach is quite different from a content management system, in which both the organization of the website and the *workflow* (the rules for creating, editing, reviewing, and approving content) are tightly controlled.[21] But with a wiki, if you see a way to improve a particular page or want to add a new page, you simply edit or write using your Web browser, and it's done. A content management system is a useful way to maintain consistent presentation on a company's primary public website, whereas wikis allow teams to collaborate with speed and flexibility.

Enterprise wiki systems extend the wiki concept with additional features for business use that ensure information quality and confidentiality without losing the speed and flexibility of a wiki. For instance, *access control* lets a team leader identify who is allowed to read and modify the wiki. *Change monitoring* alerts team members when significant changes or additions are made. And *rollback* allows a team to "travel back in time" to see all previous versions of pages.[22]

To use a wiki productively, keep these points in mind:[23]

> Contributors need to let go of traditional expectations of authorship, including individual recognition.
> Team members sometimes need to be encouraged to edit and improve each other's work.

Collaboration tools include multiauthor blogs, content management systems, and wikis.

Objective 3 Explain how wiki technology can help teams collaborate.

Benefits of wikis include simple operation and the ability to post new or revised material instantly, without a formal review process.

> Figure 2–1 Using a Wiki for Collaborative Communication

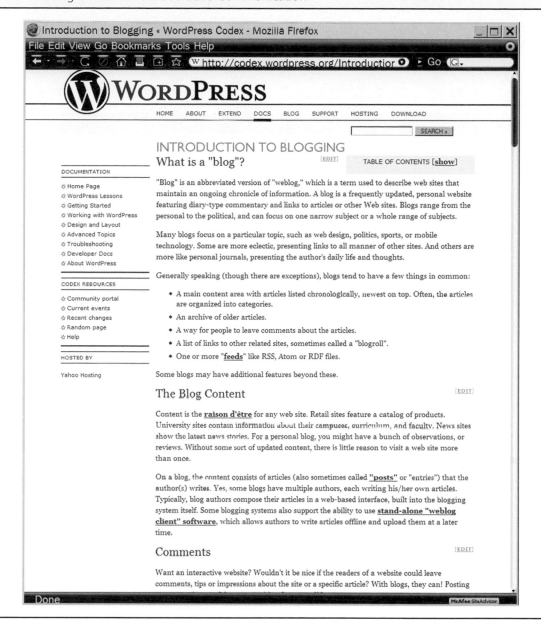

> The focus of wikis is text content; formatting and design options are usually quite limited.
> Many wikis provide both editing and commenting capabilities, and participants should use the appropriate tool for each.
> New users should take advantage of the *sandbox,* if available; this is a "safe," nonpublished section of the wiki where team members can practise editing and writing.

Of course, most teams work on a wide variety of documents and other files, from traditional word processing files to spreadsheets and so on. To facilitate collaboration on a broad scale, many teams now take advantage of **groupware**, computer-based systems that let people communicate, share files, present materials, and work on documents simultaneously. **Shared workspaces** are online "virtual offices" that give everyone on a team access to the same set of resources

Shared workspaces give team members instant access to shared resources and information.

> Figure 2–2 Shared Workspaces

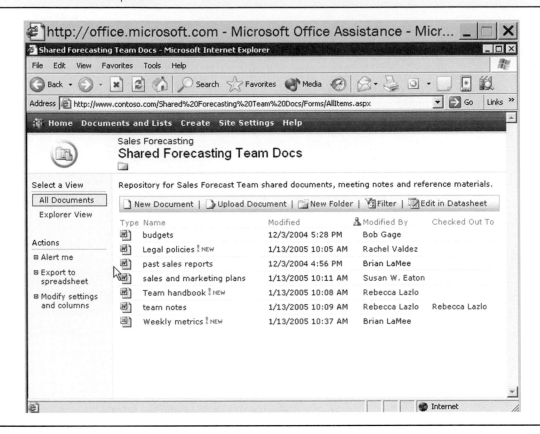

and information: databases, calendars, project plans, pertinent instant messaging and email exchanges, shared reference materials, and team-created documents (see Figure 2–2). Workspaces such as Documentum eRoom, Microsoft SharePoint, and IBM Lotus Team Workspace create a seamless environment for collaboration.

Most groupware systems also have built-in intelligence to control which team members can read, edit, and save specific files. *Revision control* goes one step further: it allows only one person at a time to check out a given file or document and records all the changes that person makes. This feature prevents two people from independently editing the same report at the same time and creating two versions of the same document.[24]

Group Dynamics

Objective 4 Explain how group dynamics can affect team effectiveness.

Group dynamics are the interactions and processes that take place in a team.

The interactions and processes that take place between the members of a team are called **group dynamics**. Some teams are more effective than others simply because the dynamics of the group facilitate member input and the resolution of differences. To keep the process moving forward, productive teams also tend to develop rules that are conducive to business. Often unstated, these rules become group **norms**—informal standards of conduct that members share and that guide member behaviour. For example, some teams may develop a casual approach to schedules, with members routinely showing up 10 or 15 minutes late for meetings, while other teams may expect strict adherence to time commitments.

> Table 2–1 Team Roles People Play

Dysfunctional		Functional
Self-Oriented Roles	Team-Maintenance Roles	Task-Facilitating Roles
Controlling: Dominating others by exhibiting superiority or authority	**Encouraging:** Drawing out other members by showing verbal and non-verbal support, praise, or agreement	**Initiating:** Getting the team started on a line of inquiry
Withdrawing: Retiring from the team either by becoming silent or by refusing to deal with a particular aspect of the team's work	**Harmonizing:** Reconciling differences among team members through mediation or by using humour to relieve tension	**Information giving or seeking:** Offering (or seeking) information relevant to questions facing the team
Attention seeking: Calling attention to oneself and demanding recognition from others	**Compromising:** Offering to yield on a point in the interest of reaching a mutually acceptable decision	**Coordinating:** Showing relationships among ideas, clarifying issues, summarizing what the team has done
Diverting: Focusing the team's discussion on topics of interest to the individual rather than on those relevant to the task		**Procedure setting:** Suggesting decision-making procedures that will move the team toward a goal

When a team has a strong identity, members observe team rules rigorously: they're upset by any deviation and feel a great deal of pressure to conform. This loyalty can be positive, giving members a strong commitment to one another and highly motivating them to see that the team succeeds. However, an overly strong identity could lead to negative conditions such as groupthink or make it difficult for new members to fit in. Group dynamics are affected by several factors: the roles that team members assume, the current phase of team development, the team's success in resolving conflict, and its success in overcoming resistance.

ASSUMING TEAM ROLES Members of a team can play various roles, which fall into three categories (see Table 2–1). Members who assume **self-oriented roles** are motivated mainly to fulfill personal needs, so they tend to be less productive than other members. Surprisingly, "dream teams" composed of multiple superstars often don't perform as well as one might expect because high-performing individuals can have trouble putting the team's needs ahead of their own.[25] In addition, highly skilled and experienced people with difficult personalities might not contribute as they could for the simple reason that other team members may avoid interacting with them.[26] Far more likely to contribute to team goals are those members who assume **team-maintenance roles** to help everyone work well together, and those who assume **task-facilitating roles** to help the team reach its goals.[27]

Roles can also change over time. For instance, in a self-directed team with no formal leader, someone may assume a task-oriented leadership role early in the team's evolution. If this person doesn't prove to be a capable leader, someone else may emerge as a leader as the group searches for more effective direction.[28]

ALLOWING FOR TEAM EVOLUTION Teams can rarely jump right to work and start making decisions; you and your fellow team members need time to establish rapport and let natural leadership roles emerge. Experts suggest that teams evolve through a number of phases on their way to becoming productive (see Figure 2–3). One common model identifies five phases:[29]

1. **Orientation.** Team members socialize, establish their roles, and begin to define their task or purpose. The leadership role can be formally assigned,

Each member of a group plays a role that affects the outcome of the group's activities.

Teams typically evolve through five phases: a common model of this growth includes orientation, conflict, brainstorming, emergence, and reinforcement.

> Figure 2–3 Phases of Group Development

1. Orientation	2. Conflict	3. Brainstorming	4. Emergence	5. Reinforcement
Team members get to know each other and establish roles	Different opinions and perspectives begin to emerge	Team members explore their options and evaluate alternatives	The team reaches a consensus on the chosen decision	Team harmony is reestablished and plans are made to put the decision into action

Personality tests, such as the excerpt below, can reveal much about a person. Do you think personality tests are a valid way of assessing a person's commitment as a team member? Check out the Myers-Briggs personality types at www.myersbriggs.org/my-mbti-personality-type/mbti-basics/. What type are you?

6. You tend to act impulsively rather than cautiously.

   Yes ❑   No ❑

7. You prefer quiet music to loud music.

   Yes ❑   No ❑

8. At parties you enjoy meeting people you don't know.

   Yes ❑   No ❑

9. You like to check how things are progressing.

   Yes ❑   No ❑

10. You feel wasting time is sometimes a good thing.

    Yes ❑   No ❑

11. You avoid being restricted by obligations.

    Yes ❑   No ❑

or it can be assumed informally by a team member as the group evolves. Establishing a "team operating agreement" that sets expectations for online meetings, communication processes, and decision making can help teams overcome the disadvantages of distance.[30]

2. **Conflict.** Team members begin to discuss their positions and become more assertive in establishing their roles. If you and the other members have been carefully selected to represent a variety of viewpoints and expertise, disagreements are a natural part of this phase. Conflict is a positive force because it helps the group to clarify both the ideas and the processes for reaching their decisions. Conflict also works against the danger of groupthink.[31]

3. **Brainstorming.** Team members air all the options and discuss the pros and cons fully. At the end of this phase, members begin to settle on a single solution to the problem. It's important to avoid judging ideas during brainstorming, so people feel free to contribute all their thoughts, rather than limiting them to ones they believe will win approval. Note that while group brainstorming remains a highly popular activity in today's companies, it may not always be the most productive way to generate new ideas. Some research indicates that having people brainstorm individually and then bring their ideas to a group meeting is more successful.[32]

4. **Emergence.** Team members reach a decision. Consensus is reached when the team finds a solution that is acceptable enough for all members to support (even if they have reservations). Consensus happens only after all members have had an opportunity to communicate their positions and feel that they have been listened to.

5. **Reinforcement.** The team clarifies and summarizes the agreed-upon solution. Members receive their assignments for carrying out the group's decision, and they make arrangements for following up on those assignments.

You may also hear the process defined as *forming*, *storming*, *norming*, *performing*, and *adjourning*, the phases identified by researcher Bruce Tuckman when he proposed one of the earliest models of group development.[33] Note that stages are a general framework for team development. Some teams may move forward and backward through several stages before they become productive, and other teams may be productive right away, even while some or all members are in a state of conflict.[34]

RESOLVING CONFLICT Conflict is a natural part of any team experience, but conflict isn't necessarily bad. When handled poorly, conflict can lead to complete failure of a group's efforts. However, the right approach to conflict can push the team to better performance.

Conflict can arise for any number of reasons. Team members may believe that they need to compete for money, information, or other resources. Or members may disagree about who is responsible for a specific task; this disagreement is usually the result of poorly defined responsibilities and job boundaries. Various members can also bring ideas that are equally good but incompatible, such as two different solutions to a given problem. Also, poor communication can lead to misunderstandings about other team members, and intentionally withholding information can undermine trust. Basic differences in values, attitudes, and personalities may lead to arguments. Power struggles may result when one member questions the authority of another or when people or teams with limited authority attempt to increase their power or exert more influence. Conflict can also arise because individuals or teams are pursuing different goals.[35]

Conflict can be both constructive and destructive to a team's effectiveness. Conflict is constructive if it forces important issues into the open, increases the involvement of team

Conflict is an inevitable part of working in teams, but an effective team knows how to keep destructive conflict from distracting the team from its objectives. How have you managed team conflict when preparing assignments with other students? In your opinion, what is the most important factor to lessen conflict?

members, and generates creative ideas for the solution to a problem. Constructive conflict can prod teams to higher performance, in fact. Teamwork isn't necessarily about happiness and harmony; even teams that have some interpersonal friction can excel with effective leadership and team players committed to strong results. As teamwork experts Andy Boynton and Bill Fischer put it, "Virtuoso teams are not about getting polite results."[36]

In contrast, conflict is destructive if it diverts energy from more important issues, destroys the morale, or polarizes or divides the team.[37] Destructive conflict can lead to win–lose or lose–lose outcomes, in which one or both sides lose, to the detriment of the entire team. If you approach conflict with the idea that both sides can satisfy their goals to at least some extent (a *win–win strategy*), no one loses. However, for the win–win strategy to work, everybody must believe that (1) it's possible to find a solution that both parties can accept, (2) cooperation is better for the organization than competition, (3) the other party can be trusted, and (4) greater power or status doesn't entitle one party to impose a solution.

One of the first steps to finding a win–win solution is to consider the other party's needs. Find out what is acceptable to the other team members. Be observant; ask questions that will help you understand their needs. Search for mutually satisfactory solutions or compromises whose results are better for the team overall.[38] In many cases, the resolution process is chiefly an exchange of opinions and information that gradually leads to a mutually acceptable solution.[39]

Conflict in teams can be either constructive or destructive.

Here are seven measures that can help team members successfully resolve conflict:

1. **Proaction.** Deal with minor conflict before it becomes major conflict.
2. **Communication.** Get those directly involved in the conflict to participate in resolving it.

3. **Openness.** Get feelings out in the open before dealing with the main issues.
4. **Research.** Seek factual reasons for the problem before seeking solutions.
5. **Flexibility.** Don't let anyone lock into a position before considering other solutions.
6. **Fair play.** Don't let anyone avoid a fair solution by hiding behind the rules.
7. **Alliance.** Get opponents to fight together for a common goal instead of against each other.

When you encounter resistance or hostility, maintain your composure and address the other person's emotional needs.

OVERCOMING RESISTANCE Part of dealing with conflict is learning how to persuade others to accept your point of view. In a business situation, reason usually prevails—that is, by explaining cost savings, increase in productivity, and other benefits of your ideas, you will probably win your colleagues' agreement. However, you might meet people who are unable to give up their personal agendas for the good of the team. Or you may encounter people who react emotionally. When you face irrational resistance, remain calm and detached, so you can avoid destructive confrontations and present your position in a convincing manner:

> **Express understanding.** Most people are ashamed of reacting emotionally in business situations. Show that you sympathize. You might say, "I can understand that this change might be difficult, and if I were in your position, I might be reluctant myself." Help the other person relax and talk about his or her anxiety, so you have a chance to offer reassurance.[40]

> **Make people aware of their resistance.** When people are noncommittal and silent, they may be tuning you out without even knowing why. Continuing with your argument is futile. Deal directly with the resistance without being accusing. You might say, "You seem cool to this idea. Have I made some faulty assumptions?" Such questions force people to face and define their resistance.[41]

> **Evaluate others' objections fairly.** Don't simply repeat yourself. Focus on what the other person is expressing, both the words and the feelings. Get the person to open up, so that you can understand the basis for the resistance. Others' objections may raise legitimate points that you'll need to discuss, or they may reveal problems that you'll need to minimize.[42]

> **Hold your arguments until the other person is ready for them.** Getting your point across depends as much on the other person's frame of mind as it does on your arguments. You can't assume that a strong argument will speak for itself. By becoming more audience-centred, you will learn to address the other person's emotional needs first.

Making Your Meetings More Productive

Much of the communication you'll participate in will take place in meetings.

Meetings are a primary communication venue for today's businesses, whether held in formal conference rooms, an informal setting such as a lunchroom, or on the internet as *virtual meetings*. Well-run meetings can help solve problems, develop ideas, and identify opportunities. Much of your workplace communication will occur in small-group meetings; therefore, your ability to contribute to the company and to be recognized for those contributions will depend on your meeting participation skills.

A single, poorly run meeting can waste thousands of dollars.

Unfortunately, many meetings are unproductive. In one study, senior and middle managers reported that only 56 percent of their meetings were actually productive and that 25 percent of them could have been replaced by a phone call or a memo.[43] The three most frequently reported problems with meetings are getting off the subject, not having an agenda, and running too long.[44] You'll help your company make better use of meetings by preparing carefully, conducting meetings efficiently, and using meeting technologies wisely.

Preparing for Meetings

Careful preparation helps you avoid the two biggest meeting mistakes: (1) holding a meeting when a blog posting or other message would do the job or (2) holding a meeting without a specific goal in mind. Before you even begin preparing for a meeting, ensure it's truly necessary. Once you're sure, proceed with four preparation tasks:

1. **Identify your purpose.** Although many meetings combine purposes, most focus on one of two types. *Informational meetings* involve sharing information and perhaps coordinating action. *Decision-making meetings* involve persuasion, analysis, and problem solving. Whatever your purpose, make sure it is clear and clearly communicated to all participants.

2. **Select participants for the meeting.** With a clear purpose in mind, it's easier to identify the right participants. If the session is purely informational and one person will do most of the talking, you can invite a large group. *Webcasts* (Chapter 14) are an increasingly popular way to reach large or geographically widespread audiences. For problem-solving and decision-making meetings, invite only those people who are in a direct position to help the meeting reach its objective. The more participants, the more comments and confusion you're likely to get and the longer the meeting will take. However, ensure that you invite all the key decision makers, or your meeting will fail to satisfy its purpose.

3. **Choose the time and the facility.** For working sessions, morning meetings are usually more productive than afternoon sessions. Also, consider the seating arrangements: are rows of chairs suitable, or do you need a conference table or some other setting? Plus, give some attention to details such as room temperature, lighting, ventilation, acoustics, and refreshments; any of these seemingly minor details can make or break a meeting.

4. **Set the agenda.** The success of any meeting depends on the preparation of the participants. Distribute a carefully written agenda to participants, giving them enough time to prepare as needed. A typical agenda format (see Figure 2–4) may seem overly formal, but it will help you start on time and stay on track. A productive agenda answers three key questions:

   > What do we need to do in this meeting to accomplish our goals?
   > What issues will be of greatest importance to all participants?
   > What information must be available in order to discuss these issues?[45]

In addition to improving productivity, this level of agenda detail shows respect for participants and the other demands on their time.

To ensure a successful meeting, decide on your purpose ahead of time, select the right participants, choose the time and facility carefully, and set a clear agenda.

Leading and Participating in Meetings

Everyone in a meeting shares the responsibility for keeping the meeting productive and making it successful. If you're the designated leader of a meeting, however, you have an extra degree of responsibility and accountability. To ensure productive meetings, be sure to do the following:

> **Keep the discussion on track.** A good meeting draws out the best ideas and information the group has to offer. Good leaders occasionally guide, mediate, probe, stimulate, and summarize, but mostly they encourage participants to share. Experience will help you recognize when to push the group forward and when to step back and let people talk. If the meeting lags, ask questions to encourage participation. Conversely, there will be times when you have no choice but to cut off discussion in order to stay on schedule.

Everyone shares the responsibility for successful meetings.

> Figure 2–4 Typical Meeting Agendas

AGENDA

PLANNING COMMITTEE MEETING

Monday, October 25, 2010
10:00 A.M. to 11:00 A.M.

Executive Conference Room

		Person	Proposed Time
I.	Call to Order		
II.	Roll Call		
III.	Approval of Agenda		
IV.	Approval of Minutes from Previous Meeting		
V.	Chairperson's Report on Site Selection Progress		
VI.	Subcommittee Reports		
	a. New Markets	Alan	5 minutes
	b. New Products	Jennifer	5 minutes
	c. Finance	Craig	5 minutes
VII.	Old Business—Pricing Policy for New Products	Terry	10 minutes
VIII.	New Business		
	a. Carson and Canfield Data on New Product Sales	Sarah	10 minutes
	b. Restructuring of Product Territories Due to New Product Introductions	Edith	10 minutes
IX.	Announcements		
X.	Adjournment		

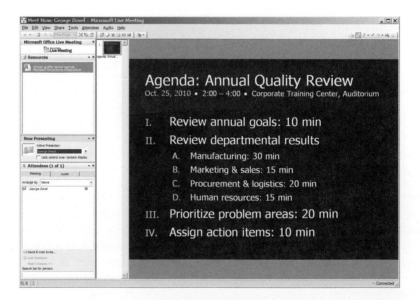

> **Follow agreed-upon rules.** Business meetings run the range from informal to extremely formal, complete with detailed rules for speaking, proposing new items to discuss, voting on proposals, and so on. The larger the meeting, the more formal you'll need to be to maintain order. Formal meetings use **parliamentary procedure**, a time-tested method for planning and running effective meetings. The best-known guide to this procedure is *Robert's Rules of Order.* Check out the online "Survival Tips on Robert's Rules of Order" at www.roberts-rules.com/index.html to help you understand and use this system.

An agenda, committee reports, and debate are all part of Canadian parliamentary procedure. Why is an established order important to both political and business meetings?

> **Encourage participation.** As the meeting begins, you'll discover that some participants are too quiet and others are too talkative. The quiet participants might be shy, they might be expressing disagreement or resistance, or they might be answering email or instant messages. Draw them out by asking for their input on issues that particularly pertain to them. For the overly talkative, simply say that time is limited and others need to be heard from.

> **Participate actively.** If you're a meeting participant, contribute to both the subject of the meeting and the smooth interaction of the group. Use your listening skills and powers of observation to size up the interpersonal dynamics of the group; then adapt your behaviour to help the group achieve its goals. Speak up if you have something useful to say, but don't monopolize the discussion.

> **Close effectively.** At the meeting's conclusion, verify that the objectives have been met; if not, arrange for follow-up work as needed. Make sure all participants agree on the outcome, and give people a chance to clear up any misunderstandings.

To review the tasks that contribute to productive meetings, refer to "Checklist: Improving Meeting Productivity."

For formal meetings, it's good practice to appoint one person to record the *minutes,* a summary of the important information presented and the decisions made during a meeting. In smaller or informal meetings, attendees often make their own notes on their copies of the agenda. In either case, a clear record of the decisions made and the people responsible for follow-up action is essential.

CHECKLIST Improving Meeting Productivity

A. Preparation
✔ Determine the meeting's objectives.
✔ Work out an agenda that will achieve your objectives.
✔ Select participants.
✔ Determine the location and reserve a room.
✔ Arrange for light refreshments, if appropriate.
✔ Determine whether the lighting, ventilation, acoustics, and temperature of the room are adequate.
✔ Determine seating needs: chairs only or table and chairs.

B. Conduct
✔ Begin and end the meeting on time.
✔ Control the meeting by following the announced agenda.

✔ Encourage full participation, and either confront or ignore those who seem to be working at cross-purposes with the group.
✔ Sum up decisions, actions, and recommendations as you move through the agenda, and restate main points at the end.

C. Follow-Up
✔ Distribute the meeting's notes or minutes on a timely basis.
✔ Take the agreed upon follow-up action.

> Figure 2–5 Typical Minutes of a Meeting

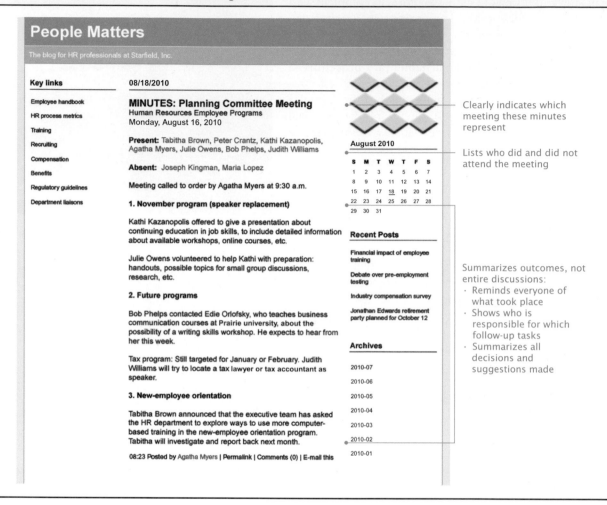

If your company doesn't have a specific format for minutes, follow the generic format shown in Figure 2–5. The specific format of the minutes is less important than making sure you record all the key information, particularly regarding responsibilities that were assigned during the meeting. Key elements include a list of those present and a list of those who were invited but didn't attend, followed by the times the meeting started and ended, all major decisions reached at the meeting, all assignments of tasks to meeting participants, and all subjects that were deferred to a later meeting. In addition, the minutes objectively summarize important discussions, noting the names of those who contributed major points. Outlines, subheadings, and lists help organize the minutes, and additional documentation (such as tables or charts submitted by meeting participants) are noted in the minutes and attached. Whichever method you use, make sure that responsibilities are clear, so all issues raised at the meeting will be addressed. Many companies today use intranets and blog postings to distribute meeting minutes.

Using Meeting Technologies

Not all teams have the luxury of meeting face to face, as employees at local Royal Bank branches do. The high cost of travel, loss of valuable work time, increased security concerns, and growing reliance on global workforces and partnerships have all stimulated a number of advances in meeting technologies. Learn how to use these tools effectively, and you'll become a more effective contributor and leader in all your meetings.

Some meeting technologies assist with local, or on-site, meetings, in which everyone is in the same room at the same time. For example, **electronic whiteboards** capture meeting notes and create files that can be printed, emailed, and archived. Electronic presentations are used extensively in business; you'll learn more about them in Chapter 14.

Most of the recent innovations in meeting technology are in support of **virtual meetings**, in which participants interact remotely. Virtual meeting technologies encompass a wide range of tools that let team members in different locations interact without the disruption, risk, and cost of travel.[46] Instant messaging (discussed in Chapter 7) and **teleconferencing**, in which three or more people are connected by phone simultaneously, are the simplest forms of virtual meetings. When you are invited to participate in a teleconference, you are typically given a special phone number and a meeting access code, which ensures the privacy of the session.

Videoconferencing combines audio communication with live video, letting team members see each other, demonstrate products, and transmit other visual information. Videoconferencing can take place either over the internet or through dedicated networks with specially built rooms in the designated locations.

The most sophisticated **Web-based meeting systems** combine the best of instant messaging, shared workspaces, and videoconferencing with other tools such as *virtual whiteboards* that let teams collaborate in real time (see Figure 2–6).

Objective 5 Describe how meeting technologies can help participants communicate more successfully.

Virtual meeting technologies connect people around the country or around the world.

> Figure 2–6 Web-Based Meetings Online workspaces provide the same productivity tools available at face-to-face meetings. What are the differences between face-to-face meetings and online workspaces? Can online workspaces always replace face-to-face meetings?

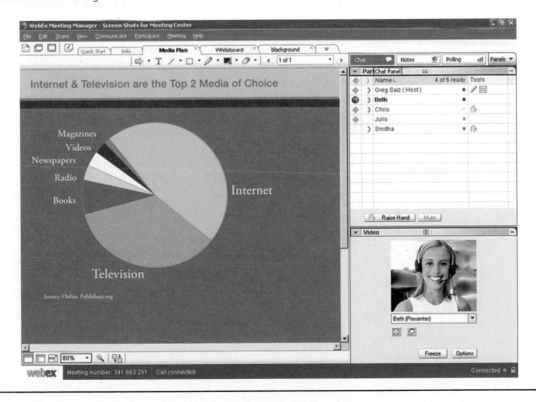

Online brainstorming is an effective choice for geographically dispersed team members. What are its benefits over face-to-face brainstorming? Its shortcomings?

Companies continue to look for innovative ways to promote communication and collaboration while reducing the cost and hassle of meetings.

Listening is one of the most important skills in the workplace.

Using such systems, attendees can log on from a desktop or laptop PC, a PDA, or even a Web-enabled mobile phone from almost anywhere in the world.

Technology continues to create intriguing opportunities for online interaction. One of the newest virtual tools is *online brainstorming*, in which companies conduct "idea campaigns" to generate new ideas from people across the organization. These range from small team meetings to huge events such as IBM's giant Innovation Jam, in which 100 000 IBM employees, family members, and customers from 160 countries were invited to brainstorm online for three days.[47] See www.collaborationjam.com for more information on this unique tool.

Companies are also beginning to experiment with virtual meetings and other communication activities in *virtual worlds* such as Second Life (www.secondlife.com). In much the same way that gamers can create and control characters (often known as *avatars*) in a multiplayer video game, professionals can create online versions of themselves to participate in meetings, training sessions, sales presentations, and other activities. For example, the computer company Sun Microsystems created the Sun Pavilion in Second Life where the virtual reality environment lets presenters transcend the limits of physical reality. For example, in one Sun Microsystems presentation, a presenter floats in front of a giant version of a computer chip. In real life, such a chip would be smaller than a postage stamp, making it impossible for the audience to see important details; in virtual reality, the enlarged chip shows its construction. This virtual arena provides a place for Sun executives and invited guests to present information and share ideas.[48]

Improving Your Listening Skills

Because listening is such a routine, everyday activity, few people think of developing their listening skills. Unfortunately, most of us aren't very good listeners. We may hear the words, but that doesn't mean we're actually listening to the message.[49] Most of us face so many distractions that we often give speakers less than our full attention. Some 80 percent of top executives say that listening is the most important skill needed to get things done in the workplace.[50]

Effective listening strengthens organizational relationships, enhances product delivery, alerts the organization to opportunities for innovation, and allows the organization to manage growing diversity both in the workforce and in the customers it serves.[51] Companies whose employees and managers listen effectively stay informed, up to date, and out of trouble. Conversely, poor listening skills can cost companies millions of dollars a year as a result of lost opportunities, legal mistakes, and other errors. Effective listening is vital to the process of building trust not only between organizations but also between individuals.[52] Throughout your own career, effective listening will give you a competitive edge, enhancing your performance and thus the influence you have within your company. At Canadian Imperial Bank of Commerce, financial advisors are evaluated for their listening skills: how effectively can they determine problems customers do not express? How well do they perceive the basic causes of a customer's concerns? At CIBC, listening skills are considered a core competency for employees.[53]

Recognizing Various Types of Listening

Understanding the nature of listening is the first step toward improving your listening skills. People listen in a variety of ways, and although how they listen is often an unconscious choice, it influences both what they hear and the meaning they extract. For example, an employee who values teamwork and relationships will naturally be inclined to look for ways to bond with a speaker. In contrast, an action-oriented listener will listen more for information related to tasks that need to be completed.

In either case, relying on a single approach to listening limits your effectiveness. A people-oriented listener might miss important information about an upcoming deadline, whereas an action-oriented listener might miss an important clue that there's a personal problem brewing between team members.[54] As you read about the major types of listening, reflect on your own inclination as a listener, and consider how learning to use several methods could make your listening more effective.

The primary goal of **content listening** is to understand and retain the speaker's message. When you're listening for content, the emphasis is on information and understanding. Ask questions to clarify the material and probe for details. Because you're not evaluating at this point, it doesn't matter whether you agree or disagree, approve or disapprove—only that you understand. Try to overlook the speaker's style and any limitations in the presentation; just focus on the information.[55] Looking for the main ideas and paraphrasing what the speaker says will help you understand and retain the information effectively.[56]

The goal of **critical listening** is to understand and evaluate the meaning of the speaker's message on several levels: the logic of the argument, the strength of the evidence, and the validity of the conclusions. You also want to analyze the implications of the message for you and your organization, the speaker's intentions and motives, and the omission of any important or relevant points. If you're skeptical, ask questions to explore the speaker's point of view and credibility. Look for bias that might colour the way the information is presented, and be careful to separate opinions from facts.[57]

The goal of **empathic listening** is to understand the speaker's feelings, needs, and wants, so that you can appreciate his or her viewpoint, regardless of whether you share that perspective. By listening in an empathic way, you help the individual vent the emotions that prevent a calm, clear-headed approach to the subject. Sometimes an upset colleague is only looking for somebody to listen, so avoid the temptation to jump in with advice unless the person specifically asks for it. Also, don't judge the speaker's feelings and don't try to tell people they shouldn't feel this or that emotion. Instead, let the speaker know that you appreciate his or her feelings and understand the situation. Once you establish that connection, you can then help the speaker move on to search for a solution.[58]

What type of listening is occurring in this picture? What listening skills must the listener apply in this situation?

To be a good listener, adapt the way you listen to suit the situation.

When you engage in empathic listening, you pay attention to feelings, needs, and wants—not just the spoken words.

Understanding the Listening Process

Listening is a far more complex process than most people think. As a consequence, most of us aren't very good at it. Given such complexity, it's no wonder most of us listen at or below a 25 percent efficiency rate, remember only about half of what's said during a 10-minute conversation, and forget half of that within 48 hours.[59] Furthermore, when questioned about material we've just heard, we're likely to get the facts mixed up.[60]

Objective 6 Describe the listening process, and explain how good listeners overcome barriers at each stage of the process.

Listening involves five steps: receiving, decoding, remembering, evaluating, and responding.

Why is such a seemingly simple activity so difficult? The answer lies in the complexity of the process. Listening follows the same sequence as the general communication process model you explored in Chapter 1 (page 11), with the added burden that it happens in real time. To listen effectively, you need to complete successfully five separate steps:[61]

1. **Receiving:** You start by physically hearing the message and acknowledging it. Physical reception can be blocked by noise, impaired hearing, or inattention. Some experts also include nonverbal messages as part of this stage, since these factors influence the listening process as well.
2. **Decoding:** Your next step is to assign meaning to sounds, which you do according to your own values, beliefs, ideas, expectations, roles, needs, and personal history.
3. **Remembering:** Before you can act on the information, you need to store it for future processing. As you learned in Chapter 1, incoming messages must first be captured in short-term memory, and then they are transferred to long-term memory for more permanent storage.
4. **Evaluating:** With the speaker's message captured, your next step is to evaluate it by applying critical thinking skills. Separate fact from opinion and evaluate the quality of the evidence. You should ask, Is the evidence credible? Why is it credible?
5. **Responding:** After you've evaluated the speaker's message, you react. If you're communicating one-on-one or in a small group, the initial response generally takes the form of verbal feedback. If you're one of many in an audience, your initial response may take the form of applause, laughter, or silence. Later on, you may act on what you have heard.

Good listeners actively overcome the barriers to successful listening.

If any one of these steps breaks down, the listening process becomes less effective or even fails entirely. As both a sender and receiver, you can reduce the failure rate by recognizing and overcoming a variety of physical and mental barriers to effective listening.

Overcoming Barriers to Effective Listening

Your mind can process information much faster than most speakers talk.

Good listeners look for ways to overcome potential barriers throughout the listening process (see Table 2–2). You are unlikely to have control over some barriers to physical reception, such as conference room acoustics, poor cell phone reception, or background music. However, you can certainly control other barriers, such as interrupting speakers or creating distractions that make it hard for others to pay attention. If you have questions for a speaker, wait until he or she has finished speaking. And don't think that you're not interrupting just because you're not talking. Rustling papers, tapping on your PDA, checking your watch, making eye contact with someone over the speaker's shoulder— these are just a few of the many nonverbal behaviours that can interrupt a speaker and hinder listening for everyone.

Selective listening is one of the most common barriers to effective listening. If your mind wanders, you often stay tuned out until you hear a word or phrase that gets your attention back. But by that time, you're unable to recall what the speaker *actually* said; instead, you remember what you *think* the speaker probably said.[62]

One reason listeners' minds tend to wander is that people think faster than they speak. Most people speak at about 120 to 150 words per minute. However, studies indicate that, depending on the subject and the individual, humans

> Table 2–2 Distinguishing Good Listeners from Bad Listeners

The Bad Listener	The Good Listener	To Listen Effectively
Tunes out dry subjects	Seeks opportunities; asks "What's in it for me?"	1. Find areas of interest.
Tunes out if delivery is poor		2. Judge content, not delivery.
Tends to enter into argument	Judges content; skips over delivery errors	3. Reserve judgment until you are sure you completely understand the speaker.
Listens for facts	Doesn't judge until comprehension is complete; interrupts only to clarify	
Takes extensive notes		4. Listen for ideas.
Fakes attention	Listens for central themes	5. Take selective notes.
Is distracted easily	Takes fewer notes	6. Work at listening.
Resists difficult material	Demonstrates interest; exhibits active body state	7. Block out competing thoughts.
Reacts to emotional words		8. Paraphrase the speaker's ideas.
Tends to daydream with slow speakers	Fights or avoids distractions; knows how to concentrate	9. Stay open-minded.
	Uses heavier material as exercise for the mind	10. Capitalize on the fact that thought is faster than speech.
	Interprets emotional words; does not get hung up on them	
	Listens between the lines; weighs the evidence; mentally summarizes	

can process audio information at around 500 words per minute.[63] In other words, your brain has a lot of free time whenever you're listening, and if left unsupervised, it will find a thousand other things to think about. Rather than listening part time, make a conscious effort to focus on the speaker and use the extra time to analyze what you hear, prepare questions you might need to ask, and engage in other relevant thinking.

Overcoming such interpretation barriers can be difficult because you might not even be aware of them. As Chapter 1 notes, selective perception leads listeners to mould a message to fit their own conceptual frameworks. Listeners sometimes make up their minds before fully hearing the speaker's message, or they engage in defensive listening—protecting their self-esteem by tuning out anything that doesn't confirm their view of themselves.

Even when your intentions are the best, you can still misinterpret incoming messages if you and the speaker don't share enough language or experience. Lack of common ground is why misinterpretation is so frequent between speakers of different native languages, even when they're trying to speak the same language. When listening to a speaker whose native language or life experience is different from yours, paraphrase that person's ideas. Give the speaker a chance to confirm what you think you heard or to correct any misinterpretation.

Overcoming memory barriers is a slightly easier problem to solve, but it takes some work. If the information is crucial, record it, write it down, or capture it in some other physical way. If you do need to memorize something, you can hold the information in short-term memory by repeating it silently to yourself or organizing a long list of items into several shorter lists. To store information in long-term memory, four techniques can help:

1. Associate new information with something closely related (such as the restaurant in which you met a new client).

CHECKLIST Overcoming Barriers to Effective Listening

✔ Control whatever barriers to physical reception you can (especially interrupting speakers by asking questions or by exhibiting disruptive nonverbal behaviours).

✔ Avoid selective listening by focusing on the speaker and analyzing what you hear.

✔ Keep an open mind by avoiding any prejudgment and by not listening defensively.

✔ Paraphrase the speaker's ideas, giving that person a chance to confirm or correct your interpretation.

✔ Don't count on your memory, but record, write down, or capture information in some physical way.

✔ Improve your short-term memory by repeating information, organizing it into patterns, or breaking it into shorter lists.

✔ Improve your long-term memory by association, categorization, visualization, and mnemonics.

2. Categorize the new information into logical groups (such as alphabetizing the names of products you're trying to remember).

3. Visualize words and ideas as pictures.

4. Create mnemonics such as acronyms or rhymes.

Note that all four techniques have an important factor in common: you have to *do* something to make the information stick.

When information is crucial and you can't record it in some way, use memory techniques to make sure you don't forget it.

If you can overcome all these barriers to effective listening, you're finally ready to evaluate what you hear and respond as needed. Your response might be simple, even automatic, such as laughing or thanking the speaker and following her directions to the office building around the corner. However, your response might require a far more rigorous process of analysis, such as interpreting the results of market research interviews before making recommendations about a potential product. For a reminder of the steps you can take to overcome listening barriers, see "Checklist: Overcoming Barriers to Effective Listening."

Improving Your Nonverbal Communication Skills

The boss walks out of the conference room after explaining that your department needs to double its sales next year. You're skeptical, though. You turn to a colleague and raise your eyebrows. She smiles and nods, sitting upright on the edge of her seat—she seems to relish the challenge. You turn to another colleague but he seems to dread what lies ahead, rolling his eyes and sighing. He is slumped so far down in his chair, you wonder how he keeps from sliding off.

Nonverbal communication supplements spoken language.

A complex conversation has just taken place without a single word being spoken. **Nonverbal communication** is the interpersonal process of sending and receiving information, both intentionally and unintentionally, without using written or spoken language. Nonverbal signals play three important roles in communication. The first is complementing verbal language. Nonverbal signals can strengthen a verbal message (when nonverbal signals match words), weaken a verbal message (when nonverbal signals don't match words), or replace words entirely.

Nonverbal cues help you ascertain the truth of spoken information.

The second role for nonverbal signals is revealing truth. People find it much harder to deceive with nonverbal signals. You might tell a client that the project is coming along nicely, but your forced smile and nervous glances send a different message. In fact, nonverbal communication often conveys more to listeners than the words you speak—particularly when they're trying to decide how you really feel about a situation or when they're trying to judge your credibility and aptitude for leadership.[64] However, even the power of nonverbal cues is not infallible when it comes to detecting truth. In one recent study, most people failed to detect dishonest speech roughly half the time; only a tiny fraction of the population are able to detect consistently when people are lying to them.[65]

The third role for nonverbal signals is conveying information efficiently. Nonverbal signals can convey both nuance and rich amounts of information in a single instant, as the previous conference room example suggests.

Recognizing Nonverbal Communication

Although you've been tuned into nonverbal communication since your first contact with other human beings, paying special attention to these signals in the workplace will enhance your ability to communicate successfully (see "Sharpening Your Career Skills—Improving Your Business Etiquette"). Moreover, as you interact with business associates from other backgrounds, you'll discover that some nonverbal signals don't translate across cultures. You'll learn more about cultural influences on nonverbal communication in Chapter 3. The range and variety of nonverbal signals is almost endless, but you can grasp the basics by studying six general categories:

Objective 7 Clarify the importance of nonverbal communication and list six categories of nonverbal expression.

1. **Facial expression.** Your face is the primary site for expressing your emotions; it reveals both the type and the intensity of your feelings.[66] Your eyes are especially effective for indicating attention and interest, influencing others, regulating interaction, and establishing dominance.[67]

2. **Gesture and posture.** By moving or not moving your body, you express both specific and general messages, some voluntary and some involuntary. Many gestures—a wave of the hand, for example—have a specific and intentional meaning. Other types of body movement are unintentional and express a more general message. Slouching, leaning forward, fidgeting, and walking briskly are all unconscious signals that reveal whether you feel confident or nervous, friendly or hostile, assertive or passive, powerful or powerless.

3. **Vocal characteristics.** Your voice also carries both intentional and unintentional messages. Consider the sentence "What have you been up to?" If you repeat that question, changing your tone of voice and stressing various words, you can consciously convey quite different messages. However, your voice can also reveal things of which you are unaware. Your tone and volume, your accent and speaking pace, and the little *ums* and *ahs* that creep into your speech say a lot about who you are, your relationship with the audience, and the emotions underlying your words.

4. **Personal appearance.** People respond to others on the basis of their physical appearance, sometimes fairly and other times unfairly. Although an individual's body type and facial features impose limitations, most people are able to control their appearance to some degree. Grooming, clothing, accessories, and style—you can control all of these. If your goal is to make a good impression, adopt the style of the people you want to impress.

5. **Touch.** Touch is an important way to convey warmth, comfort, and reassurance. Touch is so powerful, in fact, that it is governed by cultural customs

SHARPENING YOUR CAREER SKILLS

Improving Your Business Etiquette

Etiquette is knowing how to behave properly in a given situation. Knowing how to interact with people in business will help you appear polished, professional, and confident. Following proper etiquette helps you put fellow employees, business associates, and customers at ease, so they feel comfortable doing business with you.

Consider such common interactions as smiling, shaking hands, and making introductions. When you smile, do so genuinely. An artificial smile is obvious because the timing is off and the expression fails to involve all the facial muscles that a genuine smile would. Repeated false smiling may earn you the reputation of being insincere. Plus, if you smile too long, you make others uncomfortable, because they feel that you're not focused on the present. However, certain occasions require smiling:

> **When you are introduced to someone.** Smiling is courteous and suggests that you are receptive.
> **When you are feeling uncomfortable or out of place.** Smiling masks your concerns, and your confidence level will rise quickly (always being careful that your smile does not appear false).
> **When you give or receive a compliment.** Smiling punctuates your tribute when you give praise. If you're receiving praise, smiling augments the other person's position. Even if you feel embarrassed or undeserving, don't diminish the praise-giver by revealing those feelings.
> **When you applaud someone.** Smiling is the courteous, gracious thing to do.

In Canada and the United States, most business greetings include a handshake. (Other cultures may have varying approaches or completely different customs.) Extend your hand to greet business associates, regardless of gender. When seated, rise from your chair if you are physically able, and lean into the handshake. Pulling away suggests that something is wrong (people may pull away because of powerful perfume, tobacco residue on breath or clothing, or body odour). Make eye contact, smile, and nod your head to indicate that the person has your full attention. Never extend your hand while turning your head to speak to someone else.

Convey confidence, assurance, interest, and respect by using a firm handshake, without squeezing too hard. Use your right hand. Your hand should touch the other person's extended hand. Thumbs should point upward as you shake hands vertically and face one another squarely. Although your handshake should be brief, it should last long enough for both persons to speak their name and a few words of greeting.

Proper introductions are also an important part of business etiquette. The whole purpose of an introduction is to give people an opportunity to establish a connection, to get to know one another. When introducing yourself to a stranger, include a short, matter-of-fact description of your role, followed by a question about your new acquaintance. When introducing two other people, weave appropriate information into the introduction to help the individuals ease into a comfortable conversation. Suggest a subject of mutual interest. Remember that first and last names are mandatory. The people you're introducing need to know what to call each other and how to find each other later. You might say, "Henry Johnson, I would like you to meet Meredith Tucker, our new team member. Ms. Tucker, this is Mr. Johnson, senior manager at Lynco Systems. Ms. Tucker recently canoed the Nahanni River on a four-day trip. Mr. Johnson just returned from sabbatical in London, England."

When making introductions, gender is not a factor in who is introduced to whom. For example, you should mention the name of the older, more senior person first. Here are some examples of preferred forms of introduction:

> Introduce younger to older ("Mr. *Older Executive,* I would like you to meet Mr. *Younger Executive.*").
> Introduce company peer to a peer in another company ("Sam Locker, I'd like to introduce Kelly Martin, our head of engineering. Kelly, this is Sam from Brent & Moran.").
> Introduce junior executive to senior executive ("Ms. *Senior Executive,* I would like to introduce Mr. *Junior Executive.*").
> Introduce fellow executive to a client or customer ("Claire Waters, I'd like you to meet Kelly Martin, our head of engineering. Kelly, this is Mrs. Waters, one of our newest clients.").

When you're introduced to someone, take note of the person's name and use it as soon as possible. Connect the name to something common to you—perhaps the name is the same as that of a school friend or a favourite movie character. Knowing and using someone's name is a compliment, and doing so will be useful if you need to contact or refer to this person in the future.

By applying basic business etiquette, you will help create positive working relationships and gain the respect of your peers.

CAREER APPLICATIONS

1 You are introduced to a new business associate. You extend your hand expecting a handshake, but the person does not extend his. What do you do? Explain your answer.
2 Should you feel embarrassed if you don't remember someone's name after you are introduced? What should you do?

that establish who can touch whom and how in various circumstances. In Canada, the United States, and Great Britain, for example, people usually touch less frequently than people in France or Costa Rica. Even within each culture's norms, however, individual attitudes toward touch can vary widely. A manager might be comfortable using hugs to express support or congratulations, but his or her subordinates might interpret those hugs as either a show of dominance or sexual interest.[68] Touch is a complex subject. The best advice: When in doubt, don't touch.

6. **Time and space.** Like touch, time and space can be used to assert authority, imply intimacy, and send other nonverbal messages. For example, some people demonstrate their own importance or disregard for others by making people wait; others show respect by being on time. The manipulation of space works in a similar way. When top executives gather for lunch in a private dining room, they send a strong signal to all the employees crowding into the cafeteria downstairs. The decision to respect or violate someone's "private space" is another powerful nonverbal signal. Again, attitudes toward time and space vary from culture to culture (see Chapter 3).

Work to ensure that your nonverbal signals match the tone and content of your spoken communication.

Using Nonverbal Communication Effectively

Paying attention to nonverbal cues will make you both a better speaker and a better listener. Are they effective without being manipulative? Consider a situation in which an employee has come to you to talk about a raise. This situation is stressful for the employee, so don't say you're interested in what he has to tell you and then spend your time glancing at your computer or checking your watch. Conversely, if you already know you won't be able to give him the raise, be honest in expressing your emotions. Don't overcompensate for your own stress by smiling too broadly or shaking his hand too vigorously. Both nonverbal signals would raise his hopes without justification. In either case, match your nonverbal cues to the tone of the situation.

Also consider the nonverbal signals you send when you're not talking—the clothes you wear, the way you sit, or the way you walk. Are you talking like a serious business professional but dressing like you belong in a dance club or a frat house? The way you look and act sends signals too; make sure you're sending the right ones.

When you listen, be sure to pay attention to the speaker's nonverbal cues. Do they amplify the spoken words or contradict them? Is the speaker intentionally using nonverbal signals to send you a message that he or she can't put into words? Be observant, but don't assume that you can "read someone like a book." Nonverbal signals are powerful, but they aren't infallible. Just because someone doesn't look you squarely in the eye doesn't mean he or she is lying, contrary to popular belief.[69] If something doesn't feel right, ask the speaker an honest and respectful question—doing so might clear everything up, or it might uncover issues you need to explore further.

When you speak with friends, colleagues, or teachers, do you consciously analyze their body language? What do the stance, the eye contact, and the gesture suggest about the unspoken messages between the people in this photograph?

Summary of Learning Objectives

1 **Explain the advantages and disadvantages of working in teams.** Teams can achieve a higher level of performance than individuals because of the combined intelligence and energy of the group. Motivation and creativity flourish in team settings. Moreover, individuals tend to perform better in teams because they achieve a sense of purpose by belonging to a group. Teams also bring more input and a greater diversity of views, which tend to result in better decisions. And because team members participate in the decision-making process, they are committed to seeing the results succeed. Teams do have disadvantages, however. If poorly managed, teams can be a waste of everyone's time. If members are pressured to conform, they may develop groupthink, which can lead to poor-quality decisions and ill-advised actions. Some members may let their private motives get in the way. Others may not contribute their fair share, so certain tasks may not be completed.

2 **Outline an effective approach to team communication.** Effective team communication is collaborative. Although team members often come from different backgrounds with different concerns, they must accommodate others' opinions and focus on team objectives instead of individual priorities. Effective team communication includes agreeing on team goals before beginning the project, allowing for early social interaction to create a comfortable work atmosphere, clarifying the work process and schedules, and frequent checking on the group's progress. If team members use technology to share information, they must ensure the system is functional.

3 **Explain how wiki technology can help teams collaborate.** Wikis give team members the ability to post Web content without needing to learn the conventional tools and techniques for creating web pages. If a collaborator sees the need to improve a document or add content, he or she can post this material quickly, without waiting for approval. Wikis offer speed and flexibility to facilitate workflow.

4 **Explain how group dynamics can affect team effectiveness.** The roles group members assume result in either the success or failure of the group's ability to solve problems and make decisions. As teams go through the phases of group formation (orientation, conflict, brainstorming, emergence, and reinforcement) to reach consensus, members who assume team-oriented roles, instead of self-oriented roles, help create team success because they place collective goals above personal ones.

5 **Describe how meeting technologies can help participants communicate more successfully.** Meeting technologies permit group members to collaborate remotely in real time. Electronic whiteboards can store meeting notes for printing, emailing, and archiving. Shared workspaces give team members access to common resources and information, such as databases and team-created documents. Virtual meeting technology, such as videoconferencing and Web-based meeting systems, provide opportunities to communicate as well as revise documents online.

6 **Describe the listening process, and explain how good listeners overcome barriers at each stage of the process.** The listening process involves five activities: (1) receiving (physically hearing the message); (2) decoding (assigning meaning to what you hear); (3) remembering (storing the message for future reference); (4) evaluating (thinking critically about the message); (5) responding (reacting to the message, taking action, or giving feedback). Three barriers can interfere with each stage of the listening process. One is selective listening, which prevents the listener from retaining the real message; this problem can be overcome by listening actively. The second is prejudgment, which involves holding assumptions and sometimes even distorting messages if they don't conform to what you want to hear. Good listeners control prejudgment by listening with an open mind. The third is memory barriers, which good listeners overcome with such techniques as organizing information into patterns and taking notes.

7 **Clarify the importance of nonverbal communication and list six categories of nonverbal expression.** Nonverbal communication is important because actions may speak louder than words. Body language is more difficult to control than words and may reveal a person's true feelings, motivation, or character. Consequently, people tend to believe nonverbal signals over the spoken message. In addition, nonverbal communication is more efficient; with a wave of your hand or a wink, you can streamline your thoughts—and do so without much thought. Types of nonverbal expression include facial expression, gesture and posture, vocal characteristics, personal appearance, touching behaviour, and use of time and space.

On the Job PERFORMING COMMUNICATION TASKS AT ROYAL BANK FINANCIAL GROUP

Teamwork permeates all business activities at Royal Bank. New employees are introduced to the team approach right away, ensuring that everyone contributes to the company's success through effective teamwork. You have recently been promoted to assistant branch manager at your neighbourhood Royal Bank. Your responsibilities include (1) promoting the team concept among all customer service representatives in your branch, and (2) serving as a team leader on special projects that involve your staff.

Apply the concepts you have learned in this chapter to the following challenges.

1 Your district manager has asked you and three other employees at your large urban branch to find a solution to the lack of sufficient office space for the growing number of workers at your location. As leader, you schedule team meetings on Thursday afternoons for four weeks to address the problem. After two meetings with your co-workers, you notice that everyone is making vital contributions to the group's efforts—except Jane. During the meetings, she displays very poor listening skills. She often jumps ahead of the topic or interrupts a speaker's train of thought. At other times, she doodles on her notepad instead of taking constructive notes. And she remains silent after team members deliver lengthy reports about possible solutions to the office space problem. What can you do as team leader to help Jane improve her listening skills?

a Ask Jane to take extensive notes during each meeting. The process of taking detailed notes will improve her concentration and force her to listen more carefully to team members. After the meeting, she can use her notes as a reference to clarify any questions about team decisions or the nature of assignments to individual team members.

b Suggest that Jane mentally summarize the speaker's ideas—or verbally rephrase the ideas in her own words—during the meeting. With some practice, Jane should be able to focus on the topics under discussion and block out distracting thoughts.

c Schedule future team meetings for Thursday mornings instead of Thursday afternoons. After devoting most of the workday to her regular duties, Jane may be feeling tired or sluggish by the time of your team meeting.

d Prepare a detailed written summary of each meeting. The summary will clarify any points that Jane may have missed during the meeting and provide her with a complete reference of team decisions and assignments.

2 As assistant branch manager, you schedule a team meeting to discuss new methods of motivating customer service representatives to achieve their quarterly goals for selling bank products, such as guaranteed investment certificates. During the meeting, one customer service representative disagrees with every suggestion offered by team members, often reacting with a sneer on his face and a belligerent tone of voice. Which of the following strategies is the best way to overcome the rep's resistance?

a Ignore his remarks. Keep the meeting on track and avoid destructive confrontations by asking for input from other team members.

b Directly confront the sales rep's concerns. Point out the flaws in his arguments, and offer support for the opinions of other team members.

c Remain calm and try to understand his point of view. Ask him to clarify his ideas, and solicit his suggestions for motivating sales representatives.

d Politely acknowledge his opinions, and then repeat the most valid suggestions offered by other team members in a convincing manner.

3 The district manager realizes his communication skills are important for several reasons: he holds primary responsibility for the region; he needs to communicate with the branch managers who report to him; and his style sets an example for other employees in the region. He asks you to sit in on face-to-face meetings for several days to observe his nonverbal messages. You witness four habits. Which of the following habits do you think is the most negative?

a He rarely comes out from behind his massive desk when meeting people; at one point, he offered a congratulatory handshake to a branch manager, and the manager had to lean way over his desk just to reach him.

b When a manager hands him a report and then sits down to discuss it, he alternates between making eye contact and making notes on the report.

c He is consistently pleasant, even if the person he is meeting is delivering bad news.

d He interrupts meetings to answer the phone, rather than letting an assistant get the phone; then he apologizes to visitors for the interruption.

Test Your Knowledge

1 What are three ways in which an organization's decision making can benefit from teams?

2 What are the main activities that make up the listening process?

3 What questions should an effective agenda answer?

4 How do self-oriented team roles differ from team-maintenance roles and task-facilitating roles?

5 What is groupthink? How can it affect an organization?

6 How can team members successfully resolve conflict?

7 How does content listening differ from critical listening and empathic listening?

8 What are the benefits of wikis and Web-based meeting systems as meeting technologies?

9 How is nonverbal communication limited?

10 What is the purpose of using parliamentary procedure?

Apply Your Knowledge

1 How can nonverbal communication help you run a meeting? How can it help you call a meeting to order, emphasize important topics, show approval, express reservations, regulate the flow of conversation, and invite a colleague to continue with a comment?

2 Your boss frequently asks for feedback from you and her other subordinates, but she blasts anyone who offers criticism, which causes people to agree with everything she says. You want to talk to her about it, but what should you say? List some of the points you want to make when you discuss this issue with her.

3 Is conflict in a team good or bad? Explain your answer.

4 At your last department meeting, three people monopolized the entire discussion. What might you do at the next meeting to encourage other department members to participate voluntarily?

5 **Ethical Choices** Strange instant messages occasionally pop up on your computer screen during your team's virtual meetings, followed quickly by embarrassed apologies from one of your colleagues in another city. You eventually figure out that this person is working from home, even though he says he's in the office; moreover, the messages suggest that he's running a sideline business from his home. Instant messaging is crucial to your team's communication, and you're concerned about the frequent disruptions, not to mention your colleague's potential ethical violations. What should you do? Explain your choice.

Running Cases   ◉▭Watch on mycanadianbuscommlab

> CASE 1 Noreen

Noreen is planning to attend a WebEx online meeting today at 11:00 A.M. Her boss has asked her to participate in the meeting with other Petro-Go "Go Points" team leaders from around the world. The group is to compile statistics regarding the "Go Points" program as well as discuss strategies for expanding the program and improving customer retention. They are to submit a report in one week detailing their findings and suggestions.

Noreen begins the set-up and login process on her computer at 10:45 A.M. She finds that because she has never participated in a WebEx conference, she is unable to prepare her computer. She calls the technical department, and a technician comes to set it up for her. She finally connects with the group at 12:30 P.M. By this time they are ending the meeting and planning to meet tomorrow at the same time. Noreen apologizes and explains what happened, but feels rather embarrassed.

The next day Noreen connects on time, but is somewhat behind the discussion because she does not know what was discussed the day before. She tries her best to share information, but is scrambling to find the data she needs to share with the group. The group divides the workload between them and asks everyone to meet online again at 11:00 A.M. in three days to share and review their work. Noreen types her team's statistics and suggestions for expanding and finishes early. When she meets the group again she discovers that not only did everyone type their team's statistics and suggestions for expanding the program, they also compared their team's performance with two other office teams and gave suggestions for improving customer retention. Noreen was not aware they were supposed to include all of this information. One team leader volunteered to compile everything and said he would contact the others tomorrow if he had questions. Noreen knew she would be out of the office for the next three days on training. The report was finished on time, but Noreen's team's section was incomplete. Her boss was not happy.

QUESTIONS

a) Why did Noreen not know what was expected?

b) What could Noreen have done differently to ensure communication would not break down?

c) Should Noreen have alerted the others to the fact that her section was incomplete?

d) Should the group have gone ahead with the report without Noreen's completed section?

e) What could Noreen have done to ensure that she had done the task correctly?

YOUR TASK

Write an email from Noreen to her boss explaining what happened and apologizing for the errors. She should admit fault and offer suggestions for correcting the situation.

> CASE 2 Kwong

Kwong is working on a group project for his business communication class. His group members are Mohamed, Gopan, and Marie. The project is to choose a company and research its channels and methods of communication. The group will submit a formal report and deliver a presentation.

The group divides the tasks for the project: Kwong will create the PowerPoint slides, Marie and Mohamed will gather the information, and Gopan will create the formal report. Mohamed does not attend the next class. The group sends several emails to Mohamed over the course of the next four days, but they get no response. The group emails the professor to make her aware of the situation and to ask for guidance on how to proceed.

The day the project is due, Mohamed meets Gopan outside the classroom door. They have a loud argument that the class overhears. The teacher asks Kwong's group to stay after class to discuss any problems their group may have. The class begins, and Kwong's group does not allow Mohamed to present with them nor do they accept his work.

After class Gopan complains that Mohamed did his part incorrectly and did not participate. Marie says she came with Mohamed's part done and added it to their project, so they would not lose marks. Mohamed tells the group that he had family problems and apologizes for his absence. Mohamed is willing to accept a zero grade. The professor discusses appropriate behaviour with the team. Gopan apologizes for yelling at Mohamed, and they shake hands.

The next day when each member emailed the professor their peer evaluation forms, both Mohamed and Kwong said they did not wish to work in a group with Gopan again. The group members each gave Mohamed a low grade because of his lack of participation.

QUESTIONS

a) Do you think having a group contract from the beginning of the group assignment would have helped the situation? Could a contract have helped ensure that communication would not break down?

b) Was the group being mean by making the professor aware of Mohamed's non-participation? Why did they inform her?

c) Why do you think Mohamed did not wish to work with Gopan again? Why do you think Kwong did not wish to work with Gopan again?

d) What could Gopan have done differently? What could Mohamed have done differently?

e) Should the group have let Mohamed present with them?

YOUR TASK

Create an email to your professor evaluating Gopan's, Mohamed's, Marie's, and Kwong's individual performance on this group assignment. Rate them on

1 Cooperation
2 Participation
3 Contribution
4 Demonstrated interest
5 Communication

Give a brief explanation as to why you rated each member the way you did.

Practise Your Knowledge

A project leader has made notes about covering the following items at the quarterly budget meeting. Prepare a formal agenda by putting these items into a logical order and rewriting, where necessary, to give phrases a more consistent sound.

> Budget Committee Meeting to be held on December 13, 2010, at 9:30 A.M.

> I will call the meeting to order.

> Real estate director's report: A closer look at cost overruns on Greentree site.

> The group will review and approve the minutes from last quarter's meeting.

> I will ask the finance director to report on actual versus projected quarterly revenues and expenses.

> I will distribute copies of the overall divisional budget and announce the date of the next budget meeting.

> Discussion: How can we do a better job of anticipating and preventing cost overruns?

> Meeting will take place in Conference Room 3, with videoconferencing for remote employees.

> What additional budget issues must be considered during this quarter?

Exercises

2.1 Teamwork: Meeting Assessment

With a classmate, attend a local community or campus meeting where you can observe a group discussion, vote, or other group action. During the meeting, take notes individually and, afterward, work together to answer the following questions:

a. What is your evaluation of this meeting? In your answer, consider (1) the leader's ability to articulate the meeting's goals clearly, (2) the leader's ability to engage members in a meaningful discussion, (3) the group's dynamics, and (4) the group's listening skills.

b. How did group members make decisions? Did they vote? Did they reach decisions by consensus? Did those with dissenting opinions get an opportunity to voice their objections?

c. How well did the individual participants listen? How could you tell?

d. Did any participants change their expressed views or their votes during the meeting? Why might that have happened?

e. Did you observe any of the communication barriers that Chapter 1 discusses? Identify them.

f. Compare the notes you took during the meeting with those of your classmate. What differences do you notice? How do you account for these differences?

2.2 Team Communication: Overcoming Barriers

Every month, each employee in your department is expected to give a brief oral presentation on the status of his or her project. However, your department has recently hired an employee with a severe speech impediment that prevents people from understanding most of what he has to say. As department manager, how will you resolve this dilemma? Please explain.

2.3 Team Development: Resolving Conflict

Describe a recent conflict you had with a team member at work or at school, and explain how you resolved it. Did you find a solution that was acceptable to both of you and to the team?

2.4 Ethical Choices: Dealing with a Meeting Controller

During team meetings, one member constantly calls for votes before all the members have voiced their views. As the leader, you asked this member privately about his behaviour. He replied that he was trying to move the team toward its goals, but you are concerned that he is really trying to take control. How can you deal with this situation without removing the member from the group?

2.5 Online Communication: Staying on Track with Blog Replies

As the leader of a product development team, you write a daily blog to inform team members of questions, concerns, and other developments related to your project. Team members are always encouraged to reply to your online posts, but lately a number of people have been wandering off track with their replies, raising new issues in the middle of a discussion thread or posting on matters unrelated to the item to which they're replying. As a result, the blog is becoming less useful for everyone because individual message threads no longer stick to a single topic. Write a brief blog posting, three or four sentences at most, courteously reminding everyone why it's important to stick to the subject at hand when replying to blog items.

2.6 Internet: Whiteboards for Meetings

Visit the PolyVision website at www.websterboards.com and read about electronic whiteboards. What advantages do you see in using this kind of whiteboard during a meeting? Draft a short internal memo to your boss outlining the product's advantages, using the memo format described in Appendix A.

2.7 Listening Skills: Overcoming Barriers

Identify some of your bad listening habits and make a list of ways you could correct them. For the next 30 days, review your list and jot down any improvements you've noticed as a result of your effort.

2.8 Nonverbal Communication: Analyzing Written Messages

Select a business letter and an envelope that you received at work or home. Analyze their appearance. What nonverbal messages do they send? Are these messages consistent with the content of the letter? If not, what could the sender have done to make the nonverbal communication consistent with the verbal communication?

2.9 Nonverbal Communication: Analyzing Body Language

Describe what the following body movements suggest when someone exhibits them during a conversation. How do such movements influence your interpretation of spoken words?

a. Shifting one's body continuously while seated

b. Twirling and playing with one's hair

c. Sitting in a sprawled position

d. Rolling one's eyes

e. Extending a weak handshake

2.10 Listening Skills: Self-Assessment

How good are your listening skills? Use the following chart to rate yourself on each element of listening. Then, examine your ratings to identify where you are strongest and where you can improve, using the tips in this chapter.

Element of Listening	Always	Frequently	Occasionally	Never
1. I look for areas of interest when people speak.				
2. I focus on content rather than delivery.				
3. I wait to respond until I understand the content.				
4. I listen for ideas and themes, not isolated facts.				
5. I take notes only when needed.				
6. I really concentrate on what speakers are saying.				
7. I stay focused even when the ideas are complex.				
8. I keep an open mind despite emotionally charged language.				

3

Communicating Interculturally

ON THE JOB

Communicating with the Help of Graybridge Malkam
WORKING WITH CULTURAL DIVERSITY

www.graybridgemalkam.com

When making a toast at a dinner with your Czech counterparts, where would you focus your eyes? If working in India, would you shake hands when introduced to an Indian colleague?

Laraine Kaminsky, executive vice-president of Ottawa-based Graybridge Malkam International Consulting, helps her clients overcome obstacles that might interfere with their adaptation to both the Canadian and international workplace. The 40-member staff deliver cross-cultural, language, international development, and diversity training programs to new immigrants, Canadians who will work abroad, and Canadians who want to improve their communication skills in the multicultural work-place at home. The global marketplace and Canada's position as a magnet for immi-grants from around the world have provided Graybridge Malkam with many opportunities to help people communicate across cultures. Says Kaminsky, "A good people manager in Canada today has to be able to understand the changing demo-graphics of who your customers are, both internal and external."

The unique combination of influences present in one culture can condition people to think, feel, and behave quite differently from people in another culture. Some differences are dramatic, such as the importance of social status. Other differences,

Graybridge Malkam's Laraine Kaminsky says, "For organizations to succeed in attracting, retaining, and developing a diverse talent pool, they have to create a culture of inclusion where different styles of working, communicating, or managing are integrated and respected."

such as personal values and decision-making approaches, can be more subtle and more difficult to perceive. Basic language barriers often prevent employees from understanding each other, but the potential for misunderstanding goes beyond language. As one example, Kaminsky cites the employer–employee relationship. In Canada, it is often on a first-name basis. In Korea, she says, the workplace is very formal. Coming from a culture where employees and employers keep their distance, Korean immigrants will find this casual interaction startling.

Cultural differences—and the misconceptions that might result from them—can affect teamwork, productivity, and job satisfaction. If you worked for Graybridge Malkam, how would you help immigrants adapt to Canadian culture? What advice would you give to Canadians to improve their communication with colleagues from other countries?

Answers: When making a toast at a meal with Czechs, look directly into the eyes of the person you are toasting. If you don't, you will be considered impolite. In India, shaking hands is uncommon. Instead, place the palms of your hands together below your chin, bow slightly, and say "namaste."[1]

Understanding the Opportunities and Challenges of Intercultural Communication

When you enter the workplace, you will experience both the challenges of intercultural communication and the opportunities available for business professionals who know how to communicate across cultures. **Intercultural communication** is the process of sending and receiving messages between people whose cultural backgrounds could lead them to interpret verbal and nonverbal signs differently. Every attempt to send and receive messages is influenced by culture, so to communicate successfully, you'll need a basic grasp of the cultural differences you may encounter and how you might overcome them. Your efforts to recognize and surmount cultural differences will open up business opportunities throughout the world and maximize the contribution of all the employees in a diverse workforce. Laraine Kaminsky advises, "People are increasingly seeing a different side of the world. They need to know how to interact with different cultures and successfully communicate and build relationships."[2]

Objective 1 Discuss the opportunities and challenges of intercultural communication.

Effective intercultural communication
> opens up business opportunities around the world
> improves the contributions of employees in a diverse workforce

The Opportunities in a Global Marketplace

You might be a business manager looking for new customers or new sources of labour. Or you might be an employee looking for new work opportunities. Either way, chances are good that you'll be looking across international borders in the course of your career. New communication technologies allow teams from all over the world to work on projects and share information without leaving their desks. At the same time, advanced technologies allow manufacturers to produce their goods in foreign locations that offer favourable corporate tax rates and low-cost labour.[3] Natural boundaries and national borders disappear as increasing numbers of people work in multicultural settings. Even firms that once thought they were too small to expand into a neighbouring city have discovered that they can tap the sales potential of overseas markets with the help of the internet, email, fax machines, and overnight delivery services.

Thousands of Canadian businesses depend on exports for significant portions of their revenues. For example, Export Development Canada sees Brazil as a

You will communicate with people from other cultures throughout your career.

The diversity of today's workforce brings distinct advantages to businesses:
> a broader range of views and ideas
> a better understanding of diverse markets
> a broader pool of talent from which to recruit

August 2007

FM 97.9 CHIN
INTERNATIONAL RADIO · TV
OTTAWA 97.9FM CJLL

30 Murray Street, Ste. 100, Ottawa K1N 5M4   613-244-0979
www.chinradio.com

This schedule from CHIN Radio, a broadcaster of multicultural programs, reflects the diversity of Canadian society. Besides radio, what other media will help you understand different cultures?

A company's cultural diversity affects how its business messages are conceived, composed, delivered, received, and interpreted.

major market for Canadian exporters.[4] More than 3000 Canadian companies export to Japan each year, Canada's third-largest export market.[5] Indeed, domestic markets are opening to worldwide competition as businesses of all sizes look for new growth opportunities outside their own countries. In 2008, the Montreal-based engineering company Tecsult signed a $20-million contract to work on a financial mega-centre in Riyadh, Saudi Arabia.[6] Another example is SolutionInc Limited, a Halifax-based developer of internet software that sells to clients in the Middle East and the Asia Pacific region.[7] Large or small, companies know that in the global marketplace, they face cultural and language barriers among customers and employees.

Advantages of a Multicultural Workforce

Even if you never visit another country or transact business on a global scale, you will interact with colleagues from a variety of cultures and with a wide range of life experiences. Over the past few decades, many innovative companies have changed the way they approach diversity, from seeing it as a legal requirement to seeing it as a strategic opportunity to connect with customers and take advantage of the broadest possible pool of talent.[8] Diverse workforces offer a broader spectrum of viewpoints and ideas, help companies understand and identify with diverse markets, and enable companies to tap into the broadest possible talent pool. Says Gordon Nixon, president and chief executive officer of the Royal Bank Financial Group, "If we succeed at leveraging the diversity of our current and future workforce, we will have unrivalled advantage. But if we fail, we will pay a heavy opportunity cost for our citizens and will face an uphill battle to maintain, let alone enhance, our quality of life."[9]

Diversity is integral to all companies. The most recent census figures show that immigrants form almost one-fifth of the Canadian workforce. Recent immigrants—those who have arrived in Canada in the last 10 years—account for 70 percent of labour market growth.[10] The "brain gain" has brought specialists in the fields of information technology, biotechnology, and engineering from such countries as India, Japan, and the former Yugoslavia. Canadian firms have responded to the needs of these employees through training and other supportive measures to improve communication. For example, Toronto's Dalton Chemical Laboratories offers English as a Second Language classes to its diverse workforce.[11]

You and your colleagues don't need to be recent immigrants to constitute a diverse workforce. Differences in everything from age and gender to religion, ethnic heritage, geography, and military experience enrich the workplace. Both immigration and workforce diversity create advantages—and challenges—for business communicators throughout the world.

The Challenges of Intercultural Communication

Cultural diversity affects how business messages are conceived, planned, sent, received, and interpreted in the workplace. Today's increasingly diverse workforce encompasses a wide range of skills, traditions, backgrounds, experiences, outlooks, and attitudes toward work—all of which can affect employee behaviour on the job. Supervisors face the challenge of communicating with these diverse employees, motivating them, and fostering cooperation and harmony among them. Teams face the challenge of working together closely, and companies are challenged to coexist peacefully with business partners and with the community as a whole.

The interaction of culture and communication is so pervasive that separating the two is virtually impossible. The way you communicate—from the language you speak and the nonverbal signals you send to the way you perceive other people—is influenced by the culture in which you were raised. The meaning of words, the significance of gestures, the importance of time and space, the rules of human relationships—these and many other aspects of communication are defined by culture. To a large degree, your culture influences the way you think, which naturally affects the way you communicate as both a sender and a receiver.[12] So you can see how intercultural communication is much more complicated than simply matching language between sender and receiver. It goes beyond mere words to beliefs, values, and emotions.

Throughout this chapter, you'll see numerous examples of how communication styles and habits vary from one culture to another. These examples are intended to illustrate the major themes of intercultural communication, not to give an exhaustive list of styles and habits of any particular culture. With an understanding of these major themes, you'll then be prepared to explore the specifics of any culture.

> Culture influences everything about communication, including
> > language
> > nonverbal signals
> > word meaning
> > time and space issues
> > rules of human relationships

Enhancing Your Intercultural Sensitivity

You are already an expert in culture, at least in the culture you grew up with. You understand how your society works, how people are expected to communicate, what common gestures and facial expressions mean, and so on. However, because you're such an expert in your own culture, your communication is largely automatic; that is, you rarely stop to think about the communication rules you're following. An important step toward successful intercultural communication is becoming more aware of these rules and of the way they influence your communication. A good place to start is to understand what culture is.

Objective 2 Define culture and explain how culture is learned.

Culture is a shared system of symbols, beliefs, attitudes, values, expectations, and behaviour norms.

Understanding the Concept of Culture

Culture is a shared system of symbols, beliefs, attitudes, values, expectations, and norms for behaviour. People's cultural background influences the way they prioritize what is important in life, helps define their attitude toward what is appropriate in any given situation, and establishes rules for their behaviour.[13] One study suggests that people from different cultures even view the world—literally—in different ways. Shown a variety of pictures, Chinese subjects focused more on the whole picture and the harmony of elements within it, whereas North Americans of European descent focused more on the dominant, individual objects in the scene.[14]

You belong to several cultures, each of which affects the way you communicate.

Actually, everyone belongs to several cultures. The most obvious is the culture you share with all the people who live in your own country. In addition, you belong to other cultural groups, including an ethnic group, possibly a religious group, and perhaps a profession that has its own special language and customs. With its large population and history of immigration, Canada is home to a vast array of cultures. In contrast, Japan is much more homogeneous, having only a few separate cultural groups.[15]

Cultures differ widely and may vary in their rate of change, their degree of complexity, and their tolerance toward

Experts such as Laraine Kaminsky recommend that companies transacting business with people from other nationalities find out as much as possible about their customs and religions. What information about your background would be necessary for your business partners?

Cultures tend to offer views of life that are coherent (internally logical) and complete (answer all of life's big questions).

Objective 3 Define ethnocentrism and stereotyping, and then give three suggestions for overcoming these limiting mindsets.

Ethnocentrism is the tendency to judge all other groups according to the standards, behaviours, and customs of one's own group.

Xenophobia is a fear of strangers.

Stereotyping is assigning generalized attributes to an individual on the basis of membership in a particular group.

Cultural pluralism is the acceptance of multiple cultures on their own terms.

outsiders. These differences affect the level of trust and openness that you can achieve when communicating with people of other cultures.

People learn culture directly and indirectly from other members of their group. As you grow up in a culture, you are taught who you are and how best to function in that culture by the group's members. Sometimes you are explicitly told which behaviours are acceptable; at other times you learn by observing which values work best in a particular group. In these ways, culture is passed on from person to person and from generation to generation.[16]

In addition to being automatic, established cultures tend to be coherent; that is, they are fairly logical and consistent when viewed from the inside. For example, the notion of fairness is deeply embedded in Canadian culture. Those who demonstrate fairness are admired, and those who don't are sometimes viewed negatively. Such coherence generally helps a culture function more smoothly internally, although it can create disharmony between cultures that don't view the world in the same way.

Cultures also tend to be complete; that is, they provide most of their members with most of the answers to life's big questions. This idea of completeness dulls or even suppresses curiosity about life in other cultures. Therefore, such completeness can complicate communication with other cultures.[17]

Overcoming Ethnocentrism and Stereotyping

Ethnocentrism is the tendency to judge all other groups according to the standards, behaviours, and customs of one's own group. Given the automatic influence of one's own culture, when people compare their culture to others, they often conclude that their own group is superior.[18] An even more extreme reaction is **xenophobia**, a fear of strangers and foreigners. Clearly, businesspeople who take these views will not interpret messages from other cultures correctly, nor are they likely to send successful messages.

Distorted views of other cultures or groups also result from **stereotyping**, assigning a wide range of generalized attributes to an individual on the basis of membership in a particular culture or social group. Whereas ethnocentrism and xenophobia represent negative views of everyone in a particular group, stereotyping is more a matter of oversimplifying and of failing to acknowledge individuality. For example, Japanese visitors often stereotype Americans as people who walk fast, are wasteful in utilizing space, speak directly, ask too many questions in the classroom, don't respect professors, are disrespectful of age and status, lack discipline, and are extravagant.[19]

Those who want to show respect for other people and to communicate effectively in business need to adopt a more positive viewpoint in the form of **cultural pluralism**—the practice of accepting multiple cultures on their own terms. When crossing cultural boundaries, you'll be even more effective if you move beyond simple acceptance and adapt your own communication style to that of the new cultures you encounter—even integrating aspects of those cultures into your own.[20] Three simple habits can help you avoid both the negativity of ethnocentrism and the oversimplification of stereotyping:

> **Avoid assumptions.** Don't assume that others will act as you do, that they will operate from the same values and beliefs, or that they will use language and symbols the same way you do.

Participation in group activities is an important method of learning about a culture's rules and expectations. What have you learned about other cultures through groups you belong to? Has it influenced how you communicate with others?

> **Avoid judgments.** When people act differently, don't conclude that they are in error, that their way is invalid, or that their customs are inferior to your own.
> **Acknowledge distinctions.** Don't ignore the differences between another person's culture and your own.

You can avoid ethnocentrism and stereotyping by avoiding assumptions and judgments and by accepting differences.

Unfortunately, overcoming ethnocentrism and stereotyping is no simple task, even for people who are highly motivated to do so. You may need to change patterns of beliefs that you've had your entire life and even change the way you view yourself and your culture. Moreover, recent research suggests that people often have beliefs and biases that they're not even consciously aware of—and that may even conflict with the beliefs they *think* they have. (To see if you might have some of these *implicit beliefs,* visit the Project Implicit website at https://implicit.harvard.edu/implicit and take some of the simple online tests.)[21]

Recognizing Cultural Variations

When you communicate with someone from another culture, your instinct is to encode your message using the assumptions of your own culture. However, members of your audience decode your message according to the assumptions of *their* culture, so your meaning may be misunderstood (see "Communicating Across Cultures: Test Your Intercultural Knowledge"). The greater the difference between cultures, the greater the chance for misunderstanding.[22] From using brand names that are obscene slang in another language to misunderstanding attitudes about worker–manager relationships, companies around the world have made mistakes that have damaged relationships and lost sales. You can learn to avoid such blunders by recognizing and accommodating six main types of cultural differences: contextual, legal and ethical, social, nonverbal signals, gender, and age,.

Objective 4 Explain the importance of recognizing cultural variations, and list six categories of cultural differences.

Cultural differences can lead to miscommunication in the workplace.

CONTEXTUAL DIFFERENCES Every attempt at communication occurs within a **cultural context**, the pattern of physical cues, environmental stimuli, and implicit understanding that convey meaning between two members of the same culture. However, cultures around the world vary widely in the role that context plays in communication.

Cultural context is the pattern of physical cues, environmental stimuli, and implicit understanding that conveys meaning between members of the same culture.

In a **high-context culture** such as South Korea or Taiwan, people rely less on verbal communication and more on the context of nonverbal actions and environmental setting to convey meaning. For example, a Chinese speaker expects the receiver to discover the essence of a message and uses indirectness and metaphor to provide a web of meaning.[23] In high-context cultures, the rules of everyday life are rarely explicit; instead, as individuals grow up, they learn how to recognize situational cues (gestures and tone of voice) and how to respond as expected.[24] The primary role of communication is building relationships, not exchanging information.[25]

High-context cultures rely heavily on nonverbal actions and environmental setting to convey meaning; low-context cultures rely more on explicit verbal communication.

In a **low-context culture** such as Canada, the United States, or Germany, people rely more on verbal communication and less on circumstances and cues to convey meaning. A British speaker feels responsible for transmitting the meaning of the message and often places sentences in chronological sequence to establish a cause-and-effect pattern.[26] In a low-context culture, rules and expectations are usually spelled out through explicit statements such as "Please wait until I'm finished" or "You're welcome to browse."[27] The primary task of communication in low-context cultures is exchanging information.[28]

Contextual differences are apparent in the way cultures approach situations such as decision making, problem solving, and negotiating. For example, in lower-context cultures, businesspeople tend to focus on the results of the

COMMUNICATING ACROSS CULTURES

Test Your Intercultural Knowledge

Even well-intentioned businesspeople can make mistakes if they aren't aware of simple but important cultural differences. Can you spot the erroneous assumptions in these scenarios?

1. You are attending a special event at a Chinese hotel with your colleagues. The food is served buffet-style. You are in line with your Chinese associates and select from the choices displayed, expecting your counterparts to follow. Why do they look surprised?

2. You finally made the long trip overseas to meet the new German director of your division. Despite slow traffic, you arrive only four minutes late. His door is shut, so you knock on it and walk in. The chair is too far away from the desk, so you pick it up and move it closer. Then you lean over the desk, stick out your hand and say, "Good morning, Hans, it's nice to meet you." Why is his reaction so chilly?

3. Your meeting went better than you'd ever expected. In fact, you found the Japanese representative for your new advertising agency to be very agreeable; she said yes to just about everything. When you share your enthusiasm with your boss, he doesn't appear very excited. Why?

Here's what went wrong in each situation:

1. In Canada, it is expected that people selecting food from a buffet take it in the order they are in line. In China, it is con-

sidered rude to take food before inviting your colleagues to choose before you. In addition, when having tea with Chinese partners, you should pour for everyone at the table before helping yourself.

2. You've just broken four rules of German polite behaviour: punctuality, privacy, personal space, and proper greetings. In time-conscious Germany, you should never arrive even a few minutes late. Also, Germans like their privacy and space, and many adhere to formal greetings of "Frau" and "Herr," even if the business association has lasted for years.

3. The word *yes* may not always mean "yes" in the Western sense. Japanese people may say yes to confirm they have heard or understood something but not necessarily to indicate that they agree with it. You'll seldom get a direct no. Some of the ways that Japanese people say no indirectly include "It will be difficult," "I will ask my supervisor," "I'm not sure," "We will think about it," and "I see."

CAREER APPLICATIONS

1. Have you ever been on the receiving end of an intercultural communication error, such as when someone inadvertently used an inappropriate gesture or figure of speech? How did you respond?

2. If you had arrived late at the office of the German colleague, what would have been a better way to handle the situation?

---

decisions they face, a reflection of the cultural emphasis on logic and progress. Will this be good for our company? For my career? In comparison, higher-context cultures emphasize the means or the method by which the decision will be made. Building or protecting relationships can be as important as the facts and information used in making the decisions.[29] Consequently, negotiators working on business deals in such cultures may spend most of their time together building relationships, rather than hammering out contractual details.

Whether you're making a decision, solving a problem, or negotiating a business deal, the communication tactics that work well in a high-context culture may backfire in a low-context culture, and vice versa. The key to success is understanding why the other party is saying and doing particular things and then adapting your approach accordingly.

LEGAL AND ETHICAL DIFFERENCES   Cultural context also influences legal and ethical behaviour. For example, because low-context cultures value the written word, they consider written agreements binding. But high-context cultures put less emphasis on the written word and consider personal pledges more important than contracts. They also tend to take a more flexible approach regarding adherence to the law, whereas low-context cultures would adhere to the law strictly.[30]

Low-context cultures tend to value written agreements and interpret laws strictly, whereas high-context cultures view adherence to laws as being more flexible.

As you conduct business around the world, you'll find that legal systems differ from culture to culture. In the United Kingdom, Canada, and the United States, a person is presumed innocent until proven guilty, a principle rooted in English common law. However, in Mexico and Turkey, one is presumed guilty until proven innocent, a principle rooted in the Napoleonic code.[31]

As Chapter 1 discusses, making ethical choices can be difficult, even within your own culture. When communicating across cultures, ethics can be even more complicated. What happens when a certain behaviour is unethical in Canada but an accepted practice in another culture?

For example, in Canada, bribing officials is illegal, but many Kenyans consider paying such bribes a part of life. To get something done right, they pay *kitu kidogo* (or "something small"). In China businesses pay *huilu*, in Russia they pay *vzyatka*, in the Middle East it's *baksheesh*, and in Mexico it's *una mordida* ("a small bite").[32] In 1999, Canada signed an international bribery convention negotiated by nations belonging to the Organization for Economic Cooperation and Development (OECD). In the same year, federal legislation was instituted that would make bribing a foreign official a criminal offence in Canada.[33]

Making ethical choices across cultures can seem highly complicated, but doing so actually differs little from the way you choose the most ethical path in your own culture (see Chapter 1). When communicating across cultures, keep your messages ethical by applying four basic principles:[34]

In the low context cultures of Canada, the U.S., and France, for example, employees avoid socializing with fellow workers and value skill as much as position and status. In the high context cultures of Greece, China, and Japan, for example, business and social relationships mix and employees value position and status more than skills. Are these assessments of low context and high context cultures accurate, based on your experience? What are the dangers of generalizing culture?

Cultural differences can complicate ethical choices.

1. **Actively seek mutual ground.** To allow the clearest possible exchange of information, both parties must be flexible and avoid insisting that an interaction take place strictly in terms of one culture or another.
2. **Send and receive messages without judgment.** To allow information to flow freely, both parties must recognize that values vary from culture to culture, and they must trust each other.
3. **Send messages that are honest.** To ensure that the information is true, both parties must see things as they are—not as they would like them to be. Both parties must be fully aware of their personal and cultural biases.
4. **Show respect for cultural differences.** To protect the basic human rights of both parties, each must understand and acknowledge the other's needs and preserve each other's dignity by communicating without deception.

Honesty and respect are cornerstones of ethical communication, regardless of culture.

SOCIAL DIFFERENCES The nature of social behaviour varies among cultures, sometimes dramatically. These behaviours are guided by rules. Some rules are formal and specifically articulated (table manners are a good example), and some are informal and learned over time (such as the comfortable standing distance between two speakers in an office or whether it's acceptable for male and female employees to socialize outside work). The combination of both types of rules influences the overall behaviour of everyone in a society, or at least most of the people most of the time. In addition to the factors already discussed, social rules can vary from culture to culture in the following areas:

Formal rules of etiquette are explicit and well defined, but informal rules are learned through observation and imitation.

> **Roles and status.** Culture dictates how people show respect and signify rank. For example, people in Canada show respect by addressing top managers as "Mr. Roberts" or "Ms. Gutierrez." However, people in China address businesspeople according to their official titles, such as "President" or "Manager."[35] Laraine Kaminsky notes that "High-tech people speak in very casual language using first names. But many people from abroad are raised with a different level of formality." A middle-aged engineer from another country would need to adjust to working under a younger manager, particularly if the manager is female.[36]

Founded by Tomas Bata, an immigrant from the former Czechoslovakia, Bata Shoes owns over 4600 stores in more than 50 countries and employs over 40 000 people. How do you think culture influences employee interactions in Africa or the Middle East? Check out www.bata.com/us/about_us/bata_in_the_world.php to learn about the company's operations around the world.

The rules of polite behaviour vary from country to country.

Attitudes toward time, such as strict adherence to meeting schedules, can vary throughout the world.

Nonverbal differences can vary widely from culture to culture.

The "thumbs up" sign means "one" in Germany and "five" in Japan; it is an obscene gesture in Australia and some other countries. The "OK" sign means "zero" or "worthless" in France; indicates money in Japan; it is an obscene gesture in Germany, Brazil, and some other countries. Do you know of other hand signs that are interpreted differently in different countries? Should business people avoid gesturing when interacting with global partners?

> **Use of manners.** What is polite in one culture may be considered rude in another. For example, asking a colleague "How was your weekend?" is a common way of making small talk in Canada and the United States, but the question sounds intrusive to people in cultures where business and private lives are seen as totally separate. Laraine Kaminsky says, "Hospitality matters in a collectivist culture like China. It would be considered impolite to help yourself to food at an event, for example, without also explicitly inviting colleagues to partake or even offering them a serving. At dinner, pour the tea for everyone at the table before you fill your own cup."[37]

> **Concepts of time.** Business runs on schedules, deadlines, and appointments, but these matters are regarded differently from culture to culture. People in low-context cultures view time as a limited resource and tend to treat schedules as rigid requirements. However, executives from high-context cultures often see time as more flexible and often take care not to damage relationships in pursuit of deadlines. Consequently, the workday isn't expected to follow a rigid, preset schedule.[38] Trying to coax a team into staying on a strict schedule would be an attractive attribute in Canadian and U.S. companies but could be viewed as pushy and overbearing in other cultures.

NONVERBAL DIFFERENCES As Chapter 2 discusses, nonverbal communication can be a reliable guide to determining the meaning of a message. However, this notion of reliability is valid only when the communicators belong to the same culture. For example, the simplest hand gestures change meaning from culture to culture. A gesture that communicates good luck in Brazil is the equivalent of giving someone "the finger" in Colombia.[39] In fact, the area of gestures is so complicated that entire books have been written about it. Don't assume that the gestures you grew up with will translate to another culture; doing so could lead to embarrassing mistakes.

From colours to facial expression, nonverbal elements add yet another layer of richness and complexity to intercultural communication. When you have the opportunity to interact with people in another culture, the best advice is to study the culture in advance and then observe the way people behave in the following areas:

> **Greetings.** Do people shake hands, bow, or kiss lightly (on one side of the face or both)?

> **Personal space.** When people are conversing, do they stand closer together or farther away than you are accustomed to?

> **Touching.** Do people touch each other on the arm to emphasize a point or slap each other on the back to show congratulation? Or do they refrain from touching altogether?

> **Facial expressions.** Do people shake their heads to indicate "no" and nod them to indicate "yes"? This is what people are accustomed to in Canada and the United States, but it is not universal.
> **Eye contact.** Do people make frequent eye contact or avoid it? Frequent eye contact is often taken as a sign of honesty and openness in Canada, but in other cultures it can be a sign of aggressiveness or lack of respect.
> **Posture.** Do people slouch and relax in the office and in public, or do they sit up straight?
> **Formality.** In general, does the culture seem more or less formal than yours?

Following the lead of people who grew up in the culture is not only a great way to learn, but also a good way to show respect.

AGE DIFFERENCES Canada celebrates youth in general and successful young businesspeople in particular; for example, newspapers such as the *National Post* publish special supplements highlighting successful entrepreneurs under 40. Youth is associated with strength, energy, possibilities, and freedom, whereas age is too often associated with declining powers and a loss of respect and authority.[40] As a result, younger employees in Canadian companies often communicate with older colleagues as equals, even to the point of openly disagreeing with them.

In contrast, in cultures that value age and seniority, longevity earns respect and increasing power and freedom. For example, in many Asian societies, the oldest employees hold the most powerful jobs, the most impressive titles, and the greatest degree of freedom and decision-making authority. If a younger employee disagrees with one of these senior executives, the discussion is never conducted in public. The notion of "saving face," of avoiding public embarrassment, is too strong. Instead, if a senior person seems to be in error about something, other employees will find a quiet, private way to communicate whatever information they feel is necessary.[41]

As with all diversity issues, the solution to age-related conflicts can be found in respecting one another and working toward common goals. As one career counsellor from Encinitas, California, put it, "It's a real blessing to have different generations in our workplaces. There is so much we can share, if we make the effort."[42]

> *A culture's views on youth and aging affect how people communicate with one another.*

GENDER DIFFERENCES The perception of men and women in business also varies from culture to culture. In Canada, women find a much wider range of business opportunities than existed just a few decades ago. Christine Magee is the founder and CEO of Sleep Country Canada, and Barbara Stymiest is the chief operating officer of the Royal Bank of Canada. However, such opportunity is not the case in more tradition-oriented societies, where men tend to hold most or all of the positions of authority and women are expected to play a more subservient role. Female executives who visit other cultures may not be taken seriously until they successfully handle challenges to their knowledge, capabilities, and patience.[43]

Whatever the culture, evidence suggests that men and women tend to have slightly different communication styles. Broadly speaking, men tend to emphasize content in their communication efforts whereas women place a higher premium on relationship maintenance.[44] Again, these are broad generalizations that do not apply to every person in every situation, but keeping them in mind can help men and women overcome communication hurdles in the workplace.

> *Generally speaking, the communication styles of men and women can differ on several points.*

Improving Intercultural Communication Skills

The better you are at intercultural communication, the more successful you'll be in today's business environment. However, communicating successfully from one culture to another requires a variety of skills (see Figure 3–1). You can

> **Objective 5** Outline strategies for studying other cultures.

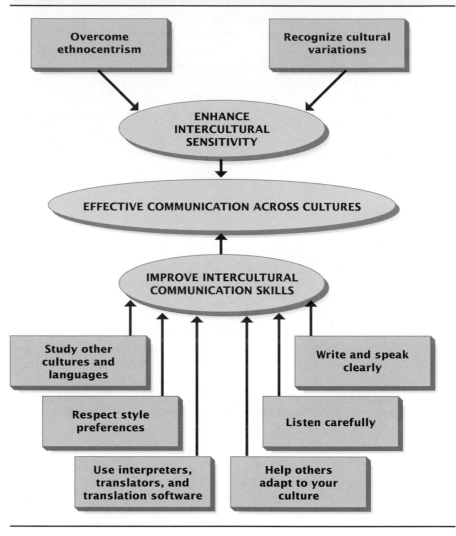

> Figure 3–1 Components of Successful Intercultural Communication

improve your intercultural skills throughout your entire career. Begin now by studying other cultures and languages, respecting preferences for communication styles, learning to write and speak clearly, listening carefully, knowing when to use interpreters and translators, and helping others adapt to your culture.

Studying Other Cultures

Effectively adapting your communication efforts to another culture requires not only knowledge about the culture, but also both the ability and the motivation to change your personal habits as needed.[45] In other words, it's not a simple task. Unfortunately, a thorough knowledge of another culture and its communication patterns (both verbal and nonverbal) can take years to acquire. Fortunately, you don't need to learn about the whole world all at once. Many companies appoint specialists for specific countries or regions, giving you a chance to focus on fewer cultures at a time. On IBM's global workforce diversity intranet site, for instance, employees can click on the "GoingGlobal" link to learn about customs in specific cultures.[46]

Components of Successful Intercultural Communication

Nor do you need to learn everything about a culture to ensure some level of communication success. Even a small amount of research and practice will help you get through many business situations. In addition, most people respond positively to honest effort and good intentions, and many business associates will help you along if you show an interest in learning more about their cultures.

Approach situations with an open mind and a healthy sense of humour. Recognize that everybody who tries to communicate across cultures makes mistakes. When it happens, simply apologize if appropriate, ask the other person to explain the accepted way, and then move on. As business becomes ever more global, even the most tradition-bound cultures are learning to deal with outsiders more patiently and overlook the occasional cultural blunder.[47]

Numerous websites and books offer advice on travelling to and working in specific cultures; they're a great place to start. Also, sample newspapers, magazines, and even the music and movies of another country. For example, a movie can demonstrate nonverbal customs even if you don't grasp the language. For some key issues to research before doing business in another country, refer to Table 3–1.

Improving intercultural skills is a career-long effort.

Mistakes will happen, and when they do, apologize (if appropriate), ask about the accepted way, and move on.

Studying Other Languages

Consider what it must be like to work at Royal Bank, where its global workforce operates in more than 30 countries worldwide. Without the ability to communicate in more than one language, how does this diverse group of people conduct business? As commerce continues to become more globalized, the demand for multilingual communicators continues to grow as well. Some countries have emphasized language diversity more than others over the years. For example, in the Netherlands, with its long history of international trade, fluency in multiple languages is considered an essential business skill.[48] Shifts in business patterns can dramatically affect language learning, too. As U.S. companies continue to outsource a variety of business functions to facilities in India, many Indians now view English skills as an important career asset. Conversely, the growing international status of China as a manufacturing powerhouse is prompting many professionals in Canada, the United States, and other countries to learn Mandarin, the official language in China.[49]

Even if your colleagues or customers in another country do speak your language, it's worth the time and energy to learn common phrases in theirs. Learning the basics not only helps you get through everyday business and social situations, but also demonstrates your commitment to the business relationship. After all, the other person probably spent years learning your language.

And don't assume that two countries speaking the same language speak it the same way. Canada and the United Kingdom are two countries divided by a common language. For example, *apartment*, *elevator*, and *gasoline* in Canada are *flat*, *lift*, and *petrol* in the United Kingdom.

English is the most prevalent language in international business, but it's a mistake to assume that everyone understands it.

If you have a long-term business relationship with people of another culture, it is helpful to learn at least some basic words and phrases of their language.

Respecting Preferences for Communication Style

Communication style—including the level of directness, the degree of formality, preferences for written versus spoken communication, and other factors—varies widely from culture to culture. Knowing what your communication partners expect can help you adapt to their particular style. Once again, watching and learning is the best way to improve your skills; however, you can infer some generalities from what you already know about a culture. For example,

> ## > Table 3–1 Doing Business Abroad

Action	Details to Consider
Understand social customs	> How do people react to strangers? Are they friendly? Hostile? Reserved? > How do people greet each other? Should you bow? Nod? Shake hands? > How do you express appreciation for an invitation to lunch, dinner, or someone's home? Should you bring a gift? Send flowers? Write a thank-you note? > Are any phrases, facial expressions, or hand gestures considered rude? > How do you attract the attention of a waiter? Do you tip the waiter? > When is it rude to refuse an invitation? How do you refuse politely? > What topics may or may not be discussed in a social setting? In a business setting? > How do social customs dictate interaction between men and women? Between younger people and older people?
Learn about clothing and food preferences	> What occasions require special clothing? > What colours are associated with mourning? Love? Joy? > Are some types of clothing considered taboo for one gender or the other? > How many times a day do people eat? > How are hands or utensils used when eating? > Where is the seat of honour at a table?
Assess political patterns	> How stable is the political situation? > Does the political situation affect businesses in and out of the country? > What are the traditional government institutions? > Is it appropriate to talk politics in social or business situations?
Understand religious and folk beliefs	> To which religious groups do people belong? > Which places, objects, actions, and events are sacred? > Do religious beliefs affect communication between men and women or between any other groups? > Is there a tolerance for minority religions? > How do religious holidays affect business and government activities? > Does religion require or prohibit eating specific foods? At specific times?
Learn about economic and business institutions	> Is the society homogeneous or heterogeneous? > What languages are spoken? > What are the primary resources and principal products? > Are businesses generally large? Family controlled? Government controlled? > What are the generally accepted working hours? > How do people view scheduled appointments? > Are people expected to socialize before conducting business?
Appraise the nature of ethics, values, and laws	> Is money or a gift expected in exchange for arranging business transactions? > Do people value competitiveness or cooperation? > What are the attitudes toward work? Toward money? > Is politeness more important than factual honesty?

Canadian and U.S. workers typically prefer an open and direct communication style; they find other styles frustrating or suspect. Directness is also valued in Sweden as a sign of efficiency; but, unlike discussions in the United States, heated debates and confrontations are unusual. Italian, German, and French executives don't soften up colleagues with praise before they criticize—doing so seems manipulative to them. However, professionals from high-context cultures, such as Japan or China, tend to be less direct.[50]

Business correspondence is often more formal in other countries than it is in Canada and the United States.

In international correspondence, Canadian and U.S. businesspeople will generally want to be somewhat more formal than they would be when writing to people in their own country. The letter in Figure 3–2 was written by a supplier in Germany to a nearby retailer; you can see how the tone is more formal than would be used in Canada. In Germany, business letters usually open with a reference to the business relationship and close with a compliment to the recipient. Of course, if you carry formality to extremes, you'll sound unnatural.

> Figure 3–2 Effective German Business Letter (Translated)

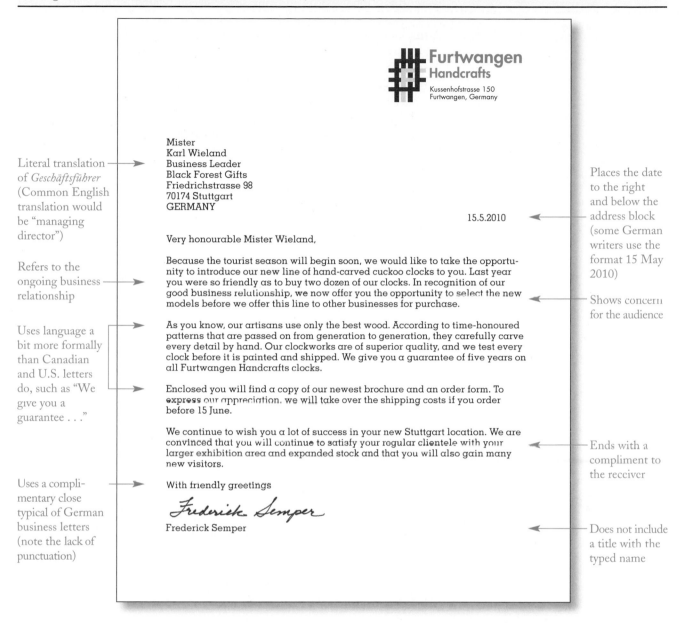

Literal translation of *Geschäftsführer* (Common English translation would be "managing director")

Refers to the ongoing business relationship

Uses language a bit more formally than Canadian and U.S. letters do, such as "We give you a guarantee . . ."

Uses a complimentary close typical of German business letters (note the lack of punctuation)

Furtwangen Handcrafts
Kussenhofstrasse 150
Furtwangen, Germany

Mister
Karl Wieland
Business Leader
Black Forest Gifts
Friedrichstrasse 98
70174 Stuttgart
GERMANY

15.5.2010

Very honourable Mister Wieland,

Because the tourist season will begin soon, we would like to take the opportunity to introduce our new line of hand-carved cuckoo clocks to you. Last year you were so friendly as to buy two dozen of our clocks. In recognition of our good business relationship, we now offer you the opportunity to select the new models before we offer this line to other businesses for purchase.

As you know, our artisans use only the best wood. According to time-honoured patterns that are passed on from generation to generation, they carefully carve every detail by hand. Our clockworks are of superior quality, and we test every clock before it is painted and shipped. We give you a guarantee of five years on all Furtwangen Handcrafts clocks.

Enclosed you will find a copy of our newest brochure and an order form. To express our appreciation, we will take over the shipping costs if you order before 15 June.

We continue to wish you a lot of success in your new Stuttgart location. We are convinced that you will continue to satisfy your regular clientele with your larger exhibition area and expanded stock and that you will also gain many new visitors.

With friendly greetings

Frederick Semper
Frederick Semper

Places the date to the right and below the address block (some German writers use the format 15 May 2010)

Shows concern for the audience

Ends with a compliment to the receiver

Does not include a title with the typed name

Writing and Speaking Clearly

In addition to learning the preferred style of your communication partners, you can help ensure successful messages by taking extra care with your writing. When sending written communication to businesspeople from another culture, familiarize yourself with their written communication preferences and adapt your approach, style, and tone to meet their expectations. Follow these recommendations[51]:

Objective 6 List seven recommendations for writing clearly in multilanguage business environments.

> **Use simple, clear language.** Use precise words that don't have the potential to confuse with multiple meanings. The word *high* has 20 meanings; the word *expensive* has one, leaving no room for ambiguity.[52]
> **Be brief.** Use simple sentences and short paragraphs, breaking information into smaller chunks that are easier for your reader to capture and translate.[53]

> **Use transitional elements.** Help readers follow your train of thought by using transitional words and phrases. Precede related points with expressions such as *in addition* and *first, second,* and *third.*

> **Address international correspondence properly.** Refer to Table 1–2 in Appendix A for an explanation of different address elements and salutations commonly used in certain foreign countries.

> **Cite dates and numbers carefully.** The Canadian Standards Association has adopted the international standard of year-month-day for dates. Thus, December 5, 2010 is written numerically as 2010–12–05 when following international usage; the arrangement follows the largest element (the year) to the smallest element (the day). However, in practice many Canadian businesses also follow British or U.S. usage, and may omit the first two numbers of the year. Consequently, December 5, 2010 may be written 05–12–10, which means 5 December 2010 (British usage) or 12–05–10, which means December 5, 2010 (U.S. usage). Dates in Japan and China typically follow the international standard. You should also be aware of international differences in number formats. For example, 1.000 means one with three decimal places in Canada, the United States, and Great Britain, but it means one thousand in many European countries.

> **Avoid slang, idiomatic phrases, and business jargon.** Everyday speech and writing is full of slang and idiomatic phrases that mean more than the sum of their literal parts. Many of these informal usages are so deeply ingrained, in fact, that you may not even be aware that you're using them. Examples from Canadian and U.S. English include phrases such as "off the top of my head," and "more bang for the buck." Your foreign correspondent may have no idea what you're talking about when you use such phrases.

> **Avoid humour and other references to popular culture.** Jokes and references to popular entertainment usually rely on subtle cultural issues that your audience may be completely unaware of.

Compare the letters shown in Figures 3–3 and 3–4, in which a Canadian is writing to a French business partner to explain why his expenses were unusually high for the previous month. Although some of the differences may seem trivial, meeting the expectations of an international audience illustrates both knowledge of and respect for other cultures.

Whether you're travelling to another country or teaming up with someone who is visiting or immigrating to your country, you're likely to speak with people whose native language is different from yours. Even when you know the vocabulary and grammar of the other person's language, the processing of everyday conversations can be difficult. Immigrants with a working knowledge of English would have difficulty understanding that "Jeat yet?" means "Did you eat yet?" and that "Cannahepya?" means "Can I help you?" Some non-native English speakers don't distinguish between the English sounds *v* and *w*, so they say "wery" for "very." At the same time, Canadians may have trouble pronouncing the German *ch.* Graybridge Malkam Cross-Cultural Training offers "natural conversation" sessions to help immigrants understand English pronunciation.

To be more effective in intercultural conversations, follow these practices:

Companies such as Toronto-based Dalton Chemical Laboratories provide on-site ESL classes. These classes not only train people in English, but also create cohesive teams. Besides language training, what other methods help people of different cultures form effective teams?

1. Speak slowly and clearly.
2. Don't rephrase until it's obviously necessary (immediately rephrasing something you've just said doubles the translation workload for the listener).

> Figure 3–3 Ineffective Intercultural Letter

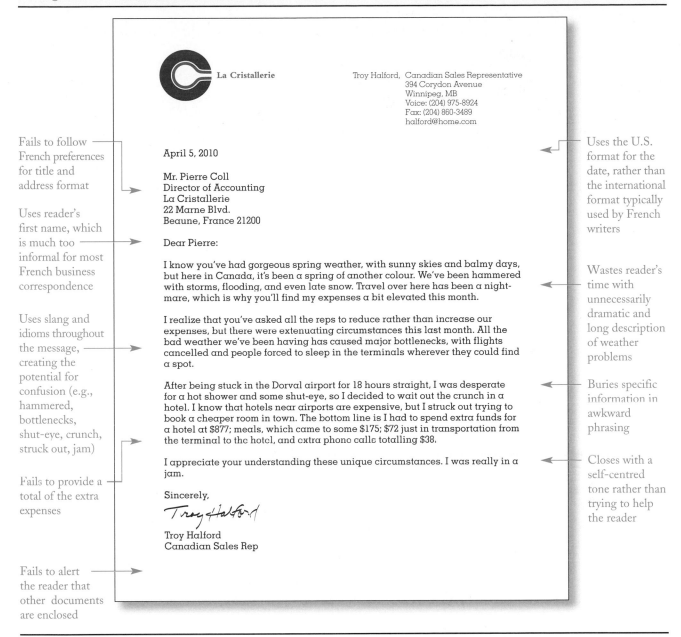

La Cristallerie

Troy Halford, Canadian Sales Representative
394 Corydon Avenue
Winnipeg, MB
Voice: (204) 975-8924
Fax: (204) 860-3489
halford@home.com

Fails to follow French preferences for title and address format

Uses reader's first name, which is much too informal for most French business correspondence

Uses slang and idioms throughout the message, creating the potential for confusion (e.g., hammered, bottlenecks, shut-eye, crunch, struck out, jam)

Fails to provide a total of the extra expenses

Fails to alert the reader that other documents are enclosed

April 5, 2010

Mr. Pierre Coll
Director of Accounting
La Cristallerie
22 Marne Blvd.
Beaune, France 21200

Dear Pierre:

I know you've had gorgeous spring weather, with sunny skies and balmy days, but here in Canada, it's been a spring of another colour. We've been hammered with storms, flooding, and even late snow. Travel over here has been a nightmare, which is why you'll find my expenses a bit elevated this month.

I realize that you've asked all the reps to reduce rather than increase our expenses, but there were extenuating circumstances this last month. All the bad weather we've been having has caused major bottlenecks, with flights cancelled and people forced to sleep in the terminals wherever they could find a spot.

After being stuck in the Dorval airport for 18 hours straight, I was desperate for a hot shower and some shut-eye, so I decided to wait out the crunch in a hotel. I know that hotels near airports are expensive, but I struck out trying to book a cheaper room in town. The bottom line is I had to spend extra funds for a hotel at $877; meals, which came to some $175; $72 just in transportation from the terminal to the hotel, and extra phone calls totalling $38.

I appreciate your understanding these unique circumstances. I was really in a jam.

Sincerely,

Troy Halford

Troy Halford
Canadian Sales Rep

Uses the U.S. format for the date, rather than the international format typically used by French writers

Wastes reader's time with unnecessarily dramatic and long description of weather problems

Buries specific information in awkward phrasing

Closes with a self-centred tone rather than trying to help the reader

3. Look for and ask for feedback to make sure your message is getting through.
4. Don't talk down to the other person by overenunciating words or oversimplifying sentences.
5. At the end of the conversation, make sure you and the listener agree on what has been said and decided.

Listening Carefully

Languages vary considerably in the significance of tone, pitch, speed, and volume. The English word *progress* can be a noun or a verb, depending on which syllable you stress. In Chinese, the meaning of the word *mà* changes depending on the speaker's tone; it can mean *mother, pileup, horse,* or *scold.*[54] Businesspeople from Japan tend to speak more softly than Westerners.

Speaking clearly and getting plenty of feedback are two keys to successful intercultural conversations.

> Figure 3–4 Effective Intercultural Letter

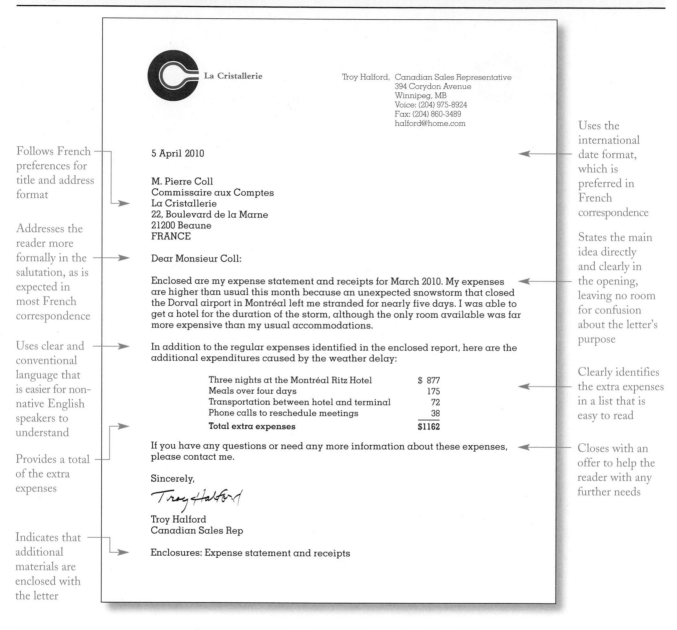

Follows French preferences for title and address format

Addresses the reader more formally in the salutation, as is expected in most French correspondence

Uses clear and conventional language that is easier for non-native English speakers to understand

Provides a total of the extra expenses

Indicates that additional materials are enclosed with the letter

Uses the international date format, which is preferred in French correspondence

States the main idea directly and clearly in the opening, leaving no room for confusion about the letter's purpose

Clearly identifies the extra expenses in a list that is easy to read

Closes with an offer to help the reader with any further needs

La Cristallerie

Troy Halford, Canadian Sales Representative
394 Corydon Avenue
Winnipeg, MB
Voice: (204) 975-8924
Fax: (204) 860-3489
halford@home.com

5 April 2010

M. Pierre Coll
Commissaire aux Comptes
La Cristallerie
22, Boulevard de la Marne
21200 Beaune
FRANCE

Dear Monsieur Coll:

Enclosed are my expense statement and receipts for March 2010. My expenses are higher than usual this month because an unexpected snowstorm that closed the Dorval airport in Montréal left me stranded for nearly five days. I was able to get a hotel for the duration of the storm, although the only room available was far more expensive than my usual accommodations.

In addition to the regular expenses identified in the enclosed report, here are the additional expenditures caused by the weather delay:

Three nights at the Montréal Ritz Hotel	$ 877
Meals over four days	175
Transportation between hotel and terminal	72
Phone calls to reschedule meetings	38
Total extra expenses	**$1162**

If you have any questions or need any more information about these expenses, please contact me.

Sincerely,

Troy Halford

Troy Halford
Canadian Sales Rep

Enclosures: Expense statement and receipts

To listen more effectively in intercultural situations, accept what you hear without judgment and let people finish what they have to say.

With some practice, you can start to get a sense of vocal patterns. The key is simply to accept what you hear first, without jumping to conclusions about meaning or motivation. Let other people finish what they have to say. If you interrupt, you may miss something important. You'll also show a lack of respect. If you do not understand a comment, ask the person to repeat it. Any momentary awkwardness you might feel in asking for extra help is less important than the risk of unsuccessful communication.

Using Interpreters, Translators, and Translation Software

You may encounter business situations that require using an interpreter (for spoken communication) or a translator (for written communication). In addition, most customers expect to be addressed in their native language, particularly concerning advertising, warranties, repair and maintenance manuals, and product labels. These documents certainly require the services of a translator. Microsoft spends several hundred million dollars a year to make virtually all of its software products, websites, and help documents available in dozens of languages; the company is believed by some to be the world's largest purchaser of translation services.[55]

Keeping up with current language usage in a given country or culture is also critical. Landor Associates, a leading international marketing agency, usually engages three native-language speakers to review translated materials to ensure that the sense of the message is compatible with current usage and slang in a given country.[56] Some companies use *back-translation* to ensure accuracy. Once a translator encodes a message into another language, a different translator retranslates the same message into the original language. This back-translation is then compared with the original message to discover any errors or discrepancies.

The time and cost required for professional translation has encouraged the development of **machine translation**, any form of computerized intelligence used to translate one language to another. Dedicated software tools and online services such as WorldLingo (www.worldlingo.com) and Montreal-based Alis Technologies (www.alis.com) offer some form of automated translation. Major search engines such as AltaVista and Google let you request a translated version of the websites you find. Don't rely on machine translation for business transactions, however, because it will not provide results on par with human translators. Machine translation will likely produce incomprehensible English when trying to handle conversational and idiomatic language, whereas specialists can render both the denotation and connotation of foreign terms. Nevertheless, machine translation can be quite useful with individual words and short phrases, and they can give you the overall gist of a message.[57]

Machine translation uses computerized intelligence (such as software on websites) to translate material from one language to another.

Helping Others Adapt to Your Culture

Now that you have a good appreciation for the complexity of getting your message across to someone in another culture, you can also appreciate the challenges faced by people from other cultures when they try to communicate with you. Whether a younger person is unaccustomed to the formalities of a large corporation, or a colleague from another country is working on a team with you, look for opportunities to help people fit in and adapt their communication style. For example, if a non-native English speaker is making mistakes that could hurt his or her credibility, you can offer advice on the appropriate words and phrases to use. Most language learners truly appreciate this sort of assistance, as long as it is offered in a respectful manner. For more ideas on how to improve communication in the workplace, see "Checklist: Improving Intercultural Communication Skills."

Remember that speaking and listening are usually much harder in a second language than writing and reading. Oral communication requires participants to process sound in addition to meaning, and it doesn't provide any time to go back and reread or rewrite. So instead of asking a foreign colleague to provide information in a conference call, you could set up an intranet site where the person can file a written report. Similarly, instant messaging, email, or blogging is often easier for colleagues with different native languages than participating in live conversations.

Whatever assistance you can provide will be greatly appreciated. Smart businesspeople recognize the value of intercultural communication skills. Moreover, while you're helping others, you'll learn something about other cultures, too.

CHECKLIST Improving Intercultural Communication Skills

✔ Study other cultures so that you can appreciate cultural variations.

✔ Study the languages of people with whom you communicate, even if you can learn only a few basic words and phrases.

✔ Help non-native speakers learn English.

✔ Respect cultural preferences for communication style.

✔ Write clearly, using brief messages, simple language, generous transitions, and appropriate international conventions.

✔ Avoid slang, humour, and references to popular culture.

✔ Speak clearly and slowly, giving listeners time to translate your words.

✔ Ask for feedback to ensure successful communication.

✔ Listen carefully and ask speakers to repeat anything you don't understand.

✔ Use interpreters and translators for important messages.

Summary of Learning Objectives

1 **Discuss the opportunities and challenges of intercultural communication.** Effective intercultural communication offers many opportunities in the global marketplace: because of technology, businesses small and large can use the internet to enlarge their customer base and sell their products both at home and abroad. The multicultural workplace offers a broad diversity of opinions and ideas, thus creating more creative companies. Cultural diversity also creates challenges to how business messages are planned, prepared, produced, and interpreted: with the broad range of skills and traditions in today's workplaces, businesspeople must be highly sensitive to how the receivers of their messages interpret language and behaviour.

2 **Define culture and explain how culture is learned.** Culture is defined as a shared system of beliefs, attitudes, values, expectations, and norms of behaviour. Culture is learned directly, through explicitly taught acceptable behaviours, and implicitly, through observing the values of your group.

3 **Define ethnocentrism and stereotyping, and then give three suggestions for overcoming these limiting mindsets.** Ethnocentrism is the tendency to judge all other groups according to one's own standards, behaviours, and customs. Stereotyping is predicting individuals' behaviour or character on the basis of their membership in a particular group or class. To overcome ethnocentrism, follow three suggestions: (1) acknowledge distinctions; (2) avoid assumptions; and (3) avoid judgments.

4 **Explain the importance of recognizing cultural variations, and list six categories of cultural differences.** It is important to recognize cultural variations to avoid communication breakdown and to demonstrate respect to members of other cultures. The six categories of cultural differences are (1) contextual differences; (2) legal and ethical differences; (3) social differences; (4) nonverbal differences; (5) age differences; and (6) gender differences.

5 **Outline strategies for studying other cultures.** Studying other cultures helps you send and receive intercultural messages more effectively. Even though you can't expect to understand another culture completely, you can increase your intercultural knowledge by reading books and articles about other cultures and by talking to people who do business in other cultures. Tips offered by successful businesspeople include the following: (1) take responsibility for communication; (2) withhold judgment; (3) show respect; (4) empathize; (5) look beyond the superficial; (6) be patient and persistent; and (7) be flexible.

6 **List seven recommendations for writing clearly in multilanguage business environments.** You can ensure successful messages across cultures by following these recommendations: (1) use simple and precise vocabulary; (2) write concisely with simple sentences and short paragraphs; (3) use transitions to guide readers through your ideas; (4) apply accepted standards of international correspondence; (5) cite numbers and dates appropriately for your audience; (6) avoid idioms and jargon; and (7) avoid humour and other references to popular culture.

PEARSON
mycanadianbuscommlab™

Visit www.mycanadianbuscommlab.ca for everything you need to help you succeed in the job you've always wanted! Tools and resources include the following:
- Composing Space and Writer's Toolkit
- Document Makeovers
- Video Case Studies
- Grammar Exercises—and much more!

On the Job PERFORMING COMMUNICATION TASKS AT GRAYBRIDGE MALKAM

Graybridge Malkam International Consulting provides diversity, cultural awareness, and language training services to individual and corporate clients. Imagine you are a trainer at Graybridge Malkam working with a class of newcomers who are learning English. You want to foster cooperation among your students and encourage them to interact effectively with each other. Use your skill in intercultural communication to choose the best response in each situation. Be prepared to explain why your choice is best.

1 It's important that students in your class for English as a second language develop their ability to speak conversational English. How do you accomplish this?
   a You have each student prepare at least two presentations in English on aspects of their culture that they will deliver to the class.
   b From time to time, you take the class to a coffee shop and have them order food in English and speak English while they are there.
   c You pair off students and have them prepare scenarios in English, such as job interviews, to present in front of the class.
   d From time to time, you invite the class to your home where you lead conversations in English.

2 Several of your students in your class for English as a second language do not make eye contact when delivering speeches because in their cultures it is considered rude to make eye contact with other people. How do you persuade them to look at the audience?

   a You gently encourage the students to make eye contact. You explain that in Canada it is common for business-people to make eye contact when giving a presentation, and that people who don't are not considered effective speakers.
   b You don't discuss the issue with the students at all and let them avoid making eye contact. You believe they will understand the importance of eye contact when they give presentations in their jobs in Canada.
   c You show videos about making effective presentations, hoping the students will be encouraged to make eye contact after watching them.
   d You set up team presentations, creating teams with students who are comfortable making eye contact with the audience and those who are not. You expect that while these teams rehearse their presentations, students who avoid looking at the audience will be persuaded to make eye contact after working with peers who do.

3 Your students are breaking into ethnically based cliques. Members of individual ethnic groups eat and socialize together and chat in their native language. Some other students feel left out and alienated. How do you encourage a unified class attitude?
   a Ban the use of languages other than English in class.
   b Do nothing. This is normal behaviour.
   c Encourage people to mingle and get to know each other better.
   d Send all of your students to diversity training classes.

Test Your Knowledge

1 How have market globalization and cultural diversity contributed to the increased importance of intercultural communication?

2 What are the basic characteristics of culture?

3 How do high-context cultures differ from low-context cultures?

4 In addition to contextual differences, what other categories of cultural differences exist?

5 What is ethnocentrism? How can it be overcome in communication?

6 Why is it a good idea to avoid slang and idioms when addressing a multicultural audience?

7 What are the benefits and disadvantages of using machine translation?

8 What are some ways to improve oral skills when communicating with people of other cultures?

9 What are some ways to improve writing skills when communicating with people of other cultures?

10 What is the purpose of back-translation when preparing a message in another language?

Apply Your Knowledge

1 What are some intercultural differences that managers of a Canada-based firm might encounter during a series of business meetings with a China-based company whose managers speak English fairly well?

2 What are some intercultural communication issues to consider when deciding whether to accept an overseas job with a firm whose headquarters are in your own country? A job in your own country with a local branch of a foreign-owned firm? Explain.

3 How do you think company managers from a country that has a relatively homogeneous culture might react when they do business with the culturally diverse staff of a com-

pany based in a less homogeneous country? Explain your answer.

4 Your company has relocated to a Canadian city where Vietnamese culture is strongly established. Many of your employees will be from this culture. What can you do to improve communication between your management and the Vietnamese Canadians you are currently hiring?

5 Your office in Turkey desperately needs the supplies that have been stuck in Turkish customs for a month. Should you bribe a customs official to speed up delivery? Explain your decision.

Running Cases

Watch on mycanadianbuscommlab

> CASE 1 Noreen

Noreen is having lunch at the Petro-Go cafeteria. She is sitting with Dan and Karen from her "Go Points" department team. An international intern who has been working in Noreen's department arrives and joins the table. After 10 minutes or so, Noreen's teammates get up and move to another table. They start giggling and whispering. The intern feels they are laughing and talking about her because she heard them mention her name, but she is not sure what they are saying.

The same afternoon Karen comes to Noreen, her team leader, and asks to speak with her in private. They go to a meeting room. Karen explains that since she moved into the cubicle next to the intern she has not been happy. She says that the intern has an unusual body odour, and others have noticed it as well.

QUESTIONS

a) What should Noreen do?
b) Does Karen have a right to ask to change seats?
c) What misunderstandings may be happening?
d) Could the intern's body odour be caused by a medical condition? Could it be the result of the cultural food she eats?
e) What can be done to prevent the intern from not being accepted by her teammates?

YOUR TASK

If you were Noreen, how would you handle this situation? Would you discuss this matter with the intern or ask your manager to? What would you say? Partner with a classmate and role-play this situation.

> CASE 2 Kwong

Kwong is on his way to an interview with A1 Accounting, the company he would like to work at during his co-op placement. Kwong arrives 10 minutes late for his interview because he had written the street name incorrectly in his notes, but the receptionist takes him into the interview room right away. There are three managers sitting, waiting at a table. They rise and introduce themselves and shake Kwong's hand. Kwong shakes each interviewer's hand with a soft, two-handed handshake. During the interview Kwong shows his respect for the managers by avoiding direct eye contact; instead, he gazes at the floor most of the time. Kwong's answers to many of the questions are vague and often ambiguous. When Kwong is asked when he would be available to start, he answers by telling the managers what he would do to get started at his job instead of when he could start work. Kwong answers a few other

questions similarly, as if he did not hear the question correctly or did not understand it. Kwong does not get the job.

QUESTIONS

a) Did Kwong communicate well and appear confident during the interview?
b) Why do you think Kwong did not get the job?
c) What do you think the managers were thinking of Kwong?
d) Why did Kwong answer the questions as if he did not hear them correctly?
e) What can Kwong do to improve his skills before the next interview?

YOUR TASK

In pairs, role-play an interview and demonstrate an appropriate introduction, handshake, questions and answers, and closing.

Assign your actors a role, such as a woman being interviewed by a man, an older person being interviewed by a younger person, a person using a wheelchair being interviewed by a person not in a wheelchair, a person from a low-context culture being interviewed by a person from a high-context culture. Have others in the class observe and give feedback on potential problems that may occur and how to handle them.

Practise Your Knowledge

Your boss wants to write a brief email message welcoming employees recently transferred to your department from your Hong Kong branch. They all speak English, but your boss asks you to review her message for clarity. What would you do to improve this message, given the intended audience—and why? Would you consider this message to be audience-centred? Why or why not?

I wanted to welcome you ASAP to our little family here north of the border. It's high time we shook hands in person and not just across the sea. I'm pleased as punch about getting to know you all, and I for one will do my level best to sell you on Canada.

Exercises

3.1 Intercultural Sensitivity: Recognizing Variations
You represent a Canadian toy company that's negotiating to buy miniature truck wheels from a manufacturer in Osaka, Japan. In your first meeting, you explain that your company expects to control the design of the wheels as well as the materials that are used to make them. The manufacturer's representative looks down and says softly, "Perhaps that will be difficult." You press for agreement, and to emphasize your willingness to buy, you show the prepared contract you've brought with you. However, the manufacturer seems increasingly vague and uninterested. What cultural differences may be interfering with effective communication in this situation? Explain.

3.2 Ethical Choices: Legal Considerations
A Canadian manager wants to export machine parts to a West African country, but an official there expects a special payment before allowing the shipment into his country. How can the two sides resolve their different approaches without violating Canadian rules against bribing foreign officials? On the basis of the information that Chapter 1 presents, would you consider this situation an ethical dilemma or an ethical lapse? Please explain.

3.3 Teamwork: Language and Culture
Working with two other students, prepare a list of 10 examples of slang (in your own language) that might be misinterpreted or misunderstood during a business conversation with someone from another culture. Next to each example, suggest other words you might use to convey the same message. Do the alternatives mean exactly the same as the original slang or idiom?

3.4 Intercultural Communication: Studying Cultures
Choose a specific country, such as India, Portugal, Bolivia, Thailand, or Nigeria, with which you are not familiar. Research the culture and write a brief summary of what a Canadian manager would need to know about concepts of personal space and rules of social behaviour to conduct business successfully in that country.

3.5 Multicultural Workforce: Bridging Differences
Differences in gender, age, and physical abilities contribute to the diversity of today's workforce. Working with a classmate, role-play a conversation in which
a. a woman is being interviewed for a job by a male personnel manager
b. an older person is being interviewed for a job by a younger personnel manager
c. an employee who is a native speaker of English is being interviewed for a job by a hiring manager who is a recent immigrant with relatively poor English skills

How did differences between the applicant and the interviewer shape the communication? What can you do to improve communication in such situations?

3.6 Intercultural Sensitivity: Understanding Attitudes
As the director of marketing for a telecommunications firm based in Germany, you're negotiating with an official in Guangzhou, China, who's in charge of selecting a new telephone system for the city. You insist that the specifications be spelled out in the contract. However, your Chinese counterpart seems to have little interest in technical and financial details. What can you do or say to break this intercultural deadlock and obtain the contract so that both parties are comfortable?

3.7 Culture and Time: Dealing with Variations

When a company knows that a scheduled delivery time given by an overseas firm is likely to be flexible, managers may buy in larger quantities or may order more often to avoid running out of product before the next delivery. Identify three other management decisions that may be influenced by differing cultural concepts of time, and make notes for a short (two-minute) presentation to your class.

3.8 Intercultural Communication: Using Interpreters

Imagine that you're the lead negotiator for a company that's trying to buy a factory in Prague, the capital of the Czech Republic. Although you haven't spent much time in the country in the past decade, your parents grew up near Prague, so you understand and speak the language fairly well. However, you wonder about the advantages and disadvantages of using an interpreter anyway. For example, you may have more time to think if you wait for an intermediary to translate the other side's position. Decide whether to hire an interpreter, and then write a brief (two- or three-paragraph) explanation of your decision.

3.9 Internet: Translation Software

Explore the powers and limitations of computer translation at Babel Fish, http://babelfish.altavista.com. In the box labelled "Translate a block of text," enter a sentence such as "We are enclosing a purchase order for four dozen computer monitors." Select "English to Spanish" and click to complete the translation. Once you've read the Spanish version, cut and paste it into the "text for translation" box, select "Spanish to English," and click to translate. Translate the same English sentence into German, French, or Italian and then back into English. How do the results of each translation differ? What are the implications for the use of automated translation services and back-translation? How could you use this website to sharpen your intercultural communication skills? Summarize your findings in a brief report.

3.10 Intercultural Communication: Improving Skills

You've been assigned to host a group of Swedish college students who are visiting your school for the next two weeks. They've all studied English but this is their first trip to your area. Make a list of at least eight slang terms and idioms they are likely to hear on campus. How will you explain each phrase? When speaking with the Swedish students, what word or words might you substitute for each slang term or idiom?

3.11 Intercultural Communication: Podcasting

Your company was one of the first to use the Apple iPod and other digital music players as business communication tools. Executives often record messages (such as monthly sales reports) as digital audio files and post them on the company's intranet site as podcasts. Employees from the 14 offices in Europe, Asia, and North America then download the files to their music players and listen to the messages while riding the train to work, eating lunch at their desks, and so on. Your boss asks you to draft the opening statement for a podcast that will announce a revenue drop caused by intensive competitive pressure. She reviews your script and then hands it back with a gentle explanation that it needs to be revised for international listeners. Improve the following statement in as many ways as you can:

Howdy, guys. Shouldn't surprise anyone that we took a beating this year, given the insane pricing moves our knucklehead competitors have been making. I mean, how those clowns can keep turning a profit is beyond me, what with steel costs still going through the roof and labour costs heating up—even in countries where everybody goes to find cheap labour—and hazardous waste disposal regs adding to operating costs, too.

4

Planning Business Messages

After studying this chapter, you will be able to

1. Describe the three-step writing process
2. Explain why it's important to define your purpose carefully, and list four questions that can help you test that purpose
3. Describe the importance of analyzing your audience, and identify the seven factors you should consider when developing an audience profile
4. Discuss gathering information for simple messages, and identify three attributes of quality information
5. List factors to consider when choosing the most appropriate medium for your message
6. Explain why good organization is important to both you and your audience
7. Summarize the process for organizing business messages effectively

ON THE JOB

Communicating at The Forzani Group
DESIGNING A GAME PLAN FOR SUCCESS

www.forzani.com

Whether it's skateboards, snowboards, skis, or sneakers, you'll probably find the gear you want at one of The Forzani Group's sporting goods stores. Founder John Forzani, a former Calgary Stampeder, created a retail empire that includes Sport Chek, Sports Experts, Coast Mountain Sports, Sports Mart, Nevada Bob's Golf, and the Hockey Experts. Since the opening of Forzani's Locker Room in 1974 with three teammates, the business has grown to include 567 corporate or franchise stores across Canada.

The success of The Forzani Group centres on management's ability to communicate effectively with employees, customers, and suppliers. To keep operations running smoothly, managers must establish good working relationships with each group. Says Forzani, "First of all, we try to hire the right person: somebody who is an outdoors or sports enthusiast. . . . We also spend a lot of time and effort training people, both in selling skills and product knowledge. . . . One of the biggest things we've done that has contributed to our success is to communicate on a daily basis what's happening and what we expect." The Forzani Retail College, an employee training facility, in-store presentations from factory reps, and sports camps, such as a four-day stay at Lake Louise, Alberta, to show employees an entire season of athletic wear, all contribute to the success of Canada's premier sporting goods business.

As Canada's largest sporting goods retailer, The Forzani Group operates stores coast to coast—with plans to expand to every Canadian city and increase product offerings. The company must keep operations running smoothly by constantly refining its communication, much of which must be in writing.

Effective communication and planning has led to the 40 000-square-foot Fitness Source megastore in Calgary. A fitness equipment, nutrition, and sporting apparel venue, it features a multipurpose area for product demonstrations and separate rooms displaying fitness equipment in home settings. "The fitness market is untapped in a prototype such as this," says Tom Quinn, president and chief operating officer, "and we set out to differentiate our megastore and give customers a reason to choose us over other retailers."

Communication planning wasn't as complex in 1974 when John Forzani opened his first store in Calgary, where he sold athletic footwear in a 1200-square-foot space and personally dealt with suppliers and trained employees. Establishing relationships with employees, suppliers of almost every major brand of athletic equipment and clothing, and millions of customers has complicated matters. And adapting messages to serve the needs of each audience requires careful planning.

If you worked at the Forzani head office, how would you plan your business messages to different audiences? What essential information do your readers need? And how would you choose the best channel and medium for each message?[1]

Understanding the Three-Step Writing Process

Like The Forzani Group's managers, you'll face a variety of communication assignments in your career, both oral and written. By following a proven process, you can learn to create effective messages that will not only satisfy audience needs but also highlight your skills as a perceptive, quality-conscious business leader. In any situation, your message must

> **Have a purpose.** Business messages provide information, solve a problem, or request the resources necessary to accomplish a goal. Every message you prepare will have a specific purpose.
> **Focus on your audience.** Business messages help audiences understand an issue, ask them to collaborate on accomplishing a goal, or take some action. Every message you prepare must consider the audience's point of view.
> **Be concise.** Business messages respect everyone's time by presenting information clearly and efficiently. Every message you prepare should be as short as possible without omitting essential facts or ideas.

The Three-Step Writing Process

Objective 1 Describe the three-step writing process.

As soon as the need to create a message appears, inexperienced communicators are often tempted to jump directly into writing. However, spending even a few minutes analyzing, organizing, adapting, and revising can often save you hours of reworking later on—and help you generate much more effective messages. Successful communicators follow a writing process that can be divided into three major steps (see Figure 4–1):

The three-step writing process consists of planning, writing, and completing your messages.

1. **Planning business messages.** To plan any message, first *analyze the situation* by defining your purpose and developing a profile of your audience. Once you're sure what you need to accomplish with your message, *gather information* that will meet your audience's needs. Next, *select the right medium* (oral, written, or electronic) to deliver your message. With those three factors in place, you're ready to *organize the information* by defining your main idea, limiting your scope, selecting a direct or an indirect approach, and outlining your content. Planning messages is the focus of this chapter.

> Figure 4–1 The Three-Step Writing Process

Planning	Writing	Completing
Analyze the Situation Define your purpose and develop an audience profile. **Gather Information** Determine audience needs and obtain the information necessary to satisfy those needs. **Select the Right Medium** Choose the best medium for delivering your message. **Organize the Information** Define your main idea, limit your scope, select a direct or an indirect approach, and outline your content.	**Adapt to Your Audience** Be sensitive to audience needs by writing with a "you" attitude, politeness, positive emphasis, and bias-free language. Build a strong relationship with your audience by establishing your credibility and projecting your company's image. Control your style with a conversational tone, plain English, and appropriate voice. **Compose the Message** Choose precise language that will help you create effective sentences and coherent paragraphs.	**Revise the Message** Evaluate content and review readability, then edit and rewrite for conciseness and clarity. **Produce the Message** Use effective design elements and suitable layout for a clean, professional appearance. **Proofread the Message** Review for errors in layout, spelling, and mechanics. **Distribute the Message** Deliver your message using the chosen medium; make sure all documents and all relevant files are distributed successfully.
1	**2**	**3**

2. **Writing business messages.** Once you've planned your message, *adapt to your audience*. Be sensitive to your audience's needs by adopting the "you" attitude, being polite, emphasizing the positive, and using bias-free language. Build strong relationships with your audience by establishing your credibility and projecting your company's image. Be sure to control your style by using a conversational tone, plain English, and the correct voice. Then, you're ready to *compose your message* by choosing precise language, creating effective sentences, and developing coherent paragraphs. Writing business messages is discussed in Chapter 5.

3. **Completing business messages.** After writing your first draft, *revise your message* by reviewing the content and organization for overall style, structure, and readability. Then edit and rewrite until your message comes across concisely and clearly, with correct grammar, proper punctuation, and effective format. Next *produce your message*. Put it into the form that your audience will receive, and review all design and layout decisions for an attractive, professional appearance. *Proofread* the final draft for typos, spelling errors, and other mechanical problems. Finally, *distribute your message* using the best combination of personal and technological tools. Completing business messages is discussed in Chapter 6.

Throughout this book, you'll learn how to apply these steps to a wide variety of business messages: short messages such as emails and blog postings (Chapters 7 through 10), longer messages such as reports (Chapters 11 through 13), oral presentations (Chapter 14), and the employment messages you can use to build a satisfying career (Chapters 15 and 16).

Optimizing Your Writing Time

The more you use the three-step writing process, the more intuitive and automatic it will become. You'll also get better at allotting your time for each task

As a starting point, use half your time for planning, one-quarter for writing, and one-quarter for completing your messages.

during a writing project. As a general rule, use roughly half your time for planning—defining your purpose, getting to know your audience, immersing yourself in your subject matter, and working out media selection and organization. Use about one-quarter of your time for writing. Reserve the remaining quarter of your time for completing the project so that you don't short-change important completion steps such as revising, producing, proofreading, and distributing.[2]

Of course, these time allotments will change significantly depending on the project; for example, if you know your material intimately, the planning step might take less than half your time. Then again, if you're delivering your message via multimedia such as DVD, where you may need to add photos and graphical support to your text, as well as oral commentary, the completion step could take far longer than a quarter of your time.

Seasoned professionals understand that there is no right or best way to write all business messages. As you work through the writing process presented in this chapter and Chapters 5 and 6, don't view it as a list of how-to directives but as a way to understand the various tasks involved in effective business writing.[3]

Planning Effectively

When deadlines loom and assignments pile up, it's tempting to rush through the planning phase and jump directly into writing. However, trying to save time up front often costs you more time as you struggle to complete a message that wasn't well thought out. Even if you have only 20 or 30 minutes to prepare and send a message, work through all three steps quickly to ensure that your time is well used. Analyzing your audience helps you find and assemble the facts they're looking for and deliver that information in a concise and compelling way. Planning your message reduces indecision as you write and helps eliminate work as you review and revise.

Is playing chess similar to planning business messages? How does the three-step process apply to this challenging game?

Trying to save time by skimping on planning usually costs you more time in the long run.

Analyzing Your Situation

A successful message starts with a clear purpose that connects the sender's needs with the audience's needs. Identifying your purpose and your audience is usually a straightforward task for simple, routine messages; however, this task can be more demanding in more intricate situations. For example, if you need to communicate about a shipping problem between your Beijing and Vancouver factories, your purpose might be simply to alert upper management to the situation, or it might involve asking the two factory managers to explore and solve the problem. These two scenarios have different purposes and different audiences; therefore, they yield dramatically different messages. If you launch directly into writing without clarifying both your purpose and your audience, you'll waste time and energy, and you'll probably generate a less effective message.

Defining Your Purpose

Objective 2 Explain why it's important to define your purpose carefully, and list four questions that can help you test that purpose.

Your general purpose may be to inform, persuade, or collaborate.

All business messages have a **general purpose**: to inform, persuade, or collaborate with an audience. This purpose helps define the overall approach you'll take, including the information you gather, your choice of media, and even the way you organize your message. The general purpose also determines both the appropriate degree of audience participation and the amount of control you have over your message.

Informing your audience requires little interaction (see Figure 4–2). Audience members absorb the information and accept or reject it, but they don't contribute

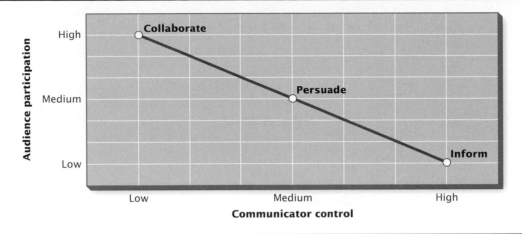

> Figure 4–2 The Relation Between the General Purpose of a Business Message and Communicator Control

to message content; you control the message. To persuade your audience, you require a moderate amount of participation, such as giving people the chance to ask questions so that you can answer any doubts; nevertheless, you need to retain a moderate amount of message control. Finally, to collaborate with audience members, you need maximum participation. Your control of the message is reduced because you must adjust to new, unexpected input and reactions.

Within the scope of its general purpose, each message also has a **specific purpose**, which identifies what you hope to accomplish with your message and what your audience should do or think after receiving your message. For example, is your goal simply to update your audience on an event, or do you want them to take immediate action? State your specific purpose as precisely as possible, even identifying which audience members should respond, how they should respond, and when.

After you have defined your specific purpose, you can decide whether that purpose merits the time and effort required for you to prepare and send the message. Test your purpose by asking four questions:

To determine the specific purpose, think of how the audience's ideas or behaviour should be affected by the message.

1. **Will anything change as a result of your message?** Don't contribute to information overload by sending messages that won't change events or actions. For example, if you don't like your company's latest advertising campaign, but you're not in a position to influence it, sending a critical message to your colleagues won't change anything and won't benefit anyone.
2. **Is your purpose realistic?** If your purpose involves a radical shift in action or attitude, go slowly. Consider proposing a first step so that your message acts as the beginning of a learning process.
3. **Is the time right?** Think through the potential impact of your message—both intentional and unintentional—to see whether this is a good time to send it. Many professions and departments have recurring cycles in their workloads, so messages sent during peak times might be ignored. Similarly, employees in departments that are in the midst of a reorganization, series of layoffs, or other changes won't be able to give your message their full attention.
4. **Is your purpose acceptable to your organization?** Your company's business objectives may dictate whether a purpose is acceptable. For example, you may be tempted to fire off a stern reply to a particularly unpleasant customer, suggesting the person take his or her business elsewhere, but this might go against your company's priorities of retaining all current customers.

When you are satisfied that (1) you have a clear and meaningful purpose and (2) now is a smart time to proceed, your next step is to understand the members of your audience and their needs.

Developing an Audience Profile

Objective 3 Describe the importance of analyzing your audience, and identify the seven factors you should consider when developing an audience profile.

Before your audiences will take the time to read or hear your messages, they need to be interested in what you're saying. They need to see what's in it for them: How will listening to your advice or doing what you ask help them, personally or professionally? The more you know about your audience, their needs, and their expectations, the more effectively you'll be able to communicate with them.

If you're communicating with someone you know well, audience analysis is relatively easy. You can identify the person's needs and predict his or her reaction to any given message without a lot of research. On the other hand, your audience could be made up of strangers—potential customers or suppliers you've never met, a new boss, or new employees. In these situations, you'll need to learn more in order to adjust your message to meet the needs of your audience. For an example of the kind of information you need to compile in an audience analysis, see the planning sheet in Figure 4–3. Completing a form will help you select the necessary content for your messages, choose the right format, and write them using an appropriate tone and style.

To conduct an audience analysis:

Ask yourself key questions about your audience to help achieve your purpose.

1. **Identify your primary audience.** For some messages, certain audience members might be more important than others. Don't ignore the needs of less influential members, but make sure you address the concerns of the key decision makers.

2. **Identify the secondary audience.** The secondary audience is composed of people who are given some details of your message—or the entire message itself—by the primary audience. For example, if your message recommends upgrading your department's computers, your manager might copy your message to the company's purchasing director, who would have to approve the decision. Although this director is not the person to whom you addressed your memo, she receives the message because she influences your proposal's outcome.

3. **Determine audience size and geographic distribution.** A report meant for wide distribution requires a more formal style, organization, and format than one directed to three or four people in your department. Also, make sure you respond to the particular concerns of key individuals. The head of marketing would need different facts than the head of production or finance would need.

4. **Determine audience composition.** Look for both similarities and differences in culture, language, age, education, organizational rank and status, attitudes, experience, motivations, and any other factors that might affect the success of your message. For example, if you're reporting the results of a market research project, the vice-president of sales will probably want to know what's happening right now. On the other hand, the vice-president of communication might be more interested in how the market will look a year or two from now, when that department's new products will be ready to sell.

If audience members have different levels of understanding of the topic, aim your message at the most influential decision makers.

5. **Gauge audience members' level of understanding.** If audience members share your general background, they'll probably understand your material without difficulty. If not, your message will need an element of education, and deciding how much information to include can be a challenge. Include only enough information to accomplish the specific purpose of your

> Figure 4–3 Audience Analysis Worksheet

Project: A report recommending that we close down the on-site exercise facility and subsidize private memberships at local health clubs.

1	Who is my primary audience?	Nicole Perazzo, vice-president of operations
2	Who is my secondary audience?	Nicole's assistants (James, Tammy) James Ngomo, vice-president of finance Felice Gonzalez, vice-president of human resources
3	What is the size of my audience? What is their location?	Five managers total All managers are located in Halifax
4	What is their level of knowledge?	All will have knowledge of the financial situation, but Felice will not have the budget. (Note: summarize budget details in the report to give Felice the financial context.)
5	What are their expectations and preferences?	All are expecting a firm recommendation, supported by a clear financial rationale. They will also want suggestions for communicating the bad news to employees. (I want to send a hard-copy memo to employees; they may prefer email.)
6	What is the probable reaction?	Staff might first resent the change, but they may prefer going to a full-service health club with personal trainers after the change is fully explained.

message. Other material will overwhelm your audience and divert attention from the important points. If the members of your audience have various levels of understanding, gear your coverage to your primary audience (the key decision makers).

6. **Understand audience expectations and preferences.** Will members of your audience expect complete details or just a summary of the main points? Do they want an email or will they expect a formal memo? (See Chapter 7 for guidelines on email etiquette.) High-level executives might prefer a three-page memo to a fifteen-page report because they have limited time to spend on the many messages they receive and act on.

7. **Forecast probable audience reaction.** As you'll read later in the chapter, audience reaction affects message organization. If you expect a favourable

response, you can state conclusions and recommendations up front and offer minimal supporting evidence. If you expect skepticism, introduce conclusions gradually, with more proof. By anticipating the primary audience's response to certain points, you can vary the amount of evidence you'll need to address those issues.

Gathering Information

Objective 4 Discuss gathering information for simple messages, and identify three attributes of quality information.

With a clear picture of your audience and their needs, your next step is to assemble the information that you will include in your message. For simple messages, you may already have all the information at hand, but more complex messages can require considerable research and analysis before you're ready to begin writing. Chapter 11 explores formal techniques for finding, evaluating, and processing information, but you can often use a variety of informal techniques to gather insights and focus your research efforts:

> **Consider other viewpoints.** Putting yourself in someone else's position helps you consider what that person might be thinking, feeling, or planning.
> **Read reports and other company documents.** Your company's files may be a rich source of the information you need for a particular memo or email message. Consider annual reports, financial statements, news releases, blogs, marketing reports, and customer surveys for helpful information. Find out whether your company has a *knowledge management system,* a centralized database that collects the experiences and insights of employees throughout the organization.
> **Talk with supervisors, colleagues, or customers.** Fellow workers and customers may have information you need, or they may know what your audience will be interested in.
> **Ask your audience for input.** If you're unsure of what audience members need from your message, ask them. Admitting that you don't know but want to meet their needs will impress an audience more than guessing and getting it wrong.

Uncovering Audience Needs

If you're given a vague request, ask questions to clarify it before you plan a response.

In many situations your audience's information needs are readily apparent, such as when a consumer sends an email asking a specific question. In other cases, your audience might be unable to articulate exactly what is needed. If someone makes a vague or broad request, ask questions to narrow the focus. If your boss says, "Find out everything you can about Interscope Records," ask which aspect of the company and its business is most important. Asking a question or two often forces the person to think through the request and define more precisely what is required.

Include any additional information that might be helpful, even though the requester didn't specifically ask for it.

Also, think of information needs of which your audience may not even be aware. Suppose your company has just hired a new employee from out of town, and you've been assigned to coordinate this person's relocation. At a minimum, you would write a welcoming letter describing your company's procedures for relocating employees. With a little extra thought, however, you might include some information about the city: perhaps a guide to residential areas, a map or two, brochures about cultural activities, or information on schools and transportation. In some cases, you may be able to tell your audience something they consider important but wouldn't have thought to ask. Although adding information of this sort lengthens your message, it can also create goodwill.

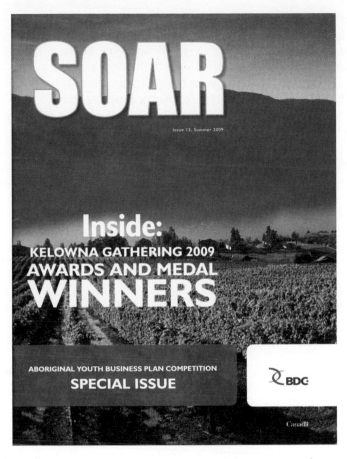

Published by the Aboriginal Banking department of the Business Development Bank of Canada (BDC), *SOAR* magazine includes inspirational stories about Aboriginal youth. How do you think staff develop story ideas for this magazine?

Providing Required Information

Once you've defined your audience's information needs, ensure that you satisfy those needs completely. One good way to test the thoroughness of your message is to use the **journalistic approach**: Check whether your message answers *who, what, when, where, why,* and *how.* Using this test, you can quickly tell whether a message fails to deliver—such as this message requesting information from employees:

We are exploring ways to reduce our office space leasing costs and would like your input on a proposed plan in which employees who telecommute on alternate days could share offices. Please let me know what you think of this proposal.

The message fails to tell employees everything they need to know in order to provide meaningful responses. The *what* could be improved by identifying the specific information points the writer needs from employees (such as whether individual telecommuting patterns are predictable enough to allow scheduling of shared offices). The writer also doesn't specify *when* the responses are needed or *how* the employees should respond. By failing to address such points, the request is likely to generate a variety of responses, some possibly helpful but some probably not.

TIPS FOR SUCCESS

"The most effective writers are those who view what they compose from the reader's vantage point. Ask yourself, Does the intended reader have your background, your education, and your experience with the subject at hand?, If not, adjust your text accordingly."

Ray Dreyfack, systems executive, Fabergé Perfumes, business writer and consultant

Test the completeness of your document by ensuring it answers all the important questions: *who, what, when, where, why,* and *how.*

To gauge the quality of the information you provide in your messages, check to ensure that the information is accurate, ethical, and pertinent.

Be certain that the information you provide is accurate and that the commitments you make can be kept.

BE SURE THE INFORMATION IS ACCURATE Inaccurate information communicated in business messages can cause a host of problems, from embarrassment and lost productivity to serious safety and legal issues. Inaccurate information may persist for months or years after you distribute it, or you may commit the organization to promises it isn't able to keep—and the error could harm your reputation as a reliable businessperson.

You can minimize mistakes by double-checking every piece of information you collect. If you consult sources outside the organization, ask yourself whether they are current and reliable. Be particularly careful when using sources you find on the internet. As you'll see in Chapter 11, the simplicity of online publishing and common lack of editorial oversight call for extra care in using online information. Be sure to review any mathematical or financial calculations. Check all dates and schedules, and examine your own assumptions and conclusions to be certain they are valid.

BE SURE THE INFORMATION IS ETHICAL By working hard to ensure the accuracy of the information you gather, you'll also avoid many ethical problems in your messages. If you do make an honest mistake, such as delivering information you initially thought to be true but later found to be false, contact the recipients of the message immediately and correct the error. No one can reasonably fault you in such circumstances, and most people will respect your honesty.

Ethics should guide your decisions when determining how much detail to include in your message.

Messages can also be unethical if important information is omitted. Of course, as a business professional, you may have legal or other sound business reasons for not including every detail about every matter. So just how much detail should you include? Make sure you include enough detail to avoid misleading your audience. If you're unsure how much information your audience needs, offer as much as you believe best fits your definition of complete, and then offer to provide more upon request.

BE SURE THE INFORMATION IS PERTINENT When gathering information for your message, try to prioritize the information your audience needs and filter out the information they don't. For example, if you're summarizing a recent conversation you had with one of your company's oldest and best customers, the emphasis you give each point of the conversation will depend on your audience's concerns. The head of engineering might be most interested in the customer's reaction to your product's new design features. The shipping manager might be most concerned about the customer's comments on recent delivery schedules. In other words, you must choose and emphasize the points that will have the most impact on your audience. By focusing on the information that concerns your audience the most, you increase your chances of accomplishing your own communication goals.

Figure out what points will especially interest your audience, then give those points the most attention.

If you don't know your audience, or if you're communicating with a large group of people with diverse interests, use common sense to identify points of particular interest. Audience factors such as age, job, location, income, and education can give you a clue. If you're trying to sell memberships in a health club, you might adjust your message for athletes, busy professionals, families, and people in different locations or in different income brackets. The comprehensive facilities and professional trainers would appeal to athletes, whereas the low monthly rates would appeal to students on tight budgets. As Figure 4–4 shows, your main goal is to tell audience members what they need to know in an accessible format and style. This corporate responsibility document from Royal Bank Financial Group uses formatting features and a question/answer approach for its student audience.

> Figure 4–4 Audience-Focused Document (selected pages)

Uses photo (cover of corporate responsibility report) to draw reader's attention

Corporate Responsibility 101:
A Resource for Students

This document has been prepared to help answer the most common questions students ask about corporate responsibility at RBC. For additional information, please visit rbc.com/responsibility and click on "Approach."

How does RBC define "corporate responsibility"?
The meaning of the term "*corporate responsibility*" is much debated. It can also be called *corporate social responsibility, corporate accountability, sustainability, the triple bottom line or corporate citizenship.*

At RBC, we tend to use the terms "corporate responsibility" and "sustainability" interchangeably, and define the concept as:

"behaving with integrity, sustaining our company's long-term viability, being transparent and accountable, and contributing to the future well- being of all our stakeholders."

At RBC, corporate responsibility is not a standalone "program." It includes, but is not limited to community relations and donations.

RBC considers corporate responsibility to have a number of elements, shown in the graphic below.

What are the hallmarks of responsible corporations?
We believe that truly responsible companies:

* operate with integrity and demonstrate sound corporate governance principles;
* provide full and plain disclosure of financial results;
* disclose reliable performance data on key non-financial items that may represent risks or opportunities;

(revised February, 2008)

* make a positive economic impact by creating employment and a well- trained workforce, paying axes, and purchasing goods and services responsibly;
* adopt fair and progressive people management practices, respect human rights, and encourage diversity in the workforce;
* support community programs through donations, sponsorships and employee volunteerism;
* work towards environmental sustainability, reducing their environmental footprint while having a positive impact through their products and services;
* Further, we also believe that financial service companies can demonstrate responsibility by contributing to economic prosperity, including support for small business, innovation and entrepreneurship, and community economic development initiatives.

Why does RBC engage in corporate responsibility activities?
The basic responsibility of a company is not about solving the problems of the world. Our job is to conduct business profitably, with integrity and in a way that aligns with societal values.

At RBC, our goal is to behave with integrity every day, in every transaction, in every part of our business, sustaining our company's long-term viability, being transparent and accountable, and contributing to the future well-being of all our stakeholders.

In this way, corporate responsibility is about good governance. It's about solid risk management. It's about delivering a good return to investors. It's about strong consumer protection, active community relations, leading-edge human resource practices and employee relations. It's about responsible supplier chain management. It's about paying a fair share of taxes and obeying the law.

The world has started to use the term "corporate responsibility" as shorthand for some or all of these things. But in many ways, we think "corporate responsibility" is just a new term for good business practices of good sustainable companies.

(continued)

Uses FAQ format to focus on specific topics

Incorporates visual support to represent the concepts in an easy-to-understand manner

> Figure 4–4 Audience-Focused Document (selected pages) (*continued*)

What is the RBC Blueprint for Doing Better?

RBC Blueprint for Doing Better™

When it comes to corporate responsibility, companies are often expected to be everything to everyone. For a company like RBC, with more than 15 million clients in 38 countries and more than 70,000 employees worldwide, managing diverse stakeholder expectations can be a challenge. Over the last few years, our stakeholders have grown in number and influence. In 2007, we developed a new strategic approach so we could better manage their expectations and continue to make a positive economic, environmental and social impact.

We started with a full assessment of RBC's global business strategy. Then we mapped out stakeholder interests, and benchmarked the practices of leading financial institutions and other industry leaders worldwide. We prioritized current and emerging issue areas.

After further evaluation, we developed an overall framework, vision and direction for managing and prioritizing the diverse elements that comprise corporate responsibility, and dubbed the plan our "RBC Blueprint for Doing Better."

Our vision: we will continue to demonstrate integrity in our business practices, and provide leadership in the workplace and the marketplace. Our two key areas of focus will be diversity and the environment. We will remain a strong supporter of the communities in which we do business and will maintain transparent sustainability reporting practices.

Why did RBC select 'diversity' as a priority?

RBC Diversity Blueprint™

Diversity can be a competitive advantage not only when it comes to developing intellectual capital, but also for ensuring the growth of companies and countries.

Financial services companies like RBC depend on intellectual capital, and no asset is more significant than people. There is a global war for talent, and we believe we must be an employer of choice for new employees by leveraging the diversity of our current and future workforce.

Of our millions of clients in Canada, the percentage of new Canadians and visible minorities is growing – and we expect much of our future growth to come from these markets   Managing and leveraging diversity is a critical issue for financial services companies, and we believe this will help us differentiate ourselves from the competition, and deliver better customer service.

Why did RBC choose the 'environment' as a priority?

RBC Environmental Blueprint™

Financial services companies aren't considered high-impact when it comes to the environment, but many of our clients are. So, as their bank, we have an indirect impact through our lending and investment activities. Like many companies, we must also manage our own footprint responsibly and know that we can have an impact through how we purchase goods and services as well.

In 2007, we unveiled the RBC Environmental Blueprint, a strategy that built on our strong history, with a new vision of how we will move forward with issues like climate change, biodiversity, forests and water. The RBC Environmental Blueprint lays out our three priorities:

- To reduce the intensity of our environmental footprint
- To promote environmentally responsible business activities
- To offer environmental products and services.

What about community relations?

RBC Community Blueprint™

While our new focus areas are diversity and the environment, we remain committed to supporting local communities through donations, sponsorships and employee participation. As one of Canada's largest corporate donors, and with a tradition of philanthropy that dates back to 1891, RBC supports the arts, athletics, health and wellness, education, social and civic causes, and we will continue to do so under the RBC Community Blueprint umbrella. In 2007, we contributed more than $82.8 million to community causes worldwide, through donations of more than $47.7 million, and an additional $35.1 million in sponsorship of community events and national organizations.

Who are your stakeholders?

At RBC, we strongly believe that a company "does well by doing good", across the broad range of elements included under the umbrella term of "corporate responsibility", while respecting and considering the needs of shareholders and stakeholders including:

- clients and consumers;
- current and prospective employees;
- investors and analysts;
- our partners in the voluntary sector, including NGOs and activists;
- government and regulators;
- suppliers and prospective suppliers.

Uses brief paragraphs to keep the information accessible and to engage the reader

Uses headings to refer to topic in the Corporate Responsibility Report

Uses bullets to draw attention to specific information

Selecting the Right Medium

Selecting the best medium for your message can make the difference between effective and ineffective communication.[4] A **medium** is the form through which you choose to communicate your message. You may choose to talk with someone face to face, leave a voice-mail message, post to a blog, send email, or create a webcast—and there are many other media to choose from.

In fact, media categories have become increasingly blurred in recent years with the advent of so many options that include multimedia formats. For the sake of discussion, you can divide media into oral, written, visual, and electronic (which often combines several media types).

Objective 5 List factors to consider when choosing the most appropriate medium for your message.

Oral Media

Primary oral media include face-to-face conversations, interviews, speeches, and in-person presentations and meetings. By giving communicators the ability to see, hear, and react to each other, traditional oral media are useful for encouraging people to ask questions, make comments, and work together to reach a consensus or decision. In particular, experts recommend that managers engage in frequent "walk-arounds," chatting with employees to get input, answer their questions, and interpret important business events and trends.[5]

Of course, if you don't want a lot of questions or interaction, oral media can be an unwise choice. However, consider your audience carefully before deciding to limit interaction by choosing a different medium. As a manager, you will encounter unpleasant situations (declining an employee's request for a raise, for example) in which sending an email message or otherwise avoiding personal contact will seem appealing. Avoiding personal interaction in difficult circumstances demonstrates weakness; in many such cases, you owe the other party the opportunity to ask questions or express concerns. Moreover, facing the tough situations in person will earn you a reputation as an honest, caring manager.

Oral communication is best when you need to encourage interaction, express emotions, or monitor emotional responses.

 Explore

Written Media

Written messages take many forms, from traditional memos to glossy reports that rival magazines in production quality. Most letters and memos are relatively brief documents, generally one or two pages, although some run much longer. Memos are used for the routine, day-to-day exchange of information within an organization. Because of their informal method of delivery (such as being placed in baskets), memos are less private than letters. In many organizations, email messages, blogs, and other electronic media have largely replaced paper memos.

Letters are sent to recipients outside the organization, so in addition to conveying a particular message, they perform an important public relations function in fostering good working relationships with customers, suppliers, and others. Letters can be sent in hard copy or as email messages. Many organizations rely on form letters, either in hard copy or sent as email, to save time and money on routine communication. Form letters are particularly handy for such one-time mass mailings as sales messages about products, information about organizational activities, and goodwill messages such as seasonal greetings. Chapters 8 through 10 discuss memos, letters, instant messages, and other short-message forms, and Appendix A explains how to format these business documents.

Reports and proposals are usually longer than letters and memos, although both can be created in memo or letter format. These documents come in a variety of lengths, ranging from a few pages to several hundred, and are usually fairly formal in tone. Chapters 11 through 13 discuss reports and proposals in detail.

Memos are short, printed messages for internal audiences; letters are short, printed messages for external audiences.

The higher you rise in an organization, the more time you spend talking and listening. Your ability to communicate with people from virtually any background will be key to your success. How can you be a sensitive communicator when you need to communicate bad news orally?

Visual Media

Although you probably won't work with many messages that are purely visual (with no text), the importance of visual elements in business communication continues to grow. Traditional business messages rely primarily on text, with occasional support from graphical elements such as charts, graphs, or diagrams to help illustrate points discussed in the text. However, many business communicators are discovering the power of messages in which the visual element is dominant and supported by small amounts of text. For the purposes of this discussion, you can think of visual media as any formats in which one or more visual elements play a central role in conveying the message content. Figure 4–5 shows how the message about CRM, customer relationship management (a category of software that helps companies manage their interactions with customers), can be presented more effectively by basing the message on a dominant visual and using text to support that image.

In some situations, a message that is predominantly visual with text used to support the illustration can be more effective than a message that relies primarily on text.

Messages that combine powerful visuals with supporting text can be effective for a number of reasons. Today's audiences are pressed for time and bombarded with messages, so anything that communicates quickly is welcome. Visuals are also effective at describing complex ideas and processes because they can reduce the work required for an audience to identify the parts and relationships that make up the whole. Also, in a multilingual business world, diagrams, symbols, and other images can lower communication barriers by requiring less language processing. Finally, visual images can be easier to remember than purely textual descriptions or explanations.

✳─[Explore Electronic Media

The range of electronic media is broad and continues to grow even broader, from telephones and podcasts to blogs and wikis to email and text messaging. When you want to make a powerful impression, using electronic media can increase the excitement and visual appeal with computer animation, video, even music.

To use many electronic media options successfully, a person must have at least some degree of technical skill.

The growth of electronic communication options is both a blessing and a curse for business communicators. On the one hand, you have more tools than ever before to choose from, with more ways to deliver rational and emotional content. On the other hand, the sheer range of choices can complicate your job because you often need to choose among multiple media, and you need to know how to use each medium successfully. You'll learn more about using electronic media throughout this book (and in Chapter 7, in particular); for now, here is a quick overview of the major electronic media now used in business:

Electronic media offer an ever-expanding array of ways to deliver oral, written, and visual messages.

> **Electronic versions of oral media.** These include telephone calls, teleconferencing (when three or more people join the same call), voice mail messages, audio recordings such as compact discs and podcasts, and even

> Figure 4–5 Visual Media

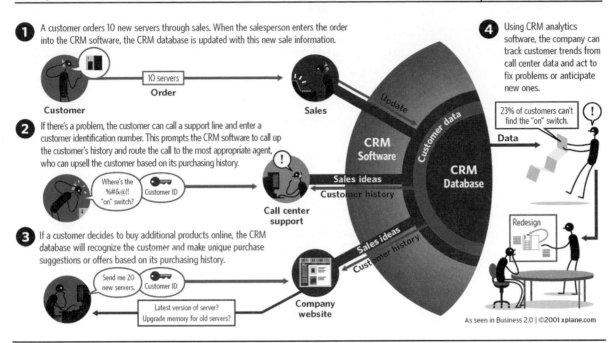

online speaking characters, sometimes called *avatars*, that help sell a company's products or services. The simple telephone call is still a vital communication link for many organizations, but it has evolved with *internet telephony,* also known by the technical term *VoIP* (which stands for *Voice over IP,* the Internet Protocol). More than 370 million people worldwide now use Skype, which offers free basic phone service over the Internet.[6] Although telephone calls can't convey all the nonverbal signals of an in-person conversation, they can convey quite a few, including tone of voice, laughter, pauses, and so on. Voice mail is a handy way to send brief messages when an immediate response isn't crucial, but it's a poor choice for lengthy messages because the information is difficult to retrieve. You'll learn about podcasts, perhaps the most significant business audio advancement of recent years, in Chapter 7.

> **Electronic versions of written media.** These range from email and instant messages to blogs, websites, and wikis. Instant messaging (IM) is rapidly overtaking email in some companies. At IBM, for instance, employees send more than 5 million instant messages a month.[7] *Text messaging* has become popular in North America.[8] Even documents that were once distributed on paper are now easily transferred electronically with Adobe's portable document format (PDF). Faxes have been replaced by other electronic options in many cases, although they still have a role in business communication. Internet-based fax services, such as eFax, lower the cost of faxing by eliminating the need for a dedicated fax line and fax machine.

Electronic written media have largely replaced traditional written media in many companies.

✳–Explore

> **Electronic versions of visual media.** These include electronic presentations (using Microsoft PowerPoint and other software), computer animation (using software such as Adobe Flash to create animated sequences for websites), and video. Businesses have made extensive use of video (particularly for training, new product promotions, and executive announcements) for

years—first on tape, then on DVD, and now online. Video is also incorporated in podcasting, creating *vidcasts,* and in blogging, including *video blogs* (*vlogs*) and *mobile blogs* (*moblogs*).[9] **Multimedia** refers to use of two or more media to craft a single message, typically some combination of audio, video, text, and visual graphics.

For a brief look at some of the other interesting communication technologies that you may encounter on the job, see "Using the Power of Technology: More Ways to Spread the Message" (p. 104).

Factors to Consider When Choosing Media

Choosing the right medium for each message is a question of balancing your needs with your audience's needs (see Table 4–1). Be sure to consider how your message is affected by the following factors:

> **Media richness.** Richness is a medium's ability to (1) convey a message through more than one *informational cue* (visual, verbal, vocal), (2) facilitate feedback, and (3) establish personal focus. The richest medium is face-to-face communication: it's personal; it provides immediate feedback (verbal and nonverbal); and it conveys the emotion behind a message.[10] Multimedia presentations and multimedia web pages are also rich, with the ability to present images, animation, text, music, and sound effects. Many electronic media are also *interactive,* in that they enable audiences to participate in the communication process. For example, a website can allow visitors to select the types of information they want to see, to provide feedback, or use a variety of online calculators or other tools. At the other end of the richness continuum are the leanest media—those that communicate in the simplest ways and provide no opportunity for audience feedback (see Figure 4–6). Use the richest media to send non-routine, complex messages, to humanize your presence throughout the organization, to communicate caring to employees, and to gain employee commitment to company goals.

> **Message formality.** Your media choice governs the style and tone of your message. For example, to share simple information with employees, you would probably send an email message or post an announcement on a blog rather than write a formal printed memo or make a face-to-face presentation.

> **Media limitations.** Every medium has limitations. Although face-to-face communication is the richest medium, it's one of the most restrictive because you and your audience must be in the same place at the same time.[11] Similarly, IM is perfect for communicating simple, straightforward messages, but it is ineffective for sending complex ones.

> **Sender intentions.** Your choice of medium influences your audience's perception of your intentions. If you want to emphasize the formality of your message, use a more formal medium, such as a memo or a letter. To convey emotion, consider a visual medium such as a personal speech or a videoconference. For immediate feedback, meet face-to-face, make a phone call, or use IM.[12]

> **Urgency and cost.** Electronic media have lowered the cost of transmitting messages, but in some instances (usually involving printed messages), you need to weigh cost versus delivery time. For instance, local couriers and delivery services such as

The richest media use more than one informational cue, facilitate feedback, and establish a personal focus on each audience member.

Your intentions heavily influence your choice of medium.

Time and cost also affect medium selection.

Many websites now feature talking animated figures, such as avatars, giving website visitors a more enhanced online experience. Do these figures serve a meaningful purpose? Do they engage potential customers or detract from the text and other visuals?

> ## Table 4–1   Media Advantages and Disadvantages

Media	Advantages	Disadvantages
Oral	> Provide opportunity for immediate feedback > Allow a certain ease of interaction > Involve rich nonverbal cues (both physical gesture and vocal inflection) > Allow you to express the emotion behind your message	> Restrict participation to those physically present > Unless recorded, provide no permanent, verifiable record of the communication > Reduce communicator's control over the message > Other than for messages that are prewritten and rehearsed, offer no opportunity to revise or edit your spoken words
Written	> Allow you to plan and control your message > Reach geographically dispersed audiences > Offer a permanent, verifiable record > Minimize the distortion that can accompany oral messages > Can be used to avoid immediate interactions > De-emphasize any inappropriate emotional components	> Usually not conducive to speedy feedback > Lack the rich nonverbal cues provided by oral media > Often take more time and more resources to create and distribute > Elaborate printed documents can require special skills in preparation and production
Visual	> Can convey complex ideas and relationships quickly > Often less intimidating than long blocks of text > Can reduce the burden on the audience to figure out how the pieces fit	> Can require artistic skills to design > Require some technical skills to create > Can require more time to create than equivalent amount of text > More difficult to transmit and store than simple textual messages
Electronic	> Deliver messages quickly > Reach geographically dispersed audiences > Offer the persuasive power of multimedia formats > Can increase accessibility and openness in an organization	> Are easy to overuse (sending too many messages to too many recipients) > Privacy risks and concerns (exposing confidential data; employer monitoring of email and IM; accidental forwarding) > Security risks (viruses; spyware) > Productivity concerns (frequent interruptions; non-business Web surfing)

FedEx, UPS, and DHL can deliver printed materials quickly, but they tend to cost much more than regular mail.

> **Audience preferences.** Make sure you consider which media your audience expects or prefers.[13] What would you think if your school tried to deliver your diploma by fax? You'd expect the college to hand it to you at graduation or mail it to you. In addition, some cultures tend to favour one channel over another. For example, Canada, the United States, and Germany emphasize written messages, whereas Japan emphasizes oral messages—perhaps because its high-context culture carries so much of the message in nonverbal cues and "between the lines" interpretation.[14]

When choosing the appropriate medium, don't forget to consider your audience's expectations.

Once you select the best medium for your purpose, situation, and audience, you are ready to start thinking about the organization of your message.

USING THE POWER OF TECHNOLOGY

More Ways to Spread the Message

Businesses invest significant amounts of money in technologies designed to improve both internal and external communication. In some instances, technologies such as electronic data interchange and its newer Web-based equivalents replace the human element in the communication process. In others, technology attempts to enhance human communication by increasing mobility, lowering cost, improving responsiveness, or creating new capabilities. Here are some of the most intriguing communication-enhancement technologies:

> **Voice synthesis and recognition.** The human voice will always be central to business communication, but that doesn't mean two human beings are required for every conversation. Voice synthesis regenerates a human speaking voice from computer files that represent words or parts of words. Voice recognition converts human speech to computer-compatible data. Both technologies continue to improve every year, with richer vocabularies and more human-sounding voices.

> **Virtual agents.** Virtual agents, also known as *bots* (derived from the word *robot*), are a class of automated tools that perform a variety of communication tasks, such as answering customer service questions and responding to requests for electronic documents. They can function in either voice-based (over the telephone) or text-based (via IM or text messaging) environments.

> **Mobile communication.** If you're accustomed to studying on the go, you'll fit right into today's untethered work environment. In some cases, mobile workers don't even have traditional offices, using temporary cubicles at work, home offices, cars, airports, and even new Internet-equipped airplanes for office space. Geographic data from a **global positioning system (GPS)** are also creating new forms of mobile communication, such as location-based advertising (getting an advertisement on your mobile phone from a store you're walking past, for instance) and remote monitoring of medical patients and trucking fleets.

> **Networking advances.** You might already be using some of the new networking technologies that help businesspeople communicate and collaborate. **Peer-to-peer (P2P)** computing lets multiple PCs communicate directly so that they can share files or work on large problems simultaneously. **Wireless networking** extends the reach of the Internet with wireless access points that connect to PCs and handheld devices via radio signals. Wireless networking extends the reach of the internet through the commonly used *Wi-Fi* technology for local area networks and the emerging *WiMAX* standard, which can cover entire metropolitan areas.

> **Cloud computing.** If you already use Google Docs, mentioned in Chapter 2, for collaborating through the internet, you are already working in the "cloud." **Cloud computing** allows companies to create and store content online, thereby giving employees a workspace they can access from the office, home, or even a Wi-Fi–enabled coffee shop. Cloud computing enhances productivity by allowing employees to share and edit documents easily, watch training videos, and access email, among other tasks. Online application hosting platforms such as Google Apps and Amazon Web Services, two of the most popular, provide these services and technical support for lower cost than company-based resources.

CAREER APPLICATIONS

1. Have you ever encountered a bot or a voice-recognition system when you expected to reach a human being (such as reaching a voice-response system when you telephoned a business)? Describe the situation and purpose of your "conversation." Were you satisfied with the outcome of the conversation? Why or why not?

2. What are the ethical implications of using GPS to track the movement of employees such as truck drivers?

> Figure 4–6 Media Richness

| Leaner:
fewer cues,
no interactivity,
no personal focus | Standard reports
Static web pages
Mass media
Posters & signs | Custom reports
Letters & memos
Email & IM
Wikis
Blogs
Podcasts | Telephone calls
Teleconferencing
Video (including
vodcasts,
vlogs,
video IM) | Face-to-face
conversations
Multimedia
presentations
Multimedia
web pages
Virtual reality | Richer:
multiple cues,
interactive,
personalized |

Organizing Your Information

For anything beyond the simplest messages, organization can make the difference between success and failure. Compare the draft and revision versions of the message in Figure 4–7, in which the writer is requesting the replacement of a faulty DVD drive. The draft version exhibits four of the most common organization mistakes:

1. **Taking too long to get to the point.** The writer, Jill Saunders, didn't introduce her topic, the faulty DVD drive, until the third paragraph. Then she waited until the final paragraph to state her purpose: requesting a replacement. *Solution:* Make the subject and purpose clear, and get to the point without wasting the reader's time.

2. **Including irrelevant material.** The first draft is full of irrelevant information: that Nutri-Veg has 3000 stores, that its online presence is growing, and so on. *Solution:* Include only information that is related to the subject and purpose.

3. **Getting ideas mixed up.** Saunders tries to make several points: (1) Her company has been a customer for a long time. (2) Her company has purchased numerous items at ComputerTime. (3) The DVD drive doesn't work. (4) Saunders wants a replacement. However, the ideas are mixed up and located in the wrong places. *Solution:* Group similar ideas and present them in a logical way, where one idea leads to the next.

4. **Leaving out necessary information.** Computer Time may want to know the make, model, and price of the DVD drive; the date of purchase; and the specific problems the device has had. Saunders also failed to say what she wants the store to do: send her a new DVD drive of the same type, send her a different model, or simply refund her money. *Solution:* Include all the information necessary for the audience to respond as the writer wishes.

> Most disorganized communication suffers from problems with clarity, relevance, grouping, and completeness.

The revised version corrects all four mistakes, and the result is a much stronger letter.

As you'll see in the following chapters, various types of messages may require different organizational schemes. Nevertheless, in every case, you can organize your message in a logical and compelling way by recognizing the importance of good organization, defining your main idea, limiting your scope, choosing either a direct or an indirect approach, and outlining your content.

> To organize a message, define your main idea, limit the scope, choose the direct or indirect approach, and group your points.

Recognizing the Importance of Good Organization

At best, poor organization creates unnecessary work for your readers, forcing them to piece your message together in a sensible way. At worst, poor organization leads readers to form inaccurate conclusions or tempts them to stop reading or listening. If you gain a reputation as a disorganized communicator, people will find ways to ignore your messages and question your thinking skills. In other words, poorly organized messages are bad for business and bad for your career.

> **Objective 6** Explain why good organization is important to both you and your audience.

Effective organizing also saves you time and consumes less of your creative energy. Your draft goes more quickly because you don't waste time putting ideas in the wrong places or composing material that you don't need. You might also use your organizational plan to get advance input from your audience. That way, you can be sure you're on the right track *before* you spend hours working on your draft. Furthermore, if you're working on a large, complex project, you can use your organization plan to divide the writing among co-workers.

> Poor organization can waste time, reduce efficiency, and damage relationships.

> Figure 4–7 Email Message with Improved Organization

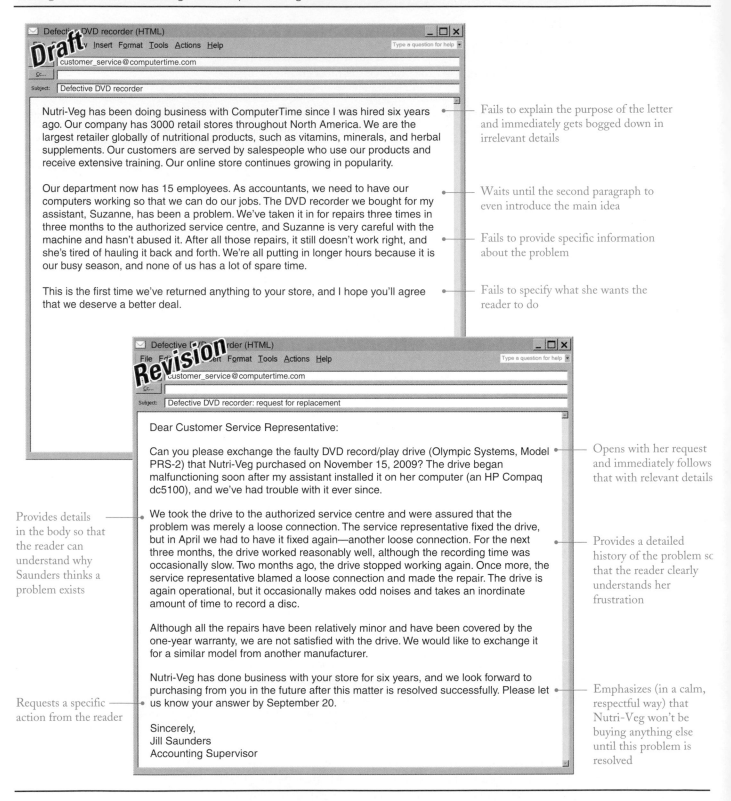

Fails to explain the purpose of the letter and immediately gets bogged down in irrelevant details

Waits until the second paragraph to even introduce the main idea

Fails to provide specific information about the problem

Fails to specify what she wants the reader to do

Provides details in the body so that the reader can understand why Saunders thinks a problem exists

Opens with her request and immediately follows that with relevant details

Provides a detailed history of the problem so that the reader clearly understands her frustration

Requests a specific action from the reader

Emphasizes (in a calm, respectful way) that Nutri-Veg won't be buying anything else until this problem is resolved

In addition to helping you, good organization helps the members of your audience in three key ways. First, it helps your audience understand your message. By making your main point clear at the outset and by presenting information logically, a well-organized message satisfies your audience's need for information.

Second, it helps your audience accept your message. Effective messages often require a bit more than simple, clear logic. A diplomatic approach helps receivers accept your message, even if it's not exactly what they want to hear. In the case of ComputerTime's response to Jill Saunders's request for a replacement product from a different manufacturer, ComputerTime isn't able to do exactly what Saunders requested (they've arranged a replacement from the same manufacturer instead). Consequently, the response letter from Linda Davis has a negative aspect to it, but the style of the letter is tactful and positive (see Figure 4–8).

Third, good organization saves your audience time. Well-organized messages are efficient. They contain only relevant ideas, and they are brief. Moreover, all the information in a well-organized message is in a logical place. Your audience receives only the information they need, and because that information is presented as accessibly and succinctly as possible, they can follow the thought pattern without a struggle. Before you can even begin arranging the information in your message, take a moment to define your main idea.

Good organization helps audience members understand your message, accept your message, and save time.

> Figure 4–8 Message Demonstrating a Diplomatic Organization Plan

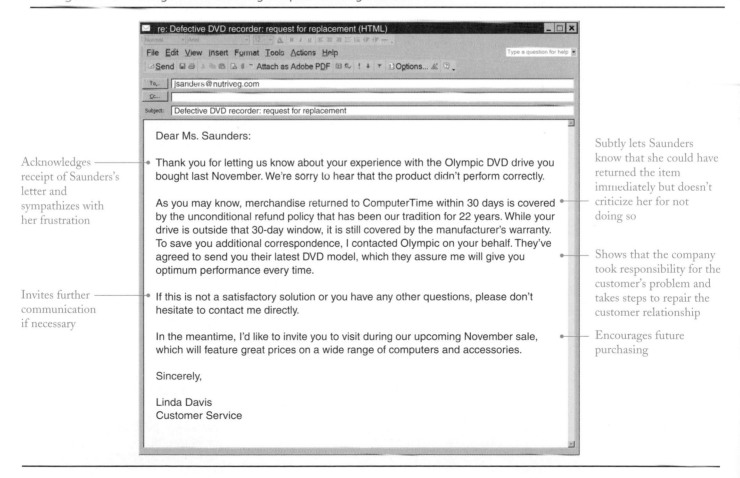

re: Defective DVD recorder: request for replacement (HTML)

File Edit View Insert Format Tools Actions Help

Send — Attach as Adobe PDF — Options...

To: jsanders@nutriveg.com
Cc:
Subject: Defective DVD recorder: request for replacement

Dear Ms. Saunders:

Thank you for letting us know about your experience with the Olympic DVD drive you bought last November. We're sorry to hear that the product didn't perform correctly.

As you may know, merchandise returned to ComputerTime within 30 days is covered by the unconditional refund policy that has been our tradition for 22 years. While your drive is outside that 30-day window, it is still covered by the manufacturer's warranty. To save you additional correspondence, I contacted Olympic on your behalf. They've agreed to send you their latest DVD model, which they assure me will give you optimum performance every time.

If this is not a satisfactory solution or you have any other questions, please don't hesitate to contact me directly.

In the meantime, I'd like to invite you to visit during our upcoming November sale, which will feature great prices on a wide range of computers and accessories.

Sincerely,

Linda Davis
Customer Service

Acknowledges receipt of Saunders's letter and sympathizes with her frustration

Invites further communication if necessary

Subtly lets Saunders know that she could have returned the item immediately but doesn't criticize her for not doing so

Shows that the company took responsibility for the customer's problem and takes steps to repair the customer relationship

Encourages future purchasing

Defining Your Main Idea

Objective 7 Summarize the process for organizing business messages effectively.

The topic is the broad subject; the main idea makes a statement about the topic.

Defining your main idea is more difficult when you're trying to persuade someone or convey disappointing information.

The broad subject, or **topic,** of every well-organized business message is condensed into one idea, whether it's soliciting the executive committee for a larger budget or apologizing to a client for an incident of poor customer service. Your entire message supports, explains, or demonstrates your **main idea**—a specific statement about the topic of your message (see Table 4–2).

Your main idea may be obvious when you're preparing a brief message with simple facts that have little emotional impact on your audience. If you're responding to a request for information, your main idea may be simply, "Here is what you wanted." However, defining your main idea is more complicated when you're not sure what to tell your audience—either because you don't fully understand the topic yourself or you're not sure what the audience needs to know. In addition, in longer documents and presentations, you often need to unify a mass of material, so you'll need to define a main idea that encompasses all the individual points you want to make. Finding a common thread through all these points can be a challenge. Sometimes you won't even be sure what your main idea is until you sort through the information. For especially challenging assignments like these, consider a variety of techniques to generate creative ideas:

> **Brainstorming.** Working alone or with others, generate as many ideas and questions as you can, without stopping to criticize or organize. After you capture all these pieces, look for patterns and connections to help identify the main idea and the groups of supporting ideas. If your assignment is to find a way to increase sales, for example, you might find a cluster of ideas relating to new products, another relating to advertising strategies, and another related to pricing. Identifying such clusters helps you see the major issues and determine the most important idea.

> **Journalistic approach.** Introduced earlier in the chapter, the journalistic approach asks *who, what, when, where, why,* and *how* questions to distill major ideas from piles of unorganized information.

> **Question-and-answer chain.** Perhaps the best approach is to look at the subject of your message from your audience's point of view. Ask yourself: "What is the audience's main question? What do audience members need to know?" Write down and examine your answers. As additional questions emerge, write down and examine those answers. Follow the chain of questions and answers until you have replied to every conceivable question that might occur to your audience. By thinking about your material from your audience's perspective, you are likely to define your main idea.

> Table 4–2 Defining Topic and Main Idea

General Purpose	Specific Purpose	Topic	Main Idea
To inform	Teach customer service representatives how to file insurance claims	Insurance claims	Proper filing saves the company time and money.
To persuade	Convince top managers to increase spending on research and development	Funding for research and development	Competitors spend more than we do on research and development.
To collaborate	Acquire technology and sales figures to devise a computer program that tracks sales by geographical region	Sales	Using a computer program that tracks sales by region will easily highlight geographical areas that need improved representation of products.

> Figure 4–9 Using the Mind-Mapping Technique to Plan a Writing Project

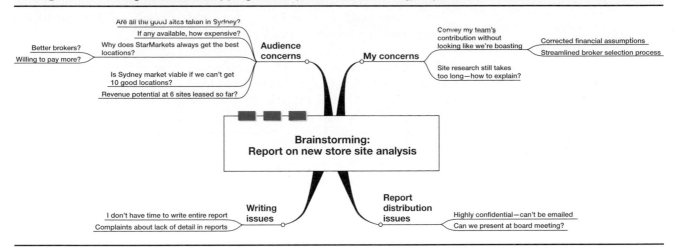

> **Storyteller's tour.** Some writers find it easier to talk through a communication challenge before they write. Pretend you're giving a colleague a guided tour of your message and record what you say. Then listen to your talk, identify ways to tighten and clarify the message, and repeat the process. Working through this recording several times will help you distill the main idea down to a single, concise message.

> **Mind mapping.** You can also generate and organize ideas using a graphic method called mind mapping. Start with a main idea and then branch out to connect every other related idea that comes to mind. For example, the map in Figure 4–9 outlines the writer's own concerns about a report, her insights into the audience's concerns, and several issues related to writing and distributing the report. You can use pen and paper or mind-mapping software such as Visual Mind (www.visual-mind.com).

Limiting Your Scope

The **scope** of your message is the range of information you present, the overall length, and the level of detail—all of which need to correspond to your main idea. For a report outlining your advice on whether to open a new restaurant in Calgary, your message, including all supporting evidence, needs to focus on that question alone. Your plan for new menu selections and your idea for a new source of financing both would be outside the scope of your message.

Whether your audience expects a one-page memo or a one-hour speech, work within that framework to develop your main idea with major points and supporting evidence. Once you have a tentative statement of your main idea, test it against the length limitations that have been imposed on your message. If you don't have enough time or space to develop your main idea fully, or if your main idea won't fill up the time and space allotted, you'll need to redefine it accordingly. If you don't have a fixed limit to work against, plan to make the document or presentation only as long as it needs to be to convey your main idea and critical support points.

Whatever the length of your message, limit the number of major support points to half a dozen or so—and if you can get your idea across with fewer points, all the better. Listing twenty or thirty support points might feel as if you're being thorough, but your audience will view such detail as disorganized and rambling. Instead, look for ways to group supporting points under major

Limit the number of support points; having fewer strong points is a better approach than using many weak points.

headings, such as finance, customers, competitors, employees, or whatever is appropriate for your subject. Just as you might need to refine your main idea, you may also need to refine your major support points so that you have a smaller number with greater impact.

If your message needs to be brief, your main idea will have to be easy to understand and easy to accept. However, if your message is long, you can develop the major points in more detail. How much space you need to communicate and support your main idea depends on your subject, your audience members' familiarity with the material, their receptivity to your conclusions, and your credibility. You'll need fewer words to present routine information to a knowledgeable audience that already knows and respects you. You'll need more words to build a consensus about a complex and controversial subject, especially if the members of your audience are skeptical or hostile strangers.

Choosing Between Direct and Indirect Approaches

After you've defined your ideas, you're ready to decide on the sequence you will use to present your points. You have two basic options:

> **Direct approach (deductive).** When you know your audience will be receptive to your message, use a direct approach: Start with the main idea (a recommendation, a conclusion, or a request) and follow that with your supporting evidence.
> **Indirect approach (inductive).** When your audience will be skeptical about or even resistant to your message, use an **indirect approach:** Start with the evidence first and build your case before presenting the main idea.

To choose between these two alternatives, analyze your audience's likely reaction to your purpose and message. Bear in mind, however, that each message is unique. No simple formula will solve all your communication problems. For example, although an indirect approach may be best when you're sending bad news to outsiders, if you're writing a memo to an associate, you may want to get directly to the point, even if your message is unpleasant. The direct approach might also be a good choice for long messages, regardless of your audience's attitude—because delaying the main idea could cause confusion and frustration. Figure 4–10 summarizes how your approach may differ depending on the likely audience reaction. The type of message also influences the choice of a direct or indirect approach.

 ROUTINE AND POSITIVE MESSAGES The most straightforward business messages are *routine* and *positive* ones. If you're inquiring about products or placing an order, your audience will usually want to comply. If you're announcing a price cut, granting an adjustment, accepting an invitation, or congratulating a colleague, your audience will most likely be pleased to hear from you. If you're providing routine information as part of your regular business, your audience will probably be neutral, neither pleased nor displeased.

Aside from being easy to understand, routine messages are easy to prepare. In most cases you use the direct approach. In the opening, you state your main idea directly, without searching for some creative introduction. By starting off with your positive idea, you emphasize the pleasing aspect of your message. You put your audience in a good frame of mind and encourage them to be receptive to whatever else you have to say. The body of your message can then provide all necessary details. The close should be cordial and emphasize your good news or make a statement about the specific action desired. Routine and positive messages are discussed in greater detail in Chapter 8.

Use a direct approach if the audience's reaction is likely to be positive and the indirect approach if it is likely to be negative.

> Figure 4–10 Choosing Between the Direct and Indirect Approaches

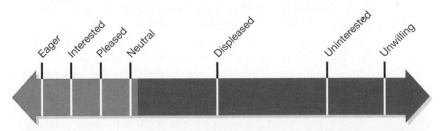

	Direct Approach	Indirect Approach	
Audience Reaction	Eager/interested/ pleased/neutral	Displeased	Uninterested/unwilling
Message Opening	Start with the main idea, the request, or the good news.	Start with a neutral statement that acts as a transition to the reasons for the bad news.	Start with a statement or question that captures attention.
Message Body	Provide necessary details.	Give reasons to justify a negative answer. State or imply the bad news, and make a positive suggestion.	Arouse the audience's interest in the subject. Build the audience's desire to comply.
Message Close	Close with a cordial comment, a reference to the good news, or a statement about the specific action desired.	Close cordially.	Request action.

NEGATIVE MESSAGES Unfortunately, being a business communicator also means you'll face situations in which you need to deliver bad news. Because your audience will be disappointed, these messages usually benefit from the indirect approach—putting the evidence first and building up to the main idea. This approach strengthens your case as you go along, not only making the receiver more receptive to the eventual conclusion but also treating the receiver in a more sensitive manner, which helps you retain as much goodwill as possible. Astute businesspeople know that every person they encounter could be a potential customer, supplier, or contributor or could influence someone who is a customer, supplier, or contributor.

Successful communicators take extra care with their negative messages. They often open with a neutral statement that acts as a transition to the reasons for the bad news. In the body, they give the reasons that justify the negative answer, announcement, or information before they state or imply the bad news. And they are always careful to close cordially.

The challenge of negative messages lies in being honest but kind. You don't want to sacrifice ethics and mislead your audience, nor do you want to be overly blunt. To achieve a good mix of candour and kindness, focus on some aspect of the situation that makes the negative news a little easier to take.

Keep in mind that the indirect approach is neither manipulative nor unethical. As long as you can be honest and reasonably brief, you're often better off opening a bad-news message with a neutral point and putting the negative information after the explanation. Then, if you can close with something fairly positive, your audience may feel able to tolerate the situation—they may not like it, but they may not be hostile either (which is often all you can hope for when you must deliver bad news). Negative messages are discussed further in Chapter 9.

  Explore

If you have bad news, try to put it somewhere in the middle, cushioned by other more positive ideas.

Using the indirect approach allows you to get your message across to an uninterested or skeptical audience.

PERSUASIVE MESSAGES Persuasive messages present a special communication challenge because you're asking your audience to give, do, or change something, whether it's contributing to a charity, buying a product, or changing a belief or an attitude. Professionals who specialize in persuasive messages such as sales letters and other advertising spend years perfecting their craft, and the best practitioners command salaries on a par with some high-ranking executives. You might not have the opportunity to take your skills to that level, but you can learn some basic techniques to improve your own persuasive messages.

> Persuasive messages can be challenging because you're generally asking your audience to give up something, such as time, money, power, and so on.

Before you try to persuade people to do something, capture their attention and get them to consider your message with an open mind. Make an interesting point and provide supporting facts that encourage your audience to continue paying attention. In most persuasive messages, the opening mentions a reader benefit, refers to a problem that the recipient might have, poses a question, or mentions an interesting statistic. Then the body builds interest in the subject and arouses audience members' desire to comply. Once you have them thinking, you can introduce your main idea. The close is cordial and requests the desired action. Persuasive messages are discussed at greater length in Chapter 10.

Outlining Your Content

Once you have chosen the right approach, it's time to figure out the most logical and effective way to present your major points and supporting details. Even if you've resisted creating outlines in your school assignments over the years, get into the habit when you're preparing business messages. You'll save time, get better results, and do a better job of navigating through complicated business situations. Whether you use the outlining features provided with word-processing software or simply jot down three or four points on the back of an envelope, making a plan and sticking to it will help you cover the important details.

> A good way to visualize how all the points will fit together is to construct an outline.

When you're preparing a longer, more complex message, an outline is indispensable, because it helps you visualize the relationships among the various parts. Without an outline, you may be inclined to ramble. As you're describing one point, another point may occur to you, so you describe it as well. One detour leads to another, and before you know it, you've forgotten the original point and wasted precious time and energy. With an outline to guide you, however, you can communicate in a more systematic way. Following an outline also helps you insert transitions so that your message is coherent and your audience can understand the relationships among your ideas.

You're no doubt familiar with the basic outline formats which (1) use numbers or numbers and letters to identify each point and (2) indent points to show which ideas are of equal status (see Figure 4–11). An effective outline divides a topic into at least two parts, restricts each subdivision to one category, and ensures that each group is separate and distinct (see Figure 4–12).

> You may want to experiment with other organizational schemes in addition to traditional outlines.

Another way to visualize the outline of your message is to create an "organization chart" similar to the charts used to show a company's management structure (see Figure 4–13). The main idea is shown in the highest-level box and, like a top executive, establishes the big picture. The lower-level ideas, like lower-level employees, provide the details. All the ideas are logically organized into divisions of thought, just as a company is organized into divisions and departments.[15] Using a visual chart instead of a traditional outline has many benefits. Charts help you (1) see the various levels of ideas and how the parts fit together, (2) develop new ideas, and (3) restructure your information flow. The mind-mapping technique used to generate ideas works in a similar way.

> Figure 4–11 Two Common Outline Forms

ALPHANUMERIC OUTLINE

I. First Major Point
  A. First subpoint
  B. Second subpoint
    1. Evidence
    2. Evidence
      a. Detail
      b. Detail
    3. Evidence
  C. Third subpoint
II. Second Major Point
  A. First subpoint
    1. Evidence
    2. Evidence
  B. Second subpoint

DECIMAL OUTLINE

1.0 First Major Point
  1.1 First subpoint
  1.2 Second subpoint
    1.2.1 Evidence
    1.2.2 Evidence
      1.2.2.1 Detail
      1.2.2.2 Detail
    1.2.3 Evidence
  1.3 Third subpoint
2.0 Second Major Point
  2.1 First subpoint
    2.1.1 Evidence
    2.1.2 Evidence
  2.2 Second subpoint

Whichever outlining or organizing scheme you use, start your message with the main idea, follow that with major supporting points, and then illustrate these points with evidence.

START WITH THE MAIN IDEA The main idea helps you establish the goals and general strategy of the message. This idea expresses two purposes: (1) what you want your audience to do or think and (2) why they should do so. Everything in your message either supports the main idea or explains its implications. As discussed earlier in this chapter, some messages state the main idea quickly and directly, whereas other messages delay the main idea until after the evidence is presented.

Major supporting points clarify your main idea.

STATE THE MAJOR POINTS Now it's time to support your main idea with the major points that clarify and explain your ideas in more concrete terms. If your purpose is to inform and the material is factual, your major points might

> Figure 4–12 Topic Division in Outlines

RIGHT:	WRONG:

I. Alternatives for Improving Profits
  A. Increasing sales
    1. Internet advertising
    2. Radio advertising
  B. Reducing production costs
    1. Modernizing plants
    2. Using more off-shore labour
	I. Alternatives for Improving Profits
	  A. Increasing sales
	    1. Internet advertising
	  B. Reducing production costs
	    1. Modernizing plants
	    2. Using more off-shore labour

When dividing a topic in an outline, be sure to divide it into at least two parts. A topic cannot be divided into only one part.

In the second (wrong) example, subtopic A is divided only once. Either the writer hasn't developed her ideas sufficiently, or has only one idea (internet advertising) for increasing sales. If she has only one idea for increasing sales, then that idea should be subtopic A (A. Increasing internet sales).

> Figure 4–13 Organization Chart Method for Outlining

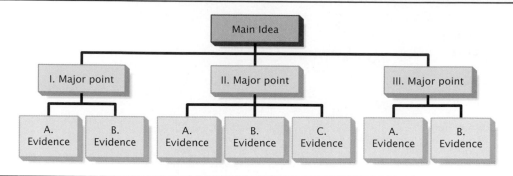

You can divide major points according to physical relationships, the description of a process, the components of an object, or a historical chronology.

be based on something physical or financial—something you can visualize or measure, such as activities to be performed, functional units, spatial or chronological relationships, or parts of a whole. When you're describing a process, the major points are almost inevitably steps in the process. When you're describing an object, the major points correspond to the components of the object. When you're giving a historical account, major points represent events in the chronological chain. If your purpose is to persuade or to collaborate, select major points that develop a line of reasoning or a logical argument that proves your central message and motivates your audience to act.

ILLUSTRATE WITH EVIDENCE After you've defined the main idea and identified supporting points, you're ready to illustrate each point with specific

> Table 4–3 Six Types of Detail

Type of Detail	Example	Comment
Facts and figures	Sales are strong this month. We have two new contracts worth $5 million and a good chance of winning another worth $2.5 million.	Adds more credibility than any other type. Can become boring if used excessively. Most common type used in business.
Example or illustration	We've spent four months trying to hire recent accounting graduates, but so far, only one person has joined our firm. One candidate told me that she would love to work for us, but she can get $5000 more a year elsewhere.	Adds life to a message, but one example does not prove a point. Idea must be supported by other evidence as well.
Description	Upscale hamburger restaurants target burger lovers who want more than the convenience and low prices of McDonald's. These places feature wine and beer, half-pound burgers, and generous side dishes (nachos, potato skins). "Atmosphere" is key.	Helps audience visualize the subject by creating a sensory impression. Does not prove a point, but clarifies it and makes it memorable. Begins with overview of function; defines its purpose, lists major parts, and explains how it operates.
Narration	Under former management, executives worked in blue jeans, meetings rarely started on time, and lunches ran long. When Jim Wilson became CEO, he completely overhauled the operation. A Queen's MBA who favours custom-tailored suits, Wilson has cut the product line in half and chopped $12 million off expenses.	Works well for attracting attention and explaining ideas, but lacks statistical validity.
Reference to authority	I discussed this idea with Jackie Loman in the Sudbury plant, and she was very supportive. As you know, Jackie has been in charge of that plant for the past six years. She is confident that we can speed up the number 2 line by 150 units an hour if we add another worker.	Bolsters a case while adding variety and credibility. Works only if "authority" is recognized and respected by audience.
Visual aids	Graphs, charts, tables	Helps audience grasp specific data. Used more in memos and reports than in letters.

evidence that helps audience members understand and remember the more abstract concepts you're presenting. For example, if you're advocating that your company increase its advertising budget, you can support your major point by providing evidence that your most successful competitors spend more on advertising than you do. You can also describe a case in which a particular competitor increased its ad budget and achieved an impressive sales gain. Then you can show that over the past five years, your firm's sales have gone up and down in response to the amount spent on advertising.

If you're developing a long, complex message, you may need to carry the outline down several levels. Remember that every level is a step along the chain from the abstract to the concrete, from the general to the specific. The lowest level contains the evidence, the individual facts and figures that tie the generalizations to the observable, measurable world. The higher levels are the concepts that reveal why those facts are significant.

Up to a point, the more evidence you provide, the more conclusive your case will be. If your subject is complex and unfamiliar, or if your audience is skeptical, you'll need a lot of facts and figures to demonstrate your points. On the other hand, if your subject is routine and your audience is positively inclined, you can be more sparing with the evidence. You want to provide enough support to be convincing but not so much that your message becomes boring or inefficient.

> Each major point must be supported with enough specific evidence to be convincing, but not so much that your message becomes long and boring.

Another way to keep your audience interested is to vary the type of detail you include. As you draft your message, incorporate the methods described in Table 4–3. Employ both facts and figures in narrative sections, add relevant description, and include some examples or a reference to authority. Where appropriate, reinforce details with visual aids. A variety of approaches adds richness and meaning to the whole.

If your schedule permits, put aside your outline for a day or two before you begin composing your first draft. Then, review it with a fresh eye, looking for opportunities to improve the flow of ideas. For a reminder of the planning tasks involved in preparing your messages, see "Checklist: Planning Business Messages."

CHECKLIST Planning Business Messages

A. Analyze your situation
- ✔ Determine whether the purpose of your message is to inform, persuade, or collaborate.
- ✔ Identify what you want your audience to think or do.
- ✔ Make sure your purpose is worthwhile and realistic.
- ✔ Make sure the time is right for your message.
- ✔ Make sure the right person is delivering your message.
- ✔ Make sure your purpose is acceptable to your organization.
- ✔ Identify the primary audience.
- ✔ Identify the secondary audience.
- ✔ Determine audience size and composition.
- ✔ Estimate your audience's level of understanding and probable reaction to your message.

B. Gather information
- ✔ Decide whether to use formal or informal techniques for gathering information.
- ✔ Find out what your audience wants to know.
- ✔ Provide all required information and make sure it's accurate, ethical, and pertinent.

C. Select the best medium for your message
- ✔ Understand the advantages and disadvantages of oral, written, and electronic media.
- ✔ Consider media richness, formality, media limitations, sender intentions, urgency, cost, and audience preference.

D. Organize your information
- ✔ Define your main idea.
- ✔ Limit your scope.
- ✔ Choose a direct or indirect approach.
- ✔ Outline content by starting with the main idea, adding major points, and illustrating with evidence.

Summary of Learning Objectives

1 **Describe the three-step writing process.** (1) Planning consists of analyzing your purpose and your audience, collecting information (whether formally or informally), and adapting your message by selecting the appropriate channel and medium and by establishing a good relationship with your audience. (2) Writing consists of organizing your ideas and actually composing words, sentences, paragraphs, and visual graphics. (3) Completing your message consists of revising your message by evaluating content and then rewriting and editing for clarity, producing your message by using effective design elements and suitable delivery methods, and proofreading your message for typos and errors in spelling and mechanics.

2 **Explain why it's important to define your purpose carefully, and list four questions that can help you test that purpose.** You must know enough about the purpose of your message to shape that message in a way that will achieve your goal. To decide whether you should proceed with your message, ask four questions: (1) Will anything change as a result of my message? (2) Is my purpose realistic? (3) Is the time right? (4) Is my purpose acceptable to my organization?

3 **Describe the importance of analyzing your audience, and identify the seven factors you should consider when developing an audience profile.** Analyzing your audience helps you predict how your audience will react to your message. It also helps you know what to include in your message and how to include it. To develop an audience profile, determine your primary audience (key decision makers) and your secondary audience, audience size and geographic distribution, audience composition, your audience's level of understanding, expectations and preferences, and their probable reaction.

4 **Discuss gathering information for simple messages, and identify three attributes of quality information.** You can collect relevant information informally by considering others' viewpoints, browsing through company files, chatting with supervisors or colleagues, or asking your audience for input. You can test the quality of your information by checking whether it is accurate, ethical, and pertinent.

5 **List factors to consider when choosing the most appropriate medium for your message.** Media richness, the value of a medium for communicating a message, is a factor to consider for message transmission. Richness is determined by the medium's ability to (1) convey a message using more than one informational cue (visual, verbal, vocal); (2) facilitate feedback; and (3) establish personal focus. Other factors to consider when selecting media include the message's formality, media limitations, sender intentions, urgency and cost, and audience preferences.

6 **Explain why good organization is important to both you and your audience.** Audiences benefit from good organization in several ways. A well-organized message saves your audience time, because they don't have to read and reread a message to make sense of it. They are also better able to understand the content, so they can accept the message more easily and can make better decisions based on its information. Communicators also benefit from good organization: well-organized messages consume less creative energy, speed the drafting stage, make it easier to get input from colleagues, and allow communicators to divide portions of the writing assignment among co-workers.

7 **Summarize the process for organizing business messages effectively.** The process for organizing messages effectively has four parts. First, define the main idea of the message by making a specific statement about the topic. Second, limit the scope of the message by adjusting the space and detail you allocate to major points. Third, choose either a direct or an indirect approach by anticipating the audience's reaction to the message and by matching the approach to message length and message type. Fourth, group the points by constructing an outline to visualize the relationship between the ideas and the supporting material.

On the Job PERFORMING COMMUNICATION TASKS AT THE FORZANI GROUP

You have been hired as an intern at The Forzani Group's corporate office in Calgary. As a major player in the Canadian sports retail scene, the company receives a lot of media attention. Your job is to respond to press inquiries about The Forzani Group Ltd. Use what you've learned in this chapter to solve the following situations and be prepared to explain why your choice is best:

1 You have received a phone call from Ann Mason, a reporter for a local Saskatchewan newspaper. She plans to write an article about The Forzani Group's recent decision to open a Sports Experts store in her community, a small city. Mason has asked you for information about the economic impact of Sport Chek, Sports Experts, and other chains in Forzani's company in other local areas. When responding to Mason's request, what should the purpose of your letter be?

   a The general purpose is to inform. The specific purpose is to provide Mason with a brief summary of the evolution of The Forzani Group over the past 20 years.

   b The general purpose is to persuade. The specific purpose is to convince Mason that The Forzani Group creates jobs within a community, and that small, existing merchants should not feel threatened by the arrival of a Sports Experts store

   c The general purpose is to collaborate. The specific purpose is to work with Mason to develop an article that examines the history of The Forzani Group's entry into new markets.

   d The general purpose is to respond. The specific purpose is to convey details requested by a journalist.

2 Assume that your purpose is to convince Mason of The Forzani Group's abilities to create new jobs and increase economic activity in small communities. Is your purpose worth pursuing at this time?

   a Yes. The purpose is realistic, the timing is right, you are the right person to send the message, and the purpose is acceptable to the organization.

   b Not completely. Realistically, many readers of Mason's newspaper may dread the arrival of a Sports Experts store in their small community, fearing that the giant retailer may force small retailers out of business.

   c The purpose is fine, but you are not the right person to send this message. Tom Quinn, the chief operating officer, should respond.

   d The timing is right for this message. Stress The Forzani Group's involvement in small communities, citing contributions to social causes in other small cities. Show how the company cares about customers on a personal basis.

3 When planning your reply to Mason, what assumptions can you make about your audience?

   a The audience includes not only Ann Mason but also the readers of the community's newspaper. Given their bias for a simple, rural lifestyle, the readers will probably be hostile to big business in general and to The Forzani Group in particular. They probably know little about large retail operations. Furthermore, they probably mistrust you because you are a Forzani Group employee.

   b Ann Mason will probably be the only person who reads the letter directly. She is the primary audience; the readers of her article are the secondary audience. Mason will be happy to hear from The Forzani Group and will read the information with an open mind. However, she may not know a great deal about the company. Although she is a stranger to you, she trusts your credibility as a Forzani Group spokesperson.

   c Ann Mason is probably the sole and primary audience for the letter. The fact that she is writing an article about The Forzani Group suggests that she already knows a great deal about the company and likes the idea of a Sports Experts outlet in her community. In all likelihood, she will respond positively to your reply and will trust your credibility as a Forzani Group representative.

   d Ann Mason may be an industrial spy working for a sporting goods retailer. She will show your reply to people who work for your competitor; they will analyze the information and use it to improve their market share of the sporting goods industry.

Test Your Knowledge

1 What are the three steps in the writing process?

2 What types of purposes do all business messages have?

3 What do you need to know to develop an audience profile?

4 How can you test the thoroughness of the information you include in a message?

5 What are the main advantages of oral media? Of written media? Of visual media? Of electronic media?

6 How do you choose the medium for your message?

7 How does the audience benefit from a well-organized message?

8 What are the steps in the process for organizing messages?

9 What elements do you consider when choosing between a direct and an indirect approach?

Apply Your Knowledge

1 Some writers argue that planning messages wastes time because they inevitably change their plans as they go along. How would you respond to this argument? Briefly explain.

2 As a member of the public relations department, what medium would you recommend using to inform the local community that your toxic-waste cleanup program has been successful? Why?

3 Would you use a direct or an indirect approach to ask employees to work overtime to meet an important deadline? Please explain.

4 Which approach would you use to let your boss know that you'll be out half a day this week to attend your uncle's funeral—direct or indirect? Why?

5 **Ethical Choices** The company president has asked you to draft a memo to the board of directors informing them that sales in a line of gourmet fruit jams the company recently acquired have far exceeded anyone's expectations. However, you happen to know that this increase reflects a trend across the industry, with many consumers switching from moderately priced jams to gourmet products. In fact, sales of your company's traditional products have slipped in recent months. You were not asked to add this information, but you think it's important for the board to be able to put the new sales data in proper context. What should you do?

Running Cases

Watch on mycanadianbuscommlab

> CASE 1 Noreen

Noreen's manager informs her of a new Petro-Go company promotion for Canadian customers owning a "Go Points" card. The first step is to prepare the service stations.

The promotion details are as follows: (1) Cardholders will now receive double points when they purchase more than $30 of gasoline in one visit (regular points up to $30 and then double points over $30). (2) Cardholders will earn a new reward redemption—Petro-Go gift certificates ($20 certificate for a 250-point redemption). (3) Cardholders will win a free 6-litre container of windshield washer fluid when their accumulated points reach each 1000-point interval.

Noreen is asked to create a letter to inform the service station owners/operators when the promotion begins, how it will be advertised, what the promotion offers, and how they will use their equipment to offer and track this promotion. An instruction booklet on where and how to place signs, how to update equipment, and how to manage card points will be attached to the letter. Noreen needs to prepare this booklet by gathering information from past promotional materials and then choosing only what she needs for this task. This letter needs to be distributed as soon as possible. There is much to be done.

QUESTIONS
a) What information must Noreen gather?
b) Why is it so important that Noreen's letter be concise and accurate?
c) What would be the best way to distribute this information to the service stations?
d) What will the audience's general attitude be toward the message?
e) How many key ideas are in this letter? How will Noreen emphasize them?

YOUR TASK
The station owners/operators need to know how and where to put up promotional signs and how to update point-of-sale machines and registers using key codes and sequences. Write two sets of instructions for the service stations—the first set will be for a reader who has never used that type of machine or provided a promotion before, and the second set will be for a reader who is familiar with that type of machine and has provided promotions in the past. Use your imagination. Briefly explain how your two audiences affect your instructions.

> CASE 2 Kwong

Kwong has done some research into Canadian business culture. He has also attended several college workshops to improve his English and speaking skills. Thanks to his efforts and improved understanding, he has now obtained a co-op placement with Accountants For All accounting firm. With the tax season quickly approaching, Kwong's manager knows that their previous customers will once again look for an accounting firm to help them file their tax returns. Kwong's manager

asks him to produce a promotional letter that will help bring back previous customers.

QUESTIONS
a) What does Kwong need to plan?
b) How should he get started?
c) What information should Kwong put in this promotional letter?

d) How should Kwong organize his letter?

e) How much detail does he need to provide?

YOUR TASK

List five messages you have received lately, such as direct-mail promotions, letters, email messages, phone solicitations, and lectures. For each, determine the general and the specific purpose; then, answer the following questions:

1 Was the message well timed?

2 Did the sender choose an appropriate medium for the message?

3 Did the appropriate person deliver the message?

4 Was the sender's purpose realistic?

Practise Your Knowledge

A writer is working on an insurance information brochure and is having trouble grouping ideas logically into an outline. Prepare the outline, paying attention to appropriate subordination of the ideas. If necessary, rewrite phrases to give them a more consistent sound.

Accident Protection Insurance Plan

> Coverage is only pennies a day

> Benefit is $100 000 for accidental death on common carriers

> Benefit is $100 a day for hospitalization as result of motor vehicle or common carrier accident

> Benefit is $20 000 for accidental death in motor vehicle accident

> Individual coverage is only $17.85 per quarter; family coverage is just $26.85 per quarter

> No physical exam or health questions

> Convenient payment—billed quarterly

> Guaranteed acceptance for all applicants

> No individual rate increases

> Free, no-obligation examination period

> Cash paid in addition to any other insurance carried

> Covers accidental death when riding as fare-paying passenger on public transportation, including buses, trains, jets, ships, trolleys, subways, or any other common carrier

> Covers accidental death in motor vehicle accidents occurring while driving or riding in or on an automobile, truck, camper, motor home, or non-motorized bicycle

Exercises

4.1 Message Planning Skills: Self-Assessment

How good are you at planning business messages? Use the chart below to rate yourself on each element of planning an audience-centred business message. Then, examine your ratings to identify where you are strongest and where you can improve, using the tips in this chapter.

4.2 Planning Messages: General and Specific Purpose

Make a list of communication tasks you'll need to accomplish in the next week or so (for example, a job application, a letter of complaint, a speech to a class, an order for a product). For each, determine a general and a specific purpose.

4.3 Planning Messages: Specific Purpose

For each of the following communication tasks, state a specific purpose (if you have trouble, begin with "I want to . . .").

a. A report to your boss, the store manager, about the outdated items in the warehouse

b. A memo to clients about your booth at the upcoming trade show

Element of Planning	Always	Frequently	Occasionally	Never
1. I start by defining my purpose.	_____	_____	_____	_____
2. I analyze my audience before writing a message.	_____	_____	_____	_____
3. I investigate what my audience wants to know.	_____	_____	_____	_____
4. I check that my information is accurate, ethical, and pertinent.	_____	_____	_____	_____
5. I consider my audience and purpose when selecting media.	_____	_____	_____	_____

c. A letter to a customer who hasn't made a payment for three months

d. A memo to employees about the department's high cell-phone bills

e. A phone call to a supplier checking on an overdue parts shipment

f. A report to future users of the computer program you have chosen to handle the company's mailing list

4.4 Planning Messages: Audience Profile

For each communication task below, write brief answers to three questions: Who is my audience? What is my audience's general attitude toward my subject? What does my audience need to know?

a. A final-notice collection letter from an appliance manufacturer to an appliance dealer, sent 10 days before initiating legal collection procedures

b. An unsolicited sales letter asking readers to purchase computer disks at near-wholesale prices

c. An advertisement for peanut butter

d. Fliers to be attached to doorknobs in the neighbourhood, announcing reduced rates for chimney lining or repairs

e. A cover letter sent along with your résumé to a potential employer

f. A request (to the seller) for a price adjustment on a piano that incurred $150 in damage during delivery to a banquet room in the hotel you manage

4.5 Meeting Audience Needs: Necessary Information

Choose a product (such as a digital music player, camera, or cell phone) that you know how to operate well. Write two sets of instructions for operating the device: one set for a reader who has never used that type of device, and one set for someone who is generally familiar with that type of device but has never operated the specific model. Briefly explain how your two audiences affect your instructions. (Limit your instructions to the basic functions, such as placing and receiving calls on a cell phone.)

4.6 Selecting Media: Identifying an Audience

Barbara Lin is in charge of public relations for a cruise line that operates out of Vancouver. She is shocked to read a letter in a local newspaper from a disgruntled passenger, complaining about the service and entertainment on a recent cruise. Lin will have to respond to these publicized criticisms in some way. What audiences will she need to consider in her response? What medium should she choose? If the letter had been published in a travel publication widely read by travel agents and cruise travellers, how might her course of action differ?

4.7 Teamwork: Audience Analysis

Your team has been studying a new method for testing the durability of your company's running shoes. Now the team needs to prepare three separate reports on the findings: first, a report for the administrator who will decide whether to purchase the equipment needed for this new testing method; second, a report for the company's designers who develop the running shoe; and third, a report for store managers who will show employees the shoe's features. To determine the audience's needs for each report, the team has listed the following questions:

1. Who are the readers?
2. Why will they read my report?
3. Do they need introductory or background material?
4. Do they need definitions of terms?
5. What level or type of language is needed?
6. What level of detail is needed?
7. What result does my report aim for?

Working with two other students, answer the questions for each of these audiences and summarize your analysis in a brief report:

a. The administrator
b. The designers
c. The store managers

4.8 Internet: Planning Your Message

Go to the TELUS website at www.telus.ca and follow the link to the latest annual report (look under Investor Info). Locate and read the CEO's letter to investors in the report. Who is the primary audience for this message? Who is the secondary audience? What is the general purpose of the message? What do you think this audience wants to know from the CEO of TELUS? Summarize your answers in a brief (one-page) memo or oral presentation.

4.9 Message Organization: Outlining Your Content

Using the Nutri-Veg email in this chapter (Figure 4–7), draw an organizational chart similar to the one shown in Figure 4–13. Fill in the main idea, the major points, and the evidence provided in this letter. (Note: Your diagram may be smaller than the one provided in Figure 4–13.)

4.10 Message Organization: Limiting Scope

Suppose you are preparing to recommend that top management install a new heating system that uses a process called cogeneration, in which production waste is used to generate heat. The following information is in your files. Eliminate topics that aren't essential; then arrange the other topics, so your report will give top managers a clear understanding of the heating system and a balanced, concise justification for installing it.

> History of the development of the cogeneration heating process
> Scientific credentials of the developers of the process
> Risks assumed in using this process
> Your plan for installing the equipment in your building
> Stories about its successful use in comparable facilities
> Specifications of the equipment that would be installed
> Plans for disposing of the old heating equipment
> Costs of installing and running the new equipment

> Advantages and disadvantages of using the new process
> Detailed 10-year cost projections
> Estimates of the time needed to phase in the new system
> Alternative systems that management might wish to consider

4.11 Message Organization: Choosing an Approach

Indicate whether a direct or an indirect approach would be best in each situation, then briefly explain why. Would any of these messages be inappropriate for email? Explain.

a. A letter asking when next year's automobiles will be put on sale locally
b. A letter from a recent graduate requesting a letter of recommendation from a former instructor
c. A letter turning down a job applicant
d. An announcement that, because of high air-conditioning costs, the plant temperature will be held at 24°C during the summer
e. A final request to settle a delinquent debt

4.12 Message Organization: Audience Focus

If you were trying to persuade people to take the following actions, how would you organize your argument?

a. You want your boss to approve your plan for hiring two additional people.
b. You want to be hired for a job.
c. You want to be granted a business loan.
d. You want to collect a small amount from a regular customer whose account is slightly past due.
e. You want to collect a large amount from a customer whose account is seriously past due.

4.13 Ethical Choices: Providing Information

Your supervisor, whom you respect, has asked you to withhold important information that you think should be included in a report you are preparing. Disobeying him could be disastrous for your relationship with him and possibly your career. Obeying him could violate your personal code of ethics. What should you do? On the basis of the discussion in Chapter 1, would you consider this situation to be an ethical dilemma or an ethical lapse? Please explain.

4.14 Three-Step Process: Other Applications

In an email message to your instructor, explain how the material discussed in this chapter can also apply to meetings, as discussed in Chapter 2. (Hint: Review the section headings in Chapter 4 and think about making your meetings more productive.)

5

Writing Business Messages

ON THE JOB

Communicating at Creative Commons
REDEFINING TWO CENTURIES OF COPYRIGHT LAW
FOR THE DIGITAL AGE

www.creativecommons.org

Have you ever noticed that tiny © symbol on books, DVDs, music CDs, and other media products? This symbol means that the person or organization who created the item has copyright protection—the exclusive legal right to produce, distribute, and sell that creation. Anyone who wants to resell, redistribute, or adapt such works usually needs to secure permission from the current copyright holder.

However, what if you want people to remix the song you just recorded? Or suppose you need a few photos for a website or a short piece of music for a training video? Other than for limited personal and educational use, a conventional copyright requires every person to negotiate a contract for every application or adaptation of every piece of work he or she wants to use.

The search for some middle ground between "all rights reserved" and simply giving your work away led U.S.-based Stanford University law professor Lawrence Lessig to co-found Creative Commons. This non-profit organization's goal is to provide a simple, free, and legal way for musicians, artists, writers, teachers, scientists, and others to collaborate and benefit through the sharing of art and ideas. Instead of the everything-or-nothing approach of traditional copyright, Creative Commons offers a more flexible range of "some rights reserved" options.

Through books, articles, and speeches, Lessig has been a tireless promoter of the Creative Commons concept, working to convince people that society benefits from

Lawrence Lessig, co-founder of Creative Commons, uses a variety of communication vehicles to convince copyright owners to explore new ways of sharing and protecting their creative works.

the free exchange of art and ideas and that overuse of the copyright law is endangering not only creative expression but also important scientific research. The message is clearly getting through: within the first year, more than a million of these innovative licence agreements were initiated for musical works, short films, educational materials, novels, and more. This approach can't solve the entire dilemma of copyrights in the digital age, but it has already created a better way for creative people to communicate and collaborate.

If you worked at Creative Commons, how would you write messages about the purpose and process of this organization? How would you adapt your message for your audience? What media would you use?[1]

Bringing Your Ideas to Life

As they work to persuade their audiences to consider new forms of copyright protection, Lawrence Lessig and his colleagues at Creative Commons realize it takes more than just a great idea to change the way people think. Expressing ideas clearly and persuasively will be key to your success as well.

With a solid plan in place (see Chapter 4), you're ready to choose the words and craft the sentences and paragraphs that will carry your ideas to their intended audiences. The second step in the three-step writing process (Figure 5–1) includes two vital tasks: adapting to your audience and composing your message.

Adapting to Your Audience

Objective 1 Explain the importance of adapting your messages to the needs and expectations of your audience

Whether consciously or not, audiences greet most incoming messages with a question: "What's in this for me?" If your intended audience thinks a message does not apply to them or doesn't meet their needs, they won't be inclined to

Audiences want to know how your messages will benefit them.

> Figure 5–1 Step Two in the Three-Step Writing Process: Write Your Messages

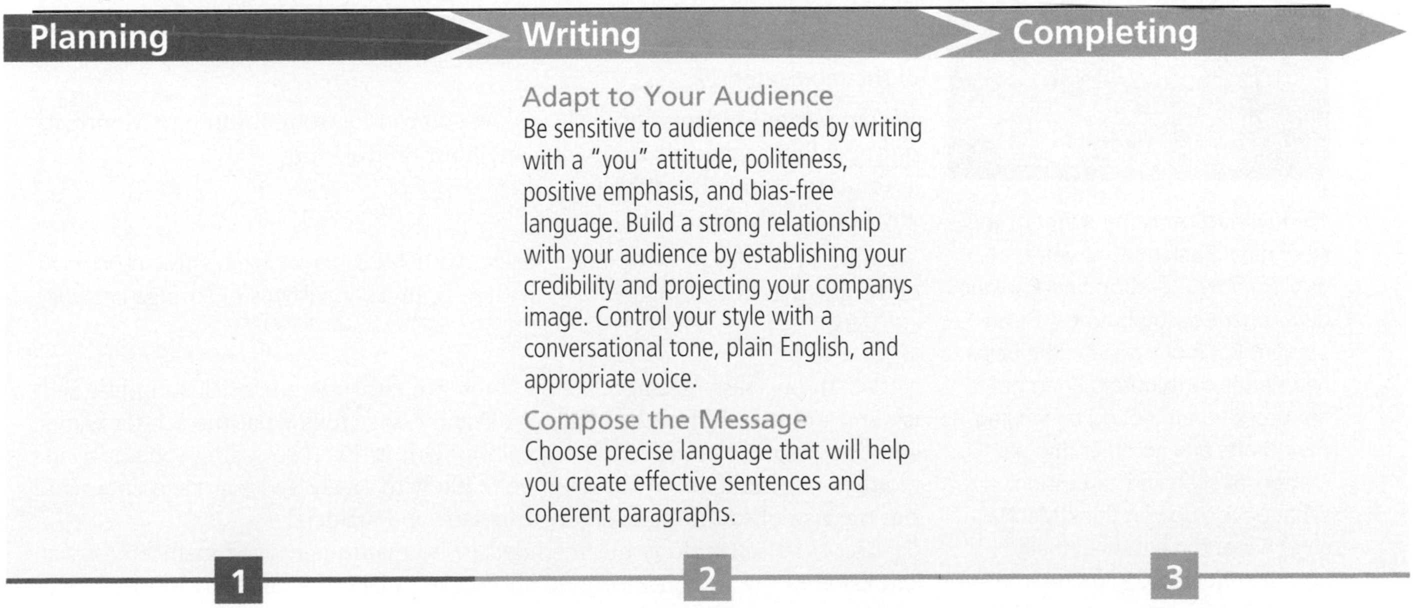

Planning > **Writing** > **Completing**

Adapt to Your Audience
Be sensitive to audience needs by writing with a "you" attitude, politeness, positive emphasis, and bias-free language. Build a strong relationship with your audience by establishing your credibility and projecting your companys image. Control your style with a conversational tone, plain English, and appropriate voice.

Compose the Message
Choose precise language that will help you create effective sentences and coherent paragraphs.

1   2   3

pay attention to it. Look at the Creative Commons website, which uses video interviews with Creative Commons employees, newsletters, and case studies, among other communication media, to engage people and educate them about Creative Commons's goals. For example, through a case study about an African sleeping sickness test, scientists can learn how to license their findings to provide free access to their research. Artists who want to provide music online can download a booklet titled "New Ways of Doing Music Business" for licensing guidance. By adapting your communication to your readers' particular needs and expectations, you'll provide a more compelling answer to "What's in this for me?" and improve the chances of your message being successful.

A good relationship with your audience is essential to effective communication.

Note that adapting your message is not always a simple task. Some situations will require you to balance competing or conflicting needs—for example, when you're trying to convince people to change their minds or when you're delivering bad news. To adapt your message to your audience, be sensitive to their needs, build a strong relationship with them, and control your style to maintain a professional tone.

Being Sensitive to Your Audience's Needs

Even in simple messages intended merely to share information, it's possible to use all the right words and still not be sensitive to your audience and their needs. You can improve your audience sensitivity by adopting the "you" attitude, maintaining good standards of etiquette, emphasizing the positive, and using bias-free language.

The "you" attitude is best implemented by expressing your message in terms of the audience's interests and needs.

USING THE "YOU" ATTITUDE You are already becoming familiar with the audience-centred approach, trying to see a subject through your audience's eyes. Now you want to project this approach in your messages by adopting a "you" attitude—speaking and writing in terms of your audience's wishes, interests, hopes, and preferences.

On the simplest level, you can adopt the "you" attitude by replacing terms that refer to yourself and your company with terms that refer to your audience. In other words, use *you* and *yours* instead of *I, me, mine, we, us,* and *ours:*

Instead of This	Use This
To help us process this order, we must ask for another copy of the requisition.	So that your order can be filled promptly, please send another copy of the requisition.
We are pleased to announce our new flight schedule from Toronto to Montreal, which is any hour on the hour.	Now you can fly from Toronto to Montreal any hour on the hour.
We offer MP3 players with 4, 8, or 16 gigabytes of storage capacity.	Select your MP3 player from three models with 4, 8, or 16 gigabytes of storage capacity.

Wendy MacNair is the editor of the Aboriginal Banking Newsletter, published by the Aboriginal Banking department of the Business Development Bank of Canada. She helps newsletter contributors bring out the best in their writing by reading their drafts and commenting on matters of style and expression. What advice do you think MacNair gives her authors to help them become effective communicators?

When business messages use an "I" or "we" attitude, they risk sounding selfish and uninterested in the audience. The message tells what the sender wants, and the audience is expected to go along with it. Even so, using *you* and *yours* requires finesse. If you overdo it, you're likely to create awkward sentences and run the risk of sounding overly enthusiastic and artificial.[2]

The "you" attitude is not intended to be manipulative or insincere. It's an extension of the audience-centred approach. In fact, the best way to implement the "you" attitude is to think sincerely about your audience when composing your message.

Nor is the "you" attitude simply a matter of using one pronoun rather than another; it's a matter of genuine empathy. You can use *you* 25 times in a single page and still ignore your audience's true concerns. In other words, it's the thought and sincerity that count, not the pronoun *you*. If you're talking to a retailer, try to think like a retailer; if you're dealing with a production supervisor, put yourself in that position; if you're writing to a dissatisfied customer, imagine how you would feel at the other end of the transaction. The important thing is your attitude toward audience members and your appreciation of their position.

Be aware that on some occasions it's better to avoid using *you*, particularly if doing so will sound overly authoritative or accusing. For instance, instead of saying, "You failed to deliver the customer's order on time," you could minimize ill will by saying, "The customer didn't receive the order on time," or "Let's figure out a system that will ensure on-time deliveries."

Instead of This	Use This
You should never use that type of paper in the copy machine.	That type of paper doesn't work very well in the copy machine.
You must correct all five copies by noon.	All five copies must be corrected by noon.

Avoid using *you* and *yours* when doing so
> makes you sound dictatorial
> makes someone else feel guilty
> goes against your organization's style

As you practise using the "you" attitude, be sure to consider the attitudes of other cultures and the policies of your organization. In some cultures, it is improper to single out one person's achievements because the whole team is responsible for the outcome; in that case, using the pronoun *we* or *our* (when you and your audience are part of the same team) would be more appropriate. Similarly, some companies have a tradition of avoiding references to *you* and *I* in their memos and formal reports.

MAINTAINING STANDARDS OF ETIQUETTE Another good way to demonstrate interest in your audience and to earn their respect is to demonstrate etiquette in your messages. You know how it feels to be treated inconsiderately; when that happens, you probably react emotionally and then pay less attention to the offending message. By being courteous to members of your audience, you show consideration for them and foster a more successful environment for communication.

On those occasions when you experience frustration with co-workers, customers, or others you deal with, you might be tempted to respond in blunt terms. However, venting your emotions rarely improves the situation and can damage your reputation. Demonstrate your diplomatic skills by controlling your emotions and communicating calmly and politely:

Although you may be tempted now and then to be brutally frank, express the facts in a kind and thoughtful manner.

Instead of This	Use This
Once again, you've managed to bring down the website through your incompetent programming.	Let's go over what went wrong with the last site update so that we can improve the process.
You've been sitting on our order for two weeks, and we need it now!	Our production schedules depend on timely delivery of parts and supplies, but we have not yet received the order you promised to deliver two weeks ago. Please respond today with a firm delivery commitment.

Use extra tact when communicating with people higher up the organization chart or outside the company.

Of course, some situations require more diplomacy than others. If you know your audience well, a less formal approach might be more appropriate. However, when you are communicating with people who outrank you or with people outside your organization, an added measure of courtesy is usually needed.

Written communication and most forms of electronic media generally require more tact than oral communication. In the "ineffective" example in Figure 5–2, notice how the customer service agent's unfortunate word choices immediately derail this instant messaging exchange. In the "effective" example, a more sensitive approach allows both people to focus on solving the problem.

Unlike writing, when you're speaking, your words are softened by your tone of voice and facial expression. In addition, you can adjust your approach according to the feedback you get. If you inadvertently offend someone in writing, you usually won't get the immediate feedback to resolve the situation. In fact, you may never know that you offended your audience.

You can communicate negative news without being negative.

EMPHASIZING THE POSITIVE During your career, you will face situations in which you need to communicate bad news—maybe dozens or hundreds of times. As you rise through the ranks of management, you will encounter situations in which unpleasant news can significantly affect the personal and financial well-being of employees, customers, and investors. However, there is a big difference between delivering negative news and being negative. When the tone of your message is negative, you put unnecessary strain on business relationships, which can cause people to distance themselves from you and your ideas.

If you're facing a potentially negative situation, seek ways to soften the blow or emphasize positive aspects of a situation. Never hide the negative news, but always try to find positive points that will foster a good relationship with your audience:[3]

Instead of This	Use This
It is impossible to repair your car today.	Your car can be ready by Tuesday. Would you like a loaner until then?
We apologize for inconveniencing you during our remodelling.	The renovations now under way will help us serve you better.
We wasted $300 000 advertising in that magazine.	Our $300 000 advertising investment did not pay off; let's analyze the experience and apply the insights to future campaigns.

When you are offering criticism or advice, focus on what the person can do to improve.

When you find it necessary to criticize or correct, don't dwell on the other person's mistakes. Avoid referring to failures, problems, or shortcomings. Focus instead on what the person can do to improve:

Instead of This	Use This
The problem with this department is a failure to control costs.	The performance of this department can be improved by tightening cost controls.
You filled out the order form wrong.	Please check your colour preferences on the enclosed card so we can process your order.

Show your audience how they will benefit from complying with your message.

If you're trying to persuade the audience to buy a product, pay a bill, or perform a service for you, emphasize what's in it for them. Don't focus on why *you*

> Figure 5–2 Fostering a Positive Relationship with an Audience

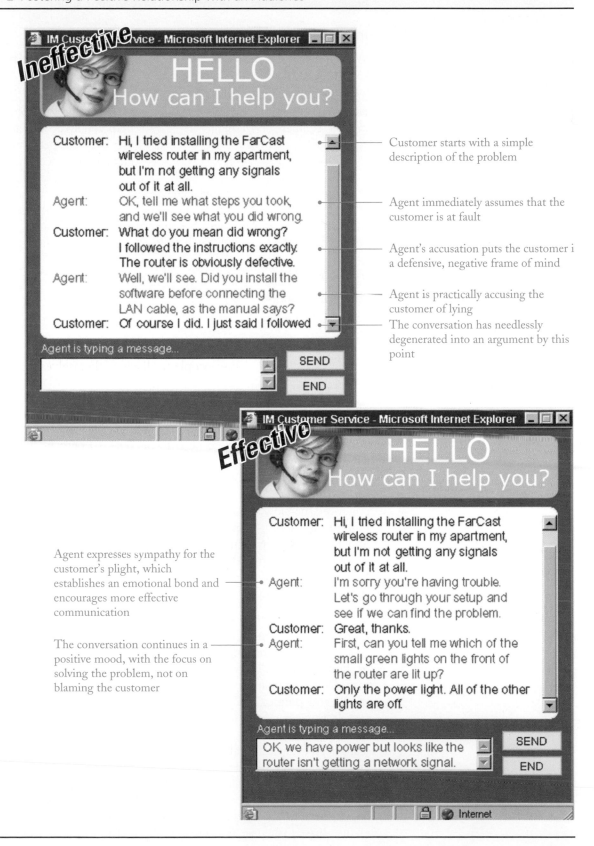

want them to do something. An individual who sees the possibility for personal benefit is more likely to respond positively to your appeal:

Instead of This	Use This
We will notify all three credit reporting agencies if you do not pay your overdue bill within 10 days.	Paying your overdue bill within 10 days will prevent a negative entry on your credit record.
I am tired of seeing so many errors in the customer-service blog.	Proofreading your blog postings will help you avoid embarrassing mistakes that generate more customer-service complaints.

In general, state your message without using words that might hurt or offend your audience. Substitute *euphemisms* (mild terms) for those that have unpleasant meanings. You can be honest without being harsh. Gentle language won't change the facts, but it will make them more acceptable:

Instead of This	Use This
cheap merchandise	economy merchandise
used cars	preowned cars
failing	underperforming
elderly	senior citizen
fake	imitation or faux

On the other hand, don't carry euphemisms to extremes, or your audience will view your efforts as insincere. And, if you're too subtle, people may miss your meaning. If employees need to become 10 percent more productive to save the company from bankruptcy, don't tell them they need to "make positive performance adjustments"—tell them they need to become 10 percent more productive. Also, when using euphemisms, you walk a fine line between softening the blow and hiding the facts. It would be unethical to speak to your community about "manufacturing by-products" when you're really talking about plans for disposing of toxic waste. Such an attempt to hide the facts would likely backfire, damaging your business image and reputation. Even if it is unpleasant, people respond better to an honest message delivered with integrity than they do to a sugar-coated message filled with empty talk.

USING BIAS-FREE LANGUAGE Chapter 3 points out that you are often unaware of the influence of your own culture on your behaviour, and this circumstance extends to the language you use. Any bias present in your culture is likely to show up in your language, often in subtle ways that you might not even recognize. However, chances are that your audience will. **Bias-free language** avoids words and phrases that unfairly and even unethically categorize or stigmatize people in ways related to gender, race, ethnicity, age, or disability. Contrary to what some might think, biased language is not simply about "labels." To a significant degree, language reflects the way we think and what we believe, and biased language may well perpetuate the underlying stereotypes and prejudices that it represents.[4] Moreover, since perception is a large part of communication, being fair and objective isn't enough; to establish a good relationship with your audience, you must also *appear* to be fair.[5] Good communicators make every effort to change biased language (see Table 5–1). Bias can come in a variety of forms:

> **Gender bias.** Avoid sexist language by using the same label for everyone (don't call a woman *chairperson* and then call a man *chairman*). Reword

Avoid words with negative connotations; use meaningful euphemisms instead.

Avoid biased language that might offend your audience.

> Table 5–1 Overcoming Bias in Language

Examples	Unacceptable	Preferable
Gender Bias		
Using words containing "man"	Mankind	Humanity, human beings, human race, people
	Man-made	Artificial, synthetic, manufactured, constructed
	Manpower	Human power, human energy, workers, workforce
	Businessman	Executive, business manager, businessperson
	Salesman	Sales representative, salesperson, clerk, sales agent
	Foreman	Supervisor
Using female-gender words	Authoress, actress, stewardess, flight attendant	Author, actor, cabin attendant
Using special designations	Woman doctor, male nurse	Doctor, nurse
Using *he* to refer to *everyone*	The average worker, he	The average worker, he or she
Identifying roles with gender	The typical executive spends four hours of his day in meetings.	Most executives spend four hours each day in meetings.
Consumer, she	Consumers, they	
The nurse/teacher, she	Nurses/teachers, they	
Identifying women by marital status	Don Harron and Catherine	Don Harron and Catherine McKinnon
	Don Harron and Ms. McKinnon	Mr. Harron and Ms. McKinnon
Racial/Ethnic Bias		
Assigning stereotypes	My black assistant speaks more articulately than I do.	My assistant speaks more articulately than I do.
	Jim Wong is an unusually tall Asian.	Jim Wong is unusually tall.
Identifying people by race or ethnicity	Frank Clementi, Italian-Canadian CEO	Frank Clementi, CEO
Age Bias		
Including age when irrelevant	Mary Kirazy, 58, has just joined our trust department.	Mary Kirazy has just joined our trust department.
Disability Bias		
Putting the disability before the person	Crippled workers face many barriers on the job.	Workers with physical disabilities face many barriers on the job.
	An epileptic, Tracy has no trouble doing her job.	Tracy's epilepsy has no effect on her job performance.

sentences to use *they* or no pronoun at all. Vary traditional patterns by sometimes putting women first (women and men, she and he, her and his). Note that the preferred title for women in business is *Ms.*, unless the individual asks to be addressed as *Miss* or *Mrs.* or has some other title, such as *Dr.*

> **Racial and ethnic bias.** Avoid language suggesting that members of a racial or ethnic group have stereotypical characteristics. The best solution is to avoid identifying people by race or ethnic origin unless such a label is relevant to the matter at hand—and it rarely is.

> **Be correct when you refer to Canada's Aboriginal peoples.** The Canadian Constitution recognizes three groups of Aboriginal peoples: Indians,

Métis, and Inuit. They each have their own heritage, language, cultural practices, and spiritual beliefs. The term "Indian" describes all the Aboriginal peoples in Canada who are not Inuit or Métis. Many Aboriginal peoples today are offended by the term "Indian" and prefer "First Nations." Many First Nations peoples have adopted the term "First Nation" to replace the term "band" to designate their community. As an accurate and ethical communicator, be sure to use the terms that Canada's Aboriginal peoples prefer.

> **Age bias.** As with gender, race, and ethnic background, mention the age of a person only when it is relevant. Moreover, be careful of the context in which you use words that refer to age. Such words carry a variety of positive and negative connotations—and not only when referring to people beyond a certain age. For example, *young* can imply youthfulness, inexperience, or even immaturity, depending on how it's used.

> **Disability bias.** No painless label exists for people with a physical, mental, sensory, or emotional impairment. Avoid mentioning a disability unless it is pertinent. However, if you must refer to someone's disability, avoid terms such as *handicapped, crippled,* or *retarded.* Put the person first and the disability second.[6] For example, by saying "employees with physical handicaps," not "handicapped employees," you focus on the whole person, not the disability. The Canadian Human Rights Commission guarantees equal opportunities for people who have or have had a condition that might handicap them. The goal of bias-free communication is to abandon stereotyped assumptions about what a person can do or will do and to focus on an individual's unique characteristics.

Building Strong Relationships with Your Audience

Objective 2 Explain why establishing credibility is vital to the success of your communication efforts

Focusing on your audience's needs is vital to effective communication, but you also have your own priorities as a communicator. Sometimes these needs are obvious and direct, such as when you're appealing for a budget increase for your department. At other times, the need may be more subtle. For example, you may want to explain your company's environmental practices when dealing with customers concerned about environmental issues. Two key efforts help you address your own needs while building positive relationships with your audience: establishing your credibility and projecting your company's image.

People are more likely to react positively to your message when they have confidence in you.

ESTABLISHING YOUR CREDIBILITY Your audience's response to every message you send depends heavily on their perception of your **credibility**, a measure of your believability based on how reliable you are and how much trust you evoke in others. With colleagues and long-term customers, you've already established some degree of credibility based on past communication efforts. As long as you haven't let people down in the past, they are inclined to accept each new message from you. However, with audiences who don't know you, you need to establish credibility before they accept—or perhaps even pay attention to—your messages. Whether you're working to build credibility with a new audience, to maintain credibility with an existing audience, or even to restore credibility after a mistake, consider emphasizing the following characteristics:

To enhance your credibility, emphasize such factors as honesty, objectivity, and awareness of audience needs.

> **Honesty.** Honesty is the cornerstone of credibility. No matter how famous, important, charming, or attractive you are, if you don't tell the truth most people will eventually lose faith in you. On the other hand, demonstrating honesty and integrity will earn you the respect of your colleagues and the trust of everyone you communicate with, even if they don't always agree with or welcome the messages you have to deliver.

> **Objectivity.** Audiences appreciate the ability to distance yourself from emotional situations and to look at all sides of an issue. They want to believe that you have their interests in mind, not just your own.

> **Awareness of audience needs.** Let your audience know that you understand what's important to them. If you've done a thorough audience analysis, you'll know what your audience cares about and their specific issues and concerns in a particular situation.

> **Credentials, knowledge, and expertise.** Every audience wants to be assured that the messages they receive come from people who know what they're talking about—that's why doctors and other medical professionals display their diplomas and certificates and why public speakers often arrange to be introduced with brief summaries of their experience and qualifications. When you need to establish credibility with a new audience, put yourself in their shoes and try to identify the credentials that would be most important to them. Is it your education, a professional certification, special training, or success on the job? Express these qualifications clearly and objectively, without overshadowing the message. Sometimes it's as simple as using the correct technical terms or mentioning your role in a successful project.

> **Endorsements.** An endorsement is a statement on your behalf by someone who is accepted by your audience as an expert. If your audience doesn't know anything about you, you might be able to get assistance from someone they do know and trust. For example, when delivering a presentation, you could quote a recognized authority on your subject, even if you don't know the authority personally. Once the audience learns that you've done your research, they'll be more receptive to your messages.

> **Performance.** Who impresses you more, the person who always says, "If you ever need me, all you have to do is call," or the one who actually shows up when you need to move or when you need a ride to the airport? It's easy to say you can do something, but following through can be much harder. That's why demonstrating impressive communication skills is not enough; people need to know they can count on you to get the job done.

> **Sincerity.** When you offer praise, don't use hyperbole, such as "you are the most fantastic employee I could ever imagine." Instead, point out specific qualities that warrant praise.

Show you are aware of a person's contributions and not making generic thanks:

Instead of This	Use This
My deepest heartfelt thanks for the excellent job you did. It's hard these days to find workers like you. You are just fantastic! I can't stress enough how happy you have made us with your outstanding performance.	Thanks for the great job you did filling in for Sean at the convention on such short notice. Despite the difficult circumstances, you managed to attract several new orders with your demonstration of the new line of coffeemakers. Your dedication and sales ability are truly appreciated.

Even though arrogance turns listeners off, displaying too much modesty or too little confidence can hurt your credibility. If you lack faith in yourself, you're likely to communicate an uncertain attitude that undermines your credibility; audiences need to know that you believe in yourself and your message. The key to being believable is to believe in yourself. If you are convinced that your message is sound, you can state your case with authority so that your audience has no doubts. Avoid vague sentiments and confidence-draining words such as *if*, *hope*, and *trust*:

Instead of This	Use This
We hope this recommendation will be helpful.	We're glad to make this recommendation.
If you'd like to order, mail us the reply card.	To order, mail the reply card.
We trust that you'll extend your service contract.	By extending your service contract, you can continue to enjoy top-notch performance from your equipment.

Finally, keep in mind that credibility can take days, months, even years to establish—and it can be wiped out in an instant. An occasional mistake or letdown is usually forgiven, but major lapses in honesty or integrity can destroy your reputation. On the other hand, when you do establish credibility, communication becomes much easier because you no longer have to spend time and energy convincing people that you are a trustworthy source of information and ideas.

PROJECTING THE COMPANY'S IMAGE When you communicate with outsiders, on even the most routine matter, you serve as the spokesperson for your organization. The impression you make can enhance or damage the reputation of the entire company. Thus, your own views and personality must be set aside, at least to some extent, to the interests and style of your company.

Many organizations have specific communication guidelines that show everything from the correct use of the company name to preferred abbreviations and other grammatical details. Specifying a desired style of communication is more difficult, however. Observe more experienced colleagues to see how they communicate, and never hesitate to ask for editorial help to make sure you're conveying the appropriate tone. For example, with clients entrusting thousands or millions of dollars to it, an investment firm communicates in a style quite different from that of a clothing retailer. And a clothing retailer specializing in high-quality business attire communicates in a style different from that of a store catering to the latest trends in casual wear.

Controlling Your Style and Tone

Your communication style involves the choices you make to express yourself: the words you select, the manner in which you use those words in sentences, and the way you build paragraphs from individual sentences. Your style creates a certain **tone,** or overall impression, in your messages. You can vary your style to sound forceful or objective, personal or formal, colourful or dry. The right choice depends on the nature of your message and your relationship with the reader. Although style can be refined during the revision phase (see Chapter 6), you'll save time and rewriting if you use a style that allows you to achieve the desired tone from the start.

USING A CONVERSATIONAL TONE The tone of your business messages can range from informal to conversational to formal. If you're in a large organization and you're communicating with your superiors or with customers, your tone would tend to be more formal and respectful.[7] However, that formal tone might sound distant and cold if used with close colleagues.

Compare the three versions of the message in Table 5–2. The first is too formal and stuffy for today's audiences, whereas the third is too casual for any audience other than close associates or friends. The second message

---

Margin notes:

Your company's interests and reputation take precedence over your personal communication style.

Your *style* involves all the choices you make to express yourself; your *tone* is the overall impression your messages create.

Most business messages aim for a conversational style that is warm but still businesslike.

> Table 5–2 Three Levels of Tone: Formal, Conversational, and Informal

Formal Tone	Conversational Tone	Informal Tone
Reserved for the most formal occasions	**Preferred for most business communication**	**Reserved for communication with friends and close associates**
Dear Ms. Navarro:	Dear Ms. Navarro:	Hi Gabriella,
Enclosed please find the information that was requested during our telephone communication of May 14. As was mentioned at that time, Lefebvre Financial Services has personal financial advisors of exceptional quality.	Here's the information you requested during our phone conversation on Friday. As I mentioned, Lefebvre Financial Services has excellent financial advisors.	Hope all is well. Just sending along the information you asked for. As I said on Friday, Lefebvre Financial Services has great financial advisors with a lot of experience.
As you were also informed, our organization has a highly trained team of pension and benefits specialists who will also assist you with your retirement planning concerns. In the event that you want one of them to provide information to a Lefebvre advisor, please inform us with your permission.	In addition, our experienced pension and benefits team will also help you with your retirement plans. They can give information to a Lefebvre advisor with your permission; please let us know.	Also, our pension and benefits team will help with your retirement plans. They'll be happy to speak with you and contact a Lefebvre rep with your permission.
In the event that you have questions or would like additional information, you may certainly contact me during regular business hours.	If you would like more information, please call any time between 9:00 and 5:00, Monday through Friday.	Just call me if you want to know more—any time from 9:00 to 5:00 is fine.
Most sincerely yours,	Sincerely,	Take care,
Samuel G. Berenz	Samuel G. Berenz	Sam

demonstrates the conversational tone used in most business communication—plain language that sounds businesslike without being stuffy or full of jargon. You can achieve a conversational tone in your messages by following these guidelines:

> **Avoid obsolete and pompous language.** Business language used to be much more formal than it is today, but some out-of-date phrases still appear. You can avoid using such language if you ask yourself, "Would I say this if I were talking with someone face to face?" Similarly, avoid using big words, trite expressions, and overly complicated sentences to impress others. Such pompous language sounds self-important (see Table 5–3).

> **Avoid preaching and bragging.** People who think that they know everything and that others know nothing can be very irritating. If you need to remind your audience of something obvious, insert the information casually, into the middle of a paragraph, where it will sound like a secondary comment rather than a major revelation. When speaking, you can preface the obvious with a comment like, "As you know." To maintain a favourable image, avoid bragging about your accomplishments or those of your organization (unless your audience is a part of your organization).

> **Be careful with intimacy.** Most business messages should avoid intimacy, such as sharing personal details or adopting a casual, unprofessional tone. However, when you do have a close relationship with your audience, such as among the members of a close-knit team, a more intimate tone is sometimes appropriate and even expected.

Before writing a letter or an email message on behalf of your company, think about how you project the company image. What image does this photo of Sara Lee Corporation's employees project? Why is image so important? How do employees project their company's image to the public?

> Table 5–3 Staying Up to Date and Accessible with Business Language

Obsolete	Accessible
in due course	today, tomorrow (or a specific time)
permit me to say that	(permission is not necessary)
we are in receipt of	we received
pursuant to	(omit)
in closing, I'd like to say	(omit)
the undersigned	I; we
kindly advise	please let me/us know
attached please find	enclosed is or I/we have enclosed
it has come to my attention	I have just learned; Ms. Garza has just told me
In closing, I'd like to say	(Omit; just say whatever you need to say.)
we wish to inform you that	(Omit; just say whatever you need to say.)
please be advised that	(Omit; just say whatever you need to say.)

Pompous	Accessible
Upon procurement of additional supplies, I will initiate fulfillment of your order.	I will fill your order when I receive more supplies.
Perusal of the records indicates a substantial deficit for the preceding accounting period due to the continued utilization of obsolete equipment.	The records show a company loss last year due to the use of old equipment.

Objective 3 Discuss how to achieve a businesslike tone with a style that is clear and concise.

> **Be careful with humour.** Humour can be an effective tool to inject interest into dry subjects or take the sting out of negative news, but it can easily backfire and divert attention from your message. The humour must be connected to the point you're trying to make. Business messages are not a forum for sharing jokes. Never use humour in formal messages or when you're communicating across cultural boundaries: your international audience may not appreciate your humour or even realize that you're trying to be funny.[8] If you don't know your audience well or you're not skilled at using humour in a business setting, don't use it at all. When in doubt, leave it out.

> **USING PLAIN ENGLISH** What do you think this sentence is trying to say?

We continually exist to synergistically supply value-added deliverables such that we may continue to proactively maintain enterprise-wide data to stay competitive in tomorrow's world.[9]

Audiences can understand and act on plain English without reading it over and over.

If you don't have any idea what it means, you're not alone. However, this is a real sentence from a real company, written in an attempt to explain what the company does and why. This sort of incomprehensible, buzzword-filled writing is driving a widespread call to use *plain English*.

Plain English is a way of presenting information in a simple, unadorned style so that your audience can easily grasp your meaning, without struggling through specialized, technical, or convoluted language. Because it's close to the way people normally speak, plain English is easily understood by anyone with a grade-eight or grade-nine education. The Plain English Campaign (a non-profit group in England campaigning for clear language) defines plain English as language "that the intended audience can read, understand and act upon the first time they read it."[10] You can see how this definition supports using the "you" attitude and shows respect for your audience.

On the Creative Commons website, for example, licensing terms are available in two versions: a complete document that spells out contractual details in specific legal terms that meet the needs of legal professionals, and a second version, labelled "human-readable," which explains the licensing terms in nontechnical language that anyone can understand.[11]

Even though readers overwhelmingly appreciate plain English and its merits have been demonstrated in a variety of audience tests,[12] the fact is that murky, pompous, and unnecessarily complex writing is still more common than it should be. One reason is that writers are unsure about their own writing skills and about the impact their messages will have. They mistakenly believe that packaging simple ideas in complex writing makes their messages seem more impressive. Another reason is inadequate planning, which results in messages that meander in search of a conclusion. A third reason is that some writers intentionally try to create distance between themselves and their audiences. Whatever the cause, the result of unnecessarily complex writing is always the same: ineffective communication that wastes time, wastes money, and annoys everyone who comes in contact with it.

As frustration builds over confusing, grandiose writing, groups such as the Plain English Campaign are raising awareness of the costs of poor communication. A number of government agencies and businesses are also working to improve matters. Revenue Canada has been improving the readability of its publications and forms.[13] The Government of Nova Scotia website has a link dedicated to communication that includes advice to government agencies (and the interested public) on plain language (see www.gov.ns.ca/cmns/plainlanguage). "The Investor Education website was revised to be jargon free," says Investor Education Fund President Tom Hamza, so that "investors can understand the content better and develop confidence with their finances" (see www.investorFD.ca).[14]

For all its advantages, plain English does have some limitations. It sometimes lacks the precision or subtlety necessary for scientific research, engineering documents, intense feeling, and personal insight. Moreover, it doesn't embrace all cultures and dialects equally. But even though it's intended for audiences who speak English as their primary language, plain English can also help you simplify the messages you prepare for audiences who speak English only as a second or even third language. For example, by choosing words that have only one interpretation, you will surely communicate more clearly with your intercultural audience.[15]

SELECTING ACTIVE OR PASSIVE VOICE Your choice of active or passive voice also affects the tone of your message. You are using **active voice** when the subject performs the action and the object receives it: "John rented the office." You're using **passive voice** when the subject receives the action: "The office was rented by John." As you can see, the passive voice combines the helping verb *to be* with a form of the verb that is usually similar to the past tense. When you use active sentences, your messages generally sound less formal and make it easier for readers to determine who performed the action (see Table 5–4). In contrast, using passive voice de-emphasizes the subject and implies that the action was done by something or someone.

Using the active voice makes your writing more direct, livelier, and easier to read. In contrast, the passive voice is not wrong grammatically, but it is often cumbersome, can be unnecessarily vague, and can make sentences longer. In most cases, the active voice is your best choice.[16] Nevertheless, using the passive voice can help you demonstrate the "you" attitude in some situations:

> When you want to be diplomatic about pointing out a problem or error (the passive version seems less like an accusation)

Active sentences are usually stronger than passive ones.

Use passive sentences to soften bad news, to put yourself in the background, or to create an impersonal tone.

> **Table 5–4** Choosing Active or Passive Voice

Avoid passive voice to make your writing lively and direct.

Dull and Indirect in Passive Voice	*Lively and Direct in Active Voice*
The new procedure was developed by the operations team.	The operations team developed the new procedure.
Legal problems are created by this contract.	This contract creates legal problems.
Reception preparations have been undertaken by our public relations people for the new CEO's arrival.	Our public relations people have begun planning a reception for the new CEO.

Passive voice is helpful when you need to be diplomatic or want to focus attention on problems or solutions rather than on people.

Accusatory or Self-Congratulatory in Active Voice	*More Diplomatic in Passive Voice*
You lost the shipment.	The shipment was lost.
I recruited seven engineers last month.	Seven engineers were recruited last month.
We are investigating the high rate of failures on the final assembly line.	The high rate of failures on the final assembly line is being investigated.

> When you want to point out what's being done without taking or attributing either the credit or the blame (the passive version leaves the actor completely out of the sentence)
> When you want to avoid personal pronouns to create an objective tone (the passive version may be used in a formal report, for example)

The second half of Table 5–4 illustrates several situations in which the passive voice helps you focus your message on your audience.

Composing Your Message

Objective 4 Briefly describe how to select words that are not only correct but also effective.

With these insights into how you can adapt to your audience, you're ready to begin composing your message. Composition is easiest if you've already figured out what to say and in what order (refer to the outlining advice in Chapter 4). You may also discover as you go along that you can improve on your outline. Feel free to rearrange, delete, and add ideas, but don't lose sight of your purpose.

As you compose your first draft, let your creativity flow. Don't draft and edit at the same time or worry about getting everything perfect. Make up words if you can't think of the correct word, draw pictures, talk out loud—do whatever it takes to get the ideas out of your head and onto your computer screen or a piece of paper. You'll have time to revise and refine the material later before showing it to anyone. In fact, many writers find it helpful to establish a personal rule of *never* showing a first draft to anyone. By working in this "safe zone," away from the critical eyes of others, your mind will stay free to think clearly and creatively. See "Sharpening Your Career Skills—Beating Writer's Block: Ten Workable Ideas to Get Words Flowing."

Correctness is the first consideration when choosing words.

TIPS FOR SUCCESS

"Use strong verbs and active voice. When you feel the need to toss in an adjective or verb, consider it a red flag that your nouns and verbs may lack precision, or you wouldn't be seeking a modifier. Make every word contribute to the information. Eliminate such redundancies as *important essentials, serious crisis, past history, previous experience, completely inaudible.*"

—Dianna Booher, CEO, Booher Consultants

Choosing Precise Words

Effective messages depend on carefully chosen words, whether you select them during your first draft or edit them in later.[17] First, pay close attention to correctness. The "rules" of grammar and usage can be a source of worry for all writers because many of these rules are complex and can evolve over time. Even professional editors and grammarians occasionally have questions about correct

SHARPENING YOUR CAREER SKILLS

Beating Writer's Block: Ten Workable Ideas to Get Words Flowing

Putting words on a page or on screen can be a real struggle. Some people get stuck so often that they develop a mental block. If you get writer's block, here are some ways to get words flowing:

> **Use positive self-talk.** Stop worrying about how well or easily you write, and stop thinking of writing as difficult, time consuming, or complicated. Tell yourself that you're capable and that you can do the job. Also, recall past examples of your writing that were successful.

> **Know your purpose.** Be specific about what you want to accomplish with this particular assignment. Without a clear purpose, writing can indeed be impossible.

> **Visualize your audience.** Picture audience backgrounds, interests, subject knowledge, and vocabulary (including the technical jargon they use). Such visualization can help you choose an appropriate style and tone for your writing.

> **Create a productive environment.** Write in a location that's meant for writing only, and make that setting pleasant. Set up "writing appointments." Scheduling a session from 9:30 A.M. to noon is less intimidating than an indefinite session. Also, keep your mind fresh with scheduled breaks.

> **Make an outline or a list.** Even if you don't create a formal outline, jot down a few notes about how your ideas fit together. As you go along, you can revise your notes so that you end up with a plan that gives direction and coherence.

> **Just start.** Put aside all worries, fears, and distractions—anything that gives you an excuse to postpone writing. Then put down any thoughts you have about your topic.

Don't worry about whether these ideas can actually be used; just let your mind range freely.

> **Write the middle first.** Start wherever your interest is greatest and your ideas are most developed. You can follow new directions, but note ideas to revisit later. When you finish one section, choose another without worrying about sequence. Just get your thoughts down.

> **Push obstacles aside.** If you get stuck at some point, don't worry. Move past the thought, sentence, or paragraph, and come back to it later. Get started simply by writing or talking about why you're stuck: "I'm stuck because . . ." Also brainstorm. Before you know it, you'll be writing about your topic.

> **Read a newspaper or magazine.** Read an article that uses a style similar to yours. Choose one you'll enjoy so that you'll read it more closely.

> **Exercise!** Simply getting out of your chair, stretching your arms, taking deep breaths, and getting outside for half an hour or so will refresh your mind and give a new perspective on your task.

When deadlines loom, don't panic. Concentrate on the major ideas first, and save the details for later, after you have something on the page. If you keep the process in perspective, you'll succeed.

CAREER APPLICATIONS

1 List the ways you procrastinate, and discuss what you can do to break these habits.

2 Analyze your own writing experiences. What negative self-talk do you use? What might you do to overcome this tendency?

---

usage, and they sometimes disagree about the answers. For example, the word *data* is the plural form of *datum,* yet some experts now prefer to treat *data* as a singular noun when it's used in non-scientific material to refer to a body of information.

Although debating the finer points of usage may seem like nitpicking, using words correctly is important. If you make grammatical or usage errors, you lose credibility with your audience—even if your message is otherwise correct. Poor grammar implies that you're uninformed, and audiences put less faith in an uninformed source. Worse still, poor grammar can imply that you don't respect your audience enough to get the details right. Even if an audience is broadminded enough to withhold such judgment, grammatical errors are distracting.

If you have doubts about what is correct, look up the answer, and use the proper form of expression. Check *Grammar on the Go,* our Grammar supplement, or consult the many special reference books and resources available

Correct grammar enhances your image.

in libraries, in bookstores, and on the internet. Most authorities agree on the basic conventions.

Just as important as selecting the correct word is selecting the most suitable word for the job at hand—the right words can make all the difference in the success of your communication efforts. Word effectiveness is generally more difficult to achieve than correctness, particularly in written communication. Even professional writers with decades of experience continue to work at their craft to use functional and content words correctly and to find words that communicate effectively.

USING FUNCTIONAL AND CONTENT WORDS CORRECTLY Words can be divided into two main categories:

Functional words express relationships and have only one unchanging meaning in any given context. They include conjunctions, prepositions, articles, and pronouns. Your main concern with functional words is to use them correctly.

Content words are multi-dimensional and therefore subject to various interpretations. They include nouns, verbs, adjectives, and adverbs. These words carry the meaning of a sentence. In your sentences, content words are the building blocks, and functional words are the mortar that holds them together. In the following sentence, all the content words are underlined:

Some objective observers of the cookie market give Christie's the edge in quality, but President's Choice is lauded for superior distribution.

Both functional words and content words are necessary, but your effectiveness as a communicator depends largely on your ability to choose the right content words for your message.

DENOTATION AND CONNOTATION Content words have both a denotative and a connotative meaning. The **denotative meaning** is the literal, or dictionary, meaning. The **connotative meaning** includes all the associations and feelings evoked by the word.

The denotative meaning of *desk* is "a table used for writing." Some desks may have drawers or compartments, and others may have a flat top or a sloping top, but the literal meaning is generally well understood. The connotative meaning of *desk* may include thoughts associated with work or study, but the word *desk* has fairly neutral connotations—neither strong nor emotional. However, some words have much stronger connotations than others. For example, the connotations of the word *fail* are negative and can carry strong emotional meaning. So if you say that a student *failed* to pass a test, the connotative meaning suggests that the person is inferior, incompetent, or below some standard of performance.

In business communication, be careful with words that have multiple interpretations and are high in connotative meaning. By saying that a student achieved a score of 65 percent, you communicate the facts and avoid a heavy load of negative connotations. If you use words that have relatively few possible interpretations, you are less likely to be misunderstood. In addition, because you are trying to communicate in an objective, rational manner, you want to avoid emotion-laden comments.

ABSTRACTION AND CONCRETENESS Words vary dramatically in the degree of abstraction or concreteness they convey. An **abstract word** expresses a concept, quality, or characteristic. Abstractions are usually broad, encompassing a category of ideas, and they are often intellectual, academic, or philosophical. *Love, honour, progress, tradition,* and *beauty* are abstractions. In contrast, a **concrete word** stands for something you can touch or see. Concrete terms are

---

Effectiveness is the second consideration when choosing words.

Functional words (conjunctions, prepositions, articles, and pronouns) express the relationships among content words (nouns, verbs, adjectives, and adverbs).

Content words have both a denotative (explicit, specific) meaning and a connotative (implicit, associative) meaning.

The more abstract a word is, the more it is removed from the tangible, objective world of things that can be perceived with the senses.

anchored in the tangible, material world. *Chair, table, horse, rose, kick, kiss, red, green,* and *two* are concrete words; they are direct, clear, and exact. Incidentally, technology continues to generate new words and new meanings that describe things that don't have a physical presence but are nonetheless concrete: *software, database, signal,* and *code* are all concrete terms as well.

You might assume that concrete words are better than abstract words because they are more precise, but this isn't always the case. Imagine talking about business without referring to such concepts as *morale, productivity, profits, quality, motivation,* and *guarantees.* Abstractions permit us to rise above the common and tangible.

Even though they're indispensable, abstractions can be troublesome. They tend to be fuzzy and subject to many interpretations. Moreover, it isn't always easy to get excited about ideas, especially if they're unrelated to concrete experience. The best way to minimize such problems is to blend abstract terms with concrete ones, the general with the specific. State the concept, and then pin it down with details expressed in more concrete terms. Save the abstractions for ideas that cannot be expressed any other way.

Because words such as *small, numerous, sizable, near, soon, good,* and *fine* are imprecise, replace them with terms that are more accurate. Instead of referring to a *sizable loss,* talk about a *loss of $32 million.*

FINDING WORDS THAT COMMUNICATE By practising your writing, learning from experienced writers and editors, and reading extensively, you'll find it easier to choose words that communicate your thoughts exactly. When you compose business messages, think carefully to find the most precise and powerful words for each situation (see Table 5–5).

> **Choose powerful words.** Choose words that express your thoughts most clearly, specifically, and dynamically. Nouns and verbs are the most concrete and should do most of the communication work in your messages. Verbs are especially powerful because they tell what's happening in the sentence, so make them dynamic and specific. For instance, you could replace *fall* with *slide, slip, plummet, drop,* or *decline* to suggest the magnitude of the decrease.

> In business communication, use concrete, specific terms whenever possible; use abstractions only when necessary.

> **Table 5–5** Finding Words That Communicate with Power

Avoid Unfamiliar Words	Use Familiar Words
ascertain	find out, learn
consummate	close, bring about
peruse	read, study
circumvent	avoid
increment	growth, increase
unequivocal	certain

Avoid Clichés and Buzzwords	Use Plain Language
an uphill battle	a challenge
writing on the wall	prediction
call the shots	be in charge
take by storm	attack
cost an arm and a leg	expensive
a new ballgame	fresh start
fall through the cracks	be overlooked
think outside the box	be creative

Here's another helpful clue: If you find yourself using a lot of adjectives and adverbs, you're probably trying to compensate for weak nouns and verbs. Saying that *sales plummeted* is stronger and more efficient than saying *sales dropped dramatically* or *sales experienced a dramatic drop*.

> **Choose familiar words.** You'll communicate best with words that are familiar to both you and your readers. Efforts to improve a situation can be *ameliorative*, but saying they are *helpful* is a lot more effective. Moreover, using an unfamiliar word for the first time in an important document can lead to embarrassing mistakes.

> **Avoid clichés and buzzwords.** Although familiar words are generally the best choice, beware of terms and phrases so common or so trendy that they have lost some of their power to communicate. Most people use these phrases not because they think it makes their message more vivid and inviting but because they don't know how to express themselves otherwise and don't invest the energy required for original writing.[18]

> **Use jargon carefully.** Handle technical or professional terms with care. Jargon is usually an efficient way to communicate within specific groups that understand their own special terms, but it will confuse people who are not members of those groups. For example, when a recording engineer wants to communicate that a particular piece of music is devoid of reverberation and other sound effects, it's a lot easier to describe the track as "dry." Of course, to people who aren't familiar with such insider terms, jargon is meaningless and intimidating—one more reason it's so important to understand your audience before you start writing.

Remember, your business writing skills will improve through imitation and practice. As you read business journals, newspapers, and even novels, make a note of the words you think are effective and keep them in a file. Doing so will expand your vocabulary and make it easier to find a precise word when you are writing.

Creating Effective Sentences

In English, words don't make much sense until they're combined in a sentence to express a complete thought. Thus the words *Jill, receptionist, the, smiles,* and *at* can be organized into "Jill smiles at the receptionist." Now that you've constructed the sentence, you can begin exploring the possibilities for improvement, looking at how well each word performs its particular function. Nouns and noun equivalents are the topics (or subjects) you're communicating about, and verbs and related words (or predicates) make statements about those subjects. In a complicated sentence, adjectives and adverbs modify the subject and predicate, and various connectors hold the words together.

CHOOSING FROM THE FOUR TYPES OF SENTENCES Sentences come in four basic varieties:

1. Simple
2. Compound
3. Complex
4. Compound–complex

A **simple sentence** has one main clause (a single subject and a single predicate), although it may be expanded by nouns and pronouns serving as objects of the action and by modifying phrases. Here's a typical example (with the subject underlined once and the predicate verb underlined twice):

<u>Profits</u> <u>increased</u> in the past year.

Avoid clichés and trendy buzzwords in your writing and use jargon only when your audience is completely familiar with it.

Objective 5 Explain how sentence style affects emphasis within your message.

A simple sentence has one main clause.

A **compound sentence** has two main clauses that express two or more independent but related thoughts of equal importance, usually joined by *and, but,* or *or.* In effect, a compound sentence is a merger of two or more simple sentences (independent clauses) that are related. For example:

Wage <u>rates</u> <u>have declined</u> by 5 percent, and employee <u>turnover</u> <u>has been</u> high.

The independent clauses in a compound sentence are always separated by a comma or by a semicolon (in which case the conjunction—*and, but, or*—is dropped).

A **complex sentence** expresses one main thought (the independent clause) and one or more subordinate thoughts (dependent clauses) related to it, often separated by a comma. The subordinate thought, which comes first in the following sentence, could not stand alone:

Although you may question Gerald's conclusions, <u>you</u> <u>must admit</u> that his research is thorough.

A **compound–complex sentence** has two main clauses, at least one of which contains a subordinate clause:

<u>Profits</u> <u>have increased</u> in the past year, and although you may question Gerald's conclusions, <u>you</u> <u>must admit</u> that his research is thorough.

When constructing a sentence, choose the form that matches the relationship of the ideas you want to express. If you have two ideas of equal importance, express them as two simple sentences or as one compound sentence. However, if one idea is less important than the other, place it in a dependent clause to form a complex sentence. For example, although the following compound sentence uses a conjunction to join two ideas, they aren't truly equal:

The chemical products division is the strongest in the company, and its management techniques should be adopted by the other divisions.

By making the first thought subordinate to the second, you establish a cause-and-effect relationship. The following complex sentence is much more effective because it clearly explains why the other divisions should adopt the chemical division's management techniques:

Because the chemical products division is the strongest in the company, its management techniques should be adopted by the other divisions.

To make your writing as effective as possible, strive for variety and balance using all four sentence types. If you use too many simple sentences, you won't be able to express the relationships among your ideas properly, and your writing will sound choppy and abrupt. If you use too many long, compound sentences, your writing will sound monotonous. On the other hand, an uninterrupted series of complex or compound–complex sentences is hard to follow.

USING SENTENCE STYLE TO EMPHASIZE KEY THOUGHTS The English language offers tremendous flexibility in saying what you want to say and in developing your own style. For business communication, however, clarity and efficiency take precedence over literary style, so strive for straightforward simplicity.

Margin notes:

A compound sentence has two main clauses.

A complex sentence has one main clause and one subordinate clause.

A compound–complex sentence has two main clauses and at least one dependent clause.

Emphasize parts of a sentence by
> devoting more words to them
> putting them at the beginning or at the end of the sentence
> making them the subject of the sentence

In every message, some ideas are more important than others. You can emphasize these key ideas through your sentence style. One obvious technique is to give important points the most space. When you want to call attention to a thought, use extra words to describe it. Consider this sentence:

The chairperson of the board called for a vote of the shareholders.

To emphasize the importance of the chairperson, you might describe her more fully:

Having considerable experience in corporate takeover battles, the chairperson of the board called for a vote of the shareholders.

You can increase the emphasis even more by adding a separate, short sentence to augment the first:

The chairperson of the board called for a vote of the shareholders. She has considerable experience in corporate takeover battles.

You can also call attention to a thought by making it the subject of the sentence. In the following example, the emphasis is on the person:

I can write letters much more quickly using a computer.

However, by changing the subject, the computer takes centre stage:

The *computer* enables me to write letters much more quickly.

Dependent clauses can determine emphasis.

Another way to emphasize an idea is to place it either at the beginning or at the end of a sentence:

Less Emphatic: We are cutting the *price* to stimulate demand.
More Emphatic: To stimulate demand, we are cutting the *price*.

In complex sentences, the placement of the dependent clause hinges on the relationship between the ideas expressed. If you want to emphasize the idea, put the dependent clause at the end of the sentence (the most emphatic position) or at the beginning (the second most emphatic position). If you want to downplay the idea, bury the dependent clause within the sentence.

Most Emphatic: The electronic parts are manufactured in Mexico, *which has lower wage rates than Canada.*
Emphatic: *Because wage rates are lower there,* the electronic parts are manufactured in Mexico.
Least Emphatic: Mexico, *which has lower wage rates,* was selected as the production point for the electronic parts.

Techniques such as these give you a great deal of control over the way your audience interprets what you have to say.

Crafting Coherent Paragraphs

 Explore
✓ Practise

After arranging precise words in effective sentences, your next step is to arrange those sentences into coherent paragraphs. Paragraphs

Even when reading online, readers expect each paragraph to address one main idea and all the paragraphs in a document to link together logically. Besides devoting one idea to each paragraph, what other methods can you use to help readers comprehend your online documents?

organize sentences related to the same general topic. Readers expect each paragraph to focus on a single unit of thought and to be a logical link in an organized sequence of the thoughts that make up a complete message. By carefully arranging the elements of each paragraph, you help your readers grasp the main idea of your document and understand how the specific pieces of support material back up that idea.

ELEMENTS OF THE PARAGRAPH The typical paragraph contains three basic elements: a topic sentence, support sentences that develop the topic, and transitional words and phrases.

Topic Sentence   Every properly constructed paragraph is unified; it deals with a single topic. The sentence that introduces that topic is called the **topic sentence.** In informal and creative writing, the topic sentence may be implied rather than stated. In business writing, the topic sentence is generally explicit and is often the first sentence in the paragraph. The topic sentence gives readers a summary of the general idea that will be covered in the rest of the paragraph. The following examples show how a topic sentence can introduce the subject and suggest the way that subject will be developed:

Most paragraphs consist of
> a topic sentence that reveals the subject of the paragraph
> related sentences that support and expand the topic
> transitional elements that help readers move between sentences and paragraphs

The medical products division has been troubled for many years by public relations problems. [In the rest of the paragraph, readers will learn the details of the problems.]

Relocating the plant to St. John's has two main disadvantages. [The disadvantages will be explained in subsequent sentences.]

To get a refund, you must supply us with some additional information. [The details of the necessary information will be described in the rest of the paragraph.]

In addition to helping your readers, topic sentences help you as a writer because they remind you of the purpose of each paragraph and thereby help you stay focused. In fact, a good way to test the effectiveness of your writing is to prepare a summary version that consists of only the first sentence of each paragraph. If this summary communicates the essence of your message in a sensible, compelling way, you've probably done a good job of presenting your information.[19]

Support Sentences In most paragraphs, the topic sentence needs to be explained, justified, or extended with one or more support sentences. These related sentences must all have a bearing on the general subject and must provide enough specific details to make the topic clear:

The medical products division has been troubled for many years by public relations problems. Since 2008 the local newspaper has published 15 articles that portray the division in a negative light. We have been accused of everything from mistreating laboratory animals to polluting the local groundwater. Our facility has been described as a health hazard. Our scientists are referred to as "Frankensteins," and our profits are considered "obscene."

The support sentences are all more specific than the topic sentence. Each one provides another piece of evidence to demonstrate the general truth of the main thought. Also, each sentence is clearly related to the general idea being developed, which gives the paragraph its unity. A paragraph is well developed when it contains (1) enough information to make the topic sentence convincing and interesting, and (2) no extraneous, unrelated sentences.

Transitional Elements In addition to being unified and well supported, effective paragraphs are *coherent;* that is, they are arranged in a logical order so that the audience can easily follow the train of thought. You achieve coherence by using transitions that show the relationship between paragraphs and among sentences within paragraphs. For example, did you notice how this paragraph began? The transitional phrase "In addition to . . ." helped move you from the previous discussion to this new topic.

Transitions are words or phrases that tie ideas together by showing how one thought is related to another and by alerting the reader to what lies ahead. They not only help readers understand the connections you're trying to make, but also improve the flow of your writing. In fact, effective transitions are one of the hallmarks of polished, effective writing.

Ideally, begin planning these transitions while you're outlining, as you decide how the various ideas and blocks of information will be arranged and connected.[20]

You can establish transitions in a variety of ways:

Transitional elements include
> connecting words (conjunctions)
> repeated words or phrases
> pronouns
> words that are frequently paired

> **Use connecting words:** *and, but, or, nevertheless, however, in addition,* and so on.
> **Echo a word or phrase from a previous paragraph or sentence:** "A system should be established for monitoring inventory levels. *This system* will provide . . ."
> **Use a pronoun that refers to a noun used previously:** "Ms. Kim is the leading candidate for the president's position. *She* has excellent qualifications."
> **Use words that are frequently paired:** "The machine has a *minimum* output of . . . Its *maximum* output is . . ."

Some transitional elements alert the reader to a change in mood from the previous paragraph. Some announce a total contrast with what's gone on before, some announce a causal relationship, and some signal a change in time. Here is a list of common transitions:

Additional detail:	moreover, furthermore, in addition, besides, first, second, third, finally
Causal relationship:	therefore, because, accordingly, thus, consequently, hence, as a result, so
Comparison:	similarly, here again, likewise, in comparison, still
Contrast:	yet, conversely, whereas, nevertheless, on the other hand, however, but, nonetheless
Condition:	although, if
Illustration:	for example, in particular, in this case, for instance
Time sequence:	formerly, after, when, meanwhile, sometimes
Intensification:	indeed, in fact, in any event
Summary:	in brief, in short, to sum up
Repetition:	that is, in other words, as I mentioned earlier

Consider using a transition whenever it might help the reader understand your ideas and follow you from point to point. You can use transitions inside paragraphs to tie related points together and between paragraphs to ease the shift from one distinct thought to another. In longer reports, a transition that links major sections or chapters is often a complete paragraph that serves as a mini-introduction to the next section or as summary of the ideas presented in the section just ending. Here's an example:

Given the nature of this product, the alternatives are limited. As the previous section indicates, we can stop making it altogether, improve it, or continue with the current model. Each alternative has advantages and disadvantages, which are discussed in the following section.

This paragraph makes it clear to the reader that the analysis of the problem (offered in the previous section) is now over and that the document is making a transition to an analysis of alternatives (to be offered in the next section).

Keep in mind that transitions are not a substitute for effective organization. Put your ideas into a strong framework first and then use transitions to link them together even more strongly.

FIVE WAYS TO DEVELOP A PARAGRAPH Unification and coherence strongly depend on how you develop your paragraphs. Use a structure that is familiar to your readers, appropriate to the idea you're trying to portray, and suited to your purpose. Five of the most common development techniques are illustration, comparison or contrast, cause and effect, classification, and problem and solution (see Table 5–6).

In practice, you'll occasionally combine two or more methods of development in a single paragraph. To add interest, you might begin by using illustration, shift to comparison or contrast, and then shift to problem and solution. However, when combining approaches, do so carefully so that you don't lose readers partway through the paragraph. In addition, before settling for the first approach that comes to mind, consider the alternatives. Think through various methods before committing yourself. By avoiding the easy habit of repeating the same old paragraph pattern time after time, you can keep your writing fresh and interesting.

Using Technology to Compose and Shape Your Messages

Careful and informed use of technology can help you compose and shape better messages in less time. As you probably know, today's software (including word processors and online publishing systems for websites and blogs) provides a wide range of tools to help writers compose documents:

> **Style sheets and templates.** *Style sheets* are master lists of predefined styles (typeface, type size, and so on) for headlines, paragraph text, and so on. (Here, the word *style* should not be confused with *writing style,* discussed earlier in the chapter.) Many organizations provide employees with approved style sheets to ensure a consistent look for all company documents. Moreover, style sheets can eliminate hours of design time by making many of your choices for you. *Templates* can go beyond style sheets by defining such factors as page design, available fonts, and other features. A template can include *boilerplate,* a section of text that is reused from document to document. (Depending on the version of Microsoft Word you're using, style sheets may have been replaced by templates.)

> **Autocompletion.** A software feature called *autocompletion* (or something similar) inserts a ready-made block of text when you type the first few characters. For example, instead of typing your company's name, address, phone number, fax number, email address, and website URL, you can set the software to enter all this information as soon as you type the first three letters of the company name.

> **Autocorrection.** Another automatic feature in some programs instantly corrects spelling and typing errors and converts text to symbols, such as

Objective 6 Cite five ways to develop coherent paragraphs.

Five ways to develop paragraphs:
> illustration
> comparison or contrast
> cause and effect
> classification
> problem and solution

Take full advantage of your software's capabilities to help you produce effective, professional messages in less time.

> Table 5–6 Five Techniques for Developing Paragraphs

Technique	Description	Example
Illustration	Giving examples that demonstrate the general idea.	Some of our most popular products are available through local distributors. For example, Everett & Lemmings carries our frozen soups and entrees. The J. B. Green Company carries our complete line of seasonings, as well as the frozen soups. Wilmont Foods, also a major distributor, now carries our new line of frozen desserts.
Comparison or contrast	Using similarities or differences to develop the topic.	When the company was small, the recruiting function could be handled informally. The need for new employees was limited, and each manager could comfortably screen and hire her or his own staff. However, our successful bid on the Owens contract means that we will be doubling our labour force over the next six months. To hire that many people without disrupting our ongoing activities, we will create a separate recruiting group within the human resources department.
Cause and effect	Focusing on the reasons for something.	The heavy-duty fabric of your Wanderer tent probably broke down for one of two reasons: 1. a sharp object punctured the fabric, and without reinforcement, the hole was enlarged by the stress of pitching the tent daily for a week, or 2. the fibres gradually rotted because the tent was folded and stored while still wet.
Classification	Showing how a general idea is broken into specific categories.	Successful candidates for our supervisor trainee program generally come from one of several groups. The largest group, by far, consists of recent graduates of accredited business management programs. The next largest group comes from within our own company, as we try to promote promising workers to positions of greater responsibility. Finally, we do occasionally accept candidates with outstanding supervisory experience in related industries.
Problem and solution	Presenting a problem and then discussing the solution.	Selling handmade toys online is a challenge because consumers are accustomed to buying heavily advertised toys from major chain stores or well-known websites such as Amazon.com. However, if we develop an appealing website, we can compete on the basis of product novelty and quality. In addition, we can provide unusual crafts at a competitive price: a rocking horse of birch, with a hand-knit tail and mane; a music box with the child's name painted on the top.

converting (c) to the © copyright symbol. However, autocorrection may make changes that you *don't* want made, such as when you type a lettered list with (a), (b), and (c)—and you really want (c), not a copyright symbol.

> **File merge and mail merge.** Today's software makes it easy to combine files—an especially handy feature when several members of a team write different sections of a report. For particularly complex reports, you can set up a master document that merges a number of subdocuments automatically

when it's time to print. *Mail merge* lets you personalize form letters by inserting names and addresses from a database.

> **Endnotes, footnotes, indexes, and tables of contents.** Your computer can help you track footnotes and endnotes, renumbering them every time you add or delete references. For a report's indexes and table of contents, you can simply flag the items you want to include, and the software assembles the lists for you.

> **Wizards.** Many programs offer wizards that guide you through the process of creating letters, résumés, web pages, and other common documents.

As with other forms of communication technology, using these tools efficiently and effectively requires some balance. You need to learn enough about the features to be handy with them, without spending so much time that the tools distract the writing process. For a reminder of the tasks involved in writing your messages, see "Checklist: Writing Business Messages."

CHECKLIST Writing Business Messages

A. Adapt to your audience.
✔ Use the "you" attitude.
✔ Maintain good etiquette through polite communication.
✔ Emphasize the positive whenever possible.
✔ Use bias-free language.
✔ Establish your credibility in the eyes of your audience.
✔ Project your company's preferred image.
✔ Use a conversational but still professional and respectful tone.
✔ Use plain English for clarity.

B. Compose your message.
✔ Choose precise words that communicate efficiently.

✔ Make sure you use functional and content words correctly.
✔ Pay attention to the connotative meaning of your words.
✔ Balance abstract and concrete terms to convey your meaning accurately.
✔ Avoid clichés and trendy buzzwords.
✔ Use jargon only when your audience understands it and prefers it.
✔ Vary your sentence structure for impact and interest.
✔ Develop coherent, unified paragraphs.
✔ Use transitional elements generously to help your audience follow your message.

Summary of Learning Objectives

1 **Explain the importance of adapting your messages to the needs and expectations of your audience.** Your audience wants to know why you are communicating with them and how your message will benefit them. By showing awareness of their needs and expectations, you are answering their question "What's in it for me?" and establishing a good relationship. Practising the "you" attitude, emphasizing the positive, and using bias-free language will also demonstrate your sensitivity to your audience.

2 **Explain why establishing credibility is vital to the success of your communication efforts.** Your audiences more likely accept your messages if you establish your credibility with them. Behaving honestly, objectively, reliably, and sincerely, and showing your awareness of your audiences' needs, demonstrate your credibility and will make your audiences more likely to respond positively to you. Establishing your credentials and expertise will communicate your credibility to audiences that don't know you, thus making them more receptive to your messages.

3 **Discuss how to achieve a businesslike tone with a style that is clear and concise.** You can achieve a businesslike tone by using plain English, which is language that is easily understood. Plain English avoids pompous and out-of-date phrases; in their place, it uses accessible

and current vocabulary that audiences with a grade-eight or grade-nine education can easily understand. Using the active voice instead of the passive voice is another way to achieve a businesslike tone. Where the passive voice tends to create a dull and indirect style, the active voice is lively and direct. However, the passive voice is useful when you must be diplomatic with your audience, because its indirect nature can create an objective tone.

4 **Briefly describe how to select words that are not only correct but also effective.** To select the best words, first make sure they are correct by checking grammar and usage guides. Next, make sure the words you select are effective by knowing how to use functional and content words. Choose words that have fewer connotations and no negative connotations. Blend abstract words with concrete ones, narrowing from the general to the specific, and select words that communicate clearly and specifically. Avoid clichés, and use jargon only if your audience will understand it.

5 **Explain how sentence style affects emphasis within your message.** The emphasis of key ideas in your message is influenced by sentence style. For example, using more words to describe ideas will give them greater stress. You can also make your ideas the subject of sentences or place them at the beginning or end of sentences; these techniques will highlight your ideas. Being familiar with the four types of sentences (simple, compound, complex, and compound–complex) will assist you in giving emphasis to your information and thoughts.

6 **Cite five ways to develop coherent paragraphs.** Each paragraph should have a topic sentence that expresses the main idea and use transitional elements for unity. Paragraphs can be developed by illustration (giving examples), by comparison and contrast (pointing out similarities or differences), by focusing on cause and effect (giving reasons), by classification (discussing categories), and by focusing on the solution to a problem (stating a problem and showing how to solve it).

---

mycanadianbuscommlab

Visit www.mycanadianbuscommlab.ca for everything you need to help you succeed in the job you've always wanted! Tools and resources include the following:
– Composing Space and Writer's Toolkit
– Document Makeovers
– Video Case Studies
– Grammar Exercises—and much more!

On the Job PERFORMING COMMUNICATION TASKS AT CREATIVE COMMONS

To achieve their mission of popularizing a new approach to copyrighting songs, artwork, literature, and other creative works, Lawrence Lessig and his staff at Creative Commons need to convince people that the traditional approach to copyright doesn't meet the needs of today's digital society. This is no small challenge: Not only do they need to persuade people to reconsider more than 200 years of legal precedent and habit, they also need to communicate with an extremely diverse audience—everyone from lawyers and business managers to artists, writers, musicians, and scientists. In the third year of your business program, you've joined Creative Commons as a communication intern. Apply your knowledge of effective writing to the following three scenarios.[21]

1. A key part of the communication challenge for Creative Commons is translating legal documents into language that musicians, artists, and others with no legal training can easily understand. Which of the following does the best job of adapting the following legal phrase (which is part of the licensing contracts) into language for a general audience?

The above rights may be exercised in all media and formats whether now known or hereafter devised. The above rights include the right to make such modifications as are technically necessary to exercise the rights in other media and formats.

a. The rights granted by this licensing contract extend to any current or future media, and you also have the right to modify the material as needed to meet the technical needs of any media.

b. You may use this material in any present or future media and modify it as needed to work with any media.

c. Be advised that your rights within the scope of this contract include the right to use this material in any media that either exists now or might be devised in the future. Moreover, you are also granted the right to modify the material as any current or future media might technically demand.

d. You are hereby granted the right to use this material in any media, including modifications required by that media.

2. The single most important concept in the Creative Commons approach is the idea of a spectrum of possibilities between *all rights reserved* (a conventional copyright) and *no rights reserved* (being in the public domain, where anybody is free to use material in any way they please). Review the structure of the following four sentences and choose the one that does the best job of emphasizing the importance of the "spectrum of possibilities."

   a. Conventional copyrights, in which the creator reserves all rights to a work, and the public domain, in which the creator gives up all rights, represent two black-and-white extremes.

   b. Between the all-or-nothing extremes of a conventional copyright and being in the public domain, Creative Commons sees a need for other possibilities.

   c. The primary contribution of Creative Commons is developing a range of possibilities between the extremes of *all rights reserved* (conventional copyright) and *no rights reserved* (public domain).

   d. The black-and-white choice of *all rights reserved* (conventional copyright) and *no rights reserved* (public domain) does not meet everyone's needs, so Creative Commons is developing a range of possibilities between these two extremes.

3. Like many other organizations these days, Creative Commons must occasionally deal with online rumours spread by bloggers who aren't always sure of their facts. You've been asked to reply to an email query from a *Wall Street Journal* reporter who read a blog rumour that Creative Commons's real objective is to destroy ownership of all copyrights. Which of the following has the right style and tone for your response?

   a. That blog posting is an absolute crock. The person who wrote it is either a liar or a fool.

   b. As our website and other materials strive to make clear, the objective of Creative Commons is to work within the framework of existing copyright law but to establish a range of possibilities for people whose needs aren't met by conventional copyright choices.

   c. You wouldn't believe how much time and energy we have to spend defending ourselves against idiotic rumours like this.

   d. Creative Commons has never expressed, in print or in online materials, nor in any speeches or presentations given by any of our current or former staff or board members, any plans or strategies that would allow anyone to reach a valid conclusion that our intent is to weaken existing copyright protections.

Test Your Knowledge

1. How is your audience likely to respond to a message that doesn't seem to be about their concerns or is written in language they don't understand?

2. What is the "you" attitude, and why is it important?

3. What contributes to a communicator's credibility?

4. What is plain English, and why is it important?

5. What are the characteristics of bias-free language?

6. How can you avoid a pompous and preachy tone in your messages?

7. What is the difference between denotative language and connotative language?

8. What is the difference between abstract words and concrete words?

9. How can different sentence types emphasize key thoughts?

10. How can word processing tools help you create your messages more efficiently?

Apply Your Knowledge

1. How can you apply the "you" approach when you don't know your audience personally?

2. When composing business messages, how can you be yourself and project your company's image at the same time?

3. What steps can you take to make abstract concepts such as *opportunity* feel more concrete in your messages?

4. Considering how fast and easy it is, should instant messaging completely replace meetings and other face-to-face communication in your company? Why or why not?

5. **Ethical Choices** In Canada it is estimated that 6 percent of children and 4 percent of adults have food allergies. Every year at least 30 000 of these people end up in the emergency room after suffering an allergic reaction, and every year approximately 200 of them die. Many of these tragic events are tied to poorly written food labels that either fail to identify dangerous allergens or use scientific terms that most consumers don't recognize.[22] Do food manufacturers have a responsibility to ensure that consumers read, understand, and follow warnings on food products? Explain your answer.

Running Cases

Watch on mycanadianbuscommlab

> CASE 1 Noreen

Now that the letter has gone to the service station owners/operators informing them of the upcoming promotion (see the case in Chapter 4) Noreen's manager at Petro-Go has asked her to send an informative promotional letter to all existing Canadian "Go Points" customers.

The promotion details are as follows:

1) Canadian cardholders will now receive double points when they purchase more than $30 of gasoline in one visit (regular points up to $30 then double points over $30).

2) There is a new reward redemption available—Petro-Go gift certificates ($20 certificate for a 250-point redemption).

3) A gift of a 6-litre container of windshield washer fluid is available when accumulated points reach each 1000-point interval.

Of course, the letter must be approved by the manager before it will be distributed.

QUESTIONS

a) Is the direct or indirect approach best for this message? Why?

b) How will Noreen use the "you" attitude in the letter?

c) Why is it so important that Noreen's letter use bias-free language?

d) How will this letter differ in tone from the one sent to the employees?

e) What considerations will Noreen think of when developing the paragraphs of the letter?

YOUR TASK

Create the letter. Apply the skills you have learned in Chapters 4 and 5. (Remember to create a company logo.)

Now, consider how Noreen would put this information into a web page. Write a list of factors she would have to consider when adding this information to the existing company website.

> CASE 2 Kwong

Kwong is working on producing a promotional letter for Accountants For All that will entice past customers to return this upcoming tax season. He has checked the database and discovered addresses and email accounts for past customers. He informs his manager of his plan to email all past customers with the promotional news as well as deliver the letter through postal mail. The main promotional points Kwong wishes to convey are these:

1) 20% discount for repeat customers

2) 10% discount for families of four or more, students, or seniors

3) Only one promotional discount may be applied

QUESTIONS

a) How should Kwong begin the letter?

b) How will Kwong emphasize the promotional discounts?

c) How will he make the message easier to read?

d) What should the subject line read in the email message?

e) Why send email and postal mail?

YOUR TASK

Create the letter. Apply the skills you have learned in Chapters 4 and 5. (Remember to create a company logo.) Once the letter is complete, create the email message. Apply the skills you have learned in Chapters 4 and 5.

Practise Your Knowledge

Read the following document, then (1) analyze the strengths and weaknesses of each sentence and (2) revise the document so that it follows this chapter's guidelines.

I am a new publisher with some really great books to sell. I saw your announcement in Publishers Weekly *about the bookseller's show you're having this summer, and I think it's a great idea. Count me in, folks! I would like to get some space to show my books. I thought it would be a neat thing if I could do some airbrushing on T-shirts live to help promote my hot new title,* T-Shirt Art. *Before I got into publishing, I was an airbrush artist, and I could demonstrate my techniques. I've done hundreds of advertising illustrations and have been a*

sign painter all my life, so I'll also be promoting my other book, hot off the presses, How to Make Money in the Sign Painting Business.

I will be starting my PR campaign about May 2010 with ads in PW and some art trade papers, so my books should be well known by the time the show comes around in August. In case you would like to use my appearance there as part of your publicity, I have enclosed a biography and photo of myself.

P.S. Please let me know what it costs for booth space as soon as possible so that I can figure out whether I can afford to attend. Being a new publisher is pretty expensive!

Exercises

5.1 Audience Relationship: Courteous Communication
Substitute a better phrase for each of the following:
a. You claim that
b. It is not our policy to
c. You neglected to
d. In which you assert
e. We are sorry you are dissatisfied
f. You failed to enclose
g. We request that you send us
h. Apparently you overlooked our terms
i. We have been very patient
j. We are at a loss to understand

5.2 Audience Relationship: The "You" Attitude
Rewrite these sentences to reflect your audience's viewpoint.
a. Your email order cannot be processed; we request that you use the order form on our website instead.
b. We insist that you always bring your credit card to the store.
c. We want to get rid of all our 15-inch LCD screens to make room in our warehouse for the new 19-, 23-, and 35-inch monitors. Thus, we are offering a 25 percent discount on all sales of 15-inch models this week.
d. I am applying for the position of bookkeeper in your office. I feel my grades prove that I am bright and capable, and I think I can do a good job for you.
e. As requested, we are sending the refund for $25.
f. If you cared about doing a good job, you would've made the extra effort required to learn how to use the machinery properly.
g. Your strategy presentation this morning absolutely blew me away; there's no way we can fail with all the brilliant ideas you've pulled together—I'm so glad you're running the company now!
h. Regarding your email message from September 28 regarding the slow payment of your invoice, it's important for you to realize that we've just undergone a massive upgrade of our accounts payable system and payments have been delayed for everybody, not just you.
i. I know I'm late with the asset valuation report, but I haven't been feeling well and I just haven't had the energy needed to work through the numbers yet.

5.3 Audience Relationship: Emphasize the Positive
Revise these sentences to be positive rather than negative.
a. To avoid the loss of your credit rating, please remit payment within 10 days.
b. We don't make refunds on returned merchandise that is soiled.
c. Because we are temporarily out of Baby Cry dolls, we won't be able to ship your order for 10 days.
d. You failed to specify the colour of the blouse that you ordered.
e. You should have realized that waterbeds will freeze in unheated houses during winter. Therefore, our guarantee does not cover the valve damage. You must pay the $22.50 valve-replacement fee (plus postage).

5.4 Audience Relationship: Emphasize the Positive
Provide euphemisms for the following words and phrases:
a. stubborn
b. wrong
c. stupid
d. incompetent
e. loudmouth

5.5 Audience Relationship: Bias-Free Language
Rewrite each of the following to eliminate bias:
a. A skilled artisan, the Indian Alice Beaver is especially known for her beadwork.
b. He needs a wheelchair, but he doesn't let his handicap affect his job performance.
c. A pilot must have the ability to stay calm under pressure and then he must be trained to cope with any problem that arises.
d. Candidate Renata Parsons, married and the mother of a teenager, will attend the debate.
e. Senior citizen Sam Nugent is still an active salesperson.

5.6 Ethical Choices
Your company has been a major employer in the local community for years, but shifts in the global marketplace have forced some changes in the company's long-term direction. In fact, the company plans to reduce local staffing by as much as 50 percent over the next 5 to 10 years, starting with a small layoff next month. The size and timing of future layoffs has not been decided, although there is little doubt more layoffs will happen at some point. In the first draft of a letter aimed at community leaders, you write that "this first layoff is part of a continuing series of staff reductions anticipated over the next several years." However, your boss is concerned about the vagueness and negative tone of the language and asks you to rewrite that sentence to read, "This layoff is part of the company's ongoing efforts to continually align its resources with global market conditions." Do you think this suggested wording is ethical, given the company's economic influence in the community? Please explain your answer.

5.7 Message Composition: Controlling Style
Rewrite the following letter to Mrs. Betty Crandall (RR #1 New Norway, AB T0B 3L0) so that it conveys a helpful, personal, and interested tone:

We have your letter of recent date to our Ms. Dobson. Owing to the fact that you neglected to include the size of the dress you ordered, please be advised that no shipment of your order was made, but the aforementioned shipment will occur at such time as we are in receipt of the aforementioned information.

5.8 Message Composition: Selecting Words
Write a concrete phrase for each of these vague phrases (make up any information you need):
  a. sometime this spring
  b. a substantial saving
  c. a large number attended
  d. increased efficiency
  e. expanded the work area
  f. flatten the website structure
  g. an incredible computer

5.9 Message Composition: Selecting Words
List terms that are stronger than the following:
  a. ran after
  b. seasonal ups and downs
  c. bright
  d. suddenly rises
  e. moves forward

5.10 Message Composition: Selecting Words
As you rewrite these sentences, replace the clichés with fresh, personal expressions:
  a. Being a jack-of-all-trades, Dave worked well in his new general manager job.
  b. Moving Truc into the accounting department, where she was literally a fish out of water, was like putting a square peg into a round hole, if you get my drift.
  c. I knew she was at death's door, but I thought the doctor would pull her through.
  d. Movies aren't really my cup of tea; as far as I am concerned, they can't hold a candle to a good book.
  e. It's a dog-eat-dog world out there in the rat race of the asphalt jungle.

5.11 Message Composition: Selecting Words
Suggest short, simple words to replace each of the following:
  a. inaugurate
  b. terminate
  c. utilize
  d. anticipate
  e. assistance
  f. endeavour
  g. ascertain
  h. procure
  i. consummate
  j. advise
  k. alteration
  l. forwarded
  m. fabricate
  n. nevertheless
  o. substantial

5.12 Message Composition: Selecting Words
Write up-to-date, less-stuffy versions of these phrases; write none if you think there is no appropriate substitute:
  a. As per your instructions
  b. Attached herewith
  c. In lieu of
  d. In reply I wish to state
  e. Please be advised that

5.13 Message Composition: Creating Sentences
Suppose that end-of-term frustrations have produced this email message to Professor Anne Brewer from a student who believes he should have received a B in his accounting class. If this message were recast into three or four clear sentences, the teacher might be more receptive to the student's argument. Rewrite the message to show how you would improve it:

I think that I was unfairly awarded a C in your accounting class this term, and I am asking you to change the grade to a B. It was a difficult term. I don't get any money from home, and I have to work mornings at the Pancake House (as a cook), so I had to rush to make your class, and those two times that I missed class were because they wouldn't let me off work because of special events at the Pancake House (unlike some other students who just take off when they choose). On the midterm examination, I originally got a 75 percent, but you said in class that there were two different ways to answer the third question and that you would change the grades of students who used the "optimal cost" method and had been counted off 6 points for doing this. I don't think that you took this into account, because I got 80 percent on the final, which is clearly a B. Anyway, whatever you decide, I just want to tell you that I really enjoyed this class, and I thank you for making accounting so interesting.

5.14 Message Composition: Creating Sentences
Rewrite each sentence so that it is active rather than passive:
  a. The raw data are entered into the customer relationship management system by the sales representative each Friday.
  b. High profits are publicized by management.
  c. The policies announced in the directive were implemented by the staff.
  d. Our computers are serviced by the Santee Company.
  e. The employees were represented by Janet Hogan.

5.15 Message Composition: Writing Paragraphs
In the following paragraph, identify the topic sentence and the related sentences (those that support the idea of the topic sentence):

Sync in a snap with Auto-Sync. By default, iTunes automatically copies your entire music library to iPod and deletes songs on iPod that are not listed in iTunes. Or you can use Playlist Sync and select the playlists you want to sync with your iPod. If you have more songs in your iTunes library than you can fit on your iPod, let iTunes create a playlist to fill your iPod, or just update your iPod by dragging over individual songs.[23]

Now add a topic sentence to this paragraph:

Our analysis of the customer experience should start before golfers even drive through the front gate here at Glencoe Meadows; it should start when they phone in or log on to our website to reserve tee times. When they do arrive, the first few stages in the process are also vital: the condition of the grounds leading up to the club house, the reception they receive when they drop off their clubs, and the ease of parking. From that point, how well are we doing with check-in at the pro shop, openings at the driving range, and timely scheduling at the first tee? Then there's everything associated with playing the course itself and returning to the clubhouse at the end of the round.

5.16 Teamwork: Paragraph Techniques

Working with four other students, divide the following five topics among yourselves and each write one paragraph on his or her selected topic. Be sure each student uses a different technique when writing his or her paragraph: One student should use the illustration technique, one the comparison or contrast technique, one a discussion of cause and effect, one the classification technique, and one a discussion of problem and solution. Then exchange paragraphs within the team and pick out the main idea and general purpose of the paragraph one of your teammates wrote. Was everyone able to correctly identify the main idea and purpose? If not, suggest how the paragraph might be rewritten for clarity.

a. types of digital cameras (or dogs or automobiles) available for sale

b. advantages and disadvantages of eating at fast-food restaurants

c. finding that first full-time job

d. good qualities of my car (or house, or apartment, or neighbourhood)

e. how to make a dessert recipe (or barbecue a steak or make coffee)

5.17 Internet: Plain English

Visit the Investor Education website (www.investorED.ca), click "Investing Basics," and review the responses to the Popular Questions. Do the answers follow the plain-English guidelines described in this chapter? Can you suggest any improvements to organization, words, sentences, or paragraphs?

5.18 Message Organization: Transitional Elements

Add transitional elements to the following sentences to improve the flow of ideas. (Note: You may need to eliminate or add some words to smooth out your sentences.)

a. Steve Case saw infinite possibilities in online business. Steve Case was determined to turn his vision into reality. The techies scoffed at his strategy of building a simple internet service for ordinary people. Case doggedly pursued his dream. He analyzed other online services. He assessed the needs of his customers. He responded to their desires for an easier way to access information over the internet. In 1992, Steve Case named his company America Online (AOL). Critics predicted the company's demise. By the end of the century, AOL was a profitable powerhouse. An ill-fated merger with Time Warner was a financial disaster and led to Case's ousting from the company.

b. Facing some of the toughest competitors in the world, Harley-Davidson had to make some changes. The company introduced new products. Harley's management team set out to rebuild the company's production process. New products were coming to market, and the company was turning a profit. Harley's quality standards were not on par with those of its foreign competitors. Harley's costs were still among the highest in the industry. Harley made a U-turn and restructured the company's organizational structure. Harley's efforts have paid off.

c. Whether you're indulging in a doughnut in Charlottetown or Vancouver, Tim Hortons wants you to enjoy the same delicious taste with every bite. The company maintains consistent product quality by carefully controlling every step of the production process. Tim Hortons tests all raw ingredients against established quality standards. Every delivery of wheat flour is sampled and measured for its moisture content and protein levels. Tim Hortons blends the ingredients. Tim Hortons tests the doughnut mix for quality. Tim Hortons delivers the mix to its stores. Financial critics have recognized Tim Hortons' success. Product innovations have shown that the company has a bright future.

5.19 Ethical Choices: Connotative Language

Under what circumstances would you consider the use of terms that are high in connotative meaning to be ethical? When would you consider it to be unethical? Explain your reasoning.

Completing Business Messages

LEARNING OBJECTIVES

After studying this chapter, you will be able to

1. Discuss the value of careful revision, and list the main tasks involved in completing a business message
2. Explain four writing techniques you can use to improve the readability of your messages
3. Describe the steps you can take to improve the clarity of your writing
4. Discuss why it's important to make your message more concise, and give four tips on how to do so
5. Explain how design elements help determine the effectiveness of your documents
6. Highlight the types of errors to look for when proofreading
7. Discuss the most important issues to consider when distributing your messages

ON THE JOB

Communicating at Free the Children
ENGAGING YOUNG AUDIENCES FOR SOCIAL CHANGE

www.freethechildren.com

How does an organization communicate its mission, particularly if it is a charity? How can an organization inspire young people to join that mission and help change the world?

Since its founding in 1995 by 12-year-old Craig Kielburger, Toronto-based Free the Children has motivated youth to raise funds or work on projects fulfilling the organization's vision of improving the lives of impoverished children around the world. Its achievements include building over 500 schools, distributing over 202 000 school and health kits, and helping more than 500 000 people get access to health care. Overall, more than one million children and young adults have become involved in programs in over 45 countries.

Kielburger was himself inspired to start Free the Children when reading about a young Pakistani boy who escaped from working 12 hours a day, six days a week in a carpet factory and began speaking out about the rights of children. To focus international attention on child labour abuses, Kielburger soon went on a fact-finding mission to Southeast Asia, drawing media attention and raising the issue of child labour to worldwide prominence. From that time, Free the Children has grown to become a major force in improving lives through "children helping children through education."

Founder of Free the Children, Craig Kielburger has received numerous awards for his work, including the Nelson Mandela Human Rights Award. His organization shows young people that they are able to help children around the world by getting involved in Free the Children's educational programs.

The challenge faced by Free the Children is to continue engaging young people, as well as expand its extensive network of corporate and non-profit partners. A key part of this effort is the Free the Children interactive website. Here visitors can learn about Free the Children by reading Craig's blog about his international projects and view videos showcasing Free the Children's projects. At the We Generation online youth hub, volunteers can post their own photos and stories, as well as questions about their current fundraising activities. Directed toward a young Web-savvy audience, the Free the Children website is an educational portal that not only explains Free the Children's mission, but inspires visitors to join in improving the global community.

To maintain Free the Children's online appeal requires attention to detail. Layout, photos, video, and interactive features all contribute to its continuing strength. If you volunteered to help Free the Children maintain its website, what details would you pinpoint for revision? What process would you follow to keep it fresh and inviting to its young audience?[1]

Moving Beyond Your First Draft

Your business messages may not require the interactive features of the Free the Children website, but they can benefit from the same rigorous attention to detail in the third step of the three-step writing process: completing your messages.

Once you've completed the first draft of your message, you may be tempted to breathe a sigh of relief and go on to the next project. Resist the temptation. Professional communicators recognize that the first draft is rarely as tight, clear, and compelling as it needs to be. Careful revision can mean the difference between a rambling, unfocused message and a lively, direct message that gets results. Figure 6–1 lists the tasks in the third step of the three-step writing process: revising your message to achieve optimum quality, then producing, proofreading, and distributing it.

First drafts are rarely as effective as they could be.

> Figure 6–1 Step Three in the Three-Step Writing Process: Complete Your Message

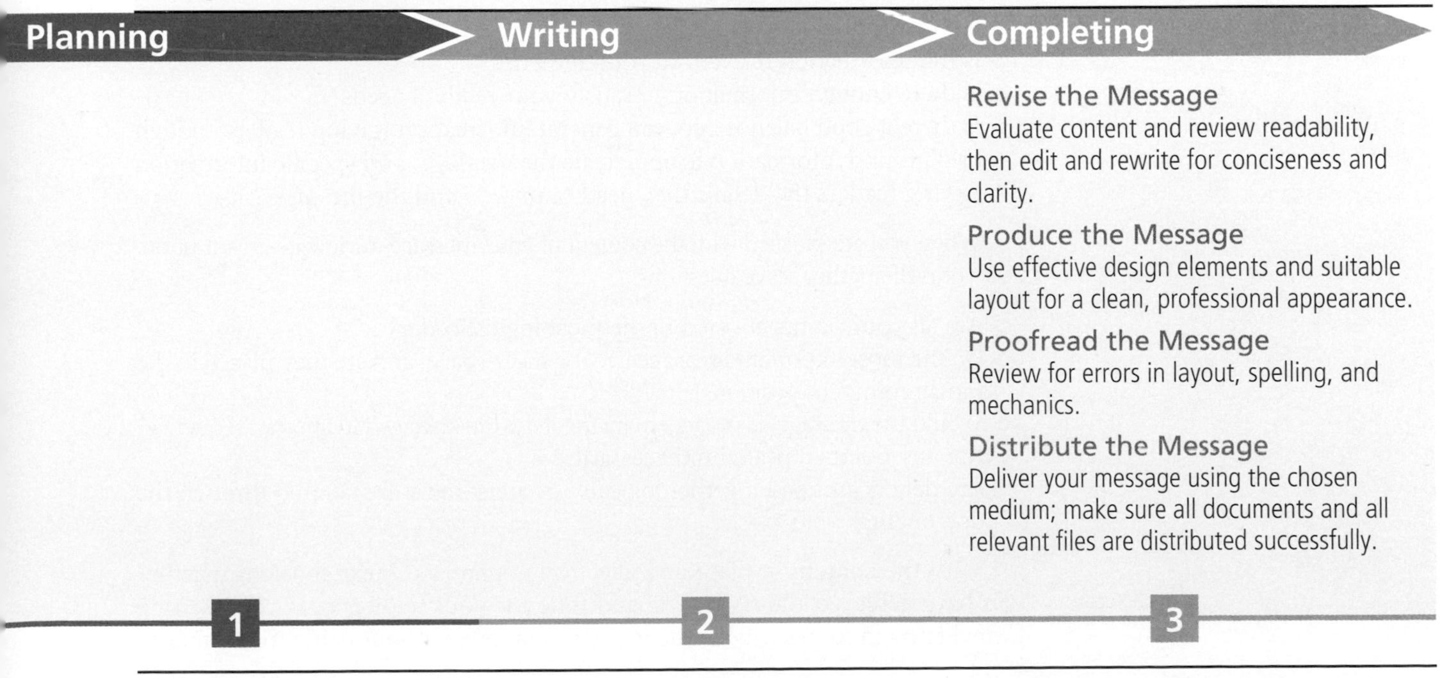

Planning > **Writing** > **Completing**

Revise the Message
Evaluate content and review readability, then edit and rewrite for conciseness and clarity.

Produce the Message
Use effective design elements and suitable layout for a clean, professional appearance.

Proofread the Message
Review for errors in layout, spelling, and mechanics.

Distribute the Message
Deliver your message using the chosen medium; make sure all documents and all relevant files are distributed successfully.

1   2   3

Revising Your Message

Even simple, short messages can usually benefit from a quick revision pass.

The nature of the revision task varies somewhat, depending on the medium you're using and the nature of your message. For informal messages to internal audiences, particularly when using instant messaging, text messaging, email, or blogging, the revision process is often as simple as quickly looking over your message to correct any mistakes before sending or posting it. However, don't fall into the common trap of thinking that these electronic media are so new and different and informal that you don't need to worry about grammar, spelling, clarity, and other fundamentals of good writing. These qualities can be even *more* important in electronic media, not less, particularly if these messages are the only contact your audience has with you. Audiences are likely to equate the quality of your writing with the quality of your thinking, decision making, and other business skills. Moreover, even minor errors can cause confusion, frustration, and costly delays.

Fortunately, revising simple messages doesn't take much time or effort. With instant messaging, for example, you need only a second or two to scan each message to make sure you haven't said something clumsy or incorrect.

If you have time, put your draft aside for a day or two before you begin the revision process.

With more complex messages, try to put your draft aside for a day or two before you begin the revision process so that you can approach the material with a fresh eye. Then start with the "big picture," making sure that the document accomplishes your overall goals. Next, move to finer points, such as readability, clarity, and conciseness. Compare the messages in Figures 6–2 and 6–3 for an example of how careful revision can improve a letter: the revised version provides the requested information more clearly, in an organized way, with a friendlier style, and with precise mechanics. The *proofreading symbols* are still widely used when printed documents are edited and revised. However, in many instances, you'll use the electronic markup features in your word processor or other software, as shown in Figure 6.5 on page 169.

Evaluating Your Content, Organization, Style, and Tone

Explore

Objective 1 Discuss the value of careful revision, and list the main tasks involved in completing a business message.

When you begin the revision process, focus your attention on content, organization, style, and tone. To evaluate the content of your message, ask yourself these questions:

> Is the information accurate?
> Is the information relevant to your audience?
> Is there enough information to satisfy your reader's needs?
> Is there a good balance between general information (giving readers enough background information to appreciate the message) and specific information (giving readers the details they need to understand the message)?

When you are satisfied with the content of your message, review its organization. Ask yourself another set of questions:

> Are all your points covered in the most logical order?
> Do the most important ideas receive the most space, and are they placed in the most prominent positions?
> Would the message be more convincing if it were arranged in another sequence?
> Are any points repeated unnecessarily?
> Are details grouped together logically, or are some still scattered through the document?

With the content in place and effectively organized, next consider whether you have achieved the right style and tone for your audience. Is your writing formal enough to meet the audience's expectations without being too formal or

> Figure 6–2 Improving a Customer Letter Through Careful Revision

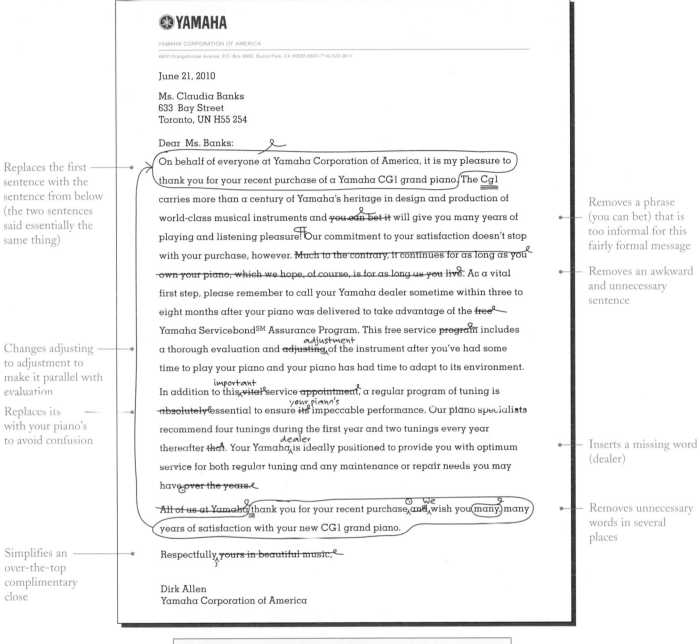

Replaces the first sentence with the sentence from below (the two sentences said essentially the same thing)

Changes adjusting to adjustment to make it parallel with evaluation

Replaces its with your piano's to avoid confusion

Simplifies an over-the-top complimentary close

Removes a phrase (you can bet) that is too informal for this fairly formal message

Removes an awkward and unnecessary sentence

Inserts a missing word (dealer)

Removes unnecessary words in several places

	Common Proofreading Symbols
~~strikethrough~~	Delete text
ℓ	Delete individual character or a circled block of text
∧	Insert text (text to insert is written above)
⊙	Insert period
⋏	Insert comma
⌐	Start new line
¶	Start new paragraph
≡	Capitalize

> Figure 6–3 Revised Customer Letter

YAMAHA CORPORATION OF AMERICA

6600 Orangethorpe Avenue, P.O. Box 6600, Buena Park, CA 90622-6600 (714) 522-9011

June 21, 2010

Ms. Claudia Banks
633 Bay Street
Toronto, UN H55 254

Dear Ms. Banks:

Thank you for your recent purchase. We wish you many years of satisfaction with your new CG1 grand piano. The CG1 carries more than a century of Yamaha's heritage in design and production of world-class musical instruments and will give you many years of playing and listening pleasure.

Our commitment to your satisfaction doesn't stop with your purchase, however. As a vital first step, please remember to call your Yamaha dealer sometime within three to eight months after your piano was delivered to take advantage of the Yamaha Servicebond℠ Assurance Program. This free service includes a thorough evaluation and adjustment of the instrument after you've had some time to play your piano and your piano has had time to adapt to its environment.

In addition to this important service, a regular program of tuning is essential to ensure your piano's impeccable performance. Our piano specialists recommend four tunings during the first year and two tunings every year thereafter. Your Yamaha dealer is ideally positioned to provide you with optimum service for both regular tuning and any maintenance or repair needs you may have.

Respectfully,

Dirk Allen
Yamaha Corporation of America

academic? Is it too casual for a serious subject? Does your message emphasize the audience's needs over your own?

Spend a few extra moments on the beginning and end of your message; these sections have the greatest impact on the audience. Be sure the opening of your document is relevant and geared to the reader's probable reaction. In longer documents, check that the first few paragraphs establish the subject, purpose, and organization of the material. Review the conclusion to ensure that it summarizes the main idea and leaves the audience with a positive impression.

The beginning and end of a message have the greatest impact on your readers.

Reviewing for Readability

When you're satisfied with the content, organization, style, and tone of your message, make a second pass to look at its readability. Most professionals are inundated with more reading material than they can ever hope to consume, and they'll appreciate your efforts to make your documents easier to read. You'll benefit from this effort, too: If you earn a reputation for well-crafted documents that respect the audience's time, people will pay more attention to your work.

You may be familiar with one of the many indexes that have been developed over the years in an attempt to measure readability. For example, the Flesch-Kincaid Grade Level score computes reading difficulty relative to grade-level achievement. Thus, a score of 10 suggests that a document can be read and understood by the average Grade 10 student. Most business documents score in the 8–11 range. Technical documents often score in the 12–14 range. A similar scoring system, the Flesch Reading Ease score, ranks documents on a 100-point scale: the higher the score, the easier the document is to read. Both measurements are built into Microsoft Word (under options in the spelling and grammar window), making them easy to use for most business communicators.

Readability indexes offer a useful reference point, but they are all limited by what they are able to measure: word length, number of syllables, sentence length, and paragraph length. They can't measure any other factors that affect readability, such as audience analysis, writing clarity, and document design. Compare these two paragraphs:

Readability formulas can give you a helpful indication, but they can't measure everything that affects readability.

Readability indexes offer a useful reference point, but they are all limited by what they are able to measure: word length, number of syllables, sentence length, and paragraph length. They can't measure any of the other factors that affect readability, from "you" orientation to writing clarity to document design.

Readability indexes can help. But they don't measure everything. They don't measure whether your writing clarity is good. They don't measure whether your document design is good or not. Reading indexes are based on word length, syllables, sentences, and paragraphs.

The first paragraph scores 12.0 on grade level and 27.4 on reading ease, meaning it is supposedly rather difficult to read. The second paragraph scores much better on both grade level (8.9) and reading ease (45.8). However, the second example is choppy, unsophisticated, and poorly organized, and much less satisfying to read. As a general rule, then, don't assume that a piece of text is readable if it scores well on a readability index—or that it is difficult to read if it doesn't score well.

Beyond shortening words and sentences for readability measurements, you can improve the readability of a message by making the document easy to skim. Most business audiences—particularly influential senior managers—skim longer documents looking for key ideas, conclusions, and recommendations. If they determine that the document contains valuable information or requires a response, they will read it more carefully when time permits. You can adopt a number of techniques to make your message easier to skim: varying sentence length, using shorter paragraphs, using lists and bullets instead of narrative, and adding effective headings and subheadings.

The effort to make your documents more readable will pay for itself in greater career success.

Objective 2 Explain four writing techniques you can use to improve the readability of your messages.

VARYING YOUR SENTENCE LENGTH Variety is a creative way to make your messages interesting and readable. By choosing words and sentence structure with care, you can create a rhythm that emphasizes important points,

To keep readers' interest, use both long and short sentences.

enlivens your writing style, and makes your information appealing to your reader. For example, a short sentence that highlights a conclusion at the end of a substantial paragraph of evidence makes your key message stand out. Effective documents, therefore, usually use a mixture of sentences that are short (up to 15 words), medium (15–25 words), and long (more than 25 words).

Each sentence length has its advantages. Short sentences can be processed quickly and are easier for non-native speakers and translators to interpret. Medium-length sentences are useful for showing the relationships among ideas. Long sentences are often the best way to convey complex ideas, list multiple related points, or summarize or preview information.

Of course, each sentence length also has disadvantages. Too many short sentences in a row can make your writing choppy. Medium-length sentences lack the punch of short sentences and the informative power of longer sentences. Long sentences are usually harder to understand than short sentences because they are packed with information that must all be absorbed at once. Because readers can absorb only a few words per glance, longer sentences are also more difficult to skim. Thus, the longer your sentence, the greater the possibility that the reader who skims it will not read enough words to process its full meaning. By choosing the best sentence length for each communication need and remembering to mix sentence lengths for variety, you'll get your message across while keeping your documents lively and interesting.

Short paragraphs are easier to read than long ones.

KEEPING YOUR PARAGRAPHS SHORT Large blocks of text can be visually daunting, so the optimum paragraph length is short to medium in most cases. Unless you break up your thoughts somehow, you'll end up with a three-page paragraph that's guaranteed to intimidate even the most dedicated reader. Short paragraphs (of 100 words or fewer; this paragraph has 88 words) are easier to read than long ones, and they make your writing look inviting. They also help audiences read more carefully. You can also emphasize an idea by isolating it in a short, forceful paragraph.

However, don't overuse short paragraphs. Be careful to use one-sentence paragraphs only occasionally and only for emphasis. Also, if you need to divide a subject into several pieces to keep paragraphs short, help your readers keep the ideas connected by guiding them with plenty of transitional elements.

Lists are effective tools for highlighting and simplifying material.

USING LISTS AND BULLETS TO CLARIFY AND EMPHASIZE An effective alternative to using conventional sentences is to set off important ideas in a list—a series of words, names, or other items. Lists can show the sequence of your ideas, heighten their impact visually, and increase the likelihood that a reader will find the key points. In addition, lists provide readers with clues, simplify complex subjects, highlight the main point, break up the page visually, ease the skimming process for busy readers, and give the reader a breather. Consider the difference between the following two approaches to the same information:

Narrative	List
Owning your own business has many advantages. One is the ease of establishment. Another advantage is the satisfaction of working for yourself. As a sole proprietor, you also have the advantage of privacy because you do not have to reveal your information or plans to anyone.	Owning your own business has three advantages: > ease of establishment > satisfaction of working for yourself > privacy of information

When creating a list, you can separate items with numbers, letters, or bullets (a general term for any kind of graphical element that precedes each item). Bullets are generally preferred over numbers, unless the list is in some logical sequence or ranking, or specific list items will be referred to later on. The following three steps need to be performed in the order indicated, and the numbers make that clear:

1. Find out how many employees would like on-site daycare facilities.
2. Determine how much space the daycare centre would require.
3. Estimate the cost of converting a conference room for the on-site facility.

Lists are easier to locate and read if the entire numbered or bulleted section is set off by a blank line before and after, as the preceding examples demonstrate. Furthermore, when using lists, make sure to introduce them clearly so that people know what they're about to read. One way to introduce lists is to make them a part of the introductory sentence:

The board of directors met to discuss the revised annual budget. To keep expenses in line with declining sales, the directors voted to

> cut everyone's salary by 10 percent
> close the employee cafeteria
> reduce travel expenses

Another way to introduce a list is to precede it with a complete introductory sentence, followed by a colon:

The decline in company profit is attributable to four factors:

> slower holiday sales
> higher employee wages
> increased transportation and fuel costs
> slower inventory turnover

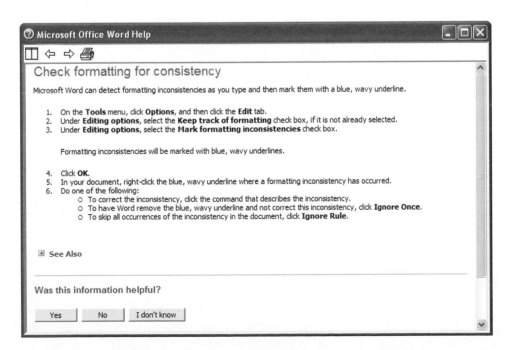

This Microsoft Word help screen uses a numbered list to explain a formatting process. Why are numbers used instead of bullets? Would the instructions be as clear in narrative form?

Regardless of the format you choose, the items in a list should be parallel; that is, they should all use the same grammatical pattern. For example, if one list item begins with a verb, all list items should begin with a verb. If one item is a noun phrase, all should be noun phrases.

Nonparallel List Items	Parallel List Items
> improve our bottom line > identification of new foreign markets for our products > global market strategies > issues regarding pricing and packaging size	> improve our bottom line > identify new foreign markets for our products > develop our global market strategies > resolve pricing and packaging issues

Parallel forms are easier to read and skim. You can create parallelism by repeating the pattern in words, phrases, clauses, or entire sentences (see Table 6–1).

ADDING HEADINGS AND SUBHEADINGS A **heading** is a brief title that tells readers about the content of the section that follows. **Subheadings** are subordinate to headings, indicating subsections within a major section. Headings and subheadings serve these important functions:

> **Organization.** Headings show your reader at a glance how the document is organized. They act as labels to group related paragraphs together and effectively organize your material into short sections.
> **Attention.** Informative, inviting, and in some cases intriguing headings grab the reader's attention, make the text easier to read, and help the reader find the parts he or she needs to read—or skip.
> **Connection.** Using headings and subheadings together helps readers see the relationship between main ideas and subordinate ones so that they can understand your message more easily. Moreover, headings and subheadings visually indicate shifts from one idea to the next.

Headings fall into two categories. **Descriptive headings,** such as "Cost Considerations," identify a topic but do little more. **Informative headings,** such as "A New Way to Cut Costs," put your reader right into the context of your message.

Informative headings guide readers to think in a certain way about the topic. They are also helpful in guiding your work as a writer, especially if written in terms of questions you plan to address in your document. Well-written informative headings are self-contained, which means that readers can read just the headings and subheadings and understand them without reading the rest of the document. For example, "Introduction" conveys little information, whereas

Use headings to grab the reader's attention and organize material into short sections.

Informative headings are generally more helpful than descriptive ones.

Use the same grammatical form for each heading.

> Table 6–1 Achieving Parallelism

Method	Example
Parallel words	The letter was approved by Nguyen, Gitlen, Merlin, and Carlucci.
Parallel phrases	We are gaining market share in supermarkets, in department stores, and in specialty stores.
Parallel clauses	I'd like to discuss the issue after Vicki gives her presentation but before Marvin shows his slides.
Parallel sentences	In 2009 we exported 30 percent of our production. In 2008 we exported 50 percent.

the heading "Staffing Shortages in Finance and Accounting Cost the Company $150 000 Last Year" provides a key piece of information and captures the reader's attention. Whatever types of headings you choose, keep them brief, and use parallel construction as you would for an outline, list, or series of words.

Editing for Clarity and Conciseness

After you've reviewed and revised your message for readability, your next step is to ensure that your message is as clear and as concise as possible. To ensure clarity, look closely at your paragraph organization, sentence structure, and word choices. Do your paragraphs have clear topic sentences? Are the transitions between ideas obvious? Then ask yourself whether your sentences are easy to decipher. Are your statements simple and direct? Perhaps a sentence is so complicated that readers can't unravel it. Next, review your word choices. You might have chosen a word that is so vague that readers can interpret it in several ways. Perhaps pronouns or tenses switch midsentence so that readers lose track of who is talking or when an event took place.[2]

See Table 6–2 for examples of the following tips:

> **Break up overly long sentences.** Don't connect too many clauses with *and* or *or*. If you find yourself stuck in a long sentence, you're probably making the sentence do more than it can reasonably do, such as expressing two dissimilar thoughts or peppering the reader with too many pieces of supporting evidence at once (did you notice how difficult this long sentence was to read?). You can often clarify your writing style by separating a string of items into individual sentences.

> **Rewrite hedging sentences.** Sometimes you have to write *may* or *seems* to avoid stating a judgment as a fact. However, when you have too many such hedges, you risk coming across as unsure of what you're saying.

> **Impose parallelism.** When you have two or more similar ideas to express, make them parallel. Repeating the same grammatical construction shows that the ideas are related, of similar importance, and on the same level of generality. Parallelism is discussed earlier in this chapter in the section on lists and bullets.

> **Correct dangling modifiers.** Sometimes a modifier is not just an adjective or an adverb but an entire phrase modifying a noun or a verb. Be careful not to leave this type of modifier dangling, with no connection to the subject of the sentence. The first unacceptable example under "Dangling Modifiers" in Table 6–2 implies that the red sports car has both an office and the legs to walk there. The second example shows one frequent cause of dangling modifiers: passive construction.

> **Reword long noun sequences.** When multiple nouns are strung together as modifiers, the resulting sentence can be hard to read. You might be trying too hard to create the desired effect. See if a single well-chosen word will do the job. If the nouns are all necessary, consider moving one or more to a modifying phrase as shown in Table 6–2. Although you may add a few more words, your audience won't have to work as hard to understand the sentence.

> **Replace camouflaged verbs.** Watch for words that end in *-ion, -tion, -ing, -ment, -ant, -ent, -ence, -ance,* and *-ency*. These endings often change verbs into nouns and adjectives, requiring you to add a verb just to get your point across. To prune and enliven your messages, use verbs instead of noun phrases.

> **Clarify sentence structure.** Keep the subject and predicate of a sentence as close together as possible. When the subject and predicate are far apart, readers may need to read the sentence twice to figure out who did what. Similarly,

Clarity is essential to getting your message across accurately and efficiently.

Objective 3 Describe the steps you can take to improve the clarity of your writing.

Don't be afraid to present your opinions without qualification.

When you use the same grammatical pattern to express two or more ideas, you show that they are comparable thoughts.

Subject and predicate should be placed as close together as possible, as should modifiers and the words they modify.

> Table 6–2 Revising for Clarity

✔•⎯Practise

Issues to Review	Unacceptable	Preferable
Overly Long Sentences Taking compound sentences too far	The magazine will be published January 1, and I'd better meet the deadline if I want my article included.	The magazine will be published January 1. I'd better meet the deadline if I want my article included.
Hedging Sentences Overqualifying sentences	I believe that Mr. Johnson's employment record seems to show that he may be capable of handling the position.	Mr. Johnson's employment record shows that he is capable of handling the position.
Unparallel Sentences Using dissimilar construction for similar ideas	Mr. Simms had been drenched with rain, bombarded with telephone calls, and his boss shouted at him.	Mr. Sims had been drenched with rain, bombarded with telephone calls, and shouted at by his boss.
	Ms. Reynolds dictated the letter, and next she signed it and left the office.	Ms. Reynolds dictated the letter, signed it, and left the office.
	To waste time and missing deadlines are bad habits.	Wasting time and missing deadlines are bad habits.
Dangling Modifiers Placing modifiers close to the wrong nouns and verbs	Walking to the office, a red sports car passed her.	A red sports car passed her while she was walking to the office.
	After a three-week slump, we increased sales.	After a three-week slump, sales increased.
Long Noun Sequences Stringing too many nouns together	The window sash installation company will give us an estimate on Friday.	The company that installs window sashes will give us an estimate on Friday.
Camouflaged Verbs Changing verbs and nouns into adjectives	The manager undertook implementation of the rules.	The manager implemented the rules.
	Verification of the shipments occurs weekly.	Shipments are verified weekly.
Changing verbs into nouns	reach a conclusion about	conclude
	make a discovery of	discover
	give consideration to	consider
Sentence Structure Separating subject and predicate	A 10% decline in market share, which resulted from quality problems and an aggressive sales campaign by Armitage, the market leader in the Maritimes, was the major problem in 2009.	The major problem in 2009 was a 10% loss of market share, which resulted from both quality problems and an aggressive sales campaign by Armitage, the market leader in the Maritimes.
Separating adjectives, adverbs, or prepositional phrases from the words they modify	Our antique desk lends an air of strength and substance with thick legs and large drawers.	With its thick legs and large drawers, our antique desk lends an air of strength and substance.
Awkward References	The Law Office and the Accounting Office distribute computer supplies for legal secretaries and beginning accountants, respectively.	The Law Office distributes computer supplies for legal secretaries; the Accounting Office distributes those for beginning accountants.
Too Much Enthusiasm	We are extremely pleased to offer you a position on our staff of exceptionally skilled and highly educated employees. The work offers extraordinary challenges and a very large salary.	We are pleased to offer you a position on our staff of skilled and well-educated employees. The work offers challenges and an attractive salary.

adjectives, adverbs, and prepositional phrases usually make the most sense when they're placed as close as possible to the words they modify.

> **Clarify awkward references.** In an effort to save words, business writers sometimes use expressions such as *the above-mentioned, as mentioned above, the aforementioned, the former, the latter,* and *respectively.* These words cause readers to jump from point to point, which hinders effective communication. You'll often be more successful using specific references (such as "as described in the second paragraph on page 22"), even if that means adding a few more words.

> **Moderate your enthusiasm.** An occasional adjective or adverb intensifies and emphasizes your meaning, but too many can degrade your writing and damage your credibility. When using an adjective or adverb to enhance your meaning, be accurate and concrete. The word "incredible" (which means "not to be believed") is often used to describe a quality. The sentence *"Your product is incredible"* would be better phrased as *"Your product's ease-of-use will please consumers."*

Showing enthusiasm for ideas is fine, but be careful not to go so far that you sound unprofessional.

In addition to clarity, readers appreciate conciseness in business messages. The good news is that most first drafts can be cut by as much as 50 percent.[3] By reorganizing your content, improving the readability of your document, and correcting your sentence structure for clarity, you will have already eliminated most of the excess. Now it is time to examine every word. As you begin editing, simplify, prune, and strive for order. See Table 6–3 for examples of the following tips:

Objective 4 Discuss why it's important to make your message more concise, and give four tips on how to do so.

> **Delete unnecessary words and phrases.** To test whether a word or phrase is essential, write the sentence without it. If the meaning doesn't change, leave it out. For example, *very* can be a useful word to achieve emphasis, but more often it's simply clutter. There's no need to call someone "very methodical." The person is either methodical or not. In addition, avoid the clutter of too many or poorly placed relative pronouns (*who, that, which*). Even articles can be excessive (mostly too many *the*s). However, well-placed relative pronouns and articles prevent confusion, so make sure you don't obscure the meaning of the sentence by removing them.

Make your documents tighter by removing unnecessary words.

> **Shorten long words and phrases.** Short words are generally more vivid and easier to read than long ones. Shorter phrases are easier to process and understand quickly. Remember, though, the idea is to use short, simple words, *not* simple concepts.[4]

> **Eliminate redundancies.** In some word combinations, the words tend to say the same thing. For example, "visible to the eye" is redundant because *visible* is enough without further clarification; "to the eye" adds nothing.

> **Recast "It is/There are" starters.** If you start a sentence with an indefinite pronoun such as *it* or *there,* you can probably rephrase the sentence to make it shorter. For example, "We believe . . . " is a stronger opening than "It is believed that . . . "

Sometimes you'll find that the most difficult problem in a sentence can be solved by simply removing the problem itself. When you come upon a troublesome element, ask yourself, "Do I need it at all?" Possibly not. In fact, you may find that it was giving you so much grief precisely because it was trying to do an unnecessary job.[5] Once you remove the troublesome element, the afflicted sentence will read correctly and smoothly. Of course, before you delete anything, you'll probably want to keep copies of your current version. Take advantage of the "undo" and "redo" functions in your software to experiment with adding and removing various elements.

What parallels can you draw between post-game analysis and editing business messages? What do coaches look for when reviewing a game that their team either won or lost? Can you adapt the process that coaches use to editing your own work?

> Table 6–3 Revising for Conciseness   ✔•─ Practise

Issues to Review	Unacceptable	Preferable
Unnecessary Words and Phrases		
Using wordy phrases	for the sum of	for
	in the event that	if
	prior to the start of	before
	in the near future	soon
	at this point in time	now
	due to the fact that	because
	in view of the fact that	because
	until such time as	when
	with reference to	about
Using too many relative pronouns	Cars that are sold after January will not have a six-month warranty.	Cars sold after January will not have a six-month warranty.
	Employees who are driving to work should park in the underground garage.	Employees driving to work should park in the underground garage.
Using too few relative pronouns	The project manager told the engineers last week the specifications were changed.	The project manager told the engineers last week that the specifications were changed.
		The project manager told the engineers that last week the specifications were changed.
Long Words and Phrases		
Using overly long words	During the preceding year, the company accelerated productive operations.	Last year the company sped up operations.
	The action was predicated on the assumption that the company was operating at a financial deficit.	The action was based on the belief that the company was losing money.
Using wordy phrases rather than infinitives	If you want success as a writer, you must work hard.	To be a successful writer, you must work hard.
	He went to the library for the purpose of studying.	He went to the library to study.
	The employer increased salaries so she could improve morale.	The employer increased salaries to improve morale.
Redundancies		
Repeating meanings	absolutely complete	complete
	basic fundamentals	fundamentals
	follows after	follows
	free and clear	free
	refer back	refer
	repeat again	repeat
	collect together	collect
	future plans	plans
	return back	return
	important essentials	essentials
	end result	result
	actual truth	truth
	final outcome	outcome
	uniquely unusual	unique
	surrounded on all sides	surrounded
Using double modifiers	modern, up-to-date equipment	modern equipment

> Table 6–3 Revising for Conciseness (continued)

Issues to Review	Unacceptable	Preferable
It Is/There Are Starters Starting sentences with *it* or *there*	It would be appreciated if you would sign the lease today.	Please sign the lease today.
	There are five employees in this division who were late to work today.	Five employees in this division were late to work today.

For a reminder of the tasks involved in revision, see "Checklist: Revising Business Messages."

Using Technology to Revise Your Message

When it's time to revise and polish your message, your word processor can help you add, delete, and move text with functions such as *cut* and *paste* (taking a block of text out of one section of a document and pasting it in somewhere else) and *find* and *replace* (tracking down words or phrases and changing them if necessary). Be careful using this feature though; choosing the "replace all" option can result in some unintended errors. For example, finding *power* and replacing all occurrences with *strength* will also change the word *powerful* to *strengthful*.

Software tools such as *revision marks* and *commenting* keep track of proposed editing changes electronically and provide a history of a document's revisions. Microsoft Word, the most commonly used word processing software in business offices, offers handy tools for reviewing draft documents. As shown

---

CHECKLIST Revising Business Messages

A. Evaluate content, organization, style, and tone.
- ✔ Ensure that the information is accurate, relevant, and sufficient.
- ✔ Check that all necessary points appear in logical order.
- ✔ Verify that you present enough support to make the main idea convincing and interesting.
- ✔ Ensure the beginning and end are effective.
- ✔ Ensure you've achieved the right tone.

B. Review for readability.
- ✔ Consider using a readability index, being sure to interpret the answer carefully.
- ✔ Use a mix of short and long sentences.
- ✔ Keep paragraphs short.
- ✔ Use bulleted and numbered lists to emphasize key points.
- ✔ Make the document easy to scan with headings and subheadings.

C. Edit for clarity.
- ✔ Break up overly long sentences and rewrite hedging sentences.
- ✔ Use parallelism to simplify reading.
- ✔ Correct dangling modifiers.
- ✔ Reword long noun sequences and replace camouflaged verbs.
- ✔ Clarify sentence structure and awkward references.
- ✔ Moderate your enthusiasm to maintain a professional tone.

D. Edit for conciseness.
- ✔ Delete unnecessary words and phrases.
- ✔ Shorten long words and phrases.
- ✔ Eliminate redundancies.
- ✔ Rewrite sentences that start with "It is" or "There are."

> Figure 6–4 Revision Marks in Microsoft Word

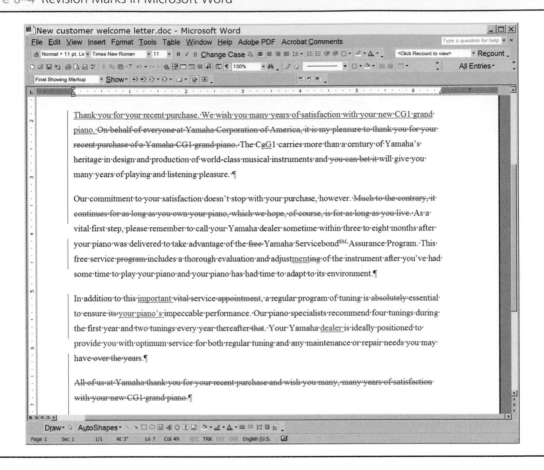

in Figure 6–4, text to be added is underlined, and text to be deleted is struck through. The writer can then choose to accept or reject each suggested change. Adobe Acrobat lets you attach comments to PDF files (see Figure 6–5). (Note that Adobe Acrobat is not the same product as the free Adobe Reader.) Using revision marks and commenting features is also a practical way to keep track of editing changes made by team members. Both Word and Acrobat let you use different colours for each reviewer, as well, so you can keep everyone's comments separate.

Spell-checkers, grammar-checkers, and computerized thesauruses can all help with the revision process, but they can't take the place of good writing and editing skills.

In addition to the many revision tools, four software functions can help bring out the best in your documents. First, a *spell-checker* compares your document with an electronic dictionary, highlights unrecognized words, and suggests correct spellings. Spell-checkers are wonderful for finding typos, but they are no substitute for good spelling skills. For example, if you use *their* when you mean to use *there,* your spell-checker won't notice, because *their* is spelled correctly. If you're in a hurry and accidentally omit the *p* at the end of *top,* the spell-checker will read *to* as correct. Plus, some "errors" that the spell-checker indicates may actually be proper names, technical words, words that you misspelled on purpose, Web addresses, or simply words that weren't included in the spell-checker's dictionary. It's up to you to decide whether each flagged word should be corrected or left alone, to find the errors that the spell-checker has overlooked, and to catch problems that the spell checker itself might introduce (such as inserting unwanted hyphens or suggesting incorrect word replacements).

You can set the default language to Canadian English in the most recent version of Microsoft Word through the Tools menu. Macintosh users can do the same through the International menu in the System Preferences.

> Figure 6–5 PDF File with Comments

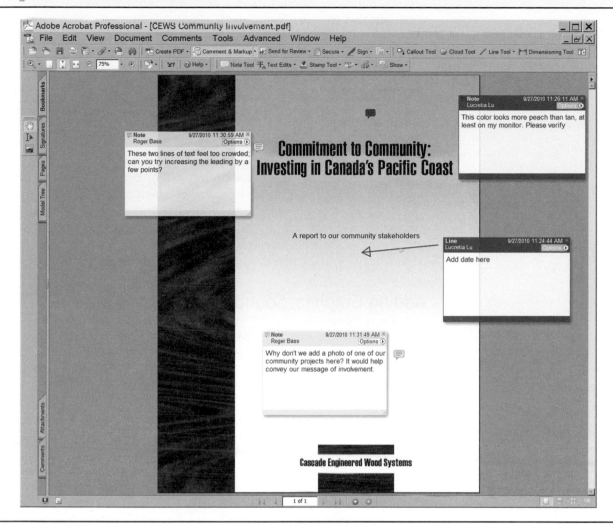

Second, a computer *thesaurus* gives you alternative words, just as a printed thesaurus does. A computer thesaurus is much faster and lets you try multiple alternatives in just a few seconds to see which works best. The best uses of any thesaurus, printed or computerized, are to find fresh, interesting words when you've been using the same word too many times and to find words that most accurately convey your intended meaning. Don't fall into the temptation of using your thesaurus to find impressive words to spice up your writing; if you're not comfortable using the word, it won't sound natural in your documents.

Third, a *grammar-checker* tries to do for your grammar what a spell-checker does for your spelling. Because the program doesn't have a clue about what you're trying to say, it can't tell whether you've said it clearly or correctly. However, grammar-checkers can highlight items you should consider changing, such as passive voice, long sentences, and words that tend to be misused.

Fourth, a *style-checker* can also monitor your word and sentence choices and suggest alternatives that might produce more effective writing. For example, the style-checking options in Microsoft Word range from basic issues, such as spelling out numbers and using contractions, to more subjective matters, such as sentence structure and the use of technical terminology.

By all means, use any software that you find helpful when revising your documents. Just remember that it's unwise to rely on them to do all your revision work, and that you are responsible for the final product.

Producing Your Message

The quality of your document or screen design affects both readability and audience perceptions of you and your message.

Now it's time to put your hard work on display. The *production quality* of your message—the total effect of page or screen design, graphical elements, typography, paper, and so on—plays an important role in the effectiveness of your message. A polished, inviting design not only makes your document easier to read but also conveys a sense of professionalism and importance.[6]

Naturally, the production task varies widely, depending on the medium you've chosen and the degree of formality you need to achieve. In the simplest media, such as text messaging, you have virtually nothing to do. With instant messaging and email, you can control a variety of aspects, such as type size and colour. With documents prepared with a word processor, your options multiply considerably—particularly if you plan to deliver the documents electronically.

Adding Graphics, Sound, Video, and Hypertext

Take advantage of your word processor's ability to incorporate other communication elements.

Today's word processors and other software tools make it easy to produce impressive documents that enliven your text with full-colour pictures, sound and video recordings, and hypertext links. The software for creating business visuals falls into two basic groups: *Presentation software,* which helps you create electronic slide shows for in-person or online meetings (see Chapter 14), and *graphics software,* which ranges from basic tools that help you create simple business diagrams to the comprehensive tools preferred by artists and graphic designers. You can create graphics yourself, add *clip art* (collections of uncopyrighted images), or scan in printed drawings or photographs.

Adding sound bites or video clips to electronic documents is an exciting new way to get your message across. Several systems let you record brief messages and attach them to particular places in a document. The reader clicks a speaker icon to play each comment.

You can also use hypertext markup language (HTML) to insert hyperlinks into your message. Readers can easily jump from one document to another by clicking such a link. They can go directly to a website, jump to another section of your document, or go to a different document altogether. Suppose you're preparing a report on this year's budget. Rather than include pages and pages of budget details from prior years, you can connect to them using hyperlinks. If readers need to access specific details, they can simply click on the appropriate links. Using hyperlinks, you can customize your documents to meet the individual information needs of your readers—just as you can on a web page. Of course, you'll have to make sure that the file (or the software program used to open that file) is included with your electronic document, installed on the recipient's computer, or accessible via a network connection.

Designing for Readability

Design affects the impression your message makes.

Design affects readability in two important ways. First, if used carefully, design elements can improve the effectiveness of your message. If done poorly, design elements can act as barriers, blocking your communication. For example, people age 65 and over are a growing segment of online consumers, but many websites don't take into account the natural changes that occur in eyesight as people age. Older people find it difficult to read the small type that is common on websites—and many websites make the even greater mistake of preventing viewers from enlarging type size in their browsers.[7] Second, the visual design itself sends a nonverbal message to the audience, influencing their perceptions of the communication before they read a single word. View any business website on the internet, and ask yourself what nonverbal message it sends, and how you are influenced by it.

Compare the two messages shown in Figures 6–6 and 6–7. They contain virtually the same information but send dramatically different messages to the reader. Figure 6–6 is uninviting and difficult to read. The amateurish use of bold type, capital letters, and italics is distracting. In contrast, Figure 6–7 is open, inviting, and easy to either read entirely or scan quickly.

> Figure 6–6 Ineffective Document Design

When Craig founded Free the Children 13 years ago, celebrating a success meant throwing a pizza party in our parents' basement, surrounded by other young volunteers.

Back then our **SUCCESSES** were small victories:

✓ an invitation to speak at a local school

✓ or the proceeds from a fundraising garage sale.

Each and every accomplishment was a big step towards the goal of helping other children through education.

Though we have grown into an international children's charity providing education to tens of thousands each day, we are still, in a sense, celebrating **many** small **victories**:

✓ each school built represents a simple but life-changing opportunity for the dozens of students it serves.

✓ And just like 13 years before, the garage sales, speeches and other heartfelt fundraisers by North American youth still drive our ability to have an impact in the field.

We chose **CELEBRATION** as the theme of this annual report in recognition of the **COMPLETION** of our **500th school**. By itself, it is one project amongst many, but as a symbol it is proof of the incredible global impact *compassionate young people* are having through Free the Children's programs.

In this report we are pleased to highlight the accomplishments of 2007 as one **outstanding** year in a long legacy worth celebrating. It is also a **call to action** for the work that still needs to be done.

> Figure 6–7 Well-Designed Document

SMALL VICTORIES BIG CHANGE

Letter from Craig and Marc

When Craig founded Free the Children 13 years ago, celebrating a success meant throwing a pizza party in our parents' basement, surrounded by other young volunteers.

Back then our successes were small victories: an invitation to speak at a local school or the proceeds from a fundraising garage sale. Each and every accomplishment was a big step towards the goal of helping other children through education.

Though we have grown into an international children's charity providing education to tens of thousands each day, we are still, in a sense, celebrating many small victories: each school built represents a simple but life-changing opportunity for the dozens of students it serves. And just like 13 years before, the garage sales, speeches and other heartfelt fundraisers by North American youth still drive our ability to have an impact in the field.

We chose celebration as the theme of this annual report in recognition of the completion of our 500th school. By itself, it is one project amongst many, but as a symbol it is proof of the incredible global impact compassionate young people are having through Free the Children's programs.

In this report we are pleased to highlight the accomplishments of 2007 as one outstanding year in a long legacy worth celebrating. It is also a call to action for the work that still needs to be done.

Sincerely,

Craig Kielburger
Founder, Free the Children
Chair, Board of Country Directors

Marc Kielburger
Chief Executive Director

Objective 5 Explain how design elements help determine the effectiveness of your documents.

For effective design, pay attention to
> consistency
> balance
> restraint
> detail

Effective design helps establish the tone of your document and helps guide your readers through your message. To achieve an effective design, pay careful attention to the following design elements:

> **Consistency**. Throughout each message, be consistent in your use of margins, typeface, type size, and spacing (paragraph indents, between columns, and around photographs). Figure 6–6 violates this rule by using type styles ineffectively and inappropriate bullets. Also be consistent when using recurring design elements, such as vertical lines, columns, and borders. In many cases, you'll want to be consistent not only within a message but also across multiple messages; that way, audiences who receive messages from you recognize your documents and know what to expect.

> **Balance.** To create a pleasing design, balance the space devoted to text, artwork, and white space. Balance is a subjective issue. One document may have a formal, rigid design in which the various elements are placed in a grid pattern, while another has a less formal design in which elements flow more freely across the page—and both could be in balance.

> **Restraint.** Strive for simplicity in design. Don't clutter your message with too many design elements, too much highlighting, too many colours, or too many decorative touches. Let "simpler" and "fewer" be your guiding concepts.

> **Detail.** Pay attention to details that affect your design and thus your message. For example, headings and subheadings that appear at the bottom of a column or a page can annoy readers when the promised information doesn't appear until the next column or page. Also, narrow columns with too much space between words can be distracting.

If you will be designing many documents that go beyond simple memos and reports, consider taking a course in page layout or graphic design to make the most of your creative efforts. However, even without special training, you can make your printed and electronic messages more effective by understanding the use of white space, margins and line justification, typefaces, and type styles.

WHITE SPACE Any space free of text or artwork, whether in print or online, is considered **white space** (note that "white space" isn't necessarily white). These unused areas provide visual contrast and important resting points for your readers. White space includes the open area surrounding headings, margins, vertical space between columns, paragraph indents or extra space between unindented paragraphs, and horizontal space between lines of text. To increase the chance that readers will read your documents, be generous with white space, which makes pages feel less intimidating and easier to read.[8]

White space separates elements in a document and helps guide the reader's eye.

MARGINS AND JUSTIFICATION Margins define the space around your text and between text columns. They're influenced by the way you place lines of type, which can be set (1) justified (flush on the left and flush on the right), (2) flush left with a ragged right margin, (3) flush right with a ragged left margin, or (4) centred. Justified type "darkens" your message's appearance, because the uniform line lengths lack the white space created by ragged margins. It also tends to make your message look more formal and less personalized. Justified type is often considered more difficult to read because large gaps can appear between words and because more words are hyphenated (excessive hyphenation is distracting and hard to follow). Even so, many magazines, newspapers, and books use justified type because it can accommodate more text in a given space. These professionally published documents also have an advantage most business communicators don't have: the time and skill needed to carefully adjust character and word spacing in order to eliminate problems caused by justification.

Most business documents use a flush left margin and a ragged right margin.

Flush-left, ragged-right type "lightens" your message's appearance. It gives a document an informal, contemporary feeling of openness. Spacing between words is the same, and only long words that fall at the ends of lines are hyphenated.

Centred type is rarely used for text paragraphs but is commonly used for headings and subheadings. Flush-right, ragged-left type is rarely used in business documents.

TYPEFACES **Typeface** or **font** refers to the physical design of letters, numbers, and other text characters. Most computers offer innumerable choices of fonts or typefaces. Each typeface influences the tone of your message, making it look authoritative or friendly, businesslike or casual, classic or modern, and so on (see Table 6–4). Choose fonts that are appropriate for your message. Most

> Table 6–4 Typeface Personalities: Serious to Casual to Playful

Serif Typefaces (best for text)	Sans Serif Typefaces (best for headlines; some work well for text)	Specialty Typefaces (for decorative purposes only)
Bookman Old Style	Arial	ANNA
Century Schoolbook	**Eras Bold**	Bauhaus
Courier	Franklin Gothic Book	*Edwardian*
Garamond	Frutiger	*Lucida Handwriting*
Rockwell	Gill Sans	Euclid Fraktur
Times Roman	Verdana	**STENCIL**

computers offer dozens of font choices, but most of these are inappropriate for general business usage.

Serif typefaces are commonly used for text; sans serif typefaces are commonly used for headings.

Serif typefaces have small crosslines (called *serifs*) at the ends of each letter stroke. Serif faces such as Times New Roman are commonly used for text; they can look busy and cluttered when set in large sizes for headings or other display treatments. Typefaces with rounded serifs can look friendly; those with squared serifs can look official.

Sans serif typefaces have no serifs (*sans* is French for "without"). Faces such as Helvetica and Arial are ideal for display treatments that use larger type. Sans serif faces can be difficult to read in long blocks of text. They look best when surrounded by plenty of white space—as in headings or in widely spaced lines of brief text (see Figure 6–7).

For most documents, you shouldn't need to use more than two typefaces, although if you want to make captions or other text elements stand out, you can use another font.[9] A sans serif typeface (such as Arial) is a good choice for heads and subheads, and a serif typeface (such as Times New Roman) works well for text and captions. Using too many typefaces clutters the document and can produce an amateurish look (as seen in Figure 6–6).

TYPE STYLES *Type style* refers to any modification that lends contrast or emphasis to type, including boldface, italic, underlining, and other highlighting and decorative styles. Using boldface type for subheads breaks up long expanses of text. You can also boldface isolated words in the middle of a text block to draw more attention to them. However, if you set too many words in boldface, you might create a "checkerboard" appearance within a paragraph, and you will darken the appearance of your entire message, making it look heavy and uninviting.

Use italic type for emphasis. Although italics are sometimes used when irony or humour is intended, quotation marks are usually best for that purpose. Italics can also be used to set off a quote and are often used in captions. Boldface type and italics are most effective when reserved for keywords—those that help readers understand the main point of the text. A good example of using boldface type effectively is found in the document-revision tips listed under the heading "Editing for Clarity and Conciseness" (p. 163). Here the boldface type draws attention to the key tips, followed by a short, regular-typeface explanation of each tip.

Avoid using any type style that inhibits your audience's ability to read your messages.

As a general rule, avoid using any style in a way that slows your audience's progress through the message. For example, underlining or using all uppercase letters can interfere with your reader's ability to recognize the shapes of words, improperly placed boldface or italicized type can slow down your reader, and shadowed or outlined type can seriously hinder legibility.

Ensure that the type size is proportionate to the importance of your message and the space allotted. For most business messages, use a type size of 10 to 12 points for regular text, and 12 to 18 points for headings and subheadings (a point is approximately 1/72 of an inch). Resist the temptation to reduce type size to squeeze in text or to enlarge it to fill up space. Type that is too small is hard to read, whereas extra-large type looks unprofessional. Be particularly careful with small type online; high-resolution computer screens can reduce this type even further, making it extremely difficult to read.

Using Technology to Produce Your Message

The production tools you'll have at your disposal might vary widely, depending on the software and systems you're using. Some IM and email systems offer limited formatting and production capabilities, whereas most word processors now offer some capabilities that rival professional publishing software for many day-to-day business needs. *Desktop publishing* software such as Quark Xpress and Adobe InDesign go beyond word processing with more advanced layout capabilities designed to accommodate photos, technical drawings, and other elements. (Quark and InDesign are used mainly by design professionals.) For online content, Web publishing and blogging systems make it easy to produce great-looking pages quickly. Multimedia production tools such as Microsoft Producer let you combine slides, audio commentary, video clips, and other features into computer-based presentations that once cost thousands of dollars to create.

Learning to use the basic features of your communication tools will help you produce better messages in less time.

No matter what system you're using, become familiar with the basic formatting capabilities. A few hours of exploration on your own or an introductory training course can dramatically improve the production quality of your documents. At a minimum, you'll benefit from being proficient with the following features:

> **Templates and style sheets.** As Chapter 5 notes, you can save a significant amount of time during production by using templates and style sheets. Many companies provide these to their employees to ensure a consistent look and feel for all print and online company documents.

> **Page setup.** Use page setup to control margins, orientation (*portrait* is vertical; *landscape* is horizontal), and the location of *headers* and *footers* (text and graphics that repeat at the top and bottom of every page).

> **Column formatting.** Most business documents use a single column of text per page, but multiple columns can be an attractive format for documents such as newsletters. Columns are also handy to format long lists.

> **Paragraph formatting.** Take advantage of the various paragraph-formatting controls to enhance the look of your documents. You can offset quotations by increasing margin width around a single paragraph, subtly compress line spacing to fit a document on a single page, or use hanging indents to offset the first line of a paragraph.

Paragraph formatting gives you greater control over the look of your documents.

> **Numbered and bulleted lists.** Let your word processor do the busywork of formatting numbered and bulleted lists. It can also automatically renumber lists when you add or remove items, saving you the embarrassment of misnumbered lists.

> **Tables.** Tables are an effective way to display any information that lends itself to rows and columns: calendars, numerical data, comparisons, and so on. Use paragraph and font formatting thoughtfully within tables.

TIPS FOR SUCCESS

" The way you present your information will increase the clarity of your message. Using bold subheadings and indents helps to highlight your points. "

Gina Cuciniello, communication trainer

> **Pictures, text boxes, and objects.** Your word processor probably lets you insert a wide variety of *pictures* (using one of the industry-standard formats such as JPEG or GIF). *Text boxes* are small blocks of text that stand apart from the main text (great for captions, callouts, margin notes, and so on). *Objects* can be anything from a spreadsheet to a sound clip to an engineering drawing. Similarly, blogging systems, wikis, and other Web development tools let you insert a variety of pictures, audio and video clips, and other multimedia elements.

By improving the appearance of your documents, you will improve your readers' impression of you.

Formatting Formal Letters and Memos

Business letters typically have the following elements:
> preprinted letterhead stationery
> date
> inside address
> salutation
> complimentary close
> signature block

Formal business letters usually follow certain design conventions, as the letter in Figure 6–3 illustrates. Most business letters are printed on *letterhead stationery*, which includes the company's name, address, and other contact information. The first thing to appear after the letterhead is the date, followed by the inside address, which identifies the person receiving the letter. Next is the salutation, usually in the form of *Dear Mr.* or *Ms. Last Name.* The message comes next, followed by the complimentary close, usually *Sincerely* or *Cordially.* And last comes the signature block: space for the signature, followed by the sender's printed name and title. Your company will probably have a standard format to follow for letters, possibly along with a template in Microsoft Word or whatever word processor is standard in the organization. For in-depth information on letter formats, see Appendix A: "Format and Layout of Business Documents."

Many companies use a printed form or word processor template for memos.

Like letters, business memos usually follow a preset design, as shown in Figure 6–8. Your employer will probably have a standard format or template for you to use. (Note that in many instances today, most information transmitted by internal memo is now sent via email.)

Most memos begin with a title such as *Memo, Memorandum,* or *Interoffice Correspondence.* Following that are usually four headings: *Date, To, From,* and *Subject.* (*Re:,* short for *Regarding,* is sometimes used instead of *Subject.*) Memos usually don't use a salutation, complimentary close, or signature, although signing your initials next to your name on the *From* line is standard practice in most companies. Bear in mind that memos are often distributed without sealed envelopes, so they are less private than most other message formats.

Proofreading Your Message

Objective 6 Highlight the types of errors to look for when proofreading.

Your credibility is affected by your attention to the details of mechanics and form.

A methodical approach to proofreading will help you find the problems that need to be fixed.

Imagine that you're a quality inspector for a car company. As each car rolls off the assembly line, you ensure that the engine runs properly, the doors close tightly, the paint shines to glossy perfection, and so on. All the work is supposedly final, but you look closely just in case. Your company's reputation is at stake, and you don't want to let a faulty product off the line. Think of proofreading as the quality inspection stage for your documents, as your last chance to ensure that your document is ready to carry your message—and your reputation—to the intended audience.

Look for two types of problems: (1) undetected mistakes from the writing, design, and layout stages and (2) mistakes that crept in during production. For the first category, you can review format and layout guidelines in Appendix A and brush up on writing basics with "*Grammar on the Go.*" The second category

> Figure 6–8 A Typical Business Memo

Uses standard company memo stationery with title indicating that this is a memo

Uses four standard headings for memos

Does not begin with a salutation

Carnival

INTERNAL MEMORANDUM

DATE: June 11, 2010
TO: Lauren Eastman
FROM: Brad Lymans
SUBJECT: Capacity for Carnival Corporation Cruise Ships

Here is the capacity data you requested along with a brief explanation of the figures:

Cruise Brand	Number of Ships	Passenger Capacity	Primary Market
Carnival	15	30,020	North America
Holland America	10	13,348	North America
Costa	7	9,200	Europe
Cunard	2	2,458	Worldwide
Seabourn	6	1,614	North America
Windstar	4	756	North America
Airtours-Sun	4	4,352	Europe
Total	48	61,748	

All passenger capacities are calculated based on two passengers per cabin, even though some cabins can accommodate three or four passengers.

Cruising capacity has grown in recent years, and management expects it to continue because all the major cruise companies are planning to introduce new ships into service. Carnival Corporation will build 18 additional cruise ships over the next five years, increasing the company's passenger capacity by 36,830, which will bring the total to 98,578.

To utilize this new capacity, we must increase our share of the overall vacation market. Keep in mind that demand for cruises may be affected by (1) the strength of the countries where the ships operate; (2) political instability in areas where the ships travel; and (3) adverse incidents involving cruise ships in general.

Please let me know if you have any further questions or need any additional data.

Does not include a complimentary close or a signature block

can include anything from computer glitches such as missing fonts or misaligned page elements to problems with the ink used in printing. Be particularly vigilant with complex documents and complex production processes that involve teams of people and multiple computers. Strange things can happen as files move from computer to computer, especially when a lot of graphics and different fonts are involved. See "Checklist: Proofing Business Messages" for a list of items to review during proofing.

Far from being a casual scan up and down the page (or screen, for online material), proofreading should be a methodical procedure in which you look for specific problems that might occur. Start by reviewing the advice in "Sharpening Your Career Skills: Proofread Like a Pro to Create Perfect Documents" (p. 179). You might also find it helpful to create a checklist of items to review; this can be a handy tool when you need to review one of your own documents or you're asked to review someone else's work.

CHECKLIST Proofing Business Messages

A. Look for writing errors.
- ✔ typographical mistakes
- ✔ misspelled words
- ✔ grammatical errors
- ✔ punctuation mistakes

B. Look for missing elements.
- ✔ missing text sections
- ✔ missing exhibits (drawings, tables, photographs, charts, graphs, online images, and so on)
- ✔ missing source notes, copyright notices, or other reference items

C. Look for design and formatting mistakes.
- ✔ incorrect or inconsistent font selections
- ✔ column sizing, spacing, and alignment

- ✔ margins
- ✔ special characters
- ✔ clumsy line and page breaks
- ✔ page numbers
- ✔ page headers and footers
- ✔ adherence to company standards
- ✔ links (make sure they're active and link to the correct pages)
- ✔ downloadable files (make sure they're stored in the appropriate folder so audiences can access them)

Plan to spend more time proofing documents that are long, complex, and important.

The amount of time you need to spend on proofing depends on both the length and complexity of the document and the situation. A typo in a memo to your team might be forgiven, but a typo in a financial report or a medical file certainly could be serious. As with every task in the writing process, practice helps—you become not only more familiar with what errors to look for but also more skilled in identifying those errors.

Distributing Your Message

Objective 7 Discuss the most important issues to consider when distributing your messages.

With the production finished, you're ready to distribute the message. As with every other aspect of business communication, your options for distribution multiply with every advance in technology. In some cases, the choice is obvious: just hit the Send button in your email program, and your message is on its way. In other cases, such as when you have a 100-page report with full-colour graphics or a complex multimedia presentation, you need to plan the distribution carefully so that your message is received by everyone who needs it—and only those who need it. When planning your distribution, consider the following factors:

Consider cost, convenience, time, security, and privacy when choosing a distribution method.

> **Cost.** Cost won't be a concern for most messages, but for lengthy reports or multimedia production, it might well be. Printing, binding, and delivering reports can be an expensive proposition, so weigh the cost versus the benefits before you decide. If you're trying to land a million-dollar client, spending $1000 on presentation materials could be a wise investment.

> **Convenience.** How much work is involved for you and your audience? Although it's easy to attach a document to an email message, the people on the other end may have trouble receiving it. They may not have access to a printer, might be accessing your message from slow wireless connections or on handheld devices with tiny screens, or might not have the software needed to open your file. If you're sending large files as IM or email attachments, consider a file compression utility such as WinZip or StuffIt to shrink the file first. For

Proofread Like a Pro to Create Perfect Documents

Before you click on "Send" or tote that stack of reports off to the shipping department, make sure your document represents the best possible work you can do. Your colleagues will usually overlook errors in everyday emails, but higher-profile mistakes in messages to outside audiences can damage your company and hinder your career.

Use these techniques from professional proofreaders to help ensure high-quality output:

> **Make multiple passes.** Go through the document several times, focusing on a different aspect each time. The first pass might be to look for omissions and errors in content; the second pass might be to check for typographical, grammatical, and spelling errors; and a final pass could be for layout, spacing, alignment, colours, page numbers, margins, and other design features.

> **Use perceptual tricks.** It's common to disregard transposed letters, improper capitalization, and misplaced punctuation when rereading your own material. Change the way you process the visual information by

1. Reading each page backward, from the bottom to the top (starting at the last word in each line)
2. Placing your finger under each word and reading it silently
3. Making a slit in a sheet of paper that reveals only one line of type at a time
4. Reading the document aloud and pronouncing each word carefully
5. Temporarily reformatting the document so that it looks fresh to your eyes

> **Double-check high-priority items.** Double-check the spelling of names and the accuracy of dates, addresses, and any number that could cause grief if incorrect (such as telling a potential employer that you'd be happy to work for $5000 a year when you meant to say $50 000).

> **Give yourself some distance.** If you have time, set the document aside and proofread it the next day. You will be able to catch your errors with a fresh review.

> **Be vigilant.** Avoid reading large amounts of material in one sitting and don't proofread when you're tired.

> **Stay focused.** Concentrate on what you're doing. Block out distractions and focus as completely as possible on your proofreading task.

> **Review complex electronic documents on paper.** Some people have trouble proofreading web pages, online reports, and other electronic documents on-screen. If you have trouble, try to print the materials so you can review them on paper.

> **Take your time.** Quick proofreading is not careful proofreading.

CAREER APPLICATIONS

1 Why is it so valuable to have other people proofread your documents?
2 Proofread the following sentence:
   aplication of thse methods in stores in Vancouver nd Winnipeg have resultted in a 30 drop in roberies an a 50 percent decling in violnce there, acording ot thedevelpers if the securty sytem, Hanover brothrs, Inc.

extremely large files, see whether your audience would prefer a CD-ROM instead.

> **Time.** How soon does the message need to reach the audience? Don't waste money on overnight delivery if the recipient won't read the report for a week.

> **Security and privacy.** The convenience offered by IM, email, blogs, and other technologies needs to be weighed against security and privacy concerns. For the most sensitive documents, your company will probably restrict both the people who can receive the documents as well as the means you can use to distribute them. In addition, most computer users are wary of opening attachments these days. Instead of sending Word files (which might be vulnerable to macro viruses and other risks), consider converting your Word documents to PDF files that can be viewed using Adobe Reader.

Chapter 7 offers more advice on distributing podcasts, blogs, and other messages in electronic formats.

Summary of Learning Objectives

1 Discuss the value of careful revision, and list the main tasks involved in completing a business message. Careful revision will produce a correctly written and professional document that will impress your readers and help them in their own tasks. Revision consists of (1) evaluating content and organization; (2) reviewing style and readability; and (3) proofreading the final version after it has been produced.

2 Explain four writing techniques you can use to improve the readability of your messages. You can help your reader easily comprehend your messages by (1) varying sentence length, which will make your message compelling by adding variety and highlighting specific ideas; (2) keeping paragraphs short to medium length to create an inviting document; (3) using headings and subheadings to guide the reader through your message and attract attention; and (4) using bullets and lists, which will clarify information through highlighting it and create a visually appealing document for complex subjects.

3 Describe the steps you can take to improve the clarity of your writing. Clear writing comes with careful and methodical revision. As you clarify your message, you should divide overly long sentences to tighten your writing and rewrite hedging sentences to sound confident. Use parallelism to highlight related ideas and correct dangling modifiers so that your meaning is accurate. Reword long noun sequences and replace camouflaged verbs to be concise. Clarify sentence structure and awkward references to enhance readability and avoid confusion. Moderate your enthusiasm to maintain your credibility.

4 Discuss why it's important to make your message more concise, and give four tips on how to do so. Businesspeople are more likely to read documents that give information efficiently. To make business messages more concise, include only necessary material and write clean sentences by (1) deleting unnecessary words and phrases; (2) shortening overly long words and phrases; (3) eliminating redundancies; and (4) recasting *It is* and *There are* starters.

5 Explain how design elements help determine the effectiveness of your documents. When selecting and applying design elements, ensure their effectiveness by being consistent throughout your document; balancing space between text, art, and white space; showing restraint in the number of elements you use; and paying attention to every detail. White space provides contrast and gives readers a resting point. Margins define the space around the text and contribute to the amount of white space. Headings and captions invite readers to become involved in the message. Fonts influence the tone of the message. Font styles provide contrast or emphasis.

6 Highlight the types of errors to look for when proofreading. When proofreading the final version of your document, always look for errors in grammar, usage, and punctuation and watch for spelling mistakes and typos. Ensure that nothing is missing, such as a source note, figure, text, or exhibit. Check for design errors, such as elements that appear in the wrong font, misaligned elements (e.g., columns in a table or figures on a page), and formatting mistakes (including uneven spacing between lines and words and incorrect line breaks). Finally, ensure that your layout conforms to company guidelines.

7 Discuss the most important issues to consider when distributing your messages. Keep in mind cost, convenience, time, security, and privacy when distributing your message. Balance cost versus benefits when selecting your distribution method for long documents, because printing, binding, and delivering long reports can be expensive. Choose a method that works best for your audience; some people might be using slow wireless connections or devices with small screens. Furthermore, ensure that your reader needs your document immediately to justify an expensive delivery method (e.g., overnight express). Finally, use secure transmission methods for sensitive documents, follow company guidelines for recipients, and use Adobe PDF instead of Word files to avoid viruses.

PEARSON
mycanadianbuscommlab

Visit www.mycanadianbuscommlab.ca for everything you need to help you succeed in the job you've always wanted! Tools and resources include the following:
– Composing Space and Writer's Toolkit
– Document Makeovers
– Video Case Studies
– Grammar Exercises—and much more!

On the Job PERFORMING COMMUNICATION TASKS AT FREE THE CHILDREN

The Free the Children website is a key communication medium for promoting the organization's programs to improve the lives of children around the world. As a recently hired volunteer in the Toronto office, you think that Free the Children should introduce audio podcasts to its site so visitors can download information and listen to it whenever they wish. You are now editing a draft of your report and need to resolve these communication situations.

1 The popularity of podcasts keeps on growing. You believe that if Free the Children posted podcasts created by volunteers who describe their experiences, more young people would be attracted to volunteering at the organization. Which of the following sentences is the best way to suggest this opportunity?

  a In just a few short years, podcasts have developed into an extremely popular communication medium, allowing anyone to create Web content for downloading on computers and MP3 players.

  b Podcasting can be audio and video, and people can find podcasts by visiting a specific organization or company or a site such as http://podcastalley.com.

  c Podcasting has grown as a way for non-profit organizations to generate interest in their activities.

  d We're going to be extremely sorry if we don't get into podcasting.

2 Like all staff at Free the Children, the communications coordinator is extremely busy, with limited time to devote to reading reports and other business documents. You've learned that headings and subheadings are an effective way to get your points across, even if your reader does nothing more than skim through one of your reports. Which is the most effective subheading to head the section about the benefits of podcasting?

  a The Explosion of Podcasting as a Communication Tool

  b The Podcasting Appeal: Attracting Volunteers through Education and Fun

  c Podcasting Appeals to Many Young Internet Surfers

  d The Great Opportunity in Podcasting on the Free the Children Website

3 You want the communications coordinator to get a real feel for podcasting, so you decide to enhance the electronic version of your report with multimedia. Which is the best way to go beyond your text to show the reader the potential of podcasting?

  a Add a sound clip with you talking about Free the Children so that the reader understands the immediacy of a podcast.

  b Include a link to the Center for Creative Leadership on iTunes U to help the reader understand how podcasts can transmit a wide variety of content about Free the Children.

  c Include a link to the podcast section in Wikipedia to give the reader a good understanding of how podcasts work.

  d Include a PowerPoint presentation that you've created about podcasting.

Test Your Knowledge

1 Why should you take care to revise messages before sending them?

2 What are the pros and cons of readability indexes?

3 How can you improve the readability of your messages?

4 How do readers benefit from white space and headings?

5 What is parallel construction? Why is it important?

6 When should you use numbered lists? Bulleted lists?

7 What are some ways you can make a document more concise?

8 What are the benefits and shortcomings of using technology to revise your messages?

9 When should you use email to distribute your messages?

10 Why are typeface and type styles important considerations when producing your messages?

Apply Your Knowledge

1 Why is it helpful to let a first draft "age" for a while before you begin the editing process?

2 Given the choice of only one, would you prefer to use a grammar-checker or a spell-checker? Why?

3 When you design a formal business letter, which design elements do you have to consider? Which are optional?

4 Which distribution method would you choose for a highly confidential strategic planning report that needs to be sent to top executives at six locations in North America, Asia, and Europe? Explain your choice.

5 **Ethical Choices** What are the ethical implications of murky, complex writing in a document explaining how customers can appeal the result of a decision made in the company's favour during a dispute?

Running Cases

●—[Watch on mycanadianbuscommlab

> CASE 1 Noreen

Petro-Go has just merged with Best Gas, and has consequently nearly doubled in size. Many staff positions have changed and will continue to change. New staff positions will become available, and others will be reassigned. Noreen has applied for and received a promotion and is now the manager of the "Go Points" team. Until a manager is assigned to the "Collections" team, Noreen has been asked to take on the acting manager role until further notice.

Noreen is asked to create a memo that will be sent to all employees of both companies informing them of the merger. There will be changes in procedures and job assignments once upper-level management determines the most effective way to handle business in this larger form. In the meantime, there is a temporary management hierarchy in place for reporting purposes.

QUESTIONS

a) What decisions will have to be made?

b) What information will have to be gathered before Noreen begins?

c) If the memo is not proofread carefully and there are errors in it, could it affect company image? How?

d) What is the best way to distribute the memo?

e) What design elements will need to be considered?

YOUR TASK

Create the memo to all employees. Apply the skills you have learned in Chapters 4, 5, and 6.

> CASE 2 Kwong

Kwong's manager at Accountants For All was very impressed with the promotional letter Kwong sent to all past customers. He has asked Kwong to revise the letter for a promotional flyer that will reach new customers. The plan is to deliver the flyer to local businesses as well as several hundred homes in the area. Kwong's manager hopes to increase new business by building credibility, emphasizing competitive prices and mentioning promotions for repeat customers, seniors, students, and families of four or more.

QUESTIONS

a) What must Kwong consider with regard to the layout or format of the flyer, graphics and fonts, sentence length and language?

b) What company contact information should Kwong include?

c) What type of company image is Kwong trying to portray?

d) How should Kwong have the flyer distributed?

e) What should Kwong look for when proofreading the flyer? Should Kwong request that another colleague also proofread the flyer?

YOUR TASK

Create the flyer from Accountants For All. Apply the skills you have learned in Chapters 4, 5, and 6.

Practise Your Knowledge

Read the following documents, and then (1) analyze the strengths and weaknesses of each sentence and (2) revise each document so that it follows the guidelines in Chapters 4 to 6.

DOCUMENT 6.A

The move to our new offices will take place over this coming weekend. For everything to run smooth, everyone will have to clean out their own desk and pack up the contents in boxes that will be provided. You will need to take everything off the walls too, and please pack it along with the boxes.

If you have a lot of personal belongings, you should bring them home with you. Likewise with anything valuable. I do not mean to infer that items will be stolen, irregardless it is better to be safe than sorry.

On Monday, we will be unpacking, putting things away, and then get back to work. The least amount of disruption is anticipated by us, if everyone does their part. Hopefully, there will be no negative affects on production schedules, and current deadlines will be met.

DOCUMENT 6.B

For delicious, air-popped popcorn, please read the following instructions: The popper is designed to pop 1/2 cup of popcorn kernels at one time. Never add more than 1/2 cup. A half cup of corn will produce three to four quarts of popcorn. More batches may be made separately after completion of the first batch. Popcorn is popped by hot air. Oil or shortening is not needed for popping corn. Add only popcorn kernels to the popping chamber. Standard grades of popcorn are recommended for use. Premium- or gourmet-type popping corns may be used. Ingredients such as oil, shortening, butter, margarine, or salt should never be added to the popping chamber. The popper, with popping chute in position, may be preheated for two minutes before adding the corn. Turn the popper off before adding the corn. Use electricity safely and wisely. Observe safety precautions when using the popper. Do not touch the popper when it is hot. The popper should not be left unattended when it is plugged into an outlet. Do not use the popper if it or its cord has been damaged. Do not use the popper if it is not working properly. Before using the first time, wash the chute and butter/measuring cup in hot soapy water. Use a dishcloth or sponge. Wipe the outside of the popper base. Use a damp cloth. Dry the base. Do not immerse the popper base in water or other liquid. Replace the chute and butter/measuring cup. The popper is ready to use.

DOCUMENT 6.C

Visit www.mycanadianbuscommlab.ca, click on the Business Communication tab, then select Textbook Resources and download Document 6.C. After analyzing and revising it, modify the formatting of the document so that its visual tone matches the tone of the message.

Dear Ms. Giraud:

Enclosed herewith please find the manuscript for your book, Careers in Woolgathering. After perusing the first two chapters of your 1500-page manuscript, I was forced to conclude that the subject matter, handicrafts and artwork using wool fibres, is not coincident with the publishing program of Framingham Press, which to this date has issued only works on business endeavours, avoiding all other topics completely.

Although our firm is unable to consider your impressive work at the present time, I have taken the liberty of recording some comments on some of the pages. I am of the opinion that any feedback that a writer can obtain from those well versed in the publishing realm can only serve to improve the writer's authorial skills.

In view of the fact that your residence is in the Montreal area, might I suggest that you secure an appointment with someone of high editorial stature at McGill-Queen's University Press, which I believe might have something of an interest in works of the nature you have produced.

Wishing you the best of luck in your literary endeavours, I remain

Arthur J. Cogswell

Editor

Exercises

6.1 Message Readability: Writing Paragraphs

Rewrite the following paragraph to vary sentence length and to shorten the paragraph so it looks more inviting to readers.

Although major league hockey remains popular, more people are attending women's league hockey games because they can spend less on admission, snacks, and parking and still enjoy the excitement of Canada's pastime. British Columbia has the Vancouver Griffins, the Richmond Steelers, and the North Island Eagles; Quebec has Laval Mistral and Montreal Wingstar; southern Ontario has the Toronto Sting, the Beatrice Aeros, and the Brampton Thunder. These teams play in relatively small arenas, so fans are close enough to see and hear everything, from the smack of the stick hitting the puck to the crash of a body check. Best of all, the cost of a family outing to see rising stars play in a local women's league game is just a fraction of what the family would spend to attend a major league game in a much larger, more crowded arena.

6.2 Message Readability: Using Bullets

Rewrite the following paragraph using a bulleted list:

Our forensic accounting services provide the insights needed to resolve disputes, recover losses, and manage risk intelligently. One of our areas of practice is insurance claims accounting and preparation services, designed to help you maximize recovery of insured value. Another practice area is dispute advisory, in which we can assist with discovery, expert witness testimony, and economic analysis. A third practice: construction consulting. This service helps our clients understand why large-scale construction projects fail to meet schedule or budget requirements. Fourth, we offer general investigative and forensic accounting services, including fraud detection and proof of loss analysis.[10]

6.3 Revising Messages: Clarity

Divide these sentences into shorter ones by adding more periods:

a. The next time you write something, check your average sentence length in a 100-word passage, and if your sentences average more than 16 to 20 words, see whether you can break up some of the sentences.

b. Don't do what the village blacksmith did when he instructed his apprentice as follows: "When I take the shoe out of the fire, I'll lay it on the anvil, and when I nod my head, you hit it with the hammer." The apprentice did just as he was told, and now he's the village blacksmith.

c. Unfortunately, no gadget will produce excellent writing, but using a readability index gives us some guideposts to follow for making writing easier to read because it reminds us to use short sentences and simple words.

d. Know the flexibility of the written word and its power to convey an idea, and know how to make your words behave so that your readers will understand.

e. Words mean different things to different people, and a word such as *block* may mean city block, butcher block, engine block, auction block, or several other things.

6.4 Revising Messages: Conciseness

Cross out unnecessary words in the following phrases:

a. consensus of opinion
b. new innovations
c. long period of time
d. at a price of $50
e. still remains

6.5 Revising Messages: Conciseness

Revise the following sentences, using shorter, simpler words:

a. The antiquated calculator is ineffectual for solving sophisticated problems.

b. It is imperative that the pay increments be terminated before an inordinate deficit is accumulated.

c. There was unanimity among the executives that Ms. Hassan's idiosyncrasies were cause for a mandatory meeting with the company's personnel director.

d. The impending liquidation of the company's assets was cause for jubilation among the company's competitors.

e. The expectations of the president for a stock dividend were accentuated by the preponderance of evidence that the company was in good financial condition.

6.6 Revising Messages: Conciseness

Use infinitives as substitutes for the overly long phrases in these sentences:

a. For living, I require money.

b. They did not find sufficient evidence for believing in the future.

c. Bringing about the destruction of a dream is tragic.

6.7 Revising Messages: Conciseness

Rephrase the following in fewer words:

a. in the near future
b. in the event that
c. in order that
d. for the purpose of
e. with regard to
f. it may be that
g. in very few cases
h. with reference to
i. at the present time
j. there is no doubt that

6.8 Revising Messages: Conciseness

Condense these sentences to as few words as possible:

a. We are of the conviction that writing is important.

b. In all probability, we're likely to have a price increase.

c. Our goals include making a determination about that in the near future.

d. When all is said and done at the conclusion of this experiment, I'd like to summarize the final windup.

e. After a trial period of three weeks, during which time she worked for a total of 15 full working days, we found her work was sufficiently satisfactory, so we offered her full-time work.

6.9 Revising Messages: Modifiers

Remove all the unnecessary modifiers from these sentences:

a. Tremendously high pay increases were given to the extraordinarily skilled and extremely conscientious employees.

b. The union's proposals were highly inflationary, extremely demanding, and exceptionally bold.

6.10 Revising Messages: Hedging

Rewrite these sentences so that they no longer contain any hedging:

a. It would appear that someone apparently entered illegally.

b. It may be possible that sometime in the near future the situation is likely to improve.

c. Your report seems to suggest that we might be losing money.

d. I believe Caitlyn apparently has somewhat greater influence over employees in the accounting department.

e. It seems as if this letter of resignation means you might be leaving us.

6.11 Revising Messages: Indefinite Starters
Rewrite these sentences to eliminate the indefinite starters:

a. There are several examples here to show that Elaine can't hold a position very long.

b. It would be greatly appreciated if every employee would make a generous contribution to Mildred Cook's retirement party.

c. It has been learned in Ottawa today from generally reliable sources that an important announcement will be made shortly by the Prime Minister's Office.

d. There is a rule that states that we cannot work overtime without permission.

e. It would be great if you could work late for the next three Saturdays.

6.12 Revising Messages: Parallelism
Present the ideas in these sentences in parallel form:

a. Mr. Luzon is expected to lecture three days a week, to counsel two days a week, and must write for publication in his spare time.

b. She knows not only accounting, but she also reads Latin.

c. Both applicants had families, university degrees, and were in their thirties, with considerable accounting experience but few social connections.

d. This book was exciting, well written, and held my interest.

e. Don is both a hard worker and he knows bookkeeping.

6.13 Revising Messages: Awkward References
Revise the following sentences to delete the awkward references:

a. The vice-president in charge of sales and the production manager are responsible for the keys to 34A and 35A, respectively.

b. The keys to 34A and 35A are in executive hands, with the former belonging to the vice-president in charge of sales and the latter belonging to the production manager.

c. The keys to 34A and 35A have been given to the production manager, with the aforementioned keys being gold embossed.

d. A laser printer and an inkjet printer were delivered to John and Megan, respectively.

e. The walnut desk is more expensive than the oak desk, the former costing $300 more than the latter.

6.14 Revising Messages: Dangling Modifiers
Rewrite these sentences to clarify the dangling modifiers:

a. Running down the railroad tracks in a cloud of smoke, we watched the countryside glide by.

b. Lying on the shelf, Ruby saw the seashell.

c. Based on the information, I think we should buy the property.

d. Being cluttered and filthy, Sandy took the whole afternoon to clean up her desk.

e. After proofreading every word, the memo was ready to be signed.

6.15 Revising Messages: Noun Sequences
Rewrite the following sentences to eliminate the long strings of nouns:

a. The focus of the meeting was a discussion of the mortgage rate issue.

b. Following the government report recommendations, we are revising our job applicant evaluation procedures.

c. The production department quality assurance program components include employee training, supplier cooperation, and computerized detection equipment.

d. The supermarket warehouse inventory reduction plan will be implemented next month.

e. The MacDonald McKenzie University business school graduate placement program is one of the best in the country.

6.16 Revising Messages: Sentence Structure
Rearrange the following sentences to bring the subjects closer to their verbs:

a. Trudy, when she first saw the bull pawing the ground, ran.

b. It was Terri who, according to Ted, who is probably the worst gossip in the office (Tom excepted), mailed the wrong order.

c. William Oberstreet, in his book *Investment Capital Reconsidered*, writes of the mistakes that bankers through the decades have made.

d. Anya Federov, after passing up several sensible investment opportunities, despite the warnings of her friends and family, invested her inheritance in a jojoba plantation.

e. The president of U-Stor-It, which was on the brink of bankruptcy after the warehouse fire, the worst tragedy in the history of the company, prepared a press announcement.

6.17 Revising Messages: Camouflaged Verbs
Rewrite each sentence so that the verbs are no longer camouflaged:

a. Adaptation to the new rules was performed easily by the employees.

b. The assessor will make a determination of the tax due.

c. Verification of the identity of the employees must be made daily.

d. The board of directors made a recommendation that Mr. Rossini be assigned to a new division.

e. The auditing procedure on the books was performed by the vice-president.

6.18 Producing Messages: Design Elements

Review a copy of the syllabus your instructor provided for this course. Which design elements were used to improve readability? Can you identify ways to make the document easier to read or more user-friendly in general? Create your own version, experimenting with different design elements and design choices. How do your changes affect readability? Exchange documents with another student and critique each other's work.

6.19 Web Design: Readability

Visit the Business News Network website at www.bnn.ca and evaluate the use of design in presenting the network's programs and features. What design improvements can you suggest to enhance readability of the information posted on this page?

6.20 Teamwork: Peer Review

Team up with another student and exchange your revised versions of Document 6.A, 6.B, or 6.C (see exercises under "Practise Your Knowledge"). Review the assignment to ensure that the instructions are clear. Then read and critique your teammate's revision to see whether it can be improved. After you have critiqued each other's work, take a moment to examine the way you expressed your comments and how you felt listening to the other student's comments. Can you identify ways to improve the critiquing process in situations such as this?

6.21 Proofreading Messages: Email

Proofread the following email message and revise it to correct any problems you find:

Our final company orrientation of the year will be held on Dec. 20. In preparation for this sesssion, please order 20 copies of the Policy handbook, the confindentiality agreenemt, the employee benefits Manual, please let me know if you anticipate any delays in obtaining these materials.

6.22 Ethical Choices: Message Distribution

Three of your company's five plants exceeded their expense budgets last month. You want all the plants to operate within their budgets from now on. You want to use email to let all five managers see the memo you're sending to the managers of the three over-budget plants. Is this a good idea? Why or why not?

Crafting Messages for Electronic Media

After studying this chapter, you will be able to

1. Compare the strengths and weaknesses of the print and electronic media available for short messages
2. Explain how overuse of email can reduce productivity
3. Identify the qualities of an effective email subject line
4. Identify guidelines for successful instant messaging (IM) in the workplace
5. Describe the role of blogging in business communication today and the importance of understanding your audience, purpose, and scope
6. Explain how to adapt the three-step writing process for podcasts
7. Describe the syndication process, and explain how it helps you distribute blog and podcast content

Communicating at Petro-Canada
EDUCATING CUSTOMERS ON GAS PRICES THROUGH BLOGGING
www.pumptalk.ca

Ask Jon Hamilton why gas prices top the weather as a subject of heated conversation—he'll tell you the industry hasn't communicated effectively about it. As Director of Downstream Communications (the refining and retail side of the business) for Petro-Canada, Hamilton and colleagues blog on pumptalk.ca, Petro-Canada's on-line forum about gasoline pricing, fuel efficiency, and the fuel industry. "Most employees are well-versed in responding to questions about gasoline pricing because, like anyone in the oil and gas industry, they usually get grilled by friends and family at barbecues and weddings," says Hamilton. "That was the inspiration for Pump Talk. Those personal backyard responses are effective because they use plain language and common comparisons to make a point."

The main contributors to Pump Talk (available separately as Pleins gaz for French-speaking readers) are Hamilton, whose focus is gas pricing; Sneh Seetal, who discusses fuel efficiency; and Michael Southern, who explains "how stuff works"— such as the refining process or pump calibration, which ensures that gas is delivered accurately to customers. The writers discuss topics in a conversational tone and use plain language and graphics to clarify technical processes and issues—all in an effort to demystify the rise in gasoline prices and help customers save money. In addition,

Petro-Canada's multiauthor blog, Pump Talk, features articles by employees who write about gas pricing and fuel efficiency in a friendly and clear manner.

two-to-three minute videos featuring Petro-Canada employees discussing carpooling or interviewing people in the street about such matters as the impact of the carbon tax on driving habits personalize Pump Talk and engage readers.

Interactivity is also a characteristic of the blog. Readers are invited to provide feedback, with the advice to "stay on topic" and "refrain from strong language." Another feature is the easy site navigation via "quicklinks," which lead readers directly to Pump Talk archives, specific categories, recent posts, a list of gas price influencers, and efficiency links, such as the Canadian Centre for Energy. Says Hamilton, "We've created an online forum where motorists can find reliable, straightforward information, ask questions, and engage in discussions on topics relevant to them." If you wrote for Pump Talk, how would you analyze its audience? How would you prepare and write your blogs?[1]

Choosing Electronic Media for Brief Messages

Today you have multiple options for sending short messages:
> printed memos
> printed letters
> email messages
> instant messages
> text messages
> blog postings
> podcasts

Petro-Canada's experience with blogging through Pump Talk is just one of many cases in which electronic media are changing business communication. In recent years, the options for sending short business messages have expanded considerably, from traditional printed memos and letters to a variety of electronic formats. When a new communication technology appears, creative businesspeople usually find a way to apply it to business challenges.

You are likely to encounter the following short-message media on the job:

> **Memos and letters.** Printed memos (for internal communication) and letters (for external communication) have been primary communication vehicles for hundreds of years. In many companies, email and other electronic media have largely replaced traditional printed memos. Letters are still used often for external communication, but electronic media are replacing many letters as well. For more on formatting printed letters and memos, see Chapter 6 and Appendix A.

> **Email.** Thanks to its high speed and low cost, email is now a primary medium for most companies. However, as technologies continue to evolve and users tire of fighting the flood of spam, viruses, and other problems related to email, this medium is in turn being replaced in many instances by instant messaging, blogging, wikis (see Chapter 2), and other tools that provide better support for instant communication and real-time collaboration.

> **Instant messaging (IM).** After consumers around the world began to adopt IM as a faster and simpler alternative to email, businesses followed; computer-based IM usage now rivals email in many companies. IM offers even greater speed than email as well as simple operation and—so far at least—fewer problems with unwanted messages or security and privacy problems.

Text messaging is taking off as an advertising and customer communication medium. What guidelines do you consider when you prepare text messages? How will you adapt your approach to text messaging to business situations?

> **Text messaging.** Phone-based text messaging offers the near-instantaneous communication of IM, with the added advantage of almost universal portability. Of course, small screen sizes and miniature keyboards on most phone devices make text messaging somewhat less convenient than computer-based IM. Text messaging is just beginning to make inroads into business communication, with marketing messages being one of the first applications.[2]

> **Blogs.** From internal communication among small teams to executive blogs with thousands of readers, blogs are now common in business communication. The ability to update content quickly and easily makes blogs a natural medium when communicators need to get messages out in a hurry; bloggers can also publish information to vast audiences with relatively little effort.

> **Microblogs.** Communicating using a strictly limited number of characters is a challenge, but microblogging has become a popular vehicle for internal communication. While you are probably most familiar with the social network site Twitter, which restricts message length to 140 characters, you might use such private work network sites as yammer (www.yammer.com) or present.ly (www.presentlyapp.com) to share information with colleagues through succinct notes.

> **Podcasts.** You may be familiar with podcasts as the online equivalent of recorded radio or video broadcasts (video podcasts are often called *vidcasts* or *vodcasts*). Businesses are now using podcasts to replace or supplement conference calls, training courses, and other communication activities. Any device capable of playing an audio or video file, including computers, PDAs, and many phones, can play podcasts. Podcasts offer a simple way for anyone to publish audio or video messages. They do require somewhat more work to create than blogs, and high-quality podcasts require a modest set of specialized equipment and plenty of network bandwidth.

Carleton University in Ottawa reaches students all over the world with its lecture vodcasts. How do educational vodcasts compare with live, face-to-face lectures? What are the benefits? The disadvantages?

When considering the various electronic media now available, it's important to recognize that they are more than just new tools in your communication toolkit. Because they (a) make it easy for almost anyone to communicate with a global audience, (b) usually provide a quick and effortless way for audiences to respond to messages, and (c) are easy to forward and link all over the internet, electronic media are changing the very nature of business communication. Customers are no longer content to be passive listeners in a one-way process controlled by business. They now expect to be active participants in a real conversation—and not only with companies but with other customers. Blogs, podcasts, bookmarking and tagging sites (such as Delicious and Digg), photo- and video-sharing sites (such as Flickr and YouTube), wikis, and other electronic tools should be viewed as **social media,** in which all participants can contribute to the conversation.[3] Today's smart companies are learning how to adapt their communication efforts to this new media landscape and to welcome customers' participation.

However, while most of your business communication is likely to be via electronic means, don't automatically dismiss the benefits of printed messages. Here are several situations in which you should use a printed message over electronic alternatives:

> **When you want to make a formal impression.** For special messages, such as sending congratulations or condolences, the formality of printed documents usually makes them a much better choice than electronic messages.

Objective 1 Compare the strengths and weaknesses of the print and electronic media available for short messages.

Consider using printed messages when you want to create a more formal impression, to accompany other physical material, to stand out from electronic messages, or when you are legally or contractually required to do so.

> **When you are legally required to provide information in printed form.** Business contracts and government regulations sometimes require that information be provided on paper. The laws that cover such disclosures continue to evolve, so make sure you consult with your firm's legal staff if you're not sure.

> **When you want to stand out from the flood of electronic messages.** Ironically, the rapid growth of electronic messages creates an opportunity for printed memos and letters. If your audience's computers are overflowing with email, IM, and newsfeeds, a printed message could stand out enough to get noticed.

Obviously, if your audience doesn't have access to electronic media or you don't have the necessary email or IM addresses, you'll also need to use a printed message.

The following sections offer advice on using email, IM, blogging, and podcasting for business communication.

Creating Effective Email Messages

You already have experience using email, but email in the workplace is a more formal medium than you are probably accustomed to for personal communication. Consequently, it's important to approach email as a professional communication medium and an important company resource, as explained in the following section.

Treating Email as a Professional Communication Medium

Business email messages are more formal than the email messages you send to family and friends.

The most important single point to recognize about email in the workplace is that the nature of business email is dramatically different from that of personal email. The expectations of writing quality are higher, and the consequences of bad writing or poor judgment in the use of email can be much more serious. For example, email and other electronic documents have the same legal weight as printed documents. In numerous instances in recent years, email and other electronic message forms have been used as evidence in lawsuits and criminal investigations involving everything from sexual harassment to financial fraud.[4] (See Using the Power of Technology: Caution! Email Can Bite, p. 191.)

Email presents considerable legal hazards, and many companies have formal email policies.

Legal hazards are only one of the serious risks that email presents. Other concerns include the possibility of disclosing confidential information and exposing company networks to security problems. To minimize the potential for trouble, many companies now have formal email policies that specify how employees can use email, including restrictions against using company email service for personal messages and sending material that might be deemed objectionable. More than one-quarter of U.S. employers have terminated employees for misuse of company email systems, according to one survey.[5] In addition, roughly the same percentage of employers now monitor internal email, and half of them monitor external email. This monitoring can involve both automated scans using software programmed to look for sensitive content and manual scans in which security staff actually read selected email messages.[6]

Regardless of formal policies, every email user has a responsibility to avoid actions that could cause trouble, from downloading virus-infected software to sending objectionable photographs. Make sure you understand what your employer expects from you.

USING THE POWER OF TECHNOLOGY

Caution! Email Can Bite

Email messages are created, sent, received, and forwarded in the blink of an eye and at the stroke of a key. Despite its benefits, this quick, efficient method of communication can cause a great deal of trouble for companies.

One of the greatest features—and dangers—of email is that people tend to treat it far more informally than they do other forms of business communication. They think of email as casual conversation and routinely make unguarded comments. Moreover, they are led to believe that "deleting" email destroys it permanently. But that's a dangerous misunderstanding of technology.

Even after you delete an email message, it can still exist on the system's hard drive and backup storage devices at both the sender's and the recipient's locations. Deleting files only signals to the computer that the space required for storing the message is no longer needed. The space is so marked, but the data that occupy it continue to exist until the computer overwrites the space with new data. Thus, deleted messages are recoverable—even though data recovery is an involved and expensive process—and they can be used as court evidence against you. Embarrassing email has played a big role in corporate battles. In the high-profile court battle between the U.S. Justice Department and Microsoft, for instance, email emerged as the star witness. Other cases using email as evidence include claims of sexual harassment, discrimination, employee productivity, information leaks, and more.

So how can companies guard against potential email embarrassment and resulting litigation? Besides restricting the use of email by employees, monitoring employees' email, developing company email policies, and reprimanding or terminating offenders, they can train employees to treat email as any other form of written communication. Perhaps one of the best ways to ensure that employees' messages won't come back to haunt the company is to teach employees that email messages are at least as permanent as, if not more so than, letters and memos.

CAREER APPLICATIONS

1 Why do most people treat email so casually? Explain in an email message to your instructor.

2 What kinds of issues should a company address in an email policy? List and explain at least three items.

Adapting the Three-Step Process for Successful Email

Objective 2 Explain how overuse of email can reduce productivity.

The three-step writing process can help you in all your email messages. With practice, you'll be able to complete the various planning, writing, and completing tasks in a matter of minutes for most—which will be a significant benefit to your career. In addition to the skills you've practised in Chapters 4 through 6, apply the guidelines in the following sections.

Attention to etiquette is vital with email communication.

PLANNING EMAIL MESSAGES The ease of email communication is its greatest strength—and its greatest weakness. Because sending email is so easy, it is often overused and misused. Consequently, attention to email etiquette is essential, and that starts in the planning stage. Many busy professionals now struggle to keep up with the flow of email messages—some report receiving as many as 50 messages an hour from colleagues and clients.[7] The flood of messages from an expanding array of electronic sources can significantly affect employees' ability to focus on their work. You can help keep electronic messages from causing problems in your organization by following the tips in Table 7–1 and these guidelines:

> **Restrict email usage to appropriate content.** In most organizations, email is used for sharing information such as goals, schedules, research, company news, and so on. An electronic message is not the medium for delivering tragic news or for disciplining people. Such messages should be reserved for face-to-face interactions.

> **Avoid sending personal messages at work.** In countless incidents, employees have been dismissed for sending personal email, including messages

TIPS FOR SUCCESS

"Don't read and answer your email all day long. You may get anywhere from a handful to hundreds of emails each day that need to be answered, but they don't need to be answered immediately, interrupting whatever else you're doing. Instead, set aside a particular time each day to review and answer your email. Schedule the hour or whatever time it takes you to answer the volume of email you get, and stick to that schedule as regularly as possible."

Susan Ward, IT consultant and founder of Cypress Technologies

> Table 7–1 Tips for Effective Email Messages

Tip	Why It's Important
When you request information or action, make it clear what you're asking for, why it's important, and how soon you need it; don't make your reader write back for details.	People will be tempted to ignore your messages if they're not clear about what you want or how soon you want it.
When responding to a request, either paraphrase the request or include enough of the original message to remind the reader what you're replying to.	Some businesspeople get hundreds of email messages a day and may need to be reminded what your specific response is about.
If possible, avoid sending long, complex messages via email.	Long messages are easier to read as printed reports or Web content.
Adjust the level of formality to the message and the audience.	Overly formal messages to colleagues are perceived as stuffy and distant; overly informal messages to customers or top executives are perceived as disrespectful.
Activate a signature file, which automatically pastes your contact information into every message you create.	You save the trouble of retyping vital information and ensure that recipients know how to reach you through other means.
Don't let unread messages pile up in your in-basket.	You'll miss important information and create the impression that you're ignoring other people.
Never type in all caps.	ALL CAPS ARE INTERPRETED AS SHOUTING.
Don't overformat your messages with background colours, coloured type, unusual fonts, and so on.	Such messages can be difficult and annoying to read on-screen.
Remember that messages can be forwarded anywhere and saved forever.	Don't let a moment of anger or poor judgment haunt you the rest of your career.
Use the "return receipt requested" feature only for the most critical messages.	This feature triggers a message back to you whenever someone receives or opens your message; many consider this an invasion of privacy.
Make sure your computer has up-to-date virus protection.	One of the worst breaches of "netiquette" is unknowingly infecting other computers because you haven't bothered to protect your own system.
Pay attention to grammar, spelling, and capitalization.	Some people don't think email needs formal rules, but careless messages make you look unprofessional and can annoy readers.
Use acronyms sparingly.	Shorthand such as IMHO (in my humble opinion) and LOL (laughing out loud) can be useful in informal correspondence with colleagues, but don't use them in other messages.

that criticize their company, discuss starting a new business, or mention a new position with another company. Moreover, many companies now archive all email. According to a U.S. study, email represents 92 percent of all business communications, and U.S. and Canadian regulations require that finance-related emails be retained for a specific number of years.[8] Consequently, any ill-considered message you send in a careless moment might live for a long time—whether personal or business related.

> **Respect the chain of command.** In many companies, any employee can email anyone else, including the president and CEO. However, take care that you don't abuse this freedom. For instance, when corresponding with superiors, don't send an email complaint straight to the top just because it's easy to do so. Your email will usually be more effective if you follow the organizational hierarchy and give each person a chance to address the situation in turn.

> **Copy only those employees who need your message.** To avoid cluttering your colleagues' mailboxes and wasting their time, decide who must read your message so that only those who require the information get it. Avoid copying multiple recipients with the *cc* (courtesy copy) function.
> **Pay attention to email hygiene.** *Email hygiene* refers to all the efforts that companies are making to keep email clean and safe—from spam blocking and virus protection to content filtering.[9] Make sure you understand what your employer expects from you, and follow those guidelines. For example, to reduce the chances that spammers can find company email addresses, some companies no longer put employee email addresses on their websites.

Of course, company policies can't cover every aspect of email or every situation. The extraordinary ease of email is also its greatest shortcoming: It's far too easy to send too many needless messages, such as jokes, vacation photos, and material that has been forwarded so many times it has multiple screens full of useless header information. Think twice before you create new messages, and think three times before you forward any. Don't contribute to the problem; let common sense be your guide.

Do your part to stem the flood of email by making sure you don't send unnecessary messages or cc people who don't really need to see particular messages.

WRITING EMAIL MESSAGES Even though email messages may seem temporary, attention to detail is just as important for these documents as for any other type of business writing. Too many people, particularly young professionals accustomed to using electronic media for personal communication, assume that the standards and expectations of business communication don't apply to email. They prepare their work messages with the same general disregard of punctuation, grammar, spelling, and other conventions that they employ in their personal email.

However, this casual approach fails to consider a number of important factors, all of which can hurt your career.[10] First, haphazard planning and sloppy writing may require less time for writers, but they usually demand *more* time from readers forced to dig the meaning out of misspelled words, confusing sentences, and disjointed paragraphs. Second, people who care about effective communication—a group that includes most senior executives, the people who often decide whether you'll get promoted and how much you'll get paid—often judge the quality of your *work* by the quality of your *writing*. Third, at the click of somebody else's mouse, email messages can travel to places you never imagined, including the CEO's computer screen, a newspaper, a lawyer's office, or any number of websites and blogs. Always assume that whatever you write in an email message could become public knowledge inside or outside the firm.

The guidelines below and in Table 7–1 list a number of other helpful tips to ensure your email messages fulfill their purpose and establish you as a knowledgeable professional when using this vital business tool.

> **Follow the PDF approach for single-screen emails.** "PDF" here means "purpose, details, and follow-through."[11] When composing an email, give your purpose in the opening paragraph, the details in the body of the message, and the desired action in the close. By using this method, you help your reader understand your point quickly and respond in a timely manner. Figure 7–1 is an internal email message that uses the PDF approach.
> **Give your messages a single purpose.** Effective emails avoid confusing readers with several purposes. Don't ask your reader to attend a meeting and also congratulate her on surpassing her sales quota in the same email; develop each purpose in separate messages.[12]
> **Make your subject line informative.** The subject line in an email might seem like a minor detail, but it's actually one of the most important parts of every email message because it helps recipients decide which messages to read

Objective 3 Identify the qualities of an effective email subject line.

A poorly written subject line could lead to a message being deleted or ignored.

> Figure 7–1 PDF Structure for Email

Flags message priority as "high."

Uses "reply to" address.

Gives purpose in first paragraph.

Provides details in body in bulleted form.

Seeks follow-through in close.

Contains signature file with sender's contact information.

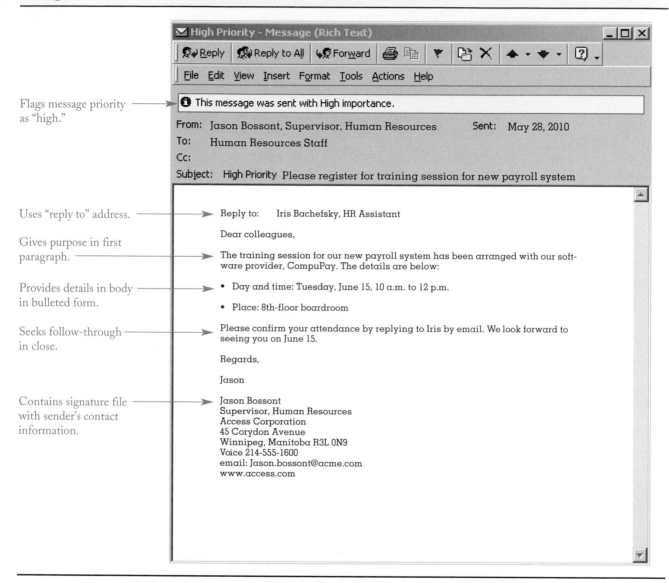

and when to read them. Missing or poorly written subject lines often result in messages being deleted without even being opened. To capture your audience's attention, make sure your subject line is informative and compelling. Go beyond simply describing or classifying your message; use the opportunity to build interest with keywords, quotations, directions, or questions:[13]

Ineffective Subject Line	Effective Subject Line
July sales results	July sales results: good news and bad news
Tomorrow's meeting	Be ready for some tough questions at Friday's meeting
Marketing reports	Marketing reports are due Monday morning
Employee parking	Revised resurfacing schedule for parking lot
Status report	Website redesign is falling behind schedule

Consider the first of these examples. "July sales results" accurately describes the content of the message, but "July sales results: good news and bad news" is more intriguing. Readers will want to know why some news is good and some is bad. "Status report" doesn't even specify which project the report is about, whereas "Website redesign is falling behind schedule" identifies the project and alerts people to a problem.

Also, if you and someone else are replying back and forth based on the same original message, periodically modify the subject line of your message to reflect the revised message content. When numerous messages have identical subject lines, trying to find a particular one can be confusing and frustrating. For instance, if you come up with a solution to the scheduling problem on the website redesign project, modify the subject line to read something like "Website redesign: staffing solution" so that people can find that specific message when they need to.

> **Make your email easy to follow.** Paragraph length, topic sentences, headings and lists, and white space will ensure your message is read. Write short, focused, logically organized paragraphs, and use topic sentences at the beginning of each paragraph to make your email easy to follow. Skip two lines between paragraphs so that each paragraph stands out. By using bulleted or numbered lists (use a hyphen if your reader's email system will not accept graphical bullets) you will also improve the readability of your message. Insert headings for lengthy emails (use capital letters so that headings are distinct) at the top of main sections to make your text easy to review.[14]

> **Keep your emotions under control.** Given the spontaneous nature of email (and other electronic media), you will sometimes need to work hard to keep your emotions from getting the best of you when you're writing. A message that contains insensitive, insulting, or critical comments is called a *flame*. If you're angry, calm down before composing an email message. If you do write an emotionally charged message, let it sit for at least a day and then revise it or even delete it. Ask yourself two questions: First, "Would I say this to my audience face to face?" And second, "Am I comfortable with this message becoming a permanent part of the company's communication history?" Remember that a living, breathing human being is on the receiving end of your communication—and that your message can be forwarded easily and stored forever.

Keep your emotions in check when you compose email messages; *flaming* can damage relationships—and your reputation.

COMPLETING EMAIL MESSAGES The revision, production, and proofing you've studied earlier all apply to email messages. Again, don't let the speed and simplicity of email lull you into thinking that careless writing is acceptable. Particularly for important messages, a few moments of revising and proofing might save you hours of headaches and damage control. Also, lean in favour of simplicity when it comes to producing your email messages. A clean, easily readable font, in black on a white background, is sufficient for nearly all email messages.

Take advantage of your email system's ability to include a *signature* (most corporate systems support this). This is a small text file that is automatically appended to your outgoing messages. Use it to include your full name, job title, company, and contact information. A signature gives your messages a more professional appearance and makes it easy for others to communicate with you through other channels.

When you're ready to distribute your message, pause to verify what you're doing before you click Send. Double-check your addressees to make sure you've included everyone necessary—and no one else. Did you click Reply All when you meant to click Reply? The difference could be embarrassing or even career threatening. Don't include people in the cc (courtesy copy) or bcc (blind courtesy copy) fields unless you know how these features work. (Everyone who receives the message can see who is on the cc line but not who is on the bcc line.) Also, don't set the message priority to "high" or "urgent" unless your message is truly urgent.

To review the tips and techniques for successful email, see "Checklist: Creating Effective Email Messages."

CHECKLIST Creating Effective Email Messages

A. Treat email as a professional communication medium.

✔ Remember that business email is more formal than personal email.

✔ Recognize that email messages carry the same legal weight as other business documents.

✔ Follow company email policy; understand the restrictions your company places on email usage.

✔ Practise good email hygiene by not opening suspicious messages, keeping virus protection up to date, and following other guidelines.

B. Adapt the three-step process for effective email.

✔ Make sure every email you send is necessary.

✔ Don't cc or bcc anyone who doesn't really need to see the message.

✔ Follow the chain of command.

✔ Pay attention to the quality of your writing and use correct grammar, spelling, and punctuation.

✔ Make your subject lines informative by clearly identifying the purpose of your message.

✔ Make your subject lines compelling by wording them in a way that signals their relevance to your audiences.

✔ Update the subject line if you reply to the same message back and forth multiple times.

✔ Follow the PDF approach (purpose, details, and follow-through).

✔ Keep your emotions under control.

✔ Don't mark messages as "urgent" unless they truly are urgent.

Creating Effective Instant Messages and Text Messages

Objective 4 Identify guidelines for successful instant messaging (IM) in the workplace.

IM is taking the place of email for routine communication in many companies.

While email is here to stay as a business medium, its disadvantages—including viruses, spam, and rampant overuse—are driving many people to explore alternatives.[15] One of the most important of those alternatives is **instant messaging (IM).** For both routine communication and exchanges during online meetings, IM is now widely used throughout the business world and is beginning to overtake and even replace email for internal communication in many companies.[16] Business-grade IM systems offer a range of capabilities, including basic chat, *presence awareness* (the ability to quickly see which people are at their desks and available to IM), remote display of documents, video capabilities, remote control of other computers, automated newsfeeds from blogs and websites, and automated bot capabilities (see Chapter 4).[17]

Phone-based text messaging is fast and portable but not as versatile as computer-based IM.

Text messaging is finding applications in business as well. Although both IM and text messaging perform the similar function of nearly instantaneous communication between devices, IM is primarily a computer-based technology, whereas text messaging is primarily a phone-based technology. (Of course, as often happens, continuing innovation blurs the lines between technologies, and now you can send a text message to a phone from your computer and so on.) Text messaging has long been popular in other parts of the world, where it is often referred to as *short messaging service (SMS)* and phones have had texting capability for years. With text messaging now well entrenched among young consumers in North America, expanded business applications are likely to follow. In addition to person-to-person communication between colleagues, text messaging is taking off in such areas as marketing (alerting customers about new sale prices, for example) and entertainment (such as letting viewers predict the outcome of sporting events or place votes on reality television programs).[18]

Because IM is currently more versatile and more widely used in business than text messaging, the following sections focus on IM. However, as text messaging evolves along with wireless devices and networking, you can expect that many of the benefits, risks, and guidelines that pertain to IM will eventually pertain to text messaging as well.

Understanding the Benefits and Risks of IM

The benefits of IM include its rapid response to urgent messages, lower cost than phone calls and email, ability to mimic conversation more closely than email, and availability on a wide range of devices, from PCs to mobile phones to PDAs.[19] In addition, because it more closely resembles real conversation, IM doesn't get misused as a broadcast method as often as email does.[20]

IM offers many benefits:
> rapid response
> lower cost
> ability to mimic conversation
> wide availability

Of course, wherever technology goes, trouble seems to follow. The potential drawbacks of IM include security problems (the risks of computer viruses and the worry that sensitive messages might be intercepted by outsiders), the need for *user authentication* (making sure that online correspondents are really who they appear to be), the challenge of logging messages for later review and archiving, and incompatibility between competing IM systems. Fortunately, with the growth of *enterprise instant messaging (EIM)*, IM systems designed for large-scale corporate use, many of these problems are being overcome. Security remains an ongoing concern, however, with attacks on IM systems, both public and corporate, continuing to rise.[21] A new breed of virus spread by bots is a particular concern. IM users who fall prey to these bots believe they are chatting with a trusted correspondent when in fact they are exchanging information with an automated bot that imitates human IM chat. The bot encourages the user to download a file or otherwise expose his or her computer to malicious software and then spreads the virus through the user's IM address book.[22]

Adapting the Three-Step Process for Successful IM

Although instant messages are often conceived, written, and sent within a matter of seconds, the principles of the three-step process still apply:

> **Planning instant messages.** View every IM exchange as a conversation; while you may not deliberately plan every individual statement you make or question you pose, take a moment to plan the overall exchange. If you're requesting something, think through exactly what you need and the most effective way to ask for it. If someone is asking you for something, consider his or her needs and your ability to meet them before you respond. And although you rarely organize instant messages in the sense of creating an outline, try to deliver information in a coherent, complete way that minimizes the number of individual messages required.

> **Writing instant messages.** As with email, the appropriate writing style for business IM is more formal than the style you may be accustomed to with personal IM or text messaging. You should generally avoid IM acronyms (such as "FWIW" for "for what it's worth" or "HTH" for "hope that helps") except when communicating with close colleagues. In the IM exchange in Figure 7–2, notice how the participants communicate quickly and rather informally but still maintain good etiquette and a professional tone. This style is even more important if you or your staff use IM to communicate with customers and other outside audiences. In the coming years, business IM writing may become less formal, but for now, the best approach is to maintain a businesslike style and tone.

> **Completing instant messages.** One of the biggest attractions of IM is that the completing step is so easy. You don't have to produce the message in the

> Figure 7–2 Instant Messaging for Business Communication

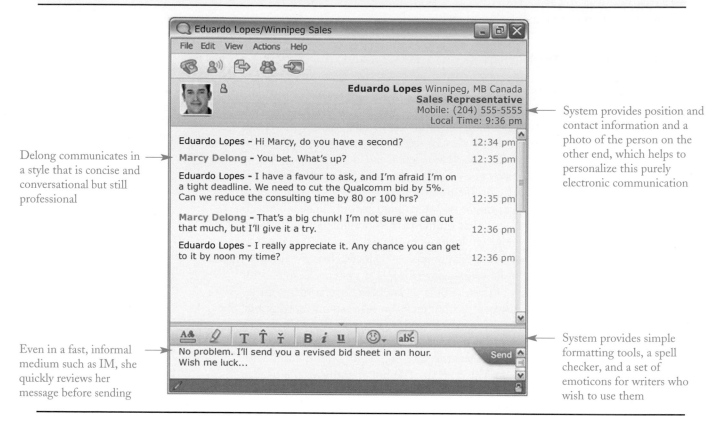

Delong communicates in a style that is concise and conversational but still professional

System provides position and contact information and a photo of the person on the other end, which helps to personalize this purely electronic communication

Even in a fast, informal medium such as IM, she quickly reviews her message before sending

System provides simple formatting tools, a spell checker, and a set of emoticons for writers who wish to use them

usual sense, and distribution is as simple as clicking the Send button. However, don't skip over the revising and proofreading tasks. Quickly scan each message before you send to make sure you don't have any missing or misspelled words and that your message is clear and complete.

When using IM, be aware of the potential for constant interruptions and wasted time.

To use IM effectively, keep in mind some important behavioural issues: the potential for constant interruptions, the ease of accidentally mixing personal and business messages, the risk of being out of the loop (if a hot discussion or an impromptu meeting flares up when you're away from your PC or other IM device), and the "vast potential for wasted time" (in the words of MIT labour economist David Autor). In addition, users are at the mercy of other people's typing abilities, which can make IM agonizingly slow.[23]

Understand the guidelines for successful business IM before you begin to use it.

Regardless of the system you're using, you can make IM more efficient and effective by following these tips:[24]

> Unless a meeting is scheduled, make yourself unavailable when you need to focus on other work.
> If you're not on a secure system, don't send confidential information.
> Be extremely careful about sending personal messages—they have a tendency to pop up on other people's computers at embarrassing moments.
> Don't use IM for important but impromptu meetings if you can't verify that everyone concerned will be available.
> Unless your system is set up for it, don't use IM for lengthy, complex messages; email is better for those.
> Try to avoid carrying on multiple IM conversations at once to minimize the chance of sending messages to the wrong people.
> If your IM system has filters for *spim*, the IM version of email spam, make sure they're active and up to date.[25]

CHECKLIST Using IM Productively

✔ Pay attention to security and privacy issues and be sure to follow all company guidelines.

✔ Treat IM as a professional communication medium, not an informal, personal tool; avoid using IM slang with all but close colleagues.

✔ Maintain good etiquette, even during simple exchanges.

✔ Protect your own productivity by making yourself unavailable when you need to focus.

✔ In most instances, don't use IM for confidential messages, complex messages, or personal messages.

To review the advice for effective IM in the workplace, see "Checklist: Using IM Productively."

Creating Effective Business Blogs

To an extent perhaps unmatched by any other medium, blogs can engage large, widely distributed audiences. In a sense, a blog combines the global reach and reference value of a conventional website with the conversational exchanges of email or IM. Good business blogs pay close attention to several important elements:

> **Communicating with personal style and an authentic voice.** Most business messages designed for large audiences are carefully scripted and written in a "corporate voice" that is impersonal and objective. In contrast, successful business blogs are written by individuals and exhibit their personal style. Audiences relate to this fresh approach and often build closer emotional bonds with the blogger's organization as a result. For instance, Microsoft's Channel 9 video blog, or *vlog* (http://channel9.msdn.com), features online informal video clips in which several of the company's technical experts answer questions and criticisms from software developers. Channel 9 and other employee blogs are credited with helping to repair Microsoft's reputation among software customers.[26]

> **Delivering new information quickly.** Today's blogging tools let you post new material within minutes of writing it or filming it. With the addition of video, blogging becomes a true multimedia experience that gives bloggers an easy way to share sights and sounds with their audiences. In Figure 7–3, Ford Motor Company integrates video blogging with elements of a conventional website. Not only does blogging allow you to respond quickly when needed—such as during a corporate crisis—it also lets your audiences know that an active conversation is taking place. Blogs that don't offer a continuous stream of new and interesting content are quickly ignored in today's online environment.

> **Choosing topics of peak interest to audiences.** Successful blogs cover topics that readers care about. For instance, General Motors's popular FastLane blog (http://fastlane.gmblogs.com) features top executives writing about GM cars and responding to questions and criticisms from car enthusiasts. The people who read the blog and write comments obviously care about cars and want the latest information from GM.[27]

> **Encouraging audiences to join the conversation.** Not all blogs invite comments, although most do. These comments can be a valuable source of news, information, and insights. In addition, the relatively informal nature

Blogs have a unique ability to encourage interaction with a large, geographically dispersed audience.

Most business blogs invite readers to leave comments.

> Figure 7–3 Video Blogging

of blogging seems to make it easier for companies to let their guard down and converse with their audiences. Of course, not all comments are helpful or appropriate, which is why many bloggers review all comments and select the most helpful or interesting ones to post.

Given the unique ability of blogs to convey topical information quickly and in a conversational format, their rapid adoption by businesses in virtually every industry should come as no surprise. The following sections offer an overview of the business applications of blogging, and Table 7–2 offers a number of suggestions for successful blogging.

Understanding the Business Applications of Blogging

Objective 5 Describe the role of blogging in business communication today and the importance of understanding your audience, purpose, and scope.

The business applications of blogs include a wide range of internal and external communication tasks.

Blogs are a potential solution whenever you have a continuing stream of information to share with an online audience—and particularly when you want the audience to have the opportunity to respond. Here are some of the many ways businesses are using blogs:[28]

> **Project management and team communication.** Using blogs is a good way to keep project teams up to date, particularly when team members are

> Table 7–2 Tips for Effective Business Blogging

Tip	Why It's Important
Have a clear plan before you start blogging.	Without a clear plan, your blog is likely to wander from topic to topic without providing compelling information or building a sense of community with your audience.
Post frequently.	The whole point of a blog is fresh material; if you don't have a constant supply of new information or new links, create a traditional website instead.
Make it about your customers and the issues that are important to them.	Readers want to know how your blog will help them, entertain them, or give them a chance to communicate with others who have similar interests.
Write in an authentic voice; never create an artificial character who supposedly writes a blog.	*Flogs*, or fake blogs, violate the spirit of blogging, show disrespect for your audience, and will turn audiences against you as soon as they uncover the truth.
Link generously—but carefully.	Providing interesting links to others' blogs and websites is a fundamental aspect of blogging, but think twice before putting these links in your blog. Make sure the links will be of value to your readers, and make sure they don't point to material that could damage your reputation.
Keep it brief.	Most online readers don't have the patience to read lengthy reports.
Don't post anything you wouldn't want the entire world to see.	Future employers, government regulators, competitors, journalists, and community critics are just a few of the people who might see what you've written. Assume that anything you write will be spread through the online world.
Don't engage in blatant product promotion.	Readers who think they're being advertised to will stop reading.
Take time to write compelling, specific headlines for your postings.	Readers usually decide within a couple of seconds whether to read your postings; boring or vague headlines will turn them away instantly.
Pay attention to spelling, grammar, and mechanics.	No matter how smart or experienced you are, poor-quality writing undermines your credibility with discriminating audiences.
Respond to criticism openly and honestly.	Hiding sends the message that you don't have a valid response to the criticism. If your critics are wrong, patiently explain why you think they're wrong. If they are right, explain how you'll fix the situation.
Listen and learn.	If you don't take the time to analyze the comments people leave on your blog or the comments other bloggers make about you, you're missing out on one of the most valuable aspects of blogging.
Respect intellectual property.	Presenting the work of others as your own is not only unethical but can violate copyright laws.
Be scrupulously honest and careful with facts.	Honesty is an absolute requirement for every ethical business communicator, of course, but you need to be extra careful online because inaccuracies (both intentional and unintentional) are likely to be discovered quickly and shared widely.

geographically dispersed. For instance, the trip reports that employees file after visiting customers or other external parties can be enhanced vividly with *mobile blogs,* or *moblogs.* Thanks to the convenience of camera phones and other multimedia wireless devices, employees on the go can send text, audio, images, and video to their colleagues. Conversely, mobile employees can also stay in touch with their team blogs using handheld devices. In addition, private network *microblogs,* such as yammer, let project teams discuss ideas and share links.

> **Company news.** On a broader scale, companies can use blogs to keep employees informed about general business matters, from facility news to benefit updates. Blogs also serve as online community forums, giving everyone in the company a chance to raise questions and voice concerns.

Moblogs are blogs adapted for display on mobile devices such as phones. What are the ethical concerns regarding moblogs?

Blogs are an ideal medium for viral marketing, the organic spread of messages from one audience member to another.

> **Customer support.** Building on the tradition of on-line customer support forums that have been around since the earliest days of the internet, customer support blogs answer questions, offer tips and advice, and inform customers about new products.

> **Public relations and media relations.** Companies now share consumer tips, company news, and industry trends with both the general public and journalists via their blogs. The "Pump Talk" blog featured at the beginning of the chapter is one example.

> **Recruiting.** Using a blog is a great way to let potential employees know more about your company, the people who work there, and the nature of the company culture.

> **Policy and issue discussions.** Executive blogs in particular provide a public forum for discussing legislation, regulations, and other broad issues of interest to an organization.

> **Crisis communication.** Using blogs is a convenient way to provide up-to-the-minute information during emergencies, correct misinformation, or respond to rumours.

> **Market research.** Blogs can be a clever way to solicit feedback from customers and experts in the marketplace. In addition to using their own blogs for research, today's companies need to monitor blogs that are likely to discuss them, their executives, and their products. Negative product reviews, rumours, and other information can spread across the globe in a matter of hours, and managers need to know what the online community is saying—whether it's positive or negative. *Reputation analysts* such as Evolve24 (www.evolve24.com) have developed ways to automatically monitor blogs and other online sources to see what people are saying about their corporate clients.[29]

> **Brainstorming.** Online brainstorming via blogs offers a way for people to toss ideas around and build on each other's contributions.

> **Viral marketing.** The interconnected nature of the blogosphere makes it a natural vehicle for spreading the word about your company and your products. Bloggers often make it a point to provide links to other blogs and websites that interest them, giving marketers a great opportunity to spread their messages. *Viral marketing* refers to the transmission of messages in much the same way that biological viruses are transmitted from person to person.

> **Email replacement.** As spam filters and message overload make it more difficult to reach people via email, many companies have turned to blogs as a way to distribute information to customers and other audiences. Using *newsfeeds* from a company's blog (see page 207), audiences can subscribe to categories of information that interest them. These messages are then delivered via an *aggregator*, bypassing the increasingly clogged email channel.

> **News syndication.** Blogging also allows both individuals and companies to become publishers of news and other information. Subscribing to a blog's news feed or update service allows you to get the latest news as soon as it's posted. Syndication is explained on pages 207–208.

> Figure 7–4 Elements of an Effective Business Blog

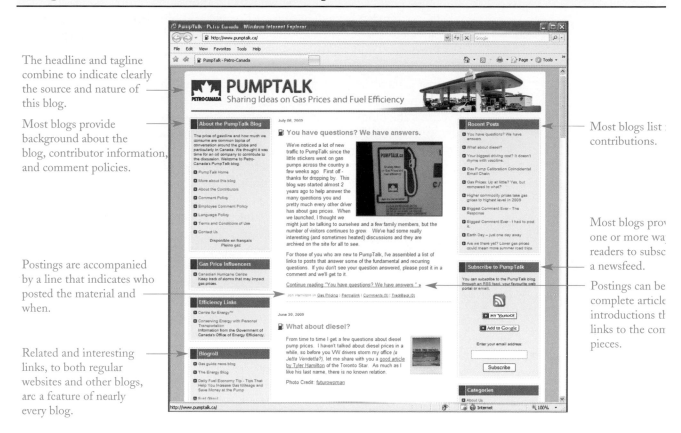

The headline and tagline combine to indicate clearly the source and nature of this blog.

Most blogs provide background about the blog, contributor information, and comment policies.

Postings are accompanied by a line that indicates who posted the material and when.

Related and interesting links, to both regular websites and other blogs, are a feature of nearly every blog.

Most blogs list contributions.

Most blogs provide one or more ways readers to subscribe a newsfeed.

Postings can be complete article introductions th links to the com pieces.

The uses of blogs are limited only by your creativity, so be on the lookout for new ways you can use them to foster positive relationships with colleagues, customers, and other important audiences. As Figure 7–4 shows, blogs exist in many forms and formats, but visitors expect a few basic elements, such as access to archives, links to related information, and a convenient way to subscribe to an automatic newsfeed.

Adapting the Three-Step Process for Successful Blogging

The three-step writing process is easy to adapt to blogging tasks. The planning step is particularly important if you're considering starting a blog because you're planning an entire communication channel, not just a single message. Pay close attention to your audience, your purpose, and your scope:

> **Audience.** Except for team blogs and other efforts with an obvious and well-defined audience, defining your target audience can be a challenge. You want an audience large enough to justify the time you'll be investing but narrow enough that you can provide a clear focus for the blog. For instance, if you

Before you launch a blog, make sure you have a clear understanding of your target audience, the purpose of your blog, and the scope of subjects you plan to cover.

work for a firm that develops computer games, would you focus your blog on "hardcore" players, the type who spend thousands of dollars on super-fast PCs optimized for video games, or would you broaden the reach to include all video gamers? The decision often comes down to business strategy.

> **Purpose.** Unlike a personal blog, in which you typically write about whatever interests you, a business blog needs to have a business-related purpose that is important to your company and to your chosen audience. Moreover, the purpose has to "have legs"—that is, it needs to be something that can drive the blog's content for months or years—rather than focus on a single event or issue of only temporary interest. Petro-Canada's Pump Talk focuses on the long-term issues of gasoline pricing and fuel efficiency—a constant consumer concern. These matters are the *general purpose* of the blog; each posting has a *specific purpose* within the context of that general purpose. Finally, if you are not writing an official company blog but rather blogging as an individual employee, make sure you understand your employer's blogging guidelines. As with email and IM, more and more companies are putting policies in place to prevent employee mistakes with blogging.[30]

> **Scope.** As with your audience, defining the scope of your blog can be a bit tricky. You want to cover a subject area that is broad enough to offer discussion possibilities for months or years but narrow enough to have an identifiable focus. Petro-Canada's Pump Talk blog is about gasoline pricing and fuel efficiency—not Petro-Canada's stock price or core businesses. Moreover, the scope of your blog needs to remain fairly stable so that you can build an audience over time. If you start out discussing product support but then shift to talking about your company's advertising programs, you'll probably lose readers along the way.

After you begin writing your blog (or posting messages to a multiauthor blog that someone else has created), the careful planning needs to continue with each message. Unless you're posting to a restricted-access blog, such as an internal blog on a company intranet, you can never be sure who might see your posts. Other bloggers might link to them months later.

Write blog postings in a comfortable—but not careless—style.

Write in a comfortable, personal style. Bear in mind, though, that *comfortable* does not mean *careless*. Sloppy writing damages your credibility. In addition, while audiences expect you to be knowledgeable in the subject area your blog covers, you don't need to know everything about a topic. If you don't have all the information yourself, provide links to other blogs and websites that supply relevant information. In fact, many blog audiences consider carefully screened links to be an essential part of blogging.

Completing messages for your blog is usually quite easy. Evaluate the content and readability of your message, proofread to correct any errors, and post using your blogging system's tools for doing so. If your blog doesn't already have one, be sure to include one or more *newsfeed* options so that your audience can automatically receive headlines (and summaries, if you choose) of new blog posts (see "Distributing Blog and Podcast Content" on page 207).

"Checklist: Blogging for Business" summarizes some of the key points to remember when creating and writing a business blog, and you can always get updated advice from some of the many blogs and websites dedicated to blogging.

Creating Effective Podcasts

Podcasting can be used to deliver a wide range of audio and video messages.

Podcasting offers a number of interesting possibilities for business communication. Its most obvious use is to replace existing audio and video messages, such as one-way teleconferences in which a speaker provides information without

CHECKLIST Blogging for Business

✓ Consider using a blog whenever you have a continuing stream of information to share with an online audience.

✓ Identify an audience that is broad enough to justify the effort but narrow enough to have common interests.

✓ Identify a purpose that is comprehensive enough to stimulate a continuing stream of posts.

✓ Consider the scope of your blog carefully; make it broad enough to attract an audience but narrow enough to keep you focused.

✓ Communicate with a personal style and an authentic voice but don't write carelessly.

✓ Deliver new information quickly.

✓ Choose topics of peak interest to your audience.

✓ Encourage audiences to join the conversation.

✓ Offer a newsfeed option so that subscribers can get automatic updates.

expecting to engage in conversation with the listeners. Training is another good use of podcasting. One of the first podcasts recorded by technical experts at IBM gave other employees advice on setting up blogs, for example.[31] Sales representatives who travel to meet with potential customers can listen to audio podcasts or view video podcasts to get the latest information on their companies' products. Podcasts are also an increasingly common feature on blogs, letting audiences listen to or watch recordings of their favourite bloggers. New services can even transcribe blogs into podcasts and vice versa.[32]

As more businesspeople become comfortable with podcasting, it should find applications in a variety of new areas, wherever audio or video content can convey business messages effectively. For instance, real estate agents can record audio podcasts that potential homebuyers can listen to while walking through houses. Marketing departments can replace expensive printed brochures with video podcasts that demonstrate new products in action. Human resources departments can offer video tours of their companies to entice new recruits.

Adapting the Three-Step Process for Successful Podcasting

Although it might not seem obvious at first, the three-step writing process adapts quite nicely to podcasting. You've already chosen the medium, so focus the planning step on analyzing the situation, gathering the information you'll need, and organizing your material. One vital planning step depends on whether you intend to create podcasts for limited use and distribution (such as a weekly audio update to your virtual team) or you plan to create a *podcasting channel* with regular recordings on a consistent theme, designed for a wider public audience. As with planning a blog, if you intend to create a podcasting channel, be sure to think through the range of topics you want to address over time to verify that you have a sustainable purpose. If you plan to comment on the stock market or breaking news in your industry, for instance, you'll have a recurring source of topics to discuss. In contrast, if you plan to share marketing ideas for small business owners, make sure you have or can find plenty of ideas over time so that your podcasting efforts don't run out of steam. If you bounce from one theme to another over time, you risk losing your audience.[33]

As you organize and begin to think about the words or images you'll use as content, pay close attention to previews, transitions, and reviews. These steering devices are especially vital in audio and video recordings because these formats lack the "street signs" (such as headings) that audiences rely on in print media. Moreover, scanning back and forth to find specific parts of an audio or video

Objective 6 Explain how to adapt the three-step writing process for podcasts.

Generous use of previews, transitions, and reviews helps podcast audiences follow the thread of your recording.

With a few upgrades beyond a basic computer, you can assemble a studio capable of producing professional-quality podcasts. What elements of vocal delivery do you have to remember when preparing podcasts?

Plan your podcast content carefully; edits are much more difficult to make in podcasts than in textual messages.

message is much more difficult than with textual messages, so you need to do everything possible to make sure your audience successfully receives and interprets your message on the first try.

One of the attractions of podcasting is the conversational, person-to-person feel of the recordings, so unless you need to capture exact wording, speaking from an outline and notes rather than a prepared script is often the best choice. However, no one wants to listen to rambling podcasts that struggle to make a point, so don't try to make up your content on the fly. Effective podcasts, like effective stories, have a clear beginning, middle, and end.

In the completing step, keep in mind that making edits is much more difficult with audio or video than with textual media. Take extra care to revise your script or think through your speaking notes before you begin to record. You don't want to get halfway through the recording process and realize that you should have said something else in the introduction.

Finally, consider integrating your podcasting efforts with a related blog. Not only can you provide additional information, you can use the commenting feature of the blog to encourage feedback from your audience.[34]

Assembling a Podcasting System

The equipment needed to record podcasts depends on the degree of production quality you want to achieve. For the most basic podcasts, such as those you might record for internal audiences, most contemporary personal computers probably have the equipment you need: a low-cost microphone (most laptop computers now have built-in microphones), a sound card to convert the microphone signal to digital format (most computers have them now), and some recording software (free versions are available online). Many handheld digital recorders can also record audio files that you can upload to a PC for editing and distribution.

For basic podcasts, your computer probably has most of the hardware you already need, and you can download recording software.

However, a basic system might not deliver the audio quality or production flexibility you need for a public podcast. For instance, the microphone built into your laptop can't reproduce sound nearly as well as a professional-quality microphone can, and because it's physically located on the computer, the built-in microphone will pick up the noise from the computer's fan. Similarly, the low-cost sound cards built into many computers can add a significant amount of noise to your signal.[35]

For higher-quality podcasts, you'll probably need additional hardware and software.

If you need higher production quality or greater flexibility, you'll need additional pieces of hardware and software, such as an audio processor (to filter out extraneous noise and otherwise improve the audio signal), a mixer (to combine multiple audio or video signals), a better microphone, and more sophisticated recording and editing software (see Figure 7–5). You may also need to improve the acoustics of the room in which you are recording, to minimize echoes, noise, and other problems. To learn more about the technical requirements of podcasting, pick up one of the many new books on the subject. Some of them even come with free recording software.[36]

> Figure 7–5 The Podcasting Process

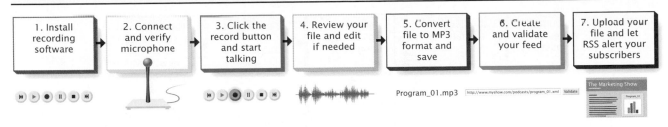

For a quick review of the key points of business podcasting, see "Checklist: Planning and Producing Business Podcasts."

Distributing Blog and Podcast Content

With today's blog and podcast technologies, you can easily reach a vast audience—an audience that can continue to grow if your "fans" spread the word for you. To distribute effectively, get into the mindset of *publishing*, rather than sending, your content.

Objective 7 Describe the syndication process, and explain how it helps you distribute blog and podcast content.

Publishing Your Content

As with newspapers and magazines, blog and podcast publishing requires some action from both the publisher and the subscriber. The publisher creates the content and submits it to a distribution channel, which delivers it to anyone who has chosen to subscribe. This process of publication for blogs and podcasts is often referred to as **syndication**.[37] The publish/subscribe model, shown in Figure 7–6, lets bloggers reach a potentially vast audience and lets audiences automatically acquire fresh content from an unlimited number of sources. As a publisher, you initiate syndication by creating a **feed**, or *newsfeed*, a file that contains information about the items you have written or recorded. In the case of podcasts, the audio or video file is enclosed within the feed file as well. Several formats now exist for these feeds; the most common is known as **RSS**, which is short for *really simple syndication*. (Although this process sounds fairly

Syndication is the process of distributing blog and podcast content via feeds.

CHECKLIST Planning and Producing Business Podcasts

✔ Consider podcasting whenever you have the opportunity to replace existing audio or video messages.

✔ If you plan a podcast channel with a regular stream of new content, make sure you've identified a theme or purpose that is rich enough to sustain your effort.

✔ Pay close attention to previews, transitions, and reviews to help prevent your audience from getting lost.

✔ Decide whether you want to improvise your podcast or speak or film from a written script.

✔ If you improvise, do enough planning and organization to avoid floundering and rambling in search of a point.

✔ Remember that editing is much more difficult to do with audio or video than with textual media and plan your content and recording carefully.

✔ Consider linking your podcast to a blog in order to provide additional information and a forum for audience feedback.

✔ Syndicate your podcast, if appropriate, via RSS enclosures.

> Figure 7–6 The Syndication Process for Blogs

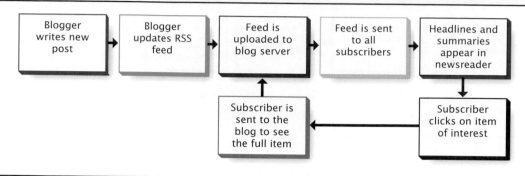

technical, popular blogging and podcasting systems take care of most of the details for you.) The benefit of syndication via an RSS feed is that you have the potential to build up a vast audience over time, provided that you offer compelling content and make that content easy to find.

On the receiving end, audiences subscribe to your content through a piece of software called an **aggregator** or a *newsreader*. (*Aggregating* is simply another word for *collecting*.) Basic aggregators can collect messages with both text and static images, and some aggregators specialize in certain types of media. Aggregators specifically for podcasts are usually called **podcatchers**. Whenever you create a feed for a new blog post or podcast, your subscribers are automatically alerted via the feed. In the case of blogs, aggregators usually display a headline and brief summary of your post. Anyone who wants to read the full item can click on the headline to be directed back to your blog to see the entire post (see Figure 7–7). In the case of podcasts, subscribers can choose to have new podcasts downloaded to their computer or other device automatically, or they can download them manually. For audiences, the key benefit of syndication is automatically collecting interesting content from many sources in a variety of formats. In a sense, it's like creating personal versions of the Internet.

> Aggregators automatically collect information about new blog postings and podcasts.

Connecting with Audiences

> Adding feed capability is the most important step in staying connected with your blog or podcast audiences.

This publish/subscribe process generally works nicely when publishers and subscribers take the necessary steps to send and receive content. Of course, both parties need to find each other in the first place. This connection can happen in a variety of ways. The most fundamental step for blog publishers is to add the feed capability to their blogs so that interested audiences can easily subscribe through their aggregators. Bloggers and podcasters can also take advantage of services such as FeedBurner, www.feedburner.com, which make sure files are properly formatted and help publicize content.[38]

Beyond that, publishers can get themselves listed in a variety of directories, some of which specialize in blogs (such as Technorati, www.technorati.com), others in podcasts (such as Juice, http://juicereceiver.sourceforge.net), some in only video feeds, and others in two or more media types (such as Mefeedia, http://mefeedia. com, which covers podcasts and vodcasts).

> Tagging involves assigning descriptive words to each post of a podcast.

Content creators can also make their material easier to find through tagging, which involves assigning descriptive words to each post or podcast. For example, for a blog posting on clever techniques for attracting new employees,

> Figure 7–7 Viewing Blog Headlines in Newsreader Software

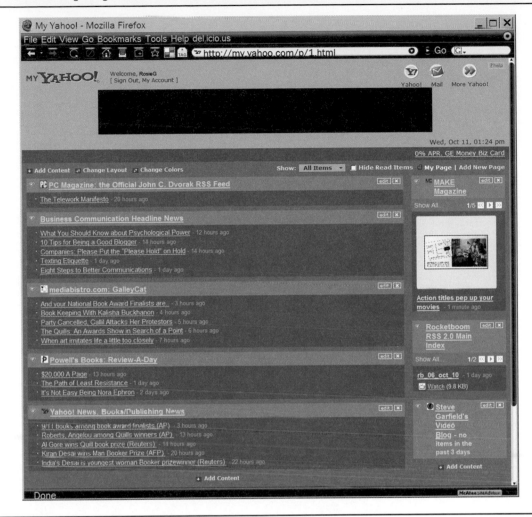

you might tag the post with the word *recruiting*. Visitors to your blog who want to read everything you've written about recruiting just click on that word to see all your posts on that subject. Tagging can also help audiences locate your posts on blog trackers such as Technorati or on *social bookmarking* or *social news* sites such as Delicious, http://delicious.com (see Figure 7–8), and Digg, www.digg.com. Sites such as Delicious also let audiences apply their own tags to items they've selected (indicated by the "to" line in each entry), making it easier for them to categorize content and share their choices with other Delicious users. You can read more about social bookmarking as a research tool in Chapter 11.

Bloggers can also help each other by identifying blogs they themselves read. This list, called a *blogroll*, can be found on many blogs. In addition, when bloggers comment on individual posts on other blogs, they can also use a feature called *trackback* to let readers of the original post know that other bloggers have commented on it. Both blogrolls and trackbacks help "spread the word" for bloggers by showing audiences other blogs they might like as well.

Bloggers can help each other find audiences by listing favourite blogs in their blogrolls.

> Figure 7–8 Tagging on a Social Bookmarking Site

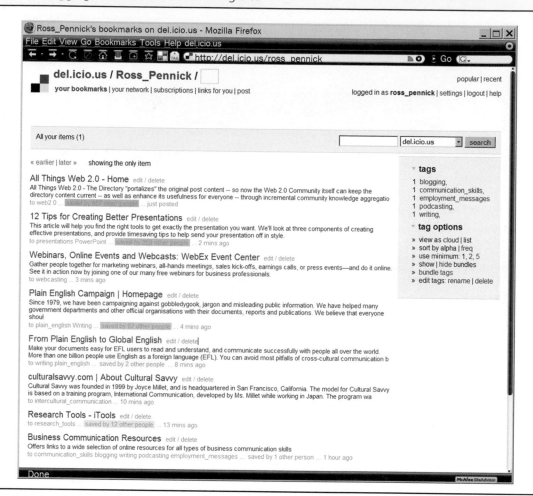

Summary of Learning Objectives

1 **Compare the strengths and weaknesses of the print and electronic media available for short messages.** You will have many choices for sending short messages, and selecting the right medium will determine the success of their reception. If you want to send messages quickly and at low cost, consider electronic media such as email, instant messages, and text messages. When you need to communicate internally or externally with a very large audience, blogs will reach thousands of readers. If your purpose is to train employees or supplement conference calls, podcasts are a simple way to spread audio or video messages. However, when you want to create a formal impression, or make your message distinct from electronic media, traditional print documents may be the better choice. In addition, when you are legally required to provide information in printed form, such as contracts, you should use print media unless advised otherwise by your company's legal department.

2 **Explain how overuse of email can reduce productivity.** Email will reduce productivity when the sender clutters the mailboxes of readers with unnecessary or personal messages. Productivity is also reduced when the sender does not respect the chain of command; messages should be transmitted to individuals who are designated to deal with specific situations according to the organizational hierarchy.

3 **Identify the qualities of an effective email subject line.** An effective email subject line is specific and concrete. To

attract your reader's attention, consider using keywords, directions, or questions.

4 **Identify guidelines for successful instant messaging (IM) in the workplace.** For successful instant messages, apply the three-step process. First, plan your message by determining its purpose. Second, use a business-like writing style and generally avoid IM acronyms except when communicating with close colleagues. Third, complete the message by revising and proofreading it before sending to ensure it is mechanically correct, clear, and complete.

5 **Describe the role of blogging in business communication today and the importance of understanding your audience, purpose, and scope.** In business, blogging can be used to communicate company news, streamline team communication, recruit employees, and update audiences quickly in crisis situations. To create effective blogs, be sure to choose topics that are relevant to your audience and encourage them to join the conversation. Your purpose should be business-related and broad enough to generate interest for months or even years. Similarly, the scope should not be too tightly focused; otherwise, discussion would be limited. Furthermore, the scope should be stable in order to keep readers interested.

6 **Explain how to adapt the three-step writing process for podcasts.** First, plan your podcast by analyzing the situation, gathering the necessary information, and organizing it. Also determine the frequency of distribution and the topics to be addressed over time. Second, prepare the podcast by thinking about the language and images of your content, and guiding devices such as previews, transitions, and reviews. Prepare a speaking outline, rather than a script, so that the podcast sounds conversational and personal. Third, because editing podcasts is more difficult than editing videocasts or written text, review your outline carefully before beginning to speak.

7 **Describe the syndication process and explain how it helps you distribute blog and podcast content.** To publish blogs and podcasts, begin the syndication process by creating a newsfeed and uploading it to the blog or podcast server. The feed is sent to subscribers, who click on headlines or summaries of interest. Syndication helps you distribute blog and podcast content because audiences subscribe to aggregators, or newsreaders, which collect the messages and permit readers to view and download entire posts.

PEARSON
mycanadianbuscommlab

Visit www.mycanadianbuscommlab.ca for everything you need to help you succeed in the job you've always wanted! Tools and resources include the following:
– Composing Space and Writer's Toolkit
– Document Makeovers
– Video Case Studies
– Grammar Exercises—and much more!

On the Job PERFORMING COMMUNICATION TASKS AT PETRO-CANADA

You recently joined the corporate communications staff at Petro-Canada, and one of your responsibilities is editing the Pump Talk blog. Study the scenarios that follow and apply what you learned about blogging in this chapter to choose the best course of action.

1 Pressure is building to stop the practice of moderating the blog by reviewing reader comments and selecting which ones will appear online. You've received a number of adamant messages saying that Pump Talk won't be a "real" blog until anyone is allowed to write any sort of comment without being "censored" by the company. However, you know that every blog is vulnerable to inappropriate and irrelevant comments, and you don't want Pump Talk to turn into a free-for-all shouting match.

Which of the following messages should you post on the blog to explain that the current policy of reviewing and filtering comments will continue?

a There are plenty of free-for-all blogs and websites on the internet; if you want to rant and rave, I suggest you try one of those.

b Please bear in mind that this blog is a Petro-Canada company commercial communication endeavour and, as such, it must adhere to company standards for communication style. I therefore regret to inform you that we cannot allow a free-form, unmonitored exchange as part of this blog.

c Our blog; our rules. Seriously, though, this is a professional communication channel designed primarily to give Petro-Canada the opportunity to share their thoughts with customers and vice versa. As such, we need to make sure that primary messaging effort doesn't get lost in the noise that can flare up in unregulated online forums.

d Every Web surfer knows that online discussions can get a little out of hand at times, degenerating into shouting matches, name calling, and off-topic rants. In order to continue providing the congenial, information-driven blog that readers have come to expect, we believe it is necessary to exercise a minimal amount of control over the content.

2 The multiauthor concept generally works well for Pump Talk. It divides the writing workload, and it gives readers the opportunity to hear from several voices discussing different aspects of gasoline pricing and fuel efficiency. One member of the team is moving to another position in the company, so you need to recruit a new blogger to replace her. Your plan is to send an email message to everyone in the company, providing a brief reminder of the blog's purpose, describing the writing style you're looking for, and inviting interested writers to submit sample blog entries for evaluation. Which of the following paragraphs is the best way to describe the preferred writing style for the blog? (This message is for employees only; it won't be seen by the public.)

a Pump Talk has connected with thousands of readers because the writing is *engaging* (people want to read and respond), *personal* (readers want to get to know real, live human beings, not a faceless corporation), *honest* (we don't sugar-coat anything or hide from criticism), and *friendly* (our readers want to enjoy the experience).

b What kind of writing are we looking for? Well, let me tell you exactly what we need. We need writing that is above all (a) engaging—it makes people *want* to read and become involved in the conversation. Plus, (b), the writing must be *personal*; we don't need anybody to repeat "the company line" here; we want *your unique* thoughts and opinions. However, (c), we, of course (!), need writing that is consistent with Pump Talk's approach that combines honesty with friendliness.

c You should be able to produce copy that meets the following criteria: Your writing must be engaging, personal, honest, and friendly. Writing that does not meet these criteria, no matter how well written in other respects, will not be accepted for online publication.

d I'll be short and to the point: the writing we want for this blog must be engaging, personal, honest, and friendly.

3 For the sample blog entries you solicited in your email message, you asked candidates to start their entries with a brief paragraph introducing themselves. Which of the following seems like the most compatible style for Pump Talk?

a Hi everyone! I'm Janice McNathan, and I couldn't be more excited to be joining the Pump Talk! I've worked at some great companies before, but nobody seems to have as much fun as the Pump Talk blog guys, so I know I'm going to have a great time writing for this blog!

b Charlie Parker here. I'm just a lowly auditor. Pretty much, I keep tabs on accounts and I make sure all the paperwork stays in order. I can't promise any exciting stories of adventure in the oil fields, but maybe something interesting will come up. Maybe you'd like some discussion of the financial side of the oil industry?

c I'm Rick Munoz, and I've always wanted to be a professional writer. My career sort of took a detour, though, and I wound up as a programmer who works behind the scenes at the Petro-Canada website. I really appreciate this opportunity to hone my craft, and who knows—maybe this will be the break I need to make it as a "real" writer. You'll be able to say "I knew that guy before he became famous!"

d Excuse me while I wipe the oil off my hands; I don't want to mess up this shiny new keyboard! Hi, I'm Kristal Yan, a field mechanic at Petro-Canada's facility in Lewis, Alberta. I've been an avid reader of Pump Talk since it started, and I really look forward to participating in this wonderful conversation. I hope to provide some interesting observations from the field. Feel free to ask any questions you may have about drilling and how things work in the oil fields.

Test Your Knowledge

1 What are key features of effective business-related blogs?

2 When should the *cc* and *bcc* features be used in email?

3 How is email use related to productivity?

4 Why is instant messaging usage overtaking email in some companies?

5 Who is the optimum audience for a blog?

6 How do aggregators and podcatchers work?

7 How do you capture your reader's attention in email?

8 When should you use podcasts?

9 When should instant messaging be used in business?

Apply Your Knowledge

1 Are instant messaging and blogging replacing many instances of email for the same reasons that email replaced many instances of printed memos and letters? Explain your answer.

2 If one of the benefits of blogging is the personal, intimate style of writing, is it a good idea to limit your creativity by adhering to conventional rules of grammar, spelling, and mechanics? Why or why not?

3 In your work as a video game designer, you know that eager players search the Web for any scrap of information they can find about upcoming releases. In fact, to build interest, your company's public relations department carefully doles out small bits of information in the months before a new title hits the market. However, you and others in the company are also concerned about competitors getting their hands on all this "prerelease" information. If they learn too much too soon, they can use the information to improve their own products more quickly. You and several other designers and programmers maintain blogs that give players insights into game design techniques and that occasionally share tips and tricks. You have thousands of readers, and you know your blog helps build customer loyalty. The company president wants to ban blogging entirely so that bloggers don't accidentally share too much

prerelease information about upcoming games. Would this be a wise move? Why or why not?

4 Should podcasting be considered as a potential replacement for your company's employee newsletter, which is currently sent by email? Why or why not?

5 **Ethical Choices** Your boss wants you to send a message to the production staff, thanking all 60 members for their hard work and overtime to get the new manufacturing line set up and running on schedule. Your boss has been working a lot of overtime herself, and she's been under a lot of pressure. She wants to send the thank-you message by email and asks you to work on the wording. You think each member of the production staff should receive a formal printed letter to keep for future promotions or other jobs. You know your boss won't like being interrupted about an issue that she thinks is off her desk, and you know how valuable her time is.

a Should you draft the letter and produce 60 copies so that you don't have to bother your boss?

b Should you simply draft the email message as requested to save everyone time?

c Should you discuss the issue with your boss, regardless of taking her away from the tasks she so desperately needs to get done?

Running Cases

Watch on mycanadianbuscommlab

> CASE 1 Noreen

Noreen has been asked to create an entry for the new blog at the Petro-Go website. All visitors to the website can read the blog, which is edited by Petro-Go's director of corporate communications. Management at all levels will post messages that focus on Petro-Go's environmental awareness, community relations, and community investment. The blog catchphrase is "We care about the communities we live and work in." Management wants to promote goodwill with current and potential customers. They want to be viewed as "the good gas company." Posts will discuss new and continuing initiatives, future goals, donations, and sponsorships.

QUESTIONS

a) Should all website visitors be allowed to add content to the blog and not just management? Why?

b) Will this blog help attract new customers and retain existing customers? Why?

c) How often should new postings be uploaded? Why?

d) Give two other blog topics that might help attract visitors to the site and that would be appropriate for this company.

e) Who would be most interested in reading the blog? Why?

YOUR TASK

As Noreen, write a posting for the blog about how your team's office is going green. Include an interesting heading for your post. Do an online search to discover ways in which business offices are becoming more eco-friendly. Incorporate some of those eco-friendly practices into your post. Email your proposed posting to your professor for approval. Remember to format the email message in a professional manner.

> CASE 2 Kwong

Kwong's manager asks him to work with the IT specialist and put together the first of a series of 52 video podcasts (also known as vidcasts or vodcasts). One podcast will be uploaded to the company website each week. The podcasts will give website visitors tips on personal and business tax planning and reporting. This first podcast will show Kwong discussing personal tax planning. Kwong's manager hopes that existing and potential customers will find value in the videos.

QUESTIONS

a) Before creating the first podcast for the series, what questions will Kwong need to ask his manager?

b) How can Kwong make the podcast interesting?

c) Why are previews, transitions, and reviews more important in video and audio recordings than they are in print media?

d) Is Kwong the right employee to represent the company on this podcast? For the podcast series? Why?

e) Could this company benefit from a blog on their website? Why?

YOUR TASK

The podcast's purpose is to offer tax planning tips to existing and potential customers. Narrow the scope of the topic for this first podcast to three personal tax tips. You will need to review government taxation guidelines before offering suggestions to your audience. You may wish to include some helpful website URLs for your audience. Prepare a document for your professor that details the information to be conveyed in the podcast and the order in which it will be presented. Use the following document headings: Plan (the podcast's setting, length, and main points), Introduction (including a preview of topics), Body (the three tips you will discuss and the information you will share), Conclusion (how you will conclude). Apply the three-step writing process and remember to use previews, transitions, and reviews in your dialogue. Email your proposed plan for the podcast to your professor for approval. Remember to format the email message in a professional manner.

Practise Your Knowledge

Review the following messages and then (1) analyze the strengths and weaknesses of each message and (2) revise as indicated.

MESSAGE 7.A: IMPROVING IM SKILLS

Review this IM exchange and explain how the customer service agent could have handled the situation more effectively:

Agent: Thanks for contacting Home Exercise Equipment. What's up?

Customer: I'm having trouble assembling my home gym.

Agent: I hear that a lot! LOL

Customer: So is it me or the gym?

Agent: Well, let's see. Where are you stuck?

Customer: The crossbar that connects the vertical pillars doesn't fit.

Agent: What do you mean doesn't fit?

Customer: It doesn't fit. It's not long enough to reach across the pillars.

Agent: Maybe you assembled the pillars in the wrong place. Or maybe we sent the wrong crossbar.

Customer: How do I tell?

Agent: The parts aren't labelled so it could be tough. Do you have a measuring tape? Tell me how long your crossbar is.

MESSAGE 7.B: DRAFTING EFFECTIVE BLOG POSTS

Revise this blog post based on what you've learned in this chapter:

[headline]

We're DOOMED!!!!!
[post]
I was at the Sikorsky plant in Stratford yesterday, just checking to see how things were going with the assembly line retrofit we did for them last year. I think I saw the future, and it ain't pretty. They were demo'ing a prototype robot from Motoman that absolutely blows our stuff out of the water. They wouldn't let me really see it, but based on the 10-second glimpse I got, it's smaller, faster, and more manoeuvrable than any of our units. And when I asked about the price, the guy just grinned. And it wasn't the sort of grin designed to make me feel good.

I've been saying for years that we need to pay more attention to size, speed, and manoeuvrability instead of just relying on our historical strengths of accuracy and payload capacity, and you'd have to be blind not to agree that this experience proves me right. If we can't at least show a design for a better unit within two or three months, Motoman is going to lock up the market and leave us utterly in the dust.

Believe me, being able to say "I told you so" right now is not nearly as satisfying as you might think!!

MESSAGE 7.C: PLANNING A BETTER PODCAST

Visit www.mycanadianbuscommlab.ca, click on the Business Communication tab, then select Textbook Resources and click on Message 7.C. Download and listen to this podcast. Identify at least three ways in which the podcast could be improved and draft a brief email message that you could send to the podcaster with your suggestions for improvement.

Exercises

7.1 Choose Your Medium: Selecting the Best Technology for a Message

For each of these message needs, choose a medium that you think would work effectively and explain your choice. (More than one medium could work in some cases; just be able to support your particular choice.)

a. A technical support service for people trying to use their digital music players

b. A message of condolence to the family of an employee who passed away recently

c. A message from the CEO of a small company, explaining that she is leaving the company to join a competitor

d. A series of observations on the state of the industry

e. A series of messages, questions, and answers surrounding the work of a project team

7.2 Email: Making Subject Lines Informative

Using your imagination to make up whatever details you need, revise the following email subject lines to make them more informative.

a. New budget figures

b. Marketing brochure—your opinion

c. Production schedule

7.3 Email: Message Outlining a New Employee Procedure

The following email message contains numerous errors related to what you've learned about planning and writing business messages. Using the information it contains, write a more effective version.

> *TO: Felicia August*
> *SUBJECT: Those are the breaks, folks*
>
> *Some of you may not like the rules about break times; however, we determined that keeping track of employees while they took breaks at times they determined rather than regular breaks at prescribed times was not working as well as we would have liked. The new rules are not going to be an option. If you do not*

follow the new rules, your pay could be docked for hours when you turned up missing, since your direct supervisor will not be able to tell whether you were on a "break" or not and will assume that you have walked away from your job. We cannot be responsible for any errors that result from your inattentiveness to the new rules. I have already heard complaints from some of you and I hope this memo will end this issue once and for all. The decision has already been made.

Starting Monday, January 1, you will all be required to take a regular 15-minute break in the morning and again in the afternoon, and a regular thirty-minute lunch at the times specified by your supervisor, NOT when you think you need a break or when you "get around to it."

There will be no exceptions to this new rule!

Felicia August
Manager
Billing and Accounting

7.4 Instant Messaging: Let's Get Professional

Your firm, which makes professional paint sprayers, uses IM extensively for internal communication and frequently for external communication with customers and suppliers as well. Several customers have recently forwarded copies of messages they've received from your staff, asking if you know how casually some employees were treating this important medium. You decide to revise parts of several messages to show your staff a more appropriate writing style. Rewrite these sentences, making up any information you need, to convey a more businesslike style and tone. (Look up the acronyms online if you need to.)

a. IMHO, our quad turbo sprayer is best model 4U.

b. No prob; happy2help!

c. FWIW, I use the L400 myself & it rocks

d. Most cust see 20–30% reduct in fumes w/this sprayer—of course, YMMV.

7.5 Blogging: Keeping Emotions Under Control

The members of the project team of which you are the leader have enthusiastically embraced blogging as a communication medium. Unfortunately, as emotions heat up during the project, some of the blog postings are getting too casual, too personal, and even sloppy. Because your boss and other managers around the company also read this project blog, you don't want the team to look unprofessional in anyone's eyes. Revise the following blog posting so that it communicates in a more businesslike manner while retaining the informal, conversational tone of a blog. (Be sure to correct any spelling and punctuation mistakes you find as well.)

Well, to the profound surprise of absolutely nobody, we are not going to be able meet the June 1 commitment to ship 100 operating tables to Southeast Surgical Supply. (For those of you who have been living in a cave the past six month, we have been fighting to get our hands on enough high-grade chromium steel to meet our production schedule.) Sure enough, we got news, this morning that we will only get enough for 30 tables. Yes, we look lik fools for not being able to follow through on promises we made to the customer, but no, this didn't have to happ-pen. Six month's ago, purchasing warned us about shrinking supplies and suggested we advance-buy as much as we would need for the next 12 months, or so. We naturally tried to followed their advice, but just as naturally were shot down by the bean counters at corporate who trotted out the policy about never buying more than three months worth of materials in advance. Of course, it'll be us- - -not the bean counters who'll take the flak when everybody starts asking why revenues are down next quarter and why Southeast is talking to our friends at Crighton Manuf!!! Maybe, some day this company will get its head out of the sand and realize that we need to have some financial flexibility in order to compete.

7.6 Blogging: Blog Post Informing Employees About an Office Relocation

From what you've learned about effective blogging as well as planning and writing business messages in general, you should be able to identify numerous errors made by the writer of the following blog posting. After identifying the flaws, draft a version that fixes them.

Get Ready!

We are hoping to be back at work soon, with everything running smoothly, same production schedule and no late projects or missed deadlines. So you need to clean out your desk, put your stuff in boxes, and clean off the walls.

You can put the items you had up on your walls in boxes, also.

We have provided boxes. The move will happen this weekend. We'll be in our new offices when you arrive on Monday.

We will not be responsible for personal belongings during the move.

Posted by David Burke at 10:42 AM 09–27–10

7.7 Podcasting: Where Are We Going with This, Boss?

You've recently begun recording a weekly podcast to share information with your large and far-flung staff. After a month, you ask for feedback from several of your subordinates, and you're disappointed to learn that some people stopped listening to the podcast after the first couple of weeks. Someone eventually admits that many staffers feel the recordings are too long and rambling, and the information they contain isn't valuable enough to justify the time it takes to listen. You aren't pleased, but you want to improve. An assistant transcribes the introduction to last week's podcast so you can review it. You immediately see two problems. Revise the introduction based on what you've learned in this chapter.

So there I am, having lunch with Anju Gill, who just joined and took over the Northeast sales region from Ryan Stroud. In walks our beloved CEO with Anju's old boss at Uni-Plex; turns out they were finalizing a deal to co-brand our products and theirs and to set up a joint distribution program in all four domestic regions. Pretty funny, huh? Anju left Uni-Plex because she wanted to sell our products instead, and now she's back selling her old stuff, too. Anyway, try to chat with her when you can; she knows the biz inside and out and probably can offer insight into just about any sales challenge you might be running up against. We'll post more info on the co-brand deal next week; should be a boost for all of us. Other than those two news items, the other big news this week is the change in commission reporting. I'll go into the details in minute, but when you log onto the intranet, you'll now see your sales results split out by product line and industry sector. Hope this helps you see where you're doing well and where you might beef things up a bit. Oh yeah, I almost forgot the most important bit. Speaking of our beloved CEO, Thomas is going to be our guest of honour, so to speak, at the quarterly sales meeting next week and wants an update on how petroleum prices are affecting customer behaviour. Each district manager should be ready with a brief report. After I go through the commission reporting scheme, I'll outline what you need to prepare.

Cases   APPLYING THE THREE-STEP WRITING PROCESS TO CASES

Apply each step to the following cases, as assigned by your instructor.

Planning > Writing > Completing

Analyze the Situation

Identify both your general purpose and your specific purpose. Clarify exactly what you want your audience to think, feel, or believe after receiving your message. Profile your primary audience, including their backgrounds, differences, similarities, and likely reactions to your message.

Gather Information

Identify the information your audience will need to receive, as well as other information you may need in order to craft an effective message.

Select the Right Medium

The medium is identified for each case here, but when on the job, make sure your medium is both acceptable to the audience and appropriate for the message.

Organize the Information

Define your main idea, limit your scope, choose a direct or indirect approach, and outline necessary support points and other evidence.

Adapt to Your Audience

Show sensitivity to audience needs by using a "you" attitude, politeness, positive emphasis, and bias-free language. Understand how much credibility you already have—and how much you may need to establish. Project your company's image by maintaining an appropriate style and tone. Consider cultural variations and the differing needs of internal and external audiences.

Compose the Message

For written messages, draft your message using clear but sensitive words, effective sentences, and coherent paragraphs. For podcasts, outline your message and draft speaking notes to ensure smooth recording; use plenty of previews, transitions, and review to help audiences follow along.

Revise the Message

Evaluate content and review readability, then edit and rewrite for conciseness and clarity.

Produce the Message

For written messages, use effective design elements and suitable layout for a clean, professional appearance. For podcasts, record your messages using whatever equipment you have available (professional podcasts may require upgraded equipment).

Proofread the Message

Review for errors in layout, spelling, and mechanics. Listen to podcasts to check for recording problems.

Distribute the Message

Deliver your message using the chosen medium; make sure all documents and all relevant files are distributed successfully.

1   2   3

Blogging SKILLS

1. Selling without selling: Blog posting about a GPS rescue Promoting products through customer success stories can be a great marketing tactic, as long as you keep the customer as the "star" of the story and don't promote the product too blatantly. You've recently joined Garmin, a leading manufacturer of electronic navigation equipment, including a popular line of handheld global positioning system (GPS) devices used by hikers, kayakers, and others who venture off the beaten path.

Your task: As a communication specialist, your responsibilities include writing blog postings that highlight dramatic stories in which people used Garmin GPS units to rescue themselves or others from potentially dangerous situations. Visit Garmin's website, at www.garmin.com, click on "Company," "What's New" and then "GPS Adventures" (or access the page directly at www8.garmin.com/whatsNew/adventures.html). Select a customer story that involves a wilderness rescue in which a Garmin product played an important role. Using the information provided by the customer, rewrite the story in the third person

(changing "I" or "we" references to "he," "she," or "they") for an audience that isn't familiar with the product in question. Subtly work in references to the product and the benefits it

provided in this scenario, but keep the focus on the customer. Limit yourself to 400 words.

Blogging SKILLS

2. Come on to Comic-Con: Explaining the benefits of attending

Comic-Con International is an annual convention that highlights a wide variety of pop culture and entertainment media, from comic books and collectibles to video games and movies. From its early start as a comic book convention that attracted several hundred fans and publishing industry insiders, Comic-Con has become a major international event with more than 100 000 attendees.

Your task: Several readers of your pop culture blog have been asking for your recommendation about visiting Comic-Con in San Diego next summer. Write a two- or three-paragraph posting for your blog that explains what Comic-Con is and what visitors can expect to experience at the convention. Be sure to address your posting to fans, not industry insiders. You can learn more at www.comic-con.org.[39]

Email SKILLS

3. Keeping the fans happy: Analyzing advertising on ESPN.com

ESPN leads the pack both online and off. Its well-known cable television sports channels are staple fare for sports enthusiasts, and ESPN.com (http://espn.go.com) is the leader in sports websites, too. Advertisers flock to ESPN.com because it delivers millions of visitors in the prime 18- to 34-year-old demographic group. With a continually refreshed offering of sporting news, columnists, video replays, and fantasy leagues (online competitions in which participants choose players for their teams, and the outcome is based on how well the real players do in actual live competition), ESPN.com has become one of the major advertising venues on the Web.

As an up-and-coming Web producer for ESPN.com, you're concerned about the rumblings of discontent you've heard from friends and read in various blogs and other sources. ESPN.com remains popular with millions of sports fans, but some say they are getting tired of all the ads—both ads on the site itself and pop-up ads. A few say they are switching to other websites with fewer advertising intrusions. Your site traffic numbers are holding fairly steady for now, but you're worried that the few visitors leaving ESPN.com might be the start of a significant exodus in the future.

Your task: Write an email message to your manager, expressing your concern about the amount of advertising content on ESPN.com. Acknowledge that advertising is a vital source of revenue, but share what you've learned about site visitors who claim to be migrating to other sites. Offer to lead a comprehensive review effort that will compare the advertising presence on ESPN.com with that of other sports websites and explore ways to maintain strong advertising sales without alienating readers.[40]

4. That's not the way things really are: Correcting economic misinformation

As a member of the corporate communications staff of a small manufacturing company, your interests and responsibilities range far beyond the four walls of the factory. You have to be in tune with the global economy, politics, taxation policies, and other external forces that affect your company and your employees. Along with your peers in other companies, you've learned to speak out on issues—particularly when you believe that misguided government policies or misinformed public opinions threaten the viability of your company, your industry, and the economy as a whole.

An item in this morning's newspaper certainly got your attention. A prominent national political leader claimed that job-growth figures in recent years prove that the government's economic policies are working. The economy is in reasonably good shape, considering the battering it has taken in recent years, but you believe the situation would improve considerably if the government would address economic issues, such as incentives for investing in manufacturing upgrades.

Your task: Write an email, limited to 250 words, to the editor of the newspaper. Correct the impression that job growth is occurring throughout the economy and encourage political leaders to address problems that you believe continue to limit growth in other industries, including taxation policies in the manufacturing sector and unfair competitive practices from companies in certain other countries. Make up whatever information you need to back up your claims.[41]

Email SKILLS

Portfolio BUILDER

5. Help is on the way: Encouraging Ford dealers

The "Big Three" U.S. automakers—General Motors, Chrysler, and Ford—haven't had much good news to share lately. Ford, in particular, has been going through a rough time, losing billions of dollars and being overtaken in sales volume by Toyota.

Your task: Write an email to be sent to all Ford dealers in North America, describing an exciting new model about to be introduced to the public. For this exercise, you can use either an upcoming Ford model you have researched in the automotive media or a fictitious car of your own imagination (make sure it's something that could conceivably be introduced by Ford).[42]

IM SKILLS

6. The very definition of confusion: Helping consumers sort out high-definition television

High-definition television can be a joy to watch—but complicated to buy. The field is filled with competing technologies and terminology that is meaningless to most consumers. Moreover, it's nearly impossible to define one technical term without invoking two or three others, leaving consumers swimming in an alphanumeric soup of confusion. The manufacturers themselves can't even agree on which of the

18 different digital TV formats truly qualify as "high definition." As a sales support manager for Crutchfield www.crutchfield.com), a leading online retailer of audio and video systems, you understand the frustration buyers feel; your staff is deluged daily by their questions.

Your task: To help your staff respond quickly to consumers who ask questions via Crutchfield's online IM chat service, you are developing a set of "canned" responses to common questions. When a consumer asks one of these questions, a sales advisor can simply click on the ready-made answer. Start by writing concise, consumer-friendly definitions of the following terms: *resolution*, *HDTV*, *1080p*, and *HDMI*. (Visit Crutchfield's educational site, www.crutchfieldadvisor.com, and click on "Learn About Home Theater & A/V" to learn more about these terms. Answers.com and CNET.com are two other handy sources.)[43]

Podcasting SKILLS

Portfolio BUILDER

7. Based on my experience: Recommending your college or university

With any purchase decision, from a restaurant meal to a college education, recommendations from satisfied customers are often the strongest promotional messages.

Your task: Write a script for a one- to two-minute podcast (roughly 150 to 250 words) explaining why your college or university is a good place to get an education. Your audience is grade 11 and 12 students. You can choose to craft a general message, something that would be useful to all prospective students, or you can focus on a specific academic discipline, the athletic program, or some other important aspect of your college or university experience. Either way, make sure your introductory comments make it clear whether you are offering a general recommendation or a specific recommendation. If your instructor asks you to do so, record the podcast and submit the file electronically.

Podcasting SKILLS

8. Based on my experience: Suggestions for improving your college or university

Every organization, no matter how successfully it operates, can find ways to improve customer service.

Your task: Write a script for a one- to two-minute podcast (roughly 150 to 250 words) identifying at least one way in which your college or university experience could have been or still could be improved through specific changes in policies, programs, facilities, or other elements. Your audience is the school's administration. Offer constructive criticism and specific arguments why your suggestions would help you—and possibly other students as well. Be sure to focus on meaningful and practical opportunities for improvement. If your instructor asks you to do so, record the podcast and submit the file electronically.

Blogging SKILLS

9. Look sharp: Travel safety tips for new employees

As the travel director for a global management consulting firm, your responsibilities range from finding the best travel deals to helping new employees learn the ins and outs of low-risk, low-stress travels. One of the ways in which you dispense helpful advice is through an internal blog.

Your task: Research advice for safe travel and identify at least six tips that every employee in your company should know. Write a brief blog posting that introduces and identifies the six tips.

Email SKILLS

10. Your work does matter: Encouraging an unhappy colleague

You certainly appreciate your company's "virtual team" policy of letting employees live wherever they want while using technology to communicate and collaborate. The company is headquartered in a large urban area, but you get to live in the mountains, only a step or two away from some of the best skiing in the world. Most of the time, this approach to work couldn't get any better.

However, the lack of face-to-face contact with your colleagues definitely has disadvantages. For example, when a teammate seems to be upset about something, you wish you could go for a walk with the person and talk it out rather than relying on phone calls, email, or IM. In the past couple weeks, Chris Grogan, the graphic designer working with you on a new e-commerce website project, seems to be complaining about everything. His negative attitude is starting to wear down the team's enthusiasm at a critical point in the project. In particular, he has complained several times that no one on the team seems to care about his design work. It is rarely mentioned in team teleconferences, and no one asks him about it. That part is true, actually, but the reason is that there is nothing wrong with his work—some critical technical issues unrelated to the graphic design are consuming everyone's attention.

Your task: After a couple of unsuccessful attempts at encouraging Grogan over the phone, you decide to write a brief email message to assure him of the importance of his work on this project and the quality of his efforts. Let him know that graphic design is a critical part of the project's success and that as soon as those technical issues are resolved and the project is completed, everyone will have a chance to appreciate his contribution to the project. Make up whatever details you need to craft your message.

Email SKILLS

11. She's one of us: Promoting a new lifestyle magazine

Consumers looking for beauty, health, and lifestyle magazines have an almost endless array of choices, but even in this crowded field, Logan Olson found her own niche. Olson, who was born with congenital heart disease, suffered a heart attack at age 16 that left her in a coma and caused serious brain damage. The active and outgoing teen had to relearn everything from sitting up to feeding herself. As she recovered, she looked for help and advice in conquering such daily challenges as finding fashionable clothes that were easier to put on and makeup that was easier to apply. Mainstream beauty magazines didn't seem to offer any information for young women with disabilities, so she started her own magazine. Oprah Winfrey has *Oprah*, and now Logan Olson has *Logan*. The magazine not only gives young women tips on buying and using a variety of products but lets women with disabilities know there are others out there like them, facing and meeting the same challenges.

Your task: Write a promotional email message to be sent to young women with disabilities as well as families and friends who might like to give gift subscriptions, promoting the benefits of subscribing to *Logan*. You can learn more about *Logan* at www.loganmagazine.com.[44]

Email SKILLS

Portfolio BUILDER

12. We're the one: Explaining why a company should hire your firm

You work for Brainbench (www.brainbench.com), one of many companies that offer employee screening services. Brainbench's offerings include a variety of online products and consulting services, all designed to help employers find and develop the best possible employees. For example, Brainbench's Pre-Hire Testing products help employers test for job skills, communication skills, personality, and employment history red flags (such as chronic absenteeism or performance problems). Employers use these test results to either screen out candidates entirely or ask focused interview questions about areas of concern.

Sonja Williamson, the human resources director of a large retail company, has just emailed your sales team. She would like an overview of the Pre-Hire Testing products and some background on your company.

Your task: Write an email response to Williamson's query. Be sure to thank her for her interest, briefly describe the Pre-Hire Testing products, and summarize Brainbench's qualifications. Include at least one hyperlink to the Brainbench website, and consider attaching one or more PDF files from the website as well.

Email SKILLS

13. Firing the customer: When a particular customer is always wrong

Many companies operate on the principle that the customer is always right, even when the customer *isn't* right. They take any steps necessary to ensure happy customers, lots of repeat sales, and a positive reputation among potential buyers. Overall, this is a smart and successful approach to business. However, most companies eventually encounter that one nightmare customer who drains so much time, energy, and profits that the only sensible option is to refuse the customer's business. For example, the nightmare customer might be someone who constantly berates you and your employees, repeatedly makes outlandish demands for refunds and discounts, or simply requires so much help that you not only lose money on this person but you also no longer have enough time to help your other customers. "Firing" a customer is an unpleasant step that should be taken only in the most extreme cases and only after other remedies have been attempted (such as talking with the customer about the problem), but it is sometimes necessary for the well-being of your employees and your company.

Your task: If you are currently working or have held a job in the recent past, imagine that you've encountered just such a customer. If you don't have job experience to call on, imagine that you work in a retail location somewhere around campus or in your neighbourhood. Identify the type of behaviour this imaginary customer exhibits and the reasons the behaviour can no longer be accepted. Write a brief email message to the customer to explain that you will no longer be able to accommodate him or her as a customer. Calmly explain why you have had to reach this difficult decision. Maintain a professional tone by keeping your emotions in check.

Podcasting SKILLS

14. Podcasting pitch: Training people to sell your favourite product

What product do you own (or use regularly) that you can't live without? It could be something as seemingly minor as a favourite pen or something as significant as a medical device that you literally can't live without. Now imagine you're a salesperson for this product; think about how you would sell it to potential buyers. How would you describe it and how would you explain the benefits of owning it? After you've thought about how you would present the product to others, imagine that you've been promoted to sales manager, and it is your job to train other people to sell the product.

Your task: Write the script for a brief podcast (200 to 300 words) that summarizes for your sales staff the most important points to convey about the product. Imagine that they'll listen to your podcast while driving to a customer's location or preparing for the day's activity in a retail store (depending on the nature of the product). Be sure to give your staffers a concise overview message about the product and several key support points.

Email SKILLS

15. Time to think: Email requesting a change in your workload

The description of your job as a global marketing manager for New Balance is full of responsibilities that require creative thinking, from predicting consumer and retailing trends to establishing seasonal priorities for the global merchandising effort. You love these challenges—in fact, they're the main reason you took the job at this respected maker of athletic shoes and apparel. Unfortunately, between department meetings, status reports, budgets, and an endless array of other required chores, you hardly have time to think at all, much less engage in the sort of unstructured, "blue sky" thinking that is crucial to creative strategizing. You have virtually no time at work for such thinking, and after 50 or 60 hours a week at the office or on the road, you're too exhausted to brainstorm on your own time.

Your task: Write an email to your boss, Alan Hed, the executive vice-president, international, persuading him that you need to reshuffle your assignments to free up more time to think. This is a tricky request because you know that Hed faces the same challenge. However, you're convinced that by spending less time on tasks that could be done by someone else (or perhaps shouldn't be done at all), you'll be able to do a better job of creating marketing strategies—and maybe even set a good example for other New Balance executives. You have a preliminary list of changes you'd like to make, but you know you need to discuss the entire scope of your job with Hed before finalizing the list. Your purpose: Invite him to lunch to begin a discussion of reshaping your responsibilities.[45]

Email SKILLS

16. Mercedes merchandise: Message announcing exclusive online gift shop
Mercedes-Benz owners take their accessories seriously, which is why you get angry letters and emails when they buy Mercedes-branded merchandise that turns out to be fake. Even though your company has nothing to do with these low-quality, unauthorized knock-offs, customers sometimes blame you anyway. To battle the problem, Mercedes has opened an online store where every item comes with a certificate of authenticity that it was manufactured by a Mercedes-approved partner and meets Mercedes quality standards. At www.mbusi.com, the website for the Mercedes-Benz manufacturing plant, shoppers can follow the "Store" link to the online gift shop. But first they need to know it exists.

Your task: As assistant to Steve Beaty, vice president of accessories marketing, draft an email message to registered Mercedes owners, telling them about the online gift shop. Visit the website to learn more about it and then write the message using a style you think suits the car manufacturer's image.

 Team Skills

17. Measuring suppliers: Email requesting reviews at Microsoft
Microsoft evaluates employees regularly to determine their performance; why not do the same with the independent contractors the company hires to perform key functions? Nearly every department uses outside providers these days—a practice called *outsourcing*. So if there's a gap between what

Microsoft expects from contractors and what the contractors actually deliver, shouldn't Microsoft tell them how they can improve their performance?

You've been discussing these questions all morning in a meeting with other members of the Employee Services Group. Your boss is convinced that regular reviews of independent contractors are essential.

"It's all about improving clarity in terms of goals and expectations," he says, adding that if contractors receive constructive feedback, Microsoft can develop good relationships with them instead of having to look for new service suppliers all the time.

Your boss assigns your team the task of informing all Microsoft departments that they'll be required to evaluate subcontractors every six months, beginning immediately. The goal of the review is to determine the performance of independent contractors so that Microsoft can (1) give them constructive feedback and continue a strong relationship or (2) end the relationship if service is substandard. Departments will need to rate each contractor on a scale of 1 (poor) to 5 (excellent) for each of several factors that your group is going to determine. Departments will be sending their reports to Roxanna Frost, group program manager for Microsoft's Executive Management and Development Group.

Your task: Working as a team with your classmates, develop a list of factors that will help you rate the overall service of independent contractors. You'll need to consider cost, quality of work, innovation, delivery, and other factors similar to those you'd encounter in a job performance review. Then compose an email to all Microsoft department managers: Explain the new review requirements and include your list of factors to be rated on the 1-to-5 scale.[46]

IM SKILLS

18. Yes, we do purple: Instant message from Lands' End
When clothing retailer Lands' End offered its 2500 telephone service representatives the chance to train on its new instant messaging system, "Lands' End Live," you jumped at the opportunity. As it turned out, so many volunteered for the new training that the company had to give preference to a few hundred who'd been on the job longest. You were one of the lucky ones.

Now you've had months of practice answering messages like the one you just received from a customer named Alicia. She wants to know if she can have a red Polartec Aircore-200 Scarf custom monogrammed—not in the standard, contrasting, wheat-coloured thread, but in radiant purple—as a gift for her husband, whose favourite colours are red and purple.

On its website, Lands' End promises to fulfill nonstandard monogram requests "if technical limitations allow." You've done a quick check and, yes, her husband can have his initials in bright purple on the red background.

Your Task: Write the instant message reply to Alicia, telling her the good news.[47]

Email SKILLS

19. No exaggeration: Short email describing internship duties

You've been labouring all summer at an internship, learning how business is conducted. You've done work nobody else wanted to do, but that's okay. Even the smallest tasks can make a good impression on your future résumé.

This morning, your supervisor asks you to write a description of the job you've been doing. "Include everything, even the filing," she suggests, "and address it to me in an email message." She says a future boss might assign such a task prior to a performance review. "You can practise describing your work without exaggeration—or too much modesty," she says, smiling.

Your task: Using good techniques for short messages and relying on your real-life work experience, write an email that will impress your supervisor. Make up any details you need.

Blogging SKILLS

20. Meet the parents: Blog posting announcing the acquisition of Prime Insurance

As the human resources director for Prime Insurance, you know how proud your fellow employees are to work for one of the most admired insurance companies in Canada. Prime Insurance, which serves customers across Canada, was founded in Montreal, Quebec, in the 1960s by the husband-and-wife team of Herbert and Marion Sandler. For decades, Prime Insurance flourished as an independent company, but in 2009, the Sandlers decided to sell Prime Insurance to Global One Insurance, an insurance-services giant based in Toronto, Ontario.

Over the coming weeks, you'll provide Prime Insurance employees with more information about the impact of the huge deal, but for now, you want them to be aware of four key points:

> The deal allows Prime Insurance to expand beyond its core offering of home mortgages to provide other financial services that its customers have requested for some time.

> The Sandlers carefully selected Global One because of its compatible values of integrity, customer-first business practices, and teamwork.

> Prime Insurance operations will continue from existing locations under the existing Prime Insurance brand name.

> The company's commitment to providing excellent career opportunities for women and visible minorities will not change.[48]

Your task: Write a short posting for Prime Financial's internal blog, announcing the deal and communicating the four afore-mentioned key points listed (in your own words). Close by telling your colleagues how excited you are about the deal and that you'll be providing more information in the days and weeks ahead.

Email SKILLS

21. Environmental planning: Email announcing a committee meeting

You've probably worked as a volunteer on a committee or with team members for class assignments. You know how hard it is to get a diverse group of individuals together for a productive meeting. Maybe you've tried different locations—one member's home or a table at the library. This time you're going to suggest a local restaurant.

The committee you're leading is a volunteer group planning a trash-clearing project at an area park. Your meeting goal is to brainstorm ways to encourage public participation in this environmental event, to be held next Earth Day.

Your task: Develop a short email message telling committee members about the meeting. Include time, date, duration, and location (choose a place you know). Mention the meeting goal to encourage attendance.

Podcasting SKILLS

22. Why me? Introducing yourself to a potential employer

While writing the many letters and email messages that are part of the job search process, you find yourself wishing that you could just talk to some of these companies so your personality could shine through. Well, you've just been given that opportunity. One of the companies that you've applied to has emailed you back, asking you to submit a two-minute podcast introducing yourself and explaining why you would be a good person to hire.

Your task: Identify a company that you'd like to work for after graduation and select a job that would be a good match for your skills and interests. Write a script for a two-minute podcast (two minutes represents roughly 250 words for most speakers). Introduce yourself and the position you're applying for, describe your background, and explain why you think you're a good candidate for the job. Make up any details you need. If your instructor asks you to do so, record the podcast and submit the file.

23. "Hi, my name is . . .": Introducing yourself on an online business network

Business networking websites such as www.linkedin.com, www.ryze.com, and www.spoke.com have become popular places for professionals to make connections that would be difficult or impossible to make without the internet. You might be familiar with MySpace.com or Friendster.com, sites that help individuals meet through networks of people they already know and trust. These business-oriented sites follow the same principle, but instead of using them to find new friends or dates, you use them to find new customers, new suppliers, or other important business connections. For instance, you might find that the ideal contact person in a company you'd like to do business with is the aunt of your boss's tennis partner.

CHAPTER 7 > CRAFTING MESSAGES FOR ELECTRONIC MEDIA 223

An important aspect of business networking is being able to provide a clear description of your professional background and interests. For example, a manufacturing consultant can list the industries in which she has experience, the types of projects she has worked on, and the nature of work she'd like to pursue in the future (such as a full-time position for a company or additional independent projects).

Your task: Write a brief statement introducing yourself, including your educational background, your job history, and the types of connections you'd like to make. Feel free to "fast forward" to your graduation and list your degree, the business specialty you plan to pursue, and any relevant experience. If you have business experience already, feel free to use that information instead. Make sure your statement is clear, concise (no more than two sentences), and compelling so that anyone looking for someone like you would want to get in touch with you after reading your introduction.

8

Writing Routine and Positive Messages

LEARNING OBJECTIVES

After studying this chapter, you will be able to

1. Apply the three-step writing process to routine and positive messages
2. Outline an effective strategy for writing routine requests
3. Describe a strategy for writing routine replies and positive messages
4. Discuss the importance of knowing who is responsible when granting claims and requests for adjustment
5. Explain how creating informative messages differs from responding to information requests
6. Describe the importance of goodwill messages and explain how to make them effective

ON THE JOB

Communicating at Indigo Books and Music
BECOMING CANADA'S BOOKSELLER

www.chapters.indigo.ca

"I've always been passionate about reading," says Heather Reisman. ". . . I still have all my childhood books. But I didn't know I was going to end up in the business."

Heather Reisman's business is her passion. The CEO of Indigo Books and Music, Reisman created Indigo in 1996 as "the world's first cultural department store," where consumers can buy books, CDs, DVDs, videos, gift items, and fine stationery. At that time, her chief competitor was Chapters Books, another superstore chain, which merged with Indigo in 2001, with Reisman becoming the controlling shareholder. Today, Indigo is Canada's largest retail bookstore, with 90 superstores under the Indigo, Chapters, and The World's Biggest Bookstore banners and 155 small-format stores, including Coles, Indigospirit, SmithBooks and The Book Company.

Reisman's challenge is to nurture Canadian interest in books. A book lover herself, she highlights her "personal picks" on the website and in-store. Yet Indigo is intended to be more than retail outlets: Reisman envisions them as "cultural havens for book lovers to meet local, national, and international artists." Online, customers can participate in a community of readers by posting and reading book reviews, viewing members' book lists, and joining book clubs. In-store, customers can also enjoy coffee in a café with friends and make book selection a social event.

As Indigo's founder and CEO (chief executive officer), Heather Reisman is the primary decision maker for her firm's image and activities. Her goal is to create an environment where book lovers can enjoy "the best of a proprietor-run shop combined with the selection of a true emporium." Indigo's position in the Canadian book market is testimony to her ability to communicate her vision clearly to Indigo executives, front-line staff, and customers.

Her company raises money for the Indigo Love of Reading Foundation, which supplies new books and learning materials to high-needs elementary schools. Reisman sees literacy as a way to raise the self-esteem of young Canadians and involves customers in this mission by encouraging donations through the website or stores. Through another program, FUNdraisers, schools and groups can hold in-store student programs with Indigo donating a portion of purchases made by invited guests.

As you read this chapter, put yourself in Heather Reisman's position. To maintain your business and social goals, you must send clear messages to customers and store managers, requesting both information and action. How can you obtain the facts you need to make your decisions? How will you communicate your goals so Indigo can maintain its stature in consumers' eyes?[1]

Using the Three-Step Writing Process for Routine and Positive Messages

✷–[Explore

Regardless of the subject matter of your business messages, you can make them more effective by staying focused on your business goals and emphasizing the audience's concerns.

Objective 1 Apply the three-step writing process to routine and positive messages.

Whether you're answering consumer correspondence, congratulating an employee on a job well done, or requesting information from another firm, during the typical business day you'll be composing a lot of routine, good-news, and goodwill messages. In fact, most business communication is about routine matters: orders, information, company policies, claims, credit, employees, products, operations, and so on. The three-step writing process still gives you a valuable way to produce effective messages.

Step 1: Plan Your Message

Even though planning routine and positive messages may take only a few minutes, the four tasks of planning still apply.

Even simple messages can benefit from thoughtful planning.

1. Analyze the situation ensuring that your purpose is clear and that you know enough about your audience to craft a successful message.
2. Gather the information your audience needs to know.
3. Select the right medium for the message and the audience.
4. Organize your information effectively. This task includes defining your main idea, limiting your scope, selecting a direct or an indirect approach, and outlining your content. Throughout this chapter, you'll learn more about performing all four of these tasks for a variety of routine and positive message types.

Step 2: Write Your Message

With all messages, you need to adapt to your audience by being sensitive to their needs: Maintain a "you" attitude, be polite, emphasize the positive, and use bias-free language. To strengthen your relationship with your audience, establish your credibility and project your company's image. And keep in mind that even if you normally use a conversational tone, some messages may need to be more formal than others. Finally, use plain English and make your writing as active as possible.

With some practice, you'll be able to compose most routine messages quickly. Your main idea is probably well defined already; just ensure that you stick to it by limiting the scope of your message.

For routine requests and positive messages
> state the request or main idea
> give necessary details
> close with a cordial request for specific action

In most cases, your readers will be interested or at least neutral, so you can usually adopt the direct approach for routine and positive messages: Open with a clear statement of the main idea, include all necessary details in the body, and then close cordially. However, even though these messages are the least complicated to write, communicating across cultural boundaries can be a challenge, especially if you're not familiar with the cultural differences involved. (See "Achieving Intercultural Communication—How Direct Is Too Direct?")

Step 3: Complete Your Message

No matter how brief or straightforward your message, maximize its impact by giving yourself plenty of time to revise, produce, proofread, and distribute it.

1. Revise your message by evaluating content and organization to ensure that you've said what you want to in the order you want to say it. Review your message's readability. Edit and rewrite to make it concise and clear.

2. Design your document to suit your purpose and your audience. Even simple messages can benefit from careful font selection, the wise use of white space, and other design choices.

ACHIEVING INTERCULTURAL COMMUNICATION

How Direct Is Too Direct?

Being direct is civil, considerate, and honest—or so say people in Canada and the United States. Others view that same directness as being abrupt, rude, and intrusive—even dishonest and offensive. Countries such as Mexico, Japan, Saudi Arabia, Italy, and the Philippines all tend to have high-context cultures (see discussion in Chapter 3). That is, the people in these countries depend on shared knowledge and inferred messages to communicate; they gather meaning more from context and less from direct statement.

Offering a little constructive criticism may actually hurt your Japanese assistant's dignity. In fact, in high-context cultures, avoid saying outright, "You are wrong." You could cause the other person to lose face. When making requests, determine whether to use a direct or an implied message by considering audience attitudes toward destiny, time, authority, and logic:

> **Destiny.** Do audience members believe they can control events themselves or do they see events as predetermined and uncontrollable? If you're supervising employees who believe that fate controls a construction deadline, your crisp email message requesting them to stay on schedule may be hard for them to understand. It may even be insulting.

> **Time.** Do audience members view time as exact, precise, and not to be wasted, or do they see time as relative, relaxed, and necessary for developing interpersonal relationships? If you see time as money and you get straight to business in your memo to your Mexican manager, your message may be overlooked in the confusion over your disregard for social propriety.

> **Authority.** Do audience members conduct business more autocratically or more democratically? In Japan, rank and status are highly valued, so when communicating downward, you may need to be even more direct than you're used to being in Canada. And when communicating upward, you may need to be much less direct than usual.

> **Logic.** Do audience members pursue logic in a straight line, from point *a* to point *b*, or do they communicate in circular or spiral patterns of logic? If you organize a speech or letter in a straightforward and direct manner, your message may be considered illogical, unclear, and disorganized.

You may want to decide not only how direct to be in written messages but also whether to write at all. Perhaps a phone call or a visit would be more appropriate. By finding out how much or how little a culture tends toward high-context communication, you'll know whether to be direct or to rely on nuance when communicating with the people there.

CAREER APPLICATIONS

1 Research a high-context culture such as Japan, Korea, or China, and write a one- or two-paragraph summary of how someone in that culture would go about requesting information.

2 When you write to someone in a high-context culture, would it be better to (a) make the request directly in the interest of clarity or (b) match your audience's unfamiliar logic and make your request indirectly? Explain your answer.

3. Proofread the final version of your message, looking for typos, errors in spelling and mechanics, alignment problems, poor print quality, and so on.
4. Choose a distribution method that balances cost, convenience, time, security, and privacy. Refer to Chapter 7 for the most common media formats for brief messages.

Making Routine Requests

☀ Explore

Making requests—for information, action, products, adjustments, or other matters—is a routine part of business. In most cases, your audience will be prepared to comply, as long as you're not being unreasonable or asking someone to do something they would expect you to do yourself. By applying a clear strategy and tailoring your approach to each situation, you'll be able to generate effective requests quickly.

Strategy for Routine Requests

Like all business messages, routine requests have three parts: an opening, a body, and a close. Using the direct approach, open with your main idea, which is a clear statement of your request. Use the body to give details and justify your request. Then close by requesting specific action (see Figure 8–1).

STATE YOUR REQUEST UPFRONT Begin routine requests by placing your request first—up front is where it stands out and gets the most attention. Of

> **Figure 8–1** Organizing Routine and Positive Messages

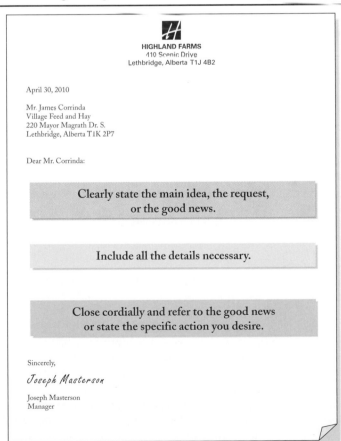

Online product ordering is simple: You merely click the item and quantity, and your purchase is added to your electronic shopping cart, with shipping and taxes automatically calculated. But how do you phrase order messages to small businesses, such as cottage industries operating out of home offices or small factories, that don't use online ordering? What medium do you select? How do you organize your message?

Objective 2 Outline an effective strategy for writing routine requests.

Take care that your direct approach doesn't come across as abrupt or tactless.

course, getting right to the point should not be interpreted as a licence to be abrupt or tactless.

> **Pay attention to tone.** Even though you expect a favourable response, the tone of your initial request is important. Instead of demanding action ("Send me your latest catalogue"), soften your request with words such as *please* and *I would appreciate.*
> **Assume your audience will comply.** An impatient demand for rapid service isn't necessary. You can generally make the assumption that your audience will comply with your request once the reason for it is clearly understood.
> **Be specific.** State precisely what you want. For example, if you request the latest market data from your research department, ensure that you say whether you want a one-page summary or a hundred pages of raw data.

EXPLAIN AND JUSTIFY YOUR REQUEST Use the body of your message to explain your initial request. Make the explanation a smooth and logical outgrowth of your opening remarks. If possible, point out how complying with the request could benefit the reader. For example, if you would like some assistance interpreting complex quality-control data, point out how a better understanding of quality-control issues would improve customer satisfaction and ultimately lead to higher profits for the entire company.

Using lists helps readers sort through multiple related items or multiple requests.

Whether you're writing a formal letter or a simple instant message, you can use the body of your request to list a series of questions. This list of questions helps organize your message and helps your audience identify the information you need. Just keep in mind a few basics:

> **Ask the most important questions first.** If cost is your main concern, you might begin with a question such as "What is the cost for shipping the merchandise by air versus truck?" Then ask more specific but related questions about, say, discounts for paying early.
> **Ask only relevant questions.** To help expedite the response to your request, ask only those questions that are central to your main request. Doing so will generate an answer sooner and make better use of the other person's time.
> **Deal with only one topic per question.** If you have an unusual or complex request, break it down into specific, individual questions so the reader can address each one separately. Don't put the burden of untangling a complicated request on your reader. This consideration not only shows respect for your audience's time but also gets you a more accurate answer in less time.

Close request messages with
> a request for some specific action
> information about how you can be reached
> an expression of appreciation

REQUEST SPECIFIC ACTION IN A COURTEOUS CLOSE Close your message with three important elements:

1. a specific request;
2. information about how you can be reached (if it isn't obvious); and
3. an expression of appreciation or goodwill.

When you ask readers to perform a specific action, ask that they respond by a specific time, if appropriate. ("Please send the figures by April 5 so I can return first-quarter results to you before the May 20 conference.") Also, by including your phone number, email address, office hours, and other contact information, you help your readers respond easily.

Conclude your message by sincerely expressing your goodwill and appreciation. However, don't thank the reader "in advance" for cooperating. If the reader's reply warrants a word of thanks, send it after you've received the reply. To review, see "Checklist: Writing Routine Requests."

CHECKLIST Writing Routine Requests

A. State your request upfront.
- ✔ Write in a polite, undemanding, personal tone.
- ✔ Use the direct approach, since your audience will probably respond favourably.
- ✔ Be specific and precise.

B. Explain and justify your request.
- ✔ Justify the request or explain its importance.
- ✔ Explain any potential benefits of responding.

- ✔ Break complex requests into individual questions that are limited to only one topic each.

C. Request specific action in a courteous close.
- ✔ Make it easy to comply by including appropriate contact information.
- ✔ Express your gratitude.
- ✔ State clearly any important deadlines.

Common Examples of Routine Requests

The various types of routine requests are innumerable, from asking favours to requesting credit. However, many of the routine messages that you'll write will likely fall into a few main categories: asking for information and action, asking for recommendations, and making claims and requesting adjustments.

ASKING FOR INFORMATION AND ACTION When you need to know about something, to elicit an opinion from someone, or to request a simple action, you usually need only ask. In essence, simple requests say

> what you want to know or what you want readers to do
> why you're making the request
> why it may be in your readers' interest to help you

If your reader is able to do what you want, such a straightforward request gets the job done quickly. Follow the direct approach by opening with a clear statement of your reason for writing. In the body, provide whatever explanation is needed to justify your request. Then close with a specific description of what you expect and include a deadline, if appropriate. In some situations, readers might be unwilling to respond unless they understand how the request benefits them, so be sure to include this information in your explanation. You can assume some shared background when communicating about a routine matter to someone in the same company.

Figure 8–2, an email request, asks district managers to fill out an attached information collection form. Although the request is not unusual and responding to it is part of the managers' responsibility, Helene Clausen asks for their help in a courteous manner and points out the benefits of responding.

In contrast to requests sent internally, those sent to people outside the organization usually adopt a more formal tone. Such requests are often in letter form, although some are sent via email. These messages are usually short and simple, but still formal and professional, such as the following request for information:

Dear Bioverse:

Please provide additional information on distribution opportunities for your Healthy Ponds product line, as mentioned on your website. Enviro Domestic is a 20-year-old firm with a well-established design, retail, and service presence in the Ottawa area, and we believe your bioremediation products would make a compelling addition to our offerings.

← Makes overall request in polite question form (no question mark)

← Identifies the writer's affiliation and reason for writing

> Figure 8–3 Effective Letter Requesting a Recommendation

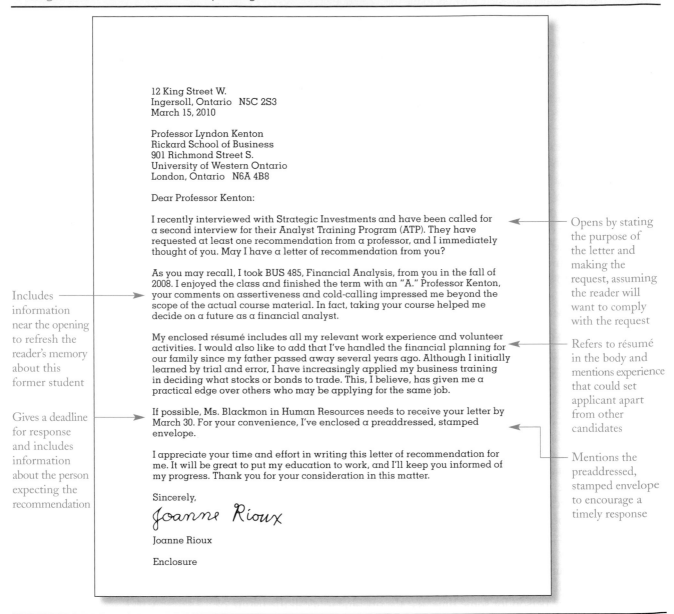

12 King Street W.
Ingersoll, Ontario   N5C 2S3
March 15, 2010

Professor Lyndon Kenton
Rickard School of Business
901 Richmond Street S.
University of Western Ontario
London, Ontario   N6A 4B8

Dear Professor Kenton:

Opens by stating the purpose of the letter and making the request, assuming the reader will want to comply with the request

I recently interviewed with Strategic Investments and have been called for a second interview for their Analyst Training Program (ATP). They have requested at least one recommendation from a professor, and I immediately thought of you. May I have a letter of recommendation from you?

Includes information near the opening to refresh the reader's memory about this former student

As you may recall, I took BUS 485, Financial Analysis, from you in the fall of 2008. I enjoyed the class and finished the term with an "A." Professor Kenton, your comments on assertiveness and cold-calling impressed me beyond the scope of the actual course material. In fact, taking your course helped me decide on a future as a financial analyst.

Refers to résumé in the body and mentions experience that could set applicant apart from other candidates

My enclosed résumé includes all my relevant work experience and volunteer activities. I would also like to add that I've handled the financial planning for our family since my father passed away several years ago. Although I initially learned by trial and error, I have increasingly applied my business training in deciding what stocks or bonds to trade. This, I believe, has given me a practical edge over others who may be applying for the same job.

Gives a deadline for response and includes information about the person expecting the recommendation

If possible, Ms. Blackmon in Human Resources needs to receive your letter by March 30. For your convenience, I've enclosed a preaddressed, stamped envelope.

Mentions the preaddressed, stamped envelope to encourage a timely response

I appreciate your time and effort in writing this letter of recommendation for me. It will be great to put my education to work, and I'll keep you informed of my progress. Thank you for your consideration in this matter.

Sincerely,

Joanne Rioux

Joanne Rioux

Enclosure

In most cases, and especially in your first letter, assume that a fair adjustment will be made, and follow the plan for direct requests. Open with a straightforward statement of the problem. In the body, give a complete, specific explanation of the details. Provide any information an adjuster would need to verify your complaint. In your close, politely request specific action or convey a sincere desire to find a solution. And if appropriate, suggest that the business relationship will continue if the problem is solved satisfactorily.

Be prepared to document your claim. Send copies and keep the original documents.

Companies usually accept the customer's explanation of what's wrong, so ethically it's important to be entirely honest when filing claims. Also, be prepared to back up your claim with invoices, sales receipts, cancelled cheques, dated correspondence, and any other relevant documents. Send copies and keep the originals for your files.

If the remedy is obvious, tell your reader exactly what you expect from the company, such as exchanging incorrectly shipped merchandise for the right item or issuing a refund if the item is out of stock. In some cases you might ask the reader to resolve a problem. However, if you're uncertain about the precise nature of the trouble, you could ask the company to make an assessment, then advise you on how the situation could be fixed. Supply your contact information so the company can discuss the situation with you if necessary.

Compare the tone of the draft version in Figure 8–4 with the revised version. If you were the person receiving the complaint, which version would you respond to more favourably?

A rational, clear, and courteous approach is best for any routine request. To review the tasks involved in making claims and requesting adjustments, see "Checklist: Making Claims and Requesting Adjustments."

> Figure 8–4 Effective and Ineffective Versions of Claim Letter

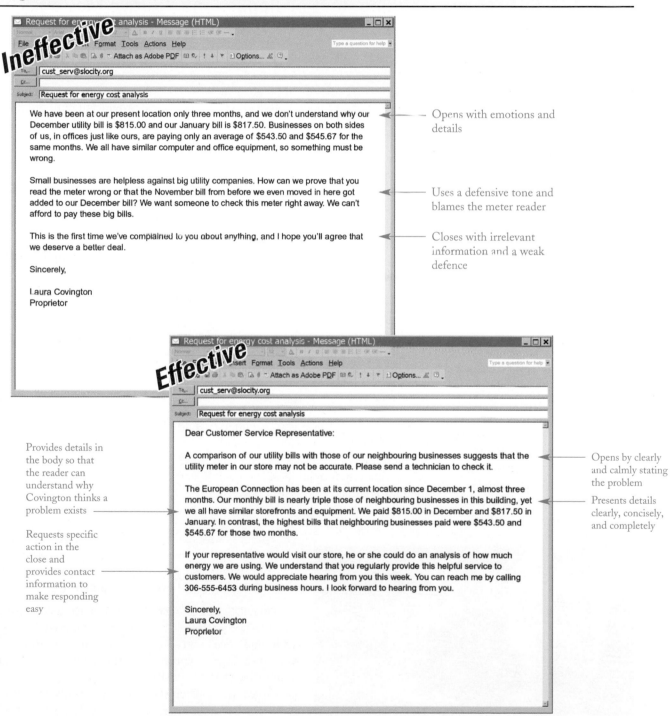

Ineffective

To: cust_serv@slocity.org
Subject: Request for energy cost analysis

We have been at our present location only three months, and we don't understand why our December utility bill is $815.00 and our January bill is $817.50. Businesses on both sides of us, in offices just like ours, are paying only an average of $543.50 and $545.67 for the same months. We all have similar computer and office equipment, so something must be wrong.

— Opens with emotions and details

Small businesses are helpless against big utility companies. How can we prove that you read the meter wrong or that the November bill from before we even moved in here got added to our December bill? We want someone to check this meter right away. We can't afford to pay these big bills.

— Uses a defensive tone and blames the meter reader

This is the first time we've complained to you about anything, and I hope you'll agree that we deserve a better deal.

— Closes with irrelevant information and a weak defence

Sincerely,

Laura Covington
Proprietor

Effective

To: cust_serv@slocity.org
Subject: Request for energy cost analysis

Dear Customer Service Representative:

Provides details in the body so that the reader can understand why Covington thinks a problem exists

A comparison of our utility bills with those of our neighbouring businesses suggests that the utility meter in our store may not be accurate. Please send a technician to check it.

— Opens by clearly and calmly stating the problem

The European Connection has been at its current location since December 1, almost three months. Our monthly bill is nearly triple those of neighbouring businesses in this building, yet we all have similar storefronts and equipment. We paid $815.00 in December and $817.50 in January. In contrast, the highest bills that neighbouring businesses paid were $543.50 and $545.67 for those two months.

— Presents details clearly, concisely, and completely

Requests specific action in the close and provides contact information to make responding easy

If your representative would visit our store, he or she could do an analysis of how much energy we are using. We understand that you regularly provide this helpful service to customers. We would appreciate hearing from you this week. You can reach me by calling 306-555-6453 during business hours. I look forward to hearing from you.

Sincerely,
Laura Covington
Proprietor

CHECKLIST Making Claims and Requesting Adjustments

- ✔ Maintain a professional tone, even if you're extremely frustrated.
- ✔ Open with a straightforward statement of the problem.
- ✔ Provide specific details in the body.
- ✔ Present facts honestly and clearly.

- ✔ Politely summarize desired action in the closing.
- ✔ Clearly state what you expect as a fair settlement, or ask the reader to propose a fair adjustment.
- ✔ Explain the benefits of complying with the request, such as your continued patronage.

Sending Routine Replies and Positive Messages

Just as you'll make numerous requests for information and action throughout your career, you'll also respond to similar requests from other people. When responding positively to a request, sending routine announcements, or sending a positive or goodwill message, you have several goals: to communicate the information or the good news, answer all questions, provide all required details, and leave your reader with a good impression of you and your firm.

Strategy for Routine Replies and Positive Messages

Objective 3 Describe a strategy for writing routine replies and positive messages.

Use a direct approach for positive messages.

Customer relationship software (CRM) stores a variety of customer information—addresses and phone numbers, previous orders, personal facts such as birthdates, hobbies, and interests. This information helps companies generate routine, good-news, and goodwill messages such as new product announcements to selected customers. While CRM software helps business retain customers and raise profits, does it also pose the danger of violating one of our most prized possessions, our privacy?

Like requests, routine replies and positive messages have an opening, a body, and a close. Since readers receiving these messages will generally be interested in what you have to say, you'll usually use the direct approach. Place your main idea (the positive reply or the good news) in the opening, use the body to explain all the relevant details, and close cordially—perhaps highlighting a benefit to your reader.

START WITH THE MAIN IDEA By opening your routine and positive messages with the main idea or good news, you're preparing your audience for the detail that follows. Make your opening clear and concise. Although the following introductory statements make the same point, one is cluttered with unnecessary information that buries the purpose, whereas the other is brief and to the point:

Instead of This	Write This
I am pleased to inform you that after careful consideration of a diverse and talented pool of applicants, each of whom did a thorough job of analyzing Bild Pharmaceuticals' training needs, we have selected your bid.	Bild Pharmaceuticals has accepted your bid to provide public speaking and presentation training to the sales staff.

The best way to write a clear opening is to have a clear idea of what you want to say. Before you put one word on paper, ask yourself, "What is the single most important message I have for the audience?"

PROVIDE NECESSARY DETAILS AND EXPLANATION Use the body to explain your point completely so that your audience won't be confused or doubtful about your meaning. As you provide the details, maintain the supportive tone established in the opening. This tone is easy to continue when your message is entirely positive, as in this example:

Your educational background and internship have impressed us, and we believe you would be a valuable addition to Green Valley Properties. As discussed during your interview, your salary will be $4600 per month, plus benefits. Please plan to meet with our benefits manager, Paula Sanchez, at 9:30 A.M. on Monday, March 22. She will assist you with all the paperwork necessary to tailor our benefit package to your family situation. She will also arrange various orientation activities to help you fit in with our company.

However, if your routine message is mixed and must convey mildly disappointing information, put the negative portion of your message into as favourable a context as possible:

Embed any negative information in a positive context.

Instead of This	Write This
No, we no longer carry the Sportsgirl line of sweaters.	The new Olympic line has replaced the Sportsgirl sweaters that you asked about. Olympic features a wider range of colours and sizes and more contemporary styling.

In this example, the more complete description is less negative and emphasizes how the audience can benefit from the change. Be careful, though: You can use negative information in this type of message *only* if you're reasonably sure the audience will respond positively. Otherwise, use the indirect approach (discussed in Chapter 9).

If you are communicating to customers, you might also want to use the body of your message to assure the customer of the wisdom of his or her purchase selection (without being condescending or self-congratulatory). Using such favourable comments, often know as *resale*, is a good way to build customer relationships. These comments are commonly included in acknowledgments of orders and other routine announcements to customers, and they are most effective when they are relatively short and specific:

The zipper on the carrying case you purchased is double-stitched and guaranteed for the life of the product.

The KitchenAid mixer you ordered is our best-selling model. It should meet your cooking needs for many years.

END WITH A COURTEOUS CLOSE Your message is most likely to succeed if your readers are left feeling that you have their best interests in mind. You can accomplish this task either by highlighting a benefit to the audience or by expressing appreciation or goodwill. If follow-up action is required, clearly state who will do what next. See "Checklist: Writing Routine Replies and Positive Messages" to review the primary tasks involved in this type of business message.

Ensure that the audience understands what to do next and how that action will benefit them.

Common Examples of Routine Replies and Positive Messages

Practise

As with routine requests, you'll encounter the need for a wide variety of routine replies and positive messages. You can expect to write letters or email messages for most routine messages directed to people outside the company, although instant messages (with live operators or automated bots) are gaining in popularity in customer-service applications. Most routine and positive messages fall into six main categories: answers to requests for information and action, grants

CHECKLIST Writing Routine Replies and Positive Messages

A. Start with the main idea.
- ✔ Be clear and concise.
- ✔ Identify the single most important message before you start writing.

B. Provide necessary details and explanation.
- ✔ Explain your point completely to eliminate any confusion or lingering doubts.
- ✔ Maintain a supportive tone throughout.

- ✔ Embed negative statements in positive contexts or balance them with positive alternatives.
- ✔ Talk favourably about the choices the customer has made.

C. End with a courteous close.
- ✔ Let your readers know that you have their personal well-being in mind.
- ✔ Tell readers how to proceed, if further action is required, and encourage them to act promptly.

of claims and requests for adjustment, recommendations, informative messages, good-news announcements, and goodwill messages.

 Practise

ANSWERING REQUESTS FOR INFORMATION AND ACTION Every professional answers requests for information and action from time to time. If the response to a request is a simple yes or some other straightforward information, the direct plan is appropriate. A prompt, gracious, and thorough response will positively influence how people think about you and the organization you represent. Figure 8–5 shows

> Figure 8–5 Effective Instant Messaging Response to Information Request

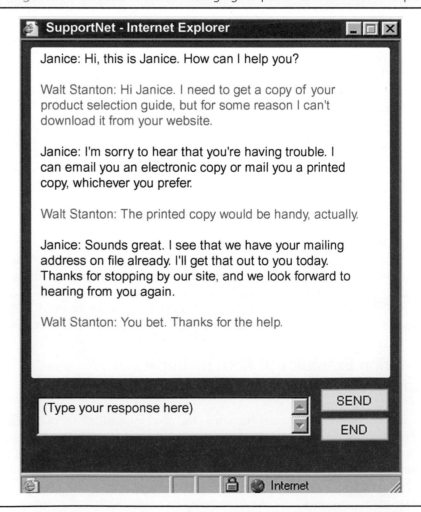

> Figure 8–6 Personalized Reply to a Request for Information

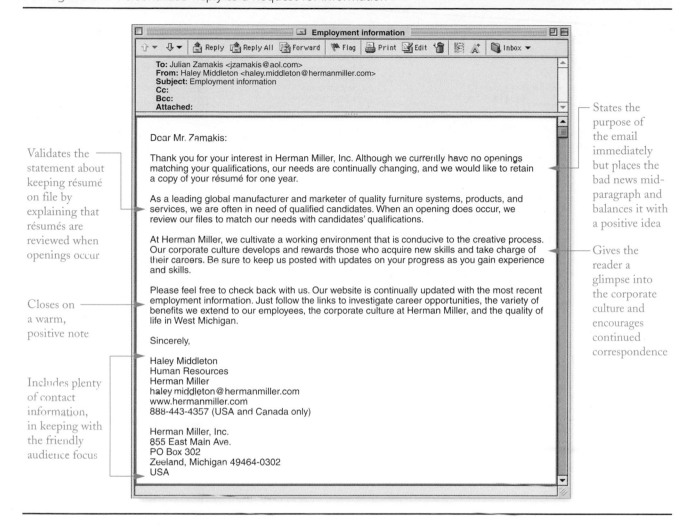

Validates the statement about keeping résumé on file by explaining that résumés are reviewed when openings occur

Closes on a warm, positive note

Includes plenty of contact information, in keeping with the friendly audience focus

States the purpose of the email immediately but places the bad news mid-paragraph and balances it with a positive idea

Gives the reader a glimpse into the corporate culture and encourages continued correspondence

Dear Mr. Zamakis:

Thank you for your interest in Herman Miller, Inc. Although we currently have no openings matching your qualifications, our needs are continually changing, and we would like to retain a copy of your résumé for one year.

As a leading global manufacturer and marketer of quality furniture systems, products, and services, we are often in need of qualified candidates. When an opening does occur, we review our files to match our needs with candidates' qualifications.

At Herman Miller, we cultivate a working environment that is conducive to the creative process. Our corporate culture develops and rewards those who acquire new skills and take charge of their careers. Be sure to keep us posted with updates on your progress as you gain experience and skills.

Please feel free to check back with us. Our website is continually updated with the most recent employment information. Just follow the links to investigate career opportunities, the variety of benefits we extend to our employees, the corporate culture at Herman Miller, and the quality of life in West Michigan.

Sincerely,

Haley Middleton
Human Resources
Herman Miller
haley_middleton@hermanmiller.com
www.hermanmiller.com
888-443-4357 (USA and Canada only)

Herman Miller, Inc.
855 East Main Ave.
PO Box 302
Zeeland, Michigan 49464-0302
USA

a quick and courteous exchange typical of IM communication in such areas as customer service and technical support. The agent (Janice) solves the problem quickly and leaves the customer with a positive impression of the company.

To handle repetitive queries quickly and consistently, companies usually develop form responses that can be customized as needed. The email message shown in Figure 8–6 personalizes a standardized response by including the recipient's name in the greeting. These ready-made message templates can be printed forms, word processor documents, email templates, or blocks of instant messaging text that can be dropped into a messaging window with the click of a mouse.

When you're answering requests and a potential sale is involved, you have three main goals: (1) to respond to the inquiry and answer all questions, (2) to leave your reader with a good impression of you and your firm, and (3) to encourage the future sale.

The letter in Figure 8–7 meets all three objectives.

GRANTING CLAIMS AND REQUESTS FOR ADJUSTMENT Even the best-run companies make mistakes, from shipping the wrong order to billing a customer's credit card inaccurately. In other cases, the customer or a third party might be responsible for the mistake, such as misusing a product or damaging

✳ Explore

Objective 4 Discuss the importance of knowing who is responsible when granting claims and requests for adjustment.

> Figure 8–7 Effective Inquiry Response Letter That Encourages a Future Sale

Piano
LIFE SAVER SYSTEM
from
DAMPP-CHASER

Phone: 800-438-1524   828-892-8271
Fax: 828-892-8272
Post Office Box 1610
Hendersonville, NC 28793 USA
www.dampp-chaser.com
e mail: piano@dampp-chaser.com

June 18, 2010

Giulio Ferrante
2 Campbell Avenue
St. John's, Newfoundland A1E 2S6

Dear Mr. Ferrante:

Thank you for visiting the Dampp-Chaser homepage. You will find enclosed the information you requested about the Dampp-Chaser Piano Climate Control System.

Opens with a clear statement of the main point

Established in 1974, Dampp-Chaser Corporation manufactures and supports products that provide climate control for small enclosed spaces. With the installation of the Dampp-Chaser Piano Climate Control System, application of Dampp-Chaser's unique technology protects pianos from the damaging effects of environmental changes.

From our headquarters and manufacturing facility in Hendersonville, North Carolina, we serve an international market. We have cultivated a corporate environment where pride in our product flourishes, where creativity and ingenuity are rewarded, and where the best interest of the customer is our primary consideration.

Presents both product and company information to educate the reader and heighten the credibility of the message

Please read through the enclosed literature. Our Piano Climate Control Systems are sold by piano dealers and piano technicians. To activate the 5-year warranty we extend on each System, it must be installed by a professional piano technician. If your piano technician is not a Dampp-Chaser installer, please call us to get the name of a technician in your area who currently installs Dampp-Chaser Systems. Or, ask your technician to contact us for detailed installation instructions. With his or her exceptional knowledge of the piano, your technician can easily follow the instructions we provide.

Provides essential information about the warranty and installation

Call us with any questions you may have at our toll-free number: 800-438-1524.

Thank you again for your interest in the Dampp-Chaser System, which extends the life of your piano, and over time, will provide you substantial cost savings for repairs and pitch adjustments.

Offers customer service for more information and cites product benefits

Best regards,
Dampp-Chaser Corporation

Brenda Robbins

Brenda Robbins
Customer Service

Enclosures

it in shipment. Each of these events represents a turning point in your relationship with your customer. If you handle the situation well, your customer will likely be even more loyal than before because you've proven that you're serious about customer satisfaction. However, if a customer believes that you mishandled a complaint, you'll make the situation even worse. Dissatisfied customers often take their business elsewhere without notice and tell numerous friends and colleagues about the negative experience. A transaction that might be worth only a few dollars by itself could cost you many times that amount in lost business. In other words, every mistake is an opportunity to improve a relationship.

Few people go to the trouble of requesting an adjustment unless they actually have a problem, so most businesses start from the assumption that the customer is correct. From there, your response to the complaint depends on both your company's policies for resolving such issues and your assessment of whether the company, the customer, or some third party is at fault.

Responding to a Claim When Your Company Is at Fault Whenever you communicate about a mistake your company has made, do so carefully. Before you respond, ensure that you know your company's policies, which might even dictate specific legal and financial steps to be taken. For serious problems that go beyond routine errors, your company should have a *crisis management plan* that outlines communication steps both inside and outside the organization (see Chapter 9).

Most routine responses should take your company's specific policies into account and address the following points:

> **Acknowledge receipt of the customer's claim or complaint.** Even if you can't solve the problem immediately, at least let the other party know that somebody is listening.
> **Take (or assign) personal responsibility for setting matters straight.** Customers want to know that someone is listening and responding.
> **Sympathize with the customer's inconvenience or frustration.** Letting the customer see that you're on his or her side helps defuse the emotional element of the situation.
> **Explain precisely how you have resolved, or plan to resolve, the situation.** If you can respond exactly as the customer requested, be sure to communicate that. If you can't, explain why.
> **Take steps to repair the relationship.** Keeping your existing customers is almost always less expensive than acquiring new customers, so look for ways to mend the relationship and encourage future business.
> **Follow up to verify that your response was correct.** Follow-up not only helps improve customer service, but also gives you another opportunity to show how much you care about your customer.

In addition to these positive steps, maintain a professional demeanour by avoiding some key negative steps: Don't blame anyone in your organization by name, don't make exaggerated, insincere apologies, don't imply that the customer is at fault, and don't promise more than you can deliver.

As with requests for information or action, companies often create customizable templates for granting claims and requests for adjustment. In the following example, a large mail-order clothing company created a form letter to respond to customers who complain that they haven't received exactly what was ordered:

Acknowledges receipt of the customer's communication → Your letter concerning your recent Ross River order has been forwarded to our director of order fulfillment. Your complete satisfaction is our goal, and a customer service representative will contact you within 48 hours to assist with the issues raised in your letter.

Explains what will happen next and when, without making promises the writer can't keep

Takes steps to repair the relationship and ensure continued business → In the meantime, please accept the enclosed $5 gift certificate as a token of our appreciation for your business. Whether youre skiing or driving a snowmobile, Ross River Gear offers you the best protection available from wind, snow, and cold—and Ross River has been taking care of customers' outdoor needs for over 27 years.

Closes with statement of company's concern for all its customers → Thank you for taking the time to write to us. Your input helps us better serve you and all our customers.

In contrast, a response letter written as a personal answer to a unique claim would open with a clear statement of the good news: the settling of the claim according to the customer's request. The following is a more personal response from Ross River Gear:

Here is your heather-blue wool-and-mohair sweater (size large) to replace the one returned to us with a defect in the knitting. Thanks for giving us the opportunity to correct this situation. Customers' needs have come first at Ross River Gear for 27 years.

I've enclosed our newest catalogue and a $5 gift certificate that's good toward any purchase from it. Whether you are skiing or driving a snowmobile, Ross River Gear offers you the best protection available from wind, snow, and cold. Please let us know how we may continue to serve you and your sporting needs.

✷⊟Explore   **Responding to a Claim When the Customer Is at Fault** Communication about a claim is a delicate matter when the customer is clearly at fault. You can (1) refuse the claim and attempt to justify your refusal, or (2) simply do what the customer asks.

If you refuse the claim, you may lose your customer—as well as many of the customer's friends and colleagues, who will hear only one side of the dispute. You must weigh the cost of making the adjustment against the cost of losing future business from one or more customers.

When granting an unjustified claim, maintain a respectful and positive tone while informing the customer that the claim was a result of misuse or mistreatment of the product.

If you choose to grant the claim, you can open with the good news: You're replacing the merchandise or refunding the purchase price. However, the body needs more attention. Your job is to make the customer realize that the merchandise was mistreated, but you want to avoid being condescending ("Perhaps you failed to read the instructions carefully") or preachy ("You should know that wool shrinks in hot water"). The dilemma is this: If the customer fails to realize what went wrong, you may commit your firm to an endless procession of returned merchandise; but if you insult the customer, your cash refund will have been wasted because you'll lose your customer anyway. Close in a courteous manner that expresses your appreciation for the customer's business. Without being offensive, the letter in Figure 8–8 educates a customer about how to treat his in-line skates.

✷⊟Explore   **Responding to a Claim When a Third Party Is at Fault** Sometimes neither your firm nor your customer is at fault. For example, ordering a DVD from Chapters.Indigo.ca involves not only the company but also a delivery service such as private courier or Canada Post, the manufacturer of the DVD, a credit card issuer, and a company that processes credit card transactions. Any one of these other partners might be at fault, but the customer is likely to blame Chapters.Indigo.ca, since that is the entity primarily responsible for the transaction.

No general scheme applies to every case involving a third party, so evaluate the situation carefully and know your company's policies before responding. For instance, an online retailer and the companies that manufacture its merchandise might have an agreement which specifies that the manufacturers automatically handle all complaints about product quality. However, regardless of who eventually resolves the problem, if customers contact you, you need to respond with messages that explain how the problem will be solved. Pointing fingers is unproductive and unprofessional; resolving the situation is the only issue customers care about. See "Checklist: Granting

> Figure 8–8 Responding to a Claim When the Buyer Is at Fault

Planning > **Writing** > **Completing**

Analyze the Situation
Verify that the purpose is to grant the customer's claim, tactfully educate him, and encourage further business.

Gather Information
Gather information on product care, warranties, and resale information.

Select the Right Medium
An email message is appropriate in this case because the customer contacted the company via email.

Organize the Information
You're responding with a positive answer, so a direct approach is fine.

Adapt to Your Audience
Show sensitivity to audience needs by using a "you" attitude, politeness, positive emphasis, and bias-free language.

Compose the Message
Maintain a style that is respectful while still managing to educate the customer on product usage and maintenance.

Revise the Message
Evaluate content and review readability; avoid unnecessary details.

Produce the Message
Emphasize a clean, professional appearance.

Proofread the Message
Review for errors in layout, spelling, and mechanics.

Distribute the Message
Email the reply.

1   **2**   **3**

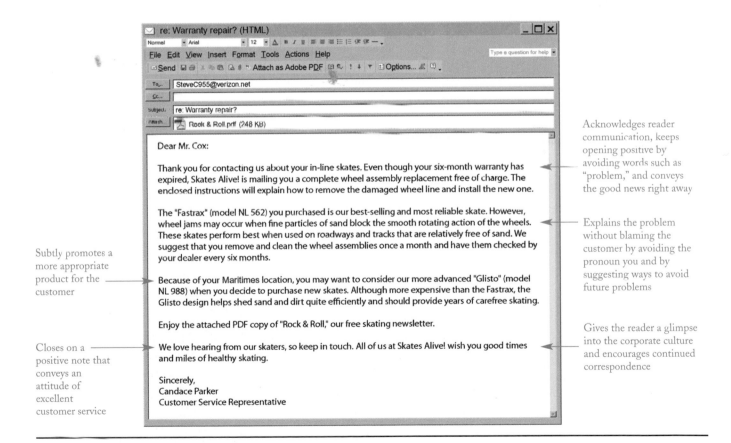

re: Warranty repair? (HTML)

To: SteveC955@verizon.net
Cc:
Subject: re: Warranty repair?
Attach: Rock & Roll.pdf (248 KB)

Dear Mr. Cox:

Thank you for contacting us about your in-line skates. Even though your six-month warranty has expired, Skates Alive! is mailing you a complete wheel assembly replacement free of charge. The enclosed instructions will explain how to remove the damaged wheel line and install the new one.

The "Fastrax" (model NL 562) you purchased is our best-selling and most reliable skate. However, wheel jams may occur when fine particles of sand block the smooth rotating action of the wheels. These skates perform best when used on roadways and tracks that are relatively free of sand. We suggest that you remove and clean the wheel assemblies once a month and have them checked by your dealer every six months.

Because of your Maritimes location, you may want to consider our more advanced "Glisto" (model NL 988) when you decide to purchase new skates. Although more expensive than the Fastrax, the Glisto design helps shed sand and dirt quite efficiently and should provide years of carefree skating.

Enjoy the attached PDF copy of "Rock & Roll," our free skating newsletter.

We love hearing from our skaters, so keep in touch. All of us at Skates Alive! wish you good times and miles of healthy skating.

Sincerely,
Candace Parker
Customer Service Representative

Acknowledges reader communication, keeps opening positive by avoiding words such as "problem," and conveys the good news right away

Explains the problem without blaming the customer by avoiding the pronoun you and by suggesting ways to avoid future problems

Subtly promotes a more appropriate product for the customer

Gives the reader a glimpse into the corporate culture and encourages continued correspondence

Closes on a positive note that conveys an attitude of excellent customer service

Claims and Adjustment Requests" (p. 242) to review the tasks involved in these kinds of business messages.

PROVIDING RECOMMENDATIONS When writing a letter of recommendation, your goal is to convince readers that the person being recommended has the characteristics necessary for the job, project assignment, or other objective the

CHECKLIST Granting Claims and Adjustment Requests

A. Responding when your company is at fault
- ✔ Be aware of your company's policies in such cases before you respond.
- ✔ Refer to the company's crisis management plan for serious situations.
- ✔ Start by acknowledging receipt of the claim or complaint.
- ✔ Take or assign personal responsibility for resolving the situation.
- ✔ Sympathize with the customer's frustration.
- ✔ Explain how you have resolved the situation (or plan to).
- ✔ Take steps to repair the customer relationship.
- ✔ Verify your response with the customer and keep the lines of communication open.

B. Responding when the customer is at fault
- ✔ Weigh the cost of complying with or refusing the request.
- ✔ Open with the good news if you choose to comply.
- ✔ Use the body of the message respectfully to educate the customer about steps needed to avoid a similar outcome in the future.
- ✔ Close with an appreciation for the customer's business.

C. Responding when a third party is at fault
- ✔ Evaluate the situation and review your company's policies before responding.
- ✔ Avoid placing blame; focus on the solution.
- ✔ Let the customer know what will happen to resolve the problem regardless of who is responsible for resolving the situation.

TIPS FOR SUCCESS

"Most professors have contact with hundreds of students a year. . . . Thus it is difficult to remember the specific accomplishments of each individual. Provide a résumé with each request, plus any other information that would be helpful."

Julie K. Henderson, APR, accredited public relations professional

A serious shortcoming cannot be ignored in letters of recommendation, but beware of being libellous:
> Include only relevant, factual information.
> Avoid value judgments.
> Balance criticisms with favourable points.

person is seeking. A successful recommendation letter contains a number of relevant details:

> The candidate's full name
> The position or other objective the candidate is seeking
> The nature of your relationship with the candidate
> An indication of whether you're answering a request from the person or taking the initiative to write
> Facts and evidence relevant to the candidate and the opportunity
> A comparison of this candidate's potential with that of peers, if available (for example, "Ms. Jonasson consistently ranked in the top 10 percent of her class.")
> Your overall evaluation of the candidate's suitability for the opportunity

As surprising as this might sound, the most difficult recommendation letters to write are often those for truly outstanding candidates. Your audience will have trouble believing uninterrupted praise for someone's talents and accomplishments. To enhance your credibility—and the candidate's—illustrate your general points with specific examples that point out the candidate's abilities and fitness for the job opening.

Most candidates aren't perfect, however, and you'll need to decide how to handle each situation that comes your way. Omitting a reference to someone's shortcomings may be tempting, especially if the shortcomings are irrelevant to the demands of the job in question. Even so, you have an obligation to refer to any serious shortcoming that could be related to job performance. You owe it to your audience, to your own conscience, and even to better-qualified candidates. You don't have to present the shortcomings as simple criticisms, however. A good option is to list them as areas for improvement, even as areas the person might be working on now.

The danger in writing a critical letter is that you might inadvertently engage in *libel*, publishing a false and malicious written statement that injures the candidate's reputation. On the other hand, if that negative information is truthful and relevant, it may be unethical and even illegal to omit it from your recommendation.

If you must refer to a shortcoming, you can best protect yourself by sticking to the facts, avoiding value judgments, and placing your criticism in the context of a generally favourable recommendation, as in Figure 8–9. In this letter, the writer supports all statements and judgments with evidence.

Recommendation letters are sensitive messages because you may need to describe the candidate's shortcomings as well as strengths. What is the ethical responsibility of the person writing the recommendation? What advice from Chapters 5 and 6 will help you write an effective and ethical letter?

> Figure 8–9 Effective Recommendation Letter

7700 Wisconsin Avenue
Bethesda, Maryland 20814-3579
301-986-1999

DISCOVERY
COMMUNICATIONS
INCORPORATED

November 15, 2010

Ms. Clarice Gailey
Director of Operations
McNally and Associates, Inc.
80 Royal Crest Drive
Markham, ON L3R 9X6

Dear Ms. Gailey:

I am pleased to recommend Talvin Biswas for the marketing position at McNally and Associates. Mr. Biswas has worked with Discovery Communications as an intern for the past two summers while working toward his degree in marketing and advertising. His duties included customer correspondence, Web content updates, and direct mail campaign planning.

As his supervisor, in addition to knowing his work here, I also know that Mr. Biswas has served as secretary for the International Business Association at the University of Michigan. He tutored other international students in the university's writing centre. His fluency in three languages (English, French, and Hindi) and thorough knowledge of other cultures will make him an immediate contributor to your international operation.

Although a quiet, introspective young man, Mr. Biswas will not hesitate to contribute ideas when invited to do so. In addition, because Mr. Biswas learns quickly, he will learn your company's routine with ease.

Mr. Biswas will make an excellent addition to your staff at McNally and Associates. If I can provide any additional information, please call or fax me at the numbers above. If you prefer to communicate by email, my address is rasmey@discovery.com.

Sincerely,

Lim Sok Rasmey
Vice-President, Strategy and Development

Specifies duration and nature of relationship in the body to give weight to the evaluation

Closes by inviting reader to discuss the candidate further

Clearly states candidate's full name and the main point of the letter in the opening

Begins the close by summarizing the supportive evaluation

You can also avoid trouble by asking yourself the following questions before mailing a recommendation letter:

> Does the party receiving this personal information have a legitimate right to it?
> Does all the information I've presented relate directly to the job or benefit being sought?
> Have I put the candidate's case as strongly and as honestly as I can?
> Have I avoided overstating the candidate's abilities or otherwise misleading the reader?
> Have I based all my statements on first-hand knowledge and provable facts?

Many human resource departments have specific guidelines for writing recommendation letters. You should always seek their expert advice when you prepare them.

Finally, before you send any recommendation letter, even for someone you know closely and respect without reservation, keep in mind that every time you write a recommendation, you're putting your own reputation on the line. If the person's shortcomings are so pronounced that you don't think he or she is a good fit for the job, the only choice is to not write the letter at all. Unless your relationship with the person warrants an explanation, simply suggest that someone else might be in a better position to provide a recommendation.[2]

✓•─Practise

Objective 5 Explain how creating informative messages differs from responding to information requests.

When writing informative messages
> State the purpose at the beginning and briefly mention the nature of the information you are providing.
> Provide the necessary details.
> End with a courteous close.

CREATING INFORMATIVE MESSAGES All companies send routine informative messages such as reminder notices and policy statements. For example, you may need to inform employees of organizational changes or tell customers about new shipping and return policies. Use the opening of informative messages to state the purpose (to inform) and briefly mention the nature of the information you are providing. Unlike the replies discussed earlier, informative messages are not solicited by your reader, so make it clear up front why the reader is receiving this particular message. In the body, provide the necessary details and end your message with a courteous close.

Most informative communications are neutral. That is, they stimulate neither a positive nor a negative response from readers. For example, when you send departmental meeting announcements and reminder notices, you'll generally receive a neutral response from your readers (unless the purpose of the meeting is unwelcome). Simply present the factual information in the body of the message and don't worry about the reader's attitude toward the information.

Some informative messages may require additional care. For example, policy statements or procedural changes may be good news for a company (perhaps by saving money). However, it may not be obvious to employees that such savings may make available additional employee resources or even pay raises. In instances where the reader may not initially view the information positively, use the body of the message to highlight the potential benefits from the reader's perspective.

✓•─Practise

ANNOUNCING GOOD NEWS To develop and maintain good relationships, smart companies, such as Indigo Books and Music, recognize that it's good business to advertise positive developments. These can include opening new facilities, appointing a new executive, introducing new products or services, or sponsoring community events. Because good news is always welcome, use the direct approach.

Writing to a successful job applicant is one of the most pleasant good-news messages you might have the opportunity to write. The following example uses the direct approach and provides information that the recipient needs:

Welcome to Lake Valley Rehabilitation Centre. A number of excellent candidates were interviewed, but your educational background and recent experience at Memorial Hospital make you the best person for the position of medical records coordinator.

Announces news in a friendly, welcoming tone

As we discussed, your salary is $38 600 a year. We would like you to begin on Monday, February 15. Please come to my office at 9 A.M. I will give you an in-depth orientation to Lake Valley and discuss the various company benefits available to you. You can also sign all the necessary employment documents.

Explains all necessary details

After lunch, Vanessa Jackson will take you to the medical records department and help you settle into your new responsibilities at Lake Valley Rehabilitation Centre. I look forward to seeing you first thing on February 15.

Explains first day's routine to ease the new employee's uncertainty

Although messages such as these are pleasant to write, they require careful planning and evaluation to avoid legal troubles. For example, messages that imply lifetime employment or otherwise make promises about the length or conditions of employment can be interpreted as legally binding contracts, even if you never intended to make such promises. Similarly, downplaying potentially negative news (such as rumours of a takeover) that turns out to affect the hired person in a negative way can be judged as fraud. Consequently, experts advise that a company's legal staff either scrutinize each offer letter or create standardized content to use in such letters.[3]

Job-offer letters should be reviewed by legal experts familiar with employment law because they can be viewed as legally binding contracts.

Good-news announcements are usually communicated via a letter or a **news release**, also known as a *press release,* a specialized document used to share relevant information with the local or national news media. (News releases are also used to announce negative news, such as plant closings.) In most companies, news releases are usually prepared (or at least supervised) by specially trained writers in the public relations department (see Figure 8–10). The content follows the customary pattern for a positive message: good news, followed by details and a positive close. However, news releases have a critical difference: You're not writing directly to the ultimate audience (such as the readers of a newspaper); you're trying to interest an editor or reporter in a story, and that person will then write the material that is eventually read by the larger audience. To write a successful news release, keep the following points in mind:[4]

> Ensure that your information is newsworthy and relevant to the specific publications or websites to which you are sending it. Editors are overwhelmed with news releases, so those without real news content are disposed of—and can damage the writer's credibility, too.
> Focus on one subject; don't try to pack a single news release with multiple, unrelated news items.
> Put your most important idea first. Don't force editors to hunt for the news.
> Be brief: Break up long sentences and keep paragraphs short.
> Eliminate clutter such as redundancy and extraneous facts.

> Figure 8–10 Online News Release

chapters.indigo.ca

Indigo love of reading foundation

Random House of Canada Donates $150,000 to Indigo Love of Reading Foundation

For Immediate Release. Toronto. January 24th, 2008. Random House of Canada President and CEO Brad Martin today announced a $150,000 charitable donation from Random House of Canada to the Indigo Love of Reading Foundation.

Created in 2004, The Indigo Love of Reading Foundation was launched by Indigo Books & Music Inc. in response to the crisis of under-resourced elementary school libraries across Canada.

Fifteen schools are selected each year by the Foundation. As of 2008, they will each receive a grant of $100,000 each over three years, $35,000 in the first two years and $30,000 in the third year. Funds are then allocated to the purchase of books or services to improve facilities, inspire students, and encourage a love of reading for elementary students within their school environments and throughout their lives.

According to Martin, "When Heather Reisman took a leadership position on this issue, illuminating the disturbing state of so many school libraries in Canada, as well as the incredible effect this grant has on the recipient schools, we at Random House of Canada decided we needed to make a significant contribution to the Love of Reading Foundation to try to help even more Canadian children."

Heather Reisman CEO of Indigo Books & Music Inc. said, "Only as a community can we draw the attention required to the chronic under-funding of so many school libraries across Canada. Random House of Canada's donation to Indigo's Love of Reading Foundation will ensure that one more Canadian elementary school will have a rich selection of books in their libraries and classrooms. We applaud their generosity and hope our entire publishing community will join in helping to make a difference in the lives of Canadian children."

Applications for the 2008 Indigo Love of Reading Foundation Grants are available at www.loveofreading.org, with the deadline for applications extended for 2008 until February 14th, 2008.

####

About Random House of Canada
Random House of Canada Limited is the Canadian division of Random House, Inc., the world's largest publisher of general interest hardcover, paperback and audio adult and children's fiction and nonfiction books. Random House of Canada Limited is home to the prestigious and long-standing Canadian imprints Doubleday Canada, Knopf Canada, Random House Canada, Vintage Canada, Anchor Canada and Seal Books. Random House is the book publishing division of Bertelsmann AG, one of the world's foremost media companies.

About the Love of Reading Foundation and Indigo Books & Music Inc.
In addition to Random House's generous contribution, the Indigo Love of Reading Foundation is supported year-round by the care and concern of Indigo customers and employees through a variety of initiatives including donations in-store at Chapters, Indigo and Coles, and online at www.loveofreading.org, the purchase of designated fundraising items.

Indigo Books and Music is a Canadian company and the largest book retailer in Canada, operating bookstores in all provinces under the names Indigo Books and Music, Chapters, and Coles. Indigo operates chapters.indigo.ca, an online retailer of books, music, videos, and DVDs. It is a publicly traded company listed on the Toronto Stock Exchange under the stock symbol IDG.

Contact info:

Tracey Turriff, SVP, Director, Corporate Communications, Random House of Canada
tturriff@randomhouse.com; 416-957-1568

Janet Eger, Director, Public Relations, Indigo Books & Music Inc.
jeger@indigo.ca; 416-342-8561

Annotations (left margin):

Focuses on one subject only; avoids unrelated news

Opens with the most important idea

Keeps paragraphs short

Includes concrete and specific information; maintains an objective tone

Keeps paragraphs short

> Be as specific as possible.
> Minimize self-congratulatory adjectives and adverbs; if the content of your message is newsworthy, the media professionals will be interested in the news on its own merits.
> Follow established industry conventions for style, punctuation, and format.

Online distribution systems such as CNW Telbec (www.cnw.ca) and PR Newswire (www.prnewswire.com) make it easy for even the smallest companies to reach editors and reporters at the most prominent publications around the world. Many companies also create special media pages on their websites that contain their latest news releases, background information on the company, and archives of past news releases.

Until recently, news releases were intended only for members of the news media and crafted in a way to provide information to reporters who would then write their own articles if the subject matter was interesting to their readers. Thanks to the internet, however, the nature of the news release is changing. Many companies now view it as a general-purpose tool for communicating directly with customers and other audiences, writing *direct-to-consumer news releases*. Some companies even forgo the traditional news release in favour of controlling and distributing such messages themselves. One form is blogs, which have become a popular mechanism for announcing positive company news (see Figure 8–11). As new-media expert David Meerman Scott puts it,

> Figure 8–11 Announcing Positive News

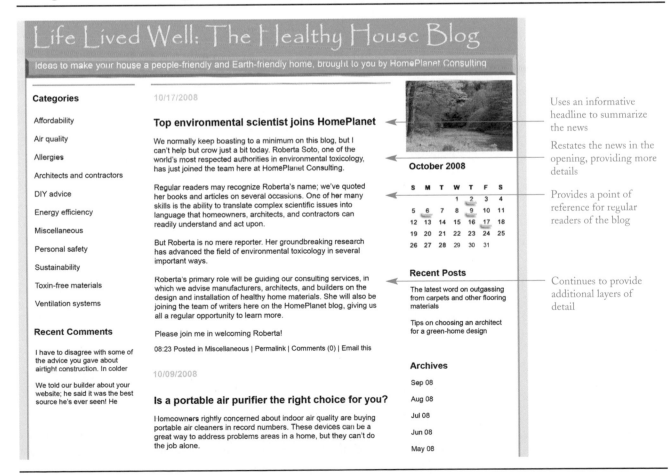

"Millions of people read press releases directly, unfiltered by the media. You need to be speaking directly to them."[5]

Explore

FOSTERING GOODWILL All business messages should be written with an eye toward fostering goodwill among business contacts, but some messages are written primarily and specifically to build goodwill. You can use these messages to enhance your relationships with customers, colleagues, and other businesspeople by sending friendly, or even unexpected notes with no direct business purpose.

Objective 6 Describe the importance of goodwill messages and explain how to make them effective.

Effective goodwill messages must be sincere and honest. Otherwise, you'll appear to be interested in personal gain rather than in benefiting customers, fellow workers, or your organization. To come across as sincere, avoid exaggerating, and back up any compliments with specific points. In addition, readers often regard more restrained praise as being more sincere:

Goodwill is the positive feeling that encourages people to maintain a business relationship.

Ensure that your compliments are both sincere and honest.

Instead of This	Write This
Words cannot express my appreciation for the great job you did. Thanks. No one could have done it better. You're terrific! You've made the whole firm sit up and take notice, and we are ecstatic to have you working here.	Thanks again for taking charge of the meeting in my absence and doing such an excellent job. With just an hour's notice, you managed to pull the legal and public relations departments together so we could present a united front in the negotiations. Your dedication and communication abilities have been noted and are truly appreciated.

Explore

Taking note of significant events in someone's personal life helps cement the business relationship.

Sending Congratulations One prime opportunity for sending goodwill messages is to congratulate someone for a significant business achievement—perhaps for being promoted or for attaining an important civic position. Compare the congratulatory notes in Figure 8–12, in which a manager at Office Supply corporate headquarters congratulates an advertising agency that was awarded a prestigious national contract. The draft version sounds vague and insincere, and it doesn't bother to actually offer congratulations until the final sentence. In contrast, the revised version moves swiftly to the subject: the good news. It gives reasons for expecting success and avoids extravagant and essentially meaningless praise such as "Only you can do the job!"

Other reasons for sending congratulations include recognizing employees for volunteer work, charity fundraising, or an athletic achievement. Figure 8–13 shows an email congratulating an organization's team that participated in the International Dragon Boat race on Lake Ontario. The highlights in people's personal lives—weddings, births, and graduations—are also occasions for such goodwill messages. You may congratulate business acquaintances on their own achievements or on the accomplishments of a spouse or child. You may also take note of personal events, even if you don't know the reader well. If you're already friendly with the reader, a more personal tone is appropriate.

Some companies even develop a mailing list of potential customers by assigning an employee to clip newspaper announcements of births, engagements,

> Figure 8–12 Poor and Improved Versions of a Letter Congratulating a Business Acquaintance

We are so pleased when companies that we admire do well. When we attended our convention in Montreal last month, we heard about your firm's recent selection to design and print media advertisements for the Canadian Association of Business Suppliers (CABS).

Sounds condescending and self-centred—expressing the reason but failing to actually congratulate the reader

We have long believed that high-visibility projects such as these should be awarded to only the top-tier companies in the industry, and Lambert, Cutchen & Browt is clearly the only company for the job.

Seems insincere because of the lack of supporting reasons and the exaggeration

We wish you the best of luck with your new ad campaign. Congratulations on a job well done!

Congratulating the reader in the close makes it seem like an afterthought

Sincerely,

Janice McCarthy

Janice McCarthy
Director, Media Relations

Draft

OFFICE SUPPLY, INC.
1659 Lower Water Street
Halifax, Nova Scotia   B3J 1R7

Phone: 902-555-8714
Fax: 902-555-8711
www.officesupply.com
info@officesupply.com

Revision

March 3, 2010

Mr. Ralph Lambert, President
Lambert, Cutchen & Browt, Inc.
85, rue Dalhousie
Québec City, QC G1K 7A7

Dear Mr. Lambert:

Opens by immediately expressing the reason for congratulating the reader

Congratulations on your firm's recent selection to design and print media advertisements for the Canadian Association of Business Suppliers (CABS). Your appointment was announced at the national convention in Montreal last month, and here at Office Supply we can think of no better firm to help our industry achieve wide recognition.

Uses body to make the compliment more effective by showing knowledge of the reader's work—without exaggeration

Over the course of many years, your firm's work for Office Supply has been nothing short of excellent. Both our corporate advertising staff here in Nova Scotia and regional promotional managers around the country continue to offer compliments on the quality of LCB's efforts. The campaign you will design for CABS is sure to yield similar positive responses.

Closes by expressing interest in following the future success of the firm

You can be sure we will follow your media campaign with great interest.

Sincerely,

Janice McCarthy

Janice McCarthy
Director, Media Relations

tw

> Figure 8–13 Email Congratulations Message

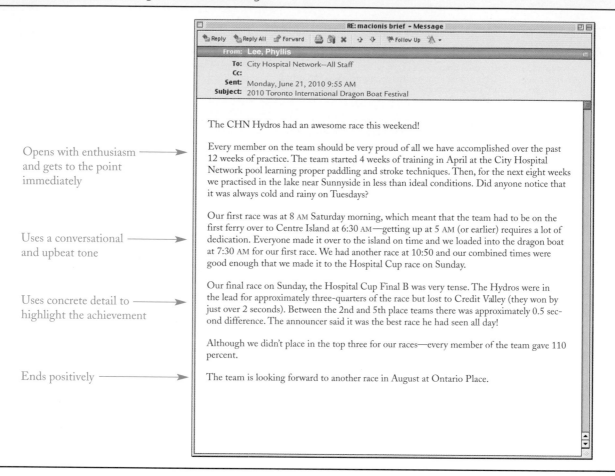

	RE: macionis brief - Message	

🖃 Reply   🖃 Reply All   🖅 Forward   🖨 📑 ✖   ⬆ ⬇   ☞ Follow Up 🖹 ▾

From: **Lee, Phyllis**
To: City Hospital Network—All Staff
Cc:
Sent: Monday, June 21, 2010 9:55 AM
Subject: 2010 Toronto International Dragon Boat Festival

The CHN Hydros had an awesome race this weekend!

Opens with enthusiasm and gets to the point immediately →

Every member on the team should be very proud of all we have accomplished over the past 12 weeks of practice. The team started 4 weeks of training in April at the City Hospital Network pool learning proper paddling and stroke techniques. Then, for the next eight weeks we practised in the lake near Sunnyside in less than ideal conditions. Did anyone notice that it was always cold and rainy on Tuesdays?

Uses a conversational and upbeat tone →

Our first race was at 8 AM Saturday morning, which meant that the team had to be on the first ferry over to Centre Island at 6:30 AM—getting up at 5 AM (or earlier) requires a lot of dedication. Everyone made it over to the island on time and we loaded into the dragon boat at 7:30 AM for our first race. We had another race at 10:50 and our combined times were good enough that we made it to the Hospital Cup race on Sunday.

Uses concrete detail to highlight the achievement →

Our final race on Sunday, the Hospital Cup Final B was very tense. The Hydros were in the lead for approximately three-quarters of the race but lost to Credit Valley (they won by just over 2 seconds). Between the 2nd and 5th place teams there was approximately 0.5 second difference. The announcer said it was the best race he had seen all day!

Although we didn't place in the top three for our races—every member of the team gave 110 percent.

Ends positively →

The team is looking forward to another race in August at Ontario Place.

Employee volunteer activities not only contribute to the community but can also bring employees together. How should management acknowledge employee volunteerism? Are notes of appreciation sufficient? What are other methods for showing recognition?

✦ Explore

weddings, and graduations or to obtain information on real estate transactions in the local community. Then they introduce themselves by sending out a form letter that might read like this:

Congratulations on your new home! All of us at Klemper Security Solutions hope it brings you and your family many years of security and happiness.

Please accept the enclosed *Homeowner's Guide to Home Security* with our compliments. It lists a number of simple steps you can take to keep your home, your family, and your possessions safe.

This simple message has a natural, friendly tone, even though the sender has never met the recipient.

Sending Messages of Appreciation An important business quality is the ability to recognize the contributions of employees, colleagues, suppliers, and other associates. Your praise does more than just make the person feel good; it encourages further excellence. Moreover, a message of appreciation may become an important part of someone's personnel file. So, when you write a message of appreciation, specifically mention the person or people you want to praise. The brief message that follows expresses gratitude and reveals the happy result:

> Thank you and everyone on your team for the heroic efforts you took to bring our servers back up after last Friday's flood. We were able to restore business right on schedule first thing Monday morning. You went far beyond the level of contractual service in restoring our data centre within 16 hours. I would especially like to highlight the contribution of networking specialist Julienne Marks, who worked for 12 straight hours to reconnect our Internet service. If I can serve as a reference in your future sales activities, please do not hesitate to ask.

An effective message of appreciation documents a person's contributions.

Offering Condolences In times of serious trouble and deep sadness, well-written condolences and expressions of sympathy can mean a great deal to people who've experienced loss. Granted, this type of message is difficult to write, but don't let the difficulty of the task keep you from responding promptly. Those who have experienced a health problem, the death of a loved one, or a business misfortune appreciate knowing that others care.

Open condolences with a brief statement of sympathy, such as "I was deeply sorry to hear of your loss." In the body, mention the good qualities or the positive contributions made by the person or business. State what the person or business meant to you or to your colleagues. In closing, offer your condolences and best wishes. One considerate way to end this type of message is to say something that will give the reader a little lift, such as a reference to a brighter future. Here are a few general suggestions for writing condolence messages:

The primary purpose of condolence messages is to let the audience know that you and the organization you represent care about the person's loss.

> **Keep reminiscences brief.** Recount a memory or an anecdote (even a humorous one), but don't dwell on the details of the loss lest you add to the reader's anguish.
> **Write in your own words.** Write as if you were speaking privately to the person. Don't quote "poetic" passages or use stilted or formal phrases. If the loss is a death, refer to it as such rather than as "passing away" or "departing."
> **Be tactful.** Mention your shock and dismay, but remember that bereaved and distressed loved ones take little comfort in lines such as "Richard was too young to die" or "Starting all over again will be so difficult." Try to strike a balance between superficial expressions of sympathy and painful references to a happier past or the likelihood of a bleak future.
> **Take special care.** Ensure that you spell names correctly and are accurate in your review of facts. Be prompt.
> **Write about special qualities of the deceased.** You may have to rely on reputation to do this, but let the grieving person know you valued his or her loved one.
> **Write about special qualities of the bereaved person.** A few kind words may help a bereaved family member feel more confident about their future during such a traumatic time.[6]

The following example, a message by a manager to his administrative assistant after learning of her husband's death, shows sensitivity and sincerity:

> My sympathy to you and your children. All your friends at Carter Electric were so very sorry to learn of John's death. Although I never had the opportunity to meet him, I do know how very special he was to you. Your tales of your family's camping trips and his rafting expeditions were always memorable.

To review the tasks involved in writing goodwill messages, see "Checklist: Sending Goodwill Messages."

CHECKLIST Sending Goodwill Messages

✔ Be sincere and honest.

✔ Don't exaggerate or use vague, grandiose language. Support positive statements with specific evidence.

✔ Use congratulatory messages to build goodwill with clients and colleagues.

✔ Send messages of appreciation to emphasize how much you value the work of others.

✔ When sending condolence messages, open with a brief statement of sympathy, followed by an expression of how much the deceased person meant to you or your firm (as appropriate), and then close by offering your best wishes for the future.

Summary of Learning Objectives

1 **Apply the three-step writing process to routine and positive messages.** Even though routine messages are usually short and simple, they benefit from the three-step writing process. First, plan your message by analyzing your situation, gathering your information, and selecting the right medium. Second, when writing your message, maintain the "you" attitude; use the direct approach as long as your readers will be positive (or neutral); write in plain English, and use the active voice. Third, completing routine messages means making them as professional as possible by (1) revising for clarity, completeness, and conciseness, (2) selecting appropriate design elements and delivery methods, and (3) proofreading carefully.

2 **Outline an effective strategy for writing routine requests.** When writing a routine request, open by stating your specific request. At the same time, avoid being abrupt or tactless: pay attention to tone, assume your audience will comply, and be specific. Use the body of a routine request to justify your request and explain its importance. Close routine requests by asking for specific action (including a deadline when possible) and expressing goodwill. Ensure that you include all contact information so your reader can respond easily.

3 **Describe a strategy for writing routine replies and positive messages.** When writing routine and positive replies, open concisely and clearly with your main idea. Follow the opening with the necessary details and explanation, ensuring that you maintain a courteous, supportive tone. End with a courteous close, incorporating an audience benefit or expressing goodwill. If reader follow-up is required, make the action detailed.

4 **Discuss the importance of knowing who is responsible when granting claims and requests for adjustment.** In messages granting a claim, the explanatory section differs depending on who is at fault. If your company is at fault, avoid reacting defensively, and be careful when referring to company errors. Rather than placing blame, explain your company's efforts to do a good job. Remember not to make any unrealistic promises or guarantees. If your customer is at fault, you must help your reader realize what went wrong so it won't happen repeatedly. However, you don't want to sound condescending, preachy, or insulting. If a third party is at fault, you can honour the claim with no explanation, or you can honour the claim and explain that the problem was not your fault.

5 **Explain how creating informative messages differs from responding to information requests.** When writing informative messages and responses to information requests, open with the main idea. However, because informative messages are not solicited by your audience, you must clarify early in your message why the reader is receiving it. Furthermore, most informative messages are neutral, unlike responses to information requests, which motivate either a positive or negative reader response. In situations where readers may not view the information positively, stress potential reader benefits in the message body to encourage a positive reaction.

6 **Describe the importance of goodwill messages and explain how to make them effective.** Goodwill messages are important for building relationships with customers, colleagues, and other businesspeople. These friendly, unexpected notes have no direct business purpose, but they make people feel good about doing business with the sender. To make goodwill messages effective, be honest and sincere. Avoid exaggerating, back up compliments with specific points, and give restrained praise.

On the Job PERFORMING COMMUNICATION TASKS AT INDIGO BOOKS AND MUSIC

Heather Reisman wants to offer Canada's book lovers "the best of a small proprietor-run shop combined with the selection of a true emporium." The impact she has made demonstrates her ability to communicate with customers and employees. You have recently taken a job at Indigo's head office as an administrative assistant on the management team. One of your jobs entails drafting emails to Indigo store managers. Using the principles outlined in this chapter for writing direct requests, handle each situation to the best of your ability. Be prepared to explain your choices.

1 You are asked to contact the store managers to find out how the company's website has affected sales in retail outlets over the last six months. Which is the best opening for this email?

  a I have recently joined Heather Reisman's staff as an administrative assistant. She has asked me to write to you to obtain your feedback on the impact on store sales of the company's website over the last six months. Please reply to the following questions within five working days. (List of questions follows.)

  b Please tell us what you think of www.chapters.indigo.ca. Ms. Reisman wants to evaluate its impact on our business. Within the next few days, can you take a few moments to jot down your thoughts on its impact. Specifically, Ms. Reisman would like to know . . . (List of questions follows.)

  c By April 14, please submit written answers to the following questions on the Indigo website. (List of questions follows.)

  d Has the website affected sales in your store over the last six months? We're polling all store managers for the impact of online retailing. Is it thumbs up or thumbs down on the Web?

2 Which is the best choice for the middle section of the email?

  a Specifically, has store business decreased because of the website? If so, what is the percentage decrease in sales over the last six months? Over the comparable period last year? Have customers mentioned the website? If so, have their comments been positive or negative? Has employee morale been affected by the site? How?

  b By replying to the following questions, you will help us decide whether to continue with the website as is or change it:

    1) Has business decreased in your store since Indigo has had the website? If it has, what is the percentage decrease in sales over the last six months? Over the comparable period last year?

    2) Have customers mentioned the site? If so, have their comments been positive or negative? Give some typical examples.

    3) Has employee morale been affected by the website? How?

  c By circling the response that most accurately reflects your store's experience, please answer the following questions regarding the company's new website:

    1) Over the last six months, sales have
      a increased
      b decreased
      c remained about the same

    2) Customers (have/have not) mentioned the website. Their comments have been primarily (positive/negative).

    3) Employee morale (has/has not) been affected by the website.

  d Ms. Reisman needs to know the following:

    1) How have overall store sales changed over the last six months because of the company's website?

    2) What do customers think of the site? Attach complimentary customer comments.

    3) What do employees think of the site? Attach complimentary employee comments.

3 For a courteous close with a request for specific action, which paragraph is the best?

  a Thank you for your cooperation. Please submit your reply in writing by April 14.

  b Ms. Reisman is meeting with her senior staff on April 16 to discuss the website. She would like to have your reaction in writing by April 14 so that she can present your views during that meeting. If you have any questions, please contact me at (416) 555-2886.

  c You may contact me at (416) 555-2886 if you have any questions or need additional information about this survey. Ms. Reisman requires your written response by April 14 so she can discuss your views with her senior staff on April 16.

  d Thank you for your input. As the frontline troops in the battle for sales, you are in a good position to evaluate the impact of the website. We here at corporate headquarters want to increase overall company sales, but we need your feedback. Please submit your written evaluation by April 14 so Ms. Reisman can use the results as ammunition in her meeting with senior staff on April 16.

Test Your Knowledge

1 What is an effective strategy for writing a routine request?

2 How does the question of fault affect what you say in a message granting a claim?

3 How do you ask for specific action in a courteous manner?

4 When is a request routine?

5 How does a claim differ from an adjustment?

6 How can you avoid sounding insincere when writing a goodwill message?

7 What are some guidelines for writing condolence messages?

8 Why is tone important in routine messages?

Apply Your Knowledge

1 When organizing request messages, why is it important to know whether any cultural differences exist between you and your audience? Explain.

2 Your company's error cost an important business customer a new client; you know it and your customer knows it. Do you apologize, or do you refer to the incident in a positive light without admitting any responsibility? Explain.

3 You've been asked to write a letter of recommendation for an employee who worked for you some years ago. You recall that the employee did an admirable job, but you can't remember any specific information at this point. Should you write the letter anyway? Explain.

4 Every time you send a direct-request memo to Ted Erasmus, who works in another department in your company, he delays or refuses to comply. You're beginning to get impatient. Should you send Erasmus a memo to ask what's wrong? Complain to your supervisor about Erasmus's uncooperative attitude? Arrange a face-to-face meeting with Erasmus? Bring up the problem at the next staff meeting? Explain.

5 **Ethical Choices** You have a complaint against one of your suppliers, but you have no documentation to back it up. Should you request an adjustment anyway? Why or why not?

Running Cases

●─┤Watch on **mycanadianbuscommlab**

> CASE 1 Noreen

Now that Petro-Go is a larger company (see Chapter 6 for the merger with Best Gas), upper management has established a new procedure: regular semi-annual bonuses will be distributed to all employees who meet performance targets. The letter announcing this development will include a list of performance expectations and bonus goals.

Noreen is asked to write the letter on her manager's behalf informing the "Go Points" and "Collections" teams of this new bonus opportunity. Petro-Go will mail the letter, once approved, to each of the team members, letting them know that, because of their hard work over the past six months, they will each receive a bonus cheque. The cheques will be enclosed with the letters. Each member will receive a bonus amount based on their individual performance and achievements captured in the Petro-Go semi-annual statistics and progress reports.

QUESTIONS

a) Is this a routine or good-news letter or both?

b) What information should Noreen begin the letter with? Why?

c) How should Noreen end the letter? Why?

d) Does Noreen need to include an announcement about the merger in this letter?

e) What tone will Noreen use in this letter?

YOUR TASK

Write the letter. Remember to use company letterhead (create it yourself) and include an enclosure notation for the two enclosures. Also thank the team for their hard work and dedication to the company over the past six months. Let the employees know they can contact Noreen if they have questions or comments.

This letter contains confidential information and should state so on the envelope and on the letter itself. Prepare the envelope. (See Appendix A for letter and envelope formats.)

> CASE 2 Kwong

Kwong's boss at Accountants For All asks him to write a letter replying to a corporate customer's request for information. Kwong needs to write to Albridge and Scranton Ltd. to give

them the details of the last five years' tax summaries. John Albridge would like to know the total expenses claimed, primarily the vehicle expense deduction, and the total amount of refund/amount owed each year. Kwong needs to attach copies of each year's summary statement as well.

This is a good opportunity for Kwong to thank Albridge and Scranton Ltd. for their past business and let them know that Accountants For All looks forward to their future business.

QUESTIONS

a) Should Kwong list the information requested in the letter or simply attach the summary statements and refer the reader to those statements?

b) Is this a routine or goodwill letter or both?

c) Is the direct or indirect approach best for this letter? Why?

d) Is it best to thank the customer for their past business in the introductory part of the letter? Why or why not?

e) Where in the letter should Kwong include the information about looking forward to doing future business with Albridge and Scranton Ltd.?

YOUR TASK

Write the letter. Remember to use company letterhead (create it yourself) and include an enclosure notation. Also thank the customer for their past and anticipated future business. Leave the customer with a contact name at Accountants For All for further inquiries.

This letter contains confidential information; the envelope and the letter itself should state this warning. Prepare the envelope. (See Appendix A for letter and envelope formats.)

Practise Your Knowledge

Read the following documents, then (1) analyze the strengths and weaknesses of each sentence and (2) revise each document so it follows this chapter's guidelines.

DOCUMENT 8.A: REQUESTING ROUTINE INFORMATION FROM A BUSINESS

Our university is closing its dining hall for financial reasons, so we want to do something to help the students prepare their own food in their residence rooms if they so choose. Your colourful ad in University Management Magazine *caught our eye. We need the following information before we make our decision.*

> *Would you be able to ship the microwaves by August 15? We realize this is short notice, but our board of trustees just made the decision to close the dining hall last week, and we're scrambling around trying to figure out what to do.*
> *Do they have any kind of a warranty? Students can be pretty hard on things, as you know, so we will need a good warranty.*
> *How much does it cost? Do you give a discount for a big order?*
> *Do we have to provide a special electrical outlet?*
> *Will students know how to use them, or will we need to provide instructions?*

As I said before, we're on a tight time frame and need good information from you as soon as possible to help us make our decision about ordering. You never know what the board might come up with next. I'm looking at several other companies, also, so please let us know ASAP.

DOCUMENT 8.B: MAKING CLAIMS AND REQUESTS FOR ADJUSTMENT

At a local business-supply store, I recently purchased your Negotiator Pro for my computer. I bought the CD because I saw your ad for it in MacWorld *magazine, and it looked as if it might be an effective tool for use in my corporate seminar on negotiation.*

Unfortunately, when I inserted it in my office computer, it wouldn't work. I returned it to the store, but since I had already opened it, they refused to exchange it for a CD that would work or give me a refund. They told me to contact you and that you might be able to send me a version that would work with my computer.

You can send the information to me at the letterhead address. If you cannot send me the correct disc, please refund my $79.95. Thanks in advance for any help you can give me in this matter.

DOCUMENT 8.C: RESPONDING TO CLAIMS AND ADJUSTMENT REQUESTS WHEN THE CUSTOMER IS AT FAULT

We read your letter requesting your deposit refund. We couldn't figure out why you hadn't received it, so we talked to our maintenance engineer as you suggested. He said you had left one of the doors off the hinges in your apartment to get a large sofa through the door. He also confirmed that you had paid him $35.00 to replace the door, since you had to turn in the U-Haul trailer and were in a big hurry.

This entire situation really was caused by a lack of communication between our housekeeping inspector and the maintenance engineer. All we knew was that the door was off the hinges when it was inspected by Sally Tarnley. You know that our policy states that if anything is wrong with the apartment, we keep the deposit. We had no way of knowing that George just hadn't gotten around to replacing the door.

But we have good news. We approved the deposit refund, which will be mailed to you from our home office in Halifax, N.S. I'm not sure how long that will take, however. If you don't receive the cheque by the end of next month, give me a call.

Next time, it's really a good idea to stay with your apartment until it's inspected as stipulated in your lease agreement. That way, you'll be sure to receive your refund when you expect it. Hope you have a good summer.

DOCUMENT 8.D: LETTER OF RECOMMENDATION

Your letter to Michael McKay, president of SoundWave Electronics, was forwarded to me because I am the human resources director. In my job as head of HR, I have access to performance reviews for all of the SoundWave employees in Canada. This means, of course, that I would be the person best qualified to answer your request for information on Nick Oshinski.

In your letter of the 15th, you asked about Nick Oshinski's employment record with us because he has applied to work for your company. Mr. Oshinski was employed with us from January 3, 2008, until February 27, 2009. During that time, Mr. Oshinski received ratings ranging from 2.5 up to 9.6, with 10 being the top score. As you can see, he must have done better reporting to some managers than to others. In addition, he took all vacation days, which is a bit unusual. Although I did not know Mr. Oshinski personally, I know that our best workers seldom use all the vacation time they earn. I do not know if that applies in this case.

In summary, Nick Oshinski performed his tasks well depending on who managed him.

Exercises

8.1 Revising Messages: Directness and Conciseness

Revise the following short email messages so they are more direct and concise; develop a subject line for each revised message.

a I'm contacting you about your recent email request for technical support on your cable internet service. Part of the problem we have in tech support is trying to figure out exactly what each customer's specific problem is so that we can troubleshoot quickly and get you back in business as quickly as possible. You may have noticed that in the online support request form, there are a number of fields to enter your type of computer, operating system, memory, and so on. While you did tell us you were experiencing slow download speeds during certain times of the day, you didn't tell us which times specifically, nor did you complete all the fields telling us about your computer. Please return to our support website and resubmit your request, being sure to provide all the necessary information; then we'll be able to help you.

b. Thank you for contacting us about the difficulty you had collecting your luggage at Fort Simpson Airport. We are very sorry for the inconvenience this has caused you. As you know, travelling can create problems of this sort regardless of how careful the airline personnel might be. To receive compensation, please send us a detailed list of the items that you lost and complete the following questionnaire. You can email it back to us.

c. Sorry it took us so long to get back to you. We were flooded with résumés. Anyway, your résumé made the final ten, and after meeting three hours yesterday, we've decided we'd like to meet with you. What is your schedule like for next week? Can you come in for an interview on June 15 at 3:00 P.M.? Please get back to us by the end of this workweek and let us know if you will be able to attend. As you can imagine, this is our busy season.

d. We're letting you know that because we use over a ton of paper a year and because so much of that paper goes into the wastebasket to become so much more environmental waste, starting Monday, we're placing green plastic bins outside the elevators on every floor to recycle that paper and in the process, minimize pollution.

8.2 Revising Messages: Directness and Conciseness

Rewrite the following sentences so that they are direct and concise. If necessary, divide your answer into two sentences.

a. We wanted to invite you to our special 40% off by-invitation-only sale. The sale is taking place on November 9.

b. We wanted to let you know that we are giving a tote bag and a voucher for five iTunes downloads with every $50 donation you make to our radio station.

c. The director planned to go to the meeting that will be held on Monday at a little before 11 A.M.

d. In today's meeting, we were happy to have the opportunity to welcome Paul Eccleson. He reviewed some of the newest types of order forms. If you have any questions about these new forms, feel free to call him at his office.

8.3 Internet: Analyzing an E-card

Visit the Career eCards section of the Blue Mountain site at www.bluemountain.com and analyze one of the electronic greeting cards bearing a goodwill message of appreciation for good performance. Under what circumstances would you send this electronic message? How could you personalize it for the recipient and the occasion? What would be an appropriate close for this message?

8.4 Teamwork: Choosing Format and Approach

With another student, identify the purpose and select the most appropriate format for communicating these written messages. Next, consider how the audience is likely to respond to each message. Based on this audience analysis, determine whether the direct or indirect approach would be effective for each message. Explain your reasoning.

a. a notice to all employees about the placement of recycling bins by the elevator doors

b. the first late-payment notice to a good customer who usually pays his bills on time

8.5 Revising Messages: Conciseness, Courteousness, and Specificity

Critique the following closing paragraphs. How would you rewrite each to be concise, courteous, and specific?

a. I need your response sometime soon so I can order the parts in time for your service appointment. Otherwise your air-conditioning system may not be in tip-top condition for the start of the summer season.

b. Thank you in advance for sending me as much information as you can about your products. I look forward to receiving your package in the very near future.

c. To schedule an appointment with one of our knowledgeable mortgage specialists in your area, you can always call our hotline at 1-800-555-8765. This is also the number to call if you have more questions about mortgage rates, closing procedures, or any other aspect of the mortgage process. Remember, we're here to make the home-buying experience as painless as possible.

8.6 Ethical Choice: Customer Service

Your company markets a line of automotive accessories for people who like to "tune" their cars for maximum performance. A customer has just written a furious email, claiming that a supercharger he purchased from your website didn't deliver the extra engine power he expected. Your company has a standard refund process to handle situations such as this, and you have the information you need to inform the customer about that. You also have information that could help the customer find a more compatible supercharger from one of your competitors, but the customer's email message is so abusive that you don't feel obligated to help. Is this an appropriate response? Why or why not?

Cases APPLYING THE THREE-STEP WRITING PROCESS TO CASES

Apply each step to the following cases, as assigned by your instructor.

Planning

Analyze the Situation
Identify both your general purpose and your specific purpose. Clarify exactly what you want your audience to think, feel, or believe after receiving your message. Profile your primary audience, including their backgrounds, differences, similarities, and likely reactions to your message.

Gather Information
Identify the information your audience will need to receive, as well as other information you may need in order to craft an effective message.

Select the Right Medium
Make sure your medium is both acceptable to the audience and appropriate for the message.

Organize the Information
Choose a direct or indirect approach based on the audience and the message; most routine requests and routine and positive messages should employ a direct approach. Identify your main idea, limit your scope, then outline necessary support points and other evidence.

Writing

Adapt to Your Audience
Show sensitivity to audience needs with a "you" attitude, politeness, positive emphasis, and bias-free language. Understand how much credibility you already have—and how much you may need to establish. Project your company's image by maintaining an appropriate style and tone.

Compose the Message
Draft your message using precise language, effective sentences, and coherent paragraphs.

Completing

Revise the Message
Evaluate content and review readability, then edit and rewrite for conciseness and clarity.

Produce the Message
Use effective design elements and suitable layout for a clean, professional appearance.

Proofread the Message
Review for errors in layout, spelling, and mechanics; verify overall document quality.

Distribute the Message
Deliver your message using the chosen medium; make sure all documents and all relevant files are distributed successfully.

1   2   3

Routine Requests

1. Step on it: Letter to Floorgraphics requesting information about underfoot advertising

You work for Mary Utanpitak, owner of Better Bike and Ski Shop. Yesterday, Mary met with the Schwinn sales representative, Tom Beeker, who urged her to sign a contract with Floorgraphics. That company leases floor space from retail stores and then creates and sells floor ads to manufacturers such as Schwinn. Floorgraphics will pay Mary a fee for leasing the floor space, as well as a percentage for every ad it sells. Mary was definitely interested and turned to you after Beeker left.

"Tom says that advertising decals on the floor in front of the product reach consumers right where they're standing when making a decision," explained Mary. "He says the ads increase sales from 25 to 75 percent."

You both look down at the dusty floor, and Mary laughs. "It seems funny that manufacturers will pay hard cash to put their names where customers are going to track dirt all over them! But if Tom's telling the truth, we could profit three ways: from the leasing fee, the increased sales of products being advertised, and the share in ad revenues. That's not so funny."

Your Task: Mary Utanpitak asks you to write a letter for her signature to CEO Richard Rebh at Floorgraphics, Inc. (1725 E. 3rd Avenue, Vancouver, BC, V5M 5R6) asking for financial details and practical information about the ads. For example, how will you clean your floors? Who installs and removes the ads? Can you terminate the lease if you don't like the ads?[7]

Email SKILLS

2. Breathing life back into your biotech career: Email requesting a recommendation

After five years of work in the human resources department at Cell Genesys (a company that is developing cancer treatment drugs), you were laid off in a round of cost-cutting moves that rippled through the biotech industry in recent years. The good

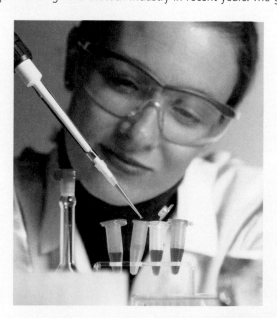

news is that you found stable employment in the grocery distribution industry. The bad news is that in the three years since you left Cell Genesys, you truly miss working in the exciting biotechnology field and having the opportunity to be a part of something as important as helping people recover from life-threatening diseases. You know that careers in biotech are uncertain, but you have a few dollars in the bank now, and you're willing to ride that roller coaster again.

Your Task: Draft an email to Calvin Morris, your old boss at Cell Genesys, reminding him of the time you worked together and asking him to write a letter of recommendation for you.[8]

Email SKILLS

3. Please tell me: Email requesting routine information about a product

As a consumer, you've probably seen hundreds of products that you'd like to buy (if you haven't, look at the advertisements in your favourite magazine for ideas). Choose a big-ticket item that is rather complicated, such as a stereo system or a vacation in the Caribbean.

Your Task: You surely have some questions about the features of your chosen product or about its price, guarantees, local availability, and so on. Write an email to the company or organization that's offering it, and ask four questions that are important to you. Ensure that you include enough background information for the reader to answer your questions satisfactorily.

Text-Messaging SKILLS

4. Tracking the new product buzz: Text message to colleagues at a trade show

The vast Consumer Electronics Show (CES) is the premier promotional event in the industry. More than 13 0000 industry insiders from all over the world come to see the exciting new products on display from nearly 1500 companies—everything from video game gadgets to internet-enabled refrigerators with built-in computer screens. You've just stumbled on a video game controller that has a built-in webcam to allow networked gamers to see and hear each other while they play. Your company also makes game controllers, and you're worried that your customers will flock to this new controller-cam. You need to know how much "buzz" is circulating around the show: Have people seen it? What are they saying about it? Are they excited about it?

Your Task: Compose a text message to your colleagues at the show, alerting them to the new controller-cam and asking them to listen for any "buzz" that it might be generating among the attendees at the Las Vegas Convention Center and the several surrounding hotels where the show takes place. Here's the catch: Your text messaging service limits messages to 160 characters, including spaces and punctuation, so your message can't be any longer than this.[9]

5. Couch potato: Letter requesting refund from House of Couches furniture store

You finally saw the couch you need: the colour is perfect (royal blue), the length just right (it could seat you, your husband, and the kids), and the style ideal for your furnishings (modern but classic). With the scratch-and-save card, you bought it at a 40-percent discount, bringing the price to a mere $600.00, plus delivery and taxes.

The salesperson who served you said that for an extra $10.00 you can have "deluxe delivery": the new couch will be taken out of its box and put into place, and the cardboard and your old couch removed. You wouldn't have to arrange removal on your own. "Deluxe delivery" sounded great, and the price was right. You decided to pay for it.

The day of delivery, your couch arrived wrapped in plastic. The deliverymen dropped it in the middle of your living room, and started to leave, with their hands out for a tip. You reminded them about "deluxe delivery." They removed the plastic covering, took your old, sagging couch to the garage after you asked them twice, saying they didn't remove couches from the owner's property. They left grumbling. You could have done everything with the help of your spouse, and saved the $10.00.

That afternoon you called customer service at House of Couches seeking a refund of the $10.00 you paid for "deluxe delivery." The representative refused to honour your request, saying that the deliverers fulfilled the "deluxe delivery" conditions.

Your Task: You feel that the salesperson lied to you and that the customer service representative was rude. You decide to write to the owner of House of Couches, Fritz Wegman, to seek satisfaction. His address is: House of Couches, 2 Broad Street, Regina, SK, S1P 1Y2.

|Email SKILLS |

6. Website: Email message from Knitsmart Yarn and Needles requesting additional information

An enjoyable hobby that whiled away cold winter evenings in Corner Brook, Newfoundland and Labrador, has given cousins Lee O'Reilly and Siobhan Gavin a local following and fame throughout the hand-knitting community in the Atlantic provinces as well as in fashionable shops in Canada's large cities. First teaching their young relatives and neighbours the art of knitting, they soon branched into selling yarn out of Lee's basement and then running small classes for different skill levels. After opening a small yarn shop in Corner Brook's shopping district, they began creating their own knitwear designs and selling them as kits, supplied with yarn and knitting needles, through their shop and catalogue. After their designs caught the eye of a Holt Renfrew buyer, their business took off beyond what the cousins ever imagined. Their colourful sweater and hat designs are worn by not only socialites but also film and stage performers attracted to their uniqueness. Little did the cousins think that their hobby would become a cottage industry and then a major business.

You've been working at Knitsmart Yarn and Needles during your summer break from university, and you think it's time that Lee and Siobhan branched into new territory: the World Wide Web. You think that the cousins should build a website where they can gain new customers, interest other people in their craft, and inspire knitters around the world with their patterns. You find an advertisement in the local newspaper for a company that creates websites (Webtech), but the classified ad gives little information beyond a phone number and an email address.

Your Task: You will set aside time next week to discuss the opportunities a Knitsmart website offers to Lee and Siobhan. Write an email message requesting more information from Webtech about what the company can do for Knitsmart Yarn and Needles.

|IM SKILLS |

7. Transglobal exchange: Instant message request for information from Chinese manufacturer

Fortunately, your company, Diagonal Imports, chose the Sametime enterprise instant messaging software produced by IBM Lotus. Other products also allow you to carry on real-time exchanges with colleagues on the other side of the planet, but Sametime supports bidirectional machine translation, and you're going to need it.

The problem is that production on a popular line of decorative lighting appliances produced at your Chinese manufacturing plant inexplicably came to a halt last month. As the product manager in Canada, you have many resources you could call on to help, such as new sources for faulty parts. But you can't do anything if you don't know the details. You've tried telephoning top managers in China, but they're not giving you the responses you need.

Finally, your friend Kuei-chen Tsao has returned from a business trip. You met her during your trip to China last year. She doesn't speak English, but she's the line engineer responsible for this particular product: a fibre-optic lighting display that features a plastic base with a rotating colour wheel. As the wheel turns, light emitted from the spray of fibre-optic threads changes colour in soothing patterns. Product #3347XM is one of Diagonal's most popular items, and you've got orders from novelty stores around Canada waiting to be filled. Kuei-chen should be able to explain the problem, determine whether you can help, and tell you how long before regular shipping resumes.

Your Task: Write the first of what you hope will be a productive instant message exchange with Kuei-chen. Remember that your words will be machine translated.[10]

Routine Messages

|Portfolio BUILDER | |Podcasting SKILLS |

8. Listening to business: Using the iPod to train employees

As a training specialist in Winnebago Industry's human resources department, you're always on the lookout for new ways to help employees learn vital job skills. While watching a production worker page through a training manual while learning how to assemble a new recreational vehicle, you get what seems to be a great idea: Record the assembly instructions as audio files that workers can listen to while performing the necessary steps. With audio instructions, they wouldn't need to keep shifting their eyes between the product and the manual—and constantly losing their place. They could focus on the product and listen for each instruction. Also, the new system wouldn't cost much at all; any computer can record the audio files, and you'd simply make them available on an intranet site for download onto iPods or other digital music players.

Your Task: You immediately run your new idea past your boss, who has heard about podcasting but doesn't think it has any place in business. He asks you to prove the practicality of the idea by recording a demonstration. Choose a process that you engage in yourself—anything from replacing the strings on a guitar to sewing a quilt to changing the oil in a car—and write a brief (one page or less) description of the process that could be recorded as an audio file. Think carefully about the limitations of the audio format as a replacement for printed text (e.g., do you need to tell people to pause the audio while they perform a time-consuming task?).

9. Got it covered? Letter from American Express about SUV rentals

You can always tell when fall arrives at American Express—you are deluged with complaints from customers who've just received their summer vacation bills. Often these angry calls are about a shock-inducing damage repair bill from a car rental agency. Vacation car rentals can be a lot more complicated than most people think. Here's what happens.

Your credit card customers are standing at the Hertz or Avis counter, ready to drive away, when the agent suggests an upgrade to, say, a Ford Expedition or another large SUV. Feeling happy-go-lucky on vacation, your customers say, "Why not?" and hand over their American Express card.

As they drive off in large vehicles that many are unaccustomed to handling, 9 out of 10 are unaware that the most common accidents among rental cars take place at low speeds in parking lots. Also, the upgraded vehicle they're driving is no longer fully covered either by their regular auto insurance or by the secondary car rental insurance they expect from American Express. If they've agreed to pay the additional $10 to $25 a day for the car rental agency's "collision and liability damage waiver fee," they will be able to walk away from any accident with no liability. Otherwise, they're running a costly risk.

Soon they pull into a shopping mall with the kids to pick up the forgotten sunscreen and sodas, where they discover that the luxury road-warrior-mobile is not so easy to park in stalls designed in the 1970s and 1980s when compact cars were all the rage. *Thwack*—there goes the door panel. *Crunch*—a rear bumper into a light post. *Wham!* There goes the family bank account, but they don't realize it yet—not until they receive the bill from the rental agency, the one that comes *after* their auto

insurance and credit card companies have already paid as much as they're going to pay for damages.

Auto insurers typically provide the same coverage for rentals as you carry on your own car. When customers use their credit card to pay for car rentals, American Express offers secondary protection that generally covers any remaining unpaid damages. But there are important exceptions.

Neither insurance nor credit card companies will pay the "loss of vehicle use fees" that car rental agencies always tack on. These fees can run into thousands of dollars, based on the agency's revenue losses while their car is in the repair shop. When your customers are billed for this fee, they invariably call you, angrily demanding to know why American Express won't pay it. And if they've rented an SUV, they're even angrier.

American Express Green and Gold cards provide secondary coverage up to $55 000, and the Platinum card extends that to $75 000. But large SUVs such as the Ford Expedition, GMC Yukon, and Chevrolet Suburban are not covered at all. Such exclusions are common. For example, Diners Club specifically excludes "high-value, special interest or exotic cars"—such as the Ferraris, Maseratis, and even Rolls-Royces that are urged on customers by rental agencies.

Your Task: As assistant vice-president of customer service, you'd like to keep the phone lines cooler this summer and fall. It's April, so there's still time. Write a form letter to be sent to all American Express customers, urging them to check their rental car coverages, advising them against renting vehicles that are larger than they really require, and encouraging them to consider paying the rental agency's daily loss waiver fees.[11]

Blogging SKILLS

10. Here's how it will work: Explaining the brainstorming process

Austin, Texas, advertising agency GSD&M Advertising brainstorms new advertising ideas using a process it calls *dynamic collaboration*. A hand-picked team of insiders and outsiders is briefed on the project and given a key question or two to answer. The team members then sit down at computers and anonymously submit as many responses as they can within five minutes. The project moderators then pore over these responses, looking for any sparks that can ignite new ways of understanding and reaching out to consumers.

Your Task: For these brainstorming sessions, GSD&M recruits an eclectic mix of participants from inside and outside the agency—figures as diverse as economists and professional video gamers. To make sure everyone understands the brainstorming guidelines, prepare a message to be posted on the project blog. In your own words, convey the following four points as clearly and succinctly as you can:

> **Be yourself.** We want input from as many perspectives as possible, which is why we recruit such a diverse array of participants. Don't try to get into what you believe is the mindset of an advertising specialist; we want you to approach the given challenge using whatever analytical and creative skills you normally employ in your daily work.
> **Create, don't edit.** Don't edit, refine, or self-censor while you're typing during the initial five-minute session. We don't care if your ideas are formatted beautifully, phrased poetically, or even spelled correctly. Just crank 'em out as quickly as you can.
> **It's about the ideas, not the participants.** Just so you know up front, all ideas are collected anonymously. We can't tell who submitted the brilliant ideas, the boring ideas, or the already-tried-that ideas. So while you won't get personal credit, you can also be crazy and fearless. Go for it!
> **The winning ideas will be subjected to the toughest of tests.** Just in case you're worried about submitting ideas that could be risky, expensive, or difficult to implement—don't fret. As we narrow down the possibilities, the few that remain will be judged, poked, prodded, and assessed from every angle. In other words, let us worry about containing the fire; you come up with the sparks.[12]

Routine Replies

|Email SKILLS|

11. Auto-talk: Email messages for Highway Bytes computers to send automatically

You are director of customer services at Highway Bytes, which markets a series of small, handlebar-mounted computers for bicyclists. These Cycle Computers do everything, from computing speed and distance travelled to displaying street maps. Serious cyclists love them, but your company is growing so fast that you can't keep up with all the customer service requests you receive every day. Your boss wants not only to speed up response time but also to reduce staffing costs and allow your technical experts the time they need to focus on the most difficult and important questions.

You've just been reading about automated response systems, and you quickly review a few articles before discussing the options with your boss. Artificial intelligence researchers have been working for decades to design systems that can actually converse with customers, ask questions, and respond to requests. Some of today's systems have vocabularies of thousands of words and the ability to understand simple sentences. For example, *chatterbots* are automated bots that can actually mimic human conversation. (You can see what it's like to carry on a conversation with some of these bots by visiting www.botspot.com, clicking Artificial Life Bots, and then selecting Chatterbots.)

Unfortunately, even though chatterbots hold a lot of promise, human communication is so complex that a truly automated customer service agent could take years to perfect (and may even prove to be impossible). However, the simplest automated systems are called autoresponders or *email-on-demand*. They are fast and extremely inexpensive. They have no built-in intelligence, so they do nothing more than send back the same reply to every message they receive.

You explain to your boss that although some messages you receive require the attention of your product specialists, many are simply requests for straightforward information. In fact, the customer service staff already answer some 70 percent of email queries with three ready-made attachments:

> **Installing Your Cycle Computer.** Gives customers advice on installing the cycle computer the first time or reinstalling it on a new bike. In most cases, the computer and wheel sensor bolt directly to the bike without modification, but certain bikes do require extra work.
> **Troubleshooting Your Cycle Computer.** Provides a step-by-step guide to figure out what might be wrong with a malfunctioning cycle computer. Most problems are simple, such as dead batteries or loose wires, but others are beyond the capabilities of your typical customer.
> **Upgrading the Software in Your Cycle Computer.** Tells customers how to attach the cycle computer to their home or office PC and download new software from Highway Bytes.

Your boss is enthusiastic when you explain that you can program your current email system to look for specific words in incoming messages and then respond based on what it finds. For example, if a customer message contains the word "installation," you can program the system to reply with the "Installing Your Cycle Computer" attachment. This reconfigured system should be able to handle a sizeable portion of the hundreds of emails your customer service group gets every week.

Your Task: First, draft a list of keywords that you'll want your email system to look for. You'll need to be creative and spend some time with a thesaurus. Identify all the words and word combinations that could identify a message as pertaining to one of the three subject areas. For example, the word *attach* would probably indicate a need for the installation material, whereas new software would most likely suggest a need for the upgrade attachment.

Second, draft three short email messages to accompany each ready-made attachment, explaining that the attached document answers the most common questions on a particular subject (e.g., installation, troubleshooting, or upgrading). Your messages should invite recipients to write back if the attached document doesn't solve the problem, and don't forget to provide the email address: support2@highwaybytes.com.

Third, draft a fourth message to be sent out whenever your new system is unable to figure out what the customer is asking for. Simply thank the customer for writing and explain that the query will be passed on to a customer service specialist who will respond shortly.

12. The special courier: Letter of recommendation for an old friend

In today's mail you get a letter from Non-Stop Messenger Service, 899 Sparks St., Ottawa, ON K3A 2G2. It concerns a friend of yours who has applied for a job. Here is the letter:

Kathryn Norquist has applied for the position of special courier with our firm, and she has given us your name as a reference. Our special couriers convey materials of considerable value or confidentiality to their recipients. It is not an easy job. Special couriers must sometimes remain alert for periods of up to 20 hours, and they cannot expect to follow the usual "three square meals and eight hours' sleep" routine because they often travel long distances on short notice. On occasion, a special courier must react quickly and decisively to threatening situations.

For this type of work, we hire only people of unquestioned integrity, as demonstrated both by their public records and by references from people such as you, who have known them personally or professionally.

We would appreciate a letter from you, supplying detailed answers to the following questions:

1) *How long and in what circumstances have you known the applicant?*

2) *What qualities does she possess that would qualify her for the position of special courier?*

3) *What qualities might be improved before she is put on permanent assignment in this job?*

As vice-president of human resources at DHL, you know how much weight a strong personal reference can carry, and you don't really mind that Kathryn never contacted you for permission to list your name—that's Kathryn. You met her during second year at Carleton University—that would have been 1996—and you two were roommates for several years after. Her undergraduate degree was in journalism, and her investigative reporting was relentless. You have never known anyone who could match Kathryn's stamina when she was on a story. Of course, when she was between stories, she could sleep longer and do less than anyone else you have ever known.

After a few years reporting, Kathryn went back to school and earned her MBA from the Rotman School of Business, and after that you lost track of her for a while. Somebody said that she had joined CSIS or travelled throughout Europe—you never really knew. You did receive a couple of postcards from Paris and one from Madrid.

Two years ago, you met Kathryn for dinner. Only in town for the evening, she was on her way to Borneo to "do the text" for a photographer friend of hers who worked for National Geographic. You read the article last year on the shrinking habitat for orangutans. It was powerful.

Although you're in no position to say much about Kathryn's career accomplishments, you can certainly recommend her energy and enthusiasm, her ability to focus on a task or assignment, her devotion to ethics, and her style. She always seems unshakable—organized, thorough, and honourable, whether digging into political corruption or trudging the jungles of Borneo. You're not sure that her free spirit would flourish in a courier's position, and you wonder if she wouldn't be a bit overqualified for the job. But knowing Kathryn, you're confident she wouldn't apply for a position unless she truly wanted it.

Your Task: Supplying any details you can think of, write as supportive a letter as possible about your friend Kathryn to Roscoe de la Penda, Human Resources Specialist, Non-Stop Messenger Service.

▌Email SKILLS▐

13. Shopping for talent: Memo at Clovine's recommending a promotion

You enjoy your duties as manager of women's sportswear at Clovine's—a growing chain of moderate to upscale department stores in British Columbia. You especially enjoy being able to recommend someone for a promotion. Today, you received a memo from Rachel Cohen, head buyer for women's apparel. She is looking for a smart, aggressive employee to become assistant buyer for Clovine's women's sportswear division. Clovine's likes to promote from within, and Rachel is asking all managers and supervisors for likely candidates. You have just the person she's looking for.

Jennifer Ramirez is a salesclerk in the designer sportswear boutique of your main store in Vancouver, and she has caught your attention. She's quick, friendly, and good at sizing up a customer's preferences. Moreover, at recent department

meetings, she's made some intelligent remarks about new trends in fashion.

Your Task: Write a memo to Rachel Cohen, head buyer, women's sportswear, recommending Jennifer Ramirez and evaluating her qualifications for the promotion. Rachel can check with the human resources department about Jennifer's educational and employment history; you're mainly interested in conveying your positive impression of Jennifer's potential for advancement.

▍Email SKILLS▍

14. Cable hiccups: Email reply to an unhappy cable internet customer

As a customer service agent working for your local cable company, you've received the occasional complaint such as the one you're looking at on your computer monitor. The writer says:

I'm fed up with your cable internet service. I've had my new computer for about a year and used the slow dial-up ISP service only because the manufacturer included it for free. I got your high-speed cable internet service because your advertising promised it was 30 times faster than dial-up. I've used it since March, and I'm very disappointed. I'm paying $39.95 a month, plus taxes, but twice in the last month I've been unable to connect and service is a lot slower than advertised. What a rip-off!

I'm a student and I work part-time. I do a lot of my research for essays and reports over the internet. Not to mention email. I have deadlines to meet. I want you to cancel my service and refund me my last two months' payments.

You know that many people complain that the cable line is shared with neighbours, which might slow down service. But slowdowns are rare with cable and happen with high-speed phone lines too. Cable internet service has a lot of capacity and can provide rapid access to the internet, even though lines are shared. You think the writer is exaggerating and just wants to get his money back because the message is dated April 6, near the end of the school term.

Your Task: You'll send a positive email to the writer indicating that your company will refund the amount he requests. Write to TopGuy@ihome.com. You've been trained to educate consumers about cable internet service.

Positive Messages

▍Blogging SKILLS▍ ▍Portfolio BUILDER▍

15. Leveraging the good news: Blog announcement of a prestigious professional award

You and your staff in the public relations department at Epson of America were delighted when the communication campaign you created for the new PictureMate Personal Photo Lab (www.epson.com/picturemate) was awarded the prestigious Silver Anvil award by the Public Relations Society of America. Now you'd like to give your team a pat on the back by sharing the news with the rest of the company.

Your Task: Write a one-paragraph message for the PR department blog (which is read by people throughout the company but is not accessible outside the company), announcing the award. Take care not to "toot your own horn" as the manager of the PR department and use the opportunity to compliment the rest of the company for designing and producing such an innovative product.[14]

16. ABCs: Form letter thanking volunteers

Working together with government, educators, labour, and business, ABC Canada, a national literacy organization, promotes awareness of literacy and works to involve the private sector in supporting literacy. Its aim is "to promote a fully literate Canadian population." People in your firm, Fine Paper Company, participated in the annual PGI Golf Tournament for Literacy, which was founded by Peter Gzowski, one of Canada's great broadcasters and writers, and best known for his morning show on the CBC. The PGI is a very successful fundraising event, having generated $5 million over more than a decade. PGI tournaments are held in every province and territory.

Statistics Canada's report, *Literary Skills for the Knowledge Society,* notes that "22 percent of adult Canadians have serious problems with printed materials" and that "24 to 26 percent of Canadians can only deal with simple reading tasks."

Not only does your firm support the PGI Golf Tournament with monetary donations—and golf lovers—but the CEO, Laurent DesLauriers, established a volunteer program for employees to donate their time at local community centres to help adults learn to read. This program has become a success at Fine Paper Company.

Your Task: As a human resources specialist at Fine Paper Company, you are sometimes asked to write goodwill letters to employees, a job you enjoy doing. Mr. DesLauriers has directed the office to send a thank-you letter to all the volunteers, those who participated in the golf tournament and those who volunteer their time at the community centres. You will compose a form letter, which will be merged with individual employees' names and addresses.[15]

17. Learn while you earn: Memo announcing Burger House's educational benefits

Your boss, Mike Andrade, owner of three Burger House restaurants in downtown Montreal, is worried about employee turnover. He needs to keep 50 people on his payroll to operate the outlets, but recruiting and retaining those people is tough. The average employee leaves after about seven months, so Andrade has to hire and train 90 people a year just to maintain a 50-person crew. At a cost of $1500 per hire, the price tag for all that turnover is approximately $62 000 a year.

Andrade knows that a lot of his best employees quit because they think that flipping burgers is a dead-end job. But what if it weren't a dead end? What if a person could really get someplace flipping burgers? What if Andrade offered to pay his employees' way through school if they remained with the store? Would that keep them behind the counter?

He's decided to give educational incentives a try. Employees who choose to participate will continue to earn their usual salary, but they will also get free books and tuition, keyed to the number of hours they work each week. Those who work 10 to 15 hours a week can take one free course at any local college or university; those who work 16 to 25 hours can take two courses; and those who work 26 to 40 hours can take three courses. The program is open to all employees, regardless of how long they have worked for Burger House, but no one is obligated to participate.

Your Task: Draft a memo for Mr. Andrade to send out announcing the new educational incentives.[16]

18. Our sympathy: Condolence letter to a Mackie Insurance underwriter

As chief administrator for the underwriting department of Mackie Health Plans in Montreal, Quebec, you're facing a difficult task. One of your best underwriters, Jean Dary, recently lost his wife in an automobile accident (he and his teenage daughter weren't with her at the time). Because you're the boss, everyone in the close-knit department is looking to you to communicate the group's sympathy and concern.

Someone suggested a simple greeting card that everyone could sign, but that seems so impersonal for someone you've worked with every day for nearly five years. So you decided to write a personal note on behalf of the whole department. Although you met Jean's wife, Rosalia, at a few company functions, you knew her mostly through Jean's frequent references to her. You didn't know her well, but you do know important things about her life, which you can celebrate in the letter.

You plan to suggest that when he returns to work, he might like to move his schedule up an hour so that he'll have more time to spend with his daughter, Lisa, after school. It's your way of helping make their lives a little easier for them during this period of adjustment.

Your Task: Write the letter to Jean Dary, who lives at 4141 rue Peel #10, Montreal, QC H3B 1B3. (Feel free to make up any details you need.)[17]

9

Writing Negative Messages

ON THE JOB

Communicating at Maple Leaf Foods
LEADING IN A CRISIS

www.mapleleaf.ca

In the summer and fall of 2008, Michael McCain, President and CEO of Maple Leaf Foods Inc., faced the severest challenge of his career: dealing with fatal food-borne bacteria in several products made by the company that was linked to the deaths of 22 people.

    Communication was the key to McCain's success in restoring public confidence in Maple Leaf Foods, a firm with more than 24 000 employees and $5.2 billion in sales in 2008. The first announcement dealing with the crisis appeared on August 17, 2008, when the company issued a health hazard alert warning the public about two meat products possibly contaminated with *Listeria monocytogenes* bacteria, especially dangerous to pregnant women, the elderly, and people with weakened immune systems. Another news release followed three days later, on August 20, announcing an expanded withdrawal of Maple Leaf products and the closure of the company's Toronto plant. On August 23, McCain taped a television statement responding to findings by government health agencies that linked the deaths of several people to the same Listeria strain found in some Maple Leaf products. In addition to the shut-down of the company's Toronto plant, McCain apologized and expressed his sympathy to the people and families affected by the crisis.

Michael McCain, President and CEO of Maple Leaf Foods, was praised by crisis management experts for his leadership during the Listeria crisis in summer and fall 2008, when 22 people died from food-borne bacteria. His prompt action, empathy, and transparency helped the company regain the confidence of consumers and maintain its prominence in the food industry.

In the weeks that followed, Maple Leaf Foods published open letters in newspapers across Canada. They described precautionary measures: recalling 191 products in addition to the three that were contaminated, contacting more than 15 000 retail and food service customers nationwide to ensure the products were removed from shelves, and engaging an outside, technical expert panel to conduct a comprehensive investigation to identify the likely source of the contamination. Furthermore, McCain recorded additional television advertisements and videos explaining Maple Leaf's plans that were made available on the company's website and YouTube. In each announcement McCain showed the human face of the company.

McCain's prompt actions and sensitivity to the victims and their families earned him the 2008 Business Newsmaker of the Year Award. Experts praised him for applying effective crisis management strategy: being proactive, speaking honestly and transparently, and maintaining constant communication with employees and the public. But McCain commented, "This is not about some contrived strategy. It's just about a tragic situation and an organization's desire to make it right."[1]

If you had to handle a business crisis, how would plan your communications? How would you deliver your messages? How would you demonstrate sensitivity to your audiences?

Using the Three-Step Writing Process for Negative Messages

Chances are slim that you'll be in a position like Michael McCain's, but communicating negative news is a fact of life for all business professionals, from rejecting job applicants to telling customers that shipments will be late to turning down speaking invitations.

Objective 1 Apply the three-step writing process to negative messages.

When you need to send a negative message, you have five goals:
> Give the bad news.
> Ensure acceptance of the bad news.
> Maintain reader's goodwill.
> Maintain organization's good image.
> Reduce future correspondence on the matter.

When you need to send a negative message, you have five goals: (1) to convey the bad news; (2) to gain acceptance for the bad news; (3) to maintain as much goodwill as possible with your audience; (4) to maintain a good image for your organization; and (5) if appropriate, to reduce or eliminate the need for future correspondence on the matter (however, in a few cases, you want to encourage discussion). Five goals are clearly a lot to accomplish in one message. However, by learning some simple techniques and following the three-step process, you can develop negative messages that reduce the stress for everyone involved and improve the effectiveness of your communication efforts.

Step 1: Plan Your Message

Analysis, investigation, and adaptation help you avoid alienating your readers.

When planning negative messages, you can't avoid the fact that your audience does not want to hear what you have to say. To minimize the damage to business relationships and to encourage the acceptance of your message, analyze the situation carefully to better understand the context in which the recipient will process your message.

Be sure to consider your purpose thoroughly—whether it's straightforward (such as rejecting a job application) or more complicated (such as drafting a negative performance review, in which you not only give the employee feedback on past performance but also help the person develop a plan to improve future performance). Similarly, your audience profile can be simple and obvious in some situations (such as rejecting a credit request) and far more complex in others (such as telling a business partner that you've decided to terminate the partnership).

With a clear purpose and your audience's needs in mind, identify and gather the information your audience will need to understand and accept your message. Negative messages can be intensely personal to the recipient, and in many cases recipients have a right to expect a thorough explanation of your answer (although that isn't always the case). For example, if one of your hardworking employees has asked for a raise, but you don't think his performance warrants it, you can carefully explain the difference between hard work and productive results to help him accept your message.

Selecting the right medium is critical. For example, experts advise that bad news for employees be delivered in person whenever possible, both to show respect for the employees and to give them an opportunity to ask questions. Of course, delivering bad news is never easy, and an increasing number of managers appear to be using email and other electronic media to convey negative messages to employees.[2] However, employees are more likely to accept messages and maintain respect for the sender if bad news is delivered in person.

Higher fees or loan refusals are two examples of bad-news messages that banks send to customers. Is it more difficult for banks to communicate bad news than other types of businesses? Are there special image or ethical concerns that banks face?

Defining your main idea in a negative message is often more complicated than simply saying *no*. For example, in the case of the hardworking employee who requested a raise, your message would go beyond saying no to explain how he can improve his performance by working smarter, not just harder. On the other hand, ensure that you limit your scope and include only the information your audience needs. For example, a credit denial is not the place to lecture customers on better financial habits.

When preparing negative messages, choose the medium with care.

Step 2: Write Your Message

When you are adapting a negative message to your audience, pay close attention to effectiveness and diplomacy. After all, your audience does not want to hear what you have to say and might disagree strongly with you; messages perceived to be unclear or unkind will amplify the audience's stress. Maintain a "you" attitude, strive for polite language that emphasizes the positive whenever appropriate, and ensure that your word choice is without bias. For more advice, see "Adapting to Your Audience" later in this chapter.

If your credibility hasn't already been established with an audience, lay out your qualifications for making the decision in question. Recipients of negative messages who don't think you are credible are more likely to challenge your decision. And as always, projecting and protecting your company's image is a prime concern; if you're not careful, a negative answer could spin out of control into negative feelings about your company.

When you use language that conveys respect and avoids an accusing tone, you protect your audience's pride. This kind of communication etiquette is always important, but it demands special care with negative messages. Moreover, you can ease the sense of disappointment by using positive words rather than negative, counterproductive ones (see Table 9–1).

You'll likely spend more time on word, sentence, and paragraph choices for negative messages than for any other type of business writing. People who receive negative messages often look for subtle shades of meaning, seeking flaws in your reasoning or other ways to challenge the decision. By writing clearly and sensitively, you can take some of the sting out of bad news and help your reader accept the decision and move on.

> Table 9–1 Choosing Positive Words

Examples of Negative Phrasings	Positive Alternatives
Your request *doesn't make any sense*.	Please clarify your request.
The *damage* won't be fixed for a week.	The item will be repaired next week.
Although it wasn't our *fault*, there will be an *unavoidable delay* in your order.	We will process your order as soon as we receive an aluminum shipment from our supplier, which we expect to happen within 10 days.
You are clearly *dissatisfied*.	We are doing what we can to correct the situation.
I was *shocked* to learn that you're unhappy.	Thank you for sharing your concerns about the service you received while shopping with us.
Unfortunately, we haven't received it.	It hasn't arrived yet.
The enclosed statement is *wrong*.	Please recheck the enclosed statement.

Step 3: Complete Your Message

Your need for careful attention to detail continues as you complete your message. Revise your content to ensure that everything is clear, complete, and concise—bearing in mind that even small flaws are magnified as readers react to your negative news. Produce clean, professional documents, and proofread carefully to eliminate mistakes. Finally, be especially sure that your negative messages are delivered promptly and successfully; waiting for bad news is difficult enough, without wondering whether a message was lost.

Developing Negative Messages

As you apply the three-step writing process to develop negative messages, keep three points in mind. First, before you organize the main points of a message, it is vital to choose a direct or an indirect approach. Second, before actually composing your message, be sensitive to variations across cultures or between internal and external audiences. And third, to fulfill the spirit of audience focus, ensure that you maintain high ethical standards.

Choosing the Best Approach

Objective 2 Explain the differences between the direct and the indirect approaches to negative messages, including when it's appropriate to use each one.

You need to consider a variety of factors when choosing between direct and indirect approaches.

You've been choosing between direct and indirect approaches to deliver negative messages your entire life. When you come right out and tell somebody bad news, you're using a direct approach. When you try to ease your way into the conversation before delivering the bad news, you're using an indirect approach. To choose an approach for negative business messages, ask yourself the following questions:

> **Will bad news come as a shock?** The direct approach is fine for business situations in which people readily acknowledge the possibility of receiving bad news. However, if bad news might come as a shock to readers, use the indirect approach to help them prepare for it.

> **Does the reader prefer short messages that get right to the point?** If you know that your boss always wants brief messages that get right to the point, even when they deliver bad news, use the direct approach.

> **How important is this news to the reader?** For minor or routine scenarios, the direct approach is nearly always best. However, if the reader has an

emotional investment in the situation or the consequences to the reader are considerable, the indirect approach is often best because it gives you a chance to prepare that reader to accept your news.

> **Do you need to maintain a close working relationship with the reader?** Pay attention to the relationship as you deliver bad news. The indirect approach makes it easier to soften the blow of bad news and can therefore be the better choice when you need to preserve a good relationship.

> **Do you need to get the reader's attention?** If someone hasn't responded to repeated messages, the direct approach can help you get his or her attention.

> **What is your organization's preferred style?** Some companies have a distinct communication style, ranging from blunt and direct to gentle and indirect. However, going against expectations can be an effective way to get people's attention in a dramatic way. When Coca-Cola CEO E. Neville Isdell wanted to let both insiders and outsiders know that the company's continuing sales slump was due to more than just temporary market factors, he issued uncharacteristically blunt statements such as saying that the company suffers from both "a people deficit and a skills deficit."[3]

> **How much follow-up communication do you want?** If you want to discourage a response from your reader, the direct approach signals the finality of your message more effectively. However, if you use the indirect approach to list your reasons before announcing a decision, you allow a follow-up response from your reader—which might actually be the best strategy at times. For example, if you're rejecting a project team's request for funding, based on the information you currently have, you might be wise to invite the team to provide any new information that could encourage you to reconsider your decision.

USING THE DIRECT APPROACH EFFECTIVELY A negative message using the direct approach opens with the bad news, proceeds to the reasons for the situation or the decision, and ends with a positive statement aimed at maintaining a good relationship with the audience (see Figure 9–1). Depending on the circumstances, the message may also offer alternatives or a plan of action to fix the situation under discussion. Stating bad news at the beginning can have two advantages: (1) It makes a shorter message possible and (2) it requires less time for the audience to reach the main idea of the message.

Use the direct approach when your negative answer or information will have minimal personal impact.

✴┤Explore

> Figure 9–1 Choosing the Indirect or Direct Approach for Negative Messages

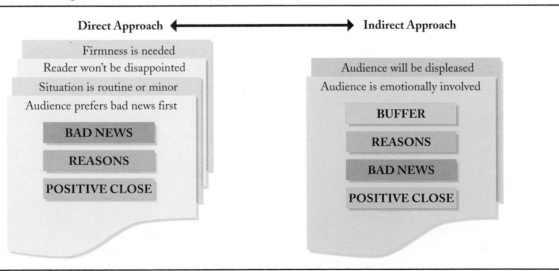

OPEN WITH A CLEAR STATEMENT OF THE BAD NEWS Whether it's something relatively minor, such as telling a supplier that you're planning to reduce the size of your orders in the future, or something major, such as telling employees that revenues dropped the previous quarter, come right out and say it. Even if the news is devastating, maintain a calm, professional tone that keeps the focus on the news and not on individual failures. Also, if necessary, remind the reader why you're writing.

Reminds the reader that your company has a standing order and announces the change immediately

> Please modify our standing order for the FL-205 shipping cases from 3000 per month to 2500 per month.

Reminds the reader that he or she applied for life insurance with your firm and announces your decision

> Transnation Life is unable to grant your application for SafetyNet term life insurance.

Eases into the bad news with a personal acknowledgment to the staff, even though it delivers the news directly and immediately

> In spite of everyone's best efforts to close more sales this past quarter, revenue fell 14 percent compared to the third quarter last year.

Notice how the third example still manages to ease into the bad news, even though it delivers the news directly and quickly. In all three instances, the recipient gets the news immediately, without reading the reasons why the news is bad.

PROVIDE REASONS AND ADDITIONAL INFORMATION In most cases, you'll follow the direct opening with an explanation of why the news is negative:

Reassures the reader that the product in question is still satisfactory but is no longer needed in the same quantity

> Please modify our standing order for the FL-205 shipping cases from 3000 per month to 2500 per month. The FL-205 continues to meet our needs for medical packaging, but our sales of that product line have levelled off.

Offers a general explanation as the reason the application was denied and discourages further communication on the matter

> Transnation Life is unable to grant your application for SafetyNet term life insurance. The SafetyNet program has specific health history requirements that your application does not meet.

Lets readers know why the news is negative and reassures them that job performance is not the reason

> In spite of everyones best efforts to close more sales this past quarter, revenue fell 14 percent compared to the third quarter last year. Reports from the field offices indicate that the economic downturn in Asia has reduced demand for our products.

The amount of detail you provide depends on your relationship with the audience.

The extent of your explanation depends on the nature of your news and your relationship with the reader. In the first example, a company wants to assure its long-time supplier that the product is still satisfactory. It's in the best interest of both parties to maintain a positive relationship even when circumstances between them are sometimes negative.

In the second example, the insurance company provides a general reason for the denial because listing a specific health issue might encourage additional communication from the applicant, and the company's decision is final. In the third example, the explanation points out why the news is bad and also reassures employees that no one in the firm is personally responsible for the failure.

In some situations, it's a good idea to follow the explanation with a statement of how you plan to correct or respond to the negative news. For example, in the case of the sales decline, follow up by telling the staff you plan to increase advertising to help stimulate sales. Alternatively, invite ideas from the staff. In any event, your readers will want to know how they should respond to the news, so additional information would be helpful.

You will encounter some situations in which explaining negative news is neither appropriate nor helpful, for example, when the reasons are confidential, excessively complicated, or irrelevant to the reader. To maintain a cordial working relationship with the reader, explain why you can't provide the information.

Should you apologize when delivering bad news? The answer isn't quite as simple as one might think. The notion of *apology* is hard to pin down. To some people, it simply means an expression of sympathy that something negative has happened to another person. At the other extreme, it means admitting fault and taking responsibility for specific compensations or corrections to atone for the mistake.

Some experts have advised that a company should never apologize, even when it knows it has made a mistake, as the apology might be taken as a confession of guilt that could be used against the company in a lawsuit.[4] The best general advice in the event of a serious mistake or accident is to immediately and sincerely express sympathy and offer help, if appropriate, without admitting guilt; then seek the advice of your company's lawyers before elaborating. As one recent survey concluded, "The risks of making an apology are low, and the potential reward is high."[5]

CLOSE ON A POSITIVE NOTE After you've explained the negative news, close the message in a positive, but still honest and respectful, manner.

Please modify our standing order for the FL-205 shipping cases from 3000 per month to 2500 per month. The FL-205 continues to meet our needs for medical packaging, but our sales of that product line have levelled off. **We appreciate the great service you continue to provide and look forward to doing business with you.**

Reinforces the relationship you have with the reader and provides a positive view toward the future without unduly promising a return to the old level of business

Transnation Life is unable to grant your application for SafetyNet term life insurance. The SafetyNet program has specific health history requirements that your application does not meet. **We wish you success in finding coverage through another provider.**

Ends on a respectful note, knowing that life insurance is an important subject for the reader, but also makes it clear that the company's decision is final

In spite of everyone's best efforts to close more sales this past quarter, revenue fell 14 percent compared to the third quarter last year. Reports from the field offices indicate that the economic downturn in Asia has reduced demand for our products. **However, I continue to believe that we have the best product for these customers, and we'll continue to explore ways to boost sales in these key markets.**

Helps readers respond to the news by letting them know that the company plans to fix the situation, even if the plan for doing so isn't clear yet

Notice how all three examples deliver bad news quickly and efficiently, without being unduly disrespectful or overly apologetic. Consider offering your readers an alternative solution, if you can. For example, if you know that another insurance company has a program for higher-risk policies, you can alert your reader to that opportunity.

USING THE INDIRECT APPROACH EFFECTIVELY The indirect approach helps readers prepare for the bad news by presenting the reasons for it first. However, don't assume that the indirect approach is meant to obscure bad news, delay it, or limit your responsibility. Rather, the purpose of this approach is to ease the blow and help readers accept the situation. When done poorly, the indirect approach can be disrespectful and even unethical. But when done well, it is a good example of audience-oriented communication crafted with attention to both ethics and etiquette.

OPEN WITH A BUFFER Messages using the indirect approach open with a **buffer**, a neutral, non-controversial statement that establishes common ground with your reader (refer to Figure 9–1). Some critics believe that using a buffer is manipulative and unethical—and even dishonest. However, buffers are unethical only if they're insincere or deceptive. Showing consideration for the feelings of others is never dishonest.

Poorly written buffers mislead or insult the reader.

A poorly written buffer might trivialize the reader's concerns, divert attention from the problem with insincere flattery or irrelevant material, or mislead the reader into thinking your message actually contains good news. A good buffer, on the other hand, can express your appreciation for being considered (if you're responding to a request), assure your reader of your attention to the request, or indicate your understanding of the reader's needs. A good buffer also needs to be relevant and sincere.

Consider these possible responses to a manager of the order fulfillment department, who requested some temporary staffing help from your department (a request you won't be able to fulfill):

Establishes common ground with the reader and validates the concerns that prompted the original request without promising a positive answer → Our department shares your goal of processing orders quickly and efficiently.

Establishes common ground, but in a negative way that downplays the recipient's concerns → As a result of the last downsizing, every department in the company is running shorthanded.

Potentially misleads the reader into concluding that you will comply with the request → You folks are doing a great job over there, and I'd love to be able to help out.

Trivializes the reader's concerns by opening with an irrelevant issue → Those new provincial labour regulations are driving me crazy over here; how about in your department?

Only the first of these buffers can be considered effective; the other three are likely to damage your relationship with the other manager—and to lower his or her opinion of you. Table 9–2 shows several types of effective buffers you could use to open a negative message tactfully.

Given the damage that a poorly composed buffer can do, consider every buffer carefully before you send it. Is it respectful? Is it relevant? Is it neutral, implying neither yes nor no? Does it provide a smooth transition to the reasons that follow? If you can answer yes to every question, you can proceed confidently to the next section of your message. However, if a little voice inside your head tells you that your buffer sounds insincere or misleading, it probably is, in which case you'll need to rewrite it.

❋ Explore

PROVIDE REASONS AND ADDITIONAL INFORMATION An effective buffer serves as a stepping stone to the next part of your message, in which you build up the explanations and information that will culminate in your negative news. The nature of the information you provide is similar to that of the direct approach—it depends on the audience and the situation—but the way you portray this information differs because your reader doesn't know your conclusion yet.

An ideal explanation section leads readers to your conclusion before you actually say it. That is, before you actually say no, the reader has followed your line of reasoning and is ready for the answer. By giving your reasons effectively, you help maintain focus on the issues at hand and defuse the emotions that always accompany significantly bad news.

Phrase your reasons to signal the negative news ahead.

As you lay out your reasons, guide your readers' responses by starting with the most positive points first and moving forward to increasingly negative ones. Provide enough detail for the audience to understand your reasons, but be concise; a long, roundabout explanation will just make your audience impatient. Your reasons need to convince your audience that your decision is justified, fair, and logical.

> ## Table 9–2 Types of Buffers

Buffer Type	Strategy	Example
Agreement	Find a point on which you and the reader share similar views.	We both know how hard it is to make a profit in this industry.
Appreciation	Express sincere thanks for receiving something.	Your cheque for $127.17 arrived yesterday. Thank you.
Cooperation	Convey your willingness to help in any way you realistically can.	Employee Services is here to smooth the way for all associates with their health insurance, retirement planning, and continuing education needs.
Fairness	Assure the reader that you've closely examined and carefully considered the problem, or mention an appropriate action that has already been taken.	For the past week, we have carefully monitored those using the photocopying machine to see whether we can detect any pattern of use that might explain its frequent breakdowns.
Good news	Start with the part of your message that is favourable.	A replacement knob for your range is on its way, shipped February 10 via Canada Post.
Praise	Find an attribute or an achievement to compliment.	The Stratford Group clearly has an impressive record of accomplishment in helping clients resolve financial reporting problems.
Resale	Favourably discuss the product or company related to the subject of the letter.	With their heavy-duty, full-suspension hardware and fine veneers, the desks and file cabinets in our Montclair line have become a hit with value-conscious professionals.
Understanding	Demonstrate that you understand the reader's goals and needs.	So you can more easily find the printer with the features you need, we are enclosing a brochure that describes all the Panasonic printers currently available.

If appropriate, use the explanation section to suggest how the negative news might in fact benefit your reader. Suppose you work for a multinational company that wants to hire an advertising agency to support your offices in a dozen different countries, and you receive a proposal from an agency that has offices in only one of those countries. In your list of reasons, indicate that you don't want to impose undue hardship on the agency by requiring significant amounts of international travel. However, use this technique with care; it's easy to insult readers by implying that they shouldn't ask for the benefits or opportunities they sought originally.

Avoid hiding behind company policy to cushion bad news. If you say, "Company policy forbids our hiring anyone who does not have two years' supervisory experience," you imply that you won't consider anyone on his or her individual merits. Skilled and sympathetic communicators explain company policy (without referring to it as "policy") so that the audience can try to meet the requirements at a later time. Consider this response to an employee:

Don't hide behind "company policy" when you deliver bad news.

Because these management positions are quite challenging, the human relations department has researched the qualifications needed to succeed in them. The findings show that the two most important qualifications are a bachelor's degree in business administration and two years' supervisory experience.

Shows the reader the decision is based on a methodical analysis of the company's needs and not on some arbitrary guideline

Establishes the criteria behind the decision and lets the reader know what to expect

The paragraph does a good job of stating reasons for the refusal:

> It provides enough detail to logically support the refusal.
> It implies that the applicant is better off avoiding a program in which he or she might fail.
> It explains the company's policy as logical rather than arbitrary.

Well-written reasons are
> detailed
> tactful
> individualized
> unapologetic
> positive

> It offers no apology for the decision because no one is at fault.
> It avoids negative personal expressions (e.g., "You do not meet our requirements").

Even valid, well-thought-out reasons won't convince every reader in every situation. However, if you've done a good job of laying out your reasoning, then you've done everything you can to prepare the reader for the main idea, which is the negative news itself.

CONTINUE WITH A CLEAR STATEMENT OF THE BAD NEWS After you've prepared the audience to receive the bad news, the next task is to present the news as clearly and as kindly as possible. Three techniques are especially useful for saying no. First, de-emphasize the bad news:

To handle bad news carefully
> De-emphasize the bad news visually and grammatically.
> Use a conditional statement if appropriate.
> Tell what you did do, not what you didn't do.

> Minimize the space or time devoted to the bad news—without trivializing it or withholding any important information.
> Subordinate bad news in a complex or compound sentence ("My department is already shorthanded, so I'll need all my staff for at least the next two months"). This construction pushes the bad news into the middle of the sentence, the point of least emphasis.
> Embed bad news in the middle of a paragraph or use parenthetical expressions ("Our profits, which are down, are only part of the picture").

However, keep in mind that it's possible to abuse de-emphasis. For example, if the primary point of your message is that profits are down, it would be inappropriate to marginalize that news by burying it in the middle of a sentence. State the negative news clearly and then make a smooth transition to any positive news that might balance the story.

Second, use a conditional (*if* or *when*) statement to imply that the audience could have received, or might someday receive, a favourable answer ("When you have more managerial experience, you are welcome to reapply"). Such a statement could motivate applicants to improve their qualifications.

Third, emphasize what you can do or have done, rather than what you cannot do. Say, "We sell exclusively through retailers, and the one nearest you that carries our merchandise is . . . " rather than "We are unable to serve you, so please call your nearest dealer." Also, by implying the bad news, you may not need to actually state it ("The five positions currently open have been filled with people whose qualifications match those uncovered in our research"). By focusing on the positive and implying the bad news, you make the impact less personal.

Don't disguise bad news when you emphasize the positive.

When implying bad news, ensure that your audience understands the entire message—including the bad news. Withholding negative information or overemphasizing positive information is unethical and unfair to your reader. If an implied message might lead to uncertainty, state your decision in direct terms. Just be sure that you avoid overly blunt statements that are likely to cause pain and anger:

Instead of This	Use This
I *must refuse* your request.	I will be out of town on the day you need me.
We *must deny* your application.	The position has been filled.
I *am unable* to grant your request.	Contact us again when you have established . . .
We *cannot afford to* continue the program.	The program will conclude on May 1.
Much as I would like to attend . . .	Our budget meeting ends too late for me to attend.
We *must turn down* your extension request.	Please send in your payment by June 14.

CLOSE ON A POSITIVE NOTE As with the direct approach, the conclusion of the indirect approach is your opportunity to emphasize your respect for your audience, even though you've just delivered unpleasant news. Express best wishes without ending on a falsely upbeat note. If you can find a positive angle that's meaningful to your audience, by all means consider adding it to your conclusion. However, don't pretend that the negative news didn't happen or that it won't affect the reader. Suggest alternative solutions if such information is available. In a message to a customer or potential customer, an ending that includes resale information or sales promotions may also be appropriate. If you've asked readers to decide between alternatives or to take some action, make sure that they know what to do, when to do it, and how to do it. Whatever type of conclusion you use, follow these guidelines:

> **Avoid a negative or uncertain conclusion.** Don't refer to, repeat, or apologize for the bad news, and refrain from expressing any doubt that your reasons will be accepted (avoid statements such as "I trust our decision is satisfactory").
> **Limit future correspondence.** Encourage additional communication *only* if you're willing to discuss your decision further (if you're not, avoid wording such as "If you have further questions, please write").
> **Be optimistic about the future.** Don't anticipate problems (avoid statements such as "Should you have further problems, please let us know").
> **Be sincere.** Steer clear of clichés that are insincere in view of the bad news (if you can't help, don't say, "If we can be of any help, please contact us").
> **Be confident.** Don't show any doubt about keeping the person as a customer (avoid phrases such as "We hope you will continue to do business with us").

A positive close
> builds goodwill
> offers a suggestion for action
> provides a look toward the future

Finally, keep in mind that the closing is the last thing the audience has to remember you by. Even though they're disappointed, leave them with the impression that they were treated with respect.

Adapting to Your Audience

Even more than other business messages, negative messages require that you maintain your audience focus and be as sensitive as possible to audience needs. Therefore, adapt your message to cultural differences or to the differences between internal and external audiences.

CULTURAL VARIATIONS Bad news is unwelcome in any language, but the conventions for conveying it to business associates can vary considerably from country to country. For example, French business letters are traditionally quite formal and writer-oriented, often without reference to audience needs or benefits. Moreover, when the news is bad, French writers take a direct approach. They open with a reference to the problem or previous correspondence and then state the bad news clearly. While they don't refer to the audience's needs, they often do apologize and express regret for the problem.[6]

In contrast, Japanese letters traditionally open with remarks about the season, business prosperity, or health. When the news is bad, these opening formalities serve as the buffer. Explanations and apologies follow and then comes the bad news or refusal. Japanese writers protect their reader's feelings by wording the bad news ambiguously. Western readers may even misinterpret this vague language as a condition of acceptance rather than as the refusal it actually is.[7] In short, if you communicate across cultures, use the tone, organization, and other cultural conventions that your audience expects. Only then can you avoid the inappropriate or even offensive approaches that could jeopardize your business relationship.[8]

Expectations for handling bad news vary from culture to culture.

Objective 4 Adapt negative messages for internal and external audiences.

Compared to external audiences, internal audiences often expect more detail in negative messages.

You may need to adjust the content of negative messages for different groups within an external audience.

INTERNAL VERSUS EXTERNAL AUDIENCES Internal audiences frequently have expectations for negative messages that differ from those of recipients outside the company. In some cases, the two groups can interpret the news in different or even opposite ways. For example, employees will react negatively to news of an impending layoff, but company shareholders might welcome the news as evidence that management is trying to control costs. In addition, if a negative message such as a layoff is being sent to internal and external audiences, employees will not only expect more detail but also expect to be informed before the general public is told.

Negative messages to outside audiences require attention to the diverse nature of your audience and the concern for confidentiality of internal information. A single message might have a half-dozen separate audiences, all with differing opinions and agendas. You may not be able to provide explanations to the level of detail that some people want if doing so would release proprietary information such as future product plans.

Maintaining High Standards of Ethics and Etiquette

Objective 5 Explain the importance of maintaining high standards of ethics and etiquette when delivering negative messages.

All business messages demand attention to ethics and etiquette, of course, but these considerations take on special importance when you are delivering bad news—for several reasons. First, a variety of laws and regulations dictate the content and delivery of many business messages with potentially negative content, such as the release of financial information by a public company. Second, negative messages can have a significant negative impact on the lives of those receiving them. Even if the news is conveyed legally and conscientiously, good ethical practice demands that these situations be approached with care and sensitivity. Third, emotions often run high when negative messages are involved, for both the sender and the receiver. Senders need to not only manage their own emotions but also consider the emotional state of their audiences.

The challenge of sending—and receiving—negative messages fosters a tendency to delay, downplay, or distort the bad news.[9] However, doing so may be unethical, if not illegal. In recent years, numerous companies have been sued by shareholders, consumers, employees, and government regulators for allegedly withholding or delaying negative information in such areas as company finances, environmental hazards, and product safety. In many of these cases, the problem was slow, incomplete, or inaccurate communication between the company and external stakeholders. In others, problems stemmed from a reluctance to send or receive negative news within the organization.

Sharing bad news effectively requires commitment from everyone in the organization.

Effectively sharing bad news within an organization requires commitment from everyone involved. Employees must commit to sending negative messages when necessary, and to doing so in a timely fashion, even when that is unpleasant or difficult. Conversely, managers must commit to maintaining open communication channels, truly listening when employees have negative information to share, and not punishing employees who deliver bad news.

The impulse to want to believe that everything is fine can be strong, and managers who are so inclined can fail to perceive or respond to negative messages from their employees. The energy company BP (formerly British Petroleum) recently experienced such breakdowns when managers didn't act on warnings from employees in the company's Alaska oil pipeline and Texas refining operations. After years of intense efforts by the company to reduce maintenance costs, corrosion and other problems led to a large oil spill along its Alaska pipeline and a tragic accident at its Texas refinery. Some employees said the emphasis on saving money was so strong that safety warnings sometimes went unheeded up the chain of command. Said one, "A scream at our level is, if anything, a whisper at their level."[10]

Although BP employees were not discouraged from reporting bad news, in corporate cultures that don't encourage open communication, employees who fear retribution may go to great lengths to avoid sending bad-news messages. In such dysfunctional environments, failure breeds still more failure because decision makers don't get the honest, objective information they need to make wise choices.[11] In contrast, managers in open cultures expect or even demand that their employees bring them bad news whenever it happens so that corrective action can be taken. Whatever the case, if you need to transmit bad news up the chain of command, don't try to pin the blame on anyone in particular. Simply emphasize the nature of the problem—and a solution, if possible. This tactic will help you earn a reputation as an alert problem solver rather than just a complainer.[12]

Finally, recognize that some negative news scenarios will also test your self-control and sense of etiquette and tempt you to respond with a personal attack. However, keep in mind that negative messages can have a lasting impact on both the people who receive them and the people who send them. As a communicator, you have a responsibility to minimize the negative impact of your negative messages through careful planning and sensitive, objective writing. As much as possible, focus on the actions or conditions that led to the negative news, not on personal shortcomings or character issues. Develop a reputation as a professional who can handle the toughest situations with dignity.

For a reminder of successful strategies for creating negative messages, see "Checklist: Creating Negative Messages."

Negative news situations can put your sense of self-control and business etiquette to the test.

CHECKLIST Creating Negative Messages

A. Choose the best approach.
✔ Consider a direct approach when the audience is aware of the possibility of negative news, when the reader is not emotionally involved in the message, when you know that the reader would prefer the bad news first, when you know that firmness is necessary, and when you want to discourage a response.
✔ Consider an indirect approach when the news is likely to come as a shock or surprise, when your audience has a high emotional investment in the outcome, and when you want to maintain a good relationship with the audience.

B. For an indirect approach, open with an effective buffer.
✔ Establish common ground with the audience.
✔ Validate the request, if you are responding to a request.
✔ Don't trivialize the reader's concerns.
✔ Don't mislead the reader into thinking the coming news might be positive.

C. Provide reasons and additional information.
✔ Explain why the news is negative.
✔ Adjust the amount of detail to fit the situation and the audience.

✔ Avoid explanations when the reasons are confidential, excessively complicated, or irrelevant to the reader.
✔ If appropriate, state how you plan to correct or respond to the negative news.
✔ Seek the advice of company lawyers if you're unsure what to say.

D. State the bad news clearly.
✔ State the bad news as positively as possible, using tactful wording.
✔ De-emphasize bad news by minimizing the space devoted to it, subordinating it, or embedding it.
✔ If your response might change in the future if circumstances change, explain the conditions to the reader.
✔ Emphasize what you can do or have done, rather than what you can't or won't do.

E. Close on a positive note.
✔ Express best wishes without being falsely positive.
✔ Suggest actions that readers might take, if appropriate, and provide them with necessary information.
✔ Encourage further communication only if you're willing to discuss the situation further.
✔ Keep a positive outlook on the future.

Exploring Common Examples of Negative Messages

In the course of your business career, you might write a wide variety of negative messages, from announcing declines in revenue to giving negative performance reviews. The following sections offer examples of the most common negative messages, dealing with topics such as routine business matters, organizational news, and employment messages.

Sending Negative Messages on Routine Business Matters

Most companies receive numerous requests for information and donations or invitations to join community or industry organizations. As you progress in your career and become more visible in your industry and community, you will receive a wide variety of personal invitations to speak at private or public functions or to volunteer your time for a variety of organizations. In addition, routine business matters such as credit applications and requests for adjustment will often require negative responses. Neither you nor your company will be able to say yes to every request; crafting negative responses quickly and graciously is an important skill for many professionals.

✓•⌐Practise

REFUSING ROUTINE REQUESTS When you are unable to meet the request, your primary communication challenge is to give a clear negative response without generating negative feelings or damaging either your personal reputation or the company's. As simple as these messages may appear to be, they can test your skills as a communicator because you often need to deliver negative information while maintaining a positive relationship with the other party.

Saying no is a routine part of business and shouldn't reflect negatively on you. The direct approach will work best for most routine negative responses. It not only helps your audience get your answer quickly and move on to other possibilities but also helps you save time, since the direct approach is often easier to write. Figure 9–2 shows how Mohammed Mansour used this approach to refuse a favour from an acquaintance.

When turning down an invitation or a request for a favour, consider your relationship with the reader.

The indirect approach works best when the stakes are high for you or for the receiver, when you or your company has an established relationship with the person making the request, or when you're forced to decline a request that you might have said yes to in the past. Lisa McKinnon used the indirect approach in her letter to Phillippe DiCastro, a financial analyst (see Figure 9–3). The tone of the letter is intended to maintain a good relationship with the reader although the favour is refused.

Consider the following points as you develop your routine negative messages:

> **Manage your time carefully.** Focus your time on the most important relationships and requests and then get in the habit of crafting quick standard responses for less important situations.

> **If the matter is closed, don't imply that it's still open.** If your answer is truly no, don't use phrases such as "Let me think about it and get back to you" as a way to delay saying no. Such delays waste time for you and the other party and project a weak image.

> **Offer alternative ideas if you can.** The letters in Figures 9–2 and 9–3 include options that might help the reader. However, remember to use your

> Figure 9–2 Letter Declining a Favour Using the Direct Strategy

Plastics Injections Inc.

33 Research Court, Saskatoon, SK, Canada S7N 3R1
Phone (306) 555-1265   Fax (306) 555-1166
www.plasticsinjections.ca   info@plasticsinj.ca

December 2, 2010

Professor Ning Wong
Department of Chemistry
Western Technical University
62 Campus Drive
Saskatoon, Saskatchewan S8N 0H2

Dear Ning,

Thank you for asking Plastics Injections Inc. to host a plant tour for your students. In past years, students have learned a great deal about how a business like ours operates. This year, however, I will have to book a date other than the one you have suggested. *(States the bad news in opening)*

Our company-wide sales meeting takes place from March 14 to 17. During this time, our auditorium is fully booked for presentations, and the staff who conduct the tours will be updating the sales reps on current projects. *(Buffers bad news by presenting reason)*

Can your class take the tour the following week, on March 21? As usual, a tour guide will meet your group at 10:00 a.m. at the main entrance. Let me know if this date is good for you and how many students to expect. As in the past, the tour lasts two hours, and the students can enjoy lunch in the staff cafeteria. Please call me at (306) 555-2232 (my direct line) to discuss the new date. *(Suggests an alternative—showing that the writer cares about the tour and has given the matter some thought)*

Ning, I appreciate your understanding and look forward to speaking with you. *(Seeks action and expresses goodwill)*

Sincerely,

Mohammed Mansour

Mohammed Mansour
Manager
Manufacturing Division

---

time wisely in such matters. Unless the relationship is important to your company, you probably shouldn't spend time researching alternatives for the other person.

> **Don't imply that other assistance or information might be available if it isn't.** Don't close your negative message with a cheery but insincere "Please contact us if we can offer any additional assistance." An empty attempt to mollify hostile feelings could simply lead to another request you'll have to refuse.

If you aren't in a position to offer additional information or assistance, don't imply that you are.

HANDLING BAD NEWS ABOUT TRANSACTIONS Bad news about transactions, the sale and delivery of products and services, is always unwelcome and usually

✳ Explore

unexpected. These messages have three goals: (1) to modify the customer's expectations regarding the transaction; (2) to explain how you plan to resolve the situation; and (3) to repair whatever damage might have been done to the business relationship.

The specific content and tone of each message can vary widely, depending on the nature of the transaction and your relationship with the customer. Telling an individual consumer that his new sweater will arrive a week later than you promised is a much simpler task than telling General Motors that 30 000 transmission parts will be a week late, especially since you know the company will be forced to idle a multimillion-dollar production facility as a result.

If you haven't done anything specific to set the customer's expectations—such as promising delivery within 24 hours—the message simply needs to inform the customer, with little or no emphasis on apologies (see Figure 9–4). (Bear in mind, though, in this age of online ordering and overnight delivery, customers have been conditioned to expect instantaneous fulfillment of nearly every transaction, even if you haven't promised anything.) Notice how the email message in Figure 9–4, which is a combination of good and bad news, uses the indirect approach to turn the good news into a buffer for the bad news. In this case, the customer wasn't promised delivery by a certain date, so the writer simply informs the customer when to expect the rest of the order. The writer also took steps to repair the relationship and encourage future business with her firm.

If you did set the customer's expectations and now find you can't meet them, your task is more complicated. In addition to resetting the customer's expectations and explaining how you'll resolve the problem, you may need to include an element of apology. The scope of the apology depends on the magnitude of the mistake. For the customer who ordered the sweater, a simple apology, followed by a clear statement of when the sweater will arrive, would probably be sufficient.

> Some negative messages regarding transactions carry significant business ramifications.

> Your approach to bad news about business transactions depends on the customer's expectations.

> If you've failed to meet expectations that you set for the customer, an element of apology should be considered.

Planning > Writing > Completing

Planning

Analyze the Situation
Verify that the purpose is to decline a request and offer alternatives; audience is likely to be surprised by the refusal.

Gather Information
Determine audience needs and obtain the necessary information.

Select the Right Medium
For formal messages, printed letters on company letterhead are best.

Organize the Information
The main idea is to refuse the request, so limit your scope to that; select an indirect approach based on the audience and the situation.

Writing

Adapt to Your Audience
Adjust the level of formality based on degree of familiarity with the audience; maintain a positive relationship by using the "you" attitude, politeness, positive emphasis, and bias-free language.

Compose the Message
Use a conversational but professional style and keep the message brief, clear, and as helpful as possible.

Completing

Revise the Message
Evaluate content and review readability to make sure the negative information won't be misinterpreted; make sure your tone stays positive without being artificial.

Produce the Message
Emphasize a clean, professional appearance on company letterhead.

Proofread the Message
Review for errors in layout, spelling, and mechanics.

Distribute the Message
Deliver your message using the chosen medium.

1   2   3

> Figure 9–3 Letter Declining a Favour Using the Indirect Strategy

Quallcom Corporation

687 Portage Ave, Suite 1700, Winnipeg, MB   R3Y 0M5
204-555-2354/fax 204-555-2349
www.quallcom.net
contact@quallcom.net

February 15, 2010

Phillippe DiCastro
Analyst
Morrissey Financial Advisors
30 Cumberland St N
Thunder Bay, ON   P7F 4K9

Dear Mr. DiCastro:

We at Quallcom Corporation appreciate and benefit from the research conducted by companies such as yours. Your study sounds interesting, and we are certainly able to help within the guidelines of our firm's policies governing outside researchers.

Sensitive data is of special concern to the company; our board requires strict confidentiality of all sales information until quarterly reports are mailed to shareholders. As you know, we release news reports at the same time quarterly reports go out. We will be happy to include you in all our future mailings.

Although we cannot release projected figures, we are, of course, able to share data that are part of the public record. I've enclosed several of our past earnings reports for your inspection.

We look forward to the results of your study. Please let us know if there is any additional way we can help.

Yours truly,

Lisa McKinnon

Lisa McKinnon
Customer Service
Investor Relations

Enclosure

Annotations:
- Buffers negative response by demonstrating respect
- States a meaningful reason for the negative response without apologizing since the company suggests an alternative, showing that McKinnon cares about the request and has given the matter some thought
- Closes by reinforcing the company's continuing commitment

An explanation is usually not required, although if a meaningful reason exists, and if stating it will help smooth over the situation without sounding like a feeble excuse, by all means include it. For example, if a snowstorm closed the highways and prevented your receiving necessary materials, say so; however, if you simply received more orders than you expected and promised more than you could deliver, the customer will be less sympathetic. For larger business-to-business transactions, the customer may want an explanation of what went wrong to determine whether you'll be able to perform as you promise in the future.

> Figure 9–4 Effective Email Advising of a Back Order

Conveys the good news first in the buffer

Implies the actual bad news by telling the reader what's being done, not what can't be done

Fosters a positive ongoing relationship by inviting inquiries and reminding the customer of a key benefit

Includes helpful contact information

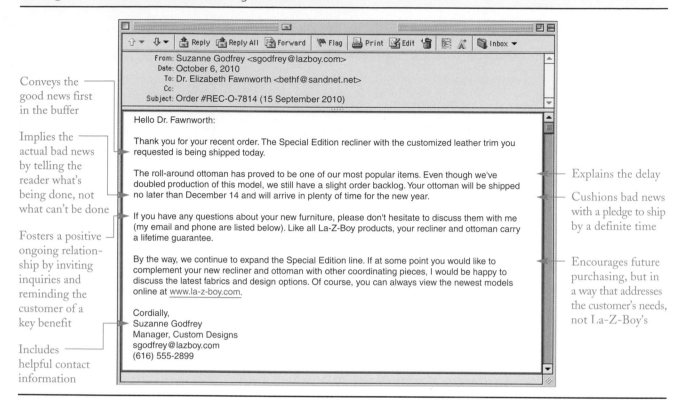

Explains the delay

Cushions bad news with a pledge to ship by a definite time

Encourages future purchasing, but in a way that addresses the customer's needs, not La-Z-Boy's

To help repair the damage to the relationship and encourage repeat business, many companies offer discounts on future purchases, free merchandise, or other considerations. Even modest efforts can go a long way to rebuilding the customer's confidence in your company. However, you don't always have a choice. Business-to-business purchasing contracts often include performance clauses that legally entitle the customer to discounts or other restitution in the event of late delivery. To review the concepts covered in this section, see "Checklist: Handling Bad News About Transactions."

Use the indirect approach in most cases of refusing a claim.

  Explore

REFUSING CLAIMS AND REQUESTS FOR ADJUSTMENT Almost every customer who makes a claim or requests an adjustment is emotionally involved; therefore, the indirect method is usually the best approach for a refusal. Your job as a writer is to avoid accepting responsibility for the unfortunate situation and yet avoid blaming or accusing the customer. To steer clear of these pitfalls, pay special attention to the tone of your letter.

CHECKLIST Handling Bad News About Transactions

✔ Reset the customer's expectations regarding the transaction.

✔ Explain what happened and why, if appropriate.

✔ Explain how you'll resolve the situation.

✔ Repair any damage done to the business relationship, perhaps offering future discounts, free merchandise, or other considerations.

✔ Offer a professional, businesslike expression of apology if your organization made a mistake.

A tactful and courteous letter can build goodwill even while denying the claim, as shown in Figure 9–5. Here, Village Electronics recently received a letter from Daniel Lindmeier, who purchased a digital video camera a year ago. He wrote to say that the unit doesn't work correctly and to inquire about the warranty. Lindmeier incorrectly believes that the warranty covers one year, when it actually covers only three months. Walter Brodie uses an indirect approach to convey the bad news and to offer additional helpful information.

When refusing a claim, avoid language that might have a negative impact on the reader. Instead, demonstrate that you understand and have considered the complaint carefully. Then, even if the claim is unreasonable, rationally explain why you are refusing the request. Remember, don't apologize and don't hide behind "company policy." End the letter on a respectful and action-oriented note.

> When refusing a claim
> > demonstrate your understanding of the complaint
> > explain your refusal
> > suggest alternative action

If you deal with enough customers over a long enough period, chances are you'll get a request that is particularly outrageous. However, you need to control your emotions and approach the situation as calmly as possible to avoid saying or writing anything that the recipient might interpret as defamation. Someone suing for defamation must prove (1) that the statement is false, (2) that the language is injurious to the person's reputation, and (3) that the statement has been published.

To avoid being accused of defamation, follow these guidelines:

> Refrain from using any kind of abusive language or terms that could be considered defamatory.
> Provide accurate information and stick to the facts.
> Never let anger or malice motivate your messages.

You can help avoid defamation by not responding emotionally.

Planning	Writing	Completing
Analyze the Situation Verify that the purpose is to refuse a warranty claim and offer repairs; audience's likely reaction will be disappointment and surprise.	**Adapt to Your Audience** Adjust the level of formality based on degree of familiarity with the audience; maintain a positive relationship by using the "you" attitude, politeness, positive emphasis, and bias-free language.	**Revise the Message** Evaluate content and review readability to make sure the negative information won't be misinterpreted; make sure your tone stays positive without being artificial.
Gather Information Gather information on warranty policies and procedures, repair services, and resale information.	**Compose the Message** Use a conversational but professional style and keep the message brief, clear, and as helpful as possible.	**Produce the Message** Emphasize a clean, professional appearance appropriate for a letter on company stationery.
Select the Right Medium Choose the best medium for delivering your message; for formal messages, printed letters on company letterhead are best.		**Proofread the Message** Review for errors in layout, spelling, and mechanics.
Organize the Information Your main idea is to refuse the claim and promote an alternative solution; select an indirect approach based on the audience and the situation.		**Distribute the Message** Deliver your message using the chosen medium; make sure the reader receives any necessary support documents as well.

1   2   3

> Figure 9–5 Effective Letter Refusing a Claim

NUMBER ONE IN ENTERTAINMENT

Village Electronics

415 Main St. • Whitehorse, YT Y1B 2X6
Voice: 867-555-1312 • Fax: 867-555-1316

May 5, 2010

Mr. Daniel Lindmeier
General Delivery
Cassiar, BC   VOC 1ED

Dear Mr. Lindmeier:

Thank you for your letter about the battery release switch on your JVC digital camera. Village Electronics believes, as you do, that electronic equipment should be built to last. That's why we stand behind our products with a one-year warranty.

Even though your JVC camera is more than a year old and therefore out of warranty, we can still help. Please package your camera carefully and ship it to our store in Whitehorse. Include your complete name, address, phone number, and a brief description of the malfunction, along with a cheque for $35 for an initial examination. After assessing the unit, we will give you a written estimate of the needed parts and labour. Then just let us know whether you want us to make the repairs—either by phone or by filling out the prepaid card we'll send you with the estimate.

If you choose to repair the unit, the $35 will be applied toward your bill, the balance of which is payable by cheque or credit card. JVC also has service centres available in your area. If you would prefer to take the unit to one of them, please see the enclosed list.

Thanks again for inquiring about our service. I've also enclosed a catalogue of our latest cameras and accessories, in which you'll find information about JVC's "Trade-Up Special." If you're ready to move up to one of the newest cameras, JVC will offer a generous trade-in allowance on your current model.

Sincerely,

Walter Brodie

Walter Brodie
Customer Service Manager
Enclosures: List of service centres
                    Catalogue

Annotations (left margin):
- Buffers the bad news by emphasizing a point the reader and writer both agree on
- States bad news indirectly, tactfully leaving the repair decision to the customer
- Closes by blending sales promotion with an acknowledgment of the customer's interests

Annotations (right margin):
- Puts company's policy in a favourable light
- Helps soothe the reader with a positive alternative

> Consult your company's legal department or a lawyer whenever you think a message might have legal consequences.
> Communicate honestly and ensure that what you're saying is what you believe to be true.
> Emphasize a desire for a good relationship in the future.

Most important, remember that nothing positive can come out of antagonizing a customer, even a customer who has verbally abused you or your colleagues. Reject the claim or request for adjustment and move on to the next challenge. For a brief review of the tasks involved when refusing claims, see "Checklist: Refusing Claims."

CHECKLIST Refusing Claims

- ✔ Use an indirect approach since the reader is expecting or hoping for a positive response.
- ✔ Indicate your full understanding of the nature of the complaint.
- ✔ Explain why you are refusing the request, without hiding behind company policy.
- ✔ Provide an accurate, factual account of the transaction.

- ✔ Emphasize ways processes and procedures should have been handled, rather than dwelling on a reader's negligence.
- ✔ Avoid any appearance of defamation.
- ✔ Avoid expressing personal opinions.
- ✔ End with a positive, friendly, helpful close.
- ✔ Make any suggested action easy for readers to comply with.

Sending Negative Organizational News

As a manager, you may need to issue negative announcements regarding some aspect of your products, services, or operations. Most of these scenarios have unique challenges that must be addressed on a case-by-case basis, but the general advice offered here applies to all of them. One key difference among all these messages is whether you have time to plan the announcement. The following section addresses those negative messages for which you do have time to plan, then "Communicating in a Crisis" offers advice on communication during emergencies.

COMMUNICATING UNDER NORMAL CIRCUMSTANCES Businesses must convey a range of negative messages regarding their ongoing operations. A company may need to make decisions that are unpopular with customers (such as price increases, product cancellations, product recalls), with employees (such as layoffs, benefit reductions, plant closings), or with other groups (such as relocating to a new community, replacing a board member, cancelling a contract with a supplier). Because you're using a single announcement to reach a variety of people, each of whom may react differently, these messages need to be planned with great care. The letter in Figure 9–6 is a mass mailing to trade customers, such as interior designers and owners of home decor stores, from a wallpaper manufacturer. It announces a change in practice that might inconvenience some readers but provides overriding benefits.

Negative organizational messages to external audiences often require extensive planning.

A more significant event, such as a plant closing, can affect hundreds or thousands of people in many organizations. Employees need to find new jobs, get training in new skills or perhaps get emergency financial help—issues that need to be addressed. School districts may have to adjust budgets and staffing levels if many of your employees plan to move in search of new jobs. Your customers need to find new suppliers. Your suppliers may need to find other customers of their own. Government agencies may need to react to everything from a decrease in tax revenues to an influx of people seeking unemployment benefits.

When making negative announcements, follow these guidelines:

> **Match your approach to the situation**. A modest price increase won't shock most customers, so the direct approach is fine. However, cancelling a product that people count on is another matter, so building up to the news through the indirect approach might be better.
> **Consider the unique needs of each group**. As the plant-closing example illustrates, various people have different information needs.
> **Give each audience enough time to react as needed**. For example, employees, particularly higher-level executives, may need as much as six months or more to find new jobs.

Give people as much time as possible to react to negative news.

> Figure 9–6 Effective Letter Describing Change in Company Practice

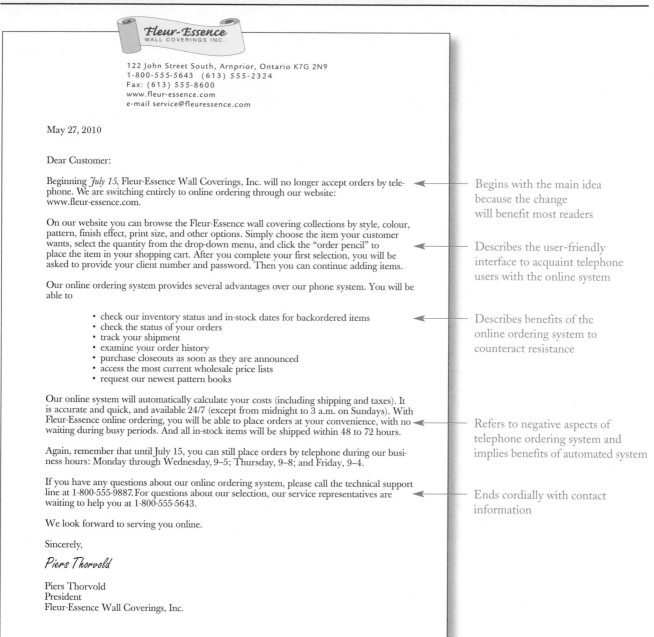

Fleur-Essence
WALL COVERINGS INC.

122 John Street South, Arnprior, Ontario K7G 2N9
1-800-555-5643   (613) 555-2324
Fax: (613) 555-8600
www.fleur-essence.com
e-mail service@fleuressence.com

May 27, 2010

Dear Customer:

Beginning *July 15*, Fleur-Essence Wall Coverings, Inc. will no longer accept orders by telephone. We are switching entirely to online ordering through our website: www.fleur-essence.com.   ◄——— Begins with the main idea because the change will benefit most readers

On our website you can browse the Fleur-Essence wall covering collections by style, colour, pattern, finish effect, print size, and other options. Simply choose the item your customer wants, select the quantity from the drop-down menu, and click the "order pencil" to place the item in your shopping cart. After you complete your first selection, you will be asked to provide your client number and password. Then you can continue adding items.   ◄——— Describes the user-friendly interface to acquaint telephone users with the online system

Our online ordering system provides several advantages over our phone system. You will be able to

- check our inventory status and in-stock dates for backordered items   ◄——— Describes benefits of the online ordering system to counteract resistance
- check the status of your orders
- track your shipment
- examine your order history
- purchase closeouts as soon as they are announced
- access the most current wholesale price lists
- request our newest pattern books

Our online system will automatically calculate your costs (including shipping and taxes). It is accurate and quick, and available 24/7 (except from midnight to 3 a.m. on Sundays). With Fleur-Essence online ordering, you will be able to place orders at your convenience, with no waiting during busy periods. And all in-stock items will be shipped within 48 to 72 hours.   ◄——— Refers to negative aspects of telephone ordering system and implies benefits of automated system

Again, remember that until July 15, you can still place orders by telephone during our business hours: Monday through Wednesday, 9–5; Thursday, 9–8; and Friday, 9–4.

If you have any questions about our online ordering system, please call the technical support line at 1-800-555-9887. For questions about our selection, our service representatives are waiting to help you at 1-800-555-5643.   ◄——— Ends cordially with contact information

We look forward to serving you online.

Sincerely,

Piers Thorvold

Piers Thorvold
President
Fleur-Essence Wall Coverings, Inc.

> **Give yourself enough time to plan and manage a response.** You will receive numerous complaints, questions, or product returns after you make your announcement, so ensure that you're ready with answers and additional follow-up information.

> **Look for positive angles but don't give false optimism.** If eliminating a seldom-used employee benefit means employees will save money, you can promote that positive angle. On the other hand, laying off 10 000 people does not give them "an opportunity to explore new horizons." It's a traumatic event that can affect employees, their families, and their communities

for years. The best you may be able to do is to thank people for their past support and wish them well in the future.

> **Minimize the element of surprise whenever possible.** This step can require considerable judgment on your part, but if you recognize that current trends are pointing toward negative results sometime in the near future, it's often better to let your audience know ahead of time. For example, a common complaint in many shareholder lawsuits is a claim that the company didn't let investors know business was deteriorating until it was too late.

> **Seek expert advice if you're not sure.** Many significant negative announcements have important technical, financial, or legal elements that require the expertise of lawyers, accountants, or other specialists. If you're not sure how to handle every aspect of the announcement, ask.

> Ask for legal help and other assistance if you're not sure how to handle a significant negative announcement.

Negative situations will test your skills as a communicator and leader. People may turn to you and say, "Okay, so things are bad; now what do we do?" Inspirational leaders try to seize such opportunities as a chance to reshape or reinvigorate the organization, and they offer encouragement to those around them. In Figure 9–7, a message to employees at Sybervantage, Frank Leslie shares the unpleasant news that a hoped-for licensing agreement with Warner Brothers has been rejected. Rather than dwell on the bad news, he focuses on options for the future. The upbeat close diminishes the effect of the bad news without hiding or downplaying the news itself.

Objective 6 Explain the role of communication in crisis management.

COMMUNICATING IN A CRISIS As the example with Maple Leaf Foods (profiled in the chapter opener) shows, some of the most critical instances of business communication occur during internal or external crises. These can range from incidents of product tampering to industrial accidents, crimes or scandals

TIPS FOR SUCCESS

" A clearly written media policy can help minimize your firm's media liabilities and promote a public perception of your firm—it's all in *what* you say and *how* you say it."

David M. Freedman and Janice E. Purtell, communication consultants

> Figure 9–7 Effective Email Providing Bad News About Company Operations

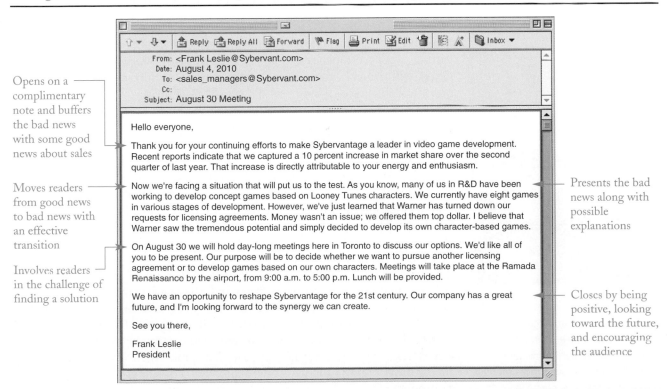

Opens on a complimentary note and buffers the bad news with some good news about sales

Moves readers from good news to bad news with an effective transition

Involves readers in the challenge of finding a solution

Presents the bad news along with possible explanations

Closes by being positive, looking toward the future, and encouraging the audience

From: <Frank Leslie@Sybervant.com>
Date: August 4, 2010
To: <sales_managers@Sybervant.com>
Cc:
Subject: August 30 Meeting

Hello everyone,

Thank you for your continuing efforts to make Sybervantage a leader in video game development. Recent reports indicate that we captured a 10 percent increase in market share over the second quarter of last year. That increase is directly attributable to your energy and enthusiasm.

Now we're facing a situation that will put us to the test. As you know, many of us in R&D have been working to develop concept games based on Looney Tunes characters. We currently have eight games in various stages of development. However, we've just learned that Warner has turned down our requests for licensing agreements. Money wasn't an issue; we offered them top dollar. I believe that Warner saw the tremendous potential and simply decided to develop its own character-based games.

On August 30 we will hold day-long meetings here in Toronto to discuss our options. We'd like all of you to be present. Our purpose will be to decide whether we want to pursue another licensing agreement or to develop games based on our own characters. Meetings will take place at the Ramada Renaissance by the airport, from 9:00 a.m. to 5:00 p.m. Lunch will be provided.

We have an opportunity to reshape Sybervantage for the 21st century. Our company has a great future, and I'm looking forward to the synergy we can create.

See you there,

Frank Leslie
President

USING THE POWER OF TECHNOLOGY ∿

Controlling Online Rumours

Business has found the internet to be an invaluable way to promote products, serve customers, provide company information, and raise its profile through media releases, executive presentations, blogs, podcasts, and more. With the internet, a business can grow globally and increase market share, thus enhancing investor value and job security for employees.

The internet is also a tool for consumers. They can share rumours and complaints through email, instant messaging, blogs, chat rooms, newsgroups, review sites such as epinions.com, complaint websites such as www.planetfeedback.com, and "corporate hate" sites such as www.paypalsucks.com. On the positive side, consumers who feel they have been treated unfairly can use the public exposure as leverage. Many companies appreciate the feedback from these sites, too, and even buy complaint summaries so they can improve products and services.

Nevertheless, many of these venues don't verify rumours or complaints. Email is probably the worst offender in this respect because messages are so easy to forward en masse. Among the classic rumours spread online: McDonald's soft-serve ice cream contains pig fat, products from Coca-Cola and PepsiCo are tainted, perfume samples arriving in the mail are poisonous, and bananas from Costa Rica carry flesh-eating bacteria. Every one of these rumours is false.

Controlling false rumours is difficult, but you can help contain them by (1) responding quickly with clear information distributed in any way you can, (2) tracking down and responding to rumours wherever they appear, (3) enlisting the help of government agencies such as the Public Health Agency of Canada (www.publichealth.gc.ca) and debunking sites such as www.snopes.com, and (4) even digging back through email threads and responding personally to everyone who passed the message along. Moreover, don't wait for bad news to find you; monitor complaint sites and newsgroups so that you can stop false information faster.

CAREER APPLICATIONS

1 A legitimate complaint about one of your products on planetfeedback.com also contains a statement that your company "doesn't care about its customers." How should you respond?

2 A few bloggers are circulating false information about your company, but the problem is not widespread—yet. Should you jump on the problem now and tell the world the rumour is false, even though most people haven't heard it yet? Explain your answer.

---

involving company employees, on-site hostage situations, or terrorist attacks. During a crisis, employees, their families, the surrounding community, and others will demand information, and rumours can spread unpredictably and uncontrollably (see "Using the Power of Technology: Controlling Online Rumours"). You can also expect the news media to descend quickly, asking questions of anyone they can find.

Although you can't predict these events, you can prepare for them. Companies that respond quickly with the information people need tend to fare much better in these circumstances than those who go into hiding or release bits and pieces of uncoordinated or inconsistent information. Companies such as Johnson & Johnson (in a Tylenol-tampering incident) and Maple Leaf Foods emerged from crisis with renewed respect for their decisive action and responsive communication. In contrast, Exxon continues to be cited as a classic example of how not to communicate in a crisis—more than a quarter century after one of its tankers spilled 250 000 barrels of oil into Alaska's Prince William Sound. The company frustrated the media and the public with sketchy, inconsistent information and an adamant refusal to accept responsibility for the full extent of the environmental disaster. The company's CEO didn't talk to the media for nearly a week; other executives made contradictory statements, which further undermined public trust. The mistakes had a lasting impact on the company's reputation and consumers' willingness to buy its products.[13]

Should you use the indirect or direct strategy when communicating all bad news? Many people in finance believe that, when communicating the falling fortunes of one's investments, the direct strategy is best. Why?

> Table 9–3 How to Communicate in a Crisis

When a Crisis Hits:

Do	Don't
Prepare for trouble ahead of time by identifying potential problems, appointing and training a response team, and preparing and testing a crisis management plan.	Don't blame anyone for anything.
Get top management involved as soon as the crisis hits.	Don't speculate in public.
Set up a news centre for company representatives and the media, equipped with phones, computers, and other electronic tools for preparing news releases and online updates. At the news centre, take the following steps:	Don't refuse to answer questions.
> Issue frequent news updates, and have trained personnel available to respond to questions around the clock.	Don't release information that will violate anyone's right to privacy.
> Provide complete information packets to the media as soon as possible.	Don't use the crisis to pitch products or services.
> Prevent conflicting statements and provide continuity, appointing a single person, trained in advance, to speak for the company.	Don't play favourites with media representatives.
> Tell receptionists and other employers to direct all media calls to the news centre.	
Tell the whole story—openly, completely, and honestly. If you are at fault, apologize.	
Demonstrate the company's concern by your statements and your actions.	

The key to successful communication efforts during a crisis is having a **crisis management plan.** In addition to defining operational procedures to deal with the crisis itself, the plan also outlines communication tasks and responsibilities, which can include everything from media contacts to news release templates (see Table 9–3). The plan should clearly specify which people are authorized to speak for the company, contact information for all key executives, and a list of the media outlets and technologies that will be used to disseminate information. Experts attribute the success of Michael McCain's handling of the Listeria contamination crisis at Maple Leaf Food to an effective crisis plan. In fact, many companies today regularly test crisis communications in realistic practice drills lasting a full day or more.[14]

Anticipation and planning are key to successful communication in a crisis.

Sending Negative Employment Messages

Most managers must convey bad news about individual employees from time to time. Recipients have an emotional stake in your message, so take an indirect approach when giving negative performance reviews to employees; they will most certainly be emotionally involved. In addition, choose the media you use for these messages with care. For example, email and other written forms let you control the message and avoid personal confrontation, but one-on-one conversations are more sensitive and facilitate questions and answers. Companies often have policies on reference letters and other negative employment messages that managers are required to follow.[15]

REFUSING REQUESTS FOR RECOMMENDATION LETTERS Negative employment messages have legal implications; that's why many former employers refuse to write recommendation letters—especially for people whose job performance has been unsatisfactory.[16] When sending refusals to prospective employers, your message may be brief and direct:

✴ Explore

Our human resources department has authorized me to confirm that Yolanda Johnson worked for Tandy, Inc., for three years, from June 2000 to July 2002. Best of luck as you interview administrative applicants.

Implies that company policy prohibits the release of any more information but does provide what information is available

Ends on a positive note

This message doesn't need to say, "We cannot comply with your request." It simply gets down to the business of giving readers the information that is allowable.

Refusing an applicant's direct request for a recommendation letter is another matter. Any refusal to cooperate may seem a personal slight and a threat to the applicant's future. Diplomacy and preparation help readers accept your refusal:

Uses the indirect approach since the other party is probably expecting a positive response →

Announces that the writer cannot comply with the request, without explicitly blaming it on "policy" ⌐

Offers to fulfill as much of the request as possible, then offers an alternative

Ends on a positive note

Thank you for letting me know about your job opportunity with Gildan Activewear. Your internship here and the MBA you've worked so hard to earn should place you in an excellent position to land the marketing job.

Although we do not send out formal recommendations here at Ferman Textiles, I can certainly send Gildan a confirmation of your employment dates. And if you haven't considered this already, be sure to ask several of your professors to write evaluations of your marketing skills. Best of luck to you in your career.

This letter deftly and tactfully avoids hurting the reader's feelings, because it makes positive comments about the reader's recent activities, implies the refusal, suggests an alternative, and uses a polite close.

Poorly written rejection letters tarnish your company's reputation and can even invite legal troubles.

✱ Explore

REJECTING JOB APPLICATIONS Tactfully telling job applicants that you won't offer them employment is another frequent communication challenge. Poorly written rejection letters have negative consequences, ranging from the loss of qualified candidates for future openings to the loss of potential customers (not only the rejected applicants but also their friends and family).[17] Poorly phrased rejection letters can even invite legal troubles. When delivering bad news to job applicants, follow three guidelines:[18]

Objective 7 Identify three guidelines for delivering negative news to job applicants, and give a brief explanation of each one.

1. **Choose your approach carefully.** Experts disagree on whether a direct or an indirect approach is best for rejection letters. On the one hand, job applicants know they won't get many of the positions for which they apply, so negative news during a job search is not generally a shock. On the other hand, people put their hopes and dreams on the line when they apply for work, so job applicants have a deep emotional investment in the process, which is one of the factors to consider in using an indirect approach. If you opt for a direct approach, don't be brutally blunt in the opening. Tell your reader that the position has been filled, rather than saying, "Your application has been rejected." If you opt for an indirect approach, be careful not to mislead the reader or delay the bad news for more than a sentence or two. A simple "Thank you for considering ABC as the place to start your career" is a quick, courteous buffer that shows your company is flattered to be considered. Don't mislead the reader in your buffer by praising his or her qualifications in a way that could suggest good news is soon to follow.
2. **Clearly state why the applicant was not selected.** Make your rejection less personal by stating that you hired someone with more experience or whose qualifications match the position requirements more closely.
3. **Close by suggesting alternatives.** If time permits, you might suggest professional organizations that could help the applicant find employment. If

the applicant is suitable for a position in your organization that fits his or her current qualifications, you can indicate that the résumé will be kept on file.

The email response in Figure 9–8 was drafted by Marvin Fichter to communicate the bad news to Carol DeCicco following her interview with Bradley & Jackson. After reviewing the first draft, Fichter made several changes to improve

> Figure 9–8 Poor and Improved Emails Rejecting a Job Application

From Marvin R. Fichter <marvin.fichter@bradleyjackson.com>
Date: October 4, 2010
To: <cldecicco@home.net>
Subject: Job Application

Draft

Dear Ms. DeCicco:

We were so impressed with your résumé and credentials. Your academic record and previous accounting experience are just what we were hoping to see. We just didn't expect to see such sterling qualifications in so many candidates. As you can imagine, with 30 applicants for this position, the selection process was quite difficult.

After much consideration, we were able to narrow down the choices to three, one of which was you. However, I'm sorry to say that you were not chosen to fill the tax accountant position.

If you wouldn't mind, we would like to keep your information on file for six months, on the off chance that another position might open up before you find another position.

Thank you for thinking of us.

Sincerely,

Marvin R. Fichter
Human Resources

Opens with an excessively positive tone that misleads the reader into thinking the answer will be positive

Includes an inappropriate apology; the company did nothing wrong so therefore has no need to apologize; also fails to explain why the candidate was not chosen

Closes with a weak, insincere request

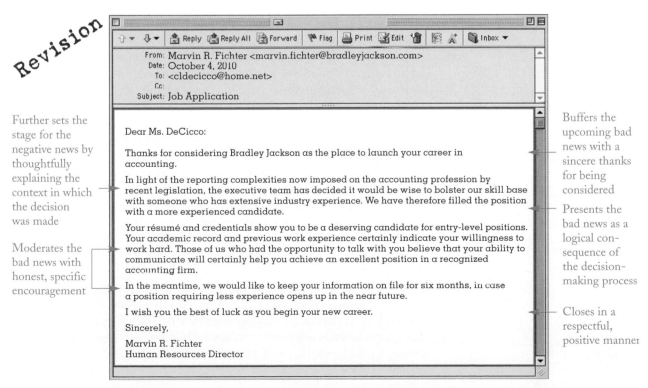

Revision

From: Marvin R. Fichter <marvin.fichter@bradleyjackson.com>
Date: October 4, 2010
To: <cldecicco@home.net>
Cc:
Subject: Job Application

Dear Ms. DeCicco:

Thanks for considering Bradley Jackson as the place to launch your career in accounting.

In light of the reporting complexities now imposed on the accounting profession by recent legislation, the executive team has decided it would be wise to bolster our skill base with someone who has extensive industry experience. We have therefore filled the position with a more experienced candidate.

Your résumé and credentials show you to be a deserving candidate for entry-level positions. Your academic record and previous work experience certainly indicate your willingness to work hard. Those of us who had the opportunity to talk with you believe that your ability to communicate will certainly help you achieve an excellent position in a recognized accounting firm.

In the meantime, we would like to keep your information on file for six months, in case a position requiring less experience opens up in the near future.

I wish you the best of luck as you begin your new career.

Sincerely,

Marvin R. Fichter
Human Resources Director

Further sets the stage for the negative news by thoughtfully explaining the context in which the decision was made

Moderates the bad news with honest, specific encouragement

Buffers the upcoming bad news with a sincere thanks for being considered

Presents the bad news as a logical consequence of the decision-making process

Closes in a respectful, positive manner

the communication. The revised email helps DeCicco understand that (1) she would have been hired if she'd had more tax experience and (2) she shouldn't be discouraged.

Always respond to job applications.

Resist the temptation to not respond to applicants. Some companies are now so swamped with emailed résumés and online applications that they no longer have time to respond to them all. However, a failure to respond to job applicants has traditionally been viewed as a fairly serious breach of business etiquette. Responding is not only good for your company's image but also initiates conversations that might lead to successful hiring when you have the right opportunities for the right people.[19]

An important goal of any performance evaluation is giving the employee a plan of action for improving his or her performance.

GIVING NEGATIVE PERFORMANCE REVIEWS The main purpose of these reviews is to improve employee performance by

 Explore

> emphasizing and clarifying job requirements
> giving employees feedback on their efforts to fulfill those requirements
> guiding continued efforts by developing a plan of action, which includes rewards and opportunities

Performance reviews help companies set organizational standards and communicate organizational values.[20]

Positive and negative performance reviews share several characteristics: The tone is objective and unbiased, the language is non-judgmental, and the focus is problem resolution.[21] Criticizing others is difficult for most people, but discussing shortcomings is a necessary first step to improvement for both an employee and an organization. When you need to give a negative performance review, follow these guidelines:[22]

> **Confront the problem right away.** Avoiding performance problems only makes them worse—and it robs the employee of the opportunity to improve. Moreover, if you don't document problems when they occur, you may make it more difficult to terminate employment later on, if the situation comes to that.[23]
> **Plan your message.** Be clear about your concerns, and include examples of the employee's specific actions. Think about any possible biases you may have, and get feedback from others. Collect and verify all relevant facts (both strengths and weaknesses).

Address performance problems in private.

> **Deliver the message in private.** Whether in writing or in person, address the performance problem privately. Don't send performance reviews by email or fax. If you're reviewing an employee's performance face to face, conduct that review in a meeting arranged expressly for that purpose, and consider holding that meeting in a conference room, the employee's office, or some other neutral area.
> **Focus on the problem.** Without attacking the employee, discuss the problems caused by his or her performance and explain how it doesn't meet expectations established for the position. Identify the consequences of continuing poor performance, and show that you're committed to help solve the problem.
> **Ask for a commitment from the employee.** Help the employee understand that planning for and making improvements are the employee's responsibility. However, finalize decisions jointly so that you can ensure that any action taken is achievable. Set a schedule for improvement and for following up with evaluations of that improvement.

Even if your employee's performance has been disappointing, you should begin by mentioning some good points in your performance review. Then clearly and tactfully state how the employee can better meet the responsibilities of the job. If the performance review is to be effective, ensure that you suggest ways the employee can improve.[24] The goal is to help the employee succeed.

TERMINATING EMPLOYMENT The decision to terminate employees is rarely easy or simple, but doing it effectively is an important managerial responsibility. When writing a termination message, you have three goals:

1. Present the reasons for this difficult action
2. Avoid statements that might expose the company to a wrongful termination lawsuit
3. Leave the relationship between the terminated employee and the firm as favourable as possible

For both legal and personal reasons, present specific justification for asking the employee to leave.[25] If the employee is working under contract, your company's lawyers can tell you whether the employee's performance is legal grounds for termination.

Ensure that all your reasons are accurate and verifiable. Avoid words that are open to interpretation, such as *untidy* and *difficult*. You can do so by telling the truth about the termination and by helping as much as you can to make the employee's transition as smooth as possible.[26] To review the tasks involved in this type of message, see "Checklist: Writing Negative Employment Messages."

Carefully word a termination letter to avoid creating undue ill will and grounds for legal action.

✴ Explore

CHECKLIST Writing Negative Employment Messages

A. Refusing requests for recommendation letters
✔ Don't feel obligated to write a recommendation letter if you don't feel comfortable doing so.
✔ Take a diplomatic approach to minimize hurt feelings.
✔ Compliment the reader's accomplishments.
✔ Suggest alternatives if available.

B. Rejecting job applications
✔ Always respond to applications.
✔ Avoid being blunt or cold if you use a direct approach.
✔ Don't mislead the reader in your buffer or delay the bad news for more than one or two sentences if you use an indirect approach.
✔ State clearly why the applicant was rejected.
✔ Suggest alternatives if possible.

C. Giving negative performance reviews
✔ Maintain an objective and unbiased tone.
✔ Use non-judgmental language.
✔ Focus on problem resolution.
✔ Ensure that negative feedback is documented and shared with the employee.
✔ Don't avoid confrontations by withholding negative feedback.
✔ Ask the employee for a commitment to improve.

D. Terminating employment
✔ State your reasons accurately and ensure that they are objectively verifiable.
✔ Avoid statements that might expose your company to a wrongful termination lawsuit.
✔ Consult company lawyers to clarify all terms of the separation.
✔ End the relationship on terms as positive as possible.

Summary of Learning Objectives

1 **Apply the three-step writing process to negative messages.** Because the way you say "no" can be far more damaging than the fact that you're saying it, planning your bad-news messages is crucial. Ensure that your purpose is specific, necessary, and appropriate for your chosen medium. Determine how your audience prefers to receive bad news. Collect all the facts necessary to support your negative decision and adapt your tone to the situation as well as to your audience. Bad-news messages may be organized according to the direct or the indirect approach, and your choice depends on audience preference as well as the situation. In addition, carefully choose positive words to construct diplomatic sentences. Finally, revision, design, and proofreading are necessary to ensure that you are saying exactly what you want to say in the best possible way.

2 **Explain the differences between the direct and the indirect approaches to negative messages, including when it's appropriate to use each one.** The direct approach to bad-news messages puts the bad news up front, follows with the reasons (and perhaps offers an alternative), and closes with a positive statement. On the other hand, the indirect approach begins with a buffer (a neutral or positive statement), explains the reasons, clearly states the bad news (de-emphasizing it as much as possible), and closes with a positive statement. Use the direct approach when you know your audience prefers receiving bad news up front or if the bad news will cause readers little pain or disappointment. Otherwise, the indirect approach is best.

3 **Identify the risks of using the indirect approach, and explain how to avoid such problems.** If used ineffectively, the indirect approach may be disrespectful and may mislead the reader. To avoid these problems, ensure that the buffer does not trivialize the reader's concerns but establishes common ground in a neutral manner. The body of the message should build up the explanation for the decision, preparing the reader through facts and logical reasoning. Give the most positive points first and, if possible, demonstrate how the negative decision might benefit the reader. End by clearly expressing the bad news, but de-emphasize the news without trivializing it. Focus on what could be done, instead of what cannot be accomplished.

4 **Adapt negative messages for internal and external audiences.** Internal and external audiences often have different needs and different expectations. Internal audiences often expect more detail than external audiences; for example, they want to know how change is going to impact them personally. When sending bad news outside the organization, you will write for a variety of audiences with different concerns; consequently you may need to adjust your content for each group.

5 **Explain the importance of maintaining high standards of ethics and etiquette when delivering negative messages.** Sending negative news is an unpleasant task, but this news must be delivered in a timely and sensitive manner. Ignoring bad news can violate laws and regulations, such as those governing financial communications; thus, an ethical communicator faces bad news head-on. Negative news can have a life-changing effect on the receiver; consequently, an ethical communicator sends this news with sensitivity to the receiver's situation and emotions. Furthermore, ethical communicators deliver bad news accurately, overcoming any reluctance to avoid the circumstances and mislead the receiver. By facing difficult situations honestly and considerately, communicators ultimately help others and are viewed with respect.

6 **Explain the role of communication in crisis management.** Communicating in a crisis can help maintain the company's reputation, instill the confidence of the public, and maintain the confidence of employees. Successful crisis communication is rooted in a crisis management plan that designates a company spokesperson and the procedures for operating and sending messages during the situation. Effective crisis communication is honest and open, and proactive rather than reactive.

7 **Identify three guidelines for delivering negative news to job applicants, and give a brief explanation of each one.** First, when delivering bad news to job applicants, choose an approach appropriate for the audience and the situation. If you choose the direct approach, which gives bad news up front, ensure that you are sensitive to the reader's emotions. If you choose the indirect approach, ensure that you do not mislead the reader through a poorly written buffer or inadequate explanation. Second, state clearly why the applicant was not selected. Depersonalize the bad news by indicating that the person hired fit the job requirements more closely. Third, if possible, close by suggesting alternatives; you will soften the reader's disappointment and you will project a positive image of your firm.

PEARSON

mycanadianbuscommlab

Visit www.mycanadianbuscommlab.ca for everything you need to help you succeed in the job you've always wanted! Tools and resources include the following:
- Composing Space and Writer's Toolkit
- Document Makeovers
- Video Case Studies
- Grammar Exercises—and much more!

On the Job PERFORMING COMMUNICATION TASKS AT MAPLE LEAF FOODS

Effective communication was one of the key skills demonstrated by Michael McCain and his team at Maple Leaf Foods during the food contamination crisis in 2008. As an administrative assistant in communications at Maple Leaf Foods, you need to send effective messages in negative situations. Your current task is to respond to proposals from graphic designers who want to produce Maple Leaf Foods' annual report. Although a company's proposal may be rejected, Maple Leaf Foods still wants to maintain the firm's goodwill and keep opportunities open for the future. Use this chapter's strategies to face the challenge of saying no with tact and understanding.

1 You have received a proposal from a graphic design company that, you believe, would create an effective and engaging annual report. But the applicant has not effectively discussed his company's previous work, one of the key questions in the proposal package. You'd like the applicant to resubmit the proposal, but he will have to wait an additional six weeks for a response. Which paragraph does the best job of presenting the bad news?

a It's too bad you neglected to answer fully the key question about the previous work your company did. If you want us to consider your firm as a candidate for producing our annual report, you'd better fill out the questionnaire completely.

b We know completing the proposal is a demanding and time-consuming process. As the instructions indicate, all key questions must be fully answered if the proposal is to receive consideration. We are returning your proposal package so you can review your answer to Question 4, dealing with previous design work.

c We appreciate the work you put into completing your supplier proposal. You did a thorough job, but please expand on Question 4.

2 Continuing with the case of the incomplete proposal, which closing paragraph would you choose? Why?

a We do appreciate that you took a lot of time to work on the proposal, but we can't read it until you complete it. And you won't hear from us for another six weeks.

b If you need further assistance in completing your proposal, please consult the internet bookmarks listed in the guidebook. We look forward to receiving your revised supplier proposal.

c Thank you for your attention to this matter.

3 Personal contacts are an important source of new business opportunities in many industries. In some cases, businesspeople develop these contacts through active participation in industry or professional groups and visits to trade shows, alumni societies, and other groups. You've recently received a request from a former classmate (Marcia DeLancey) who owns her own graphic design firm. She wants to visit your office to present her portfolio. However, your supervisor is already familiar with her work when she was an employee at another firm and knows her style would not fit Maple Leaf Foods' requirements. You didn't know DeLancey all that well; in fact, you had to think for a minute to remember who she was (this is the first contact you've had with her since you both graduated five years ago). Which opening would be most appropriate, keeping in mind she can't make the grade?

a Congratulations on owning your own company! I hope you enjoy your work as much as I enjoy mine. Thank you for your recent inquiry— evaluating such requests is one of my key responsibilities.

b Great to hear from you. I'd love to catch up on old times with you and find out how you're doing in your new job. I bounced around a bit after university, but I really feel that I've found my niche here at Maple Leaf Foods.

c I'm sorry to say that Maple Leaf Foods has already evaluated your work through submissions by your previous firm and found it did not fit our style. However, I do appreciate your getting in touch, and I hope all is well with you.

Test Your Knowledge

1 Why is it particularly important to adapt your medium and tone to your audience's needs and preferences when writing a bad-news message?

2 What are the main goals in delivering bad news?

3 What are the advantages of using the direct approach to deliver bad news at the beginning of a message?

4 What is the sequence of elements in a bad-news message organized using the indirect approach?

5 What is a buffer? Why do some critics consider it unethical?

6 When using an indirect approach to announce a negative decision, what is the purpose of presenting your reasons before explaining the decision itself?

7 What are the techniques for de-emphasizing bad news?

8 What are the ethical considerations for delivering bad news?

9 What are the characteristics of effective crisis communication?

10 When giving a negative review to an employee, what five guidelines should you follow?

Apply Your Knowledge

1 Why is it important to end negative messages on a positive note?

2 If company policy changes, should you explain those changes to employees and customers at about the same time? Why or why not?

3 If your purpose is to convey bad news, such as refusing a request, should you take the time to suggest alternatives to your reader? Why or why not?

4 When a company suffers a setback, should you soften the impact by letting out the bad news a little at a time? Why or why not?

5 Why is choice of medium important when delivering performance reviews?

6 **Ethical Choices:** Is intentionally de-emphasizing bad news the same as distorting graphs and charts to de-emphasize unfavourable data? Why or why not?

Running Cases

◉─ Watch on mycanadianbuscommlab

> CASE 1 Noreen

In her role as collections manager, Noreen has to write a letter informing customers with overdue accounts that the interest rate has risen by 1 percent, effective 30 days from the date on the letter. This policy means Petro-Go's current interest rate is 14 percent and in 30 days will increase to 15 percent. Overdue accounts are charged with compounding interest (i.e., interest on both the previous month's balance and the interest already charged on that month's balance).

QUESTIONS

a) What does it mean to use the "you" attitude in this type of message?

b) Is the direct or indirect approach best for this bad-news message? Why?

c) What must be considered to avoid defamation of the customer's character or reputation?

d) How will Noreen end this message on a positive note?

e) Should Noreen suggest ways for the customer to avoid paying late payment charges in this letter?

YOUR TASK

Write the letter. Remember to use company letterhead (create it yourself) and include an enclosure notation. Include a 1-800 number customers can call for further information.

Both the letter and the envelope should indicate the information is confidential. Prepare the envelope. (See Appendix A for letter and envelope formats.)

> CASE 2 Kwong

Kwong has returned to Accountants For All to complete his third co-op work term required by his college diploma. The owner, being very impressed with Kwong's past work performance and knowing that he has completed the required courses, promotes Kwong to corporate accountant status. He asks Kwong to write a letter to an important corporate client, Trisix, informing Marion Beattie, chief financial officer, that the quote Accountants For All gave them for this year's tax services was incorrect. The actual charge will be $500 more than discussed previously in an office meeting with Accountants For All's owner. The increased fee is due to the fact that Trisix's ledger was not accurate and Accountants For All's staff had to review receipts and adjust ledger entries manually. The initial price quote did not include manual handling of receipts. The letter should attempt to maintain a good customer relationship.

QUESTIONS

a) What facts must Kwong gather before writing the letter?

b) How will he choose positive words for this bad news?

c) Kwong has chosen the indirect approach for this letter. Suggest a reasonable buffer.

d) Should Kwong apologize?

e) How will Kwong end this message on a positive note? Why is this important?

YOUR TASK

Write the letter. Apply the guidelines for writing bad-news messages that Chapter 9 discusses.

Practise Your Knowledge

Read the following documents, then (1) analyze the strengths and weaknesses of each sentence and (2) revise each document so it follows this chapter's guidelines.

DOCUMENT 9.A: PROVIDING NEGATIVE NEWS ABOUT TRANSACTIONS

Your spring fraternity party sounds like fun. We're glad you've again chosen us as your caterer. Unfortunately, we have changed a few of our policies, and I wanted you to know about these changes in advance so we won't have any misunderstandings on the day of the party.

We will arrange the delivery of tables and chairs as usual the evening before the party. However, if you want us to set up, there is now a $100 charge for that service. Of course, you might want to get some of the brothers and pledges to do it, which would save you money. We've also added a small charge for cleanup. This is only $3 per person (you can estimate because I know a lot of people come and go later in the evening).

Other than that, all the arrangements will be the same. We'll provide the skirting for the band stage, tablecloths, bar set-up, and, of course, the barbecue. Will you have the tubs of ice with soft drinks again? We can do that for you as well, but there will be a fee.

Please let me know if you have any problems with these changes, and we'll try to work them out. I know it's going to be a great party.

DOCUMENT 9.B: REFUSING REQUESTS FOR CLAIMS AND ADJUSTMENTS

I am responding to your letter of about six weeks ago asking for an adjustment on your wireless hub, model WM39Z. We test all our products before they leave the factory; therefore, it could not have been our fault that your hub didn't work.

If you or someone in your office dropped the unit, it might have caused the damage. Or the damage could have been caused by the shipper if he dropped it. If so, you should file a claim with the shipper. At any rate, it wasn't our fault. The parts are already covered by warranty. However, we will provide labour for the repairs for $55, which is less than our cost, since you are a valued customer.

We will have a booth at the upcoming trade show there and hope to see you or someone from your office. We have many new models of office machines that we're sure you'll want to see. I've enclosed our latest catalogue. Hope to see you there.

DOCUMENT 9.C: REJECTING JOB APPLICATIONS

I regret to inform you that you were not selected for our summer intern program at Equifax. We had over a thousand résumés and cover letters to go through and simply could not get to them all. We have been asked to notify everyone that we have already selected students for the 25 positions based on those who applied early and were qualified.

We're sure you will be able to find a suitable position for summer work in your field and wish you the best of luck. We deeply regret any inconvenience associated with our reply.

Exercises

9.1 Selecting the Approach: Various Scenarios
Select the approach you would use (direct or indirect) for these negative messages:

a. an email message to your boss informing her that one of your key clients is taking its business to a different accounting firm

b. an email message to a customer informing her that one of the books she ordered over the internet is temporarily out of stock

c. an instant message to a customer explaining that the DVD recorder he ordered for his new computer is on back order and that, as a consequence, the shipping of the entire order will be delayed

d. a blog post to all employees notifying them that the company parking lot will be repaved during the first week of June and that the company will provide a shuttle service from a remote parking lot during that period

e. a letter from a travel agent to a customer stating that the airline will not refund her money for the flight she missed but that her tickets are valid for one year

f. a form letter from a Canadian airline to a customer explaining that they cannot extend the expiration date of the customer's frequent flyer miles even though the customer was living overseas for the past three years and unable to use the miles during that time

g. a letter from an insurance company to a policyholder denying a claim for reimbursement for a special dental procedure that is not covered under the terms of the customer's policy

h. a letter from an electronics store stating that the customer will not be reimbursed for a malfunctioning cell phone still under warranty (the terms of the warranty do not cover damages to phones that were accidentally dropped from a moving car)

i. an announcement to the repairs department listing parts that are on back order and will be three weeks late

9.2 Teamwork: Communicating Bad News

Working alone, revise the following statements to de-emphasize the bad news. (*Hint:* Minimize the space devoted to the bad news, subordinate it, embed it, or use the passive voice.) Then team up with a classmate and read each other's revisions. Did you both use the same approach in every case? Which approach seems to be more effective for each revised statement?

a. The airline can't refund your money. The "Conditions" segment on the back of your ticket states that there are no refunds for missed flights. Sometimes the airline makes exceptions, but only when life and death are involved. Of course, your ticket is still valid and can be used on a flight to the same destination.

b. I'm sorry to tell you, we can't supply the custom decorations you requested. We called every supplier and none of them can do what you want on such short notice. You can, however, get a standard decorative package on the same theme in time. I found a supplier that stocks these. Of course, it won't have quite the flair you originally requested.

c. We can't refund your money for the malfunctioning MP3 player. You shouldn't have immersed the unit in water while swimming; the user's manual clearly states the unit is not designed to be used in adverse environments.

9.3 Using Buffers: Practice

Answer the following questions pertaining to buffers:

a. You have to tell a local restaurant owner that your plans have changed and you have to cancel the 90-person banquet scheduled for next month. Do you need to use a buffer? Why or why not?

b. Write a buffer for a letter declining an invitation to speak at an association's annual fund-raising event. Show your appreciation for being asked.

c. Write a buffer declining a high-school group visit to your factory because it does not provide access to the two students who are in wheelchairs.

d. Write a memo cancelling the office end-of-year party because the company does not have enough money to hold it this year. Do you need to use a buffer? Why or why not?

e. Write a buffer for a letter cancelling a school group's reservation to attend a theatre's musical show in two months. It's been cancelled because box office sales have been generally poor.

9.4 Internet: Bad News Strategy

Public companies occasionally need to issue news releases announcing or explaining downturns in sales, profits, demand, or other business factors. Search the Web to locate a company that has issued a press release that recently reported lower earnings or other bad news, and access the news release on that firm's website. Alternatively, find the type of press release you're seeking by reviewing press releases at www.cnw.ca (CNW Telbec) or www.prnewswire.com. How does the headline relate to the main message of the release? Is the release organized according to the direct or the indirect approach? What does the company do to present the bad news in a favourable light—and does this effort seem sincere and ethical to you?

9.5 Ethical Choices: Communicating Escalating Rates

The insurance company where you work is planning to raise all premiums for health-care coverage. Your boss has asked you to read a draft of her letter to customers announcing the new higher rates. The first two paragraphs discuss some exciting medical advances and the expanded coverage offered by your company. Only in the final paragraph do customers learn that they will have to pay more for coverage starting next year. What are the ethical implications of this draft? What changes would you suggest?

Cases APPLYING THE THREE-STEP WRITING PROCESS TO CASES

Apply each step to the following cases, as assigned by your instructor.

> **Planning** > **Writing** > **Completing**

Analyze the Situation
Identify both your general purpose and your specific purpose. Clarify exactly what you want your audience to think, feel, or believe after receiving your message. Profile your primary audience, including their backgrounds, differences, similarities, and likely reactions to your message.

Gather Information
Identify the information your audience will need to receive, as well as other information you may need in order to craft an effective message.

Select the Right Medium
Make sure your medium is both acceptable to the audience and appropriate for the message. Realize that written media are inappropriate for some negative messages.

Organize the Information
Choose a direct or indirect approach based on the audience and the message; many negative messages are best delivered with an indirect app-roach. If you use the indirect approach, carefully consider which type of buffer is best for the situation. Identify your main idea, limit your scope, and then outline necessary support points and other evidence.

Adapt to Your Audience
Show sensitivity to audience needs by using a "you" attitude, politeness, positive emphasis, and bias-free language. Understand how much credibility you already have—and how much you may need to establish. Project your company's image by maintaining an appropriate style and tone. Consider cultural variations and the differing needs of internal and external audiences.

Compose the Message
Draft your message using clear but sensitive words, effective sentences, and coherent paragraphs.

Revise the Message
Evaluate content and review readabil-ity, then edit and rewrite for concise-ness and clarity.

Produce the Message
Use effective design elements and suit-able layout for a clean, professional appearance.

Proofread the Message
Review for errors in layout, spelling, and mechanics.

Distribute the Message
Deliver your message using the chosen medium; make sure all documents and all relevant files are distributed successfully.

1 **2** **3**

Negative Replies to Routine Requests
1. No deal: Letter from Home Depot to faucet manufacturer
As assistant to the vice-president of sales for Home Depot, you were present at Home Depot's biannual product-line review. Also present were hundreds of vendor hopefuls, eager to become one of the huge retail chain's 25 303 North American suppliers. These suppliers did their best to win, keep, or expand their spot in the Home Depot product lineup, in individual meetings with a panel of regional and national merchandisers for the chain.

Product suppliers know that Home Depot has the upper hand, so if they want to do business, they have to follow Home Depot rules, offering low wholesale prices and swift delivery. Once chosen, they're constantly re-evaluated—and quickly dropped for infractions such as requesting a price increase or planning to sell directly to consumers via the internet. They'll also hear sharp critiques of their past performance, which are not to be taken lightly.

A decade ago, General Electric failed to keep Home Depot stores supplied with light bulbs, causing shortages. Co-founder

Bernard Marcus immediately stripped GE of its exclusive 80-foot shelf space and flew off to negotiate with its Netherlands competitor, Philips. Two years later, after high-level negotiations, GE bulbs were back on Home Depot shelves—but in a position inferior to Philips's.

Such cautionary tales aren't lost on vendors. But they know that, despite tough negotiating, Home Depot is always looking for variety to please its customers' changing tastes and demands. The sales potential is so enormous that the compromises and concessions are worthwhile. If selected, vendors get immediate distribution in more than 1000 stores (a number that Home Depot plans to double in the next few years).

Still, you've seen the stress on reps' faces as they explain product enhancements and on-time delivery ideas in the review sessions. Their only consolation for this gruelling process is that, although merchandisers won't say yes or no on the spot, they do let manufacturers know where they stand within a day or two. And the company is always willing to reconsider at the next product-line review—wherever it's held.

Your Task: You're drafting some rejection letters, and the next one on your stack is to a faucet manufacturer, Brightway Manufacturing, 2401 Lasalle Blvd., Sudbury, ON P3A 2A3. "Too expensive," "substandard plastic handles," and "a design not likely to appeal to Home Depot customers," say the panel's notes. (And knowing what its customers want has put Home Depot in the top 10 of the Fortune 500 list, with $40 billion in annual sales.) Find a way to soften the blow in your rejection letter to Brightway. After all, consumer tastes do change. Direct your letter to Pamela Wilson, operations manager.[27]

2. Suffering artists: Memo declining high-tech shoes at Centennial Ballet Theatre

Here at the Centennial Ballet Theatre (CBT), where you're serving as assistant to Artistic Director Kenneth MacLachlan, the notion of suffering for the art form has been ingrained since the early 1800s, when the first ballerina rose up en pointe. Many entrepreneurs are viewing this painful situation with hopeful enthusiasm, especially when they discover that dancers worldwide spend about $150 million annually on their shoes—those "tiny torture chambers" of cardboard and satin (with glued linen or burlap to stiffen the toes). The pink monstrosities (about $75 a pair) rarely last beyond a single hard performance.

A company the size of CBT spends about $500 000 a year on ballet slippers—plus the cost of their staff physical therapist and all those trips to chiropractors, podiatrists, and surgeons to relieve bad necks, backs, knees, and feet. Entrepreneurs believe there must be room for improvement, given the current advantages of orthopedics, space-age materials, and high-tech solutions for contemporary athletes. There's no denying that ballerinas are among the hardest-working athletes in the world.

The latest entrepreneur to approach CBT is Melinda Ellis of Grey Ellis, Inc. No one in the ballet company blames her for wanting to provide a solution to the shoe problem. She buttonholed Marvin King, executive director and a member of CBT's Board of Governing Trustees, with a proposal for providing new, high-performance pointe shoes in exchange for an endorsement. It truly is a good idea. It's just a hard sell among the tradition-oriented dancers.

Ellis' alternative pointe shoes offer high-impact support and toe cushions. They're only $70 a pair, and supposedly they can be blow-dried back into shape after a performance. When the cost-conscious board member urged the company to give them a try, you were assigned to collect feedback from dancers.

So far, not good. For example, principal ballerina Grace Durham: She'd rather numb her feet in icy water, dance through "zingers" of toe pain, and make frequent visits to the physical therapist than wear Ellis' shoes, she insisted after a brief trial. The others agree. Apparently, they like breaking in the traditional satin models with hammers and door slams and throwing them away after a single performance of Swan Lake. Too stiff, they say of the new shoes. Adds Durham, "I'm totally settled into what I'm doing."

You've seen those sinewy, wedge-shaped feet bleeding backstage. You feel sorry for Ellis; it was a good idea. Maybe she should try younger dancers.

Your Task: MacLachlan has asked you to write an internal memo in his name to Marvin King, executive director of the CBT, explaining the dancers' refusal to use the new high-tech Grey Ellis pointe shoes. In your memo ensure that you include the dancers' reasons as well as your own opinion regarding the matter. You'll need to decide whether to use the direct or the indirect approach; include a separate short note to your instructor justifying your selection.[28]

3. Cyber-surveillance: Memo refusing claim from Silent Watch victim

Your business is called Advertising Inflatables, and your specialty is designing and building the huge balloon replicas used for advertising atop retail stores, tire outlets, used car lots, fast-food outlets, fitness clubs, and so on. You've built balloon re-creations of everything from a 50-foot King Kong to a "small" 10-foot pizza.

Not long ago, you installed the "cyber-surveillance" software Silent Watch to track and record employees' computer usage. At the time, you sent out a memo informing all employees that they should limit their computer use and email to only work projects. You also informed them that their work would be monitored. You did not mention that Silent Watch would record every keystroke of their work or that they could be monitored from a screen in your office.

As expected, Silent Watch caught two of the sales staff spending between 50 and 70 percent of their time surfing internet sites unrelated to their jobs. You withheld their pay accordingly, without warning. You sent them a memo notifying them that they were not fired but were on probation. You considered this wise, because when they work, both employees are very good at what they do, and talent is hard to find.

But now salesman Jarod Harkington has sent you a letter demanding reinstatement of his pay and claiming he was "spied on illegally." On the contrary, company attorneys have assured you that the courts almost always side with employers on this issue, particularly after employees receive a warning such as the one you wrote. The computer equipment belongs to Advertising Inflatables, and employees are paid a fair price for their time.

Your Task: Write a letter refusing Mr. Harkington's claim.[29]

4. Photo finish: No credit to Todd Rooker, photographer

You've dealt with Todd Rooker, a photographer of weddings and family events, for the last 13 years with no problem. He's sent numerous jobs to you for developing and has always paid on time. But for the last two jobs he has asked your company, Best Photo Labs, to extend credit. He says the wedding and special events market is drying up in his neighbourhood, and he's getting few referrals from old customers. He has to work as an industrial photographer during the day for a friend's firm and can only work evenings at his own business. He isn't making the money he used to, but he hopes to get enough cash flowing from his day job to pay Best Labs for developing his photos. He sure can't ask for money from his customers until they see the finished pictures.

But Best Photo Labs has a business to run, and they can't rely on goodwill to pay their technicians, rent, and utilities, as well as for developing chemicals and photographic paper.

Your Task: As the office manager for Best Photo Labs, you've dealt with Todd Rooker's account for several years. You know he's a nice guy and a good photographer. Write Todd a tactful letter refusing credit. Todd's address is Todd Rooker, Professional Photographer, 195 Argyle St., Fredericton, NB E3B 1T6.

Email SKILLS   **Portfolio** BUILDER

5. Message to the boss: Refusing a project on ethical grounds

A not-so-secret secret is getting more attention than you'd really like after an article in *BusinessWeek* gave the world an inside look at how much money you and other electronics retailers make from extended warranties (sometimes called service contracts). The article explained that typically half of the warranty price goes to the salesperson as a commission and that only 20 percent of the total amount customers pay for warranties eventually goes to product repair.

You also know why extended warranties are such a profitable business. Many electronics products follow a predictable pattern of failure: a high failure rate early in their lives, then a "midlife" period during which failures go way down, and concluding with an "old age" period when failure rates ramp back up again (engineers refer to the phenomenon as the bathtub curve because it looks like a bathtub from the side—high at both ends and low in the middle). Those early failures are usually covered by manufacturers' warranties, and the extended warranties you sell are designed to cover that middle part of the life span. In other words, many extended warranties cover the period of time during which consumers are least likely to need them and offer no coverage when consumers need them most. (Consumers can actually benefit from extended warranties in a few product categories, including laptop computers and plasma TVs. Of course, the more sense the warranty makes for the consumer, the less financial sense it makes for your company.)

Your Task: Worried that consumers will start buying fewer extended warranties, your boss has directed you to put together a sales training program that will help cashiers sell the extended warranties even more aggressively. The more you ponder this challenge, though, the more you're convinced that your company should change its strategy so that it doesn't rely on profits from these warranties so much. In addition to offering questionable value to the consumer, they risk creating a consumer backlash that could lead to lower sales of all your products. You would prefer to voice your concerns to your boss in person, but both of you are travelling on hectic schedules for the next week. You'll have to write an email instead. Draft a brief message explaining why you think the sales training specifically and the warranties in general are both bad ideas.[30]

6. Pay or sell: Last chance to settle condo management fees

You don't like writing such letters, but during your five years as a property manager for Provide Corporation, you've had to tell condo owners that if they don't pay their monthly maintenance fees, Provide will attach a lien to their bank accounts, as they are permitted to do by provincial law. The problem you're having now is with Mrs. Edith Bookman, a recent widow who has fallen behind two months in her maintenance fees. The money she—and all the other apartment owners—pay each month goes toward maintaining the building and grounds to keep the property healthy and attractive. Without the monthly maintenance fee from each owner, the condo would fall into disrepair, and everyone would have to pay a special assessment to bring it back to standard. No one wants that to happen.

You know that things are difficult for Mrs. Bookman right now. You've consulted with the condo's board of directors, made up of owners who give direction to the property manager when needed. They've told you not to attach Mrs. Bookman's account now, although provincial law says you could. Instead, they want to give her another month to pay the arrears.

Your Task: Write a letter to Mrs. Bookman following the board's direction. Explain that she must pay her two months' arrears with her third payment, and why doing so is important. If she doesn't, Provide will attach her bank account for the balance owed as well as a $500 administrative lien fee, which they are legally allowed to do. Mrs. Bookman lives at 1335 St. Albert Trail NW, Suite 3E, Edmonton, AB T5L 4R3.

7. More to come: Letter explaining delay of Anne of Green Gables T-shirt
Each year thousands of people attend the Charlottetown Festival to see plays featuring Lucy Maud Montgomery's fictional characters. Montgomery's stories have been loved by Canadians and by millions around the world since the publication of her first novel, *Anne of Green Gables*, in 1908. Prince Edward Island has benefited immensely from tourists who travel there during the festival season to enjoy not only the theatre but also the sea, beaches, and Montgomery's birthplace. Souvenirs are popular among both Canadian and foreign visitors, who buy them for friends and relatives back home.

This summer's festival was so successful that your local store, Little Things, has sold out its stock of child- and youth-sized T-shirts featuring Anne's image. You've received a letter from a German tourist explaining that when his nieces and nephews saw his daughter's T-shirt, they each wanted one, too. He's included his credit card number and expiry date, and wants two green T-shirts in size 6X, three white shirts in size 10–12, and two in size 14–16. His letter is dated October 6, 2010, and he is hoping to get the shirts in time for Christmas. Your problem is that you have only two blue shirts, size 6X—no green—in stock, and one white shirt, size 10–12. You do have lots of white shirts in size 14–16. More T-shirts won't be available until March 2011 as the product is seasonal. You also have some other items in stock, such as stickers, always popular with kids, and buttons.

Your Task: Write to Josef Mandelheim, Sonnenstrasse 4, 86669 Erlingshofen, Germany. Explain what you can do. Child-sized shirts are $8.95 each, youth-sized $10.95, duty is 12 percent of the total, there is no GST, and shipping is $32.00.

Negative Organizational News

Email SKILLS   **Portfolio BUILDER**
8. Sorry, but we don't have a choice: Email about monitoring employee blogs
You can certainly sympathize with employees when they complain about having their email and instant messages monitored, but you're only implementing a company policy that all employees agree to abide by when they join the company. Your firm, Nebcor Builders of Ottawa, Ontario, is one of the growing number of Canadian companies with such monitoring systems in place. More and more companies use these systems (which typically operate by scanning messages for keywords that suggest confidential, illegal, or otherwise inappropriate content) in an attempt to avoid instances of sexual harassment and other problems.

As the chief information officer, the manager in charge of computer systems in the company, you're often the target when employees complain about being monitored. Consequently, you know you're really going to hear it when employees learn that the monitoring program will be expanded to personal blogs as well.

Your Task: Write an email to be distributed to the entire workforce, explaining that the automated monitoring program is about to be expanded to include employees' personal blogs. Explain that while you sympathize with employee concerns regarding privacy and freedom of speech, the management team's responsibility is to protect the company's intellectual property and the value of the company name. Therefore, employees' personal blogs will be added to the monitoring system to ensure that employees don't intentionally or accidentally expose company secrets or criticize management in a way that could harm the company.[31]

Blogging SKILLS   **Portfolio BUILDER**
9. Removing the obstacles on the on-ramp: Blog posting to Ernst & Young employees
Like many companies these days, the accounting firm Ernst & Young is fighting a brain drain as experienced executives and professionals leave in mid-career to pursue charitable interests, devote more time to family matters, or pursue a variety of other dreams or obligations. The problem is particularly acute among women, since on average they step off the career track more often than men do. As general manager of the largest division in the company, you've been tapped to draft a set of guidelines to make it easier for employees who've taken some time off to move back into the company.

However, as soon as word gets out about what you're planning, several of your top performers, people who've never left the company for personal time off—or "taken the off-ramp," in current buzzword-speak—march into your office to complain. They fear that encouraging the "off-rampers" to return isn't fair to the employees who've remained loyal to the firm, as they put it. One goes so far as to say that anyone who leaves the company doesn't deserve to be asked back. Two others claim that the additional experience and skills they've gained as they continued to work should guarantee them higher pay and more responsibilities than employees who took time off for themselves.

Your Task: As unhappy as these several employees are, the program needs to be implemented if Ernst & Young hopes to bring "off-rampers" back into the company—thereby ensuring that they don't go to work for competitors instead. However, you also can't afford to antagonize the existing workforce, and if the people who've already complained are any indication, you have a sizable morale problem on your hands. You decide that your first step is to explain clearly why the program is necessary, including how it will benefit everyone in the company by making Ernst & Young more competitive. Write a short posting for the company's internal blog, explaining that in spite of the objections some employees have raised, the firm is going ahead with the program as planned. Balance this news (which some employees will obviously view as negative) with positive reassurances that all current employees will be treated fairly in terms of both compensation and promotion opportunities. Close with a call for continued communication on this issue, inviting people to meet with you in person or to post their thoughts on the blog.[32]

| Email SKILLS |

10. Low-carb impact: Email announcing losses and new products at Palermo Pasta
As marketing planning manager for Palermo Pasta Company, you're responsible for spotting social trends that could affect your company. Months ago, you suggested that your employer seriously consider the new low-carb diet craze, but your colleagues thought you were exaggerating the impact this trend would have on pasta sales. Now the figures bear you out: Nationwide pasta sales have fallen dramatically as dieters in record numbers are avoiding high-carbohydrate and especially flour-based foods.

At Wal-Mart and Costco, the warehouse-style retail stores that make up Palermo Pasta's largest buyers, sales plummeted nearly 30 percent in the last few months. Your company is not alone; other traditional pasta makers are also showing losses because of the new diet preferences. In contrast, your major competitor, Canadian Italian Pasta, introduced a line of low-carb pastas months ago. Their sales are still climbing.

Now management has asked you to issue a revised forecast for fourth-quarter earnings. Previous predictions were for fourth-quarter sales to increase over last year's figures by 7 to 10 percent. Today's forecast from chief financial officer Scott S. Wheeler is for a 3 to 5 percent decrease in revenue from last year's fourth-quarter earnings.

However, in the same message, management wants you to announce the release of Palermo Pasta's new "CARB-SMART" line of fresh pastas, sauces, and prepared entrees. In a company meeting, Palermo Pasta president and CEO Sergio Ferrano announced, "Canadians love fresh pasta, but the current wave of low-carb diets has many consumers watching the amount of carbohydrates they consume. CARB-SMART responds to that trend by delivering the flavour and convenience of traditional fresh pasta, but with half the carbs. So, carb-counting pasta lovers can now have their ravioli . . . and eat it, too."

The new products include three prepared ravioli varieties, plus tortellini, linguine, fettuccine, and a new low-carb, four-cheese sauce. Complete CARB-SMART product information will be posted on the Palermo Pasta website, www.palermopasta.com.

Your Task: Write an email to announce both the good news and the bad news. Your message will go to shareholders, retail customers, distributors, and other interested parties.[33]

11. The cheque's in the mail—almost: Letter from Sun Microsystems explaining late payments
You'd think that a computer company could install a new management information system without a hitch, wouldn't you? The people at Sun Microsystems thought so too, but they were wrong. When they installed their own new computerized system for getting information to management, a few things, such as payments to vendors, fell through the cracks.

It was embarrassing when Sun's suppliers started clamouring for payment. Terence Lenaghan, the corporate controller, found himself in the unfortunate position of having to tell 6000 vendors why Sun Microsystems had failed to pay its bills on time—and why it might be late with payments again. "Until we get these bugs ironed out," Lenaghan confessed, "we're going to have to finish some accounting work by hand. That means that some payments to vendors will probably be late next month, too. We'd better write to our suppliers and let them know that there's nothing wrong with the company's financial performance. The last thing we want is for our vendors to think our business is going down the tubes."

Your Task: Write a form letter to Sun Microsystems' 6000 vendors explaining that bugs in their new management information system are responsible for the delays in payment.[34]

| Portfolio BUILDER |

12. Listen to the music, partner: Delivering an ultimatum to a business associate
You're a marketing manager for Stanton, one of the premier suppliers of DJ equipment (turntables, amplifiers, speakers, mixers, and related accessories). Your company's latest creation, the FinalScratch system, has been flying off retailers' shelves. Both professional and amateur DJs love the way that FinalScratch gives them the feel of working with vinyl records by letting them control digital music files from any analogue turntable or CD player, while giving them access to the endless possibilities of digital music technology. (For more information about the product, go to www.stantondj.com.) Sales are strong everywhere except in Music99 stores, a retail

chain in the Ontario–Quebec region. You suspect the cause: The owners of this chain refused to let their salespeople attend the free product training you offered when FinalScratch was introduced, claiming their people were smart enough to train themselves.

To explore the situation, you head out from Stanton headquarters in Markham, Ontario, on an undercover shopping mission. After visiting a few Music99 locations, you're appalled by what you see. The salespeople in these stores clearly don't understand the FinalScratch concept, so they either give potential customers bad information about it or steer them to products from your competitors. No wonder sales are so bad at this chain.

Your Task: You're tempted to pull your products out of this chain immediately, but based on your experience in this market, you know how difficult and expensive it is to recruit new retailers. However, this situation can't go on; you're losing thousands of dollars of potential business every week. Write a letter to Gil Atami, the CEO of Music99 (1108 Sherbrooke St. East, Montreal, QC H2L 1M2), expressing your disappointment in what you observed and explaining that the Music99 sales staff will need to agree to attend product training or else your company's management team will consider terminating the business relationship. You've met Mr. Atami in person once and talked on the phone several times, and you know him well enough to know that he will not be pleased by this ultimatum. Music99 does a good job selling other Stanton products—and he'll probably be furious to learn that you were "spying" on his sales staff.[35]

Email SKILLS

13. Cell phone violations: Email message to associates at Smith Rooney law firm

"Company policy states that personnel are not to conduct business using cell phones while driving," David Finch reminds you. He's a partner at the law firm of Smith Rooney in St. John's, Newfoundland, where you work as his administrative assistant.

You nod, waiting for him to explain. He already issued a memo about this rule last year, after that 15-year-old girl was hit and killed by an attorney from another firm. Driving back from a client meeting, the attorney was distracted while talking on her cell phone. The girl's family sued the firm and won $10 million, but that's not the point. The point is that cell phones can cause people to be hurt, even killed.

Finch explains, "Yesterday one of our associates called his secretary while driving his car. We can't allow this. Recently in Windsor a driver caused a fatal accident when reaching for his cell phone; his van turned over, and the accident killed his nephew and two friends. The van caught fire because they were transporting a canister of gasoline to a farm. From now on, any violation of our cell phone policy will result in suspension without pay, unless the call is a genuine health or traffic emergency."

Your Task: Finch asks you to write an email message to all employees, announcing the new penalty for violating company policy.[36]

14. Product recall: Letter from Perrigo to retailers about children's painkiller

Discovering that a batch of your company's cherry-flavoured children's painkiller contains more than the label-indicated amount of acetaminophen was not a happy occasion around Perrigo Company. But such errors do happen, and the best move is to be immediate and direct and completely honest with retailers and the public—so say your superiors in the Customer Support and Service Department. Full and prompt disclosure is especially crucial when consumers' health is involved, as it always is in your line of business.

Perrigo is the leading manufacturer of store-brand, over-the-counter pharmaceuticals and nutritional products, producing more than 900 products. These are the items found beside brand-name products such as Tylenol, Motrin, Aleve, Benadryl, NyQuil, Centrum, or Ex-Lax, but they're packaged under the name of the store in which customers are shopping. They're priced a bit lower and offer "comparable quality and effectiveness," as your sales literature proclaims.

For retailers, selling Perrigo products yields a higher profit margin than name brands. For consumers, buying the store brands can mean significant savings.

As of this morning, your marketing department calculates that 6500 113-millilitre bottles of the "children's non-aspirin elixir" (a Tylenol look-alike) are already in the hands of consumers. That leaves some 1288 bottles still on store shelves.

The problem is that the acetaminophen contained in the painkilling liquid is up to 29 percent more than labels state—enough to cause an overdose in the young children for whom the product is designed. Such overdoses can cause liver failure. No one is telling you how this error happened, and it's been found only in lot number 1AD0228, but frankly, finding a guilty party is not so important to your job. You're more concerned about getting the word out fast.

The painkiller has been sold under the T-Mart label at stores in British Columbia, the Northwest Territories, Saskatchewan, Manitoba, and Alberta. It was sold under the Good Life label in Ontario, Quebec, Newfoundland and Labrador, New Brunswick, Nova Scotia, and Prince Edward Island. It was sold under the Healthy Living label in independent retail chains throughout Canada. Perrigo needs to notify consumers throughout Canada that they should not give the product to children but rather should check the lot number and return the bottle to the store from which they bought it for a refund if it's from the affected batch.

Your Task: As Perrigo's customer service supervisor, you must notify retailers by letter. They've already been told verbally, but legal requirements mandate a written notification. That's good, because a form letter to your retail customers can also include follow-up instructions. Explain the circumstances behind the recall, and instruct stores to pull bottles from the shelves immediately for return to your company. Perrigo will, of course, reimburse refunds provided to consumers. Questions should be directed to Perrigo at 1-800-555-0206—and it's okay if they give that number to consumers. Ensure that you mention all that your company is doing, and use resale information.[37]

Negative Employment Messages

15. Bad news for 80: Form letter to unsuccessful job candidates
The Dean's Selection Committee screened 85 applications for the position of dean of arts and sciences at your campus. After two rounds of eliminations, the top five candidates were invited to two-hour interviews with the committee. Then the top three candidates were invited to the campus to meet with students, faculty, and administrators.

The committee recommended to the university president that the job be given to Constance Pappas, who has a doctorate in Canadian studies and has been chairperson of the history department at the University of Western Ontario for the past three years. The president agreed, and Dr. Pappas accepted the offer.

One final task remained before the work of the Dean's Selection Committee was finished: Letters must be sent to the 84 unsuccessful candidates. The four who were invited to the two-hour interviews will receive personal letters from the chairperson of the committee. Your job, as secretary of the committee, is to draft the form letter that will be sent to the other 80 applicants.

Your Task: Draft a letter of 100 to 200 words. All copies will be individually addressed to the recipients but will carry identical messages.

Email SKILLS

16. Career moves: Email refusing to write a recommendation
Tom Weiss worked in the office at Opal Pools and Patios for four months, under your supervision (you're office manager). On the basis of what he told you he could do, you started him off as a file clerk. However, his organizational skills proved inadequate for the job, so you transferred him to logging in accounts receivable, where he performed almost adequately. Then he assured you that his "real strength" was customer relations, so you moved him to the complaint department. After he spent three weeks making angry customers even angrier, you were convinced that no place in your office was appropriate for the talents of Mr. Weiss. Five weeks ago, you encouraged him to resign before being formally fired.

Today's email brings a request from Weiss asking you to write a letter recommending him for a sales position with a florist shop. You can't assess Weiss's sales abilities, but you do know him to be an incompetent file clerk, a careless bookkeeper, and an insensitive customer service representative. Someone else is more likely to deserve the sales job, so you decide that you have done enough favours for Tom Weiss for one lifetime and plan to refuse his request.

Your Task: Write an email reply to Mr. Weiss (tomweiss@yahoo.com) indicating that you have chosen not to write a letter of recommendation for him.

IM SKILLS

17. Midair let-down: Instant message about flight cancellations at Premier Airlines
It used to be that airline passengers didn't learn about cancelled connecting flights until after they'd landed. Sometimes a captain would announce cancellations just before touching down at a major hub, but how were passengers to notify waiting relatives or business associates on the ground?

As a customer service supervisor for Premier Airlines, you've just received information that all Premier flights from New York's LaGuardia Airport to Toronto's Pearson Airport have been cancelled until further notice. A late winter storm has already blanketed New York with snow and freezing rain is expected overnight. The way the weather report looks, Premier will probably lodge New York-bound connecting passengers in Toronto-area hotels tonight.

Meanwhile, you'll use some of Premier's newest communication tools to notify travellers of the bad news.

Premier Airlines partners with InterUse Communications to provide JetConnect information services, giving travellers access to instant messaging and other resources while they're

airborne. For a small fee, they can plug their laptop computers into the Airfone jack, activating their own instant messaging software to send and receive messages. If they've signed up for Premier's EasyUpdate flight status notification service, they'll also receive instant message alerts for flight cancellations, delays, seating upgrades, and so on.

Your Task: Write the cancellation alert, staying within the 65-word limit of many instant-messaging programs. Mention the airline's policy of providing overnight lodging for passengers who planned to use the New York route as a connecting flight to complete journeys in progress.[38]

IM SKILLS

18. Quick answer: Instant message turning down employee request at Hewlett-Packard
If she'd asked you a week ago, Branka Bilic might have been granted her request to attend a conference on the use of blogging for business, which is being held in Boston next month. Instead, Bilic waited until you were stuck in this meeting, and she needs your response within the hour. She'll have to take no for an answer: With travel budgets under tight restrictions, you would need at least three days to send her request up the chain of command. Furthermore, Bilic hasn't given you sufficient justification for her attendance, since she's already familiar with blogging.

Your Task: Write a 60- to 75-word instant message to Branka Bilic, declining her request. Decide whether the direct or indirect approach is appropriate.[39]

19. Performance review
Team up with someone in your class and interview each other about a job you currently have or had in the past. Get details about the organization that employed your partner, the organization's objectives and goals, and your partner's responsibilities and duties. Ask your partner about the strengths and weaknesses of his or her performance in that job (be sure to get concrete details). Using the guidelines in this chapter, write a performance review for your partner in memo format.

10

Writing Persuasive Messages

LEARNING OBJECTIVES

After studying this chapter, you will be able to

1. Apply the three-step writing process to persuasive messages
2. Identify seven ways to establish credibility in persuasive messages
3. Describe the AIDA model for persuasive messages
4. Distinguish between emotional and logical appeals, and discuss how to balance them
5. Explain why it is important to identify potential objections before you start writing persuasive messages
6. Explain an effective approach to identifying selling points and audience benefits
7. Identify steps you can take to avoid ethical lapses in marketing and sales messages

ON THE JOB

Communicating at the Canadian Youth Business Foundation
GEARING UP FOR BUSINESS
www.cybf.ca

A good idea must be matched with a sound and persuasive business plan to obtain mentorship and financial support from the Canadian Youth Business Foundation. Since 1996 the CYBF has been helping young entrepreneurs launch and sustain their unique businesses.

The CeliCase, a PDA/cell phone holder that's a fashion statement . . . the Flying Pigs, roadside recyclers in Canmore, Alberta . . . the Be'ato Coffee Company, an online retailer of organic and fair trade coffee beans—these are just three innovative business ventures nourished with support and funding from the Canadian Youth Business Foundation (CYBF).

A nationwide charity valuing "character, not collateral," the CYBF offers potential entrepreneurs between 18 and 34 personal guidance, online resources, and start-up financing to help them transform their ideas into reality. With the motto "driving Canada's business success by helping youth help themselves," the CYBF assists young people unable to get advice and funding through customary sources. Since its founding in 1996, the Canadian Youth Business Foundation has aided more than 2700 promising entrepreneurs, whose businesses have created more than 14 000 new jobs and generated almost $300 million in sales revenue.

To benefit from the CYBF, people with a great business idea first visit the website, where they can view videos, read real-life success stories, and take a self-assessment quiz to determine if starting their own business is right for them. They can learn about the CYBF program, which includes pre-launch coaching, loan programs, and a close mentoring relationship with volunteer business leaders. At this point, they can register as a CYBF entrepreneur and access services such as the online interactive business planner. With a solid business plan in place, three references, and experience or training in their business idea, they can apply for a CYBF loan of up to $15 000. Eligible applicants attend a face-to-face interview before their business plan is approved and they are matched with a mentor, a successful businessperson in their region. Over the course of two years they work closely together to market and expand the venture.

With a lot of effort and good advice, a budding entrepreneur can become one of CYBF's success stories. If you had an idea for a new business, how would you persuade the Canadian Youth Business Foundation of its value? What strategies would you use to gain its interest and support?[1]

Using the Three-Step Writing Process for Persuasive Messages

All businesspeople realize that successful businesses rely on persuasive messages in both internal and external communication. Whether you're convincing your boss to open a new office in Europe or encouraging potential customers to try your products, you'll use many of the same techniques of **persuasion**—the attempt to change an audience's attitudes, beliefs, or actions.[2] Persuasive techniques are a cornerstone of marketing and selling, but even if you never work in those fields, you'll still need good persuasion skills to advance in your career. Successful professionals understand that persuasion is not about trickery or getting people to make choices that aren't in their best interest; rather, it lets your audience know they have a choice and helps them choose to agree with you.[3]As with every type of business message, the three-step writing process improves persuasive messages.

Step 1: Plan Your Message

In today's information-saturated business environment, having a great idea or a great product is no longer enough. Every day, untold numbers of good ideas go unnoticed and good products go unsold simply because the messages meant to promote them aren't compelling enough to rise above the competitive noise. Even if audiences agree that your idea or product is attractive, they usually have other options to consider as well, so you will need to convince them that your choice is the best of all the attractive alternatives. Creating successful persuasive messages in these challenging situations demands careful attention to all four tasks in the planning step, starting with an insightful analysis of your purpose and your audience.

ANALYZING YOUR SITUATION A clear purpose is important in every message, of course, but clarity is doubly important in persuasive messages because you are asking the audience to do something—to take action, make decisions, and so on. Let's say you want to persuade members of top management to support a particular research project. But what does "support" mean? Do you want them to pat you on the back and wish you well? Or do you want them to pull

Persuasion is the attempt to change someone's attitudes, beliefs, or actions.

Objective 1 Apply the three-step writing process to persuasive messages.

In today's message-saturated environment, it's not enough to have a great idea or a great product; you also need a compelling message.

Failing to clarify your purpose is a common mistake with persuasive messages.

five researchers off another project and assign them to your project? With a clear, specific goal in mind, you'll find it much easier to craft effective persuasive messages.

In addition to having a clear purpose, the best persuasive messages are closely connected to the audience's desires and interests.[4] Consider both the positives and the negatives—the wants, needs, and motivations of your audience (the reasons they might respond favourably to your message) as well as their concerns and objections (the reasons they might *not* respond favourably). With these two insights as guides, you can then work to find common ground with your audience, while emphasizing positive points and minimizing negative ones.

To persuade successfully, consider both the positive and negative aspects of your proposed solution.

To understand and categorize audience needs, refer to specific information such as **demographics** (the age, gender, occupation, income, education, and other quantifiable characteristics of the people you're trying to persuade) and **psychographics** (personality, attitudes, lifestyle, and other psychological characteristics). Both types of information are strongly influenced by culture. When analyzing your audience members, take into account their cultural expectations and practices so that you don't undermine your persuasive message by using an inappropriate appeal or by organizing your message in a way that seems unfamiliar or uncomfortable to your audience.

Demographics include characteristics such as age, gender, occupation, income, and education.

Psychographics include characteristics such as personality, attitudes, and lifestyle.

If you aim to change someone's attitudes, beliefs, or actions through a persuasive message, it is vital to understand his or her motivation—the combination of forces that drive people to satisfy their needs. Table 10–1 identifies some of the needs that psychologists have identified or suggested as being important in influencing human motivation. Obviously, the more closely a persuasive message aligns with a recipient's existing motivation, the more effective the message is likely to be. For example, if you try to persuade consumers to purchase a product on the basis of its fashion appeal, that message will connect with consumers who are motivated by a desire to be in fashion but probably won't connect with consumers driven more by practical function or financial concerns.

Motivation is a complex psychological subject, and researchers have proposed a variety of theories to help explain why humans are driven to behave as they do. For instance, some theories suggest a process in which people take action to fulfill perceived needs and then evaluate the outcomes of those actions to determine whether the effort was worthwhile:

1. **Need.** The individual senses a need of some sort, from the basic need to earn enough money for food to a need for recognition or self-respect. We are all born with certain needs but can acquire other needs as we grow up, such as a need for achievement, a need for power, or a need to affiliate with compatible friends and colleagues.[5]

2. **Action.** To fulfill the need, the individual takes actions or adopts behaviours that he or she believes will result in the need being satisfied. The quality of the action is a matter of choosing which action to take, deciding how much effort to put into the action, and deciding how long to sustain that effort.[6]

3. **Outcome.** The individual observes the outcome of the action (sometimes called the *reward*) and determines whether the effort was worthwhile. Actions that result in positive outcomes are likely to be repeated; those that result in negative outcomes are less likely to be repeated.

Although this is a simplified view of motivation and not all theorists endorse this model, it helps emphasize the importance of understanding your audience's needs and why they would be driven to satisfy those needs. If you don't understand what motivates your audience, you won't be able persuade them to take the actions you'd like them to take. In addition, you can see why following

> Table 10–1 Human Needs That Influence Motivation

Need	Implications for Communication
Basic physiological requirements: The needs for food, water, sleep, oxygen, etc.	Everyone has these needs, but the degree of attention an individual gives to them often depends on whether the needs are being met; for instance, an advertisement for sleeping pills will have greater appeal to someone suffering from insomnia than to someone who has no problem sleeping.
Safety and security: The need for protection from bodily harm; the need to know that loved ones are safe; needs for financial security, protection of personal identity, career security, etc.	These needs influence both consumer and business decisions in a wide variety of ways; for instance, advertisements for life insurance often encourage parents to think about the financial security of their children and other loved ones.
Affiliation and belonging: The needs for companionship, acceptance, love, popularity, etc.	The need to feel loved, accepted, or popular drives a great deal of human behaviour, from the desire to be attractive to potential mates to wearing the clothing style that a particular social group is likely to approve.
Power and control: The need to feel in control of situations or to exert authority over others	You can see many examples appealing to this need in advertisements: Take control of your life, your finances, your future, your career, and so on. Many people who lack power want to know how to get it, and people who have power often want others to know they have it.
Achievement: The need to feel a sense of accomplishment—or to be admired by others for accomplishments	This need can involve both knowing (when people experience a feeling of accomplishment) and showing (when people are able to show others that they've achieved success); advertising for luxury consumer products frequently appeals to this need.
Adventure and distraction: The need for excitement or relief from daily routine	People vary widely in their need for adventure; some crave excitement— even danger—while others value calmness and predictability. Some needs for adventure and distraction are met virtually, such as through horror movies, thriller novels, etc.
Knowledge, exploration, and understanding: The need to keep learning	For some people, learning is usually a means to an end, a way to fulfill some other need; for others, acquiring new knowledge is the goal.
Aesthetic appreciation: The desire to experience beauty, order, symmetry, etc.	Although this need may seem "noncommercial" at first glance, advertisers appeal to it frequently, from the pleasing shape of a package to the quality of the gemstones in a piece of jewelry.
Self-actualization: The need to reach one's full potential as a human being	Psychologists Kurt Goldstein and Abraham Maslow popularized self-actualization as the desire to make the most of one's potential, and Maslow identified it as one of the higher-level needs in his classic hierarchy; even if people met most or all of their other needs, they would still feel the need to self-actualize. A frequently-heard phrase that summarizes this feeling is "be all that you can be."
Helping others: The need to believe that one is making a difference in the lives of other people	This need is the central motivation in fundraising messages and other appeals to charity.

through on the claims or promises made in your message is so vital. If a manager agrees to fund a project that ultimately fails, or a customer buys a product that doesn't perform as you said it would, those people are going to be less likely to be persuaded by messages from you in the future.

GATHERING INFORMATION Once your situation analysis is complete, gather the information necessary to close the gap between what your audience knows, believes, or feels right now and what you want them to know, believe, or feel as a result of receiving your message. Most persuasive messages are a combination of logical and emotional factors, but the ratio varies dramatically from message to message. You can get a sense of this variation by comparing the websites of

Research in Motion (telecommunication products, www.rim.com), Chrysler (automobiles, www.chrysler.ca), and Lancôme (beauty products, www.lancome.ca). Research in Motion relies primarily on straightforward product information to convince buyers, whereas Lancôme tries to evoke a more emotional response through its visual and verbal imagery. Chrysler is somewhere in the middle, providing plenty of facts and figures about its cars but also including strong emotional messages about the joy of driving. By identifying the mix of factors that will most likely persuade your audience, you'll know what sort of information you need to gather.

You'll learn more about the types of information to offer when you read "Developing Persuasive Business Messages" later in the chapter. Chapter 11 presents advice on how to find the information you need.

SELECTING THE RIGHT MEDIUM Persuasive messages can be found in virtually every communication medium ever devised, from instant messages and computer animations to radio ads and skywriting. For persuasive business messages, your choice of medium will closely follow the guidelines that Chapter 4 presents. However, for marketing and sales messages, your options are far more numerous. In fact, advertising agencies employ media specialists whose only job is to analyze the media options available and select the most cost-effective combination for each client and each ad campaign.

To further complicate matters, various members of your audience might prefer different media for the same message. Some consumers like to do all their car shopping in person, whereas others do most of their car-shopping research online. Some people don't mind promotional emails for products they're interested in; others resent every piece of commercial email they receive. If you can't be sure you can reach most or all of your audience with a single medium, you need to use two or more, such as following up an email campaign with printed letters.

ORGANIZING YOUR INFORMATION Successful persuasion requires close attention to all four aspects of organizing your information—defining your main idea, limiting your scope, choosing a direct or indirect approach, and grouping your points in a meaningful way. The most effective main ideas for persuasive messages have one element in common: They are about the receiver, not the sender. For example, if you're trying to convince others to join you in a business venture, explain how it will help them, not how it will help you.

To limit the scope of each message effectively, include only the information needed to help your audience take the next step toward making the ultimate decision or taking the ultimate action you want. In simple scenarios such as persuading teammates to attend a special meeting, you might put everything you have to say into a single, short message. But if you want your company to invest several million dollars in your latest product idea, the scope of your first message might be limited to securing 10 minutes at the next executive committee meeting so you can introduce your idea and get permission to explore it.

As with routine and negative messages, the best organizational approach is based on your audience's likely reaction to your message. However, because the nature of persuasion is to convince your audience to change their attitudes, beliefs, or actions, most persuasive messages use an indirect approach. That means you'll want to explain your reasons and build interest before asking for a decision

Businesses continue to find creative new ways to reach target audiences with persuasive messages. If you're a video gamer, you've probably noticed the brand-name products that appear in many of today's games. Is it ethical to include these products when young children play video games?

You may need to use multiple media to reach your entire audience.

Limit your scope to include only the information needed to help your audience take the next step toward making a favourable decision.

or for action—or perhaps even before revealing your purpose. You'll see several examples of the indirect approach in action later in this chapter.

> Use the direct approach if your audience is ready to hear your proposal.

Consider using the direct approach whenever you know your audience is ready to hear your proposal. If your boss wants to change shipping companies and asks for your recommendation, you'll probably want to open with your choice and then provide your reasons as backup. Similarly, if there's a good chance your audience will agree with your message, don't force them to wade through pages of reasoning before seeing your main idea. If they happen not to agree with your pitch, they can move into your reasoning to see why you're promoting that particular idea. The direct approach is also called for if you've been building your case through several indirect messages, and it's now time to make your request.

In the email message in Figure 10–1, Bette McGiboney, an administrative assistant to the athletic director of Central Alberta Institute of Technology, presented a solution to the problem of high phone bills during the month of August. She already has a close relationship with her boss, who is likely to welcome the money-saving idea, so the direct approach is a fast, efficient way to communicate her proposal.

If you use the direct approach as McGiboney does in Figure 10–1, keep in mind that even though your audience may be easy to convince, you'll still want to include at least a brief justification or explanation. Don't expect your reader

> Figure 10–1 Proposal Email Using a Direct Approach

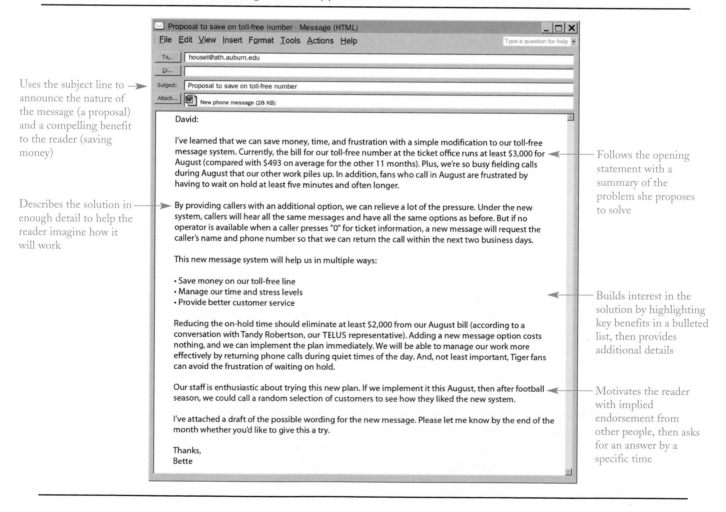

Uses the subject line to announce the nature of the message (a proposal) and a compelling benefit to the reader (saving money)

Describes the solution in enough detail to help the reader imagine how it will work

Follows the opening statement with a summary of the problem she proposes to solve

Builds interest in the solution by highlighting key benefits in a bulleted list, then provides additional details

Motivates the reader with implied endorsement from other people, then asks for an answer by a specific time

to accept your idea on blind faith. For example, consider the following two openers:

Less Effective	More Effective
I recommend building our new retail outlet on the West Main Street site.	After comparing the four possible sites for our new retail outlet, I recommend West Main Street as the only site that fulfills our criteria for visibility, proximity to mass transportation, and square footage.

Your choice between the direct and indirect approaches is also influenced by the extent of your authority, expertise, or power in an organization. Generally, the more of these qualities you have in a given situation, the more likely that the direct approach will work for you because audience members are more apt to accept whatever you have to say. Conversely, if you're writing on a subject outside your recognized expertise, or if you're trying to persuade higher-level managers, the indirect approach is usually better because it allows you to build credibility as you present your reasoning.

> Your choice of approach is influenced by your authority, expertise, or power within the organization.

Step 2: Write Your Message

Persuasive messages are often uninvited and occasionally even unwelcome, so adopting the "you" attitude is particularly critical when you write them. Most people won't even pay attention to your message, much less respond to it, if it isn't about them. You can encourage a more welcome reception by (1) using positive and polite language, (2) understanding and respecting cultural differences, (3) being sensitive to organizational cultures, and (4) taking steps to establish your credibility.

> Persuasive messages are often unexpected or even unwelcome, so the "you" attitude is crucial.

Positive language usually happens naturally with persuasive messages, since you're promoting an idea or product you believe in. However, polite language isn't as automatic, surprisingly enough. Don't inadvertently insult the readers by implying that they are incapable of making smart decisions without your wise advice.

Demonstrating an understanding and respect for cultural differences is crucial to persuasion. For example, an aggressive, hard-sell technique is likely to antagonize a French audience. In Germany, where people tend to focus on technical matters, make sure you provide solid supporting evidence for all messages. In Sweden, audiences tend to focus on theoretical questions and strategic implications, whereas Canadian and U.S. audiences are usually concerned with more practical matters.[7]

> Cultural differences influence your persuasion attempts.

Just as culture within various social groups affects the success of persuasive messages, so too does the culture within various organizations. For example, some organizations handle disagreement and conflict in an indirect, behind-the-scenes way, whereas others accept and even encourage open discussion and sharing of viewpoints. When you accept and follow these traditions, even if they don't reflect your personal preferences, you show the audience that you understand them and respect their values.

Finally, when trying to persuade a skeptical or hostile audience, you must convince people that you know what you're talking about and that you're not trying to mislead them. Your credibility is even more important in persuasive messages than it is in other business messages (see Chapter 5). Without it, your efforts to persuade will seem ineffective at best and manipulative at worst. Research suggests that most managers overestimate their own credibility.[8] Establishing your credibility in persuasive messages takes time. Chapter 5 lists characteristics

Audiences often respond unfavourably to over-the-top language, so keep your writing simple and straightforward.

Objective 2 Identify seven ways to establish credibility in persuasive messages.

essential to building and maintaining your credibility, including honesty, objectivity, awareness of audience needs, knowledge and expertise, endorsements, performance, and communication style. In addition to those elements, you can improve your credibility in persuasive messages with these techniques:

> **Using simple language.** In most persuasive situations, your audience will be cautious, watching for fantastic claims, insupportable descriptions, and emotional manipulation. Express yourself plainly and simply.

> **Supporting your message with facts.** Documents, statistics, and research results all provide objective evidence for what you have to say, which adds to your credibility. The more specific and relevant your proof, the better.

> **Identifying your sources.** Telling your audience where your information comes from improves your credibility, especially if your audience already respects these sources.

> **Establishing common ground.** Those beliefs, attitudes, and background experiences that you have in common with your audience members will help them identify with you.

> **Being objective.** Your ability to understand and acknowledge all sides of an issue helps you present fair and logical arguments in your persuasive message. Top executives often ask if their employees have considered all the possibilities before committing to a single choice.

> **Displaying your good intentions.** Show your audience your genuine concern, good faith, and truthfulness. Let them see how you are focusing on their needs. Your willingness to keep your audience's best interests at heart helps you create persuasive messages that are not only more effective but also more ethical.

> **Avoiding the "hard sell."** You've no doubt experienced a "hard sell," an aggressive approach that uses strong, emotional language and high-pressure tactics to convince people to make a firm decision in a hurry. Audiences tend to instinctively resist this approach. No one likes being pressured into making a decision, and communicators who take this approach can come across as being more concerned with meeting their own goals than with satisfying the needs of their audiences. In contrast, a "soft sell" is more like a comfortable conversation in which the sender uses calm, rational persuasion to help the recipient make a smart choice.

Step 3: Complete Your Message

Professionals know from experience that the details can make or break a persuasive message, so they're careful not to shortchange this part of the writing process. Advertisers may have a dozen or more people review a message before it's released to the public. Ads and commercial websites are often tested extensively with representative recipients to ensure that the intended audience gets the information the sender intends.

When you evaluate your content, judge your argument objectively and don't overestimate your credibility. When revising for clarity and conciseness, carefully match the purpose and organization to audience needs. If possible, ask an experienced colleague who knows your audience well to review your draft. Your design elements must complement, not detract from, your argument. In addition, meticulous proofreading will identify any mechanical or spelling errors that would weaken your persuasive potential. Finally, ensure that your distribution methods fit your audience's expectations and preferences as well as your purpose. Don't start your persuasive efforts on the wrong foot by annoying your audience with an unwelcome delivery method.

With the three-step model in mind, you're ready to begin composing persuasive messages, starting with *persuasive business messages* (such as those that try to convince readers to approve new projects or enter into business partnerships), followed by *marketing and sales messages* (such as those that try to convince readers to consider and then purchase products and services).

Developing Persuasive Business Messages

Persuasive business messages comprise a broad and diverse category, with audiences that range from a single person in your own department to government agencies, investors, business partners, community leaders, and other external groups.

Your success as a businessperson is closely tied to your ability to convince others to accept new ideas, change old habits, or act on your recommendations. Even early in your career, you might have the opportunity to convince your manager to let you join an exciting project or to improve an important process. As you move into positions of greater responsibility, your persuasive messages could start to influence multimillion-dollar investments and the careers of hundreds or thousands of employees. Obviously, the increase in your persuasive skills needs to be matched by the care and thoroughness of your analysis and planning so that the ideas you convince others to adopt are sound.

> Your success in business will depend on writing persuasive messages effectively.

Strategies for Persuasive Business Messages

The goal of your persuasive business message is to convince your reader that your request or idea is reasonable and that it will benefit him or her in some way. Within the context of the three-step process, effective persuasion involves four essential strategies: framing your arguments, balancing emotional and logical appeals, reinforcing your position, and anticipating objections. (Note that all these concepts in this section apply as well to marketing and sales messages, covered later in the chapter.)

 Explore

STRUCTURING PERSUASIVE BUSINESS MESSAGES As noted earlier, most persuasive messages use the indirect approach. Experts in persuasive communication have developed a number of indirect models for such messages. One of the best known is the **AIDA model,** which organizes messages into these four phases: (1) attention, (2) interest, (3) desire, and (4) action (see Table 10–2).

> **Objective 3** Describe the AIDA model for persuasive messages.

> Organize persuasive messages using the AIDA model:
> > Attention
> > Interest
> > Desire
> > Action

> Table 10–2 The AIDA Model

Phase	Objective
Attention	Get the reader's attention with a benefit that is of real interest or value.
Interest	Build the reader's interest by further explaining benefits and appealing to his or her logic or emotions.
Desire	Build desire by providing additional supporting details and answering potential questions.
Action	Motivate the reader to take the next step by closing with a compelling call to action and providing a convenient means for the reader to respond.

The purpose of the first phase is to get your audience members' attention with a compelling introduction. In the second phase, you raise audience members' interest in your product or idea, and in the third, you increase the audience's desire for the product or willingness to accept your idea. In the fourth phase, you motivate readers to take specific action. Other models exist, but they all follow a pattern similar to this one:

> **Attention.** Your first objective is to encourage your audience to want to hear about your problem, idea, or new product—whatever your main idea is. Write a brief and engaging opening sentence, with no extravagant claims or irrelevant points. And ensure that you find some common ground on which to build your case. In the memo in Figure 10–2 Randy Thumwolt uses the AIDA model in a persuasive memo about his program that would try to reduce Host Marriott's annual plastics costs and try to curtail consumer complaints about the company's recycling record. Note also how Thumwolt "sells the problem" before attempting to sell the solution. Few people are interested in hearing about solutions to problems they don't know about or don't believe exist.

> **Interest.** Explain the relevance of your message to your audience. Continuing the theme you started with, paint a more detailed picture of the problem you propose to solve with the solution you're offering (whether it's a new idea, a new process, a new product, or whatever). In Figure 10–2 Thumwolt's interest section introduces an additional, unforeseen problem with plastic product containers. Also, Thumwolt breaks out his suggestions into an easy-to-read list, a format which engages the reader's notice.

Planning	Writing	Completing
Analyze the Situation The purpose is to solve an ongoing problem, so the audience will be receptive.	**Adapt to Your Audience** Adjust the level of formality based on degree of familiarity with the audience; maintain a positive relationship by using the you " attitude, politeness, positive emphasis, and bias-free language.	**Revise the Message** Evaluate content and review readability to make sure the information is clear and complete without being overwhelming.
Gather Information Determine audience needs and obtain the necessary information on recycling problem areas.		**Produce the Message** Emphasize a clean, professional appearance on company letterhead.
Select the Right Medium A printed memo is appropriate for this formal communication.	**Compose the Message** Use a conversational but professional style and keep the message brief, clear, and as helpful as possible.	**Proofread the Message** Review for errors in layout, spelling, and mechanics.
Organize the Information Your main idea is to propose a recycling solution, so limit the scope to the problem at hand; use an indirect approach to lay out the extent of the problem.		**Distribute the Message** Deliver your message using the chosen medium.

1   2   3

> Figure 10–2 Persuasive Memo Using the AIDA Model to Propose Procedural Changes

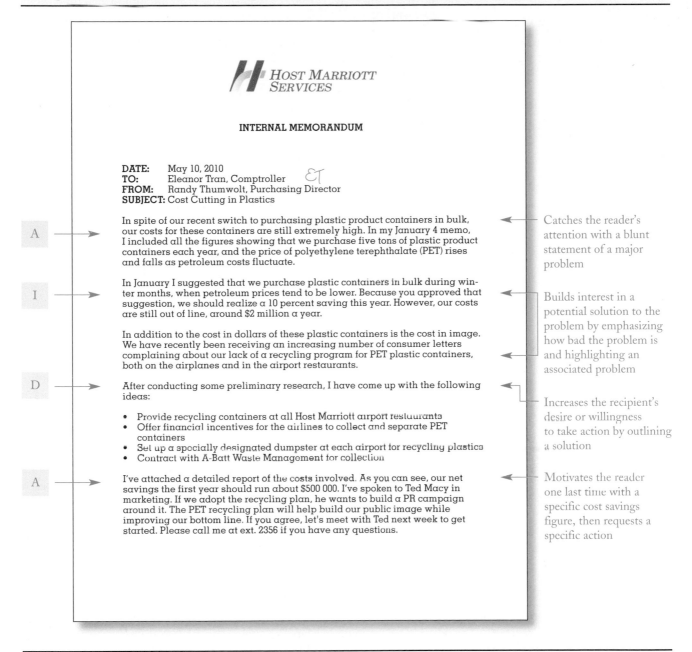

HOST MARRIOTT SERVICES

INTERNAL MEMORANDUM

DATE: May 10, 2010
TO: Eleanor Tran, Comptroller   *ET*
FROM: Randy Thumwolt, Purchasing Director
SUBJECT: Cost Cutting in Plastics

A → In spite of our recent switch to purchasing plastic product containers in bulk, our costs for these containers are still extremely high. In my January 4 memo, I included all the figures showing that we purchase five tons of plastic product containers each year, and the price of polyethylene terephthalate (PET) rises and falls as petroleum costs fluctuate.   ← Catches the reader's attention with a blunt statement of a major problem

I → In January I suggested that we purchase plastic containers in bulk during winter months, when petroleum prices tend to be lower. Because you approved that suggestion, we should realize a 10 percent saving this year. However, our costs are still out of line, around $2 million a year.   ← Builds interest in a potential solution to the problem by emphasizing how bad the problem is and highlighting an associated problem

In addition to the cost in dollars of these plastic containers is the cost in image. We have recently been receiving an increasing number of consumer letters complaining about our lack of a recycling program for PET plastic containers, both on the airplanes and in the airport restaurants.   ←

D → After conducting some preliminary research, I have come up with the following ideas: ← Increases the recipient's desire or willingness to take action by outlining a solution

- Provide recycling containers at all Host Marriott airport restaurants
- Offer financial incentives for the airlines to collect and separate PET containers
- Set up a specially designated dumpster at each airport for recycling plastics
- Contract with A-Batt Waste Management for collection

A → I've attached a detailed report of the costs involved. As you can see, our net savings the first year should run about $500 000. I've spoken to Ted Macy in marketing. If we adopt the recycling plan, he wants to build a PR campaign around it. The PET recycling plan will help build our public image while improving our bottom line. If you agree, let's meet with Ted next week to get started. Please call me at ext. 2356 if you have any questions.   ← Motivates the reader one last time with a specific cost savings figure, then requests a specific action

> **Desire.** Help audience members embrace your idea by explaining how the change will benefit them, either personally or professionally. Reduce resistance by identifying and answering in advance any questions the audience might have. If your idea is complex, you may need to explain how you would implement it. Back up your claims to increase audience willingness to take the action that you suggest in the next section.

> **Action.** Suggest the action you want readers to take. Make it more than a statement such as "Please institute this program soon" or "Send me a refund." This is the opportunity to remind readers of the benefits of taking action. The secret of a successful action phase is making the action easy, so

if possible, give your readers a couple of options for responding, such as a toll-free number to call and a website to visit. Include a deadline when applicable.

The AIDA model is ideal for the indirect approach.

The AIDA plan is tailor-made for using the indirect approach, allowing you to save your main idea for the action phase. However, it can also be used for the direct approach, in which case you use your main idea as an attention-getter, build interest with your argument, create desire with your evidence, and emphasize your main idea in the action phase with the specific action you want your audience to take.

When your AIDA message uses an indirect approach and is delivered by memo or email, keep in mind that your subject line usually catches your reader's eye first. Your challenge is to make it interesting and relevant enough to capture reader attention without revealing your main idea. If you put your request in the subject line, you're likely to get a quick "no" before you've had a chance to present your arguments.

Less Effective	More Effective
Proposal to install new phone message	Reducing the cost of our toll-free number system

You can also see from the AIDA model why it's so important to have a concise, focused purpose for your persuasive messages. If you don't, you'll find it nearly impossible to guide your reader through each phase from attention to action. Focus on your primary goal when presenting your case, and concentrate your efforts on accomplishing that one goal. For example, if your main idea is to convince your company to install a new phone-messaging system, leave discussions about switching long-distance carriers until another day—unless it's relevant to your argument.

✓•─Practise

Objective 4 *Distinguish between emotional and logical appeals, and discuss how to balance them.*

BALANCING EMOTIONAL AND LOGICAL APPEALS Few persuasive appeals are purely logical or purely emotional. Research in Motion bolsters its fact-based website presentation with stylish images of its product, the BlackBerry, and a smiling businessperson demonstrating the cell phone's convenience and ease of use. Without coming right out and saying so, the website depicts the Black-Berry's dependability and elegance. Conversely, even though Lancôme's website is packed with emotional imagery, its product presentations are laced with facts and advice, from the vitamin content of moisturizing lipsticks to application techniques for various makeup products.

Imagine you're sitting at a control panel, with one knob labelled "logic" and another labelled "emotion." As you prepare your persuasive message, you carefully adjust each knob, tuning the message for maximum impact. Too little emotion, and your audience might not care enough to respond. Too much emotion, and your audience might think you haven't thought through the tough business questions.

Generally speaking, persuasive business messages rely more heavily on logical appeals than on emotional appeals because the main idea is usually to save money, increase quality, or improve some other practical, measurable aspect of business. To find the optimum balance, consider four factors: (1) the actions you hope to motivate, (2) your reader's expectations, (3) the degree of resistance you need to overcome, and (4) how far you feel empowered to go to sell your point of view.[9]

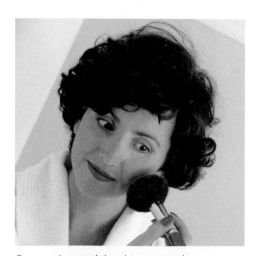

Companies work hard to persuade consumers to buy their products. What appeals do manufacturers of cosmetics make? Are these appeals successful?

Emotional Appeals As its name implies, an **emotional appeal** calls on feelings, basing the argument on audience needs or sympathies. For example, you can make use of the emotion surrounding certain words. The word *freedom* evokes strong feelings, as do words such as *success, prestige, compassion, free, value,* and *comfort.* Such words put your audience in a certain frame of mind and help them accept your message. However, emotional appeals aren't necessarily effective by themselves because the audience wants proof that you can solve a business problem. Even if your audience reaches a conclusion based on emotions, they'll look to you to provide logical support as well.

Emotional appeals attempt to connect with the reader's feelings or sympathies.

Logical Appeals   A **logical appeal** calls on reasoning and evidence. The basic approach with a logical appeal is to make a claim based on a rational argument supported by solid evidence. When appealing to your audience's logic, use three types of reasoning:

Logical appeals are based on the reader's notions of reason; these appeals can use analogy, induction, or deduction.

> **Analogy.** With analogy, you reason from specific evidence to specific evidence. For example, to persuade reluctant employees to attend a planning session, use a town meeting analogy, comparing your company to a small community and your employees to valued members of that community.
> **Induction.** With inductive reasoning, work from specific evidence to a general conclusion. To convince your team to change a certain production process, you could point out that every company that adopted it showed an increase in profits, so it must be a smart idea.
> **Deduction.** With deductive reasoning, you work from a generalization to a specific conclusion. To persuade your boss to hire additional customer support staff, point to industry surveys that show how crucial customer satisfaction is to corporate profits.

Every method of reasoning is vulnerable to misuse, both intentional and unintentional, so verify your rational arguments carefully. For example, in the case of the production process, are there any other factors that affect the integrity of your reasoning? What if that process works well only for small companies with few products, and your firm is a multinational giant with 10 000 products? To avoid faulty logic, practise the following guidelines:[10]

> **Avoid hasty generalizations.** Ensure that you have plenty of evidence before drawing conclusions.

Logical flaws include hasty generalizations, circular reasoning, attacks on opponents, oversimplifications, false assumptions of cause and effect, faulty analogies, and illogical support.

> **Avoid circular reasoning.** *Circular reasoning* is a logical flaw in which you try to support your claim by restating it in different words. The statement "We know temporary workers cannot handle this task because temps are unqualified for it" doesn't prove anything because the claim and the supporting evidence are essentially identical. It doesn't prove *why* the temps are unqualified.
> **Avoid attacking an opponent.** If your persuasive appeal involves countering a competitive appeal made by someone else, make sure you attack the argument your opponent is making, not his or her character or qualifications.
> **Avoid oversimplifying a complex issue.** Make sure you present all the factors and don't reduce a wide range of choices to a simple "either/or" scenario if that isn't the case.
> **Avoid mistaken assumptions of cause and effect.** If you can't isolate the impact of a specific factor, you can't assume it's the cause of whatever effect you're discussing. The weather improves in spring, and people start playing baseball in spring. Does good weather cause baseball? No. There is a *correlation* between the two—meaning the data associated with them tend to rise and fall at the same time, but there is no *causation*—no proof that one causes the other. The complexity of many business situations makes cause and effect a particular challenge. You lowered prices and sales went up. Were lower prices the cause? Maybe, but it might have been caused by a better advertising campaign, a competitor's delivery problems, or some other factor.

> **Avoid faulty analogies.** Be sure that the two objects or situations being compared are similar enough for the analogy to hold. Even if A resembles B in one respect, it may not hold true in other important respects.
> **Avoid illogical support.** Ensure that the connection between your claim and your support is truly logical and not based on a leap of faith, a missing premise, or irrelevant evidence.

Choose your words carefully and use abstractions to enhance emotional content.

REINFORCING YOUR POSITION After you've worked out the basic elements of your argument, step back and look for ways to bolster the strength of your position. Can you find more powerful words to convey your message? For example, if your company is in serious financial trouble, talking about *survival* is more powerful than talking about *continued operations*. Using vivid abstractions such as this along with basic facts and figures can bring your argument to life. As with any powerful tool, though, use vivid language and abstractions carefully and honestly. If the company's survival isn't on the line, don't state or imply that it is.

In addition to individual word choices, consider using *metaphors* and other figures of speech. If you want to describe a quality-control system as being designed to catch every possible product flaw, call it a *spider web* to imply that it catches everything that comes its way. Similarly, anecdotes and stories can help your audience grasp the meaning and importance of your arguments. Instead of just listing the number of times the old laptop computers your department uses have failed, you could describe what happened when your computer broke down during a critical presentation.

Highlight the direct and indirect benefits of complying with your request.

Beyond specific words and phrases, look for other factors that can reinforce your position. When you're asking for something, your audience will find it easier to grant your request if they stand to benefit from it as well. For example, if you're asking for more money to increase your staff, you might offer to lend those new employees to other managers during peak workloads in other departments. The timing of your message can also help. Virtually all organizations operate in cycles of some sort—incoming payments from major customers, outgoing tax payments, seasonal demand for products, and so on. Study these patterns to see whether they might work for or against you. For example, the best time to ask for additional staff might be right after a period of intense activity that prompted multiple customers to complain about poor service, when the experience is still fresh in everyone's mind. If you wait several months for the annual budgeting cycle, the emotional aspect of the experience will have faded, and your request will look like just another cost increase.

Objective 5 Explain why it is important to identify potential objections before you start writing persuasive messages.

ANTICIPATING OBJECTIONS Even the most powerful persuasive messages can expect to encounter some initial resistance. The best way to deal with audience resistance is to anticipate as many objections as you can and address them in your initial message before your audience can even bring them up. By doing so you not only address such issues right away, but you demonstrate a broad appreciation of the issue and imply confidence in your message.[11] This anticipation is particularly important in written messages, when you don't have the opportunity to detect and respond to objections on the spot.

Even powerful persuasive messages can encounter resistance from the audience.

For example, if you know that your proposal to switch to lower-cost materials will raise concerns about product quality, address these issues head-on in your message. If you wait until people raise the concern after reading your message, chances are they will already have gravitated toward a firm no before you have a chance to address their concerns. At the very least, waiting until people object will introduce additional rounds of communication that will delay the response you want to receive.

Present both sides of an issue when you expect to encounter strong resistance.

If you expect a hostile audience, one biased against your plan from the beginning, present all sides. As you cover each option, explain the pros and cons. You'll gain additional credibility if you present these options before presenting your recommendation or decision.[12]

To uncover potential audience objections, try some "What if?" scenarios. Poke holes in your own theories and ideas before your audience does. Then find solutions to the problems you've uncovered.

Furthermore, people are more likely to support what they help create, so ask your audience for their thoughts on the subject before you put your argument together. If appropriate, let your audience recommend some solutions. With enough thought and effort, you could turn problems into opportunities; for example, show how your proposal will be more economical in the long run, even though it may cost more now. Just be sure that you are thorough, open, and objective about all the facts and alternatives.

Keep in mind that compromise might be your best path to success. Rather than automatically countering audience objections or discounting alternative ideas, listen carefully and then engage your audience in discussion. Chances are, you'll end up with a solution that is even better than your original.

Persuasion is a process, not a one-time event. More often than not, persuasion involves listening to people, testing a position, developing a new position that reflects new input, more testing, more compromise, and so on.

To review the steps involved in developing persuasive messages, refer to "Checklist: Developing Persuasive Messages."

Common Examples of Persuasive Business Messages

Throughout your career, you'll have numerous opportunities to write persuasive messages within your organization: selling a supervisor on a cost-cutting idea, suggesting more efficient operating procedures, eliciting cooperation from competing departments, winning employee support for a new benefits package, requesting money for new equipment or funding for a special project. Similarly, you may send a variety of persuasive messages to people outside the organization: websites promoting products, proposals soliciting investment funds, or letters requesting adjustments that go beyond a supplier's contractual obligations. In addition, many of the routine requests you studied in Chapter 8 can become persuasive messages if you want a non-routine result or believe that you haven't received fair treatment.

CHECKLIST Developing Persuasive Messages

A. Get your reader's attention.
- ✔ Open with a reader benefit, a stimulating question, a problem, or an unexpected statement.
- ✔ To establish common ground, discuss something your audience can agree with.
- ✔ Show that you understand the audience's concerns.

B. Build your reader's interest.
- ✔ Expand and support your opening claim or promise.
- ✔ Emphasize the relevance of your message to your audience.

C. Increase your reader's desire.
- ✔ Make audience members want to change by explaining how the change will benefit them.
- ✔ Back up your claims with relevant evidence.

D. Motivate your reader to take action.
- ✔ Suggest the action you want readers to take.
- ✔ Stress the positive results of the action.
- ✔ Make the desired action clear and easy.

E. Balance emotional and logical appeals.
- ✔ Use emotional appeals to help the audience accept your message.
- ✔ Use logical appeals when presenting facts and evidence for complex ideas or recommendations.
- ✔ Avoid faulty logic.

F. Reinforce your position.
- ✔ Provide additional evidence of the benefits of your proposal and your own credibility in offering it.
- ✔ Use abstractions, metaphors, and other figures of speech to bring facts and figures to life.

G. Anticipate objections.
- ✔ Anticipate and answer potential objections.
- ✔ Present the pros and cons of all options if you anticipate a hostile reaction.

Practise

Explore

When making a persuasive request for action, use the AIDA plan to frame your argument.

Most messages can be divided into persuasive requests for action, persuasive presentation of ideas, and persuasive claims and requests for adjustment.

PERSUASIVE REQUESTS FOR ACTION The bulk of your persuasive business messages will involve requests for action. In some cases, your request will be anticipated or will require minimal effort on the recipient's part, so the direct approach is fine. In others, you'll need to introduce your intention indirectly, and the AIDA model is ideal for this purpose. Open with an attention-getting device and show readers that you know something about their concerns. Use the interest and desire sections of your message to demonstrate that you have good reason for making such a request and to cover what you know about the situation: the facts and figures, the benefits of helping, and any history or experience that will enhance your appeal. Your goals are (1) to gain credibility and (2) to make your readers believe that helping you will indeed help solve a significant problem. Once you've demonstrated that your message is relevant to your reader, you can close with a request for some specific action.

Leslie Jorgensen applies the AIDA strategy in the memo in Figure 10–3. She believes the new Airbus A380 could help Oceana Pacific Airways meet its

> Figure 10–3 Persuasive Memo Using the AIDA Model to Request Action

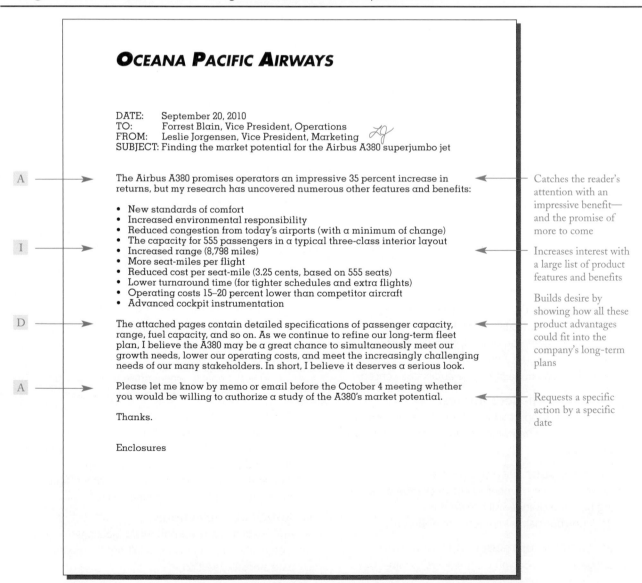

growth needs while lowering its operating costs. She now needs her boss's approval for a study of the plane's market potential. Note that because she also wants to provide some printed materials to support her argument, she opted for a printed memo rather than an email message.

When requesting a favour that is routine (for example, asking someone to attend a meeting in your absence), use the direct approach and the format for routine messages (see Chapter 8). However, when asking for a special favour (for example, asking someone to chair an event or to serve as the team leader because you can no longer fill that role), use persuasive techniques to convince your reader of the value of the project. Include all necessary information about the project and any facts and figures that will convince your reader that his or her contribution will be enjoyable, easy, important, and of personal benefit.

A direct approach is usually best for routine requests.

PERSUASIVE PRESENTATION OF IDEAS Most internal persuasive messages focus on getting the audience to make a specific decision or take some specific action. However, you will encounter situations in which you simply want to change attitudes or beliefs about a particular topic, without asking the audience to decide or do anything—at least not yet. In complicated, multistep persuasive efforts, the goal of your first message might be nothing more than convincing your audience to re-examine long-held opinions or admit the possibility of new ways of thinking.

Sometimes the objective of persuasive messages is simply to encourage people to consider a new idea.

For example, you think your company is spending too much time processing payroll, and you've found an outside firm that can do it for less money than you now spend on internal staff and systems (a practice known as *outsourcing*). However, your company president is philosophically opposed to outsourcing any critical business function, saying that something as important as payroll should never be entrusted to outsiders. Until and unless you can bring about a change in the president's way of thinking, there is no point in pushing for a decision about outsourcing.

Another example is the effort to improve internet access for people with visual and other disabilities. A campaign called the Web Accessibility Initiative has been launched by the Worldwide Web Consortium (a global association that defines many guidelines and technologies behind the World Wide Web). Although the Consortium's ultimate goal is making websites more accessible, a key interim goal is simply making website developers more aware of the need. As part of this effort, the Consortium has developed a presentation that highlights issues such as the following:[13]

> the Web's growing importance as a source of everything, including news and entertainment, workplace interaction, and government services
> the Web's gradual displacement of traditional sources of these services

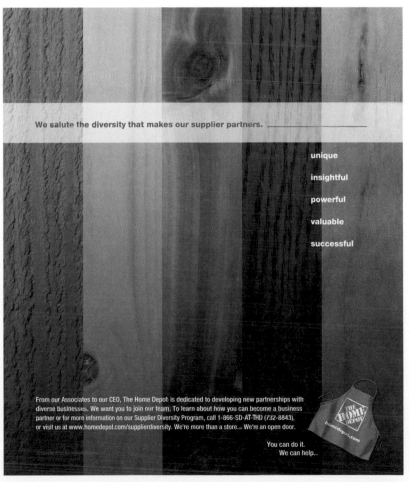

We salute the diversity that makes our supplier partners.

unique
insightful
powerful
valuable
successful

From our Associates to our CEO, The Home Depot is dedicated to developing new partnerships with diverse businesses. We want you to join our team. To learn about how you can become a business partner or for more information on our Supplier Diversity Program, call 1-866-SD-AT-THD (732-8843), or visit us at www.homedepot.com/supplierdiversity. We're more than a store.... We're an open door.

You can do it.
We can help...

This Home Depot magazine ad promotes the idea of the company's commitment to an ethnically diverse supplier base. What metaphor communicates the idea? Is it effective? What are the emotional appeals in this metaphor?

> the presence of barriers on the Web for many types of disabilities
> the number of people whose disabilities affect their access to the Web (the number is in the millions)
> the fact that accessible Web designs can also help other users

Information on these specific issues can help open the eyes of website operators who may assume that standard Web practices are sufficient for their audiences.

PERSUASIVE CLAIMS AND REQUESTS FOR ADJUSTMENT Although persuasive claims and adjustment requests are sometimes referred to as *complaint letters*, you don't write them merely to get a complaint off your chest. Your goal is to persuade someone to make an adjustment in your favour. You work toward this goal by demonstrating the difference between what you expected and what you actually got.

Most claim letters are routine messages and use the direct approach discussed in Chapter 8. However, both consumers and business professionals sometimes encounter situations in which they believe they haven't received a fair deal. For example, suppose you purchase something and, after the warranty expires, discover that the item was defective. You write the company a routine request asking for a replacement, but your request is denied. You're not satisfied, and you still believe you have a strong case. Perhaps you just didn't communicate it well enough the first time. Persuasion is necessary in such cases.

Because you've already paid for the product, you can't threaten to withhold payment. Instead, try to convey the essentially negative information in a way that will get positive results. Fortunately, most people in business are open to settling your claim fairly. It's to their advantage to maintain your goodwill and to resolve your problem quickly.

The key ingredients of a good persuasive claim are a complete and specific review of the facts and a confident and positive tone. Assume that the other person is not trying to cheat you but that you also have the right to be satisfied with the transaction. Your goal is to solve a particular problem, and your audience is most likely to help if you focus on the audience benefits of doing so (rather than focusing on the disadvantages of neglecting your complaint).

Begin persuasive claims by stating the basic problem or reviewing what has been done about the problem so far. Include a statement that both you and your audience can agree on or that clarifies what you wish to convince your audience about. Be as specific as possible about what you want to happen. Next, give your reader a good reason for granting your claim. Show how your audience is responsible for the problem and appeal to your reader's sense of fair play, goodwill, or moral responsibility. Explain how you feel about the problem, but don't get carried away, don't complain too much, and don't make threats. People generally respond more favourably to requests that are both calm and reasonable.

Developing Marketing and Sales Messages

Marketing and sales messages use many of the same techniques as persuasive business messages.

Marketing and sales messages use the same basic techniques as other persuasive messages, with the added emphasis of encouraging someone to participate in a commercial transaction. Although the terms *marketing message* and *sales message* are often used interchangeably, they do represent separate but related efforts. Marketing messages usher potential buyers through the purchasing process without asking them to make an immediate decision; that's when sales messages take over. Marketing messages focus on such tasks as introducing new brands to the public, providing competitive comparison information, encouraging customers to visit websites for more information, and reminding buyers that a particular product or service is available. In contrast, a sales message makes a specific request for people to place an order for a particular product or service.

Most marketing and sales messages, particularly in larger companies, are created and delivered by professionals with specific training in marketing, advertising, sales, or public relations. However, you may be called on to review the work of these specialists or even to write such messages in smaller companies, so a good understanding of how these messages work will help you be a more effective manager. The basic strategies to consider include assessing customer needs, analyzing your competition, determining key selling points and benefits, anticipating purchase objections, applying the AIDA model, and maintaining high standards of ethics, legal compliance, and etiquette.

Assessing Audience Needs

As with every other business message, successful marketing and sales messages start with an understanding of audience needs. For some products and services, this assessment is a simple matter. For example, customers compare only a few basic attributes when purchasing copy or printer paper, including weight, brightness, colour, and finish. In contrast, they might consider dozens of features when shopping for real estate, cars, professional services, and other complex purchases.

 Explore

Purchasing decisions often involve more than just the basic product or service.

In addition, customer needs often extend beyond the basic product or service. Clothes do far more than simply keep you warm. What you wear makes a statement about who you are, which social groups you want to be associated with (or not), and how you view your relationship with the people around you.

Begin by assessing audience needs, interests, and emotional concerns—just as you would for any business message. Form a mental image of the typical buyer for the product you wish to sell. Ask yourself what audience members might want to know about this product. How can your product help them? Are they driven by bottom-line pricing, or is quality more important to them?

Note the ads you're exposed to every day. They often focus on just one or two attributes or issues, even if the product or service has many different facets to consider. The purpose of these narrow marketing messages is to grab your attention and then raise your interest level enough to encourage you to conduct further research.

Analyzing Your Competition

Marketing and sales messages nearly always compete with messages from other companies trying to reach the same audience. When Chrysler plans a sales letter to introduce a new model to current customers, the company knows that its audience has also been exposed to messages from Ford, Honda, Volkswagen, and numerous other car companies. In crowded markets, writers sometimes have to search for words and phrases that other companies aren't already using. They might also want to avoid themes, writing styles, or creative approaches that are too similar to those of competitors' messages.

Most marketing and sales messages have to compete for the audience's attention.

Determining Key Selling Points and Benefits

With some insight into audience needs and existing messages from the competition, you're ready to decide which benefits and features of your product or service to highlight. For all but the simplest products, you'll want to prioritize the items you plan to discuss. You'll also want to distinguish between the features of the product and the benefits that those features offer the customers.

As Table 10–3 shows, **selling points** are the most attractive features of an idea or product, whereas **benefits** are the particular advantages that readers will realize

Objective 6 Explain an effective approach to identifying selling points and audience benefits.

Selling points focus on the product; benefits focus on the user.

> Table 10–3 Features Versus Benefits

Product Feature	Customer Benefit
Our easy financing plan includes no money down, no interest, and no payments for 24 months.	You can buy what you want right now, even if you have limited cash on hand.
Our marketing communication audit accurately measures the impact of your advertising and public relations efforts.	You can find out whether your message is reaching the target audience and whether you're spending your marketing budget in the best possible manner.
The spools in our fly fishing reels are machined from solid blocks of aircraft-grade aluminum.	Go fishing with confidence: These lightweight reels will stand up to the toughest conditions.

from those features. Selling points focus on the product. Benefits focus on the user. For example, if you say that your snow shovel has "an ergonomically designed handle," you've described a good feature. But to persuade someone to buy that shovel, say "The ergonomically designed handle will reduce your risk of back injury." That's a benefit. For your message to be successful, your product's distinguishing benefit must correspond to your readers' primary needs or emotional concerns.

Consider how SecureAbel Alarms uses the AIDA model to persuade students to buy its residence-room alarm system (see Figure 10–4). The features of the system include its portability, piercing alarm, and programmable control units. The benefits include simple installation, simple operation, and a sense of security.

Anticipating Purchase Objections

As with persuasive business messages, marketing and sales messages often encounter objections, and once again, the best way to handle them is to identify them up front and address as many as you can. Objections can range from high price to low quality to a lack of compatibility with existing products. Perceived risk is another common objection. Consumers might worry that a car won't be safe enough for a family, that a jacket will make them look unattractive, or that a hair salon will botch a haircut. Business buyers might worry about disrupting operations or failing to realize the financial returns on a purchase.

Price can be a particularly tricky issue in any message, whether audience members are consumers or business customers. Whether you highlight or downplay the price of your product, prepare your readers for it. Words such as *luxurious* and *economical* provide unmistakable clues about how your price compares with that of competitors. Such words will help your readers accept your price when you finally state it.

If price is a major selling point, give it a position of prominence, such as in the headline or as the last item in a paragraph. If price is not a major selling point, you can handle it in several ways. You could leave the price out altogether or de-emphasize it by putting the figure in the middle of a paragraph that comes well after you've presented the benefits and selling points.

Anticipating objections is crucial to effective marketing and sales messages.

Emphasizes the rarity of the edition to signal value and thus prepare the reader for the big-ticket price that follows

Buries the actual price in the middle of a sentence and ties it in with another reminder of the exclusivity of the offer

Only 100 prints of this exclusive, limited-edition lithograph will be created. On June 15, they will be made available to the general public, but you can reserve one now for only $350, the special advance reservation price. Simply rush the enclosed reservation card back today so that your order is in before the June 15 publication date.

> Figure 10–4 Effective Letter Using the AIDA Model to Sell a Product

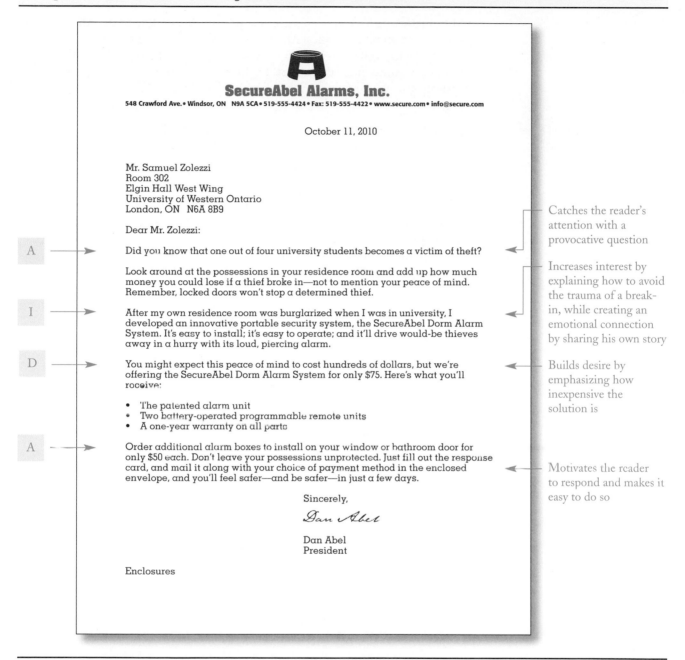

The pros also use two other techniques for minimizing price. One is to break a quantity price into units. Instead of saying that a case of motor oil costs $24, you might say that each bottle costs $2. The other technique is to compare your product's price with the cost of some other product or activity: "The cost of owning your own exercise equipment is less than you'd pay for a health-club membership." Your aim is to make the cost seem as small and affordable as possible, thereby minimizing price as a possible objection.

If you've done your homework up front and assessed your audience thoroughly, you should be aware of most concerns. You might not be able to address every one of them in your message—if the product or service isn't ideal for the customer, your message can't fix that—but you will be prepared to do the best you can with the product or service you have to promote.

Applying the AIDA Model

Most marketing and sales messages are prepared according to the AIDA plan or some variation of it. A typical AIDA-organized message begins with an attention-getting device, generates interest by describing some of the product's or service's unique features, increases desire by highlighting the benefits that are most appealing to your audience, and closes by suggesting the action you want the audience to take.

You can employ a variety of attention-getting devices in marketing and sales messages.

GETTING ATTENTION You can use a wide range of techniques to attract the audience's attention:

> **Your product's strongest benefit.** "Millions of Songs. Thousands of Games. Countless Hours of Fun. (for Apple iPod touch)[14]
> **A piece of genuine news.** "Bundle and Save." (Promoting a Bell Canada plan where customers save money by combining selected telecommunication services.)[15]
> **A point of common ground with the audience.** "An SUV adventurous enough to accommodate your spontaneity and the gear that comes with it."[16]
> **A personal appeal to the reader's emotions and values.** "The only thing worse than paying taxes is paying taxes when you don't have to."
> **The promise of insider information.** "You may be one of those people who dreams of working and living in France and don't know how to go about simply doing it. This guide tells—from the inside out—how others like yourself have managed to work within the French system."[17]
> **The promise of savings.** "Enjoy the best of TV. Order Bell TV and save $10/mo. for 12 months."[18]
> **A sample or demonstration of the product.** "Here's your free sample of the new Romalite packing sheet."
> **A solution to a problem.** "This backpack's designed to endure a kid's dropping and dragging."[19]

Of course, words aren't the only attention-getting device at your disposal. You can grab your audience by using special sizes or styles of type, underlining, bullets, colour, or indentations, as Figure 10–5, a magazine's subscription renewal letter, shows.

Strong, evocative images are also a common attention getter. With online messages, you have even more options, including audio, animation, and video.

To build interest, expand on and support the promises in your attention-getting opening.

BUILDING INTEREST Use the interest section of your message to build on the intrigue you created with your opening. This section should also offer support for whatever claims or promises you might have made in the opening. For example, when Apple introduced a redesigned iPod nano in a choice of nine colours, it used the headline "Rockalicious. Colour isn't the only brilliant new iPod nano feature" and then continued with several support points, including the feature of screen size:[20]

Puts screen size in a position of emphasis, since that—not price—is the major selling point

World's biggest small screen. Watching movies, TV shows, and videos is big fun on iPod nano. And the high-resolution picture looks crisp and vivid on the 2-inch widescreen display. So you can always have a little video with you.

Planning	Writing	Completing
Analyze the Situation The purpose is to sell a product, so the audience will be neutral, uninterested, or perhaps unwilling.	**Adapt to Your Audience** Adjust the level of formality based on degree of familiarity with the audience; maintain a positive relationship by using the "you" attitude, politeness, positive emphasis, and bias-free language.	**Revise the Message** Evaluate content and review readability to make sure the information is clear and complete without being overwhelming.
Gather Information Determine audience needs and obtain the necessary information to present a persuasive message.	**Compose the Message** Use a conversational but professional style, and keep the message brief, clear, and as helpful as possible.	**Produce the Message** Emphasize a clean, professional appearance on company letterhead.
Select the Right Medium A printed letter is appropriate for this formal communication.		**Proofread the Message** Review for errors in layout, spelling, and mechanics.
Organize the Information Your main idea is to offer a product for sale, so limit your scope to that issue; use the AIDA approach to propose the solution.		**Distribute the Message** Deliver your message using the chosen medium.

1   **2**   **3**

> Figure 10–5 Sales Letter with Formatting Devices

Keep Rockin' On—Renew Today!

Dear John Hendricks,

Renew your subscription today . . . and you won't miss a single issue of *Rock On!* magazine, your number-one source for information about your favourite bands and your favourite music.

As a member of the *Rock On!* family, you already know that each issue is loaded with news, interviews, and photos of today's number-one musical movers and shakers. We take you into the studio and onto the stage. You see behind the scenes at every concert, from set-up to strike-down. We're always there . . . for *YOU!*

So renew now. It's easy. Just return your subscription form today, and you'll continue to receive *Rock On!* at 35% off the newsstand price!

Don't miss a single issue!

Cordially.

Mike Garcia

Miki Garcia

P.S. Call our operators at 1-800-435-ROCK, and ask for our two- or three-year subscription rates, and save even more! Check us out at www.rockon.com.

Uses italics and boldface to stress key words

Uses underlining to stress main action and benefit

Add details and audience benefits to increase desire for the product or service.

At this point in the message, Apple has substantiated the claim made in the headline and has whetted readers' appetites with some intriguing features and benefits.

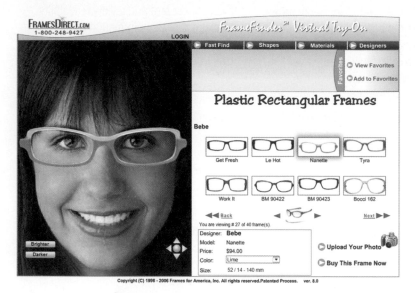

FramesDirect.com is an interactive website that lets you upload a photo of yourself and then see how you look in a variety of eyeglass styles. Flexible media technologies make it easy to adapt promotional messages to the interests of individual audience members. Why might this technology have a strong appeal to consumers? Does it have any disadvantages?

INCREASING DESIRE To build desire for the product, continue to expand and explain what it offers, how it works, and how customers can use it. On the iPod nano page, Apple continues with more details about the features summarized in the first paragraph of text, such as describing the game and photo display functions. Take advantage of whatever medium you are using to continue to offer additional information that will increase audience desire for the product and help you prepare for the action stage. For example, after reading this much about the iPod, some users might want to know more about the iTunes music store, whereas others will want to know about using iPods in their cars. Apple makes it easy to find the information each individual wants. This ability to provide flexible access to information is just one of the reasons the Web is such a powerful medium for marketing and sales.

Throughout the body of your message, remember to keep the focus on the audience, not on your company or your product. When you talk about product features, remember to stress the benefits and talk in terms that make sense to users. Listing the capacity of the iPod classic as 30 000 songs and 150 hours of video is a lot more meaningful for most readers than saying it has 120 gigabytes of memory. Action words give strength to any business message, but they are especially important in sales letters. Compare the following:

Less Effective	More Effective
The NuForm desk chair is designed to support your lower back and relieve pressure on your legs.	The NuForm desk chair supports your lower back and relieves pressure on your legs.

The second version expresses the idea in fewer words and emphasizes what the chair does for the user ("supports") rather than the intentions of the design team ("is designed to support").

To keep readers interested, use strong, colourful language without overdoing it.

To keep readers interested, use colourful verbs and adjectives that convey a dynamic image. Be careful, however, not to overdo it: If you say "Your factory floors will sparkle like diamonds," your audience will find it hard to believe, which may prevent them from believing the rest of your message.

To increase desire, as well as boost your credibility, provide support for your claims. You can't assume your audience will believe what you say just because you've said it in writing. You'll have to give them proof. Support is especially important if your product is complicated, costs a lot, or represents some unusual approach.

Creative marketers find many ways to provide support: testimonials from satisfied users, articles written by industry experts, competitive comparisons, product samples and free demonstrations, independent test results, even movies or computer animations that show a product in action. You can also highlight guarantees that demonstrate your faith in your product and your willingness to back it up.

MOTIVATING ACTION   After you have raised enough interest and built up the reader's desire for your offering, you're ready to ask your audience to take action. Whether you want people to pick up the phone to place an order or visit your website to download a free demo version of your software, persuade them to do it right away with an effective *call to action*. You might offer a discount for the first 1000 people to order, put a deadline on the offer, or simply remind them that the sooner they order, the sooner they'll be able to enjoy the product's benefits. Even potential buyers who want the product can get distracted or forget to respond, so encouraging immediate action is important. Make the response action as simple and as risk-free as possible.

> After you've generated sufficient interest and desire, you're ready to persuade readers to take the preferred action.

Take care to maintain the respectful, professional tone you've been using up to this point. Don't resort to gimmicks and desperate-sounding pleas for the customer's business. Ensure that your final impression is compelling and positive. For example, in a printed sales letter, the postscript (P.S.) below your signature is often one of the first and last parts people read. Use this valuable space to emphasize the key benefit you have to offer and to emphasize the advantages of ordering soon.

Maintaining High Standards of Ethics, Legal Compliance, and Etiquette

The word *persuasion* has negative connotations for some people, especially in a marketing or sales context. They associate persuasion with dishonest and unethical practices that lead unsuspecting audiences into accepting unworthy ideas or buying unneeded products. However, effective businesspeople view persuasion as a positive force, aligning their own interests with what is best for their audiences. They influence audience members by providing information and aiding understanding, which allows audiences the freedom to choose.[21] Ethical businesspeople inform audiences of the benefits of an idea, an organization, a product, a donation, or an action so that these audiences can recognize just how well the idea, organization, product, donation, or action will satisfy a need they truly have. They don't try to trick people into making choices that are not in their best interest.

To maintain the highest standards of business ethics, make every attempt to persuade without manipulating. Choose words that won't be misinterpreted, and ensure that you don't distort the truth. Adopt the "you" attitude by showing honest concern for your audience's needs and interests. Your consideration of audience needs is more than ethical; it's the proper use of persuasion. That consideration is likely to achieve the response you intend and to satisfy your audience's needs.

> **Objective 7**   Identify steps you can take to avoid ethical lapses in marketing and sales messages.

As marketing and selling grow increasingly complex, so do the legal ramifications of marketing and sales messages. In Canada, the Competition Bureau has the authority to administer and enforce the *Competition Act* and

> Marketing and sales messages are covered by a wide range of laws and regulations.

the *Consumer Packaging and Labelling Act* (as well as other consumer-related legislation). The legal aspects of promotional communication can be complex, and most companies require marketing and sales people to obtain clearance from company lawyers before sending messages. In any event, pay close attention to the following legal aspects of marketing and sales communication:[22]

> **Marketing and sales messages must be truthful and non-deceptive.** The *Competition Act* considers messages to be deceptive if they include statements that are likely to mislead reasonable customers, and the statement is an important part of the purchasing decision. Failing to include important information is also considered deceptive. The *Competition Act* also looks at *implied claims,* those you don't explicitly make but that can be inferred from what you do or don't say.

> **You must back up your claims with evidence.** According to the *Competition Act,* offering a money-back guarantee or providing letters from satisfied customers is not enough; you must still be able to support your claims with objective evidence such as a survey or scientific study. According to the *Consumer Packaging and Labelling Act,* if you claim that your food product lowers cholesterol, you must have scientific evidence to support that claim.

> **Complaints about misleading marketing and sales messages may lead to prosecution.** If you imply or make an offer and can't fulfill it, the practices may be reviewed by the Federal Court, or a provincial superior court.

> **In most cases, you can't use a person's name, photograph, or other identity without permission.** Doing so is considered an invasion of privacy. You can use images of people considered to be public figures, as long as you don't unfairly imply that they endorse your message.

Before you launch a marketing or sales campaign, ensure that you're up to date on the latest regulations affecting spam (or *unsolicited bulk email,* as it's officially known), customer privacy, and data security. The electronic marketplace is of special concern to the government.[23]

Meeting your ethical and legal obligations will go a long way toward maintaining good communication etiquette as well. However, you may still face etiquette decisions within ethical and legal boundaries. For example, you can produce a marketing campaign that complies with all applicable laws and yet is still offensive or insulting to your audience. An audience-centred approach, involving respect for your readers and their values, should help you avoid any such etiquette missteps.

Technology also gives communicators new ways to demonstrate sensitivity to user needs. One example is automated updates from blogs and websites, alerting customers to information in which they've expressed an interest. *Opt-in* email newsletters are another technology that shows the "you" attitude at work. Unlike the unwelcome spam messages that litter email in-boxes these days, opt-in messages are sent only to those people who have specifically requested information. Consider the email newsletter in Figure 10–6. It's part of an *opt-in* mailing that Aeroplan sends only to those customers who specifically request it. The newsletter itself combines friendly and informative text that addresses typical customer concerns and convenient links to the company's and partners' websites.

Maintaining high ethical standards is a key aspect of good communication etiquette.

Communication technologies such as opt-in email and blog syndication can help you be sensitive to audience needs.

TIPS FOR SUCCESS

"Newsletters can be great relationship builders, but the content should be varied. Otherwise, they become tedious and lose their customer value."

Edmund O. Lawler, Professor of Journalism and writer on advertising

> Figure 10–6 Opt-In Email Newsletter

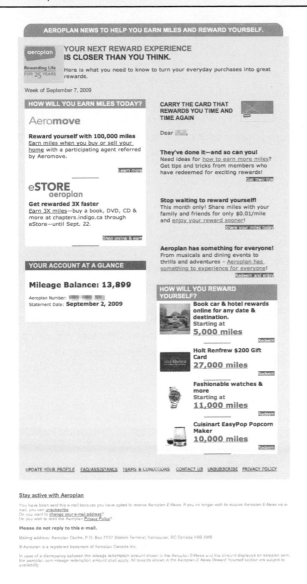

PROMOTING WORKPLACE ETHICS

Selling Ethically Online

Before you sell products online, become familiar with the *Canadian Code of Practice for Consumer Protection in Electronic Commerce.* Developed by professional associations such as the Retail Council of Canada, federal and provincial government agencies, and corporations, its intent is to protect consumers during any online transaction. By subscribing to these guidelines, you will conduct your business ethically and avoid complaints and lawsuits.

> **Provide complete and current contact and policy information.** Customers often need to contact companies to ask questions, learn about their warranties, change orders, and complain. Your website should include all contact information (postal address, email address, phone and fax numbers) and details regarding payment methods, return policies, warranties, and the complaint process. You should also state your policies on privacy and

unsolicited email. As the *Code of Practice* states, all information should be "clearly presented in plain language, truthful, conspicuous and easily accessible . . . at appropriate stages of consumers' decision making, particularly before consumers confirm transactions or provide any personal information."

> **Describe products fully.** Customers want to know what they are buying. You should describe your products accurately and in detail, and include any information that customers would see if they bought the product in a store, such as health and safety warnings or suggestions for parental supervision. If you neglect to disclose product information fully or deliver a product materially different from that described, you must honour any refund request, including charges the buyer incurred for returning the product.

> **Respect consumers' right to privacy.** As an online vendor, you must make your privacy policy easily accessible on your website. Tell your customers the kind of information you collect, its purpose, how it will be used, and to whom it may be disclosed. Consumers must know how they can review their personal information, and, when necessary, how they can correct or remove it. You cannot require your customers to disclose personal data as a condition of sale

beyond that needed to complete the transaction. Your customers' right to privacy also extends to unsolicited email. The *Code of Practice* notes that online vendors should not send email to customers without their consent, and that marketing messages should include a provision, in plain language, for removal from electronic marketing messages, with a return email address for that purpose.

You can learn more about the *Canadian Code of Practice for Consumer Protection in Electronic Commerce* at http://cmcweb.ca/epic/site/cmc-cmc.nsf/en/fe00064e.html.

CAREER APPLICATIONS

1 Review two websites that sell products online, such as www.canadiantire.com or www.mec.ca (Mountain Equipment Co-op). In what areas do they follow the guidelines set in the *Canadian Code of Practice for Consumer Protection in Electronic Commerce*? How can these websites be improved in terms of consumer protection?

2 Do you think that following the guidelines in the *Canadian Code of Practice for Consumer Protection in Electronic Commerce* improves the potential of commercial websites to sell products? Justify your answer.

Summary of Learning Objectives

1 **Apply the three-step writing process to persuasive messages.** Because persuasive messages can be complicated and sensitive, several planning tasks need extra attention. You'll be persuading people to take action that they probably wouldn't have taken without your message, so analyzing your purpose is crucial. In addition, audience analysis may be more detailed for persuasive messages, so gauge psychological and social needs in addition to cultural differences. Also, when persuading a skeptical audience, your credibility must be unquestionable, so spend some extra effort to establish it. Since your attempts to persuade could be viewed by some as manipulative, strive for the highest ethical standards.

2 **Identify seven ways to establish credibility in persuasive messages.** When persuading your audience, ensure that you speak simply and avoid exaggeration. Support your message with objective evidence and name your sources. Understand your audience's beliefs and attitudes so that you can establish common ground. Present all sides of the argument, show honest interest in your audience's concerns, and avoid pressuring your audience.

3 **Describe the AIDA model for persuasive messages.** When using the AIDA plan, open your message by getting *attention* with a reader benefit, a problem, a stimulating

question, a piece of news, or an unexpected statement. You build *interest* with facts, details, and additional reader benefits. You increase *desire* by providing more evidence and reader benefits and by anticipating and answering possible objections. You conclude by motivating a specific *action*, emphasizing the positive results of that action, and making it easy for the reader to respond.

4 **Distinguish between emotional and logical appeals, and discuss how to balance them.** Emotional appeals call on human feelings, using arguments based on audience needs or sympathies. However, these appeals aren't effective by themselves. Logical appeals call on human reason (whether using analogy, induction, or deduction). Use logic together with emotion, thereby supplying rational support for an idea that readers have already embraced emotionally. In general, logic will be your strongest appeal, with only subtle emotion. However, when persuading someone to purchase a product, join a cause, or make a donation, you can heighten emotional appeals.

5 **Explain why it is important to identify potential objections before you start writing persuasive messages.** Being aware of specific audience objections to your persuasive purpose will help you gain the support of audience members. You can address your audience's

opposition, thus demonstrating your understanding of their particular concerns. You heighten your credibility because you show you are not biased, so you may influence your audience to agree with your viewpoint.

6 **Explain an effective approach to identifying selling points and audience benefits.** Identify selling points as the most striking features of a product or service; identify benefits as the advantages the reader will gain from these features. In other words, selling points focus on the product; benefits focus on the user.

7 **Identify steps you can take to avoid ethical lapses in marketing and sales messages.** Avoid ethical lapses in marketing and sales messages by ensuring they are honest and accurate. Use language precisely, and support your claims with objective facts. Do not use any identifying features of an individual without permission. Being familiar with legislation such as the *Competition Act* is an important part of preparing marketing and sales messages.

PEARSON mycanadianbuscommlab™

Visit www.mycanadianbuscommlab.ca for everything you need to help you succeed in the job you've always wanted! Tools and resources include the following:
- Composing Space and Writer's Toolkit
- Document Makeovers
- Video Case Studies
- Grammar Exercises—and much more!

On the Job PERFORMING COMMUNICATION TASKS AT THE CANADIAN YOUTH BUSINESS FOUNDATION

As an aspiring entrepreneur, you believe there are others like you who want to launch their own business but need the advice of local business leaders. Indeed, you have consulted with students in your new venture start-up class, and you all agree that a monthly networking group, where you can meet with CYBF coaches in your area, would provide you all with valuable guidance. Your first step is getting a central meeting place. You decide to contact the chairperson of your school's business program, seeking her support. Use your knowledge of persuasive messages to choose the best alternative in each of the following situations. Be prepared to explain why your choice is the most effective one.

1 You are drafting an email to be sent to the chairperson. She is not familiar with the CYBF's programs. Which version is the best attention-getter for this email?
   a No, this isn't a letter asking for a higher grade. We know that you have a valuable resource you may be able to share with us: meeting room space.
   b Don't let that unused meeting room time go to waste! Let enterprising students use that time! We're looking for a meeting room in the Business department. If you let us have any unscheduled time, you'll be giving your students a chance to network with coaches who can help us start our own business.
   c If you could put available meeting room time to productive use by helping your students, wouldn't you be interested? Donate some of our department's unscheduled meeting room time to students in the entrepreneurial classes who want to meet with CYBF coaches. You'll gain the satisfaction of helping your students by giving them a central place to meet and to learn from the success of other businesspeople.

2 Which version is the most effective interest and desire section for your letter?
   a You may have unused meeting room time after 4:00 P.M. Just two hours a month would be enough time for students to meet with CYBF coaches and gain valuable knowledge about starting up a business. We would bring our own computers to access the school's wireless network. By giving us regular meeting room time, you will enhance your students' studies and careers by providing a location where they can share ideas and information with business leaders in a relaxed and quiet atmosphere. You will see them take into the classroom the enthusiasm they've developed from seeing how entrepreneurs started their own businesses and became successful.
   b All we need is two hours a month. So please check the meeting room schedule. Just two hours a month, ideally in the late afternoon or early evening, is all we need. You will be proud of your department's donation, which will help serve your students. Help the next generation of entrepreneurs by donating unscheduled meeting time today!
   c Your entrepreneurial students need your help. Any unused meeting time—just two hours a month—will help us meet with local business leaders and get real-life knowledge about starting up a small business. Please take a moment to check the schedule.

   If you give us the meeting room once a month, the business department will benefit by further educating their students with real-world advice. But the people who will really benefit will be your students, because they will be enhancing what they learn in the classroom with real-world advice and become more successful when they graduate.

3 Newspapers managed and written by students are common on many university and college campuses. Imagine that you have created an advertisement seeking students who would like to meet with CYBF coaches. Because of limited funds, you would like the advertising space to be donated. Which appeal to your audience would be most effective in a letter seeking free advertising space?

a an entirely emotional appeal stressing the needs of the students and the satisfaction of helping a worthy cause

b an entirely logical appeal stressing that the advertisements can be inserted whenever the newspapers have unused space, thus saving editors the trouble of rearranging articles and other advertisements to make the page look good, or using meaningless filler

c a combination of emotional and logical appeals, stressing both the satisfaction of helping a worthy cause and the rationale behind printing the advertisement wherever the editors have available space

Test Your Knowledge

1 How do emotional appeals differ from logical appeals?

2 What is the AIDA plan? How does it apply to persuasive messages?

3 What mistakes should you avoid when developing a persuasive message to overcome resistance?

4 What are some similarities between sales messages and bad-news messages?

5 What are some questions to ask when gauging the audience's needs during the planning of a persuasive message?

6 How can you build credibility with an audience when planning a persuasive message?

7 What types of reasoning can you use in logical appeals?

8 How can semantics affect a persuasive message?

9 How do benefits differ from features?

10 What ethical and legal responsibilities influence sales and marketing messages?

Apply Your Knowledge

1 Why is it important to present both sides of an argument when writing a persuasive message to a potentially hostile audience?

2 How are persuasive messages different from routine messages?

3 When is it appropriate to use the direct organizational approach in persuasive messages?

4 What is likely to happen if your persuasive message starts immediately with a call to action? Why?

5 As an employee, how many of your daily tasks require persuasion? List as many as you can think of. Who are your audiences? How do their needs and characteristics affect the way you develop your persuasive messages at work?

6 **Ethical Choices** Are emotional appeals ethical? Why or why not?

Running Cases   ⊙─[Watch on **mycanadianbuscommlab**

> CASE 1 Noreen

Noreen is reviewing overdue accounts. At 30-days (first notice) and again at 60-days (second notice) past due a reminder letter is sent to customers. At 90-days (third and final notice) past due a letter is sent to customers informing them of the fact that at 120-days past due legal action will be taken. At 120-days overdue an account is sent out for legal proceedings.

Petro-Go also asks the customers to contact the company to discuss payment arrangements and offers to help them devise an affordable and manageable payment plan before legal action takes place. Petro-Go has many strategies for helping customers manage their debts efficiently. The letter is an attempt to persuade the customer to make at least the minimum payments to avoid legal action. Legal action will hurt the customer's credit score and future ability to obtain credit.

QUESTIONS

a) How will Noreen apply the "you" attitude?

b) How will she balance emotional and logical appeals? Give examples.

c) What must Noreen avoid doing in the letter?

d) What are some persuasive tools Noreen will use?

e) Is it ethical for Noreen to threaten legal action?

YOUR TASK

Write the letter. Apply the guidelines for writing persuasive messages that Chapter 10 discusses.

> CASE 2 Kwong

Kwong sees the announcement below on his college's website offering scholarships. He decides to apply. He needs to write a persuasive letter to the college's Financial Aid office convincing the selection committee that he should be one of the two students chosen to receive this scholarship money. Kwong wants to put the $5000 toward starting his own accounting firm once he graduates. Kwong will graduate at the end of this semester thereby gaining advanced standing in the CGA program. The CGA program should take Kwong only one year to complete.

ASSOCIATION OF ENTREPRENEURS
SCHOLARSHIPS 2 × $5000.00—Awarded to two final-year business students who demonstrate community service and entrepreneurial experience or goals and show successful academic progression of study.

QUESTIONS

a) What tone and approach should Kwong use for this persuasive letter?

b) What are some questions Kwong needs to ask himself about his audience?

c) How will Kwong establish his credibility?

d) What supporting facts or evidence should Kwong include with his application letter?

e) How will Kwong get his audience's attention?

YOUR TASK

Write the letter. Apply the guidelines for writing persuasive messages that Chapter 10 discusses.

Practise Your Knowledge

Read the following documents and then (1) analyze the strengths and weaknesses of each sentence and (2) revise each document so that it follows this chapter's guidelines.

DOCUMENT 10.A: WRITING PERSUASIVE REQUESTS FOR ACTION

At Tolson Auto Repair, we have been in business for over 25 years. We stay in business by always taking into account what the customer wants. That's why we are writing. We want to know your opinions to be able to better conduct our business.

Take a moment right now and fill out the enclosed questionnaire. We know everyone is busy, but this is just one way we have of ensuring that our people do their jobs correctly. Use the enclosed envelope to return the questionnaire.

And again, we're happy you chose Tolson Auto Repair. We want to take care of all your auto needs.

DOCUMENT 10.B: WRITING PERSUASIVE CLAIMS AND REQUESTS FOR ADJUSTMENT

Dear TechStar Computing:

I'm writing to you because of my disappointment with my new multimedia PC display. The display part works all right, but the audio volume is set too high and the volume knob doesn't turn it down. It's driving us crazy. The volume knob doesn't seem to be connected to anything but simply spins around. I can't believe you would put out a product like this without testing it first.

I depend on my computer to run my small business and want to know what you are going to do about it. This reminds me of every time I buy electronic equipment from what seems like any company. Something is always wrong. I thought quality was supposed to be important, but I guess not.

Anyway, I need this fixed right away. Please tell me what you want me to do.

DOCUMENT 10.C: WRITING SALES LETTERS

We know how awful dining hall food can be, and that's why we've developed the "Mealaweek Club." Once a week, we'll deliver food to your dormitory or apartment. Our meals taste great. We have pizza, buffalo wings, hamburgers, curly fries, veggie wraps, and more!

When you sign up for just six months, we will ask what day you want your delivery. We'll ask you to fill out your selection of meals. And the rest is up to us. At Mealaweek, we deliver! And payment is easy. We accept MasterCard and Visa or a personal cheque. It will save money especially when compared to eating out.

Simply fill out the enclosed card and indicate your method of payment. As soon as we approve your credit or cheque, we'll begin delivery. Tell all your friends about Mealaweek. We're the best idea since sliced bread!

Exercises

10.1 Teamwork: Analyzing the Persuasive Strategy
With another student, analyze the persuasive memo to Eleanor Tran at Host Marriott (Figure 10–2) by answering the following questions:
a. What techniques are used to capture the reader's attention?
b. Does the writer use the direct or the indirect organizational approach? Why?
c. Is the subject line effective? Why or why not?
d. Does the writer use an emotional or a logical appeal? Why?
e. What reader benefits are included?
f. How does the writer establish credibility?
g. What tools does the writer use to reinforce his position?

10.2 Composing Subject Lines: Capturing Attention
Compose effective subject lines for the following persuasive messages:
a. an email request to your supervisor to purchase a new high-speed colour laser printer for your office. You've outsourced quite a bit of your printing to AlphaGraphics, and you're certain this printer will pay for itself in six months.
b. a letter to area residents soliciting customers for your new business, "Meals à la Car," a carryout dining service that delivers from most local restaurants. All local restaurant menus are on the internet. Mom and Dad can dine on egg rolls and chow mein while the kids munch on pepperoni pizza.
c. a memo to the company president requesting that managers be allowed to carry over their unused vacation days to the following year. Apparently, many managers cancelled their fourth-quarter vacation plans to work on the installation of a new company computer system. Under their current contract, vacation days not used by December 31 can't be carried over to the following year.

10.3 Ethical Choices: Persuasion or Manipulation?
Your boss has asked you to post a message on the company's internal blog urging everyone in your department to donate money to the company's favourite charity, an organization that operates a special summer camp for physically challenged children. You wind up writing a lengthy posting packed with facts and heartwarming anecdotes about the camp and the children's experiences. When you must work that hard to persuade your audience to take an action such as donating money to a charity, aren't you being manipulative and unethical? Explain.

10.4 Focusing on Benefits: Features vs. Benefits
Determine whether the following sentences focus on features or benefits; rewrite as necessary to focus all the sentences on benefits.
a. All-Cook skillets are coated with a durable, patented non-stick surface.
b. You can call anyone and talk as long as you like on Saturdays and Sundays with our new FamilyTalk wireless plan.
c. With 8-millisecond response time, the Samsung LN-S4095D 40-inch LCD TV delivers fast video action that is smooth and crisp.[24]

10.5 Internet: Telemarketing and Deceptive Practices
Visit the *Canadian Consumer Handbook* website at www.ic.gc.ca/eic/site/oca-bc.nsf/eng/h_ca02349.html and open the PDF version. Read the section on telemarketing (p. 40). Think about telemarketing calls you've recently received and consider whether they used deceptive practices. What does the *Canadian Consumer Handbook* suggest you do before purchasing a telemarketer's products or services?

Cases APPLYING THE THREE-STEP WRITING PROCESS TO CASES

Apply each step to the following cases, as assigned by your instructor.

Planning	Writing	Completing

Analyze the Situation
Identify both your general purpose and your specific purpose. Clarify exactly what you want your audience to think, feel, or believe after receiving your message. Profile your primary audience, including their backgrounds, differences, similarities, and likely reactions to your message.

Gather Information
Identify the information your audience will need to receive, as well as other information you may need in order to craft an effective message.

Select the Right Medium
Make sure your medium is both acceptable to the audience and appropriate for the message.

Organize the Information
Choose a direct or indirect approach based on the audience and the message; most persuasive messages employ an indirect approach (often following the AIDA model). Identify your main idea, limit your scope, then outline necessary support points and other evidence.

Adapt to Your Audience
Show sensitivity to audience needs with a "you" attitude, politeness, positive emphasis, and bias-free language. Understand how much credibility you already have—and how much you may need to establish with any particular audience. Project your company's image by maintaining an appropriate style and tone.

Compose the Message
Draft your message using precise language, effective sentences, and coherent paragraphs. Support your claims with objective evidence; balance emotional and logical arguments.

Revise the Message
Evaluate content and review readability, then edit and rewrite for conciseness and clarity.

Produce the Message
Use effective design elements and suitable layout for a clean, professional appearance.

Proofread the Message
Review for errors in layout, spelling, and mechanics.

Distribute the Message
Deliver your message using the chosen medium; make sure all documents and all relevant files are distributed successfully.

1   **2**   **3**

Persuasive Requests for Action
| Blogging SKILLS | | Portfolio BUILDER |

1. That's the point: Email encouraging your boss to blog
You've tried for months to convince your boss, Will Florence, to start blogging. You've told him that top executives in numerous industries now use blogging as a way to connect with customers and other stakeholders without going through the filters and barriers of formal corporate communications. He was just about convinced—until he looked at the GM Fast-Lane blog site, where General Motors executives and managers write about current GM products and issues.

"Look at this!" he calls from his office. "Some of the most respected executives in the world, and all these people are criticizing them. Sure, a lot of the responses are positive, but quite a few are openly hostile, disagreeing with GM strategy, criticizing the products, criticizing the subjects he chooses for his blog—you name it. If blogging is all about opening yourself up to criticism from every bystander with a keyboard, no way am I going to start a blog."

Your Task: Write Florence an email (w_florence@sprenco .com) persuading him that the freewheeling nature of blog communication is its key advantage, not a disadvantage at all.

While they may not always agree with what he has to say, automotive enthusiasts and car buyers respect Lutz for communicating in his own words—and for giving them the opportunity to respond. For background information, read some postings by GM executives at http://fastlane. gmblogs.com.[25]

Email SKILLS

2. Give a little to get a lot: Suggesting free wireless at Starbucks
Like many students at your school, you like to escape from your cramped apartment to work on projects at local coffee shops. With your wireless-equipped laptop, you hunt for places that offer free wireless so that you can access course websites, do research, and check out your friends on Facebook. But there's a problem: At the Starbucks right around the corner, you have to pay for wireless access through the service offered by C-Mobile. Several locally owned coffee houses offer free wireless, but the closest one is two kilometres from your apartment. That's a long walk in winter.

Your Task: Write a persuasive message to Starbucks suggesting that the company drop its agreement with C-Mobile and offer free wireless instead. Convince the firm that free wireless will attract enough additional coffee-buying customers to offset the loss of revenue from wireless—and help Starbucks overcome the "big corporation" image that prompts some coffee drinkers to patronize locally owned establishments instead. While you don't have the data to prove that the cost of offering free wireless would be more than offset by increased coffee sales, at least make a convincing argument that Starbucks should consider making the change. You'll send an email to Starbucks through its contact page at www. starbucks.ca. Keep your message to 2600 characters to ensure conciseness.[26]

3 Always urgent: Memo pleading case for hosting a Canadian Blood Services mobile clinic
This morning as you drove to your job as desk clerk at the Midwood Community Centre in Saint John, New Brunswick, you were concerned to hear on the radio that the local Canadian Blood Services chapter put out a call for blood because national supplies have fallen dangerously low. During highly publicized disasters, people are emotional and eager to help out by donating blood. But in calmer times, only 5 percent of eligible donors think of giving blood. You're one of those few.

Not many people realize that donated blood lasts for only 72 hours. Consequently, the mainstay of emergency blood supplies must be replenished in an ongoing effort.

Donated blood helps victims of accidents and disease, as well as surgery patients. Just yesterday you were reading about a girl named Melissa, who was diagnosed with multiple congenital heart defects and underwent her first open-heart surgery at one week old. Now 5, she's used well over 50 units of donated blood, and she wouldn't be alive without them. In a thank-you letter, her mother lauded the many strangers who had "given a piece of themselves" to save her precious daughter— and countless others. You also learned that a donor's pint of blood can benefit up to four other people.

Today, you're going to do more than just roll up your own sleeve. You know the local CBS chapter sets up a mobile clinic at fire stations, schools, and community centres. What if you could convince Midwood's board of directors to support a blood clinic? The meeting rooms and fitness centre are usually full, and people who've never visited before might come out to donate blood. With materials from CBS, you're confident you can organize the Centre's hosting effort and handle the promotion. (Last year you headed Midwood's successful Toys for Tots drive.)

To give blood, one must be healthy, at least 17 years old (with an age limit of 71), and weigh at least 110 pounds. Donors can give every 56 days. You will distribute information about donating, urging potential donors to make an appointment and to eat well, drink water, and be rested before the clinic is set up.

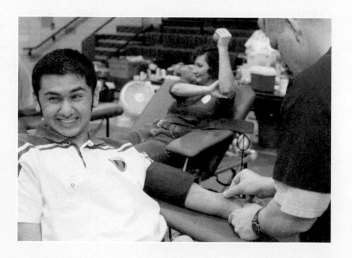

The CBS's mission statement says that "Canadian Blood Services operates Canada's blood supply in a manner that gains the trust, commitment, and confidence of all Canadians by providing a safe, secure, cost-effective, affordable, and accessible supply of quality blood, blood products, and their alternatives."

Your Task: Write a memo persuading the Midwood Community Centre's board of directors to host a public Canadian Blood Services blood drive. You can learn more about what's involved in hosting a blood drive at www.bloodservices.ca (click "How Can I Get Involved?"). Ask the board to provide bottled water, orange juice, and snacks for donors. You'll organize food service workers to handle the distribution, but you'll need the board's approval to let your team volunteer during work hours. Use a combination of logical and emotional appeals.[27]

Email SKILLS

4. Caribbean Recognition: Email to city council

The request seems simple enough: members of the Caribbean Business Association of your city have asked the city council to erect two signs designating the neighbourhood where many Caribbean businesses are located as the Caribbean Business District. The area has been home to your family's restaurant, Island Tastes, for many years.

But some members of the community complained when the issue was brought up during a city council session. "We should be focusing on unifying the community as a whole and its general diversity," they argued, "not dividing the city up into small ethnic districts." Some council members had been intrigued, however, by the prospect of creating a new tourist destination by marking the Caribbean Business District officially—that's what it actually is and has been for as long as you can remember. However, the issue was tabled for later consideration.

As the manager of your family's restaurant, you agree with those council members who think the designation would attract visitors. Moreover, the Caribbean Business Association has returned to the city council with an offer to pay for the cement structures that will designate the neighbourhood as the Caribbean Business District. The Association is willing to spend up to $30 000 for the design and installation of the signs.

Your Task: As a member of the Caribbean Business Association, you've been asked to support the request with an email message to Cathy Stanford, your city's deputy mayor, at cstandford@council.yc.[28]

5. No more driving: Memo about telecommuting to Bachman, Trinity, and Smith

Sitting in your Toronto office at the accounting firm of Bachman, Trinity, and Smith, clacking away on your computer, it seems as though you could be doing this work from your home. You haven't spoken to any co-workers in more than two hours. As long as you complete your work on time, does your location matter?

As an entry-level accountant, you've participated in on-location audits at major companies for nearly a year now. If your bosses trust you to work while staying at a hotel, why not let you work from home, where you already have an office with a computer, phone, and fax machine? You'd love to regain those two hours you lose commuting to and from work every day.

Your Task: To support this idea, visit the website of the International Telework Association and Council at www.telecommute.org (ensure that you check out the "Telework Facts" page). You'll find statistics and other support for a memo persuading your boss, senior partner Marjorie Bachman, to grant you a six-month trial as a telecommuter.[29]

6. Helping out: Persuasive memo to Good Eats store managers

Good Eats is a chain of organic food stores with locations in Ottawa. The stores are big and well lit, like their more traditional grocery store counterparts. They are also teeming with a wide variety of attractively displayed foods and related products.

However, Good Eats is different from the average supermarket. Its products include everything from granola sold in bulk to environmentally sensitive household products. The meats sold come from animals that were never fed antibiotics, and the cheese is from cows said to be raised on small farms and treated humanely.

Along with selling these products to upscale shoppers, the company has been giving food to homeless shelters. Every third weekend, Good Eats donates non-perishable food to three soup kitchens downtown. Company executives believe they are in a unique position to help others.

You work for the chief operating officer of Good Eats. You've been asked to find ways to expand the donation program by involving the company's eight branches, most of which are in the suburbs. Ideally, the company would be able to increase the number of people it helps and to get more of its employees involved.

You don't have a great deal of extra money for the program, so the emphasis has to be on using resources already available to the stores. One idea is to use trucks from suburban branches to make the program mobile. Another idea is to join forces with a retail chain to give food and clothing to individuals. The key is to be original and not exclude any idea, no matter how absurd it might seem. The only stipulation is to keep ideas politically neutral. Good Eats executives do not want to be seen as supporting any party or candidate. They just want to be good corporate citizens.

Your Task: Send persuasive memos to all managers at Good Eats requesting ideas to expand the program. Invite employees to contribute ideas, for this or any other charitable project for the company.[30]

Persuasive Claims and Requests for Adjustment

| Email SKILLS |

7. Too good to be true: Email to Western Tel requesting adjustment

Western Tel offered its pager services for a mere $5 a month. You purchased an inexpensive pager and signed a contract for two years. After you thought your pager phone number was up and running for two weeks, you heard from co-workers and clients that they repeatedly got a busy signal when dialling your pager number. You call Western Tel, and they resolve the problem—but doing so takes an additional week. You don't want to be charged for the time the pager wasn't in service. After discussing the situation with the local manager, she asks you to contact Judy Hinkley at the company's regional business office.

Your Task: Send an email message to Hinkley at Judy@westerntel.com and request an adjustment to your account. Request credit or partial credit for one month of service. Remember to write a summary of events in chronological order, supplying exact dates for maximum effectiveness.

8. Endless trouble: Claim letter to Abe's Pool Installation

As chief administrator, you worked hard to convince the board of directors of Westlake Therapy and Rehabilitation Centre that a small 2.5-by-4.5–metre Endless Pool would be a wonderful addition to the facility.

Because the pool produces an adjustable current flow, a swimmer can swim "endlessly" against it, never reaching the pool's edge. With this new invention by a Philadelphia manufacturer, your patients could experience a complete range of water therapy in a year-round indoor pool small enough to fit in a standard living room! The board agreed, choosing the optional two-metre depth, which would allow for additional therapeutic uses but would require a special platform and installation in a room with a high ceiling.

The old gymnasium would become your new Water Therapy Pavilion. Total cost with custom features: $20 080, plus $8000 budgeted for installation.

According to the manufacturer, "The Endless Pool has been designed as a kit for bolt-together assembly. It can be assembled by two reasonably handy people with no prior installation experience following detailed procedural videos." You can do it yourself, they proclaim, or hire a local contractor.

You've hired Abe's Pool Installation, which will build the special access platform and install the pool. You passed along the instructional videos, along with the manufacturer's hotline numbers. They've offered a pre-installation engineering consultation for your customized pool, without additional charge, as you told Abe. They'll also be glad to help determine whether the planned site can handle the pool's 10-tonne filled weight. Abe nodded and told you not to worry.

Finally, Abe's crew completed the platform and amid much excitement from your staff, assembled the galvanized steel pool. At a grand ribbon-cutting dedication ceremony, you personally flipped the switch.

Immediately the hydraulic motor began moving 140 000 litres of water per minute through a grille at the front, which smoothes and straightens the current. Everyone's excitement grew as the first wave of water washed down the centre of the pool. But instead of entering the turning vane arrays (which were supposed to recirculate the water through hidden channels back to the front of the pool), the water kept going, splashing out the back of the pool onto the platform and the gathered onlookers . . . at 140 000 litres per minute. Panic and shouts erupted as you fumbled quickly to turn the thing off.

Final damage included a collapsed platform, a ruined floor, an incorrectly installed pool, and numerous dry-cleaning bills from onlookers. Fortunately, no one was hurt. Estimated cost, including floor repair: $10 000. Abe is not returning your phone calls. But local reporters are coming to film the damage tomorrow, and it's your job to conduct their tour.

Your Task: Write a claim letter to Abe Hanson, Owner, Abe's Pool Installation, 7650 Fort Sheppard Dr., Nelson, British Columbia, V1L 6A5.[31]

| Email SKILLS |

9. Tangled Web: Email to PurelySoftware regarding an online order duplication

Last week you ordered new design software for your boss, Martin Soderburgh, at ArtAlive, the small art consulting business where you work. As he requested, you used his Visa card to order Adobe InDesign and Adobe Photoshop from an internet vendor, PurelySoftware.com.

When you didn't receive the usual email order confirmation, you called the company's toll-free number. The operator said the company's website was having problems, and he took a second order over the phone: $649.00 for Adobe InDesign and $564.00 for Adobe Photoshop, including tax and shipping. Four days later, ArtAlive received two shipments of the software, and your boss's credit card was charged $1213.00 twice, for a total of $2426.00.

Your Task: Technically, you authorized both orders. But you understood during the phone call that the first order was cancelled, although you have no written proof. Send a persuasive email to customerservice@purelysoftware.com, requesting (1) an immediate credit to your boss's Visa account and (2) a postage-paid return label for the duplicate order.[32]

Marketing and Sales Messages
| Podcasting SKILLS |

10. Listen up: Podcast promoting a podcast station

Podcasting, the technique of recording individual sound files that people download from the internet to listen to on their computers or music players, is quickly redefining the concept of radio. A growing crowd of musicians, essayists, journalists, and others with compelling content use podcasting to reach audiences they can't get to through traditional broadcast radio. The good news is that anyone with a microphone and a computer can record podcasts. That's also the bad news, at least from your perspective as a new podcaster: With so many podcasters now on the internet, potential listeners have thousands and thousands of audio files to select from.

Your new podcast, School2Biz, offers advice to business students making the transition from college or university to career. You provide information on everything from preparing résumés to interviewing to finding one's place in the business world and building a successful career. As you expand your audience, you'd eventually like to turn School2Biz into a profitable operation (perhaps by selling advertising time during your podcasts). For now, you're simply offering free advice.

Your Task: You've chosen The Podcast Bunker (www.podcastbunker.com) as the first website on which to promote School2Biz. The site lets podcasters promote their feeds with brief text listings, such as this description of Pet Talk Radio: "A weekly lifestyle show for people with more than a passing interest in pets. Hosted by Brian Pickering and Kaye Browne with Australia's favourite vet Dr. Harry Cooper and animal trainer Steve Austin."

Write a 50-word description of your new podcast, making up any information you need to describe School2Biz. Ensure that you mention who you are and why the information you present is worth listening to.[33]

11. Letter promoting your province for business
Your provincial government works hard to attract businesses that are considering expanding or relocating entirely from another province. Your office has services and resources that reach out to these companies and oversee the incentive programs the province offers to both new and established businesses.

Your Task: As an assistant in the communication office of your provincial government, you play an important role in reaching out to companies that want to expand or relocate to your area. Research the business pages on your provincial government's website and review the reasons why a business would find it desirable to relocate to your province. Summarize these reasons in a form letter that will be sent to business executives throughout the country. Ensure that you introduce yourself and your purpose in the letter, and close with a compelling call to action (have them reach you by telephone at 800-555-2930 or by email at your office, e.g., yourname@yourprovince.ca). As you plan your letter, imagine yourself as the CEO of a company and consider what a complex choice it would be to move to another province.

Portfolio BUILDER
12. Outsourcing: Letter from Kelly Services offering solutions
In 1946, with his dynamic vision and pioneering spirit, William Russell Kelly started a new company to meet the office and clerical needs of Detroit-area businesses. Kelly temporary employees with skills in calculating, inventory, typing, and copying were soon in great demand. During the 1960s, the Kelly Girl became an American icon, synonymous with high-quality

temporary employees. The company changed its name to Kelly Services, Inc. in 1966, reflecting the increasing diversity of its services, customers, and employees.

Today, Kelly Services is a global Fortune 500 company offering staffing solutions that include temporary services, staff leasing, outsourcing, vendor on-site, and full-time placement, including global services in Canada. Kelly provides employees who have a wide range of skills across many disciplines including office services, accounting, engineering, information technology, law, science, marketing, light industrial, education, health care, and home care.

Workforce needs, in terms of quantity and skills mix, fluctuate greatly. At the same time, employees have adaptable skills and are far more mobile. The result is that more employers and employees alike want flexible staffing arrangements, and temporary staffing is often the best solution.

Companies use Kelly Services to strategically balance workload and workforces during peaks and valleys of demand, to handle special projects, and to evaluate employees prior to making a full-time hiring decision. This dramatic change in business has spurred the rapid growth of the contingent employment industry.

In turn, many individuals are choosing the flexibility of personal career management, increasing options of where, when, and how to work. It is now the desire of many employees to fit their work into their lifestyles, rather than fitting their lifestyles into their work. Therefore, more and more workers are becoming receptive to being a contract, temporary, or consulting employee.

This flexibility offers advantages to both the company and the employee. Both have the opportunity to evaluate one another prior to making a long-term commitment. Kelly Services earns a fee when its employees are hired permanently, but employers find that it's a small price to pay for such valuable preview time, which saves everyone the cost and pain of a bad hiring decision.

Kelly has received many supplier awards for providing outstanding and cost-efficient staffing services, including Daimler-Chrysler's Gold Award, Ford Motor Company's Q1 Preferred Quality Award, Intel Corporation's Supplier Continuous Quality Improvement (SCQI) Award, and DuPont Legal's Challenge Award.

A job as a marketing manager with Kelly holds challenge and promise. With 2500 offices in 26 countries, Kelly provides its customers nearly 650 000 employees annually, generating revenue of $5.5 billion in 2008. The company provides staffing solutions to more than 90 percent of the Fortune 500 companies.

As companies increasingly face new competitive pressures to provide better service and quality at lower prices, many are turning to outsourcing suppliers to deliver complete operational management of specific functions or support departments, allowing the company the necessary time to focus on its core competencies. One solution is to choose a single supplier such as the Kelly Management Services (KMS) division to deliver "full-service" outsourcing.

KMS combines management experience, people process improvements, technology enhancements, and industry expertise to optimize customer operations and reduce cost. KMS understands the unique challenges companies face in today's increasingly fast-paced business world and can provide customers with services across multiple functional offerings including Call Centre Operations, Warehousing, Distribution and Light Assembly, Back Office and Administrative functions, and Mail and Reprographic services. The result is a department staffed by employees that can fluctuate as a company's needs change.

KMS customers who have implemented one service often add others when they see KMS-managed employees performing at high levels and producing substantial cost savings and operational efficiencies. By partnering with an outsourcing supplier such as KMS, companies will experience a greater value and cost savings than with in-house operations.

Your Task: Write a sales letter to companies similar to DaimlerChrysler, Ford, Intel, and DuPont explaining what Kelly has to offer. For current information, visit the Kelly website at www.kellyservices.ca.[34]

Portfolio BUILDER

13. Greener cleaners: Letter promoting "environmentally sound" franchise

When you told everyone you aspired to work for an environmentally responsible business, you didn't imagine you'd be in dry-cleaning. But now that you are director of franchise development for Hangers Cleaners, you go home every night with a "clean conscience" (your favourite new pun).

Co-founders Joseph DeSimone, James McClain, and Timothy Romack established Micell Technologies, Inc. in 1995 after research resulted in the first breakthrough in dry-cleaning technology in nearly 50 years. They developed a cleaning process, called Micare, which uses liquid carbon dioxide (CO_2) and specially developed detergents to clean clothes. There's no heat required and no further need for the toxic perchloroethylene (perc) or petroleum traditionally used in dry cleaning.

In 2001 Micell sold all licensing, all intellectual property, and all interest in Hangers cleaners to Cool Clean Technologies, which now manufactures the "CO2OL Clean" dry-cleaning machine that your franchise relies on. Hangers franchise owners don't have to deal with regulatory paperwork, zoning restrictions, or expensive insurance and taxes for hazardous waste disposal. And unlike petroleum-based solvents, the CO_2 used in the CO2OL Clean machine is non-combustible. It's the same substance that carbonates beverages, and it's captured from the waste stream of industries that produce it as a by-product. Moreover, 98 percent of the CO_2 used in a Hangers outlet is recycled and used again, which helps keep prices competitive. A leading consumer products group recently rated the CO2OL Clean machine the best dry-cleaning alternative.

You've already sold franchises in three provinces and 23 states. Customers love the fact that their clothes don't carry toxic fumes after cleaning, and employees are happy to be working in a safe and cool environment. The process is actually gentler on clothes (no strong solvents or heat), reducing fading and shrinking and helping them last longer. You aren't dry cleaners, you're "garment care specialists."

And beyond the progressive corporate atmosphere, you simply love the design of Hangers stores. When Micell originally established the chain, it hired dry-cleaning experts and architects alike to come up with a sleek, modern, high-end retail "look" that features a cool, clean, light-filled interior and distinctive signage out front. It's more akin to a Starbucks than the overheated, toxic-smelling storefront most customers associate with dry cleaning. This high-end look is making it easier to establish Hangers as a national brand, attracting investors and franchisees rapidly as word spreads about the new "greener cleaner."

Your Task: Develop a sales letter that can be mailed in response to preliminary inquiries from potential franchise owners. You'll include brochures covering franchise agreements and CO2OL Clean specifics, so focus instead on introducing and promoting the unique benefits of Hangers Cleaners. Your contact information is Hangers Cleaners, 3505 County Road 42 West, Burnsville, MN 55306-3803; phone 952-882-5000; toll-free 866-262-9274.[35]

IM SKILLS

14. Instant promotion: Text message from Hilton Hotels to frequent guests

Hilton Hotels now uses an SMS (short messaging service) to send instant text promotions to customers who've signed up as "HHonors" members. But you work in marketing, and that means you're often struggling to condense elaborate travel packages into 65 enticing words (system maximum).

For example, today's promotion offers "A Golfer's Dream Come True: 'I just played a round of golf by the pyramids!'" For $575 per person per day (double room), valid through January 18, 2009, travellers can stay in the Hilton Pyramids Golf Resort in Cairo, Egypt, for 7 nights/8 days, including breakfast, service charge, and tax. They'll be met at the airport, given transportation to the resort, plus two rounds of golf per person at Dreamland Golf course and two rounds of golf per person at Soleimaneia Pyramids Golf & Country Club course. That's 88 words so far.

But you also need to convey that the Dreamland course wraps like a serpent around the Hilton resort. Its lush greens and lakes, designed by Karl Litten, contrast sharply with the golden desert, culminating in a stunning view of the great Pyramids of Giza, one of the Seven Wonders of the World. The Soleimaneia course features the "biggest floodlit driving course in Egypt." The travel package provides free transportation to this nearby course.

Rates, of course, are subject to availability and other restrictions may apply. But interested travellers should mention code G7 Pyramids Golf Special when they call Hilton Reservations Worldwide. They can also email RM_PYRAMIDS_GOLF@hilton.com, or call the Cairo hotel directly at 20 2 8402402. That is, if you can entice them in 65 words.

Your Task: Write the persuasive instant message.[36]

| IM SKILLS |

15. Helping children: Instant message holiday fund drive at IBM

At IBM, you're one of the coordinators for the annual Employee Charitable Contributions Campaign. Since 1978, the company has helped employees contribute to more than 2000 health and human service agencies. These groups may offer child care, treat substance abuse, provide health services, or fight illiteracy, homelessness, and hunger. Some offer disaster relief or care for the elderly. All deserve support. They're carefully screened by IBM, one of the largest corporate contributors of cash, equipment, and people to non-profit organizations and educational institutions, in Canada, the United States, and around the world. As your literature states, the program "has engaged our employees more fully in the important mission of corporate citizenship."

During the winter holidays, you target agencies that cater to the needs of displaced families, women, and children. It's not difficult to raise enthusiasm. The prospect of helping children enjoy the holidays—children who otherwise might have nothing—usually awakens the spirit of your most distracted workers. But some of them wait until the last minute and then forget.

They have until Wednesday, December 16, to come forth with cash contributions. To make it in time for holiday deliveries, they can also bring in toys, food, and blankets through Monday, December 21. They shouldn't have any trouble finding the collection bins; they're everywhere, marked with bright red banners. But some will want to call you with questions or (hopefully) to make credit card contributions; they can reach you at 800-555-3899, ext. 3342.

Your Task: It's December 14. Write a 75- to 100-word instant message encouraging last-minute gifts.[37]

Planning Reports and Proposals

LEARNING OBJECTIVES

After studying this chapter, you will be able to

1. Distinguish between informational reports, analytical reports, and proposals
2. Describe an effective process for conducting business research
3. Define primary and secondary research, and explain when you use each method
4. Evaluate the credibility of an information source, and conduct an effective online search
5. Outline an effective process for planning and conducting information interviews
6. Explain the differences between drafting a summary, drawing a conclusion, and developing a recommendation
7. Discuss three major ways to organize analytical reports

ON THE JOB

Communicating at Dell Inc.
STAYING ON TOP OF THE COMPUTER WORLD
www.dell.com

Ranked number one in North America and number two globally, Dell Inc. maintains its prominence by listening to customers to understand how technology can address their business requirements. Founded by Michael Dell in 1984, the company is renowned as the fastest growing computer firm in history, serving the public sector, large enterprise, small business and individual consumers. As recent financial reports show, over the ten-year period from 1998 to 2008, revenue rose from $12 billion to $61 billion—in Michael Dell's words, "a remarkable achievement by any count."

Flexibility is one reason for Dell's market prominence. For example, in the early 1990s, the company briefly experimented with selling consumer computers in retail outlets. But after studying retail sales reports that were based on careful data analysis, Michael Dell determined that selling directly to consumers online and by phone were the most profitable approaches for his business and, in 1994, abandoned the in-store venture. However, in 2007, Dell re-established retail partnerships with Wal-Mart, Staples, Best Buy, and other major chains, such as Gome in China. New reports examining market trends indicated that the "walk model," as Michael Dell calls traditional shopping, was now a profitable complement to the click and talk methods. In 2009, Dell consumer products were available in more than 40 000 retail outlets worldwide, contributing to the company's financial success.

Dell Inc., a leading global computer systems company, designs, manufactures, and customizes products and services to customer requirements, offering an extensive selection of hardware, software, and peripherals. In the fast-paced world of computer technology, the company relies on reports to keep up with industry trends, statistics, and issues.

Reports written at Dell Inc. must do more than simply summarize and present carefully researched data. They must analyze data to identify and discuss such pertinent issues as customer preferences, market trends, and industry developments. The company's 2008 interactive online annual report to shareholders is one example. Here, Dell discusses such matters as entry into emerging countries to gain new customers, environmental sustainability, and new services for consumers and business, such as online storage of digital records. This interactive report also features a video of Dell introducing the new media format, where visitors can jump to specific sections, follow links to further information, and connect to the DellShares blog to read more investor news.

If you wrote reports for Dell, you would need to decide on your reporting medium, focus your problem, plan your overall strategy, and conduct research. How would you break down your tasks and approach writing reports for Dell Inc.?[1]

Applying the Three-Step Writing Process to Reports and Proposals

Reports play a significant role in Dell Inc.'s success, as they do for all high-achieving companies. Whether you prepare or receive them, reports are the foundation of sound decisions and solutions. Reports fall into three basic categories:

Objective 1 Distinguish between informational reports, analytical reports, and proposals.

1. **Informational reports** provide data, facts, feedback, and other types of information, without analysis or recommendations.
2. **Analytical reports** provide both information and analysis, and they can also include recommendations.
3. **Proposals** provide a structured, persuasive rationale for internal or external audiences.

The nature of these reports varies widely, from one-page trip reports that follow a standard format to detailed business plans and proposals that can run hundreds of pages. Figure 11–1 shows the major subcategories within each of the three major report categories, along with examples of the more common types. No matter what the circumstances, view every business report as an opportunity to demonstrate your understanding of your audience's challenges and your ability to contribute to your organization's success.

The purpose and content of business reports varies widely; in some cases you'll follow a strict guideline, but in others the organization and format will be up to you.

The three-step process you studied (see Chapters 4 to 6) and applied to short messages (see Chapters 7 to 10) is easy to adapt to longer message formats (see Figure 11–2). This chapter addresses the planning step, focusing on two major areas that require special attention in long documents: gathering and organizing information. Chapter 12 covers the writing step and also includes advice on creating effective visuals for your reports and proposals. Chapter 12 describes the tasks involved in completing reports and proposals.

Analyzing the Situation

The complexity of many reports and the amount of work involved put a premium on carefully analyzing the situation before you begin to write. Pay special attention to your **statement of purpose**, which explains *why* you are preparing the report and *what* you plan to deliver in the report (see Table 11–1).

Given the length and complexity of many reports, it's crucial to define your purpose clearly, so you don't waste time with unnecessary rework.

> Figure 11–1 Common Types of Business Reports and Proposals

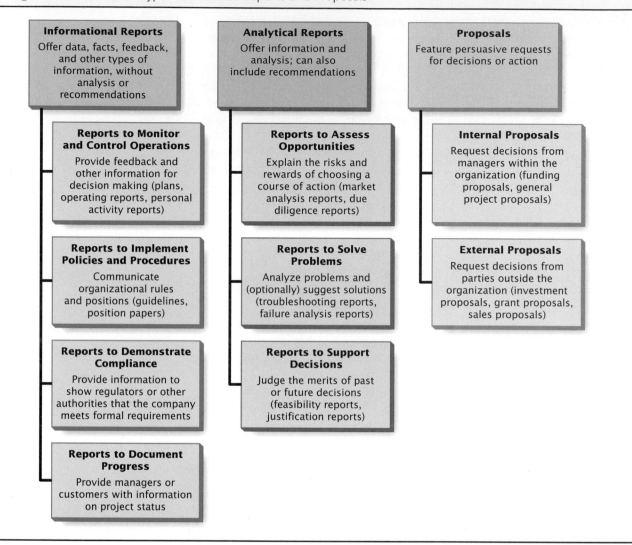

The most useful way to phrase your purpose statement is to begin with an infinitive phrase (*to* plus a verb), which helps pin down your general goal (e.g., *to inform, to identify, to analyze*). For example, in an informational report, your statement of purpose can be as simple as one of these:

To identify potential markets for our new phone-based video games

To update the board of directors on the progress of the research project

To submit required information to the Canadian Bankers Association

Longer reports may have several related purposes.

Your statement of purpose for an analytical report often needs to be more comprehensive. When Linda Moreno, the cost accounting manager for Electrovision, a high-tech company, was asked to find ways to reduce employee travel and entertainment costs, she phrased her statement of purpose accordingly:

. . . to analyze the T&E (travel and entertainment) budget, evaluate the impact of recent changes in airfares and hotel costs, and suggest ways to tighten management's control over T&E expenses.

> Figure 11–2 Three-Step Writing Process for Reports and Proposals

Planning	Writing	Completing
Analyze the Situation Clarify the problem or opportunity at hand, define your purpose, develop an audience profile, and develop a work plan. **Gather Information** Determine audience needs and obtain the information necessary to satisfy those needs; conduct a research project if necessary. **Select the Right Medium** Choose the best medium for delivering your message; consider delivery through multiple media. **Organize the Information** Define your main idea, limit your scope, select a direct or an indirect approach, and outline your content using an appropriate structure for an informational report, analytical report, or proposal.	**Adapt to Your Audience** Be sensitive to audience needs by using a "you" attitude, politeness, positive emphasis, and bias-free language. Build a strong relationship with your audience by establishing your credibility and projecting your company's image. Control your style with a tone and voice appropriate to the situation. **Compose the Message** Choose precise language that will help you create effective sentences and coherent paragraphs throughout the introduction, body, and close of your report or proposal.	**Revise the Message** Evaluate content and review readability; edit and rewrite for conciseness and clarity. **Produce the Message** Use effective design elements and suitable layout for a clean, professional appearance; seamlessly combine textual and graphical elements. **Proofread the Message** Review for errors in layout, spelling, and mechanics. **Distribute the Message** Deliver your report using the chosen medium; make sure all documents and all relevant files are distributed successfully.
1	**2**	**3**

Because Moreno was assigned an analytical report rather than an informational report, she had to go beyond merely collecting data; she had to draw conclusions and make recommendations. See her complete report in Chapter 13.

> Table 11–1 Problem Statements Versus Purpose Statements

Problem Statement	Statement of Purpose
Our company's market share is steadily declining.	To explore new ways of promoting and selling our products and to recommend the approaches most likely to stabilize our market share
Our current computer network lacks sufficient bandwidth and cannot be upgraded to meet our future needs.	To analyze various networking options and to recommend the system that will best meet our company's current and future needs
We need $2 million to launch our new product.	To convince investors that our new business would be a sound investment, so we can obtain desired financing
Our current operations are too decentralized and expensive.	To justify the closing of the Sudbury plant and the transfer of Ontario operations to a single Eastern location to save the company money

When writing a proposal, you must also be guided by a clear statement of purpose to help you focus on crafting a persuasive message. Here are several examples:

To secure funding in next year's budget for new conveyor systems in the warehouse

To get management approval to reorganize the North American sales force

To secure $2 million from outside investors to start production of the new titanium mountain bike

Remember, the more specific your purpose statement, the more useful it will be as a guide to planning your report. Furthermore, if you've been assigned the report by someone else, always double-check your statement of purpose with that person to ensure that you've interpreted the assignment correctly.

In addition to considering your purpose carefully, you will also want to prepare a *work plan* for most reports and proposals to make the best use of your time. For simpler reports, the work plan can be an informal list of tasks and a simple schedule. However, if you're preparing a lengthy report, particularly when you're collaborating with others, develop a more detailed work plan. This plan might include the following elements:

> **Statement of the problem or opportunity (for analytical reports and proposals):** The problem statement clarifies the challenge you face and helps you and anyone working with you stay focused on the core problem.

> **Statement of the purpose and scope of your investigation:** The purpose statement describes what you plan to accomplish with this report and, thus, the boundaries of your work. Stating which issues you'll cover and which issues you won't cover is especially important with complex, lengthy investigations.

> **Discussion of the tasks that need to be accomplished to complete the report:** Ensure that you indicate your sources of information, the research necessary, and any constraints (for example, on time, money, personnel, or data). This section helps establish your credibility as a researcher and the validity of your information.

> **Review of project assignments, schedules, and resource requirements:** Indicate who will be responsible for specific tasks, when tasks will be completed, any special needs, such as equipment and technical advice, and how much the investigation will cost. (Collaborative writing is discussed in detail in Chapter 2.)

> **Plans for following up after delivering the report:** Follow-up can be as simple as ensuring that people received the information they needed or as complex as conducting additional research to evaluate the outcome of the recommendations you made. Follow-up signals that you care about your work's effectiveness and its impact on the organization.

Some work plans also include a tentative outline, if the author has had the opportunity to think through the organization of the report. The work plan in Figure 11–3, which was developed for a report assessing whether to launch a company newsletter, includes such an outline. A formal work plan such as this is a vital tool for planning and managing complex writing projects. The preliminary outline here helps guide the research; the report writers may modify the outline when they begin writing the report.

In addition, project management charts are useful tools for scheduling and tracking tasks from start to finish. With graphical representation of project timelines and workflow, these charts are strong visual aids that can keep you and your collaborators organized. You can find many examples online, from simple to complex, by entering "project management software" in a search engine. Figure 11–4 is a simple example that can be adapted to your needs.

A detailed work plan saves time and often produces more effective reports.

> Figure 11–3 Work Plan for a Report

States the problem clearly enough for anyone to understand without additional research

Identifies the tasks to be accomplished and does so in clear, simple terms

Offers a preliminary outline to help readers understand the issues that will be addressed in the report

Identifies who is responsible for each task and when it will be completed

STATEMENT OF THE PROBLEM
The rapid growth of our company over the past five years has reduced the sense of community among our staff. People no longer feel like part of an intimate organization that values teamwork.

PURPOSE AND SCOPE OF WORK
The purpose of this study is to determine whether a company newsletter would help rebuild a sense of community within the workforce. The study will evaluate the impact of newsletters in other companies and will attempt to identify features that might be desirable in our own newsletter. Such variables as length, frequency of distribution, types of articles, and graphic design will be considered. Costs will be estimated for several approaches, including print and electronic versions. In addition, the study will analyze the personnel and procedures required to produce a newsletter.

SOURCES AND METHODS OF DATA COLLECTION
Sample newsletters will be collected from 10–20 companies similar to ours in size, growth rate, and types of employees. The editors will be asked to comment on the impact of their publications on employee morale. Our own employees will be surveyed to determine their interest in a newsletter and their preferences for specific features. Production procedures and costs will be analyzed through conversations with newsletter editors, printers, and our website development team.

PRELIMINARY OUTLINE
The preliminary outline for this study is as follows:
I. Do newsletters affect morale?
   A. Do people read them?
   B. How do employees benefit?
   C. How does the company benefit?
II. What are the features of good newsletters?
   A. How long are they?
   B. What do they contain?
   C. How often are they published?
   D. How are they designed?
III. How should a newsletter be produced?
   A. Should it be written and edited internally or externally?
   B. Should it be printed or produced electronically?
   C. If electronic, should it be formatted as email, a blog, or regular Web content?
IV. What would a newsletter cost?
   A. What would the personnel cost be?
   B. What would the material cost be?
   C. What would outside services cost?
V. Should we publish a company newsletter?
VI. If so, what approach should we take?

TASK ASSIGNMENTS AND SCHEDULE
Each phase of this study will be completed by the following dates:

Collect/analyze newsletters	Hank Waters	September 17, 2010
Interview editors by phone	Hank Waters	September 24, 2010
Survey employees	Julienne Cho	October 1, 2010
Develop sample	Hank Waters	October 8, 2010
Develop cost estimate	Julienne Cho	October 8, 2010
Prepare report	Hank Waters	October 22, 2010
Submit final report	Hank Waters	October 26, 2010

Explains exactly what will be covered by the research and included in the final report

> Figure 11–4 Project Management Chart

PROJECT: EMPLOYEE NEWSLETTER STUDY							
Collect & analyze newsletters	Hank Waters						
Interview editors by phone		Hank Waters					
Survey employees		Julienne Cho					
Develop sample				Hank Waters			
Develop cost estimate		Julienne Cho					
Prepare report					Hank Waters		
Submit final report							Hank Waters
	Sept. 1–17	Sept. 17–24	Sept. 24–Oct. 1	Oct. 1–Oct. 8	Oct. 8–15	Oct. 15–22	Oct. 22–26

Gathering Information

Some reports require formal research projects to gather all the necessary information.

The sheer volume of information needed for many reports and proposals requires careful planning—and may even require a separate research project just to acquire the data and information you need (see "Supporting Your Messages with Reliable Information" on page 354). To stay on schedule and on budget, ensure that you review both your statement of purpose and your audience's needs, so you collect all the information you need without wasting time on false leads or digressions. In some cases, you won't be able to collect every piece of information you'd like—for example, a primary source for an interview may be unavailable—so prioritize your needs before you begin your research and focus on the most important questions.

Selecting the Right Medium

The best medium for any given report might be anything from a professionally printed and bound document to an online executive dashboard that displays nothing but report highlights.

Just as you would for other business messages, select the medium for your report based on the needs of your audience and the practical advantages and disadvantages of the choices available to you. In addition to the general media selection criteria discussed in Chapter 4, consider several points for reports and proposals:

> **Audiences have specific media requirements.** You will have to follow company culture for distributing your report. Executives in many corporations now expect to review reports via their in-house intranets, sometimes in conjunction with an *executive dashboard,* a customized online presentation of key operating variables such as revenue, profits, quality, customer satisfaction, and project progress.
> **Audiences may want to provide written feedback on your report or proposal.** You will have to determine if your readers prefer to write comments on a printed document or to use the commenting and markup features in a word processing program or Adobe Acrobat.
> **Audiences may need to search through your document frequently or update it in the future.** Delivering a report as a word processor file makes both tasks far easier.
> **Audiences will assess your professional image according to your choice of media.** Technology provides a wide array of products and features for enhancing reports; however, any special effects you choose must suit the message. For example, a routine sales report dressed up in expensive multimedia will look like a waste of valuable company resources—and will affect how your readers view your abilities as an employee.

Organizing Your Information

The direct approach is by far the most popular and convenient for business reports; it saves time, makes the report easier to follow, and produces a more forceful report. You project confidence when you state your conclusions at the outset.

However, if the audience is unsure about your credibility or is not ready to accept your main idea without first seeing some reasoning or evidence, the indirect approach is a better choice because it gives you a chance to prove your points and gradually overcome audience reservations. You introduce your complete findings and discuss all supporting details before presenting your conclusions and recommendations. By deferring the conclusions and recommendations to the end of the report, you imply that you've weighed

> Figure 11–5 Direct Approach Versus Indirect Approach in an Introduction

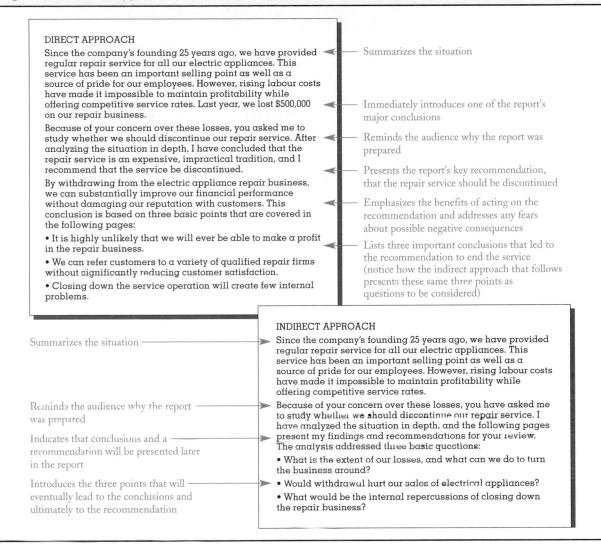

DIRECT APPROACH

Since the company's founding 25 years ago, we have provided regular repair service for all our electric appliances. This service has been an important selling point as well as a source of pride for our employees. However, rising labour costs have made it impossible to maintain profitability while offering competitive service rates. Last year, we lost $500,000 on our repair business.

Because of your concern over these losses, you asked me to study whether we should discontinue our repair service. After analyzing the situation in depth, I have concluded that the repair service is an expensive, impractical tradition, and I recommend that the service be discontinued.

By withdrawing from the electric appliance repair business, we can substantially improve our financial performance without damaging our reputation with customers. This conclusion is based on three basic points that are covered in the following pages:

• It is highly unlikely that we will ever be able to make a profit in the repair business.

• We can refer customers to a variety of qualified repair firms without significantly reducing customer satisfaction.

• Closing down the service operation will create few internal problems.

— Summarizes the situation

— Immediately introduces one of the report's major conclusions

— Reminds the audience why the report was prepared

— Presents the report's key recommendation, that the repair service should be discontinued

— Emphasizes the benefits of acting on the recommendation and addresses any fears about possible negative consequences

— Lists three important conclusions that led to the recommendation to end the service (notice how the indirect approach that follows presents these same three points as questions to be considered)

Summarizes the situation ——————

Reminds the audience why the report was prepared ——————

Indicates that conclusions and a recommendation will be presented later in the report ——————

Introduces the three points that will eventually lead to the conclusions and ultimately to the recommendation ——————

INDIRECT APPROACH

Since the company's founding 25 years ago, we have provided regular repair service for all our electric appliances. This service has been an important selling point as well as a source of pride for our employees. However, rising labour costs have made it impossible to maintain profitability while offering competitive service rates.

Because of your concern over these losses, you have asked me to study whether we should discontinue our repair service. I have analyzed the situation in depth, and the following pages present my findings and recommendations for your review. The analysis addressed three basic questions:

• What is the extent of our losses, and what can we do to turn the business around?

• Would withdrawal hurt our sales of electrical appliances?

• What would be the internal repercussions of closing down the repair business?

the evidence objectively without prejudging the facts. You also imply that you're subordinating your judgment to that of the audience, whose members are capable of drawing their own conclusions when they have access to all the facts.

However, the longer the message, the less effective an indirect approach is likely to be. Therefore, consider report length before deciding on the direct or indirect approach.

Both approaches have merit, so businesspeople often combine them, revealing their conclusions and recommendations as they go along, rather than putting them first or last. Figure 11–5 presents the introductions from two reports with the same general outline. In the direct version, a series of statements summarizes the conclusion reached about each main topic in the outline. In the indirect version, the same topics are introduced in the same order but without drawing any conclusions about them. Instead, the conclusions appear in the body of the report.

When you outline your content, use informative ("talking") headings rather than simple descriptive ("topical") headings (see Table 11–2). When in question or summary form, informative headings force you to think through the content carefully, rather than simply identify the general topic area. Using informative

> Table 11–2 Types of Outline Headings

Descriptive (Topical) Outline	Informative (Talking) Outline	
	Question Form	Summary Form

I. Industry Characteristics
  A. Annual sales
  B. Profitability
  C. Growth rate
    1. Sales
    2. Profit
	I. What is the nature of the industry?
	  A. What are the annual sales?
	  B. Is the industry profitable?
	  C. What is the pattern of growth?
	    1. Sales growth?
	    2. Profit growth?
		I. Flour milling is a mature industry.
		  A. Market is large.
		  B. Profit margins are narrow.
		  C. Growth is modest.
		    1. Sales growth averages less
		      than 3 percent a year.
		    2. Profits are flat.

You don't have to become an expert on every subject you undertake, but you must learn enough about the subject you're exploring to pose intelligent questions. How is research like exploration or detective work?

headings will not only help you plan more effectively but will also facilitate collaborative writing because it establishes common understanding of ideas and information. A heading such as "Industry characteristics" could have different meanings to each of the five people on your writing team, so use a heading that conveys a single, unambiguous meaning, such as "Flour milling is a mature industry."

For a quick review of adapting the three-step process to long reports, refer to "Checklist: Adapting the Three-Step Writing Process to Informational and Analytical Reports." The following sections provide specific advice on how to plan informational reports, analytical reports, and proposals.

Supporting Your Messages with Reliable Information

No matter what the subject of your report, audiences expect you to support your message with solid research. As you've probably discovered while doing school projects, research involves a lot more than simply typing a few terms into a search engine. Good research requires a clear process:

1. **Plan your research.** Planning is the most important step of any research project; a solid plan yields better results in less time.

CHECKLIST Adapting the Three-Step Writing Process to Informational and Analytical Reports

A. Analyze the situation.
✔ Define your purpose clearly before you start writing.
✔ Identify all of your goals in advance if you need to accomplish several in the report.
✔ Prepare a work plan to guide your efforts.

B. Gather information.
✔ Determine whether you need to launch a separate research project to collect the necessary information.
✔ Reuse or adapt existing material whenever possible.

C. Select the right medium.
✔ Base your decision on audience expectations (or requirements, as the case may be).

✔ Consider the need for commenting, revising, distributing, and storing.
✔ Remember that the medium you choose also sends a message.

D. Organize your information.
✔ Use a direct approach if your audience is receptive.
✔ Use an indirect approach if your audience is skeptical.
✔ Use an indirect approach when you don't want to risk coming across as arrogant.
✔ Combine approaches if that will help build support for your primary message.

2. **Locate the data and information you need.** The research plan tells you *what* to look for; your next step is to figure out *where* the data and information are and *how* to access them.

3. **Process the data and information you located.** The data and information you find probably won't be in a form you can use immediately and will require some processing, which might involve anything from statistical analysis to resolving the differences between two or more expert opinions.

4. **Apply your findings.** You can apply your research findings in three ways: summarizing information for someone else's benefit, drawing conclusions based on what you've learned, or developing recommendations.

5. **Manage information efficiently.** Many companies today try to maximize the return on the time and money they invest in business research by collecting and sharing research results in a variety of computer-based systems, known generally as **knowledge management systems**. At the very least, be sure to share your results with any colleagues who may be able to benefit from it.

You can see the sequence of these steps in Figure 11–6; the following sections offer more details, starting with planning your research.

Planning Your Research

With so much information online, it's tempting just to enter some keywords into a search engine and then dig through the results looking for something, anything, that looks promising. However, this haphazard approach limits both your effectiveness (you might not find the right information) and your efficiency (you might spend too much time and money on research).

To avoid expensive and embarrassing mistakes that can occur with poorly planned research, start by familiarizing yourself with the subject, so you can frame insightful questions. As you explore the general subject area, try to identify basic terminology, significant trends, important conflicts, influential people, and potential sources of information, such as industry publications, experts within your organization, and competitors' websites. Next, develop a **problem statement** that will define the purpose of your research—the decision you need to make or the conclusion you need to reach at the end of the process.

Then identify the most critical *information gaps*. An information gap is simply the difference between what you currently know and what you need to know. For example, if you had the problem statement of "find out what

Many of your business reports will require some level of research.

Objective 2 Describe an effective process for conducting business research.

Explore

Researching without a plan wastes time and usually produces unsatisfactory results.

> Figure 11–6 The Research Process

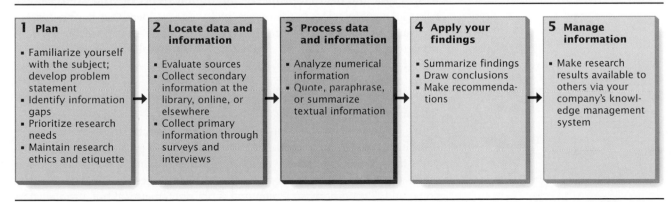

1 Plan	2 Locate data and information	3 Process data and information	4 Apply your findings	5 Manage information
• Familiarize yourself with the subject; develop problem statement • Identify information gaps • Prioritize research needs • Maintain research ethics and etiquette	• Evaluate sources • Collect secondary information at the library, online, or elsewhere • Collect primary information through surveys and interviews	• Analyze numerical information • Quote, paraphrase, or summarize textual information	• Summarize findings • Draw conclusions • Make recommendations	• Make research results available to others via your company's knowledge management system

percentage of new computers purchased in the last 30 days were Dell XPS laptops," you would need two key pieces of information: (1) the total number of laptop computers purchased and (2) the number of Dell XPS laptops purchased.

You can easily find the second piece of information by asking Dell's product management department. However, you might not have immediate access to the total number of laptops purchased. To fill this information gap, your company could subscribe to an independent research service that tracks the industry. Using the information-gap approach focuses your research on just those topics that you need to know about, and it saves you the time and expense of searching for answers that somebody in the organization already has.

> You'll never have enough time or money to answer every question that comes to mind, so setting priorities is a must.

As you begin listing questions to ask, compile more questions than you have time or money to answer. Moreover, if you interview or survey people to gather information, you'll need to limit the number of questions you ask, so you don't consume more time than people are willing to give. Consequently, you'll usually need to prioritize your information needs and concentrate on the most vital set of questions.

Being an Ethical Researcher

With a prioritized list of questions, you're almost ready to start your research. Before taking that step, however, it's important to be aware that research carries some significant ethical responsibilities. Your research tactics affect the people from whom you gather data and information, the people who read your results, and the people who are affected by the way you present those results. Refer to Appendix B, "Documentation of Report Sources," to learn how to cite your secondary and primary sources. To avoid ethical lapses, keep the following points in mind:

> Privacy is one of the most important issues in the research field today.

> **Don't force a specific outcome by skewing your research.** If you go in with strong biases or opinions, you're more likely to favour information that supports your position and gloss over information that doesn't. If you go in with an open mind and are willing to accept whatever you find, your research will be more valuable.

> **Respect the privacy of your research participants.** For example, don't observe people without their consent or publicly disclose personal information that you promised to keep private.[2]

> **Document sources and give appropriate credit.** Whether you use published documents, personal interviews, or company records, citing your sources is not only fair to the people who created and provided the information, but doing so also builds your credibility as a writer.

> **Respect the intellectual property and digital rights of your sources.** *Intellectual property* refers to the ownership of unique ideas that have commercial value in the marketplace.[3] Intellectual property laws cover everything from artists' works to industrial processes, so ensure that you can legally use the information you uncover.

> **Don't distort information from your sources.** For example, if an industry expert says that a sales increase is *possible*, don't quote her as saying that a sales increase is *probable*.

> **Don't misrepresent who you are or what you intend to do with the research results.** One prominent example of misrepresentation in recent years is known as *pretexting*, which is essentially lying about who you are (such as posing as a journalist) in order to gain access to information that you couldn't get otherwise. Pretexting is not only unethical but also illegal in many instances.[4]

In addition to ethics, research etiquette deserves careful attention, too. For example, respect the time of anyone who agrees to be interviewed or to be a research participant, and maintain courtesy throughout the interview or research process.

Locating Data and Information

The range of sources available to business researchers today is remarkable, almost overwhelming at times. If you have a question about an industry, company, market, new technology, or financial topic, it's likely somebody else has already researched the subject. Research conducted previously for another purpose is considered **secondary research** when the results are reused in a new project. These sources include magazines, newspapers, public websites, books, and other reports. Start with secondary research for your project: It will give you a grounding in the area, and it can save considerable time and money for the overall assignment. Before you use any secondary sources, however, you need to know whether you can trust them, as the following section explains. In contrast, **primary research** is new research done specifically for your current project and includes surveys, interviews, observations, and experiments.

EVALUATING SOURCES In every research project, you have the responsibility to verify the quality of the sources you use. The internet has made this challenge easier in one respect, since it's usually possible to cross-check information by referring to multiple sources. At the same time, online research is more difficult because so much bad information exists on the internet, from doctored photos to unverified "facts" to biased sources. To avoid tainting your results and damaging your reputation, ask yourself the following questions about each piece of material:

> **Does the source have a reputation for honesty and reliability?** For example, find out how a publication accepts articles and whether it has an editorial board, peer review, or fact-checking procedures. Most traditional offline publishers have such quality-control procedures in place, but many online sources do not.
> **Is the source potentially biased?** To interpret an organization's information, you need to know its point of view.
> **What is the purpose of the material?** For example, was the material designed to inform others of new research, advance a political position, or promote a product?
> **Is the author credible?** Is the author a professional journalist? An informed amateur? Merely someone with an opinion?
> **Where did the source get *its* information?** Find out who collected the data, the methods they used, their qualifications, and their professional reputation.
> **Can you verify the material independently?** Verification can uncover biases or mistakes, which is particularly important when the information goes beyond simple facts to include projections, interpretations, and estimates.
> **Is the material current?** Ensure that you use the most current information available by checking the publication date of a source.
> **Is the material complete?** Have you accessed the entire document or only a selection from it? If it's a selection, which parts were excluded? Do you need more detail?

You probably won't have time to conduct a thorough background check on all your sources, so focus your efforts on the most important or most suspicious pieces of information. See "Sharpening Your Career Skills: Evaluating World Wide Web Resources" for guidelines on internet sources.

Objective 3 Define primary and secondary research, and explain when you use each method.

Primary research consists of information that you gather specifically for a new research project; secondary research consists of information that others have gathered (and published, in many cases).

Objective 4 Evaluate the credibility of an information source, and conduct an effective online search.

Evaluate your sources carefully to avoid embarrassing and potentially damaging mistakes.

Statistics Canada, is a credible source of information. Explore www.statcan. gc.ca to see the breadth of research in Canada's national statistical agency. How can Statistics Canada help you complete assignments you are currently writing?

SHARPENING YOUR CAREER SKILLS

Evaluating World Wide Web Resources

Anyone who has gone online will agree that the internet offers the benefits of high speed and enormous scope for people who want both convenience and wide access to a variety of information sources. A quick entry into an online search engine may harvest dozens, hundreds, or thousands of hits, confronting internet researchers with data ranging from essential to just plain worthless. If you are just starting to acquire research skills, or wish to refine them further, developing a critical sense of internet resources will help you become a better researcher. Your reports could be more credible and beneficial to your audiences.

Analyzing the reliability of your internet information is not that much different from determining the trustworthiness of your secondary print sources, a topic already discussed in this chapter (see Evaluating Sources). You must consider the source's reputation and potential bias. You must determine where your sources got their information, thereby providing yourself with a further check for reliability. You must also see if you can verify your source's information independently and if your source's claims meet the test of thoughtful scrutiny—in other words, do they make sense? With information you have accessed electronically, you should also ask yourself the following questions:

> **What is the URL (Universal Resource Locator)?** If the URL is a corporation or a political party, the information on the website may be particularly slanted. For example, if you are doing a study of the popularity of a certain snack food, the manufacturer's website will likely not include information you should know about competing products. And if the URL is a personal web page, the information is more likely to be opinion rather than fact.

> **Who is the author?** What are the author's qualifications? An unsolicited book review downloaded from a major online e-bookseller, such as Chapters.Indigo.ca, may be written by a fan of the author, or even a friend, who wants to promote the book by writing a favourable review. If you have obtained an article from a private or organizational website, look for a biography of the author and a list of his or her publications and affiliations. Check these carefully for clues to the author's attitudes and interests, which may betray a particular viewpoint. Sometimes the author is anonymous, often a clue that the information may not be reliable.

> **Who is the audience?** Noting the URL and investigating the website and its links will help you determine if the information is directed toward a particular group of people with common interests. If it is, the information you have obtained may be slanted. For example, information on websites established by environmental associations or associations that promote the interests of the tobacco industry should be analyzed carefully for signs of bias.

Are you an efficient researcher? How do you organize your notes and information during this critical report-writing phase?

> **Is the information in its original format?** If not, is the original source cited? You must determine if the information is taken out of context, different from the original, or plagiarized. If the source isn't documented, it may not be trustworthy.

> **Has the information been filtered?** Filtering means that an author's article has undergone review by external readers. The author's peers, a publisher, or an editor has read it and probably asked the author for improvements in content and writing style. Look for an author's acknowledgments of reviewers and editors. Acknowledgments suggest that the work was subjected to this kind of quality control, which results in a more authoritative and reliable electronic document than one that wasn't.

> **How current is the website?** Websites include a "last-updated" feature that indicates the last time the site was revised. Stale-dated sites may contain out-of-date information. Be aware of the site's date, which can usually be found on the website's first page.

For information that is current and has undergone the peer-review process, your best bet is to search your school library's electronic journals or those located at your public library. Spending the time analyzing your internet sources will help you become a credible and reliable researcher and writer. Your audiences will value your skills and respect you for your integrity.

CAREER APPLICATIONS

1 Look at two websites for manufacturers of your favourite products. What kinds of bias do you see on these sites? How is the bias displayed?

2 You are writing a research paper on the advantages and disadvantages of snack foods. How can you use information you find through commercial databases to evaluate information on company websites?

KEEPING TRACK OF YOUR RESEARCH Before doing research, you should think about how you will keep track of the information you gather. The following strategies will streamline the research stage:

> **Bookmark, download, or print out pages from library databases.** Most library databases give you the option to set up a folder of "marked" articles that you can review later. You can email the list to yourself, either as citations, citations with abstracts, or full articles.
> **Write down the complete bibliographic information when recording information manually.** Spending an extra minute or two double-checking your handwritten or keyboarded citation against your source will prevent backtracking later on as you near your deadline.
> **Mark up computer printouts or photocopies.** Highlight key phrases, facts, or sections, and write comments in the margins. You can then record your notes on cards or enter them directly into a computer.
> **Consider taking notes on three-by-five-inch index cards.** Note cards are easy to use, carry, sort, and arrange. You can also take notes by computer. By recording notes in electronic format instead of on handwritten cards, you can easily search for words (using the "find" function), sort the notes by column headings, and copy information directly into the document draft.
> **Read topic sentences first.** The topic sentence, generally the first sentence of a paragraph), will help you decide whether the source may contain useful information. If it does, then read the entire paragraph.

CONDUCTING SECONDARY RESEARCH Even if you intend to eventually conduct primary research, most projects start with a review of secondary research. In your company, you might be able to find a variety of reports, memos, and other documents that could help. Outside the company, business researchers can choose from a wide range of print and online resources. Table 11–3 provides a small sample of the many secondary resources available.[5]

Finding Information at the Library Public, corporate, and university libraries offer an enormous array of business books, electronic databases, newspapers, periodicals, directories, almanacs, and government publications. Some of these printed sources provide information that is not available online, and some of the online sources provide information that is available by subscription. Don't assume you can find everything you need through your own online research. Libraries are also where you'll find one of your most important resources: librarians. Reference librarians are trained in research techniques and can often help you find obscure information you can't find on your own. They can also direct you to many sources of business information:

> **Newspapers and periodicals.** Libraries offer access to a wide variety of popular magazines, general business magazines, *trade journals* (which provide information about specific professions and industries), and *academic journals* (which provide research-oriented articles from researchers and educators). Check with a librarian to see which periodicals are available in print or electronic formats.
> **Business books.** Although less timely than newspapers and periodicals, business books provide in-depth coverage of a variety of business topics. Many libraries now offer online access to their card catalogues, so you can see if they have specific titles in their collections.
> **Directories.** Thousands of directories are published in print and electronic formats in Canada, and many include membership information for all kinds of professions, industries, and special-interest groups. Directories

Before you conduct primary research, see if there is any secondary research you can take advantage of first.

Even in the internet age, libraries offer information and resources you can't find anywhere else—including experienced research librarians.

> Table 11–3 Major Business Resources

Company, Industry, and Product Resources (Print)

> *Brands and Their Companies/Companies and Their Brands.* Data on over 281 000 consumer products and 51 000 manufacturers, importers, marketers, and distributors
> *Corporate and Industry Research Reports (CIRR).* Collection of industry reports produced by industry analysts for investment purposes; unique coverage includes industry profitability, comparative company sales, market share, profits, and forecasts
> *Directory of Canadian Manufacturers.* (Dun & Bradstreet). Information on contacts and commercial products. Lists more than 50 000 businesses
> *Manufacturing USA.* Data series listing nearly 25 000 companies, including detailed information on over 450 manufacturing industries
> *Moody's Industry Review.* Data on 4000 companies in about 150 industries; ranks companies within industry by five financial statistics (revenue, net income, total assets, cash and marketable securities, and long-term debt) and includes key performance ratios
> *Moody's Manuals.* Weekly manual of financial data in each of six business areas: industrials, transportation, public utilities, banks, finance, and over-the-counter (OTC) industrials
> *Report on Business Magazine Top 1000.* Contact, financial, and product information on Canada's largest corporations
> *Scott's Industrial Directory.* Sales and marketing profiles of Canadian companies; includes list of companies by NAICS code
> *Service Industries USA.* Comprehensive data on 2100 services grouped into over 150 industries
> *Standard & Poor's Industry Surveys.* Concise investment profiles for a broad range of industries; coverage is extensive, with a focus on current situation and outlook; includes some summary data on major companies in each industry
> *Standard & Poor's Register of Corporations, Directors, and Executives.* Index of major U.S. and international corporations; lists officers, products, sales volume, and number of employees
> *Thomas's Register of American Manufacturers.* Information on thousands of U.S. manufacturers indexed by company name and product
> *U.S. Industrial Outlook.* Annual profiles of several hundred key U.S. industries; each industry report covers several pages and includes tables, graphs, and charts that visually demonstrate how an industry compares with similar industries, including important component growth factors and other economic measures

Company, Industry, and Product Resources (Online)

> **AnnualReports.com.** Free access to annual reports from thousands of public companies
> **Canadian Business Resource.** www.cbr.ca. Corporate and executive profiles from over 6000 Canadian companies, including stock ranking; website updated several times a week; subscription-based
> **Canadian Company Capabilities.** http://strategis.ic.gc.ca/sc_coinf/ccc/engdoc/homepage.html. Profiles of 50 000 Canadian businesses, by manufacturing, service, and product-specific business directories
> **Canadian Market Research.** www.statslinkcanada.com/index.html. User-friendly site providing strategies and sources for researching the Canadian market. Links to Statistics Canada and Industry Canada. Free and low-cost services.
> **Canadian Trade Index.** www.ctidirectory.com. Searchable by company name, product description, and keyword; profiles of manufacturers and exporters
> *Fraser's Canadian Trade Directory.* www.frasers.com. Directory of Canadian Companies, products, and brands; free
> *Hoover's Online.* www.hoovers.com. Database of 12 million companies worldwide, including in-depth coverage of 35 000 leading companies around the world; basic information available free; in-depth information requires subscription
> *SEC filing.* www.sec.gov. SEC filings including 10Ks, 10Qs, annual reports, and prospectuses for 35 000 U.S. public firms

Directories and Indexes (Print and online)

> *Books in Print.* Index of 425 000 books in 62 000 subject categories currently available from U.S. publishers; indexed by author and title
> *Canadian Books in Print.* Contains more than 52 000 titles; author and title index is extensively cross-referenced; subject index lists titles under 800 different subject categories
> **Canadian Information Centre for International Credentials.** www.cicic.ca/en/profess.aspx?sortcode=2.19.21.21. Extensive list of Canadian professional organizations covering all sectors and industries
> *Encyclopaedia of Associations.* Index of thousands of associations listed by broad subject category, specific subject, association, and location
> *Reader's Guide to Periodical Literature.* Periodical index categorized by subject and author
> *Ulrich's International Periodicals Directory.* Listings by title, publisher, editor, phone, and address of over 140 000 publications such as popular magazines, trade journals, government documents, and newspapers; great for locating hard-to-find trade publications

> Table 11–3 Major Business Resources (*continued*)

People (Print)

> *Dun & Bradstreet's Reference Book of Corporate Management.* Professional histories of people serving as the principal officers and directors of more than 12 000 U.S. companies
> *Who's Who in Canadian Business.* Comprehensive guide to Canada's business leaders with more than 5400 entries. Contains detailed biographical information

Trademarks (Print/Online)

> **Canadian Patents Database.** http://patents1.ic.gc.ca/intro-e.html. Access to over 75 years of patent descriptions and images in over 1 500 000 patent documents
> **Canadian Trade-Marks Database.** http://strategis.ic.gc.ca/app/cipo/trademarks/search/tmSearch.do?language=eng. Trademark information, including designs, wares, and services
> *United States Patent and Trademark Office.* www.uspto.gov. Trademark and patent information records

Statistics and Facts (Print)

> *Canadian Almanac and Directory.* Wide-ranging statistics and facts about Canada, including financial institutions, media, transportation, and Canada's chief trading partners
> *Dun & Bradstreet Canadian Industry Norms and Key Ratios.* Canadian industry, performance, and performance ratios
> *Industry Norms and Key Business Ratios (Dun & Bradstreet).* Industry, financial, and performance ratios
> *Statistical Abstract of the United States.* U.S. economic, social, political, and industrial statistics
> *Statistics Canada Publications.* Large collection of comprehensive business, census, and other data
> *The World Almanac and Book of Facts.* Facts on economic, social, educational, and political events for major countries

Statistics and Facts (Online)

> **Bureau of Economic Analysis.** www.bea.gov. Large collection of economic and government data
> **Canadian Human Rights Commission.** www.chrc-ccdp.ca. Legislation and policies regarding employment equity and other human rights legislation
> **Canadian Legislature.** www.parl.gc.ca. Information about bills, committees, and the Canadian Parliament
> **Department of Finance online.** www.fin.gc.ca/access/fininst-eng.asp. Comprehensive directory to resources about Canada's financial institutions and markets
> **Europa—The European Union Online.** www.europa.eu. A portal that provides up-to-date coverage of current affairs, legislation, policies, and EU statistics
> **Human Resources and Social Development Canada.** www.hrsdc.gc.ca. Comprehensive labour and employment information
> **Industry Canada.** www.ic.gc.ca. Wide-ranging information about the Canadian economy, business, and employment; includes company directories and consumer information
> **Statistics Canada.** www.statcan.gc.ca. Online collection of comprehensive business, census, and other data
> **STAT-USA.** www.stat-usa.gov. Large collection of U.S. economic and government data
> **U.S. Census Bureau.** www.census.gov. Demographic data on both consumers and businesses based on census data
> **U.S. Bureau of Labour Statistics.** www.bls.gov. Extensive national and regional information on labour and business, including employment, industry growth, productivity, Consumer Price Index (CPI), and overall U.S. economy

International Business Resources (Print and Online)

> *Bank of Canada Review.* www.bankofcanada.ca/en/review/index.html. Includes charts and statistics on external trade
> *D&B Million Dollar Databases.* www.dnbmdd.com/mddi. Lists over 1 600 000 international companies, with information on total employees, legal status, annual U.S. sales dollar equivalent
> *Dictionary of International Business Terms.* Definitions relating to international dimensions of accounting, business policy and strategy, information systems and technology, marketing, management, finance, and trade
> *Inter-Corporate Ownership Directory.* Index of which corporation owns and/or controls other corporations in Canada; data include country of residence, country of control, and percentage of voting rights held
> *World Development Report.* www.worldbank.org. Analyzes major international economic conditions and trends for International Monetary Fund and World Bank countries; produced annually

Commercial Databases (Require Subscriptions)

> **Academic Search Premier.** Database of over 1500 scholarly and trade journals in business, management, industry, and economics (full text and abstracts)
> **CBCA Complete—Canadian Business & Current Affairs.** Database of over 700 Canadian industry and professional periodicals and newsletters; covers business, science, and technology.
> **CPI.Q—Canadian Periodical Index.** Citations, abstracts, and full-text articles from periodicals published in or providing major coverage of Canadian business, technology, arts, and other areas
> **LexisNexis.** Several thousand databases covering legal, corporate, government, and academic subjects
> **ProQuest Research Library.** More than 5000 journals, magazines, newspapers, and other information sources

are considered invaluable for marketers, job seekers, and others who need to establish a prospect list.

> **Almanacs and statistical resources.** Almanacs are convenient guides to factual and statistical information about countries, politics, the labour force, and so on. Also check out the various Canadian government websites, such as Statistics Canada, Human Resources and Social Development Canada, and Industry Canada. These resources contain statistics about life, work, government, population patterns, business, and the environment.

> **Government publications.** Information on laws, court decisions, tax questions, regulatory issues, and other governmental concerns can often be found in collections of government documents. A librarian can direct you to the information you want.

> **Electronic databases.** Databases offer vast collections of computer-searchable information, often in specific areas such as business, law, science, technology, and education. Some libraries offer remote online access to some or all databases; for others you'll need to visit in person. The following section offers more information on using databases.

Government agencies publish a huge array of information that is helpful to business researchers.

Finding Information Online The internet can be a valuable source of business information, provided you know where to look and how to use the tools available. **Search engines** identify individual web pages that contain a specific word or phrase you've asked for. Search engines have the advantage of scanning millions or billions of individual web pages, and the best engines present the pages that are probably the most relevant to your search request. For all their ease and power, search engines have three disadvantages you should be aware of: (1) no human editors are involved to evaluate the quality of the content on these pages; (2) various engines use different search techniques, so one engine might miss a site that another one finds; and (3) search engines can't reach the content on restricted websites (such as the back issues of many professional journals). These out-of-reach pages are sometimes called the *hidden internet* or the *deep Web* because conventional search techniques can't access them. Web pages can be hidden from search engines for a variety of reasons, including password protection, links that some search engines can't follow (such as the links created with Adobe Flash animation software), pages that webmasters block from search engines, and dynamic pages that exist only when a visitor submits a query or request on a website. The hidden internet is estimated to be at least several times larger than the visible internet, and much of the material you might want to find for some reports could be unreachable through standard search engines.[6]

Conduct online research with extreme care; much of the information online has not been subjected to the same quality controls common in traditional offline publishing.

The good news is that you can get around all three shortcomings when conducting research—although doing so is sometimes expensive. **Web directories** address the first major shortcoming of search engines by using human editors to categorize and evaluate websites. Directories such as those offered by Yahoo!, *About.com*, and the Open Directory at www.dmoz.org present lists of websites chosen by a team of editors. And as Chapter 7 points out, a number of directories (and search engines) specialize in specific media types, such as Technorati's focus on blogs.

Web directories rely on human editors to evaluate and select websites.

Metasearch engines, or *metacrawlers,* address the second shortcoming of search engines by formatting your search request for the specific requirements of multiple search engines. These versatile tools produce displays that tell you how many hits each engine was able to find for you. Table 11–4 lists some of the more popular search engines, metacrawlers, and directories.

Metacrawlers can save you time by employing multiple search engines at once.

Online databases give you access to the most important resource that search engines usually can't reach: millions of newspaper, magazine, and journal articles.

Online databases help address the third shortcoming of search engines by offering access to the newspapers, magazines, and journals that you're likely to

Specialized search capabilities such as Google Book can help you locate texts that might be of value in your research efforts. Is consulting Google Book enough to qualify as good research?

need for many research projects. Some databases, such as **High Beam** (www.highbeam.com), are priced to attract individual users, whereas others, such as **LexisNexis** (www.lexisnexis.ca) and **ProQuest** (www.proquest.com), are intended for use by companies, libraries, and other institutions. In addition to databases that primarily feature content from newspapers and periodicals, specialized databases such as **Industry Canada** (http://strategis.ic.gc.ca) and **Fraser's Canadian Trade Directory** (www.frasers.com) offer detailed information on thousands of individual companies. You can obtain company news releases at no charge from **CNWTelbec** (www.cnw.ca/en), Canada's premier resource for up-to-the-minute news and information from more than 10 000 Canadian and global sources, including public companies, associations, unions, not-for-profits, and all levels of government. Ask your librarian for advice on accessing all these resources.

As search engines, metacrawlers, and databases continue to multiply and offer new ways to find information, using them can become a challenge. No two of them work in exactly the same way. Make sure you understand what the search tool expects from you before you enter your query. With a *keyword search*, the engine or database attempts to find items that include all of the words you enter. A *Boolean search* lets you define a query with greater precision, using such operators as *AND* (the search must include the two terms linked by the *AND*), *OR* (it can include either or both words), or *NOT* (the search ignores items with whatever word comes after *NOT*). Other common Boolean capabilities include searching for a particular word in close proximity to other words and wildcards that search for similar spellings. In contrast to both keyword and Boolean searches, *natural language* searches let you ask questions in everyday English. For example, "Which video game companies are the most profitable?" is a natural language query. *Forms-based searches* help

Make sure you know how each search engine, directory, database, or metacrawler works; they work in different ways, and you can get unpredictable results if you don't know how each one operates.

> Table 11–4 Best of Internet Searching

Major Search Engines

A9	www.a9.com
Alta Vista	www.altavista.com
Google	www.google.com
Lycos	www.lycos.com

Metacrawlers and Hybrid Sites

DogPile	www.dogpile.com
MetaCrawler	www.metacrawler.com
Search.com	www.search.com
WebCrawler	www.webcrawler.com
Yahoo!	www.yahoo.com

Web Directories and Online Libraries

Library and Archives Canada	www.collectionscanada.gc.ca/
Digital Librarian	www.digital-librarian.com/business.html
Internet Public Library	www.ipl.org
Librarians' Internet Index	http://lii.org
Library of Congress	www.loc.gov/rr/business

News Search Engines

AltaVista News	http://news.altavista.com
Google News	http://news.google.com
World News Network	www.wn.com
Yahoo! News	http://news.yahoo.com

Blog and Podcast Search Engines and Directories

Blogdigger	www.blogdigger.com
Google video search	http://video.google.com
Technorati	www.technorati.com
Podcast Alley	www.podcastalley.com

Magazine and Periodical Search Engines

FindArticles.com	www.findarticles.com
Google Scholar	http://scholar.google.ca

you create powerful queries by simply filling out an online form that lets you specify such parameters as date ranges, language, internet domain name, and even file and media types.[7] See Table 11–5 to learn how to conduct productive and time-saving searches.

As you conduct research throughout your career, keep an eye out for the latest technologies that can help you research more effectively and more efficiently, including these four innovations:

> **Desktop and enterprise search engines.** Unlike conventional search engines, which look for content on the Web, **desktop search engines** look for content on a particular computer. These tools are designed to identify and organize the many information and message fragments that most people have stored in various forms on their computers—email messages, IM, PowerPoint presentations, audio and video clips, word processing files, and

Take advantage of the latest research technologies, including desktop and enterprise searches, research and content managers, social bookmarking sites, and newsfeeds.

> Table 11–5 Using Search Engines and Databases

Read the instructions.	Check the Help page for advice on how to use a particular tool; each search engine has its own set of instructions.
Pay attention to the details.	Treat search operators carefully. Most search engines treat *AND* (upper case) as a Boolean search operator and look only for pages or entries that contain both words connected by *AND*. For example, if you typed "business AND communication" into the search bar, the search engine would return entries that included only the words "business" and "communication."
	In contrast, *and* (lower case) and similar basic words (called *stopwords*) are excluded from many searches because they are so common they'll show up in every web page or database entry.
	Use question marks and asterisks only after checking the Help page. Various engines and databases interpret question marks and asterisks in special ways.
Review the search and display options.	Review all the options presented before submitting a search. Some article databases search through only the title unless you specifically ask them to search through the article text as well; this distinction will dramatically affect your results.
	Verify the presentation order when the results are displayed: Items could be listed by date, relevancy, or some other criteria. Choose the presentation order that best serves your purposes.
Vary your terms.	Try alternatives of your term to pinpoint data, such as > abbreviations (*CEO, CPA*) > synonyms (*man, male*) > related terms (*child, adolescent, youth*) > different spellings (*dialog, dialogue*) > singular and plural forms (*woman, women*) > nouns and adjectives (*management, managerial*) > open and compound forms (*online, on line, on-line*)
Adjust the scope of your search.	If a search yields little or no information, broaden it by specifying fewer terms. If you're inundated with too many hits, use more terms to narrow your search.

so on.[8] **Enterprise search engines** perform a similar task but across an entire network of computers.

> **Research and content managers.** A variety of tools known as research managers, or content managers, can be particularly helpful when your research involves numerous websites. These tools offer such features as letting you save and organize stored website links, providing permanent access to web pages you've visited even if the pages later change or disappear, and automatically generating parts of reports such as tables of contents and bibliographies.[9]

> **Social bookmarking sites.** The social bookmarking sites introduced in Chapter 7 can also assist with research. By highlighting websites, news articles, and other online items that other people find useful, bookmarking sites such as www.digg.com and http://delicious.com can alert you to helpful resources and offer some indication of what online audiences are interested in at a particular moment in time. When using bookmarking sites for research, don't assume that all voters use the same terminology to identify things or that the rankings represent any particular segment of the population.[10]

> **Newsfeeds.** Newsfeeds, also discussed in Chapter 7, are an ideal way to stay up to date on fast-moving topics. For example, to stay on top of competitive moves in your industry, you can subscribe to newsfeeds from stock analysts who cover the industry, product user blogs, and blogs published by your competitors.

Desktop search engines are part of the new generation of software tools that can help businesspeople find vital information on company computers. In this example showing Copernic Desktop Search (www.copernic.com), a user searching for "agreements" found 127 documents in a variety of formats. Are desktop search engines a sufficient resource for research?

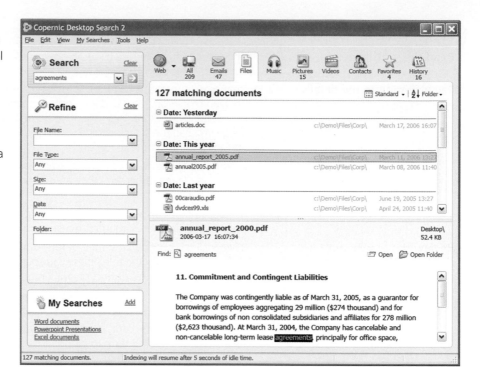

Proper documentation of the sources you use is both ethical and an important resource for your readers.

Documenting Your Sources Documenting the secondary sources you use in your writing serves three important functions: It properly and ethically credits the person who created the original material, it shows your audience that you have credible support for your message, and it helps your readers explore your topic in more detail, if desired. Be sure to take advantage of the source documentation tools in your word processing or specialized note-management software, such as Microsoft's OneNote.[11] Thorough documentation is particularly important if you're working in a large organization; your reports might be used by colleagues for years after you originally wrote them, and these people won't always have the opportunity to query you in person for more information.

You may document your sources through footnotes, endnotes, or some similar system (see Appendix B, "Documentation of Report Sources"). Whatever method you choose, documentation is necessary for such sources as books, articles, tables, charts, diagrams, song lyrics, scripted dialogue, letters, speeches—anything that you take from someone else, including ideas and information that you've re-expressed through paraphrasing or summarizing. However, you do not have to cite a source for general knowledge or for specialized knowledge that's generally known among your readers, such as the fact that Microsoft is a large software company.

Copyright law covers the expression of creative ideas, and copyrights can cover a wide range of materials, including reports and other documents, Web content, movies, musical compositions, lectures, computer programs, and even choreographed dance routines. Copyright protection is initiated the moment the expression is put into fixed form. Copyright law does not protect such elements as titles, names, short phrases, slogans, familiar symbols, or lists of ingredients or contents. It also doesn't protect ideas, procedures, methods, systems, processes, concepts, principles, discoveries, or devices, although it does cover their description, explanation, or illustration.[12] However, many of the entities not covered under copyright law are covered under other legal protections, such as patents for devices and processes and trademarks for slogans.

Merely crediting the source is not always enough. According to the fair use doctrine, you can use other people's work only as long as you don't unfairly prevent them from benefiting as a result. For example, if you reproduce someone else's copyrighted questionnaire in a report you're writing, even if you identify the source thoroughly, you may be preventing the author from selling a copy of that questionnaire to your readers.

In an age when instant global connectivity makes it effortless to copy and retransmit electronic files, the protection of intellectual property has become a widespread concern. **Intellectual property (IP)** includes patents, copyrighted materials, trade secrets, and internet domain names.[13] Bloggers need to be particularly careful about IP protection, given the carefree way that some post the work of others without offering proper credit.[14] Copyright law can be a complicated issue, so consult your company's legal department if you have any questions about material you plan to use.

CONDUCTING PRIMARY RESEARCH If secondary research can't provide the information and insights you need, your next choice is to gather the information yourself with primary research. The two most common primary research methods are surveys and interviews. (Other primary techniques are observations and experiments in special situations such as test marketing, but they're not commonly used for day-to-day business research.)

Conducting Surveys A carefully prepared and conducted survey can provide invaluable insights, but only if it is *reliable* (would produce identical results if repeated) and *valid* (measures what it's supposed to measure). To avoid errors in design and implementation, consider hiring a research specialist for important surveys. The two most common sources of errors are in the sample, the people selected to participate in the survey, and in the questions themselves.

When selecting the people who'll participate in your survey, the most critical task is getting a representative *sample* of the entire population in question. For example, if you want to know how Canadian consumers feel about something, you can't just randomly survey people in a mall and assume these opinions represent the entire population. Different types of consumers shop at different times of the day and different days of the week; some consumers don't shop at malls regularly, and many who do won't stop to talk with researchers. The online surveys you see on many websites today potentially suffer from the same *sampling bias:* They capture the opinions only of people who visit the sites and want to participate, which might not be a representative sample of the population. A good handbook on survey research will help you select the right people for your survey, including selecting enough people to have a statistically valid result.[15]

To develop an effective survey questionnaire, start with the prioritized information gaps you identified at the beginning of the research process. Then break these points into specific questions, choosing an appropriate type of question for each point (Figure 11–7 shows various types of survey questions). The following guidelines will help you produce results that are both valid and reliable:[16]

> **Provide clear instructions.** Respondents need to know exactly how to fill out your questionnaire. Entry mistakes will distort your results.
> **Don't ask for information that people can't be expected to remember.** For example, a question such as "How many times did you go grocery shopping last year" will generate unreliable answers.
> **Keep the questionnaire short and easy to answer.** Don't make any individual questions difficult to answer, and don't expect people to give you more than 10 or 15 minutes of their time.

Surveys and interviews are the most common primary research techniques.

For a survey to produce valid results, it must be based on a representative sample of respondents.

Provide clear instructions to prevent mistaken answers.

Marketing surveys are a common way to gather data directly from customers. What ethical guidelines should marketers follow when interviewing subjects?

> Figure 11–7 Types of Survey Questions

QUESTION TYPE	EXAMPLE
Open-ended	How would you describe the flavour of this ice cream?
Either-or	Do you think this ice cream is too rich? _____ Yes _____ No
Multiple-choice	Which description best fits the taste of this ice cream? (Choose only one.) a. Delicious b. Too fruity c. Too sweet d. Too intensely flavoured e. Bland f . Stale
Scale	Please mark an X on the scale to indicate how you perceive the texture of this ice cream. Too light Light Creamy Too creamy
Checklist	Which of the following ice cream brands do you recognize? (Check all that apply.) _____ Ben & Jerry's _____ Breyers _____ President's Choice _____ Chapman's _____ Häagen-Dazs
Ranking	Rank these flavours in order of your preference, from 1 (most preferred) to 5 (least preferred): _____ Vanilla _____ Cherry _____ Strawberry _____ Chocolate _____ Coconut
Short-answer	In the past two weeks, how many times did you buy ice cream in a grocery store? _____ In the past two weeks, how many times did you buy ice cream in an ice cream shop? _____

> **Formulate questions, whenever possible, to provide answers that are easy to analyze.** Numbers and facts are easier to summarize than opinions, for example.

> **Avoid leading questions that could bias your survey.** If you ask, "Do you prefer that we stay open in the evenings for customer convenience?" you'll no doubt get a "yes." Instead, ask, "What time of day do you normally do your shopping?"

> **Avoid ambiguous questions.** If you ask "Do you shop at the mall often?" some people might interpret *often* to mean "every day," whereas others might think it means "once a week" or "once a month."
> **Ask only one question at a time.** A compound question such as "Do you read books and magazines?" doesn't allow for the respondent who reads one but not the other.

The internet is quickly becoming the preferred survey mechanism for many researchers, and dozens of companies now offer online survey services.[17] Compared to traditional mail and in-person techniques, online surveys are usually faster to create, easier to administer, quicker to analyze, and less expensive overall. The interactive capabilities of the Web can enhance all kinds of surveys, from simple opinion polls to complex purchase simulations. However, online surveys require the same care as any other type of survey, including being on guard against sampling bias.[18]

Conducting Interviews Getting in-depth information straight from an expert can be a valuable method for collecting primary information. Although interviews are relatively easy to conduct, they require careful planning to get the best results and make the best use of the other person's time. Planning an interview is similar to planning any other form of communication. You begin by analyzing your purpose, learning about the other person, and formulating your main idea. Then you decide on the length, style, and organization of the interview.

Objective 5 Outline an effective process for planning and conducting information interviews.

The answers you receive are influenced by the types of questions you ask, by the way you ask them, and by your subject's cultural and language background. Other potentially significant factors include the person's race, gender, age, educational level, and social status, so know your subject before you start writing questions.[19]

Ask **open-ended questions** to invite the expert to offer opinions, insights, and information, such as "Why do you believe that South America represents a better opportunity than Europe for this product line?" Bear in mind that although open-ended questions can extract significant amounts of information, they do give you less control over the interview. Someone might take 10 seconds or 10 minutes to answer a question, so plan to be flexible.

Choose question types that will generate the specific information you need.

Ask **closed-ended questions** to elicit a specific answer, such as yes or no. However, including too many closed-ended questions in an interview will make the experience feel more like a simple survey and won't take full advantage of the interview setting. When you do ask a question that implies a straightforward answer, such as "Do you think we should expand distribution in South America?" explore the reasoning behind the expert's answer with follow-up questions.

Think carefully about the sequence of your questions and the subject's potential answers, so you can arrange them in an order that helps uncover layers of information. Also consider providing the other person with a list of questions at least a day or two before the interview, especially if you'd like to quote your subject in writing or if your questions might require your subject to conduct research or think extensively about the answers. If you want to record the interview, ask the person ahead of time and respect his or her wishes.

As soon as possible after the interview, take a few moments to write down your thoughts, go over your notes, and organize your material. Look for important themes, helpful facts or statistics, and direct quotes. If you made a tape recording, *transcribe* it (take down word for word what the person said) or take notes from the tape just as you would while listening to someone in person.

A successful interview requires careful planning and organization to ensure that you get the information you really need. How have you planned interviews? How can you improve your approach?

Face-to-face interviews give you the opportunity to gauge nonverbal responses.

Face-to-face interviews allow you to gauge the reaction to your questions and observe the nonverbal signals that accompany the answers, but interviews don't necessarily have to take place in person. Email interviews have become common, partly because they give subjects a chance to think through their responses thoroughly, rather than rushing to fit the time constraints of a face-to-face interview.[20] Also, email interviews might be the only way you can access some experts.

In addition to individual interviews, business researchers can also use a form of group interview known as the **focus group.** In this format, a moderator guides a group through a series of discussion questions while the rest of the research team observes through a one-way mirror. The key advantage of focus groups is the opportunity to learn from group dynamics as the various participants bounce ideas and questions off each other. By allowing a group to discuss topics and problems in this manner, the focus group technique can uncover much richer information than a series of individual interviews.[21]

As a reminder of the tasks involved in interviews, see "Checklist: Conducting Effective Information Interviews."

✳ Explore Using Your Research Results

After you collect your data, the next step is converting it into usable information.

After you've collected all the necessary secondary and primary information, the next step is transforming it into the specific content you need. For simpler projects, you may be able to insert some material, such as statistics from secondary sources and brief quotations from experts in the field, directly into your report, presentation, or other application. However, when you've gathered a significant amount of information or raw data from surveys, you'll need to process the material before you can use it. This step can involve analyzing numerical data; quoting, paraphrasing, or summarizing textual material; drawing conclusions; and making recommendations.

ANALYZING DATA Business research often produces numerical data—everything from sales figures to population statistics to survey answers. By themselves, these numbers might not provide the insights you or your audience require. Are sales going up or going down? What percentage of employees surveyed are so dissatisfied that they're ready to look for new jobs? These are the insights managers need to make good business decisions.

Mean, median, and mode provide insight into sets of data.

Even without advanced statistical techniques, you can use simple arithmetic to extract powerful insights from sets of research data. Table 11–6 shows several insights you can gain about a collection of numbers, for example. The **mean** (which is what most people refer to when they use the term "average") is the sum of all the items in the group divided by the number of items in that group. The **median** is the "middle of the road," or the midpoint of a series with an

CHECKLIST Conducting Effective Information Interviews

- ✔ Learn about the person you're interviewing.
- ✔ Formulate your main idea to ensure effective focus.
- ✔ Choose the length, style, and organization of the interview.
- ✔ Select question types to elicit the specific information you want.
- ✔ Design each question carefully to collect useful answers.
- ✔ Limit the number of questions you ask.
- ✔ Consider recording the interview if the subject permits.
- ✔ Review your notes as soon as the interview ends.

> Table 11–6 Three Types of Data Measures: Mean, Median, and Mode

Salesperson	Sales ($)	
Simpson	3 000	
Chu	5 000	
Carrick	6 000	
Sharma	7 000 ——— Mean	
Kuszaj	7 500 ——— Median	
Kemble	8 500 —	
O'Toole	8 500	Mode
Caruso	8 500 —	
Harari	9 000	
Total	$63 000	

equal number of items above and below. The **mode** is the number that occurs more often than any other in your sample. It's the best answer to a question such as "What is the usual amount?" Each measure will help you interpret a set of data.

It's also helpful to look for **trends,** any repeatable patterns taking place over time, including growth, decline, and cyclical trends that vary between growth and decline. Trend analysis is common in business. By looking at data over a period of time, you can detect patterns and relationships that will help you answer important questions. In addition, researchers frequently explore the relationships between subsets of data using a technique called **cross-tabulation.** For example, if you want to figure out why total sales rose or fell, look separately at sales data by age, gender, location, and product type.

> Trends suggest patterns that repeat over time.

Whenever you process numerical data, keep in mind that numbers are easy to manipulate and misinterpret, particularly with spreadsheets and other computer tools. Ensure that you double-check all of your calculations and document the operation of any spreadsheets you plan to share with colleagues. Also, step back and look at your entire set of data before proceeding with any analysis. Do the numbers make sense based on what you know about the subject? Are there any individual data points that stand out as suspect? Have you made any comparisons that don't really make sense? Have you read more into the data than is really there? Business audiences make decisions based on the clarity of numbers; it's your responsibility to deliver numbers that are reliable.

QUOTING, PARAPHRASING, AND SUMMARIZING INFORMATION You can use textual information from sources in three ways. *Quoting* a source means you reproduce it exactly as you found it, and you either set it off with quotation marks (for shorter passages) or extract it in an indented paragraph (for longer passages). Use direct quotations when the original language will enhance your argument or when rewording the passage would lessen its impact. However, don't quote sources at great length. Too much quoting creates a choppy patchwork of varying styles and gives the impression that all you've done is piece together the work of other people.

> Quoting a source means reproducing the content exactly and indicating who created the information originally.

You can often maximize the impact of secondary material in your own writing by *paraphrasing* it, restating it in your own words and with your own sentence structures.[22] Paraphrasing helps you maintain consistent tone while using vocabulary familiar to your audience. Of course, you still need to credit

> Paraphrasing is expressing someone else's ideas in your own words.

> Table 11–7 Summarizing Effectively

Original Material (110 Words)	45-Word Summary	22-Word Summary
Our facilities costs spiralled out of control last year. **The 23% jump** was far ahead of every other cost category in the company and many times higher than the 4% average rise for commercial real estate in the Winnipeg metropolitan area. The rise can be attributed to many factors, but the major factors include repairs (mostly electrical and structural problems at the downtown office), energy (most of our offices are heated by electricity, the price of which has been increasing much faster than for oil or gas), and last but not least, the loss of two sublease tenants whose rent payments made a substantial dent in our cost profile for the past five years. **Main idea** Major support points Details	**Our facilities costs jumped 23% last year,** far ahead of every other cost category in the company and many times higher than the 4% local average. The major factors contributing to the increase are repairs, energy, and the loss of two sublease tenants.	**Our facilities costs jumped 23% last year,** mainly because of rising repair and energy costs and the loss of sublease income.

Summarizing is similar to paraphrasing but distills the content into fewer words.

Objective 6 Explain the differences between drafting a summary, drawing a conclusion, and developing a recommendation.

All universities penalize students for committing plagiarism—claiming the words, ideas, artistic works, and research data of others as your own. Penalties may range from zero on the assignment to expulsion. What are your school's penalties for plagiarism? To prevent plagiarism, document your sources using one of the systems explained in Appendix B, "Documentation of Report Sources."

the originator of the information, but not with quotation marks or indented paragraphs.

To paraphrase effectively, follow these tips:[23]

> Reread the original passage until you fully understand its meaning.
> Record your paraphrase on a note card or in an electronic format.
> Use language with which your audience is familiar.
> Check your version with the original source to verify that you have not altered the meaning.
> Use quotation marks to identify any unique terms or phrases you have borrowed exactly from the source.
> Record the source (including the page number) so that you can give proper credit if you use this material in your report.

Summarizing is similar to paraphrasing but presents the gist of the material in fewer words than the original. An effective summary identifies the main ideas and major support points from your source material, but leaves out most details, examples, and other information that is less critical to your audience. Like quotations and paraphrases, summaries also require complete documentation of your sources. Summarizing is not always a simple task, and your audience will judge your ability to separate significant issues from less significant details. Identify the main idea and the key support points, and separate these from details, examples, and other supporting evidence (see Table 11–7). Focus your efforts on your audience, highlighting the information that is most important to the person who assigned the project or to those who will read the report.

Of course, all three approaches require careful attention to ethics. When quoting directly, don't distort the original intent of the material by quoting selectively or out of context. And never succumb to **plagiarism,** presenting someone else's words or ideas as your own.

DRAWING CONCLUSIONS A conclusion is a logical interpretation of the facts and other information in a report. A sound conclusion is not only logical but flows from the information included in a report, meaning that it should be based on the information included in the report and shouldn't rely on information that isn't in the report. Moreover, if you or the organization you represent have certain biases that influence your conclusion, you are ethically obligated to inform the audience accordingly.

Reaching good conclusions based on the evidence at hand is one of the most important skills you can develop in your business career. In fact, the ability to see patterns and possibilities that others can't see is one of the hallmarks of innovative business leadership. Consequently, take your time with this part of the process. Play "devil's advocate" against yourself; attacking your conclusion as an audience might to ensure it stands up to rigorous scrutiny.

MAKING RECOMMENDATIONS Whereas a conclusion interprets information, a **recommendation** suggests action—what to do in response to the information. The following example illustrates the difference between a conclusion and a recommendation:

Conclusion	Recommendation
On the basis of its track record and current price, I conclude that this company is an attractive buy.	I recommend that we write a letter to the board of directors offering to buy the company at a 10-percent premium over the current market value of its stock.

If you've been asked to take the final step and translate your conclusions into recommendations, make the relationship between them clear. To be credible, recommendations must be based on logical analysis and sound conclusions. They must also be practical and acceptable to the people who have to make them work. Finally, when making a recommendation, be certain that you have adequately described the steps needed to implement your recommendation. Don't leave your readers wondering what they need to do in order to act on it.

Planning Informational Reports

Informational reports provide the feedback that employees, managers, and others need to make decisions, take action, and respond to dynamic conditions both inside and outside the organization. Although these reports come in dozens of particular formats, they can be grouped into four general categories:

> **Reports to monitor and control operations.** Managers rely on a wide range of reports to see how well their companies are functioning. *Plans* establish expectations and guidelines to direct future action. The most important of these are *business plans,* which summarize a proposed business venture, communicate the company's goals, highlight how management intends to achieve those goals, and explain why customers will be motivated to buy the company's products or services. Many business plans are actually a combination of an informational report (describing conditions in the marketplace), an analytical report (analyzing threats and opportunities and recommending specific courses of action), and a proposal (persuading investors to put money into the firm in exchange for a share of ownership). *Operating reports* provide feedback on a wide variety of an organization's functions, including sales, inventories, expenses, shipments, and so on. *Personal activity reports* provide information regarding an individual's experiences during sales calls, industry conferences, market research trips, and so on.

> **Reports to implement policies and procedures.** Reports are the most common vehicle for conveying guidelines, approved procedures, and other

Informational reports are used to monitor and control operations, implement policies and procedures, demonstrate compliance, and document progress.

 Explore

 Explore
Practise

> Figure 11–8 Building Access Policy Excerpt

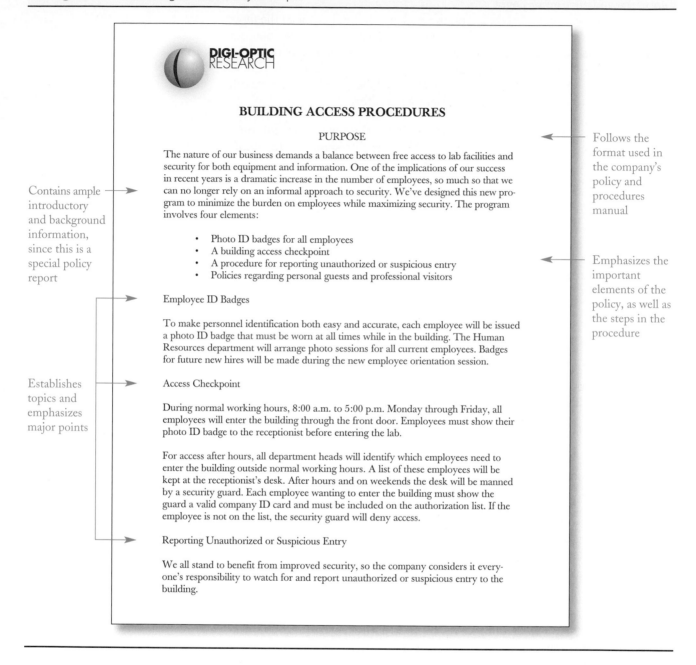

Contains ample introductory and background information, since this is a special policy report

Establishes topics and emphasizes major points

DIGI-OPTIC RESEARCH

BUILDING ACCESS PROCEDURES

PURPOSE

The nature of our business demands a balance between free access to lab facilities and security for both equipment and information. One of the implications of our success in recent years is a dramatic increase in the number of employees, so much so that we can no longer rely on an informal approach to security. We've designed this new program to minimize the burden on employees while maximizing security. The program involves four elements:

- Photo ID badges for all employees
- A building access checkpoint
- A procedure for reporting unauthorized or suspicious entry
- Policies regarding personal guests and professional visitors

Employee ID Badges

To make personnel identification both easy and accurate, each employee will be issued a photo ID badge that must be worn at all times while in the building. The Human Resources department will arrange photo sessions for all current employees. Badges for future new hires will be made during the new employee orientation session.

Access Checkpoint

During normal working hours, 8:00 a.m. to 5:00 p.m. Monday through Friday, all employees will enter the building through the front door. Employees must show their photo ID badge to the receptionist before entering the lab.

For access after hours, all department heads will identify which employees need to enter the building outside normal working hours. A list of these employees will be kept at the receptionist's desk. After hours and on weekends the desk will be manned by a security guard. Each employee wanting to enter the building must show the guard a valid company ID card and must be included on the authorization list. If the employee is not on the list, the security guard will deny access.

Reporting Unauthorized or Suspicious Entry

We all stand to benefit from improved security, so the company considers it everyone's responsibility to watch for and report unauthorized or suspicious entry to the building.

Follows the format used in the company's policy and procedures manual

Emphasizes the important elements of the policy, as well as the steps in the procedure

organizational decisions. Policy reports range from brief descriptions of business procedures to manuals that run dozens or hundreds of pages. *Position papers* outline an organization's official position on issues that affect the company's success. Figure 11–8 explains a building access policy for a firm where many scientists work irregular hours, especially when a deadline approaches or when experiments need constant monitoring.

> **Reports to demonstrate compliance.** Businesses are required to submit a variety of *compliance reports,* from tax returns and corporate financial statements to reports describing the proper handling of hazardous materials.

> **Reports to document progress.** Supervisors, investors, and customers frequently expect to be informed of the progress of projects and other

✱ Explore

activities. *Progress reports* range from simple updates in memo form to comprehensive status reports.

Organizing Information Reports

In most cases, the direct approach is the best choice for informational reports, since you are simply conveying information. However, if the information is disappointing, such as a project that is behind schedule or over budget, you might consider building up to the bad news through an indirect approach. In general, let the nature of whatever you're describing dictate your structure.

Most informational reports use a **topical organization**, arranging material in one of the following ways:

> **Comparison.** If you need to show similarities and differences (or advantages and disadvantages) between two or more entities, organize your report in a way that helps your readers see those similarities and differences clearly.
> **Importance.** Build up from the least important item to most important if you expect that the audience will read the entire report, or start with the most important item and progress to the least important if you suspect the readers are interested in only the more important items.
> **Sequence.** Any information that concerns a process or procedure is a good candidate for organizing by sequence. Discuss the steps or stages in the order in which they occur.
> **Chronology.** Describe a development or an event by the order in which incidents occurred. For example, when discussing a sales trend over time, you can organize the study according to what happened in January, what happened in February, and so on.
> **Spatial orientation.** If you're explaining how a physical object works or a physical space looks, describe it from left to right (or right to left in some cultures), top to bottom, or outside to inside—in whatever order makes the most sense.
> **Geography.** If location is important, organize your study according to geography, perhaps by region of the world or by area of a city.
> **Category.** If you're asked to review several distinct aspects of a subject, look at one category at a time, such as sales, profit, cost, or investment.

Whichever pattern you choose, use it consistently, so readers can easily follow your discussion from start to finish. Bear in mind, however, that in many instances you might be expected to follow a standard organization.

Of course, effective informational reports must also be audience-centred, logical, focused, and easy to follow, with generous use of previews and summaries. Your audience expects you to sort out the details and separate major points from minor points. In other words, readers expect you to put in all the thought and effort it takes to make the best use of their time. In addition, effective reports are honest and objective without being unduly harsh whenever negative information must be conveyed.

Compare the two versions of Carrie Andrews's personal activity report in Figures 11–9 and 11–10. At a quick glance, Figure 11–9 may seem to do a good job of meeting audience needs, but this report has a number of weaknesses that distract from the writer's intent and make readers struggle to extract the main points. The version of the report in Figure 11–10 is much easier to read and presents pertinent information in a clear, concise way.

The messages conveyed by informational reports can range from extremely positive to extremely negative, so the approach you take warrants careful consideration.

> Figure 11–9 Ineffective Informational Report

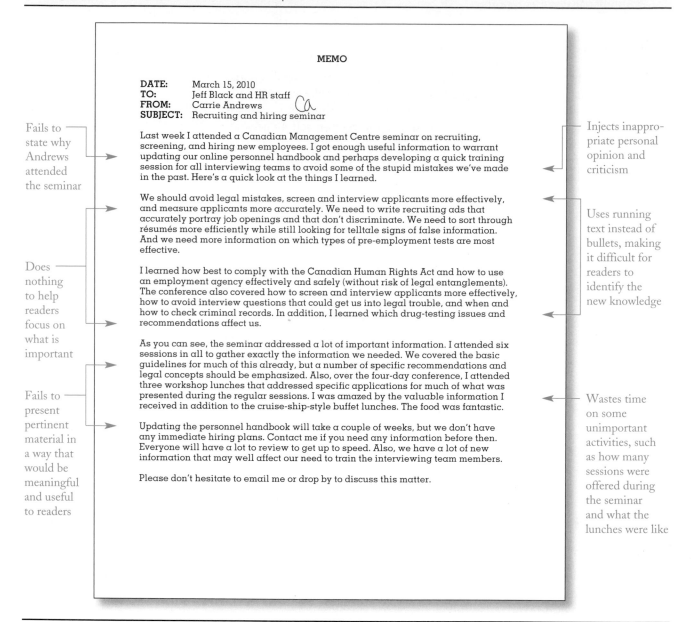

Fails to state why Andrews attended the seminar

Does nothing to help readers focus on what is important

Fails to present pertinent material in a way that would be meaningful and useful to readers

Injects inappropriate personal opinion and criticism

Uses running text instead of bullets, making it difficult for readers to identify the new knowledge

Wastes time on some unimportant activities, such as how many sessions were offered during the seminar and what the lunches were like

MEMO

DATE: March 15, 2010
TO: Jeff Black and HR staff
FROM: Carrie Andrews
SUBJECT: Recruiting and hiring seminar

Last week I attended a Canadian Management Centre seminar on recruiting, screening, and hiring new employees. I got enough useful information to warrant updating our online personnel handbook and perhaps developing a quick training session for all interviewing teams to avoid some of the stupid mistakes we've made in the past. Here's a quick look at the things I learned.

We should avoid legal mistakes, screen and interview applicants more effectively, and measure applicants more accurately. We need to write recruiting ads that accurately portray job openings and that don't discriminate. We need to sort through résumés more efficiently while still looking for telltale signs of false information. And we need more information on which types of pre-employment tests are most effective.

I learned how best to comply with the Canadian Human Rights Act and how to use an employment agency effectively and safely (without risk of legal entanglements). The conference also covered how to screen and interview applicants more effectively, how to avoid interview questions that could get us into legal trouble, and when and how to check criminal records. In addition, I learned which drug-testing issues and recommendations affect us.

As you can see, the seminar addressed a lot of important information. I attended six sessions in all to gather exactly the information we needed. We covered the basic guidelines for much of this already, but a number of specific recommendations and legal concepts should be emphasized. Also, over the four-day conference, I attended three workshop lunches that addressed specific applications for much of what was presented during the regular sessions. I was amazed by the valuable information I received in addition to the cruise-ship-style buffet lunches. The food was fantastic.

Updating the personnel handbook will take a couple of weeks, but we don't have any immediate hiring plans. Contact me if you need any information before then. Everyone will have a lot to review to get up to speed. Also, we have a lot of new information that may well affect our need to train the interviewing team members.

Please don't hesitate to email me or drop by to discuss this matter.

Organizing Website Content

Many websites, particularly company websites, function as informational reports, offering sections with information about the company, its history, its products and services, its executive team, and so on. While most of what you've already learned about informational reports applies to website writing, the online experience requires some special considerations and practices.

As you begin to plan a website, start by recognizing the unique nature of online communication:

> **Web readers are demanding.** Most site visitors won't bother to dig through poorly organized information. They quickly scan navigation buttons, headings, images, and hyperlinks, looking for possibilities. If nothing looks promising, they're gone.[24]

> Figure 11–10 Effective Informational Report

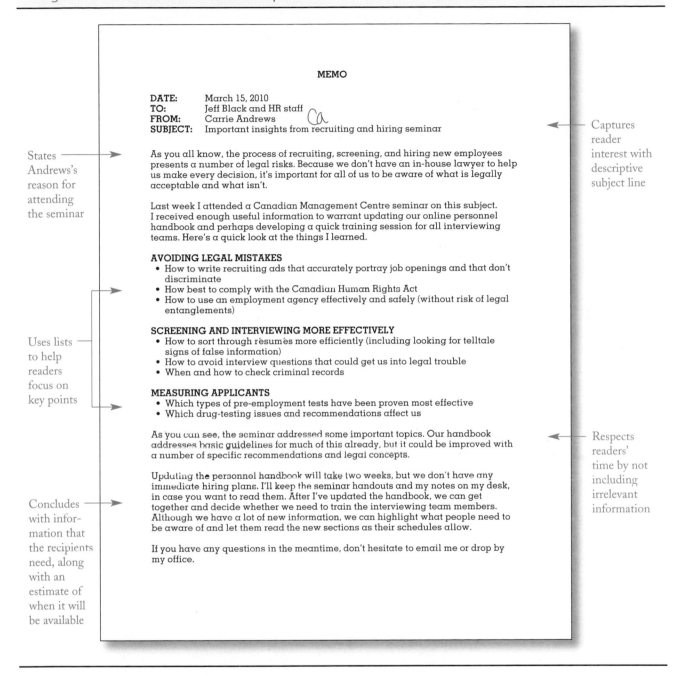

States Andrews's reason for attending the seminar

Uses lists to help readers focus on key points

Concludes with information that the recipients need, along with an estimate of when it will be available

MEMO

DATE: March 15, 2010
TO: Jeff Black and HR staff
FROM: Carrie Andrews
SUBJECT: Important insights from recruiting and hiring seminar

As you all know, the process of recruiting, screening, and hiring new employees presents a number of legal risks. Because we don't have an in-house lawyer to help us make every decision, it's important for all of us to be aware of what is legally acceptable and what isn't.

Last week I attended a Canadian Management Centre seminar on this subject. I received enough useful information to warrant updating our online personnel handbook and perhaps developing a quick training session for all interviewing teams. Here's a quick look at the things I learned.

AVOIDING LEGAL MISTAKES
- How to write recruiting ads that accurately portray job openings and that don't discriminate
- How best to comply with the Canadian Human Rights Act
- How to use an employment agency effectively and safely (without risk of legal entanglements)

SCREENING AND INTERVIEWING MORE EFFECTIVELY
- How to sort through résumés more efficiently (including looking for telltale signs of false information)
- How to avoid interview questions that could get us into legal trouble
- When and how to check criminal records

MEASURING APPLICANTS
- Which types of pre-employment tests have been proven most effective
- Which drug-testing issues and recommendations affect us

As you can see, the seminar addressed some important topics. Our handbook addresses basic guidelines for much of this already, but it could be improved with a number of specific recommendations and legal concepts.

Updating the personnel handbook will take two weeks, but we don't have any immediate hiring plans. I'll keep the seminar handouts and my notes on my desk, in case you want to read them. After I've updated the handbook, we can get together and decide whether we need to train the interviewing team members. Although we have a lot of new information, we can highlight what people need to be aware of and let them read the new sections as their schedules allow.

If you have any questions in the meantime, don't hesitate to email me or drop by my office.

Captures reader interest with descriptive subject line

Respects readers' time by not including irrelevant information

> **Reading online can be difficult.** Studies show that reading speeds are about 25 percent slower on a monitor than on paper.[25] Reading from computer screens can also be tiring on the eyes, even to the point of causing headaches, double vision, blurred vision, and other physical problems.[26]

> **The Web is a nonlinear, multidimensional medium.** Readers of online material move around in any order they please; there often is no beginning, middle, or end. As a Web writer, you need to anticipate the various paths your readers will want to follow and to make sure you provide the right hyperlinks in the right places to help readers explore successfully.

Further compounding a Web writer's challenge is the fact that many websites have to perform more than one communication function and therefore have more than one purpose. Each of these individual purposes needs to be carefully defined and then integrated into an overall statement of purpose for the entire website. Then, as you develop the site, you need to identify clearly the specific purpose of each section so that readers always know where to find the information they need.[27]

Just as you probably have a number of purposes for a single website, you're likely to have a number of audiences as well. The global reach of the Web further complicates the audience analysis issue because you may get visitors from all parts of the world. After you've identified your multiple audiences, you then need to analyze each group's unique information needs and then find a logical way to organize all that material. Professional website designers often use the term **information architecture** to describe the structure and navigational flow of all the parts of a website. In a sense, the information architecture is a three-dimensional outline of the site, showing (1) the vertical hierarchy of pages from the homepage down to the lower level, (2) the horizontal division of pages across the various sections of the site, and (3) the links that tie all these pages together, both internally (between various pages on the site) and externally (between your site and other websites).

As you develop the site architecture, you can begin to simulate how various audiences will use the site and refine the plan to meet everyone's needs. For instance, can potential customers find new product information quickly? In

> ### Figure 11–11 Information Architecture

contrast, can existing customers get support or warranty information quickly, without wading through pages of promotion for new products? You can also get a sense of how you need to assist visitors who enter the site at points other than the homepage, as often happens with search engine links. Accommodating these multiple entry points is one of the most difficult tasks in site design.[28] In Figure 11–11, thanks to careful consideration of information architecture, virtually every site visitor can quickly link to the information in which he or she might be interested.

To organize your site effectively, keep the following advice in mind:

> **Plan your navigation first.** Don't make the mistake of writing a traditional printed report and then adding links to make it a website. Most likely, you will need a different structure for the information, so plan your site structure and navigation before you write.[29]

> **Let your readers be in control.** Most readers want to navigate using paths they establish themselves, so create links and pathways that let them explore on their own. Help your readers by starting with a homepage that clearly points the way to various sections of the site and then offer plenty of descriptive labels, subheads, and previews that let readers figure out where to go next.

> **Break your information into chunks.** Help online readers scan and absorb information by breaking it into self-contained, easily readable chunks that are linked together logically.

Planning Analytical Reports

The purpose of analytical reports is to analyze, understand, and explain—to think through a problem or an opportunity and figure out how it affects the company and how the company should respond. In many cases, you'll also be expected to make a recommendation based on your analysis. As you saw in Figure 10-7, analytical reports fall into three basic categories:

Analytical reports are used to assess opportunities, to solve problems, and to support decisions.

> **Reports to assess opportunities.** Every business opportunity carries some degree of risk and also requires a variety of decisions and actions in order to capitalize on the opportunity. You can use analytical reports to assess both risk and required decisions and actions. For example, *market analysis reports* are used to judge the likelihood of success for new products or sales. *Due diligence reports* examine the financial aspects of a proposed decision, such as acquiring another company.

> **Reports to solve problems.** Managers often assign *troubleshooting reports* when they need to understand why something isn't working properly and what needs to be done to fix it. A variation, the *failure analysis report,* studies events that happened in the past, with the hope of learning how to avoid similar failures in the future.

> **Reports to support decisions.** *Feasibility reports* are called for when managers need to explore the ramifications of a decision they're about to make, such as switching materials used in a manufacturing process. *Justification reports* explain a decision that has already been made.

Writing analytical reports presents a greater challenge than writing informational reports, for three reasons: the quality of your reasoning, the quality of your writing, and the responsibility that comes with persuasion. First, you're doing more than simply delivering information—you're also thinking through a problem or opportunity and presenting your conclusions. The best writing in the world can't compensate for shaky analysis. Second, when your analysis is complete, you need to present your thinking in a compelling and persuasive manner. Third, analytical reports often convince other people to make significant financial and personnel decisions, so your reports carry the added responsibility of the consequences of these decisions.

Clarify the problem in an analytical report by determining what you need to analyze, why the issue is important, who is involved, where the trouble is located, and how and when it started.

To help define the problem that your analytical report will address, answer these questions:

> What needs to be determined?
> Why is this issue important?
> Who is involved in the situation?
> Where is the trouble located?
> How did the situation originate?
> When did it start?

Not all these questions apply in every situation, but asking them helps you define the problem being addressed and limit the scope of your discussion.

Use problem factoring to divide a complex problem into more manageable pieces.

Break down the perceived problem into a series of logical, connected questions that identify cause and effect. This process is sometimes called **problem factoring.** You probably subconsciously approach most problems this way, identifying cause-and-effect relationships that might pinpoint the source of the problem. When you speculate on the cause of a problem, you're forming a **hypothesis,** a potential explanation that needs to be tested. By subdividing a problem and forming hypotheses based on available evidence, you can tackle even the most complex situations.

Before you choose an approach, determine whether your audience is receptive or skeptical.

As with all business messages, the best organizational structure for each analytical report depends largely on your audience's likely reaction. The three basic structures involve focusing on conclusions, focusing on recommendations, and focusing on logic.

Focusing on Conclusions

Objective 7 Discuss three major ways to organize analytical reports.

Focusing on conclusions is often the best approach when you're addressing a receptive audience.

When writing for audiences that are likely to accept your conclusions—either because they've asked you to perform an analysis or they trust your judgment—consider using a direct approach that focuses immediately on your conclusions. This structure communicates the main idea quickly, but it does present some risks. Even if audiences trust your judgment, they may have questions about your data or the methods you used. Moreover, starting with a conclusion may create the impression that you have oversimplified the situation. To give readers the opportunity to explore the thinking behind your conclusion, support that conclusion with solid reasoning and evidence. Figure 11–12 presents an outline of a report analyzing the success of an outsourced training program. The writer opened with the conclusion but supported it with clear evidence, not personal opinion. Readers who accept the conclusion can stop reading, and those who desire more information can continue.

Focusing on Recommendations

When readers want to know what you think they should do, organize your report to focus on recommendations.

A slightly different approach is useful when your readers want to know what they ought to do in a given situation (as opposed to what they ought to conclude). You'll often be asked to solve a problem or assess an opportunity, rather than just study it. The actions you want your readers to take become the main subdivisions of your report.

When structuring a report around recommendations, use the direct approach as you would for a report that focuses on conclusions. Then, unfold your recommendations using a series of five steps:

1. Establish the need for action in the introduction by briefly describing the problem or opportunity.
2. Introduce the benefit(s) that can be achieved if the recommendation is adopted, along with any potential risks.

> Figure 11–12 Preliminary Outline of a Research Report Focusing on Conclusions

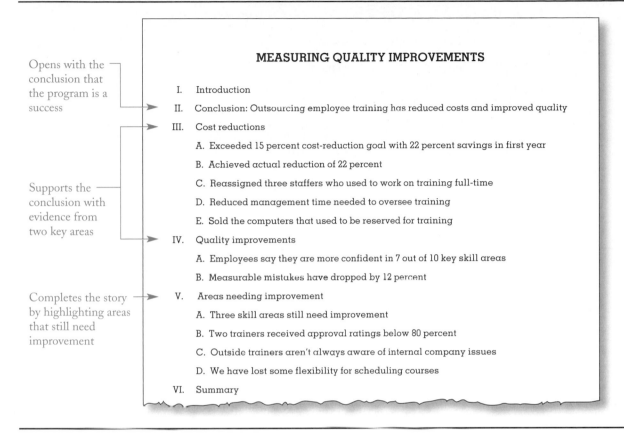

MEASURING QUALITY IMPROVEMENTS

Opens with the conclusion that the program is a success

I.   Introduction

II. Conclusion: Outsourcing employee training has reduced costs and improved quality

III. Cost reductions

    A. Exceeded 15 percent cost-reduction goal with 22 percent savings in first year

    B. Achieved actual reduction of 22 percent

    C. Reassigned three staffers who used to work on training full-time

    D. Reduced management time needed to oversee training

    E. Sold the computers that used to be reserved for training

Supports the conclusion with evidence from two key areas

IV. Quality improvements

    A. Employees say they are more confident in 7 out of 10 key skill areas

    B. Measurable mistakes have dropped by 12 percent

Completes the story by highlighting areas that still need improvement

V.   Areas needing improvement

    A. Three skill areas still need improvement

    B. Two trainers received approval ratings below 80 percent

    C. Outside trainers aren't always aware of internal company issues

    D. We have lost some flexibility for scheduling courses

VI. Summary

3. List the steps (recommendations) required to achieve the benefits, using action verbs for emphasis.

4. Explain each step more fully, giving details on procedures, costs, and benefits; if necessary, also explain how risks can be minimized.

5. Summarize your recommendations.

Focusing on Logical Arguments

When readers are skeptical or hostile to the conclusion or recommendation you plan to make, use an indirect approach that logically builds toward your conclusion or recommendation. If you guide the audience along a rational path toward the answer, they are more likely to accept it when they encounter it. The two most common logical approaches are known as the *2 + 2 = 4 approach* and the *yardstick approach* (see Table 11–8).

Logical arguments can follow two basic approaches: 2 + 2 = 4 (adding everything up) and the yardstick method (comparing ideas against a predetermined set of standards).

THE 2 + 2 = 4 APPROACH The **2 + 2 = 4 approach** is so named because it convinces readers of your point of view by demonstrating that everything adds up. The main points in your outline are the main reasons behind your conclusions and recommendations. You support each reason with the evidence you collected during your analysis. With its natural feel and versatility, the 2 + 2 = 4 approach is generally the most persuasive and efficient way to develop an analytical report for skeptical readers, so try this structure first. You'll find that most of your arguments fall naturally into this pattern.

Use the 2 + 2 = 4 approach; it's familiar and easy to develop.

As national sales manager of a sporting goods company, Binh Phan was concerned about his firm's ability to sell to its largest customers. His boss, the

> Table 11–8 Common Ways to Structure Analytical Reports

Element	Focus on Conclusions or Recommendations	Focus on Logical Argument	
		Use 2 + 2 = 4 Model	Use Yardstick Model
Readers	Are likely to accept	Hostile or skeptical	Hostile or skeptical
Approach	Direct	Indirect	Indirect
Writer credibility	High	Low	Low
Advantages	Readers quickly grasp conclusions or recommendations	Works well when you need to show readers how you built toward an answer by following clear, logical steps	Works well when you have a list of criteria (standards) that must be considered in a decision; alternatives are all measured against same criteria
Drawbacks	Structure can make topic seem too simple	Can make report longer	Readers must agree on criteria; can be lengthy because of the need to address each criterion for every alternative

vice-president of marketing, shared these concerns and instructed Phan to analyze the situation and recommend a solution.

Phan's troubleshooting report appears in Figure 11–13. The main idea is that the company should establish separate sales teams for these major accounts, rather than continuing to service them through the company's four regional divisions. However, Phan knew his plan would be controversial because it required a big change in the company's organization and in the way sales reps are paid. His thinking had to be clear and easy to follow, so he used the 2 + 2 = 4 approach to focus on his reasons.

The yardstick approach compares alternatives to a set of predetermined standards, without conducting experiments or evaluating hypotheses.

THE YARDSTICK APPROACH The **yardstick approach** is useful when you need to use a number of criteria to decide which option to select from two or more possibilities. With this approach, you begin by discussing the problem or opportunity and then list the criteria that will guide the decision. The body of the report then evaluates the alternatives against those criteria. Figure 11–14 is an outline of a feasibility report that uses the yardstick approach, using five criteria to evaluate two alternative courses of action. The report was provided by a market analyst for a large company that makes irrigation equipment for farms and ranches. Because the company was successful in the agricultural market, it started to run out of customers. To keep the company growing, the firm needed to find another market. Two alternatives considered were commercial buildings and residences. The author of the report was determined to make careful recommendations because, even though she didn't make the final decision, the information and the professional opinions that she provided weighed heavily on the decision process.

The yardstick approach has two potential drawbacks. First, your audience needs to agree with the criteria you're using in your analysis. If they don't, they won't agree with the results of the evaluation. If you have any doubt about your audience's agreement, build consensus before you start your report, if possible, or take extra care to explain why the criteria you're using are the best ones in this particular case. Second, the yardstick approach can get tedious when you have many options to consider or many criteria to compare them against. One way to minimize the repetition is to compare the options in tables and then highlight the more unusual or important aspects of each alternative in the text, so you balance the commentary with visual representation. This approach allows you to compare all the alternatives against the same yardstick while calling attention to the most significant differences among them.

Planning Proposals

The specific formats for proposals are innumerable, but they can be grouped into two general categories. *Internal proposals* request decisions from managers within the organization, such as proposals to buy new equipment or launch new research projects. *External proposals* request decisions from parties outside the organization. Examples of external proposals include *investment proposals,* which request funding from external investors; *grant proposals,* which request funds from government agencies and other sponsoring organizations; and *sales proposals,* which suggest individualized solutions for potential customers and request purchase decisions.

The most significant factor in planning a proposal is whether the recipient has asked you to submit a proposal. *Solicited proposals* are generally prepared at

❋⎯Explore

Buyers solicit proposals by publishing a request for proposals (RFP).

> Figure 11–13 Analytical Report Using the 2 + 2 = 4 Approach

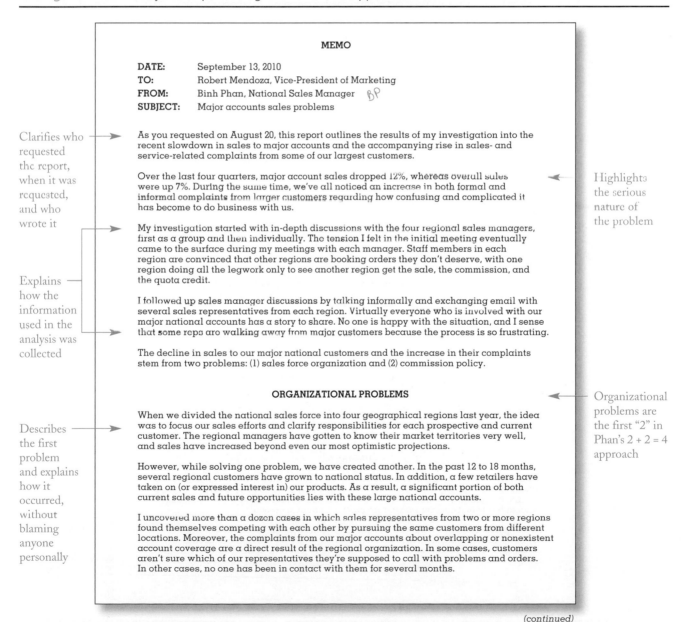

Clarifies who requested the report, when it was requested, and who wrote it

Explains how the information used in the analysis was collected

Describes the first problem and explains how it occurred, without blaming anyone personally

Highlights the serious nature of the problem

Organizational problems are the first "2" in Phan's 2 + 2 = 4 approach

MEMO

DATE: September 13, 2010
TO: Robert Mendoza, Vice-President of Marketing
FROM: Binh Phan, National Sales Manager
SUBJECT: Major accounts sales problems

As you requested on August 20, this report outlines the results of my investigation into the recent slowdown in sales to major accounts and the accompanying rise in sales- and service-related complaints from some of our largest customers.

Over the last four quarters, major account sales dropped 12%, whereas overall sales were up 7%. During the same time, we've all noticed an increase in both formal and informal complaints from larger customers regarding how confusing and complicated it has become to do business with us.

My investigation started with in-depth discussions with the four regional sales managers, first as a group and then individually. The tension I felt in the initial meeting eventually came to the surface during my meetings with each manager. Staff members in each region are convinced that other regions are booking orders they don't deserve, with one region doing all the legwork only to see another region get the sale, the commission, and the quota credit.

I followed up sales manager discussions by talking informally and exchanging email with several sales representatives from each region. Virtually everyone who is involved with our major national accounts has a story to share. No one is happy with the situation, and I sense that some reps are walking away from major customers because the process is so frustrating.

The decline in sales to our major national customers and the increase in their complaints stem from two problems: (1) sales force organization and (2) commission policy.

ORGANIZATIONAL PROBLEMS

When we divided the national sales force into four geographical regions last year, the idea was to focus our sales efforts and clarify responsibilities for each prospective and current customer. The regional managers have gotten to know their market territories very well, and sales have increased beyond even our most optimistic projections.

However, while solving one problem, we have created another. In the past 12 to 18 months, several regional customers have grown to national status. In addition, a few retailers have taken on (or expressed interest in) our products. As a result, a significant portion of both current sales and future opportunities lies with these large national accounts.

I uncovered more than a dozen cases in which sales representatives from two or more regions found themselves competing with each other by pursuing the same customers from different locations. Moreover, the complaints from our major accounts about overlapping or nonexistent account coverage are a direct result of the regional organization. In some cases, customers aren't sure which of our representatives they're supposed to call with problems and orders. In other cases, no one has been in contact with them for several months.

(continued)

> Figure 11–13 Analytical Report Using the 2 + 2 = 4 Approach (*continued*)

2

An example should help illustrate the problem. CanSport, with retail outlets in the Maritimes and on the west coast, was being pitched by reps from our West, Central, and East regions. Because we give our regional offices a lot of negotiating freedom, the three reps were offering the client different prices. But all of CanSport's buying decisions are made at their headquarters in Montreal, so all we did was confuse the customer. A critical problem with the current organization is that we're often giving our weakest selling and support efforts to the largest customers in the country.

Brings the first problem to life by complementing the general description with a specific example

COMMISSION PROBLEMS

Commission problems are the second "2" in Phan's 2 + 2 = 4 approach

The regional organization problems are compounded by the way we assign commissions and quota credit. Salespeople in one region can invest a lot of time in pursuing a sale, only to have the customer place the order in another region. So some sales rep in the second region ends up with the commission on a sale that was partly or even entirely earned by someone in the first region. Therefore, sales reps sometimes don't pursue leads in their regions, thinking that a rep in another region will get the commission.

Simplifies the reader's task by maintaining a parallel structure for the discussion of the second problem: a general description followed by a specific example

For example, Athletic Express, with outlets in four provinces spread across all four regions, finally got so frustrated with us that the company president called our headquarters. Athletic Express has been trying to place a large order for tennis and golf accessories, but none of our local reps seem interested in paying attention. I spoke with the rep responsible for Winnipeg, where the company is headquartered, and asked her why she wasn't working the account more actively. Her explanation was that last time she got involved with Athletic Express, the order was actually placed from their Vancouver regional office, and she didn't get any commission after more than two weeks of selling time.

RECOMMENDATIONS

Phan concludes the 2 + 2 = 4 approach: organizational problems + commission problems = the need for a new sales structure

Our sales organization should reflect the nature of our customer base. To accomplish that goal, we need a group of reps who are free to pursue accounts across regional borders— and who are compensated fairly for their work. The most sensible answer is to establish a national account group. Any customers whose operations place them in more than one region would automatically be assigned to the national group.

Explains how the new organizational structure will solve both problems

In addition to solving the problem of competing sales efforts, the new structure will also largely eliminate the commission-splitting problem because regional reps will no longer invest time in prospects assigned to the national accounts team. However, we will need to find a fair way to compensate regional reps who are losing long-term customers to the national team. Some of these reps have invested years in developing customer relationships that will continue to yield sales well into the future, and everyone I talked to agrees that reps in these cases should receive some sort of compensation. Such a "transition commission" would also motivate the regional reps to help ensure a smooth transition from one sales group to the other. The exact nature of this compensation would need to be worked out with the various sales managers.

Acknowledges that the recommended solution does create a temporary compensation problem, but expresses confidence that a solution to that can be worked out

3

SUMMARY

Neatly summarizes both the problem and the recommended solution

The regional sales organization is effective at the regional and local levels but not at the national level. We should establish a national accounts group to handle sales that cross regional boundaries. Then we'll have one set of reps who are focused on the local and regional levels and another set who are pursuing national accounts.

To compensate regional reps who lose accounts to the national team, we will need to devise some sort of payment to reward them for the years of work invested in such accounts. This can be discussed with the sales managers once the new structure is in place.

> Figure 11–14 Outline of an Analytical Report Using the Yardstick Approach

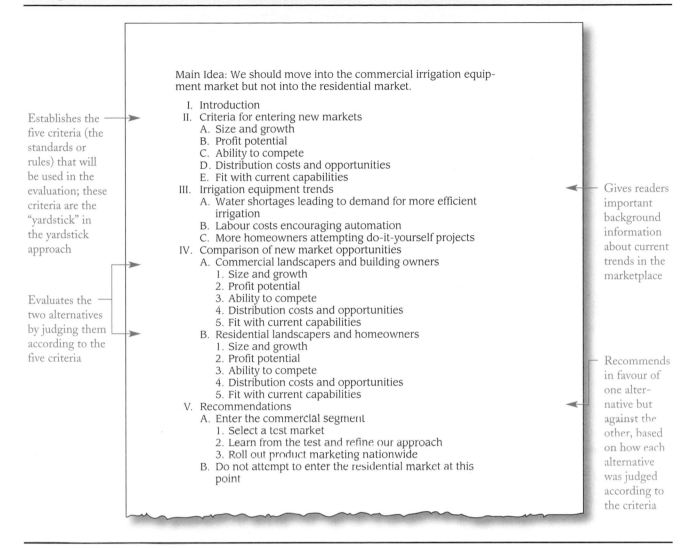

Establishes the five criteria (the standards or rules) that will be used in the evaluation; these criteria are the "yardstick" in the yardstick approach

Evaluates the two alternatives by judging them according to the five criteria

Gives readers important background information about current trends in the marketplace

Recommends in favour of one alternative but against the other, based on how each alternative was judged according to the criteria

Main Idea: We should move into the commercial irrigation equipment market but not into the residential market.

I. Introduction
II. Criteria for entering new markets
   A. Size and growth
   B. Profit potential
   C. Ability to compete
   D. Distribution costs and opportunities
   E. Fit with current capabilities
III. Irrigation equipment trends
   A. Water shortages leading to demand for more efficient irrigation
   B. Labour costs encouraging automation
   C. More homeowners attempting do-it-yourself projects
IV. Comparison of new market opportunities
   A. Commercial landscapers and building owners
      1. Size and growth
      2. Profit potential
      3. Ability to compete
      4. Distribution costs and opportunities
      5. Fit with current capabilities
   B. Residential landscapers and homeowners
      1. Size and growth
      2. Profit potential
      3. Ability to compete
      4. Distribution costs and opportunities
      5. Fit with current capabilities
V. Recommendations
   A. Enter the commercial segment
      1. Select a test market
      2. Learn from the test and refine our approach
      3. Roll out product marketing nationwide
   B. Do not attempt to enter the residential market at this point

the request of external parties that require a product or a service, but they may also be requested by such internal sources as management or the board of directors. Some external parties prepare a formal invitation to bid on their contracts, called a **request for proposals (RFP)**, which includes instructions that specify the exact type of work to be performed or products to be delivered, along with budgets, deadlines, and other requirements. Suppose that a municipal transit commission wants to purchase new, accessible buses to improve service for their elderly and physically challenged customers. Companies respond by preparing proposals that show how they would meet the stated needs. In most cases, organizations that issue RFPs also provide strict guidelines on what the proposals should include, and you need to follow these guidelines carefully to be considered. RFPs can seem surprisingly demanding, even to the point of specifying the size of paper to use, but you must follow every detail.

Unsolicited proposals offer more flexibility but a completely different sort of challenge than solicited proposals since recipients aren't expecting to receive them. In fact, your audience may not be aware of the problem or opportunity you are addressing, so before you can propose a solution, you might first need to convince your readers that a problem or opportunity exists. Consequently, an indirect approach is often the wise choice for unsolicited proposals.

Regardless of its format and structure, a good proposal explains what a project or course of action will involve, how much it will cost, and how the recipient and his or her organization will benefit. You can see all of these elements in Figure 11–15, Shandel Cohen's internal proposal for an automatic email response system that would replace a labour-intensive process of mailing out printed brochures every time a potential customer requests information.

Cohen manages the customer-response section of the marketing department at a personal computer manufacturer. Her section sends out product information requested by customers and the field sales force. Cohen has

> Figure 11–15 An Internal Proposal

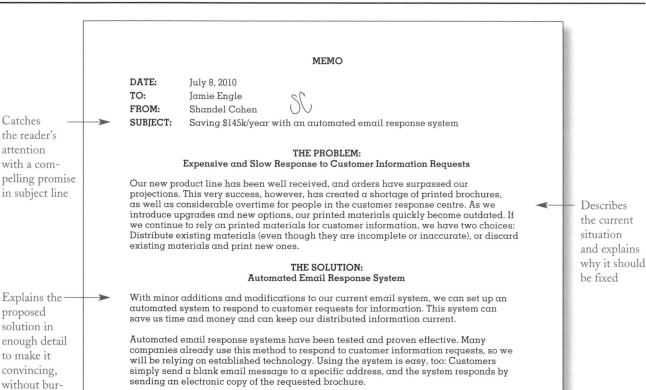

Catches the reader's attention with a compelling promise in subject line

Explains the proposed solution in enough detail to make it convincing, without burdening the reader with excessive detail

Describes the current situation and explains why it should be fixed

Builds reader interest in the proposed solution by listing a number of compelling benefits

MEMO

DATE: July 8, 2010
TO: Jamie Engle
FROM: Shandel Cohen
SUBJECT: Saving $145k/year with an automated email response system

THE PROBLEM:
Expensive and Slow Response to Customer Information Requests

Our new product line has been well received, and orders have surpassed our projections. This very success, however, has created a shortage of printed brochures, as well as considerable overtime for people in the customer response centre. As we introduce upgrades and new options, our printed materials quickly become outdated. If we continue to rely on printed materials for customer information, we have two choices: Distribute existing materials (even though they are incomplete or inaccurate), or discard existing materials and print new ones.

THE SOLUTION:
Automated Email Response System

With minor additions and modifications to our current email system, we can set up an automated system to respond to customer requests for information. This system can save us time and money and can keep our distributed information current.

Automated email response systems have been tested and proven effective. Many companies already use this method to respond to customer information requests, so we will be relying on established technology. Using the system is easy, too: Customers simply send a blank email message to a specific address, and the system responds by sending an electronic copy of the requested brochure.

Benefit #1: Always-Current Information

Rather than discard and print new materials, we would need to keep only the electronic files up to date on the server. We could be able to provide customers and our field sales organization with up-to-date, correct information as soon as the upgrades or options are available.

Benefit #2: Instantaneous Delivery

Almost immediately after requesting information, customers would have that information in hand. Electronic delivery would be especially advantageous for our international customers. Regular mail to remote locations sometimes takes weeks to arrive, by which time the information may already be out of date. Both customers and field salespeople will appreciate the automatic mail-response system.

Benefit #3: Minimized Waste

With our current method of printing every marketing piece in large quantities, we discard thousands of pages of obsolete catalogues, data sheets, and other materials every year. By maintaining and distributing the information electronically, we would eliminate this waste. We would also free up a considerable amount of expensive floor space and shelving that is required for storing printed materials.

(continued)

> Figure 11–15 An Internal Proposal (*continued*)

Acknowledges one potential shortcoming with the new approach but provides a convincing solution

Itemizes the cost savings in order to support the $145k/year claim made in the subject line

Summarizes the benefits and invites further discussion

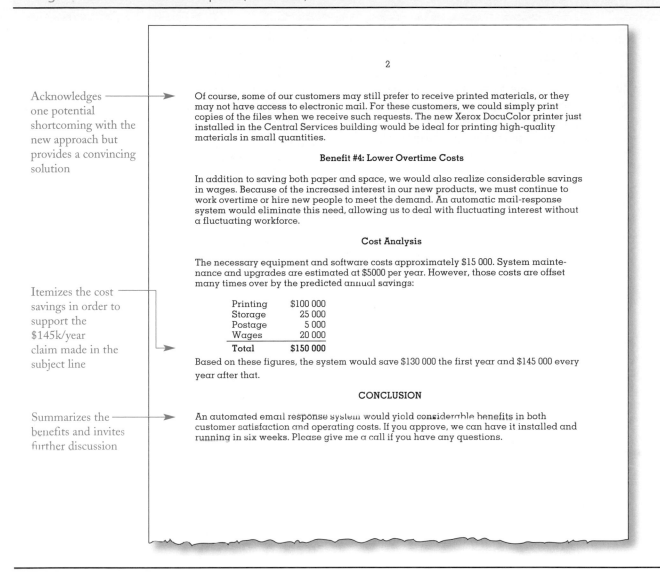

2

Of course, some of our customers may still prefer to receive printed materials, or they may not have access to electronic mail. For these customers, we could simply print copies of the files when we receive such requests. The new Xerox DocuColor printer just installed in the Central Services building would be ideal for printing high-quality materials in small quantities.

Benefit #4: Lower Overtime Costs

In addition to saving both paper and space, we would also realize considerable savings in wages. Because of the increased interest in our new products, we must continue to work overtime or hire new people to meet the demand. An automatic mail-response system would eliminate this need, allowing us to deal with fluctuating interest without a fluctuating workforce.

Cost Analysis

The necessary equipment and software costs approximately $15 000. System mainte-nance and upgrades are estimated at $5000 per year. However, those costs are offset many times over by the predicted annual savings:

Printing	$100 000
Storage	25 000
Postage	5 000
Wages	20 000
Total	**$150 000**

Based on these figures, the system would save $130 000 the first year and $145 000 every year after that.

CONCLUSION

An automated email response system would yield considerable benefits in both customer satisfaction and operating costs. If you approve, we can have it installed and running in six weeks. Please give me a call if you have any questions.

observed that the demand for information increases when a new product is released and that it diminishes as a product matures. This fluctuating demand causes drastic changes in her section's workload. Employees either have more work than they can handle, or they don't have enough to keep consistently busy. A cycle of layoffs and hiring was not a desired option. Cohen is also concerned about the amount of printed material that's discarded when products are upgraded or replaced.

Cohen's internal proposal seeks management's approval to install an automatic mail-response system. Because the company manufactures computers, she knows that her boss won't object to a computer-based solution. Also, since profits are always a concern, her report emphasizes the financial benefits of her proposal. Her report describes the problem, the proposed solutions, the benefits to the company, and the projected costs.

Summary of Learning Objectives

1 **Distinguish between informational reports, analytical reports, and proposals.** Informational reports focus on facts and are intended mainly to inform and educate readers, not to persuade them. Informational reports include those for monitoring and controlling operations (plans, operating reports, and personal activity reports), implementing policies and procedures (guidelines or position papers), demonstrating compliance (reports to regulators), and documenting progress. Analytical reports analyze and interpret data and may make recommendations based on the data. Many analytical reports are intended to persuade readers to accept a decision, action, or recommendation. Troubleshooting, failure analysis, feasibility, and justification reports are examples of analytical reports. Proposals persuade readers to make decisions and take action; proposals may be internal (funding and project proposals) or external (investment, grant, and sales proposals).

2 **Describe an effective process for conducting business research.** To plan your research effectively, develop a problem statement that defines the purpose of the research. Identify gaps in your information to help you use your time well. Locate data and information effectively by evaluating your sources, determining such qualities as credibility, currency, and completeness.

3 **Define primary and secondary research, and explain when you use each method.** Primary research is new research; it is undertaken specifically for your study. This research includes surveys, interviews, observations, and experiments. Secondary research is characterized by research materials previously created for another purpose: These sources include magazines, newspapers, public websites, and books. Use secondary research to fill in the gaps in your knowledge and to enhance the credibility of your report.

4 **Evaluate the credibility of an information source, and conduct an effective online search.** Judge the credibility of sources by exploring their reputations for honesty and objectivity. Assess the qualifications of the author, and determine if the material can be verified independently and is complete. To conduct an effective online search, determine and assess the owner of the URL (is it a corporation or political party promoting its own goals?), the author's qualifications, the context of the information (is it original or plagiarized? is it documented?), and how current the site is.

5 **Outline an effective process for planning and conducting information interviews.** Plan information interviews by analyzing your purpose, learning about the person you're interviewing, and formulating your main idea. Determine the interview duration, style, and structure. Conduct interviews by asking open-ended questions for opinions, insights, and information. Ask closed-ended questions for specific answers. Use follow-up questions to encourage your subjects to elaborate on brief responses.

6 **Explain the differences between drafting a summary, drawing a conclusion, and developing a recommendation.** A summary provides the essence of the material by presenting the main ideas but omits most details and supporting information. A conclusion is a logical interpretation from the information in the report. A recommendation advises how the reader should act on the information.

7 **Discuss three major ways to organize analytical reports.** Focusing on conclusions is one way to organize analytical reports: In this approach, you present the main idea quickly, but you risk the audience questioning your data or methodology. The audience may also believe you oversimplified the situation. To overcome such problems, ensure that you support your conclusions with logical reasoning and firm evidence. Focusing on recommendations, another report structure, also requires the direct approach: Begin by describing the problem and follow with benefits if your audience accepts your recommendations. The report then describes the steps needed to attain the benefits. A third way to structure reports is by focusing on logical arguments. A useful method for dealing with skeptical readers, this approach uses indirection and logically builds to your conclusions and recommendations.

On the Job PERFORMING COMMUNICATION TASKS AT DELL INC.

To keep its position in the computer industry, Dell Inc. must continue to improve customer service. You are a manager in customer relations, and your supervisor has asked you to plan a report that will outline ways to increase customer satisfaction. You'll need to conduct the necessary research, analyze the findings, and present your recommendations. From the following, choose the best responses, and be prepared to explain why your choices are best.

1 Which represents the most appropriate statement of purpose for this study?

   a The purpose of this study is to identify any customer service problems at Dell.

   b This study answers the following question: "What improvements in customer service can Dell make to increase overall customer satisfaction?"

   c This study identifies the Dell customer service representatives who are most responsible for poor customer satisfaction.

   d This study identifies steps that Dell's customer service representatives should undertake to change customer service practices at Dell.

2 You have tentatively identified the following factors for analysis:

   I To improve customer service, we need to hire more customer service representatives.

     A Compute competitors' employee-to-sales ratios.

     B Compute our employee-to-sales ratio.

   II To improve customer service, we need to hire better customer service representatives.

     A Assess skill level of competitors' customer service representatives.

     B Assess skill level of our customer service representatives.

   III To improve customer service, we need to retrain our customer service representatives.

     A Review competitors' training programs.

     B Review our training programs.

   IV To improve customer service, we need to compensate and motivate our people differently.

     A Assess competitors' compensation levels and motivational techniques.

     B Assess our compensation levels and motivational techniques.

   Should you proceed with the investigation on the basis of this preliminary outline, or should you consider other approaches to factoring the problem?

   a Proceed with this outline.

   b Do not proceed. Factor the problem by asking customers how they perceive current customer service efforts at Dell. In addition, ask customer service representatives what they think should be done differently.

   c Do not proceed. Factor the problem by surveying non-buyers to find out if current customer service efforts influenced their decision not to buy from Dell. In addition, ask non-buyers what they think should be done differently.

   d Do not proceed. Factor the problem by asking customer service representatives for suggestions on how to improve customer service. In addition, ask non-buyers and current customers what they think should be done differently.

3 Which work plan is the best option for guiding your study of ways to improve customer service?

   a Version 1

   Statement of Problem: As part of Dell Inc.'s continuing efforts to offer the most attractive computers in the world, management wants to improve customer service. The challenge here is to identify service improvements that are meaningful and valuable to the customer without being too expensive or time consuming.

   Purpose and Scope of Work: The purpose of this study is to identify ways to increase customer satisfaction by improving customer service at Dell. A four member study team, composed of the vice-president of customer relations and three customer service representatives, has been appointed to prepare a written service-improvement plan. To accomplish this objective, this study will survey customers to learn what changes they'd like to see in terms of customer service. The team will analyze these potential improvements in terms of cost and time requirements and then will design new service procedures that customer service representatives can use to better satisfy customers.

   Sources and Methods of Data Collection and Analysis: The study team will assess current customer service efforts by

   1 querying customer service representatives regarding their customer service

   2 observing representatives in action dealing with customers through email responses and telephone calls

   3 surveying current Dell owners regarding their purchase experiences

   4 surveying visitors to the Dell website who decide not to purchase from Dell (by intercepting a sample of these people as they leave the website)

   The team will also view competitive websites to determine first-hand how they treat customers, and the team will submit online questionnaires to a sample of computer owners and classify the results by brand name. Once all these data have been collected, the team will analyze them to determine where buyers and potential buyers consider customer service to be lacking. Finally, the team will design procedures to meet their expectations.

Schedule:

Jan. 11–Jan. 31:	Query customer service representatives.
	Observe representatives in action.
	Survey current Dell owners.
	Survey non-buyers at the Dell website.
Feb. 1–Feb. 15:	Visit competitive websites.
	Conduct online survey of computer owners.
Feb. 16–Mar. 15:	Analyze data.
	Draft new procedures.
Mar. 16–Mar. 25:	Prepare final report.
Mar. 29:	Present to management/customer service committee.

b Version 2

Statement of Problem: Dell's customer service representatives need to get on the ball in terms of customer service, and we need to tell them what to do to fix their customer service shortcomings.

Purpose and Scope of Work: This report will address how we plan to solve the problem. We'll design new customer service procedures and prepare a written report from which customer service representatives can learn.

Sources and Methods of Data Collection: We plan to employ the usual methods of collecting data, including direct observation and surveys.

Schedule:

Collect data.	Jan. 11–Feb. 15
Analyze data.	Feb. 16–Mar. 1
Draft new procedures.	Mar. 2–Mar. 15
Prepare final report.	Mar. 16–Mar. 25
Present to management/customer service committee.	Mar. 29

c Version 3

Task 1—Query customer service representatives: We will interview a sampling of customer service representatives to find out what steps they take to ensure customer satisfaction. Dates: Jan. 11–Jan. 20

Task 2—Observe representatives in action: We will observe a sampling of customer service representatives as they work with potential buyers and current owners to learn first hand what steps employees typically take. Dates: Jan. 21–Jan. 29

Task 3—Survey current Dell owners: Using a sample of names from Dell's database of current owners, we'll ask owners how they felt about the purchase process when they bought their computer and how they feel

they've been treated since then. We'll also ask them to suggest steps we could take to improve service. Dates: Jan. 15–Feb. 15

Task 4—Survey non-buyers at Dell: While we are observing customer service representatives, we will also approach visitors to the Dell website who leave the site without making a purchase. As visitors exit the site, we'll present a quick online survey, asking them what they think about Dell's customer service policies and practices and whether these had any bearing on their decision not to buy a Dell product. Dates: Jan. 21–Jan. 31

Task 5—Visit competitive websites: Under the guise of shoppers looking for new computers, we will visit a selection of competitive websites to discover how they treat customers and whether they offer any special service that Dell doesn't. Dates: Feb. 1–Feb. 15

Task 6—Conduct online survey of computer owners: Using internet-based technology, we will survey a sampling of computer owners (of all brands). We will then sort the answers by brand of computer owned to see which dealers are offering which services. Dates: Jan. 15–Feb. 15

Task 7—Analyze data: Once we've collected all these data, we'll analyze them to identify (1) services that customers would like to see Dell offer, (2) services offered by competitors that aren't offered by Dell, and (3) services currently offered by Dell that may not be all that important to customers. Dates: Feb. 16–Mar. 1

Task 8—Draft new procedures: From the data we've analyzed, we'll select new services that should be considered by Dell. We'll also assess the time and money burdens that these services are likely to present, so management can see whether each new service will yield a positive return on investment. Dates: Mar. 2–Mar. 15

Task 9—Prepare final report: This is essentially a documentation task, during which we'll describe our work, make our recommendations, and prepare a formal report. Dates: Mar. 16–Mar. 25

Task 10—Present to management/customer relations committee: We'll summarize our findings and recommendations and make the full report available to dealers at the quarterly meeting. Date: Mar. 29

d Version 4

Problem: To identify meaningful customer service improvements that can be implemented by Dell.

Data Collection: Use direct observation and online surveys to gather details about customer service at the Dell website and at competing websites. Have the study team survey current Dell owners and people who visited dell.ca but did not buy, and send an online questionnaire to computer owners.

Schedule:

Step 1: Data collection. Work will begin on January 11 and end on February 15.

Step 2: Data analysis. Work will start on February 16 and end on March 1.

Step 3: Drafting new procedures. Work will start on March 2 and end on March 15.

Step 4: Preparation of the final report. Work will start on March 16 and end on March 25.

Step 5: Presentation of the final report. The report will be presented to management and the customer service committee on March 29.

Test Your Knowledge

1 How do informational reports differ from analytical reports?

2 What is included in a work plan for a report, and why is it important?

3 How does primary information differ from secondary information?

4 What are the disadvantages of using search engines?

5 What is the difference between the mean, the median, and the mode?

6 What are the guidelines for conducting effective surveys?

7 What types of questions can be posed during an interview?

8 What is paraphrasing, and what is its purpose?

9 What are the characteristics of a sound conclusion?

10 How does a conclusion differ from a recommendation?

Apply Your Knowledge

1 Why must you be careful when using information from a web page in a business report?

2 Why do you need to evaluate the sources you uncover in your research?

3 If you were writing a recommendation report for an audience that doesn't know you, would you use a direct approach focusing on the recommendation or an indirect approach focusing on logic? Why?

4 Why are unsolicited proposals more challenging to write than solicited proposals?

5 **Ethical Choices:** Companies occasionally make mistakes that expose confidential information, such as when employees lose laptop computers containing sensitive data files or webmasters forget to protect confidential web pages from search engine indexes. If you conducted an online search that turned up competitive information on web pages that were clearly intended to be private, what would you do? Explain your answer.

Running Cases

Watch on mycanadianbuscommlab

> CASE 1 Noreen

Noreen would like to propose a new project to upper-level management: reorganizing two departments into one.

Currently, the "Go Points" department is on the 4th floor and is staffed by 20 sales/service reps. They (1) make sales calls to existing Petro-Go credit card holders to offer the points program, (2) receive calls from existing points program customers who have enquiries, and (3) call existing points customers to announce promotions, offers, and so on.

The Petro-Go credit card department is on the 3rd floor and is staffed by 30 sales/service reps. They (1) make sales calls to recruit new credit card customers, (2) receive calls from existing credit card holders who have enquiries, and (3) call existing credit card customers to announce promotions, offers, and so on.

Noreen thinks that by joining the credit card sales/service department with the "Go Points" department, customers will be better served by one-stop shopping. She also feels that the credit card sales/service staff could easily modify their call routines to include information about the "Go Points" program, and the "Go Points" staff could easily be trained on the credit card policies and procedures.

QUESTIONS

a) Is this a solicited proposal?

b) How will Noreen use the "you" attitude in this proposal?

c) What costs might be involved?

d) What supporting facts or evidence do you think might help Noreen justify this proposal?

e) What are some concerns or problems that may arise during this project?

YOUR TASK

Create a work plan for Noreen to use as a guide (see Figures 11–2 and 11–3) in writing her proposal. Include the following elements:

> statement of the problem
> statement of the purpose and scope
> discussion of the tasks to be accomplished, and
> review of timelines and resources required

> CASE 2 Kwong

Kwong applies to and gets hired by a large national telephone service provider, ET Canada, in the accounting department. He plans to complete his CGA studies part-time because he finds his expenses increasing and he needs to have more income. His goal of opening his own accounting firm is still alive but will take a little longer to achieve.

One of his first tasks is to work on the company's annual report with a team from the finance department. The annual report will be posted on the internet and distributed to all shareholders.

QUESTIONS

a) Which type of report best describes an annual report—an analytical report, an operating report, or a progress report?

b) What information is included in a company annual report?

c) Where will Kwong find the information he needs for the annual report?

d) What teamwork skills will Kwong need to be an effective team member?

e) How will Kwong format the headings in the report so the reader knows where each new section begins and which sub topics relate to which heading?

YOUR TASK

Research a public Canadian utility company. Public companies usually have more information available than private companies. Use the SEDAR (System for Electronic Document Analysis and Retrieval) website to find a list of Canadian public companies and their annual reports. Review several company annual reports for utility service providers. Make a list of the common headings and sections within the annual reports. Create a table of contents that Kwong might use in ET Canada's annual report.

Practise Your Knowledge

The Canadian Securities Regulatory System (CSRA) requires all public companies to file a comprehensive financial annual report electronically. Many companies post links to these reports on their websites along with links to other company reports. Visit the website of the Montreal sport shirt manufacturer Gildan Activewear at www.gildan.com and find the company's most recent annual financial reports. (Click "Corporate" on the homepage and then click the "Investor Relations" link. Then click "Financial Information and Reports".) Analyze the style and format of the annual report. For which audience(s) is the annual report targeted? Who besides members of the CSRA might be interested in the annual report? Do you find this report easy to read? Interesting? Detailed?

Exercises

11.1 Understanding Business Reports and Proposals: How Companies Use Reports

Interview several people working in a career you might like to enter, and ask them about the written reports they receive and prepare. How do these reports tie in to the decision-making process? Who reads the reports they prepare? Summarize your findings in writing, give them to your instructor and be prepared to discuss them with the class.

11.2 Understanding Business Reports and Proposals: Report Classification

Using the information presented in this chapter, identify the report type represented by each example. In addition, write a brief paragraph about each, explaining who the audience is likely to be, what type of data would be used, and whether conclusions and recommendations would be appropriate.

a. a statistical study of the pattern of violent crime in a large city during the last five years

b. a report prepared by a seed company demonstrating the benefits of its seed corn for farmers

c. a report prepared by an independent testing agency evaluating various types of non-prescription cold remedies

d. a trip report submitted at the end of a week by a travelling salesperson

e. a report indicating how 45 acres of undeveloped land could be converted into an industrial park

f. an annual report to be sent to the shareholders of a large corporation

g. a written report by a police officer who has just completed an arrest

11.3 Informational Reports: Personal Activity Report

Imagine you're the manager of campus recruiting for Manulife Financial, a major Canadian financial services company. Each of your four recruiters interviews up to 11 fourth-year university students every day. What kind of personal activity report can you design to track the results of these interviews? List the areas you would want each recruiter to report on, and explain how each would help you manage the recruiting process (and the recruiters) more effectively.

11.4 Understanding Your Topic: Sub-Questions

Your supervisor has asked you to do some research on franchising. Actually, he's thinking about purchasing a few Subway franchises, and he needs some information. Visit www.amazon.ca and perform a keyword search on "franchises." Explore some of the books that you find by reading reviews and using the "search inside" feature.

a. Use the information to develop a list of sub-questions to help you narrow your focus.

b. Write down the names of three books you might purchase for your boss.

c. How can this website assist you with your research efforts?

11.5 Finding Secondary Information: Major Business Resources

Using online, database, or printed sources, find the following information. Ensure that you properly cite your sources using the formats discussed in Appendix B. (Hint: Start with Table 11–3, Major Business Resources.)

a. contact information for the Chartered Accountants of Canada

b. median weekly earnings of men and women by occupation

c. current market share for Perrier water

d. performance ratios for office supply retailers

e. annual stock performance for Ballard Power Systems

f. number of franchise outlets in Canada

g. composition of the Canadian workforce by profession

11.6 Finding Information: Company Information

Select any public company and find the following information:

a. names of the company's current officers

b. list of the company's products or services (if the company has a large number of products, list the product lines instead)

c. current issues in the company's industry

d. outlook for the company's industry as a whole

11.7 Finding Information: Secondary Information

You'd like to know if it's a good idea to buy banner ads on other websites to drive more traffic to your company's website. You're worried about the expense and difficulty of running an experiment to test banner effectiveness, so you decide to look for some secondary data. Using databases available through your library, identify three secondary sources that might offer helpful data on this question.

11.8 Finding Information: Search Techniques

Analyze any recent school or work assignment that required you to conduct research. How did you approach your investigation? Did you rely mostly on sources of primary information or mostly on sources of secondary information? Now that you have studied this chapter, can you identify two ways to improve the research techniques you used during that assignment? Explain.

11.9 Finding Information: Surveys

You work for a movie studio that is producing a young director's first motion picture, the story of a group of unknown musicians finding work and making a reputation in a competitive industry. Unfortunately, some of your friends leave the screening, saying that the 182-minute movie is simply too long. Others said they couldn't imagine any sequences to cut out. Your supervisor wants to test the movie on a regular audience and ask viewers to complete a questionnaire that will help the director decide whether edits are needed and, if so, where. Design a questionnaire that you can use to solicit valid answers for a report to the director about how to handle the audience's reaction to the movie.

11.10 Finding Information: Interviews

You're conducting an information interview with a manager in another division of your company. Partway through the interview, the manager shows clear signs of impatience. How should you respond? What might you do differently to prevent this from happening in the future? Explain your answers.

11.11 Teamwork: Evaluating Sources

Break into small groups and surf the internet to find websites that provide business information such as company or industry news, trends, analysis, facts, or performance data. Use the criteria discussed under "Evaluating Your Sources" to evaluate the credibility of the information presented at these websites.

11.12 Processing Information: Reading and Taking Notes

Select an article from a business magazine such as *Canadian Business, Report on Business Magazine, or Fortune*. Read the article and highlight the key points. Summarize the article in less than 100 words, paraphrasing the key points.

11.13 Analyzing Data: Calculating the Mean

Your boss has asked you to analyze and report on your division's sales for the first nine months of this year. Use the following data from company invoices to calculate the mean for each quarter and all averages for the year to date. Then, identify and discuss the quarterly sales trends.

January	$24 600	April	$21 200	July	$29 900
February	25 900	May	24 600	August	30 500
March	23 000	June	26 800	September	26 600

11.14 Teamwork: Unsolicited Proposal

Break into small groups and identify an operational problem occurring at your campus involving either registration, university housing, food services, parking, or library services. Then, develop a workable solution to that problem. Finally, develop a list of pertinent facts that your team will need to gather to convince the reader that the problem exists and that your solution will work.

11.15 Analyzing the Situation: Statement of Purpose

Sales at The Style Shop, a clothing store for men, have declined for the third month in a row. The owner is not sure if this decline is due to a weak economy or if it's due to another unknown reason. She has asked you to investigate the situation and to submit a report to her highlighting some possible reasons for the decline. Develop a statement of purpose for your report.

11.16 Ethical Choices

Your company operates a website featuring children's games and puzzles. The vice-president of marketing needs to know more about the children who visit the site, so she can plan new products. She has asked you to develop an online survey questionnaire to collect the data. What ethical issues do you see in this situation? What should you do?

12

Writing Reports and Proposals

ON THE JOB

Communicating at FedEx
DELIVERING ON TIME, EVERY TIME

www.FedEx.com

Imagine collecting, transporting, and delivering more than 7.5 million letters and packages every day. Now imagine that every one of these parcels absolutely, positively has to arrive at its destination when expected. That's the standard against which Federal Express managers—and customers—measure performance. Living up to this exacting standard day in and day out presents founder and chief executive officer Frederick W. Smith and his entire management team with a variety of communication challenges.

When FedEx began operations in 1973, its services covered 22 U.S. cities. Today it delivers throughout the United States and Canada, and to 220 countries around the world. FedEx operates more than 670 airplanes, maintains a fleet of 80 000 trucks and vans, and employs more than 290 000 people; in Canada, FedEx employees number 5000 across the country and the company operates hub facilities in Vancouver, Toronto, and Montreal.

FedEx must battle a host of rivals, including United Parcel Service (UPS), Purolator (owned by Canada Post), Airborne Express, and DHL. Competition is fierce, so FedEx must constantly introduce new methods or ideas to maintain its industry position and serve its customers better. The firm offers a host of online business tools, including address books, an address checker, complete international shipping documents, and

At FedEx, many kinds of reports are used to track both system and employee performance, as well as to assemble information needed for making managerial decisions. Not only does Frederick Smith read innumerable reports now, but as a university student he wrote a very famous one that detailed the idea of his air express delivery service and persuaded investors to fund him.

customizable portals where FedEx customers can track shipments and access signature proofs of delivery. Businesses can also add common FedEx functions to their retail websites and link directly to their own order management systems.

With competitors offering more and customers expecting more, Smith and his management team have their work cut out for them. Monitoring and controlling company operations, training new employees, tracking competitor service and performance, making a host of decisions about how to serve customers better—all these activities require the communication of timely, accurate information, and much of that information comes in the form of reports. To keep the business running smoothly, maintain satisfied customers, and hold competitors at bay, FedEx managers receive and prepare reports of all kinds. So how do Smith and his managers use reports for internal communication? How can FedEx writers make their reports readable and convenient to use? What makes one report better than another?[1]

Crafting Reports and Proposals

Report writers, including FedEx managers, will be the first to tell you how important the writing stage is in the development of successful reports and proposals. This chapter builds on the writing techniques and ideas you learned in Chapter 5 and examines issues that are particularly important when preparing longer message formats (see Figure 12–1). In addition, you'll get an introduction to creating effective visuals, which are a vital aspect of many reports and proposals.

As with shorter messages, take a few moments before you start writing to ensure that you're ready to adapt your approach to your audience.

> Figure 12–1 Step Two in the Three-Step Writing Process for Reports and Proposals

Planning > **Writing** > **Completing**

Adapt to Your Audience

Be sensitive to audience needs by using a "you" attitude, politeness, positive emphasis, and bias-free language. Build a strong relationship with your audience by establishing your credibility and projecting your companys image. Control your style with a tone and voice appropriate to the situation.

Compose the Message

Choose precise language that will help you create effective sentences and coherent paragraphs throughout the introduction, body, and close of your report or proposal.

1   2   3

Adapting to Your Audience

Like all successful business messages, effective reports and proposals are adapted to the intended audience as much as possible. To ensure your success with reports, be sensitive to audience needs, build strong relationships with your audience, and control your style and tone.

Chapter 5 introduced four aspects of audience sensitivity, and all four apply to reports and proposals: adopting the "you" attitude, maintaining a strong sense of etiquette, emphasizing the positive, and using bias-free language. Reports and proposals that are highly technical, complex, or lengthy can put heavy demands on your readers, so the "you" attitude takes on even greater importance with these long messages. As you'll see later in this chapter, part of that attitude includes helping your readers find their way through your material, so they can understand critical information.

Whether your report is intended for people inside or outside the company, plan how you will adapt your style and your language to reflect the image of your organization. Many companies have specific guidelines for communicating with public audiences; be sure you're aware of these preferences before you start writing (see Figure 12–2).

If you know your readers reasonably well and your report is likely to meet with their approval, you can generally adopt a fairly informal tone (as long as this is appropriate in your organization, of course). To make your tone less formal, speak to readers in the first person, refer to them as *you*, and refer to yourself as *I* (or *we* if there are multiple report authors).

Objective 1 Explain how to adapt to your audiences when writing reports and proposals.

Long or complex reports demand a lot from readers, making the "you" attitude even more important.

Many companies have specific guidelines for reports, particularly those intended for external audiences.

> Figure 12–2 Choosing the Right Tone for Business Reports

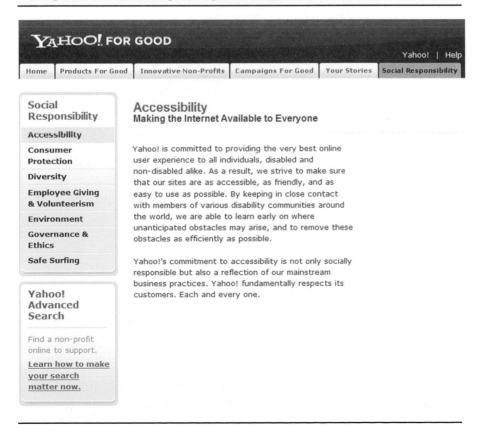

Committed

Clear. Capable. Committed.

PETRO-CANADA'S 2006–2007 REPORT TO THE COMMUNITY

Corporate reports to the community require a writing style and tone appropriate to the audience. What audiences read community reports? Should the writing style be formal or informal? What level of language should be used? Why are images important for these reports?

Reports destined for audiences outside Canada and the United States often require a more formal tone to match the expectations of audiences in many other countries.

To make your tone more formal, use the impersonal style: Emphasize objectivity, ensure that content is free from personal opinion, and build your argument on provable facts. When creating a formal tone, eliminate all references to *you* and *I* (including *we, us,* and *our*). Your tone should also be businesslike and unemotional. Be careful to avoid jokes, similes, and metaphors, and minimize the use of colourful adjectives or adverbs.

A more formal tone is appropriate for longer reports, especially those dealing with controversial or complex information. You'll also need a more formal tone when your report will be sent to other parts of the organization or to outsiders, such as customers, suppliers, or members of the community. Loblaws, for example, will use an informal tone in its advertising, but, as Figure 12–2 shows, the company's tone is formal when communicating with the public on more serious matters.

Communicating with people in other cultures often calls for more formality, for two reasons. First, the business environment outside Canada and the United States tends to be more formal in general, and that formality must be reflected in your communication. Second, the techniques you use to make a document informal (e.g., employing humour and idiomatic language) tend to translate poorly or not at all from one culture to another. Using a less formal tone in cross-cultural reports and proposals increases the risk of offending people and the chance of miscommunicating information.

Composing Reports and Proposals

With a clear picture of how you need to adapt to your audience, you're ready to begin composing your first draft. This section offers advice on drafting content for both reports and proposals, along with several strategies for making your content more readable. When you compose reports and proposals, follow the advice Chapter 5 offered: Use the most precise vocabulary, create the most effective sentences, and develop the most coherent paragraphs.

As with other written business communications, the text of reports and proposals has three main sections: an introduction (or *opening*), a body, and a close. The content and length of each section varies with the type and purpose of the document, the document's organizational structure, and the length and depth of the material. The document's degree of formality and your relationship with your audience will also influence the document's subject matter and extent.

Your introduction needs to put the report in context for the reader, introduce the subject, preview main ideas, and establish the tone of the document.

The *introduction* (or *opening*) is the first section in the text of any report or proposal. An effective introduction fulfills at least four aims:

> Puts the report or proposal in a broader context by tying it to a problem or an assignment
> Introduces the subject or purpose of the report or proposal and indicates why the subject is important
> Previews the main ideas and the order in which they'll be covered
> Establishes the tone of the document and the writer's relationship with the audience

The body of your report presents, analyzes, and interprets the information you gathered during your investigation.

The *body*, or main section, usually consists of the major divisions or sections with various levels of headings. These divisions present, analyze, and interpret the information gathered during your investigation, and they support the recommendations or conclusions discussed in your document. The body contains the proof, the detailed information necessary to support your conclusions and recommendations. Note how the recommendation report in Figure 12–3 uses the report body to articulate a recommendation—a move to a fully interactive

> Figure 12–3 Effective Problem-Solving Report Focusing on Recommendations

Reminds readers of the origin and purpose of the report

Presents logical reasons for recommending that the firm expand its website to include e-commerce

Clarifies the recommendation by listing the necessary actions in clear, direct language

Supports the reasoning with evidence

DATE: July 7, 2010
TO: Board of Directors, Executive Committee members
FROM: Alycia Jenn, Business Development Manager
SUBJECT: Website expansion

In response to your request, my staff and I investigated the potential for expanding our website from its current "brochureware" status (in which we promote our company and its products but don't provide any way to place orders online) to full e-commerce capability (including placing orders and checking on order delivery status). After analyzing the behaviour of our customers and major competitors and studying the overall development of electronic retailing, we have three recommendations:

1. We should expand our online presence from "brochureware" to e-commerce capability within the next six months.

2. We should engage a firm that specializes in online retailing to design and develop the new e-commerce capabilities.

3. We must take care to integrate online retailing with our store-based and mail-order operations.

1. WE SHOULD EXPAND THE WEBSITE TO FULL E-COMMERCE CAPABILITY

First, does e-commerce capability make sense today for a small company that sells luxury housewares? Even though books and many other products are now commonly sold online, in most cases this enterprise involves simple, low-cost products that don't require a lot of hands-on inspection before purchasing. As we've observed in our stores, shoppers like to interact with our products before purchasing them. However, a small but growing number of websites do sell specialty products, using such tactics as "virtual product tours" (in which shoppers can interactively view a product in three dimensions, rather than simply looking at a static photograph) and generous return policies (to reduce the perceived risk of buying products online).

Second, do we need to establish a presence now in order to remain competitive in the future? The answer is an overwhelming "yes." The initial steps taken by our competitors are already placing us at a disadvantage among those shoppers who are already comfortable buying online, and every trend indicates our minor competitive weakness today will turn into a major weakness in the next few years:

• Several of our top competitors are beginning to implement full e-commerce, including virtual product tours. Our research suggests that these companies aren't yet generating significant financial returns from these online investments, but their online sales are growing.

• Younger consumers who grew up with the World Wide Web will soon be reaching their peak earning years (ages 35-54). This demographic segment expects e-commerce in nearly every product category, and we'll lose them to the competition if we don't offer it.

• The Web is erasing geographical shopping limits, presenting both a threat and an opportunity. Even though our customers can now shop websites from anywhere in the world (so that we have thousands of competitors instead of a dozen), we can now target customers anywhere in the world.

(continued)

e-commerce website—to a company's board of directors. This report section provides enough information to support the argument, without burdening the high-level readership with a lot of tactical details.

The *close* is the final section in the text of your report or proposal. It has three important functions:

> Emphasizes the main points of the message
> Summarizes the benefits to the reader if the document suggests a change or some other course of action
> Brings all the action items together in one place and gives the details about who should do what, when, where, and how

> Figure 12–3 Effective Problem-Solving Report Focusing on Recommendations (*continued*)

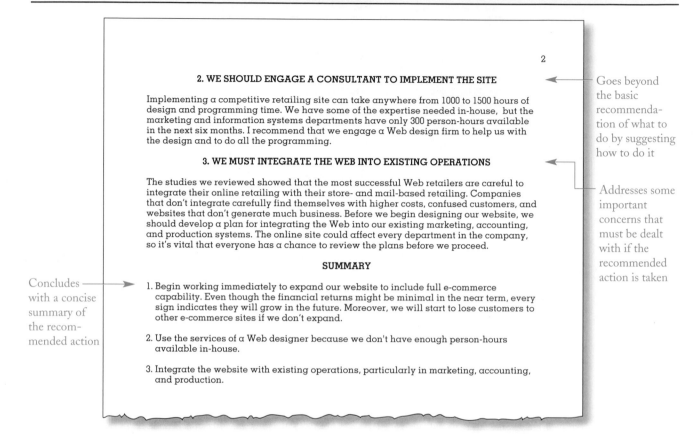

Goes beyond the basic recommendation of what to do by suggesting how to do it

Addresses some important concerns that must be dealt with if the recommended action is taken

Concludes with a concise summary of the recommended action

The close might be the only part of your report some readers have time for, so ensure that it conveys the full weight of your message.

Research shows that the final section of a report or proposal leaves a lasting impression. The close gives you one last chance to ensure that your report says what you intended.[2] In fact, readers who are in a hurry might skip the body of the report and read only the summary, so ensure that it carries a strong, clear message.

Drafting Report Content

Objective 2 Describe five characteristics of effective report content.

Your credibility and career advancement potential are underscored with every business report you write, so ensure that your content is

> **Accurate.** Double-check your facts and references in addition to checking for typographical errors. If an audience even senses that your information is shaky, they'll start to view all your work with a skeptical eye.

> **Complete.** To help colleagues or supervisors make an informed decision, include everything necessary for readers to understand the situation, problem, or proposal. Support all key assertions using an appropriate combination of illustrations, explanations, and facts.[3] In a recent Fedex annual report, for example, Frederick Smith and his team provided a concise and easily understandable overview of the company's global operations. The subject matter is presented in a way that any investor interested in the company's stock can comprehend.[4]

> **Balanced.** Present all sides of the issue fairly and equitably, and include all the essential information, even if some information doesn't support your

line of reasoning. Omitting relevant information or facts creates an incomplete and partial argument. Your audience will believe your report is one-sided, and your credibility will suffer.

> **Clear and logical.** Clear sentence structure and good transitions are essential.[5] Save your readers time by ensuring that your sentences are uncluttered, contain well-chosen words, and proceed logically. To help your readers move from one point to the next, make your transitions clear and logical. For a successful report, identify the ideas that belong together, and organize them in a way that's easy to understand.[6]

> **Documented properly.** If you use primary and secondary sources for your report or proposal, ensure that you properly document and give credit to your sources, as Chapter 11 explains.

Keeping these points in mind will help you draft the most effective introduction, body, and close for your report. Note how the report excerpt in Figure 12–4 offers the client a complete, but concise update of the company's landscaping services. In addition to providing routine information, the writer also informs her client of progress on two problem areas, one that her firm has been able to resolve and one that they've just discovered. In the case of the problem with the soil, you might be tempted not to share any information with the client until you've resolved the problem, but doing so could affect the client's budgets and other plans. The writer behaves in an ethical manner by telling the client about the problem at an early stage.

REPORT INTRODUCTION The specific elements you should include in an introduction depend on the nature and length of the report, the circumstances under which you're writing it, and your relationship with the audience. An introduction could contain all of the following topics, although you'll want to choose the most relevant ones for each report you write:

> **Authorization.** The person who assigned the report and the date he or she assigned it; in long reports, this material appears in a *letter of transmittal* for external audiences and a transmittal memo for internal audiences (see Chapter 13) to accompany the report

> **Problem/opportunity/purpose.** The reason the report was written and its practical outcomes and accomplishments

> **Scope.** What is and what isn't covered in the report. The scope also helps with the critical job of setting the audience's expectations

> **Background.** The historical conditions or factors that led up to the report; this section enables readers to understand how the problem, situation, or opportunity developed and what has been done about it so far

> **Sources and methods.** The primary and secondary sources of information used; as appropriate, this section explains how samples were selected, how questionnaires were constructed (which should be included in an appendix with any cover letters), what follow-up was done, and other matters related to methodology. This section builds reader confidence in the work and in the sources and methods used

> **Definitions.** A list of terms that might be unfamiliar to your audience, along with brief definitions; this section is unnecessary if readers are familiar with the terms you've used in your report—and they all agree on what the terms mean, which isn't always the case. If you have any question about reader knowledge, define any terms that might be misinterpreted; terms may also be defined in the body, explanatory notes, or glossary

> **Limitations.** Factors beyond your control that affect report quality, such as budgets, schedule constraints, or limited access to information or people; if appropriate, this section can also express any doubts you have about any

Carefully select the elements to include in your introduction; strive for a balance between necessary, expected information and brevity.

> Figure 12–4 Effective Progress Report Offering Complete Content (Excerpt)

Johnson Landscaping

2430 Grafton Street, Halifax, NS B3S 2W1 (902) 555-1961 / Fax (902) 555-0742
E-mail: info@johnscape.com

May 31, 2010
Mr. Steve Gamvrellis, Facilities Manager
United Food Processing
255 Sackville Street
Halifax, NS B2M SV1

Dear Mr. Gamvrellis:

This report will bring you up to date on the work done for your company by
Johnson Landscaping during the month of May 2010.

GROUND PREPARATION AND SPRINKLER INSTALLATION

Initial ground preparation and sprinkler system installation is complete. We
cleared, tilled, levelled, and raked 25 000 square metres for lawn and beds.
Installation of the sprinkler system for 15 000 square metres of lawn and beds
was completed on May 19.

BED PLANTING

From May 22 to May 30, shrubs and ornamental perennials were planted in
7000 square metres of beds. Beds were prepared for 3000 square metres of
annuals.

SPECIAL ISSUES AND SOLUTIONS

We've resolved the flooding discovered last month near the south end of the
shipping and receiving dock. It appears that an old plumbing repair had failed
under the employee cafeteria, causing water to flow under the building and
occasionally flood a small portion of the new lawn area.

In several of the perennial borders we've created along the east side of the
main building, a series of soil samples indicates an extremely high level of
acidity, much higher than would occur under natural conditions. We suspect
that the problem may have been caused by a small chemical spill at some
point in the past. We'll try to resolve this issue next month with soil
amendments. I'll contact you if this solution is likely to affect your budget
planning.

PLANS FOR JUNE

1. Distribute beauty bark and plant remaining annuals.
2. Resolve the soil quality issue in the perennial bed and make soil
   amendments as needed.
3. Monitor and adjust the automated sprinkling system to ensure adequate
   watering.

Annotations:

Uses letter format, which is appropriate for a simple interim progress report

Introduces the purpose of the report

Uses clear headings to help the reader find items of interest

Doesn't hesitate to bring up problems that need to be solved, but offers possible solutions for further investigation

Outlines plans for the next reporting period (the month of June)

aspect of your report. Such candour may be uncomfortable to you, but it
helps your readers assess your information accurately, and it helps establish
your report's integrity

> **Report organization.** The organization of the report (what topics are cov-
ered and in what order), along with a rationale for following this plan; this
section is a road map that guides the reader through the report

In a relatively brief report, these topics may be discussed in only a paragraph
or two. Here's an example of a brief indirect opening, taken from the introduction of a memo on why a new line of luggage has failed to sell well. The writer's
ultimate goal is to recommend a shift in marketing strategy.

The performance of the Venturer line can be improved. In the two years since its introduction, this product line has achieved a sales volume lower than we expected, resulting in a drain on the company's overall earnings. The purpose of this report is to review the luggage-buying habits of consumers in all markets where the Venturer line is sold so that we can determine where to focus our marketing campaign.

This paragraph quickly introduces the subject (disappointing sales), tells why the problem is important (drain on earnings), and indicates the main points to be addressed in the body of the report (review of markets where the Venturer line is sold), without revealing what the conclusions and recommendations will be.

In a longer formal report, the discussion of these topics may span several pages and constitute a significant section within the report.

REPORT BODY As with the introduction, the body of your report can require some tough decisions about which elements to include and how much detail to offer. Here again, your decisions depend on many variables, including the needs of your audience. Some situations require detailed coverage; others can be handled with more concise treatment. Provide only enough detail in the body to support your conclusions and recommendations; you can put additional detail in tables, charts, and appendixes. If you were writing a report that would be read by both high-level executives (who need only summaries and "big picture" information) and functional staff (who need specific details), you could address major points in the body and refer readers to specific places in an appendix for more details.

As with the introduction, the report body should contain only enough information to convey your message in a convincing fashion; don't overload the body with interesting but unnecessary material.

The topics commonly covered in a report body include

> explanations of a problem or opportunity
> facts, statistical evidence, and trends
> results of studies or investigations
> discussion and analysis of potential courses of action
> advantages, disadvantages, costs, and benefits of a particular course of action
> procedures or steps in a process
> methods and approaches
> criteria for evaluating alternatives and options
> conclusions and recommendations
> supporting reasons for conclusions or recommendations

For analytical reports using the direct organizational approach, you'll generally state your conclusions or recommendations in the introduction and use the body of your report to provide your evidence and support (as illustrated in Figures 12–3 and 12–4). If you're using an indirect approach, you'll likely use the body to discuss your logic and reserve your conclusions or recommendations until the very end.

REPORT CLOSE The content and length of your report close depend on your choice of direct or indirect order, among other variables. If you're using a direct approach, you can end with a summary of key points (usually not necessary in short memo-style reports) listed in the order they appear in the report body. If you're using an indirect approach, you can use the close to present your conclusions or recommendations if you didn't end the body with them. Keep in mind that a conclusion or recommendation isn't the place to introduce new facts; your audience should have all the information they need by the time they reach this point in your report.

The nature of your close depends on the type of report (informational or analytical) and the approach (direct or indirect).

> Figure 12–5 Effective Report Expressing Action Plan in the Close

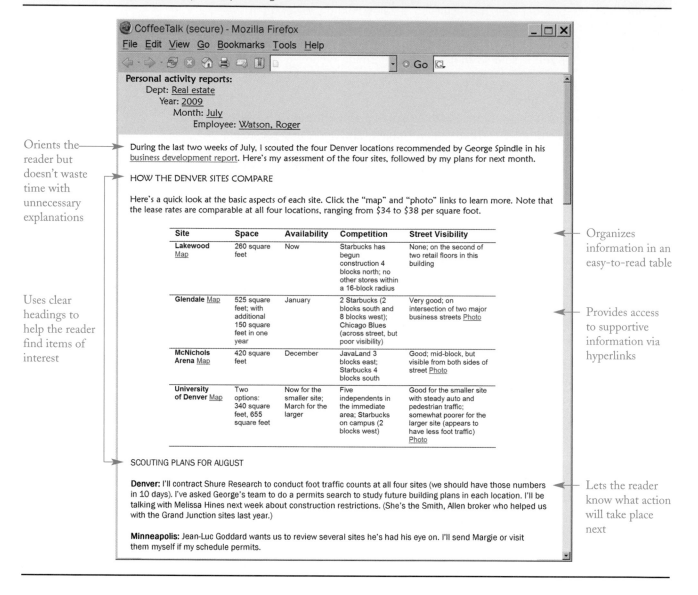

Orients the reader but doesn't waste time with unnecessary explanations

Uses clear headings to help the reader find items of interest

Organizes information in an easy-to-read table

Provides access to supportive information via hyperlinks

Lets the reader know what action will take place next

If your report is intended to prompt others to action, use the ending to spell out exactly what should happen next. Readers may agree with everything you say in your report but still fail to take any action if you're vague about the outcomes. Providing a schedule and specific task assignments is helpful because concrete plans tend to motivate action. If you'll take all the actions yourself, ensure that your readers understand this fact so that they'll know what to expect from you. The personal activity report in Figure 12–5 is a good example of efficiently conveying key information points, including a clear plan of action in the close. Note the use of hyperlinks to maps, photos, and a related report, all of which are stored on the same secure intranet site.

In a short report, the close may be only a paragraph or two. However, the close of a long report may have separate sections for conclusions, recommendations, and actions. Using separate sections helps your reader locate this material and focus on each element. Such an arrangement also gives you a final opportunity to emphasize this important content.

For long reports, you may need to divide your close into separate sections for conclusions, recommendations, and actions.

If you have multiple conclusions, recommendations, or actions, you may want to number and list them. An appropriate lead-in to such a list might be,

"The findings of this study lead to the following conclusions." A statement that could be used for a list of recommendations might be, "Based on the conclusions of this study, we make the following recommendations." A statement that could be used for actions might be, "To accomplish our goals on time, we must complete the following actions before the end of the year."

Drafting Proposal Content

✖ Explore

With proposals, the content for each section is governed by many variables—the most important being the source of your proposal. If your proposal is unsolicited, you have some latitude in the scope and organization of content. However, if you are responding to a request for proposals, you need to follow the instructions in the request for proposal (RFP) in every detail. Most RFPs spell out precisely what you should cover and in what order, so all bids will be similar in form and therefore easier to compare.

The general purpose of any proposal is to persuade readers to take an action, such as purchase goods or services, fund a project, or implement a program. Thus, your approach to writing a proposal is similar to that used for persuasive sales messages (see Chapter 10). As with other persuasive messages, the AIDA method of gaining attention, building interest, creating desire, and motivating action is an effective structure. Here are some additional strategies to strengthen your argument:[7]

Approach proposals the same way you approach persuasive messages.

> **Demonstrate your knowledge and credibility.** Show your reader that you have the knowledge and experience to solve the problem or address the opportunity outlined in your proposal.

Objective 3 Explain six strategies to strengthen your proposal argument.

> **Provide concrete information and examples.** Avoid vague, unsupported generalizations such as "We are losing money on this program." Instead, provide quantifiable details such as the amount of money being lost, how, and why. Explain how much money your proposed solution will save. Spell out your plan and give details on how the job will be done. Such concrete information persuades readers; unsupported generalizations do not.

> **Research the competition.** If you're competing against other companies for a potential customer's business, use trade publications, newspaper articles, industry directories, and the internet to become familiar with the products, services, and prices of these other companies.

> **Prove that your proposal is workable.** Your proposal must be appropriate and feasible for your audience. It should be consistent with your audience's capabilities.

Business proposals need to provide more than just attractive ideas—readers look for evidence of practical, achievable solutions.

> **Adopt a "you" attitude.** Relate your product, service, or personnel to the reader's exact needs, either as stated in the RFP for a solicited proposal or as discovered through your own investigation for an unsolicited proposal.

> **Package your proposal attractively.** Ensure that your proposal is letter perfect, inviting, and readable. Readers will prejudge the quality of your products, services, and capabilities by the quality of the proposal you submit. Errors, omissions, or inconsistencies will work against you—and maybe even cost you important career and business opportunities.

PROPOSAL INTRODUCTION The introduction presents and summarizes the problem you want to solve (or the opportunity you want to exploit), along with your proposed solution. It orients readers to the remainder of the text. If your proposal is solicited, its introduction should refer to the RFP, so readers know which RFP you're responding to. If your proposal is unsolicited, your introduction should mention any factors that led you to submit your proposal,

Objective 4 Determine the topics commonly covered in a proposal introduction, body, and closing.

such as previous conversations you've had with readers. The following topics are commonly covered in a proposal introduction:

> **Background or statement of the problem.** This is a brief review of the reader's situation and establishes a need for action. Readers may not perceive a problem or opportunity the same way you do. In unsolicited proposals, you need to convince them that a problem or opportunity exists before you can convince them to accept your solution. In a way that is meaningful to your reader, discuss the current situation and explain how the reader's circumstances can be improved.

> **Solution.** Briefly describes the change you propose and highlights your key selling points and their benefits, showing how your proposal will help readers meet their business objectives. In a sales proposal, the solution would be the products or services you offer, along with any accessories, warranties, professional services such as installation, and other enhancements. In other types of proposals, the solution would be defined by the nature of the proposal.

> **Scope.** States the boundaries of the proposal—what you will and will not do

> **Proposal organization.** Orients the reader to the structure of the proposal and calls attention to the major divisions of information

In short proposals, your discussion of these topics will be brief—perhaps only a sentence or two for each one. For long, formal proposals, each topic may warrant separate subheadings and several paragraphs of discussion.

PROPOSAL BODY The proposal's body has the same purpose as the body of other reports: It gives complete details on the proposed solution and specifies what the anticipated results will be. Because a proposal is by definition a persuasive message, your audience expects you to promote your plan in a confident but professional manner. Even when you're expressing an idea that you believe in passionately, maintain an objective tone so that you don't risk overselling your message.

In addition to providing facts and evidence to support your conclusions, an effective body covers this information:

> **Proposed solution.** This part describes what you have to offer: your concept, product, or service. Stress the benefits of your product, service, or investment opportunity that are relevant to your readers' needs and point out any advantages that you have over your competitors.

> **Work plan.** This section describes how you'll accomplish what must be done. Explain the steps you'll take, their timing, the methods or resources you'll use, and the person(s) responsible. Specifically include when the work will begin, how it will be divided into stages, when you will finish, and whether any follow-up is involved. For solicited proposals, ensure that your dates match those specified in the RFP. Keep in mind that if your proposal is accepted, the work plan is contractually binding, so don't promise more than you can deliver.

> **Statement of qualifications.** This describes your organization's experience, personnel, and facilities—all in relation to reader needs. The qualifications section can be an important selling point, and it deserves to be handled carefully. You can supplement your qualifications by including a list of client references, but get permission ahead of time to use these references.

> **Costs.** This section covers pricing, reimbursable expenses, discounts, and so on. Coverage can vary widely, from a single price amount to detailed breakdowns by part number, service category, and so on. If you're responding to an RFP, follow the instructions it contains. In other cases, your firm probably has a set policy for discussing costs.

In an unsolicited proposal, your introduction needs to convince readers that a problem or opportunity exists.

Readers understand that a proposal is a persuasive message, so they're willing to accommodate a degree of promotional emphasis in your writing—as long as it is professional and focused on their needs.

The work plan indicates exactly how you will accomplish the solution presented in the proposal.

> Figure 12–6 Effective Solicited Proposal in Letter Form

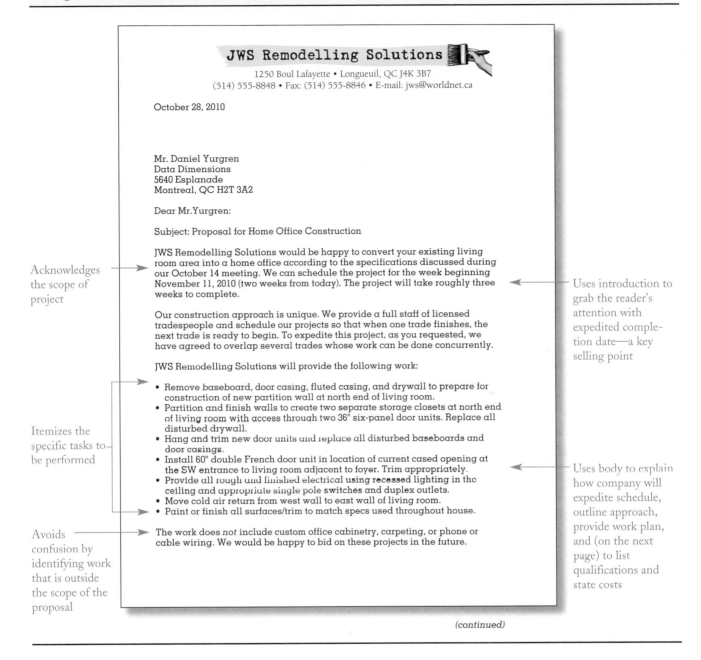

Acknowledges the scope of project

Itemizes the specific tasks to be performed

Avoids confusion by identifying work that is outside the scope of the proposal

Uses introduction to grab the reader's attention with expedited completion date—a key selling point

Uses body to explain how company will expedite schedule, outline approach, provide work plan, and (on the next page) to list qualifications and state costs

(continued)

In an informal, short proposal, discussion of some or all of these elements may be grouped together. If the proposal is directed toward an audience outside your organization, use a letter format, as the proposal in Figure 12–6 does. In a long, formal proposal, the discussion of these elements will be extensive and thorough. In this case, the proposal will be presented as a long report with multiple parts, accompanied by a memo or letter of transmittal as Chapter 13 discusses.

PROPOSAL CLOSE The final section of a proposal generally summarizes the key points, emphasizes the benefits that readers will realize from your solution, summarizes the merits of your approach, restates why you and your firm are a good choice, and asks for a decision from the client. The close is your last opportunity to persuade readers to accept your proposal. In both formal and

The close is your last chance to convince the reader of the merits of your proposal, so make doubly sure it's clear, compelling, and audience-oriented.

Objective 5 Identify five characteristics of effective writing in online reports

> Figure 12–6 Effective Solicited Proposal in Letter Form (*continued*)

Mr. Daniel Yurgren   October 28, 2010   Page 2

JWS Remodelling Solutions has been in business in the Montreal area for over 17 years. We have a strong reputation for being a quality builder. We take great pride in our work and we treat all projects with the same high-level attention, regardless of their size or scope. Our tradespeople are all licensed, insured professionals with years of experience in their respective crafts. Enclosed is a copy of our company brochure discussing our qualifications in greater detail, along with a current client list. Please contact any of the names on this list for references.

Increases desire by highlighting qualifications

Helps reader accept the cost total by breaking it down into specific categories

The total cost for this project is $6800, broken down as follows:

Materials and supplies	$3800
Labour	2700
Disposal fees	300
Total	$6800

An initial payment of $3800 is due upon acceptance of this proposal. The remaining $3,000 is due upon completion of the work.

If you would like to have JWS Remodelling Solutions complete this work, please sign one copy of this letter and return it to us with your deposit in the enclosed envelope. We currently anticipate no construction delays, since the materials needed for your job are in stock and our staff of qualified workers is available during the period mentioned. If you have any questions regarding the terms of this proposal, please call me.

Sincerely,

Jordan W. Spurrier
President

Enclosures (3)

Makes letter a binding contract, if signed

Accepted by:

_____   _____
Daniel Yurgren   Date

informal proposals, make this section relatively brief, assertive (but not brash or abrupt), and confident.

Drafting Online Content

When you're writing for an audience online, follow the basic guidelines for writing a report presented earlier in this chapter along with these five additional steps to make your Web content as effective as possible. First, take special care to build trust with your intended audiences because careful readers can be skeptical of online content. Make sure your content is accurate, current, complete, and authoritative. Indicate the date that material was originally posted and when it is updated so that readers can judge your content's currency.

Second, even though it can be complicated and expensive, adapt your content for a global audience. Translating content is expensive, and going a step beyond—to localizing it so that it reflects not only the native language of your readers but their cultural norms, weights, measures, time, money, and so on—costs even more. Some companies compromise by localizing the homepage and key secondary pages while keeping the deeper, more detailed content in its original language.

Third, compose Web-friendly content. In an environment that presents many reading challenges, careful attention to composition is critical. Compelling, reader-oriented content is the key to success for any website.[8] Most readers don't return to websites that don't offer interesting, helpful content—it's too easy to find websites that serve them better. Wherever possible, use the inverted pyramid style, in which you cover the most important information briefly at first, then gradually reveal successive layers of detail—letting readers choose to see those additional layers if they want to. (Links to subpages are ideal for this.) Also, make sure your writing is compact and efficient; material on the Web needs to be short because online readers tend to skip over long chunks of text.

Fourth, present your information in a concise, skimmable format. Effective websites use a variety of means to help readers skim pages quickly, including lists, careful use of colour and boldface, informative headings (clever headings with lots of wordplay are usually more annoying than effective), and helpful summaries that give readers a choice of learning more if they want to.

Fifth, write effective links that serve for both site navigation and content skimming. Above all else, clearly identify where a link will take readers; don't force them to click through and try to figure out where they're going. If necessary, include a brief summary that explains what readers will experience if they click on the link—particularly if the link downloads or opens a file or does anything else that might be unexpected. Also, try to avoid using directional words such as back, forward, next, above, below, bottom, or top. Such words are meaningful in a linear document but not necessarily in a hypertext document, where visitors can enter your site at many places and from many directions. Instead, use absolute directions such as Return to Tables, Next Learning Step, or Beginning of Tutorial.[9]

> Localizing Web content involves both translating the content and adapting it to local cultural norms and practices.

> Effective links in online reports let readers know exactly what to expect before they click on them.

Establishing a Time Perspective

In what time frame will your report exist? Will you write in the past or present tense? The person who wrote this paragraph never decided:

Of those interviewed, 25 percent *report* that they *are* dissatisfied with their present brand. The wealthiest participants *complained* most frequently, but all income categories *are* interested in trying a new brand. Only 5 percent of the interviewees *say* they *had* no interest in alternative products.

By switching from tense to tense when describing the same research results, you can confuse your readers. They wonder whether the shift is significant or whether you are just being careless. Eliminate the potential for such confusion by using tense consistently.

Also ensure that you observe the chronological sequence of events in your report. If you describe the history or development of something, start at the beginning and cover each event in the order of its occurrence. If you explain the steps in a process, take each step in proper sequence.

> Unexplained shifts in time perspective can both confuse readers and lead them to question the thinking behind your report or proposal.

Helping Readers Find Their Way

Navigational aids help your readers appreciate the organization of your thoughts—and can help you convey your message.

As you begin to compose the text for your report, remember that readers have no concept of how the various pieces of your report relate to one another. Because you have done the work, you have a sense of your document's wholeness and can see how each page fits into the overall structure. But readers see the report one page at a time. Experienced report writers know that good writers give their readers a preview, or road map, of a report's structure, clarifying how the various parts are related. These directions are particularly important for people from other cultures and countries, whose language skills and business expectations may differ from yours.

To help readers find what they're looking for and stay on track as they navigate through your documents, make good use of headings and links, smooth transitions, and previews and reviews:

> **Headings and links.** Readers should be able to follow the structure of your document and pick up the key points of your message from the headings and subheadings (see Chapter 6 for a review of what makes an effective heading). Follow a simple, consistent arrangement that clearly distinguishes levels, as shown in Figure 12–7. For online reports, where the difficulty of reading onscreen makes clear headings crucial, make generous use of hyperlinks to help your readers navigate the report and access additional information.

Transitions connect ideas by helping readers move from one thought to the next.

> **Transitions.** Chapter 5 defines transitions as words or phrases that tie ideas together and show how one thought is related to another. In a long report, an entire paragraph might be used to highlight transitions from one section to the next, such as in this example:

. . . *As you can see,* our profits have decreased by 12 percent over the past eight months.

To counteract *this decline in profits,* we have three alternatives. *First,* we can raise our selling prices of existing products. *Second,* we can increase our offering by adding new products. *Third,* we can reduce our manufacturing costs. *However,* each alternative has both advantages and disadvantages.

The phrase *As you can see* alerts readers to the fact that they are reading a summary of the information just presented. The phrase *this decline in profits* lets readers know that the text will include something else about that previous topic. The words *first, second,* and *third* help readers stay on track as the three alternatives are introduced, and the word *however* alerts readers to the fact that evaluating the three alternatives requires some additional discussion. Effective transitions such as these can help readers grasp what they've learned so far while preparing to receive new information.

Previews help readers prepare for upcoming information, and reviews help them verify and clarify what they've just read.

> **Previews and reviews.** *Preview sections* introduce important topics by helping readers get ready for new information. Previews are particularly helpful when the information is complex, unexpected, or unfamiliar. In contrast, *review sections* come after a body of material and summarize the information for your readers. Reviews help readers absorb details while keeping track of the big picture. Previews and reviews can be written in sentence format, bulleted lists (see Chapter 6), or a combination of the two. Both are effective, but bullets can increase your document's readability by adding white space to the document design:

> Figure 12–7 Heading Format for Reports

TITLE

The title is centred at the top of the page in all-capital letters, usually boldfaced, often in a large font, and often using a sans serif typeface. When the title runs to more than one line, the lines are usually double-spaced and arranged as an inverted pyramid (longer line on the top).

FIRST-LEVEL HEADING

A first-level heading indicates what the following section is about, perhaps by describing the subdivisions. All first-level headings are grammatically parallel, with the possible exception of such headings as "Introduction," "Conclusions," and "Recommendations." Some text appears between every two headings, regardless of their levels. Still boldfaced and serif, the font may be smaller than that used in the title but still larger than the typeface used in the text and still in all capital letters.

Second-Level Heading

Like first-level headings, second-level headings indicate what the following material is about. All second-level headings within a section are grammatically parallel. Still boldfaced and serif, the font may either remain the same or shrink to the size used in the text, and the style is now initial capitals with lower case. Never use only one second-level heading under a first-level heading. (The same is true for every other level of heading.)

Third-Level Heading
A third-level heading is worded to reflect the content of the material that follows. All third-level headings beneath a second-level heading should be grammatically parallel.

Fourth-Level Heading. Like all the other levels of heading, fourth-level headings reflect the subject that will be developed. All fourth-level headings within a subsection are parallel. Fourth-level headings are generally the lowest level of heading used. However, you can indicate further breakdowns in your ideas by using a list:

1. *The first item in a list*. You may indent the entire item in block format to set it off visually. Numbers are optional.

2. *The second item in a list*. All lists have at least two items. An introductory phrase or sentence may be italicized for emphasis, as shown here.

Sentence Format	Bulleted List
The next section discusses the advantages of advertising on the internet. Among them are currency, global reach, affordability, and interactivity.	As the next section shows, advertising on the internet has four advantages: > currency > global reach > affordability > interactivity

To review the tasks discussed in this section, see "Checklist: Composing Business Reports and Proposals."

CHECKLIST Composing Business Reports and Proposals

A. Review and fine-tune your outline.
✔ Match your parallel headings to the tone of your report.
✔ Understand how the introduction, body, and close work together to convey your message.

B. Draft report content.
✔ Use the introduction to establish the purpose, scope, and organization of your report.
✔ Use the body to present and interpret the information you gathered.
✔ Use the close to summarize major points, discuss conclusions, or make recommendations.

C. Draft proposal content.
✔ Use the introduction to discuss the background or problem, your solution, the scope, and organization.
✔ Use the body to explain persuasively the benefits of your proposed approach.

✔ Use the close to emphasize reader benefits and summarize the merits of your approach.

D. Establish a consistent time frame.
✔ Avoid switching from tense to tense.
✔ Observe the chronological sequence of events.

E. Help readers find their way.
✔ Provide headings to improve readability and clarify the framework of your ideas.
✔ Use hyperlinks online to allow readers to jump from section to section.
✔ Create transitions that tie ideas together and show how one thought relates to another.
✔ Preview important topics to help readers get ready for new information.
✔ Review key information to help readers absorb details and keep the big picture in mind.

Using Technology to Craft Reports and Proposals

Look for ways to utilize technology to reduce the mechanical work involved in writing long reports.

Creating lengthy reports and proposals can be a huge task, so take advantage of technological tools to help throughout the process. You've read about some of these tools in earlier chapters; here are some of the most important ones for developing reports and proposals:

> **Templates.** Beyond simply formatting documents, report templates can identify the specific sections required for each type of report. For example, a marketing plan could include such sections as a competitive analysis, market analysis, launch plans, financial analysis, and promotional and customer support plans. The template could automatically insert headings for each section, with reminders of the content to include.

> **Linked and embedded documents.** In many reports and proposals, you need to include graphics, spreadsheets, databases, and other elements produced in other software programs. Make sure you know how the software handles the files, or you may receive some unpleasant surprises. For example, in Microsoft Office, you can choose to either *link* or *embed* an incoming element, such as a table from a spreadsheet. If you link, the element will be updated whenever you or someone else updates the spreadsheet. In contrast, if you embed it, the files are no longer connected; changes in the spreadsheet will not show up in the report document.

> **Electronic forms.** For recurring forms such as sales reports and compliance reports, consider creating a word processing file that combines *boilerplate* text for material that doesn't change from report to report. To accommodate information that does change (such as last week's sales results), use *form tools* such as text boxes (in which users can type new text) and check boxes (which can be used to select from a set of predetermined choices). The completed file can then be printed, emailed, or posted to a website.

> **Electronic documents.** Portable Document Format (PDF) files have become a universal replacement for printed reports and proposals. With a copy of Adobe Acrobat (a separate product from the free Acrobat Reader), you can quickly convert reports and proposals to PDF files that are easy and safe to share electronically.

> **Multimedia documents.** When the written word isn't enough, combine your report with video clips, animation, presentation software slides, and other elements.

> **Proposal-writing software.** Basic features of proposal-writing software include the ability to automatically personalize proposals, ensure proper structure (making sure you don't forget any sections, for example), and organize storage of all your boilerplate text. At a more advanced level, products such as Pragmatech's RFP Machine and Sant's RFPMaster can scan RFPs to identify questions and requirements and fill in potential answers from a centralized knowledge base that contains input from all the relevant experts in your company.[10]

Today's computer technology also makes it easy to add a wide variety of compelling visuals to reports, which you'll learn more about in the next section.

Illustrating Your Reports with Effective Visuals

Well-designed visual elements can enhance the communication power of textual messages and, in some instances, even replace textual messages. Visuals can often convey some message points (such as spatial relationships, correlations, procedures, and emotions) more effectively and more efficiently than words. Generally speaking, in a given amount of time, well-designed images can convey much more information than text.[11] In the numbers-oriented world of work, people rely heavily on trend lines, distribution curves, and visual presentations of numeric quantities. Visuals attract and hold people's attention, helping your audience understand and remember your message. Busy readers often jump to visuals to try to get the gist of a message, and attractive visuals can draw readers more deeply into your reports and presentations. Using pictures is also an effective way to communicate with the diverse audiences that are common in today's business environment.

Carefully crafted visuals enhance the power of your words.

In addition to their direct information value, visuals often have connotative meaning as well. As you read in Chapter 5, many words and phrases carry connotative meanings, which are all the mental images, emotions, and other impressions that the word or phrase evokes in audience members. A significant part of the power—and risk—of visual elements derives from their connotative meanings as well. Even something as simple as a watermark symbol embedded in letterhead stationery can boost reader confidence in whatever message is printed on the paper.[12] Many colours, shapes, and other design elements have visual symbolism; and their symbolic, connotative meaning can evolve over time and have different meanings to different cultures. For example, a red cross on a white background stands for emergency medical care in many countries. But the cross is also a Christian symbol, so the International Federation of Red Cross and Red Crescent Movement uses a red crescent in Islamic countries— even though the original Red Cross symbol is based on the flag of Switzerland and not on any religious icons. In 2007, the red crystal was adopted as a third emblem intended to avoid specific religious associations. Being aware of these symbolic meanings and using them to your advantage are important aspects of being an effective business communicator.

Like words, visuals often carry connotative or symbolic meanings.

Understanding Visual Design Principles

Visual literacy is the ability to create and interpret visual messages.

Given the importance of visuals in today's business environment, **visual literacy**—the ability (as a sender) to create effective images and (as a receiver) to correctly interpret visual messages—has become a key business skill.[13] Just as creating effective sentences, paragraphs, and documents requires working knowledge of the principles of good writing, creating effective visuals requires some knowledge of the principles of good design. For example, the slide in Figure 12.8a

> Figure 12–8 Ineffective and Effective Visual Designs

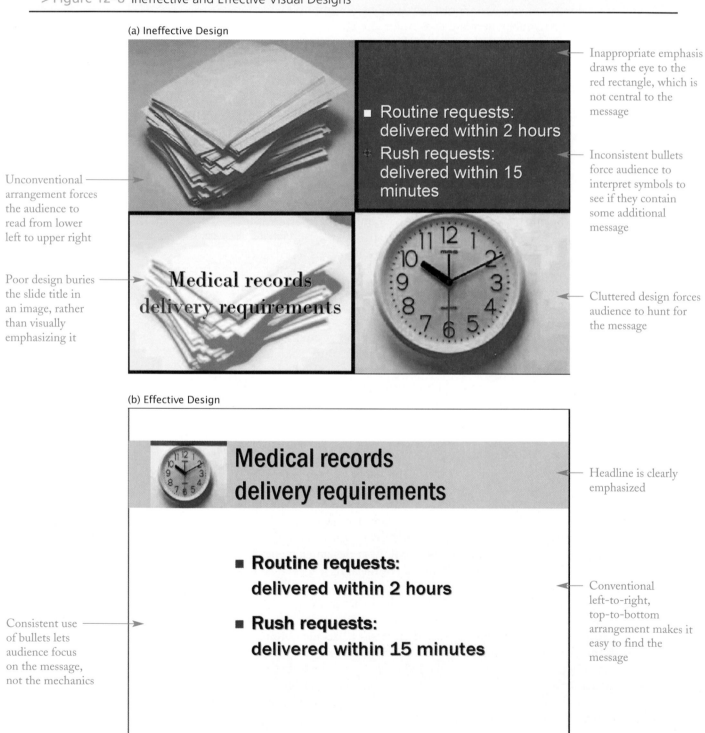

(a) Ineffective Design

Unconventional arrangement forces the audience to read from lower left to upper right

Poor design buries the slide title in an image, rather than visually emphasizing it

Inappropriate emphasis draws the eye to the red rectangle, which is not central to the message

Inconsistent bullets force audience to interpret symbols to see if they contain some additional message

Cluttered design forces audience to hunt for the message

(b) Effective Design

Consistent use of bullets lets audience focus on the message, not the mechanics

Headline is clearly emphasized

Conventional left-to-right, top-to-bottom arrangement makes it easy to find the message

violates numerous principles of effective design, as you can see in the annotations. Figure 12.8b will never win any awards for exciting or innovative design, but it does its job efficiently and effectively.

Even without any formal training in design, being aware of the following six principles will help you be a more effective visual communicator:

Objective 6 Discuss six principles of graphic design that can improve the quality of your visuals.

> **Consistency.** Readers view a series of visuals as a whole, assuming that design elements will be consistent from one page to the next. Think of continuity as *visual parallelism,* in the same way that textual parallelism helps audiences understand and compare a series of ideas.[14] You can achieve visual parallelism in a variety of ways, through the consistent use of colour, shape, size, texture, position, scale, or typeface. For example, if your first chart shows results for Division A in blue, the audience will expect Division A to be shown in blue throughout the report or presentation.

> **Contrast.** Readers expect visual distinctions to match verbal ones. To emphasize differences, depict items in contrasting colours, such as red and blue or black and white. To emphasize similarities, make colour differences more subtle. In a pie chart, you might show two similar items in two shades of blue and a dissimilar item in yellow. Keep in mind that accent colours draw attention to key elements, but they lose their effect if you overdo them.

> **Balance.** The human eye tends to compare visual images with physical structures, and images that appear to be out of balance can be as unsettling as a building that looks like it's about to tip over. Balance can be either *formal,* in which the elements in the images are arranged symmetrically around a central point or axis, or *informal,* in which elements are not distributed evenly but stronger and weaker elements are arranged in a way that achieves an overall effect of balance. A common approach to informal balance is weighing one visually dominant element against several smaller or weaker elements.[15] Generally speaking, formal balance is calming and serious, whereas informal balance tends to feel dynamic and engaging (which is why most advertising uses this approach, for example).

> **Emphasis.** Audiences usually assume that the dominant element in a design is the most important, so make sure that the visually dominant element really does represent the most important information. You can do this through colour, position, size, or placement, for example. Conversely, be sure to downplay visually less important items. For example, avoid using strong colours for minor support points, and de-emphasize background features such as the grid lines on a chart.

> **Convention.** Just as written communication is guided by an array of spelling, grammar, punctuation, and usage conventions, visual communication is guided by a variety of generally accepted rules or conventions that dictate virtually every aspect of design.[16] Moreover, many conventions are so ingrained that people don't even realize they are following conventions. For example, if English is your native language, you assume that ideas progress across the page from left to right because that's the direction in which English text is written. Whether it's the sequence of steps in a process diagram or elapsed time along the bottom of a graph, you automatically expect this left-to-right flow. However, if you are a native Arabic or Hebrew speaker, you might automatically assume that flow on a page or screen is from right to left because that is the direction in which those languages are written. Flouting conventions often causes breakdowns in communication, but in some cases, it can be done to great effect.[17] For example, flipping an organization chart upside down—putting the customers at the top, with frontline employees directly beneath them and on down to the chief executive at the bottom—can be an effective way to emphasize that customers

When designing visuals, observe the principles of consistency, contrast, balance, emphasis, convention, and simplicity.

OPERATING REVIEW

Our production facilities are located in four countries and span over three continents. As for our products, they are distributed in more than 30 countries and six continents around the world.

We maintain our commitment to excellence

With 52 years of experience, Saputo has always been dedicated to crafting the highest quality dairy and bakery products. To do this, Saputo has relied on ancestral techniques and innovation since its inception. Saputo is the sum of the efforts and expertise of thousands of craftsmen who put their passion to work on a daily basis.

Saputo's operating structure is divided into two sectors: Dairy Products and Grocery Products. It is further divided into five divisions: the Dairy Products Division (Canada), the Dairy Products Division (Argentina), the Dairy Products Division (Germany), the Cheese Division (USA) and the Bakery Division.

Our production facilities are located in four countries and span three continents. As for our products, they are distributed in more than 30 countries and six continents around the world. They are sold in all three food market segments: retail, foodservice and industrial. Saputo processes over 4 billion litres of raw milk into various dairy products, of which approximately 400 million kilograms of cheese is produced every year.

During fiscal 2006, we continued to deploy our efforts to find new ways of improving our manufacturing efficiencies and lowering our costs. Furthermore, the excellence of our products and service was recognized by our clients, consumers and also by international and national industry associations. Always with an expert hand, we maintain our commitment to excellence.

Number of employees per sector*

- **1,067** Grocery Products Sector
- **1,948** US Dairy Products Sector
- **5,401** Canadian and Other Dairy Products Sector

*As of May 1, 2006

Number of plants per sector

- **1** Grocery Products Sector
- **13** US Dairy Products Sector
- **30** Canadian and Other Dairy Products Sector

Revenues (%) per sector

- **4** Grocery Products Sector
- **30** US Dairy Products Sector
- **66** Canadian and Other Dairy Products Sector

As this page shows, graphics play an important role in the Saputo 2006 annual report. What information does the variety of visuals communicate? Are all the visuals necessary? Are they arranged in an effective manner?

come first and the responsibility of managers is supporting employees in their efforts to satisfy customers.

> **Simplicity.** As Figure 12.8 indicates, simpler is usually better when using visuals for business communication. When you're designing graphics for your documents, remember that you're conveying information, not creating artwork. Limit the number of colours and design elements you use and take care to avoid *chartjunk,* a term coined by visual communication specialist Edward R. Tufte for decorative elements that clutter documents and potentially confuse readers without adding any relevant information.[18] Computers make it far too easy to add chartjunk, from clip art illustrations to three-dimensional bar charts that display only two dimensions of data. When you need to show distinctions between visual elements, follow Tufte's strategy of the smallest effective difference. In his words, "Make all visual distinctions as subtle as possible, but still clear and effective."[19] For example, the slices in a pie chart don't need to be distinguished by both colour and texture; one or the other will do the job more efficiently.

Understanding the Ethics of Visual Communication

The potential power of visuals places an ethical burden on every business communicator. This responsibility involves not only the obvious requirement of avoiding intentional ethical lapses but the more complicated and often more subtle requirement of avoiding unintentional lapses as well. Ethical problems can range from photos that play on racial or gender stereotypes to images that imply cause-and-effect relationships that may not exist to graphs that distort data.

When you communicate with visuals, you must do so ethically.

For example, photographs can influence perceptions of physical size (and perhaps of quality, value, danger, or other associated variables), depending on the way the various elements are arranged in the picture. To increase the perceived size of a product, an advertiser might show a close-up of it being held by someone with smaller-than-average hands. Conversely, a large hand would make the product seem smaller.

You can take many steps to emphasize or de-emphasize specific elements in your visuals, but make sure you don't inadvertently commit an ethical lapse while doing so.

You can work to avoid ethical lapses in your visuals by following these guidelines:[20]

> Consider all possible interpretations—and misinterpretations; will audience biases, beliefs, or backgrounds lead them to different conclusions than you intend?
> Provide enough background information to help audiences interpret the visual information correctly.
> Don't hide or minimize visual information that runs counter to your argument— and don't exaggerate visual information that supports your argument.
> Don't oversimplify complex situations by hiding complications that are important to the audience's understanding of the situation.
> Don't imply cause-and-effect relationships without providing proof that they exist.
> Avoid emotional manipulation or other forms of coercion.
> Be careful with the way you aggregate, or group, data. For example, aggregating daily sales data by weeks or months can obscure daily fluctuations that could be meaningful to your audience.

Visuals can't always speak for themselves; make sure your audience has enough context to interpret your visuals correctly.

Identifying Points to Illustrate

To help identify which parts of your message can benefit from visuals, step back and consider the flow of the entire message from the audience's point of view. Which parts might seem complex, open to misinterpretation, or even just a little bit dull? Are there any connections between ideas or data sets that might not be obvious if they are addressed only in text? Is there a lot of numeric data or other discrete factual content that would be difficult to read if presented in paragraph form? Is there a chance the main idea won't jump off the page if it's covered only in text? Will readers greet the message with skepticism and therefore look for plenty of supporting evidence?

Objective 7 Explain how to choose which points in your message to illustrate.

If you answer yes to any of these questions, you probably need one or more visuals. When you're deciding which points to present visually, think of the five Cs:

Effective visuals are clear, complete, concise, connected, and compelling.

> **Clear.** The human mind is extremely adept at processing visual information, whether it's something simple, such as the shape of stop sign, or complicated, such as the floor plan for a new factory. If you're having difficultly conveying an idea in words, take a minute to brainstorm some visual possibilities.

> **Complete.** Visuals, particularly tables, often serve to provide the supporting details for your main idea or recommendation. Moreover, the process of summarizing, concluding, or recommending often requires you to narrow down your material or exclude details; a table or another visual can provide such details without getting in the way of your main message.

> **Concise.** You've probably heard the phrase "A picture is worth a thousand words." If a particular section of your message seems to require extensive description or explanation, see whether there's a way to convey that information visually in order to reduce your word count.

> **Connected.** A key purpose of many business messages is to show connections of some sort—similarities or differences, correlations, cause-and-effect relationships, and so on. Whenever you want readers to see such a connection, consider whether a chart, diagram, or another illustration can help.

> **Compelling.** Your readers live in a highly visual world. Will one or more illustrations make your message more persuasive, more interesting, more likely to get read? You never want to insert visuals simply for decorative purposes, but even if a particular point can be expressed equally well via text or visuals, consider adding the visual to make your report or presentation more compelling.

As you identify which points in your document would benefit from visuals, make sure that each visual you decide on has a clear purpose (see Table 12–1).

> Table 12–1 When to Use Visuals

Purpose	Example Applications
To clarify	Support text descriptions of quantitative or numerical information, trends, spatial relationships, physical constructions.
To simplify	Break complicated descriptions into components that can be depicted with conceptual models, flowcharts, organization charts, or diagrams.
To emphasize	Call attention to particularly important points by illustrating them with line, bar, pie and other types of charts.
To summarize	Review major points in the narrative by providing a chart or table that summarizes key items.
To reinforce	Present information in both visual and written forms to increase readers' retention.
To attract	Engage readers visually and emotionally; provide visual relief from long blocks of text.
To impress	Build credibility by putting ideas into visual form to convey the impression of authenticity and precision.
To unify	Depict the relationship among points, such as visually integrating the steps in a process by presenting them in a flowchart.

Selecting the Right Type of Visual

Once you've identified which points would benefit most from visual presentation, your next decision is to choose which type of visual to use for each message point. As you see in Figure 12–9, you have many choices for business graphics. For certain types of information, the decision is usually obvious. If you want to present a large set of numerical values or detailed textual information, a table is the obvious choice in most cases. However, if you're presenting data broken down geographically, a colour-coded map might be more effective to show overall patterns rather than individual data points. Also, certain visuals are used more commonly for certain applications; for example, your audience is likely to expect line charts to show trends and bar charts to show comparisons. Line charts usually show data

> Figure 12–9 Selecting the Best Visual

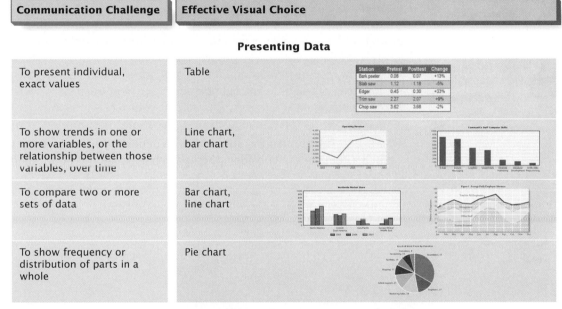

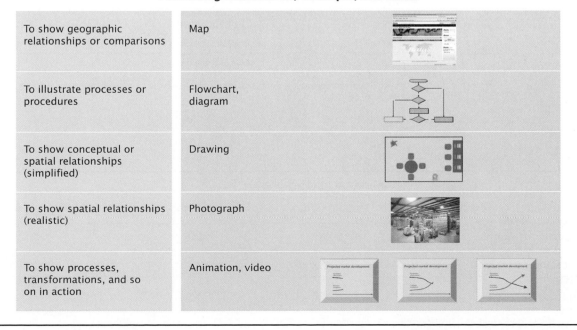

Printed tables can display extensive amounts of data, but tables for online display and electronic presentations need to be simpler.

variations relative to a time axis (such as sales month by month), whereas bar charts more often compare discrete groups (such as sales by demographic segment). Similarly, although a bar chart can show the percentages that make up a whole, this job is usually reserved for pie charts.

The following sections explore the most common types of visuals in more detail, starting with visuals designed to present data.

VISUALS FOR PRESENTING DATA Business professionals have a large number of choices for presenting data, from general purpose line, bar, and pie charts to specialized charts for product portfolios, financial analysis, and other professional functions. The visuals most commonly used to present data include tables, line and surface charts, bar charts, pictograms, Gantt charts, and pie charts.

Tables When you need to present detailed, specific information, choose a table, a systematic arrangement of data in columns and rows. Tables are ideal when your audience needs information that would be either difficult or tedious to handle in the main text.

Most tables contain the standard parts illustrated in Table 12–2. Every table includes vertical columns and horizontal rows, with useful headings along the top and side. The number of columns and rows you can comfortably fit in a table depends on the medium. For printed documents, you can adjust font size and column/row spacing to fit a considerable amount of information on the page and still maintain readability. For online documents, you often need to reduce the number of columns and rows to ensure that your tables are easily readable online. Tables for oral presentations usually need to be the simplest of all because you can't expect audiences to read detailed information from the screen.

Although complex information may require formal tables that are set apart from the text, you can present some data more simply within the text. You make the table, in essence, a part of the paragraph, typed in tabular format. Such text tables are usually introduced with a sentence that leads directly into the tabulated information. Here's an example from the Scotiabank 2008 Corporate Social Responsibility report:

	Total loans	Average loan size	# of customers
Chile (Banco del Desarrollo)	US$110 million	US$2,500	45,000
Peru	US$280 million	US$2,750	100,000
Guatemala	US$20 million	US$3,000	6,000
Dominican Republic	US$8 million	US$4,000	2,000
Jamaica **	US$2.5 million	US$713	2,500
Total	**US$420.5 million**		**155,500**

* We define microfinance clients as self-employed or micro-business owners with annual revenues below US$100,000.
** As of September, 2008.

> Table 12–2 Parts of a Table

	Multicolumn Heading			
Subheading	Subheading	Subheading	Subheading	Single-Column Heading
Row heading	XXX	XXX	XXX*	XXX
Row heading				
Subheading	XXX	XXX	XXX	XXX
Subheading	XXX	XXX	XXX	XXX
Total	XXX	XXX	XXX	XXX

Source: (In the same format as a text footnote; see Appendix B)

*Footnote (For an explanation of elements in the table, a superscript number or small letter may be used instead of an asterisk or other symbol.)

> Figure 12–10 Line Chart

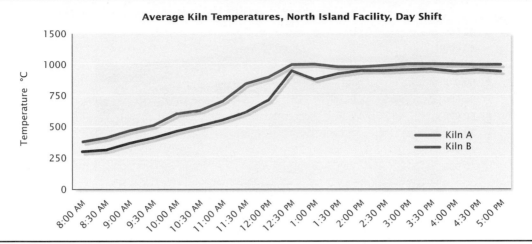

Average Kiln Temperatures, North Island Facility, Day Shift

When you prepare tables, follow these guidelines to make your tables easy to read:

> Use common, understandable units, and clearly identify the units you use, whether dollars, percentages, price per ton, and so on.
> Express all items in a column in the same unit and round off for simplicity.
> Label column headings clearly and use a subhead if necessary.
> Separate columns or rows with lines or extra space to make the table easy to follow; in complex tables, consider highlighting every other row or column in a pale, contrasting colour.
> Provide totals or averages of columns or rows when relevant.
> Document the source of the data using the same format as a text footnote (see Appendix B).

Although numerical tables are more common, tables can also contain words, symbols, or other facts and figures. Word tables are particularly appropriate for presenting survey findings or for comparing various items against a specific standard.

Line Charts and Surface Charts A **line chart,** or *line graph,* illustrates trends over time or plots the relationship of two variables. In line charts showing trends, the vertical, or *y-*, axis shows the amount, and the horizontal, or *x-*, axis shows the time or other quantity against which the amount is measured. Moreover, you can plot just a single line or overlay multiple lines to compare different entities. The line chart in Figure 12–10 shows the fluctuations in operating revenue over four years.

A **surface chart,** also called an **area chart,** is a form of line chart with a cumulative effect; all the lines add up to the top line, which represents the total (see Figure 12–11). This form of chart helps you illustrate changes in the composition of something over time. When preparing a surface chart, put the most important segment against the baseline, and restrict the number of strata to four or five.

Bar Charts and Pie Charts A **bar chart,** or *bar graph,* portrays numbers by the height or length of its rectangular bars, making a series of numbers easy to read or understand. Bar charts are particularly valuable when you want to (1) compare the size of several items at one time; (2) show changes in one item

Line charts are commonly used to show trends over time or the relationship between two variables.

> Figure 12–11 Surface Chart

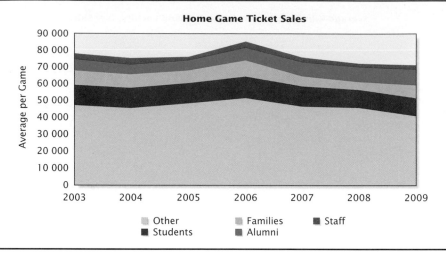

over time; (3) indicate the composition of several items over time; and (4) show the relative size of components of a whole.

As the charts in Figure 12–12 suggest, bar charts can appear in various forms. *Grouped* bar charts compare more than one set of data, using a different colour or pattern for each set. *Deviation* bar charts identify positive and negative

> Figure 12–12 The Versatile Bar Chart

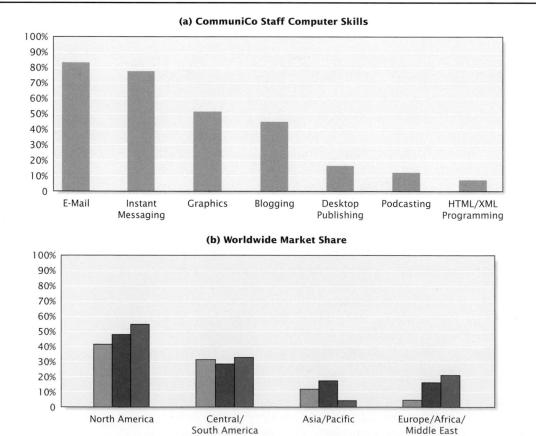

(continued)

> Figure 12–12 The Versatile Bar Chart (*continued*)

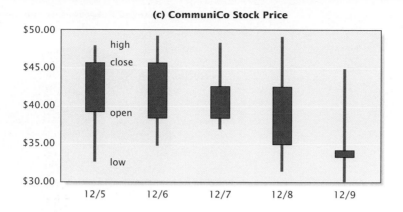

(c) CommuniCo Stock Price

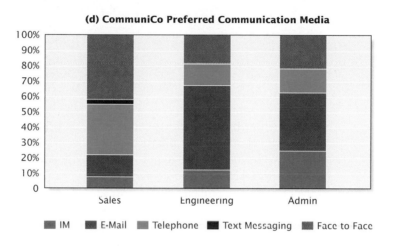

(d) CommuniCo Preferred Communication Media

IM   E-Mail   Telephone   Text Messaging   Face to Face

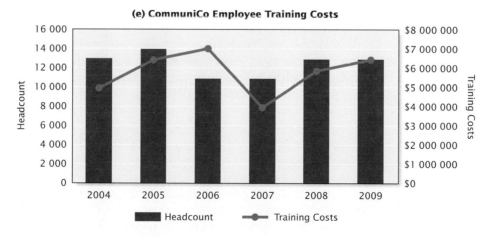

(e) CommuniCo Employee Training Costs

Headcount   Training Costs

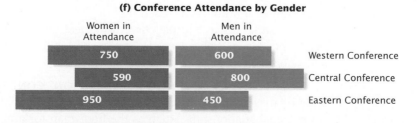

(f) Conference Attendance by Gender

Women in Attendance	Men in Attendance	
750	600	Western Conference
590	800	Central Conference
950	450	Eastern Conference

> Figure 12–13 Pie Chart

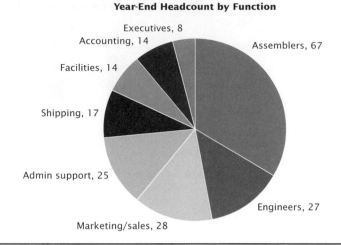

Year-End Headcount by Function

Most readers expect pie charts to show the distribution of parts within a whole.

values, or winners and losers. *Segmented* bar charts, also known as stacked bar charts, show how individual components contribute to a total number, using a different colour or pattern for each component. *Combination* bar and line charts compare quantities that require different intervals. *Paired* bar charts show the correlations between two items.

Like segmented bar charts and area charts, a **pie chart** shows how the parts of a whole are distributed. However, pie charts have the advantage of familiarity; most people expect parts-of-a-whole to be displayed via a pie chart. Each segment represents a slice of a complete circle, or *pie*. As you can see in Figure 12–13, pie charts are an effective way to show percentages or to compare one segment with another.

When creating pie charts, restrict the number of slices in the pie to 8 or less. Otherwise, the chart looks cluttered and is difficult to label. If necessary, combine the smallest pieces together in a "miscellaneous" category. Ideally, the largest or most important slice of the pie, the segment you want to emphasize, is placed at the twelve o'clock position; the rest are arranged clockwise either in order of size or in some other logical progression.

Use different colours or patterns to distinguish the various pieces. If you want to draw attention to the segment that is of the greatest interest to your readers, use a brighter colour for that segment, draw an arrow to the segment, or explode it; that is, pull the segment away from the rest of the pie. In any case, label all the segments and indicate their values in either percentages or units of measure, so your readers will be able to judge the value of the wedges. Remember, the segments must add up to 100 percent if percentages are used or to the total number if numbers are used.

Line, surface, bar, and pie charts will meet most of your data presentation needs, but for specialized needs, explore the other chart options available in software such as Microsoft Excel.

VISUALS FOR PRESENTING INFORMATION, CONCEPTS, AND IDEAS In addition to facts and figures, you can present other types of information visually, from spatial relationships (such as the floor plan for a new office building) to abstract ideas (such as progress or competition). The most common types of

> Figure 12–14 Flowchart

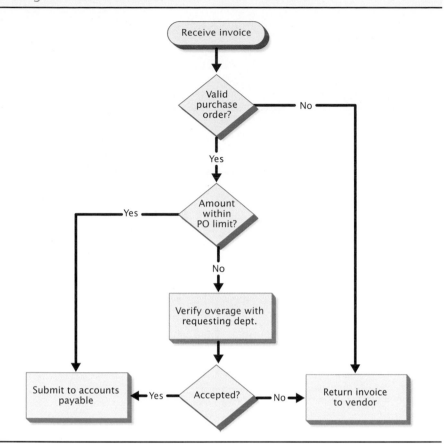

visuals for these applications include flowcharts, organization charts, maps, drawings, diagrams, photographs, animation, and video.

Flowcharts and Organization Charts A **flowchart** (see Figure 12–14) illustrates a sequence of events from start to finish; it is an indispensable tool for illustrating processes, procedures, and sequential relationships. For general business purposes, you don't need to be too concerned about the specific shapes in a flowchart, but use them consistently. However, you should be aware of the formal flowchart "language," in which each shape has a specific meaning (diamonds are decision points and rectangles are process steps). If you're communicating with computer programmers and others accustomed to formal flowcharting, ensure that you use the correct symbols in each case to avoid confusion.

As the name implies, an **organization chart** illustrates the positions, units, or functions of an organization and the way they interrelate. An organization's normal communication channels are almost impossible to describe without the benefit of a chart like the one in Figure 12–15. These charts aren't limited to organizational structures, of course; as you saw in Chapter 4, they can also be used to outline messages.

Maps, Drawings, Diagrams, and Photographs When your information has a geographic aspect, maps are often an ideal visual device. For example, the Bata in the World map in Chapter 3 shows the company's global operations. Maps are useful for showing market territories, distribution routes, facilities locations, and other geographically significant data.

Use maps to represent statistics by geographic area and to show spatial relationships.

> Figure 12–15 Organization Chart

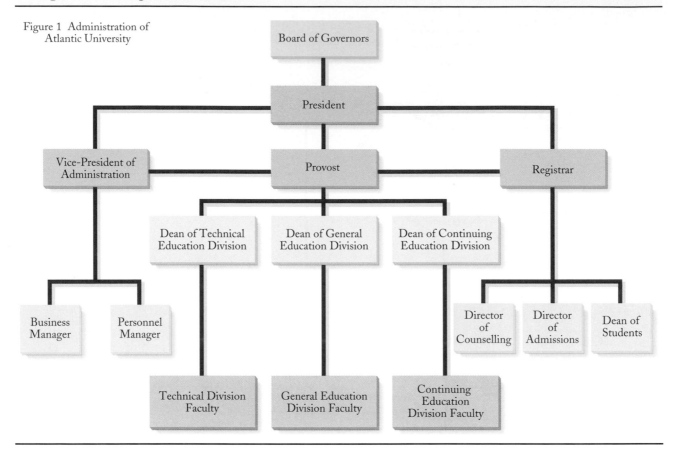

Figure 1 Administration of
Atlantic University

Use drawings and diagrams to show how something works or how it is made or used; drawings are sometimes better than photographs because they let you focus on the most important details.

Simple maps are available via clip art libraries for word processor and presentation software, but more powerful uses (such as automatically generating colour-coded maps based on data inputs) usually require the specialized capabilities of *geographic information systems*. You may also want to explore online resources such as Google Earth (http://earth.google.com) and Bing (www.bing.com/maps), which offer a variety of mapping and aerial photography features.

Although drawings, diagrams, and photographs are often created by people working in communication specialties such as web design or technical writing, all managers encounter situations in which such images can help get their messages across (see Figure 12–16). Simple drawings can show the network of suppliers in an industry, the flow of funds through a company, or the process for completing the payroll each week. More complex diagrams can convey technical topics such as the operation of a machine or repair procedures.

Word processors and presentation software provide basic drawing capabilities, but for more precise and professional illustrations you'll need a specialized package like Microsoft Visio or Adobe Illustrator. Moving to a level beyond those programs, computer-aided design (CAD) systems such as Autodesk's AutoCAD can produce extremely detailed architectural and engineering drawings.

This map is a simple version of a geographic information system (GIS), in this case showing hotels and motels in a neighbourhood near New York's LaGuardia Airport. How can a real estate company use this type of map? How can a GIS map help a chain of restaurants find locations in new areas?

Photographs offer both functional and decorative value. In the past their use was limited to specialized documents such as annual reports and product brochures; however, with low-cost digital photography now widely available, virtually all writers can have the ability to add photographs to print documents, presentations, and web pages. In addition, photo libraries such as Getty Images (www.gettyimages.com) and photo search engines such as the one provided by AltaVista (www.altavista.com/image) make it easy to find digital photographs. Some photos are available for free, but the professional collections, such as Getty Images, require either a one-time payment for unlimited use (often called *royalty free*) or an annual payment or other limited-use purchase (often called *rights managed*).

Nothing else can demonstrate the exact appearance of a new facility, a piece of property, a new product, or even a retiring co-worker the way a photograph can. However, in some situations a photograph may show too much detail, which is one reason that repair manuals frequently use drawings instead of photos, for example. With a drawing, you can select how much detail to show, and you can focus the reader's attention on particular parts or places. The disadvantage of such technical illustrations is the time, skill, and special tools often required to create them.

Technology makes it easier to use photographs in reports and presentations, but it also presents an important ethical concern. Software tools such as

Use photographs for visual appeal and to show exact appearances.

> Figure 12–16 Diagram

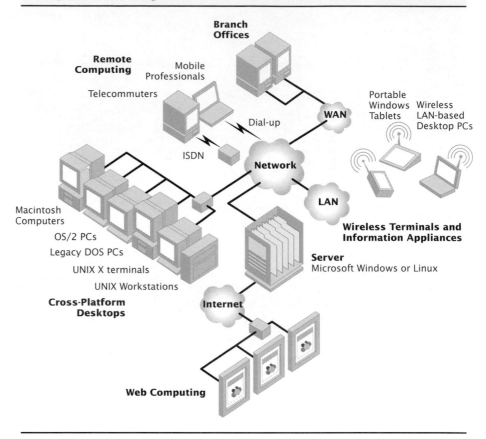

Photoshop and Paint Shop Pro allow you to make dramatic changes to photos easily—without leaving a clue that they've been altered. Altering photos in small ways has been possible for a long time (more than a few people have had blemishes airbrushed out of their yearbook photos), but computers make drastic changes easy and undetectable. You can remove people from photographs, put Person A's head on Person B's body, and make products look more attractive than they really are. Most people would agree that it's acceptable to make cosmetic improvements, such as brightening an underexposed photo to make it easier to view. But to avoid ethical lapses, don't make any alterations that mislead the viewer or substantially change the message conveyed by the photo—at least not without informing your audience of the changes.[21]

Animation and Video Computer animation and video are among the most specialized forms of business visuals. When they are appropriate and done well, they offer unparalleled visual impact. At a simple level, you can animate shapes and text within Microsoft PowerPoint, although the possibilities are somewhat limited. At a more sophisticated level, software programs, such as Adobe Flash, enable the creation of multimedia files that include computer animation, digital video, and other elements. A wide variety of tools are also available for digital video production. Chances are you won't have to use these tools yourself, but if you do employ a specialist to create animation or video for websites or presentations, ensure that the results follow all the guidelines for effective business messages.

To show investors what a new building would look like in its environment, an artist combined a photograph of a scale model of the building with a photograph of the actual street scene. Because the target audience clearly understands that the building doesn't exist, this sort of image manipulation is not unethical. Why is it important to alert your audience to photographic manipulation?

Producing and Integrating Visuals

Now that you understand the communication power of visuals and have chosen the best visuals to illustrate key points in your report, website, or presentation, it's time to get creative. This section offers advice on creating visuals, integrating them with your text, and verifying the quality of your visual elements.

Creating Visuals

Computers make it easy to create visuals, but they also make it easy to create ineffective, distracting, and even downright ugly visuals. However, by following the basic design principles discussed on pages 414 to 417, you can create all the basic visuals you need—visuals that are attractive and effective. If possible, have a professional designer set up a *template* for the various types of visuals you and your colleagues need to create. In addition to helping ensure an effective design, using templates saves you the time of making numerous design decisions every time you create a chart or graphic.

> Computer software offers a variety of tools but doesn't automatically give you the design sensibility that is needed for effective visuals.

Remember that the style and quality of your visuals communicates a subtle message about your relationship with the audience. A simple sketch might be fine for a working meeting but inappropriate for a formal presentation or report. On the other hand, elaborate, full-colour visuals may be viewed as extravagant for an informal report but may be entirely appropriate for a message to top management or influential outsiders.

Integrating Visuals with Text

For maximum effectiveness and minimum disruption for the reader, visual elements need to be carefully integrated with the text of your message so that readers can move back and forth between text and visuals with as little disruption as possible. Successful integration involves four decisions: maintaining a balance between visuals and text, referring to visuals in the text, placing the visuals in the document, and writing titles and other descriptions.

The use of colour in visuals accelerates learning, retention, and recall by 55 percent to 78 percent, and it increases motivation and audience participation by up to 80 percent. Is colour suitable for all visuals? On what occasions is it appropriate to use black and white instead of colour?

Maintain a balance between text and visuals and pace your visuals in a way that emphasizes your key points.

BALANCING ILLUSTRATIONS AND WORDS Strong visuals enhance the descriptive and persuasive power of your writing, but putting too many visuals into a report can distract your readers. Constantly referring to visuals makes it difficult for readers to maintain focus on the thread of your message. The space occupied by visuals can also disrupt the flow of text on the page or screen. The pacing of visuals throughout the text is also an important consideration. Although it isn't always possible to have perfect distribution throughout the report, try to have a fairly even flow of text and visuals from page to page or screen to screen.

As always, take your readers' specific needs into account. If you're addressing an audience with multiple language backgrounds or widely varying reading skills, you can shift the balance toward more visual elements to help overcome any language barriers. The professional experience, education, and training of your audience should influence your approach as well. For example, detailed statistical plots and mathematical formulas are everyday reading material for quality-control engineers but not for most salespeople or top executives.

REFERENCING VISUALS Unless a visual element clearly stands on its own, as in the *sidebars* you often see in magazines or the captioned photographs in this textbook, visuals should be clearly referred to by number in the text of your report. Some report writers refer to all visuals as "exhibits" and number them consecutively throughout the report; many others number tables and figures separately (everything that isn't a table is regarded as a figure). In a long report with numbered sections, illustrations may have a double number (separated by a period or a hyphen) representing the section number and the individual illustration number within that section. Whichever scheme you use, make sure it's clear and consistent.

To tie visuals to the text, introduce them in the text and place them near the points they illustrate. Help your readers understand the significance of visuals by referring to them before readers encounter them in the document or onscreen. The following examples show how you can make this connection in the text:

Figure 1 summarizes the financial history of the motorcycle division over the past five years, with sales broken into four categories.

Total sales were steady over this period, but the mix of sales by category changed dramatically (see Figure 2).

The underlying reason for the remarkable growth in our sales of youth golf apparel is suggested by Table 4, which shows the growing interest in junior golf around the world.

When describing the data shown in your visuals, ensure that you emphasize the main point you want to make. Don't make the mistake of simply repeating the data to be shown. Paragraphs that do are guaranteed to put the reader to sleep:

Among women who replied to the survey, 17.4 percent earn less than $9 per hour; 26.4 percent earn $9 to $11; 25.7 percent, $12 to $14; 18.0 percent, $15 to $24; 9.6 percent, $25 to $49; and 2.9 percent, $50 and over.

The visual will provide all these details; there is no need to repeat them in the text. Instead, use round numbers that summarize the core message:

Over two-thirds of the women who replied earn less than $12 per hour.

PLACING VISUALS Position your visuals so that your audience won't have to flip back and forth (in printed documents) or scroll (onscreen) between the visuals and the text. Ideally, it's best to place each visual within, beside, or immediately after the paragraph it illustrates so that readers can consult the explanation and the visual at the same time. If possible, try to avoid bunching several visuals in one section of the document.

Writing Titles, Captions, and Legends Titles, captions, and legends provide more opportunities to connect your visual and textual messages. A **title** provides a short description that identifies the content and purpose of the visual, along with whatever label and number you're using to refer to the visual. As with headings and subheadings, a *descriptive* title simply identifies the topic of the illustration, whereas an *informative* title calls attention to the conclusion that ought to be drawn from the data. Here's an example of the difference:

Descriptive Title	Informative Title
Relationship Between Petroleum Demand and Refinery Capacity in Canada	Shrinking Refinery Capacity Results from Stagnant Petroleum Demand

A **caption** usually offers additional discussion of the visual's content and can be several sentences long, if appropriate. Captions can also alert readers that additional discussion is available in the accompanying text. Titles usually appear above visuals and captions appear below, but effective designs can place these two elements in other positions. Sometimes titles and captions are combined in a single block of text as well. As with all design decisions, be consistent throughout your report or website. A **legend** helps readers decode the visual by explaining what various colours, symbols, or other design choices mean. Legends aren't necessary for simple graphs, such as a line chart or bar chart with only one series of data, but they are invaluable with more complex graphics.

Don't assume that titles, captions, and legends are minor details. They are often the first elements that people read in a document—and sometimes the only elements that people read—so use them effectively to communicate your key points. For a review of the important points to remember when creating visuals, see "Checklist: Creating Effective Visuals."

> The title of a visual functions in the same way as a subheading, whereas the caption provides additional detail if needed.

CHECKLIST Creating Effective Visuals

- ✔ Emphasize visual consistency to connect parts of a whole and minimize audience confusion.
- ✔ Avoid arbitrary changes of colour, texture, typeface, position, or scale.
- ✔ Highlight contrasting points through colour, position, and other design choices.
- ✔ Decide whether you want to achieve formal or informal balance.
- ✔ Emphasize dominant elements and de-emphasize less important pieces in a design.
- ✔ Understand and follow (at least most of the time) the visual conventions your audience expects.
- ✔ Strive for simplicity and clarity; don't clutter your visuals with meaningless decoration.
- ✔ Follow the guidelines for avoiding ethical lapses.

- ✔ Carefully consider your message, the nature of your information, and your audience to choose which points to illustrate.
- ✔ Select the proper types of graphics for the information at hand and for the objective of the message.
- ✔ Be sure the visual contributes to overall understanding of the subject.
- ✔ Understand how to use your software tools to maximize effectiveness and efficiency.
- ✔ Integrate visuals and text by maintaining a balance between illustrations and words, clearly referring to visuals within the text, and placing visuals carefully.
- ✔ Verify the quality of your visuals by checking for accuracy, proper documentation, and honesty.

PROMOTING WORKPLACE ETHICS

Ethical Communication and Distorting the Data

Take a quick look at these three line charts, which display the level of impurities found in a particular source of drinking water. Chart A suggests that the source has a consistently high level of impurities throughout the year, Chart B indicates that the level of impurities jumps up and down throughout the year, and Chart C shows an impurity level that is fairly consistent throughout the year—and fairly low.

Here's the problem: All three charts are displaying the *exact same data.*

Look again at Chart A. The vertical scale is set from 0 to 120, sufficient to cover the range of variations in the data. However, what if you wanted to persuade an audience that the variations from month to month were quite severe? In Chart B, the scale is "zoomed in" on 60 to 110, making the variations look much more dramatic. The result could be a stronger emotional impact on the reader, creating the impression that these impurities are out of control.

On the other hand, what if you wanted to create the impression that the situation was fine, with low levels of impurities and no wild swings from month to month. You would follow the example in Chart C, where the scale is expanded from 0 to 200, which appears to minimize the variations in the data. This graph is visually "calmer," potentially creating the opposite impression—that there's really nothing to worry about.

If all three graphs show the same data, is any one of them more honest than the others? The answer to this question depends on your intent and your audience's information needs. For example, if dramatic swings in the measurement from month to month suggest a problem with the quality of your product or the safety of a process that affects the public, then visually minimizing the swings might well be considered dishonest.

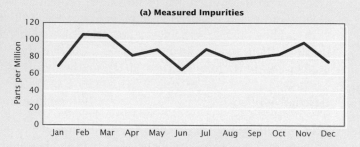

(a) Measured Impurities

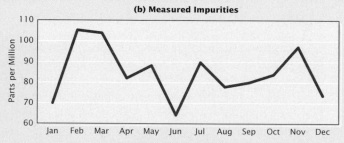

(b) Measured Impurities

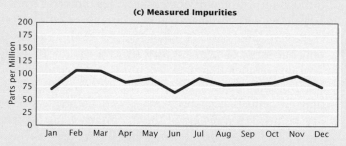

(c) Measured Impurities

CAREER APPLICATIONS

1 What sort of quick visual impression would such a chart give if the vertical scale were set to 0–500? Why?

2 If the acceptable range of impurities in this case is from 60 to 120 parts per million, which chart is the fairest way to present the data? Why?

Verifying the Quality and Integrity of Your Visuals

Proof visuals as carefully as you proof text.

Visuals have a particularly strong impact on your readers and on their perceptions of you and your work. Ensure that you check visuals for mistakes such as typographical errors, inconsistent colour treatment, confusing or undocumented symbols, and misaligned elements. Ensure that your computer hasn't done something unexpected, such as arranging pie chart slices in an order you don't want or plotting line charts in unusual colours. Also take a few extra minutes to ensure that your visuals are absolutely accurate, properly documented, and honest.

> **Is the visual accurate?** Be sure to check visuals for mistakes such as typographical errors, inconsistent colour treatment, confusing or undocumented symbols, and misaligned elements. Does each visual deliver your message

accurately? Have you inserted the right visuals in the right places? Also verify that information in visuals and accompanying text matches. For data presentations, particularly if you're producing charts with a spreadsheet, verify any formulas used to generate the numbers and make sure you've selected the right numbers for each chart.

> **Is the visual properly documented?** As with the textual elements in your reports and presentations, visuals based on other people's research, information, and ideas require full citation. (Note that in many books, including this one, source notes for visuals are collected in one place at the end of the book.) Also, anticipate any questions or concerns your audience may have and address them with additional information as needed. For example, if you're presenting the results of survey research, many readers will want to know who participated in the survey, how many people responded, and when the questions were asked. You could answer these questions with a note in the caption along the lines of "652 accountants, surveyed the week of January 17." Similarly, if you found a visual in a secondary source, list that source on or near the graphic to help readers assess the information. To avoid cluttering your graphic, use a shortened citation or note on the graphic itself and include a complete citation elsewhere in the report.

> **Is the visual honest?** As a final precaution, step back and make sure your visuals communicate truthful messages (see "Promoting Workplace Ethics: Ethical Communication and Distorting the Data"). Make sure they don't hide information the audience needs, imply conclusions that your information doesn't support, or play on audience emotions in manipulative or coercive ways.

Review each visual to ensure that it doesn't intentionally or unintentionally distort the meaning of the underlying information.

Summary of Learning Objectives

1 **Explain how to adapt to your audiences when writing reports and proposals.** Successful reports and proposals require careful use of language and tone. You may use personal pronouns if you are familiar with your audience, but use an impersonal style if you are not. A more formal tone is appropriate when reports are sent to outsiders or when they contain controversial or complex information. When writing for people of other cultures, avoid humour and idiomatic language because they do not translate effectively from one culture to the next.

2 **Describe five characteristics of effective report content.** Effective reports represent your credibility to both internal and external readers. To ensure that your credibility is maintained, your reports must (1) be factually accurate; (2) contain all necessary information that is well supported with evidence; (3) present the issues fairly, representing all sides of your argument; (4) flow logically and clearly; and (5) be properly documented.

3 **Explain six strategies to strengthen your proposal argument.** Write compelling proposals by showcasing your knowledge and experience, which demonstrate your ability to tackle the problem or opportunity. Additionally, support the proposal with concrete and specific examples.

Supply information about the competition if relevant, and prove that the proposal is realistic. You should also highlight how the product or service will benefit the reader. Finally, check your proposal for correctness and format it in an inviting way.

4 **Determine the topics commonly covered in a proposal introduction, body, and closing.** The proposal introduction summarizes the problem, provides the recommended solution, states the document's scope, and previews its organization. The proposal body develops the solution, describes a work plan, states the qualifications of the writer and his or her organization, and covers the solution's implementation costs. The proposal close provides a general summary and reinforces reader benefits and the writer's capabilities.

5 **Identify five characteristics of effective writing in online reports.** Online reports require special features in addition to those of hard-copy reports. First, because readers may mistrust online content, build trust through accurate and current information and include the date material was posted. Second, adapt your content for a global audience; one way is through localizing the home page for cultural practices while keeping more detailed content in the

original language. Third, be sure content is structured to attract and maintain interest by using the inverted pyramid style. Fourth, write concisely so readers can skim pages easily. Fifth, identify where links will take readers, so they understand they can access information easily.

6 **Discuss six principles of graphic design that can improve the quality of your visuals.** To design the most effective visuals for business reports, keep the following principles in mind. First, to avoid confusing readers, be consistent in your use of design elements such as colour, shape, size, position, scale, and typeface. Second, use strong contrasting colours to show difference and subtle colours to show similarity. Third, ensure that your document is balanced to avoid a jarring appearance. Fourth, give visual emphasis to the most important points, as your reader expects. Fifth, take into account your audience's culture, education, and other background experiences, because your readers may have specific associations with certain symbols and images. Sixth, avoid clutter and chartjunk to maintain clarity and project professionalism.

7 **Explain how to choose which points in your message to illustrate.** Ideas and information that are too complicated to describe in words are prime candidates for visual illustration; so is information that is connected in some way (such as cause-and-effect relationships). In addition, points that should have an impact on readers can be shown visually to heighten their importance.

PEARSON mycanadianbuscommlab

Visit www.mycanadianbuscommlab.ca for everything you need to help you succeed in the job you've always wanted! Tools and resources include the following:
- Composing Space and Writer's Toolkit
- Document Makeovers
- Video Case Studies
- Grammar Exercises—and much more!

On the Job PERFORMING COMMUNICATION TASKS AT FEDEX

Reports are essential to maintaining FedEx's prominence in the courier industry. They are written by internal auditors, for example, to justify expenditures for equipment intended to improve procedures and practices, by human resources managers to recommend training programs, by technical staff to explain potential innovations, and by many others to ensure that FedEx continues to run smoothly and provide value to its customers.

You have recently been hired as an administrative assistant at FedEx Canada's head office to help with a variety of special projects. In each situation, choose the best communication alternative from among those listed. Be prepared to explain your choice.

1 To keep track of the industry, you have been instructed to research two online services offered by FedEx's top competitors: online pickup requests and online package tracking. How should you introduce your report? Choose the best opening from the four shown below.

a Begin by introducing the purpose of the study (to review what online services competitors are offering) and making recommendations about how FedEx can better compete with these offerings.

b Begin by introducing the purpose of the study (to review what online services competitors are offering) and outlining how you will present your data.

c Begin by giving a brief history of the rivalry between FedEx and its top three competitors.

d Begin by summarizing FedEx efforts to stay on top of the technology wave and how important such technology will be to the company's future.

2 As you work on your report about competitors' online services, you want to include a visual that compares FedEx Canada's online statistics with those of its major rivals. For example, in your research you learn how many people visit the FedEx.ca website each month and how many online tracking requests FedEx.ca receives each day. You also locate the same information for all major competitors. What is the best way to present this information?

a Use a table to present the numbers for each company.

b Use a line chart to present the numbers for each company.

c Use a bar chart to present the numbers for each company.

d Use a pie chart to present the numbers for each company.

3 CEO Frederick W. Smith wants to celebrate the company's achievements by creating a special advertising insert on FedEx's history. He wants to distribute this insert inside the April issue of a national business magazine. The magazine's publisher is excited about the concept and has asked Smith to send her "something in writing." You are asked to draft the proposal, which should be no more than 10 pages long. Which outlines should you use?

a Version 1

I An overview of FedEx's history

A How company was founded

B Overview of company services

C Overview of markets served

D Overview of transportation operations

II The FedEx magazine insert
  A Historic events to be included
  B Employees to be interviewed
  C Customers to be discussed
  D Production schedule
III Pros and cons of FedEx magazine insert
  A Pros: Make money for magazine, draw new customers for FedEx
  B Cons: Costs, questionable audience interest
b Version 2
  I Introduction: Overview of the FedEx special insert
  A Purpose
  B Content
  C Timing
  II Description of the insert
  A Text
    1 Message from CEO
    2 History of FedEx
    3 Interviews with employees
    4 Customer testimonials
  B Advertising
    1 Inside front and back covers
    2 Colour spreads
    3 Congratulatory ads placed by customers
  III Next steps
  IV Summary

c Version 3
  Who: FedEx
  What: Special magazine insert
  When: Inserted in April issue
  Where: Coordinated by magazine's editors
  Why: To celebrate FedEx's anniversary
  How: Overview of content, production responsibilities, and schedule
d Version 4
  I Introduction: The rationale for producing a magazine insert promoting FedEx
  A Insert would make money for magazine.
  B Insert would boost morale of FedEx employees.
  C Insert would attract new customers.
  II Insert description
  A Interview with founder Frederick Smith
  B Interviews with employees
  C Description of historic moments
  D Interviews with customers
  E Advertisements
  III Production plan
  A Project organization
  B Timing and sequence of steps
  C FedEx's responsibilities
  D Magazine's responsibilities
  IV Detailed schedule
  V Summary of benefits and responsibilities

Test Your Knowledge

1 Why is the "you" attitude particularly important with long or complex reports and proposals?
2 Where would you list action items in a report? Why?
3 How are audiences likely to react if they spot several errors in your reports?
4 What strategies strengthen your proposal arguments?
5 How do online reports differ from hard-copy reports?
6 How do visuals enhance the communication impact of your writing?
7 How do you select report content for visual representation?
8 How do you verify the accuracy of the visuals in your report?
9 What tools can you use to help readers follow the structure and flow of information in a long report?
10 What ethical issue is raised by the use of technology to alter photographs in reports?

Apply Your Knowledge

1 Should a report always explain the writer's method of gathering evidence or solving a problem? Why or why not?
2 Besides telling readers why an illustration is important, why refer to it in the text of your document?
3 When you read a graph, how can you ensure that the visual impression you receive is an accurate reflection of reality? Please explain.
4 If you want your audience to agree to a specific course of action, should you exclude any references to alternatives that you don't want the audience to consider? Why or why not?
5 **Ethical Choices** If a company receives a solicited formal proposal outlining the solution to a particular problem, is it ethical for the company to adopt the proposal's recommendations without hiring the firm that submitted the proposal? Why or why not?

Running Cases

Watch on mycanadianbuscommlab

> CASE 1 Noreen

Noreen's boss likes the idea Noreen proposed to merge the "Go Points" department with the Petro-Go credit card sales/service department. The boss would like Noreen to write an analysis and justification report to support the idea and plan to merge the two departments into one.

Currently, the "Go Points" department is on the 4th floor and staffed by 20 sales/service reps. They (1) make sales calls to existing Petro-Go credit card holders to offer the points program, (2) receive calls from existing points program customers who have enquiries, and (3) call existing points customers to announce promotions and offers.

The Petro-Go credit card department is on the 3rd floor and staffed by 30 sales/service reps. They (1) make sales calls to recruit new credit card customers, (2) receive calls from existing credit card holders who have enquiries, and (3) call existing credit card customers to announce promotions and offers.

Noreen thinks that by joining the credit card sales/service department with the "Go Points" department, customers will be better served by one-stop shopping. She also feels that the credit card sales/service staff could easily modify their call routines to include information about the "Go Points" program, and the "Go Points" staff could easily be trained on the credit card policies and procedures.

QUESTIONS

a) What information must Noreen gather?
b) What logical arguments can Noreen use?
c) What are the five steps Noreen should follow to focus her report around recommendations?
d) What type of visuals might Noreen include in the report?
e) How will Noreen leave a strong and lasting impression on the reader at the end of her report?

YOUR TASK

With a partner, use your imagination to write an analytical memo report from Noreen to her managers (use your names) that gives an analysis of the situation and justifies the merger. When structuring a report around recommendations, follow the five steps listed on page 381 in your textbook. Include at least one visual in your report (you will need to use your imagination).

> CASE 2 Kwong

Kwong is working with the annual report project team to gather, summarize, and compile the annual report for ET Canada. The annual report will be posted on the internet and distributed to all shareholders. The report will include several charts and tables. Revenue will be reported in the annual report, and Kwong will use a table to show product lines offered by ET Canada and the revenue for each over the past few years.

QUESTIONS

a) Why will placing the information in a table help the reader?
b) Would this annual report best be organized in chronological, geographical, or category order?
c) Should the company's annual report use the direct approach or the indirect approach?
d) Would the 2 + 2 = 4 approach help with this annual report?
e) List three factors Kwong should consider when he is deciding how many and what type of visuals to include in the annual report.

YOUR TASK

Create an internal memo to Kwong showing ET Canada's product line analysis for this year and last year. The memo is from the chief information officer. The memo contains a table showing revenues for each product line for this year and last year. Product lines are Local and Access, Long Distance, Wireless, Data, Video, Terminal Sales, and Other. The table also includes a column for percentage of change between this year and last year as well as column totals. The memo also contains a bar/column chart that displays the revenues for each product line for the two years. Kwong plans to add this information to the company annual report.

Practise Your Knowledge

Documents for Analysis

DOCUMENT 12.A

Examine the pie charts in Figure 12–17 below and point out any problems or errors you notice.

> Figure 12–17 Pie Chart for Analysis (Document 12.A)

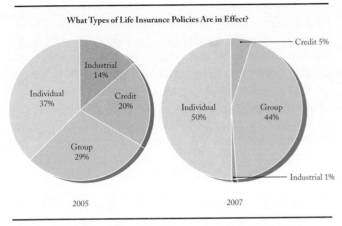

DOCUMENT 12.B

Examine the line chart in Figure 12–18 below and point out any problems or errors you notice.

> Figure 12–18 Line Chart for Analysis (Document 12.B)

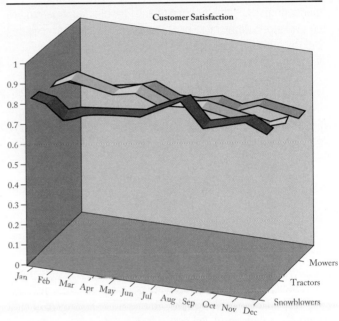

Exercises

12.1 Business Reports: Building Audience Rapport

Review the reports shown in Figures 12–3 and 12–4. Give specific examples of how each report establishes a good relationship with the audience. Consider such things as using the "you" attitude, emphasizing the positive, establishing credibility, being polite, using bias-free language, and projecting a good company image.

12.2 Composing Reports: Report Content

You are writing an analytical report on the Canadian sales of your newest product. Of the following topics, identify those that should be covered in the report introduction, body, and close. Briefly explain your decisions:

a. regional breakdowns of sales across the country
b. date the product was released in the marketplace
c. sales figures from competitors selling similar products worldwide
d. predictions of how the Canadian economy will affect sales over the next six months
e. method used for obtaining the above predictions

f. the impact of similar products being sold in Canada by Chinese competitors
g. your recommendation as to whether the company should sell this product internationally
h. actions that must be completed by year end if the company decides to sell this product internationally

12.3 Teamwork: Graphic Design

Team up with a classmate to design graphics based on a comparison of the total tax burden of the Canadian taxpayer with that of people in other nations. One teammate should sketch a horizontal bar chart and the other should sketch a vertical one from the estimates that follow. Then, exchange visual aids and analyze how well each conveys the situation of the Canadian taxpayer. Would the bar chart look best with vertical or horizontal bars? Why? What scale is best? How does the direction used in the bar chart enhance or obscure the meaning or impact of the data? What suggestions can you make for improving your teammate's visual aid?

Estimates show that Swedish taxpayers spend 47 percent of their incomes on taxes, British taxpayers spend 34 percent, French taxpayers spend 50 percent, Japanese taxpayers spend 28 percent, and U.S. taxpayers spend 27 percent. In Canada, the average is estimated at 32 percent.

12.4 Composing Reports: Supporting a Solution

Find an article in a business newspaper or journal (in print or online) that recommends a solution to a problem. Identify the problem, the recommended solution(s), and the supporting evidence provided by the author to justify his or her recommendation(s). Did the author cite any formal or informal studies as evidence? What facts or statistics did the author include? Did the author cite any criteria for evaluating possible options? If so, what were they?

12.5 Composing Reports: Navigational Clues

Review a long business article in a journal or newspaper. Highlight examples of how the article uses headings, transitions, previews, and reviews to help the readers find their way.

12.6 Ethical Choices: Survey Questions

Your boss has asked you to prepare a feasibility report to determine whether the company should advertise its custom-crafted cabinetry in the weekly neighbourhood newspaper. Based on your primary research, you think they should. As you draft the introduction to your report, however, you discover that the survey administered to the neighbourhood newspaper subscribers was flawed. Several questions were poorly written and misleading. You used the survey results, among other findings, to justify your recommendation. The report is due in three days. What actions should you take, if any, before you complete your report?

12.7 Improving Visuals: Applying the Six Principles of Graphic Design

Find a communication example that you believe could be improved by applying the visual design principles you learned in this chapter. It can be from any medium—a web page, a magazine ad, a promotional email message, an illustration from a report—anything that you can either copy or scan into a word processing file. With the image in your word processing program, annotate it with notes that identify visual weaknesses and describe ways to fix those weaknesses. (In Microsoft Word, for example, you can use the "AutoShapes Callouts" feature to place notes wherever you'd like on the page.) In a paragraph of accompanying text, explain why you believe the message isn't as effective as it could be and how your suggestions would make it more effective.

12.8 Writing Reports: Pie Charts

As director of new business development for a growing advertising agency, you're interested in how companies spend their advertising dollars. Create a pie chart based on the information that shows national advertising spending by media category. Summarize these findings (in two or three sentences) for publication in a report to top management.[22]

Media type	Expenditure (in $ billions)
Television	42.5
Newspaper	38.4
Direct mail	38.4
Miscellaneous	22.6
Radio	12.3
Yellow Pages	10.8
Magazines	9.0
Business papers	3.8
Outdoor	1.3
Total	$179.1

12.9 Annual Report: Selecting the Right Visual

You're preparing the annual report for FretCo Guitar Corporation. For each type of information, select the right chart or visual to illustrate the text. Explain your choices.

a. data on annual sales for the past 20 years
b. comparison of FretCo sales, product by product (electric guitars, bass guitars, amplifiers, acoustic guitars), for this year and last year
c. explanation of how a FretCo acoustic guitar is manufactured
d. explanation of how the FretCo Guitar Corporation markets its guitars
e. data on sales of FretCo products in each of 12 countries
f. comparison of FretCo sales figures with sales figures for three competing guitar makers over the past 10 years

12.10 Sales Trends: Selecting the Right Chart

Here are last year's sales figures for the appliance and electronics megastore where you work. Construct charts based on these figures that will help you explain to the store's general manager seasonal variations in each department.

Store Sales in 2009 (in $ thousands)

Month	Home Electronics	Computers	Appliances
January	$68	$39	$36
February	72	34	34
March	75	41	30
April	54	41	28
May	56	42	44
June	49	33	48
July	54	31	43
August	66	58	39
September	62	58	36
October	66	44	33
November	83	48	29
December	91	62	24

12.11 Company Expansion: Creating Maps

You work for C & S Holdings, a company that operates coin-activated, self-service car washes. Research shows that the farther customers live from a car wash, the less likely they are to visit. You know that 50 percent of customers at each of your car washes live within a 4-kilometre radius of the location, 65 percent live within 6 kilometres, 80 percent live within

8 kilometres, and 90 percent live within 10 kilometres. C & S's owner wants to open two new car washes in your city and has asked you to prepare a report recommending locations. Using a map of your city (try www.mapquest.com), choose two possible locations for car washes and create a visual depicting the customer base surrounding each location (make up whatever population data you need).

11.12 Internet: Financial Reporting
Visit the internet site www.sedar.com and review the annual reports recently released by two corporations in the same industry (go to the "public company documents" search page). Analyze each report and be prepared to discuss the following questions in class:

a. What differences do you see in the way each corporation reports its financial data? Are the data presented clearly, so shareholders can draw conclusions about each corporation's financial results?

b. What goals, challenges, and plans do top managers emphasize in their discussion of results?

c. How do the format and organization of each report enhance or detract from the information being presented?

Cases APPLYING THE THREE-STEP WRITING PROCESS TO CASES

Apply each step to the following cases, as assigned by your instructor.

Informational Reports
1. My progress to date: Interim progress report on your academic career
As you know, the bureaucratic process involved in getting a degree or certificate is nearly as challenging as any course you could take.

Your Task: Prepare an interim progress report detailing the steps you've taken toward completing your graduation or certification requirements. After examining the requirements listed in your school catalogue, indicate a realistic schedule for completing those that remain. In addition to course requirements, include steps such as completing the residency requirement, filing necessary papers, and paying necessary fees. Use memo format for your report and address it to anyone who is helping or encouraging you through school.

Planning

Analyze the Situation
Clarify the problem or opportunity at hand, define your purpose, develop an audience profile, and develop a work plan.

Gather Information
Determine audience needs and obtain the information necessary to satisfy those needs; conduct a research project if necessary.

Select the Right Medium
Choose the best medium for delivering your message; consider delivery through multiple media.

Organize the Information
Define your main idea, limit your scope, select a direct or an indirect approach, and outline your content using an appropriate structure for an informational report, analytical report, or proposal.

Writing

Adapt to Your Audience
Be sensitive to audience needs by using a "you" attitude, politeness, positive emphasis, and bias-free language. Build a strong relationship with your audience by establishing your credibility and projecting your company's image. Control your style with a tone and voice appropriate to the situation.

Compose the Message
Choose precise language that will help you create effective sentences and coherent paragraphs throughout the introduction, body, and close of your report or proposal.

Completing

Revise the Report
Evaluate content and review readability; edit and rewrite for conciseness and clarity.

Produce the Report
Use effective design elements and suitable layout for a clean, professional appearance; seamlessly combine textual and graphical elements.

Proofread the Report
Review for errors in layout, spelling, and mechanics.

Distribute the Report
Deliver your report using the chosen medium; make sure all documents and all relevant files are distributed successfully.

1   2   3

2. Gavel to gavel: Personal activity report of a meeting
Meetings, conferences, and conventions abound in the academic world. You've probably attended meetings to complete group projects for your classes, and you may have attended trade conventions or academic conferences.

Your Task: Prepare a personal activity report on a meeting, convention, or conference that you recently attended. Use memo format and direct the report to other students in your field who were not able to attend.

3. Check that price tag: Informational report on trends in costs
Your university's administration has asked you to compare your school's tuition costs with those of one nearby and determine which has risen more quickly. Research the trend by checking your university's annual tuition costs for each of the most recent four years. Then, research the four-year tuition trends for neighbouring universities. For both universities, calculate the percentage change in tuition costs from year to year and between the first and fourth year.

Your Task: Prepare an informal report (using the letter format) presenting your findings and conclusions to the president of your school. Include graphics to explain and support your conclusions.

4. Get a move on it: Lasting guidelines for moving into university residences
Moving into a university residence is one experience you weren't quite prepared for. In addition to lugging all your earthly belongings up four flights of stairs in 30-degree heat, channelling cables to the one outlet tucked in the corner of the room, and negotiating with your roommate over who gets the bigger closet, you had to hug your parents goodbye in the parking lot in front of the entire first-year class—or so it seemed. Now that you are a pro, you've offered to write some lasting guidelines for future first-year students so that they know what is expected of them on moving day.

Your Task: Prepare an informational report for future incoming classes outlining the rules and procedures to follow when moving into a university residence. Lay out the rules such as starting time, handling trash and empty boxes, items permitted and not permitted in residence rooms, common courtesies, and parking. Ensure that you mention what the policy is for removing furniture from the room, lofting beds, and overloading electrical circuits. Of course, any recommendations on how to handle disputes with roommates would be helpful; so would some brief advice on how to cope with anxious parents. Direct your memo report to the director of student affairs.

Analytical Reports

5. My next career move: Feasibility report organized around recommendations
If you've ever analyzed your career objectives, you'll be quite comfortable with this project.

Your Task: Write a memo report directed to yourself and signed with a fictitious name. Indicate a possible job that your education will qualify you for, mention the advantages of the position in terms of your long-range goals, and then outline the actions you must take to get the job.

6. Staying the course: Unsolicited proposal using the $2 + 2 = 4$ approach
Think of a course you believe will add value to the core curriculum at your school. Conversely, if you would like to see a course offered as an elective rather than being required, write your email report accordingly.

Your Task: Write a short email proposal using the $2 + 2 = 4$ approach (refresh your memory in Chapter 11, if necessary). Prepare your proposal to be submitted to the academic dean by email. Ensure that you include all the reasons supporting your idea.

7. Planning my program: Problem-solving report using the yardstick approach
Assume that you will have time for only one course next term.

Your Task: List the pros and cons of four or five courses that interest you and use the yardstick approach to settle on the course that is best for you to take at this time. Write your report in memo format, addressing it to your academic advisor.

8. Restaurant review: Troubleshooting report on a restaurant's food and operations
Visit any restaurant, possibly your school cafeteria. The workers and fellow customers will assume that you are an ordinary customer, but you are really a spy for the owner.

Your Task: After your visit, write a short report to the owner, explaining (a) what you did and what you observed, (b) any violations of policy that you observed, and (c) your recommendations for improvement. The first part of your report (what you did and what you observed) will be the longest. Include a description of the premises, inside and out. Tell how long it took for each step of ordering and receiving your meal. Describe the service and food thoroughly. You are interested in both the good and bad aspects of the establishment's décor, service, and food. For the second section (violations of policy), use some common sense. If all the servers but one have their hair covered, you may assume that policy requires hair to be covered; a dirty window or restroom obviously violates policy. The last section (recommendations for improvement) involves professional judgment. What management actions will improve the restaurant?

9. On the books: Troubleshooting report on improving the campus bookstore

Imagine that you are a consultant hired to improve the profits of your campus bookstore.

Your Task: Visit the bookstore and look critically at its operations. Then draft a letter to the bookstore manager offering recommendations that would make the store more profitable, perhaps suggesting products it should carry, hours that it should remain open, or added services that it should make available to students. Ensure that you support your recommendations.

10. Day and night: Problem-solving report on stocking a 24 hour convenience store

When a store is open all day, every day, when's the best time to restock the shelves? That's the challenge at Store 24, a retail chain that never closes. Imagine you're the assistant manager of a Store 24 branch that just opened near your campus. You want to set up a restocking schedule that won't conflict with prime shopping hours. Think about the number of customers you're likely to serve in the morning, afternoon, evening, and overnight hours. Consider, too, how many employees you might have during these four periods.

Your Task: Using the scientific approach, write a problem-solving report in letter form to the store manager (Isabel Chu) and the regional manager (Eric Angstrom), who must agree on a solution to this problem. Discuss the pros and cons of each period and include your recommendation for restocking the shelves.

Proposals

11. "Would you carry it?" Unsolicited sales proposal recommending a product to a retail outlet

Select a product you are familiar with and imagine that you are the manufacturer trying to get a local retail outlet to carry it. Use the internet and other resources (see the sources in Table 11–3) to gather information about the product.

Your Task: Write an unsolicited sales proposal in letter format to the owner (or manager) of the store, proposing that the

item be stocked. Use the information you gathered to describe some product features and benefits to the store. Then, make up some reasonable figures, highlighting what the item costs, what it can be sold for, and what services your company provides (e.g., return of unsold items, free replacement of unsatisfactory items, or necessary repairs).

12. Where is everybody? Proposal to sell GPS fleet tracking system

As a sales manager for Air-Trak, one of your responsibilities is writing sales proposals for potential buyers of your company's Air-Trak tracking system. The Air-Trak uses the Global Positioning System (GPS) to track the location of vehicles and other assets. For example, the dispatcher for a trucking company can simply click a map display on a computer screen to find out where all the company's trucks are at that instant. Air-Trak lists the following as benefits of the system:

> Making sure vehicles follow prescribed routes with minimal loitering time
> "Geofencing," in which dispatchers are alerted if vehicles leave
> Route optimization, in which fleet managers can analyze routes and destinations to find the most time- and fuel-efficient path for each vehicle
> Comparisons between scheduled and actual travel
> Enhanced security to protect both drivers and cargos

Your Task: Write a brief proposal to Doneta Zachs, fleet manager for First Place Van Lines Inc. (Head Office) 2014 Miners Avenue, Saskatoon, SK S7K 4Z7. Introduce your company, explain the benefits of the Air-Trak system, and propose a trial deployment in which you would equip five Saskatchewan division trucks. For the purposes of this assignment, you don't need to worry about the technical details of the system; focus on promoting the benefits and asking for a decision regarding the test project. (You can learn more about Air-Trak at www.air-trak.com.)[23]

13

Completing Reports and Proposals

ON THE JOB

Communicating at the Bill & Melinda Gates Foundation

CREATING EFFECTIVE PARTNERSHIPS TO TACKLE SOME OF THE WORLD'S MOST CHALLENGING PROBLEMS

www.gatesfoundation.org

Microsoft co-founder Bill Gates is accustomed to creating change on a global scale, and he now applies the same energy and strategic thinking to charitable causes. Backed by billions of dollars in endowments, the Bill & Melinda Gates Foundation acts as a catalyst, bringing resources together in a way that "increases the momentum, scale, and sustainability of change." The strategy is applied to such important social challenges as containing the AIDS epidemic, eradicating malaria, improving high schools, and making sure people everywhere have access to the digital revolution made possible by the internet.

Meeting challenges of such staggering complexity and coordinating the resources of organizations all over the world is obviously no small task, and communication plays a vital role in this effort. In particular, reports and proposals link the various groups involved in the foundation's activities and inform the public about ongoing challenges and progress.

The foundation is staffed with people who have demonstrated effective leadership and communication skills, including Patty Stonesifer, a former Microsoft executive, who serves as chief executive officer. Stonesifer is deeply involved in reports and proposals, both as a writer and a reader. In addition to co-authoring the foundation's annual report, she reads numerous proposals from organizations asking for part of the $1.5 billion the foundation provides every year. The foundation receives some 3000 formal grant requests every month, and the review process is thorough.

For Patty Stonesifer, co-chair and president of the Bill & Melinda Gates Foundation, much of her communication effort involves one-on-one conversations with both the people the foundation helps and the researchers who create solutions to health and education challenges. However, written reports and proposals play an equally important role in her work.

Stonesifer examines proposals from various angles, listening to her colleagues' perspectives and asking all sorts of questions: Is this really the best approach? What's going to make the biggest difference? Could this proposal be a catalyst that attracts other organizations to participate?

Stonesifer and her colleagues recognize that they are tackling problems of almost unimaginable complexity, but with systematic thinking, unstoppable optimism, unmatched financial resources, and effective communication skills, they remain committed to improving life for people the world over. If you worked at the Gates Foundation, how would you assess proposals? What elements would you look for to select groups for funding?[1]

Putting the Final Touches on Reports and Proposals

Experienced business communicators such as Patty Stonesifer recognize that the process of writing a report or proposal doesn't end with a first draft. This chapter addresses all four tasks involved in completing longer messages: revising, producing, proofreading, and distributing (see Figure 13–1). Although the tasks covered in this chapter are similar in concept to those you studied for short messages in Chapter 6, completing reports and proposals can require considerably more work. As you've probably experienced with school reports already, computers, copiers, and other resources break down at the last minute, when you're frantic to finish and have no time to spare. When completing an important report on the job, try to leave yourself double or even triple the amount of time you think you'll need so that last-minute glitches don't compromise the quality of all your hard work.

Objective 1 Characterize the four tasks involved in completing business reports and proposals.

Most of the discussion in this chapter applies to *formal* reports and proposals, those documents that require an extra measure of polish and professionalism. Few reports and proposals require every component described in this chapter, but ensure that you carefully select the elements you want to include in each of your documents.

Formal reports have a higher degree of polish and production quality, and they often contain elements not found in informal reports.

> Figure 13–1 Step Three in the Three-Step Writing Process for Reports

Planning	Writing	Completing

Revise the Message
Evaluate content and review readability, then edit and rewrite for conciseness and clarity.

Produce the Message
Use effective design elements and suitable layout for a clean, professional appearance; seamlessly combine text and graphical elements.

Proofread the Message
Review for errors in layout, spelling, and mechanics.

Distribute the Message
Deliver your report using the chosen medium; make sure all documents and all relevant files are distributed successfully.

1   2   3

Revising Your Reports and Proposals

The revision process is essentially the same for reports as for any business message, although it may take considerably longer, depending on the length of your document. Evaluate your organization, style, and tone, ensuring that you've said what you want to say in the most logical order and in a way that responds to your audience's needs. Then work to improve the report's readability by varying sentence length, keeping paragraphs short, using lists and bullets, and adding headings and subheadings. Keep revising the content until it is clear, concise, and compelling.

Revising for clarity and conciseness is especially important for online reports because reading online can be difficult.

Tight, efficient writing that is easy to skim is always a plus, but it's especially important for impatient online audiences.[2] Review online report content carefully; strip out all information that doesn't meet audience needs and condense everything else as much as possible. Audiences will gladly return to sites that deliver quality information quickly—and they'll avoid sites that don't.

The virtually unlimited graphical and technical possibilities of Web design have had the unfortunate side effect of producing too many websites that are difficult to read. You've no doubt visited some of these hard-to-read sites yourself—web pages with backgrounds so busy that you can't make out the words, tiny type that has you reaching for a magnifying glass, quirky fonts that are difficult to read at any size, lines of text that are stretched and wrapped around images, unlabelled graphical hyperlinks that force you to click on them to see what each page is about, and so on. Even when these sites are visually attractive, which isn't often, they fail to meet the primary objective of providing information to the reader. Web-design expert Dean Allen put it perfectly when he wrote that "the primary goal of communication design is to make vital, engaging work intended above all to be read."[3]

Producing Your Reports and Proposals

When you are satisfied with your text, you're ready to produce your report by incorporating the design elements discussed in Chapter 6. At this point you also start to add in charts, graphs, and other visuals, as well as any missing textual elements such as previews and reviews.

Objective 2 Explain how computers have both simplified and complicated the report-production process.

In some organizations, you'll be able to rely on the help of specialists in design and production, particularly when you are working on important, high-visibility reports or proposals. You may also have clerical help available to assist with the mechanical assembly and distribution. However, for most reports in many of today's lean-staffed companies, you should count on doing most or all of the production work yourself.

Computer tools have made it easy for virtually anyone to create handsome reports, but they've also raised the expectations of business audiences.

The good news is that computer tools are now generally easy enough for the average businessperson to use productively. A software suite such as Microsoft Office or Word Perfect Office lets you produce reports that incorporate graphics, tables, spreadsheet data, and database records. Even features such as photography are relatively simple these days, with low-cost digital cameras, colour desktop scanners, and inexpensive colour printers with near-photo-quality output.

The bad news is that continually improving computer tools increase your audience's expectations. People are influenced by packaging, so a handsomely bound report with full-colour graphics will impress your audience more than a plain, typewritten-style report, even though the two documents contain the

> Figure 13–2 Parts of a Formal Report

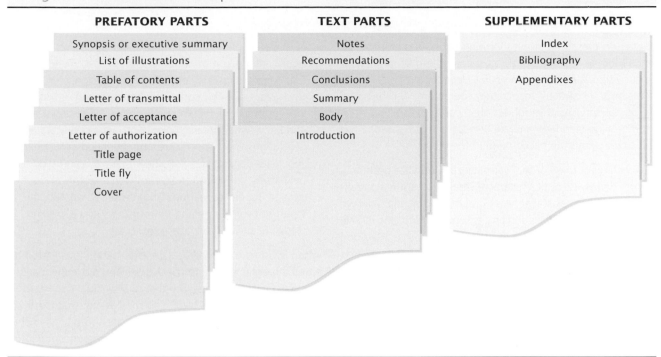

PREFATORY PARTS	TEXT PARTS	SUPPLEMENTARY PARTS
Synopsis or executive summary	Notes	Index
List of illustrations	Recommendations	Bibliography
Table of contents	Conclusions	Appendixes
Letter of transmittal	Summary	
Letter of acceptance	Body	
Letter of authorization	Introduction	
Title page		
Title fly		
Cover		

same information. In other words, you may find yourself spending more time on production just to keep up with the competition.

Components of a Formal Report

The parts you include in a report depend on the type of report you are writing, how long it is, what your audience expects and requires, and what your organization dictates. The components listed in Figure 13–2 fall into three categories, depending on where they are found in a report: *prefatory parts* (pieces belonging at the front of the report), *text* of the report, and *supplementary parts*. Depending on the level of formality you need to achieve, you can select from these elements to complete your formal report. For an illustration of how the various parts fit together, see Linda Moreno's Electrovision report in the "Report Writer's Notebook: Analyzing a Formal Report."

Many of the components in a formal report start on a new page, but not always. Inserting page breaks consumes more paper and adds to the bulk of your report. On the other hand, starting a section on a new page helps your readers navigate the report and recognize transitions between major sections or features.

When you want a particular section to stand apart, you'll generally start it and the material after it on new pages (in the same way that each chapter in this book starts on a new page). Most prefatory parts, such as the table of contents, should also be placed on their own pages. However, the various parts in the report text are often run together and seldom stand alone. If your introduction is only a paragraph long, don't bother with a page break before moving into the body of your report. If the introduction runs longer than a page, however, a page break can signal the reader that a major shift is about to occur in the flow of the report.

Length, audience expectations, and organizational traditions all dictate what you should include in a formal report.

REPORT WRITER'S NOTEBOOK

Analyzing a Formal Report

The report presented in the following pages was prepared by Linda Moreno, manager of the cost accounting department at Electrovision, a high-tech company. Electrovision's main product is optical character recognition equipment, which is used by postal services throughout the world for sorting mail. Moreno's job is to help analyze the company's costs. She has this to say about the background of the report:

> For the past three or four years, Electrovision has been on a roll. Our A-12 optical character reader was a real breakthrough, and postal services grabbed up as many as we could make. Our sales and profits kept climbing, and morale was fantastic. Everybody seemed to think that the good times would last forever. Unfortunately, everybody was wrong. When one of our major clients announced that it was postponing all new equipment purchases because of cuts in its budget, we woke up to the fact that we are essentially a one-product company with one customer. At that point, management started scrambling around looking for ways to cut costs until we could diversify our business a bit.
>
> The vice president of operations, Dennis McWilliams, asked me to help identify cost-cutting opportunities in travel and entertainment. On the basis of his personal observations, he felt that Electrovision was overly generous in its travel policies and that we might be able to save a significant amount by controlling these costs more carefully. My investigation confirmed his suspicion.
>
> I was reasonably confident that my report would be well received. I've worked with Dennis for several years and know what he likes: plenty of facts, clearly stated conclusions, and specific recommendations for what should be done next. I also knew that my report would be passed on to other Electrovision executives, so I wanted to create a good impression. I wanted the report to be accurate and thorough, visually appealing, readable, and appropriate in tone.

When writing the analytical report that follows, Moreno based the organization on conclusions and recommendations presented in direct order. The first two sections of the report correspond to Moreno's two main conclusions: that Electrovision's travel and entertainment costs are too high and that cuts are essential. The third section presents recommendations for achieving better control over travel and entertainment expenses. As you review the report, analyze both the mechanical aspects and the way Moreno presents her ideas. Be prepared to discuss the way the various components convey and reinforce the main message.

Puts the title all in capital letters

Puts all lines other than title in uppercase and lower-case letters

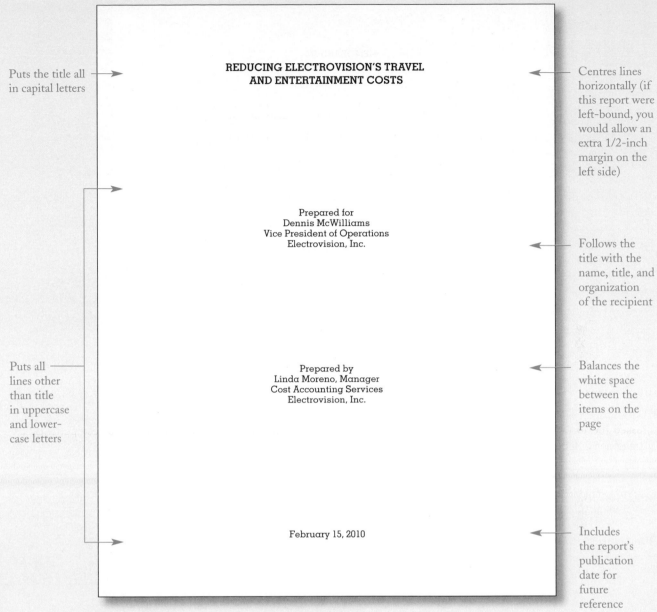

**REDUCING ELECTROVISION'S TRAVEL
AND ENTERTAINMENT COSTS**

Prepared for
Dennis McWilliams
Vice President of Operations
Electrovision, Inc.

Prepared by
Linda Moreno, Manager
Cost Accounting Services
Electrovision, Inc.

February 15, 2010

Centres lines horizontally (if this report were left-bound, you would allow an extra 1/2-inch margin on the left side)

Follows the title with the name, title, and organization of the recipient

Balances the white space between the items on the page

Includes the report's publication date for future reference

The "how to" tone of Moreno's title is appropriate for an action-oriented report that emphasizes recommendations. A neutral title, such as "An Analysis of Electrovision's Travel and Entertainment Costs," would be more suitable for an informational report.

Uses memo format for transmitting this internal report (see page 462); letter format would be used for transmitting external reports

Uses a conversational style

Acknowledges help that has been received

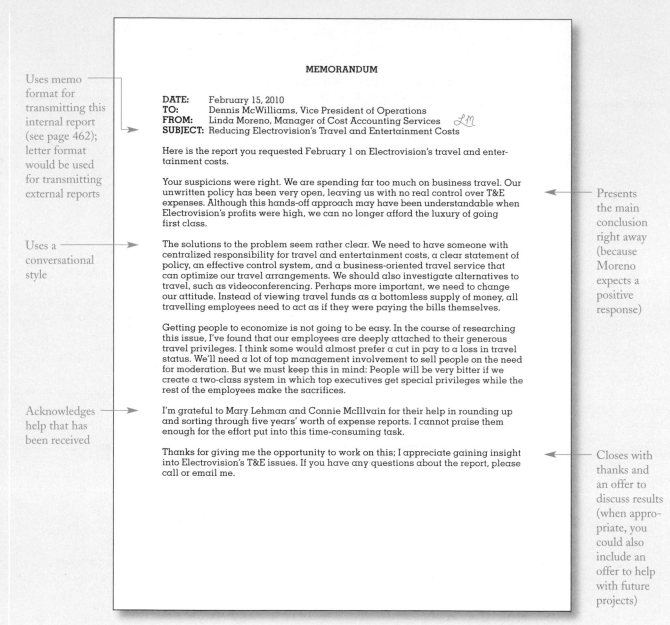

MEMORANDUM

DATE: February 15, 2010
TO: Dennis McWilliams, Vice President of Operations
FROM: Linda Moreno, Manager of Cost Accounting Services   *LM*
SUBJECT: Reducing Electrovision's Travel and Entertainment Costs

Here is the report you requested February 1 on Electrovision's travel and entertainment costs.

Your suspicions were right. We are spending far too much on business travel. Our unwritten policy has been very open, leaving us with no real control over T&E expenses. Although this hands-off approach may have been understandable when Electrovision's profits were high, we can no longer afford the luxury of going first class.

The solutions to the problem seem rather clear. We need to have someone with centralized responsibility for travel and entertainment costs, a clear statement of policy, an effective control system, and a business-oriented travel service that can optimize our travel arrangements. We should also investigate alternatives to travel, such as videoconferencing. Perhaps more important, we need to change our attitude. Instead of viewing travel funds as a bottomless supply of money, all travelling employees need to act as if they were paying the bills themselves.

Getting people to economize is not going to be easy. In the course of researching this issue, I've found that our employees are deeply attached to their generous travel privileges. I think some would almost prefer a cut in pay to a loss in travel status. We'll need a lot of top management involvement to sell people on the need for moderation. But we must keep this in mind: People will be very bitter if we create a two-class system in which top executives get special privileges while the rest of the employees make the sacrifices.

I'm grateful to Mary Lehman and Connie McIllvain for their help in rounding up and sorting through five years' worth of expense reports. I cannot praise them enough for the effort put into this time-consuming task.

Thanks for giving me the opportunity to work on this; I appreciate gaining insight into Electrovision's T&E issues. If you have any questions about the report, please call or email me.

Presents the main conclusion right away (because Moreno expects a positive response)

Closes with thanks and an offer to discuss results (when appropriate, you could also include an offer to help with future projects)

In this report, Moreno decided to write a brief memo of transmittal and include a separate executive summary. Short reports (fewer than 10 pages) often combine the synopsis or executive summary with the memo or letter of transmittal.

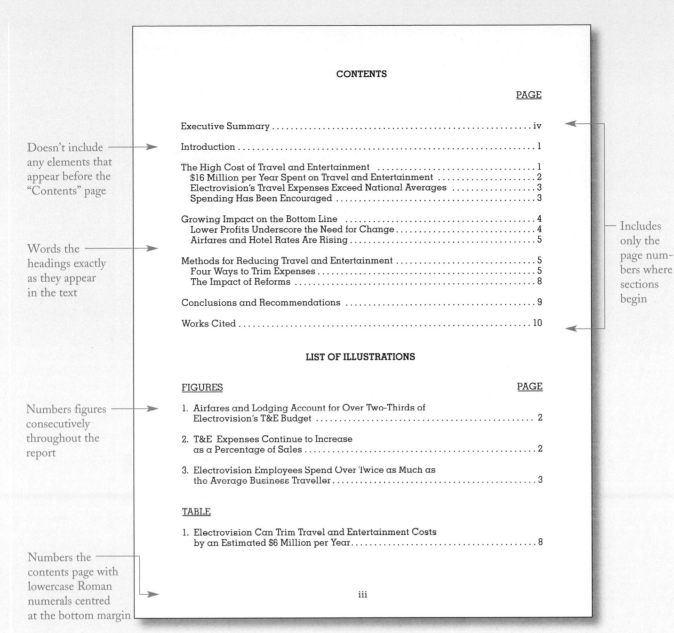

Doesn't include any elements that appear before the "Contents" page

Words the headings exactly as they appear in the text

Numbers figures consecutively throughout the report

Numbers the contents page with lowercase Roman numerals centred at the bottom margin

Includes only the page numbers where sections begin

CONTENTS

LIST OF ILLUSTRATIONS

iii

Moreno included only first- and second-level headings in her table of contents, even though the report contains third-level headings. She prefers a shorter table of contents that focuses attention on the main divisions of thought. She used informative titles, which are appropriate for a report to a receptive audience.

Begins by stating the purpose of the report

Presents the points in the executive summary (see page 463) in the same order as they appear in the report, using subheadings that summarize the content of the main sections of the report

Continues numbering the executive summary pages with lowercase Roman numerals

Targets a receptive audience with a hard-hitting tone in the executive summary (a more neutral approach would be better for hostile or skeptical readers)

Executive summary uses the same font and paragraph treatment as the text of the report

EXECUTIVE SUMMARY

This report analyzes Electrovision's travel and entertainment (T&E) costs and presents recommendations for reducing those costs.

Travel and Entertainment Costs Are Too High

Travel and entertainment is a large and growing expense category for Electrovision. The company spends over $16 million per year on business travel, and these costs have been increasing by 12 percent annually. Company employees make roughly 1880 trips each year at an average cost per trip of $8500. Airfares are the biggest expense, followed by hotels, meals, and rental cars.

The nature of Electrovision's business does require extensive travel, but the company's costs are excessive: Our employees spend almost three times more than the average business traveller. Although the location of the company's facilities may partly explain this discrepancy, the main reason for our high costs is a management style that gives employees little incentive to economize.

Cuts Are Essential

Electrovision management now recognizes the need to gain more control over this element of costs. The company is currently entering a period of declining profits, prompting management to look for every opportunity to reduce spending. At the same time, rising airfares and hotel rates are making T&E expenses more significant.

Electrovision Can Save $6 Million per Year

Fortunately, Electrovision has a number of excellent opportunities for reducing T&E costs. Savings of up to $6 million per year should be achievable, judging by the experience of other companies. A sensible travel management program can save companies 9 to 18 percent a year simply on accommodation, food, and car rental (Baker, "SLA Use Spreading" 14; Baker, "Study Eyes Expense Tactics"; *Expense Management Strategies*, 6). Given that we purchase many more business-class tickets than the average, we should be able to achieve these, or greater, savings— at least 25 percent to 35 percent (McDougall 45). Four steps will help us cut costs:

1. Hire a director of travel and entertainment to assume overall responsibility for T&E spending, policies, and technologies, including the hiring and management of a national travel agency.
2. Educate employees on the need for cost containment, both in avoiding unnecessary travel and reducing costs when travel is necessary.
3. Negotiate preferential rates with travel providers.
4. Implement technological alternatives to travel, such as virtual meetings.

As necessary as these changes are, they will likely hurt morale, at least in the short term. Management will need to make a determined effort to explain the rationale for reduced spending. By exercising moderation in their own travel arrangements, Electrovision executives can set a good example and help other employees accept the changes. On the plus side, using travel alternatives such as web conferencing will reduce the travel burden on many employees and help them balance their business and personal lives.

iv

Moreno decided to include an executive summary because her report is aimed at a mixed audience, some of whom are interested in the details of her report and others who just want the "big picture." The executive summary is aimed at the second group, giving them enough information to make a decision without burdening them with the task of reading the entire report.

Her writing style matches the serious nature of the content without sounding distant or stiff. Moreno chose the formal approach because several members of her audience are considerably higher up in the organization, and she did not want to sound too familiar. In addition, her company prefers the impersonal style for formal reports.

Centres the title of the report on the first page of the text, 5 cm from the top of the page

REDUCING ELECTROVISION'S TRAVEL AND ENTERTAINMENT COSTS

INTRODUCTION

Electrovision has always encouraged a significant amount of business travel. To compensate employees for the stress and inconvenience of frequent trips, management has authorized generous travel and entertainment (T&E) allowances. This philosophy has been good for morale, but last year Electrovision spent $16 million on travel and entertainment—$7 million more than it spent on research and development.

Opens by establishing the need for action

This year's T&E costs will affect profits even more, because of increases in airline fares and hotel rates. Also, the company anticipates that profits will be relatively weak for a variety of other reasons. Therefore, Dennis McWilliams, Vice President of Operations, has asked the accounting department to explore ways to reduce the T&E budget.

The purpose of this report is to analyze T&E expenses, evaluate the effect of recent hotel and airfare increases, and suggest ways to tighten control over T&E costs. The report outlines several steps that could reduce Electrovision's expenses, but the precise financial impact of these measures is difficult to project. The estimates presented here provide a "best guess" view of what Electrovision can expect to save.

In preparing this report, the accounting department analyzed internal expense reports for the past five years to determine how much Electrovision spends on travel and entertainment. These figures were then compared with average travel business costs reported in the 2009 Accenture/American Express *Expense Management Study* and the *Business Travel News Corporate Travel Index 2009,* and by investigating fee structures of air carriers, hotels, and car rental agencies. We also analyzed trends and suggestions published in a variety of business journal articles to see how other companies are coping with the high cost of business travel.

Mentions sources and methods to increase credibility and to give readers a complete picture of the study's background

THE HIGH COST OF TRAVEL AND ENTERTAINMENT

Although many companies view travel and entertainment as an incidental cost of doing business, the dollars add up. At Electrovision the bill for airfares, hotels, rental cars, meals, and entertainment totalled $16 million last year. Our T&E budget has increased by 12 percent per year for the past five years. Compared to the average Canadian business traveller, Electrovision's expenditures are high, largely because of management's generous policy on travel benefits.

Uses the Arabic numeral 1 for the first page, centring the number about 2.5 cm from the bottom of the page

In her brief introduction, Moreno counts on topic sentences and transitions to indicate that she is discussing the purpose, scope, and limitations of the study.

2

Uses Arabic numerals to number the second and succeeding pages of the text in the upper right-hand corner where the top and right-hand margins meet

$16 Million per Year Spent on Travel and Entertainment

Electrovision's annual budget for travel and entertainment is only 8 percent of sales. Because this is a relatively small expense category compared with such items as salaries and commissions, it is tempting to dismiss T&E costs as insignificant. However, T&E is Electrovision's third-largest controllable expense, directly behind salaries and information systems.

Last year Electrovision personnel made about 1880 trips at an average cost per trip of $8500. The typical trip involved a round-trip flight of 8000 km, meals, hotel accommodations for four or five days, and a rental car. Roughly 80 percent of trips were made by 20 percent of the staff—top management and sales personnel travelled most, averaging 17 trips per year.

Figure 1 illustrates how the T&E budget is spent. The largest categories are airfares and lodging, which together account for $7 out of $10 that employees spend on travel and entertainment. This spending breakdown has been relatively steady for the past five years and is consistent with the distribution of expenses experienced by other companies.

Figure 1
Airfares and Lodging Account for Over
Two-Thirds of Electrovision's T&E Budget

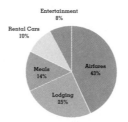

Although the composition of the T&E budget has been consistent, its size has not. As mentioned earlier, these expenditures have increased by about 12 percent per year for the past five years, roughly twice the rate of the company's sales growth (see Figure 2). This rate of growth makes T&E Electrovision's fastest-growing expense item.

Figure 2
T&E Expenses Continue to Increase as a
Percentage of Sales

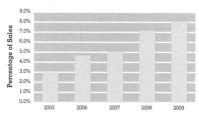

Moreno opens the first main section of the body with a topic sentence that introduces an important fact about the subject of the section. Then she orients the reader to the three major points developed in the section.

Places the visual as close as possible to the point it illustrates

Gives each visual a title that clearly indicates what it's about; titles are consistently placed to the left of each visual

3

Electrovision's Travel Expenses Exceed National Averages

Much of our travel budget is justified. Two major factors contribute to Electrovision's high T&E budget:

- With our headquarters in Kanata, Ontario, and our major customers in the U.S., Central and South America, and Western Europe, we naturally spend a lot of money on cross-country and international flights.

- A great deal of travel takes place between our headquarters here in Kanata and the manufacturing operations in Salt Lake City, Utah; Seattle, Washington; and Dublin, Ireland. Corporate managers and division personnel make frequent trips to coordinate these disparate operations.

However, even though a good portion of Electrovision's travel budget is justifiable, the company spends considerably more on T&E than the average business traveller (see Figure 3).

Introduces visuals before they appear and indicates what readers should notice about the data

Numbers the visuals consecutively and refers to them in the text by their numbers

Figure 3
Electrovision Employees Spend
Three Times More than the Average
Business Traveller

Source: *Business Travel News Corporate Travel Index 2009*t and company records.

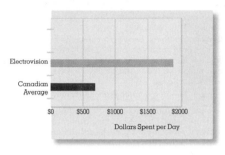

Basing my calculations on the *Business Travel News Corporate Travel Index 2009* and my own research into airfares, Canadian companies spend an average of $2900 for each traveller, based on airfare, hotel rates, meals, and rental car rates. For a 4.5 day trip, the daily rate is about $644 per day. In contrast, Electrovision's average daily expense over the past year has been about $1888 per day, or about three times higher than average. This figure is based on the average trip cost of $8500 listed earlier and an average trip length of 4.5 days.

Spending Has Been Encouraged

Although a variety of factors may contribute to this differential, Electrovision's relatively high T&E costs are at least partially attributable to the company's philosophy and management style. Since many employees do not enjoy business travel, management has tried to make the trips more pleasant by authorizing business-class airfare, luxury hotel accommodations, and full-size rental cars. The sales staff is encouraged to entertain clients at top restaurants and to invite them to cultural and sporting events.

The chart in Figure 3 is simple but effective; Moreno includes just enough data to make her point. Notice how she is as careful about the appearance of her report as she is about the quality of its content.

4

The cost of these privileges is easy to overlook, given the weakness of Electrovision's system for keeping track of T&E expenses:

Uses a bulleted list to make it easy for readers to identify and distinguish related points

- The monthly financial records do not contain a separate category for travel and entertainment; the information is buried under Cost of Goods Sold and under Selling, General, and Administrative Expenses.

- Each department head is given authority to approve any expense report, regardless of how large it may be.

- Receipts are not required for expenditures of less than $100.

- Individuals are allowed to make their own travel arrangements.

- No one is charged with the responsibility for controlling the company's total spending on travel and entertainment.

GROWING IMPACT ON THE BOTTOM LINE

Uses informative headings to focus reader attention on the main points (such headings are appropriate when a report uses direct order and is intended for a receptive audience; however, descriptive headings are more effective when a report is in indirect order and readers are less receptive)

During the past three years, the company's healthy profits have resulted in relatively little pressure to push for tighter controls over all aspects of the business. However, as we all know, the situation is changing. We're projecting flat to declining profits for the next two years, a situation that has prompted all of us to search for ways to cut costs. At the same time, rising airfares and hotel rates have increased the impact of T&E expenses on the company's financial results.

Leaves an extra line of white space above headings to help readers associate each heading with the text it describes

Lower Profits Underscore the Need for Change

The next two years promise to be difficult for Electrovision. After several years of steady increases in spending, many of our clients are tightening procurement policies for automated mail-handling equipment. Funding for the A-12 optical character reader has been cancelled. As a consequence, the marketing department expects sales to drop by 15 percent. Although Electrovision is negotiating several other promising R&D contracts, the marketing department does not foresee any major procurements for the next two to three years.

At the same time, Electrovision is facing cost increases on several fronts. As we have known for several months, the new production facility now under construction in Montreal is behind schedule and over budget. Labour contracts in Salt Lake City and Seattle will expire within the next six months, and plant managers there anticipate that significant salary and benefits concessions may be necessary to avoid strikes.

Moreover, marketing and advertising costs are expected to increase as we attempt to strengthen these activities to better cope with competitive pressures. Given the expected decline in revenues and increase in costs, the Executive Committee's prediction that profits will fall by 12 percent in the coming fiscal year does not seem overly pessimistic.

Moreno designed her report to include plenty of white space so even those pages that lack visuals are still attractive and easy to read.

5

Airfares and Hotel Rates Are Rising

Business travellers have grown accustomed to frequent fare wars and discounting in the travel industry in recent years. Excess capacity and aggressive price competition, particularly in the airline business, made travel a relative bargain.

Documents the facts to add weight to Moreno's argument → However, that situation has changed as weaker competitors have been forced out and the remaining players have grown stronger and smarter. Airlines and hotels are better at managing inventory and keeping occupancy rates high, which translates into higher costs for Electrovision. Last year saw some of the steepest rate hikes in years. Business airfares (tickets most likely to be purchased by business travellers) jumped more than 40 percent in many markets. The trend is expected to continue, with rates increasing another 5 to 10 percent overall ("American Express Business Travel Announces Adjusted Results"; McDougall 45–46; "Travel Trends" 33).

Given the fact that air and hotel costs account for 70 percent of our T&E budget, the trend toward higher prices in these two categories will have serious consequences, unless management takes action to control these costs.

METHODS FOR REDUCING T&E COSTS

Gives recommendations an objective flavour by pointing out both the benefits and the risks of taking action → By implementing a number of reforms, management can expect to reduce Electrovision's T&E budget by as much as 35 percent. This estimate is based on the general assessment made by *Business Travel News*, American Express, and consulting firm HRG (Baker; Accenture/American Express " Travel Trends" 33) and on the fact that we have an opportunity to significantly reduce air travel costs by eliminating business-class travel. However, these measures are likely to be unpopular with employees. To gain acceptance for such changes, management will need to sell employees on the need for moderation in T&E allowances.

Four Ways to Trim Expenses

By researching what other companies are doing to curb T&E expenses, the accounting department has identified four prominent opportunities that should enable Electrovision to save about $6 million annually in travel-related costs.

Institute Tighter Spending Controls

A single individual should be appointed director of travel and entertainment to spearhead the effort to gain control of the T&E budget. More than 30 percent of North American companies employ travel managers (Bochmer 11). The director should be familiar with the travel industry and should be well versed in both accounting and information technology. The director should report to the vice president of operations. The director's first priorities should be to establish a written T&E policy and a cost-control system.

Electrovision currently has no written policy on travel and entertainment, a step that is widely recommended by air travel experts; in fact, more than 75 percent of respondents to an American Express study of Canadian corporations said that they have established travel policies (Craig-Bourdin). Creating a policy

Moreno creates a forceful tone by using action verbs in the third-level subheadings of this section. This approach is appropriate to the nature of the study and the attitude of the audience. However, in a status-conscious organization, the imperative verbs might sound presumptuous coming from a junior member of the staff.

6

would clarify management's position and serve as a vehicle for communicating the need for moderation. At a minimum, the policy should include the following:

- All travel and entertainment should be strictly related to business and should be approved in advance.

- Except under special circumstances to be approved on a case-by-case basis, employees should travel by coach and stay in mid-range business hotels.

- The T&E policy should apply equally to employees at all levels.

To implement the new policy, Electrovision will need to create a system for controlling T&E expenses. Each department should prepare an annual T&E budget as part of its operating plan. These budgets should be presented in detail so that management can evaluate how T&E dollars will be spent and can recommend appropriate cuts. To help management monitor performance relative to these budgets, the director of travel should prepare monthly financial statements showing actual T&E expenditures by department.

The director of travel should also be responsible for retaining a business-oriented travel service that will schedule all employee business trips and look for the best travel deals, particularly in airfares. In addition to centralizing Electrovision's reservation and ticketing activities, the agency will negotiate reduced group rates with hotels and rental car firms. The agency selected should have offices nationwide so that all Electrovision facilities can channel their reservations through the same company. This is particularly important in light of the dizzying array of often wildly different airfares available between some cities. It's not uncommon to find dozens of fares along commonly travelled routes ("BTN Quantifies" 1; Wan, Zou, and Dressner 629). In addition, the director can help coordinate travel across the company to secure group discounts whenever possible (McDougall 45).

Reduce Unnecessary Travel and Entertainment

One of the easiest ways to reduce expenses is to reduce the amount of travelling and entertaining that occurs. An analysis of last year's expenditures suggests that as much as 30 percent of Electrovision's travel and entertainment is discretionary. The professional staff spent $2.8 million attending seminars and conferences last year. Although these gatherings are undoubtedly beneficial, the company could save money by sending fewer representatives to each function and perhaps by eliminating some of the less valuable seminars.

Similarly, Electrovision could economize on trips between headquarters and divisions by reducing the frequency of such visits and by sending fewer people on each trip. Although there is often no substitute for face-to-face meetings, management could try to resolve more internal issues through telephone, electronic, and written communication.

Electrovision can also reduce spending by urging employees to economize. Instead of flying business class, employees can fly coach class or take advantage

---

Breaks up text with bulleted lists, which not only call attention to important points but also add visual interest

Specifies the steps required to implement recommendations

Moreno takes care not to overstep the boundaries of her analysis. For instance, she doesn't analyze the value of the seminars that employees attend every year, so she avoids any absolute statements about reducing travel to seminars.

7

of discount fares. Rather than ordering a $75 bottle of wine, employees can select a less expensive bottle or dispense with alcohol entirely. People can book rooms at moderately priced hotels and drive smaller rental cars.

Obtain Lowest Rates from Travel Providers

Apart from urging employees to economize, Electrovision can also save money by searching for the lowest available airfares, hotel rates, and rental car fees. Currently, few employees have the time or knowledge to seek out travel bargains. When they need to travel, they make the most convenient and comfortable arrangements. A professional travel service will be able to obtain lower rates from travel providers.

Judging by the experience of other companies, Electrovision may be able to trim as much as 35% from the travel budget simply by looking for bargains in airfares and negotiating group rates with hotels and rental car companies. Electrovision should be able to achieve these economies by analyzing its travel patterns, identifying frequently visited locations, and selecting a few hotels that are willing to reduce rates in exchange for guaranteed business. At the same time, the company should be able to save up to 40 percent on rental car charges by negotiating a corporate rate.

The possibilities for economizing are promising; however, making the best travel arrangements often requires trade-offs such as the following:

- The best fares might not always be the lowest. Indirect flights are usually cheaper, but they take longer and may end up costing more in lost work time.

- The cheapest tickets often require booking 14 or even 30 days in advance, which is often impossible for us.

- Discount tickets are usually nonrefundable, which is a serious drawback when a trip needs to be cancelled at the last minute.

Replace Travel with Technological Alternatives

Less-expensive travel options promise significant savings, but the biggest cost reductions over the long term might come from replacing travel with virtual meeting technology. Both analysts and corporate users say that the early kinks that hampered online meetings have largely been worked out, and the latest systems are fast, easy to learn, and easy to use (Brady 41; Merritt 16). For example, Webex (a leading provider of webconferencing services) offers everything from simple, impromptu team meetings to major online events with up to 300 participants (*Cisco Webex Meeting Centre* Product Overview).

One of the first responsibilities of the new travel director should be an evaluation of these technologies and a recommendation for integrating them throughout Electrovision's operations.

[Margin annotation] Points out possible difficulties to show that all angles have been considered and to build confidence in her judgment

---

Note how Moreno makes the transition from section to section. The first sentence under the second heading on this page refers to the subject of the previous paragraph and signals a shift in thought.

8

The Impact of Reforms

By implementing tighter controls, reducing unnecessary expenses, negotiating more favourable rates, and exploring alternatives to travel, Electrovision should be able to reduce its T&E budget significantly. As Table 1 illustrates, the combined savings should be in the neighbourhood of $6 million, although the precise figures are somewhat difficult to project.

Table 1
Electrovision Can Trim Travel and Entertainment Costs
by an Estimated $6 Million per Year

SOURCE OF SAVINGS	ESTIMATED SAVINGS
Switching from business-class to coach airfare	$2 300 000
Negotiating preferred hotel rates	940 000
Negotiating preferred rental car rates	460 000
Systematically searching for lower airfares	375 000
Reducing interdivisional travel	675 000
Reducing seminar and conference attendance	1 250 000
TOTAL POTENTIAL SAVINGS	**$6 000 000**

To achieve the economies outlined in the table, Electrovision will incur expenses for hiring a director of travel and for implementing a T&E cost-control system. These costs are projected at $115 000: $105 000 per year in salary and benefits for the new employee and a one-time expense of $10 000 for the cost-control system. The cost of retaining a full-service travel agency is negligible, even with the service fees that many are now passing along from airlines and other service providers.

The measures required to achieve these savings are likely to be unpopular with employees. Electrovision personnel are accustomed to generous T&E allowances, and they are likely to resent having these privileges curtailed. To alleviate their disappointment

- Management should make a determined effort to explain why the changes are necessary.

- The director of corporate communication should be asked to develop a multifaceted campaign that will communicate the importance of curtailing T&E costs.

- Management should set a positive example by adhering strictly to the new policies.

- The limitations should apply equally to employees at all levels in the organization.

Uses informative title in the table, which is consistent with the way headings are handled in this report and is appropriate for a report to a receptive audience

Uses complete sentence to help readers focus immediately on the point of the table

Includes financial estimates to help management envision the impact of the suggestions, even though estimated savings are difficult to project

Note how Moreno calls attention in the first paragraph to items in the following table, without repeating the information in the table.

Uses a descriptive heading for the last section of the text (in informational reports, this section is often called "Summary"; in analytical reports, it is called "Conclusions" or "Conclusions and Recommendations")

Emphasizes the recommendations by presenting them in list format

9

CONCLUSIONS AND RECOMMENDATIONS

Electrovision is currently spending $16 million per year on travel and entertainment. Although much of this spending is justified, the company's costs are high relative to competitors' costs, mainly because Electrovision has been generous with its travel benefits.

Electrovision's liberal approach to travel and entertainment was understandable during years of high profitability; however, the company is facing the prospect of declining profits for the next several years. Management is therefore motivated to cut costs in all areas of the business. Reducing T&E spending is particularly important because the bottom-line impact of these costs will increase as airline fares increase.

Electrovision should be able to reduce T&E costs by as much as 40 percent by taking four important steps:

1. *Institute tighter spending controls.* Management should hire a director of travel and entertainment who will assume overall responsibility for T&E activities. Within the next six months, this director should develop a written travel policy, institute a T&E budget and a cost-control system, and retain a professional, business-oriented travel agency that will optimize arrangements with travel providers.

2. *Reduce unnecessary travel and entertainment.* Electrovision should encourage employees to economize on T&E spending. Management can accomplish this by authorizing fewer trips and by urging employees to be more conservative in their spending.

3. *Obtain lowest rates from travel providers.* Electrovision should also focus on obtaining the best rates on airline tickets, hotel rooms, and rental cars. By channelling all arrangements through a professional travel agency, the company can optimize its choices and gain clout in negotiating preferred rates.

4. *Replace travel with technological alternatives.* With the number of computers already installed in our facilities, it seems likely that we could take advantage of desktop videoconferencing and other distance-meeting tools. Technological alternatives won't be quite as feasible with customer sites. since these systems require compatible equipment at both ends of a connection, but such systems are certainly a possibility for communication with Electrovision's own sites.

Because these measures may be unpopular with employees, management should make a concerted effort to explain the importance of reducing travel costs. The director of corporate communication should be given responsibility for developing a plan to communicate the need for employee cooperation.

Summarizes conclusions in the first two paragraphs—a good approach because Moreno organized her report around conclusions and recommendations, so readers have already been introduced to them

Moreno doesn't introduce any new facts in this section. In a longer report she might have divided this section into subsections, labelled "Conclusions" and "Recommendations," to distinguish between the two.

10

WORKS CITED

Accenture/American Express. "Expense Management Strategies for an Economic Downturn." Accenture 2009. Web. 2 June 2009.

American Express. "American Express Business Travel Announces Adjusted Results of Forecast in Anticipation of Global Economic Slowdown." 22 Oct. 2009. News release. Web. 2 June. 2009.

"AMEX Business Travel 2007 Forecasts and Trends." *Daily Travel & Tourism Newsletter* 2007. Web. 21 Oct. 2007. <http://www.traveldailynews.com/makeof.asp?central_id+1363_id=12>.

Baker, Michael B. "SLA Use Spreading, Especially for TMC Services." *Business Travel News* 17 May 2007: 14. Print.

Baker, Michael B. "Study Eyes Expense Tactics." *Business Travel News* (BTNOnline). 20 Jan. 2009. Web. 2 June 2009.

Boehmer, Jay. "Procurement Gains Corporate Ground Service Appreciation." *Business Travel News* 21 May 2007: 11. Print.

Brady, Paul. "Simplified Airfares that Aren't." *Arthur Frommer's Budget Travel* 8.10 (2006): 41. Print.

"BTN Quantifies '07 Road Warrior Norms in 100 Cities." *The Controller's Report* May 2007: 1. Print.

Business Travel News. Business Travel News Corporate Index 2009. Web. 2 June 2009.

Craig-Bourdin, Margaret. "Business Travel Survey Roundup." *CA Magazine* Jan.–Feb. 2007. Web. 17 Oct. 2007 <http://www.camagazine.com/3/7/8/5/7/index1.shtml>.

McDougall, Diane. "Travel - Managing the Cost Crunch." *CMA Management* 80.5 (2006): 44. Print.

Meritt, Jennifer. "Execs See Travel Tool Efficacy." *Business Travel News* 20 Nov. 2006: 16. Print.

"Travel Trends: Marshal Your Buying Power." *Canadian Business* 79.20 (2006): 33. Print.

Wan, Xiang, Li Zou, and Martin Dresner, "Assessing the Price Effects of Airline Alliances on Parallel Routes," *Transportation Research Part E* 45 (2009): 619–620. Print.

WebEx. *Cisco Webex Meeting Center*. Product Overview. Web. 2 June 2004.

Lists references alphabetically by the author's last name, and when the author is unknown, by the title of the reference (see Appendix B for additional details on preparing reference lists)

Moreno's list of references follows the style recommended in the 7th edition of the *MLA Handbook for Writers of Research Papers*. The box below shows how these sources would be cited following the style prescribed in the 6th edition of the *Publication Manual of the American Psychological Association*.

10

REFERENCES

Accenture/American Express. (2009). Expense Management Strategies for an Economic Downturn. Accenture, 2009. Retrieved from http://home3.americanexpress.com/corp/pc/2009/pdf/bestpractices.pdf

American Express. (2009, October 22). American Express Business Travel announces adjusted results of forecast in anticipation of global economic slowdown.

AMEX Business Travel 2007 forecasts and trends. (2007). *Daily Travel & Tourism Newsletter*. Retrieved from http://www.traveldailynews.com/makeof.asp?central_id+1363_id=12

Baker, M. B. (2007, May 21). SLA use spreading, especially for TMC services. *Business Travel News*, 14.

Baker, M. B. (2009, January 20). Study eyes expense tactics. *Business Travel News* (BTNOnline). Retrieved from http://www.btnonline.com

Boehmer, J. (2007, May 21). Procurement gains corporate ground service appreciation, *Business Travel News*, 11.

Brady, P. (2006). Simplified airfares that aren't. *Arthur Frommer's Budget Travel, 8*(10), 41.

BTN quantifies '07 road warrior norms in 100 cities. (2007 May). *The Controller's Report*, 1.

Business Travel News. (2009). Business Travel News corporate travel index 2009. Retrieved from http://www.com/nxtbooks/niclsen/btn_cti09/#/2

Craig-Bourdin, M. (2007, October 17). Business travel survey roundup [Electronic version]. *CA Magazine*.

McDougall, D. (2006). Travel—managing the cost crunch. *CMA Management, 80*(5), 44.

Merritt, J. (2006, November 20). Execs see travel tool efficacy, *Business Travel News*, 16.

Travel Trends: Marshal your buying power. (2006). *Canadian Business, 79*(20), 33.

Wan, X., Zou, L., & Dresner, M. (2009). Assessing the price effects of airline alliances on parallel routes. *Transportation Research Part E 45*, 619–620.

Webex. (2009). Cisco Webex Meeting Center. Product Overview. Retrieved from http://www.webex.com/product-overview/meeting-center.html

PREFATORY PARTS Prefatory parts are front-end materials that provide key preliminary information, so readers can decide whether and how to read the report.[4] Note that many of these parts—such as the table of contents, list of illustrations, and executive summary—are easier to prepare after the text has been completed, because they directly reflect the contents. When your text is complete, use your word processor to compile the table of contents and the list of illustrations automatically. Other parts can be prepared at almost any time.

Cover Many companies have standard covers for reports, made of heavy paper and imprinted with the company's name and logo. If your company has no standard covers, you can usually find something suitable in a good stationery store. Look for a cover that is attractive, convenient, and appropriate to the subject matter. Also, make sure it can be labelled with the report title, the writer's name (optional), and the submission date (also optional).

Only about 30 years ago, report writers commonly prepared their reports on manual or electric typewriters. What are the differences between using old-fashioned typewriters to prepare reports and using computers with word-processing software? Are there any advantages to typewriters? Any disadvantages to using computers? What are they?

Think carefully about the title you put on the cover. A business report is not a mystery novel, so give your readers all the information they need: the who, what, when, where, why, and how of the subject. At the same time, be concise. You don't want to intimidate your audience with a title that's too long or awkward. You can reduce the length of your title by eliminating phrases such as *A Report of, A Study of,* or *A Survey of.*

Title Fly and Title Page The **title fly** is a single sheet of paper with only the title of the report on it. It's not essential, but it adds a touch of formality.

The **title page** includes four blocks of information, as shown in Moreno's Electrovision report:

Formal reports can contain a variety of prefatory parts, from a cover page to a synopsis or executive summary.

1. The title of the report
2. The name, title, and address of the person, group, or organization that authorized the report (if anyone)
3. The name, title, and address of the person, group, or organization that prepared the report
4. The date on which the report was submitted

On some title pages the second block of information is preceded by the words *Prepared for* or *Submitted to,* and the third block of information is preceded by *Prepared by* or *Submitted by.* In some cases the title page serves as the cover of the report, especially if the report is relatively short and is intended solely for internal use.

Letter of Authorization and Letter of Acceptance If you received written authorization to prepare the report, you may want to include that letter or memo in your report. This **letter of authorization** (or *memo of authorization*) is a document you received, asking or directing you to prepare the report. If you wrote a **letter of acceptance** (or *memo of acceptance*) in response to that communication, accepting the assignment and clarifying any conditions or limitations, you might also include that letter here in the report's prefatory parts. If there is any chance that your audience's expectations might not align with the actual work you did on the report, the letter of acceptance can remind your readers what you agreed to do and why.

A letter of authorization is the document that instructed you to produce a report; a letter of acceptance is your written agreement to produce the report.

In general, the letters of authorization and acceptance are included in only the most formal reports. However, in any case where a significant amount of time has passed since you received the letter of authorization, or you do not have a close working relationship with the audience, consider including both letters to ensure that everyone is clear about the report's intent and the approach you took to create it. You don't want your weeks or months of work to be diminished by any misunderstandings.

Objective 3 Explain the functions of the letter of transmittal.

Letter of Transmittal The **letter of transmittal** (or *memo of transmittal*), a specialized form of a cover letter, introduces your report to your audience. (In a book, this section is called the preface.) The letter of transmittal says what you'd say if you were handing the report directly to the person who authorized it, so the style is less formal than the rest of the report. For example, the letter would use personal pronouns (*you, I,* and *we*) and conversational language. Moreno's Electrovision report includes a one-page transmittal memo from Moreno to her boss (the person who requested the report).

The transmittal letter usually appears right before the table of contents. If your report will be widely distributed, however, you may decide to include the letter of transmittal only in selected copies, so you can make certain comments to a specific audience. If your report discusses layoffs or other issues that affect people in the organization, you may want to discuss your recommendations privately in a letter of transmittal to top management. If your audience is likely to be skeptical of or even hostile to something in your report, the transmittal letter is a good opportunity to acknowledge their concerns and explain how the report addresses the issues they care about.

Depending on the nature of your report, your letter of transmittal can follow either the direct approach for routine or positive messages described in Chapter 8 or the indirect approach for negative messages described in Chapter 9. Open by officially conveying the report to your readers and summarizing its purpose. Such a letter typically begins with a statement such as "Here is the report you asked me to prepare on . . ." The rest of the introduction includes information about the scope of the report, the methods used to complete the study, limitations, and any special messages you need to convey.

In the body of the transmittal letter, you may also highlight important points or sections of the report, give suggestions for follow-up studies, and offer any details that will help readers understand and use the report. You may also wish to acknowledge help given by others—if your report is extensive, you probably received assistance from many people, and this letter is a high-visibility way to show your appreciation. The conclusion of the transmittal letter is a note of thanks for having been given the report assignment, an expression of willingness to discuss the report, and an offer to assist with future projects.

If you don't include a synopsis, you can summarize the report's contents in your letter of transmittal.

If the report does not have a synopsis, the letter of transmittal may summarize the major findings, conclusions, and recommendations. This material would be placed after the opening of the letter.

Table of Contents The table of contents (usually titled simply *Contents*) indicates in outline form the coverage, sequence, and relative importance of the information in the report. The headings used in the text of the report are the basis for the table of contents. Depending on the length and complexity of the report, you may need to decide how many levels of headings to show in the contents; you want to strike a balance between simplicity and completeness. Contents that show only first-level heads are easy to scan but could frustrate people looking for specific subsections in the report. Conversely, contents that show every level of heading—down to fourth or fifth level in detailed reports—identify all the sections but can intimidate readers and blur the focus by detracting from your most important message points. In extreme cases, where the detailed table of contents could have dozens or even hundreds of entries, consider including two tables: a high-level table that shows only major headings, followed by a detailed table that includes everything (as this and many other textbooks do). No matter how many levels you include, ensure that readers can easily distinguish between them.

To save time and reduce errors, use the table of contents generator in your word processor.

Also, take extra care to verify that your table of contents is accurate, consistent, and complete. Even minor errors could damage your credibility if readers turn to a given page expecting to find something that isn't there, or if they find headings that seem similar to the table of contents but aren't worded quite the same. To ensure accuracy, construct the table of contents after your report is complete, thoroughly edited, and proofed. This way, the headings and subheadings aren't likely to change or move from page to page. If possible, use the automatic features in your word processor to generate the table of contents. Not only does this help improve accuracy by eliminating typing mistakes, but it also keeps your table current in the event you do have to repaginate or revise headings late in the process.

List of Illustrations If you have more than a handful of illustrations in your report, or you want to call attention to your illustrations, include a list of illustrations after the table of contents. For simplicity's sake, some reports refer to all visuals as *illustrations* or *exhibits*. In other reports, as in Moreno's Electrovision report, tables are labelled separately from other types of visuals, which are called *figures*. Regardless of the system you use, ensure that you include titles and page numbers.

If you have enough space on a single page, include the list of illustrations directly beneath the table of contents. Otherwise, put the list on the page after the contents page. When tables and figures are numbered separately, they should also be listed separately. The two lists can appear on the same page if they fit; otherwise, start each list on a separate page.

Synopsis or Executive Summary A **synopsis** is a brief overview (one page or less) of a report's most important points, designed to give readers a quick preview of the contents. It's often included in long informational reports dealing with technical, professional, or academic subjects and can also be called an **abstract**. Because it's a concise representation of the whole report, it may be distributed separately to a wide audience; then interested readers can request a copy of the entire report. The synopsis or abstract can also be indexed as a separate entry in electronic databases, so think carefully about the best way to preview the report's contents.

The phrasing of a synopsis can be either informative or descriptive. An informative synopsis presents the main points of the report in the order in which they appear in the text. A descriptive synopsis, on the other hand, simply tells what the report is about, using only moderately greater detail than the table of contents; the actual findings of the report are omitted. Here are examples of statements from each type:

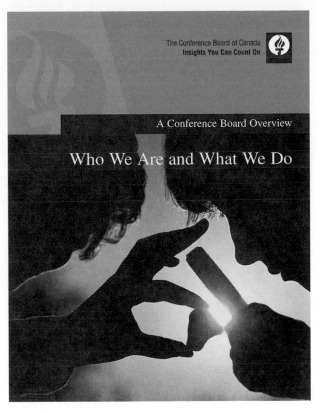

The Conference Board of Canada, a research organization, prepares numerous reports on a variety of subjects. View some of the reports at www.conferenceboard.ca. Click "e-library" and download reports on topics that interest you (your school's library probably has electronic access to the site). What do you notice about the writing style of these reports? Who are the audiences? How is visual support incorporated into the reports?

✓ **Practise**
✳ **Explore**

Objective 4 Explain the difference between a synopsis and an executive summary.

Take time writing your synopsis or executive summary; it's one of the most important parts of your report.

Informative Synopsis	Descriptive Synopsis
Sales of super-premium ice cream make up 11 percent of the total ice cream market.	This report contains information about super-premium ice cream and its share of the market.

The way you handle a synopsis reflects the approach you use in the text. If you're using an indirect approach in your report, you're better off with a descriptive synopsis. An informative synopsis, with its focus on conclusions and key points, may be too confrontational if your audience is skeptical. You don't want to disrupt the communication process by providing a controversial beginning.

No matter which type of synopsis you use, be sure to present an accurate picture of the report's contents.[5]

A synopsis and an executive summary both summarize a report's content, but an executive summary is more comprehensive.

Many business report writers prefer to include an **executive summary** instead of a synopsis or an abstract. Whereas a synopsis is a prose table of contents that outlines the main points of the report, an executive summary is a fully developed "mini" version of the report itself. Executive summaries are more comprehensive than a synopsis; many contain headings, well-developed transitions, and even visual elements. A good executive summary opens a window into the body of the report and allows the reader to quickly see how well you have managed your message. It is often organized in the same way as the report, using a direct or an indirect approach, depending on the audience's receptivity.

Executive summaries are intended for readers who lack the time or motivation to study the complete text. As a general rule, keep the length of an executive summary proportionate to the length of the report. A brief business report may have only a one-page or shorter executive summary. Longer business reports may have a two- or three-page summary. Anything longer, however, might cease to be a summary.[6]

Linda Moreno's Electrovision report provides one example of an executive summary. After reading the summary, audience members know the essentials of the report and are in a position to make a decision. Later, when time permits, they may read certain parts of the report to obtain additional detail. However, from daily newspapers to websites, businesspeople are getting swamped with more and more data and information. They are looking for ways to cut through all the clutter, and reading executive summaries is a popular shortcut. Because you can usually assume that many of your readers will not read the main text of your report, ensure that you cover all your important points (along with significant supporting information) in the executive summary.

Many reports require neither a synopsis nor an executive summary. Length is usually the determining factor. Most reports of fewer than 10 pages either omit such a preview or combine it with the letter of transmittal. However, if your report is over 20 pages long, include either a synopsis or an executive summary as a convenience for readers. Which one you provide depends on the traditions of your organization.

TEXT OF THE REPORT Although reports may contain a variety of components, the heart of a report is always composed of three main parts: an introduction, a body, and a close (which may consist of a summary, conclusions, or recommendations, or some combination of the three). As Chapter 12 points out, the length and content of each part varies with the length and type of report, the organizational structure, and the reader's familiarity with the topic. Following is a brief review of the three major parts of the report text.

Introduction A good introduction prepares your readers to follow and comprehend the information in the report body. It invites the audience to continue reading by telling them what the report is about, why they should be concerned, and how the report is organized. If your report has a synopsis or an executive summary, minimize redundancy by balancing the introduction with the material in your summary—as Linda Moreno does in her Electrovision report. For example, Moreno's executive summary is fairly detailed, so she keeps her introduction brief. If you believe that your introduction needs to repeat information that has already been covered in one of the prefatory parts, vary the wording to minimize the feeling of repetition.

Body This section contains the information that supports your conclusions and recommendations as well as your analysis, logic, and interpretation of the information. See the body of Linda Moreno's Electrovision report for an example of the types of supporting detail commonly included in this section. Pay close attention to her effective use of visuals. Most inexperienced writers have a tendency to include too much data in their reports or place too much data in paragraph format instead of using tables and charts. Such treatment increases the chance of boring or losing an audience. If you find yourself with too much information, include only the essential supporting data in the body, use visuals, and place any additional information in an appendix.

Close The close of your report should summarize your main ideas, highlight your conclusions or recommendations (if any), and list any courses of action that you expect readers to take or that you will be taking yourself. In a long report, this section may be labelled "Summary" or "Conclusions and Recommendations." If you have organized your report in a direct pattern, your close should be relatively brief, such as Linda Moreno's. With an indirect organization, you may be using this section to present your conclusions and recommendations for the first time, in which case this section might be fairly extensive.

SUPPLEMENTARY PARTS Supplementary parts follow the text of the report and provide information for readers who seek more detailed discussion. For online reports, put supplements on separate web pages and allow readers to link to them from the main report pages. Supplements are more common in long reports than in short ones, and they typically include appendixes, a bibliography, and an index.

Appendixes An **appendix** contains materials related to the report but not included in the text because they are too lengthy, are too bulky, or perhaps not relevant to everyone in the audience. If your company has an intranet or other means of storing and accessing information online, consider putting your detailed supporting evidence there and referring readers to those sources for more detail.

The content of report appendixes varies widely, including any sample questionnaires and cover letters, sample forms, computer printouts, statistical formulas, financial statements and spreadsheets, copies of important documents, and complex illustrations. You might also include a glossary as an appendix or as a separate supplementary part. Of course, the best place to include visual aids is in the text body nearest the point of discussion, but if any visuals are too large to fit on one page or are only indirectly relevant to your report, they too may be put in an appendix.

If you have multiple categories of supporting material, give each type a separate appendix. Appendixes are usually identified with a letter and a short, descriptive title—for example, "Appendix A: Questionnaire," "Appendix B: Computer Printout of Raw Data." All appendixes should be mentioned in the text and listed in the table of contents.

Bibliography To fulfill your ethical and legal obligation to credit other people for their work, and to assist readers who may wish to research your topic further, include a **bibliography**, a list of the secondary sources you consulted when preparing your report. In her Electrovision report, Linda Moreno labelled her bibliography "Works Cited" because she listed only the works that were mentioned in the report. Call this section "Sources" or "References" if it includes works consulted but not mentioned in your report. Moreno uses the author–date system to format her bibliographic sources. An alternative is to use numbered footnotes (bottom of the page) or endnotes (end of the report). For more information on citing sources, see Appendix B "Documentation of Report Sources."

In addition to providing a bibliography, some authors prefer to cite references in the report text. Acknowledging your sources in the body of your report demonstrates that you have thoroughly researched your topic. Furthermore,

---

Objective 5 Describe the three supplementary parts of a formal report.

The supplementary parts provide additional detail and reference materials.

Use an appendix for materials that are too lengthy for the body or not directly relevant to all audience members.

A bibliography fulfills your ethical obligation to credit your sources, and it allows readers to consult those sources for more information.

mentioning the names of well-known or important authorities on the subject helps build credibility for your message. On the other hand, you don't want to make your report read like an academic treatise, dragging along from citation to citation. The source references should be handled as conveniently and inconspicuously as possible. One approach, especially for internal reports, is simply to mention a source in the text:

> According to Dr. Lewis Morgan of Northwestern Hospital, hip replacement operations account for 7 percent of all surgery performed on women age 65 and over.

However, if your report will be distributed to outsiders, include additional information on where you obtained the data. Most students are familiar with citation methods suggested by the Modern Language Association (MLA) or the American Psychological Association (APA). *The Chicago Manual of Style* is a reference often used by typesetters and publishers. All of these sources encourage the use of in-text citations (inserting the author's last name and a year of publication or a page number directly into the text).

If your report is lengthy, an index can help readers locate specific topics quickly.

Index An **index** is an alphabetical list of names, places, and subjects mentioned in your report, along with the pages on which they occur (see the indexes in this book for examples). If you think your readers will need to access specific points of information in a lengthy report, consider including an index that lists all key topics, product names, markets, important persons—whatever is relevant to your subject matter. As with your table of contents, accuracy is critical. The good news is that you can also use your word processor to compile the index. Just ensure that you update the index (and any automatically generated elements, for that matter), right before you print the report or convert it to PDF (Portable Document Format) or other electronic format. In addition, have another person spot-check the index to ensure that your entries are correct and easy to follow.

Components of a Formal Proposal

Formal proposals must be produced with a high degree of polish and professionalism.

The goal of a proposal is to impress readers with your professionalism and to make your offering and your company stand out from the competition. Consequently, proposals addressed to external audiences, including potential customers and investors, are nearly always formal. For smaller projects and situations where you already have a working relationship with the audience, the proposal can be less formal and omit some components described in this section.

Formal proposals contain many of the same components as other formal reports (see Figure 13–3). The difference lies mostly in the text, although a few of the prefatory parts are also different. With the exception of an occasional appendix, most proposals have few supplementary parts. As always, if you're responding to a request for proposal (RFP) follow its specifications to the letter, ensuring that you include everything it asks for and nothing it doesn't ask for.

✴—⎾Explore

Objective 6 Explain how prefatory parts of a proposal differ, depending on whether the proposal is solicited or unsolicited.

An RFP may require you to include a copy of the RFP in your prefatory section; just be sure to follow instructions carefully.

PREFATORY PARTS The cover, title fly, title page, table of contents, and list of illustrations are handled the same as in other formal reports. However, you'll want to handle other prefatory parts a bit differently, such as the copy of the RFP, the synopsis or executive summary, and the letter of transmittal.

Copy of the RFP RFPs usually have specific instructions for referring to the RFP itself in the proposal because the organizations that issue RFPs need a methodical way to track all their active RFPs and the incoming responses. Some organizations require that you include a copy of the entire RFP in your proposal; others simply want you to refer to the RFP by name or number or perhaps include just the introductory section of the RFP. Make sure you follow the

> Figure 13–3 Parts of a Formal Proposal

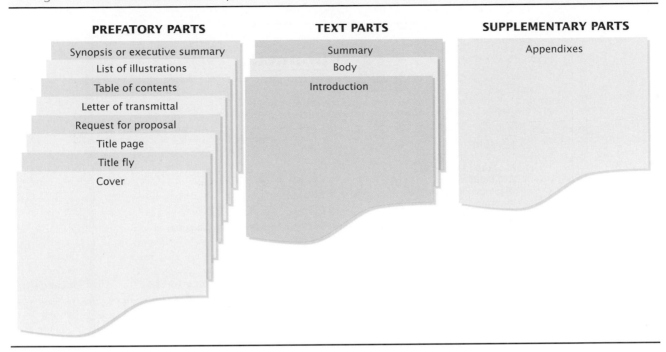

instructions in every detail. If there are no specific instructions, use your best judgment, based on the length of the RFP and whether you received a printed copy or accessed it online. In any event, make sure your proposal refers to the RFP in some way so that the audience can associate your proposal with the correct RFP.

Synopsis or Executive Summary Although you may include a synopsis or an executive summary for your reader's convenience when your proposal is long, these components are often less useful in a formal proposal than they are in a formal report. If your proposal is unsolicited, your transmittal letter will already have caught the reader's interest, making a synopsis or an executive summary redundant. It may also be less important if your proposal is solicited, because the reader is already committed to studying your proposal to find out how you intend to satisfy the terms of a contract. The introduction of a solicited proposal would provide an adequate preview of the contents.

Letter of Transmittal The way you handle the letter of transmittal depends on whether the proposal is solicited or unsolicited. If the proposal is solicited, the transmittal letter follows the pattern for positive messages, highlighting those aspects of your proposal that may give you a competitive advantage. If the proposal is unsolicited, approach the transmittal letter as a persuasive message. The letter must persuade the reader that you have something worthwhile to offer, something that justifies the time required to read the entire proposal.

TEXT OF THE PROPOSAL As with reports, the text of a proposal is composed of three main parts: an introduction, a body, and a close. The content and depth of each part depend on whether the proposal is solicited or unsolicited, formal or informal. Here's a brief review:[7]

✳ Explore

> **Introduction.** This section presents and summarizes the problem you intend to solve and your solution to that problem, including any benefits the reader will receive from your solution.
> **Body.** This section explains the complete details of the solution: how the job will be done, how it will be divided into tasks, what method will be used to do

> Figure 13–4 Dixon O'Donnell's Informal Solicited Proposal

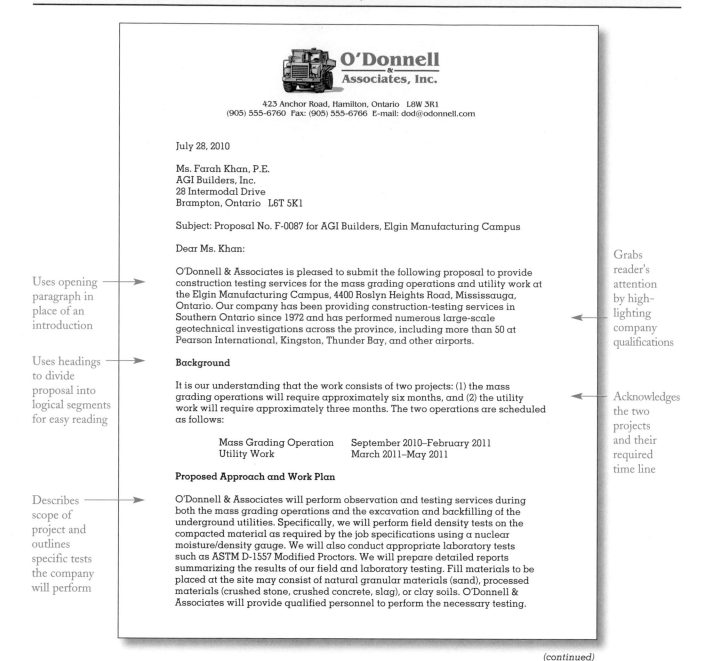

O'Donnell & Associates, Inc.

423 Anchor Road, Hamilton, Ontario L8W 3R1
(905) 555-6760 Fax: (905) 555-6766 E-mail: dod@odonnell.com

July 28, 2010

Ms. Farah Khan, P.E.
AGI Builders, Inc.
28 Intermodal Drive
Brampton, Ontario L6T 5K1

Subject: Proposal No. F-0087 for AGI Builders, Elgin Manufacturing Campus

Dear Ms. Khan:

Uses opening paragraph in place of an introduction

O'Donnell & Associates is pleased to submit the following proposal to provide construction testing services for the mass grading operations and utility work at the Elgin Manufacturing Campus, 4400 Roslyn Heights Road, Mississauga, Ontario. Our company has been providing construction-testing services in Southern Ontario since 1972 and has performed numerous large-scale geotechnical investigations across the province, including more than 50 at Pearson International, Kingston, Thunder Bay, and other airports.

Grabs reader's attention by high-lighting company qualifications

Background

Uses headings to divide proposal into logical segments for easy reading

It is our understanding that the work consists of two projects: (1) the mass grading operations will require approximately six months, and (2) the utility work will require approximately three months. The two operations are scheduled as follows:

Acknowledges the two projects and their required time line

| Mass Grading Operation | September 2010–February 2011 |
| Utility Work | March 2011–May 2011 |

Proposed Approach and Work Plan

Describes scope of project and outlines specific tests the company will perform

O'Donnell & Associates will perform observation and testing services during both the mass grading operations and the excavation and backfilling of the underground utilities. Specifically, we will perform field density tests on the compacted material as required by the job specifications using a nuclear moisture/density gauge. We will also conduct appropriate laboratory tests such as ASTM D-1557 Modified Proctors. We will prepare detailed reports summarizing the results of our field and laboratory testing. Fill materials to be placed at the site may consist of natural granular materials (sand), processed materials (crushed stone, crushed concrete, slag), or clay soils. O'Donnell & Associates will provide qualified personnel to perform the necessary testing.

(continued)

it (including the required equipment, material, and personnel), when the work will begin and end, how much the entire job will cost (including a detailed breakdown, if required or requested), and why your company is qualified.

> **Close.** This section emphasizes the benefits that readers will realize from your solution, and it urges readers to act.

Figure 13–4 is an informal proposal submitted by Dixon O'Donnell, vice-president of O'Donnell & Associates, a geotechnical engineering firm that conducts a variety of environmental testing services. The company is bidding on the mass grading and utility work specified by AGI Builders. As you review this document, pay close attention to the specific items addressed in the proposal's introduction, body, and close.

> Figure 13–4 Dixon O'Donnell's Informal Solicited Proposal *(continued)*

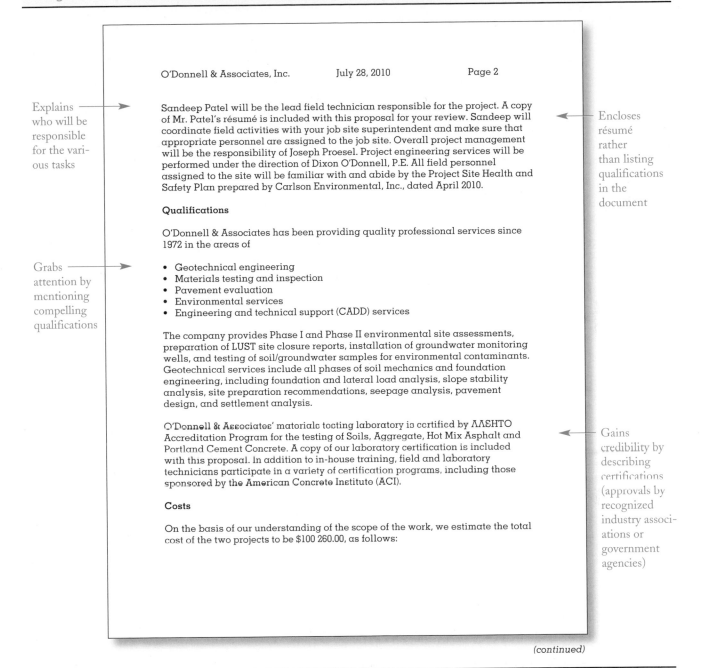

Explains who will be responsible for the various tasks

Grabs attention by mentioning compelling qualifications

Encloses résumé rather than listing qualifications in the document

Gains credibility by describing certifications (approvals by recognized industry associations or government agencies)

O'Donnell & Associates, Inc.   July 28, 2010   Page 2

Sandeep Patel will be the lead field technician responsible for the project. A copy of Mr. Patel's résumé is included with this proposal for your review. Sandeep will coordinate field activities with your job site superintendent and make sure that appropriate personnel are assigned to the job site. Overall project management will be the responsibility of Joseph Proesel. Project engineering services will be performed under the direction of Dixon O'Donnell, P.E. All field personnel assigned to the site will be familiar with and abide by the Project Site Health and Safety Plan prepared by Carlson Environmental, Inc., dated April 2010.

Qualifications

O'Donnell & Associates has been providing quality professional services since 1972 in the areas of

- Geotechnical engineering
- Materials testing and inspection
- Pavement evaluation
- Environmental services
- Engineering and technical support (CADD) services

The company provides Phase I and Phase II environmental site assessments, preparation of LUST site closure reports, installation of groundwater monitoring wells, and testing of soil/groundwater samples for environmental contaminants. Geotechnical services include all phases of soil mechanics and foundation engineering, including foundation and lateral load analysis, slope stability analysis, site preparation recommendations, seepage analysis, pavement design, and settlement analysis.

O'Donnell & Associates' materials testing laboratory is certified by AASHTO Accreditation Program for the testing of Soils, Aggregate, Hot Mix Asphalt and Portland Cement Concrete. A copy of our laboratory certification is included with this proposal. In addition to in-house training, field and laboratory technicians participate in a variety of certification programs, including those sponsored by the American Concrete Institute (ACI).

Costs

On the basis of our understanding of the scope of the work, we estimate the total cost of the two projects to be $100 260.00, as follows:

(continued)

Proofreading Your Reports and Proposals

After you have assembled all the various components of your report or proposal, revised the entire document's content for clarity and conciseness, and designed the document to ensure readability and a positive impression on your readers, you have essentially produced your document in its final form. Now you need to review it thoroughly one last time, looking for inconsistencies, errors, and missing components. For example, if you changed a heading in the report's text part, ensure that you also changed the corresponding heading in the table of contents and in all references to that heading in your report. Proofing can catch minor flaws that might diminish your credibility—and major flaws that might damage your career.

> Figure 13–4 Dixon O'Donnell's Informal Solicited Proposal (continued)

O'Donnell & Associates, Inc.   July 28, 2010   Page 3

Cost Estimates

Cost Estimate: Mass Grading	Units	Rate ($)	Total Cost ($)
Field Inspection			
Labour	1320 hours	$38.50	$ 50 820.00
Nuclear Moisture Density Metre	132 days	35.00	4 620.00
Vehicle Expense	132 days	45.00	5 940.00
Laboratory Testing			
Proctor Density Tests (ASTM D-1557)	4 tests	130.00	520.00
Engineering/Project Management			
Principal Engineer	16 hours	110.00	1 760.00
Project Manager	20 hours	80.00	1 600.00
Administrative Assistant	12 hours	50.00	600.00
Subtotal			$ 65 860.00

Cost Estimate: Utility Work	Units	Rate ($)	Total Cost ($)
Field Inspection			
Labour	660 hours	$ 38.50	$ 25 410.00
Nuclear Moisture Density Meter	66 days	5.00	2 310.00
Vehicle Expense	66 days	45.00	2 970.00
Laboratory Testing			
Proctor Density Tests (ASTM D-1557)	2 tests	130.00	260.00
Engineering/Project Management			
Principal Engineer	10 hours	110.00	1 100.00
Project Manager	20 hours	80.00	1 600.00
Administrative Assistant	15 hours	50.00	750.00
Subtotal			$ 34 400.00

Total Project Costs			**$100 260.00**

This estimate assumes full-time inspection services. However, our services may also be performed on an as-requested basis, and actual charges will reflect time associated with the project. We have attached our standard fee schedule for your review. Overtime rates are for hours in excess of 8.0 hours per day, before 7:00 a.m., after 5:00 p.m., and on holidays and weekends.

Itemizes costs by project and gives supporting detail

Provides alternative option in case full-time service costs exceed client's budget

(continued)

Proofreading the textual part of your report is essentially the same as proofreading any business message—you check for typos, spelling errors, and mistakes in punctuation. Proof your visuals thoroughly, as Chapter 12 points out, and ensure that they are positioned correctly. If you need specific tips on proofreading documents, look back at Chapter 6 for some reminders on what to look for when proofreading text and how to proofread like a pro.

Whenever possible, arrange for someone with "fresh eyes" to proofread the report, somebody who hasn't been involved with the text so far. At this point in the process, you are so familiar with the content that your mind is likely to fill in missing words, fix misspelled words, and subconsciously compensate for other flaws without you even being aware of it. Someone with fresh eyes might see mistakes that you've passed over a dozen times without noticing. An ideal

Ask for proofreading assistance from someone who hasn't been involved in the development of your proposal; he or she might see errors that you've overlooked.

> Figure 13–4 Dixon O'Donnell's Informal Solicited Proposal *(continued)*

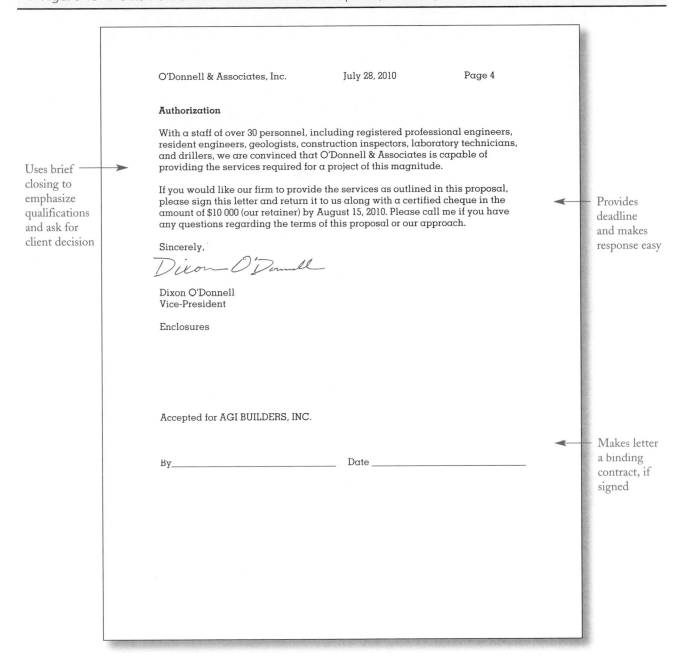

Uses brief closing to emphasize qualifications and ask for client decision

O'Donnell & Associates, Inc.   July 28, 2010   Page 4

Authorization

With a staff of over 30 personnel, including registered professional engineers, resident engineers, geologists, construction inspectors, laboratory technicians, and drillers, we are convinced that O'Donnell & Associates is capable of providing the services required for a project of this magnitude.

If you would like our firm to provide the services as outlined in this proposal, please sign this letter and return it to us along with a certified cheque in the amount of $10 000 (our retainer) by August 15, 2010. Please call me if you have any questions regarding the terms of this proposal or our approach.

Sincerely,

Dixon O'Donnell
Vice-President

Enclosures

Accepted for AGI BUILDERS, INC.

By_____   Date _____

Provides deadline and makes response easy

Makes letter a binding contract, if signed

approach is to have two people review it, one who is an expert in the subject matter and one who isn't. The first person can ensure its technical accuracy, and the second can ensure that a wide range of readers will understand it.[8]

Distributing Your Reports and Proposals

All of the distribution issues you explored in Chapter 6 apply to reports and proposals, as long as you take into account the length and complexity of your documents. For physical distribution, consider spending the few extra dollars for a professional courier or package delivery service, if that will help your document stand apart from the crowd. The online tracking offered by Canada Post, FedEx, UPS, and other services can verify that your document arrived safely. On

Adobe's PDF is a safe and common way to distribute reports electronically.

the other hand, if you've prepared the document for a single person or small group, delivering it in person can be a nice touch. Not only can you answer any immediate questions about it, but you can also promote the results in person—reminding the recipient of the benefits contained in your report or proposal.

For electronic distribution, unless your audience specifically requests a word processor file, provide documents as Portable Document Format (PDF) files. Most people are reluctant to open word processor files these days, particularly from outsiders, given the vulnerability of such files to macro viruses and other contaminations. Moreover, PDFs let you control how your document is displayed on your audience's computers, ensuring that your readers see your document as you intended. In addition, making documents available as downloadable PDF files is almost universally expected these days, if only for the sake of convenience.

If your company or client expects you to distribute your reports via a Web-based content management system, intranet, or extranet, ensure that you upload the correct file(s) to the correct online location. Verify the onscreen display of your report after you've posted it, too; ensure that graphics, charts, links, and other elements are in place and operational.

When you've completed your formal report and sent it off to your audience, your next task is to wait for a response. If you don't hear from your readers within a week or two, you might want to ask politely whether the report arrived. (Some RFPs specify a response time frame. In such a case, *don't* pester the recipient ahead of schedule, or you'll hurt your chances.) In hope of stimulating a response, you might ask a question about the report, such as "How do you think accounting will react to the proposed budget increase?" You might also offer to answer any questions or provide additional information. To review the ideas presented in this chapter, see "Checklist: Completing Formal Reports and Proposals."

CHECKLIST Completing Formal Reports and Proposals

A. Prefatory parts
✓ Use your company's standard report covers, if available.
✓ Include a concise, descriptive title on the cover.
✓ Include a title fly only if you want an extra-formal touch.
✓ List on the title page
   1. report title
   2. name, title, and address of the group or person who authorized the report
   3. name, title, and address of the group or person who prepared the report
   4. date of submission
✓ Include a copy of the letter of authorization, if appropriate.
✓ Include a copy of the RFP (or its introduction only if the document is long) if appropriate.
✓ Include a letter of transmittal that introduces the report.
✓ Provide a table of contents in outline form, with headings worded exactly as they appear in the body of the report.

✓ Include a list of illustrations if the report contains a large number of them.
✓ Include a synopsis (brief summary of the report) or executive summary (a condensed "mini" version of the report) for longer reports.

B. Text of the report
✓ Draft an introduction that prepares the reader for the content that follows.
✓ Provide the information that supports your conclusions, recommendations, or proposals in the body of the report.
✓ Don't overload the body with unnecessary detail.
✓ Close with a summary of your main idea.

C. Supplementary parts
✓ Use appendixes to provide supplementary information or supporting evidence.
✓ List any secondary sources you used in a bibliography.
✓ Provide an index if your report contains a large number of terms or ideas and is likely to be consulted over time.

Summary of Learning Objectives

1 **Characterize the four tasks involved in completing business reports and proposals.** To complete business reports and proposals, revise, produce, proofread, and distribute the document, as you would with any other business message. Revising reports and proposals involves evaluating content and organization, reviewing style and readability, and editing for conciseness and clarity. After revision, produce your report by designing it with appropriate graphical features and white space and adding visual support and any missing transitional elements. Proofread your report for correct spelling, grammar, and punctuation, and, if distributing it electronically, use PDFs for reader convenience and document security.

2 **Explain how computers have both simplified and complicated the report-production process.** Computers have assisted report and proposal writers through software suites such as Microsoft Office and WordPerfect Office that facilitate incorporating graphics with the written text and creating an impressive document. Computers have complicated the report-writing process because their wide variety of electronic features such as multimedia and hypertext links raise readers' expectations for a more impressive document.

3 **Explain the functions of the letter of transmittal.** The letter of transmittal (or memo of transmittal) serves as a cover letter for a proposal. Written in a personal style, it typically presents the reader with the proposal's key ideas, explains how the proposal addresses the audience's concerns, highlights important issues, and advises readers on how to understand and apply the proposal's contents. The letter of transmittal also provides an opportunity for the proposal's author to acknowledge the help of others and establish good will with the audience.

4 **Explain the difference between a synopsis and an executive summary.** A synopsis is a brief outline of a report's contents; it is usually no longer than a page. A synopsis can be either informative (presenting the main points in the order in which they appear in the report body) or descriptive (telling generally what the report is about). Typically, if the report follows the indirect approach, a descriptive synopsis is the better, more tactful choice. If the report follows the direct approach, an informative synopsis that focuses on conclusions and key points is better. The executive summary is a capsule version of the entire report, listing key details and benefits and using headings, transitions, and even visual support to communicate the full contents of the report text.

5 **Describe the three supplementary parts of a formal report.** Three supplementary parts of the formal report are the appendix, bibliography, and index. The appendix contains materials related to the report but too lengthy to include or lacking direct relevance. These materials may include sample questionnaires, financial statements, and complex illustrations. The bibliography lists the secondary sources you consulted to prepare the report and fulfills your ethical and legal obligation to acknowledge the work of others. The index lists alphabetically the names, places, and subjects mentioned in the report, with corresponding page numbers. To help the reader access specific information, the index must be accurate and contain all key topics.

6 **Explain how prefatory parts of a proposal differ, depending on whether the proposal is solicited or unsolicited.** First, a proposal solicited through an RFP should refer to it so the soliciting organization can manage the responses systematically. Because an unsolicited proposal does not respond to an RFP, this element does not appear in the proposal. Secondly, in an unsolicited proposal, the transmittal letter may eliminate the need for a synopsis, because the letter has piqued the reader's interest in the proposal itself. Similarly, in a solicited proposal, the synopsis may play a minor role, because readers are already interested in how you want to help them. Finally, in an unsolicited proposal, the transmittal letter should follow the persuasive strategy, because you are approaching the organization through your own incentive. In a solicited proposal, the transmittal letter should follow the strategy for positive messages, by emphasizing the proposal contents that differentiate you from the competition.

mycanadianbuscommlab

On the Job PERFORMING COMMUNICATION TASKS AT THE BILL & MELINDA GATES FOUNDATION

A decade into your business career, you've decided to put your communication skills to use in an effort to improve global health. You recently joined the Gates Foundation as a program officer in global health strategies.

Malaria is one of the foundation's primary health concerns. This mosquito-borne disease has been largely eradicated in many parts of the world, but it remains an active and growing menace in other areas (particularly sub-Saharan Africa). Worldwide, malaria kills more than a million people every year, most of whom are children.

You are writing an informational report that will be made available on the foundation's website, summarizing the current crisis and progress being made toward the eventual control and eradication of malaria. How will you handle the following challenges?[9]

1 A wide variety of people visit the foundation's website, from researchers who are interested in applying for grants to reporters writing about health and education issues to members of the general public. Consequently, you can't pin down a specific audience for your report. In addition, because people will simply download a PDF file of the report from the website, you don't have the opportunity to write a traditional letter or memo of transmittal. How should you introduce your report to website visitors?

  a Write a brief description of the report, explaining its purpose and content; post this information on the website, above the link to the PDF file so that people can read it before they decide whether to download the file.

  b Provide an email link that people can use to send you an email message if they'd like to know more about the report before reading it.

  c Write a news release describing the report and post this document on the website's "Newsroom" section.

  d Count on the title of the report to introduce its purpose and content; don't bother writing an introduction.

2 Which of the following report titles would do the best job of catching readers' attention with an emotional "hook"

that balances the urgency of the crisis with the reasons for hope?

  a Children Who Don't Need to Die: The Urgent Global Malaria Crisis

  b Preventing a Million Malaria Deaths Every Year: The Urgent Global Challenge—And Reasons for Hope

  c Malaria: It Killed Two Thousand More Children Today

  d Malaria: Progress Toward Eradicating This Global Disease

3 The Gates Foundation is known around the world for the quality of its work, and that includes the quality of its communication efforts. Which of the following proofreading strategies should you use to make sure your report is free of errors?

  a Take advantage of technology. Double-check the settings in your word processor to make sure every checking tool is activated as you type, including the spell checker, grammar checker, and style checker. When you're finished with the first draft, run each of these tools again, just to make sure the computer didn't miss anything.

  b Recognize that no report, particularly a complex 48-page document with multiple visuals and more than 60 sources, is going to be free of errors. Include a statement on the title page apologizing for any errors that may still exist in the report. Provide your email address and invite people to send you a message when they find errors.

  c As soon as you finish typing the first draft, immediately review it for accuracy while the content is still fresh in your mind. After you have done this, you can be reasonably sure that the document is free from errors. If you wait a day or two, you'll start to forget what you've written, thereby lowering your chances of catching errors.

  d Put the report aside for at least a day and then proofread it carefully. Also, recruit two colleagues to review it for you—one who can review the technical accuracy of the material and one you has a good eye for language and clarity.

Test Your Knowledge

1 What are the four tasks involved in completing business reports and proposals?

2 In what circumstances should you include letters of authorization and letters of acceptance in your reports?

3 What is the difference between a synopsis and an executive summary?

4 What are the functions of the supplementary parts of a formal report?

5 How should you handle the RFP for an unsolicited proposal?

6 How should you handle the letter of transmittal for an unsolicited proposal?

Apply Your Knowledge

1 Is an executive summary a persuasive message? Explain your answer.

2 Under what circumstances would you include more than one index in a lengthy report?

3 If you were submitting a solicited proposal to build an indoor pool, would you include as references the names and addresses of other clients for whom you recently built similar pools? Would you include these references in an unsolicited proposal? Where in either proposal would you include these references? Why?

4 If you included a bibliography in your report, would you also need to include in-text citations? Explain.

5 **Ethical Choices** How would you report on a confidential survey in which employees rated their managers' capabilities? Both employees and managers expect to see the results. Would you give the same report to employees and managers? What components would you include or exclude for each audience? Explain your choices.

Running Cases

Watch on **mycanadianbuscommlab**

> CASE 1 Noreen

Noreen has an assignment to complete for her Business Communications class: to research the social and business customs of a foreign country and then submit a report on her findings.

Noreen is excited about this assignment because her employer, Petro-Go, is considering new gas stations and offices in another country. She plans to do a thorough investigation and hopes to share her findings and report with her manager. She feels that having an understanding of the social and business customs of the country where Petro-Go intends to do business will help the company prosper.

QUESTIONS

a) List three sources of information Noreen can use to research foreign business and social customs.

b) Does Noreen have to acknowledge the sources of information she uses even if she does not quote the authors?

c) How will Noreen know that the sources are trustworthy?

d) What correlation will Noreen need to make between the headings in her report and the table of contents?

e) Should the report include an executive summary?

YOUR TASK

Choose a non-English-speaking country and write a long formal report summarizing the country's social and business customs. Include at least one visual. Review Chapter 3 and use Table 3–1 as a guide for the types of information you should include in your report.

> CASE 2 Kwong

Kwong needs to prepare a business plan, so he can apply for a business grant and licence to open his accounting firm, which he has named CG Accounting.

QUESTIONS

a) Is this business plan a formal or informal report?

b) List three sources where Kwong can find sample business plans or information on how to prepare a business plan.

c) The business plan, like any report, must appear professionally formatted. What formats will Kwong need to apply throughout the report?

d) Where can Kwong find information about competitors in the industry?

e) Which prefatory and supplementary report parts may be required in this business plan?

YOUR TASK

Team up with a partner in your class. Conduct some research and review several business plans. Create a business plan for Kwong's company, CG Accounting.

Include the following sections:

> Executive summary, Table of Contents, References, and other prefatory and supplementary sections as required. Include at least one visual.

> Business Overview
  • description of business
  • major demographic, economic, social, and cultural factors
  • major players (e.g., suppliers, distributors, and clients)
  • nature of the industry, trends in the industry
  • government regulations
  • market segment, market trends
  • products and services

- pricing and distribution
- implications of risk factors
- competitors and type of competition
- competitors' strengths and weaknesses
- competitive advantage
> Sales and Marketing Plan
> Operating Plan

- business location and requirements, advantages, lease details, equipment, technology, research and development, and environmental aspects
> Human Resources Plan
> Action Plan And Timetable
> Financial Plan
- projected profit and loss

Practise Your Knowledge

Visit the Citizenship and Immigration Canada publications page at www.cic.gc.ca/english/index.asp, click "Multiculturalism" and "Publications," and open the *Annual Report on the Operation* *of the Canadian Multiculturalism Act* 2007–2008. Use the information in this chapter on the executive summary to analyze and explain how this section functions in the report.

Exercises

13.1 Teamwork: Creating an Informational Report

You and a classmate are helping Linda Moreno prepare her report on Electrovision's travel and entertainment costs (see "Report Writer's Notebook: Analyzing a Formal Report"). This time, however, the report is to be informational rather than analytical, so it will not include recommendations. Review the existing report and determine what changes would be needed to make it an informational report. Be as specific as possible. For example, if your team decides the report needs a new title, what title would you use? Now draft a transmittal memo for Moreno to use in conveying this informational report to Dennis McWilliams, Electrovision's vice president of operations.

13.2 Producing Reports: Letter of Transmittal

You are president of the Friends of the Library, a non-profit group that raises funds and provides volunteers to support your local library. Every February, you send a report of the previous year's activities and accomplishments to the County Arts Council, which provides an annual grant of $1000 toward your group's summer reading festival. Now it's February 6, and you've completed your formal report. Here are the highlights:

> Back-to-school book sale raised $2000.
> Holiday craft fair raised $1100.
> Promotion and prizes for summer reading festival cost $1450.
> Materials for children's program featuring local author cost $125.
> New reference databases for library's career centre cost $850.
> Bookmarks promoting library's website cost $200.

Write a letter of transmittal to Erica Maki, the council's director. Because she is expecting this report, use the direct approach.

Ensure that you express gratitude for the council's ongoing financial support.

13.3 Internet: Analyzing a Proposal

Follow the step-by-step hints and examples for writing a funding proposal at www.learnerassociates.net/proposal. Review the writing hints and the entire sample proposal online. What details did the author decide to include in the appendixes? Why was this material placed in the appendixes and not the main body of the report?

13.4 Ethical Choices: Team Challenge

You submitted what you thought was a masterful report to your boss over three weeks ago. The report analyzes current department productivity and recommends several steps that you think will improve employee output without increasing individual workloads. Brilliant, you thought. But you haven't heard a word from your boss. Did you overstep your boundaries by making recommendations that might imply that she has not been doing a good job? Did you overwhelm her with your ideas? You'd like some feedback. In your last email to her, you asked if she had read your report. So far you've received no reply. Then yesterday, you overheard the company vice-president talk about some productivity changes in your department. The changes were ones that you had recommended in your report. Now you're worried that your boss submitted your report to senior management and will take full credit for your terrific ideas. What, if anything, should you do? Should you confront your boss about this? Should you ask to meet with the company vice-president? Discuss this situation among your teammates and develop a solution to this sticky situation. Present your solution to the class, explaining the rationale behind your decision.

Cases SHORT FORMAL REPORTS REQUIRING NO ADDITIONAL RESEARCH

|Portfolio BUILDER|

1. Giving it the online try: Report analyzing the advantages and disadvantages of corporate online learning

As the newest member of the corporate training division of Paper Products, Inc., you have been asked to investigate and analyze the merits of creating online courses for the company's employees. The president of your company thinks so-called e-learning might be a good employee benefit as well as a terrific way for employees to learn new skills that they can use on the job. You've already done your research; here's a copy of your notes:

Online courses open up new horizons for working adults, who often find it difficult to juggle conventional classes with jobs and families.

Adults over 25 now represent nearly half of higher-ed students; most are employed and want more education to advance their careers.

Some experts believe that online learning will never be as good as face-to-face instruction.

Online learning requires no commute and is appealing for employees who travel regularly.

Enrollment in courses offered online by postsecondary institutions is expected to increase from 2 million students in 2003 to 5 million students in 2008.

E-learning is a cost-effective way to get better-educated employees.

More than one-third of the $50 billion spent on employee training every year is spent on e-learning.

At IBM, some 200 000 employees received education or training online last year, and 75 percent of the company's Basic Blue course for new managers is online. E-learning cut IBM's training bill by $350 million last year—mostly because online courses don't require travel.

There are no national statistics, but a recent report from the *Chronicle of Higher Education* found that institutions are seeing dropout rates that range from 20 to 50 percent for online learners. The research does not adequately explain why the dropout rates for e-learners are higher.

A recent study of corporate online learners reported that employees want the following from their online courses: university credit or a certificate; active correspondence with an online facilitator who has frequent virtual office hours; access to 24-hour, seven-day-a-week technical support; and the ability to start a course anytime.

Corporate e-learners said that their top reason for dropping a course was lack of time. Many had trouble completing courses from their desktops because of frequent distractions caused by co-workers. Some said they could only access courses through the company's intranet, so they couldn't finish their assignments from home.

Besides lack of time, corporate e-learners cited the following as e-learning disadvantages: lack of management oversight, lack of motivation, problems with technology, lack of student support, individual learning preferences, poorly designed courses, and substandard/inexperienced instructors.

A recent study by GE Capital found that finishing a corporate online course was dependent on whether managers gave reinforcement on attendance, how important employees were made to feel, and whether employee progress in the course was tracked.

Sun Microsystems found that interactivity can be a critical success factor for online courses. Company studies showed that only 25 percent of employees finish classes that are strictly self-paced. But 75 percent finish when given similar assignments and access to tutors through email, phone, or online discussion.

Company managers must supervise e-learning just as they would any other important initiative.

For online learning to work, companies must develop a culture that takes online learning just as seriously as classroom training.

For many e-learners, studying at home is optimal. Whenever possible, companies should offer courses through the internet or provide intranet access at home. Having employees studying on their own time will more than cover any added costs.

Corporate e-learning has grown into a $2.3 billion market, making it one of the fastest-growing segments of the education industry.

Rather than fly trainers to 7000 dealerships, General Motors University now uses interactive satellite broadcasts to teach salespeople the best way to highlight features on their new models.

Fast and cheap, e-training can shave companies' training costs while it saves employees travel time.

Pharmaceutical companies such as Merck are conducting live, interactive classes over the web, allowing sales reps to learn about the latest product information at home rather than flying them to a conference centre.

McDonald's trainers can log on to Hamburger University to learn such skills as how to assemble a made-to-order burger or properly place the drink on a tray.

One obstacle to the spread of online corporate training is the mismatch between what employees really need—customized courses that are tailored to a firm's products and its unique corporate culture—and what employers can afford.

Eighty percent of companies prefer developing their own online training courses in-house. But creating even one customized e-course can take months, involve armies of experts, and cost anywhere from $25 000 to $50 000. Thus, most companies either stick with classroom training or buy generic courses on such topics as how to give performance appraisals, understanding basic business ethics, and so on. Employers can choose from a wide selection of noncustomized electronic courses.

For online learning to be effective, content must be broken into short "chunks" with lots of pop quizzes, online discussion groups, and other interactive features that let students demonstrate what they've learned. For example, Circuit City's tutorial on digital camcorders consists of three 20-minute segments. Each contains audio demonstrations of how to handle customer product queries, tests on terminology, and "try-its" that propel trainees back onto the floor to practise what they've learned.

Dell expects 90 percent of its learning solutions to be totally or partially technology enabled.

The Home Depot has used e-training to cut a full day from the time required to train new cashiers.

Online training has freed up an average of 17 days every year for Black & Decker's sales representatives.

Your Task: Write a short (3- to 5-page) memo report to the director of human resources, Kerry Simmons, presenting the advantages and disadvantages of e-learning and making a recommendation as to whether Paper Products, Inc. should invest time and money in training its employees this way. Ensure that you organize your information, so that it is clear, concise, and logically presented. Simmons likes to read "the bottom line" first, so be direct: Present your recommendation up front and support your recommendation with your findings.[10]

|Portfolio BUILDER|

2. Building a new magazine: Finding opportunity in the remodelling craze

Spurred on in part by the success of such hit shows as *Changing Rooms, Trading Spaces*, and *Designers' Challenge*, homeowners across the country are redecorating, remodelling, and rebuilding. Many people are content with superficial changes, such as new paint or new accessories, but some are more ambitious. These homeowners want to move walls, add rooms, redesign kitchens, and convert garages to home theatres—the big stuff.

As with many consumer trends, publishers try to create magazines that appeal to carefully identified groups of potential readers and the advertisers who'd like to reach them. The do-it-yourself (DIY) market is already served by numerous magazines, but you see an opportunity in those homeowners who tackle the heavy-duty projects. Tables 13–1 through 13–3 summarize the results of some preliminary research you asked your company's research staff to conduct.

> **Table 13–1** Rooms Most Frequently Remodelled by DIYers

Room	Percentage of homeowners surveyed who have tackled or plan to tackle at least a partial remodel
Kitchen	60
Bathroom	48
Home office/ study	44
Bedroom	38
Media room/ home theatre	31
Den/recreation room	28
Living room	27
Dining room	12
Sun room/ solarium	8

> **Table 13–2** Average Amount Spent on Remodelling Projects

Estimated amount	Percentage of surveyed homeowners
Under $5k	5
$5–10k	21
$10–20k	39
$20–50k	22
More than $50k	13

> **Table 13–3** Tasks Performed by Homeowner on a Typical Remodelling Project

Task	Percentage of surveyed homeowners who perform or plan to perform most or all of this task themselves
Conceptual design	90
Technical design/ architecture	34
Demolition	98
Foundation work	62
Framing	88
Plumbing	91
Electrical	55
Heating/ cooling	22
Finish carpentry	85
Tile work	90
Painting	100
Interior design	52

Your Task: You think the data show a real opportunity for a "big projects" DIY magazine, although you'll need more extensive research to confirm the size of the market and refine the editorial direction of the magazine. Prepare a brief analytical report that presents the data you have, identifies the opportunity or opportunities you've found (suggest your own ideas based on the Tables 13–1 through 13–3), and requests funding from the editorial board to pursue further research.

Short Formal Reports Requiring Additional Research

|Portfolio BUILDER|

3. Selling overseas: Research report on the prospects for marketing a product in another country

Select a fairly inexpensive product that you currently own and a country with which you're not familiar. The product could be a moderately priced watch, radio, or other device. Now imagine that you are with the international sales department of the company that manufactures and sells the item and that you are proposing to make it available in the country you have selected.

First, learn as much as possible about the country where you plan to market the product. Check almanacs, encyclopedias, the internet, and library databases for the most recent information, paying particular attention to descriptions of the social life of the inhabitants, their economic conditions, and cultural traditions that would encourage or discourage use of the product.

Your Task: Write a short report that describes the product you plan to market abroad, briefly describes the country you have selected, indicates the types of people in this country who would find the product attractive, explains how the product would be transported into the country (or possibly manufactured there if materials and labour are available), recommends a location for a regional sales centre, and suggests how the product should be sold. Your report is to be submitted to the chief operating officer of the company, whose name you can either make up or find in a corporate directory. The report should include your conclusions (how the product will do in this new environment) and your recommendations for marketing (steps the company should take immediately and those it should develop later).

|Portfolio BUILDER|

4. A ready-made business: Finding the right franchise opportunity

After 15 years in the corporate world, you're ready to strike out on your own. Rather than building a business from the ground up, however, you think that buying a franchise is a better idea. Unfortunately, some of the most lucrative franchise opportunities, such as the major fast-food chains, require significant start-up costs—some more than a half million dollars. Fortunately, you've met several potential investors who seem willing to help you get started in exchange for a share of ownership. Between your own savings and these investors, you estimate that you can raise from $350 000 to $600 000, depending on how much ownership share you want to concede to the investors.

You've worked in several functional areas already, including sales and manufacturing, so you have a fairly well-rounded business résumé. You're open to just about any type of business, too, as long as it provides the opportunity to grow; you don't want to

be so tied down to the first operation that you can't turn it over to a hired manager and expand into another market.

Your Task: To convene a formal meeting with the investor group, you need to first draft a report outlining the types of franchise opportunities you'd like to pursue. Write a brief report identifying five franchises that you would like to explore further (choose five based on your own personal interests and the criteria identified above). For each possibility, identify the nature of the business, the financial requirements, the level of support the company provides, and a brief statement of why you could run such a business successfully (based on your own experience, education, and personal qualities). Ensure that you carefully review the information you find about each franchise company to ensure that you can qualify for it. For example, McDonald's doesn't allow investment partnerships to buy franchises, so you won't be able to start up a McDonald's outlet until you have enough money to do it on your own.

For a quick introduction to franchising, see How Stuff Works (www.howstuffworks.com/franchising). You can learn more about the business of franchising at Franchising.com (www.franchising.com) and search for specific franchise opportunities at FranCorp Connect (www.francorpconnect. com). In addition, many companies that sell franchises, such as Subway, offer additional information on their websites.

5. Picking the better path: Research report assisting a client in a career choice

You are employed by Open Options, a career-counselling firm, where your main function is to help clients make career choices. Today a client with the same name as yours (a truly curious coincidence!) came to your office and asked for help deciding between two careers, careers that you yourself had been interested in (an even greater coincidence!).

Your Task: Do some research on the two careers and then prepare a short report that your client can study. Your report should compare at least five major areas, such as salary, working conditions, and education required. Interview the client to understand his or her personal preferences regarding each of the five areas. For example, what is the minimum salary the client will accept? By comparing the client's preferences with the research material you collect, such as salary data, you will have a basis for concluding which of the two careers is better. The report should end with a career recommendation. (Note: One good place for career-related information is the Training and Careers page on the Services Canada website at www.jobsetc.gc.ca/eng).

Long Formal Reports Requiring No Additional Research

6. Customer service crisis: Report summarizing and explaining customer service problems

You are the operations manager for Continental Security Systems (CSS), a mail-order supplier of home-security systems and components. Your customers are do-it-yourself homeowners who buy a wide range of motion sensors, automatic telephone diallers, glass breakage detectors, video cameras, and other devices.

The company's aggressive pricing has yielded spectacular growth in the last year, and everyone is scrambling to keep up with the orders arriving every day. Unfortunately, customer service has often taken a back seat to filling those orders. Your boss, the company's founder and president, knows that service is slipping, and she wants you to solve the problem. You started with some internal and external surveys to assess the situation. Some of the most significant findings from the research are presented in Tables 13–4 through 13–6.

> Table 13–4 Customer Complaints over the Last 12 Months

Type of Complaint	Number of Occurrences	Percentage of Total
Delays in responding	67	30%
Product malfunction	56	25
Missing parts	45	20
No answer when calling for help	32	14
Rude treatment	18	8
Overcharge	5	2

Note: Percentages don't add to 100 because of rounding.

> Table 13–5 Customer Perceptions and Opinions

Statement	Agree	Disagree
CSS offers a competitive level of customer service.	12%	88%
I recommended CSS to friends and colleagues.	4	96
I plan to continue buying from CSS.	15	85
I enjoy doing business with CSS.	9	91

> Table 13–6 How Complaints Were Resolved

Resolution	Percentage
Employee receiving the phone call	20% solved the problem
Employee referred customer to manager	30
Customer eventually solved the problem by himself or herself	12
Unable to solve problem	23
Resolution unknown	15

Portfolio BUILDER

7. Moving the workforce: Understanding commute patterns

Your company is the largest private employer in your metropolitan area, and the 43 500 employees in your workforce have a tremendous impact on local traffic. A group of city and district transportation officials recently approached your CEO with a request to explore ways to reduce this impact. The CEO has assigned you the task of analyzing the workforce's transportation habits and attitudes as a first step toward identifying potential solutions. He's willing to consider anything from subsidized bus passes to company-owned shuttle buses to telecommuting, but the decision requires a thorough understanding of employee transportation needs. Tables 13–7 through 13–11 summarize data you collected in an employee survey.

Your Task: Present the results of your survey in an informational report using the data provided in Tables 13–7 through 13–11.

> Table 13–7 Employee Carpool Habits

Frequency of Use: Carpooling	Portion of Workforce
Every day, every week	10 138 (23%)
Certain days, every week	4 361 (10%)
Randomly	983 (2%)
Never	28 018 (64%)

> Table 13–8 Use of Public Transportation

Frequency of Use: Public Transportation	Portion of Workforce
Every day, every week	23 556 (54%)
Certain days, every week	2 029 (5%)
Randomly	5 862 (13%)
Never	12 053 (28%)

> Table 13–9 Effect of Potential Improvements to Public Transportation

Which of the Following Would Encourage You to Use Public Transportation More Frequently (check all that apply)	Portion of Respondents
Increased perceptions of safety	4 932 (28%)
Improved cleanliness	852 (5%)
Reduced commute times	7 285 (41%)
Greater convenience: fewer transfers	3 278 (18%)
Greater convenience: more stops	1 155 (6%)
Lower (or subsidized) fares	5 634 (31%)
Nothing could encourage me to take public transportation	8 294 (46%)

Note: This question was asked of those respondents who use public transportation randomly or never, a subgroup that represents 17 915 employees or 41 percent of the workforce.

> Table 13–10 Distance Travelled to/from Work

Distance You Travel to Work (one way)	Portion of Workforce
Less than 2 km	531 (1%)
2 to 5 km	6 874 (16%)
6 to 15 km	22 951 (53%)
16 to 30 km	10 605 (24%)
More than 30 km	2 539 (6%)

> Table 13–11 Is Telecommuting an Option?

Does the Nature of Your Work Make Telecommuting a Realistic Option?	Portion of Workforce
Yes, every day	3 460 (8%)
Yes, several days a week	8 521 (20%)
Yes, random days	12 918 (30%)
No	18 601 (43%)

Long Formal Reports Requiring Additional Research

8. Travel opportunities: Report comparing two destinations
You plan to take a two-week trip abroad sometime within the next year. Because a couple of destinations appeal to you, you will have to do some research before you can make a decision.

Your Task: Prepare a lengthy comparative study of two countries that you would like to visit. Begin by making a list of important questions you will need to answer. Do you want a relaxing vacation or an educational experience? What types of services will you require? What will your transportation needs be? Where will you have the least difficulty with the language? Using resources in your library, the internet, and perhaps travel agencies, analyze the suitability of these two destinations with respect to your own travel criteria. At the end of the report, recommend the better country to visit this year.

|Portfolio BUILDER|
9. Secondary sources: Report based on library and online research
As a student and active consumer, you may have considered one or more of the following questions at some point in the past few years:
a. What criteria distinguish the top-rated MBA programs in the country? How well do these criteria correspond to the needs and expectations of business? Are the criteria fair for students, employers, or business schools?
b. Which of three companies you might like to work for has the strongest corporate ethics policies?
c. What will the music industry look like in the future? What's next after online stores such as Apple iTunes and digital players such as the iPod?
d. Which industries and job categories are forecast to experience the greatest growth—and therefore the greatest demands for workers—in the next 10 years?
e. What has been the impact of Starbucks' aggressive growth on small, independent coffee shops? On mid-sized chains or franchises? In Canada or in another country?
f. How large is the "industry" of university sports? How much do football or basketball programs contribute—directly or indirectly—to other parts of a typical university?
g. How much have minor league sports—soccer, hockey, and arena football—grown in small- and medium-market cities? What is the local economic impact when these municipalities build stadiums and arenas?

Your Task: Answer one of those questions using secondary research sources for information. Ensure that you document your sources in the correct form. Give conclusions and offer recommendations where appropriate.

Formal Proposals

|Portfolio BUILDER|
10. Polishing the presenters: Offering your services as a presentation trainer
Presentations can make—or break—both careers and businesses. A good presentation can bring in millions of

dollars in new sales or fresh investment capital. A bad presentation might cause any number of troubles, from turning away potential customers to upsetting fellow employees to derailing key projects. To help business professionals plan, create, and deliver more effective presentations, you offer a three-day workshop that covers the essentials of good presentations:

> Understanding your audience's needs and expectations
> Formulating your presentation objectives
> Choosing an organizational approach
> Writing openings that catch your audience's attention
> Creating effective graphics and slides
> Practising and delivering your presentation
> Leaving a positive impression on your audience
> Avoiding common mistakes with Microsoft PowerPoint
> Making presentations online using web-casting tools
> Handling questions and arguments from the audience
> Overcoming the top 10 worries of public speaking (including *How can I overcome stage fright?* and *I'm not the performing type; can I still give an effective presentation?*)

Workshop benefits: Students will learn how to prepare better presentations in less time and deliver them more effectively.

Who should attend: Top executives, project managers, employment recruiters, sales professionals, and anyone else who gives important presentations to internal or external audiences.

Your qualifications: 12 years of business experience, including 8 years in sales and 6 years in public speaking; experience speaking to audiences as large as 300 people; 6 speech-related articles published in professional journals; experience conducting successful workshops for 75 companies.

Workshop details: Three-day workshop (9 A.M. to 3:30 P.M.) that combines lectures, practice presentations, and both individual and group feedback. Minimum number of students per workshop: 6. Maximum number of students: 12.

Pricing: The cost is $3500, plus $100 per student; 10 percent discount for additional workshops.

Other information: Each attendee will have the opportunity to give three practice presentations that will last from three to five minutes. Everyone is encouraged to bring PowerPoint files containing slides from actual business presentations. Each attendee will also receive a workbook and a digital video recording of his or her final class presentation on DVD. You'll also be available for phone or email coaching for six months after the workshop.

Your Task: Identify a company in your local area that might be a good candidate for your services. Learn more about them by visiting their website, so you can personalize your proposal. Using the information listed above, prepare a sales proposal that explains the benefits of your training and what students can expect during the workshop.

Portfolio BUILDER

11 Healthy alternatives: Proposal to sell snacks and beverages at local high schools

For years, a controversy has been brewing over the amount of junk food and soft drinks being sold through vending machines in local schools. Schools benefit from revenue-sharing arrangements, but many parents and health experts are concerned about the negative effects of these snacks and beverages. You and your brother have almost a decade of experience running juice stands in malls, and you'd love to find some way to expand your business into schools. After a quick brainstorming session, the two of you craft a plan that makes good business sense while meeting the financial concerns of school administrators and the nutritional concerns of parents and dieticians. Here are the notes from your brainstorming session:

> Set up portable juice bars in local schools offering healthy fruit and vegetable drinks along with simple, healthy snacks.
> Offer schools 30 percent of profits in exchange for free space and long-term contracts.
> Provide job training opportunities for students (e.g., during athletic events).
> Provide detailed dietary analysis of all products sold.
> Establish a nutritional advisory board composed of parents, students, and at least one certified health professional.
> Assure schools and parents that all products are safe (e.g., no stimulant drinks, no dietary supplements)
> Support local farmers and specialty food preparers by buying locally and giving these vendors the opportunity to test market new products at your stands

Your Task: Based on the ideas listed, draft a formal proposal to the local school board, outlining your plan to offer high schools healthier alternatives to soft drinks and pre-packaged snack foods. Invent any details you need to complete your proposal.

‖Portfolio BUILDER‖

12. Career connections: Helping employees get the advice they need to move ahead

It seems like everybody in your firm is frustrated. On the one hand, top executives complain about the number of lower-level employees who want promotions but just don't seem to "get it" when it comes to dealing with customers and the public, recognizing when to speak out and when to be quiet, knowing how to push new ideas through the appropriate channels, and performing other essential but difficult-to-teach tasks. On the other hand, ambitious employees who'd like to learn more feel that they have nowhere to turn for career advice from people who've been there. In between, a variety of managers and mid level executives are overwhelmed by the growing number of mentoring requests they're getting, sometimes from employees they don't even know.

You've been assigned the challenge of proposing a formal mentoring program—and a considerable challenge it is:

> The number of employees who want mentoring relationships far exceeds the number of managers and executives willing and able to be mentors; how will you select people for the program?

> The people most in demand for mentoring also tend to be some of the busiest people in the organization.

> After several years of belt tightening and staff reductions, the entire company feels overworked; few people can imagine adding another recurring task to their seemingly endless to-do lists.

> What's in it for the mentors? Why would they be motivated to help lower-level employees?

> How will you measure the success or failure of the mentoring effort?

Your Task: Identify potential solutions to the issues (make up any information you need) and draft a proposal to the executive committee for a formal, company-wide mentoring program that would match selected employees with successful managers and executives.

Designing and Delivering Oral and Online Presentations

After studying this chapter, you will be able to

1. Explain the importance of oral presentations in your career success
2. Explain how to adapt the three-step writing process to oral presentations
3. Discuss the three functions of an effective introduction
4. Identify six ways to keep your audience's attention during your presentation
5. Explain how visuals enhance oral presentations, and discuss the importance of design consistency in visual support
6. Highlight six major issues to consider when you're preparing to give a presentation online
7. Identify six ways that effective speakers use to handle questions responsively

ON THE JOB

Communicating at Telefilm Canada
PROMOTING CANADA'S FILM INDUSTRY

www.telefilm.gc.ca

Wayne Clarkson promotes the Canadian film and multimedia industry at home and around the world. As executive director of Telefilm Canada, a Crown corporation reporting to the Minister of Canadian Heritage, Clarkson manages an agency of 200 employees and a multi-million-dollar budget that supports Canadian movies, television, new media, and special programs, such as *Écrire au long,* directed toward French-language filmmakers outside Quebec. In Clarkson's own words, Telefilm has "invested in over 1000 features, over 1000 documentaries, and over 1000 dramas, making it possible for tens of thousands of talented producers, writers, directors, editors, musicians, cinematographers, performers, and technicians to pursue their careers in Canada."

Raising the profile of the Canadian film industry is a challenging task. In addition to overseeing the planning of numerous reports and industry conferences, Clarkson himself communicates directly with Telefilm's many stakeholders through press conferences, keynote addresses at professional forums and film festivals, and speeches to a variety of government and industry audiences. Meeting with the Standing Committee on Canadian Heritage, Clarkson has highlighted the need for an increased budget, including support for video game production, so Canada, "recognized internationally for its highly skilled game production talent," can nurture a homegrown game industry.

As Telefilm's executive director, Wayne Clarkson speaks to a variety of audiences to raise the profile of the Canadian film industry and ensure its growth. Oral communication is an essential part of Clarkson's job.

A talk to the Director's Guild of Canada reinforced the benefits of working with Telefilm by showing how agency funding contributed to the success of such Canadian-made films as *Bon Cop, Bad Cop*, a 2006 box-office hit. A speech to Canadian film and television producers praised both English and French Canadian feature film achievements but also underlined the need for more Canadian-based productions in both official languages.

Explaining Telefilm's mandate clearly and convincingly is a large part of Wayne Clarkson's job. Analyzing his audiences and understanding how to appeal to them are essential to his success as Telefilm's executive director—and the growth of Canada's film industry. If you worked with Wayne Clarkson, how would you approach planning and developing speeches and presentations for Telefilm Canada? How would you prepare your text and visual support? And how would you polish your delivery style and platform manner?[1]

Building Your Career with Presentations

Wayne Clarkson's experience shows that presentation skills are vital in today's business environment. Oral presentations offer important opportunities to put all your communication skills on display—not just in research, planning, writing, and visual design, but also in interpersonal and nonverbal communication. Presentations can also let you demonstrate your ability to think on your feet, grasp complex issues, and handle challenging situations—all attributes that executives look for when searching for talented employees to promote.

If the thought of giving a speech or presentation makes you nervous, keep three points in mind. First, everybody gets nervous when speaking in front of a group. Even professional speakers and entertainers get nervous after years of experience. Second, being nervous is actually good; it means you care about the topic, your audience, and your career success. With practice, you can convert those nervous feelings into positive energy. Third, you don't have to be a victim of your own emotions when it comes to oral presentations. You can take control of the situation by using the planning and development techniques that you'll learn in this chapter—starting with how to adapt the three-step writing process to the unique challenges of oral presentations.

Objective 1 Explain the importance of oral presentations in your career success.

Oral presentations involve all of your communication skills, from research through nonverbal communication.

Feeling nervous is perfectly normal when you're faced with an oral presentation; the good news is there are positive steps you can take to reduce your anxiety.

Adapting the Three-Step Process for Oral Presentations

Although you don't often write out presentations word for word, nearly every task in the three-step writing process applies to oral presentations, with some modifications (see Figure 14–1). In addition, a few extra steps will help you prepare both your material and yourself for the actual presentation. As with written reports, people often judge the quality of the content by the quality of the presentation, so your delivery style and the packaging of any visual support materials can be as important as your message.

Objective 2 Explain how to adapt the three-step writing process to oral presentations.

While you don't usually write your oral presentations word for word, the three-step writing process is easily adaptable to oral presentations.

Step 1: Planning Your Presentation

Planning oral presentations is much like planning any other business message: You (1) analyze the situation, (2) gather information, (3) select the right medium, and (4) organize the information. Gathering information for oral

ACHIEVING INTERCULTURAL COMMUNICATION

Five Tips for Making Presentations Around the World

When making presentations to international audiences, language fluency might vary widely. So take special care to ensure clear communication:

1. **Speak slowly and distinctly.** The most common complaint of international audiences is that English speakers talk too fast. If you speak too rapidly, your less-fluent listeners will be lost. Articulate every word carefully, emphasize consonants for clarity, and pause frequently.

2. **Repeat keywords and phrases.** When audiences are less familiar with your language, they need to hear important information more than once. Also, they may not be familiar with various synonyms, so word key points in the same way throughout your presentation. If you introduce the concept of *benefits,* for example, continue to use the same word. Don't refer to *advantages* later on.

3. **Aim for clarity.** Keep your message simple. Eliminate complex sentence structure, abbreviations, and acronyms. Replace two-word verbs with one-word alternatives (e.g., *review* instead of *look over* and *examine* instead of *check out*). Such verbs are confusing because the definition of each separate word differs from the meaning of the two words combined. Avoid cultural idioms, such as *once in a blue moon,* which may be unfamiliar to an international audience.

4. **Communicate with body language.** Establish a relationship with your audience through strong eye contact. And don't forget to smile! Smiles and other facial expressions are universally recognized. Moreover, multilingual audiences pay close attention to a speaker's body language to get clues about the meanings of unfamiliar words. For example, prepositions can often be confusing to multilingual listeners, so use gestures to illustrate the meaning of words such as up, down, or under.

5. **Support your oral message with visuals.** For most audiences, visual messages support and clarify spoken words. Develop handouts or slides for your presentation, using simple words to describe your key points. To eliminate problems with rapid speech, unclear pronunciations, or strange accents, prepare captions both in English and in your audience's native language.

CAREER APPLICATIONS

1. One of the most important changes speakers need to make when addressing audiences in other cultures is to avoid figures of speech. Replace each phrase with wording that is more likely to be understood by non-native English speakers or audiences in other countries: "hit one out of the park," "go for broke," and "get your ducks lined up in a row."

2. Make a list of 10 two-word verbs. How does the meaning of each separate word differ from the definition of the combined words? Replace each two-word verb with a single, specific word that will be clearer to an international audience.

Table 14–1 offers a summary of the key steps in analyzing an audience for oral presentations. For even more insight into audience evaluation (including emotional and cultural issues), consult a good public-speaking textbook.

Selecting the Right Medium

Expect to give many presentations via electronic media in your career.

The task of selecting the right medium might seem obvious—after all, you are speaking, so it's an oral medium. However, technology offers an array of choices these days, ranging from live, in-person presentations to webcasts that people view on your website whenever it fits their individual schedules. Explore these options early on so that you can take full advantage of the ones at your disposal. For example, to reach an international audience, you might want to conduct a live presentation with a question-and-answer session for the audience members in your home office and then post a video archive of this meeting on your website for audience members in other time zones. Planning is the key to media selection.

> Table 14–1 Analyzing Audiences for Oral Presentations

Task	Actions
To determine audience size and composition	1. Estimate how many people will attend. 2. Consider whether they share professional interests or other affiliations that can help you establish common ground with them. 3. Analyze the mix of men and women, age ranges, socioeconomic and ethnic groups, occupations, and geographic regions represented.
To predict the audience's probable reaction	1. Analyze why audience members are attending the presentation. 2. Determine the audience's general attitude toward the topic: interested, moderately interested, unconcerned, open-minded, or hostile. 3. Analyze the mood that people will be in when you speak to them. 4. Find out what kind of backup information will most impress the audience: technical data, historical information, financial data, demonstrations, samples, and so on. 5. Consider whether the audience has any biases that might work against you. 6. Anticipate possible objections or questions.
To gauge the audience's experience	1. Analyze whether everybody has the same background and level of understanding. 2. Determine what the audience already knows about the subject. 3. Decide what background information the audience will need to better understand the subject. 4. Consider whether the audience is familiar with the vocabulary you intend to use. 5. Analyze what the audience expects from you. 6. Think about the mix of general concepts and specific details you will need to present.

Organizing Your Presentation

 Explore

Organizing a presentation involves the same tasks as organizing a written message: Define your main idea, limit your scope, select a direct or an indirect approach, and outline your content. As you work through these tasks, keep in mind that audiences for oral presentations are more or less trapped in your time frame and sequence. When reading written reports, audiences can skip back and forth, backing up if they miss a point or become confused and jumping ahead if they aren't interested in a particular part or are already familiar with the content. However, other than interrupting you, presentation audiences have no choice but to listen to your content in the exact order in which you present it.

For example, say that your presentation is a proposal and that you believe your audience will be hostile to the idea. You plan to structure your proposal using an indirect approach. Simple enough, until you suddenly realize that the members of your audience have already heard of your idea through other channels, and they like it. Now they have to sit through an extended presentation of your reasons so that you can convince them to accept an idea they already accept. With a printed report, your audience would simply skip ahead, but they can't do that with an oral presentation. Fortunately, you can use hyperlinks (see page 505) to build flexibility into your presentation, but only if you plan ahead.

DEFINE YOUR MAIN IDEA If you've ever heard a speaker struggle to get his or her main point across ("What I really mean to say is . . . "), you know how frustrating such an experience can be for an audience. To avoid that struggle, figure out the one message you want audience members to walk away with. Then compose a one-sentence summary that links your subject and purpose to your audience's frame of reference, much as an advertising slogan points out how a product can benefit consumers. Here are some examples:

If you can't express your main idea in a single sentence, you probably haven't defined it clearly enough.

Organizations such as the Hong Kong Trade Development Council, Nike, Sears, and Avon use webcast speeches to make live announcements of financial news, new products, and management changes. Unlike ordinary speeches that address a particular audience at a particular time and place, webcast speeches can be viewed and listened to long after the speaker has left the podium. How should speakers prepare presentations for this technology? Is preparation different for live audiences?

> Convince management that reorganizing the technical support department will improve customer service and reduce employee turnover.
> Convince the board of directors that they should build a new plant in New Brunswick to eliminate manufacturing bottlenecks and improve production quality.
> Address employee concerns regarding a new health-care plan by showing how the plan will reduce costs and improve the quality of their care.

Each statement puts a particular slant on the subject, one that directly relates to the audience's interests. By focusing on your audience's needs and using the "you" attitude, you help keep their attention and convince them that your points are relevant. For example, a group of new employees will be much more responsive to your discussion of plant safety procedures if you focus on how the procedures can save lives and prevent injuries, rather than focusing on company rules, saving the company money, or conforming to government guidelines.

LIMIT YOUR SCOPE Effective presentations not only focus on the audience's needs but also tailor the material to the time allowed, which is often strictly regulated. Moreover, in many situations, multiple presenters are scheduled to speak one right after the other, so time allotments are rigid, permitting little or no flex-

Limiting your scope is important for two reasons: to ensure that your presentation fits the allotted time and to ensure that your content meets audience needs and expectations.

ibility. If you overestimate the amount of material you can cover within your allotted time, you're left with only unpleasant alternatives: rushing through your presentation, skipping some information you've so carefully prepared, or trying to steal a few minutes from the next presenter. Or if you don't have enough material prepared to fill your time slot, you might be left standing in front of the audience trying to ad lib information you haven't prepared.

Limiting your scope also involves matching your message with your audience's needs and expectations. Studies show that audience attention levels and retention rates drop sharply after 20 minutes, and venture capitalists (investors who fund many new companies) expect entrepreneurs to get to the point within 15 minutes.[2] In addition, if you cover too many details in a presentation, you can leave the audience feeling confused and frustrated. Often a better approach is to explain important concepts in your oral presentation and refer your audience to printed documents or websites for supporting details.

The only sure way to measure the length of your presentation is to complete a practice run.

When you've decided on the right amount of information to cover, do your best to estimate the time required to present that material or to estimate the amount of material you can cover within a fixed amount of time. The only sure way to do this is to practise. As an alternative to a complete practice run, try several techniques for estimating time requirements. First, if you're in one of those rare situations in which you're reciting your material verbatim or reading from a prepared script (more on this later in the chapter), you can divide your word count by 125 (if you speak slower than average) or 150 (if you're faster than average) to get a rough idea of how many minutes you'll need. Most speakers can comfortably deliver between 125 and 150 words per minute. Second, you can measure how long it takes to talk through a small portion of your presentation and then extrapolate how long the entire presentation will take. This method isn't terribly accurate, but it can help identify major timing problems. Third, after you get some experience giving presentations with either overhead transparencies or electronic slides, you'll get a feel for the time you typically need to cover a single slide. As a general guideline, figure on three or even four minutes per slide.[3] For example, if you have 20 minutes, plan on roughly six or seven slides. If you're whipping through slides faster than that, chances are your slides are too simple or you're not engaging the audience with enough discussion about each one.

Of course, ensure that you factor in time for introductions, coffee breaks, demonstrations, question-and-answer sessions, and anything else that takes away from your speaking time.

CHOOSE YOUR APPROACH With a well-defined main idea to guide you and a clear idea about the scope of your presentation, you can begin to arrange your message. If you have 10 minutes or less to deliver your message, organize your presentation much as you would a letter or a brief memo: Use the direct approach if the subject involves routine information or good news, and use the indirect approach if the subject involves bad news or persuasion. Plan your introduction to arouse interest and to give a preview of what's to come. For the body of the presentation, be prepared to explain the who, what, when, where, why, and how of your subject. In the final section, review the points you've made, and close with a statement that will help your audience remember the subject of your speech. Figure 14–2 presents an

> Organize short presentations the same way you would a letter or brief memo.

> Figure 14–2 Effective Outline for a 10-Minute Progress Report

Progress Report: August 2010

Purpose: To update the Executive Committee on our product development schedule.

I. Review goals and progress
   A. Mechanical design:
      1. Goal: 100%
      2. Actual: 80%
      3. Reason for delay: Unanticipated problems with case durability
   B. Software development:
      1. Goal: 50%
      2. Actual: 60%
   C. Material sourcing:
      1. Goal: 100%
      2. Actual: 45% (and materials identified are at 140% of anticipated costs)
      3. Reason for delay: Purchasing is understaffed and hasn't been able to research sources adequately
II. Discuss schedule options
   A. Option 1: Reschedule product launch date
   B. Option 2: Launch on schedule with more expensive materials
III. Suggest goals for next month
IV. Q&A

outline of a short presentation that updates management on the status of a key project; the presenter has some bad news to deliver, so she opted for an indirect approach to lay out the reasons for the delay before sharing the news of the schedule slip.

Longer presentations are organized like reports. If the purpose is to motivate or inform, use a direct order and a structure imposed naturally by the subject: importance, sequence, chronology, spatial orientation, geography, or category (as discussed in Chapter 11). If your purpose is to analyze, persuade, or collaborate, organize your material around conclusions and recommendations or around a logical argument. Use a direct order if the audience is receptive and indirect if you expect resistance.

Regardless of the length of your presentation, remember that simplicity of organization is especially valuable in oral communication. If listeners lose the thread of your presentation, they'll have a hard time catching up and following your message in the remainder of your speech. Look for the most obvious and natural way to organize your ideas, using a direct approach whenever possible. Explain at the beginning how you've organized your material, and limit the number of main points to three or four—even when the speech or presentation is lengthy.

Finally, remind yourself that just like every other good business message, an effective presentation has a clear introduction, body, and close. In fact, one noted presentation expert even advises a three-act storytelling structure (the approach used in many novels, movies, and TV shows). Act I introduces the "story" you're about to tell and grabs the audience's attention. Act II explores the complications, evidence, support points, and other information needed to understand the story and its conclusion. Act III resolves all the complications and presents a solution that addresses the problem introduced in Act I and that is strongly supported by all the evidence introduced in Act II.[4]

PREPARE YOUR OUTLINE A presentation outline performs the same all-important function as an outline for a written report: helping you organize the message in a way that maximizes its impact on your audience. To ensure effective organization, prepare your outline in several stages:[5]

> State your purpose and main idea and then use these to guide the rest of your planning.
> Organize your major points and subpoints in logical order, expressing each major point as a single, complete sentence.
> Identify major points in the body first and then outline the introduction and close.
> Identify transitions between major points or sections and then write these transitions in full-sentence form.
> Prepare your bibliography or source notes; highlight the sources you want to identify by name during your talk.
> Choose a compelling title; even if the title won't be published, it will help you focus your thoughts around your main idea.

Figure 14–3 is an outline for a 30-minute analytical presentation. Based on Chapter 13's Electrovision report, written by Linda Moreno, it is organized around conclusions and presented in direct order. The outline clearly identifies the purpose and the distinct points to be made in the introduction, body, and close. Notice also how the speaker wrote her major transitions in full-sentence form to be sure she can clearly phrase these critical passages when it's time to speak.

Simplicity is critical in the organization of oral presentations.

In addition to planning your speech, a presentation outline helps you plan your speaking notes.

> Figure 14–3 Effective Outline for a 30-Minute Progress Report

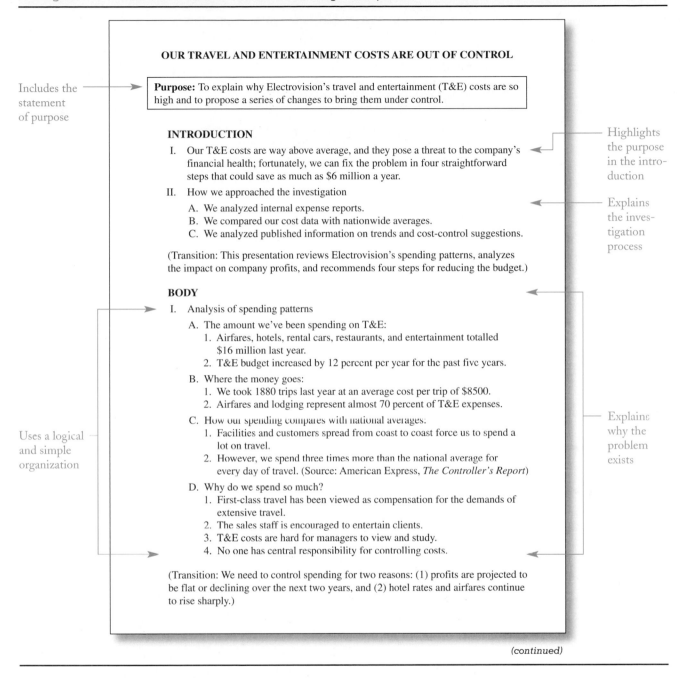

Includes the statement of purpose

OUR TRAVEL AND ENTERTAINMENT COSTS ARE OUT OF CONTROL

Purpose: To explain why Electrovision's travel and entertainment (T&E) costs are so high and to propose a series of changes to bring them under control.

INTRODUCTION

I. Our T&E costs are way above average, and they pose a threat to the company's financial health; fortunately, we can fix the problem in four straightforward steps that could save as much as $6 million a year.

II. How we approached the investigation
   A. We analyzed internal expense reports.
   B. We compared our cost data with nationwide averages.
   C. We analyzed published information on trends and cost-control suggestions.

(Transition: This presentation reviews Electrovision's spending patterns, analyzes the impact on company profits, and recommends four steps for reducing the budget.)

BODY

I. Analysis of spending patterns
   A. The amount we've been spending on T&E:
      1. Airfares, hotels, rental cars, restaurants, and entertainment totalled $16 million last year.
      2. T&E budget increased by 12 percent per year for the past five years.
   B. Where the money goes:
      1. We took 1880 trips last year at an average cost per trip of $8500.
      2. Airfares and lodging represent almost 70 percent of T&E expenses.
   C. How our spending compares with national averages:
      1. Facilities and customers spread from coast to coast force us to spend a lot on travel.
      2. However, we spend three times more than the national average for every day of travel. (Source: American Express, *The Controller's Report*)
   D. Why do we spend so much?
      1. First-class travel has been viewed as compensation for the demands of extensive travel.
      2. The sales staff is encouraged to entertain clients.
      3. T&E costs are hard for managers to view and study.
      4. No one has central responsibility for controlling costs.

(Transition: We need to control spending for two reasons: (1) profits are projected to be flat or declining over the next two years, and (2) hotel rates and airfares continue to rise sharply.)

Highlights the purpose in the introduction

Explains the investigation process

Uses a logical and simple organization

Explains why the problem exists

(continued)

Many speakers like to prepare both a detailed *planning outline* and a simpler *speaking outline* that provides all the cues and reminders they need to present their material.[6] To prepare an effective speaking outline, follow these steps:[7]

You may find it helpful to create a simpler speaking outline from your planning outline.

> Start with the planning outline and then strip away anything you don't plan to say to your audience (statement of general purpose, main idea, bibliography, and so on).
> Condense points and transitions to key words or phrases, choosing words that will prompt you to remember what each point is about. However, write out statistics, quotations, and other specifics so that you don't stumble over them.
> Add delivery cues, such as places in your outline where you plan to pause for emphasis or use a visual. Consider using coloured ink to highlight them.

> Figure 14–3 Effective Outline for a 30-Minute Progress Report (*continued*)

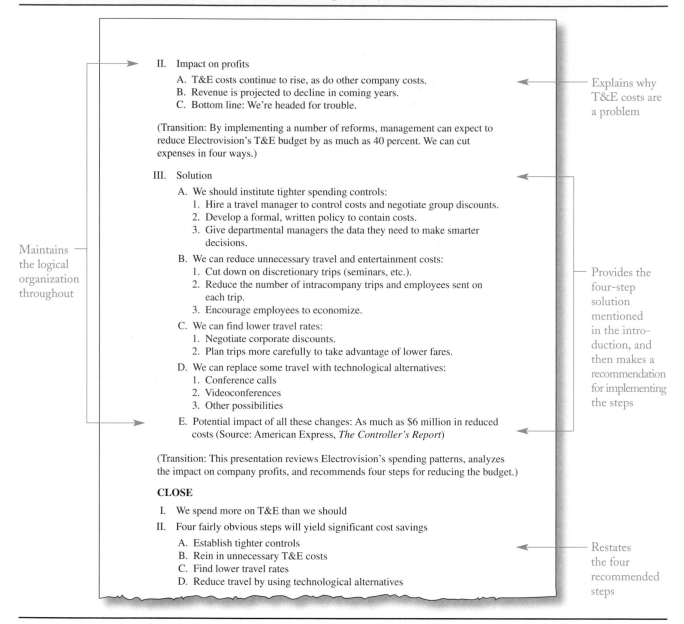

Maintains the logical organization throughout

II. Impact on profits
    A. T&E costs continue to rise, as do other company costs.
    B. Revenue is projected to decline in coming years.
    C. Bottom line: We're headed for trouble.

(Transition: By implementing a number of reforms, management can expect to reduce Electrovision's T&E budget by as much as 40 percent. We can cut expenses in four ways.)

III. Solution
    A. We should institute tighter spending controls:
      1. Hire a travel manager to control costs and negotiate group discounts.
      2. Develop a formal, written policy to contain costs.
      3. Give departmental managers the data they need to make smarter decisions.
    B. We can reduce unnecessary travel and entertainment costs:
      1. Cut down on discretionary trips (seminars, etc.).
      2. Reduce the number of intracompany trips and employees sent on each trip.
      3. Encourage employees to economize.
    C. We can find lower travel rates:
      1. Negotiate corporate discounts.
      2. Plan trips more carefully to take advantage of lower fares.
    D. We can replace some travel with technological alternatives:
      1. Conference calls
      2. Videoconferences
      3. Other possibilities
    E. Potential impact of all these changes: As much as $6 million in reduced costs (Source: American Express, *The Controller's Report*)

(Transition: This presentation reviews Electrovision's spending patterns, analyzes the impact on company profits, and recommends four steps for reducing the budget.)

CLOSE

I. We spend more on T&E than we should
II. Four fairly obvious steps will yield significant cost savings
    A. Establish tighter controls
    B. Rein in unnecessary T&E costs
    C. Find lower travel rates
    D. Reduce travel by using technological alternatives

Explains why T&E costs are a problem

Provides the four-step solution mentioned in the intro-duction, and then makes a recommendation for implementing the steps

Restates the four recommended steps

> Arrange your notes on cards (or sheets of paper, if you prefer); number your cards (or sheets of paper) so that you can keep them in order. (If you plan to use PowerPoint or other presentation software, you can also use the "notes" field on each slide for speaking notes.)

✓• Practise ## Step 2: Writing Your Presentation

Although you may never actually write out a presentation word for word, you still engage in the writing process—developing your ideas, structuring support points, phrasing your transitions, and so on. Depending on the situation and your personal style, your actual presentation might follow these initial words closely or might express your thoughts in fresh, spontaneous language. Before you get to the actual writing phase, consider how you should adapt your style to your audience.

Adapting to Your Audience

Your audience's size, your subject, your purpose, your budget, and the time available for preparation all influence the style of your presentation. If you're speaking to a small group, particularly people you already know, you can use a casual style that encourages audience participation. A small conference room, with your audience seated around a table, may be appropriate. Use simple visuals, and invite your audience to interject comments. Deliver your remarks in a conversational tone, using notes to jog your memory if necessary.

If you're addressing a large audience and the event is an important one, establish a more formal atmosphere. During formal presentations, speakers are often located on a stage or platform, standing behind a lectern and using a microphone, so their remarks can be heard throughout the room or captured for broadcasting or webcasting. These presentations are often accompanied by slides and other visuals showcasing major products, technological breakthroughs, and other information that the speakers want audience members to remember.

Whether your presentation is formal or informal, always choose your words carefully. If you try to impress your audience with obscure or unfamiliar vocabulary, your message will be lost. Make sure you can define all the words you use, and be sure you can pronounce them. If you repeatedly stumble over a word as you rehearse, use a different one.[8]

Finally, when you're pondering how you'll adapt to your audience, take public speaking etiquette into account. Show consideration for your audience by making good use of their time, addressing them respectfully, and maintaining a professional presence during your speech.

> Adapting to your audience involves a number of issues, from speaking style to technology choices.

Composing Your Presentation

Just like written documents, oral presentations are composed of distinct elements: the introduction, body, and close.

INTRODUCTION A good introduction arouses the audience's interest in your topic, establishes your credibility, and prepares the audience for what will follow. That's a lot to pack into the first few minutes of your presentation, so give yourself plenty of time to develop the words and visuals you'll use to get your presentation off to a great start.

> **Objective 3** Discuss the three functions of an effective introduction.
>
> An effective introduction arouses interest in your topic, establishes your credibility, and prepares the audience for the body of your presentation.

Arousing Audience Interest   Some subjects are naturally interesting; others call for more imagination. How do you get people to listen if you're explaining your pension program to a group of new clerical employees, none of whom will be fully eligible for the program for another five years and many of whom might leave the company within two? The best approach to dealing with an uninterested audience is to appeal to human nature and encourage people to take the subject personally. Show them how they'll be affected as individuals. For example, you might begin by addressing the new clerical employees like this:

If somebody offered to give you $200 000 in exchange for $40 per week, would you be interested? That's the amount you can expect to collect during your retirement years if you choose to contribute to the voluntary pension plan. During the next two weeks, you will have to decide whether you want to participate. Although retirement is many years away for most of you, it is an important financial decision. During the next 20 minutes, I hope to give you the information you need to make a decision that's best for you and your families.

> Table 14–2 Six Ways to Get Attention and Keep It

> Unite the audience around a common goal.	Invite them to help solve a problem, capitalize on an opportunity, or otherwise engage in the topic of your presentation.
> Tell a story.	Slice-of-life stories are naturally interesting and can be compelling. Be sure your story illustrates an important point.
> Pass around a sample.	Psychologists say that you can get people to remember your points by appealing to their senses. The best way to do so is to pass around a sample. If your company is in the textile business, let the audience handle some of your fabrics. If you sell chocolates, give everybody a taste.
> Ask a question.	Asking questions will get the audience actively involved in your presentation and, at the same time, will give you information about them and their needs.
> State a startling statistic.	People respond to details. If you can interject an interesting statistic, you can often wake up your audience.
> Use humour.	Even though the subject of most business presentations is serious, including a light comment now and then can perk up the audience. Just ensure that the humour is relevant to the presentation and not offensive to the audience. In general, avoid humour when you and the audience don't share the same native language.

Table 14–2 suggests several techniques you can use to arouse audience interest during your introduction, and "Holding Your Audience's Attention" on page 497 lists six ways to keep audience members' attention throughout your presentation. Regardless of which technique you choose, make sure you can give audience members a reason to care and to believe that the time they're about to spend listening to you will be worth their while.[9]

Building Your Credibility   In addition to grabbing the audience's attention, your introduction has to establish your credibility. If you're a well-known expert in the subject matter or have earned your audience's trust in other situations, you've already gained their confidence. However, if you have no working relationship with your audience or if you're speaking in an area outside your presumed expertise, you need to establish your credibility and do so quickly; people tend to decide within a few minutes whether you're worth listening to.[10]

Techniques for building credibility vary depending on whether you introduce yourself or someone else introduces you. If a master of ceremonies, conference chair, or other person introduces you, he or she can present your credentials so that you won't appear boastful. If you will be introducing yourself, keep your comments simple but don't be afraid to mention your accomplishments. Your listeners will be curious about your qualifications, so tell them briefly who you are and why you're there. Generally, you need to mention only a few aspects of your background: your position in an organization, your profession, and the name of your company. You might say something like this:

> I'm Petra Maly, a market research analyst with Information Resources Corporation. For the past five years, I've specialized in studying high-technology markets. Your director of engineering, John LaBarre, has asked me to talk to you about recent trends in computer-aided design, so you'll have a better idea of how to direct your research efforts.

This speaker establishes credibility by tying her credentials to the purpose of her presentation. By mentioning her company's name, her specialization and position, and the name of the audience's boss, she lets her listeners know immediately that she is qualified to tell them something they need to know. She connects her background to their concerns.

If someone else introduces you to the audience, you can ask this person to present your credentials as well.

Previewing Your Message In addition to arousing audience interest and building your credibility, a good introduction gives your audience a preview of what's ahead. A reader can get an idea of the structure and content of a report by looking at the table of contents and scanning the headings. However, in an oral presentation, you provide that framework with a preview. Without cues from the speaker, the audience may be unable to figure out how the main points of the message fit together.

Your preview should summarize the main idea of your presentation, identify major supporting points, and indicate the order in which you'll develop those points. Tell your listeners in so many words, "This is the subject, and these are the points I will cover." Once you've established the framework, you can be confident that the audience will understand how the individual facts and figures are related to your main idea as you move into the body of your presentation.

BODY The bulk of your speech or presentation is devoted to a discussion of the main points in your outline. Use the same organizational patterns you'd use in a letter, memo, or report, but keep things simple. Your goals are to ensure that (1) the organization of your presentation is clear and (2) your presentation holds the audience's attention.

Connecting Your Ideas In written documents, you can show how ideas are related on the page or screen by employing a variety of design clues: headings, paragraph indentions, white space, and lists. However, with oral communication—particularly when you aren't using visuals for support—you have to rely primarily on words to link various parts and ideas.

For the small links between sentences and paragraphs, use one or two transitional words: *therefore, because, in addition, in contrast, moreover, for example, consequently, nevertheless,* or *finally.* To link major sections of a presentation, use complete sentences or paragraphs, such as "Now that we've reviewed the problem, let's take a look at some solutions." Every time you shift topics, ensure that you stress the connection between ideas. Summarize what's been said and then preview what's to come.

The longer your presentation, the more important your transitions become. If you will be presenting many ideas, audience members may have trouble absorbing them and seeing the relationships among them. Your listeners need clear transitions to guide them to the most important points. Furthermore, they'll appreciate brief, interim summaries to pick up any ideas they may have missed. By repeating key ideas in your transitions, you can compensate for lapses in your audience's attention. When you actually give your presentation, you might also want to call attention to the transitions by using gestures, changing your tone of voice, or introducing a new visual.

> Use the preview to help your audience understand the importance, the structure, and the content of your message.

> Use transitions to repeat key ideas, particularly in longer presentations.

Holding Your Audience's Attention An important part of helping your audience connect your ideas is to hold their attention from start to finish. In addition to the general challenge of keeping readers interested, you have to compensate for another inescapable fact of oral presentations: Your audience can think and read faster than you can speak. If you don't keep their minds engaged, they'll start thinking of other pressing subjects, reading ahead through your handouts, checking email on wireless handhelds, or doing a thousand other things besides paying attention to you. Here are several helpful tips for keeping the audience tuned into your message:

> **Objective 4** Identify six ways to keep your audience's attention during your presentation.

> **Relate your subject to your audience's needs.** People are interested in topics and issues that affect them personally. As much as possible, present every point in light of your audience's needs and values.
> **Anticipate your audience's questions.** Anticipate as many questions as you can and address these questions in the body of your presentation.
> **Use clear, vivid language.** People become bored quickly when they don't understand the speaker. If your presentation involves abstract ideas, show

> The most important way to hold an audience's attention is to show how your message relates to their individual needs and concerns.

Short, simple messages help speakers hold an audience's attention in noisy, distracting environments, such as trade shows. What other techniques can speakers use to keep audiences interested at these and similar venues?

Plan your close carefully, so your audience leaves with your main idea fresh in their minds.

how those abstractions connect with everyday life. Use familiar words, short sentences, and concrete examples. Ensure that you vary vocabulary as well; repeating the same words and phrases over and over puts people to sleep.

> **Explain the relationship between your subject and familiar ideas.** Show how your subject is related to ideas that audience members already understand, and give people a way to categorize and remember your points.[11]

> **Ask for opinions or pause occasionally for questions or comments.** Audience feedback helps you determine whether your listeners understand a key point before you launch into another section. Feedback also gives your audience a chance to switch for a time from listening to participating, which helps them engage with your message and develop a sense of shared ownership.

> **Illustrate your ideas with visuals.** Visuals enliven your message, help you connect with audience members, and help them remember your message more effectively (see "Enhancing Your Presentation with Effective Visuals," on the following page).

CLOSE The close of a speech or presentation is critical for two reasons: Audiences tend to focus more carefully as they wait for you to wrap up, and they will leave with your final words ringing in their ears. Before closing your presentation, tell listeners that you're about to finish, so they'll make one final effort to listen intently. Don't be afraid to sound obvious. Consider saying something such as "In conclusion" or "To sum it all up." You want people to know that this is the final segment of your presentation.

Restating Your Main Points After you announce your close, repeat your main idea and reinforce it with your key support points. Emphasize what you want your audience to do or to think, and stress the key motivating factor that will encourage them to respond that way. For example, to conclude a presentation on your company's executive compensation program, you can repeat the recommendations and finish with a memorable statement to motivate your audience to take action:

We can all be proud of the way our company has grown. However, if we want to continue that growth, we need to adjust our executive compensation program to reflect competitive practices. If we don't, our best people will look for opportunities elsewhere.

In summary, our survey has shown that we need to take four steps to improve executive compensation:

> Increase the overall level of compensation.
> Install a cash bonus program.
> Offer a variety of stock-based incentives.
> Improve our health insurance and pension benefits.

By making these improvements, we can help our company cross the threshold of growth to face our industry's largest competitors.

Such repetition of key ideas greatly improves the chance that your audience will hear your message in the way you intended.

Describing Next Steps Some presentations require the audience to reach a decision or agree to take specific action, in which case the close provides a clear wrap-up. If the audience agrees on an issue covered in the presentation, briefly review the consensus. If they don't agree, make the lack of consensus clear by saying something such as "We seem to have some fundamental disagreement on this question." Then be ready to suggest a method to resolve the differences. If you're not sure in advance how your audience will respond, prepare alternative closes. Few public speaking episodes are more embarrassing than trying to launch into a rousing, positive finish when you know you've lost your audience somewhere along the way.

If you expect any action to occur as a result of your speech, ensure that you explain who is responsible for each activity. One effective technique is to list the action items, with an estimated completion date and the name of the person or team responsible. You can present this list in a visual and ask each person on the list to agree to accomplish his or her assigned task by the target date. This public commitment to action is good insurance that something will happen.

If the required action is likely to be difficult, ensure that everyone understands the problems involved. You don't want people to leave the presentation thinking their tasks will be easy, only to discover later that the jobs are quite demanding. You'll want everyone to have a realistic attitude and to be prepared to handle whatever arises. So when composing your presentation, use the close to alert people to potential difficulties or pitfalls.

Ending on a Strong Note Make sure your final remarks are upbeat and memorable. After summarizing the key points of your presentation, conclude with a quote, a call to action, or some encouraging words. For example, you might stress the benefits of action or express confidence in the listeners' ability to accomplish the work ahead. An alternative is to end with a question or a statement that will leave your audience thinking.

At the completion of your presentation, your audience should feel satisfied. The close is not the place to introduce new ideas or to alter the mood of the presentation. Even if parts of your presentation are downbeat, close on a positive note. As with everything else in your oral presentation, compose your closing remarks carefully. You don't want to wind up on stage with nothing to say but "Well, I guess that's it."

Enhancing Your Presentations with Effective Visuals

Visuals can improve the quality and impact of your oral presentation by creating interest, illustrating points that are difficult to explain in words alone, adding variety, and increasing the audience's ability to absorb and remember information. Behavioural research has shown that visuals can improve learning by up to 400 percent because humans can process visuals 60 000 times faster than text.[12]

You can select from a variety of visuals to enhance oral presentations, each with unique advantages and disadvantages:

> **Overhead transparencies.** Overhead transparencies have been the work-horses of business presentations for decades, and some professionals still prefer them to electronic presentations. Transparencies don't require the latest computer or projection equipment, you can write on them during a presentation, and they never crash on you—as computers have been known to do. However, they're limited to static displays and are impossible to edit once you've printed them.

> **Electronic presentations.** Electronic presentations are the visual of choice in most business situations today. An **electronic presentation,** or *slide show,* consists of a series of electronic slides composed using popular computer software such as

---

If you need to have the audience make a decision or agree to take action, make sure the responsibilities for doing so are clear.

Plan your final statement carefully, so you can end on a strong, positive note.

Objective 5 Explain how visuals enhance oral presentations, and discuss the importance of design consistency in visual support.

Thoughtfully designed visuals create interest, illustrate complex points in your message, add variety, and help the audience absorb and remember information.

In most businesses, electronic presentations are now the presentation technology of choice, although they're certainly not the only option.

Electronic whiteboards let you capture notes and feedback during presentations and then print them out or email them to audience members. Are electronic whiteboards suitable for all speaking situations? Are they appropriate for all audiences?

Microsoft PowerPoint or Apple Keynote. To display an electronic presentation, you simply connect your computer to a portable projector (some are now small enough to carry around in your pocket) or a built-in unit that's part of a multimedia system in a conference room. Electronic presentations are easy to edit and update; you can add sound, photos, video, and animation; they can be incorporated into online meetings, webcasts, and *webinars* (a common term for Web-based seminars); and you can record self-running presentations for trade shows, websites, and other uses. The primary disadvantage is the complexity involved in relying on a computer and a display projector.

> **Chalkboards and whiteboards.** Chalkboards and whiteboards are effective tools for the flexible, spontaneous nature of workshops and brainstorming sessions. Electronic whiteboards let you capture the information written on them; you can print a hardcopy or distribute an electronic version via email.

> **Flip charts.** Flip charts are great for recording comments and questions during your presentation or for keeping track of ideas during a brainstorming session.

> **Other visuals.** Be creative when choosing visuals to support your presentation. A video recording of a group of customers talking about your company can have a lot more impact than a series of slides that summarize what they said. Sample products or materials let your audience experience your subject directly. Designers and architects use mock-ups and models to help people envision what a final creation will look like. For software products, *screencasting* lets presenters capture software operation in action and replay it for audiences.

This chapter focuses on electronic presentations, the mainstay of business presentations today, although most of these design tips apply to overhead transparencies as well.

Once you've decided on the form your visuals will take, think through your presentation plan carefully before you start creating anything. Visuals are powerful devices, and that power can just as easily harm your efforts as help. Above all, remember that visuals support your spoken message; they should never replace it or overshadow it. A discerning audience—the sort of people who can influence the direction of your career—is not easily fooled by visual razzle-dazzle. If your analysis is shaky or your conclusions are suspect, an over-the-top visual production won't help your presentation succeed.

Think through your presentation outline carefully before designing your visuals.

 Explore

Accuracy and simplicity are keys to effective visuals.

Packing slides with too much information is a common beginner's mistake; use slide text to emphasize key points, not to convey your entire message.

CREATING EFFECTIVE SLIDES When it's time to make design choices, from selecting fonts to deciding whether to include a photo, let accuracy and simplicity guide you. Doing so has several advantages. First, simple materials take less time to create than complex materials. Second, simple visuals reduce the chances of distraction and misinterpretation. Third, the more "bells and whistles" you have in your presentation, the more likely it is that something will go wrong.

Writing Readable Content Effective text slides supplement your words and help the audience follow the flow of ideas. They are simplified outlines of your presentation and are used to highlight key points, summarize and preview your message, signal major shifts in thought, illustrate concepts, or help create interest in your oral message. Slides are not intended to display your entire script or highlight every single point you plan to make.[13] Keep your message short and simple:

> Limit each slide to one thought, concept, or idea.
> Limit the content to about 40 words—with no more than 6 lines of text containing a maximum of 6 or 7 words per line.
> Write short bulleted phrases rather than long sentences or blocks of text.
> Phrase list items in parallel grammatical form to facilitate quick reading.
> Make your slides easy to read by using the active voice.
> Include short informative titles.

Figure 14–4 is a good example of text slides that have been revised according to these principles to make their content more readable.

Modifying Graphics for Slides The visual design principles you learned in Chapter 12 apply to presentation visuals as well, but with an important caution: Visuals for oral presentations need to be much simpler than visuals for printed documents. Detailed visuals that might look fine on the printed page can be too dense and complicated for presentations.

Visuals created for printed documents may need to be simplified for use in presentations.

If you're adapting visuals originally created for a written report, start by reducing the level of detail, eliminating anything that is not absolutely essential to the message. If necessary, break information into more than one graphic illustration. Whenever you can do so without confusing the audience, look for shorter variations of numerical values. For example, round off a number such as $12 500.72 to $12 or $12.5 and then label the axis to indicate thousands.

With the basic design in place, use graphical elements to highlight key points. Leave plenty of white space, use colours that stand out from the slide's background, and choose a font that's clear and easy to read. Use arrows, boldface type, and colour to direct your audience's eyes to the main point of a visual.

Selecting Design Elements Chapter 12 highlights six principles of effective design: consistency, contrast, balance, emphasis, convention, and simplicity. Pay close attention to these principles as you select the colour, background and foreground designs, artwork, fonts, and type styles for your slides.

To design effective slides, you need to consider six principles of effective design: consistency, contrast, balance, emphasis, convention, and simplicity.

> **Colour.** Colour is a critical design element that can grab attention, emphasize important ideas, and create contrast. Research shows that colour visuals can account for 60 percent of an audience's acceptance or rejection of an idea. Colour can increase willingness to read by up to 80 percent, and it can enhance learning and improve retention by more than 75 percent.[14] Your colour choices can also stimulate various emotions, as Table 14–3 suggests. For example, if you wish to excite your audience, add some warm colours such as red and orange to your slides. If you wish to achieve a more relaxed and receptive environment, blue would be a better choice.[15] When selecting colour, limit your choices to a few complementary ones, and keep in mind that some colours work better together than others. Contrasting colours, for example, increase readability. So, when selecting colour for backgrounds, titles, and text, avoid choosing colours that are close in hue, such as brown on green or blue on purple.[16]

Colour is more than just decoration; colours have meanings themselves, based on both cultural experience and the relationships that you established between the colours in your designs.

When changing colours from slide to slide, don't switch back and forth from very dark to very bright; the effect is jarring to the audience's eyes.[17] Last, remember that colour may have a different meaning in certain cultures (see Chapter 3). So, if you are creating slides for international audiences, be sensitive to cultural differences.

> **Background designs and artwork.** Electronic slides have two layers or levels of graphic design: the background and foreground. The *background* is the equivalent of paper in a printed report. Keep the background simple;

> Figure 14–4 Writing Readable Content

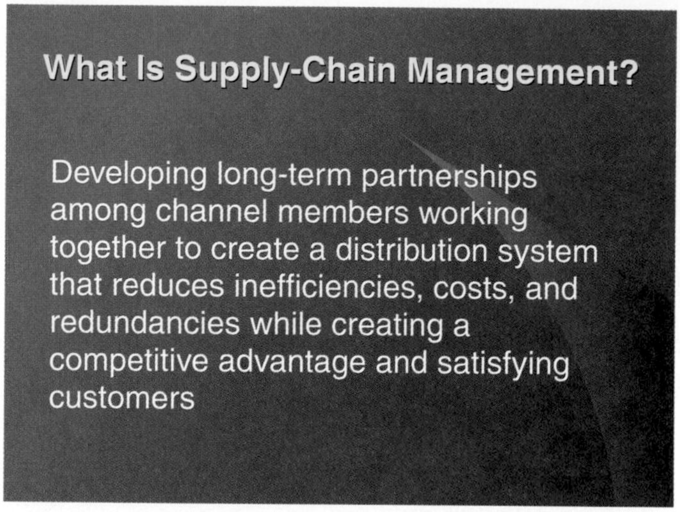

What Is Supply-Chain Management?

Developing long-term partnerships among channel members working together to create a distribution system that reduces inefficiencies, costs, and redundancies while creating a competitive advantage and satisfying customers

> Figure 14–4a Inappropriate paragraph style

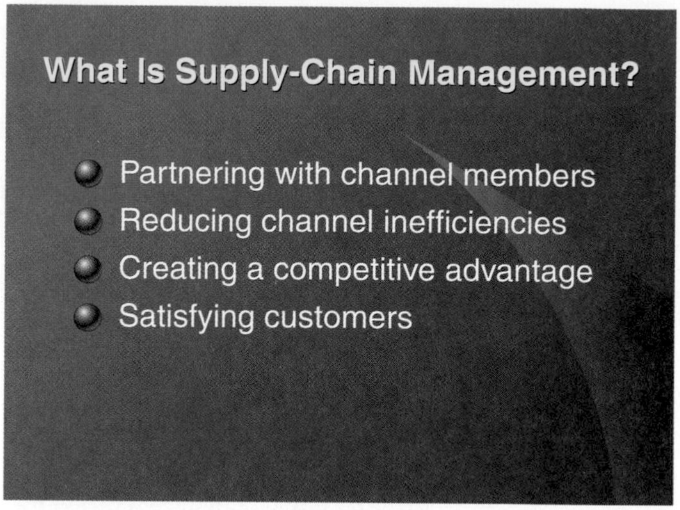

What Is Supply-Chain Management?

- Partnering with channel members
- Reducing channel inefficiencies
- Creating a competitive advantage
- Satisfying customers

> Figure 14–4b Appropriate bulleted phrases

The paragraph style in Figure 14–4a is much more difficult to read, particularly from a distance, than the bulleted style in Figure 14–4b. The speaker will explain these bullet points while showing the slide.

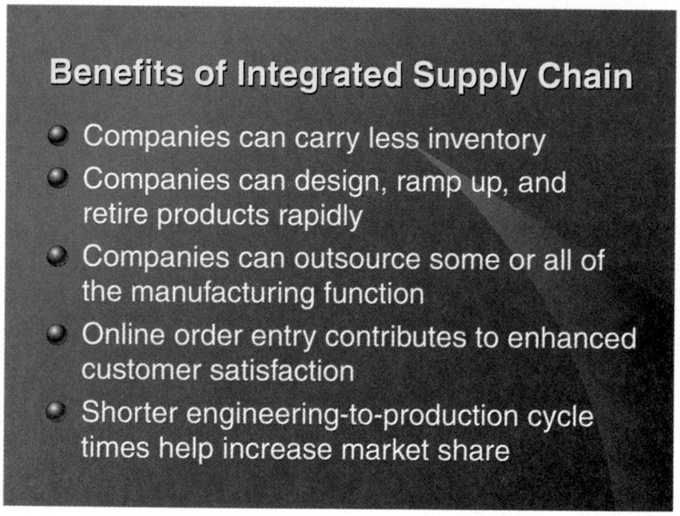

Benefits of Integrated Supply Chain

- Companies can carry less inventory
- Companies can design, ramp up, and retire products rapidly
- Companies can outsource some or all of the manufacturing function
- Online order entry contributes to enhanced customer satisfaction
- Shorter engineering-to-production cycle times help increase market share

> Figure 14–4c Inappropriate wordy bullets

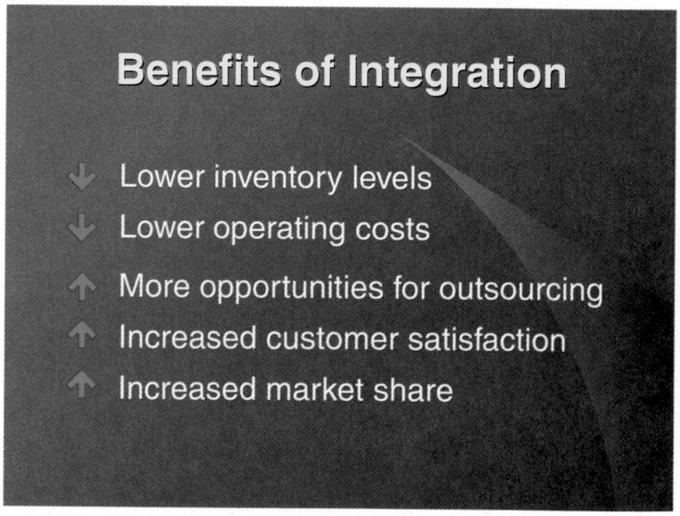

Benefits of Integration

- Lower inventory levels
- Lower operating costs
- More opportunities for outsourcing
- Increased customer satisfaction
- Increased market share

> Figure 14–4d Appropriate concise bullets

Unnecessary words in Figure 14–4c make these bullets harder to read. With the concise bullets in Figure 14–4d, the audience can quickly grasp key message points as the speaker provides additional information. Note also how the phrases in Figure 14–4d are parallel and the font is larger, both of which make this slide easier to read.

cluttered or flashy backgrounds tend to distract from your message. As part of the background, you may want to add a company logo, the date, the presentation title, and a slide number. Just be sure to keep all these elements small and unobtrusive.

Artwork in the foreground of your slides can be either decorative or functional; use decorative artwork sparingly.

> **Foreground designs and artwork.** The *foreground* contains the unique text and graphic elements that make up each individual slide. In the foreground, artwork can be either functional or decorative. *Functional artwork* includes photos, technical drawings, charts, and other visual elements containing information that's part of your message. In contrast, *decorative artwork* simply enhances the look of your slides. Decorative artwork is the least important

> Table 14–3 Colour and Emotion

Colour	Emotional Associations	Best Uses
Blue	Peaceful, soothing, tranquil, cool, trusting	Background for electronic business presentations (usually dark blue); safe and conservative
White	Neutral, innocent, pure, wise	Font colour of choice for most electronic business presentations with a dark background
Yellow	Warm, bright, cheerful, enthusiastic	Text bullets and subheadings with a dark background
Red	Passionate, dangerous, active, painful	Promote action or stimulate audience; seldom used as a background ("in the red" specifically refers to financial losses)
Green	Assertive, prosperous, envious, relaxed	Highlight and accent colour (green symbolizes money in the United States but not in other countries).

element of any slide, but it tends to cause the most trouble for anyone inexperienced in designing slides. *Clip art* and other pieces of purely decorative artwork must be used with great care to avoid distracting your audience members by giving them extra visual elements to decode—particularly if the artwork is inconsistent from piece to piece or slide to slide. The clip art in Figure 14–5 doesn't add any information value, and it creates a cartoonish, unprofessional look.

> **Fonts and type styles.** Type is harder to read on screen than on the printed page because projectors have lower *resolution* (the ability to display fine details) than most printed pages. Sans serif fonts are usually easier to read than serif fonts (see Figure 14–6). In general, avoid script or decorative fonts and italicized type. Use both uppercase and lowercase letters, with extra white space between lines of text, and limit the number of fonts to two or three. Choose font sizes that are easy to read from anywhere in the

> Figure 14–5 Distractions from Decorative Artwork

> Figure 14–6 Selecting Readable Fonts and Type Styles

> Figure 14–6a Times New Roman font

> Figure 14–6b Arial font

Times New Roman is a standard font for many print documents; however, as Figure 14–6a demonstrates, the serifs at the end of each letter make it difficult to read on screen, as does the italicized type. Figure 14–6b shows that sans serif fonts such as Arial are a better choice for slides; they are cleaner and easier to read from a distance.

room, usually between 24 and 36 points. Headings of the same level of importance should use the same font, type size, and colour. Once you have selected your fonts and type styles, test them for readability by viewing sample slides from a distance.

Design inconsistencies confuse and annoy audiences; don't change colours and other design elements randomly throughout your presentation.

With so many choices at your fingertips, maintaining consistency in your design is critical. Audiences start to assign meaning to visual elements beginning with the first slide. For example, if the first slide presents the most important information in bright yellow, 36-point Arial font, your audience will expect the same font treatment for the most important information on the second and third slides as well. So, when choosing fonts and point size, be consistent. Also be consistent in your layout. Make sure items that repeat on every slide, such as the date and the company logo, are in the same location on every slide.

Fortunately, the *slide master* (Figure 14–7) provides a predefined layout from those available in your software, which ensures that bulleted lists, charts, graphics, and other elements show up in predictable places on each slide. The less that readers have to work to interpret your slide designs, the more attention they can pay to your message.

You can animate just about everything in an electronic presentation; resist the temptation to do so—ensure that the animation has a purpose.

Adding Animation and Special Effects   Today's presentation software offers a wide array of options for livening up your slides, including sound, animation, video clips, transition effects, and hyperlinks. Think about the impact that all these effects will have on your audience and use only those special effects that support your message.[18]

Functional animation involves motion that is directly related to your message, such as a highlight arrow that moves around the screen to emphasize specific points in a technical diagram. Such animation is also a good way to demonstrate sequences and procedures. For a training session on machinery repair, for example, you can show a schematic diagram of the machinery and walk your audience through each step of the troubleshooting process, highlighting each step onscreen as you address it verbally. In contrast, *decorative animation*, such as having a block of text cartwheel in from offscreen, needs to

> Figure 14–7 PowerPoint Slide Master

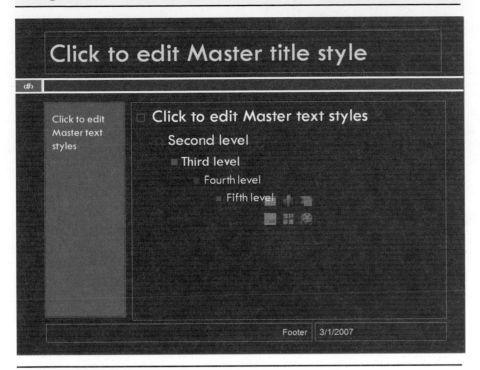

be used with great care. These effects don't add any functional value, and they easily distract audiences.

Transitions control how one slide replaces another, such as having the current slide gently fade out before the next slide fades in. Subtle transitions like this can ease your viewers' gaze from one slide to the next. However, many transition effects now available (e.g., checkerboards, pinwheels, and spinning "newsflashes") not only disrupt the flow of your presentation, but also can make your entire presentation seem amateurish. **Builds** control the release of text, graphics, and other elements on individual slides. With builds you can make your bullet points appear one at a time rather than having all of them appear on a slide at once, thereby making it easier for you and the audience to focus on each new message point.

A **hyperlink** instructs your computer to jump to another slide in your presentation, to a website, or to another program entirely. Hyperlinks can also be assigned to **action buttons,** which are a variety of pre-programmed icons available in PowerPoint. Action buttons let you perform such common tasks as jumping forward or backward to a specific slide or opening a document or spreadsheet. Using hyperlinks and action buttons is also an effective way to build flexibility into your presentations. For example, if you need to adapt one presentation for a variety of audiences and situations, you can create a menu of action buttons that launch whatever subset of the presentation is appropriate for each scenario.

Multimedia elements offer the ultimate in active presentations. Say that a few words from your company president would help bolster your argument, but she's not available to speak at your presentation. However, keep these clips short; audiences dislike being forced to sit through long speeches online.[19] For more advanced digital video, use such specialized products as Adobe Premiere Pro or Macromedia Director (samples of which can be viewed at the respective company's website).

Some slide transitions available in presentation software are distracting and can quickly begin to annoy audiences.

You can increase the flexibility of your presentation slides with hyperlinks that let you jump to different slides, websites, or other displays at will.

Video clips can add memorable, engaging content to your presentations; just make sure they are relevant, interesting, and brief.

Online presentations let you reach a wide audience, but are characterized by lack of direct contact. What should you do to engage your audience when delivering an online presentation?

Online presentations give you a way to reach more people in less time, but they require special preparation and skills.

Objective 6 Highlight six major issues to consider when you're preparing to give a presentation online.

GIVING PRESENTATIONS ONLINE

With the global reach of today's business organizations, you can expect to deliver a presentation online at some point in your career. In some companies, online presentations have already become a routine matter, conducted via internal groupware, virtual meeting systems, or webcast systems designed specifically for online presentations. In most cases, you'll communicate through some combination of audio, video, and data presentations (with PowerPoint slides, for example). Your audience will view your presentation either on their individual computer screens or via a projector in a conference room.

The benefits of online presentations are considerable, including the opportunity to communicate with a geographically dispersed audience at a fraction of the cost of travel and the ability for a project team or an entire organization to meet at a moment's notice. Online presentations can also be less disruptive for the members of your audience, giving them the options of viewing your presentation from their desks and listening to only those parts that apply to them. However, the challenges for a presenter can be significant, thanks to that layer of technology between you and your audience. Many of those "human moments" that guide and encourage you through an in-person presentation won't travel across the digital divide. For example, it's often difficult to tell whether your audience is bored or confused because your view of them is usually confined to small video images. Moreover, the technology itself can be a source of trouble from time to time, with dropped internet connections, untrained users, and other problems. However, online systems continue to improve, and presenters who master this new mode of communication will definitely have an advantage in tomorrow's business environment.

To ensure successful online presentations, regardless of the system you're using, keep the following advice in mind:

> **Consider sending preview study materials ahead of time.** If your presentation covers complicated or unfamiliar material, consider sending a brief message ahead of time, so your audience can familiarize itself with any important background information.

> **Keep your content—and your presentation of it—as simple as possible.** Break down complicated slides into multiple slides if necessary, and keep the direction of your discussion clear so that no one gets lost. Moreover, make sure any streaming video presentations are short; audiences dislike being forced to sit through long speeches online.[20]

> **Ask for feedback frequently.** You won't have as much of the visual feedback that alerts you when audience members are confused, and many online viewers will be reluctant to call attention to themselves by interrupting you to ask for clarification. So, to ensure that your audience is on track, draw out feedback as you go.

> **Consider the viewing experience from the audience's side.** Will they be able to see what you think they can see? For example, webcast video is typically displayed in a small window onscreen, so viewers may miss important details.

> **Make sure your audience can receive the sort of content you intend to use.** For example, some corporate *firewalls* don't allow *streaming media*, so your webcast video might not survive the trip.[21]

> **Allow plenty of time for everyone to get connected and familiar with the screen they're viewing.** Build extra time into your schedule to ensure that everyone is connected and ready to start.

Last but not least, don't get lost in the technology. Use these tools whenever they'll help, but remember that the most important aspect of any presentation is getting the audience to receive, understand, and embrace your message.

When you master the technology, you can spend less time thinking about it and more time thinking about the most important elements of the presentation: your message and your audience.

Step 3: Completing Your Presentation

With a draft of your presentation in hand, you're ready to complete the development of your presentation. As with written communication, this third step starts with the all-important task of revising your message to ensure appropriate content. Edit your presentation for clarity and conciseness as you would any business message. If you're using electronic slides, make sure they are readable, concise, consistent from slide to slide, and fully operational (including transitions, builds, and animations). The first step in completing your presentation is finalizing your slides and support materials.

Finalizing Slides and Support Materials

Electronic presentation software can help you throughout the editing and revision process. As Figure 14–8 shows, the *slide sorter view* lets you see some or all of the slides in your presentation on a single screen. Use this view to add and delete slides, reposition slides, check slides for design consistency, and verify the operation of animation and transition effects.

Use the slide sorter view to verify and modify the organization of your slides.

In addition to the content slides that you've already created, help your audience follow the flow of your presentation by creating slides for your title, agenda and program details, and navigation flow:

Navigational slides help your audience keep track of what you've covered already and what you plan to cover next.

> **Title slide(s).** Make a good first impression on your audience with one or two title slides, the equivalent of a report's title page (the first slide in Figures 14–9a and 14–9b). A title slide should contain the title of your presentation (and subtitle, if appropriate), your name, your department affiliation (for internal audiences), your company affiliation (for external audiences), and the date of your presentation.

> **Agenda and program details.** These slides communicate both the agenda for your presentation and any additional information your audience might need, such as lunch plans (see Figures 14–9c and 14–9d).

> **Navigation slides.** To tell your audience where you're going and where you've been, you can use a series of **navigation slides** based on your outline or agenda. This technique is most useful in longer presentations with several major sections. As you complete each section, repeat the slide but indicate which material has been covered and which section you are about to begin (see Figure 14–10). This sort of slide is sometimes referred to as a *moving blueprint*. You can use the original slide again in the close of your presentation to review the points you've covered. As an alternative to the repeating agenda slide, you can insert a simple *bumper slide* at each major section break, announcing the title of the section you're about to begin.[22]

With your slides working properly and in clear, logical order, consider whether some additional material will help your audience either during or after your presentations. *Handouts* are an efficient way to offer your audience additional material without overloading your slides with information. Possibilities for good

Use handout materials to support the points made in your presentation and to offer the audience additional information on your topic.

> Figure 14–8 Slide Sorter View

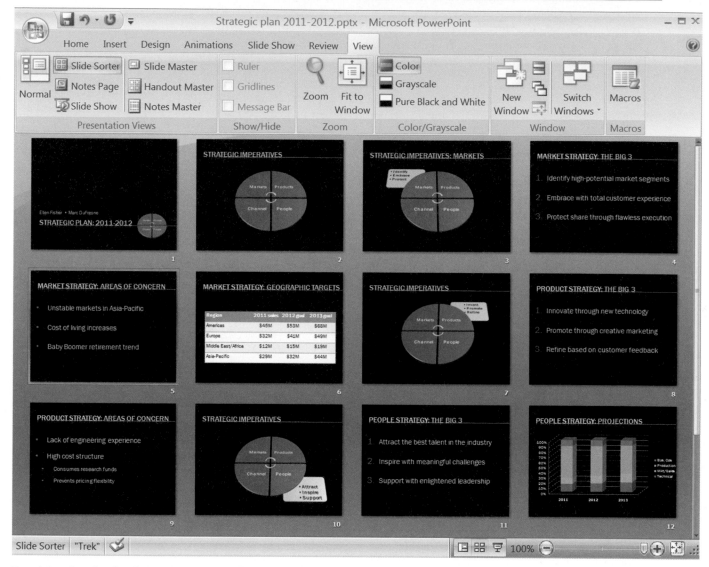

Examining thumbnails of slides on one screen is the best way to check the overall design of your final product. The slide sorter also makes it easy to review the order and organization of your presentation; you can change the position of any slide simply by clicking and dragging it to a new position.

handout materials include complex charts and diagrams that are too unwieldy for the screen, articles and technical papers, case studies, lists of websites, and printed copies of your slides.[23]

Finally, think about a backup plan. What will you do if your laptop won't boot up or the projector dies? Can you get by without your slides? For important presentations, consider having backup equipment on standby, loaded with your presentation, and ready to go. Having a backup copy of your presentation slides on a CD-ROM or flash drive is often a good idea, too. At the very least, have enough printed handouts ready to give the audience so that, as a last resort, you can give your presentation "on paper."

Preparing to Speak

With all your materials ready, your next step is to decide which method of speaking you want to use. You have three options: memorizing your material

> Figure 14–9 Navigation and Support Slides

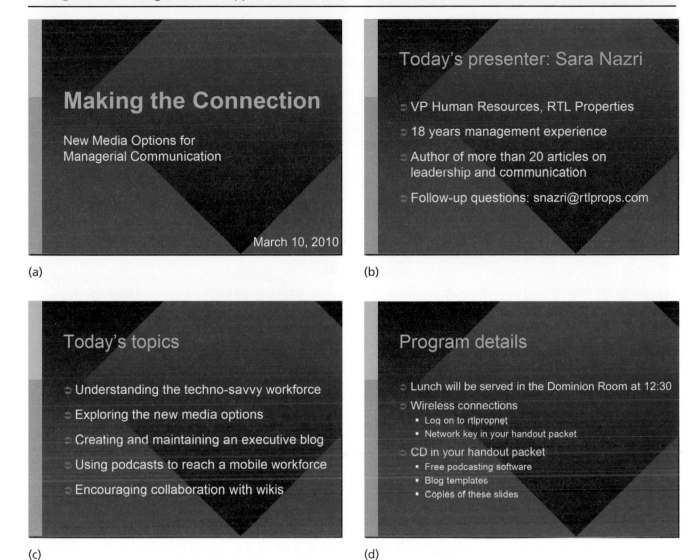

(a)

(b)

(c)

(d)

You can use a variety of navigation and support slides to introduce yourself and your presentation, to let the audience know what your presentation will cover, and to provide essential details.

word for word, reading a printout of your material, or speaking from notes. Memorizing is usually not a good choice. In the best of circumstances you'll probably sound stilted; in the worst, you might forget your lines. Besides, you'll often need to address audience questions during your speech, so you must be flexible enough to adjust your speech as you go. However, memorizing a quotation, an opening paragraph, or a few concluding remarks can bolster your confidence and strengthen your delivery.

Reading your speech is sometimes necessary, such as when delivering legal information, policy statements, or other messages that must be conveyed in an exact manner. However, for most business presentations, reading is a poor choice because it limits your interaction with the audience and lacks the fresh, dynamic feel of natural talking. (In any event, *never* stand in front of an audience and simply read the text on your slides.) If you do plan to read a prepared speech, practise enough so that you can still maintain eye contact with

> Figure 14–10 Moving Blueprint Slides

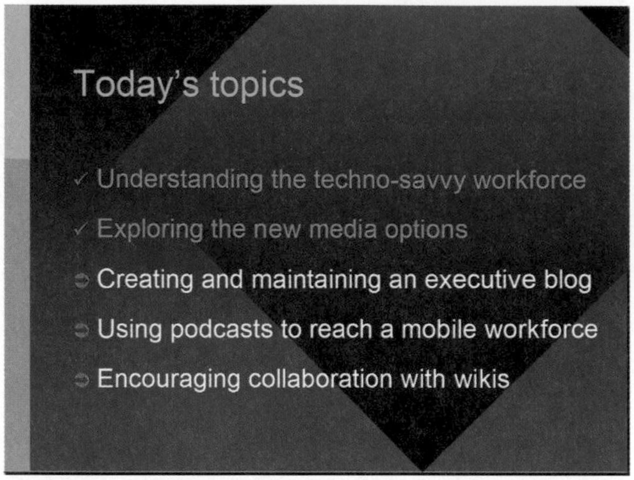

(a) 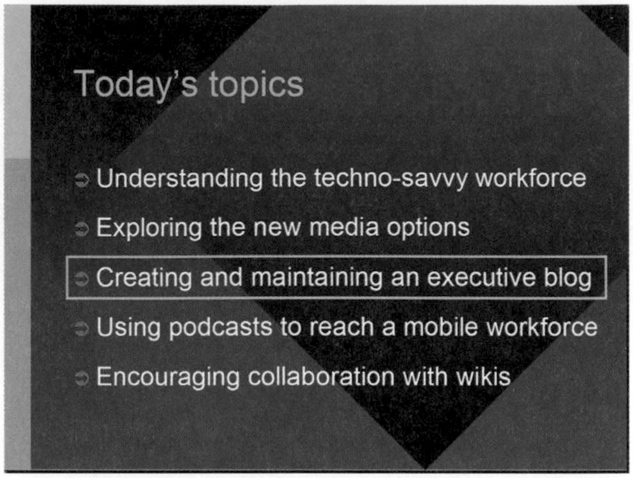   (b)

Here are two of the ways you can use a *blueprint slide* as a navigational aid to help your audience stay on track with the presentation. Figure 14–10a visually "mutes" and checks off the sections of the presentation that have already been covered. In contrast, Figure 14–10b uses a sliding highlight box to indicate the next section to be covered.

your audience. Print your speech with triple-spaced lines, wide margins, and large type. You might even want to include stage cues, such as *pause, raise hands, lower voice.*

Speaking from notes, with the help of an outline, note cards, or visuals, is usually the most effective and easiest delivery mode. This approach gives you something to refer to and still allows for plenty of eye contact, interaction with the audience, and improvisation in response to audience feedback.

Speaking from carefully prepared notes is the easiest and most effective delivery mode for most speakers.

From time to time, you may have to give an *impromptu,* or unrehearsed, speech when you have virtually no time at all to prepare. If you have the option, avoid speaking unprepared unless you're well versed in the topic or have lots of experience at improvising in front of a live audience. When you're asked to speak "off the cuff," take a moment to think through what you'll say and then focus on your key points. If you absolutely cannot say something intelligent and effective on the subject at hand, it's usually better to explain that you can't and ask for an opportunity to prepare some remarks for a later time or date.

Practising Your Delivery

The more you practise, the more confidence you'll have in yourself and your material.

You're now just one step away from giving your presentation, and it's a step that too many novice presenters overlook: practising the delivery of your presentation. Many things can go wrong in a major presentation, including equipment glitches, timing problems, and that sinking feeling that you don't know what to say next. That's why experienced speakers always practise important presentations. If you can arrange an audience of several helpful colleagues, by all means do so. They can tell you if your slides are understandable and whether your delivery is effective. A day or two before you're ready to step on stage for an important talk, ensure that you can give a positive response to the following questions:

> Can you present your material naturally, without reading your slides word for word?

> Is the equipment working—and do you know how to work it?
> Is your timing on track?
> Can you easily pronounce all the words you plan to use?
> Have you decided how you're going to introduce your slides?
> Have you anticipated likely questions and objections?

With experience, you'll get a feel for how much practice is enough in any given situation. For an important presentation, four or five practice runs is not excessive. Your credibility is dramatically enhanced when you move seamlessly through your presentation, matching effective words with each slide. Practising helps keep you on track, helps you maintain a conversational tone with your audience, and boosts your confidence and composure.

If you're addressing an audience that doesn't speak your language, consider using an interpreter. Working with an interpreter does constrain your presentation somewhat. For one thing, you must speak slowly enough for the interpreter to keep up with you; however, don't speak so slowly that the rest of your audience loses interest. Send your interpreter a copy of your speech and visuals as far in advance of your presentation as possible. If your audience is likely to include persons with hearing impairments, be sure to team up with a sign-language interpreter as well.

Any time you deliver an oral presentation to people from other cultures, you may need to adapt the content of your presentation. It is also important to take into account any cultural differences in appearance, mannerisms, and other customs. Your interpreter or host will be able to suggest appropriate changes for a specific audience or particular occasion.

Practising your oral presentation with a co-worker or a friend is an effective way to polish your public speaking skills in a relaxed setting. What should your audience look for to help you improve as a speaker?

You'll know you've practised enough when you can present the material at a comfortable pace and in a conversational tone, without the need to read your slides or constantly refer to your notes.

Overcoming Anxiety

If you're nervous about facing an audience, you're not alone: Even speakers with years of experience feel some anxiety about getting up in front of an audience. Polished speakers know how to use that nervous energy to their advantage. As you practise your speech, think of nervousness as an indication that you care about your audience, your topic, and the occasion. If your palms get wet or your mouth goes dry, don't think of it as nerves—think of it as excitement. Such stimulation can give you the extra energy you need to make your presentation sparkle. Here are some ways to harness your nervous energy to become a more confident speaker:[24]

> **Prepare more material than necessary.** Combined with a genuine interest in your topic, extra knowledge will reduce your anxiety.
> **Practise.** The more familiar you are with your material, the less panic you'll feel.
> **Think positively.** See yourself as polished and professional, and your audience will too.
> **Visualize your success.** Use the few minutes before you actually begin speaking to tell yourself you're on and

Preparation is the best antidote for anxiety.

Learning to focus on and interact with the audience while using electronic slides or other visuals takes practice. How do you adapt your platform manner for this type of situation?

you're ready. Visualize yourself in front of the audience, feeling confident, prepared, and able to handle any situation that might arise.[25]

> **Take a few deep breaths.** Before you begin to speak, remember that your audience wants you to succeed, too.

> **Be ready.** Have your first sentence memorized and on the tip of your tongue.

> **Be comfortable.** Dress appropriately for the situation but as comfortably as possible. Drink plenty of water before your scheduled presentation time to ensure that your voice is well hydrated (bring a bottle of water with you, too). If possible, adjust the temperature in the room to your personal preference. The fewer physical distractions you have, the better you'll perform.

> **Don't panic.** If you sense that you're starting to race—a natural response when you're nervous—stop for a second and arrange your notes or perform some other small task while taking several deep breaths. Then, start again at your normal pace. If you feel that you're losing your audience, pull them back by involving them in the action; ask for their opinions or pause for questions.

> **Concentrate on your message and your audience, not on yourself.** When you're busy thinking about your subject and observing your audience's response, you tend to forget your fears.

> **Maintain eye contact with friendly audience members.** Once your presentation is under way, be particularly careful to maintain eye contact with your audience, shifting your gaze periodically around the room. Looking directly at your listeners will make you appear sincere, confident, and trustworthy. It also helps you get an idea of the impression you're creating.

> **Keep going.** Your confidence level will increase as you continue, with each successful minute giving you more and more self-assurance.

Handling Questions Responsively

Objective 7 Identify six ways that effective speakers use to handle questions responsively.

Don't leave the question-and-answer period to chance: Anticipate likely questions and think through your answers.

The question-and-answer period is one of the most important parts of an oral presentation. Questions give you a chance to obtain important information, to emphasize your main idea and supporting points, and to build enthusiasm for your point of view. When you're speaking to high-ranking executives in your company, the question-and-answer period will often consume most of the time allotted for your presentation.[26]

Preparation is essential. Even if you can't anticipate every single question, learn enough about your audience to get an idea of their concerns. Think through answers to questions you're likely to get, even those to which you don't have a complete answer. Don't assume that you can handle whatever comes up.[27]

Pay attention to the questioner's body language and facial expression to help determine what the person really means (assuming that you can see your audience). Repeat the question to confirm your understanding and to ensure that the entire audience has heard it. If the question is vague or confusing, ask for clarification; then give a simple, direct answer. If you're asked to choose between two alternatives, don't feel you must do so. Offer your own choice instead, if it makes more sense.[28]

Be sure to answer the question you're asked. Don't sidestep it, ignore it, laugh it off, or get so caught up in the situation that you forget to respond. If giving an adequate answer would take too long, simply say, "I'm sorry, we don't have time to get into that issue right now, but if you'll see me after the presentation, I'll be happy to discuss it with you." If you don't know the answer, don't pretend that you do. Instead, say something like "I don't have those figures. I'll get them for you as quickly as possible."

You have less control over the proceedings during the question-and-answer session than during the rest of your presentation, but establish some ground rules up front. If appropriate—and it wouldn't be appropriate to do so if your audience consists of potential investors or your company's top managers—announce a time limit or a question limit per person. Plus, give as many audience members as possible a chance to participate by calling on people from different parts of the room.

If audience members try to turn a question into an opportunity to make their own mini-presentations, remember that it's up to you to stay in control. You might admit that you and the questioner have differing opinions and, before calling on someone else, offer to get back to the questioner once you've done more research. Or you might simply respond with a brief answer, avoiding a lengthy debate or additional questions.[29]

The question-and-answer session is often the most valuable part of a presentation. How should you prepare for it? How can the question-and-answer session enhance your reputation before your audience?

If a question ever puts you on the hot seat, respond honestly but keep your cool. Look the person in the eye, answer the question as well as you can, and keep your emotions under control. Avoid getting into a heated argument. Defuse hostility by paraphrasing the question and asking the questioner to confirm that you've understood it correctly. Maintain a businesslike tone of voice and a pleasant expression.[30]

When the time allotted for your presentation is up, call a halt to the question-and-answer session. Prepare the audience for the end by saying something such as, "Our time is almost up. Let's have one more question." After you've made your reply, summarize the main idea of the presentation and thank people for their attention. Conclude the way you opened: by looking around the room and making eye contact. Then, gather your notes and leave the podium, maintaining the same confident demeanour you've had from the beginning. For a reminder of the steps to take in developing an oral presentation, refer to "Checklist: Developing Oral Presentations."

Maintaining control during the question-and-answer session can be a challenge, particularly if any audience members outrank you in the corporate hierarchy.

If you ever face hostile questions, don't duck; respond honestly and directly while keeping your cool.

CHECKLIST Developing Oral Presentations

A. Plan your oral presentation.
✔ Analyze the situation by defining your purpose and developing an audience profile.
✔ Select the right medium.
✔ Organize your presentation by defining the main idea, limiting the scope, choosing your approach, and preparing your outline.

B. Write your oral presentation.
✔ Adapt to your audience by tailoring your style and language.
✔ Compose your presentation by preparing an introduction, body, and close.
✔ Use your introduction to arouse audience interest, build your credibility, and preview your message.

✔ Use the body to connect your ideas and hold your audience's attention.
✔ Use the close to restate your main points and describe the next steps.

C. Complete your oral presentation.
✔ Master the art of delivery by choosing a delivery method, knowing your material, and practising your delivery.
✔ Check the location and equipment in advance.
✔ Determine whether you should use an interpreter.
✔ Overcome anxiety by preparing thoroughly.
✔ Handle questions responsively.

Summary of Learning Objectives

1 **Explain the importance of oral presentations in your career success.** Oral presentations give you the opportunity to highlight all of your communication skills, from planning and researching a project to producing and delivering it. Executives will note your ability to deal with audiences, react spontaneously to questions, and present information through effective visuals—all qualities that will show your ability to handle challenging assignments.

2 **Explain how to adapt the three-step writing process to oral presentations.** Both written and oral communication require analyzing the situation, determining your purpose, doing research, and organizing information. However, in most cases, you won't write out every word of a presentation, but rather think through key phrases and perhaps draft your opening and closing statements. Keep in mind that, unlike a written document, an oral presentation is a one-time event, so audience members cannot browse through the speaker's comments to verify something said earlier. Consequently, unlike document writers, presenters must find ways to capture audience attention and keep it so listeners will remember what is said. The completion stage for presentations involves a wider range of tasks, including testing your presentation slides, verifying equipment operation, practising your speech, and creating handout materials.

3 **Discuss the three functions of an effective introduction.** An effective introduction arouses audience interest, sometimes in imaginative ways, such as by uniting the audience around a common goal, asking a question, telling a story, or stating a startling statistic. An effective introduction also builds the speaker's credibility to gain the audience's trust and previews the message to keep the audience on track.

4 **Identify six ways to keep your audience's attention during your presentation.** Keep your audience's attention by relating your information to their needs. In addi-

tion, anticipate your audience's questions, use concrete and familiar language to keep your audience engaged, explain the relationship between your subject and familiar ideas, pause for feedback as needed to promote audience interest, and illustrate your ideas with visuals.

5 **Explain how visuals enhance oral presentations, and discuss the importance of design consistency in visual support.** Visuals enhance presentations by adding interest, illustrating and clarifying important points, and helping your audience absorb and understand information. Consistency simplifies the viewing and listening process for your audience and enables them to pay closer attention to your message, rather than spending time trying to figure out your visuals.

6 **Highlight six major issues to consider when you're preparing to give a presentation online.** Online presentations lack the immediacy and nuances of face-to-face communication, so ensure that you ask questions frequently to gauge your audience's level of understanding. Furthermore, your audience may have trouble following complex material, so consider sending information before the presentation and simplifying slide content. The resolution of your audience's monitor may be low, so consider the level of detail in your visual support. Corporate firewalls may prevent streaming video from reaching your audience, and some people in remote locations may have slow connections; consequently, add extra time for start-up.

7 **Identify six ways that effective speakers use to handle questions responsively.** Effective speakers predict questions, so they can give informed answers. They are also sensitive to the questioner's body language to determine any deeper meanings to the questions. Furthermore, effective speakers answer the question asked, limit the length of their responses, establish time limits or other rules for questions, and respond to hostile questions honestly, directly, and calmly.

PEARSON mycanadianbuscommlab™

Visit www.mycanadianbuscommlab.ca for everything you need to help you succeed in the job you've always wanted! Tools and resources include the following:
- Composing Space and Writer's Toolkit
- Document Makeovers
- Video Case Studies
- Grammar Exercises—and much more!

On the Job PERFORMING COMMUNICATION TASKS AT TELEFILM CANADA

Wayne Clarkson speaks to a variety of industry and government audiences. To succeed with each one, he must focus his purpose and tailor his content to reach them successfully. As an intern with Telefilm Canada's head office, you are asked to help plan a speech Clarkson will deliver to an audience of directors, producers, and actors as well as journalists at the Toronto International Film Festival. Clarkson's topic is Telefilm's recent successes, and he is allocated about 10 minutes for his talk. For the following situations choose the best solution and explain your answer.

1 How should Clarkson begin his speech?
 a Clarkson should immediately list films supported by Telefilm that have been box-office hits.
 b Clarkson should discuss the history of Telefilm.
 c Clarkson should show some brief video clips of successful Telefilm-supported productions.
 d Clarkson should ask the audience what they know about Telefilm.

2 You are considering including statistics in Clarkson's speech, such as the number of awards Telefilm-supported films have won, the amount of worldwide distribution, and profits. What is the best way of presenting this quantitative information?
 a Clarkson should use electronic slides to highlight this information.
 b Clarkson should express this information orally.
 c Clarkson should use overhead transparencies.
 d Statistical information should not be used.

3 How should Clarkson end his speech?
 a Clarkson should discuss the need for more funding for Telefilm Canada and ask Canadian audience members to write to the Standing Committee on Canadian Heritage, Telefilm's supervisory body.
 b Show brief film clips of Telefilm-sponsored movies.
 c Make positive, unifying remarks, thank the audience, and distribute handouts about Telefilm Canada.
 d Make positive, unifying remarks, thank the audience, but do not distribute handouts about Telefilm Canada.

Test Your Knowledge

1 What is an effective way to respond if you feel nervous right before giving a presentation?

2 How does the completion stage of the three-step writing process differ between reports and presentations?

3 Why do you have to limit your scope when planning a presentation?

4 What do you want to achieve with the introduction to your speech? With the close of your speech?

5 If you suspect that your audience doesn't really care about the topic you plan to discuss, how can you generate interest in your presentation?

6 If you're giving a presentation in a subject area that you've researched thoroughly but in which you don't have any hands-on experience, how do you build credibility?

7 What are the advantages of electronic presentations over transparencies?

8 What are the key rules for designing effective text visuals? Graphic visuals?

9 As a speaker, what nonverbal signals can you send to appear more confident?

10 What can speakers do to maintain control during the question-and-answer period of a presentation?

Apply Your Knowledge

1 Would you rather (a) deliver an oral presentation to an outside audience, (b) be interviewed for a news story, or (c) make a presentation to a departmental meeting? Why? How do the communication skills differ among those situations? Explain.

2 How might the audience's attitude affect the amount of audience interaction during or after a presentation? Explain your answer.

3 If you were giving an oral presentation on the performance of a company product, what three attention-getters might you use to enliven your speech?

4 How can you use the slide master to enhance the effectiveness of your slides?

5 **Ethical Choices** Is it ethical to use design elements and special effects to persuade an audience? Why or why not?

Running Cases

Watch on mycanadianbuscommlab

> CASE 1 Noreen

The Petro-Go senior management team has decided to move forward with the merger of the "Go Points" department and the credit card sales/service department. They approved Noreen's proposal and report and decided to implement this plan across all national and international centres.

Noreen is about to deliver a business presentation to the staff in both departments. She needs to introduce herself, explain how the departments have merged, and discuss how job roles will change. She plans to show the new organizational chart during her presentation and mention that all centres will merge the two departments, so all credit card sales/service staff will also market the points program and all "Go Points" staff will now conduct credit card sales and offer service to existing credit card customers. Staff will be provided with product, systems, and service training as well as new phone scripts and procedures manuals.

QUESTIONS

a) What features will Noreen's audience have in common?

b) When creating visual slides what principles must Noreen remember?

c) Is the direct or indirect approach best?

d) How can Noreen arouse the audience's interest on this topic?

e) In the event the equipment fails during Noreen's speech, what backup plan should she have?

YOUR TASK

Prepare this presentation. Assume you are Noreen. Create a speech outline and an electronic slide show. Deliver the presentation to a group.

> CASE 2 Kwong

Kwong has to prepare a presentation for his final course in his CGA program and seeks his manager's permission to use ET Canada as his case study. Kwong will have to gather some company information and get approval to use it for his course project. Kwong's manager would like to see his project before Kwong presents it to his class. Kwong plans to discuss the software systems used at ET Canada and the policies and procedures the company follows to gather information electronically from the national branches into the head office. System screen shots (pictures of data screens) will be used and charts, graphs or other reported information may be included in Kwong's presentation.

QUESTIONS

a) What must Kwong consider when sharing company data with the public?

b) How can Kwong arouse the audience's interest on this topic?

c) Should Kwong prepare handouts for the audience? If so, when should he hand them out?

d) How will Kwong ensure that the audience can clearly see the screen shots and other visuals in the slide show?

e) What should Kwong include in the introductory part of the speech?

YOUR TASK

Create a similar presentation. Investigate how your college or university computer labs work. How are they networked? What software is loaded? How can students get access? Where can students get help? How much does it cost? Who maintains the network and software licences/upgrades? Take some screen shots and include them in an electronic slide show. Prepare a speech outline and then present your findings to a group.

Practise Your Knowledge

DOCUMENT 14.A

Examine the slide in Figure 14–11 and point out any problems you notice. How would you correct these problems?

DOCUMENT 14.B

Examine the graph in Figure 14–12 and explain how to modify it for an electronic presentation using the guidelines discussed in this chapter.

> Figure 14–11 Piece of Cake Bakery Electronic Slide #8

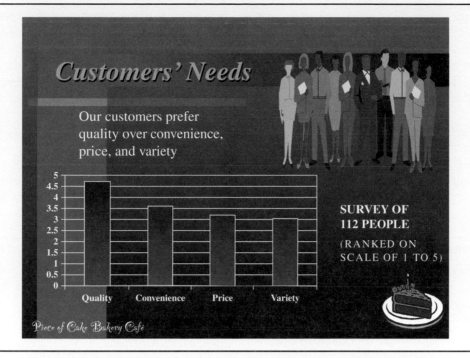

> Figure 14–12 CommuniCo Employee Training Costs

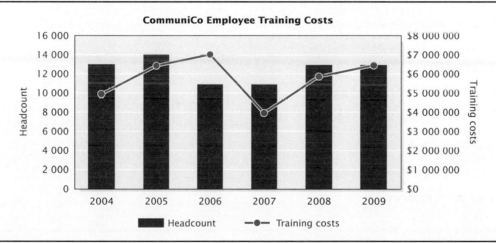

DOCUMENT 14.C

Visit www.mycanadianbuscommlab.ca, click on the Business Communication tab, then select Textbook Resources and download Document 14.C. Watch the presentation in slide show mode. After you've watched the presentation, identify at least three ways in which various animations, builds, and transitions either enhanced or impeded your understanding of the subject matter.

Exercises

14.1 Mastering Delivery: Analysis

Attend a presentation at your school or in your area, or watch a speech on television. Categorize the speech as one that motivates or entertains, one that informs or analyzes, or one that persuades or urges collaboration. Then, compare the speaker's delivery with this chapter's "Checklist: Developing Oral Presentations." Write a two-page report analyzing the speaker's performance and suggesting improvements.

14.2 Mastering Delivery: Nonverbal Signals

Observe and analyze the delivery of a speaker in a school, at work, or in another setting. What type of delivery did the speaker use? Was this delivery appropriate for the occasion? What nonverbal signals did the speaker use to emphasize key points? Were these signals effective? Which nonverbal signals would you suggest to further enhance the delivery of this oral presentation—and why?

14.3 Ethical Choices

Think again about the oral presentation you observed and analyzed in Exercise 14.2. How could the speaker have used nonverbal signals unethically to manipulate the audience's attitudes or actions?

14.4 Teamwork

You've been asked to give an informative 10-minute presentation on vacation opportunities in your home province. Draft your introduction, which should last no more than 2 minutes. Then, pair off with a classmate and analyze each other's introductions. How well do these two introductions arouse the audience's interest, build credibility, and preview the presentation? Suggest how these introductions might be improved.

14.5 Completing Oral Presentations: Self-Assessment

How good are you at planning, writing, and delivering oral presentations? Rate yourself on each of the following elements of the oral presentation process. Then, examine your ratings to identify where you are strongest and where you can improve, using the tips in this chapter.

Element of Presentation Process	Always	Frequently	Occasionally	Never
1. I start by defining my purpose.				
2. I analyze my audience before writing an oral presentation.				
3. I match my presentation length to the allotted time.				
4. I begin my oral presentations with an attention-getting introduction.				
5. I look for ways to build credibility as a speaker.				
6. I cover only a few main points in the body of my presentation.				
7. I use transitions to help listeners follow my ideas.				
8. I review main points and describe next steps in the close.				
9. I practise my presentation beforehand.				
10. I prepare in advance for questions and objections.				
11. I conclude oral presentations by summarizing my main idea.				

14.6 Creating Effective Slides: Content

Look through recent issues (print or online) of *Canadian Business*, *BusinessWeek*, *Fortune*, or other business publications for articles discussing challenges that a specific company or industry is facing. Using the articles and the guidelines discussed in this chapter, create three to five slides summarizing these issues.

14.7 Creating Effective Slides: Content and Design

You've been asked to give an informative 10-minute talk to a group of conventioneers on great things to see and do while visiting your hometown. Write the content for three or four slides (including a cover slide). Then, think about the design elements for your slides. Describe design choices you would make, particularly in terms of colours, fonts, drawings, and photography.

14.8 Completing Electronic Presentations: Slide Sorter View

Visit www.mycanadianbuscommlab.ca, click on the Business Communication tab, select Textbook Resources, then select PowerPoints. Download any one of the presentations listed. Then, use the *slide sorter view* to critique the content, layout, and design elements of this presentation. Edit and revise the slides to improve their overall effectiveness.

14.9 Internet

Creating hyperlinks to live websites can add life to an electronic presentation, but it also means being prepared for the unexpected. What are some obstacles you might encounter when creating live internet links? How can you prepare in advance to overcome such obstacles?

Building Careers and Writing Résumés

After studying this chapter, you will be able to

1. Explain the importance and features of an employment portfolio
2. Describe the approach most employers take to finding potential new employees
3. Discuss how to choose the appropriate résumé organization, and list the advantages and disadvantages of the three common options
4. Describe the problem of résumé fraud
5. Outline the major sections of a traditional résumé
6. Describe what you should do to adapt your résumé to a scannable format

ON THE JOB

Communicating at Tim Hortons

RECRUITING TOP TALENT

www.timhortons.com

With 3000 locations nationally and such programs as the Tim Horton Children's Foundation Camp, Smile Cookie charity donations, Community Clean-Up, and Earn-a-Bike, Tim Hortons is both Canada's most recognized fast-food chain and an influential corporate citizen. Supporting the famous franchise is the TDL Group, the operator of the Tim Hortons chain that manages its continuing growth across Canada and the United States. Through such areas as distribution, purchasing, owner training, real estate, and financial planning, this behind-the-scenes company administers the entire Tim Hortons system.

TDL looks for people who like challenges, approach their job with a "can do" attitude, enjoy working on a team, and "appreciate the freedom to develop their skills and move ahead." By searching under "corporate opportunities" on the Tim Horton's website, applicants will find a variety of challenging jobs. These include bilingual customer service agent: liaising between store owners and centralized shipping and operations, the applicant must be fluent in both French and English as well as have high-level computer skills, particularly in warehouse management software. The position of employee relations representative requires up-to-date knowledge of human resources practices and employment law. The work of district supervisor demands extensive experience in the hospitality industry and strong problem-solving skills. All positions require high interpersonal, organizational, and communication competence.

Through effective workforce recruiting, Tim Hortons has achieved a dominant position in the fast-food business. Managed by the TDL Group, the renowned Canadian franchise offers job seekers opportunities in finance, marketing, human resources, property management, and other fields that support the growth of the retail chain.

Job seekers are asked to complete an online application by entering a cover letter and résumé, answering a series of questions about their experience in the food service field, their education, and salary expectations. They are required to list skills they feel are relevant to the position, noting their proficiency level on a scale from "no knowledge" to "expert," and the number of years they've used that skill. TDL makes contact after reviewing the submission.

Tuition reimbursement, training programs, and opportunities to be involved with the Tim Horton Children's Foundation are some of the benefits of working for TDL. The company prides itself on innovation, excellence, hard work—and respect for its employees. If you were interested in working at TDL, how would you do research for a corporate-level position? How would you plan and prepare your résumé to be noticed by recruiters?[1]

Building a Career with Your Communication Skills

Successful job hunters view the search as a comprehensive process—and put all of their communication skills to work.

Obtaining the job that's right for you takes more than sending out a few résumés and application letters. As you get ready to enter (or re-enter) the workplace, explore the wide range of actions you can take to maximize your perceived value and find the ideal career opportunities. The skills you've learned in research, planning, and writing will help you every step of the way.

Understanding Today's Dynamic Workplace

Social, political, and financial events continue to change workplace conditions from year to year, so the job market you read about this year might not be the same market you try to enter a year or two from now. However, you can count on a few forces that are likely to affect your entry into the job market and your career success in years to come:[2]

For many workers, the employment picture is less stable today than it was in years past.

> **Stability.** Your career probably won't be as stable as careers were in your parents' generation. In today's business world, your career will be affected by globalization, mergers and acquisitions, short-term mentality driven by the demands of stockholders, ethical upheavals, and the relentless quest for lower costs. On the plus side, new opportunities, new companies, and even entire industries can appear almost overnight, so while your career might not be as predictable as careers used to be, it could well be more of an adventure.

> **Lifetime employment.** The idea of *lifetime employment,* in which employees spend their entire working lives with a single firm that takes care of them throughout their careers, is all but gone in many industries. Boeing, the aerospace giant, speaks of lifetime *employability,* rather than lifetime employment, putting the responsibility on employees to track market needs and keep their skills up to date—even changing careers if necessary.

> **Growth of small business.** Small business is a major engine of job creation in Canada, so chances are good that you'll work for a small firm at some point. The corporate layoffs of 2009 produced an increase in small-business startups, as former executives and managers turned their skills toward fulfilling the needs of consumers through their own independent companies.[3] Furthermore, it is predicted that retirees will be an entrepreneurial force as consultants and other service-sector providers instead of pursuing such traditional retirement activities as golf and travel.[4]

> **Increase in independent contractors.** The nature of employment itself is changing for many people. As companies try to become more flexible, more employees are going solo and setting up shop as independent contractors, sometimes selling their services back to the very companies they just left.
> **Changing view of job-hopping.** Given all these changes, job-hopping doesn't have quite the negative connotation it once had. Even so, you still need to be careful about jumping at every new opportunity that promises more money or prestige. Recruiting and integrating new employees takes time and costs money, and most employers are reluctant to invest in someone who has a history of switching jobs numerous times.

What do all these forces mean to you? First, take charge of your career—and stay in charge of it. Understand your options, have a plan, and don't count on others to watch out for your future. Second, as you've learned throughout this course, understanding your audience is key to successful communication, starting with understanding how employers view today's job market.

HOW EMPLOYERS VIEW TODAY'S JOB MARKET From the employer's perspective, the employment process is always a question of balance. Maintaining a stable workforce can improve practically every aspect of business performance, yet many employers feel they need the flexibility to shrink and expand payrolls as business conditions change. Employers obviously want to attract the best talent, but the best talent is more expensive and more vulnerable to offers from competitors, so there are always financial trade-offs to consider.

Employers also struggle with the ups and downs of the economy, just as employees do. When unemployment is low, the balance of power shifts to employees, and employers have to compete to attract and keep top talent. When unemployment is high, the power shifts back to employers, who can afford to be more selective and less accommodating. In other words, pay attention to the economy whenever you're job-hunting; at times you can be more aggressive but at other times you should be more accommodating.

Rather than looking for lifelong employees for every position, many employers now fill some needs by hiring temporary workers or engaging contractors on a project-by-project basis. Many Canadian and U.S. employers are now also more willing to move jobs to cheaper labour markets outside the country and to recruit globally to fill local positions. Both trends have stirred controversy, especially in the technology sector, as firms recruit top engineers and scientists from abroad while shifting mid- and low-range jobs to India, China, Russia, and other countries with lower wage structures.[5]

WHAT EMPLOYERS LOOK FOR IN JOB APPLICANTS Given the forces in the contemporary workplace, employers are looking for people who can adapt to the new dynamics of the business world, can survive and thrive in fluid and uncertain situations, and can continue to learn throughout their careers. Companies want team players with strong work records, leaders who are versatile, and employees with diversified skills and varied job experience.[6] In addition, most employers expect college and university graduates to be sensitive to intercultural differences and to have a sound understanding of international affairs.[7] In fact, in some cases, your chances of being hired are better if you've studied abroad, learned another language, or can otherwise demonstrate an appreciation of other cultures.

Adapting to Today's Job Market

Adapting to the workplace is a lifelong process of seeking the best fit between what you want to do and what employers are willing to pay you to do. For example, if money is more important to you than anything else, you can certainly

Computer capabilities and internet access have fuelled the growth of small business. Would you like to pursue a career in business but have the flexibility to work from home? What special communication skills might be needed to be a successful entrepreneur?

Changes in the job market mean you need to take charge of your career, rather than counting on a single employer to look out for you.

The nature of the job market fluctuates with the ups and downs of the economy.

Most employers value employees who are flexible, adaptable, and sensitive to the complex dynamics of today's business world.

pursue jobs that promise high pay; just be aware that most of these jobs require years of experience, and many produce a lot of stress, require frequent travel, or have other drawbacks you'll want to consider. In contrast, if location, lifestyle, intriguing work, or other factors are more important to you, you may well have to sacrifice some level of pay to achieve them. To find a satisfying job, ensure that you know what you want to do, what you have to offer, and how to make yourself more attractive to employers.

WHAT DO YOU WANT TO DO? Economic necessities and the vagaries of the marketplace will influence much of what happens in your career, of course; nevertheless, it's wise to start your employment search by examining your own values and interests. Identify what you want to do first and then see whether you can find a position that satisfies you at a personal level while also meeting your financial needs.

> Have you thought long and hard about what you really want to do in your career? The choices you make now could influence your life for years to come.

> **What would you like to do every day?** Research occupations that interest you. Find out what people really do every day. Ask friends, relatives, or alumni from your school.
> **How would you like to work?** Consider how much independence you want on the job, how much variety you like, and whether you prefer to work with products, machines, people, ideas, figures, or some combination thereof. Do you want constant change or a predictable role?
> **What specific compensation do you expect?** What do you hope to earn in your first year? What's your ultimate earnings goal? Are you willing to settle for less money to do something you really love?
> **Can you establish some general career goals?** Consider where you'd like to start, where you'd like to go from there, and the ultimate position you'd like to attain.
> **What size company would you prefer?** Do you like the idea of working for a small, entrepreneurial operation or a large corporation?
> **What sort of corporate culture are you most comfortable with?** Would you be happy in a formal hierarchy with clear reporting relationships or a less structured environment? Do you prefer teamwork or individualism? Do you like a competitive environment?
> **What location would you like?** Would you like to work in a city, a suburb, a small town, or an industrial area? Do you favour a particular part of the country? Another country? (See "Achieving Intercultural Communication: Looking for Work Around the World.")

WHAT DO YOU HAVE TO OFFER? Knowing what you *want* to do is one thing. Knowing what you *can* do is another. You may already have a good idea of what you can offer employers. If not, some brainstorming can help you identify your skills, interests, and characteristics. Start by jotting down 10 achievements you're proud of, such as learning to ski, taking a prize-winning photo, tutoring a child, or editing your school paper. Think carefully about what specific skills these achievements demanded of you. For example, leadership skills, speaking ability, and artistic talent may have helped you coordinate a winning presentation to your school's administration. As you analyze your achievements, you'll begin to recognize a pattern of skills. Which of them might be valuable to potential employers?

Next, look at your educational preparation, work experience, and extracurricular activities. What do your knowledge and experience qualify you to do? What have you learned from volunteer work or class projects that could benefit you on the job? Have you held any offices, won any awards or scholarships, mastered a second language?

Take stock of your personal characteristics. Are you aggressive, a born leader? Or would you rather follow? Are you outgoing, articulate, great with people? Or do

> No matter what profession you're in, you are a valuable package of skills and capabilities; ensure that you have a clear picture of your own strengths.

TIPS FOR SUCCESS

"The best way to get started is to brainstorm about your natural talents and abilities. Write down everything you've accomplished, even as far back as childhood. This is a confidence boost and also can help you get everything out on paper that you could possibly include in your résumé."

Hallie Crawford, professional coach

ACHIEVING INTERCULTURAL COMMUNICATION

Looking for Work Around the World

If your goal is a career with an international focus, check out your school's office of international affairs for work abroad opportunities. You will find extensive information on its website and access to advisors and students who have international work experience. You'll be able to sign on with an organization that offers students assistance with foreign work permits and provides housing and job leads.

To help ensure success in your own search for employment abroad, keep these points in mind:

> **Give yourself plenty of time.** Finding a job in another country is a complicated process that requires extensive and time-consuming research.

> **Research thoroughly, both online and off.** In addition to your school's resources, you can find numerous websites that offer advice, job listings, and other information. For a good look at the range of international opportunities, visit www.InternAbroad.com, www.VolunteerAbroad.com, www.TeachAbroad.com, and www.JobsAbroad.com However, people with international experience will tell you that you can't limit your research to the Web. Like any job search, networking is crucial, so join cultural societies with international interests, volunteer with exchange student programs, or find other ways to connect with people who have international experience.

> **Consider all the possibilities.** Keep an open mind when you're exploring your options; you'll probably run across situations you hadn't considered at the beginning of your search. For example, you might find that an unpaid internship in your future profession would help your career prospects more than a paying position in some other industry.

> **Be flexible.** If you have to settle for something less than that dream job, focus on the big picture, which for most students is the cultural opportunity.

Finding a job in another country can be a lot of work, but the rewards can be considerable. As many students have found, working in a culture is the best way to get a true sense of it.

CAREER APPLICATIONS

1 How might international work experience help you in a career in Canada, even if you never work abroad again?

2 If your work history involves political activities, either paid or volunteer, explain how you might present this information on a résumé intended for international readers.

---

you prefer working alone? Make a list of what you believe are your four or five most important qualities. Ask a relative or friend to rate your traits as well.

If you're having difficulty figuring out your interests, characteristics, or capabilities, consult your school's placement office. Many campuses administer a variety of tests to help you identify interests, aptitudes, and personality traits. These tests won't reveal your "perfect" job, but they'll help you focus on the types of work best suited to your personality.

Your school's placement office can point you to a variety of tests to gauge your interest and suitability for a variety of career possibilities.

HOW CAN YOU MAKE YOURSELF MORE VALUABLE? While you're figuring out what you want from a job and what you can offer an employer, you can take positive steps now toward building your career.

Take an active approach to making yourself a more attractive job candidate—and it's never too early to start.

> **Take interim assignments.** As you search for a permanent job, consider temporary jobs, freelance work, volunteer projects, or internships. These temporary assignments not only help you gain valuable experience and relevant contacts but also provide you with important references and with items for your portfolio (see the following section).[8]

> **Consider applying your talents to crowdsourcing projects.** To accomplish these projects, companies and non profit organizations invite the public to contribute solutions to various challenges. For example, Fellowforce (www.fellowforce.com) posts projects involving advertising, business writing, photography, graphic design, programming, strategy development, and other skills.[9] Even if your contributions aren't chosen, you still have solutions to real business problems that you can show to potential employers as examples of your work.

> **Learn more about the industry or industries in which you want to work.** Stay on top of new developments by joining networks of professional colleagues and friends who can help you keep up with your occupation and industry. Many professional societies have student chapters or offer students discounted memberships. Take courses and pursue other educational or life experiences that would be hard to get while working full-time.

Keep your eyes and your mind open as you approach every experience in school, part-time jobs, and social engagements.

Even after an employer hires you, it's a good idea to continue improving your skills, to distinguish yourself from your peers and to make yourself more valuable to current and potential employers. Acquire as much technical knowledge as you can, build broad-based life experience, and develop your social skills. Learn to respond to change in positive, constructive ways; doing so will help you adapt if your "perfect" career path eludes your grasp. Learn to see each job, even so-called entry-level jobs, as an opportunity to learn more and to expand your knowledge, experience, and social skills. Share what you know with others instead of hoarding knowledge in the hope of becoming indispensable; helping others excel is a skill, too.[10]

Building an Employment Portfolio

Objective 1 Explain the importance and features of an employment portfolio.

Employers want proof that you have the skills to succeed on the job, but even if you don't have much relevant work experience, you can use your university and college classes to assemble that proof. Simply create and maintain an employment portfolio, which is a collection of projects that demonstrate your skills and knowledge. You can create both a print portfolio and an e-portfolio; both can help with your career effort. A print portfolio gives you something tangible to bring to interviews, and it lets you collect project results that might not be easy to show online, such as a handsomely bound report.

An e-portfolio is a multimedia presentation of your skills and experiences.[11] Think of it as a website that contains your résumé, work samples, letters of recommendation, articles you may have written, and other information about you and your skills. You can be creative. For example, a student who was pursuing a degree in meteorology added a video clip of himself delivering a weather forecast.[12] The portfolio can be burned on a CD-ROM for physical distribution or, more commonly, posted online—whether it's a personal website, your school's site (if student pages are available), or a networking site such as www.collegegrad.com or www.portfolios.com. To see a selection of student e-portfolios, visit MyCanadianBusCommLab.

Pay close attention to the activities and cases marked "Portfolio Builder" in Chapters 7–10. These items will make particularly good samples of not only your communication skills but your ability to understand and solve business-related challenges. By combining these projects with samples from your other courses, you can create a compelling portfolio by the time you're ready to start interviewing. Your portfolio is also a valuable resource for writing your résumé because it reminds you of all the great work you've done over the years. Moreover, you can continue to refine and expand your portfolio throughout your career; many professionals, such as graphic designers, use e-portfolios to advertise their services.

As you assemble your portfolio, collect anything that shows your ability to perform, whether it's in school, on the job, or in other venues. However, you must check with an employer before including any items you created while you were an employee. Many business documents contain confidential information that companies don't want distributed to outside audiences.

For each item you add to your portfolio, write a brief description that helps other people understand the meaning and significance of the project. Include items such as these:

> **Background.** Why did you undertake this project? Was it a school project, an article you wrote on your own initiative, or something else?
> **Project objectives.** Explain the project's goals, if relevant.
> **Collaborators.** If you worked with others, be sure to mention that and discuss team dynamics, if appropriate. For instance, if you led the team or worked with others long distance as a virtual team, point that out.
> **Constraints.** Sometimes the most impressive thing about a project is the time or budget constraints under which it was created. If these apply to a project, consider mentioning them in a way that doesn't sound like an excuse for poor quality. If you had only one week to create a website, for example, you might say, "One of the intriguing challenges of this project was the deadline; I had only one week to design, compose, test, and publish this material."
> **Outcomes.** If the project's goals were measurable, what was the result? For example, if you wrote a letter soliciting donations for a charitable cause, how much money did you raise?
> **Learning experience.** If appropriate, describe what you learned during the course of the project.

Keep in mind that the portfolio itself is a communication project, too, so be sure to apply everything you learn in this course about effective communication and good design. Also, assume that every potential employer will find your e-portfolio site (even if you don't tell them about it), so don't include anything that could come back to haunt you.

To get started, first check with the career centre at your university or college; many schools now offer e-portfolio systems for their students. (Some schools now require e-portfolios, so you may already be building one.) You can also find plenty of advice online; search for "e-portfolio" or "student portfolio." Finally, consider reading *Portfolios for Technical and Professional Communicators* by Herb J. Smith and Kim Haimes-Korn. This book is intended for communication specialists, but it offers valuable advice for anyone who wants to create a compelling employment portfolio.

Securing Employment in Today's Job Market

Understanding how employers approach the hiring process is just one of many insights and skills you need to conduct a successful job search. After you've armed yourself with knowledge of today's workplace and your potential role in it, it's time to launch an efficient, productive process to find that ideal position. Finding the ideal job opportunity is a six-step process that you might repeat a number of times during your career; Figure 15–1 shows the most important tasks in the search process. This chapter discusses the first two, and Chapter 16 explores the final four.

Understanding Employers' Approach to the Employment Process

You can save considerable time and effort by understanding how employers approach the recruiting process (see Figure 15–2). Generally, employers prefer to look for candidates within their own organization or through referrals from people they know and trust. Overall, personal contacts appear to be the prime

Objective 2 Describe the approach most employers take to finding potential new employees.

> Figure 15–1 The Employment Search

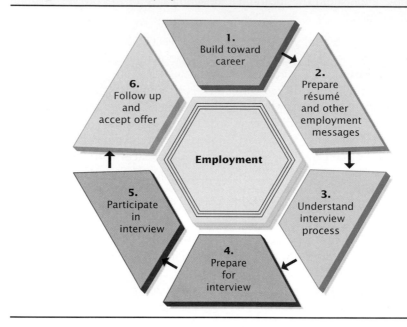

source of jobs, regardless of whether a candidate has just graduated from college or has been out of school for several years.[13] Increasingly, these personal referrals can come through social networking websites, a fact that highlights the importance of networking (see page 529).

Many employers send representatives to campuses to conduct student interviews, which are usually coordinated by the campus placement office. In addition, many employers accept unsolicited résumés, and most keep unsolicited résumés on file or in a database. **Applicant tracking systems,** such as the one used by Tim Hortons for online applications, help employers sift through the hundreds or thousands of résumés they receive each year. Employers also recruit candidates through employment agencies, government employment services, temporary staffing services, and the employment bureaus operated by some trade associations. They also post jobs through ads in newspapers, trade magazines, campus publications, their own websites, and job sites such as Monster.ca, www.workopolis.com, and www.careerowl.ca, where employers can search by occupation or by region. In fact, major job boards such as Monster.ca and CareerBuilder.ca have grown so popular that some employers feel deluged with résumés, and some job seekers fear it's becoming impossible to stand out from the crowd when hundreds or thousands of people are applying for the same jobs. As a result, many specialized websites are now springing up to focus on narrow

> Figure 15–2 How Organizations Prefer to Find New Employees

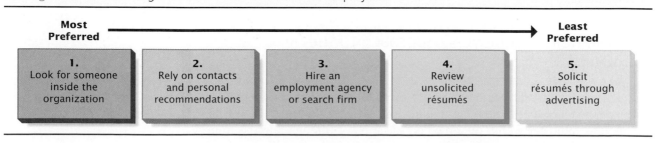

parts of the job market or offer technology that promises to do a better job of matching employers and job searchers. For example, the PublicPac.ca service offers specialized job networks for Canadians, including www.jobwings.com, which focuses on finance and accounting jobs in Canada, and nicejob.ca, a Canadian bilingual job search engine.[14]

Look again at Figure 15–2, and you'll notice that the easiest way for you to find out about new opportunities—through the employer's outside advertising—is the employer's least-preferred way of finding new employees. As many as 80 percent of all job openings are never advertised, a phenomenon known as the *hidden job market*.[15] In other words, employers have looked in quite a few other places before they come looking for you. To find the best opportunities, it's up to you to take action to get yourself noticed. But be confident; throughout this course, you've developed the communication skills to present yourself to the world effectively.

It's important to understand that the easiest way for you to find jobs (through companies' help-wanted advertising) is the least-preferred channel for many companies to find new employees.

Organizing Your Approach to the Employment Process

The employment process can be time-consuming, so organize your efforts carefully to save time and maximize your chances. Begin by finding out where the job opportunities are, which industries are strong, and which specific job categories offer the best prospects for the future. From there you can investigate individual organizations, doing your best to learn as much about them as possible. If you plan to search in another country, heed the advice in "Communicating Across Cultures: Looking for Work Around the World."

With so many print and electronic resources available today, it's easy to stay in touch with what's happening in the business world.

STAYING ABREAST OF BUSINESS AND FINANCIAL NEWS Thanks to the internet, staying on top of business news is easy today. In fact, your biggest challenge will be selecting new material from the many available sources. To help you get started, here is a selection of websites that offer business news (in some cases, you need to be a subscriber to access all the material, including archives):

> *The Globe and Mail:* www.globeandmail.com
> *The National Post:* www.nationalpost.com
> *Canadian Business:* www.canadianbusiness.com
> *Wall Street Journal:* http://online.wsj.com
> *New York Times:* www.nytimes.com
> *Business 2.0:* www.business2.com
> *BusinessWeek:* www.businessweek.com
> *Fast Company:* www.fastcompany.com
> *Fortune:* www.fortune.com
> *Forbes:* www.forbes.com

In addition, thousands of bloggers and podcasters offer news and commentary on the business world. To identify those you might find helpful, start with directories such as Technorati (www.technorati.com/blogs/business) for blogs or Podcast Alley (www.podcastalley.com; select the "Business" genre) for podcasts. For all these online resources, use a newsfeed aggregator (see Chapter 7) to select the type of stories you're interested in and have them delivered to your screen automatically.

Of course, with all the business information available today, it's easy to get lost in the details. Don't get too caught up in the daily particulars of business. Start by examining "big picture" topics—trends, issues, industry-wide challenges, and careers—before delving into specific companies that look attractive.

Would you like a career that keeps you on your feet and out of an office? Specialized job boards offer unique short- and long-term opportunities in the food industry, building trades, and the environment. Check out www.canadiancareers.com for jobs such as these. How would you sell yourself for this kind of employment?

RESEARCHING SPECIFIC COMPANIES Chapter 11 discusses how to find information on individual industries and companies, and it provides a list of popular business resources. Review those sources, as well as professional and trade journals in the fields that interest you. Once you've identified a promising industry and career field, consult directories of employers at your school library, at your career centre, or on the internet, and compile a list of specific organizations that appeal to you.

Go beyond every company's own communication materials; find out what others in their industries and communities think about them.

In addition to using the Web to find detailed information about prospective employers, you can use it to look for and respond to job openings. Most companies, even small firms, offer at least basic information about themselves on their websites. Look for the "About Us" or "Company" part of the site to find a company profile, executive biographies, press releases, financial information, and information on employment opportunities. You'll often find information about an organization's mission, products, annual reports, and employee benefits. Plus, you can often download annual reports, descriptive brochures, or newsletters. Any company's website is going to present the firm in the most positive light possible, of course, so look for outside sources as well, including the business sections of local newspapers and trade publications that cover the company's industries and markets.

Table 15–1 lists some websites where you can learn more about companies and find job openings. Start with Service Canada's Job Bank www.jobbank.gc.ca,

> Table 15–1 Netting a Job on the Web

Website*	URL	Highlights
Job Bank (Service Canada)	www.jobbank.gc.ca	Comprehensive site for government and private-sector jobs. Create a job account and save it on the site with a personalized service code. You can create a job profile and receive job alerts by email that match it. French and English.
Monster	www.monster.ca	One of the most popular job sites, with hundreds of thousands of openings, many from hard-to-find smaller companies; extensive collection of advice on the job search process.
Workopolis	www.workopolis.com	Billed as "Canada's biggest job site," Workopolis contains tips and advice from experts in addition to an extensive job list classified by province and career track.
MonsterTrak	www.monstertrak.ca	Focused on job searches for new grads; your school's career centre site probably links here
Yahoo! Canada Hotjobs	http://ca.hotjobs.yahoo.com	Another leading job board, formed by the recent merger of Hotjobs and Yahoo! Careers
CareerBuilder	www.careerbuilder.ca	Fast-growing site affiliated with more than 100 local newspapers around the country that include career advice.
CareerOwl	www.careerowl.ca	Browse by occupation and read recent articles about the Canadian job scene. Contains numerous job search resources.
Dice.com	www.dice.com	One of the best sites for high-technology jobs for both Canada and the U.S.
Net-Temps	www.net-temps.ca	Popular site for contractors and freelancers looking for short-term assignments.

*This list represents only a fraction of the hundreds of job-posting sites and other resources available online; ensure that you check with your school's career centre for the latest information.

where you can search jobs and find links to other job sites. Your school's career centre placement office probably maintains an up-to-date list as well.

NETWORKING **Networking** is the process of making informal connections with a broad sphere of mutually beneficial business contacts. According to one recent survey, networking is the most common way that employees find jobs.[16] Networking takes place wherever and whenever people talk, for example, at industry functions, at social gatherings, at sports events and recreational activities, in online newsgroups, or at alumni reunions. Increasingly, business-oriented social networking sites such as LinkedIn (www.linkedin.com) and Ryze (www.ryze.com) have become important ways to get connected with job openings. Some of these sites are even linked to job-posting websites, and when you apply for a job at a particular company, you can see a list of people in your network who work at that company. The website PartnerUp (www.partnerup.com) offers opportunities to entrepreneurs seeking work with small businesses. Facebook (www.facebook.com), best known as a social networking site, is fast becoming a job-recruitment site for employers, who can use a software product such as Jobvite (www.jobvite.com) to survey personal profiles for potential employees.[17]

To find helpful networks, both the in person and online variety, read news sites, blogs, and other online sources. Participate in student business organizations, especially those with ties to professional organizations such as the Canadian Marketing Association or an affiliate of the Canadian Council of Human Resources Associations. Visit *trade shows* that cater to an industry you're interested in. You will learn plenty about that sector of the workplace and meet people who actually work in the industry.[18] Hundreds of trade shows are held every year around the country, and many are open to the public for free or for a nominal fee. Don't overlook volunteering in social, civic, and religious organizations. As a volunteer, you not only meet people but also demonstrate your ability to solve problems, plan projects, and so on.

> Start thinking like a networker now; your classmates could turn out to be some of your most important business contacts.

Novice job seekers sometimes misunderstand networking and unknowingly commit breaches of etiquette. Networking isn't a matter of walking up to strangers at social events, handing over your résumé, and asking them to find you a job. Rather, it involves the sharing of information between people who might be able to offer mutual help at some point in the future. Think of it as an organic process, in which you cultivate the possibility of finding that perfect opportunity. Networking can take time, so start early and make it part of your lifelong program of career management.

> Remember that you need to contribute to the networking process, too.

To become a valued network member, you need to be able to help others in some way. You may not have any influential contacts yet, but because you're actively researching a number of industries and trends in your own job search, you probably have valuable information you can share. Or you might simply be able to connect one person with another person who can help. The more you network, the more valuable you become in your network—and the more valuable your network becomes to you.

Job fairs are good places to start your job search. How should you prepare to attend a job fair? What should you bring with you? How should you dress?

Don't overlook the many resources available through your college or university's placement office.

SEEKING CAREER COUNSELLING College and university placement offices offer individual counselling, credential services, job fairs, on-campus interviews, and job listings. They can give you advice on résumé-writing software and provide workshops in job search techniques, résumé preparation, interview techniques, and more.[19] You can also find job counselling online. You might begin your self-assessment, for example, with the Keirsey Temperament Sorter, an online personality test at www.keirsey.com. For excellent job-seeking pointers and counselling, visit your school's career centre. Major online job boards such as Monster.ca also offer a variety of career-planning resources.

Preparing Résumés

The job search process involves many forms of communication, but the centrepiece of this effort is a well-written résumé. In fact, your success in finding a job will depend on how carefully you plan, write, and complete your résumé. Some job searchers are intimidated by the prospect of writing a résumé, but it is really just another specialized business message. Follow the three-step writing process, and you will be able to create a résumé that effectively presents your qualifications and achievements (see Figure 15–3). Remember to pay particular attention to the "you" attitude and presentation quality; your résumé will probably get tossed aside if it doesn't speak to audience needs or if it contains mistakes.

> Figure 15–3 Three-Step Writing Process for Résumés

Planning

Analyze the Situation
Recognize that the purpose of your résumé is to get an interview, not to get a job.

Gather Information
Research target industries and compa- nies so you know what they're looking for in new hires; learn about various jobs and what to expect.

Select the Right Medium
Start with a traditional paper résumé and develop scannable, plain-text, or HTML versions as needed.

Organize the Information
Choose an organizational model that highlights your strengths and downplays your shortcomings.

Writing

Adapt to Your Audience
Plan your wording carefully so you can catch a recruiters eye within seconds; translate your education and experience into attributes that target employers find valuable.

Compose the Message
Write clearly and succinctly, using active, precise language that is appropriate to the industries and companies you're targeting; use a professional tone in all communications, even when using email.

Completing

Revise the Message
Evaluate your content and review readability, clarity, and accuracy.

Produce the Message
Use effective design elements and suitable layout for a clean, professional appearance.

Proofread the Message
Review for errors in layout, spelling, and mechanics; mistakes can cost you interview opportunities.

Distribute the Message
Deliver your résumé following the specific instructions of each employer or job-board website.

1   2   3

Planning Your Résumé

Your résumé must be more than a simple list of the jobs you've held. It needs to tell the "story of you"—who you are, what you've accomplished, and, most importantly, what you can contribute to any organization that hires you. As with other business messages, planning a résumé means analyzing your purpose and your audience, gathering information, choosing the best medium, and organizing your content. Be prepared to craft several or perhaps many versions of your résumé. By making some simple changes in wording or organization, you'll probably be able to match your value more closely to the specific opportunities offered by particular employers.

ANALYZING YOUR PURPOSE AND AUDIENCE A résumé is a structured, written summary of a person's education, employment background, and job qualifications. Recognize that your résumé is a persuasive business message intended to stimulate an employer's interest in meeting you and learning more about you. (Table 15–2 lists some common misconceptions about résumés.) A successful résumé inspires a prospective employer to invite you to interview with the company. In other words, your purpose in writing your résumé is to create interest—*not* to tell readers every little detail.[20]

When you view your résumé as a persuasive business message, it's easier to decide what should and shouldn't be in it.

Because you've already completed a good deal of research on specific companies, you should know quite a bit about the organizations you'll apply to. But take some time now to learn what you can about the individuals who may read your résumé. For example, if you learned of an opportunity through your networking efforts, chances are you'll have both a contact name and some personalized advice to help fine-tune your writing. Search online using the person's name; you might find him or her mentioned in a news release, magazine article, or blog. Any bit of information can help you craft a more effective message. Even if you can't identify a specific hiring manager, put yourself in your audience's position, so you'll be able to tailor your résumé to satisfy your audience's needs. Why would they be interested in learning more about you?

By the way, if employers ask to see your "CV," they're referring to your *curriculum vitae*, the term used instead of *résumé* in some professions and in many countries outside Canada and the United States. Résumés and CVs are essentially the same, although CVs can be more detailed. If you need to adapt a Canadian-style résumé to CV format, or vice versa, see Monster.ca, which has helpful guidelines on the subject.

> Table 15–2 Fallacies and Facts About Résumés

Fallacy	Fact
The purpose of a résumé is to list all your skills and abilities.	The purpose of a résumé is to generate interest and an interview.
A good résumé will get you the job you want.	All a résumé can do is get you in the door.
Your résumé will be read carefully and thoroughly.	In most cases, your résumé needs to make a positive impression within 30 or 45 seconds; moreover, it may be screened by a computer looking for keywords first, and if it doesn't contain the right keywords, a human being may never see it.
The more good information you present about yourself in your résumé, the better.	Recruiters don't need that much information about you at the initial screening stage, and they probably won't read it.
If you want a really good résumé, have it prepared by a résumé service.	You have the skills needed to prepare an effective résumé, so prepare it yourself—unless the position is especially high-level or specialized. Even then, you should check carefully before using a service.

GATHERING PERTINENT INFORMATION If you haven't been building an employment portfolio thus far, you may need to do some research on yourself. Gather all the pertinent personal history you can think of, including all the specific dates, duties, and accomplishments of any previous jobs you've held. Collect every piece of relevant educational experience that adds to your qualifications—formal degrees, skills certificates, academic awards, or scholarships. Also, gather any relevant information about personal endeavours: dates of your membership in an association, offices you may have held in a club or professional organization, any presentations you might have given to a community group. You probably won't use every piece of information you come up with, but you'll want to have it at your fingertips before you begin composing your résumé.

SELECTING THE BEST MEDIUM Selecting the medium for your résumé used to be a simple matter: You typed on paper. These days, though, your job search might involve various forms, including an uploaded Word document, a plain-text document that you paste into an online form, or a multimedia résumé that is part of your online e-portfolio. Explore all your options and choose those that (a) meet the requirements of target employers and (b) allow you to present yourself in a compelling fashion. For example, if you're applying for a sales position, in which your personal communication skills would be a strong point, a vidcast showing you making a sales presentation (even a mock presentation) could be a strong persuader.

No matter how many different media you eventually use, it's always a good idea to prepare a basic paper résumé and keep copies on hand. You'll never know when someone might ask for it, and not all employers want to bother with electronic media when all they want to know is your basic profile. In addition, starting with a traditional paper résumé is a productive way to organize your background information and identify your unique strengths.

ORGANIZING YOUR RÉSUMÉ AROUND YOUR STRENGTHS The most successful résumés convey seven qualities that employers seek: They demonstrate that you (1) think in terms of results, (2) know how to get things done, (3) are well rounded, (4) show signs of career progress and professional development, (5) have personal standards of excellence,(6) are flexible and willing to try new things, and (7) communicate effectively.

The key to organizing a résumé is aligning your personal strengths with both the general and specific qualities that your target employers are looking for.

Although you may want to include a little information in all categories, you'll naturally want to emphasize the information that does the best job of aligning your career objectives with the needs of your target employers—and that does so without distorting or misrepresenting the facts.[21] Do you have something in your history that might trigger an employer's red flag? Here are some common problems and some quick suggestions for overcoming them:[22]

Frequent job changes and gaps in your work history are two of the more common issues that employers may perceive as weaknesses, so plan to address these if they pertain to you.

> **Frequent job changes.** If you've had a number of short-term jobs of a similar nature, such as independent contracting and temporary assignments, see if you can group them under a single heading. Also, if past job positions were eliminated as a result of mergers or other factors beyond your control, find a subtle way to convey that information (if not in your résumé, then in your cover letter). Reasonable employers understand that many otherwise stable employees have been forced to hold short-term jobs in recent years.

> **Gaps in work history.** Mention relevant experience and education you gained during employment gaps, such as volunteer or community work. If gaps are due to personal problems such as drug or alcohol abuse or mental illness, offer honest but general explanations about your absences ("I had serious health concerns and had to take time off to fully recover").

> **Inexperience.** Mention related volunteer work. List relevant course work and internships. If appropriate, offer hiring incentives such as "willing to work nights and weekends."

> **Over-qualification.** Tone down your résumé, focusing exclusively on the experience and skills that relate to the position.

> **Long-term employment with one company.** Itemize each position held at the firm to show career progress with increasing responsibilities.

> **Job termination for cause.** Be honest with interviewers. Show that you're a hard-working employee and counter their concerns with proof, such as recommendations and examples of completed projects.

> **Criminal record.** You don't necessarily need to disclose a criminal record or time spent incarcerated on your résumé, but you may be asked about it on a job application form. Laws regarding what employers may ask vary by jurisdiction, and what might be done with or in reliance upon the results can also vary by jurisdiction.[23] If you are asked about a criminal record and the question applies to you, you must answer truthfully, or you risk being terminated later if the employer finds out. Use the interview process to explain any mitigating circumstances and to emphasize your rehabilitation and commitment to being a law-abiding, trustworthy employee.[24]

To focus attention on your strongest points, adopt the appropriate organizational approach for your résumé, based on your background and your goals.

The Chronological Résumé In a **chronological résumé**, the work-experience section dominates and is placed in the most prominent slot, immediately after the name and address and optional objective. Develop this section by listing your jobs sequentially in reverse order, beginning with the most recent position. Under each listing, describe your responsibilities and accomplishments, giving the most space to the most recent positions. If you're just graduating from college or university with limited professional experience, you can vary this chronological approach by putting your educational qualifications before your experience, thereby focusing attention on your academic credentials.

The chronological approach is the most common way to organize a résumé, and many employers prefer it. This approach has three key advantages: (1) Employers are familiar with it and can easily find information, (2) it highlights growth and career progression, and (3) it highlights employment continuity and stability.[25] As vice-president with Korn/Ferry International, Robert Nesbit speaks for many recruiters: "Unless you have a really compelling reason, don't use any but the standard chronological format. Your résumé should not read like a treasure map, full of minute clues to the whereabouts of your jobs and experience. I want to be able to grasp quickly where a candidate has worked, how long, and in what capacities."[26]

The chronological approach is especially appropriate if you have a strong employment history and are aiming for a job that builds on your current career path. This is the case for Roberto Cortez. Compare the ineffective and effective versions of Cortez's résumé in Figures 15–4 and 15–5. The ineffective résumé exhibits a wide range of problems: The language is self-centred and unprofessional, and the organization forces the reader to dig out essential details—and today's recruiters don't have the time or the patience for that. The improved version does a much better job of presenting the candidate's ability to contribute to a new employer. Notice in particular how easy it is to scan through this résumé to find sections of interest.

The Functional Résumé A **functional résumé**, sometimes called a *skills résumé*, emphasizes your skills and capabilities while identifying employers and academic experience in subordinate sections. This pattern stresses individual

Explore

Objective 3 Discuss how to choose the appropriate résumé organization, and list the advantages and disadvantages of the three common options.

The chronological résumé is the most common approach, but it might not be right for you at a particular stage in your career.

The functional résumé is often used by people with little employment history to show or gaps in their work history, but some employers suspect that people who use this approach are trying to hide weaknesses in their backgrounds.

> Figure 15–4 Ineffective Chronological Résumé

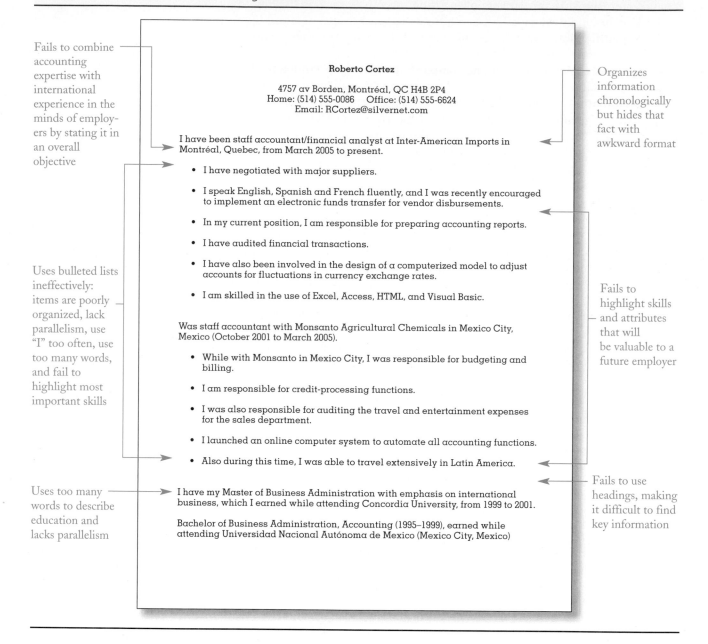

Fails to combine accounting expertise with international experience in the minds of employers by stating it in an overall objective

Organizes information chronologically but hides that fact with awkward format

Uses bulleted lists ineffectively: items are poorly organized, lack parallelism, use "I" too often, use too many words, and fail to highlight most important skills

Fails to highlight skills and attributes that will be valuable to a future employer

Uses too many words to describe education and lacks parallelism

Fails to use headings, making it difficult to find key information

Roberto Cortez

4757 av Borden, Montréal, QC H4B 2P4
Home: (514) 555-0086   Office: (514) 555-6624
Email: RCortez@silvernet.com

I have been staff accountant/financial analyst at Inter-American Imports in Montréal, Quebec, from March 2005 to present.

- I have negotiated with major suppliers.

- I speak English, Spanish and French fluently, and I was recently encouraged to implement an electronic funds transfer for vendor disbursements.

- In my current position, I am responsible for preparing accounting reports.

- I have audited financial transactions.

- I have also been involved in the design of a computerized model to adjust accounts for fluctuations in currency exchange rates.

- I am skilled in the use of Excel, Access, HTML, and Visual Basic.

Was staff accountant with Monsanto Agricultural Chemicals in Mexico City, Mexico (October 2001 to March 2005).

- While with Monsanto in Mexico City, I was responsible for budgeting and billing.

- I am responsible for credit-processing functions.

- I was also responsible for auditing the travel and entertainment expenses for the sales department.

- I launched an online computer system to automate all accounting functions.

- Also during this time, I was able to travel extensively in Latin America.

I have my Master of Business Administration with emphasis on international business, which I earned while attending Concordia University, from 1999 to 2001.

Bachelor of Business Administration, Accounting (1995–1999), earned while attending Universidad Nacional Autónoma de Mexico (Mexico City, Mexico)

areas of competence, so it's useful for people who are just entering the job market, who want to redirect their careers, or who have little continuous career-related experience. The functional approach also has three advantages: (1) Without having to read through job descriptions, employers can see what you can do for them; (2) you can emphasize earlier job experience; and (3) you can de-emphasize any lack of career progress or lengthy unemployment. However, you should be aware that because the functional résumé can obscure your work history, many employment professionals are suspicious of it—and some assume that candidates who use it are trying to hide something. In fact, Monster.com lists the functional résumé as one of employers' "Top 10 Pet Peeves."[27] If you don't have a strong, uninterrupted history of relevant work, the combination résumé might be a better choice.

> Figure 15–5 Effective Chronological Résumé

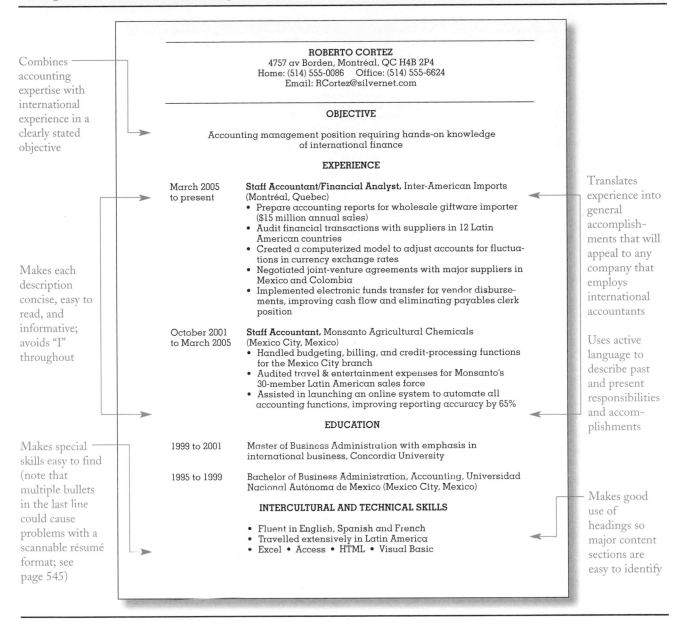

Combines accounting expertise with international experience in a clearly stated objective

Makes each description concise, easy to read, and informative; avoids "I" throughout

Makes special skills easy to find (note that multiple bullets in the last line could cause problems with a scannable résumé format; see page 545)

ROBERTO CORTEZ
4757 av Borden, Montréal, QC H4B 2P4
Home: (514) 555-0086   Office: (514) 555-6624
Email: RCortez@silvernet.com

OBJECTIVE

Accounting management position requiring hands-on knowledge
of international finance

EXPERIENCE

March 2005
to present

Staff Accountant/Financial Analyst, Inter-American Imports
(Montréal, Quebec)
- Prepare accounting reports for wholesale giftware importer
($15 million annual sales)
- Audit financial transactions with suppliers in 12 Latin
American countries
- Created a computerized model to adjust accounts for fluctuations in currency exchange rates
- Negotiated joint-venture agreements with major suppliers in
Mexico and Colombia
- Implemented electronic funds transfer for vendor disbursements, improving cash flow and eliminating payables clerk
position

October 2001
to March 2005

Staff Accountant, Monsanto Agricultural Chemicals
(Mexico City, Mexico)
- Handled budgeting, billing, and credit-processing functions
for the Mexico City branch
- Audited travel & entertainment expenses for Monsanto's
30-member Latin American sales force
- Assisted in launching an online system to automate all
accounting functions, improving reporting accuracy by 65%

EDUCATION

1999 to 2001   Master of Business Administration with emphasis in
international business, Concordia University

1995 to 1999   Bachelor of Business Administration, Accounting, Universidad
Nacional Autónoma de Mexico (Mexico City, Mexico)

INTERCULTURAL AND TECHNICAL SKILLS

- Fluent in English, Spanish and French
- Travelled extensively in Latin America
- Excel • Access • HTML • Visual Basic

Translates experience into general accomplishments that will appeal to any company that employs international accountants

Uses active language to describe past and present responsibilities and accomplishments

Makes good use of headings so major content sections are easy to identify

The Combination Résumé A **combination résumé** includes the best features of the chronological and functional approaches. Nevertheless, it is not commonly used, and it has two major disadvantages: (1) It tends to be longer and (2) it can be repetitive if you have to list your accomplishments and skills in both the functional section and the chronological job descriptions.[28] With her limited work experience in her field of interest, Erica Vorkamp opted for a combination résumé to highlight her skills (see Figure 15–6). Her employment history is complete and easy to find, but it isn't featured to the same degree as the other elements. Also, because she created an HTML version and posted it on her personal website, she is able to provide instant links to other information, such as samples of her work and testimonials from people who have worked with her in the past.

✳ Explore

If you don't have a lot of work history to show, consider a combination résumé to highlight your skills while still providing a chronological history of your employment.

> Figure 15–6 Combination Resume

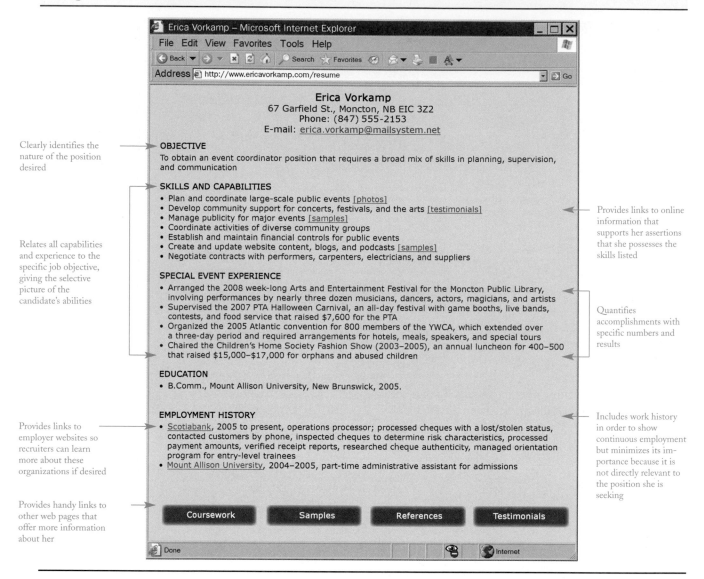

Clearly identifies the nature of the position desired

Relates all capabilities and experience to the specific job objective, giving the selective picture of the candidate's abilities

Provides links to employer websites so recruiters can learn more about these organizations if desired

Provides handy links to other web pages that offer more information about her

Provides links to online information that supports her assertions that she possesses the skills listed

Quantifies accomplishments with specific numbers and results

Includes work history in order to show continuous employment but minimizes its importance because it is not directly relevant to the position she is seeking

Writing Your Résumé

Until employers meet you in person, your résumé (and perhaps your cover letter) is usually the only information they have about you, so ensure that the information is clear and compelling.

Your résumé is one of the most important documents you'll ever write. Follow the three-step process and help ensure success by remembering four key points:

> **First, treat your résumé with the respect it deserves.** Until you're able to meet with employers in person, you *are* your résumé, and a single mistake or oversight can cost you interview opportunities.

> **Second, give yourself plenty of time.** Don't put off preparing your résumé until the last second and then try to write it in one sitting.

> **Third, learn from good models.** You can find thousands of sample résumés online at job sites such as Monster.ca.

> **Fourth, don't get frustrated by the conflicting advice you'll read about résumés; they are more art than science.** Consider the alternatives and choose the approach that makes the most sense to you, given everything you know about successful business communication.

You can take some comfort in the fact that many people, even accomplished writers, find it difficult to write their own résumés. Part of this problem stems from the challenge of writing a compelling message in limited space, and part from the awkward feeling of talking about oneself to strangers. You might find it helpful to distance yourself emotionally from the task; you can even pretend you're writing about someone else. You might also find a classmate or friend who's also writing a résumé and swap projects for a while. By working on each other's résumés, you might be able to speed up the process for both of you.

KEEPING YOUR RÉSUMÉ HONEST At some point in the writing process, you're sure to run into the question of honesty. A claim may be clearly wrong ("So what if I didn't get those last two credits—I got the same education as people who did graduate, so it's OK to say that I graduated too"). Or a rationalization may be more subtle ("Even though the task was to organize the company picnic—that qualifies as 'project management'"). Either way, the information is dishonest.

Objective 4 Describe the problem of résumé fraud.

Somehow, the idea that "everybody lies on their résumés" has crept into popular consciousness, and résumé fraud has reached epidemic proportions. As many as half of the résumés now sent to employers contain false information. And it's not just the simple fudging of a fact here and there. Dishonest applicants are getting bolder—buying fake diplomas online, paying computer hackers to insert their names into prestigious universities' graduation records, and signing up for services that offer phony employment verification.[29]

Applicants with integrity know they don't need to lie to compete in the job market. If you are tempted to stretch the truth, bear in mind that professional recruiters have seen every trick and deception, and employers who are fed up with the dishonesty are getting more aggressive at uncovering the truth. Roughly 80 percent now contact references and conduct criminal background checks, and many do credit checks when the job involves financial responsibility.[30] In a recent survey in Great Britain, 25 percent of employers reported withdrawing job offers after discovering that applicants lied on their résumés.[31] And even if you were to get past these filters, you'd probably be exposed on the job when you couldn't live up to your own résumé. Résumé fabrications have been known to catch up to people many years into their careers, with embarrassing consequences.

Applicants with integrity know they don't need to lie on their résumés to catch the attention of potential employers.

If you're not sure whether to include something in your résumé, ask yourself this: Would you be willing to say the same thing to the interviewer in person? If you wouldn't be comfortable saying in it person, don't say it in your résumé. Keep your résumé honest so it represents who you really are and leads you toward jobs that are truly right for you.

ADAPTING YOUR RÉSUMÉ TO YOUR AUDIENCE Your résumé needs to make a positive impression in a matter of seconds, so be sure to adopt a "you" attitude and think about your résumé from the employer's perspective. Ask yourself: What key qualifications will this employer be looking for? Which of these qualifications are your greatest strengths? What quality would set you apart from other candidates in the eyes of a potential employer? What are three or four of your greatest accomplishments, and what resulted from these accomplishments? No matter which format you use or what information you include, the single most important concept to keep in mind as you write is to translate your past accomplishments into perceived future potential. In other words, employers are certainly interested in what you've done in the past, but they're more interested in what you can do for them in the future. If necessary, customize your résumé for individual companies, too.

One of the biggest challenges in writing a résumé is to make your unique qualities apparent to readers *quickly;* they won't search through details if you don't look like an appealing candidate.

You may also need to translate your skills and experiences into the terminology of the hiring organization. For example, military experience can develop a number of skills that are valuable in business, but military terminology can sound like a foreign language to people who aren't familiar with it. Isolate the important general concepts and present them in common business language. Similarly, educational achievements in other countries might not align with the standard Canadian definitions of high schools, colleges, polytechnics, and universities. If necessary, include a brief statement explaining how your degree or certificate relates to Canadian expectations—or how your Canadian degree relates to expectations in other countries, if you're applying for work abroad.

Regardless of your background, it's up to you to combine your experiences into a straightforward message that communicates what you can do for your potential employer.[32] Think in terms of an image or a theme you'd like to project. Are you academically gifted? A campus leader? A well-rounded person? A creative genius? A technical wizard? By knowing yourself and your audience, you'll focus successfully on the strengths needed by potential employers.

> Although your résumé is a highly factual document, it should still tell the "story of you," giving readers a clear picture of the sort of employee you are.

COMPOSING YOUR RÉSUMÉ To save readers time and to state your information as forcefully as possible, write your résumé using a simple and direct style. (You may need to modify your approach for other countries.) Use short, crisp phrases instead of whole sentences, and focus on what your reader needs to know. Avoid using the word *I*, which can sound both self-involved and repetitious by the time you outline all your skills and accomplishments. Instead, start your phrases with strong action verbs such as these:[33]

> Draft your résumé using short, crisp phrases built around strong verbs and nouns.

accomplished	achieved	administered	approved	arranged
assisted	assumed	budgeted	chaired	changed
complied	completed	coordinated	created	demonstrated
developed	directed	established	explored	forecast
generated	identified	implemented	improved	initiated
installed	introduced	investigated	joined	launched
maintained	managed	motivated	operated	organized
oversaw	participated	performed	planned	presented
proposed	raised	recommended	reduced	reorganized
resolved	saved	served	set up	simplified
sparked	streamlined	strengthened	succeeded	supervised
systematized	targeted	trained	transformed	upgraded

For example, you might say, "Created a campus organization for students interested in entrepreneurship" or "Managed a fast-food restaurant and four employees." Whenever you can, quantify the results so that your claims don't come across as empty puffery. Don't just say you're a team player or detail oriented—show who you are by offering concrete proof.[34] Here are some additional examples of how to phrase your accomplishments using active statements that show results:

Avoid Weak Statements	Use Active Statements That Show Results
Responsible for developing a new filing system	Developed a new filing system that reduced paperwork by 50 percent
I was in charge of customer complaints and all ordering problems.	Handled all customer complaints and resolved all product order discrepancies
I won a trip to Europe for opening the most new customer accounts in my department.	Generated the highest number of new customer accounts in my department
Member of special campus task force to resolve student problems with existing cafeteria assignments	Assisted in implementing new campus dining program that balances student wishes with cafeteria capacity

In addition to presenting your accomplishments effectively, think carefully about the way you provide your name and contact information, educational credentials, employment history, activities and achievements, and relevant personal data.

Name and Contact Information An employer first needs to know who you are and where you can be reached. Your name and contact information constitute the heading of your résumé, so include the following:

> Your name
> Physical address (both permanent and temporary if you're likely to move during the job search process; however, if you're posting a résumé in an unsecured location online, leave off your physical address for security purposes)
> Email address
> Phone number(s)
> The URL of your personal web page or e-portfolio (if you have one)

Be sure that everything in your résumé heading is well organized and clearly laid out on the page.

If the only email address you have is through your current employer, get a free personal email address from one of the many services that offer them, such as Hotmail or Yahoo!. It's not fair to your current employer to use company resources for a job search; moreover, it sends a bad signal to potential employers. Also, if your personal email address is anything like precious.princess@something.com or HeyMe@something.com, get a new email address for your business correspondence.

Career Objective or Summary of Qualifications Experts disagree about the need to state a career objective on your résumé. Some argue that your objective is obvious from your qualifications, so stating your objective seems redundant. Some also maintain that such a statement labels you as having only one focus and thus limits your possibilities as a candidate (especially if you want to be considered for a variety of openings). Other experts argue that employers will try to categorize you anyway, so you might as well ensure that they attach the right label. They maintain that stating your objective up front gives employers an immediate idea of what you're all about.

Objective 5 Outline the major sections of a traditional résumé.

Be sure to provide complete and accurate contact information; mistakes in this section of the résumé are surprisingly common.

Get a professional-sounding email address for business correspondence (such as *firstname.lastname@something.com*), if you don't already have one.

Remember to check your college or university's career office for help in writing your résumé. Why is it important to speak with a career expert at your school?

Whether you choose to open with a career objective or a summary of qualifications, remember that the important point is to generate interest immediately.

Remember, your goal is to generate interest immediately. Consider the situation and the qualities the employer is looking for. If a stated objective will help you look like the perfect fit, then you should definitely consider adding it. Consider the following objectives:

A software sales position in a growing company requiring international experience.

Advertising assistant with print media emphasis requiring strong customer-contact skills.

With some careful writing, you can phrase your career objective in terms that highlight the reader's needs.

Both these objectives have an important aspect: Even though they are stating "your" objective, they are really about the employer's needs. Avoid self-absorbed (but all too common) statements such as "A fulfilling position that provides ample opportunity for career growth and personal satisfaction." Writers who include such statements have completely forgotten about audience focus and the "you" attitude.

A good alternative to a simple statement of career objectives is to highlight your strongest points in a brief *summary of qualifications*. A good summary of qualifications not only identifies the type of job you're interested in but also gives employers a compelling reason to consider you. Use short, direct phrases that highlight what you can bring to a new employer, such as in this example:

Summary of qualifications: Ten years of experience in commission selling, consistently meeting or exceeding sales goals through creative lead generation, effective closing techniques, and solid customer service.

The career objective or summary of qualifications may be the only section that employers read fully, so if you include either one, make it strong, concise, and convincing.

Your education might be one of your strongest selling points, so think carefully about how you will present it.

Education If you're still in school, education is probably your strongest selling point. Present your educational background in depth, choosing facts that support your "theme." Give this section a heading such as "Education," "Technical Training," or "Academic Preparation," as appropriate. Then, starting with the most recent, list the name and location of each school you attended, along with the term of your enrolment (in months and years), your major and minor fields of study, significant skills and abilities you've developed in your course work, and the degrees or certificates you've earned. If you're still working toward a degree, include in parentheses the expected date of completion. Showcase your qualifications by listing courses that have directly equipped you for the job you seek, and indicate any scholarships, awards, or academic honours you've received.

The education section also includes off-campus training sponsored by business or government. Include any relevant seminars or workshops you've attended, as well as the certificates or other documents you've received. Mention high school or military training only if the associated achievements are pertinent to your career goals.

Whether you list your grade-point average (GPA) depends on the job you want and the quality of your grades. If you choose to show a grade-point average, ensure that you mention the scale, especially if a five-point scale is used instead of a four-point scale. If you don't show your GPA on your résumé—and there's no rule saying you have to—be prepared to answer questions about it during the interview process because many employers will assume that your GPA is not spectacular if you didn't show it on your résumé. If your grades are better within your major than in other courses, you can also list your GPA as "Major GPA" and include only those courses within your major.

Education is usually given less emphasis in a résumé after you've worked in your chosen field for a year or more. If work experience is your strongest qualification, save the section on education for later in the résumé and provide less detail.

Work Experience, Skills, and Accomplishments As in the education section, the work-experience section should focus on your overall theme. Align your past with the employer's future. Call attention to the skills you've developed on the job and to your ability to handle increasing responsibility.

List your jobs (including military service) in reverse chronological order and include any part-time, summer, or intern positions, even if unrelated to your current career objective. Employers will see that you have the ability to get and hold a job—an important qualification in itself. If you have worked your way through school and contributed significantly to your education expenses, say so. Many employers interpret this accomplishment as a sign of both character and the ability to manage your time.

In each listing include the name and location of the employer. If readers are unlikely to recognize the organization, briefly describe what it does. When you want to keep the name of your current employer confidential, you can identify the firm by industry only ("a large video-game developer"). Alternatively, you might use the firm's name and request confidentiality in your application letter or include an underlined note at the top or bottom of your résumé: "Résumé submitted in confidence."

Before or after each job listing, state your functional title, such as "records clerk" or "salesperson." Don't make your role seem more important by glamourizing your job title, functions, or achievements. List the years you worked in the job and use the phrase "to present" to denote current employment. If a job was part time, say so.

Devote the most space to the jobs that are related to your target position. If you were personally responsible for significant achievements, be sure to mention it ("Devised a new collection system that accelerated payment of overdue receivables"). Facts about your skills and accomplishments are the most important information you can give a prospective employer, so quantify them whenever possible:

Designed a new ad that increased sales by 9 percent.

Raised $2500 in 15 days for cancer research.

One helpful exercise is to write a 30-second "commercial" for each major skill you want to highlight. The commercial should offer proof that you really do possess the skill. For your résumé, distill the commercials down to brief phrases; you can use the more detailed proof statements in cover letters and as answers to interview questions.[35]

You may also include information describing other aspects of your background that pertain to your career objective, such as fluency in another language. If you have an array of special skills, group them together and include them near your education or work-experience section. You might categorize such additional information as "Special Skills," "Work-Related Skills," "Other Experience," "Language Skills," or "Computer Skills." If samples of your work might increase your chances of getting the job, insert a line at the end of your résumé offering to supply them on request, or indicate they're available in your e-portfolio.

Activities and Achievements Many employers look beyond your formal employment to assess your total character and personality. Your activities and achievements outside work speak volumes about who you are and what you

When you describe past job responsibilities, ensure that you relate them to potential employers' needs—identify the skills and knowledge from these previous jobs that you can apply to a future job.

Whenever you can, quantify your accomplishments in numerical terms: sales increases, customer satisfaction scores, measured productivity, and so on.

Don't overlook personal accomplishments that indicate special skills or qualities, but ensure that they are relevant to the jobs you're seeking.

value. Use this section to list volunteer activities that demonstrate important abilities such as leadership, organization, teamwork, and cooperation. Emphasize career-related activities such as "member of the Student Marketing Association." List skills you learned in these activities and explain how these skills are related to your target job. Include speaking, writing, or tutoring experience; participation in athletics or creative projects; fundraising or community-service activities; and offices held in academic or professional organizations.

Note any awards you've received. Again, quantify your achievements whenever possible. Instead of saying that you addressed various student groups, state how many and the approximate audience sizes. If your activities have been extensive, you may want to group them into divisions such as "School Activities," "Community Service," "Professional Associations," "Seminars and Workshops," and "Speaking Activities."

Personal Data The question of what personal data to provide is a common source of confusion with résumés. Most experts advise you to skip personal interests unless including them enhances the employer's understanding of why you would be the best candidate for the job.[36] Just make sure that any personal interests and accomplishments relate to the employer's business, culture, or customers. For example, your achievements as an amateur artist could appeal to an advertising agency, even if you're applying for a technical or business position, because it shows an appreciation for the creative process. Similarly, an interest in sports and outdoor activities could show that you'll fit in nicely at a company such as Mountain Equipment Co-op.

Some information is best excluded from your résumé. Human rights legislation prohibits employers from discriminating on the basis of gender, marital or family status, age, race, colour, religion, national origin, and physical or mental disability. So ensure that you exclude any items that could encourage discrimination, even subconsciously. Experts also recommend excluding salary information, reasons for leaving jobs, and personal identification codes; save these items for the interview and then offer them only if the employer specifically requests them. Supply your social insurance number only when you are offered the job and are completing the required Revenue Canada and company benefit forms.

The availability of references is usually assumed, so you don't necessarily need to put "References available upon request" at the end of your résumé. Whether you include this line or not, be sure to have a list of several references available when you begin applying for jobs. You will probably be asked for it at some point in the selection process. Prepare your reference sheet with your name and contact information at the top. For a finished look, use the same design and layout you use at the top of your résumé. Then list three or four people who have agreed to serve as references. (Don't list anyone who hasn't agreed to be listed.) Include each person's name, job title, organization, address, telephone number, and email address (if the reference prefers to be contacted by email).

✓•⎯Practise ## Completing Your Résumé

When you're creating your résumé, the last step in the three-step writing process is no less important than the other two. As with any other business message, you need to revise your résumé, produce it in an appropriate form, and proofread it for any errors before distributing it to your target employers.

As a general guideline, if you have less than 10 years of professional experience, try to keep your résumé to one page. If you have a great deal of experience and are applying for a higher-level position, prepare a somewhat longer résumé.

For highly technical positions, longer résumés are often the norm as well because the qualifications for these jobs can require more space to describe.

REVISING YOUR RÉSUMÉ   Ask professional recruiters to list the most common mistakes they see on résumés, and you'll hear the same complaints over and over again. Keep your résumé out of the recycling bin by avoiding these flaws:

> **Too long.** The résumé is not concise, relevant, and to the point.
> **Too short or sketchy.** The résumé does not give enough information for a proper evaluation of the applicant.
> **Hard to read.** The résumé lacks enough white space and devices such as indentions and boldfacing to make the reader's job easier.
> **Wordy.** Descriptions are verbose, using numerous words describing simple concepts.
> **Too slick.** The résumé appears to have been written by someone other than the applicant, which raises the question of whether the qualifications have been exaggerated.
> **Amateurish.** The résumé includes the wrong information or presents it awkwardly, which indicates that the applicant has little understanding of the business world or of a particular industry.
> **Poorly produced.** The print is faint and difficult to read, or the paper is cheap and inappropriate.
> **Misspelled words and ungrammatical writing throughout.** The document contains spelling and grammar mistakes that indicate the candidate lacks the verbal skills that are so important on the job.
> **Boastful.** The overconfident tone makes the reader wonder whether the applicant's self-evaluation is realistic.
> **Gimmicky.** The words, structure, decoration, or material used in the résumé depart so far from the usual as to make the résumé ineffective.

PRODUCING YOUR RÉSUMÉ   Good design is a must, and it's not hard to achieve. As you can see in Figures 15–5 and 15–6, good designs feature simplicity, order, plenty of white space, and straightforward typefaces such as Times New Roman or Arial. (Keep in mind that many of the fonts on your computer are not appropriate for a résumé). Make your subheadings easy to find and easy to read, placing them either above each section or in the left margin. Use lists and leave plenty of white space, even if doing so forces you to use two pages rather than one. Colour is not necessary by any means, but if you add colour, make it subtle and sophisticated, such as in a thin horizontal line under your name and address. If any part of the design "jumps out at you," tone it down. To see how jarring and unprofessional a truly poor design looks to an employer, compare Figures 15–5 and 15–6 to the "creative" design in Figure 15–7, where the approach exhibits numerous flaws, including distracting lines, bad font choices, and unprofessional colours. The well-written information is completely lost in all the visual "noise." In fact, an amateurish design could end your chances of getting an interview. One experienced recruiter says, "At our office, these résumés are rejected without even being read."[37]

Depending on the companies you apply to, you might want to produce your résumé in as many as six forms (all are explained in the following sections):

Avoid the common errors that will get your résumé excluded from consideration.

Effective résumé designs are simple, clean, and professional—not gaudy, clever, or cute.

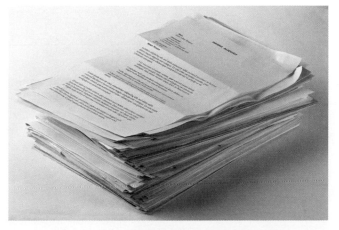

Job recruiters can receive hundreds of résumés a month. A well-formatted résumé makes their job easier and helps yours get noticed. How much time have you put into résumé preparation? What techniques can you use to streamline the process?

> Figure 15–7 Ineffective Résumé Design

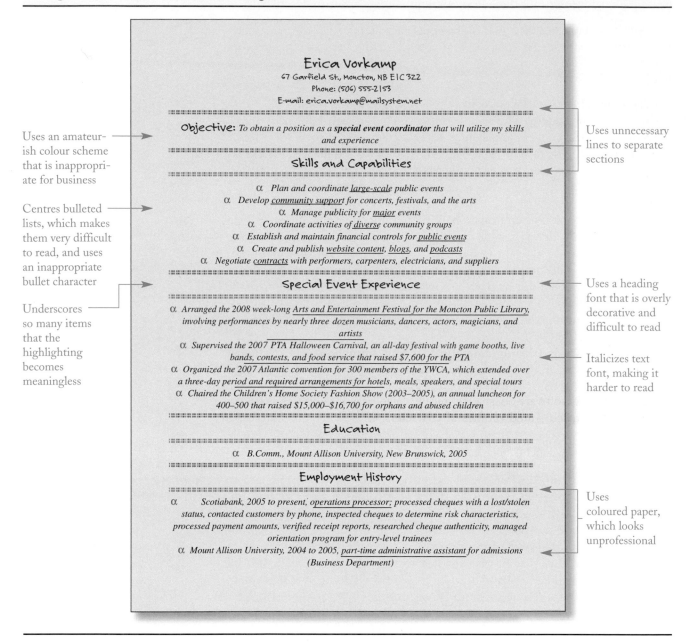

Uses an amateurish colour scheme that is inappropriate for business

Centres bulleted lists, which makes them very difficult to read, and uses an inappropriate bullet character

Underscores so many items that the highlighting becomes meaningless

Uses unnecessary lines to separate sections

Uses a heading font that is overly decorative and difficult to read

Italicizes text font, making it harder to read

Uses coloured paper, which looks unprofessional

Erica Vorkamp
67 Garfield St., Moncton, NB E1C 3Z2
Phone: (506) 555-2153
E-mail: erica.vorkamp@mailsystem.net

Objective: *To obtain a position as a* **special event coordinator** *that will utilize my skills and experience*

Skills and Capabilities

α *Plan and coordinate* <u>large-scale</u> *public events*
α *Develop* <u>community support</u> *for concerts, festivals, and the arts*
α *Manage publicity for* <u>major</u> *events*
α *Coordinate activities of* <u>diverse</u> *community groups*
α *Establish and maintain financial controls for* <u>public events</u>
α *Create and publish* <u>website content</u>, <u>blogs</u>, *and* <u>podcasts</u>
α *Negotiate* <u>contracts</u> *with performers, carpenters, electricians, and suppliers*

Special Event Experience

α *Arranged the 2008 week-long* <u>Arts and Entertainment Festival for the Moncton Public Library</u>, *involving performances by nearly three dozen musicians, dancers, actors, magicians, and artists*
α *Supervised the 2007 PTA Halloween Carnival, an all-day festival with game booths, live bands, contests, and food service that raised $7,600 for the PTA*
α *Organized the 2007 Atlantic convention for 300 members of the YWCA, which extended over a three-day period and required arrangements for hotels, meals, speakers, and special tours*
α *Chaired the Children's Home Society Fashion Show (2003–2005), an annual luncheon for 400–500 that raised $15,000–$16,700 for orphans and abused children*

Education

α *B.Comm., Mount Allison University, New Brunswick, 2005*

Employment History

α *Scotiabank, 2005 to present,* <u>operations processor</u>; *processed cheques with a lost/stolen status, contacted customers by phone, inspected cheques to determine risk characteristics, processed payment amounts, verified receipt reports, researched cheque authenticity, managed orientation program for entry-level trainees*
α *Mount Allison University, 2004 to 2005,* <u>part-time administrative assistant</u> *for admissions (Business Department)*

> Printed traditional résumé
> Printed scannable résumé
> Electronic plain-text file
> Microsoft Word file
> HTML format
> PDF file

Start with a traditional printed résumé, but realize that you may need to create several other versions during your job search.

Most of these versions are easy to create, as you'll see in the following sections. In addition to these six common options, you might consider creating a résumé slide show in Microsoft PowerPoint. Two key advantages of a PowerPoint résumé are the flexibility and multimedia capabilities. For instance, you can present a menu of choices on the opening screen and allow viewers to click through to such items as a brief biography, photos that document important accomplishments (such as an event you planned or a project you created for a class), or screen shots of websites that you were involved in creating. Be creative— and make sure you don't simply re-create your résumé in PowerPoint; doing so would result in a rather dull presentation that is actually harder to read than a regular printed version.

Printing a Traditional Résumé The traditional paper résumé still has a place in this world of electronic job searches, if only to have a few ready whenever one of your networking contacts asks for a copy. Avoid basic, low-cost white bond paper intended for general office use and gimmicky papers with borders and backgrounds. Choose a heavier, higher-quality paper designed specifically for résumés and other important documents. White or slightly off-white is the best colour choice. This paper is more expensive, but you don't need much, and it's a worthwhile investment.

When you're ready to print your résumé, find a well-maintained, quality printer. Don't tolerate any streaks, stray lines, or poor print quality. You wouldn't walk into an interview looking messy, so make sure your résumé doesn't look that way, either.

Printing a Scannable Résumé To cope with the flood of unsolicited paper résumés in recent years, many companies now optically scan incoming résumés into a database that hiring managers can search for attractive candidates. Whether they use simpler keyword matching or sophisticated linguistic analysis, these systems display a list of possible candidates, each with a percentage score indicating how closely the résumé reflects the employer's requirements.[38] Nearly all large companies now use these systems, as do many mid-sized companies and even some smaller firms.[39]

The emergence of such scanning systems has important implications for your résumé. First, computers are interested only in matching information to search parameters, not in artistic attempts at résumé design. In fact, complex designs can cause errors in the scanning process. Second, optical character recognition (OCR) software doesn't technically "read" anything; it merely looks for shapes that match stored profiles of characters. If the OCR software can't make sense of your fancy fonts or creative page layout, it will enter gibberish into the database (for example, your name might go in as "W<$..3r?00# instead of "Walter Jones"). Third, even the most sophisticated databases cannot conduct a search with the nuance and intuition of an experienced human recruiter.

For job searchers, this situation creates two requirements for a successful scannable résumé: (1) Use a plain font and simplified design and (2) compile a **keyword summary** that lists all the terms that could help match your résumé to the right openings. Other than the keyword summary, a scannable résumé contains the same information as your traditional résumé but is formatted to be OCR-friendly:[40]

> Use a clean, common sans serif font such as Optima or Arial, and size it between 10 and 14 points.
> Ensure that characters do not touch one another (whether numbers, letters, or symbols—including the slash [/]).
> Don't use side-by-side columns (the OCR software reads one line all the way across the page).
> Don't use ampersands (&), percent signs (%), foreign-language characters (such as é and ö), or bullet symbols (use a dash—not a lower-case 'o'—in place of a bullet symbol).
> Put each phone number and email address on its own line.
> Print on white, plain paper (speckles and other background colouration can confuse the OCR software).

Figure 15–8, a version of the chronological résumé from Figure 15–5, shows the changes necessary for it to be successfully scanned. Notice that it doesn't have any special characters or design elements that are likely to confuse the scanning software.

Your scannable résumé will probably be longer than your traditional résumé because you can't compress text into columns and because you need plenty of

Strive for a clean, classy look in your printed résumé, using professional-grade paper and a clean, high-quality printer.

Objective 6 Describe what you should do to adapt your résumé to a scannable format.

Converting your résumé to scannable format is easy to do—and extremely important.

> Figure 15–8 Scannable Résumé

Removes all boldfacing, nontext characters such as bullets, and two-column formatting

Includes carefully selected keyword list derived from descriptions of target jobs

Uses a dash instead of bullet point character in bulleted lists

Uses ample white space to help ensure accurate scanning

Roberto Cortez
4757 av Borden
Montréal, QC H4B 2P4
Home phone: (514) 555-0086
Office phone: (514) 555-6624
Email: RCortez@silvernet.com

KEYWORDS

Financial executive, accounting management, international finance, financial analyst, accounting reports, financial audit, computerized accounting model, exchange rates, joint-venture agreements, budgets, billing, credit processing, online systems, MBA, fluent English, fluent French, Excel, Access, Visual Basic, team player, willing to travel

OBJECTIVE

Accounting management position requiring hands-on knowledge of international finance

EXPERIENCE

Staff Accountant/Financial Analyst, Inter-American Imports (Montreal, Quebec), March 2005 to present
— Prepare accounting reports for wholesale giftware importer ($15 million annual sales)
— Audit financial transactions with suppliers in 12 Latin American countries
— Created a computerized model to adjust for fluctuations in currency exchange rates
— Negotiated joint-venture agreements with major suppliers in Mexico and Colombia
— Implemented electronic funds transfer for vendor disbursements, improving cash flow and eliminating payables clerk position

Staff Accountant, Monsanto Agricultural Chemicals (Mexico City, Mexico), October 2001 to March 2005
— Handled budgeting, billing, and credit-processing functions for the Mexico City branch
— Audited travel & entertainment expenses for Monsanto's 30-member Latin American sales force
— Assisted in launching an online system to automate all accounting functions, improving reporting accuracy by 65%

EDUCATION

Master of Business Administration with emphasis in international business, Concordia University, 1999-2001

Bachelor of Business Administration, Accounting, Universidad Nacional Autónoma de Mexico (Mexico City, Mexico), 1995-1999

INTERCULTURAL AND TECHNICAL SKILLS

— Fluent in Spanish and German
— Travelled extensively in Latin America
— Excel, Access, HTML, Visual Basic

Think carefully about the keywords you include in your scannable résumé; they need to appeal to recruiters and reflect your qualities accurately.

white space between headings and sections. If your scannable résumé runs more than one page, ensure that your name appears on every subsequent page (in case the pages become separated). Before sending a scannable résumé, check the company's website or call the human resources department to see whether it has any specific requirements other than those discussed here.

When adding a keyword summary to your résumé, keep your audience in mind. Employers generally search for nouns (since verbs tend to be generic rather than specific to a particular position or skill), so make your keywords nouns as well. Use abbreviations sparingly and only when they are well known and unambiguous, such as *MBA*. List 20 to 30 words and phrases that define your skills, experience, education, professional affiliations, and so on. Place this list right after your name and address. Figure 15–8 offers an example of a keyword summary for an accountant.

One good way to identify which keywords to include in your summary is to underline all the skills listed in ads for the types of jobs you're interested in.

(Another advantage of staying current by reading periodicals, networking, and so on is that you'll develop a good ear for current terminology.) Avoid the temptation to toss in impressive keywords that don't really apply to you. Increasingly sophisticated résumé analysis systems can now detect whether your keywords truly relate to the job descriptions and other information on your résumé. If a system suspects that you've padded your keyword list, it could move you to the bottom of the ranking or delete your résumé.[41]

Creating a Plain-Text File of Your Résumé An increasingly common way to get your information into an employer's database is by entering a *plain-text* version (sometimes referred to as an *ASCII text version*) of your résumé into an online form. This approach has the same goal as a scannable résumé, but it's faster and less prone to errors than the scanning process. If you have the option of mailing a scannable résumé or submitting plain text online, go with plain text.

In addition, when employers or networking contacts ask you to email your résumé, they'll often want to receive it in plain-text format in the body of your email message. Thanks to the prevalence of computer viruses these days, many employers will refuse to open an email attachment. Plain text is also helpful when you're completing online application forms; simply copy and paste from your plain-text file into the appropriate fields.

Plain text is just what it sounds like: no font selections, no bullet symbols, no colours, no lines or boxes, and so on. A plain-text version is easy to create with your word processor. Start with the file you used to create your traditional printed résumé, use the *save as* choice to save it as "plain text" or whichever similarly labelled option your software has, and then verify the result.

The verification step is crucial because you need to be sure what happens to your layout. Open the text file to view the layout, but don't use your word processor; instead, open the file with a basic text editor (such as Microsoft's Notepad) so that the text doesn't get reformatted in any way. If necessary, adjust the page manually, moving text and inserting spaces as needed. For simplicity's sake, left justify all your headings, rather than centring them manually. You can put headings in all caps or underline them with a row of hyphens to separate them from blocks of text.

Creating a Word File of Your Résumé In some cases, an employer or job-posting website will let you upload a Microsoft Word file directly. (Although there are certainly other word processors on the market, Microsoft Word is the most frequently used in business today.) Read the instructions on each site carefully. For example, you can upload a Word résumé to Monster.com, but the site asks you to follow some specific formatting instructions to ensure that your file isn't garbled.[42]

Before you submit a Word file to anyone, ensure that your system is free from computer viruses. Infecting a potential employer's PC is probably not the way to make a good first impression.

Creating an HTML Version of Your Résumé You can probably find several uses for an HTML (web page) version of your résumé, including sending it as a fully formatted email message and including it in your e-portfolio. A key advantage of an HTML version is that you can provide links to supporting details and other materials from within your résumé. Even if you don't have HTML experience, you can save your résumé as a web page from within Word. This method won't necessarily create the most spectacularly beautiful web page, but it should at least be functional.

As you design your HTML résumé, think of important keywords to use as hyperlinks—words that will grab an employer's attention and make the recruiter want to click that hyperlink to learn more about you. You can link to papers you've written, recommendations you've received, and sound or video clips that directly support your résumé. However, be sure to have permission to publish or link to material created for a previous employer.

✳ Explore

A plain-text version of your résumé is simply a computer file without any formatting that you typically apply using a word processor.

Make sure you verify the plain-text file that you create with your word processor and adjust it as needed.

You have many options for posting your résumé online. Remember that you could be displaying your personal information for all the world to see, so think carefully about privacy and security.

Creating a PDF Version of Your Résumé Creating a PDF version of your résumé is a simple procedure, but you need the right software. Adobe Acrobat (not the free Acrobat Reader) is the best-known program, but many others are available, including some free versions. You can also use Adobe's online service at http://createpdf.adobe.com to create PDFs without buying software.

PROOFREADING YOUR RÉSUMÉ Employers view your résumé as a concrete example of how you will prepare material on the job. It doesn't need to be good or pretty good; it needs to be *perfect*. Job seekers have committed every error from forgetting to put their own names on their résumés to misspelling "Education."[43] Even seemingly tiny errors signal that you don't pay attention to details.[44] Not only is your résumé one of the most important documents you'll ever write, it's also one of the shortest, so there's every reason to make it perfect. Check all headings and lists for clarity and parallelism, and ensure that your grammar, spelling, and punctuation are correct. Ask at least three or four other people to read it, too. As the creator of the material, you could stare at a mistake for weeks and not see it.

You also need to ensure that your résumé works in every format you create, so double- and triple-check your scannable and plain-text résumés closely. Many personal computer users now have low-cost scanners with OCR software, so you can even test the scannability of your résumé. These OCR tools aren't as accurate as commercial systems, but you'll get a rough idea of what your résumé will look like on the other end of the scanning process. Test your plain-text version by copying it into an email message and sending it to yourself and several friends on different email systems. Doing so will tell you if previously hidden characters are suddenly showing up or if your formatting fell apart.

DISTRIBUTING YOUR RÉSUMÉ What you do to distribute your résumé depends on the number of employers you target and their preferences for receiving résumés. Employers usually list their preferences on their websites, so verify this information to ensure that your résumé ends up in the right format and in the right channel. Beyond that, here are some general delivery tips:

> **Mailing your traditional and scannable résumés.** Take some care with the packaging. Spend a few extra cents to mail these documents in a flat 9" 12" envelope, or better yet, use Priority Post with a sturdy cardboard mailer and faster delivery for just a few more dollars. Consider sending both formats to each employer. In your cover letter, explain that, for the employer's convenience, you're sending both standard and scannable versions.

> **Faxing your traditional and scannable résumés.** If you know that an employer prefers résumés via fax, be sure to include a standard fax cover sheet, along with your cover letter, followed by your résumé. Set the fax machine to "fine" mode to help ensure a high-quality printout on the receiving end.

> **Emailing your résumé.** Unless someone specifically asks for a Word document as an attachment, don't send it—it probably won't be opened. Instead, insert plain text into the body of the email message, attach a PDF file, or include a hyperlink in the email that links back to your HTML résumé. If you know a reference number or a job ad number, include it in your email subject line.

> **Submitting your résumé online.** The details of submitting résumés online vary from site to site, so be sure to read the instructions thoroughly. Some sites let you upload files directly from your computer; others instruct you to cut and paste blocks of plain text into specific fields in an online form. Whenever you do this, ensure that you cut and paste, rather than retyping information; you've already proofed this material, and you don't want to create any new mistakes while rekeying it.

Your résumé can't be "pretty good" or "almost perfect"—it needs to be perfect, *so proofread it thoroughly and ask several other people to verify it, too.*

When distributing your résumé, pay close attention to the specific wishes of each employer.

> **Posting a résumé on your website.** If you wish to post your résumé on your website, you need to find some way of providing potential employers with your URL; recruiters won't take the time to use search engines to find your site.[45]
> **Posting your résumé with an index service or job site.** Make sure you explore all your online options. Websites such as Monster.ca and Workopolis.ca have rapidly become a major force in recruiting. Don't forget to check specialty sites as well, such as those maintained by professional societies in your fields of interest. However, before you upload your résumé to any site, learn about its confidentiality protection. Some sites allow you to specify levels of confidentiality, such as letting employers search your qualifications without seeing your personal contact information or preventing your current employer from seeing your résumé. In any case, carefully limit the amount of personal information you provide online. Never put your home address, social insurance number, student ID number, or driver's licence number online.

For a quick summary of the steps to take when planning, writing, and completing your résumé, refer to "Checklist: Writing an Effective Résumé."

CHECKLIST Writing an Effective Résumé

A. Plan your résumé.
✔ Analyze your purpose and audience carefully to ensure that your message meets employers' needs.
✔ Gather pertinent information about your target companies.
✔ Select the best medium by researching the preferences of each employer.
✔ Organize your résumé around your strengths, choosing the chronological, functional, or combination structure. (Be careful about using the functional structure.)

B. Write your résumé.
✔ Keep your résumé honest.
✔ Adapt your résumé to your audience to highlight the qualifications each employer is looking for.

✔ Use precise language to convey your name and contact information, career objective or summary of qualifications, education, work experience, skills, work or school accomplishments, and personal activities and achievements.

C. Complete your résumé.
✔ Revise your résumé until it is clear, concise, and compelling.
✔ Produce your résumé in all the formats you might need: traditional printed résumé, scannable, plain-text file, Microsoft Word file, HTML format, or PDF.
✔ Proofread your résumé to ensure that it is letter perfect.
✔ Distribute your résumé using the means that each employer prefers.

Summary of Learning Objectives

1 **Explain the importance and features of an employment portfolio.** An employment portfolio, either in hard copy or multimedia format, shows potential employers evidence of your skills and abilities. Containing your résumé, work samples, recommendation letters, school projects, and other information highlighting your skills, this portfolio can be expanded throughout your career as you seek work opportunities.

2 **Describe the approach most employers take to finding potential new employees.** Most employers look inside the company for likely candidates, relying on personal knowledge and referrals from colleagues. Many also send

representatives to job fairs and will use job agencies and government employment services. In addition, employers post job positions on their own websites and such online sites as Workopolis.ca.

3 **Discuss how to choose the appropriate résumé organization and list the advantages and disadvantages of the three common options.** Each organizational approach emphasizes different strengths. If you have a lot of employment experience, choose the chronological approach because it focuses on your work history. The advantages of the chronological résumé are that (1) it helps employers easily locate necessary information, (2) it highlights

your professional growth and career progress, and (3) it emphasizes continuity and stability in your employment background. The functional approach focuses on particular skills and competencies you've developed. The advantages of the functional résumé are that (1) it helps employers easily see what you can do for them, (2) it allows you to emphasize earlier job experience, and (3) it lets you downplay any lengthy periods of unemployment or a lack of career progress. The combination approach uses the best features of the other two, but it has two disadvantages: (1) It tends to be longer and (2) it can be repetitious if you must list accomplishments and skills in the functional section as well as in the individual job descriptions.

4   **Describe the problem of résumé fraud.** Approximately 50 percent of résumés currently sent to potential employers contain false information. Although it may be tempting to exaggerate qualifications, recruiters will use various methods, including reference and background checks, to confirm a candidate's skills and qualifications. Even if an employee serves an employer for many years,

discovery of fraud will lead to severe consequences. An honest résumé truly represents whether a candidate is the right fit for the position.

5   **Outline the major sections of a traditional résumé.** Your résumé must include three sections: (1) your name and address, (2) your educational background (with related skills and accomplishments), and (3) your work experience (with related skills and accomplishments). Options include listing your career objective or summary of qualifications, describing related activities and achievements, and perhaps (although not necessarily recommended) explaining relevant personal data.

6   **Describe what you should do to adapt your résumé to a scannable format.** Begin by eliminating all fancy printing, graphics, and formatting such as boldface, italics, and tabs. Save the résumé as a plain-text (ASCII) document, adding some blank spaces, blank lines, and asterisks to make it more readable. Finally, provide a keyword summary that define your skills, experience, and education. Ensure that your résumé also includes important jargon that is characteristic of the language in your field.

mycanadianbuscommlab

Visit www.mycanadianbuscommlab.ca for everything you need to help you succeed in the job you've always wanted! Tools and resources include the following:
- Composing Space and Writer's Toolkit
- Document Makeovers
- Video Case Studies
- Grammar Exercises—and much more!

On the Job   PERFORMING COMMUNICATION TASKS AT TIM HORTONS

You recently joined the recruiting team at the TDL Group, the operators of the Tim Hortons chain. Your responsibilities include analyzing résumés and applications to help the company identify the most promising candidates to be interviewed. Your current task is finding candidates to fill a staff accountant position in the finance department.[46]

1   You've learned to pay close attention to the career objectives on résumés to ensure that you match applicants' interests with appropriate job openings. You've selected four résumés for the accountant position; from them, which of the following is the most compelling statement of objectives for this position?

   a   an entry-level financial position in a large company
   b   to invest my accounting and financial talent and business savvy in shepherding Tim Hortons toward explosive growth
   c   a position in which my degree in business administration and my experience in cash management will make a valuable contribution
   d   to learn all I can about back office operations in an exciting environment with a company whose reputation is as outstanding as Tim Hortons

2   Of the education sections included in the résumés, which of the following is the most effective?

   a   **University of Calgary, Calgary, AB, 2002–06.** Received B.A. degree with a major in Business Administration and a minor in Finance. Graduated with a 3.65 grade-point average. Played varsity football and basketball. Worked 15 hours per week in the library. Coordinated the local student chapter of the Canadian Management Association. Member of Alpha Phi Alpha social fraternity.
   b   I attended Mohawk College in Hamilton for two years and then transferred to Ryerson University, Toronto, where I completed my studies. My program of study was economics, but I also took many business management courses, including human resources, small business administration, introduction to marketing, and organizational behaviour. I selected courses based on the professors' reputation for excellence, and I received mostly As and Bs. Unlike many students, I viewed the acquisition of knowledge—rather than career preparation—as my primary goal. I believe I have received a well-rounded education that has prepared me to approach management situations as problem-solving exercises.

c **St. Francis Xavier University, Antigonish, NS.** Graduated with a B.A. degree in 2006. Majored in Physical Education. Minored in Business Administration. Graduated with a 2.85 average.

d **University of Regina, Regina, SK.** Received BA and MBA degrees. I majored in business as an undergraduate and concentrated in manufacturing management during my MBA program. Received a special $2500 scholarship offered by Rotary International recognizing academic achievement in business courses. I also won the MEGA award in 2003. Honour student.

3 While you would naturally prefer to hire someone with directly relevant experience in accounting, you recognize that this isn't always possible. When you can't find a candidate with such experience, you look for people who are able to translate their work experience into terms that are relevant to the positions they're applying for. Which of the following candidates does the best job of describing his or her work experience in a way that reflects the "Background and Experience" section of the staff accountant job description?

a **McDonald's, The Pas, MB, 2005–09.** Part-time cook. Worked 15 hours per week while attending high school. Prepared hamburgers, chicken nuggets, and french fries. Received employee-of-the-month award for outstanding work habits.
University Grill, Saskatoon, SK, 2001–05. Part-time cook. Worked 20 hours per week while attending university. Prepared hot and cold sandwiches. Helped manager purchase ingredients. Trained new kitchen workers. Prepared work schedules for kitchen staff.

b Although I have never held a full-time job, I have worked part-time and during summer vacations throughout my high school and university years. During my first and second years in high school, I bagged groceries at the Loblaws store three afternoons a week. The work was not terribly challenging, but I liked the customers and the other employees. During my third and fourth years, I worked at the YMCA as an after-school counsellor for elementary school children. The kids were really sweet, and I still get letters from some of them. During summer vacations while I was in university, I did construction work for a local home-builder. The job paid well, and I also learned a lot about carpentry. The guys I worked with were a mixed bag who expanded my vocabulary and knowledge of the world. I also worked part-time in university in the student cafeteria, where I scooped food onto plates. This did not require much talent, but it taught me a lot about how people behave when standing in line.

c **The Broadway Department Store, Moncton, NB, Summers 2003–08.** Sales Consultant, Furniture Department. I interacted with a diverse group of customers, including suburban matrons, teenagers, career women, and professional couples. I endeavoured to satisfy their individual needs and make their shopping experience memorable, efficient, and enjoyable. Under the direction of the sales manager, I helped prepare employee schedules and fill out departmental reports. I also helped manage the inventory, worked the cash register, and handled a variety of special orders and customer complaints with courtesy and aplomb. During the 2006 annual storewide sale, I sold more merchandise than any other salesperson in the entire furniture department.

d **Medicine Hat, AB, Civilian Member of Public Safety Committee, January–December 2008.**
> Organized and promoted a lecture series on vacation safety and home security for the residents of Medicine Hat; recruited and trained seven committee members to help plan and produce the lectures; persuaded local businesses to finance the program; designed, printed, and distributed flyers; wrote and distributed press releases; attracted an average of 120 people to each of three lectures
> Developed a questionnaire to determine local residents' home security needs; directed the efforts of 10 volunteers working on the survey; prepared written report for city council and delivered oral summary of findings at town meeting; helped persuade city to fund new home security program
> Initiated the Business Security Forum as an annual meeting at which local business leaders could meet to discuss safety and security issues; created promotional flyers for the first forum; convinced 19 business owners to fund a business security survey; arranged press coverage of the first forum

Test Your Knowledge

1 What is the purpose of maintaining an employment portfolio? How does a portfolio influence employers?

2 What is a résumé? Why is it important to adopt a "you" attitude when preparing one?

3 In what ways can job seekers use the internet during their career and employment search?

4 How does a chronological résumé differ from a functional résumé? When is each appropriate?

5   What elements are commonly included in a résumé?

6   Why do some experts recommend against including a career objective in your résumé?

7   What are some of the most common problems with résumés?

8   Should a summary of qualifications focus on the past or the future?

9   Why is it important to provide a keyword summary in a scannable or electronic résumé?

10 How do you convert a traditional résumé to scannable format?

Apply Your Knowledge

1   If you're still a year or two away from graduation, should you worry about your job search? Explain your answer.

2   One of the disadvantages of computerized résumé scanning is that some qualified applicants will be missed because the technology isn't perfect. However, many companies use this approach to deal with the flood of résumés they receive. Do you think that scanning is a good idea? Please explain.

3   Stating your career objective on a résumé or application might limit your opportunities by labelling you too narrowly. Not stating your objective, however, might lead an employer to categorize you incorrectly. Which outcome is riskier? Do summaries of qualifications overcome such drawbacks? If so, how? Explain briefly.

4   Some people don't have a clear career path when they enter the job market. If you're in that situation, how would your uncertainty affect the way you write your résumé?

5   **Ethical Choices** Between your second and third years in university, you quit school for a year to earn the money to complete your education. You worked as a loan-processing assistant in a finance company, checking references on loan applications, typing, and filing. Your manager made a lot of the fact that he had never attended university. He seemed to resent you for pursuing your education, but he never criticized your work, so you thought you were doing okay. After you'd been working there for six months, he fired you, saying that you failed to be thorough enough in your credit checks. You were actually glad to leave, and you found another job right away at a bank doing similar duties. Now that you've graduated from university, you're writing your résumé. Will you include the finance company job in your work history? Please explain.

Running Cases

●—[Watch on **mycanadianbuscommlab**

> CASE 1 Noreen

The "Go Points" department and the credit card sales/service department have merged, and Petro-Go plans to combine these two departments in all their international centres. The senior management team is hiring for a new position of Merger Project Manager and Noreen wants to apply. The project is expected to last two years and the chosen candidate will travel to 12 countries and 40 call centres to implement the merger.

QUESTIONS
a) What is the purpose of the cover letter and résumé?
b) What skills should Noreen emphasize?

c) How many pages long should her résumé be?
d) What is the best organizational style for Noreen's résumé? Why?
e) What common mistakes with résumé fonts must Noreen be sure not to make?

YOUR TASK
Create a cover letter and résumé for Noreen. Refer to the cases for Noreen at the back of each chapter to read about her skills and background. You may use your imagination to add skills and experience to Noreen's résumé as you see fit.

> CASE 2 Kwong

Kwong has obtained his CGA credentials and opened an accounting firm. His firm, CG Accounting, has been operating for three months and has 20 corporate account customers and 167 personal account customers. His sister is working in his office as the office administrator, and he has one other tax preparer working on the accounts with him. His sister is leaving, and he needs to hire a new administrative assistant who will answer phones, advise customers, prepare forms for signature, email, file, and so on. He has placed a job advertisement in the newspaper and is now reviewing résumés.

QUESTIONS

a) List three main skills for which Kwong will look.
b) Is past experience necessary?
c) What skills should the cover letter emphasize?
d) List two questions Kwong might ask an over-qualified candidate.
e) List two questions Kwong might ask an under-qualified candidate.

YOUR TASK

Create a cover letter for this position. Use your résumé and fit it to this position. Work in pairs and exchange your cover letter and résumé with another student. Each of you will give feedback and suggestions for improvement to the other.

Practise Your Knowledge

Read the following résumé information, and then (1) analyze the strengths or weaknesses of the information and (2) create a résumé that follows the guidelines presented in this chapter.

DOCUMENT 15.A: WRITING A RÉSUMÉ

Sylvia Manchester
66 Bernick Drive
Barrie, ON L4M 2V6
(705) 111-5254
smanchester@rcnmail.com

PERSONAL: Single, excellent health, 5'8", 116 lbs.; hobbies include cooking, dancing, and reading.

JOB OBJECTIVE: To obtain a responsible position in marketing or sales with a good company.

EDUCATION: BA degree in biology, Memorial University, 1999. Graduated with a 3.0 average. Member of the varsity cheerleading squad.

WORK EXPERIENCE *Fisher Scientific Instruments, 2005 to present, field sales representative.* Responsible for calling on customers and explaining the features of Fisher's line of laboratory instruments. Also responsible for writing sales letters, attending trade shows, and preparing weekly sales reports.

Fisher Scientific Instruments, 2001–2004, customer service representative. Was responsible for handling incoming phone calls from customers who had questions about delivery, quality, or operation of Fisher's line of laboratory instruments. Also handled miscellaneous correspondence with customers.

Medical Electronics, Inc., 1998–2001, administrative assistant to the vice-president of marketing. In addition to handling typical secretarial chores for the vice-president of marketing, I was in charge of compiling the monthly sales reports, using figures provided by members of the field sales force. I also was given responsibility for doing various market research activities.

Visitors Bureau, 1995–1998, summers, tour guide. During the summers of my university years, I led tours of St. John's for tourists visiting the city. My duties included greeting conventioneers and their spouses at hotels, explaining the history and features of the city during an all-day sight-seeing tour, and answering questions about St. John's and its attractions. During my fourth summer with the Bureau, I was asked to help train the new tour guides. I prepared a handbook that provided interesting facts about the various tourist attractions, as well as answers to the most commonly asked tourist questions. The Bureau was so impressed with the handbook they had it printed up so that it could be given as a gift to visitors.

Memorial University, 1996–1999, part-time clerk in admissions office. While I was a student in university, I worked 15 hours a week in the admissions office. My duties included filing, processing applications, and handling correspondence with high-school students and administrators.

Exercises

15.1 Work-Related Preferences: Self-Assessment
What work-related activities and situations do you prefer? Evaluate your preferences in each using the questionnaire below. Use the results as a good start for guiding your job search.

Activity or Situation	Strongly Agree	Agree	Disagree	No Preference
1. I want to work independently.	_____	_____	_____	_____
2. I want variety in my work.	_____	_____	_____	_____
3. I want to work with people.	_____	_____	_____	_____
4. I want to work with technology.	_____	_____	_____	_____
5. I want physical work.	_____	_____	_____	_____
6. I want mental work.	_____	_____	_____	_____
7. I want to work for a large organization.	_____	_____	_____	_____
8. I want to work for a non-profit organization.	_____	_____	_____	_____
9. I want to work for a small family business.	_____	_____	_____	_____
10. I want to work for a service business.	_____	_____	_____	_____
11. I want regular, predictable work hours.	_____	_____	_____	_____
12. I want to work in a city location.	_____	_____	_____	_____
13. I want to work in a small town or suburb.	_____	_____	_____	_____
14. I want to work in another country.	_____	_____	_____	_____
15. I want to work outdoors.	_____	_____	_____	_____
16. I want to work in a structured environment.	_____	_____	_____	_____

15.2 Internet: Career Match
Based on the preferences you identified in the self-assessment (Exercise 15.1) and the academic, professional, and personal qualities you have to offer, perform an online search for a career that matches your interests (starting with the websites listed in Table 15–1). Draft a brief report for your instructor, indicating how the career you select and the job openings you find match your strengths and preferences.

15.3 Teamwork: Action Verbs
Working with another student, change the following statements to make them more effective for a résumé by using action verbs.
a. Have some experience with database design.
b. Assigned to a project to analyze the cost accounting methods for a large manufacturer.
c. I was part of a team that developed a new inventory control system.
d. Am responsible for preparing the quarterly department budget.
e. Was a manager of a department with seven employees working for me.
f. Was responsible for developing a spreadsheet to analyze monthly sales by department.
g. Put in place a new program for ordering supplies.

15.4 Résumé Preparation: Work Accomplishments
Use your team's answers to Exercise 15.3 to make the statements stronger by quantifying them (make up any numbers you need).

15.5 Ethical Choices: Describing Teamwork
Assume that you achieved all the tasks shown in Exercise 15.3 not as an individual employee but as part of a work team. In your résumé, must you mention other team members? Explain your answer.

15.6 Résumé Preparation: Electronic Plain-Text Version

Using your revised version of Document for Analysis 15.A, prepare a web page version. Your instructor may direct you to a particular HTML editing tool, or you can use the "Save as Web Page" function in Microsoft Word. Word also lets you insert hyperlinks, so somewhere in the Work Experience section, create a hyperlink that takes the reader to a secondary page in order to show a work sample. For this new page, you can either use one of your own assignments from this course or simply create a blank page titled "Work Sample for Sylvia Manchester." On this page, create a hyperlink that takes the reader back to the main résumé page. Be sure to test your finished files using a Web browser. Adjust your formatting as necessary to ensure a clean, professional design. When your files are complete, submit as your instructor indicates.

15.7 It's Show Time: Creating a Vidcast to Supplement Your Application

Imagine that you are applying for work in a field that involves speaking in front of an audience, such as sales, consulting, management, or training. Using material you created for any of the exercises or cases in Chapter 14, plan a 2- to 3-minute video demonstration of your speaking and presentation skills. Using a digital camcorder, a digital camera with video capability, or a webcam, record yourself speaking to an imaginary audience. If possible, use PowerPoint slides or other visuals. As your instructor directs, either submit this movie clip or use it to create a video podcast. For a good tutorial on creating vidcasts on Apple computers running Mac OS X, visit www.apple.com/quicktime/tutorials/videopodcasts.html; for Windows computers, visit www.apple.com/quicktime/tutorials/videopodcasts_win.html.

Cases APPLYING THE THREE-STEP WRITING PROCESS TO CASES

Apply each step to the following cases, as assigned by your instructor.

1. Taking stock and taking aim: Résumé tailored for the right job

Think about yourself. What are some things that come easily to you? What do you enjoy doing? In what part of the country would you like to live? Do you like to work indoors? Outdoors? A combination of the two? How much do you like to travel? Would you like to spend considerable time on the road? Do you like to work closely with others or more independently? What conditions make a job unpleasant? Do you delegate responsibility easily, or do you like to do things yourself? Are you better with words or numbers? Better at speaking or writing? Do you like to work under fixed deadlines? How important is job security to you? Do you want your supervisor to state clearly what is expected of you, or do you like the freedom to make many of your own decisions?

Your Task: After answering these questions, gather information about possible jobs that suit your profile by consulting reference materials (from your college or university library or placement centre) and by searching the internet (using some search strategies that Chapter 11 discusses). Next, choose a location, a company, and a job that interests you. With guidance from your instructor, decide whether to apply for a job you're qualified for now or one you'll be qualified for with additional education. Then, as directed by your instructor, write a résumé.

2. Scanning the possibilities: Résumé for the internet

In your search for a position, you discover Career Magazine, a website that lists hundreds of companies advertising on the internet. Your chances of getting an interview with a leading company will be enhanced if you submit your résumé and cover letter electronically. On the Web, explore www.careermag.com.

Your Task: Prepare a scannable résumé that could be submitted to one of the companies advertising at the Career Magazine website. Print out the résumé for your instructor.

3. "Help wanted": Application for a job listed in the classified section

Among the jobs listed in today's *Province* (301 Granville Street, Vancouver, BC V6C 2N4) are the following:

> **Accounting Assistant** Established leader in the vacation ownership industry, Nelson Corp., has immediate opening in its accounting dept. for an Accounting Assistant. Responsibilities include bank reconciliation, preparation of deposits, AP, and cash receipt posting. Join our fast-growing company and enjoy our great benefits package. Flex work hours, medical, dental insurance. Fax résumé to Lisa: 604-555-3876.

> **Administrative Assistant** Fast-paced Burnaby office seeks professional with strong computer skills. Proficient in MS Word & Excel, PowerPoint a plus. Must be detail oriented, able to handle multiple tasks, and possess strong communication skills. Excellent benefits, salary, and work environment. Fax résumé to 604-555-8649.

> **Customer Service** A nationally known computer software developer has an exciting opportunity in customer service and inside sales support in its fast-paced downtown Vancouver office. You'll help resolve customer problems over the phone, provide information, assist in account management, and administer orders. If you're friendly, self-motivated, energetic, and have 2 years of experience, excellent problem-solving skills, organizational, communication, and PC skills, and communicate well over the

phone, send résumé to J. Haber, 2359 Venables St., Vancouver, BC V5K 1J5.

> **Sales-Account Manager** MidCity Baking Company is seeking an Account Manager to sell and coordinate our programs to major accounts in the Vancouver market. The candidate should possess strong analytical and selling skills and demonstrate computer proficiency. Previous sales experience with major account level assignment desired. A degree in business or equivalent experience preferred. For confidential consideration, please mail résumé to Steven Crane, Director of Sales, MidCity Baking Company, PO Box 23727, Vancouver, BC V7C 1X9.

Your Task: Write a résumé for one of these potential employers (make up any information you need or adapt your résumé).

16

Applying and Interviewing for Employment

LEARNING OBJECTIVES

After studying this chapter, you will be able to

1. Define the purpose of application letters and explain how to apply the AIDA organizational approach to them
2. Describe the typical sequence of job interviews
3. Describe briefly what employers look for during an employment interview and pre-employment testing
4. Outline six tasks you need to complete to prepare for a successful job interview
5. Explain the three stages of a successful employment interview
6. Identify the most common employment messages that follow an interview, and explain when you would use each one

ON THE JOB

Communicating at Google
GOOGLING THE BEST TALENT ON THE WEB
www.google.com

Are you looking for a company that's fun and stimulating? One that inspires you to stretch your mind? A workplace with a global reach but a small-town, friendly atmosphere? You might try Google, rated by *Fortune* magazine in 2008 as the number one company to work for.

With its strong corporate identity and specific ideas about hiring and management, Google has maintained its lead in search-engine technology and continues developing new tools that range from digital libraries to geographic information systems such as Google Earth. To keep its prominence, Google pursues exceptionally talented software engineers. Most are either young risk-takers with adventurous outside interests or experienced superstars from top research labs or respected technology firms. Googlers, as employees are informally known, come from every corner of the business world—and beyond. As the company puts it, "Googlers have been Olympic athletes and Jeopardy champions; professional chefs and independent filmmakers."

Interviews are challenging. As Google states, candidates will face in-depth questions "intended to let us get a peek at how you think about complicated things." They are asked to write code and discuss the intricacies of their technical work. The

Arnnon Geshuri heads Google's recruiting effort as the company looks to hire thousands of the most innovative online business and technical specialists in the world.

goal is to hire people who will drive the company forward in its mission: "to organize the world's information and make it universally accessible and useful."

But Google is more than engineers. Performing routine business functions and sustaining Google's global profile requires managers, communicators, and marketers. Non-technicians, such as facilities managers, make Google work by maintaining building and mechanical systems, overseeing vendor contracts, and coordinating space planning. Account planners provide sales support by running such events as "Getting to Know Google" and by cultivating client contacts. Along with software engineers, professionals such as these have made Google the primary internet search engine around the world.

You may never apply to Google, but it's important to gain insights about the companies you want to work for: Your research will definitely give you a competitive edge. Google provides a great deal of information on its website about its work life, but not all companies do. You may have to do some extra digging through magazines, newsgroups, employment-related blogs, and other sources. When you start your job search, how will you prepare?[1]

Writing Application Letters and Other Employment Messages

Whether you plan to apply to Google or any other company, your résumé (see Chapter 15) is the centrepiece of your job search package, but it needs support from several other employment messages, including application letters, job-inquiry letters, application forms, and follow-up notes.

✱ Explore

Application Letters

Use the three-step process to create attention-getting application letters.

Whenever you submit your résumé, accompany it with an application letter (also known as a *cover letter*) to let readers know what you're sending, why you're sending it, and how they can benefit from reading it. The three-step process of planning, writing, and completing an application letter involves the same steps you've been using throughout this course. Start by researching the organization and then focus on your audience so that you can show you've done your homework. During your research, try to find out the name, title, and department of the person you're writing to. If a company does not provide a specific contact, it often provides a department, usually Human Resources; you can insert the department name in an attention line in place of a salutation to an individual. If you're applying for work in another country, be sure to research the hiring practices prevalent in that culture and adjust your letter format as needed.

Impress your reader with knowledge and professionalism—not gimmicks.

Remember that your reader's in-box is probably overflowing with résumés and cover letters, so respect his or her time. Avoid gimmicks and don't repeat information that already appears in your résumé. Keep your letter straightforward, fact-based, short, upbeat, and professional. Here are some quick tips to help you write effective cover letters:[2]

> **Be as clear as possible about the kind of opportunity you seek.** Show that you understand the company and the position by echoing the key messages you picked up from the job ad, company brochure, or other information source.

> **Never volunteer salary information unless an employer asks for it.** And even if you are asked, you probably don't want to pin down a specific number at this point in the process. See "Discussing Salary" later in this chapter for more information.
> **Keep it short—and keep email cover letters even shorter.** In just two or three paragraphs, convey how your strengths and character would fit the position. If you find you need more space, you probably haven't thought through the opportunity sufficiently. When sending a cover letter by email, make it even shorter than traditional application letters. Remember, email readers want the gist as quickly as possible.
> **Show some personality.** Because your application letter is in your own style (rather than the choppy, shorthand style of your résumé), make the most of your chance to reveal not only your excellent communication skills, but also some of your personality. Keep it professional, of course.
> **Aim for high quality**. Meticulously check your spelling, mechanics, and grammar; errors will send your message directly to the recycling bin. And be aware that potential employers will treat your email messages every bit as seriously as formal, printed letters.[3]

If you're sending a solicited application letter in response to an announced job opening, you'll usually know what qualifications the organization is seeking. You'll also face more competition for the position because hundreds of other job seekers will have seen the listing and may be sending applications, too. The letter in Figure 16–1 was written in response to a help-wanted ad. Notice how Kenneth Sawyer highlights his qualifications and mirrors the requirements specified in the ad. He grabs attention by focusing on the phrase "proven skills," which was used in the ad: He not only elaborates on his own proven skills throughout the letter, but also mentions the term in his closing paragraph.

If you're sending an **unsolicited letter** to an organization that has not announced an opening, you'll need to do some research to identify the requirements the position is likely to have. (Note that even though these documents are referred to as letters, they can be email messages as well.) In her unsolicited application letter in Figure 16–2, Glenda Johns gives a snapshot of her qualifications and skills without repeating what is said in her résumé. She gains attention by focusing on the needs of the employer.

Both solicited and unsolicited application letters present your qualifications similarly. The main difference is in the opening paragraph. In a solicited letter, you need no special attention-getter because you have been invited to apply. In an unsolicited letter, you need to start by capturing the reader's attention and interest.

GETTING ATTENTION   Like your résumé, your application letter is a form of advertising, so organize it as you would a sales letter: Use the AIDA approach, focus on your audience, and emphasize reader benefits (as discussed in Chapter 10). Make sure your style projects confidence, without being arrogant. To sell a potential employer on your merits, you must believe in yourself and sound as though you do.

The opening paragraph of your application letter has two important tasks to accomplish: (1) clearly stating your reason for writing and (2) giving the recipient a reason to keep reading. Why would a recruiter want to keep reading your letter instead of the hundred others piling up on his or her desk? Because you show some immediate potential for meeting the company's needs. You've researched the company and the position, and you know something about the industry and its current challenges. Consider this opening:

✱ Explore

Objective 1 Define the purpose of application letters and explain how to apply the AIDA organizational approach to them.

The opening paragraph of your application letter needs to convey clearly the reason you're writing and give the recipient a compelling reason to keep reading.

> Figure 16–1 Effective Solicited Application Letter

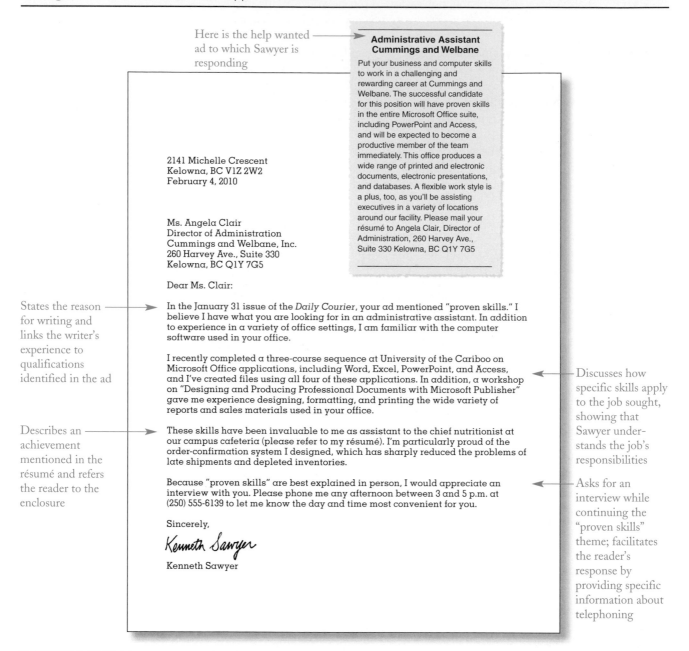

Here is the help wanted ad to which Sawyer is responding

Administrative Assistant Cummings and Welbane

Put your business and computer skills to work in a challenging and rewarding career at Cummings and Welbane. The successful candidate for this position will have proven skills in the entire Microsoft Office suite, including PowerPoint and Access, and will be expected to become a productive member of the team immediately. This office produces a wide range of printed and electronic documents, electronic presentations, and databases. A flexible work style is a plus, too, as you'll be assisting executives in a variety of locations around our facility. Please mail your résumé to Angela Clair, Director of Administration, 260 Harvey Ave., Suite 330 Kelowna, BC Q1Y 7G5

2141 Michelle Crescent
Kelowna, BC V1Z 2W2
February 4, 2010

Ms. Angela Clair
Director of Administration
Cummings and Welbane, Inc.
260 Harvey Ave., Suite 330
Kelowna, BC Q1Y 7G5

Dear Ms. Clair:

States the reason for writing and links the writer's experience to qualifications identified in the ad

In the January 31 issue of the *Daily Courier*, your ad mentioned "proven skills." I believe I have what you are looking for in an administrative assistant. In addition to experience in a variety of office settings, I am familiar with the computer software used in your office.

I recently completed a three-course sequence at University of the Cariboo on Microsoft Office applications, including Word, Excel, PowerPoint, and Access, and I've created files using all four of these applications. In addition, a workshop on "Designing and Producing Professional Documents with Microsoft Publisher" gave me experience designing, formatting, and printing the wide variety of reports and sales materials used in your office.

Discusses how specific skills apply to the job sought, showing that Sawyer understands the job's responsibilities

Describes an achievement mentioned in the résumé and refers the reader to the enclosure

These skills have been invaluable to me as assistant to the chief nutritionist at our campus cafeteria (please refer to my résumé). I'm particularly proud of the order-confirmation system I designed, which has sharply reduced the problems of late shipments and depleted inventories.

Because "proven skills" are best explained in person, I would appreciate an interview with you. Please phone me any afternoon between 3 and 5 p.m. at (250) 555-6139 to let me know the day and time most convenient for you.

Asks for an interview while continuing the "proven skills" theme; facilitates the reader's response by providing specific information about telephoning

Sincerely,

Kenneth Sawyer

Kenneth Sawyer

With the recent slowdown in corporate purchasing, I can certainly appreciate the challenge of new fleet sales in this business environment. With my high energy level and 16 months of new-car sales experience, I believe I can produce the results you listed as vital in your September 23 ad in the *St. John's Evening Telegram*.

This applicant does a smooth job of mirroring the company's stated needs while highlighting his personal qualifications along with evidence that he understands the broader market. Although 16 months may not be considered a lot of experience, the letter balances that shortfall with enthusiasm and genuine interest in the position.

> Figure 16–2 Effective Unsolicited Application Letter

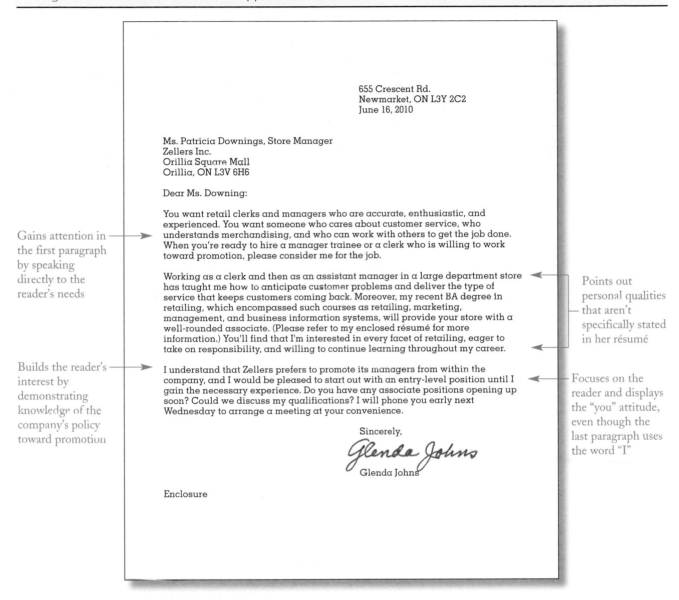

Gains attention in the first paragraph by speaking directly to the reader's needs

Builds the reader's interest by demonstrating knowledge of the company's policy toward promotion

Points out personal qualities that aren't specifically stated in her résumé

Focuses on the reader and displays the "you" attitude, even though the last paragraph uses the word "I"

655 Crescent Rd.
Newmarket, ON L3Y 2C2
June 16, 2010

Ms. Patricia Downings, Store Manager
Zellers Inc.
Orillia Square Mall
Orillia, ON L3V 6H6

Dear Ms. Downing:

You want retail clerks and managers who are accurate, enthusiastic, and experienced. You want someone who cares about customer service, who understands merchandising, and who can work with others to get the job done. When you're ready to hire a manager trainee or a clerk who is willing to work toward promotion, please consider me for the job.

Working as a clerk and then as an assistant manager in a large department store has taught me how to anticipate customer problems and deliver the type of service that keeps customers coming back. Moreover, my recent BA degree in retailing, which encompassed such courses as retailing, marketing, management, and business information systems, will provide your store with a well-rounded associate. (Please refer to my enclosed résumé for more information.) You'll find that I'm interested in every facet of retailing, eager to take on responsibility, and willing to continue learning throughout my career.

I understand that Zellers prefers to promote its managers from within the company, and I would be pleased to start out with an entry-level position until I gain the necessary experience. Do you have any associate positions opening up soon? Could we discuss my qualifications? I will phone you early next Wednesday to arrange a meeting at your convenience.

Sincerely,

Glenda Johns

Glenda Johns

Enclosure

Table 16–1 highlights some other ways that you can spark interest and grab attention in your opening paragraph. All these openings demonstrate the "you" attitude, and many indicate how the applicant can serve the employer.

BUILDING INTEREST AND INCREASING DESIRE The middle section of your application letter presents your strongest selling points in terms of their potential benefit to the organization, thereby building interest in you and creating a desire to interview you. As with the opening, the more specific you can be, the better. And back up your assertions with some convincing evidence of your ability to perform:

Use the middle section of your letter to expand on your opening, presenting a more complete picture of your strengths.

Poor: I completed three university courses in business communication, earning an A in each course, and have worked for the past year at Imperial Construction.

> Table 16–1 Tips for Getting Attention in Application Letters

Tip	Example
Unsolicited Application Letters	
> Show how your strongest skills will benefit the organization	If you need a regional sales specialist who consistently meets sales targets while fostering strong customer relationships, please consider my qualifications.
> Describe your understanding of the job's requirements and then show how well your qualifications fit them	Your annual report stated that improving manufacturing efficiency is one of the company's top priorities for next year. Through my postgraduate research in systems engineering and consulting work for several companies in the industry, I've developed reliable methods for quickly identifying ways to cut production time while reducing resource usage.
> Mention the name of a person known to and highly regarded by the reader	When Janice McHugh of your franchise sales division spoke to our business communication class last week, she said you often need promising new marketing graduates at this time of year.
> Refer to publicized company activities, achievements, changes, or new procedures	Today's issue of the *Winnipeg Free Press* reports that you may need the expertise of computer programmers versed in robotics when your Elmwood tire plant automates this spring.
> Use a question to demonstrate your understanding of the organization's needs	Can your fast-growing market research division use an interviewer with two years of field survey experience, a BA in public relations, and a real desire to succeed? If so, please consider me for the position.
> Use a catchphrase opening if the job requires ingenuity and imagination	*Haut monde*—whether said in French, Italian, or Arabic—still means "high society." As an interior designer for your Yorkville showroom, not only could I serve and sell to your distinguished clientele, but I could do it in all these languages. I speak, read, and write them fluently.
Solicited Application Letters	
> Identify where you discovered the job opening; describe what you have to offer	Your ad in the April issue of *Travel & Leisure* for a cruise-line social director caught my eye. My eight years of experience as a social director in the travel industry would allow me to serve your new Caribbean cruise division well.

Improved: Using the skills gained from three semesters of university training in business communication, I developed a collection system for Imperial Construction that reduced annual bad-debt losses by 25 percent. By emphasizing a win–win scenario for the company and its clients with incentives for on-time payment, the system was also credited with improving customer satisfaction.

When writing a solicited letter in response to an advertisement, ensure that you discuss each requirement specified in the ad. If you are deficient in any of these requirements, stress other solid selling points to help strengthen your overall presentation.

Don't restrict your message to just core job duties, either. Also highlight personal characteristics, as long as they apply to the targeted position, such as your diligence or your ability to work hard, learn quickly, handle responsibility, or get along with people:

While attending university full-time, I trained 3 hours a day with the varsity track team. In addition, I worked part-time during the school year and up to 60 hours a week each summer to be totally self-supporting. I can offer your organization the same level of effort and perseverance.

Another matter you might bring up in this section is your salary requirements— but *only* if the organization has asked you to state them. If you don't know the salary that's appropriate for the position and someone with your qualifications, you can find salary ranges for hundreds of jobs at the Service Canada website, www.labourmarketinformation.ca, or a number of commercial sites, including workopolis.com. If you do state a target salary, tie it to the benefits you would bring to the organization:

Don't bring up salary in your application letter unless the recipient has previously asked you to include your salary requirements.

> For the past two years, I have been helping a company similar to yours organize its database marketing efforts. I would therefore like to receive a salary in the same range (the mid-40s) for helping your company set up a more efficient customer database.

Toward the end of this section, refer the reader to your résumé by citing a specific fact or general point covered there:

> As you can see in the attached résumé, I've been working part-time with a local publisher since my second year in university. During that time, I've used client interactions as an opportunity to build strong customer-service skills.

MOTIVATING ACTION The final paragraph of your application letter has two important functions: to ask the reader for a specific action and to facilitate a reply. Don't demand an interview, however; sound natural and appreciative. Offer to come to the employer's office at a convenient time or, if the firm is some distance away, to meet with its nearest representative or arrange a telephone interview. Make the request easy to fulfill by stating your phone number and the best time to reach you—or, if you wish to be in control, by mentioning that you will follow up with a phone call in a few days. Refer again to your strongest selling point and, if desired, your date of availability:

In the final paragraph of your application letter, respectfully ask for specific action and make it easy for the reader to respond.

> After you have reviewed my qualifications, could we discuss the possibility of putting my marketing skills to work for your company? Since I will be on spring break the week of March 8, I would like to arrange a time to talk then. I will call in February to schedule a convenient time when we could discuss employment opportunities at your company.

After you have edited and proofread your application letter, give it a final quality check by referring to "Checklist: Writing Application Letters." Then print it and send it (or email it) along with your résumé promptly, especially if you are responding to an ad or online job posting.

CHECKLIST Writing Application Letters

- ✔ Open the letter by capturing the reader's attention in a businesslike way.
- ✔ Use specific language to state your interests and objectives clearly.
- ✔ Build interest and desire in your potential contribution by presenting your key qualifications for the job.
- ✔ Link your education, experience, and personal qualities to the job requirements.
- ✔ Outline salary requirements only if the organization has requested that you provide them.
- ✔ Request an interview at a time and place that is convenient for the reader.
- ✔ Make it easy to comply with your request by providing your complete contact information and good times to reach you.
- ✔ Adapt your style for cultural variations if required.

Application Follow-Ups

If your application letter and résumé fail to bring a response within a month or so, follow up with a second letter to keep your file active. This follow-up letter also gives you a chance to update your original application with any recent job-related information:

Since applying to you on May 5 for an executive assistant position, I have completed three courses in business and management at Coquitlam College and received straight As.

Please keep my application in your active file, and let me know when you need a skilled executive assistant.

Even if you've received a letter acknowledging your application and saying that it will be kept on file, don't hesitate to send a follow-up letter three months later to show that you are still interested:

Three months have elapsed since I applied to you for an underwriting position, but I want to let you know that I am still very interested in joining your company.

I recently completed a four-week temporary work assignment at a large local insurance agency. I learned several new verification techniques and gained experience in using the online computer system. This experience could increase my value to your underwriting department.

Please keep my application in your active file, and let me know when a position opens for a capable underwriter.

Think creatively about a follow-up letter; show that you've continued to add to your skills or that you've learned more about the company or the industry.

You can still write this sort of follow-up message even if you have no new accomplishments to share. Do some quick research on the company and its industry to find something that you can feature in your message ("I've been reading about the new technical challenges facing your industry . . . "). Your initiative and knowledge will impress recruiters. Without a follow-up communication from you, the human resources office is likely to assume that you've already found a job and are no longer interested in the organization. Moreover, a company's requirements change. A follow-up letter can demonstrate that you're sincerely interested in working for the organization, persistent in pursuing your goals, and committed to upgrading your skills. And it might just get you an interview.

Understanding the Interviewing Process

Asking questions of your own is as important as answering the interviewer's questions. Not only do you get vital information, but you also show initiative and curiosity. How can you prepare your own questions for a job interview?

Like Google, all companies have a list of qualities and accomplishments they look for in job candidates. An **employment interview** is a formal meeting during which both you and the prospective employer ask questions and exchange information. These meetings have a dual purpose: (1) The organization's main objective is to find the best person available for the job by determining whether you and the organization are a good match, and (2) your main objective is to find the job best suited to your goals and capabilities. While recruiters such as those at Google try to decide whether you are right for them, you must decide whether Google or any other company is right for you.

Large organizations that hire hundreds of new employees every year typically take a more systematic approach to the recruiting and interviewing process than small local businesses that hire only a few new people each year. You'll need to adjust your job search according to the company's size and hiring practices. In general, the easiest way to connect with a big company is through your campus placement office; the most efficient way to approach a smaller business is often contacting the company directly.

Regardless of which path you choose, interviewing takes time, so start seeking jobs well in advance of the date you want to start work. Some students begin their job search as much as nine months before graduation. During downturns in the economy, early planning is even more crucial. Many employers become more selective and many corporations reduce their campus visits and campus hiring programs, so more of the job-search burden falls on you. Whatever shape the economy is in, secure as many interviews as you can, both to improve the chances of receiving a job offer and to give yourself more options when you do get offers.

The Typical Sequence of Interviews

Not all organizations interview potential candidates the same way. At Southwest Airlines in the U.S., for example, a candidate undergoes a rigorous interview process that can take as long as six weeks.[4] However, most employers interview an applicant two or three times before deciding to make a job offer. Applicants often face a sequence of interviews, each with a different purpose.

Objective 2 Describe the typical sequence of job interviews.

Most organizations interview an applicant several times before extending a job offer

First is the preliminary *screening stage,* which may be conducted in person (at a company site or on campus for new college or university hires), over the telephone, or online. Those candidates who best meet the organization's requirements are invited to visit company offices for further evaluation. Interviews at the screening stage are fairly structured, so applicants are often asked roughly the same questions. Many companies use standardized evaluation sheets to "grade" the applicants so that all the candidates are measured against the same criteria. In some cases, technology has transformed the initial, get-to-know-you interview, allowing employers to screen candidates by phone, video interview, or computer.[5]

Your best approach to an interview at the screening stage is to follow the interviewer's lead. Keep your responses short and to the point. Time is limited, so talking too much can be a big mistake. However, to give the interviewer a way to differentiate you from other candidates and to demonstrate your strengths and qualifications, emphasize the "theme" you used in developing your résumé.

During the screening stage of interviews, differentiate yourself from other candidates.

The next stage of interviews helps the organization narrow the field a little further. Typically, if you're invited to visit a company, you will talk with several people: a member of the human resources department, one or two potential colleagues, and one or more managers, including your potential supervisor. You might face a *panel interview,* during which several interviewers ask questions during a single session. Your best approach during this *selection stage* of interviews is to show interest in the job, relate your skills and experience to the organization's needs, listen attentively, ask insightful questions, and display enthusiasm.

During the selection stage of interviews, you may interview with several people, perhaps at the same time.

If the interviewers agree that you're a good candidate, you may receive a job offer, either on the spot or a few days later by phone or mail. In other cases, you may be invited back for a final evaluation by a higher-ranking executive who has the authority to make the hiring decision and to decide on your compensation. An underlying objective of the *final stage* is often to sell you on the advantages of joining the organization.

During the final stage, the interviewer may try to sell you on working for the firm.

Common Types of Interviews

Organizations use various types of interviews to discover as much as possible about you and other applicants. A **structured interview** is generally used in the screening stage. The employer controls the interview by asking a series of prepared questions in a set order. Working from a checklist, the interviewer asks

The goal of a structured interview is to gather facts.

you each question, staying within an allotted time period. All answers are noted. Although useful for gathering facts, the structured interview is generally regarded as a poor measure of an applicant's personal qualities. Nevertheless, some companies use structured interviews to create uniformity in their hiring process.[6]

By contrast, the **open-ended interview** is less formal and unstructured, with a relaxed format. The interviewer poses broad, open-ended questions and encourages you to talk freely. This type of interview is good for bringing out your personality and for testing professional judgment. However, some candidates reveal too much, rambling on about personal or family problems that have nothing to do with their qualifications for employment, their ability to get along with co-workers, or any personal interests that could benefit their performance on the job. So be careful. You need to strike a balance between being friendly and remembering that you're in a business situation.

Some organizations perform **group interviews,** meeting with several candidates simultaneously to see how they interact. This type of interview isn't as common as the other types, but some companies use it to assess interpersonal skills and the ability to work as part of a team.[7] In contrast, the **panel interview,** in which a single candidate faces a panel of interviewers, is becoming more common. One key advantage of this approach for employers is the chance for everyone on the interview team to see the candidate's response to every question rather than relying on reports from each interviewer. To succeed in a panel interview, keep in mind that the panel is made up of individuals who represent different parts of the organization and therefore have different concerns about job candidates. Address each interviewer individually in your answers, tailoring each response to that person's concerns.[8]

The most unnerving type of interview is the **stress interview,** during which you might be asked pointed questions designed to irk or unsettle you, or you might be subjected to long periods of silence, deliberate interruptions, and abrupt or even hostile reactions by the interviewer. The theory behind this approach is that you'll reveal how well you handle stressful situations, although some experts find the technique of dubious value—particularly if the stress induced during the interview has no relationship to the job in question.[9] If you find yourself in a stress interview, pause for a few seconds to collect your thoughts, then continue, knowing what the interviewer is up to.

Many companies have learned that no strong correlation exists between how well people answer interview questions in a traditional interview and how well they perform on the job. In response, these firms have adopted a variety of new interviewing strategies. In the **situational interview,** various on-the-job scenarios are described, and candidates are asked how they would respond. Similarly, a *behavioural interview* asks candidates to describe real situations in the past and explain how they responded.[10] The most realistic approach is the **working interview,** in which the candidate is asked to perform the actual work that he or she would be doing on the job. For instance, a copywriting candidate in an advertising agency could be asked to write text for a web page.[11]

Interview Media

In addition to encountering a variety of interview formats, expect to be interviewed through a variety of media. Employers trying to cut travel costs and the demands on staff time now interview candidates via telephone, email, instant messaging, virtual online systems, and videoconferencing. These alternative media options are used most frequently in the screening stage but can be used into the selection stage as well.

In an open-ended interview, the recruiter encourages you to speak freely.

Group interviews help recruiters see how candidates interact with one another.

Panel interviews allow a group of staff to meet and question each candidate.

Stress interviews help recruiters see how you handle yourself under pressure.

In situational interviews, you're asked to explain how you would handle a specific set of circumstances.

In behavioural interviews, you're asked to relate how you responded to real situations in the past.

In working interviews, you're asked to perform actual job tasks.

To succeed at a telephone interview, make sure you treat it as seriously as an in-person interview. Be prepared with a copy of all the materials you have sent the employer, including your résumé and any correspondence. In addition, prepare some note cards with key message points you'd like to make and your supporting evidence (such as an impressive success story from your current job). If possible, arrange to speak on a landline so you don't have to worry about mobile phone reception problems. And remember that you won't be able to use a pleasant smile, a firm handshake, and other nonverbal signals to create a good impression. A positive, alert tone of voice is therefore vital.[12]

Treat a telephone interview as seriously as you would an in-person interview.

Email and IM are also sometimes used in the screening stage. While you have even less opportunity to send and receive nonverbal signals with these formats, you do have the major advantage of being able to review and edit each response before you send it. Maintain a professional style in your responses and be sure to ask questions that demonstrate your knowledge of the company and the position.[13]

When interviewing via email or IM, be sure to take a moment to review your responses before sending them.

Virtual online interviews can range from simple structured interviews to sophisticated job simulations that are similar to working interviews. People applying for teller positions at a bank, for example, may be asked to interact with video-game-like characters while performing job-related tasks.[14] The latest innovation in simulators uses prerecorded video of real people asking questions and records the candidate's answers on video as well.[15] And as one might expect from an innovator in search technology, Google is testing an extensive online interview system that measures attitudes, behaviours, personality, and personal history in an attempt to find candidates who match the profiles of successful Google employees.[16]

Computer-based virtual interviews range from simple structured interviews to realistic job simulations.

Many large companies use videoconferencing systems to screen middle-management candidates or to interview new recruits at universities. Experts recommend that candidates prepare a bit differently for a video interview than for an in-person meeting:[17]

In a video interview, speak to the camera as though you are addressing the interviewer in person.

> Ask for a preliminary phone conversation to establish rapport with the interviewer.
> Dress conservatively, in solid colours with minimal jewelry.
> Arrive early enough to get used to the equipment and setting.
> During the interview, speak clearly but not more slowly than normal.
> Sit straight.
> Talk to the camera.
> Keep your mannerisms lively without looking forced or fake.

Following these guidelines will help you feel comfortable yet project a professional appearance.

What Employers Look For in an Interview

Chapter 15 points out the attributes employers look for when reviewing résumés. The interview gives them a chance to go beyond this basic data to answer two essential questions: Will the candidate be a good fit with the organization? and Can he or she handle the responsibilities of the position? For example, TechTarget, an interactive media company, gives employees an unusual amount of freedom, including the freedom to set their own hours and take as many days off for illness, personal matters, and vacation as they want or need—provided that they meet their work objectives. It may sound like a wonderful arrangement, but CEO Greg Strakosch recognizes that some people can't handle the responsibility that comes with such independence. As a result, TechTarget's hiring process is focused on filtering out candidates who need a more structured environment.[18]

Objective 3 Describe briefly what employers look for during an employment interview and pre-employment testing.

Suitability for a specific job is judged on the basis of

> *academic preparation*
> *work experience*
> *job-related personality traits*

Compatibility with the organization is judged on the basis of personal background, attitudes, and style.

Some interviewers believe that personal background indicates how well the candidate will fit in, so they might ask about your interests, hobbies, awareness of world events, and so forth. You can expand your potential along these lines by reading widely, making an effort to meet new people, and participating in discussion groups, seminars, and workshops. For example, Google values diverse interests and experiences, and far-reaching curiosity about virtually any subject is always welcome.

Beyond your organizational fit, interviewers are likely to consider your personal style as well. You're likely to impress an employer by being open, enthusiastic, and interested. Some interviewers also look for courtesy, sincerity, willingness to learn, and a style that is positive and self-confident. All of these qualities help a new employee adapt to a new workplace and new responsibilities.

TIPS FOR SUCCESS

"Employers are looking for better-rounded workers these days. If you're just a grabber, looking for what you can get for yourself, you just might be seen as a bright spark in the beginning, but it won't carry you through your career."
—Marilyn Edelson, CEO, OnTrack Coaching and Consulting Inc.

Pre-employment Testing

Pre-employment tests attempt to provide objective, quantitative information about a candidate's skills, attitudes, and habits.

In an effort to improve the predictability of the selection process and reduce the reliance on the brief interaction that an interview allows, many employers now conduct a variety of pre-employment tests.[19] These tests attempt to assess such factors as integrity, personality, and job skills. Google uses testing in creative ways not only to measure the skills of potential hires but also to build interest in the company as a fun place to work. Thousands of computer programmers compete in the annual Google Code Jam, vying for valuable prizes and the chance to visit Google to explore job opportunities.[20]

Testing is a complex topic that varies widely by industry and position. Here is an overview of the most common types of tests:

> **Personality tests.** Personality tests are used to assess either general character or suitability for the demands of a specific profession. General tests attempt to profile overall intellectual ability, attitudes toward work, interests, and managerial potential as well as such characteristics as dependability, commitment, honesty, and motivation.[21] The specific tests evaluate whether a candidate is suited to the emotional rigours of demanding positions, such as flight crews, RCMP Aircraft Protective Officers, and police and fire services.

> **Job skills tests.** The most common type of pre-employment tests are those designed to assess the competency or specific abilities needed to perform a job. The skills you might be tested on vary according to the position, naturally, but the most frequently tested include basic computer skills, clerical tasks, basic business financial tasks, and legal and medical terminology.[22]

> **Background checks.** Although not a test in the usual sense, a background check also helps employers learn more about you. A background check might be used to verify the credentials on your résumé, to see how well you manage credit, or even to learn if you have a criminal history. These investigations can generate considerable controversy, since some people consider them an invasion of privacy. However, many employers believe they have no choice, given the magnitude of the risks they now face. It is a sad fact that lying on résumés and in interviews is prevalent. Employers know that they can be held liable for the actions of employees who obtained jobs under false pretences (in fact, for the actions of all their employees, including those who obtained their positions honestly).

When recruiters interview potential employees, they look for people who communicate well. How do your interview skills rank? Where are your strengths? What are your areas for improvement?

If you're concerned about any pre-employment test, ask the employer for more information or ask your campus placement office for advice. You can also get more information from both the federal and your provincial or territorial human rights commissions. Academically, you should check up on yourself before applying for work: Ensure that school transcripts are correct and up to date, so any errors don't cause problems when a potential employer looks into your background.[23]

Preparing for a Job Interview

The more prepared you are, the less nervous you'll be about the interviewing process. Be sure to consider any cultural differences when preparing for interviews, and base your approach on what your audience expects. To prepare for a successful interview, learn about the organization, think ahead about questions, bolster your confidence, polish your interview style, plan to look good, and be ready when you arrive.

Just as written messages need planning, employment interviews need preparation

Objective 4 Outline six tasks you need to complete to prepare for a successful job interview.

1. Learn About the Organization

Today's companies expect serious candidates to demonstrate an understanding of the company's operations, its markets, and its strategic and tactical challenges.[24] When you were planning your employment search, you probably already researched the companies you sent your résumé to. But now that you've been invited for an interview, you'll want to fine-tune your research and brush up on the facts you've collected. Table 16–2 offers tips on researching both companies and jobs.

> ### Table 16–2 Finding Out About an Organization and a Job Opportunity

Where to Look and What You Can Learn

> Company website: Overall information about the company, including key executives, products and services, locations and divisions, employee benefits, job descriptions
> Competitors' websites: Similar information from competitors, including the strengths these companies claim to have
> Industry-related websites: Objective analysis and criticism of the company, its products, its reputation, and its management
> Marketing materials (brochures, catalogues, etc.): The company's marketing strategy and customer communication style
> Company publications (both print and electronic): Key events, stories about employees, new products
> Blogs: Analysis and criticism (not always fair or unbiased) of the company, its products and services, its reputation, and its management
> Periodicals (newspapers and trade journals, both print and online): In-depth stories about the company and its strategies, products, successes, and failures; you may find profiles of top executives
> Career centre at your college: Often provides wide array of information about companies that hire graduates
> Current and former employees: Insights into the work environment

Points to Learn About the Organization

> Full name
> Location (headquarters and divisions, branches, subsidiaries, or other units)
> Age and brief history
> Products and services
> Industry position (is the company a leader or a minor player; is it an innovator or more of a follower)
> Key financial points (such as stock price and trend, if a public company)
> Growth prospects (is the company investing in its future through research and development; is it in a thriving industry)

Points to Learn About the Position

> Title
> Functions and responsibilities
> Qualifications and expectations
> Career path
> Salary range
> Travel expectations and opportunities
> Relocation expectations and opportunities

✓•Practise

The library is an excellent place to learn about employment interviews. How would you organize a search to find relevant material?

As you plan your responses to potential interview questions, be prepared to relate your qualifications to the organization's needs.

2. Think Ahead About Questions

Planning ahead for the interviewer's questions will help you handle them more confidently and successfully. As you consider answers to questions you might encounter, think about how you can relate your qualifications to the organization's needs. In addition, you will want to prepare insightful questions of your own.

PLANNING FOR THE EMPLOYER'S QUESTIONS Employers usually gear their interview questions to specific organizational needs. You can expect to be asked about your skills, achievements, and goals, as well as about your attitude toward work and school, your relationships with others (work supervisors, colleagues, and fellow students), and occasionally your hobbies and interests. You'll also need to anticipate and give a little extra thought to a few particularly tough questions, such as these:

> **What was the hardest decision you ever had to make?** Be prepared with a good example, explaining why the decision was difficult and how you finally made it.

> **What are your greatest weaknesses?** This question seems to be a favourite of some interviewers, although it probably rarely yields useful information. The standard ways to reply are to describe a weakness so that it sounds like a virtue—such as driving yourself too hard—or to describe a relatively minor shortcoming and explain how you're working to improve. Of course, interviewers who have asked this question many times have heard similar responses many times as well.

> **What didn't you like about previous jobs you've held?** State what you didn't like and discuss what the experience taught you. Avoid making negative references to former employers or colleagues. Be aware that when employers ask this question, they're trying to predict if you'll be an unhappy or difficult employee in the event they hire you, so plan your answer with care.[25]

> **Where do you want to be five years from now?** This question tests (1) whether you're merely using this job as a stopover until something better comes along and (2) whether you've given thought to your long-term goals. Whatever you plan to say, your answer should reflect your desire to contribute to the employer's long-term goals, not just your own goals.

> **Tell me something about yourself.** Answer that you'll be happy to talk about yourself, and ask what the interviewer wants to know. If this point is clarified, respond. If it isn't, explain how your skills can contribute to the job and the organization. This is a great chance to sell yourself.

Practise answering typical interview questions so that you can respond with confidence and complete answers.

For a look at the types of questions often asked, see Table 16–3. Jot down a brief answer to each one. Then read over the answers until you feel comfortable with each of them. You might also give a list of interview questions to a friend or relative and have that person ask you various questions at random. This method helps you learn to articulate answers and to look at the person as you answer.

PLANNING QUESTIONS OF YOUR OWN Remember that the interview is a two-way conversation: The questions you ask are just as important as the answers you provide. By asking insightful questions, you can demonstrate your understanding of the organization, you can steer the discussion into those areas that allow you to present your qualifications to best advantage, and you can verify for yourself whether this is the right opportunity for you. Before the interview, prepare a list of about a dozen questions you need answered to evaluate the organization and the job.

> Table 16–3 Twenty-Five Common Interview Questions

Questions About College and University

1. What courses did you like most? Least? Why?
2. Do you think your extracurricular activities were worth the time you spent on them? Why or why not?
3. When did you choose your program of study? Did you ever change it? If so, why?
4. Do you feel you did the best scholastic work you are capable of?
5. Which college or university year was the toughest? Why?

Questions About Employers and Jobs

1. What jobs have you held? Why did you leave?
2. What percentage of your school expenses did you earn? How?
3. Why did you choose your particular field of work?
4. What are the disadvantages of your chosen field?
5. Have you served in the military? What rank did you achieve? What jobs did you perform?
6. What do you think about how this industry operates today?
7. Why do you think you would like this particular type of job?

Questions About Personal Attitudes and Preferences

1. Do you prefer to work in any specific geographic location? If so, why?
2. How much money do you hope to earn in 5 years? In 10 years?
3. What do you think determines a person's progress in a good organization?
4. What personal characteristics do you feel are necessary for success in your chosen field?
5. Tell me a story.
6. Do you like to travel?
7. Do you think grades should be considered by employers? Why or why not?

Questions About Work Habits

1. Do you prefer working with others or by yourself?
2. What type of boss do you prefer?
3. Have you ever had any difficulty getting along with colleagues or supervisors? With instructors? With other students?
4. Would you prefer to work in a large or a small organization? Why?
5. How do you feel about overtime work?
6. What have you done that shows initiative and willingness to work?

Don't limit your questions to those you think will impress the interviewer, or you won't get the information you'll need to make a wise decision if you're offered the job. Craft questions to help you explore such issues as these:

> **Are these my kind of people?** Will the corporate atmosphere suit my personality and temperament?
> **Can I do this work?** Compare your qualifications with the requirements described by the interviewer.
> **Will I enjoy the work?** Know yourself and what's important to you. Will you find the work challenging? Will it give you feelings of accomplishment, of satisfaction, and of making a real contribution?
> **Is the job what I want?** You may never find a job that fulfills all your wants, but the position you accept should satisfy at least your primary ones. Will it make use of your best capabilities? Does it offer a career path to the long-term goals you've set?
> **Does the job pay what I'm worth?** By comparing jobs and salaries before you're interviewed, you'll know what's reasonable for someone with your skills in your industry.
> **What kind of person would I be working for?** If the interviewer is your prospective boss, watch how others interact with that person, tactfully query other employees, or pose a careful question or two during the interview. If

Plan questions that will help you decide whether the work and the organization are compatible with your goals and values.

> ## > Table 16–4 Ten Questions to Ask the Interviewer

1. What are the job's major responsibilities?
2. What qualities do you want in the person who fills this position?
3. How do you measure success for someone in this position?
4. What is the first problem that needs the attention of the person you hire?
5. Would relocation be required now or in the future?
6. Why is this job now vacant?
7. What makes your organization different from others in the industry?
8. How would you define your organization's managerial philosophy?
9. What additional training does your organization provide?
10. Do employees have an opportunity to continue their education with help from the organization?

your prospective boss is someone else, ask for that person's name, job title, and responsibilities. Learn all you can.

> > **What sort of future can I expect with this organization?** How healthy is the organization? Can you look forward to advancement? Does the organization offer insurance, pension, vacation, or other benefits?

Rather than bombarding the interviewer with questions the minute you walk in the room, work them into the conversation naturally, without trying to take control of the interview. For a list of good questions you might use as a starting point, see Table 16–4.

You don't necessarily have to wait until the interviewer asks if you have any questions of your own; look for smooth ways to work prepared questions into the conversation.

Impress the interviewer with your ability to organize and be thorough by bringing a list of questions to the job interview.

Write your list of questions on a notepad and take it to the interview. If you need to, jot down brief notes during the meeting, and ensure that you record answers in more detail afterward. Having a list of questions should impress the interviewer with your organization and thoroughness. It will also show that you're there to evaluate the organization and the job as well as to promote yourself.

3. Bolster Your Confidence

By building your confidence, you'll make a better impression and make the whole process less stressful. The best way to counteract any apprehension is to remove its source. You may feel shy or self-conscious because you think you have some flaw that will prompt others to reject you. Bear in mind, however, that you're often much more conscious of your limitations than other people are.

If some aspect of your appearance or background makes you uneasy, correct it or offset it by emphasizing positive traits such as warmth, wit, intelligence, or charm. Instead of dwelling on your weaknesses, focus on your strengths. Instead of worrying about how you will perform in the interview, focus on how you can help the organization succeed. Remember that all the other candidates for the job are just as nervous as you are. The interviewers may be nervous, too; after all, they're judged on how well they assess candidates, so help them see your positive qualities clearly.

4. Polish Your Interview Style

Competence and confidence are the foundation of your interviewing style, and you can enhance those by giving the interviewer an impression of poise, good manners, and good judgment. Some job seekers hire professional coaches and image consultants to create just the right impression. These experts teach clients how to adopt appropriate communication styles, and to do so they use role-playing, videotaping, and audiotaping.[26] You can use these techniques too.

You can develop an adept style by staging mock interviews with a friend. You can record these practice sessions and then evaluate them yourself. The taping process can be intimidating, but it helps you work out any problems before you begin actual job interviews. You can also see if your career centre has a computer-based interview simulator. You can search online for "practice interviews" or "interview simulators."

After each practice session, identify opportunities for improvement. Have your mock interview partner critique your performance, or critique yourself if you're able to record your practice interviews, using the list of warning signs shown in Table 16–5.

As you stage your mock interviews, pay particular attention to your nonverbal behaviour. In Canada and the United States, you are more likely to have a successful interview if you maintain eye contact, smile frequently, sit in an attentive position, and use frequent hand gestures. These nonverbal signals convince the interviewer that you're alert, assertive, dependable, confident, responsible, and energetic.[27] Some companies based in the North America are owned and managed by people from different cultures, so during your research, find out about the company's cultural background and preferences regarding nonverbal behaviour.

The sound of your voice can also have a major impact on your success in a job interview.[28] You can work with a tape recorder to overcome voice problems. If you tend to speak too rapidly, practise speaking more slowly. If your voice sounds too loud or too soft, practise adjusting it. Work on eliminating speech mannerisms such as *you know, like,* and *um,* which might make you sound inarticulate.

Interview simulators, such as this system from Perfect Interview, let you interact with a virtual interviewer and then review and improve your responses. Is this a useful tool to help you relax in job interviews? Why? Why not?

Staging mock interviews with a friend is a good way to hone your style.

Nonverbal behaviour has a significant effect on the interviewer's opinion of you.

The way you speak is almost as important as what you say.

> Table 16–5 Warning Signs: Twenty-Five Attributes That Interviewers Don't Like to See

> poor personal appearance	> poor scholastic record; just got by
> overbearing, overaggressive, conceited demeanour; a "superiority complex" or "know-it-all" attitude	> unwillingness to start at the bottom; expecting too much too soon
> inability to express ideas clearly; poor voice, diction, grammar	> tendency to make excuses
> lack of knowledge or experience	> evasive answers; hedges on unfavourable factors in record
> poor preparation for the interview	> lack of tact
> lack of interest in the job	> lack of maturity
> lack of planning for career; lack of purpose, goals	> lack of courtesy; poor manners
> lack of enthusiasm; passive and indifferent demeanour	> condemnation of past employers
> lack of confidence and poise; appearance of being nervous and ill at ease	> lack of social skills
> insufficient evidence of achievement	> marked dislike for schoolwork
> failure to participate in extracurricular activities	> lack of vitality
> overemphasis on money; interested only in financial aspects of the job	> failure to look interviewer in the eye
	> limp, weak handshake

5. Plan to Look Good

Make a positive first impression with careful grooming and attire. Why is it important to look clean, prepared, and professional? How can you evaluate and improve your professional image?

Dress conservatively and be well groomed for every interview; there's plenty of time to be casual after you get the job.

Be ready to go the minute you arrive at the interviewing site; don't fumble around for your résumé or your list of questions.

Physical appearance is important because clothing and grooming reveal something about a candidate's personality, professionalism, and ability to sense the unspoken "rules" of a situation. When it comes to clothing, the best policy is to dress conservatively. Wear the best-quality businesslike clothing you can, preferably in a dark, solid colour. Wearing clothes that are appropriate and clean is far more important than wearing clothes that are expensive. Avoid flamboyant styles, colours, and prints. Even in companies where interviewers may dress casually, it's important to show good judgment by dressing—and acting—in a professional manner. Even minor points of etiquette can make a lasting impression on recruiters.

Some candidates ask interviewers ahead of time what they should wear. One human resources executive tells job seekers to dress business casual because dressing in a suit, for example, looks awkward at his company.[29] However, in other companies, business casual would be completely out of place in a job interview. Your research into various industries and professions should give you insight into expectations for business attire, too. If you're not sure, being a little too formal is a better guess than being too casual.

Good grooming makes any style of clothing look better. Make sure your clothes are clean and unwrinkled, your shoes unscuffed and well shined, your hair neatly styled and combed, your fingernails clean, and your breath fresh. If possible, check your appearance in a mirror before entering the room for the interview. Finally, remember that one of the best ways to look good is to smile at appropriate moments.

Make professional appearance and habits a routine part of your day after you land that first job, too. Some students fail to recognize the need to adjust their dress and personal habits when they make the transition to professional life. Behaviours you may not think about, such as showing up five minutes late to every meeting or wearing a T-shirt to a client's office, could limit your career potential. Again, these may seem like minor issues, but many people are sensitive to these points of business etiquette and consider them signs of mutual respect.

6. Be Ready When You Arrive

When you go to your interview, take a small notebook, a pen, a list of the questions you want to ask, two copies of your résumé (protected in a folder), an outline of what you have learned about the organization, and any past correspondence about the position. You may also want to take a small calendar, a transcript of your college or university grades, a list of references, and a portfolio containing samples of your work, performance reviews, and certificates of achievement.[30]

Be sure you know when and where the interview will be held. The worst way to start any interview is to be late. Check the route you will take, even if it means phoning ahead to ask. Find out how much time it takes to get there; then plan to arrive early. Allow a little extra time in case you run into a problem on the way.

When you arrive, remind yourself that you are fully prepared and confident and then try to relax. You may have to wait a little while, so bring along something business-oriented to read. If company literature is available in the lobby, read it while you wait. In every case, show respect for everyone you encounter. If the opportunity presents itself, ask a few questions about the organization or express enthusiasm for the job. Refrain from smoking before the interview

CHECKLIST Planning for a Successful Job Interview

✔ Learn about the organization, including its operations, markets, and challenges.

✔ Plan for the employer's questions, including questions about tough decisions you've made, your weaknesses, what you didn't like about previous jobs, and your career plans.

✔ Plan questions of your own to find out whether this is really the job and the organization for you, and to show that you've done your research.

✔ Bolster your confidence by removing as many sources of apprehension as you can.

✔ Polish your interview style by staging mock interviews.

✔ Plan to look good with appropriate dress and grooming.

✔ Be ready when you arrive, and bring along a pen, paper, list of questions, two résumés, an outline of your research on the company, and any correspondence you've had regarding the position.

✔ Double-check the location and time of the interview and map out the route beforehand.

✔ Relax and be flexible; the schedule and interview arrangements may change when you arrive.

(nonsmokers can smell smoke on the clothing of interviewees), and avoid chewing gum or otherwise eating in the waiting room. Anything you do or say while you wait may well get back to the interviewer, so be sure your best qualities show from the moment you enter the premises. That way, you'll be ready for the interview itself once it actually begins. To review the steps for planning a successful interview, see "Checklist: Planning for a Successful Job Interview."

Interviewing for Success

Your approach to interviews evolves as you move through each stage of the process. The techniques for success are similar throughout, even though the focus and purpose of the interviews change—both for you and the employer. To increase your chances of success, follow the tips from successful interviewers about how to make a positive impression by avoiding mistakes (see "Sharpening Your Career Skills: Don't Talk Yourself Right Out of a Job").

If you're being interviewed for the first time, your main objective is to differentiate yourself from the many other candidates who are also being screened. Without resorting to gimmicks, call attention to one key aspect of your personal or professional background, so the recruiter can say, "Oh yes, I remember Brenda Jones—the one who built a computerized home weather station to wake her up a few minutes early whenever it snowed overnight." Just ensure that the trait you accentuate is relevant to the job in question. In addition, you'll want to be prepared in case an employer expects you to demonstrate a particular skill (perhaps problem solving) during the screening interview.

> Present a memorable "headline" during an interview at the screening stage.

If you progress to the initial selection interview, broaden your promotional message. Instead of telegraphing the "headline," give the interviewer the whole story. Touch briefly on all your strengths, but explain three or four of your best qualifications in depth. At the same time, probe for information that will help you evaluate the position objectively.

> Cover all your strengths during an interview at the selection stage.

If you're asked back for a final visit, your chances of being offered a position have improved considerably. At this point, you'll probably talk to a person who has the authority to make an offer and negotiate terms. This individual may have already concluded that your background is right for the job and may be most concerned with sizing up your personality. Both you and the employer need to find out whether there is a good psychological fit. Be honest about your motivations and values. If the interview goes well, your objective should be to clinch the deal on the best possible terms.

> Emphasize your personality, motivations, and values during a final interview.

SHARPENING YOUR CAREER SKILLS

Don't Talk Yourself Right Out of a Job

Even well-qualified applicants sometimes talk themselves right out of an opportunity by making avoidable blunders during the job interview. As you develop your interviewing style, avoid these all-too-common mistakes:

> **Being defensive.** An interview isn't an interrogation, and the interviewer isn't out to get you. Treat interviews as business conversations, an exchange of information in which both sides have something of value to share. You'll give (and get) better information that way.

> **Failing to ask questions.** Interviewers expect you to ask questions, both during the interview and at its conclusion when they ask if you have any questions. If you have nothing to ask, you come across as someone who isn't really interested in the job or the company. Prepare a list of questions before every interview.

> **Failing to answer questions—or bluffing your way through difficult questions.** If you simply can't answer a question, don't talk your way around it or fake your way through it. Remember that sometimes interviewers ask strange questions just to see how you'll respond. What kind of fish would you like to be? How would you go about nailing jelly to the ceiling? Why are manhole covers round? Some of these questions are designed to test your grace under pressure, whereas others actually expect you to think through a logical answer (manhole covers are round because that's the only shape that can't fall through an open hole of slightly smaller size, by the way). Don't act like the question is stupid or refuse to answer it. Sit quietly for a few seconds, imagine why the interviewer has asked the question, and then frame an answer that links your strengths to the company's needs.

> **Freezing up.** The human brain seems to have the capacity to just freeze up under stressful situations. An interviewer might have asked you a simple question, or perhaps you were halfway through an intelligent answer, and suddenly all your thoughts disappear and you can't organize words in any logical order. Quickly replay the last few seconds of the conversation in your mind to see if you can recapture the conversational thread. If that fails, you're probably better off explaining to the reviewer that your mind has gone blank and asking him or her to repeat the question. Doing so is embarrassing, but not as embarrassing as chattering on and on with no idea of what you're saying, hoping you'll stumble back onto the topic.

> **Failing to understand your potential to contribute to the organization.** Interviewers care less about your history than about how you can help their organization in the future. Unless you've inventoried your own skills, researched their needs, and found a match between the two, you won't be able to answer these questions quickly and intelligently.

CAREER APPLICATIONS

1 What should you do if you suddenly realize that something you said earlier in the interview is incorrect or incomplete? Explain your answer.

2 How would you answer the following question: "How do you respond to colleagues who make you angry?" Explain your answer.

Objective 5 Explain the three stages of a successful employment interview.

Regardless of where you are in the interview process, every interview will proceed through three stages: the warm-up, the question-and-answer session, and the close.

1. The Warm-Up

The first minute of the interview is crucial, so be ready and alert.

Of the three stages, the warm-up is the most important, even though it may account for only a small fraction of the time you spend in the interview. Studies suggest that many interviewers, particularly those who are poorly trained in interviewing techniques, make up their minds within the first 20 seconds of contact with a candidate.[31] Don't let your guard down if it appears the interviewer wants to engage in what feels like small talk; these exchanges are every bit as important as structured questions.

Body language is important at this point. Because you won't have time to say much in the first minute or two, you must sell yourself nonverbally. Begin by using the interviewer's name if you're sure you can pronounce it correctly. If the interviewer extends a hand, respond with a firm but not overpowering handshake; don't sit down until you're asked to be seated or the interviewer has taken his or her own seat. Let the interviewer start the discussion and listen for cues that tell you what he or she is interested in knowing about you as a potential employee.

2. The Question-and-Answer Stage

Questions and answers will consume the greatest part of the interview. The interviewer will ask you about your qualifications and discuss many points mentioned in your résumé. You'll also ask questions of your own.

DEALING WITH QUESTIONS Let the interviewer lead the conversation, and never answer a question before he or she has finished asking it—the last few words of the question might alter how you respond. As questions are asked, tailor your answers to make a favourable impression. Don't limit yourself to yes or no answers. If you're asked a difficult question, ensure that you pause to think before responding. The recruiter may know that you can't answer a question and only wants to know how you'll respond.

Tailor your answers to emphasize your strengths.

If you periodically ask a question or two from the list you've prepared, you'll not only learn something but also demonstrate your interest. Probe for what the company is looking for in its new employees so that you can show how you meet the firm's needs. Also zero in on any reservations the interviewer might have about you so that you can dispel them.

LISTENING TO THE INTERVIEWER Paying attention when the interviewer speaks can be as important as giving good answers or asking good questions. Review the tips on listening offered in Chapter 2.

The interviewer's facial expressions, eye movements, gestures, and posture may tell you the real meaning of what is being said. Be especially aware of how your comments are received. Does the interviewer nod in agreement or smile to show approval? If so, you're making progress. If not, you might want to introduce another topic or modify your approach.

Paying attention to both verbal and nonverbal messages can help you turn the question-and-answer stage to your advantage.

FIELDING DISCRIMINATORY QUESTIONS Employers cannot legally discriminate against a job candidate on the basis of race, ancestry, place of origin, colour, ethnic origin, citizenship, creed, sex, sexual orientation, age, record of offences, marital status, same-sex partnership status, family status, and handicap. As the Ontario Human Rights Code states, "Employment decisions should be based on the applicant's ability to do the job and not on factors that are unrelated to the job." Employers must be familiar with the employment and hiring policies enshrined in their province's or territory's human rights code.

Well-trained interviewers are aware of questions they shouldn't ask.

If your interviewer asks personal questions, how you respond depends on how badly you want the job, how you feel about revealing the information asked for, what you think the interviewer will do with the information, and whether you want to work for a company that asks such questions. Remember that you always have the option of simply refusing to answer or of telling the interviewer that you think a particular question is unethical.[21] If you do want the job, you might (1) ask how the question is related to your qualifications, (2) explain that the information is personal, (3) respond to what you think is the interviewer's real concern, or (4) answer both the question and the concern.

Think about how you might respond if you are asked a potentially unlawful question.

If you believe an interviewer's questions are unreasonable, unrelated to the job, or an attempt to discriminate, you may complain to your province's or territory's human rights commission. The commission's website will have a link to the complaint-filing process where you will find information to assist you in completing the complaint form.

3. The Close

Like the warm-up, the end of the interview is more important than its brief duration would indicate. In the last few minutes, evaluate how well you've done and correct any misconceptions the interviewer might have.

Conclude an interview with courtesy and enthusiasm.

CONCLUDING GRACEFULLY You can generally tell when the interviewer wants to conclude the session. He or she may ask whether you have any more questions, sum up the discussion, change position, or indicate with a gesture that the interview is over. When you get the signal, respond promptly, but don't rush. Ensure that you thank the interviewer for the opportunity and express an interest in the organization. If you can do so comfortably, pin down what will happen next, but don't press for an immediate decision.

Research salary ranges in your job, industry, and geographic region before you negotiate salary.

If this is your second or third visit to the organization, the interview may culminate with an offer of employment. You have two options: Accept it or request time to think it over. The best course is usually to wait. If no job offer is made, the interviewer may not have reached a decision yet, but you may tactfully ask when you can expect to know the decision.

DISCUSSING SALARY If you receive an offer during the interview, you'll naturally want to discuss salary. However, let the interviewer raise the subject. If asked your salary requirements during the interview or on a job application, you can say that your salary requirements are open or negotiable or that you would expect a competitive compensation package.[32] If you have added qualifications, point them out: "With my 18 months of experience in the field, I would expect to start in the middle of the normal salary range." You can find industry salary ranges at the Service Canada website www.labourmarketinformation.ca, or at several of the popular job websites.

Negotiating benefits may be one way to get more value from an employment package.

If you don't like the offer, you might negotiate, provided you're in a good bargaining position and the organization has the flexibility to accommodate you. You'll be in a fairly strong position if your skills are in short supply and you have several other offers. It also helps if you're the favourite candidate and the organization is booming. However, many organizations are relatively rigid in their salary practices, particularly at the entry level. In Canada, the United States, and some European countries, it is perfectly acceptable to ask, "Is there any room for negotiation?"

Salary will probably be the most important component of your compensation and benefits package, but it's not the only factor by any means. And even if salary isn't negotiable, you may find flexibility in a signing bonus, profit sharing, pension and other retirement benefits, health coverage, vacation time, stock options, and other valuable elements in the overall compensation and benefits package.[33]

It's good practice to jot down the questions you were asked, and your answers, while the interview is fresh in your mind. Should you keep handwritten notes, or transfer them into a computer file? What are the advantages of maintaining an electronic record of your interviews?

CHECKLIST Making a Positive Impression in Job Interviews

A. The warm-up

✔ Be alert; even initial small talk is part of the interviewing process.

✔ Greet the interviewer by name, with a smile and direct eye contact.

✔ Offer a firm (not crushing) handshake if the interviewer extends a hand.

✔ Take a seat only after the interviewer invites you to sit or has taken his or her own seat.

✔ Listen for cues about what the questions reveal about you and your qualifications.

B. The question-and-answer stage

✔ Let the interviewer lead the conversation.

✔ Never answer a question before the interviewer finishes asking it.

✔ Listen carefully to the interviewer and watch for nonverbal signals.

✔ Don't limit yourself to simple yes or no answers; expand on the answer to show your knowledge of the company (but don't ramble on).

✔ If you encounter a potentially discriminatory question, decide how you want to respond before you say anything

✔ When you have the opportunity, ask questions from the list you've prepared when you have the opportunity; remember that interviewers expect you to ask questions.

C. The close

✔ Watch and listen for signs that the interview is about to end.

✔ Quickly evaluate how well you've done and correct any misperceptions the interviewer might have.

✔ If you receive an offer and aren't ready to decide, it's entirely appropriate to ask for time to think about it.

✔ Don't bring up salary, but be prepared to discuss it if the interviewer raises the subject.

✔ End with a warm smile and a handshake, and thank the interviewer for meeting with you.

To review the important tips for successful interviews, see "Checklist: Making a Positive Impression in Job Interviews."

Interview Notes

If yours is a typical job search, you'll have many interviews before you accept an offer. For that reason, keeping a notebook or simple database of interview notes can help you refresh your memory of each conversation. As soon as you leave the interview facility, jot down the names and titles of the people you met. Briefly summarize the interviewer's answers to your questions. Then quickly evaluate your performance during the interview, listing what you handled well and what you didn't. Going over these notes can help you improve your performance in the future.[34] In addition to improving your performance during interviews, your interview notes will help you keep track of any follow-up messages you'll need to send.

Keep a written record of your job interviews, and keep your notes organized so that you can compare companies and opportunities.

Following Up After the Interview

Touching base with the prospective employer after the interview, either by phone or in writing, shows that you really want the job and are determined to get it. This contact also gives you another chance to demonstrate your communication skills and sense of business etiquette. Following up brings your name to the interviewer's attention once again and reminds him or her that you're actively looking and waiting for the decision.

The two most common forms of follow-up are the thank-you message and the inquiry. These messages are often handled by letter, but an email or a phone call can be just as effective, particularly if the employer seems to favour a casual,

Objective 6 Identify the most common employment messages that follow an interview, and explain when you would use each one.

Six types of follow-up messages:
- *> thank-you message*
- *> message of inquiry*
- *> request for a time extension*
- *> letter of acceptance*
- *> letter declining a job offer*
- *> letter of resignation*

personal style. Other types of follow-up messages—letters requesting a time extension, letters of acceptance, letters declining a job offer, and letters of resignation—are best handled in writing to document any official actions relating to your employment.

✳-[Explore

Thank-You Message

A note or phone call thanking the interviewer should be organized like a routine message and close with a request for a decision or future consideration.

Express your thanks within two days after the interview, even if you feel you have little chance for the job. Not only is this good etiquette, but it leaves a positive impression. Acknowledge the interviewer's time and courtesy, and convey your continued interest, then ask politely for a decision. In Figure 16–3, Michael Espinosa accomplishes all this in three brief paragraphs.

Keep your thank-you message brief (less than five minutes for a phone call or just two or three paragraphs for a letter or an email message) and organize it as a routine message. Demonstrate the "you" attitude, and sound positive without sounding overconfident. Even if the interviewer has said that you are unqualified for the job, a thank-you message may keep the door open to future opportunities.

✳-[Explore

Message of Inquiry

To inquire about a hiring decision, follow the model for a direct request.

If you're not advised of the interviewer's decision by the promised date or within two weeks, you might make an inquiry. A message of inquiry is particularly appropriate if you've received a job offer from a second firm and don't want to accept it before you have an answer from the first. The following message illustrates the general plan for a direct request; the writer assumes

> Figure 16–3 Email Thank-You Message

Indicates the writer's flexibility and commitment to the job if hired

Closes on a confident, "you"-oriented note with a request for a decision

Reminds the interviewer of the reasons for meeting and graciously acknowledges the consideration shown to the applicant

Reminds the recruiter of special qualifications

Dear Ms. Reynolds:

After talking with you yesterday, touring your sets, and watching the television commercials being filmed, I remain enthusiastic about the possibility of joining your staff as a television/film production assistant. Thanks for taking so much time to show me around.

During our meeting, I said that I would prefer not to relocate, but I've reconsidered the matter. I would be pleased to relocate wherever you need my skills in set decoration and prop design.

Now that you've explained the details of your operation, I feel quite strongly that I can make a contribution to the sorts of productions you're lining up. You can also count on me to be an energetic employee and a positive addition to your crew. Please let me know your decision as soon as possible.

Sincerely,

Michael Espinosa
201 College Blvd.
Red Deer, AB T7N 5A5
(403) 555-3113
espinosam@newm.com

that a simple oversight or routine delay, and not outright rejection, is the reason for the delay:

When we talked on April 7 about the fashion coordinator position in your Design Walk showroom, you indicated that a decision would be made by May 1. I am still enthusiastic about the position and eager to know what conclusion you have reached. ← Identifies the position and introduces the main idea

To complicate matters, another firm has now offered me a position and has asked that I reply within the next two weeks. ← Places the reason for the request second

Because your company seems to offer a greater challenge, I would appreciate knowing about your decision by Thursday, May 10. If you need more information before then, please let me know. ← Makes a courteous request for specific action last, while clearly stating a preference for this organization

Request for a Time Extension

If you receive a job offer while other interviews are still pending, you'll probably want more time to decide, so write to the offering organization and ask for a time extension. Employers understand that candidates often interview with several companies. They want you to be sure that you're making the right decision, so most are happy to accommodate you with a reasonable extension.

✳ Explore

Preface your request with a friendly opening. Ask for more time, stressing your enthusiasm for the organization. Conclude by allowing for a quick decision if your request for additional time is denied. Ask for a prompt reply confirming the time extension if the organization grants it. This type of message is, in essence, a direct request. However, because the recipient may be

Your job search will require dealing with voice mail. When leaving a message, first state your name and phone number, then describe the purpose of your call, and end by restating your name and number. Write down and rehearse what you want to say, so your delivery is smooth and clear. Why are voice-mail skills important to employers?

> Figure 16–4 Effective Request for a Time Extension

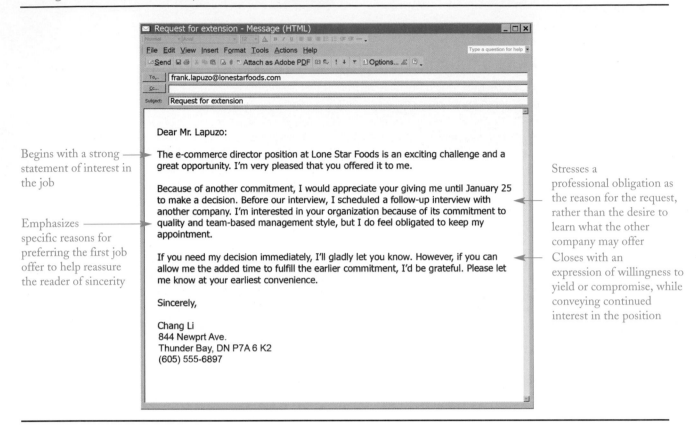

Begins with a strong statement of interest in the job

Emphasizes specific reasons for preferring the first job offer to help reassure the reader of sincerity

Stresses a professional obligation as the reason for the request, rather than the desire to learn what the other company may offer

Closes with an expression of willingness to yield or compromise, while conveying continued interest in the position

---

disappointed, ensure that you temper your request for an extension with statements indicating your continued interest. The letter in Figure 16–4 is a good example.

Use the model for positive messages when you write a letter of acceptance.

Letter of Acceptance

When you receive a job offer that you want to accept, reply within five days. Begin by accepting the position and expressing thanks. Identify the job that you're accepting. In the next paragraph, cover any necessary details. Conclude by saying that you look forward to reporting for work. As always, a positive message should convey your enthusiasm and eagerness to cooperate:

Confirms the specific terms of the offer with a good-news statement at the beginning

Covers miscellaneous details in the middle

Closes with another reference to the good news and a look toward the future

I'm delighted to accept the graphic design position in your advertising department at the salary of $2975 a month.

Enclosed are the health insurance forms you asked me to complete and sign. I've already given notice to my current employer and will be able to start work on Monday, January 18.

The prospect of joining your firm is exciting. Thank you for giving me this opportunity for what I'm sure will be a challenging future.

Be aware that a job offer and a written acceptance of that offer can constitute a legally binding contract, for both you and the employer. Before you write an acceptance letter, ensure that you want the job.

Letter Declining a Job Offer

After all your interviews, you may find that you need to write a letter declining a job offer. Use the techniques for negative messages (see Chapter 9): Open warmly, state the reasons for refusing the offer, decline the offer explicitly, and close on a pleasant note, expressing gratitude. By taking the time to write a sincere, tactful letter, you leave the door open for future contact:

✳️⎯Explore

A letter declining a job offer follows the model for negative messages.

Thank you for your hospitality during my interview at your Montreal facility last month. I'm flattered that you would offer me the computer analyst position that we talked about.

During my job search, I applied to five highly rated firms like your own, each one a leader in its field. Both your company and another offered me a position. Because my desire to work abroad can more readily be satisfied by the other company, I have accepted that job offer.

I deeply appreciate the time you spent talking with me. Thank you again for your consideration and kindness.

Uses a buffer in the opening paragraph

Precedes the bad news with tactfully phrased reasons for the applicant's unfavourable decision and leaves the door open

Lets the reader down gently with a sincere and cordial ending

Letter of Resignation

If you get a job offer and are currently employed, you can maintain good relations with your current employer by writing a letter of resignation to your immediate supervisor. Follow the approach for negative messages and make the letter sound positive, regardless of how you feel. Say something favourable about the organization, the people you work with, or what you've learned on the job. Then state your intention to leave and give the date of your last day on the job. Ensure that you give your current employer at least two weeks' notice:

✳️⎯Explore

Letters of resignation should always be written in a gracious and professional style that avoids criticism of your employer or your colleagues.

My sincere thanks to you and to all the other Emblem Corporation employees for helping me learn so much about serving the public these past two years. You have given me untold help and encouragement.

You may recall that when you first interviewed me, my goal was to become a customer relations supervisor. Because that opportunity has been offered to me by another organization, I am submitting my resignation. I will miss my friends and colleagues at Emblem, but I want to take advantage of this opportunity.

I would like to terminate my work here two weeks from today but can arrange to work an additional week if you want me to train a replacement.

Best wishes to all of you.

Uses an appreciative opening to serve as a buffer

States reasons before the bad news itself, using tactful phrasing to help keep the relationship friendly, should the writer later want letters of recommendation

Discusses necessary details in an extra paragraph

Tempers any disappointment with a cordial close

To verify the content and style of your follow-up messages, consult the tips in "Checklist: Writing Follow-Up Messages."

CHECKLIST Writing Follow-Up Messages

A. Thank-you messages
- ✔ Write a brief thank-you letter within two days of the interview.
- ✔ Acknowledge the interviewer's time and courtesy.
- ✔ Restate the specific job you're applying for.
- ✔ Express your enthusiasm about the organization and the job.
- ✔ Add any new facts that may help your chances.
- ✔ Politely ask for a decision.

B. Messages of inquiry
- ✔ If you haven't heard from the interviewer by the promised date, write a brief message of inquiry.
- ✔ Use a direct approach: main idea, necessary details, and specific request.

C. Requests for a time extension
- ✔ Request an extension if you have pending interviews and need time to decide about an offer.
- ✔ Open on a friendly note.
- ✔ Explain why you need more time and express continued interest in the company.
- ✔ In the close, promise a quick decision if your request is denied and ask for a confirmation if your request is granted.

D. Letters of acceptance
- ✔ Send this message within five days of receiving the offer.
- ✔ State clearly that you accept the offer, identify the job you're accepting, and confirm vital details such as salary and start date.
- ✔ Make sure you want the job; an acceptance letter can be treated as a legally binding contract.

E. Letters declining a job offer
- ✔ Use the model for negative messages.
- ✔ Open on a warm and appreciative note and then explain why you refuse the offer.
- ✔ End on a sincere, positive note.

F. Letters of resignation
- ✔ Send a letter of resignation to your current employer as soon as possible.
- ✔ Begin with an appreciative buffer.
- ✔ In the middle section, state your reasons for leaving and actually state that you are resigning.
- ✔ Close cordially.

Summary of Learning Objectives

1 Define the purpose of application letters and explain how to apply the AIDA organizational approach to them. The purpose of an application letter is to convince readers to look at your résumé. This makes application letters a type of sales letter, so you'll want to use the AIDA organizational approach. Get attention in the opening paragraph by showing how your work skills could benefit the organization, by explaining how your qualifications fit the job, or by demonstrating an understanding of the organization's needs. Build interest and desire by showing how you can meet the job requirements, and ensure that you refer your reader to your résumé near the end of this section. Finally, motivate action by making your request easy to fulfill and by including all necessary contact information.

2 Describe the typical sequence of job interviews. Most companies interview a candidate two or three times before making the job offer. The first stage in the sequence is the screening stage, when applicants are asked the same questions, so they are all measured against the same criteria. The second is the selection stage: Here, applicants will meet with several interviewers, who will decide if you are a good fit with the organization. The final interview stage further determines if you will get along with your future colleagues as they learn more about your personality. In this stage, your interviewers will persuade you to join the company if they want to hire you.

3 Describe briefly what employers look for during an employment interview and pre-employment testing. Employers want to see if you will fit with the corporate culture and if you can handle the responsibilities of the position. They might ask you about your personal interests and knowledge of current events to determine your personal background. They may also ask you to discuss your education and work experience in more depth to understand how your skills match the job requirements.

4 **Outline six tasks you need to complete to prepare for a successful job interview.** To prepare for a successful job interview, begin by (1) refining the research you did when planning your résumé. Knowing as much as you can about the company and its needs helps you highlight the aspects of your background and qualifications that will appeal to the organization. (2) Next, think ahead about questions—both those you'll need to answer and those you'll want to ask. (3) Bolster your confidence by focusing on your strengths to overcome any apprehension. (4) Polish your style by staging mock interviews and paying close attention to nonverbal behaviours, including voice problems. (5) Plan to look your best with businesslike clothing and good grooming. (6) Finally, arrive on time and ready to begin.

5 **Explain the three stages of a successful employment interview.** All employment interviews have three stages. The warm-up stage is the most important because first impressions greatly influence an interviewer's decision. The question-and-answer stage is the longest: Here you will answer and ask questions. Listening carefully and watching the interviewer's nonverbal clues help you determine how the interview is going. The close is also important because you need to evaluate your performance to see whether the interviewer has any misconceptions that you must correct.

6 **Identify the most common employment messages that follow an interview and explain when you would use each one.** The two most common types of follow-up messages are usually in letter form but can also be effective by phone or email. You send the thank-you message within two days after your interview to show appreciation, express your continued interest in the job, and politely ask for a decision. You send an inquiry if you haven't received the interviewer's decision by the date promised or within two weeks of the interview—especially if you've received a job offer from another firm. The remaining four employment messages are best sent in letter form, to document any official action. You request a time extension if you receive a job offer while other interviews are pending and you want more time to complete those interviews before making a decision. You send a letter of acceptance within five days of receiving a job offer that you want to take. You send a letter declining a job offer when you want to refuse an offer tactfully and leave the door open for future contact. You send a letter of resignation when you receive a job offer that you want to accept while you are currently employed.

mycanadianbuscommlab

Visit www.mycanadianbuscommlab.ca for everything you need to help you succeed in the job you've always wanted! Tools and resources include the following:
- Composing Space and Writer's Toolkit
- Document Makeovers
- Video Case Studies
- Grammar Exercises—and much more!

On the Job PERFORMING COMMUNICATION TASKS AT GOOGLE

Google recruiters work year-round arranging career fairs, booking speaking engagements, and responding to inquiries—all to attract the best students for the company. As a member of Google's human resources department at its Toronto location, you are responsible for screening job candidates and arranging for candidates to interview with members of Google's professional staff. Your responsibilities include developing interview questions and participating in evaluation interviews. In each of the following situations, choose the best alternative and be prepared to justify your choice.

1 During the on-campus screening interviews, you ask several candidates, "Why do you want to work for Google?" Of the following responses, which would you rank the highest?

a "I'd like to work here because I'm interested in the computer software industry. I've always been fascinated by technology. In addition to studying computer programming, I have taken courses in marketing and finance. I also have some personal experience in building computers. I enjoy helping my friends construct computer systems for their needs."

b "I'm an independent person with a lot of internal drive. I do my best work when I'm given a fairly free rein to use my creativity. From what I've read about your corporate culture, I think my working style would fit very well with your management philosophy. I'm also the sort of person who identifies very strongly with my job. For better or worse, I define myself through my affiliation with my employer. I get a great sense of pride from being part of a first-rate operation, and I think Google is first-rate. I've read about your selection as one of North America's best companies to work for. The articles say that Google is a well-managed company. I think I would learn a lot working here, and I think my drive and creativity would be appreciated."

c "There are a couple of reasons why I'd like to work for Google. I have friends who work here, and they both say it's terrific. I've also heard good things about your compensation and benefits."

d "My ultimate goal is to start my own company, but first I need to learn more about managing a business. I read in *Fortune* that Google is one of North America's best companies to work for. I think I could learn a lot by joining your software development group and observing your operations."

2 You are preparing questions for the professional staff to use when conducting follow-up interviews. You want a question that will reveal something about the candidates' probable loyalty to the organization. Which of the following questions is the best choice?

a If you knew you could be one of the world's most successful people in a single occupation, such as music, politics, medicine, or business, what occupation would you choose? If you knew you had only a 10 percent chance of being so successful, would you still choose the same occupation?

b We value loyalty among our employees. Tell me something about yourself that demonstrates your loyalty as a member of an organization.

c What would you do if you discovered that a co-worker routinely made personal, unauthorized long-distance phone calls from work?

d What other companies are you interviewing with?

3 In concluding an evaluation interview, you ask the candidate, "Do you have any questions?" Which of the following answers would you respond most favourably to?

a "No. I can't think of anything. You've been very thorough in describing the job and the company. Thank you for taking the time to talk with me."

b "Yes. I have an interview with one of your competitors, next week. How would you sum up the differences between your two firms?"

c "Yes. If I were offered a position here, what would my chances be of getting promoted within the next 12 months?"

d "Yes. Do you think Google will be a better or worse company 15 years from now?"

Test Your Knowledge

1 What are key tips for writing application letters?

2 How does a structured interview differ from an open-ended interview and a situational interview?

3 What typically occurs during a stress interview?

4 Why do employers conduct pre-employment testing?

5 Why are the questions you ask during an interview as important as the answers you give to the interviewer's questions?

6 What are the three stages of every interview? Which is the most important?

7 How should you respond if an interviewer at a company where you want to work asks you a question that seems too personal or unethical?

8 What should you say in a thank-you message after an interview?

9 What is the purpose of sending a letter of inquiry after an interview?

10 What organizational plan is appropriate for a letter of resignation? Why?

Apply Your Knowledge

1 How can you distinguish yourself from other candidates in a screening interview and still keep your responses short and to the point? Explain.

2 What can you do to make a favourable impression when you discover that an open-ended interview has turned into a stress interview? Briefly explain your answer.

3 If you want to switch jobs because you can't work with your supervisor, how can you explain this situation to a prospective employer? Give an example.

4 During a group interview you notice that another candidate is trying to monopolize the conversation. He's always the first to answer, his answer is the longest, and he even interrupts the other candidates while they are talking. The interviewer doesn't seem to be concerned about his behaviour, but you are. You would like to have more time to speak, so the interviewer could get to know you better. What should you do?

5 **Ethical Choices** Why is it important to distinguish unethical or illegal interview questions from acceptable questions? Explain.

Running Cases

Watch on mycanadianbuscommlab

> CASE 1 Noreen

After submitting her cover letter and résumé for the position of Merger Project Manager, Noreen is selected for an interview. Noreen arrives 10 minutes early. She remains in the waiting area until she is asked to enter the meeting room. She walks in and sees six senior management staff sitting around a large table. She is asked to sit down. The managers introduce themselves to Noreen. Noreen knows two of them already.

QUESTIONS

a) What should Noreen wear to the interview?
b) What questions might she be asked?
c) What questions might she have?
d) Since this is an internal interview (she already works for the company) should she assume this will be an informal or casual interview?

e) List three topics that Noreen should not discuss during the interview.

YOUR TASK

Form a group to role-play this interview. First, select one person to be Noreen. Noreen needs to prepare answers and questions for the interview. The group needs to prepare questions and answers for Noreen. Second, in this role-play Noreen gets a call after the interview and is offered the position. Noreen then needs to negotiate more money than offered as well as a written guarantee that she may return to her previous position or equivalent upon completion of the merger project.

> CASE 2 Kwong

Kwong is interviewing potential candidates for the administrative assistant position in his firm, CG Accounting. Some are overqualified and some have no work experience at all, which in his opinion makes them underqualified. One job applicant is very impressive and answers Kwong's questions confidently and accurately during the interview. Kwong feels this person has the right college education but has no work experience. He decides to hire this job applicant anyway.

QUESTIONS

a) Will the job applicant do well in the job without work experience?
b) What would the "right college education" be in this case?
c) Should Kwong discuss salary during the interview?
d) Is Kwong legally allowed to ask the applicant if he or she is able to work overtime?
e) List three ways the applicant can demonstrate his or her interest in the position during the interview.

YOUR TASK

Role-play this interview in a group of three students. One student can play Kwong, one can play his sister, and the other can play the job applicant. The job applicant needs to prepare answers for the interviewers, and Kwong and his sister need to prepare questions for the job applicant.

In this role-play ask the job applicant if he or she feels over- or underqualified for this position and have the applicant explain his or her answer. Have Kwong ask the applicant why he or she is applying for this position and how long he or she plans to stay in this position. Have Kwong's sister ask if the applicant is married and what religion the applicant practises. Kwong's sister should explain that she is asking because there is overtime work during tax season and the company wants to ensure the availability of employees. These are illegal questions to ask during a job interview in Canada, so have the actors in the role-play deal with them.

Practise Your Knowledge

Read the following documents and then (1) analyze the strengths or weaknesses of each document and (2) revise each document so that it follows this chapter's guidelines.

DOCUMENT 16.A: WRITING AN APPLICATION LETTER

I'm writing to let you know about my availability for the brand manager job you advertised. As you can see from my enclosed résumé, my background is perfect for the position. Even though

I don't have any real job experience, my grades have been outstanding considering that I went to a top-ranked business school.

I did many things during my undergraduate years to prepare me for this job:

> *Earned a 3.4 out of a 4.0 with a 3.8 in my business courses*
> *Elected to the student governing association*
> *Selected to receive the Lamar Franklin Award*
> *Worked to earn a portion of my tuition*

I am sending my résumé to all the top firms, but I like yours better than any of the rest. Your reputation is tops in the industry, and I want to be associated with a business that can really say it's the best.

If you wish for me to come in for an interview, I can come on a Friday afternoon or anytime on weekends when I don't have classes. Again, thanks for considering me for your brand manager position.

DOCUMENT 16.B: WRITING APPLICATION FOLLOW-UP MESSAGES

Did you receive my résumé? I sent it to you at least two months ago and haven't heard anything. I know you keep résumés on file, but I just want to ensure that you keep me in mind. I heard you are hiring health-care managers and certainly would like to be considered for one of those positions.

Since I last wrote you, I've worked in a variety of positions that have helped prepare me for management. You'll want to know I've become lunch manager at the restaurant where I work, which involved a raise in pay. I now manage a wait staff of 12 girls and take the lunch receipts to the bank every day.

Of course, I'd much rather be working at a real job, and that's why I'm writing again. Is there anything else you would like to know about my background or me? I would really like to know more about your company. Is there any literature you could send me? If so, I would really appreciate it.

I think one reason I haven't been hired yet is that I don't want to leave Winnipeg. So I hope when you think of me, it's for a position that wouldn't require moving. Thanks again for considering my application.

DOCUMENT 16.C: THANK-YOU MESSAGE

Thank you for the really awesome opportunity to meet you and your colleagues at Starret Engine Company. I really enjoyed

touring your facilities and talking with all the people there. What an awesome group! Some of the other companies I have visited have been so rigid and uptight that I can't imagine how I would fit in. It's a relief to run into a group of people who seem to enjoy their work as much as all of you do.

I know that you must be looking at many other candidates for this job, and I know that some of them will probably be more experienced than I am. But I do want to emphasize that my hitch in the Navy involved a good deal of engineering work. I don't think I mentioned all my shipboard responsibilities during the interview.

Please give me a call within the next week to let me know your decision. You can usually find me at my dormitory in the evening after dinner (phone: 614-555-9080).

DOCUMENT 16.D: LETTER OF INQUIRY

I have recently received a very attractive job offer from the Warrington Company. But before I let them know one way or another, I would like to consider any offer that your firm may extend. I was quite impressed with your company during my recent interview, and I am still very interested in a career there.

I don't mean to pressure you, but Warrington has asked for my decision within 10 days. Could you let me know by Tuesday whether you plan to offer me a position? That would give me enough time to compare the two offers.

DOCUMENT 16.E: LETTER DECLINING A JOB OFFER

I'm writing to say that I must decline your job offer. Another company has made me a more generous offer, and I have decided to accept. However, if things don't work out for me there, I will let you know. I sincerely appreciate your interest in me.

Exercises

16.1 Internet: Company Research

Select a large company (one that you can easily find information on) where you might like to work. Use internet sources to gather some preliminary research on the company; don't limit your search to the company's own website.

a. What did you learn about this organization that would help you during an interview there?

b. What internet sources did you use to obtain this information?

c. Armed with this information, what aspects of your background do you think might appeal to this company's recruiters?

d. Based on what you've learned about this company's culture, what aspects of your personality should you try to highlight during an interview?

16.2 Teamwork: Qualification Analysis

Divide the class into two groups. One group will be recruiters for a large chain of national department stores looking to fill manager trainee positions (there are 15 openings). The other group will be candidates for the job. The company is specifically looking for candidates who demonstrate these three qualities: initiative, dependability, and willingness to assume responsibility.

a. Have each recruiter select and interview an applicant for 10 minutes.

b. Have all the recruiters discuss how they assessed the applicant in each of the three desired qualities. What questions did they ask or what did they use as an indicator to determine whether the candidate possessed the quality?

c. Have all the applicants discuss what they said to convince the recruiters that they possessed each quality.

16.3 Interviews: Understanding Qualifications

Write a short email to your instructor, discussing what you believe are your greatest strengths and weaknesses from an employment perspective. Next, explain how these strengths and weaknesses would be viewed by interviewers evaluating your qualifications.

16.4 Interviews: Being Prepared

Prepare written answers to 10 of the questions listed in Table 16–3 "Twenty-Five Common Interview Questions."

16.5 Ethical Choices: Leaving Your Employer

You have decided to accept a new position with a competitor of your company. Write a letter of resignation to your supervisor, announcing your decision.

  a. Will you notify your employer that you are joining a competing firm? Please explain.

  b. Will you use the direct or the indirect approach? Please explain.

  c. Will you send your letter by email, send it by regular mail, or place it on your supervisor's desk?

Cases PREPARING OTHER TYPES OF EMPLOYMENT MESSAGES

1. Online application: Electronic cover letter introducing a résumé

While researching a digital camera purchase, you stumble on the webzine *Megapixel* (www.megapixel.net), which offers product reviews on a wide array of camera models. The quality of the reviews and the stunning examples of photography on the site inspire you with a new part-time business idea—you'd like to write a regular column for *Megapixel*. The webzine does a great job addressing the information needs of experienced camera users, but you see an opportunity to write for "newbies," people who are new to digital photography and need a more basic level of information.

Your Task: Write an email message that will serve as your cover letter and address your message to Denys Bouton, who edits the English edition of *Megapixel* (it is also published in French). Limit your message to one screen (generally 20 to 25 lines). You'll need a creative "hook" and a reassuring approach that identifies you as the right person to launch this new feature in the webzine (make up any details about your background that you may need to complete the letter).

2. All over the map: Application letter to Google Earth

You've applied yourself with vigour and resolve for four years, and you're just about to graduate with your business degree. While cruising the Web to relax one night, you decide to explore Google Earth. You're hooked instantly by the ability to zoom all around the globe and look at detailed satellite photos of places you've been to or dreamed of visiting. You can even type in the address of your apartment and get an aerial view of your neighbourhood. You're amazed at the three-dimensional renderings of major Canadian cities. Plus, the photographs and maps are linked to Google's other search technologies, allowing you to locate everything from ATMs to coffee shops in your neighbourhood.

You've loved maps since you were a kid, and discovering Google Earth is making you wish you had majored in geography instead. Knowing how important it is to follow your heart, you decide to apply to Google anyway, even though you don't have a strong background in geographic information systems.

What you do have is a passion for maps and a good head for business.

Your Task: Visit http://earth.google.com and explore the system's capabilities (you can download a free copy of the software). In particular, look at the business and government applications of the technology, such as customized aerial photos and maps for real estate sales, land use and environmental impact analysis, and emergency planning. Ensure that you visit the Community pages as well, where you can learn more about the many interesting applications of this technology. Now draft an application email to Google (address it to jobs@google.com) asking to be considered for the Google Earth team. Think about how you could help the company develop the commercial potential of this product line, and ensure that your enthusiasm shines through in the message.

Interviewing with Potential Employers

3. Interviewers and interviewees: Classroom exercise in interviewing

Interviewing is clearly an interactive process involving at least two people. The best way to practise for interviews is to work with others.

Your Task: You and all other members of your class are to write letters of application for an entry-level or management-trainee position requiring a pleasant personality and intelligence but a minimum of specialized education or experience. Sign your letter with a fictitious name that conceals your identity. Next, polish (or create) a résumé that accurately identifies you and your educational and professional accomplishments.

Now, three members of the class who volunteer as interviewers divide up all the anonymously written application letters. Then, each interviewer selects a candidate who seems the most pleasant and convincing in his or her letter. At this time the selected candidates identify themselves and give the interviewers their résumés.

Each interviewer then interviews his or her chosen candidate in front of the class, seeking to understand how the items on the résumé qualify the candidate for the job. At the end of the interviews, the class may decide who gets the job and discuss why this candidate was successful. Afterward, retrieve your letter, sign it with the right name, and submit it to the instructor for credit.

4. Internet interview: Exercise in interviewing
Locate the website of a company in an industry in which you might like to work, and then identify an interesting position within the company. Study the company, using any of the online business resources discussed in Chapter 11 and prepare for an interview with that company.

Your Task: Working with a classmate, take turns interviewing each other for your chosen positions. Interviewers should take notes during the interview. Once the interview is complete, critique each other's performance (interviewers should critique how well candidates prepared for the interview and answered the questions; interviewees should critique the quality of the questions asked). Write a follow-up letter thanking your interviewer and submit the letter to your instructor.

Following Up After the Interview

5. A slight error in timing: Letter asking for delay of an employment decision
Thanks to a mix-up in your job application scheduling, you accidentally applied for your third-choice job before going after what you really wanted. What you want to do is work in retail marketing with the upscale department store Holt Renfrew in Victoria; what you have been offered is a similar job with Zellers in Regina.

You review your notes. Your Regina interview was three weeks ago with the human resources manager, R. P. Bronson, a congenial person who has just written to offer you the position. The store's address is P.O. Box 79801, Regina, SK S4N 0A0. Mr. Bronson notes that he can hold the position open for 10 days. You have an interview scheduled with Holt Renfrew next week, but it is unlikely that you will know the store's decision within this 10-day period.

Your Task: Write to R. P. Bronson, requesting a reasonable delay in your consideration of his job offer.

6. Job hunt: Set of employment-related letters to a single company
Where would you like to work? Choose one of your favourite products, find out which company either manufactures it or sells it in Canada (if it's manufactured in another country). Assume that a month ago you sent your résumé and application letter. Not long afterward, you were invited to come for an interview, which seemed to go very well.

Your Task: Use your imagination to write the following: (a) a thank-you letter for the interview, (b) a note of inquiry, (c) a request for more time to decide, (d) a letter of acceptance, and (e) a letter declining the job offer.

Appendix A
FORMAT AND LAYOUT OF BUSINESS DOCUMENTS

The format and layout of business documents vary from country to country. In addition, many organizations develop their own variations of standard styles, adapting documents to the types of messages they send and the kinds of audiences they communicate with. The formats described here are more common than others.

First Impressions

Your documents tell readers a lot about you and about your company's professionalism. All your documents must look neat, present a professional image, and be easy to read. Your audience's first impression of a document comes from the quality of its paper, the way it is customized, and its general appearance.

Paper

To give a quality impression, businesspeople consider carefully the paper they use. Several aspects of paper contribute to the overall impression:

> **Weight.** Paper quality is judged by the weight of four reams (each a 500-sheet package) of letter-size paper. The weight most commonly used by Canadian and U.S. businesses is 20-pound paper, but 16- and 24-pound versions are also used.
> **Cotton content.** Paper quality is also judged by the percentage of cotton in the paper. Cotton doesn't yellow over time the way wood pulp does, plus it's both strong and soft. For letters and outside reports, use paper with a 25-percent cotton content. For memos and other internal documents, you can use a lighter-weight paper with lower cotton content. Airmail-weight paper may save money for international correspondence, but ensure that it isn't too flimsy.[1]
> **Size.** In Canada and the United States, the standard paper size for business documents is 8½ by 11 inches. Standard legal documents are 8½ by 14 inches. Executives sometimes have heavier 7-by-10-inch paper on hand (with matching envelopes) for personal messages such as congratulations and recommendations.[2] They may also have a box of notecards imprinted with their initials and a box of plain folded notes for condolences or for acknowledging formal invitations.
> **Colour.** White is the standard colour for business purposes, although neutral colours such as grey and ivory are sometimes used. Memos can be produced on pastel-coloured paper to distinguish them from external correspondence. In addition, memos are sometimes produced on various colours of paper for routing to separate departments. Light-coloured papers are appropriate, but bright or dark colours make reading difficult and may appear too frivolous.

Customization

For letters to outsiders, Canadian and U.S. businesses commonly use letterhead stationery, which may be either professionally printed or designed in-house using word-processing templates and graphics. The letterhead includes the company's name and address, usually at the top of the page but sometimes along the left side or even at the bottom. Other information may be included in the letterhead as well: the company's telephone number, fax number, cable address, website address, product lines, date of establishment, officers and directors, slogan, and symbol (logo). Well-designed letterhead gives readers[3]

> pertinent reference data
> a favourable image of the company
> a good idea of what the company does

For as much as it's meant to accomplish, the letterhead should be as simple as possible. Too much information makes the page look cluttered, occupies space needed for the message, and might become outdated before all the stationery can be used. If you correspond frequently with people abroad, your letterhead must be intelligible to foreigners. It must include the name of your country in addition to your cable, email, website, or fax information.

In Canada and the United States, businesses always use letterhead for the first page of a letter. Successive pages are usually plain sheets of paper that match the letterhead in colour and quality. Some companies use a specially printed second-page letterhead that bears only the company's name. Other countries have other conventions.

Many companies also design and print standardized forms for memos and frequently written reports that always require the same sort of information (such as sales reports and expense reports). These forms may be printed in sets for use with carbon paper or in carbonless-copy sets that produce multiple copies automatically. Many organizations use computers to generate their standardized forms, such as fillable PDF forms that can be completed online, which can save them both money and time.

Appearance

Produce almost all of your business documents using a laser printer; make sure to use a clean, high-quality printer. Certain documents, however, should be hand-written (such as a short informal memo or a note of condolence). Be sure to handwrite, print, or type the envelope to match the document. However, even a letter on the best-quality paper with the best-designed letterhead may look unprofessional if it's poorly produced. So pay close attention to all the factors affecting appearance, including the following:

> **Margins.** Companies in Canada and the United States ensure that documents (especially external ones) are centred on the page, with margins of at least an inch all around. Using word-processing software, you can achieve this balance simply by defining the format parameters.

> **Line length.** Lines are rarely justified, because the resulting text looks too much like a form letter and can be hard to read (even with proportional spacing). Varying line length makes the document look more personal and interesting.

> **Line spacing.** You can adjust the number of blank lines between elements (such as between the date and the inside address) to ensure that a short document fills the page vertically or that a longer document extends at least two lines of the body onto the last page.

> **Character spacing.** Use proper spacing between characters and after punctuation. For example, Canadian conventions include leaving one space after commas, semicolons, colons, and sentence-ending periods. Each letter in a person's initials is followed by a period and a single space. However, abbreviations such as U.S.A. or MBA may or may not have periods, but they never have internal spaces.

> **Special symbols.** Take advantage of the many special symbols available with your computer's selection of fonts. (In Microsoft Word, click the Insert menu and then select Symbol.) Table A–1 shows some of the more common symbols used in business documents. In addition, see if your company has a style guide for documents, which may include other symbols you are expected to use.

> **Corrections.** Messy corrections are unacceptable in business documents. If you notice an error after printing a document with your word processor, correct the mistake and reprint. (With informal memos to members of your own team or department, the occasional small correction in pen or pencil is acceptable, but never in formal documents.)

> Table A–1 Special Symbols on Computer

	Computer Symbol
Case fraction	½
Copyright	©
Registered trademark	®
Cent	¢
British pound	£
Euro	€
Paragraph	¶
Bullets	●,◆,■,□, ✓,☑,⊗
Em dash	—
En dash	–

Letters

All business letters have certain elements in common. Several of these elements appear in every letter; others appear only when desirable or appropriate. In addition, these letter parts are usually arranged in one of three basic formats.

Standard Letter Parts

The letter in Figure A–1 shows the placement of standard letter parts. The writer of this business letter had no letterhead available but correctly included a heading. All business letters typically include these seven elements.

HEADING Letterhead (the usual heading) shows the organization's name, full address, website, telephone number (almost always), and email address (often). Executive letterhead also bears the name of an individual within the organization. Computers allow you to design your own letterhead (either one to use for all correspondence or a new one for each piece of correspondence). If letterhead stationery is not available, the heading includes a return address (but no name) and starts 13 lines from the top of the page, which leaves a 2-inch top margin.

DATA If you're using letterhead, place the date at least one blank line beneath the lowest part of the letterhead. Without letterhead, place the date immediately below the return address. The standard method of writing the date in Canada uses the full name of the month (no abbreviations), followed by the day (in numerals, without *st, nd, rd,* or *th*), a comma, and then the year: July 14, 2010. Some organizations follow other conventions (see Table A–2). To maintain the utmost clarity in international correspondence, always spell out the name of the month in dates.[4]

> Figure A–1 Standard Letter Parts

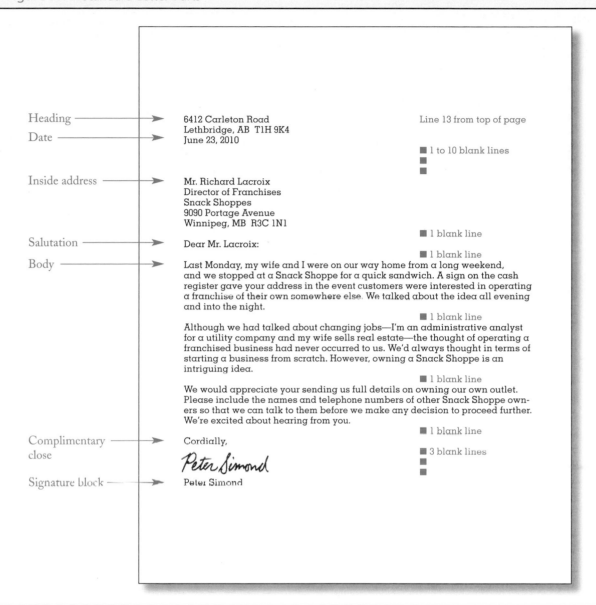

Heading ——————▶ 6412 Carleton Road   Line 13 from top of page
Lethbridge, AB T1H 9K4
Date ——————————▶ June 23, 2010

■ 1 to 10 blank lines
■
■

Inside address ————▶ Mr. Richard Lacroix
Director of Franchises
Snack Shoppes
9090 Portage Avenue
Winnipeg, MB R3C 1N1

■ 1 blank line

Salutation ——————▶ Dear Mr. Lacroix:

■ 1 blank line

Body ——————————▶ Last Monday, my wife and I were on our way home from a long weekend, and we stopped at a Snack Shoppe for a quick sandwich. A sign on the cash register gave your address in the event customers were interested in operating a franchise of their own somewhere else. We talked about the idea all evening and into the night.

■ 1 blank line

Although we had talked about changing jobs—I'm an administrative analyst for a utility company and my wife sells real estate—the thought of operating a franchised business had never occurred to us. We'd always thought in terms of starting a business from scratch. However, owning a Snack Shoppe is an intriguing idea.

■ 1 blank line

We would appreciate your sending us full details on owning our own outlet. Please include the names and telephone numbers of other Snack Shoppe owners so that we can talk to them before we make any decision to proceed further. We're excited about hearing from you.

■ 1 blank line

Complimentary ———▶ Cordially,
close

■ 3 blank lines
■
■

Signature block ————▶ Peter Simond
Peter Simond

> Table A–2 Common Date Forms

Convention	Description	Date—Mixed	Date—All Numerals
Canadian standard	Month (spelled out) day, year	July 14, 2010	7/14/10
Canadian government and some Canadian industries	Day (in numerals) month (spelled out) year	14 July 2010	14/7/10
European	Replace Canadian solidus (diagonal line) with periods	14 July 2010	14.7.2010
International standard	Year month day	2010 July 14	2010,7,14

When communicating internationally, you may also experience some confusion over time. Some Canadian companies refer to morning (A.M.) and afternoon (P.M.), dividing a 24-hour day into 12-hour blocks, so they refer to four o'clock in the morning as 4:00 A.M. and four o'clock in the afternoon as 4:00 P.M. The Canadian military and European companies refer to one 24-hour period, so 0400 hours (4:00 A.M.) is always in the morning and 1600 hours (4:00 P.M.) is always in the afternoon.[5] Ensure that your references to time are as clear as possible, and ensure that you clearly understand your audience's time references.

INSIDE ADDRESS The inside address identifies the recipient of the letter. For Canadian correspondence, begin the inside address at least one line below the date. Precede the addressee's name with a courtesy title, such as *Dr., Mr.,* or *Ms.* The accepted courtesy title for women in business is *Ms.,* although a woman known to prefer the title *Miss* or *Mrs.* is always accommodated. If you don't know whether a person is a man or a woman (and you have no way of finding out), omit the courtesy title. For example, *Terry Smith* could be either a man or a woman. The first line of the inside address would be just *Terry Smith,* and the salutation would be *Dear Terry Smith.* The same is true if you know only a person's initials, as in *S. J. Adams.*

Spell out and capitalize titles that precede a person's name, such as *Professor* or *General* (see Table A–3 for the proper forms of address). The person's organizational title, such as *Director,* may be included on this first line (if it is short) or on the line below; the name of a department may follow. In addresses and signature lines, don't forget to capitalize any professional title that follows a person's name:

Mr. Ray Johnson, Dean
Ms. Patricia T. Higgins
Assistant Vice-President

However, professional titles not appearing in an address or signature line are capitalized only when they directly precede the name.

President Kenneth Johanson will deliver the speech.
Maria Morales, president of ABC Enterprises, will deliver the speech.
The Honourable Laurie Hawn, member of Parliament for Edmonton Centre, Alberta, will deliver the speech.

If the name of a specific person is unavailable, you may address the letter to the department or to a specific position within the department. Also, ensure that you spell out company names in full, unless the company itself uses abbreviations in its official name.

> Table A–3 Forms of Address

Person	In Address	In Salutation
Personal Titles		
Man	Mr. [first & last name]	Dear Mr. [last name]:
Woman*	Ms. [first & last name]	Dear Ms. [last name]:
Two men (or more)	Mr. [first & last name] and Mr. [first & last name]	Dear Mr. [last name] and Mr. [last name] Messrs. [last name] and [last name]:
Two women (or more)	Ms. [first & last name] and Ms. [first & last name] *or* Mrs. [first & last name] and Mrs. [first & last name]	Dear Ms. [last name] and Ms. [last name] Mses. [last name] and [last name]: Dear Mrs. [last name] and Mrs. [last name]: *or* Dear Mesdames [last name] and [last name] or Mesdames:
	Miss [first & last name] Mrs. [first & last name]	Dear Miss [last name] and Mrs. [last name]:
One woman and one man	Ms. [first & last name] and Mr. [first & last name]	Dear Ms. [last name] and Mr. [last name]:
Couple (married)	Mr. and Mrs. [husband's first & last name]	Dear Mr. and Mrs. [last name]:

> Table A–3 Forms of Address (*continued*)

Person	In Address	In Salutation
Couple (married with different last names)	[title] [first & last name of husband] [title] [first & last name of wife]	Dear [title] [husband's last name] and [title] [wife's last name]:
Couple (married professionals with same title and same last name)	[title in plural form] [husband's first name] and [wife's first & last name]	Dear [title in plural form] [last name]:
Couple (married professionals with different titles and same last name)	[title] [first & last name of husband] and [title] [first & last name of wife]	Dear [title] and [title] [last name]:
Professional Titles		
President of a college or university (doctor)	Dr. [first & last name], President	Dear Dr. [last name]:
Dean of a school, college, or faculty	Dean [first & last name] *or* Dr., Mr., Ms., Mrs., *or* Miss [first & last name] Dean of (title)	Dear Dean [last name]: Dear Dr., Mr., Ms., Mrs., *or* Miss [last name]:
Professor	Professor [first & last name]	Dear Professor [last name]:
Physician	[first & last name], M.D.	Dear Dr. [last name]:
Lawyer	Mr., Ms., Mrs., *or* Miss [first & last name]	Dear Mr., Ms., Mrs., *or* Miss [last name]:
Armed forces personnel	[full rank, first & last name, abbreviation of service designation] (add Retired if applicable)	Dear [rank] [last name].
Company or corporation	[name of organization]	Ladies and Gentlemen or Gentlemen and Ladies
Governmental Titles		
Prime Minister of Canada	The Right Honourable [name]	Dear Prime Minister
Federal Minister	The Honourable [name], MP	Dear Mr. *or* Ms. [name] *or* Dear Minister
Member of Parliament	Mr. *or* Ms. [name], MP	Dear Mr. *or* Ms. [last name]
Judge	The Honourable [name]	Dear Mr. Justice [last name] Dear Madame Justice [last name]
Mayor	Mayor [name]	Dear Mr. *or* Ms. Mayor
Councillor	Councillor [name]	Dear Mr. *or* Ms. [name]

*Use *Mrs.* or *Miss* only if the recipient has specifically requested that you use one of these titles; otherwise *always* use *Ms.* in business correspondence. Also, never refer to a woman by her husband's name (e.g., Mrs. Robert Washington) unless she specifically requests that you do so.

Other address information includes the treatment of buildings, house numbers, and compass directions (see Table A–4). The following example shows all the information that may be included in the inside address and its proper order for Canadian correspondence:

Dr. H. C. Armstrong
Research and Development
Commonwealth Mining Consortium
The Chelton Building, Suite 301
585 Second St. SW
Calgary, Alberta T2P 2P5

U.S. addresses are similar:

Ms. Linda Coolidge, Vice-President
Corporate Planning Department
Midwest Airlines
Kowalski Building, Suite 21-A
7279 Bristol Ave.
Toledo, Ohio 43617

The order and layout of address information vary from country to country. So when addressing correspondence for other countries, carefully follow the format and information that appear in the company's letterhead. However, when you're sending mail from Canada, ensure that the name of the destination country appears on the last line of the address in capital letters. Use the English version of the country name so that your mail is routed from Canada to the right country. Then, to ensure that your mail is routed correctly *within* the destination country, also include the foreign spelling of the city name (using the characters and diacritical marks, signs indicating phonetical differences, that would be commonly used in the region). For example, the following address uses *Köln* instead of *Cologne*:

H. R. Veith, Director	Addressee
Eisfieren Glaswerk	Company name
Blaubachstrasse 13	Street address
Postfach 10 80 07	Post office box
d-5000 Köln I	District, city
GERMANY	Country

For additional examples of international addresses, see Table A–5.

Ensure that you use organizational titles correctly when addressing international correspondence. Job designations vary around the world. In England, for example, a managing director is often what a Canadian company would call its chief executive officer or president, and a British deputy is the equivalent of a vice-president. In France, responsibilities are assigned to individuals without regard to title or organizational structure, and in China the title *project manager* has meaning, but the title *sales manager* may not.

Businesspeople in some countries sign correspondence without their names typed below. In Germany, for example, the belief is that employees represent the company, so it's inappropriate to emphasize personal names. Use the examples in Table A–5 as guidelines when addressing correspondence to countries outside Canada.

SALUTATION In the salutation of your letter, follow the style of the first line of the inside address. If the first line is a person's name, the salutation is *Dear Mr.* or *Ms. Name*. The formality of the salutation depends on your relationship with the addressee. If in conversation you would say "Mary," your letter's salutation should be *Dear Mary*, followed by a comma. Otherwise, include the courtesy title and last name, followed by a colon. Presuming to write *Dear Lewis* instead of *Dear Professor Chang* demonstrates a disrespectful familiarity that the recipient will probably resent.

If the first line of the inside address is a position title such as *Director of Personnel*, then use *Dear Director*. If the addressee is unknown, use a polite description, such as *Dear Alumnus, Dear SPCA Supporter,* or *Dear Voter*. If the first line is plural (a department or company), then use *Ladies and Gentlemen* (look again at Table A–3). When you do not know whether you're writing to an individual or a group (for example, when writing a reference or a letter of recommendation), use *To whom it may concern*.

In Canada some letter writers use a "salutopening" on the salutation line. A salutopening omits *Dear* but

> Table A–4 Inside Address Information

Description	Example
Capitalize building names.	Royal Bank Plaza
Capitalize locations within buildings (apartments, suites, and rooms).	Suite 1073
Use numerals for all house or building numbers, except the number one.	One Trinity Lane 637 Adams Ave., Apt. 7
Spell out compass directions that fall within a street address	1074 West Connover St.
Abbreviate compass directions that follow the street address	27–783 Main St., N.E.,

> Table A–5 International Addresses and Salutations

Country	Postal Address	Address Elements	Salutations
Argentina	Sr. Juan Pérez Editorial Internacional S.A. Av. Sarmiento 1337, 8° P. C C1035AAB BUENOS AIRES – CF ARGENTINA	S.A. = Sociedad Anónima (corporation) Av. Sarmiento (name of street) 1337 (building number) 8° = 8th. P = Piso (floor) C (room suite) C1035AAB (postcode + city) CF = Capital Federal (federal capital)	Sr. = Señor (Mr.) Sra. = Señora (Mrs.) Srta. = Señorita (Miss) Don't use given names except with people you know well.
Australia	Mr. Roger Lewis International Publishing Pty Ltd. 166 Kent Street, Level 9 GPO Box 3542 SYDNEY NSW 2001 AUSTRALIA	Pty. Ltd. = Proprietory Limited (corp.) 166 (building number) Kent Street (name of street) Level (floor) GPO Box (post office box) city + state (abbrev.) + postcode	Mr. and Mrs. used on first contact. Ms. not common (avoid use). Business is informal—use given name freely.
Austria	Herrn Dipl.-Ing.J.Gerdenitsch International Verlag Ges.m.b.H. Glockengasse 159 1010 WIEN AUSTRIA	Herrn = To Mr. (separate line) Dipl.-Ing. (engineering degree) Ges.m.b.H. (a corporation) Glockengasse (street name) 159 (building number) 1010 (postcode + city) WIEN (Vienna)	Herr (Mr.) Frau (Mrs.) Fräulein (Miss) obsolete in business, so do not use. Given names are almost never used in business.
Brazil	Ilmo. Sr. Gilberto Rabello Ribeiro Editores Internacionais S.A. Rua da Ajuda, 228-6° Andar Caixa Postal 2574 20040-000 RIO DE JANEIRO – RJ BRAZIL	Ilmo. = Ilustrissimo (honorific) Ilma. = Ilustrissima (hon. female) S.A. = Sociedade Anônima (corporation) Rua = street, da Ajuda (street name) 228 (building number) 6° = 6th. Andar (floor) Caixa Postal (P.O. box) 20040-000 (postcode + city) – RJ (state abbrev.)	Sr. = Senhor (Mr.) Sra. = Senhora (Mrs.) Srta. = Senhorita (Miss) Family name at end, e.g., Senhor Ribeiro (Rabello is mother's family—as in Portugal) Given names readily used in business.
China	Xia Zhiyi International Publishing Ltd. 14 Jianguolu Chaoyangqu BEIJING 100025 CHINA	Ltd. (limited liability corporation) 14 (building number) Jianguolu (street name), lu (street) Chaoyangqu (district name) (city + postcode)	Family name (single syllable) first. Given name (2 syllables) second, sometimes reversed. Use Mr. or Ms. at all times (Mr. Xia).
France	Monsieur LEFÈVRE Alain Éditions Internationales S.A. Siège Social Immeuble Le Bonaparte 64–68, av. Galliéni B.P. 154 75942 PARIS CEDEX 19 FRANCE	S.A. = Société Anonyme Siège Social (head office) Immeuble (building + name) 64–68 (building occupies 64, 66, 68) av. = avenue (no initial capital) B.P. = Boîte Postale (P.O. box) 75942 (postcode) CEDEX (postcode for P.O. box)	Monsieur (Mr.) Madame (Mrs.) Mademoiselle (Miss) Best not to abbreviate. Family name is sometimes in all caps with given name following.
Germany	Herrn Gerhardt Schneider International Verlag GmbH Schillerstraße 159 44147 DORTMUND GERMANY	Herrn = To Herr (on a separate line) GmbH (inc.—incorporated) -straße (street—'ß' often written 'ss') 159 (building number) 44147 (postcode + city)	Herr (Mr.) Frau (Mrs.) Fräulein (Miss) obsolete in business, so do not use. Business is formal: (1) do not use given names unless invited, and (2) use academic titles precisely.

(continued)

> Table A–5 International Addresses and Salutations *(continued)*

Country	Postal Address	Address Elements	Salutations
India	Sr. Shyam Lal Gupta International Publishing (Pvt.) Ltd. 1820 Rehaja Centre 214, Darussalam Road Andheri East BOMBAY – 400049 INDIA	(Pvt.) (privately owned) Ltd. (limited liability corporation) 1820 (possibly office #20 on 18th floor) Rehaja Centre (building name) 214 (building number) Andheri East (suburb name) (city + hyphen + postcode)	Shri (Mr.), Shrimati (Mrs.) but English is common business language, so use Mr., Mrs., Miss. Given names are used only by family and close friends.
Italy	Egr. Sig. Giacomo Mariotti Edizioni Internazionali S.p.A. Via Terenzio, 21 20138 MILANO ITALY	Egr. = Egregio (honorific) Sig. = Signor (not nec. a separate line) S.p.A. = Società per Azioni (corp.) Via (street) 21 (building number) 20138 (postcode + city)	Sig. = Signore (Mr.) Sig.ra = Signora (Mrs.) Sig.a = (Ms.) Women in business are addressed as Signora. Use given name only when invited.
Japan	Mr. Taro Tanaka Kokusai Shuppan K.K. 10–23, 5-chome, Minamiazabu Minato-ku TOKYO 106 JAPAN	K.K. = Kabushiki Kaisha (corporation) 10 (lot number) 23 (building number) 5-chome (area #5) Minamiazabu (neighbourhood name) Minato-ku (city district) (city + postcode)	Given names not used in business. Use family name + job title. Or use family name + "-san" (Tanaka-san) or more used respectfully, add "-sama" or "-dono."
Korea	Mr. KIM Chang-ik International Publishers Ltd. Room 206, Korea Building 33-4 Nonhyon-dong Kangnam-ku SEOUL 135-010 KOREA	English company names common Ltd. (a corporation) 206 (office number inside the building) 33-4 (area 4 of subdivision 33) -dong (city neighbourhood name) -ku (subdivision of city) (city + postcode)	Family name is normally first but sometimes placed after given name. A two-part name is the given name. Use Mr. or Mrs. in letters, but use job title in speech.
Mexico	Sr. Francisco Pérez Martínez Editores Internacionales S.A. Independencia No.322 Col. Juárez 06050 MEXICO D.F.	S.A. = Sociedad Anónima (corporation) Independencia (street name) No. = Número (number) 322 (building number) Col. = Colonia (city district) Juárez (locality name) 06050 (postcode + city) D.F. = Distrito Federal (federal capital)	Sr. Señor (Mr.) Sra. = Señora (Mrs.) Srta. = Señorita (Miss) Family name in middle: e.g., Sr. Pérez (Martínez is mother's family). Given names are used in business.
South Africa	Mr. Mandla Ntuli International Publishing (Pty.) Ltd. Private Bag X2581 JOHANNESBURG 2000 SOUTH AFRICA	Pty. = Proprietory (privately owned) Ltd. (a corporation) Private Bag (P.O. box) (city + postcode) or (postcode + city)	Mnr = Meneer (Mr.) Mev. = Mevrou (Mrs.) Mejuffrou (Miss) is not used. Business is becoming less formal, so the use of given names is possible.
United Kingdom	Mr. N. J. Lancaster International Publishing Ltd. Kingsbury House 12 Kingsbury Road EDGEWARE Middlesex HA8 9XG ENGLAND	N. J. (initials of given names) Ltd. (limited liability corporation) Kingsbury House (building name) 12 (building number) Kingsbury Road (name of street/road) EDGEWARE (city—all caps) Middlesex (county—not all caps) HA8 9XG (postcode—after 6 spaces, or on a separate line)	Mr. and Ms. used mostly. Mrs. and Miss sometimes used in North and by older women. Given names are used in business after some time. Wait to be invited.

includes the first few words of the opening paragraph along with the recipient's name.

After this line, the sentence continues a double space below as part of the body of the letter, as in these examples:

Thank you, Mr. Brown,	Salutopening
for your prompt payment of your bill.	Body
Congratulations, Ms. Lake!	Salutopening
Your promotion is well deserved.	Body

Whether your salutation is informal or formal, be especially careful that names are spelled right. A mis-spelled name is glaring evidence of carelessness, and it belies the personal interest you're trying to express.

BODY The body of the letter is your message. Almost all letters are single-spaced, with one blank line before and after the salutation or salutopening, between para-graphs, and before the complimentary close. The body may include indented lists, entire paragraphs indented for emphasis, and even subheadings. If it does, all similar ele-ments should be treated in the same way. Your depart-ment or company may select a format to use for all letters.

COMPLIMENTARY CLOSE The complimentary close begins on the second line below the body of the letter. Alternatives for wording are available, but currently the trend seems to be toward using one-word closes, such as *Sincerely* and *Cordially*. In any case, the complimentary close reflects the relationship between you and the per-son you're writing to. Avoid cute closes, such as *Yours for bigger profits*. If your audience doesn't know you well, your sense of humour may be misunderstood.

SIGNATURE BLOCK Leave three blank lines for a written signature below the complimentary close and then include the sender's name (unless it appears in the letterhead). The person's title may appear on the same line as the name or on the line below:

Cordially,

Raymond Brodsky
Director of Personnel

Your letterhead indicates that you're representing your company. However, if your letter is on plain paper or runs to a second page, you may want to emphasize that you're speaking legally for the company. The accepted way of doing that is to place the company's name in capital letters a double space below the complimentary close and then include the sender's name and title four lines below that:

Sincerely,

WENTWORTH INDUSTRIES

(Mrs.) Helen B. Yamaguchi
President

If your name could be taken for either a man's or a woman's, a courtesy title indicating gender should be included, with or without parentheses. Also, women who prefer a particular courtesy title should include it:

Mrs. Nancy Winters
(Miss) Juana Flores
Ms. Pat Li
(Mr.) Jamie Saunders

Additional Letter Parts

Letters vary greatly in subject matter and thus in the identifying information they need and the format they adopt. The letter in Figure A–2 shows how these addi-tional parts should be arranged. The following elements may be used in any combination, depending on the requirements of the particular letter:

> **Addressee notation.** Letters that have a restricted readership or that must be handled in a special way should include such addressee notations as *Personal, Confidential,* or *Please Forward.* This sort of notation appears a double space above the inside address, in all-capital letters.

> **Attention line.** Although not frequently used today, an attention line can be used if you know only the last name of the person you're writing to. It can also direct a letter to a position title or department. Place the attention line on the first line of the inside address and put the company name on the second.[6] Match the address on the envelope with the style of the inside address. An attention line may take any of the following forms or variants of them:

Attention: Dr. McHenry

Attention Director of Marketing

Attention Marketing Department

> **Subject line.** The subject line tells recipients at a glance what the letter is about (and indicates where to file the letter for future reference). It usually appears below the salutation, either against the left margin, indented (as a paragraph in the body), or centred. It can be placed above the salutation or at the very top of the page, and it can be highlighted in boldface or underscored. Some businesses omit the word *Subject,* and some organizations replace it with *Re:* or *In re:* (meaning "concerning" or "in the matter of"). The subject line may take a variety of forms, including the following:

Subject: RainMaster Sprinklers

About your February 4, 2010 order

FALL 2010 SALES MEETING

Reference Order No. 27920

>Figure A–2 Additional Letter Parts

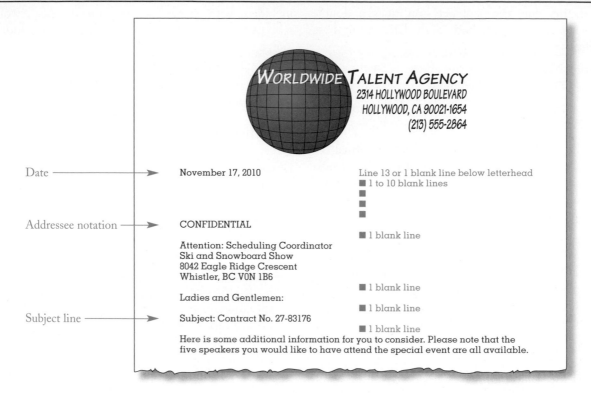

Date — CONFIDENTIAL
Addressee notation —
Subject line —

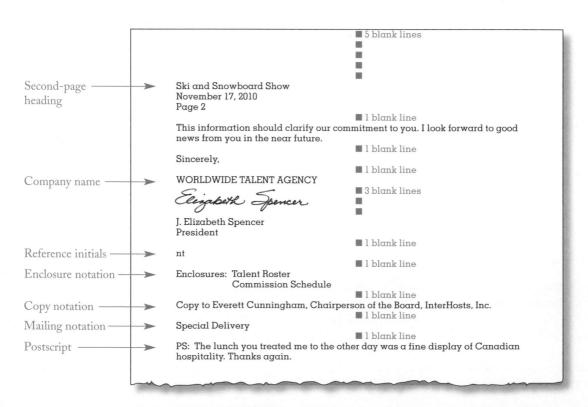

Second-page heading —
Company name —
Reference initials —
Enclosure notation —
Copy notation —
Mailing notation —
Postscript —

> **Second-page heading.** Use a second-page heading whenever an additional page is required. Some companies have second-page letterhead (with the company name and address on one line and in a smaller typeface). The heading bears the name (person or organization) from the first line of the inside address, the page number, the date, and perhaps a reference number. Leave two blank lines before the body. Ensure that at least two lines of a continued paragraph appear on the first and second pages. Never allow the closing lines to appear alone on a continued page. Precede the complimentary close or signature lines with at least two lines of the body. Also, don't hyphenate the last word on a page. All the following are acceptable forms for second-page headings:

Ms. Melissa Baker

May 9, 2010

Page 2

Ms. Melissa Baker, May 9, 2010, Page 2

Ms. Melissa Baker -2- May 9, 2010

> **Company name.** If you include the company name in the signature block, put it all in capital letters a double space below the complimentary close. You usually include the company name in the signature block only when the writer is serving as the company's official spokesperson or when letterhead has not been used.

> **Reference initials.** When businesspeople keyboard their own letters, reference initials are unnecessary, so they are becoming rare. When one person dictates a letter and another person produces it, reference initials show who helped prepare it. Place initials at the left margin, a double space below the signature block. When the signature block includes the writer's name, use only the preparer's initials. If the signature block includes only the department, use both sets of initials, usually in one of the following forms: *RSR/sm, RSR:sm,* or *RSR:SM* (writer/preparer). When the writer and the signer are different people, at least the file copy should bear both their initials as well as the typist's: *JFS/RSR/sm* (signer/writer/preparer).

> **Enclosure notation.** Enclosure notations appear at the bottom of a letter, one or two lines below the reference initials. Some common forms include the following:

Enclosure

Enclosures (2)

Enclosures: Résumé

      Photograph

      Attachment

> **Copy notation.** Copy notations may follow reference initials or enclosure notations. They indicate who's receiving a *courtesy copy* (cc). Some companies indicate copies made on a photocopier (pc), or they simply use *copy* (c). Recipients are listed in order of rank or (rank being equal) in alphabetical order. Among the forms used are the following:

cc: David Wentworth, Vice-President

pc: Dr. Martha Littlefield

Copy to Peter Simond
      6412 Carleton Rd.
      Lethbridge, AB T1H 9K4

c: Joseph Martinez with brochure and technical sheet

When sending copies to readers without other recipients knowing, place *bc, bcc,* or *bpc* (blind copy, blind courtesy copy, or blind photocopy, respectively) along with the name and any other information only on the copy, not on the original.

> **Mailing notation.** You may place a mailing notation (such as *Special Delivery* or *Registered Mail*) at the bottom of the letter, after reference initials or enclosure notations (whichever is last) and before copy notations. Or you may place it at the top of the letter, either above the inside address on the left side or just below the date on the right side. For greater visibility, mailing notations may appear in capital letters.

> **Postscript.** A postscript is an afterthought to the letter, a message that requires emphasis, or a personal note. It is usually the last element on any letter and may be preceded by *P.S., PS., PS:,* or nothing at all. A second afterthought would be designated *P.P.S.* (post postscript). Since postscripts usually indicate poor planning, generally avoid them. However, they're common in sales letters as a punchline to remind readers of a benefit for taking advantage of the offer.

Letter Formats

A letter format is the way of arranging all the basic letter parts. Sometimes a company adopts a certain format as its policy; sometimes the individual letter writer or preparer is allowed to choose the most appropriate format. In Canada, three major letter formats are commonly used:

> **Block format.** Each letter part begins at the left margin. The main advantage is quick and efficient preparation (see Figure A–3).

> **Modified block format.** Same as block format, except that the date, complimentary close, and signature block start near the centre of the page (see

> Figure A–3 Block Letter Format

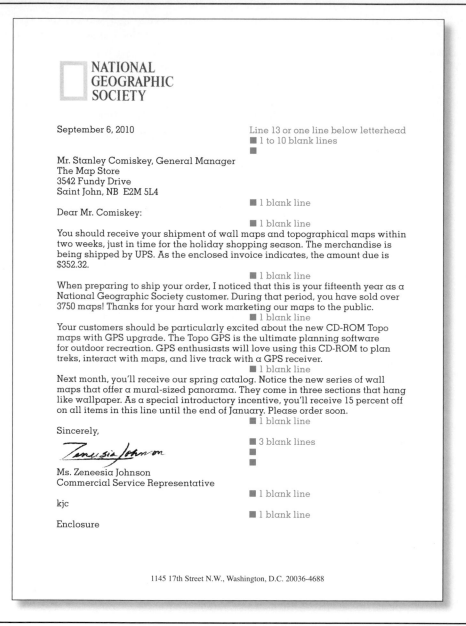

NATIONAL GEOGRAPHIC SOCIETY

September 6, 2010

Line 13 or one line below letterhead
■ 1 to 10 blank lines
■

Mr. Stanley Comiskey, General Manager
The Map Store
3542 Fundy Drive
Saint John, NB E2M 5L4

■ 1 blank line

Dear Mr. Comiskey:

■ 1 blank line

You should receive your shipment of wall maps and topographical maps within two weeks, just in time for the holiday shopping season. The merchandise is being shipped by UPS. As the enclosed invoice indicates, the amount due is $352.32.

■ 1 blank line

When preparing to ship your order, I noticed that this is your fifteenth year as a National Geographic Society customer. During that period, you have sold over 3750 maps! Thanks for your hard work marketing our maps to the public.

■ 1 blank line

Your customers should be particularly excited about the new CD-ROM Topo maps with GPS upgrade. The Topo GPS is the ultimate planning software for outdoor recreation. GPS enthusiasts will love using this CD-ROM to plan treks, interact with maps, and live track with a GPS receiver.

■ 1 blank line

Next month, you'll receive our spring catalog. Notice the new series of wall maps that offer a mural-sized panorama. They come in three sections that hang like wallpaper. As a special introductory incentive, you'll receive 15 percent off on all items in this line until the end of January. Please order soon.

■ 1 blank line

Sincerely,

■ 3 blank lines
■
■

Ms. Zeneesia Johnson
Commercial Service Representative

■ 1 blank line

kjc

■ 1 blank line

Enclosure

1145 17th Street N.W., Washington, D.C. 20036-4688

Figure A–4). The modified block format does permit indentions as an option. This format mixes preparation speed with traditional placement of some letter parts. It also looks more balanced on the page than the block format does.

> **Simplified format.** Instead of using a salutation, this format often weaves the reader's name into the first line or two of the body and often includes a subject line in capital letters (see Figure A–5). With no complimentary close, your signature appears after the body, followed by your printed (or typewritten) name (usually in all capital letters). This format is convenient when you don't know the reader's name;

however, some people object to it as mechanical and impersonal (a drawback you can overcome with a warm writing style). Because certain letter parts are eliminated, some line spacing is changed.

These three formats differ in the way paragraphs are indented, in the way letter parts are placed, and in some punctuation. However, the elements are always separated by at least one blank line, and the printed (or typewritten) name is always separated from the line above by at least three blank lines to allow space for a signature. If paragraphs are indented, the indention is normally five spaces. The most common formats for intercultural business letters are the block style and the modified block style.

> Figure A–4 Modified Block Letter Format

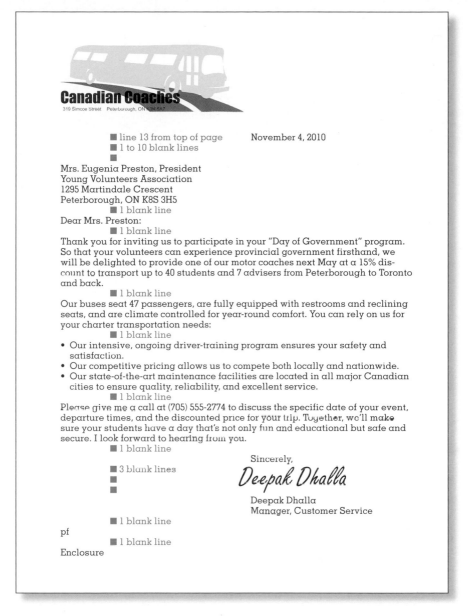

In addition to these three letter formats, letters may also be classified according to their style of punctuation. *Standard,* or *mixed, punctuation* uses a colon after the salutation (a comma if the letter is social or personal) and a comma after the complimentary close. *Open punctuation* uses no colon or comma after the salutation or the complimentary close. Although the most popular style in business communication is mixed punctuation, either style of punctuation may be used with block or modified block letter formats. Because the simplified letter format has no salutation or complimentary close, the style of punctuation is irrelevant.

Envelopes

For a first impression, the quality of the envelope is just as important as the quality of the stationery. Letterhead and envelopes should be of the same paper stock, have the same colour ink, and be imprinted with the same address and logo. Most envelopes used by Canadian businesses are No. 10 envelopes (9½ inches long), which are sized for an 8½-by-11-inch piece of paper folded in thirds. Some occasions call for a smaller, No. 6¾, envelope or for envelopes proportioned to fit special stationery. Figure A–6 shows the two most common sizes.

> Figure A–5 Simplified Letter Format

PERFORMANCETOOLS INTERNATIONAL
9553 Tecumseh Road, Windsor, ON N8R 3Z9

May 5, 2010   Line 13 from top of page
                                                        ■ 1 to 10 blank lines
                                                        ■
                                                        ■

Mr. Michael Ferraro
Pacific Coast Appliances
595 Briceland Street
Kingston, ON K7K 9L3
                                                        ■ 1 blank line

NEW PRODUCT INFORMATION
                                                        ■ 1 blank line

Thank you, Mr. Ferraro, for your recent inquiry about our product line. We appreciate your
enthusiasm for our products, and we are confident that your customers will enjoy the
improved performance of the new product line.
                                                        ■ 1 blank line

I have enclosed a package of information for your review, including product specifications,
dealer prices, and an order form. The package also contains reprints of PerformanceTools
reviews and a comparison sheet showing how our products measure up against competing
brands.
                                                        ■ 1 blank line

Please call with any questions you may have about shipping or payment arrangements.
                                                        ■ 3 blank lines
Joanna Davis   ■
                                                        ■

Joanna Davis
Product Specialist
                                                        ■ 1 blank line

ek
                                                        ■ 1 blank line

Enclosures

Addressing the Envelope

No matter what size the envelope, the address is always single-spaced with all lines aligned on the left. The address on the envelope is in the same style as the inside address and presents the same information. The order to follow is from the smallest division to the largest:

1. Name and title of recipient
2. Name of department or subgroup
3. Name of organization
4. Name of building

5. Street address and suite number, or post office box number
6. City, province or state, and postal or ZIP code
7. Name of country (if the letter is being sent abroad)

Figure A–6 also shows the proper spacing for addresses and return addresses.

Canada Post's optical scanning equipment can read both handwritten and typed addresses, and their addressing guidelines accommodate the requirements of French and English and the preferences of their customers. Businesses can use upper and lower case letters

> Figure A–6 Prescribed Envelope Format

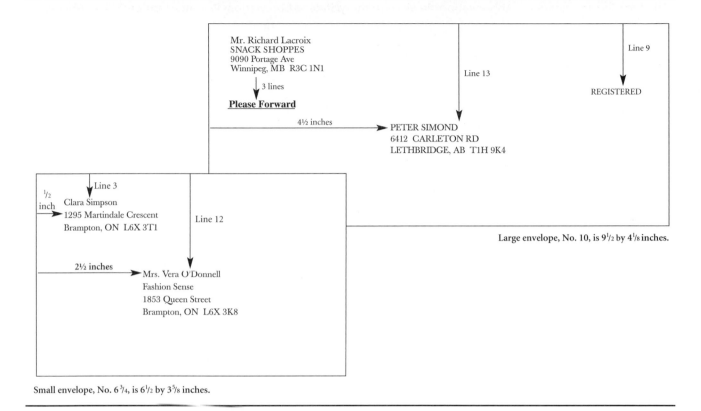

Small envelope, No. 6³/₄, is 6¹/₂ by 3⁵/₈ inches.

and accents when addressing envelopes and spell out and punctuate all address elements if they want. However, Canada Post does encourage customers to follow specific formats because their mail will be handled more efficiently. For example:

> When a civic number suffix is present in the address, do not insert a space when it is a letter (123A), but insert one space when it is a fraction (123½). (A civic number is the official number a municipality assigns to an address.)
> Use common abbreviations for street types (e.g., ST and AVE). The only street types that may be translated are ST (RUE), AVE (AV), and BLVD (BOUL).
> Always place a French street type before the street name, unless it is an ordinal number (1er, 2e,) (PREMIÈRE, DEUXIÈME).
> Do not translate the French street name: it is the official name recognized by each municipality and should remain in the original form (e.g., "Main" is not "Principale").

Canada Post also prefers customers to use the recognized two-letter province abbreviation (see Table A–6). In addition, write the postal code in upper case and place it two spaces to the right of the province, with one space between the first three and the last three characters. Review the Canada Post Addressing Guidelines PDF document, available on the Canada Post home page (www.canadapost.ca) for the details governing address format.

Follow U.S. Postal Service guidelines when addressing envelopes to customers in the United States. As with Canada Post, the U.S. Postal Service prefers the two-character state abbreviation over the full state name. The ZIP code must be separated from the state short form by two spaces. The ZIP code may be five or nine digits. A hyphen separates the fifth and sixth digits. For example,

Mr. Damon Smith
1277 Morris Ave., Apt. 7-B
Bronx, NY 10451-4598

Folding to Fit

The way a letter is folded also contributes to the recipient's overall impression of your organization's professionalism. When sending a standard-size piece of paper in a No. 10 envelope, fold it in thirds, with the bottom folded up first and the top folded down over it (see Figure A–7); the open end should be at the top of the envelope and facing out. Fit smaller stationery neatly into the appropriate envelope simply by folding it in half or in thirds. When sending a standard-size letterhead in

> **Table A–6** Two-Letter Mailing Abbreviations for Canada and the United States

Province/Territory/State	Abbreviation	Province/Territory/State	Abbreviation	Province/Territory/State	Abbreviation
Canada		District of Columbia	DC	New York	NY
Alberta	AB	Florida	FL	North Carolina	NC
British Columbia	BC	Georgia	GA	North Dakota	ND
Labrador	NL	Guam	GU	Northern Mariana	CM
Manitoba	MB	Hawaii	HI	Ohio	OH
New Brunswick	NB	Idaho	ID	Oklahoma	OK
Newfoundland and Labrador	NL	Illinois	IL	Oregon	OR
Northwest Territories	NT	Indiana	IN	Pennsylvania	PA
Nova Scotia	NS	Iowa	IA	Puerto Rico	PR
Nunavut	NU	Kansas	KS	Rhode Island	RI
Ontario	ON	Kentucky	KY	South Carolina	SC
Prince Edward Island	PE	Louisiana	LA	South Dakota	SD
Quebec	QC	Maine	ME	Tennessee	TN
Saskatchewan	SK	Maryland	MD	Trust Territories	TT
Yukon Territory	YT	Massachusetts	MA	Texas	TX
United States		Michigan	MI	Utah	UT
Alabama	AL	Minnesota	MN	Vermont	VT
Alaska	AK	Mississippi	MS	Virginia	VA
American Samoa	AS	Missouri	MO	Virgin Islands	VI
Arizona	AZ	Montana	MT	Washington	WA
Arkansas	AR	Nebraska	NE	West Virginia	WV
California	CA	Nevada	NV	Wisconsin	WI
Colorado	CO	New Hampshire	NH	Wyoming	WY
Connecticut	CT	New Jersey	NJ		
Delaware	DE	New Mexico	NM		

a No. 6¾ envelope, fold it in half from top to bottom and then in thirds from side to side.

International Mail

Postal service differs from country to country. It's usually a good idea to send international correspondence by airmail and to ask that responses be sent that way as well. Also, remember to check the postage; rates for sending mail to most other countries differ from the rates for sending mail within your own country.

Canada Post offers four methods for sending mail internationally:

> Priority Worldwide, the most expensive service, offers next-day delivery to the United States and timely delivery to 220 countries.
> Xpresspost International delivers in 4 to 9 business days to major centres in selected countries.

> Figure A–7 Folding Standard-Size Letterhead

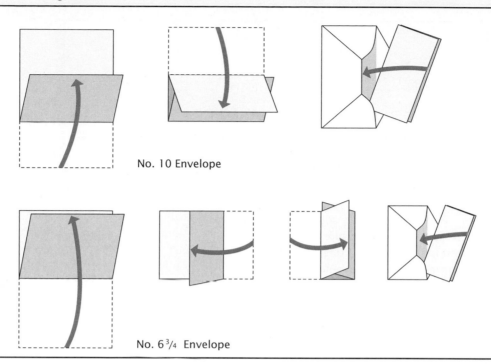

No. 10 Envelope

No. 6³/₄ Envelope

> Air parcels, a medium-priced option, provides 6 to 10 day delivery to available destinations.
> Surface parcel, the economy service, offers 4 to 6 weeks delivery to most international destinations.

When preparing material for international destinations, follow Canada Post's instructions, available at www.canadapost. ca/business/tools/pg/downloads/downPG-e.asp, for detailed information about size and weight limitations of letters and packages. Canada Post stresses that the name of the country must be spelled in full (e.g., UK is not acceptable; United Kingdom is). In addition, observe customs requirements to avoid delays; you can access Canada Border Services Agency at www.cbsa-asfc.gc.ca.

Memos

Many organizations have memo forms preprinted, with labelled spaces for the recipient's name (or sometimes a checklist of all departments in an organization or all persons in a department), the sender's name, the date, and the subject (see Figure A–8). If such forms don't exist, you can use a memo template (which comes with word-processing software and provides margin settings, headings, and special formats), or you can use plain paper.

On your document, include a title such as *MEMO* or *INTEROFFICE CORRESPONDENCE* (all in capitals) centred at the top of the page or aligned with the left margin. Also at the top, include the words *To, From, Date,* and *Subject*—followed by the appropriate information— with a blank line between, as shown here:

MEMO

TO:

FROM:

DATE:

SUBJECT:

Sometimes the heading is organized like this:

MEMO

TO: DATE:

FROM: SUBJECT:

You can arrange these four pieces of information in almost any order. The date sometimes appears without the heading *Date*. The subject may be presented with the letters *Re:* (in place of *SUBJECT:*) or may even be presented without any heading (but in capital letters, so it stands out clearly). You may want to include a file or reference number, introduced by the word *File*.

The following guidelines will help you effectively format specific memo elements:

> **Addressees.** When sending a memo to a long list of people, include the notation *See distribution list* or *See below* in the *To* position at the top; then list the names at the end of the memo. Arrange this list alphabetically, except when high-ranking officials deserve more prominent placement. You can also address memos to groups of people—*All Sales Representatives, Production Group, New Product Team.*

> Figure A–8 Preprinted Memo Form

> **Courtesy titles.** You need not use courtesy titles anywhere in a memo; first initials and last names, first names, or even initials alone are often sufficient. However, use a courtesy title if you would use one in a face-to-face encounter with the person.
> **Subject line.** The subject line of a memo helps busy colleagues quickly find out what your memo is about. Although the subject "line" may overflow onto a second line, it's most helpful when it's short (but still informative).
> **Body.** Start the body of the memo on the second or third line below the heading. Like the body of a letter, it's usually single-spaced with blank lines between paragraphs. Indenting paragraphs is optional. Handle lists, important passages, and subheadings as you do in letters. If the memo is very short, you may double-space it.
> **Second page.** If the memo carries over to a second page, head the second page just as you head the second page of a letter.
> **Writer's initials.** Unlike a letter, a memo doesn't require a complimentary close or a signature, because your name is already prominent at the top. However, you may initial the memo—either beside the name appearing at the top of the memo or at the bottom of the memo—or you may even sign your name at the bottom, particularly if the memo deals with money or confidential matters.
> **Other elements.** Treat elements such as reference initials, enclosure notations, and copy notations just as you would in a letter.

Memos may be delivered by hand, by the post office (when the recipient works at a different location), or through interoffice mail. Interoffice mail may require the use of special reusable envelopes that have spaces for the recipient's name and department or room number; the name of the previous recipient is simply crossed out. If a regular envelope is used, the words *Interoffice Mail* appear where the stamp normally goes, so it won't accidentally be stamped and mailed with the rest of the office correspondence.

Informal, routine, or brief reports for distribution within a company are often presented in memo form (see Chapter 11). Don't include report parts, such as a table of contents and appendixes, but write the body of the memo report just as carefully as you'd write a formal report.

Email

Because email messages can act both as memos (carrying information within your company) and as letters (carrying information outside your company and around the world), their format depends on your audience and purpose. You may choose to have your email resemble a formal letter or a detailed report, or you may decide to keep your email as simple as an interoffice memo. A modified memo format is appropriate for most email messages. All email programs include two major elements: the header and the body (see Figure A–9).

Header

The email header depends on the particular program you use. Some programs even allow you to choose between a shorter and a longer version. However, most headers contain similar information.

> **To:** Contains the audience's email address (see Figure A–10). Most email programs also allow you to send mail to an entire group of people all at once.

First, you create a distribution list. Then, you type the name of the list in the *To:* line instead of typing the addresses of every person in the group. The most common email addresses are addresses such as

info@gallery.ca (National Gallery of Canada)
info@schimmel-piano.de (Schimmel Piano, Braunschweig, Germany)
advqueries@nationalpost.com (print advertising sales at the *National Post*)

> Figure A–9 A Typical Email Message

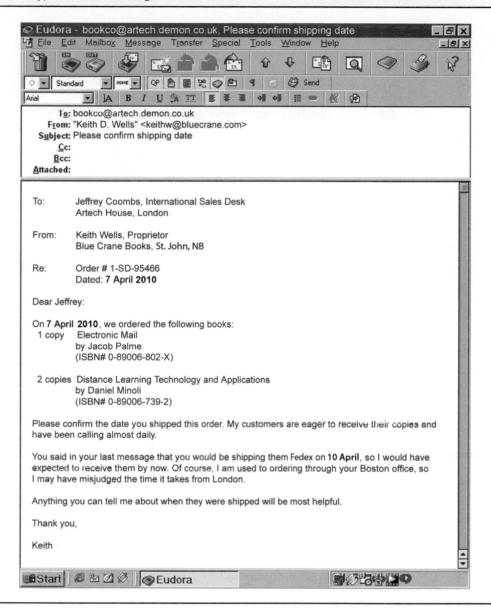

> **From:** Contains your email address.
> **Date:** Contains the day of the week, date (day, month, year), time, and time zone.
> **Subject:** Describes the content of the message and presents an opportunity for you to build interest in your message.
> **Cc:** Allows you to send copies of a message to more than one person at a time. It also allows everyone on the list to see who else received the same message.
> **Bcc:** Lets you send copies to people without the other recipients knowing—a practice considered unethical by some.[7]
> **Attachments:** Contains the name(s) of the file(s) you attach to your email message. The file can be a word-processing document, a digital image, an audio or video message, a spreadsheet, or a software program. Most email programs now allow you the choice of hiding or revealing other lines that contain more detailed information, including

> **Message-Id:** the exact location of this email message on the sender's system
> **X-mailer:** the version of the email program being used
> **Content type:** a description of the text and character set that is contained in the message
> **Received:** information about each system your email passed through en route to your mailbox

> Figure A–10 Anatomy of an Email Address

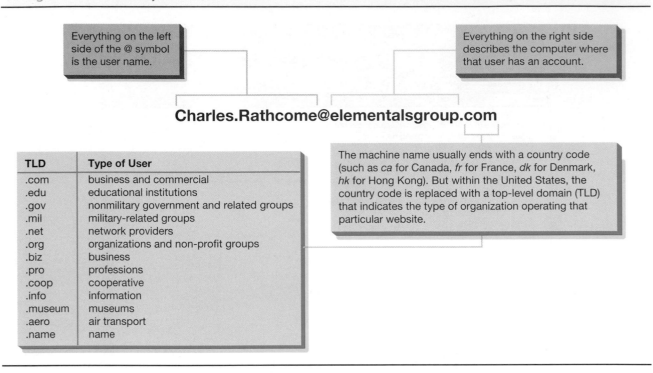

Everything on the left side of the @ symbol is the user name.

Everything on the right side describes the computer where that user has an account.

Charles.Rathcome@elementalsgroup.com

The machine name usually ends with a country code (such as *ca* for Canada, *fr* for France, *dk* for Denmark, *hk* for Hong Kong). But within the United States, the country code is replaced with a top-level domain (TLD) that indicates the type of organization operating that particular website.

TLD	Type of User
.com	business and commercial
.edu	educational institutions
.gov	nonmilitary government and related groups
.mil	military-related groups
.net	network providers
.org	organizations and non-profit groups
.biz	business
.pro	professions
.coop	cooperative
.info	information
.museum	museums
.aero	air transport
.name	name

Body

The rest of the space below the header is for the body of your message. In the *To:* and *From:* lines, some headers actually print out the names of the sender and receiver (in addition to their email addresses). Other headers do not. If your mail program includes only the email addresses, you might consider including your own memo-type header in the body of your message, as in Figure A–9. The writer even included a second, more specific subject line in his memo-type header. Some recipients may endorse the clarity of such second headers; however, others will criticize the space it takes. Your decision depends on how formal you want to be.

Do include a greeting in your email. As pointed out in Chapter 7, greetings personalize your message. Leave one line space above and below your greeting to set it off from the rest of your message. You may end your greeting with a colon (formal), a comma (conversational), or even two hyphens (informal)—depending on the level of formality you want.

Your message begins one blank line space below your greeting. Just as in memos and letters, skip one line space between paragraphs and include headings, numbered lists, bulleted lists, and embedded lists when appropriate. Limit your line lengths to a maximum of 80 characters by inserting a hard return at the end of each line.

One blank line space below your message, include a simple closing, often just one word. A blank line space below that, include your signature. Whether you type your name or use a signature file, including your signature personalizes your message.

Reports

Enhance your report's effectiveness by paying careful attention to its appearance and layout. Follow whatever guidelines your organization prefers, always being neat and consistent throughout. If it's up to you to decide formatting questions, the following conventions may help you decide how to handle margins, headings, spacing and indention, and page numbers.

Margins

All margins on a report page are at least 1 inch wide. For double-spaced pages, use 1-inch margins; for single-spaced pages, set margins between 1¼ and 1½ inches. The top, left, and right margins are usually the same, but the bottom margins can be 1½ times deeper. Some special pages also have deeper top margins. Set top margins as deep as 2 inches for pages that contain major titles: prefatory parts (such as the table of contents or the executive summary), supplementary parts (such as the reference notes or bibliography), and textual parts (such as the first page of the text or the first page of each chapter).

> Figure A–11 Margins for Formal Reports

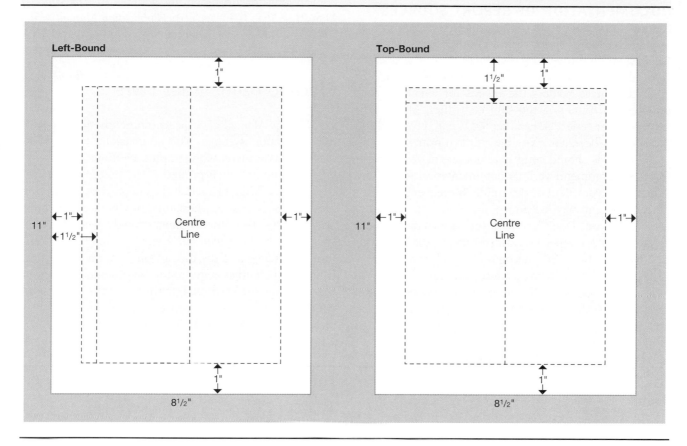

If you're going to bind your report at the left or at the top, use a 1½ inch margin on the bound edge (see Figure A–11). The space taken by the binding on left-bound reports shifts the centre point of the text ¼ inch to the right of the centre of the paper. Ensure that you centre headings between the margins, not between the edges of the paper. Computers can do this for you automatically. Other guidelines for report formats are in the Chapter 13 samples.

Headings

Headings of various levels provide visual clues to a report's organization. Figure 12–7 illustrates one good system for showing these levels, but many variations exist. No matter which system you use, ensure that you are consistent.

Spacing and Indentions

If your report is double-spaced (perhaps to ease comprehension of technical material), indent the first line of all paragraphs five character spaces (or about a ½ inch). In single-spaced reports, block the paragraphs (no indentions) and leave one blank line between them.

Ensure that the material on the title page is centred and well balanced, as on the title page of the sample report in Chapter 13.

Page Numbers

Remember that every page in the report is counted; however, not all pages show numbers. The first page of the report, normally the title page, is unnumbered. All other pages in the prefatory section are numbered with a lowercase roman numeral, beginning with *ii* and continuing with *iii, iv, v,* and so on. The unadorned (no dashes, no period) page number is centred at the bottom margin.

Number the first page of the text of the report with the unadorned arabic numeral 1, centred at the bottom margin (double- or triple-spaced below the text). In left-bound reports, number the following pages (including the supplementary parts) consecutively with unadorned arabic numerals (2, 3, and so on), placed at the top right-hand margin (double- or triple-spaced above the text). For top-bound reports and for special pages having 2-inch top margins, centre the page numbers at the bottom margin.

Appendix B
DOCUMENTATION OF REPORT SOURCES

Documenting a report is too important a task to undertake haphazardly. By providing information about your sources, you improve your own credibility as well as the credibility of the facts and opinions you present. Documentation gives readers the means for checking your findings and pursuing the subject further. Also, documenting your report is the accepted way to give credit to the people whose work you have drawn from.

What style should you use to document your report? Experts recommend various documentation forms, depending on your field or discipline. Moreover, your employer or client may use a form different from those the experts suggest. Don't let this discrepancy confuse you. If your employer specifies a form, use it; the standardized form is easier for colleagues to understand. However, if the choice of form is left to you, adopt one of the styles described here. Whatever style you choose, be consistent within any given report, using the same order, punctuation, and format from one reference citation or bibliography entry to the next.

A wide variety of style manuals provide detailed information on documentation. The three main resources are

> American Psychological Association, *Publication Manual of the American Psychological Association,* 6th ed. (Washington, DC: American Psychological Association, 2010). Details the author-date system, which is preferred in the social sciences and often in the natural sciences as well.
> *The Chicago Manual of Style,* 15th ed. (Chicago: University of Chicago Press, 2003). Often referred to only as "Chicago" and widely used in the publishing industry; provides detailed treatment of source documentation and many other aspects of document preparation.
> Joseph Gibaldi, *MLA Handbook for Writers of Research Papers,* 7th ed. (New York: Modern Language Association, 2009). Serves as the basis for the note and bibliography style used in much academic writing and is recommended in many university and college textbooks on writing term papers; provides many examples in the humanities.

Although many systems have been proposed for organizing the information in source notes, all of them break the information into parts:

1. Information about the author (name)
2. Information about the work (title, edition, volume number)
3. Information about the publication (place, publisher)
4. Information about the date
5. Information on relevant page ranges

In the following sections, we summarize the major conventions for documenting sources in *The Chicago Manual of Style* (Chicago), the *Publication Manual of the American Psychological Association* (APA), and the *MLA Handbook for Writers of Research Papers* (MLA).

Chicago Humanities Style

The Chicago Manual of Style recommends two types of documentation systems. The *documentary-note,* or *humanities,* style gives bibliographic citations in notes—either footnotes (when printed at the bottom of a page) or endnotes (when printed at the end of the report). The humanities system is often used in literature, history, and the arts. The other system strongly recommended by Chicago is the *author-date* system, which cites the author's last name and the date of publication in the text, usually in parentheses, reserving full documentation for the reference list (or bibliography). For the purpose of comparing styles, we will concentrate on the humanities system, which is described in detail in Chicago.

In-Text Citation—Chicago Humanities Style

To document report sources in text, the humanities system relies on superscripts—arabic numerals placed just above the line of type at the end of the reference:

Toward the end of his speech, Myers sounded a note of caution, saying that even though the economy is expected to grow, it could easily slow a bit.[10]

The superscript lets the reader know how to look for source information in either a footnote or an endnote (see Figure B–1). Some readers prefer footnotes so that they can simply glance at the bottom of the page for information. Others prefer endnotes so that they can read the text without a clutter of notes on the page. Also, endnotes relieve the writer from worrying about how long each note will be and how much space it will take away from the page. Both footnotes and endnotes are handled automatically by today's word-processing software.

For the reader's convenience, you can use footnotes for **content notes** (which may supplement your main text with asides about a particular issue or event, provide a cross-reference to another section of your report, or direct the reader to a related source). Then, you can use endnotes for **source notes** (which document direct quotations, paraphrased passages, and visual aids). Consider which type of note is most common in your report and then choose whether to present these notes all as endnotes or all as footnotes. Regardless of the method you choose for referencing textual information in your

> Figure B–1 Sample Endnotes—Chicago Humanities Style

	NOTES
Journal article with volume and issue numbers	1. Michael E. Porter and Mark R. Kramer, "The Competitive Advantage of Corporate Philanthropy," *Harvard Business Review* 80, no. 12 (December 2002): 59.
Brochure	2. Apple Inc., *iPhone user Guide for iPhone OS 3.0 Software* (Cupertino, CA: Apple Inc., 2009), 122.
Newspaper article, no author	3. "Toyota Sets Sights on Sales Record," *Globe and Mail Report on Business*, 1 September 2007, sec. B, 10.
Annual report	4. Suncor, *2009 Annual Report* (Calgary, AB), 5.
Magazine article	5. Denis Sequin, "A Hollywood Ending?" *Canadian Business*, 13 August 2007, 11.
Television broadcast	6. Wendy Mesley, "How Not to Get Nailed," *Marketplace* (Toronto, ON: CBC TV, 17 August 2007).
Internet, World Wide Web	7. "Intel—Company Report," Hoover's Online http://www.hoovers.com/intel-corp./ –ID_13787–/free-co-factsheet.xhtml (accessed 22 July 2009).
Book, component parts	8. Julia C. Gluesing, Tara C. Alcordo, and Margaret A. Neale, "The Development of Global Virtual Teams," in *Virtual Teams that Work: Creating Conditions for Virtual Team Effectiveness*, ed. Cristina B. Gibson and Susan G. Cohen (San Francisco: Jossey-Bass, 2003), 356.
Unpublished dissertation or thesis	9. Changhui Zhou, "Transnational Flow of Knowledge in Multinational Corporations: R&D Co-Practice as an Integrating Force" (PhD diss, University of Western Ontario, 2002), 34–43.
Paper presented at a meeting	10. Jeanette S. Martin and Lillian H. Chaney, "Integrating Global Conversational Customs into Business Courses" (paper presented at the Association for Business Communication 70th Annual Convention, Irvine, CA, October, 2005), 2–3.
Online magazine article	11. Liz Murphy, "Online Marketing: Getting What You Pay For?" *CMA Management*, June/July 2007, http://www.managementmag.com (accessed 18 September 2007).
Article from an electronic database	12. Steven V. Davis and Andrew Gilman, "Communication Coordination," *Risk Management* 49, no.8 (August 2002): 38–40, Proquest, Document ID 148778291 (accessed 27 October 2008).
CD-ROM encyclopedia article, one author	13. *The Concise Columbia Encyclopedia*, s.v. "Eastman, George" (by Robert Parkings), CD-ROM (New York: Columbia University Press, 1998).
Interview	14. Ian Hamilton (manager, Corporate Communications, Dofasco Inc.), email interview by author, 15 January 2002.
Newspaper article, one author	15. Nathan VanderKlippe, "B.C. Salmon Industry in Rough Water," *Financial Post*, 1 September 2007, sec. FP, 3.
Book, two authors	16. Paul A. Argenti and Janis Forman, *The Power of Corporate Communication: Crafting the Voice and Image of Your Business* (New York: McGraw Hill, 2006), 102–3.
Government publication	17. Office of Consumer Affairs, Industry Canada, *Canadian Consumer Handbook* (Ottawa, ON: Office of Consumer Affairs, 2009), 17.

report, notes for visual aids (both content notes and source notes) are placed on the same page as the visual.

Bibliography—Chicago Humanities Style

The humanities system may or may not be accompanied by a bibliography (because the notes give all the necessary bibliographic information). However, endnotes are arranged in order of appearance in the text, so an alphabetical bibliography can be valuable to your readers. The bibliography may be titled *Bibliography, Reference List, Sources, Works Cited* (if you include only those sources you actually cited in your report), or *Works Consulted* (if you include uncited sources as well). This list of sources may also serve as a reading list for those who want to pursue the subject of your report further, so consider annotating each entry—that is, comment on the subject matter and viewpoint of the source, as well as on its usefulness to readers. Annotations may be written in either complete or incomplete sentences. (See the annotated list of style manuals early in this appendix.) A bibliography may also be more manageable if you subdivide it into categories (a classified bibliography), either by type

> Figure B–2 Sample Bibliography—Chicago Humanities Style

Brochure	BIBLIOGRAPHY
	Apple Inc. *iPhone User Guide for iPhone OS 3.0 Software*. Cupertino, CA: Apple Inc., 2009.
Book, two authors	Argenti, Paul A., and Janis Forman. *The Power of Corporate Communication: Crafting the Voice and Image of Your Business*. New York: McGraw Hill, 2006.
Article from an electronic database	Davis, Steven V., and Andrew Gilman. "Communication Coordination." *Risk Management* 49, no. 8 (August 2002): 38–43. Proquest, Document ID 148778291 (accessed 27 October 2008).
Book, component parts	Gluesing, Julia C., Tara C. Alcordo, and Margaret A. Neale. "The Development of Global Virtual Teams." In *Virtual Teams that Work: Creating Conditions for Virtual Team Effectiveness*, edited by Cristina B. Gibson and Susan G. Cohen. San Francisco: Jossey-Bass, 2003.
Interview	Hamilton, Ian, manager, Corporate Communications, Dofasco Inc. Email interview by author, 15 January 2002.
Internet, World Wide Web	Hoover's Online, "Intel—Company Report." http://www.hoovers.com/intel-corp./--ID_13787--/free-co-factsheet.xhtml (accessed 22 July 2009).
Paper presented at a meeting	Martin, Jeanette S., and Lillian H. Chaney. "Integrating Global Conversational Customs into Business Courses." Paper presented at the Association for Business Communication 70th Annual Convention, Irvine, CA., October 2005.
Television broadcast	Mesley, Wendy. "How Not to Get Nailed." *Marketplace*. Toronto: CBC TV, 17 August 2007.
Online magazine article	Murphy, Liz. "Online Marketing: Getting What You Pay For?" *CMA Management*, June/July 2007. http://www.managementmag.com (accessed 18 September 2007).
Government publication	Office of Consumer Affairs. Industry Canada. *Canadian Consumer Handbook*. Ottawa, ON: Office of Consumer Affairs, 2009.
Journal article with volume and issue numbers	Porter, Michael E., and Mark R. Kramer. "The Competitive Advantage of Corporate Philanthropy," *Harvard Business Review* 80, no. 12 (December 2002): 56–68.
Magazine article	Sequin, Denis. "A Hollywood Ending?" *Canadian Business*, 13 August 2007, 11–12.
Annual report	Suncor. *2009 Annual Report*. Calgary: AB.
CD-ROM encyclopedia article, one author	*The Concise Columbia Encyclopedia*. s.v. "Eastman, George" (by Robert Parkings). CD-ROM, 1998.
Newspaper article, no author	"Toyota Sets Sights on Sales Record." *Globe and Mail Report on Business*, 1 September 2007, sec. B, 10.
Newspaper article, one author	VanderKlippe, Nathan. "B.C. Salmon Industry in Rough Water." *Financial Post*, 1 September 2007, sec. FP, 3.
Unpublished dissertation or thesis	Zhou, Changhui. "Transnational Flow of Knowledge in Multinational Corporations: R&D Co-Practice as an Integrating Force." PhD diss., University of Western Ontario, 2002.

of reference (e.g., books, articles, and unpublished material) or by subject matter (e.g., government regulations or market forces). The major conventions for developing a bibliography according to Chicago style (see Figure B–2) are as follows:

> Exclude any page numbers that may be cited in source notes, except for journals, periodicals, and newspapers.
> Alphabetize entries by the last name of the lead author (listing last name first). The names of second and succeeding authors are listed in normal order.

Entries without an author name are alphabetized by the first important word in the title.
> Format entries as hanging indents (indent second and succeeding lines 3 to 5 spaces).
> Arrange entries in the following general order:

1. author name
2. title information
3. publication information
4. date
5. periodical page range

> Use quotation marks around the titles of articles from magazines, newspapers, and journals. Capitalize the first and last words, as well as all other important words (except prepositions, articles, and coordinating conjunctions).
> Use italics to set off the names of books, newspapers, journals, and other complete publications—capitalizing the first and last words, as well as all other important words.
> Include the volume number and the issue number (if necessary) for journal articles. Include the year of publication inside parentheses and follow with a colon and the page range of the article: *Harvard Business Review* 80, no. 12 (December 2002): 56–68. (In this source, the volume is 80, the number is 12, and the page range is 56 to 68.)
> Use brackets to identify all electronic references: [Online database] or [CD-ROM].
> Explain how electronic references can be reached: Available from www.spaceless.com/WWWVL.
> Give the citation date for online references: Cited 23 August 2009.

APA Style

The American Psychological Association (APA) recommends the author-date system of documentation, which is popular in the physical, natural, and social sciences. When using this system, you simply insert the author's last name and the year of publication within parentheses following the text discussion of the material cited. Include a page number if you use a direct quote. This approach briefly identifies the source, so readers can locate complete information in the alphabetical reference list at the end of the report. The author-date system is both brief and clear, saving readers time and effort.

In-Text Citation—APA Style

To document report sources in text using APA style, insert the author's surname and the date of publication at the end of a statement. Enclose this information in parentheses. If the author's name is referred to in the text itself, then the name can be omitted from parenthetical material.

Some experts recommend that corporations partner with charities and educational institutions to benefit society and raise their company profiles (Porter & Kramer, 2002).

Porter and Kramer (2002) make a strong case for corporations partnering with charities and educational institutions to benefit society and raise their company profiles.

Personal communications and interviews conducted by the author would not be listed in the reference list at all. Such citations would appear in the text only.

Relating to all stakeholders is high on the list of Dofasco's Environmental and Energy reports, according to Ian Hamilton, a Dofasco corporate communications manager (personal communication, January 15, 2002).

List of References—APA Style

For APA style, list only those works actually cited in the text (so you would not include works for background or for further reading). Report writers must choose their references judiciously. The major conventions for developing a reference list according to APA style (see Figure B–3) are as follows:

> Format entries as hanging indents.
> List all author names in reversed order (last name first), and use only initials for the first and middle names.
> Arrange entries in the following general order:

1. author name
2. date
3. title information
4. publication information
5. periodical page range

> Follow the author name with the date of publication in parentheses.
> List titles of articles from magazines, newspapers, and journals without underlines or quotation marks. Capitalize only the first word of the title, any proper nouns, and the first word to follow an internal colon.
> Italicize titles of books, capitalizing only the first word, any proper nouns, and the first word to follow a colon.
> Italicize names of magazines, newspapers, journals, and other complete publications. Capitalize all the important words.
> For journal articles, include the volume number (in italics) and, if necessary, the issue number (in parentheses). Finally, include the page range of the article: *Harvard Business Review, 80*(12), 56–68. (In this example, the volume is 80, the number is 12, and the page range is 56 to 68.)
> Include personal communications (e.g., letters, memos, email, and conversations) only in text, not in reference lists.
> Electronic references include author, date of publication, title of article, name of publication (if one), volume, and source.
> For electronic references, specify the URL. Leave periods off the ends of URLs.

> Figure B–3 Sample References—APA Style

REFERENCES

Brochure

Apple Inc. (2009). *iPhone User Guide for iPhone OS 3.0 Software*. Cupertino, CA: Apple Inc.

Book, two authors

Argenti, P. A., & Forman, J. (2006). *The power of corporate communication: Crafting the voice and image of your business*. New York, NY: McGraw Hill.

Article from an electronic database

Davis, S. V., & Gilman, A. (2002, August). Communication coordination. *Risk Management 49*(8), 38–43. Retrieved from Proquest database.

Book, component parts

Gluesing, J. C., Alcordo, T. C., & Neale, M. A. (2003). The development of global virtual teams. In C.B. Gibson & S.G. Cohen (Eds.), *Virtual teams that work: Creating conditions for virtual team effectiveness* (pp. 353–380). San Francisco, CA: Jossey-Bass.

Internet, World Wide Web

Hoover's Online. (2009). *Intel—Company capsule*. Retrieved July 22, 2009, from www.hoovers.com/intel-corp./--ID_13787--/free-co-factsheet.xhtml

Paper presented at a meeting

Martin, J. S., & Chaney, L. H. (2005, October). *Integrating global conversational customs into business courses*. Paper presented at the Association for Business Communication 70th Annual Convention, Irvine, CA.

Television broadcast

Mesley, W. (Writer). (2007, August 17). How not to get nailed. [Television series episode]. In J. Fowler (Producer), *Marketplace*. Toronto, ON: CBC TV.

Online magazine article

Murphy, L. (2007, June/July). Online marketing: Getting what you pay for? *CMA Management*. Retrieved from www.managementmag.com

Government publication

Office of Consumer Affairs. Industry Canada. (2009). *Canadian consumer handbook*. Ottawa, ON: Office of Consumer Affairs.

CD-ROM encyclopedia article, one author

Parkings, R. (1998). George Eastman. *The concise Columbia encyclopaedia* [CD-ROM]. New York, NY: Columbia University Press.

Journal article with volume and issue numbers

Porter, M. E., & Kramer, M. R. (2002, December). The competitive advantage of corporate philanthropy. *Harvard Business Review, 80*(12), 56–68.

Magazine article

Sequin, D. (2007, August 13). A Hollywood ending? *Canadian Business*, 11–12.

Annual report

Suncor. (2009). *2008 Annual report*. Calgary, AB: Author.

Newspaper article, no author

Toyota sets sights on sales record. (2007, September 1). *Globe and Mail Report on Business*, p. B10.

Newspaper article, one author

VanderKlippe, N. (2007, September 1). B.C. salmon industry in rough water. *Financial Post*, p. FP3.

Unpublished dissertation or thesis

Zhou, C. (2002). *Transnational flow of knowledge in multinational corporations: R&D co-practice as an integrating force*. Unpublished doctoral dissertation, University of Western Ontario, London, Ontario, Canada.

Interview

[cited in text only, not in the list of references]

MLA Style

The style recommended by the Modern Language Association of America is used widely in the humanities, especially in the study of language and literature. Like APA style, MLA style uses brief parenthetical citations in the text. However, instead of including author name and year, MLA citations include author name and page reference.

In-Text Citation—MLA Style

To document report sources in text using MLA style, insert the author's last name and a page reference inside parentheses following the cited material: (Porter and Kramer 63). If the author's name is mentioned in the text reference, the name can be omitted from the parenthetical citation: (63). The citation indicates that the reference came from page 63 of an article by Michael Porter and Mark Kramer. With the author's name, readers can find complete publication information in the alphabetically arranged list of works cited that comes at the end of the report.

Some experts recommend that corporations partner with charities and educational institutions to benefit society and raise their company profiles (Porter and Kramer 61).

Porter and Kramer (61) make a strong case for corporations partnering with charities and educational institutions to benefit society and raise their company profiles.

List of Works Cited—MLA Style

The *MLA Handbook for Writers of Research Papers* recommends preparing the list of works cited first, so you will know what information to give in the parenthetical citation (for example, whether to add a short title if you're citing more than one work by the same author, or whether to give an initial or first name if you're citing two authors who have the same last name). The list of works cited appears at the end of your report, contains all the works that you cite in your text, and lists them in alphabetical order. The major conventions for developing a reference list according to MLA style (see Figure B–4) are as follows:

> Format entries as hanging indents.
> Arrange entries in the following general order:

1. author name
2. title information
3. publication information
4. date
5. periodical page range
6. medium of publication

> List the lead author's name in reverse order (last name first), using either full first names or initials. List second and succeeding author names in normal order.
> Use quotation marks around the titles of articles from magazines, newspapers, and journals. Capitalize all important words.
> Italicize the names of books, newspapers, journals, reports, websites, broadcasts, films, plays, CDs, and other complete publications, capitalizing all main words in the title.
> For journal articles, include the volume number and the issue number (if necessary). Include the year of publication inside parentheses and follow with a colon and the page range of the article: *Harvard Business Review* 80.12 (2002): 56–68. (In this source, the volume is 80, the number is 12, and the pages are 56 to 68.)
> The medium of publication must be included for every entry (e.g., print, Web, television, personal interview, etc.).
> For electronic sources, the date of access must follow the medium of publication.
> Include a URL only when readers are unlikely to find your source without it. If you do give a URL, make sure it is as accurate and complete as possible (including access-mode identifier such as http, ftp, gopher, or telnet), enclose it in angle brackets, and insert it after the access date. Follow this with a period. Do not hyphenate the URL; break it after a slash, if necessary: <http://www.hoovers.com/intel-corp./—ID_1378/—/free-co-factsheet.xhtml>.

> Figure B–4 Sample Works Cited—MLA Style

WORKS CITED

Brochure

Apple Inc. *iPhone User Guide for iPhone OS 3.0 Software*. Cupertino, CA: Apple, Inc., 2009. Print.

Book, two authors

Argenti, Paul A., and Janis Forman. *The Power of Corporate Communication: Crafting the Voice and Image of Your Business*. New York: McGraw Hill, 2006. Print.

Article from an electronic database

Davis, Steven V., and Andrew Gilman. "Communication Coordination." *Risk Management* 49.8 (Aug. 2002): 38–43. *Proquest*, 148778291. Web. 27 Oct. 2008.

Book, component parts

Gluesing, Julia C., Tara C. Alcordo, and Margaret A. Neale. "The Development of Global Virtual Teams." *Virtual Teams that Work: Creating Conditions for Virtual Team Effectiveness*. Ed. Cristina B. Gibson and Susan G. Cohen. San Francisco: Jossey-Bass, 2003. 353–80. Print.

Interview

Hamilton, Ian. Personal interview. 15 Jan. 2002.

Internet, World Wide Web

Hoover's. "Intel Corporation: Company Report." *Hoover's*. Hoover's, 2009. 22 July 2009. Web. 15 Sept. 2009.

Paper presented at a meeting

Martin, Jeanette S., and Lillian H. Chaney. "Integrating Global Conversational Customs into Business Courses." Association for Business Communication 70th Annual Convention. Irvine, CA. 20–25 Oct. 2005. Paper.

Television broadcast

"How Not to Get Nailed." Narr. Mesley, Wendy. *Marketplace*. CBC TV, Toronto. 17 Aug. 2007. Television.

Online magazine article

Murphy, Liz. "Online Marketing: Getting What You Pay For?" *CMA Management* (June/July 2007): n. pag. Web. 18 Sept. 2007.

Government publication

Canada. Industry Canada. Office of Consumer Affairs. *Canadian Consumer Handbook*. Ottawa, ON: Office of Consumer Affairs, 2009. Print.

CD-ROM encyclopedia article, one author

Parkings, Robert. "George Eastman." *The Concise Columbia Encyclopedia*. New York: Columbia UP, 1998. CD-ROM.

Journal article with volume and issue numbers

Porter, Michael E., and Mark R, Kramer. "The Competitive Advantage of Corporate Philanthropy." *Harvard Business Review* 80.12 (2002): 56–68. Print.

Magazine article

Sequin, Denis. "A Hollywood Ending?" *Canadian Business* 13 Aug. 2007: 11–12. Print.

Annual report

Suncor. *2009 Annual Report*. Calgary, AB: Suncor, 2009. Print.

Newspaper article, no author

"Toyota Sets Sights on Sales Record." *Globe and Mail Report on Business* 1 Sept. 2007: B10. Print.

Newspaper article, one author

VanderKlippe, Nathan. "B.C. Salmon Industry in Rough Water." *Financial Post* 1 Sept. 2007: FP 3. Print.

Unpublished dissertation or thesis

Zhou, Changhui. "Transitional Flow of Knowledge in Multinational Corporations: R&D Co-Practice as an Integrating Force." Diss. U of Western Ontario, 2002. Print.

Endnotes

Chapter 1

1. Suncor website [accessed 25 Sept. 2008] www.suncor.ca; Suncor Energy, *Suncor 2007 Annual Report* [accessed 28 Sept. 2008] www.suncor.ca; Suncor Energy, *Suncor 2007 Report on Sustainability* [accessed 2 Aug. 2006] www.suncor.ca; Suncor Energy, *Stakeholder Relations Policy*, Suncor.com 2003 [accessed 4 Aug. 2006] www.suncor.com; Suncor Energy, *Harvesting the Wind: The Business of Wind Power* at Suncor Energy, Suncor.com 2004 [accessed 4 Aug. 2006] www.suncor.com; Sue Lee, "How Human Resources, Communications Help Drive Corporate Growth," *Canadian Speeches* 12.9 (Jan.–Feb. 1999): 65–71; Andrew Nikiforuk, "Saint or Sinner? Rick George Has Engineered a Dramatic Turnaround at Suncor, While Making Peace with the Greens," *Canadian Business* 13 May 2002: 54–56, 59+.

2. Ann Kerr, "Hard Lessons in Soft Skills: It's Not Enough to Be an IT Whiz Any More. Grads Are Being Told They Need Management and Communication Skills to Find a Job," *Globe and Mail* 21 Feb. 2003: C1; Julie Connelly, "Youthful Attitudes, Sobering Realities," *New York Times* 28 Oct. 2003: E1, E6; Nigel Andrews and Laura D'Andrea Tyson, "The Upwardly Global MBA," *Strategy 1 Business* 36: 6069; Jim McKay, "Communication Skills Found Lacking," *Pittsburgh Post-Gazette* 28 Feb. 2005 [accessed 28 Feb. 2005] www.delawareonline.com.

3. Richard L. Daft, *Management*, 6th ed. (Cincinnati: Thomson South-Western, 2003) 580.

4. Joan L. Milne, "Do You Hear What I Hear? Survey Finds Poor Communication Devours Nearly Eight Workweeks Per Year," *Canadian Manager* 24.1 (1999): 5.

5. Milne, "Do You Hear What I Hear?" 5.

6. Gareth R. Jones and Jennifer M. George, *Contemporary Management*, 3rd ed. (New York: McGraw-Hill Irwin, 2003) 512, 517.

7. Philip C. Kolin, *Successful Writing at Work*, 6th ed. (Boston: Houghton Mifflin, 2001) 17–23.

8. "Did You Hear It Through the Grapevine?" *Training and Development* 48.10 (1994): 20.

9. J. David Johnson, William A. Donohoe, Charles K. Atkin, and Sally Johnson, "Differences Between Formal and Informal Communication Channels," *Journal of Business Communication* 31.2 (1994): 111–122.

10. Lorenzo Sierra, "Tell It to the Grapevine," *Communication World* 19.4 (2002): 28.

11. Tim Laseter and Rob Cross, "The Craft of Connection," *Strategy + Business* Autumn 2006: 26–32.

12. Richard L. Daft, *Management*, 4th ed. (Fort Worth: Dryden, 1997) 107.

13. Lillian H. Chaney and Jeanette S. Martin, *Intercultural Business Communications* (Upper Saddle River, N.J.: Prentice Hall, 2000) 1–2.

14. "World at Home," *Maclean's* 3 Feb. 2003: 13.

15. "Canada's Multiculturalism Aids Trade Efforts, Pettigrew Says," *Canada Newswire* 25 May 2000 [accessed 8 Mar. 2003].

16. Suncor, *Suncor 2007 Annual Report*, 3; Nikiforuk, "Saint or Sinner?"

17. Jeff Davidson, "Fighting Information Overload," *Canadian Manager* Spring 2005: 161.

18. Sherry Sweetnam, "Email Tactics," *T&D* 60.1 (Jan. 2006): 13.

19. Chuck Williams, *Management*, 2nd ed. (Cincinnati: Thomson/SouthWestern, 2002) 690.

20. Don Hellriegel, Susan E. Jackson, and John W. Slocum, Jr., *Management: A Competency-Based Approach* (Cincinnati: Thomson/South-Western, 2002) 447.

21. Gillian Flynn, "Pillsbury's Recipe Is Candid Talk," *Workforce* Feb. 1998: 556–571.

22. Bruce W. Speck, "Writing Professional Codes of Ethics to Introduce Ethics in Business Writing," *Bulletin of the Association for Business Communication* 53.3 (1990): 21–26; H. W. Love, "Communication, Accountability and Professional Discourse: The Interaction of Language Values and Ethical Values," *Journal of Business Ethics* 11 (1992): 883–892; Kathryn C. Rentz and Mary Beth Debs, "Language and Corporate Values: Teaching Ethics in Business Writing Courses," *Journal of Business Communication* 24.3 (1987): 37–48.

23. Debbie Weil, *The Corporate Blogging Book* (New York: Portfolio, 2006) 60.

24. Hellriegel et al., *Management: A Competency-Based Approach*, 451.

25. Paul Martin Lester, *Visual Communication: Images with Messages* (Belmont, Calif.: Thomson South-Western, 2006) 6–8.

26. Michael R. Solomon, *Consumer Behavior: Buying, Having, and Being*, 6th ed. (Upper Saddle River, N.J.: Pearson Prentice Hall, 2004) 65.

27. Anne Field, "What You Say, What They Hear," *Harvard Management Communication Letter* Winter 2005: 3–5.

28. Charles G. Morris and Albert A. Maisto, *Psychology: An Introduction*, 12th ed. (Upper Saddle River, N.J.: Pearson Prentice Hall, 2005) 226–239; Saundra K. Ciccarelli and Glenn E. Meyer, *Psychology* (Upper Saddle River, N.J.: Prentice Hall, 2006) 210–229; Mark H. Ashcraft, *Cognition*, 4th ed. (Upper Saddle River, N.J.: Prentice Hall, 2006) 44–54.

29. John Owens, "Good Communication in Workplace Is Basic to Getting Any Job Done," *Knight Ridder Tribune Business News* 9 July 2003: 1.

30. Tamar Lewin, "Study Finds Widespread Neglect of Writing Skills," *Desert Sun* 26 Apr. 2003: A12.

31. Williams, *Management*, 706–707.

32. "Employers, Beware: 'Techno Addicts' May Be More Liability Than Boon," Lockergnome.com 18 Aug. 2006 [accessed 23 Aug. 2006] www.lockergnome.com.

33. Eric J. Sinrod, "Perspective: It's My Internet—I Can Do What I Want," News.com 29 Mar. 2006 [accessed 12 Aug. 2006] www.news.com.

34. "The Hidden Dangers of Instant Messaging," Newsfactor.com 5 July 2006 [accessed 12 Aug. 2006] www.newsfactor.com, Kenny Brian, "Privacy: Using Employee Emails as Grounds for Discipline," *Canadian Employment Law Today* 16 Jul 2008: 514.

35. Eric J. Sinrod, "Time to Crack Down on Tech at Work?" *News.com* 14 June 2006 [accessed 12 Aug. 2006] www.news.com; Brian, "Privacy: Using Employee Emails as Grounds for Discipline": 514.

36. Thomas A. Young, "Ethics in Business: Business of Ethics," *Vital Speeches* 15 Sept. 1992: 725–730.

37. "Undercover Marketing Uncovered," CBSnews.com 25 July 2004 [accessed 11 Apr. 2005] www.cbsnews.com; Stephanie Dunnewind, "Teen Recruits Create Word-of-Mouth 'Buzz' to Hook Peers on Products," *Seattle Times* 20 Nov. 2004 [accessed 11 Apr. 2005] www.seattletimes.com.

38. Kolin, *Successful Writing at Work*, 24–30.

39. Nancy K. Kubasek, Bartley A. Brennan, and M. Neil Browne, *The Legal Environment of Business*, 3rd ed. (Upper Saddle River, N.J.: Prentice Hall, 2003) 172.

40. Mary Beth Debs, "Recent Research on Collaborative Writing in Industry," *Technical Communication* Nov. 1991: 476–484.

41. Daft, *Management*, 155.

42. Bell Canada Enterprises, *Bell Canada Enterprises Code of Business Conduct* (Bell Canada: 2005) 6.

43. Based in part on Robert Kreitner, *Management*, 9th ed. (Boston: Houghton Mifflin, 2004) 163.

Chapter 2

1. Adapted from Royal Bank Financial Group website. *Royal Bank Annual Report 2007*; www.rbc.com/aboutus/20081002top100. html [accessed 19 Oct. 2008]; *Facts about Royal Bank*. No date. [accessed 22 Aug. 2006] www.royalbank.com; Royal Bank Financial Group website. Royal Bank, *2005 Community Report* [accessed 26 Aug. 2006] www.royalbank.com; Charles Coffey, "Investing in People: Work/Life Solutions." Speech delivered to the Robert Half International Breakfast Session, (Toronto, ON) 15 Jan. 2003 [accessed 22 Feb. 2003]; www.rbc.com/newsroom/news5-2002-2005.html#2003; Kristi Nelson, "Royal Bank of Canada Optimizes Work Force," *Bank Systems + Technology* 39.6 (2002): 42 [accessed 5 Nov. 2006]; Jay Sanford, "A Royal Return," *Canadian Business* 79.10 (Summer 2006), [accessed 27 Oct. 2006] Proquest Document ID: 105051531; www.eluta.ca, *Employer Review: RBC/Royal Bank of Canada,* www.eluta.ca/top-employer-rbc [accessed 19 Oct. 2008].

2. Courtland L. Bovée and John V. Thill, *Business in Action* (Upper Saddle River, N.J.: Pearson Prentice Hall, 2005) 175.

3. "Teamwork Translates into High Performance," *HR Focus* July 1998: 7.

4. Greg Crone, "Welcome to the Other Web: Loose Clusters, Not Rigid Contracts, Are the Future in Business," *Financial Post* 22 Jan. 1998: 11.

5. Glenn Parker, "Leading a Team of Strangers: Most Teams Now Are Diverse or Virtual," *T&D* 57.2 (2003): 21.

6. Sue Nador, "The Fine Art of Team Selection," *Canadian HR Reporter* 22 Oct. 2001: 15, 19.

7. Ellen Neuborne, "Companies Save, But Workers Pay," *USA Today* 25 Feb. 1997: B2; Richard L. Daft, *Management*, 4th ed. (Fort Worth: Dryden, 1997) 338; Richard Moderow, "Teamwork Is the Key to Cutting Costs," *Modern Healthcare* 29 Apr. 1996: 138.

8. Stephen R. Robbins, *Essentials of Organizational Behavior,* 6th ed. (Upper Saddle River, N.J.: Prentice Hall, 2000) 98.

9. Max Landsberg and Madeline Pfau, "Developing Diversity: Lessons from Top Teams," *Strategy + Business* Winter 2005: 10–12.

10. Groups Best at Complex Problems," *Industrial Engineer* June 2006: 14.

11. Lynda McDermott, Bill Waite, and Nolan Brawley, "Executive Teamwork," *Executive Excellence* May 1999: 15; "Five Case Studies on Successful Teams," *HR Focus* Apr. 2002: 18+.

12. Nicola A. Nelson, "Leading Teams," *Defense AT&L* July–Aug. 2006: 26–29; Larry Cole and Michael Cole, "Why Is the Teamwork Buzz Word Not Working?" *Communication World* Feb.–Mar. 1999: 29; Patricia Buhler, "Managing in the 90s: Creating Flexibility in Today's Workplace," *Supervision* Jan. 1997: 24+; Allison W. Amason, Allen C. Hochwarter, Wayne A. Thompson, and Kenneth R. Harrison, "Conflict: An Important Dimension in Successful Management Teams," *Organizational Dynamics* Autumn 1995: 20+.

13. Richard L. Daft, *Management*, 6th ed. (Cincinnati: Thomson South-Western, 2003) 614.

14. Geoffrey Colvin, "Why Dream Teams Fail," *Fortune* 12 June 2006: 87–92.

15. Vijay Govindarajan and Anil K. Gupta, "Building an Effective Global Business Team," *MIT Sloan Management Review* Summer 2001: 63+.

16. Louise Rehling, "Improving Teamwork Through Awareness of Conversational Styles," *Business Communication Quarterly* Dec. 2004: 475–482.

17. Jon Hanke, "Presenting as a Team," *Presentations* Jan. 1998: 74–82.

18. William P. Galle, Jr., Beverly H. Nelson, Donna W. Luse, and Maurice F. Villere, *Business Communication: A Technology-Based Approach* (Chicago: Irwin, 1996) 260.

19. Mary Beth Debs, "Recent Research on Collaborative Writing in Industry," *Technical Communication* Nov. 1991: 476–484.

20. "TWiki Success Stories," TWiki website [accessed 18 Aug. 2006] www.twiki.org.

21. Mark Choate, "What Makes an Enterprise Wiki?" CMS Watch website, 28 Apr. 2006 [accessed 18 Aug. 2006] www.cmswatch.com.

22. Choate, "What Makes an Enterprise Wiki?"

23. "Codex: Guidelines," WordPress website [accessed 18 Aug. 2006] www.wordpress.org; Michael Shanks, "Wiki Guidelines," Traumwerk website [accessed 18 Aug. 2006] http://metamedia.stanford.edu/projects/traumwerk/home; Joe Moxley, M. C. Morgan, Matt Barton, and Donna Hanak, "For Teachers New to Wikis," *Writing Wiki* [accessed 18 Aug. 2006] http://writingwiki.org; "Wiki Guidelines," *PsiWiki* [accessed 18 Aug. 2006] http://psi-im.org.

24. Tony Kontzer, "Learning to Share," *InformationWeek* 5 May 2003: 28; Jon Udell, "Uniting Under Groove," *InfoWorld* 17 Feb. 2003 [accessed 9 Sept. 2003] www.elibrary.com; Alison Overholt, "Virtually There?" *Fast Company* 14 Feb. 2002: 108.

25. Colvin, "Why Dream Teams Fail," 87–92.

26. Tiziana Casciaro and Miguel Sousa Lobo, "Competent Jerks, Lovable Fools, and the Formation of Social Networks," *Harvard Business Review* June 2005: 92–99.

27. Stephen P. Robbins and David A. DeCenzo, *Fundamentals of Management*, 4th ed. (Upper Saddle River, N.J.: Prentice Hall, 2004) 266–267; Jerald Greenberg and Robert A. Baron, *Behavior in Organizations*, 8th ed. (Upper Saddle River, N.J.: Prentice Hall, 2003) 279–280.

28. "Team Building: Managing the Norms of Informal Groups in the Workplace," Accel-Team.com [accessed 16 Aug. 2006] www.accelteam.com.

29. B. Aubrey Fisher, *Small Group Decision Making: Communication and the Group Process*, 2nd ed. (New York: McGraw-Hill, 1980) 145–149; Steven P. Robbins and David A. DeCenzo, *Fundamentals of Management,* 3rd. ed. (Upper Saddle River, NJ: Prentice Hall, 2001) 334–335; Daft, *Management*, 602–603.

30. Claire Sookman, "Building Your Virtual Team," *Network World* 21 June 2004: 91.

31. Lawrence Magid, "Groupthink Can Be Fatal," *Information Week* 14 Apr. 1997: 114.

32. Jared Sandberg, "Brainstorming Works Best If People Scramble for Ideas on Their Own," *Wall Street Journal* 13 June 2006: B1.

33. Mark K. Smith, "Bruce W. Tuckman—Forming, Storming, Norming, and Performing in Groups," Infed.org [accessed 5 July 2005] www.infed.org.

34. Robbins and DeCenzo, *Fundamentals of Management*, 258–259.

35. Daft, *Management*, 609–612.

36. Andy Boynton and Bill Fischer, *Virtuoso Teams: Lessons from Teams That Changed Their Worlds* (Harrow, England: FT Prentice Hall, 2005) 10.

37. Thomas K. Capozzoli, "Conflict Resolution—A Key Ingredient in Successful Teams," *Supervision* Nov. 1999: 14–16.

38. Janis Graham, "Sharpen Your Negotiating Skills," *Sylvia Porter's Personal Finance* Dec. 1985: 54–58.

39. Amason, Hochwarter, Thompson, and Harrison, "Conflict."

40. Jesse S. Nirenberg, *Getting Through to People* (Paramus, N.J.: Prentice Hall, 1973) 134–142.

41. Nirenberg, *Getting Through to People.*

42. Nirenberg, *Getting Through to People.*

43. "Better Meetings Benefit Everyone: How to Make Yours More Productive," *Working Communicator Bonus Report* July 1998: 1.

44. Ken Blanchard, "Meetings Can Be Effective," *Supervisory Management* Oct. 1992: 5.

45. "Better Meetings Benefit Everyone."

46. Nicole Ridgway, "A Safer Place to Meet," *Forbes* 28 Apr. 2003: 97.

47. IBM InnovationJam website [accessed 4 Jan. 2009] www.globalinnovationjam.com; "Big Blue Brainstorm," *BusinessWeek* 7 Aug. 2006 [accessed 15 Aug. 2006] www.businessweek.com.

48. Linda Zimmer, "Second Life: What Is It Good For?" Business Communicators of Second Life blog, 24 Jan. 2007 [accessed 7 Feb. 2007] http://freshtakes.typepad.com/sl_communicators; Robert D. Hof, "My Virtual Life," *BusinessWeek* 1 May 2006 [accessed 7 Feb. 2007] www.businessweek.com; David Needle, "Sun Finds a Home in Second Life," Internetnews.com, 11 Oct. 2006 [accessed 7 Feb. 2007] www.internetnews.com.

49. Robyn D. Clarke, "Do You Hear What I Hear?" *Black Enterprise* May 1998: 129; Dot Yandle, "Listening to Understand," *Pryor Report Management Newsletter Supplement* 15.8 (1998): 13.

50. Judi Brownell, *Listening*, 2nd ed. (Boston: Allyn & Bacon, 2002) 9, 10.

51. Augusta M. Simon, "Effective Listening: Barriers to Listening in a Diverse Business Environment," *Bulletin of the Association for Business Communication* 54.3 (Sept. 1991): 73–74.

52. Clarke, "Do You Hear What I Hear?"

53. Laura Fowlie, "Gauging Success by One's Attributes, Not Resume: More Companies Are Using the Competency Profile as a Benchmark in Assessing an Employee's Performance," *Financial Post* 17 Oct. 1998: R8.

54. Larry Barker and Kittie Watson, *Listen Up* (New York: St. Martin's, 2000) 24–27.

55. Dennis M. Kratz and Abby Robinson Kratz, *Effective Listening Skills* (New York: McGraw-Hill, 1995) 45–53; J. Michael Sproule, *Communication Today* (Glenview, Ill.: Scott, Foresman, 1981) 69.

56. Ronald B. Adler and George Rodman, *Understanding Human Communication*, 8th ed. (New York: Oxford University Press, 2003) 126–130.

57. Judi Brownell, *Listening*, 2nd ed. (Boston: Allyn and Bacon, 2002) 230–231.

58. Kratz and Kratz, *Effective Listening Skills*, 78–79; Sproule, *Communication Today.*

59. Bob Lamons, "Good Listeners Are Better Communicators," *Marketing News* 11 Sept. 1995: 131; Phillip Morgan and H. Kent Baker, "Building a Professional Image: Improving Listening Behavior," *Supervisory Management* Nov. 1985: 35–36.

60. Clarke, "Do You Hear What I Hear?"; Dot Yandle, "Listening to Understand," *Pryor Report Management Newsletter Supplement* 15.8 (Aug. 1998): 13.

61. Brownell, *Listening*,14; Kratz and Kratz, *Effective Listening Skills*, 8–9; Sherwyn P. Morreale and Courtland L. Bovée, *Excellence in Public Speaking* (Orlando, Fla.: Harcourt Brace, 1998) 72–76; Lyman K. Steil, Larry L. Barker, and Kittie W. Watson, *Effective Listening: Key to Your Success* (Reading, Mass.: Addison-Wesley, 1983) 21–22.

62. Patrick J. Collins, *Say It with Power and Confidence* (Upper Saddle River, N.J.: Prentice Hall, 1997) 40–45.

63. Morreale and Bovée, *Excellence in Public Speaking*, 296.

64. Judee K. Burgoon, David B. Butler, and W. Gill Woodall, *Nonverbal Communication: The Unspoken Dialog* (New York: McGraw-Hill, 1996) 137.

65. "Study: Human Lie Detectors Rarely Wrong," CNN.com 14 Oct. 2004 [accessed 14 Oct. 2004] www.cnn.com.

66. Dale G. Leathers, *Successful Nonverbal Communication: Principles and Applications* (New York: Macmillan, 1986) 19.

67. Gerald H. Graham, Jeanne Unrue, and Paul Jennings, "The Impact of Nonverbal Communication in Organizations: A Survey of Perceptions," *Journal of Business Communication* 28.1 (Winter 1991): 45–62.

68. Virginia P. Richmond and James C. McCroskey, *Nonverbal Behavior in Interpersonal Relations* (Boston: Allyn and Bacon, 2000) 153–157.

69. Richmond and McCroskey, *Nonverbal Behavior in Interpersonal Relations*, 2–3.

Chapter 3

1. Based on information from the Malkam Cross-Cultural Training website, www.malkam.com [accessed 4 July 2000, 31 Mar. 2003, 18 May 2003, and 6 Jan. 2009] www.malkam.com, www.malkam.com/en/CultureShock/Issue02.asp, www.malkam.com/en/CultureShock/Issue07.asp; Janet Baine, "Softening the Culture Shock: As Companies Begin Recruiting Abroad, the Need for Cultural Trainers Is on the Rise," *SVN Canada* 6.6 (2001): B25; "Sharpening One's Soft Skills," *Computing Canada* 24 Aug. 2001: 25; Laraine Kaminsky, "Changing Attitudes Towards Diversity Training: Fighting Resistance, Cynicism a Common Reality," *Canadian HR Reporter* 4 Dec. 2006: 21; Kristrin Harald, "Training Firm Capitalizing on NOT Being American," *Ottawa Business Journal* 24 Aug. 2005: 8–9.

2. Harald, "Training Firm Capitalizing on NOT Being American," 9.

3. Hed N. Seelye and Alan Seelye-James, *Culture Clash* (Chicago: NTC Business Books, 1995) xv, xviii.

4. "EDC Expands Its Operations in Brazil." Export Development Canada. [accessed 6 Jan 2009] http://www.edc.ca/english/mediaroom_10499.htm.

5. Peter MacArthur, "Japan: Land of Rising Opportunities for Canadian Companies," *CanadaExport* 26 May 2008 [accessed 6 Jan. 2009] http://www.international.gc.ca/canadexport/articles/386220.aspx?lang=eng.

6. "Tecsult Turns the Bid Around." *CanadaExport* news release, 3 Dec. 2008 [accessed 6 Jan. 2009] http://www.international.gc.ca/canadexport/ articles/81203b.aspx.

7. SolutionInc.Com [accessed 6 Jan. 2009].

8. Nancy R. Lockwood, "Workplace Diversity: Leveraging the Power of Difference for Competitive Advantage," *HR Magazine* June 2005: special section 1–10.

9. Gordon Nixon, "Canada's Diversity Imperative: 2010 and Beyond." Speech delivered to the Vancouver Board of Trade, 10 May 2006. Royal Bank of Canada website [accessed 28 Jan. 2007] http://www.rbc.com/newsroom/20060510nixon.html.

10. Renee Huang, "The Fine Art of Canadian Conversation: More Firms are Offering On-Site Language Classes for Immigrant Staff," *Globe and Mail* 17 Mar. 2003: C3.

11. Huang, "The Fine Art of Canadian Conversation"; Dalton Pharma Services: Benefits [accessed 7 Jan. 2009] www.dalton.com/benefits.htm.

12. Tracy Novinger, *Intercultural Communication, A Practical Guide* (Austin, TX: University of Texas Press, 2001) 15.

13. Linda Beamer and Iris Varner, *Intercultural Communication in the Workplace*, 2nd ed. (New York: McGraw-Hill Irwin, 2001) 3.

14. Randolph E. Schmid, "Asians, Americans See World Differently," *SF Gate* 22 Aug. 2005 [accessed 23 Aug. 2006] http://chineseculture.about.com.

15. Philip R. Harris and Robert T. Moran, *Managing Cultural Differences*, 3rd ed. (Houston: Gulf, 1991) 394–397, 429–430.

16. Lillian H. Chaney and Jeanette S. Martin, *Intercultural Business Communication* (Upper Saddle River, N.J.: Prentice Hall, 2000) 6.

17. Beamer and Varner, *Intercultural Communication in the Workplace*, 4.

18. Chaney and Martin, *Intercultural Business Communication*, 9.

19. Guo-Ming Chen and William J. Starosta, *Foundations of Intercultural Communication* (Boston: Allyn & Bacon, 1998) 39–40.

20. Richard L. Daft, *Management*, 6th ed. (Cincinnati: Thomson South-Western, 2003) 455.

21. Project Implicit website [accessed 12 July 2005] https://implicit.harvard.edu/implicit.

22. Larry A. Samovar and Richard E. Porter, eds., "Basic Principles of Intercultural Communication," in *Intercultural Communication: A Reader*, 6th ed. (Belmont, Calif.: Wadsworth, 1991) 12.

23. Linda Beamer, "Teaching English Business Writing to Chinese-Speaking Business Students," *Bulletin of the Association for Business Communication* 57.1 (1994): 12–18.

24. Edward T. Hall, "Context and Meaning," in *Intercultural Communication*, ed. Samovar and Porter: 46–55.

25. Richard L. Daft, *Management*, 4th ed. (Fort Worth: Dryden, 1997) 459.

26. Beamer, "Teaching English Business Writing to Chinese-Speaking Business Students."

27. Charley H. Dodd, *Dynamics of Intercultural Communication*, 3rd ed. (Dubuque, Iowa: Brown, 1991) 69–70.

28. Daft, *Management*, 459.

29. Beamer and Varner, *Intercultural Communication in the Workplace*, 230–233.

30. James Wilfong and Toni Seger, *Taking Your Business Global* (Franklin Lakes, N.J.: Career Press, 1997) 277–278.

31. Harris and Moran, *Managing Cultural Differences*, 260.

32. Skip Kaltenheuser, "Bribery Is Being Outlawed Virtually Worldwide," *Business Ethics* May–June 1998: 11; Thomas Omestad, "Bye-Bye to Bribes," *U.S. News & World Report* 22 Dec. 1997: 39, 42–44.

33. Claudia Cattaneo, "An Exporter of Ethics," *Financial Post (National Post)* 13 Feb. 1999: D1, D6; Neville Nankivell, "New Legislation Forces Companies to Take Foreign Bribery Seriously: But Enforcing Anti-Corruption Law Will Be Tricky," *Financial Post (National Post)* 11 Feb. 1999: C7.

34. Guo-Ming Chen and William J. Starosta, *Foundations of Intercultural Communication* (Boston: Allyn & Bacon, 1998) 288–289.

35. Robert O. Joy, "Cultural and Procedural Differences That Influence Business Strategies and Operations in the People's Republic of China," *SAM Advanced Management Journal* (1989): 29–33.

36. "Home Away from Home," *Ottawa HR* July 2000: 18, May 2003 [accessed 31 May 2003] www.malkam.com.

37. Laraine Kaminsky, "Preparing for Life, and Business, in China," *Canadian HR Reporter 26* Sept. 2005: 8–9.

38. Chaney and Martin, *Intercultural Business Communication*, 2nd ed., 122–123.

39. Novinger, *Intercultural Communication: A Practical Guide*, 54.

40. Beamer and Varner, *Intercultural Communication in the Workplace*, 107–108.

41. Beamer and Varner, *Intercultural Communication in the Workplace*, 107–108.

42. Michael Kinsman, "Respect Helps Mix of Generations Work Well Together," *San Diego Union-Tribune* 19 Sept. 2004: H2.

43. Tonya Vinas, "A Place at the Table," *Industry Week* 1 July 2003: 22.

44. John Gray, *Mars and Venus in the Workplace* (New York: Harper Collins, 2002) 10, 25–27, 61–63.

45. P. Christopher Earley and Elaine Mosakowsi, "Cultural Intelligence," *Harvard Business Review* Oct. 2004: 139–146.

46. Wendy A. Conklin, "An Inside Look at Two Diversity Intranet Sites: IBM and Merck," *The Diversity Factor* Summer 2005.

47. Craig S. Smith, "Beware of Green Hats in China and Other Cross-Cultural Faux Pas," *New York Times* 30 Apr. 2002: C11.

48. Francesca Bargiela-Chiappini, Anne Marie Bülow-Møller, Catherine Nickerson, Gina Poncini, and Yunxia Zhu, "Five Perspectives on Intercultural Business Communication," *Business Communication Quarterly* Sept. 2003: 73–96.

49. Paul Johnson, "Must the Whole World Speak English?" *Forbes* 29 Nov. 2004: 39; Randolph E. Schmid, "Study Says English Language Is Losing Cultural Dominance," *Desert Sun* 29 Feb. 2004: A25.

50. Bob Nelson, "Motivating Workers Worldwide," *Global Workforce* Nov. 1998: 25–27.

51. Mona Casady and Lynn Wasson, "Written Communication Skills of International Business Persons," *Bulletin of the Association for Business Communication* 57.4 (1994): 36–40.

52. Chaney and Martin, *Intercultural Business Communication*, 130.

53. "From Plain English to Global English," Quickit Limited website [accessed 24 Aug. 2006] www.webpagecontent.com.

54. Myron W. Lustig and Jolene Koester, *Intercultural Competence*, 4th ed. (Boston: Allyn & Bacon, 2003) 196.

55. Daren Fonda, "Selling in Tongues," *Time* 26 Nov. 2001: B121.

56. Mark Lasswell, "Lost in Translation," *Business 2.0* Aug. 2004: 68–70.

57. Sheridan Prasso, ed., "It's All Greek to These Sites," *Business Week* 22 July 2002: 18.

Chapter 4

1. The Forzani Group, *Annual Report 2008*, The Forzani Group [accessed 15 Jan. 2009] www.forzani.com; Ian Portsmouth, "Get in the Game," *Profit Magazine* Apr. 2002: 27–28; Norman Ramage, "Forzani Covers the Field," *Marketing* 9 Sept. 2002: 14–15; Rhea Seymour, "Touchdown! John Forzani of Forzani Group Ltd," *Profit Magazine* Nov. 2001: 12; "The Forzani Group Unveils New Store Concept," *Marketwire* (newswire) Toronto 16 Dec. 2008; "Ask the Legends," *Profit Magazine* Jun 2007:112–113.

2. Sanford Kaye, "Writing Under Pressure," *Soundview Executive Book Summaries* 10.12, part 2 (Dec. 1988): 1–8.

3. Peter Bracher, "Process, Pedagogy, and Business Writing," *Journal of Business Communication* 24.1 (Winter 1987): 43–50.

4. Laurey Berk and Phillip G. Clampitt, "Finding the Right Path in the Communication Maze," *IABC Communication World* Oct. 1991: 28–32.

5. Linda Duyle, "Get Out of Your Office," *HR Magazine* July 2006: 99–101.

6. Skype website [accessed 25 Jan. 2009] www.skype.com.

7. Kris Maher, "The Jungle," *Wall Street Journal* 5 Oct. 2004: B10.

8. Kevin Maney, "Surge in Text Messaging Makes Cell Operators :-)," *USA Today* 28 July 2005: B1–B2.

9. David Kirkpatrick, "It's Hard to Manage If You Don't Blog," *Fortune* 4 Oct. 2004: 46; Lee Gomes, "How the Next Big Thing in Technology Morphed into a Really Big Thing," *Wall Street Journal* 4 Oct. 2004: B1; Jeff Meisner, "Cutting Through the Blah, Blah, Blah," *Puget Sound Business Journal* 19–25 Nov. 2004: 27–28; Lauren Gard, "The Business of Blogging," *BusinessWeek* 13 Dec. 2004: 117–119; Heather Green, "Online Video: The Sequel," *BusinessWeek* 10 Jan. 2005: 40; Michelle Conlin and Andrew Park, "Blogging with the Boss's Blessing," *BusinessWeek* 28 June 2004: 100–102.

10. Berk and Clampitt, "Finding the Right Path in the Communication Maze."

11. Berk and Clampitt, "Finding the Right Path in the Communication Maze."

12. Berk and Clampitt, "Finding the Right Path in the Communication Maze."

13. Raymond M. Olderman, *10 Minute Guide to Business Communication* (New York: Alpha Books, 1997) 19–20.

14. Mohan R. Limaye and David A. Victor, "Cross-Cultural Business Communication Research: State of the Art and Hypotheses for the 1990s," *Journal of Business Communication* 28.3 (Summer 1991): 277–299.

15. Holly Weeks, "The Best Memo You'll Ever Write," *Harvard Management Communication Letter* Spring 2005: 3–5.

Chapter 5

1. Creative Commons website [accessed 2 Feb. 2009] www.creativecommons.org; Ariana Eunjung Cha, "Creative Commons Is Rewriting Rules of Copyright," *Washington Post* 15 Mar. 2005 [accessed 3 Aug. 2005] www.washingtonpost.com; Steven Levy, "Lawrence Lessig's Supreme Showdown," *Wired* Oct. 2002

[accessed 3 Aug. 2005] www.wired.com; "Happy Birthday: We'll Sue," Snopes.com [accessed 3 Aug. 2005] www.snopes.com.

2. Elizabeth Blackburn and Kelly Belanger, "You-Attitude and Positive Emphasis: Testing Received Wisdom in Business Communication," *Bulletin of the Association for Business Communication* 56.2 (June 1993): 1–9.

3. Annette N. Shelby and N. Lamar Reinsch, Jr., "Positive Emphasis and You Attitude: An Empirical Study," *Journal of Business Communication* 32.4 (1995): 303–322.

4. Sherryl Kleinman, "Why Sexist Language Matters," *Qualitative Sociology* 25.2 (Summer 2002): 299–304.

5. Judy E. Pickens, "Terms of Equality: A Guide to Bias-Free Language," *Personnel Journal* Aug. 1985: 24.

6. Lisa Taylor, "Communicating About People with Disabilities: Does the Language We Use Make a Difference?" *Bulletin of the Association for Business Communication* 53.3 (Sept. 1990): 65–67.

7. Susan Benjamin, *Words at Work* (Reading, Mass.: Addison-Wesley, 1997) 136–137.

8. Mary A. DeVries, *Internationally Yours* (Boston: Houghton Mifflin, 1994) 61.

9. Stuart Crainer and Des Dearlove, "Making Yourself Understood," *Across the Board* May–June 2004: 23–27.

10. Plain English Campaign website [accessed 5 Feb. 2009] www.plainenglish.co.uk.

11. Creative Commons website [accessed 5 Feb. 2009] www.creativecommons.org.

12. Joseph Kimble, "Answering the Critics of Plain Language," The Plain Language Network website, 12 Apr. 2003 [accessed 22 Sept. 2006] www.plainlanguagenetwork.org.

13. Anon., "In Plain View," *Saturday Night* Sept. 1999: 11.

14. "Investor Education Fund Web-Site Offers Investors Valuable Information, Tools and Resources," *Canada NewsWire* (2007): 1.

15. Peter Crow, "Plain English: What Counts Besides Readability?" *Journal of Business Communication* 25. 1 (Winter 1988): 87–95.

16. Susan Jaderstrom and Joanne Miller, "Active Writing," *Office Pro* Nov./Dec. 2003: 29.

17. Portions of this section are adapted from Courtland L. Bovée, *Techniques of Writing Business Letters, Memos, and Reports* (Sherman Oaks, Calif.: Banner Books International, 1978) 13–90.

18. Janice Obuchowski, "Communicate to Inform, Not Impress," *Harvard Management Communication Letter* Winter 2006: 3–4; Robert Hartwell Fiske, *The Dimwit's Dictionary* (Oak Park, Ill.: Marion Street Press, 2002) 1620.

19. Beverly Ballaro and Christina Bielaszka-DuVernay, "Building a Bridge over the River Boredom," *Harvard Management Communication Letter* Winter 2005: 3–5.

20. David A. Fryxell, "Lost in Transition?" *Writers Digest* Jan. 2005: 24–26.

21. Adapted from Creative Commons website [accessed 18 Feb. 2007] www.creativecommons.org.

22. Food Allergy Initiative website [accessed 23 Sept. 2006] www.foodallergyinitiative.org; Diana Keough, "Snacks That Can Kill; Schools Take Steps to Protect Kids Who Have Severe Allergies to Nuts," *Plain Dealer* 15 July 2003: E1; "Dawdling Over Food Labels," *New York Times* 2 June 2003: A16; Sheila McNulty, "A Matter of Life and Death," *Financial Times* 10 Sept. 2003: 14; "Food Allergies and Intolerances," Health Canada website [accessed 8 Feb 2009] http://www.hc-sc.gc.ca/fn-an/securit/allerg/index-eng.php.

23. Apple iTunes website [accessed 23 Sept. 2006] www.apple.com/itunes.

Chapter 6

1. Free the Children website [accessed 14 Feb. 2009] www.freethechildren.com; *Free the Children 2007 Annual Report*; Free the Children Media Kit (www.freethechildren.com/mediaroom/mediakits.php) [accessed 14 Feb. 2009].

2. William Zinsser, *On Writing Well*, 5th ed. (New York: Harper-Collins, 1994) 9.

3. Zinsser, *On Writing Well*, 7, 17.

4. Mary A. DeVries, *Internationally Yours* (Boston: Houghton Mifflin, 1994) 160.

5. Zinsser, *On Writing Well*, 126.

6. Deborah Gunn, "Looking Good on Paper," *Office Pro* Mar. 2004: 10–11.

7. Jennifer Saranow, "Memo to Web Sites: Grow Up!" *Wall Street Journal* 15 Nov. 2004: R14–R15.

8. Jacci Howard Bear, "Desktop Publishing Rules of Page Layout," About.com [accessed 22 Aug. 2005] www.about.com.

9. Jacci Howard Bear, "Desktop Publishing Rules for How Many Fonts to Use," About.com [accessed 22 Aug. 2005] www.about.com.

10. The writing sample in this exercise was adapted from material on the Marsh Risk Consulting website [accessed 2 Oct. 2006] www.marshriskconsulting.com.

Chapter 7

1. Adapted from Pump Talk website [accessed 2 Sept. 2008].

2. Dave Carpenter, "Companies Discover Marketing Power of Text Messaging," *Seattle Times* 25 Sept. 2006 [accessed 25 Sept. 2006] www.seattletimes.com.

3. "A Definition of Social Media," Technology in Translation blog, 6 Apr. 2007 [accessed 11 June 2007] http://technologyintranslation.blockwork.org; Robert Scoble, "What Is Social Media?" Scobleizer blog, 16 Feb. 2007 [accessed 11 June 2007] www.scobleizer.com; Paul Gillin, *The New Influencers* (Sanger, Calif.: Quill Driver Books, 2007) xi–xii.

4. Joanna Pachner, "Archiving Old E-mail and Compliance and Legal Issue," *Globe and Mail* 12 Apr. 2007: B8; Hilary Potkewitz and Rachel Brown, "Spread of E-mail Has Altered Communication Habits at Work," *Los Angeles Business Journal* 18 Apr. 2005 [accessed 30 Apr. 2006] www.findarticles.com; Nancy Flynn, *Instant Messaging Rules* (New York: AMACOM, 2004) 47–54.

5. Sandra Gittlen, "Big Boss Is Reading Your E-mail," *Network World Canada* 16.25 (2006): n.p. [accessed 7 Sept. 2008] Proquest Database, Ryerson University Library; "Employee Communication Is Cause for Concern," Duane Morris LLP website, 23 Aug. 2006 [accessed 4 Oct. 2006] www.duanemorris.com.

6. Daryl-Lynn Carlson, "Spying Bosses Must Forewarn Employees," *National Post Financial Post* 23 June 2008: FP13; Greg Burns, "For Some, Benefits of E-mail Not Worth Risk," *San Diego Union-Tribune* 16 Aug. 2005: A1, A8; Pui-Wing Tam, Erin White, Nick Wingfield, and Kris Maher, "Snooping E-mail by Software Is Now a Workplace Norm," *Wall Street Journal* 9 Mar. 2005, B1+.

7. Lizette Alvarez, "Got 2 Extra Hours for Your E-mail?" *New York Times* 10 Nov. 2005 [accessed 10 Nov. 2005] www.nytimes.com.

8. Pachner, "Archiving Old E-mail and Compliance and Legal Issue," B8.

9. Matt Cain, "Managing E-mail Hygiene," *ZD Net Tech Update* 5 Feb. 2004 [accessed 19 Mar. 2004] www.techupdate.zdnet.com.

10. Reid Goldsborough, "'Creeping Informality' Can Be Big Mistake in Business E-mails," *New Orleans City Business* 14 Mar. 2005: 18; Jack E. Appleman, "Bad Writing Can Cost Insurers Time & Money," *National Underwriter* 27 Sept. 2004: 34; Adina Genn, "RE: This Is an Important Message, Really," *Long Island Business News* 5–11 Dec. 2003: 21A; Lynn Lofton, "Regardless of What You Thought, Grammar Rules Do Apply to E-mail," *Mississippi Business Journal* 23–29 May 2005:1.

11. Phillip Vassallo, "Egad! Another E-mail: Using E-mail Sensibly" (book review), *ETC: A Review of General Semantics* 59.4 (2002): 448–453.

12. Vassallo, "Egad! Another E-mail: Using E-mail Sensibly," 448–453.

13. Mary Munter, Priscilla S. Rogers, and Jone Rymer, "Business E-mail: Guidelines for Users," *Business Communication Quarterly* Mar. 2003: 26+; Renee B. Horowitz and Marian G. Barchilon, "Stylistic Guidelines for E-mail," *IEEE Transactions on Professional Communication* 37.4 (Dec. 1994): 207–212.

14. Jack Powers, Electric Pages, "Writing for the Web, Part I" [accessed 28 June 2000] www.electric-pages.com/articles/wftwl.htm.

15. "E-mail Is So Five Minutes Ago," *BusinessWeek Online* 28 Nov. 2005 [accessed 3 May 2006] www.businessweek.com.

16. Robert J. Holland, "Connected—More or Less," Richmond.com, 8 Aug. 2006 [accessed 5 Oct. 2006] www.richmond.com.

17. Vayusphere website [accessed 22 Jan. 2006] www.vayusphere.com; Christa C. Ayer, "Presence Awareness: Instant Messaging's Killer App," *Mobile Business Advisor* 1 July 2004 [accessed 22 Jan. 2006] www.highbeam.com; Jefferson Graham, "Instant Messaging Programs Are No Longer Just for Messages," *USA Today* 20 Oct. 2003: 5D; Todd R. Weiss, "Microsoft Targets Corporate Instant Messaging Customers," *Computerworld* 18 Nov. 2002: 12; "Banks Adopt Instant Messaging to Create a Global Business Network," *Computer Weekly* 25 Apr. 2002: 40; Michael D. Osterman, "Instant Messaging in the Enterprise," *Business Communications Review* Jan. 2003: 59–62; John Pallato, "Instant Messaging Unites Work Groups and Inspires Collaboration," *Internet* World Dec. 2002: 14+.

18. Paul Kedrosky, "Why We Don't Get the (Text) Message," *Business 2.02* Oct. 2006 [accessed 4 Oct. 2006] www.business2.com; Carpenter, "Companies Discover Marketing Power of Text Messaging."

19. Mark Gibbs, "Racing to Instant Messaging," *NetworkWorld* 17 Feb. 2003: 74.

20. "E-mail Is So Five Minutes Ago."

21. Elizabeth Millard, "Instant Messaging Threats Still Rising," *Newsfactor.com* 6 July 2005 [accessed 5 Oct. 2006] www.newsfactor.com.

22. Walaika K. Haskins, "New Virus Spreads by Chatting with You," *Newsfactor.com* 9 Dec. 2005 [accessed 5 Oct. 2006] www.newsfactor.com.

23. Clint Boulton, "IDC: IM Use Is Booming in Business," *InstantMessagingPlanet.com* 5 Oct. 2005 [accessed 22 Jan. 2006] www.instantmessagingplanet.com; Jenny Goodbody, "Critical Success Factors for Global Virtual Teams," *Strategic Communication Management* Feb./Mar. 2005: 18–21; Ann Majchrzak, Arvind Malhotra, Jeffrey Stamps, and Jessica Lipnack, "Can Absence Make a Team Grow Stronger?" *Harvard Business Review* May 2004:131–137; Christine Y. Chen, "The IM Invasion," *Fortune* 26 May 2003: 135–138; Yudhijit Bhattacharjee, "A Swarm of Little Notes," *Time* Sept. 2002: A3–A8; Mark Bruno, "Taming the Wild Frontiers of Instant Messaging," *Bank Technology News* Dec. 2002: 30–31; Richard Grigonis, "Enterprise-Strength Instant Messaging," Convergence.com, 10–15 [accessed Mar. 2003] www.convergence.com.

24. Pallato, "Instant Messaging Unites Work Groups and Inspires Collaboration," 14+.

25. Anita Hamilton, "You've Got Spim!" *Time* 2 Feb. 2004 [accessed 1 Mar. 2004] www.time.com.

26. Robert Scoble and Shel Israel, *Naked Conversations* (Hoboken, N.J.: Wiley, 2006) 15–18.

27. GM FastLane blog [accessed 4 May 2006] http://fastlane.gmblogs.com.

28. Fredrik Wackå, "Six Types of Blogs—A Classification," Corporate-Blogging.Info website, 10 Aug. 10 2004 [accessed 5 Oct. 2006] www.corporateblogging.info; Stephen Baker, "The Inside Story on Company Blogs," *BusinessWeek* 14 Feb. 2006 [accessed 15 Feb. 2006] www.businessweek.com; Jeremy Wright, *Blog Marketing* (New York: McGraw-Hill, 2006) 45–56; Paul Chaney, "Blogs: Beyond the Hype!" 26 May 2005 [accessed 4 May 2006] http://radiantmarketinggroup.com.

29. Evolve24 website [accessed 5 Oct. 2006] www.evolve24.com.

30. Stephen Baker and Heather Green, "Blogs Will Change Your Business," *BusinessWeek* 2 May 2005: 57–67.

31. Julie Moran Alterio, "Podcasts a Hit Inside and Outside IBM," *The Journal News* (White Plains, N.Y.) 9 Jan. 2006 [accessed 5 May 2006] www.thejournalnews.com.

32. "Turn Your Feed into a Podcast," Lifehacker blog, 12 Jan. 2006 [accessed 6 May 2006] www.lifehacker.com.

33. "Set Up Your Podcast for Success," FeedForAll website [accessed 4 Oct. 2006] www.feedforall.com.

34. Shel Holtz, "Ten Guidelines for B2B Podcasts," *Webpronews.com* 12 Oct. 2005 [accessed 9 Mar. 2006] www.webpronews.com.

35. Todd Cochrane, Podcasting: The Do-It-Yourself Guide (Indianapolis, Ind.: Wiley, 2005),107–109.

36. Michael W. Goeghegan and Dan Klass, *Podcast Solutions: The Complete Guide to Podcasting* (Berkeley, Calif.: Friends of Ed, 2005) 57–86; Cochrane, *Podcasting:* The Do-It-Yourself Guide,87–136.

37. "Syndication Format," Answers.com [accessed 5 Oct. 2006] www.answers.com.

38. FeedBurner website [accessed 5 Oct. 2006] www.feedburner.com.

39. Adapted from Comic-Con website [accessed 16 Jan. 2007] www.comic-con.org; Tom Spurgeon, "Welcome to Nerd Vegas: A Guide to Visiting and Enjoying Comic-Con International in San Diego, 2006!" *The Comics Reporter* 11 July 2006 [accessed 16 Jan. 2007] www.comicsreporter.com; Rebecca Winters Keegan, "Boys Who Like Toys," *Time* 19 Apr. 2007 [accessed 15 May 2007] www.time.com.

40. Adapted from Tom Lowry, "ESPN.COM: Guys and Dollars," *BusinessWeek* 17 Oct. 2005 [accessed 16 Jan. 2007] www.businessweek.com.

41. Adapted from Michael Mandel, "What's Really Propping Up the Economy," *BusinessWeek* 25 Sept. 2006 [accessed 16 Jan. 2007] www.businessweek.com.

42. Adapted from Sharon Terlep, "UAW: Expect Sacrifice," *Detroit News* 16 Jan. 2007 [accessed 17 Jan. 2007] www.detnews.com; Ford Motor Company website [accessed 17 Jan. 2007] www.ford.com.

43. Adapted from Crutchfield website [accessed 17 Jan. 2007] www.crutchfield.com.

44. Adapted from Logan website [accessed 16 Jan. 2007] www.loganmagazine.com.

45. Adapted from job description for Global Marketing Manager–Apparel, New Balance website [accessed 24 Aug. 2005] www.newbalance.com.

46. Adapted from "How Microsoft Reviews Suppliers," *Fast Company* 17 [accessed 3 Sept. 2003] http://fastcompany.com.

47. Adapted from Davide Dukcevich, "Instant Business: Retailer Lands' End Profits from Online Chat," Forbes.com, Special to ABCNEWS.com, 29 July 2002 [accessed 21 July 2003] http://abcnews.go.com; Lands' End website [accessed 5 Dec. 2003] www.landsend.com; Forbes.com staff, "Instant Messaging at Work," Forbes.com, 26 July 2002 [accessed 21 July 2003] www.forbes.com; Tischelle George and Sandra Swanson with Christopher T. Heun, "Not Just Kid Stuff," *InformationWeek* 3 Sept. 2001 [accessed 21 July 2003] www.informationweek.com.

48. Adapted from Liz Moyer, "California Dreaming," *Forbes* 8 May 2006 [accessed 8 May 2006] www.forbes.com; "Wachovia to Acquire Golden West Financial, Nation's Most Admired and 2nd Largest Savings Institution," 7 May 2006, Wachovia website [accessed 8 May 2006] www.wachovia.com.

Chapter 8

1. Based on Indigo Books and Music website. Investor Relations: Article [accessed 23 Feb. 2009] www.chapters.indigo.ca.; John Lorinc, "The Indigo Way: Stylish and Savvy, Canada's #2 Chain Marches to Its Own Beat," *Quill & Quire* 66.2 (2000): 22–23; Katherine Macklem, "The Book Lady," *Maclean's* 26 Feb. 2001:

40–45; Hollie Braun, "Indigo Pens Next Chapter," *National Post* 22 June 2007: FP3; Holly Braun, "Winning on the Web," *National Post* 26 June 2007: FP3; Thomas Watson, "Live and Learn: Heather Reisman," *Canadian Business* 29 Sept. 2008: 114.

2. Adapted from Brian Smeek, "Bad References Can Be Bad News for Employers," *Canadian Employment Law Today* 5 Dec. 2007: 5–6; "No Obligation to Provide Glowing Reference Letter," *Canadian Employment Law Today* 28 Sept. 2005: 3493; Diane Cadrain, "HR Professionals Stymied by Vanishing Job References," *HR Magazine* Nov. 2004: 31–40; "*Five (or More) Ways You Can Be Sued for Writing (or Not Writing) Recommendation Letters," Fair Employment Practice Guidelines* July 2006: 1, 3–4; Rochelle Kaplan, "Writing a Recommendation Letter," National Association of Colleges and Employers website [accessed 12 Oct. 2006] www.naceweb.org; Maura Dolan and Stuart Silverstein, "Court Broadens Liability for Job References," *Los Angeles Times* 28 Jan. 1997: A1, A11; David A. Price, "Good References Pave Road to Court," *USA Today* 13 Feb. 1997: 11A; Frances A. McMorris, "Ex-Bosses Face Less Peril Giving Honest Job References," *Wall Street Journal* 8 July 1996: B1, B8; Dawn Gunsch, "Gray Matters: Centralize Control of Giving References," *Personnel Journal* Sept. 1992: 114, 116–117; Betty Southard Murphy, Wayne E. Barlow, and D. Diane Hatch, "Manager's Newsfront: Job Reference Liability of Employees," *Personnel Journal* Sept. 1991: 22, 26; Ross H. Fishman, "When Silence Is Golden," *Nation's Business* July 1991: 48–49.

3. "Review Offer Letters Carefully to Avoid Binding Promises," *Fair Employment Practices Guidelines* 15 May 2001: 5–6.

4. Fraser P. Seitel, *The Practice of Public Relations*, 9th ed. (Upper Saddle River, N.J.: Pearson Prentice-Hall, 2004) 402–411; *Techniques for Communicators* (Chicago: Lawrence Ragan Communication, 1995) 34, 36.

5. David Meerman Scott, *The New Rules of Marketing and PR* (Hoboken, N.J.: Wiley, 2007) 62.

6. Mary Mitchell, "The Circle of Life—Condolence Letters," LiveandLearn.com [accessed 18 July 2005] www.liveandlearn.com; Donna Larcen, "Authors Share the Words of Condolence," *Los Angeles Times* 20 Dec. 1991: E11.

7. Adapted from Floorgraphics website [accessed 18 June 2001] www.floorgraphics.com; John Grossman, "It's an Ad, Ad, Ad, Ad World," *Inc.* Mar. 2000: 23–26; David Wellman, "Floor 'Toons," *Supermarket Business* 15 Nov. 1999: 47; "Floorshow," *Dallas Morning News* 4 Sept. 1998: 11D.

8. Adapted from Tom Abate, "Need to Preserve Cash Generates Wave of Layoffs in Biotech Industry," *San Francisco Chronicle* 10 Feb. 2003 [accessed 18 July 2005] www.sfgate.com.

9. Adapted from CES website [accessed 18 July 2005] www.cesweb.org.

10. Adapted from Lisa DiCarlo, "IBM Gets the Message—Instantly," Forbes.com, 7 July 2002 [accessed 22 July 2003] www.forbes.com; "IBM Introduces Breakthrough Messaging Technology for Customers and Business Partners," *M2 Presswire* 19 Feb. 2003 [accessed 24 July 2003] www.proquest.com; "IBM and America Online Team for Instant Messaging Pilot," *M2 Presswire* 4 Feb. 2003 [accessed 24 July 2003] www.proquest.com.

11. Adapted from Jane Costello, "Check Your Insurance Before Renting an SUV," *Wall Street Journal* 13 June 2001 [accessed 14 June 2001] http://interactive.wsj.com/articles/SB991402678854239871.htm.

12. Adapted from Burt Helm, "Wal-Mart, Please Don't Leave Me," *BusinessWeek* 9 Oct. 2006: 84–89.

13. Adapted from Davide Dukcevich, "Instant Business: Retailer Lands' End Profits from Online Chat," Forbes.com (Special to ABCNEWS.com), 29 July 2002 [accessed 21 July 2003] http://abcnews.go.com/sections/business/DailyNews/forbes_landsend.com; Lands' End website [accessed 5 Dec. 2003] www.landsend.com; Forbes.com staff, "Instant Messaging at Work," Forbes.com,

26 July 2002 [accessed 21 July 2003] www.forbes.com/2002/07/23/0723im/html; Tischelle George and Sandra Swanson with Christopher T. Heun, "Not Just Kid Stuff," *InformationWeek* 3 Sept. 2001 [accessed 21 July 2003] www.informationweek.com/story/IWK20010830S0030.

14. Public Relations Society of America website [accessed 18 June 2005] www.prsa.org.

15. Based on ABC Canada Literacy Foundation website [accessed 18 Dec. 2000].

16. Sal D. Rinalla and Robert J. Kopecky, "Recruitment: Burger King Hooks Employees with Educational Incentives," *Personnel Journal* Oct. 1989: 90–99.

Chapter 9

1. Based on Maple Leaf Foods Action website [accessed 9 Mar. 2009] www.mapleleafaction.com; "Health Hazard Alert Sure Slice Brand Roast Beef and Corned Beef May Contain Listeria Monocytogenes," Maple Leaf Foods news release, 17 Aug. 2008 [accessed 9 Mar. 2009] www.mapleleaf.com; "Maple Leaf Broadens Product Recall from Toronto Plant as a Precautionary Measure," Maple Leaf Foods news release, 20 Aug. 2008 [accessed 9 Mar. 2009] www.mapleleaf.com; "Maple Leaf CEO Michael H. McCain Responds to Determination of Link to Plant," Maple Leaf Foods news release, 23 Aug. 2008 [accessed 9 Mar. 2009] www.mapleleaf.com; Kristine Owram, "Maple Leaf Foods CEO Michael McCain Named Business Newsmaker of the Year," *The Canadian Press* 1 Jan. 2009 [n.p.]; Gordon Pitts, "The Testing of Michael McCain," *Report on Business Magazine* (*Globe and Mail*) Nov. 2008: 60+ [accessed 19 Feb. 2009] Proquest Database; Misty Harris, "Maple Leaf Winning the Battle to Bring Customers Back," *CanWest News* 22 Jan. 2009 [n.p.].

2. Katie Grasso, "Deliver Bad News to Workers Face-to-Face, with Empathy," *Courier-Post* (Camden, N.J.) 8 Feb. 2006 [accessed 14 May 2006] www.courierpostonline.com

3. Chad Terhune, "CEO Says Things Aren't Going Better with Coke," *Wall Street Journal* 16 Sept. 2004: A1, A10.

4. Ian McDonald, "Marsh Can Do $600 Million, But Apologize?" *Wall Street Journal* 14 Jan. 2005: C1, C3; Adrienne Carter and Amy Borrus, "What If Companies Fessed Up?" *BusinessWeek* 24 Jan. 2005: 59–60; Patrick J. Kiger, "The Art of the Apology," *Workforce Management* Oct. 2004: 57–62.

5. Ameeta Patel and Lamar Reinsch, "Companies Can Apologize. Corporate Apologies and Legal Liability," *Business Communication Quarterly* Mar. 2003 [accessed 1 Dec. 2003] www.elibrary.com.

6. Iris I. Varner, "A Comparison of American and French Business Correspondence," *Journal of Business Communication* 24.4 (Fall 1988): 55–65.

7. Susan Jenkins and John Hinds, "Business Letter Writing: English, French, and Japanese," *TESOL Quarterly* 21.2 (June 1987): 327–349; Saburo Haneda and Hiosuke Shima, "Japanese Communication Behavior As Reflected in Letter Writing," *Journal of Business Communication* 19.1 (1982): 19–32.

8. James Calvert Scott and Diana J. Green, "British Perspectives on Organizing Bad-News Letters: Organizational Patterns Used by Major U.K. Companies," *Bulletin of the Association for Business Communication* 55.1 (Mar. 1992): 17–19.

9. "Advice from the Pros on the Best Way to Deliver Bad News," *Report on Customer Relationship Management* 1 Feb. 2003 [accessed 1 Dec. 2003] www.elibrary.com.

10. Nelson D. Schwartz, "Can BP Recover?" *Fortune* 16 Oct. 2006: 90–96.

11. Jeffrey Pfeffer, "The Whole Truth and Nothing But," *Business 2.0* Oct. 2004: 78.

12. Walter Kiechel III, "Breaking Bad News to the Boss," *Fortune* 9 Apr. 1990 [accessed 2 Dec. 2003] www.elibrary.com.

13. Courtand L. Bovée, John V. Thill, George P. Dovel, and Marian Burk Wood, *Advertising Excellence* (New York: McGraw-Hill,

1995) 508–509; John Holusha, "Exxon's Public-Relations Problem," *New York Times* 12 Apr. 1989: D1.

14. "Throw Out the Old Handbook in Favor of Today's Crisis Drills," *PR News* 27 Jan. 2003: 1.

15. "Protecting Your Firm," *Canadian HR Reporter* 24 Mar. 2003: 5.

16. See Brian Smeek, "Bad References Can Be Bad News for Employers," *Canadian Employment Law Today* 5 Dec. 2009: 1, 6; "Case Notes," *Focus on Canadian Employment & Equality Rights* 5.24 (1999): 188; Stacey Ball, "Employers Should Exercise Care When Writing References for Former Employees," *Financial Post* 1–3 June 1996: 21; Howard Levitt, "If You Can't Say Something Good, Say Something Bad," *Financial Post* (National Post) 27 Nov. 1998: C17.

17. Thomas S. Brice and Marie Waung, "Applicant Rejection Letters: Are Businesses Sending the Wrong Message?" *Business Horizons* Mar.–Apr. 1995: 59–62.

18. Gwendolyn N. Smith, Rebecca F. Nolan, and Yong Dai, "Job-Refusal Letters: Readers' Affective Responses to Direct and Indirect Organizational Plans," *Business Communication Quarterly* 59.1 (1996): 67–73; Brice and Waung, "Applicant Rejection Letters."

19. John Zappe, "Building on Brand to Attract Top Employees," *Workforce Management* 27 Feb. 2006: 31.

20. Judi Brownell, "The Performance Appraisal Interviews: A Multipurpose Communication Assignment," *Bulletin of the Association for Business Communication* 57.2 (1994): 11–21.

21. Brownell, "The Performance Appraisal Interviews."

22. Fred Pamenter, "Moving from Appraisals to Employee Enhancement," *The Canadian Manager* 55.1 (Spring 2000): 13–15; Patricia A. McLagan, "Advice for Bad-News Bearers: How to Tell Employees They're Not Hacking It and Get Results," *Industry Week* 15 Feb. 1993: 42; Michael Lee Smith, "Give Feedback, Not Criticism," *Supervisory Management* 1993: 4; "A Checklist for Conducting Problem Performer Appraisals," *Supervisory Management* Dec. 1993: 7–9.

23. Smeek, "Bad References Can Be Bad News for Employers"; Carrie Brodzinski, "Avoiding Wrongful Termination Suits," *National Underwriter Property & Casualty—Risk & Benefits Management* 13 Oct. 2003 [accessed 2 Dec. 2003] www.elibrary.com.

24. Jane R. Goodson, Gail W. McGee, and Anson Seers, "Giving Appropriate Performance Feedback to Managers: An Empirical Test of Content and Outcomes," *Journal of Business Communication* 29.4 (1992): 329–342.

25. Craig Cox, "On the Firing Line," *Business Ethics* May–June 1992: 33–34.

26. Cox, "On the Firing Line."

27. Adapted from Michael H. Mescon, Courtland L. Bovée, and John V. Thill, *Business Today,* 10th ed. (Upper Saddle River, N.J.: Prentice-Hall, 2002) 369; Bruce Upbin, "Profit in a Big Orange Box," *Forbes* 24 Jan. 2000: 122.

28. Based on Michelle Higgins, "The Ballet Shoe Gets a Makeover, But Few Yet See the Pointe," *The Wall Street Journal* 8 Aug. 1998: A1, A6.

29. Adapted from Wolf Blitzer, "More Employers Taking Advantages of New Cyber-Surveillance Software," CNN.com 10 July 2000 [accessed 11 July 2000] www.cnn.com/2000/US/07/10/workplace.eprivacy/index.html.

30. Adapted from "Bathtub Curve," *Engineering Statistics Handbook,* National Institute of Standards and Technology website [accessed 16 Apr. 2005] www.nist.gov; Robert Berner, "The Warranty Windfall," *BusinessWeek* 20 Dec. 2004: 84–86; Larry Armstrong, "When Service Contracts Make Sense," *BusinessWeek* 20 Dec. 2004: 86.

31. Adapted from Pui-Wing Tam, Erin White, Nick Wingfield, and Kris Maher, "Snooping E-mail by Software Is Now a Workplace Norm," *Wall Street Journal* 9 Mar. 2005: B11.

32. Adapted from Sylvia Ann Hewlett and Carolyn Buck Luce, "Off-Ramps and On-Ramps," *Harvard Business Review* Mar. 2005: 43–54.

33. Adapted from Alyce Lomax, "Monterey's High-Carb Woes," *The Motley Fool* 23 Dec. 2003 [accessed 23 Dec. 2003] www.fool.com/News/mft/2003/mft03122312.htm; "Monterey Pasta Announces Quarterly Sales Decline of 3%–5% Expected When Compared to Fourth Quarter, 2002," Monterey Pasta corporate press release, 23 Dec. 2003 [accessed 23 Dec. 2003] www.montereypasta.com/Company/Press Releases/index.cfm?ID584; "Monterey Pasta Company Introduces Reduced Carbohydrate Product Line," Monterey Pasta corporate press release, 23 Dec. 2003 [accessed 23 Dec. 2003] www.montereypasta.com/Company/PressReleases.

34. Adapted from Pascal Zachary, "Sun Microsystems Apologizes in Letter for Late Payments," *The Wall Street Journal* 11 Oct. 1989: B4.

35. Adapted from Stanton website [accessed 18 Aug. 2005] www.stanton.com.

36. Based on "No Cell Calls on Nfld. Roads," *The Gazette* (Montreal) 24 Aug. 2003: A4; Ellen van Wangeningen, "Fatal Driver Pleads Guilty," *Windsor Star* 25 Feb. 2003: A5.

37. Adapted from Associated Press, "Children's Painkiller Recalled," CNN.com/Health website, 16 Aug. 2001 [accessed 22 Aug. 2001] www.cnn.com/2001/HEALTH/parenting/08/16/kids.drug.recalled.ap/index.html; Perrigo Company website [accessed 29 Aug. 2001] www.perrigo.com.

38. Adapted from United Airlines website [accessed 31 Dec. 2003] www.united.com; "United Airlines First to Offer Inflight Email on Domestic Flights: Verizon Airfone® Outfits UAL's Fleet with JetConnect^sm," United Airlines press release [accessed 21 July 2003] www.ual.com/press/detail/o,1442,51106,00.html; "Laptops Sprout Wings with Verizon Airfone JetConnect Service," PR Newswire 24 Sept. 2002 [accessed 21 July 2003] www.proquest.com; "Verizon Hopes Data Flies with Airfone JetConnect," *Wireless Data News* 7 May 2003 [accessed 24 July 2003] www.proquest.com.

39. Adapted from Sean Doherty, "Dynamic Communications," *Network Computing* 3 Apr. 2003: 26 [accessed 24 July 2003] search. epnet.com/direct.asp?an-9463336&db5bsh&tg5AN; Todd Wasserman, "Post-Merger HP Invents New Image to Challenge Tech Foes IBM and Dell," *Brandweek* 18 Nov. 2002: 9 [accessed 24 July 2003] search. epnet.com/direct.asp?an58887152&db5bsh&tg5AN; R. P. Srikanth, "IM Tools Are Latest Tech Toys for Corporate Users," *Express Computer* 1 July 2002 [accessed 21 July 2003] www.expresscomputeronline. com/20020701/indtrend1.shtml.

Chapter 10

1. Based on the Canadian Youth Business Foundation website [accessed 22 Mar. 2009]; Canadian Youth Business Federation 2008 Annual Report [accessed 22 Mar. 2009] www.cybf.ca; Daryl-Lynn Carlson, "Advice Helps Snap Up Funding," *Financial Post* 15 Dec. 2008 [accessed 22 Mar. 2009] www.financialpost.com; Daryl-Lynn Carlson, "Finance: Be Resourceful in Hard Times," *Financial Post* 26 Jan. 2009 [accessed 22 Mar. 2009] www.financialpost. com; Daryl-Lynn Carlson, "Good Applications Get Stamp of Approval" *Financial Post* 9 Feb. 2009 [accessed 22 Mar. 2009] www.financialpost.com; Daryl-Lynn Carlson, "Recessions Breed New Generation of Entrepreneurs," *Financial Post* 20 Mar. 2009 [accessed 22 Mar. 2009] www.financialpost.com.

2. Jay A. Conger, "The Necessary Art of Persuasion," *Harvard Business Review* May–June 1998: 84–95; Jeanette W. Gilsdorf, "Write Me Your Best Case for . . . ," *Bulletin of the Association for Business Communication* 54.1 (Mar. 1991): 7–12.

3. "Vital Skill for Today's Managers: Persuading, Not Ordering Others," *Soundview Executive Book Summaries* Sept. 1998: 1.

4. Mary Cross, "Aristotle and Business Writing: Why We Need to Teach Persuasion," *Bulletin of the Association for Business Communication* 54.1 (Mar. 1991): 3–6.

5. Stephen P. Robbins and David A. DeCenzo, *Fundamentals of Management,* 4th ed. (Upper Saddle River, N.J.: Prentice Hall, 2004) 284.

6. Edwin A. Locke and Gary P. Latham, "What Should We Do About Motivation Theory? Six Recommendations for the Twenty-First Century," *Academy of Management Review* July 2004: 388+.

7. Robert T. Moran, "Tips on Making Speeches to International Audiences," *International Management* Apr. 1980: 58–59.

8. Conger, "The Necessary Art of Persuasion."

9. Raymond M. Olderman, *10-Minute Guide to Business Communication* (New York: Macmillan Spectrum/Alpha Books, 1997) 57–61.

10. John D. Ramage and John C. Bean, *Writing Arguments: A Rhetoric with Readings,* 3rd ed. (Boston: Allyn & Bacon, 1995) 430–442.

11. Philip Vassallo, "Persuading Powerfully: Tips for Writing Persuasive Documents," *et Cetera* Spring 2002: 65–71.

12. Dianna Booher, *Communicate with Confidence* (New York: McGraw-Hill, 1994) 102.

13. Overview of the Web Accessibility Initiative, W3C website [accessed 15 July 2007] www.w3.org.

14. iPod touch product page, Apple website [accessed 28 July 2009] www.apple.com/ca/ipodtouch.

15. Bell Canada website [accessed 1 Apr. 2009] http://bundle.bell.ca/en/on/home.

16. Saturn VUE product page, Saturn website [accessed 8 Dec. 2003] www.saturn.com.

17. Working and Living in France: The Ins and Outs product page, Insider Paris Guides website [accessed 8 Dec. 2003] www.insiderparisguides.com.

18. Bell Canada Bell TV product page, Bell Canada website [accessed 1 Apr. 2009] www.bell.ca.

19. Fast Break Backpack product page, Lands' End website [accessed 8 Dec. 2003] www.landsend.com.

20. iPod nano product page [accessed 2 Apr. 2009] www.apple.ca.

21. Gilsdorf, "Write Me Your Best Case for . . ."

22. "Law and Litigation: About the Acts," Competition Bureau Canada website [accessed 15 July 2007] www.competitionbureau.gc.ca/internet/index.cfm?itemID=148&lg=e#packaging.

23. "Competition Bureau Participates in Worldwide Blitz on Hidden Traps Online," news release, 3 Mar. 2006, Competition Bureau Canada, News and Resources website [accessed 15 July 2007] www.competitionbureau.gc.ca/internet/index.cfm?itemID=2031&lg=e.

24. Adapted from Samsung website [accessed 22 Oct. 2006] www.samsung.com.

25. Adapted from GM Fastlane Blog [accessed 6 Apr. 2009] http://fastlane.gmblogs.com.

26. Adapted from Starbucks website [accessed 23 Aug. 2005] www.starbucks.com.

27. Adapted from Canadian Blood Services website [accessed 6 Apr. 2009] www.bloodservices.ca.

28. Adapted from Cathy Werblin, "Korean Business Owners Want Signs to Mark Area," *Los Angeles Times* 29 Mar. 1997: B3.

29. Adapted from Courtland L. Bovée and John V. Thill, *Business In Action,* 3rd ed. (Upper Saddle River, N.J.: Pearson Prentice Hall, 2005) 236–237; International Telework Association & Council website [accessed 24 Aug. 2005] www.telecommute.org; Jason Roberson, "Rush-hour Rebellion," *Dallas Business Journal* 22 June 2001: 31; Carole Hawkins, "Ready, Set, Go Home," *Black Enterprise* Aug. 2001: 118–124; Wayne Tompkins, "Telecommuting in Transition," *Courier-Journal* (Louisville, KY) 9 July 2001: C10.

30. Adapted from Andrew Ferguson, "Supermarket of the Vanities," *Fortune* 10 June 1996: 30, 32.

31. Adapted from advertisement, *The Atlantic Monthly* Jan. 2000: 119; Endless Pools, Inc. website [accessed 31 Aug. 2000] www.endlesspools.com.

32. Adapted from CNET Shopper.com [accessed 1 Oct. 2001] http://shopper.cnet.com.

33. Adapted from The Podcast Bunker website [accessed 25 Aug. 2005] www.podcastbunker.com.

34. Adapted from Kelly Services website [accessed 6 Apr. 2009], www.kellyservices.com.

35. Adapted from Hangers Cleaners website [accessed 9 Jan. 2004] www.hangersdrycleaners.com; Charles Fishman, "The Greener Cleaners," *Fast Company* 36, 54 [accessed 11 July 2000] fastcompany.com/online/36/greenclean.html; Micell Technologies website [accessed 1 Sept. 2000] www.micell.com/08142000.htm; Cool Clean Technologies, Inc., website [accessed 9 Jan. 2004] www.co2olclean.com.

36. Adapted from Sarah Plaskitt, "Case Study: Hilton Uses SMS With Success," *B&T Marketing & Media* 27 June 2002 [accessed 22 July 2003] www.bandt.com.au/articles/ce/0c00eace.asp; "Wireless Messaging Briefs," *Instant Messaging Planet,* 4 Oct. 2002 [accessed 22 July 2003] www.instantmessagingplanet.com/wireless/print.php/10766_1476111; Hilton Hotels Corporation, *Hoover's Company Capsules* 1 July 2003 [accessed 24 July 2003] www.proquest.com; Matthew G. Nelson, "Hilton Takes Reservations Wireless," *InformationWeek* 25 June 2001: 99 [accessed 24 July 2003] www.web22.epnet.com; Hilton Hotels website [accessed 15 Jan. 2004] www.hilton.com.

37. Adapted from IBM website [accessed 15 Jan. 2004] www.ibm.com/ibm/ibmgives; IBM website, "DAS faces an assured future with IBM" [accessed 16 Jan. 2004] www-306.ibm.com/software/success/cssdb.nsf/CS/DNSD-5S6KTF; IBM website, "Sametime" [accessed 16 Jan. 2004] www.lotus.com/products/lotussametime.nsf/wdocs/homepage.

Chapter 11

1. Dell Inc., *Annual Report 2008* [accessed 12 Apr. 2009] www.dell.com; Michael Dell, speech delivered at University of Toronto, Toronto, ON, 27 Feb. 2008 [accessed 12 Apr. 2009] http://content.dell.com/us/en/corp/about-dell-speeches.aspx; Reena Jana, "Taking the Dull Out of Dell," *BusinessWeek* 10 Nov. 2008: 32, Paolo Del Nibletto, "Dell to Enter the Retail Channel," *Computer Dealer News* 8 June 2007 [accessed 12 Apr. 2009] www.itbusiness.ca/IT/client/en/CDN/News.asp?id=44115; Jaikumar Vayajan, "Dell Forsakes Retail for Direct Approach," *Computerworld* 18 July 1994: 32.

2. Courtland L. Bovée, Michael J Houston, and John V. Thill, *Marketing,* 2nd ed. (New York: McGraw-Hill, 1995) 194–196.

3. Legal-Definitions.com [accessed 17 Dec. 2003] www.legal-definitions.com.

4. Tom Krazit, "FAQ: The HP 'Pretexting' Scandal," ZDNet.com, 6 Sept. 2006 [accessed 26 Oct. 2006] www.zdnet.com.

5. Information for this section was obtained from the Ryerson University Library Web site Guides [accessed 14 Apr. 2009] www.ryerson.ca/library/guides.html; "Finding Industry Information" [accessed 3 Nov. 1998] www.pitt.edu/buslibry/industries.htm; Thomas P. Bergman, Stephen M. Garrison, and Gregory M. Scott, *The Business Student Writer's Manual and Guide to the Internet* (Upper Saddle River, N.J.: Prentice Hall, 1998) 67–80; Ernest L. Maier, Anthony J. Faria, Peter Kaatrude, and Elizabeth Wood, *The Business Library and How to Use It* (Detroit: Omnigraphics, 1996) 53–76; Sherwyn P. Morreale and Courtland L. Bovée, *Excellence in Public Speaking* (Fort Worth: Harcourt Brace College Publishers, 1998) 166–171.

6. Joe Barker, "Invisible or Deep Web: What It Is, Why It Exists, How to Find It, and Its Inherent Ambiguity," 1 Aug. 2006, UC Berkeley—Teaching Library Internet Workshops [accessed 25 Oct. 2006] www.lib.berkeley.edu.

7. AllTheWeb.com advanced search page [accessed 27 Aug. 2005] www.alltheweb.com; Google advanced search page [accessed 27 Aug. 2005] www.google.com; Yahoo! advanced search page [accessed 27 Aug. 2005] www.yahoo.com.

8. "About Google Desktop," Google website [accessed 3 Nov. 2006] www.google.com; "Desktop Search Tools Matrix," Goebel Group website [accessed 3 Nov. 2006] www.goebelgroup.com.

9. Net Snippets website [accessed 3 Nov. 2006] www.netsnippets.com.

10. Antone Gonsalves, "Digg Dogged by Allegations of Manipulation," *TechWeb* 7 Sept. 2006 [accessed 3 Nov. 2006] www.techweb.com; Alex Iskold, "The Social Bookmarking Face-off," *Read/WriteWeb* 18 Sept. 2006 [accessed 1 June 2007] www.readwriteweb.com.

11. "Top 10 Benefits of OneNote 2003," Microsoft website [accessed 21 June 2004] www.microsoft.com.

12. University of Ottawa, Canadian Internet Policy and Public Interest Clinic, "Copyright Law," www.cippic.ca/copyright-law [accessed 14 Apr. 2009]; Copyright Board of Canada, "Copyright Act," www.cb-cda.gc.ca/info/act-e.html [accessed 14 Apr. 2009].

13. Henry R. Cheeseman, *Contemporary Business and E-Commerce Law*, 4th ed. (Upper Saddle River, N.J.: Prentice Hall, 2003) 325.

14. Eric Badartscher and Kathy Reese, "Taking the Confusion Out of Copyright in an Internet Age," *Information Outlook* 12:6 (June 2008): 62–67; "The Apple Case Isn't Just A Blow to Bloggers: Why Should Bloggers Be Denied Rights Given a Pamphleteer in the Past?" (editorial) *BusinessWeek* 28 Mar. 2005:128.

15. A. B. Blankenship and George Edward Breen, *State of the Art Marketing Research* (Chicago: NTC Business Books, 1993) 136.

16. Naresh K. Malhotra, Basic Marketing Research (Upper Saddle River, N.J.: Prentice-Hall, 2002) 314–317; "How to Design and Conduct a Study," *Credit Union Magazine* Oct. 1983: 36–46.

17. American Marketing Association [accessed 14 Dec. 2003] www.marketingpower.com.

18. Karen J. Bannan, "Companies Save Time, Money with Online Surveys," *B to B* 9 June 2003: 11; Allen Hogg, "Online Research Overview," American Marketing Association website [accessed 15 Dec. 2003] www.marketingpower.com.

19. Morreale and Bovée, *Excellence in Public Speaking*, 177.

20. Morreale and Bovée, *Excellence in Public Speaking*, 182.

21. Blankenship and Breen, *State of the Art Marketing Research*, 225.

22. Lynn Quitman Troyka, *Simon & Schuster Handbook for Writers*, 6th ed. (Upper Saddle River, NJ: Simon & Schuster, 2002) 481.

23. "How to Paraphrase Effectively: 6 Steps to Follow," Research Paper.com [accessed 26 Oct. 1998] www.researchpaper.com/writing_center/30.html.

24. Jakob Nielsen, "How Users Read on the Web" [accessed 11 Nov. 2004] www.useit.com/alertbox/9710a.html.

25. Reid Goldsborough, "Words for the Wise," *Link-Up* Sept.–Oct. 1999: 25–26.

26. Julie Rohovit, "Computer Eye Strain: The Dilbert Syndrome," Virtual Hospital website [accessed 9 Nov. 2004] www.vh.org.

27. Nick Usborne, "Two Pillars of a Successful Site," *Excess Voice* May 2004 [accessed 8 Nov. 2004] www.excessvoice.com.

28. Shel Holtz, "Writing for the Wired World," *International Association of Business Communicators* 1999: 6–9.

29. Holtz, "Writing for the Wired World," 28–29.

Chapter 12

1. Federal Express website [accessed 22 Apr. 2009] www.fedex.com, www.fedex.ca; "A Budding Network," *Forbes* 7 May 2007: 64; FedEx Corp. Company Overview, Hoover's Online. 27 Oct. 1997 [accessed 19 Jan. 2001]; "All Strung Up," *The Economist* 17 Apr. 1993: 70; Gary M. Stern, "Improving Verbal Communications," *Internal Auditor* Aug. 1993: 49–54; Gary Hoover, Alta Campbell, and Patrick J. Spain, *Hoover's Handbook of American Business 1994* (Austin, TX: Reference Press, 1993) 488–489; "Pass the Parcel," *The Economist* 21 Mar. 1992: 73–74; "Federal Express," *Personnel Journal* Jan. 1992: 52.

2. A. S. C. Ehrenberg, "Report Writing—Six Simple Rules for Better Business Documents," *Admap* June 1992: 39–42.

3. Michael Netzley and Craig Snow, *Guide to Report Writing* (Upper Saddle River, N.J.: Prentice Hall, 2001) 15.

4. "Message to our Shareholders," *FEDEX 2008 Annual Report* [accessed 22 Apr. 2009] www.fedex.com.

5. Claudia Mon Pere McIsaac, "Improving Student Summaries Through Sequencing," *Bulletin of the Association for Business Communication* Sept. 1987: 17–20.

6. David A. Hayes, "Helping Students GRASP the Knack of Writing Summaries," *Journal of Reading* Nov. 1989: 96–101.

7. Philip C. Kolin, *Successful Writing at Work*, 6th ed. (Boston: Houghton Mifflin, 2001) 552–555.

8. "Web Writing: How to Avoid Pitfalls," *Investor Relations Business* 1 Nov. 1999: 15.

9. Shel Holtz, "Writing for the Wired World," *International Association of Business Communicators* 1999: 6–9.

10. Sant Corporation website [accessed 16 Aug. 2007] www.santcorp.com; Pragmatech Software website [accessed 16 Aug. 2007] www.pragmatech.com.

11. Alexis Gerard and Bob Goldstein, *Going Visual* (Hoboken, N.J.: Wiley, 2005) 18.

12. Charles Kostelnick and Michael Hassett, *Shaping Information: The Rhetoric of Visual Conventions* (Carbondale, Ill.: Southern Illinois University Press, 2003) 177.

13. Gerard and Goldstein, *Going Visual*, 103–106.

14. Edward R. Tufte, *Visual Explanations: Images and Quantities, Evidence and Narrative* (Cheshire, Conn.: Graphics Press, 1997) 82.

15. Joshua David McClurg-Genevese, "The Principles of Design," *Digital Web Magazine* 13 June 2005 [accessed 23 Nov. 2006] www.digital-web.com.

16. Kostelnick and Hassett, *Shaping Information: The Rhetoric of Visual Conventions*, 17.

17. Kostelnick and Hassett, *Shaping Information: The Rhetoric of Visual Conventions*, 216.

18. Edward R. Tufte, *The Visual Display of Quantitative Information* (Cheshire, Conn.: Graphic Press, 1983) 113.

19. Tufte, *Visual Explanations: Images and Quantities, Evidence and Narrative*, 73.

20. Based in part on Tufte, *Visual Explanations: Images and Quantities, Evidence and Narrative*, 29–37, 53; Paul Martin Lester, *Visual Communication: Images with Messages*, 4th ed. (Belmont, Calif.: Thomson Wadsworth, 2006) 95–105, 194–196.

21. Sheri Rosen, "What Is Truth?" *IABC Communication World* Mar. 1995: 40.

22. R. Craig Endicott, "Leaders Back Brands with $51.2 Billion in Ads" (100 Leading National Advertisers Supplement), *Advertising Age* 29 Sept. 1997: S63.

23. Adapted from Air-Trak website [accessed 12 Sept. 2005] www.air-trak.com.

Chapter 13

1. Gates Foundation website [accessed 13 Nov. 2006] www.gatesfoundation.org; Richard Klausner and Pedro Alonso, "An Attack on All Fronts," *Nature* 19 Aug. 2004: 930–931; "Richard Klausner Spends to Save Lives," *Fast Company* Nov. 2002: 128; Kent Allen, "The Gatekeeper," *U.S. News & World Report* 8 Dec. 2003: 64–66.

2. John Morkes and Jakob Nielsen, "Concise, Scannable, and Objective: How to Write for the Web," UseIt.com [accessed 13 Nov. 2006] www.useit.com.

3. Dean Allen, "Reading Design," *A List Apart* 23 Nov. 2001 [accessed 9 Nov. 2004] www.alistapart.com.

4. Michael Netzley and Craig Snow, *Guide to Report Writing* (Upper Saddle River, N.J.: Prentice Hall, 2001) 57.

5. Oswald M. T. Ratteray, "Hit the Mark with Better Summaries," *Supervisory Management* Sept. 1989: 43–45.

6. Netzley and Snow, *Guide to Report Writing*, 43.

7. Alice Reid, "A Practical Guide for Writing Proposals" [accessed 31 May 2001] http://members.dca.net/areid/proposal.htm.

8. Liz Hughes, "Enhancing Communication Skills," *WIB* Sept./Oct. 2003: 21.

9. See Note 1.

10. Adapted from "Home Depot Says E-Learning Is Paying for Itself," *Workforce Management* 25 Feb. 2004 [accessed 28 Feb. 2004] www.workforce.com; Robert Celashi, "The Insider: Training," *Workforce Management* Aug. 2004: 67–69; Joe Mullich, "A Second Act for E-Learning," *Workforce Management* Feb. 2004: 51–55, Gail Johnson, "Brewing the Perfect Blend," *Training* Dec. 2003: 30+; Tammy Galvin, "2003 Industry Report," *Training* Oct. 2003: 21+; William C. Symonds, "Giving It the Old Online Try," *BusinessWeek* 3 Dec. 2001: 76–80; Karen Frankola, "Why Online Learners Drop Out," *Workforce* Oct. 2001: 52–60; Mary Lord, "They're Online and on the Job: Managers and Hamburger Flippers Are Being E-trained at Work,: *U.S. News & World Report* 15 Oct. 2001: 72–77.

Chapter 14

1. Based on Telefilm Canada website [accessed 6 Aug. 2007, 7 June 2009] www.telefilm.ca; Wayne Clarkson, and Charles Bélanger, "Modernizing Telefilm in the Multiplatform Era," Standing Committee on Canadian Heritage, Ottawa, Ontario, 29 Nov. 2006; Wayne Clarkson, "Artistic Directions: The Challenge of English Canadian Cinema Past, Present and Future," Directors Guild of Canada, Toronto, Ontario, 25 Nov. 2006; Wayne Clarkson, "General Admissions: How to Maintain Success and Meet Our Challenges," Prime Time in Ottawa 2007, Ottawa, Ontario, 22 Feb. 2007; Telefilm Canada, *Annual Report 2005–2006*, Telefilm Canada, 2006 [accessed 5 Aug. 2007] www.telefilm.gc.ca.

2. Carmine Gallo, "Loaded for Bore," *BusinessWeek Online* 5 Aug. 2005 [accessed 19 Sept. 2005] www.businessweek.com.

3. Sarah Lary and Karen Pruente, "Powerless Point: Common PowerPoint Mistakes to Avoid," *Public Relations Tactics* Feb. 2004: 28.

4. Cliff Atkinson, *Beyond Bullet Points: Using Microsoft PowerPoint to Create Presentations That Inform, Motivate, and Inspire* (Redmond, Wash.: Microsoft Press, 2005) 29, 55, 65.

5. Sherwyn P. Morreale and Courtland L. Bovée, *Excellence in Public Speaking* (Fort Worth: Harcourt Brace, 1998) 234–237.

6. Morreale and Bovée, *Excellence in Public Speaking*, 230.

7. Morreale and Bovée, *Excellence in Public Speaking*, 241–243.

8. "Choose and Use Your Words Deliberately," *Soundview Executive Book Summaries* 20.6, pt. 2 (June 1998): 3.

9. Carmine Gallo, "Grab Your Audience Fast," *BusinessWeek* 13 Sept. 2006: 19.

10. Walter Kiechel III, "How to Give a Speech," *Fortune* 8 June 1987: 180.

11. *Communication and Leadership Program* (Santa Ana, Calif.: Toastmasters International, 1980) 44, 45.

12. "Polishing Your Presentation," 3M Meeting Network [accessed 8 June 2001] www.mmm.com/meetingnetwork/readingroom/meetingguide_pres.html.

13. Claudyne Wilder and David Fine, *Point, Click & Wow* (San Francisco: Jossey-Bass Pfeiffer, 1996) 50.

14. Margo Halverson, "Choosing the Right Colors for Your Next Presentation," 3M Meeting Network [accessed 8 June 2001] www.mmm.com/meetingnetwork/readingroom/meetingguide_right_color.html.

15. Carol Klinger and Joel G. Siegel, "Computer Multimedia Presentations," *CPA Journal* June 1996: 46.

16. Jon Hanke, "Five Tips for Better Visuals," 3M Meeting Network [accessed 8 June 2001] www.mmm.com/meetingnetwork/presentations/pmag_better_visuals.html.

17. Hanke, "Five Tips for Better Visuals."

18. Sarah Lary and Karen Pruente, "Powerless Point: Common PowerPoint Mistakes to Avoid," *Public Relations Tactics* Feb. 2004: 28.

19. Jeff Yocom, "TechRepublic Survey Yields Advice on Streaming Video," TechRepublic website [accessed 16 Feb. 2004] www.techrepublic.com.

20. Yocom, "TechRepublic Survey Yields Advice on Streaming Video."

21. "Webcasting Tips & Advice," Spider Eye Studios [accessed 13 Feb. 2004] www.spidereye.com.

22. Jerry Weissman, *Presenting to Win: The Art of Telling Your Story* (Upper Saddle River, N.J.: Pearson Prentice-Hall, 2006) 162.

23. Ted Simons, "Handouts That Won't Get Trashed," *Presentations* Feb. 1999: 47–50.

24. Morreale and Bovée, *Excellence in Public Speaking* 24–25.

25. Jennifer Rotondo and Mike Rotondo, Jr., *Presentation Skills for Managers* (New York: McGraw-Hill, 2002) 9.

26. Rick Gilbert, "Presentation Advice for Boardroom Success," *Financial Executive* Sept. 2005: 12.

27. Rotondo and Rotondo, Jr., *Presentation Skills for Managers*, 151.

28. "Control the Question-and-Answer Session," *Soundview Executive Book Summaries* 20.6, pt. 2 (June 1998): 4.

29. Teresa Brady, "Fielding Abrasive Questions During Presentations," *Supervisory Management* Feb. 1993: 6.

30. Robert L. Montgomery, "Listening on Your Feet," *The Toastmaster* July 1987: 14–15.

Chapter 15

1. Based on Tim Hortons website [accessed 5 July 2009] www.timhortons.com.

2. Maureen Jenkins, "Yours for the Taking," *Boeing Frontiers Online* June 2004 [accessed 25 Sept. 2005] www.boeing.com; "Firm Predicts Top 10 Workforce/Workplace Trends for 2004, *Enterprise* 8–14 Dec. 2003: 1–2; Scott Hudson, "Keeping Employees Happy," *Community Banker* Sept. 2003: 341; Marvin J. Cetron and Owen Davies, "Trends Now Changing the World: Technology, the Workplace, Management, and Institutions," *Futurist* 35.2 (Mar.–Apr. 2001): 27–42.

3. Daryl-Lynn Carlson, "The New Generation of Entrepreneurs: A Paradigm Shift Is Underway That Has Business Startups Rising on the Heels of Corporate Layoffs," *National Post* 23 Mar 2009: FP5.

4. Tony Wanless, "Get Set for Wave of Boomer Startups," *National Post* 30 June 2009: FP7.

5. Jim Puzzanghera, "Coalition of High-Tech Firms to Urge Officials to Help Keep U.S. Competitive," *San Jose Mercury News* 8 Jan. 2004 [accessed 14 Feb. 2004] www.ebscohost.com.

6. Amanda Bennett, "GE Redesigns Rungs of Career Ladder," *Wall Street Journal* 15 Mar. 1993: B1, B3.

7. Robin White Goode, "International and Foreign Language Skills Have an Edge," *Black Enterprise* May 1995: 53.

8. Nancy M. Somerick, "Managing a Communication Internship Program," *Bulletin of the Association for Business Communication* 56.3 (1993): 10–20.

9. Fellowforce website [accessed 8 July 2007] www.fellowforce.com.

10. Joan Lloyd, "Changing Workplace Requires You to Alter Your Career Outlook," *Milwaukee Journal Sentinel* 4 July 1999: 1; Camille DeBell, "Ninety Years in the World of Work in America," *Career Development Quarterly* 50 (Sept. 2001): 77–88.

11. Jeffrey R. Young, "'E-Portfolios' Could Give Students a New Sense of Their Accomplishments," *The Chronicle of Higher Education* 8 Mar. 2002: A31.

12. Brian Carcione, e-portfolio [accessed 20 Dec. 2006] http://eportfolio.psu.edu.

13. Robert J. Gerberg, *Robert Gerberg's Job Changing System*, summarized by Macmillan Book Clubs, Inc., in the "Macmillan Executive Summary Program," Apr. 1987, 4.

14. Jobwings website [accessed 5 July 2009] www.jobwings.com; Nicejob.ca website [accessed 5 July 2009]; "JobWings.com Ranked Among Top 100 Employment Sites on the Web," *Marketwire* (Toronto) 30 June 2009. Online.

15. Caroline A. Drakeley, "Viral Networking: Tactics in Today's Job Market," *Intercom* Sept.–Oct. 2003: 4–7.

16. Drakeley, "Viral Networking: Tactics in Today's Job Market": 5.

17. Julie Weed, "Finding New Employees, via Social Networks," *New York Times* 30 May 2009 (online edition) www.nytimes.com [accessed 7 June 2009].

18. Anne Fisher, "Greener Pastures in a New Field," *Fortune* 26 Jan. 2004: 48.

19. Cheryl L. Noll, "Collaborating with the Career Planning and Placement Center in the Job-Search Project," *Business Communication Quarterly* 58.3 (1995): 53–55.

20. Rockport Institute, "How to Write a Masterpiece of a Résumé" [accessed 25 Sept. 2005] www.rockportinstitute.com.

21. Pam Stanley-Weigand, "Organizing the Writing of Your Resume," *Bulletin of the Association for Business Communication* 54.3 (Sept. 1991): 11–12.

22. Susan Vaughn, "Answer the Hard Questions Before Asked," *Los Angeles Times* 29 July 2001: W1–W2.

23. Colin Gibson, "Ask an Expert with Colin Gibson," *Canadian Employment Law Today* 30 Aug. 2006: 3668; Tim Mitchell, "Ask an Expert with Tim Mitchell," *Canadian Employment Law Today* 3 Aug. 2005: 3468; Stuart Rudner, "Conducting Criminal Background Checks," *Canadian HR Reporter* 14 Aug. 2006: 5.

24. John Steven Niznik, "Landing a Job with a Criminal Record," About.com [accessed 12 Dec. 2006] http://jobsearchtech.about.com.

25. Richard H. Beatty and Nicholas C. Burkholder, *The Executive Career Guide for MBAs* (New York: Wiley, 1996) 133.

26. Adapted from Burdette E. Bostwick, *How to Find the Job You've Always Wanted* (New York: Wiley, 1982) 69–70.

27. Norma Mushkat Gaffin, "Recruiters' Top 10 Resume Pet Peeves," Monster.com [accessed 19 Feb. 2004] www.monster.com; Beatty and Burkholder, *The Executive Career Guide for MBAs*, 151.

28. Rockport Institute, "How to Write a Masterpiece of a Résumé."

29. "Resume Fraud Gets Slicker and Easier," CNN.com [accessed 11 Mar. 2004] www.cnn.com.

30. "Resume Fraud Gets Slicker and Easier"; Employment Screening Resources website [accessed 18 Mar. 2004] www.erscheck.com.

31. "Employers Turn Their Fire on Untruthful CVs," *Supply Management* 23 June 2005: 13.

32. Sal Divita, "If You're Thinking Résumé, Think Creatively," *Marketing News* 14 Sept. 1992: 29.

33. Rockport Institute, "How to Write a Masterpiece of a Résumé."

34. Lora Morsch, "25 Words That Hurt Your Resume," CNN.com, 20 Jan. 2006 [accessed 20 Jan. 2006] www.cnn.com.

35. Karl L. Smart, "Articulating Skills in the Job Search," *Business Communication Quarterly* 67.2 (June 2004): 198–205.

36. Rockport Institute, "How to Write a Masterpiece of a Résumé."

37. Ed Tazzia, "Wanted: A Résumé That Really Works," *Brandweek* 15 May 2006: 26.

38. Ellen Joe Pollock, "Sir: Your Application for a Job Is Rejected; Sincerely, Hal 9000," *Wall Street Journal* 30 July 1998: A1, A12.

39. "Scannable Resume Design," ResumeEdge.com [accessed 19 Feb. 2004] www.resumeedge.com.

40. Kim Isaacs, "Tips for Creating a Scannable Resume," Monster.com [accessed 19 Feb. 2004] www.monster.com.

41. Sarah E. Needleman, "Why Sneaky Tactics May Not Help Resume; Recruiters Use New Search Technologies to Ferret Out Bogus Keywords," *Wall Street Journal* 6 Mar. 2007: B8.

42. Kim Isaacs, "Enhance Your Resume for Monster Upload," Monster.com [accessed 19 Feb. 2004] www.monster.com.

43. "The Rogue's Gallery of 25 Awful Résumé Mistakes," CareerExplorer.net [accessed 19 Feb. 2004] www.careerexplorer.net.

44. Lore Croghan, "Recruiters Cite Litany of Mistakes They've Seen on Résumés," *Seattle Times* 20 Nov. 2005 [accessed 20 Nov. 2005] www.seattletimes.com.

45. Regina Pontow, "Electronic Résumé Writing Tips," ProvenRésumés .com [accessed 18 Oct. 1998] www.provenresumes.com/reswkshps/electronic/scnres.html.

46. See note 1.

Chapter 16

1. "What's It Like to Work At Google?" Google website [accessed 14 July 2009] www.google.com; Fred Vogelstein, "Can Google Grow Up?" *Fortune* 8 Dec. 2003: 102; Quentin Hardy, "All Eyes on Google," *Forbes* 26 May 2003: 100; Keith H. Hammonds, "Growth Search," *Fast Company* Apr. 2003: 74–81; Stanley Bing, "How Not To Success (sic) in Business," *Fortune* 30 Dec. 2002: 210; Pierre Mornell, "Zero Defect Hiring," *Inc.* Mar. 1998: 74; Adam Lashinsky, "Search and Enjoy," *Fortune* 22 Jan. 2007: 70; "100 Best Companies to Work For," *Fortune* 4 Feb. 2008 [accessed 14 July 2009] www.cnnmoney.com.

2. Toni Logan, "The Perfect Cover Story," *Kinko's Impress* 2 (2000): 32, 3.

3. James Gonyea, "Money Talks: Salary History Versus Salary Requirements," Monster.com [accessed 19 Oct. 2004] www.monster. com; Marguerite Higgins, "Tech-Savvy Job Hunters Not So Suave in Writing; E-mail Résumés Appall Employers," *Washington Times* 17 Dec. 2002 [accessed 22 Feb. 2004] www.highbeam.com; "Keep Goal in Mind When Crafting a Résumé," *Register-Guard* (Eugene, Ore.) 3 Aug. 2003 [accessed 22 Feb. 2004] www.highbeam.com; Anis F. McClin, "Effects of Spelling Errors on the Perception of Writers," *Journal of General Psychology* Jan. 2002 [accessed 22 Feb. 2004] www.highbeam.com.

4. George Donnelly, "Recruiting, Retention & Returns," cfonet Mar. 2000 [accessed 10 Apr. 2000] www.cfonet.com/html/Articles/CFO/2000/00Marecr.html.

5. Stephanie Armour, "The New Interview Etiquette," *USA Today* 23 Nov. 1999: B1, B2.

6. Samuel Greengard, "Are You Well Armed to Screen Applicants?" *Personnel Journal* Dec. 1995: 84–95.

7. Caroline Levchuck, "Survival Tips for Group Interviews," Yahoo! HotJobs [accessed 16 Dec. 2006] http://hotjobs.yahoo.com.

8. "Panel Interview," Job-Employment-Guide.com [accessed 2 June 2007] www.job-employment-guide.com; Carole Martin, "The Panel Interview," JobBank USA [accessed 2 June 2007] www.jobbankusa.com.

9. William Poundstone, "Beware the Interview Inquisition," *Harvard Business Review* May 2003: 181.

10. "Interview Preparation," Madison MacArthur website [accessed 13 Dec. 2006] www.mmsearch.com.

11. Lynda M. Bassett, "Work the Working Interview," Monster.com [accessed 13 Dec. 2006] www.monster.com.

12. Peter Vogt, "Mastering the Phone Interview," Monster.com [accessed 13 Dec. 2006] www.monster.com; Nina Segal, "The Global Interview: Tips for Successful, Unconventional Interview Techniques," Monster.com [accessed 13 Dec. 2006] www.monster.com.

13. Segal, "The Global Interview: Tips for Successful, Unconventional Interview Techniques."

14. Connie Winkler, "Job Tryouts Go Virtual," *HR Magazine* Sept. 2006: 131–134.

15. Steven Isbitts, "Virtual Interview," *Tampa Tribune* 20 Mar. 2006 [accessed 13 Dec. 2006] www.ebscohost.com.

16. Saul Hansell, "Google Answer to Filling Jobs Is an Algorithm," *New York Times* 3 Jan. 2007 [accessed 3 Jan. 2007] www.nytimes.com.

17. Carole Martin, "Smile, You're on Camera: Videoconference Interviews," Monster.com [accessed 13 Dec. 2006] www.monster.com; Marcia Vickers, "Don't Touch That Dial: Why Should I Hire You?" *New York Times* 13 Apr. 1997: F11.

18. Patrick J. Sauer, "Open-Door Management," *Inc.* June 2003: 44.

19. Dino di Mattia, "Testing Methods and Effectiveness of Tests," *Supervision* Aug. 2005: 4–5.

20. John Sullivan, "A Case Study of Google Recruiting," *Electronic Recruiting Exchange* 5 Dec. 2005 [accessed 16 Dec. 2006] www.ere.net.

21. David W. Arnold and John W. Jones, "Who the Devil's Applying Now?" *Security Management* Mar. 2002: 86.

22. Adam Agard, "Preemployment Skills Testing: An Important Step in the Hiring Process," *Supervision* June 2003: 71.

23. "Check Yourself Before Employer Does," *CA Magazine* June–July 2005: 12.

24. Nancy K. Austin, "Goodbye Gimmicks," *Incentive* May 1996: 241.

25. Katherine Spencer Lee, "Tackling Tough Interview Questions," *Certification Magazine* May 2005: 35.

26. Leigh Dyer, "Job Hunters Should Think Carefully Before Using Job Counselor," *Charlotte Observer* 30 July 2001 [accessed 29 Sept. 2005] www.ebsco.com; Anne Field, "Coach, Help Me Out with This Interview," *BusinessWeek* 22 Oct. 2001: 134E2, 134E4.

27. Robert Gifford, Cheuk Fan Ng, and Margaret Wilkinson, "Nonverbal Cues in the Employment Interview: Links Between Applicant Qualities and Interviewer Judgments," *Journal of Applied Psychology* 70.4 (1985): 729.

28. Dale G. Leathers, *Successful Nonverbal Communication* (New York: Macmillan, 1986) 225.

29. Armour, "The New Interview Etiquette."

30. William S. Frank, "Job Interview: Pre-Flight Checklist," *The Career Advisor* [accessed 28 Sept. 2005] http://careerplanning.about.com.

31. T. Shawn Taylor, "Most Managers Have No Idea How to Hire the Right Person for the Job," *Chicago Tribune* 23 July 2002 [accessed 29 Sept. 2005] www.ebsco.com.

32. "Negotiating Salary: An Introduction," *InformationWeek* online [accessed 22 Feb. 2004] www.infoweek.com.

33. "Negotiating Salary: An Introduction."

34. Harold H. Hellwig, "Job Interviewing: Process and Practice," *Bulletin of the Association for Business Communication* 55.2 (1992): 8–14.

Appendix A

1. Mary A. De Vries, *Internationally Yours* (Boston: Houghton Mifflin, 1994) 9.

2. Patricia A. Dreyfus, "Paper That's Letter Perfect," *Money* May 1985: 184.

3. "When Image Counts, Letterhead Says It All," *Stamford (Conn.) Advocate and Greenwich Times* 10 Jan. 1993: F4.

4. Linda Driskill, *Business and Managerial Communication: New Perspectives* (Orlando, Fla.: Harcourt Brace Jovanovich, 1992) 470.

5. Driskill, *Business and Managerial Communication*, 475.

6. De Vries, *Internationally Yours*, 8.

7. Renee B. Horowitz and Marian G. Barchilon, "Stylistic Guidelines for E-mail," *IEEE Transactions on Professional Communications* 37.4 (1994): 207–212.

Name Index

Subject Index

Credits

Tables and Figures

4 Figure 1–2 Conference Board of Canada. **5** Paul Hébert, "Career Hunting Tips," *CIM Bulletin*, September/October 2005, 44. **37** Stephen M. Powell, "Benefits to Team Briefings," *Healthcare Executive*, July/August 2007, 54. **53** (Table 2–2): Source: Madelyn Burley-Allen, *Listening: The Forgotten Skill,* (New York: Wiley, 1995), 70–71, 119–120; Judi Brownell, *Listening: Attitudes, Principles, and Skills,* (Boston: Allyn and Bacon, 2002); 3, 9, 83, 89, 125; Larry Barker and Kittie Watson, *Listen Up,* (New York: St. Martin's, 2000), 8, 9, 64. **74** Quoted in Wallace Immen, "Earn Global Stripes Without Leaving Home," *Globe and Mail*, 8 November 2006: C1. **89** (Figure 4–1): Kevin J. Harty and John Keenan, *Writing for Business and Industry: Process and Product* (New York: Macmillan Publishing Company, 1987), 3–4; Richard Hatch, *Business Writing* (Chicago: Ill., Science Research Associates, 1983), 88–89; Richard Hatch, *Business Communication Theory and Technique* (Chicago, Ill., Science Research Associates, 1983), 74–75; Center for Humanities, *Writing as a Process: A Step-by-Step Guide, Four Filmstrips and Cassettes.* Mount Kisko, New York, 1987; Michael L. Keene, *Effective Professional Writing* (New York:D.C. Heath, 1987), 28–34. **95** Ray Dreyfack, "Take Steps to Travel the Write Road to Success," *Plant Engineering* 54, no.7: 34. **136** Dianna Booher, "Ten Writing Principles to Improve Your Training," Training & Development 53.1 (January 1999), 17–18. **172** (Figure 6–7) Free the Children, the largest network of children helping children through education. **175** Gina Cuciniello, "Writing for Global Audiences," *Training Journal*, January 2007, 42. **191** Susan Ward, "Basic Email Management," *About.com: Small Business Canada,* [accessed 24 June 2007] http://sbinfocanada.about.com/cs/management/qt/email1.htm. **201** (Table 7.2): Robert Scoble and Shel Israel, *Naked Conversations* (Hoboken, N.J.: John Wiley & Sons, 2006), 78–81, 190–194; Paul McFedries, *The Complete Idiot's Guide to Creating a Web Page & Blog*, 6th ed. (New York: Alpha, 2004), 206–208, 272–276; Shel Holtz and Ted Demopoulos, *Blogging for Business* (Chicago: Kaplan, 2006), 54–59, 113–114: Denise Wakeman, "Top 10 Blog Writing Tips," Blogarooni.com [accessed 1 February 2006] www.blogarooni.com; Dennis A. Mahoney, "How to Write a Better Weblog," 22 February 2002, A List Apart [accessed 1 February 2006] www.alistapart.com. **237** (Figure 8–6): Source: Courtesy Herman Miller. **238** (Figure 8–7) Courtesy of Dampp-Chaser Corporation. **242** Julie K. Henderson, "How to Get that Glowing Letter of Recommendation," *Public Relations Tactics* 8.9, September 2001, 20. **243** (Figure 8–9): Source: Courtesy Discover Communications. **246** Reprinted with permission from Indigo Books & Music Inc. **287** Quoted in Wilma Mathews, "What Should I Tell Them? Why Every Organization Should Have an Official Policy for Communicating," *Communication World*, May/June 2004, 50. **310** (Table 10.1): Source: Adapted from Saundra K. Ciccarelli and Glenn E. Meyer, *Psychology* (Upper Saddle River, N.J.: Prentice Hall, 2006), 336–346; Courtland L. Bovée, John V. Thill, and Michael H. Mescon, *Excellence In Business*, 3rd ed. (Upper Saddle River, N.J.: Prentice Hall, 2006), 327–333; Abraham H. Maslow, "A Theory of Human Motivation," *Psychological Review* 50 (1943): 370–396. **332** Edmund O. Lawlor, "Fine Line between Added Value, Spam," *Advertising Age*, 29 October 2001: S4. **360–361** (Table 11–3): Source: Adapted from Subscribed Sites page, Sno-Isle Regional Library System [accessed 28 August 2005] www.sno-isle.org; "Finding Industry Information" [accessed 3 November 1998] www.pitt.edu/~buslibry/industries.htm; Thomas P. Bergman, Stephen M. Garrison, and Gregory M. Scott, *The Business Student Writer's Manual and Guide to the Internet* (Paramus, N.J.: Prentice Hall, 1998), 67–80; Ernest L. Maier, Anthony J. Faria, Peter Kaatrude, and Elizabeth Wood, *The Business Library and How to Use It* (Detroit: Omnigraphics, 1996), 53–76. **370** Linda M. Cummins, "What Every Young Communicator Needs to Know," *Public Relations Tactics*, April 2004: 29. **420** Lori Guidry, "What's the Big I-DEA?" *Online*, January/February 2003: 33–34. **469** Liz Hughes, "Enhancing Communication Skills," *WIB*, September/October 2003, 21. **445** Jim Gray, "When It's Your Turn to Speak: No Sweat," *Globe and Mail*, 13 June 2007: C2. **496** (Table 13–2): Source: Adapted from Carmen Matthews, "Speaker's Notes," *Presentations*, April 2005, 42; Eric J. Adams, "Management Focus: User-Friendly Presentation Software," *World Trade*, March 1995, 92. **505** (Figure 14–7): Source: Microsoft PowerPoint 2002 software. **522** Hallie Crawford, "Polishing Your Résumé," *Contract Management*, May 2007: 4. **526** (Figure 15–1), (Figure 15–2): Source: Adapted from Richard Nelson Bolles, *What Color Is Your Parachute?* (Berkeley, CA.: Ten Speed Press, 1997), 67. **487** (Table 15–1): Source: The Riley Guide [accessed 22 September 2005] www.rileyguide.com; Bethany McLean, "A Scary Monster," *Fortune,* 22 December 2003, 19; Alan Cohen, "Best Job Hunting Sites," *Yahoo! Internet Life,* May 2002, 90–92; Richard N. Bolles, "Career Strategizing or, What Color Is Your Web Parachute?" *Yahoo! Internet Life,* May 1998, 116, 121; Tara Weingarten, "The All-Day, All-Night, Global, No-Trouble Job Search," *Newsweek,* 6 April 1998, 14; Michele Himmelberg, "Internet an Important Tool in Employment Search," *San Diego Union-Tribune,* 7 September 1998, D2; Gina Imperato, "35 Ways to Land a Job Online," *Fast Company,* August 1998, 192–197; Roberta Maynard, "Casting the Net for Job Seekers," *Nation's Business,* March 1997, 28–29. **496** (Table 14.2): Source: Adapted from Carmen Matthews, "Speaker's Notes," *Presentations*, April 2005, 42; Eric J. Adams, "Management Focus: User-Friendly Presentation Software," *World Trade*, March 1995, 92. **503** (Table 14.3): Source: Adapted from Claudyne Wilder and David Fine, *Point, Click & Wow* (San Francisco: Jossey-Bass Pfeiffer, 1996), 63, 527. **526** Quoted in Erica Noonan, "Forget IQ, How's Your EQ?" *Globe and Mail*, 13 September 2006: C10. **529** (Table 16–4): Source: Adapted from Marilyn Sherman, "Questions R Us: What to Ask at a Job Interview," *Career World,* January 2004, 20; H. Lee Rust, *Job Search: The Completion Manual for Jobseekers* (New York: American Management Association, 1979), 56. **531** (Table 15.2): Source: Adapted from Richard Nelson Bolles, *What Color Is Your Parachute?* (Berkeley, Calif.: Ten Speed Press, 1997), 67. **568** Quoted in Erica Noonan, "Forget IQ, How's Your EQ?" *Globe and Mail*, 13 September 2006: C10. **571** (Table 16–3): Source: Adapted from

The Northwestern Endicott Report (Evanston, Ill.: Northwestern University Placement Center). **572** (Table 16.4): Source: Adapted from Marilyn Sherman, "Questions R Us: What to Ask at a Job Interview," *Career World*, January 2004, 20; H. Lee Rust, *Job Search: The Complete Manual for Jobseekers* (New York: American Management Association, 1979), 56. **573** (Table 16–5): Source: Adapted from *The Northwestern Endicott Report* (Evanston: Ill.: Northwestern University Placement Center).

Photo Credits

t=top, b=bottom

1 © Wenher Krutein/CORBIS. **6** Yellow Dog Productions/The Image Bank/Getty Images. **9** TELUS materials at p. 9 used with permission. © TELUS. **13** 3M. **15** Stockbyte. **23** Masterfile Corporation. **26** Courtesy of © BCE/Bell Canada. All rights reserved. **33** Steve Smith/Getty Images. **36** Jeffery Greenberg/Photo Researchers Inc. **43** Getty Images, Stone Allstock. **47** Library of Parliament/Bibliothèque du Parlement–Stephen Fenn. **50t** Photodisc/Getty Images. **50b** PhotoAlto/James Hardy/Getty Images. **51** Getty Images, Photodisk. **57** ©Dorling Kindersley. **64** Courtesy Laraine Kaminsky. **66** Courtesy of CHIN Radio/TV International. **67** Paul Chesley/Getty Images. **68** Mark Gibson/Mark and Audra Gibson Photography. **72** Bata Brands S.A.R.L. **78** Courtesy of Dalton Chemical Laboratories, Inc. **87** ©Dorling Kindersley. **90** Shutterstock. **95** Courtesy of Business Development Bank of Canada. **97–98** Courtesy RBC. **100** Walter Hodges/Getty Images. **122** Stanford Law School. **124** Courtesy of Business Development Bank of Canada. **133** © 2000 Chip Williams/Ward-Williams Inc. **142** © Tetra Images/Alamy. **154** Free the Children, the largest network of children helping children through education. **161** Microsoft product screen shot(s) reprinted with permission from Microsoft Corporation. **165** Nick Daly/Getty Images. **187** Shutterstock. **188** Chung Sung-Jun/Getty Images. **189** Chris Strangemore/Craig Strangemore. **202** Ric Feld/AP Wide World Photos . **206** Promethius Consulting, LLC. **217** Bill Stevenson/The Stock Connection. **224** Reprinted with permission from Indigo Books & Music Inc. **227** Shutterstock. **234** ©redsnapper/Alamy. **243** ©Dorling Kindersley. **246** Reprinted with permission from Indigo Books & Music Inc. **250** Courtesy of Cancer Care Ontario. **258** Andrew Brooks/CORBIS-NY. **260** Mark Jenkinson/CORBIS-NY. **262** AP Wide World Photos. **265** Courtesy Maple Leaf Foods. **267** John Riley/Getty Images. **288** © Dick Hemingway. **300** Tom Raymond/Getty Images, Stone Allstock. **304** Reggie Casagrande/Getty Images. **306** CORBIS-NY. **307** Shutterstock. **311** Paul Sakuma/AP Wide World Photos. **318** Photodisc/Getty Images. **323** courtesy of Home Depot. **333** Aeroplan. **340t** Todd Bigelow/Aurora & Quanta Productions Inc. **340b** AP Wide World Photos, Alex Wong/Getty Images, Inc.–Liaison. **344** AP Wide World Photos. **346** Shutterstock. **354** © Rob Bartee/Alamy. **357** Reprinted with permission of Statistics Canada. **358** © George Steinmetz/CORBIS. **367** ImageWorks. **369** CORBIS/Bettmann. **395** B. Roland/The Image Works. **398** Courtesy of Petro Canada. All Rights Reserved. **416** Saputo, Inc. **429** Alan Gough/Alan Gough Photography. **430** Getty Images. **440** Corbis/Bettmann. **441** John Decker/Landov LLC. **442** Corbis/Sygma. **461** Photodisc/Getty Images. **463** Employability Skills 2000+ Brochure 2000 E/F (Ottawa: the Conference Board of Canada, 2000). **479** Shutterstock. **482** SuperStock, Inc. **484** © Sarah Hadley/Alamy. **498** AP Wide World Photos. **500** Lance Davies Photography/Polyvision, A Steelcase Company. **506** CORBIS-NY. **511t** ©Dorling Kindersley. **511b** Dennis MacDonald/PhotoEdit Inc. **513** Noel Hendrickson/Getty Images. **519** Richard B. Levine/Frances M. Roberts. **521** Patti McConville / Alamy. **527** David de Lossy/Getty Images. **539** SuperStock, Inc. **543** © Dorling Kindersley. **557** Google Inc. **564** Photolibrary.com. **568** Istock. **570** The Image Works. **574** Jon Feingersh/zefa-CORBIS-NY. **578** Photolibrary.com. **581** Jack Hollingsworth/Photodisc/Getty Images.